Hoover's Handbook of

Emerging Companies

2010

HOOVERS™

A D&B COMPANY

Austin, Texas

Hoover's Handbook of Emerging Companies 2010 is intended to provide readers with accurate and authoritative information about the enterprises covered in it. Hoover's researched all companies and organizations profiled, and in many cases contacted them directly so that companies represented could provide information. The information contained herein is as accurate as we could reasonably make it. In many cases we have relied on third-party material that we believe to be trustworthy, but were unable to independently verify. We do not warrant that the book is absolutely accurate or without error. Readers should not rely on any information contained herein in instances where such reliance might cause financial loss. The publisher, the editors, and their data suppliers specifically disclaim all warranties, including the implied warranties of merchantability and fitness for a specific purpose. This book is sold with the understanding that neither the publisher, the editors, nor any content contributors are engaged in providing investment, financial, accounting, legal, or other professional advice.

The financial data (Historical Financials sections) in this book are from a variety of sources. Morningstar, Inc., provided selected data for the Historical Financials sections of publicly traded companies. For private companies and for historical information on public companies prior to their becoming public, we obtained information directly from the companies or from trade sources deemed to be reliable. Hoover's, Inc., is solely responsible for the presentation of all data.

Many of the names of products and services mentioned in this book are the trademarks or service marks of the companies manufacturing or selling them and are subject to protection under US law. Space has not permitted us to indicate which names are subject to such protection, and readers are advised to consult with the owners of such marks regarding their use. Hoover's is a trademark of Hoover's, Inc.

HOOVERS™
A D&B COMPANY

10 9 8 7 6 5 4 3 2 1

Publishers Cataloging-in-Publication Data

Hoover's Handbook of Emerging Companies 2010

   Includes indexes.

   ISBN 978-1-57311-139-3

   ISSN 1069-7519

   1. Business enterprises — Directories. 2. Corporations — Directories.

HF3010 338.7

Hoover's Company Information is also available on the Internet at Hoover's Online (www.hoovers.com). A catalog of Hoover's products is available on the Internet at www.hooversbooks.com.

The Hoover's Handbook series is produced for Hoover's Business Press by:

Sycamore Productions, Inc.
5808 Balcones Drive, Suite 205
Austin, Texas 78731
info@sycamoreproductions.com

Cover design is by John Baker. Electronic prepress and printing are by Sheridan Books, Inc., Ann Arbor, Michigan.

U.S. AND WORLD BOOK SALES

Hoover's, Inc.
5800 Airport Blvd.
Austin, TX 78752
Phone: 512-374-4500
Fax: 512-374-4538
e-mail: orders@hoovers.com
Web: www.hooversbooks.com

EUROPEAN BOOK SALES

William Snyder Publishing Associates
5 Five Mile Drive
Oxford OX2 8HT
England
Phone & fax: +44-186-551-3186
e-mail: snyderpub@aol.com

Hoover's, Inc.

Founder: Gary Hoover
President: Hyune Hand
EVP Marketing and Business Development: Peter Poulin
VP Business Excellence: Jeffrey A. (Jeff) Cross
VP Technology: Mamie Jones
VP Business Development: Heidi Tucker
VP Advertising Sales and Operations: Mark Walters
VP Sales: Tom Wickersham
Leader e-Commerce and Books: Dan Tharp
Leader New Business Acquisitions: Amy Bible
Leader Human Resources: Robin Pfahler

(For the latest updates on Hoover's, please visit: http://hoovers.com/global/corp)

EDITORIAL

Managing Editor: Margaret L. Harrison
Senior Editors: Adrianne Argumaniz, Larry Bills, Jason Cother, Barbara-Anne Mansfield, Greg Perliski, Barbara Redding, Dennis Sutton
Team Leads: Danny Cummings and Matt Saucedo
Editors: Chelsea Adams, Adam Anderson, Jenn Barnier, Victoria Bernard, Alex Biesada, Joe Bramhall, James Bryant, Anthony Buchanan, Ryan Caione, Jason Cella, Catherine Colbert, Tami Conner, Nancy Daniels, Jeff Dorsch, Bobby Duncan, Lesley Epperson, Rachel Gallo, Jenni Gilmer, Chris Hampton, Stuart Hampton, Jim Harris, Laura Huchzermeyer, Chris Huston, Donna Iroabuchi, Ellen Jacobs, Jessica Jimenez, Linnea Anderson Kirgan, Sylvia Lambert, Anne Law, Josh Lower, John MacAyeal, Kathryn Mackenzie, Rebecca Mallett, Erin McInnis, Michael McLellan, Barbara Murray, Nell Newton, Lynett Oliver, Tracey Panek, Peter Partheymuller, Rachel Pierce, David Ramirez, Diane Ramirez, Mark Richardson, Melanie Robertson, Patrice Sarath, Amy Schein, Nikki Sein, Seth Shafer, Lee Simmons, Paula Smith, Anthony Staats, Tracy Uba, Vanessa Valencia, Ryan Wade, Randy Williams, David Woodruff
QA Editors: Carrie Geis, Rosie Hatch, Diane Lee, John Willis
Editorial Customer Advocates: Adi Anand and Kenny Jones

HOOVER'S BUSINESS PRESS

Distribution Manager: Rhonda Mitchell
Customer Support and Fulfillment Manager: Michael Febonio

ABOUT HOOVER'S, INC. — THE BUSINESS INFORMATION AUTHORITY™

Hoover's, a D&B company, provides its customers the fastest path to business with insight and actionable information about companies, industries, and key decision makers, along with the powerful tools to find and connect to the right people to get business done. Hoover's provides this information for sales, marketing, business development, and other professionals who need intelligence on U.S. and global companies, industries, and the people who lead them. Hoover's unique combination of editorial expertise and one-of-a-kind data collection with user-generated and company-supplied content gives customers a 360-degree view and competitive edge. This information, along with powerful tools to search, sort, download, and integrate the content, is available through Hoover's (http://www.hoovers.com), the company's premier online service. Hoover's is headquartered in Austin, Texas.

Abbreviations

AFL-CIO – American Federation of Labor and Congress of Industrial Organizations

AMA – American Medical Association

AMEX – American Stock Exchange

ARM – adjustable-rate mortgage

ASP – application services provider

ATM – asynchronous transfer mode

ATM – automated teller machine

CAD/CAM – computer-aided design/computer-aided manufacturing

CEO – chief executive officer

CFO – chief financial officer

COO – chief operating officer

DAT – digital audiotape

DOD – Department of Defense

DOE – Department of Energy

DOT – Department of Transportation

DRAM – dynamic random-access memory

DSL – digital subscriber line

EPA – Environmental Protection Agency

EPS – earnings per share

ESOP – employee stock ownership plan

EU – European Union

EVP – executive vice president

FCC – Federal Communications Commission

FDA – Food and Drug Administration

FDIC – Federal Deposit Insurance Corporation

FTC – Federal Trade Commission

FTP – file transfer protocol

GATT – General Agreement on Tariffs and Trade

GDP – gross domestic product

HMO – health maintenance organization

HR – human resources

ICC – Interstate Commerce Commission

IPO – initial public offering

IRS – Internal Revenue Service

ISP – Internet service provider

kWh – kilowatt-hour

LAN – local-area network

LBO – leveraged buyout

LCD – liquid crystal display

LNG – liquefied natural gas

LP – limited partnership

Ltd. – limited

MW – megawatt

NAFTA – North American Free Trade Agreement

NASA – National Aeronautics and Space Administration

Nasdaq – National Association of Securities Dealers Automated Quotations

NATO – North Atlantic Treaty Organization

NYSE – New York Stock Exchange

OCR – optical character recognition

OECD – Organization for Economic Cooperation and Development

OEM – original equipment manufacturer

OPEC – Organization of Petroleum Exporting Countries

OS – operating system

OSHA – Occupational Safety and Health Administration

OTC – over-the-counter

PBX – private branch exchange

P/E – price to earnings ratio

RAID – redundant array of independent disks

RAM – random-access memory

R&D – research and development

RISC – reduced instruction set computer

REIT – real estate investment trust

ROA – return on assets

ROE – return on equity

ROI – return on investment

ROM – read-only memory

SEC – Securities and Exchange Commission

SEVP – senior executive vice president

SIC – Standard Industrial Classification

SOC – system on a chip

SVP – senior vice president

USB – universal serial bus

VAR – value-added reseller

VAT – value-added tax

VC – venture capitalist

VoIP – Voice over Internet Protocol

VP – vice president

WAN – wide-area network

WWW – World Wide Web

Contents

Companies Profiled

Companies Profiled (continued)

Companies Profiled (continued)

About Hoover's Handbook of Emerging Companies 2010

Hoover's Handbook of Emerging Companies enters its 17th year as one of America's premier sources of business information on younger, growth-oriented enterprises. Given our current economic realities, finding value in the marketplace becomes ever more difficult, and so we are particularly pleased to present this edition of *Hoover's Handbook of Emerging Companies 2010* — the result of a search of our extensive database of business information for companies with demonstrated growth and the potential for future gains.

The 600 companies in this book were chosen from the universe of public US companies with sales between $10 million and $1 billion. Their selection was based primarily on sales growth and profitability, although in a few cases we made some rather subjective decisions about which companies we chose to include. They all have reported at least three years of sales and have sustained annualized sales growth of at least 10% during that time. Also, they are profitable (through year-end September 2009).

HOOVER'S ONLINE FOR BUSINESS NEEDS

In addition to the 2,550 companies featured in our handbooks, comprehensive coverage of more than 40,000 business enterprises is available in electronic format on our Web site, Hoover's Online (www.hoovers.com). Our goal is to provide one site that offers authoritative, updated intelligence on US and global companies, industries, and the people who shape them. Hoover's has partnered with other prestigious business information and service providers to bring you all the right business information, services, and links in one place.

Hoover's Handbook of Emerging Companies is one of our four-title series of handbooks that covers, literally, the world of business. The series is available as an indexed set, and also includes *Hoover's Handbook of American Business*, *Hoover's Handbook of World Business*, and *Hoover's Handbook of Private Companies*. This series brings you information on the biggest, fastest-growing, and most influential enterprises in the world.

We believe that anyone who buys from, sells to, invests in, lends to, competes with, interviews with, or works for a company should know as much as possible about that enterprise. Taken together, *Hoover's Handbook of Emerging Companies 2010* and the other Hoover's products represent the most complete source of basic corporate information readily available to the general public.

HOW TO USE THIS BOOK

This book has four sections:

1. "Using Hoover's Handbooks" describes the contents of our profiles.

2. "A List-Lover's Compendium" contains lists of the fastest-growing and most profitable companies. The lists are based on the information in our profiles, or compiled from well-known sources.

3. The company profiles section makes up the largest and most important part of the book — 600 profiles arranged alphabetically. Each profile features an overview of the company; some larger and more visible companies have an additional History section. All companies have up to five years of financial information, product information where available, and a list of company executives and key competitors.

4. At the end of this volume are the combined indexes from our 2010 editions of all Hoover's Handbooks. The information is organized into three separate sections. The first sorts companies by industry groups, the second by headquarters location. The third index is a list of all the executives found in the Executives section of each company profile. For a more thorough description of our indexing style, see page xii.

As always, we hope you find our books useful. We invite your comments via phone (512-374-4500), fax (512-374-4538), mail (5800 Airport Boulevard, Austin, Texas 78752), or e-mail (custsupport@hoovers.com).

The Editors
Austin, Texas
February 2010

Using Hoover's Handbooks

ORGANIZATION

The profiles in this volume are presented in alphabetical order. This alphabetization is generally word by word, which means that Bridge Bancorp precedes Bridgepoint Education. You will find the commonly used name of the enterprise at the beginning of the profile; the full, legal name is found in the Locations section. If a company name starts with initials, such as BJ's Restaurants or L. B. Foster, look for it under the combined initials (in the above example, BJ or LB, respectively).

Basic financial data is listed under the heading Historical Financials; also included is the exchange on which the company's stock is traded, the ticker symbol used by the stock exchange, and the company's fiscal year-end. The annual financial information contained in the profiles is current through fiscal year-ends occurring as late as September 2009. We have included certain nonfinancial developments, such as officer changes, through January 2010.

OVERVIEW

In the first section of the profile, we have tried to give a thumbnail description of the company and what it does. The description will usually include information on the company's strategy, reputation, and ownership. We recommend that you read this section first.

HISTORY

This extended section, which is available for some of the larger and more well-known companies, reflects our belief that every enterprise is the sum of its history and that you have to know where you came from in order to know where you are going. While some companies have limited historical awareness, we think the vast majority of the enterprises in this book have colorful backgrounds. We have tried to focus on the people who made the enterprises what they are today. We have found these histories to be full of twists and ironies; they make fascinating reading.

EXECUTIVES

Here we list the names of the people who run the company, insofar as space allows. In the case of public companies, we have shown the ages and pay of key officers. The published data is for the previous fiscal year, although the company may have announced promotions or retirements since year-end. The pay represents cash compensation, including bonuses, but excludes stock option programs.

Although companies are free to structure their management titles any way they please, most modern corporations follow standard practices. The ultimate power in any corporation lies with the shareholders, who elect a board of directors, usually including officers or "insiders," as well as individuals from outside the company. The chief officer, the person on whose desk the buck stops, is usually called the chief executive officer (CEO). Often, he or she is also the chairman of the board.

As corporate management has become more complex, it is common for the CEO to have a "right-hand person" who oversees the day-to-day operations of the company, allowing the CEO plenty of time to focus on strategy and long-term issues. This right-hand person is usually designated the chief operating officer (COO) and is often the president of the company. In other cases one person is both chairman and president.

A multitude of other titles exists, including chief financial officer (CFO), chief administrative officer, and vice chairman. We have always tried to include the CFO, the chief legal officer, and the chief human resources or personnel officer. Our best advice is that officers' pay levels are clear indicators of who the board of directors thinks are the most important members of the management team.

The people named in the Executives section are indexed at the back of the book.

The Executives section also includes the name of the company's auditing (accounting) firm, where available.

LOCATIONS

Here we include the company's full legal name and its headquarters, street address, telephone and fax numbers, and Web site, as available. The back of the book includes an index of companies by headquarters locations.

In some cases we have also included information on the geographic distribution of the company's business, including sales and profit data. Note that these profit numbers, like those in the Products/Operations section below, are usually operating or pretax profits rather than net profits. Operating profits are generally those before financing costs (interest income and payments) and before taxes, which are considered costs attributable to the whole company rather than to one division or part of the world. For this reason the net income figures (in the Historical Financials section) are usually much lower, since they are after interest and taxes. Pretax profits are after interest but before taxes.

PRODUCTS/OPERATIONS

This section lists as many of the company's products, services, brand names, divisions, subsidiaries, and joint ventures as we could fit. We have tried to include all its major lines and all familiar brand names. The nature of this section varies by company and the amount of information available. If the company publishes sales and profit information by type of business, we have included it.

COMPETITORS

In this section we have listed companies that compete with the profiled company. This feature is included as a quick way to locate similar companies and compare them. The universe of competitors includes all public companies and all private companies with sales in excess of $500 million. In a few instances we have identified smaller private companies as key competitors.

HISTORICAL FINANCIALS

Here we have tried to present as much data about each enterprise's financial performance as we could compile in the allocated space. Although the information varies somewhat from industry to industry, the following is generally present.

A five-year table, with relevant annualized compound growth rates, covers:

- Sales — fiscal year sales (year-end assets for most financial companies)
- Net income — fiscal year net income (before accounting changes)

- Net profit margin — fiscal year net income as a percent of sales (as a percent of assets for most financial firms)
- Employees — fiscal year-end or average number of employees
- Stock price — the fiscal year closing price
- P/E — high and low price/earnings ratio
- Earnings per share — fiscal year earnings per share (EPS)
- Dividends per share — fiscal year dividends per share
- Book value per share — fiscal year-end book value (common shareholders' equity per share)

The information on the number of employees is intended to aid the reader interested in knowing whether a company has a long-term trend of increasing or decreasing employment. As far as we know, we are the only company that publishes this information in print format.

The numbers on the left in each row of the Historical Financials section give the month and the year in which the company's fiscal year actually ends. Thus, a company with a September 30, 2009, year-end is shown as 9/09.

In addition, we have provided in graph form a stock price history for each company. The graphs, covering up to five years, show the range of trading between the high and the low price, as well as the closing price for each fiscal year.

Key year-end statistics in this section generally show the financial strength of the enterprise, including:

- Debt ratio (long-term debt as a percent of shareholders' equity)
- Return on equity (net income divided by the average of beginning and ending common shareholders' equity)
- Cash and cash equivalents
- Current ratio (ratio of current assets to current liabilities)
- Total long-term debt (including capital lease obligations)
- Number of shares of common stock outstanding
- Dividend yield (fiscal year dividends per share divided by the fiscal year-end closing stock price)
- Dividend payout (fiscal year dividends divided by fiscal year EPS)
- Market value at fiscal year-end (fiscal year-end closing stock price multiplied by fiscal year-end number of shares outstanding)
- Research and development as a percentage of sales
- Advertising as a percentage of sales

Per-share data has been adjusted for stock splits. The data for public companies has been provided to us by Morningstar, Inc. Other public company information was compiled by Hoover's, which takes full responsibility for the content of this section.

Using the Master Index to Hoover's Handbooks

PAGE NUMBERS

The letter preceding each page number of an index entry indicates the handbook volume that is being referenced:

A=American Business
E=Emerging Companies
P=Private Companies
W=World Business

(For convenience, this list of handbook titles and the corresponding letters are also included at the top of every index page.)

ALPHABETIZATION

English-language articles (a, an, the) are ignored when they appear at the beginning of a company name, but foreign articles are not ignored and are alphabetized as they appear. Ampersands are treated as though they are spelled out, as are the abbreviations Ft., Mt., and St.

If a company name is also a person's name, such as Edward J. DeBartolo or Mary Kay, it will be alphabetized under the first name; if the company name starts with initials, for example, L.L. Bean or S.C. Johnson, look for it under the combined initials (in the above examples, LL and SC, respectively).

Initials or words indicating limited liability appearing at the beginning of international company names (AB, A/S, NV, P.T., S.A., AS, Industrias, Gesellschaft, Koninklijke, Kongl, and Oy) are ignored and the company is sorted on the following word. Similarly, foreign-language words (Grupo, Gruppo, Compagnie, Sociedad, etc.) that begin foreign company names are ignored and the names are sorted by the key word that follows.

INDUSTRY INDEX

Companies are listed alphabetically within industry types. Similar types are grouped under industry categories. For example, Appliances and Housewares are found under the category Consumer Products Manufacturers, while Dairy Products and Fish and Seafood are found under the category Food. For your convenience, a listing of Hoover's industry categories and the pages on which each begins can be found on page 424.

Hoover's Handbook of

Emerging Companies

A List-Lover's Compendium

The Top 100 Companies in Five-Year Sales Growth
in *Hoover's Handbook of Emerging Companies 2010*

Rank	Company	Five-Year Annualized Sales Growth (%)	Rank	Company	Five-Year Annualized Sales Growth (%)	Rank	Company	Five-Year Annualized Sales Growth (%)
1	Aircastle Limited	773.7	36	Duff & Phelps	89.3	71	CyberSource Corporation	52.8
2	Infinera Corporation	442.4	37	Prospect Capital	87.7	72	Hill International	52.7
3	Summer Infant	427.9	38	Cavium Networks	85.0	73	CardioNet, Inc.	52.6
4	Genco Shipping & Trading	282.2	39	iRobot Corporation	83.5	74	LoopNet, Inc.	52.3
5	Genoptix, Inc.	258.9	40	Illumina, Inc.	82.9	75	Bill Barrett Corporation	52.3
6	Concho Resources	249.0	41	GeoResources, Inc.	81.5	76	Double Eagle Petroleum	52.1
7	NewStar Financial	217.2	42	Legacy Reserves	80.3	77	TransMontaigne Partners	51.7
8	Rackspace Hosting	215.6	43	BreitBurn Energy Partners	80.2	78	Netezza Corporation	50.9
9	Alexion Pharmaceuticals	210.3	44	Virtual Radiologic	78.4	79	VSE Corporation	50.7
10	Echo Global Logistics	202.9	45	DuPont Fabros Technology	78.0	80	Southern National Bancorp	50.6
11	Bridgepoint Education	201.1	46	American CareSource	76.6	81	Perficient, Inc.	50.3
12	Digital Ally	182.0	47	Grand Canyon Education	76.5	82	SolarWinds, Inc.	49.4
13	IMPAX Laboratories	181.0	48	Cbeyond, Inc.	75.5	83	Allion Healthcare	47.9
14	GT Solar	178.4	49	Penn Virginia Resource Partners	73.8	84	Immunomedics, Inc.	47.5
15	ViroPharma Incorporated	170.6	50	Superior Well Services	72.4	85	Contango Oil & Gas	47.1
16	Cubist Pharmaceuticals	159.3	51	EV Energy Partners	71.9	86	American Public Education	46.7
17	True Religion Apparel	157.2	52	Under Armour	71.1	87	Shutterfly, Inc.	46.7
18	Cornerstone Therapeutics	130.4	53	Deltek, Inc.	68.4	88	IPG Photonics	46.7
19	Arena Resources	124.1	54	LHC Group	67.7	89	Questcor Pharmaceuticals	46.5
20	Houston American Energy	121.2	55	Life Partners Holdings	66.1	90	Vocus, Inc.	46.5
21	Energy Recovery	120.7	56	DivX, Inc.	64.9	91	Natural Gas Services	46.4
22	SeaBright Insurance	119.1	57	Accuray Incorporated	64.2	92	Western Gas Partners	46.3
23	Transcept Pharmaceuticals	115.6	58	Rosetta Stone	62.9	93	Monolithic Power Systems	46.0
24	Dice Holdings	108.9	59	salesforce.com	62.2	94	Goodrich Petroleum	45.9
25	Diamond Hill Investment	108.2	60	AmTrust Financial	62.0	95	ExlService Holdings	45.6
26	Hiland Partners	105.4	61	DigitalGlobe, Inc.	61.4	96	Tower Group	45.3
27	NightHawk Radiology	104.4	62	NetLogic Microsystems	59.6	97	IntercontinentalExchange	45.3
28	Acme Packet	103.9	63	Allegiant Travel	58.7	98	Masimo Corporation	45.0
29	Argan, Inc.	100.6	64	Intuitive Surgical	57.0	99	Cal Dive International	44.6
30	SXC Health Solutions	97.5	65	Hansen Natural	56.4	100	DealerTrack Holdings	44.4
31	Idera Pharmaceuticals	96.5	66	Basic Energy Services	56.0			
32	Sucampo Pharmaceuticals	93.8	67	Pinnacle Financial Partners	55.8			
33	Approach Resources	93.5	68	Ultra Petroleum	54.9			
34	InnerWorkings, Inc.	91.7	69	ATP Oil & Gas	54.5			
35	BioMarin Pharmaceutical	89.6	70	Alkermes, Inc.	52.9			

Note: These rates are compounded annualized increases in sales growth for the most current fiscal years and may have resulted from acquisitions or one-time gains. If the company has been public for less than six years, sales growth is for the years available.

SOURCE: HOOVER'S, INC., DATABASE, JANUARY 2010

The Top 100 Companies in One-Year Sales Growth
in *Hoover's Handbook of Emerging Companies 2010*

Rank	Company	One-Year Sales Growth (%)	Rank	Company	One-Year Sales Growth (%)	Rank	Company	One-Year Sales Growth (%)
1	BreitBurn Energy Partners	969.9	36	Questcor Pharmaceuticals	91.2	71	True Religion Apparel	55.8
2	SXC Health Solutions	825.9	37	Ultralife Corporation	85.1	72	American Public Education	55.0
3	Immunomedics, Inc.	710.8	38	NewStar Financial	83.0	73	Deckers Outdoor	53.6
4	Cornerstone Therapeutics	403.1	39	DigitalGlobe, Inc.	81.4	74	NASB Financial	53.1
5	Maxygen, Inc.	334.1	40	Concho Resources	81.4	75	BofI Holding	53.1
6	Transcept Pharmaceuticals	262.9	41	Spire Corporation	78.9	76	Aircastle Limited	52.9
7	Alexion Pharmaceuticals	259.9	42	Image Sensing Systems	75.5	77	TeleCommunication Systems	52.6
8	IMPAX Laboratories	257.3	43	Hi-Tech Pharmacal	75.3	78	Rosetta Stone	52.5
9	Infinity Pharmaceuticals	240.4	44	Ebix, Inc.	74.8	79	Repligen Corporation	52.3
10	Idera Pharmaceuticals	230.0	45	Greatbatch, Inc.	71.5	80	Odyssey HealthCare	52.1
11	Double Eagle Petroleum	188.4	46	Digital Ally	68.0	81	Pinnacle Financial Partners	51.6
12	DuPont Fabros Technology	183.4	47	Equinix, Inc.	68.0	82	SolarWinds, Inc.	50.9
13	Western Gas Partners	168.4	48	Coinstar, Inc.	66.9	83	NuStar GP Holdings	50.6
14	Bridgepoint Education	154.7	49	STR Holdings	65.9	84	Jefferson Bancshares	50.4
15	GeoResources, Inc.	150.3	50	DXP Enterprises	65.8	85	Eagle Bulk Shipping	48.6
16	American CareSource	148.1	51	CNX Gas	65.4	86	Superior Well Services	48.5
17	BioMarin Pharmaceutical	143.8	52	Southside Bancshares	65.1	87	MedAssets, Inc.	48.4
18	Isramco, Inc.	128.9	53	CardioNet, Inc.	65.1	88	Netezza Corporation	48.2
19	GT Solar	121.6	54	Continental Resources	65.0	89	Cubist Pharmaceuticals	47.2
20	Genco Shipping & Trading	118.7	55	Lannett Company	64.4	90	Energy Recovery	47.2
21	Quicksilver Gas Services	117.5	56	StellarOne Corporation	64.3	91	Rackspace Hosting	46.9
22	Echo Global Logistics	112.4	57	Contango Oil & Gas	63.7	92	Monarch Financial Holdings	46.3
23	Houston American Energy	112.0	58	Grand Canyon Education	62.4	93	Pioneer Southwest Energy Partners	46.3
24	Infinera Corporation	111.1	59	Innophos Holdings	61.5	94	Intuitive Surgical	45.6
25	Arena Resources	108.7	60	Almost Family	60.9	95	Symmetry Medical	45.5
26	Approach Resources	104.3	61	DG FastChannel	60.8	96	InnerWorkings, Inc.	45.3
27	Petroleum Development	99.7	62	Green Mountain Coffee Roasters	60.5	97	Hudson City Bancorp	45.2
28	EV Energy Partners	99.3	63	Penn Virginia Resource Partners	60.5	98	ITC Holdings Corp.	45.0
29	Genoptix, Inc.	96.0	64	Washington Federal	60.3	99	Hawkins, Inc.	44.8
30	CyberSource Corporation	95.7	65	VSE Corporation	59.8	100	Black Hills Corporation	44.5
31	Intrepid Potash	94.5	66	Cavium Networks	59.8			
32	Summer Infant	94.4	67	Titan Machinery	59.4			
33	Goodrich Petroleum	94.2	68	NetScout Systems	58.3			
34	Legacy Reserves	92.0	69	Bill Barrett Corporation	58.3			
35	Ultra Petroleum	91.4	70	Illumina, Inc.	56.3			

Note: These rates are for sales growth for the most current fiscal year and may have resulted from acquisitions or one-time gains.

SOURCE: HOOVER'S, INC., DATABASE, JANUARY 2010

The Top 100 Companies in Five-Year Net Income Growth
in *Hoover's Handbook of Emerging Companies 2010*

Rank	Company	Five-Year Net Income Growth (%)	Rank	Company	Five-Year Net Income Growth (%)	Rank	Company	Five-Year Net Income Growth (%)
1	DuPont Fabros Technology	388.6	36	DXP Enterprises	65.3	71	Calgon Carbon	53.5
2	GulfMark Offshore	229.9	37	TransDigm Group	64.3	72	Allscripts-Misys Healthcare Solutions	53.0
3	Innophos Holdings	221.8	38	Pinnacle Financial Partners	64.1	73	ENGlobal Corporation	52.8
4	Genco Shipping & Trading	213.2	39	LSB Industries	63.8	74	Bare Escentuals	52.7
5	Energy Recovery	210.9	40	Dril-Quip, Inc.	63.6	75	Allegiant Travel	52.4
6	Summer Infant	153.7	41	Hiland Holdings	63.5	76	Deckers Outdoor	51.7
7	Arena Resources	153.4	42	Sun Hydraulics	63.5	77	Contango Oil & Gas	51.1
8	Somanetics Corporation	153.2	43	Buffalo Wild Wings	63.3	78	Almost Family	50.7
9	EV Energy Partners	142.3	44	American Public Education	62.9	79	MedAssets, Inc.	50.6
10	Newpark Resources	138.4	45	Western Gas Partners	62.8	80	Informatica Corporation	50.3
11	AmTrust Financial	126.2	46	Perficient, Inc.	61.9	81	RPC, Inc.	50.2
12	Holly Energy Partners	111.5	47	AeroVironment, Inc.	61.5	82	Astronics Corporation	50.2
13	LHC Group	106.7	48	Life Partners Holdings	61.2	83	Medallion Financial	50.0
14	Legacy Reserves	103.8	49	LoopNet, Inc.	60.8	84	Cabot Oil & Gas	49.8
15	Goodrich Petroleum	103.5	50	Hornbeck Offshore Services	59.9	85	EZCORP, Inc.	49.7
16	Atwood Oceanics	101.2	51	Double Eagle Petroleum	59.7	86	Hittite Microwave	49.5
17	American Italian Pasta	96.7	52	Servotronics, Inc.	59.5	87	Optical Cable	49.0
18	GeoResources, Inc.	93.3	53	Cal Dive International	58.9	88	Superior Well Services	48.9
19	Titan Machinery	93.2	54	MWI Veterinary Supply	58.4	89	Green Mountain Coffee Roasters	48.3
20	BreitBurn Energy Partners	91.7	55	Layne Christensen	57.9	90	Spartan Motors	48.1
21	InnerWorkings, Inc.	87.0	56	AZZ incorporated	57.9	91	K-Tron International	47.5
22	Infinity Pharmaceuticals	84.8	57	L. B. Foster	57.0	92	The Navigators Group	46.4
23	PHI, Inc.	84.5	58	VSE Corporation	56.9	93	Capella Education	45.6
24	Hansen Natural	78.9	59	Virtual Radiologic	56.7	94	Sykes Enterprises	45.5
25	Signature Bank	77.0	60	NightHawk Radiology	56.5	95	Rick's Cabaret	45.4
26	Ebix, Inc.	74.2	61	HMS Holdings	56.2	96	Willis Lease Finance	44.7
27	Innodata Isogen	72.3	62	Northwest Pipe	56.0	97	Clayton Williams Energy	44.1
28	American Science and Engineering	71.8	63	Ultra Petroleum	55.7	98	Dolby Laboratories	43.6
29	Under Armour	68.6	64	Tower Group	55.6	99	Immucor, Inc.	43.6
30	Cumberland Pharmaceuticals	68.2	65	Intrepid Potash	55.5	100	Hill International	43.5
31	Forrester Research	67.7	66	Lufkin Industries	55.5			
32	Boardwalk Pipeline	67.2	67	SWS Group	54.3			
33	Natural Gas Services	67.0	68	VASCO Data Security	54.1			
34	Concur Technologies	66.6	69	IntercontinentalExchange	54.0			
35	salesforce.com	65.5	70	Tennessee Commerce Bancorp	54.0			

Note: These rates are compounded annualized increases in net income for the most current fiscal years and may have resulted from acquisitions or one-time gains. If the company has been public for less than six years, net income growth is for the years available.

SOURCE: HOOVER'S, INC., DATABASE, JANUARY 2010

The Top 100 Companies in One-Year Net Income Growth
in *Hoover's Handbook of Emerging Companies 2010*

Rank	Company	One-Year Net Income Growth (%)	Rank	Company	One-Year Net Income Growth (%)	Rank	Company	One-Year Net Income Growth (%)
1	Internet Brands	3,766.7	36	Hiland Partners	223.8	71	CARBO Ceramics	104.6
2	Volterra Semiconductor	2,283.3	37	Energy Conversion Devices	220.5	72	On Assignment	104.3
3	EV Energy Partners	2,273.7	38	Wright Medical Group	220.0	73	NASB Financial	101.1
4	Clayton Williams Energy	2,241.7	39	Quicksilver Gas Services	218.1	74	Orchids Paper Products	100.0
5	Addus HomeCare	1,900.0	40	AboveNet, Inc.	206.5	75	Lumber Liquidators	95.6
6	Netezza Corporation	1,475.0	41	SonoSite, Inc.	198.6	76	Sucampo Pharmaceuticals	89.4
7	CTI Industries	1,100.0	42	Ecology and Environment	188.9	77	KMG Chemicals	88.9
8	Continental Resources	1,022.4	43	Maine & Maritimes Corporation	187.5	78	Metro Bancorp	84.3
9	Duff & Phelps	940.0	44	Datalink Corporation	183.3	79	American Public Education	84.1
10	Genoptix, Inc.	851.5	45	Harmonic Inc.	173.5	80	Southside Bancshares	83.8
11	OPNET Technologies	840.0	46	Western Gas Partners	172.1	81	Willis Lease Finance	83.4
12	Approach Resources	766.7	47	Hawkins, Inc.	161.5	82	Ormat Technologies	81.8
13	Bridgepoint Education	700.0	48	Monolithic Power Systems	160.2	83	Natus Medical	78.6
14	Thoratec Corporation	603.1	49	Clearfield, Inc.	153.3	84	Chart Industries	78.5
15	Vocus, Inc.	590.0	50	Calgon Carbon	151.0	85	CNX Gas	76.2
16	CEVA, Inc.	561.5	51	Green Mountain Coffee Roasters	150.7	86	Furmanite Corporation	75.2
17	STR Holdings	485.4	52	ATP Oil & Gas	150.4	87	Synaptics Incorporated	74.6
18	Microtune, Inc.	481.8	53	Jacksonville Bancorp	150.0	88	Spartan Motors	74.3
19	Image Sensing Systems	455.6	54	Wright Express	147.3	89	El Paso Pipeline Partners	73.5
20	Rosetta Stone	434.6	55	Ultralife Corporation	144.6	90	TransMontaigne Partners	73.0
21	Intrepid Potash	380.5	56	GT Solar	143.8	91	Stifel Financial	72.4
22	CryoLife, Inc.	370.0	57	Arena Resources	143.0	92	Echo Global Logistics	70.6
23	American Italian Pasta	362.3	58	Penn Virginia Resource Partners	136.4	93	Optical Cable	69.2
24	Grand Canyon Education	346.7	59	salesforce.com	135.9	94	Pegasystems Inc.	66.7
25	CyberSource Corporation	345.8	60	Albany Molecular Research	131.5	95	United Financial Bancorp	65.9
26	GeoResources, Inc.	335.5	61	Allion Healthcare	127.3	96	Innodata Isogen	65.2
27	Sapient Corporation	311.2	62	Hiland Holdings	125.0	97	Berkshire Hills Bancorp	64.4
28	Bill Barrett Corporation	301.5	63	Align Technology	124.1	98	StoneMor Partners	64.3
29	Fuel Systems Solutions	291.5	64	Spectra Energy Partners	123.6	99	SolarWinds, Inc.	64.0
30	Neutral Tandem	281.0	65	Skilled Healthcare Group	117.5	100	eResearchTechnology	63.4
31	Titan Machinery	254.9	66	Jefferson Bancshares	116.7			
32	Cubist Pharmaceuticals	253.0	67	Ebix, Inc.	115.0			
33	SeaChange International	244.8	68	Almost Family	114.5			
34	Petroleum Development	241.3	69	Natural Resource Partners	109.9			
35	American Medical Systems	230.2	70	Terra Nitrogen	107.4			

Note: These rates are for net income for the most current fiscal year and may have resulted from acquisitions or one-time gains.

SOURCE: HOOVER'S, INC., DATABASE, JANUARY 2010

The Top 100 Companies in Five-Year Employment Growth
in *Hoover's Handbook of Emerging Companies 2010*

Rank	Company	Five-Year Annualized Employment Growth (%)	Rank	Company	Five-Year Annualized Employment Growth (%)	Rank	Company	Five-Year Annualized Employment Growth (%)
1	Summer Infant	284.1	36	Monolithic Power Systems	41.0	71	Lifeway Foods	29.5
2	Eagle Bulk Shipping	233.5	37	Allegiant Travel	40.9	72	Huron Consulting	29.3
3	AboveNet, Inc.	187.1	38	Bare Escentuals	40.9	73	Concur Technologies	29.2
4	CKX, Inc.	163.0	39	Cavium Networks	40.5	74	Buffalo Wild Wings	28.9
5	Echo Global Logistics	125.7	40	AGA Medical Holdings	40.3	75	Titan Machinery	28.6
6	True Religion Apparel	125.1	41	BreitBurn Energy Partners	39.3	76	Netezza Corporation	28.4
7	Grand Canyon Education	94.4	42	Prospect Capital	38.4	77	Team, Inc.	28.0
8	Rackspace Hosting	89.4	43	Aircastle Limited	37.9	78	FLIR Systems	28.0
9	Digital Ally	77.8	44	Genoptix, Inc.	36.8	79	Sucampo Pharmaceuticals	28.0
10	InnerWorkings, Inc.	70.3	45	SXC Health Solutions	36.3	80	Southern National Bancorp	28.0
11	CyberSource Corporation	70.2	46	Hampton Roads Bankshares	36.2	81	Cornerstone Therapeutics	27.3
12	SonoSite, Inc.	66.5	47	Rosetta Stone	36.1	82	Health Grades	26.9
13	Under Armour	65.9	48	Argan, Inc.	35.7	83	Somanetics Corporation	26.8
14	Onyx Pharmaceuticals	65.2	49	First Mercury Financial	35.5	84	NetLogic Microsystems	26.7
15	GT Solar	64.3	50	GeoResources, Inc.	34.1	85	Cumberland Pharmaceuticals	26.7
16	Arena Resources	58.9	51	Sapient Corporation	33.8	86	comScore, Inc.	26.7
17	Hill International	55.6	52	Otelco Inc.	33.6	87	AngioDynamics, Inc.	26.6
18	Double Eagle Petroleum	54.0	53	DXP Enterprises	32.8	88	Medicis Pharmaceutical	26.4
19	First Clover Leaf Financial	53.4	54	Energy Recovery	32.8	89	Intuitive Surgical	26.4
20	Perficient, Inc.	51.8	55	VASCO Data Security	32.8	90	ITC Holdings Corp.	26.3
21	Superior Well Services	50.7	56	Red Hat	32.7	91	Syntel, Inc.	26.2
22	Pinnacle Financial Partners	50.0	57	Diamond Hill Investment	32.4	92	Integra LifeSciences	26.0
23	Allscripts-Misys Healthcare Solutions	49.2	58	Vocus, Inc.	32.1	93	Advanced Battery Technologies	25.9
24	Hansen Natural	49.0	59	Coinstar, Inc.	31.7	94	Transcend Services	25.7
25	salesforce.com	47.1	60	CNX Gas	31.7	95	Goodrich Petroleum	25.7
26	Riverbed Technology	46.8	61	Quality Systems	31.7	96	NewStar Financial	25.4
27	Dolan Media	46.7	62	Monarch Financial Holdings	31.5	97	Shutterfly, Inc.	25.4
28	AmTrust Financial	46.5	63	Cbeyond, Inc.	31.5	98	Cogent, Inc.	25.1
29	Illumina, Inc.	45.4	64	IntercontinentalExchange	31.3	99	Iconix Brand Group	24.9
30	Concho Resources	45.2	65	Fuel Systems Solutions	31.2	100	Image Sensing Systems	24.8
31	Prospect Medical Holdings	44.2	66	Natural Gas Services	31.0			
32	IMPAX Laboratories	43.8	67	Natus Medical	30.9			
33	Legacy Reserves	43.7	68	VSE Corporation	30.9			
34	Atheros Communications	42.4	69	SolarWinds, Inc.	30.7			
35	Deckers Outdoor	42.2	70	NightHawk Radiology	30.2			

Note: These rates are compounded annualized increases in employment growth for
the most current fiscal years and may have resulted from acquisitions or one-time gains.
If the company has been public for less than six years, employment growth is for the
years available.

SOURCE: HOOVER'S, INC., DATABASE, JANUARY 2010

The Top 40 Companies in Five-Year Stock Appreciation
in *Hoover's Handbook of Emerging Companies 2010*

Rank	Company	Five-Year Annualized Stock Appreciation (%)	Rank	Company	Five-Year Annualized Stock Appreciation (%)	Rank	Company	Five-Year Annualized Stock Appreciation (%)
1	CKX, Inc.	161.5	16	Intuitive Surgical	49.4	31	ViroPharma Incorporated	36.3
2	Hansen Natural	99.9	17	Illumina, Inc.	49.1	32	Houston American Energy	35.9
3	ArcSight, Inc.	96.4	18	DXP Enterprises	48.1	33	Hawk Corporation	35.4
4	Terra Nitrogen	80.2	19	Clean Harbors	48.1	34	Life Partners Holdings	35.0
5	Green Mountain Coffee Roasters	73.7	20	Contango Oil & Gas	44.9	35	VASCO Data Security	34.6
6	Dynamic Materials	66.7	21	VSE Corporation	42.7	36	K-Tron International	34.0
7	Advocat Inc.	64.2	22	Sun Hydraulics	42.4	37	Alexion Pharmaceuticals	33.9
8	Almost Family	58.7	23	Ebix, Inc.	42.3	38	Iconix Brand Group	33.5
9	Diamond Hill Investment	56.4	24	Goodrich Petroleum	41.8	39	Graham Corp.	33.4
10	Arena Resources	56.2	25	LMI Aerospace	41.7	40	Sterling Construction	32.5
11	Capella Education	55.7	26	VAALCO Energy	39.7			
12	Advanced Battery Technologies	54.7	27	Isramco, Inc.	38.3			
13	IEC Electronics	51.8	28	L. B. Foster	36.9			
14	True Religion Apparel	51.5	29	EZCORP, Inc.	36.3			
15	HMS Holdings	51.0	30	Stifel Financial	36.3			

Note: These rates are compounded annualized increases based on fiscal year-end closing prices. If the company has been public for less than six years, stock appreciation is for the years available.

SOURCE: HOOVER'S, INC., DATABASE, JANUARY 2010

The Top 40 Companies in Market Value
in *Hoover's Handbook of Emerging Companies 2010*

Rank	Company	Market Value ($ mil.)	Rank	Company	Market Value ($ mil.)	Rank	Company	Market Value ($ mil.)
1	Hudson City Bancorp	8,384	16	Green Mountain Coffee Roasters	3,224	31	Interactive Data	2,325
2	People's United Financial	6,209	17	Alexion Pharmaceuticals	3,205	32	IHS Inc.	2,295
3	IntercontinentalExchange	6,039	18	F5 Networks	3,142	33	Atwood Oceanics	2,266
4	Ultra Petroleum	5,226	19	ResMed Inc.	3,053	34	ITC Holdings Corp.	2,217
5	Intuitive Surgical	4,850	20	Cree, Inc.	3,047	35	Onyx Pharmaceuticals	2,123
6	FLIR Systems	4,657	21	Strayer Education	3,004	36	IDEXX Labs	2,114
7	Stericycle, Inc.	4,387	22	Hansen Natural	2,987	37	Gen-Probe Incorporated	2,103
8	Dolby Laboratories	4,355	23	Cabot Oil & Gas	2,695	38	Equinix, Inc.	2,074
9	CNX Gas	4,122	24	FactSet Research Systems	2,604	39	Wesco Financial	2,050
10	TFS Financial	3,670	25	Akamai Technologies	2,585	40	UMB Financial	1,986
11	Continental Resources	3,518	26	Red Hat	2,571			
12	ITT Educational Services	3,509	27	Waste Connections	2,485			
13	Boardwalk Pipeline	3,424	28	ANSYS, Inc.	2,474			
14	salesforce.com	3,324	29	TransDigm Group	2,440			
15	Illumina, Inc.	3,259	30	Capitol Federal Financial	2,439			

Note: These values are based on the latest available fiscal year-end stock price and the number of shares outstanding.

SOURCE: HOOVER'S, INC., DATABASE, JANUARY 2010

The Top 40 Companies with the Highest Profit Margin
in *Hoover's Handbook of Emerging Companies 2010*

Rank	Company	Profit Margin (%)	Rank	Company	Profit Margin (%)	Rank	Company	Profit Margin (%)
1	EV Energy Partners	108.8	16	Terra Nitrogen	46.8	31	Intrepid Potash	34.4
2	NuStar GP Holdings	95.3	17	Atwood Oceanics	42.7	32	Quicksilver Gas Services	33.8
3	El Paso Pipeline Partners	81.1	18	Questcor Pharmaceuticals	42.5	33	Dolby Laboratories	33.8
4	Spectra Energy Partners	81.1	19	NVE Corporation	41.9	34	Continental Resources	33.4
5	Legacy Reserves	73.4	20	Arena Resources	40.0	35	Eagle Bulk Shipping	33.2
6	TC PipeLines	69.8	21	Alkermes, Inc.	39.9	36	Wright Express	32.4
7	Goodrich Petroleum	63.0	22	Cubist Pharmaceuticals	39.2	37	Iconix Brand Group	32.4
8	Pioneer Southwest Energy Partners	62.0	23	Ultra Petroleum	38.2	38	Capitol Federal Financial	32.3
9	Natural Resource Partners	58.3	24	Versant Corporation	37.5	39	CryoLife, Inc.	31.3
10	Transcept Pharmaceuticals	57.4	25	Boardwalk Pipeline	37.5	40	CNX Gas	30.3
11	Royal Gold	51.9	26	IntercontinentalExchange	37.0			
12	GulfMark Offshore	47.5	27	Ebix, Inc.	36.5			
13	BreitBurn Energy Partners	47.1	28	Cogent, Inc.	36.0			
14	Medallion Financial	46.9	29	Advanced Battery Technologies	35.6			
15	Hudson City Bancorp	46.9	30	Prospect Capital	34.9			

Note: These values are based on the latest available fiscal year-end net income and sales.

SOURCE: HOOVER'S, INC., DATABASE, JANUARY 2010

The Top 40 Companies with the Highest Return on Equity
in *Hoover's Handbook of Emerging Companies 2010*

Rank	Company	Return on Equity (%)	Rank	Company	Return on Equity (%)	Rank	Company	Return on Equity (%)
1	Immunomedics, Inc.	749.8	16	Spire Corporation	43.2	31	Alkermes, Inc.	35.3
2	ITT Educational Services	157.1	17	Intrepid Potash	43.1	32	The Gymboree Corporation	34.5
3	Innophos Holdings	144.2	18	Bidz.com, Inc.	42.7	33	American Italian Pasta	34.4
4	Corporate Executive Board	105.7	19	Ultra Petroleum	42.6	34	Quality Systems	34.2
5	GT Solar	101.4	20	Align Technology	42.1	35	Versant Corporation	33.7
6	Cubist Pharmaceuticals	82.7	21	Ebix, Inc.	41.9	36	LSB Industries	33.4
7	Life Partners Holdings	81.4	22	Continental Resources	40.8	37	Cumberland Pharmaceuticals	33.2
8	TeleCommunication Systems	72.8	23	CryoLife, Inc.	40.6	38	Unify Corporation	32.6
9	Vascular Solutions	72.6	24	Syntel, Inc.	39.9	39	Synaptics Incorporated	32.4
10	Questcor Pharmaceuticals	65.0	25	ATP Oil & Gas	38.9	40	PetMed Express	32.4
11	Clayton Williams Energy	59.1	26	Cornerstone Therapeutics	38.7			
12	Transcept Pharmaceuticals	53.6	27	Advocat Inc.	37.6			
13	CSG Systems International	53.2	28	True Religion Apparel	37.4			
14	Wright Express	51.2	29	American Public Education	37.2			
15	Strayer Education	44.3	30	Health Grades	35.8			

Note: These values are based on the latest available fiscal year-end net income and average total equity.

SOURCE: HOOVER'S, INC., DATABASE, JANUARY 2010

The Top 40 Companies with the Highest P/E Ratios
in *Hoover's Handbook of Emerging Companies 2010*

Rank	Company	P/E High	Rank	Company	P/E High	Rank	Company	P/E High
1	Onyx Pharmaceuticals	1,945	16	Luminex Corporation	338	31	Medicis Pharmaceutical	150
2	Accuray Incorporated	908	17	Cbeyond, Inc.	330	32	Brooklyn Federal Bancorp	148
3	DealerTrack Holdings	759	18	Mac-Gray Corporation	322	33	Fox Chase Bancorp	147
4	iRobot Corporation	747	19	Energy Conversion Devices	287	34	Signature Bank	145
5	Cavium Networks	665	20	Hampden Bancorp	283	35	BioMarin Pharmaceutical	141
6	Epicor Software	632	21	BancTrust Financial	281	36	Lifeway Foods	141
7	Houston American Energy	599	22	TFS Financial	275	37	PMFG, Inc.	140
8	PrimeEnergy Corporation	588	23	Idera Pharmaceuticals	260	38	Abington Bancorp	138
9	Power Integrations	583	24	NetLogic Microsystems	252	39	CyberSource Corporation	136
10	FalconStor Software	525	25	First Capital Bancorp	238	40	Shutterfly, Inc.	132
11	NeuStar, Inc.	509	26	JDA Software Group	233			
12	Blackboard Inc.	500	27	salesforce.com	215			
13	TheStreet.com, Inc.	492	28	Tejon Ranch	193			
14	TechTarget, Inc.	387	29	Riverbed Technology	184			
15	Wright Medical Group	370	30	Rubicon Technology	184			

Note: These values are based on the latest available fiscal year earnings per share and the highest stock price for that fiscal year.

SOURCE: HOOVER'S, INC., DATABASE, JANUARY 2010

The Top 40 Companies with the Lowest P/E Ratios
in *Hoover's Handbook of Emerging Companies 2010*

Rank	Company	P/E Low	Rank	Company	P/E Low	Rank	Company	P/E Low
1	Clearfield, Inc.	1	16	TeleCommunication Systems	2	31	Willis Lease Finance	3
2	Transcept Pharmaceuticals	1	17	Genco Shipping & Trading	2	32	Hornbeck Offshore Services	3
3	EV Energy Partners	1	18	Chart Industries	2	33	Air T, Inc.	3
4	BreitBurn Energy Partners	1	19	Hiland Partners	2	34	Tennessee Commerce Bancorp	3
5	Cornerstone Therapeutics	1	20	KMG Chemicals	2	35	Atwood Oceanics	3
6	Innophos Holdings	1	21	GT Solar	3	36	Diodes Incorporated	3
7	ATP Oil & Gas	1	22	Clayton Williams Energy	3	37	Broadway Financial	3
8	Legacy Reserves	1	23	Wright Express	3	38	Infinity Pharmaceuticals	3
9	Petroleum Development	2	24	American Italian Pasta	3	39	ENGlobal Corporation	3
10	Spartan Motors	2	25	GulfMark Offshore	3	40	Bidz.com, Inc.	4
11	Advocat Inc.	2	26	American Dental Partners	3			
12	Aircastle Limited	2	27	Bare Escentuals	3			
13	IEC Electronics	2	28	American Railcar Industries	3			
14	Eagle Bulk Shipping	2	29	World Acceptance Corporation	3			
15	Berry Petroleum	2	30	DuPont Fabros Technology	3			

Note: These values are based on the latest available fiscal year earnings per share and the lowest stock price for that fiscal year.

SOURCE: HOOVER'S, INC., DATABASE, JANUARY 2010

FORTUNE SMALL BUSINESS 100

Rank	Company	Total Return to Investors* (%)	Rank	Company	Total Return to Investors* (%)	Rank	Company	Total Return to Investors* (%)
1	Life Partners Holdings	121.0	36	Elecsys Corp.	0.9	71	Spectrum Control	-0.4
2	Universal Insurance Holdings	56.3	37	Integral Systems	9.1	72	Nathan's Famous	6.6
3	HMS Holdings Corp.	60.3	38	Mercer Insurance Group	-4.7	73	Eagle Bulk Shipping	-16.5
4	Ebix Inc.	53.6	39	Bitstream Inc.	6.9	74	Pericom Semiconductor	-11.7
5	DG Fastchannel	32.2	40	Chase Corp.	18.1	75	IntegraMed America	-7.3
6	American Physicians	18.2	41	United States Lime & Mineral	-3.3	76	Amrep Corp.	8.0
7	Transcend Services	64.3	42	Versant Corp.	39.8	77	NIC Inc.	-9.3
8	Female Health	27.3	43	Bolt Technology	-9.4	78	Span-America	5.7
9	Bankrate Inc.	8.8	44	Met-Pro Corp.	16.5	79	Financial Federal Corp.	-5.7
10	Royal Gold Inc.	13.3	45	Abaxis Inc.	-0.9	80	RF Industries	1.9
11	American Ecology	14.3	46	Globecomm Systems	-3.8	81	Specialty Underwriters	-24.7
12	North American Galvanizing	54.7	47	UFP Technologies Inc.	30.7	82	ClearOne Communications	18.0
13	NVE Corp.	21.4	48	WSI Industries	-3.1	83	Somanetics Corp.	-19.8
14	Versar Inc.	5.1	49	Vicon Industries	22.3	84	Actuate Corp.	-1.9
15	Vasco Data Security International	1.6	50	Ecology & Environment Inc.	16.0	85	Anaren Inc.	-8.6
16	Interactive Intelligence	7.9	51	Atrion Corp.	12.9	86	Amtec Systems	-22.0
17	Hittite Microwave	8.4	52	Sifco Industries	15.1	87	Amerigon Inc.	-17.7
18	Mesa Laboratories Inc.	7.4	53	Simulation Plus	-10.8	88	Digi International Inc.	-8.2
19	Willis Lease	4.4	54	StoneMor Partners	-8.2	89	Middlesex Water	3.2
20	Phase Forwad Inc.	8.7	55	Intricon Corp.	-5.3	90	Shenandoah Telephone	30.0
21	Neogen Corp.	21.3	56	KMG Chemicals	-13.6	91	OYO Geospace	-15.0
22	Hi-Shear Tech	53.0	57	Transcat Inc.	13.4	92	Breeze-Eastern	2.8
23	CryoLife Inc.	42.7	58	Datalink Corp.	-6.2	93	CTI Industries	-10.3
24	Exactech Inc.	13.8	59	American Medical Alert	-8.2	94	Image Sense Systems	-21.8
25	Apco Argentina	29.0	60	Ramtron International Corp.	-3.2	95	TGC Industries	-29.8
26	Medifast Inc.	1.8	61	Medtox Scientific	2.7	96	Kewaunee Scientific	1.4
27	Graham Corp.	6.9	62	Landauer Inc.	20.9	97	Artesian Resources	-3.9
28	National Research	21.0	63	HickoryTech	-6.0	98	Electro-Rent	-7.8
29	Key Technology	13.7	64	Connecticut Water Service	2.4	99	Holly Energy Partners	-10.4
30	Sun Hydraulics	15.2	65	Cass Information Systems	16.4	100	Xeta Technologies Inc.	-10.5
31	Natus Medical	-7.1	66	Pennichuck Corp.	3.1			
32	Henry Brothers Electronics	10.2	67	Stratasys Inc.	-4.9			
33	HealthStream	0.0	68	Lacrosse Footwear	5.8			
34	Meridian Bioscience	26.3	69	Angiodynamics	-18.8			
35	Orchids Paper	8.6	70	Dialysis Corp.	-11.3			

*Three-year annualized rate, to 12/31/08.

SOURCE: *FORTUNE SMALL BUSINESS*, JULY/AUGUST 2009

FORTUNE 100 Fastest-Growing Companies

Rank	Company	Three-Year EPS Annual Growth Rate (%)	Rank	Company	Three-Year EPS Annual Growth Rate (%)	Rank	Company	Three-Year EPS Annual Growth Rate (%)
1	Research In Motion	84	36	Guess	78	71	Iconix Brand Group	31
2	Sigma Designs	338	37	LKQ	34	72	Huron Consulting Group	28
3	Sohu.com	78	38	Ctrip.com International	28	73	China Medical Technologies	32
4	Ebix	78	39	Apple	46	74	Royal Gold	21
5	DG FastChannel	308	40	AsiaInfo Holdings	51	75	Ralcorp Holdings	53
6	CF Industries Holdings	328	41	Monsanto	77	76	Team	46
7	Shanda Interactive Entertainment	91	42	NASDAQ OMX Group	67	77	WebMD Health	169
8	Arena Resources	69	43	Synaptics	35	78	Precision Castparts	49
9	Bruker	126	44	GameStop	66	79	Cameron International	48
10	Potash Corp. of Saskatchewan	94	45	Atwood Oceanics	78	80	Amedisys	35
11	Green Mountain Coffee Roasters	52	46	General Cable	87	81	Syntel	40
12	IntercontinentalExchange	47	47	National Oilwell Varco	73	82	Buffalo Wild Wings	37
13	Darling International	169	48	Intuitive Surgical	32	83	Chipotle Mexican Grill	40
14	Millicom International Cellular	151	49	ICON	53	84	Garmin	36
15	Open Text	132	50	BlackRock	27	85	Zoll Medical	56
16	VistaPrint	52	51	TransDigm Group	77	86	Gulfmark Offshore	53
17	Elbit Systems	72	52	Amazon.com	34	87	Atlantic Tele-Network	30
18	ITC Holdings	45	53	GigaMedia	55	88	Sapient	44
19	Pegasystems	73	54	Schering-Plough	73	89	Vasco Data Security International	44
20	HMS Holdings	39	55	PriceSmart	66	90	Cognizant Technology Solutions	37
21	AZZ	70	56	Teva Pharmaceutical Industries	61	91	McDermott International	34
22	Celgene	93	57	FLIR Systems	35	92	Diamond Offshore Drilling	35
23	Natus Medical	127	58	Gilead Sciences	36	93	Catalyst Health Solutions	29
24	Diana Shipping	43	59	Dolby Laboratories	50	94	Helmerich & Payne	40
25	Stifel Financial	39	60	NRG Energy	94	95	True Religion Apparel	26
26	Spartan Motors	56	61	FTI Consulting	30	96	TreeHouse Foods	39
27	Bucyrus International	55	62	Balchem	21	97	Western Digital	34
28	M & F Worldwide	44	63	DreamWorks Animation SKG	59	98	Psychiatric Solutions	42
29	Foster Wheeler	118	64	Marvel Entertainment	48	99	Enbridge	38
30	Transocean	73	65	Quanta Services	53	100	Infosys Technologies	34
31	Lindsay	80	66	Noble	67			
32	Force Protection	35	67	Activision Blizzard	40			
33	ANSYS	62	68	Google	39			
34	LSB Industries	92	69	Thermo Fisher Scientific	25			
35	Deckers Outdoor	41	70	Telvent GIT	32			

Ranked by composite score based on profit and sales growth and three-year total return.

SOURCE: *FORTUNE*, AUGUST 31, 2009

Forbes 200 Best Small Companies

Rank	Company	Five-Year Average ROE (%)	Rank	Company	Five-Year Average ROE (%)	Rank	Company	Five-Year Average ROE (%)
1	Lumber Liquidators	32	51	Dril-Quip	16	101	TIBCO Software	7
2	Allegiant Travel	16	52	NCI	26	102	Digital River	16
3	Quality Systems	35	53	Computer Programs & Systems	37	103	RTI International Metals	11
4	LHC Group	33	54	AeroVironment	23	104	Diodes	19
5	Green Mountain Coffee Roasters	17	55	Meridian Bioscience	25	105	BJ's Restaurants	6
6	Transcend Services	27	56	Dynamic Materials	32	106	Obagi Medical Products	34
7	Rackspace Hosting	17	57	Concur Technologies	16	107	Ladish Company	14
8	NVE	21	58	Aaon	20	108	Quest Software	7
9	American Public Education	29	59	DXP Enterprises	30	109	Raven Industries	28
10	American Science & Engineering	19	60	Portfolio Recovery Associates	20	110	Air T	18
11	Dolby Laboratories	22	61	Air Methods	14	111	Jack Henry & Associates	17
12	HMS Holdings	11	62	Bolt Technology	20	112	Rick's Cabaret International	11
13	Synaptics	21	63	j2 Global Communications	26	113	Anaren	6
14	Jos. A. Bank Clothiers	23	64	Balchem	19	114	Perficient	11
15	PetMed Express	36	65	Citi Trends	21	115	Monro Muffler Brake	12
16	Medifast	14	66	Pre-Paid Legal Services	97	116	Universal Electronics	11
17	Orion Marine Group	22	67	American Physicians Service Group	17	117	MTS Systems	21
18	MSCI	17	68	Sterling Construction	18	118	J&J Snack Foods	11
19	InterDigital	34	69	Team	18	119	Nathan's Famous	11
20	Capella Education	17	70	Hornbeck Offshore Services	13	120	CBIZ	11
21	AZZ	17	71	Lincoln Educational Services	16	121	Volcom	41
22	Middleby	62	72	Powell Industries	6	122	Bovie Medical	14
23	Emergent Biosolutions	22	73	Lufkin Industries	19	123	Landauer	37
24	Hittite Microwave	31	74	Berry Petroleum	29	124	Cass Information Systems	18
25	Almost Family	21	75	K-Tron International	21	125	Knight Transportation	16
26	Wright Express	29	76	Cogent	15	126	Rocky Mountain Chocolate Factory	31
27	Syntel	30	77	Genesee & Wyoming	19	127	Insituform Technologies	5
28	FactSet Research Systems	29	78	Steven Madden	14	128	Shenandoah Telecommunications	13
29	IEC Electronics	24	79	L.B. Foster	21	129	Exponent	13
30	Deckers Outdoor	21	80	ICU Medical	10	130	Twin Disc	16
31	Strayer Education	38	81	Houston Wire & Cable	62	131	Computer Task Group	7
32	Bio-Reference Laboratories	19	82	Carbo Ceramics	16	132	Calavo Growers	11
33	Hawkins	14	83	Royal Gold	9	133	Cantel Medical	6
34	Natural Gas Services Group	13	84	Rochester Medical	19	134	Hibbett Sporting Goods	24
35	GulfMark Offshore	15	85	Ansys	15	135	Argon ST	9
36	F5 Networks	13	86	GeoResources	17	135	ViaSat	9
37	Ensign Group	31	87	Neogen	11	137	Graco	53
38	ICF International	16	88	Liquidity Services	23	138	Gen-Probe	14
39	Buffalo Wild Wings	13	89	Informatica	5	139	Haemonetics	12
40	Chattem	26	90	NIC	12	140	Anika Therapeutics	19
41	LSB Industries	43	91	Sport Supply Group	10	141	Healthcare Services Group	14
42	Pros Holdings	57	92	Dionex	25	142	Comtech Telecommunications	18
43	Somanetics	29	93	Spectrum Control	8	143	Peet's Coffee & Tea	8
44	Arena Resources	22	94	Astronics	16	144	Chase	16
45	NutriSystem	49	95	United States Lime & Minerals	16	145	Integra LifeSciences	10
46	Hi-Shear Technology	21	96	Friedman Industries	18	145	Tyler Technologies	11
47	Atlantic Tele-Network	15	97	Badger Meter	23	147	U.S. Physical Therapy	15
48	Energy Recovery	27	98	Heico	10	148	Ampco-Pittsburgh	11
49	Red Hat	11	99	Zumiez	22	149	II-VI	16
50	National Presto Industries	10	100	Techne	23	150	Heartland Express	18

Ranked by composite score based on growth in sales, earnings, and ROE for the past five years and the latest 12 months.

SOURCE: *FORBES*, NOVEMBER 2, 2009

Forbes 200 Best Small Companies (continued)

Rank	Company	Five-Year Average ROE (%)	Rank	Company	Five-Year Average ROE (%)	Rank	Company	Five-Year Average ROE (%)
151	Adtran	18	171	Multi-Color	16	191	WD-40	20
152	American Reprographics	58	172	Gorman-Rupp	13	192	California Pizza Kitchen	9
153	CoStar Group	7	173	Inter Parfums	13	192	Quidel	9
154	Darling International	18	174	DG FastChannel	3	194	ESCO Technologies	11
155	Cornell	5	175	Pike Electric	12	195	Franklin Electric	15
156	Dorman Products	12	176	Rimage	14	196	Stratasys	12
157	Advisory Board	20	177	Tessco Technologies	10	197	National Healthcare	13
158	Forward Air	24	178	Boston Beer	16	198	Supertex	11
159	Portec Rail Products	11	179	Dover Downs Gaming & Entertainment	26	199	Asset Acceptance Capital	13
160	Forrester Research	7	180	Marten Transport	10	200	Gulf Island Fabrication	12
161	Lindsay	12	181	Eastern	13			
162	Tekelec	7	182	World Wrestling Entertainment	13			
163	JDA Software Group	2	183	National Instruments	13			
164	Rentrak	15	184	Northwest Pipe	10			
165	Amsurg	12	185	Matrix Service	2			
166	Oil-Dri Corp of America	9	186	Kaydon	14			
167	Books-A-Million	11	187	QLogic	13			
168	Young Innovations	13	188	Exactech	11			
169	AngioDynamics	4	189	Communications Systems	7			
170	CPI International	14	190	Navigant Consulting	13			

BusinessWeek's 25 Fastest-Growing Inner City Companies

Rank	Company	City	Five-Year Compound Annual Growth Rate* (%)
1	VisionIT	Detroit	103
2	Pinnacle Technical Resources	Dallas	96
3	Sensis	Los Angeles	97
4	Red Door Interactive	San Diego	75
5	NewBath	New Orleans	70
6	FutureNet Group	Detroit	70
7	Global Technology Resources	Denver	69
8	Navigator Management Partners	Columbus, OH	69
9	AEP Books	Buffalo, NY	64
10	Ascellon Corp.	Baltimore	64
11	Kauffman & Associates	Spokane, WA	63
12	EnviroWaste Services Group	Miami	62
13	Avencia Inc.	Philadelphia	60
14	PepperDash Technology	Allston, MA	59
15	SLR Contracting & Services Co.	Buffalo, NY	59
16	ARS International	Port Allen, LA	58
17	Horizon Staffing Services	East Hartford, CT	58
18	Tucker Technology	Oakland, CA	57
19	Yerba Buena Engineering & Constr	San Francisco	56
20	Percipio Consulting Group	Portland, OR	55
21	comCables	Denver	54
22	Ellicott Dredge Enterprises	Baltimore	53
23	Xantrion	Oakland, CA	52
24	Melissa Joy Manning	Oakland, CA	51
25	Numi Organic Tea	Oakland, CA	50

*From 2003 to 2007

SOURCE: *BUSINESSWEEK SMALLBIZ*, JUNE/JULY 2009

Hoover's Handbook of

Emerging Companies

The Companies

Abaxis, Inc.

Abaxis makes a praxis of analyzing blood. Its two types of point-of-care blood analyzers (one for humans and one for animals) can each perform more than a dozen types of tests. The analyzers are portable, require little training, provide on-the-spot results, and offer built-in quality control and calibration. The company also sells reagent discs used to perform common blood tests. Abaxis markets the systems under the VetScan name in the veterinary market (where it makes most of its sales) and Piccolo in the human medical market. It is developing a wider range of tests to penetrate the human diagnostic market. Abaxis sells its products to veterinarians, hospitals, managed care organizations, and the military.

A direct sales force markets the company's products in the US. Abaxis primarily uses distributors outside the US, though it does have a sales office in Germany.

About 70% of the company's sales are made to veterinarians, though that percentage has been declining, as the company expands its foothold in the human diagnostics market. To that end, Abaxis has introduced some oncology-related tests for the Piccolo xpress, including one that analyzes liver function in patients undergoing chemotherapy. It has also launched a comprehensive metabolic test, as well as a test marketed toward radiology and imaging centers that checks kidney function prior to injection of contrast agents.

In 2007 the company introduced next-generation versions of its blood analyzers, branded VetScan VS2 and Piccolo xpress. Abaxis then supplemented its product line two years later with a veterinary coagulation analyzer under the name Vetscan Vspro and a canine heartworm rapid test.

McKesson Medical-Surgical, Cardinal Health, Henry Schein, and PSS World Medical are among the company's distributors to the human medical market. Animal health distributor DVM Resources (part of Animal Health International) is Abaxis' largest single customer, accounting for more than 10% of sales.

EXECUTIVES

Chairman, President, and CEO:
Clinton H. (Clint) Severson, age 61, $1,056,701 total compensation
COO: Donald P. (Don) Wood, age 57
CTO: Kenneth P. Aron, age 56, $485,431 total compensation
VP Government Affairs and Marketing, Pacific Rim:
Vladimir E. Ostoich, age 64, $482,322 total compensation
VP Finance and CFO: Alberto R. Santa Ines, age 62, $465,180 total compensation
Director Marketing, Medical Diagnostics: Rick Betts
VP North American Medical Sales and Marketing:
Brenton G.A. Hanlon, age 63
Director, Business Development Veterinary Diagnostics: Michael Solomon
VP Veterinary Sales and Marketing, North America:
Martin V. (Marty) Mulroy, age 49, $466,151 total compensation
Auditors: Burr, Pilger & Mayer LLP

LOCATIONS

HQ: Abaxis, Inc.
3240 Whipple Rd., Union City, CA 94587
Phone: 510-675-6500 **Fax:** 510-441-6150
Web: www.abaxis.com

2009 Sales

	$ mil.	% of total
North America	87	83
Europe	15	13
Asia/Pacific & other	4	4
Total	**106**	**100**

PRODUCTS/OPERATIONS

2009 Sales

	$ mil.	% of total
Reagent discs & kits	69	65
Instruments	29	27
Other products	5	5
Development & licensing	3	3
Total	**106**	**100**

2009 Sales by Customer Group

	$ mil.	% of total
Veterinary market	74	70
Medical market	25	24
Other	7	6
Total	**106**	**100**

Selected Products

Piccolo xpress (human blood analyzer)
VetScan VS2 (veterinary blood analyzer)
VetScan i-STAT (handheld analyzer for veterinarians)
VetScan HM5 (blood cell counter)
VetScan VSpro (point-of-care coagulation analyzer)

COMPETITORS

Abbott Labs
Beckman Coulter
Hemagen Diagnostics
Heska
IDEXX Labs
Immucor
Johnson & Johnson
Ortho-Clinical Diagnostics
Quidel
Roche Diagnostics

HISTORICAL FINANCIALS

Company Type: Public

Income Statement

FYE: March 31

	REVENUE ($ mil.)	NET INCOME ($ mil.)	NET PROFIT MARGIN	EMPLOYEES
3/09	105.6	12.0	11.4%	339
3/08	100.6	12.5	12.4%	321
3/07	86.2	10.1	11.7%	265
3/06	68.9	7.5	10.9%	217
3/05	52.8	4.9	9.3%	184
Annual Growth	**18.9%**	**25.1%**	**—**	**16.5%**

2009 Year-End Financials

Debt ratio: —
Return on equity: 10.4%
Cash ($ mil.): 49.2
Current ratio: 9.82
Long-term debt ($ mil.): —
No. of shares (mil.): 22.0
Dividends
Yield: —
Payout: —
Market value ($ mil.): 379.7
R&D as % of sales: —
Advertising as % of sales: —

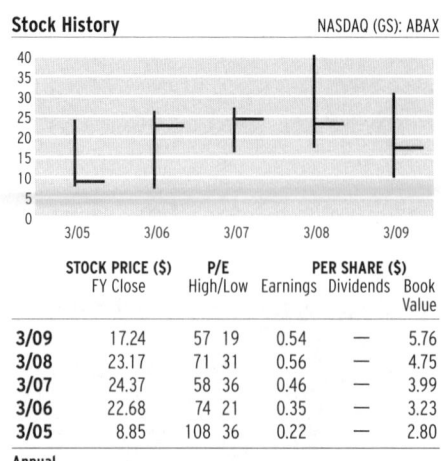

	STOCK PRICE ($) FY Close	P/E High/Low	PER SHARE ($) Earnings	Dividends	Book Value
3/09	17.24	57 19	0.54	—	5.76
3/08	23.17	71 31	0.56	—	4.75
3/07	24.37	58 36	0.46	—	3.99
3/06	22.68	74 21	0.35	—	3.23
3/05	8.85	108 36	0.22	—	2.80
Annual Growth	**18.1%**	**— —**	**25.2%**	**—**	**19.8%**

Abington Bancorp

Abington Bancorp is young, but its bank is old. Formed in 2004, the holding company (formerly Abington Community Bancorp) owns Abington Bank, which was established in 1867. The community bank has about 20 branches in southeastern Pennsylvania, north of Philadelphia. The bank offers such standard products as checking and savings accounts, debit cards, and loans. Residential mortgages account for more than half of the company's loan portfolio, which also includes construction loans, commercial and multi-family real estate loans, and home equity lines of credit.

Abington Bancorp has full-service, limited-service, and loan processing offices in Montgomery, Bucks, and Delaware counties, and is expanding by opening new banking locations.

In 2007 the company completed its conversion from a two-tier mutual holding company structure to a stock holding company structure in order to provide more liquidity of its stock.

EXECUTIVES

Chairman, President, and CEO, Abington Bancorp and Abington Bank: Robert W. White, age 64, $1,016,658 total compensation
SVP and CFO, Abington Bancorp; SVP, CFO, and Treasurer, Abington Bank: Jack J. Sandoski, age 65, $426,338 total compensation
SVP, Abington Bancorp and Abington Bank:
Frank Kovalcheck, age 51, $357,683 total compensation
SVP and Secretary, Abington Bancorp and Abington Bank: Edward W. Gormley, age 60, $183,787 total compensation
VP and Controller: Eric L. Golden, age 34, $135,068 total compensation

LOCATIONS

HQ: Abington Bancorp, Inc.
180 Old York Rd., Jenkintown, PA 19046
Phone: 215-887-3200 **Fax:** 215-887-4100
Web: www.abingtonbankonline.com

COMPETITORS

The Bancorp	Metro Bancorp
Bank of America	PNC Financial
Beneficial Mutual Bancorp	QNB Corp.
Bryn Mawr Bank Corp.	Republic First Bank
Citizens Financial Group	Royal Bancshares
Commerce Group	Sovereign Bank
First Keystone Financial	TF Financial
Firstrust Savings Bank	VIST Financial
Harleysville Savings	WSFS Financial

HISTORICAL FINANCIALS

Company Type: Public

Income Statement
FYE: December 31

	ASSETS ($ mil.)	NET INCOME ($ mil.)	INCOME AS % OF ASSETS	EMPLOYEES
12/08	1,189.8	2.1	0.2%	177
12/07	1,079.7	7.1	0.7%	170
12/06	925.2	6.8	0.7%	148
12/05	844.1	6.3	0.7%	144
12/04	718.0	4.6	0.6%	117
Annual Growth	13.5%	(17.8%)	—	10.9%

2008 Year-End Financials

Equity as % of assets: 20.0%
Return on assets: 0.2%
Return on equity: 0.9%
Long-term debt ($ mil.): 257.1
No. of shares (mil.): 21.5
Market value ($ mil.): 198.7
Dividends
  Yield: 1.6%
  Payout: 166.7%
Sales ($ mil.): 32.8
R&D as % of sales: —
Advertising as % of sales: —

Stock History
NASDAQ (GS): ABBC

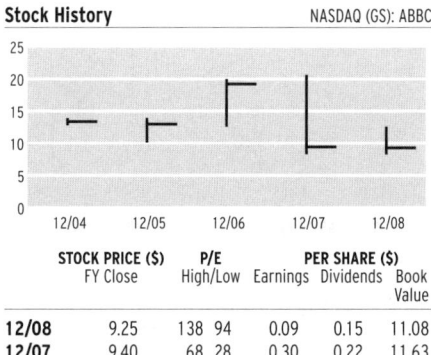

	STOCK PRICE ($) FY Close	P/E High/Low		PER SHARE ($) Earnings	Dividends	Book Value
12/08	9.25	138	94	0.09	0.15	11.08
12/07	9.40	68	28	0.30	0.22	11.63
12/06	19.18	44	28	0.45	0.23	5.31
12/05	12.97	34	25	0.41	0.15	5.46
12/04	13.37	—	—	—	—	5.73
Annual Growth	(8.8%)	—	—	(39.7%)	0.0%	17.9%

AboveNet, Inc.

AboveNet wants to light the way to faster communications. The company operates metro and long-haul fiber-optic networks, providing service to more than a dozen metropolitan markets in the US. It leases dark fiber and provides managed network services to communications carriers and government agencies, as well as high-usage enterprise customers in such industries as financial services, health care, media, and retail. The company also operates a Tier 1 IP network over its metro and long-haul infrastructure that provides customers in North America, Europe, and Japan with data transport and virtual private network (VPN) services.

AboveNet's primary business has historically been the leasing of dark fiber (fiber not yet connected to telecom transmission equipment) to customers who operate their own networks. The company has increasingly looked to its metro transport services, including building custom optical networks for enterprise customers, to grow its revenue.

In addition to its US-based facilities, AboveNet operates a metro network in London. About 10% of its revenues were generated in the UK market in 2008.

EXECUTIVES

President, CEO, and Director: William G. (Bill) LaPerch, age 54, $2,038,628 total compensation
SVP Sales and Marketing: John H. (Joc) Jacquay, age 57, $1,454,763 total compensation
SVP Operations: Douglas M. (Doug) Jendras, age 42, $1,211,540 total compensation
SVP and CFO: Joseph P. Ciavarella, age 54, $876,448 total compensation
SVP and CTO: Rajiv Datta, age 38, $1,217,384 total compensation
SVP, General Counsel, Chief Administrative Officer, and Secretary: Robert J. Sokota, age 45, $1,222,207 total compensation
VP Marketing and Customer Service: Michael A, Brown
Executive Director Business Development and Marketing: MaryBeth Nance
Managing Director, AboveNet Communications UK Ltd.: John Donaldson
Auditors: BDO Seidman, LLP

LOCATIONS

HQ: AboveNet, Inc.
360 Hamilton Ave., White Plains, NY 10601
Phone: 914-421-6700   **Fax:** 914-421-6777
Web: www.above.net

2008 Sales

	$ mil.	% of total
US	288.5	89
UK	36.1	11
Adjustments	(4.7)	—
Total	**319.9**	**100**

COMPETITORS

AT&T
BT
Cable & Wireless
Cinedigm
Cogent Communications
COLT Telecom
Equinix
FiberNet Telecom
Global Crossing
Level 3 Communications
Qwest Communications
Switch and Data Facilities
Verio
Verizon
XO Holdings

HISTORICAL FINANCIALS

Company Type: Public

Income Statement
FYE: December 31

	REVENUE ($ mil.)	NET INCOME ($ mil.)	NET PROFIT MARGIN	EMPLOYEES
12/08	319.9	42.3	13.2%	615
12/07	253.6	13.8	5.4%	549
12/06	236.7	46.4	19.6%	—
Annual Growth	16.3%	(4.5%)	—	12.0%

2008 Year-End Financials

Debt ratio: 11.5%
Return on equity: 16.7%
Cash ($ mil.): 87.1
Current ratio: 1.11
Long-term debt ($ mil.): 32.8
No. of shares (mil.): 24.2
Dividends
  Yield: —
  Payout: —
Market value ($ mil.): 350.8
R&D as % of sales: —
Advertising as % of sales: —

Stock History
NYSE: ABVT

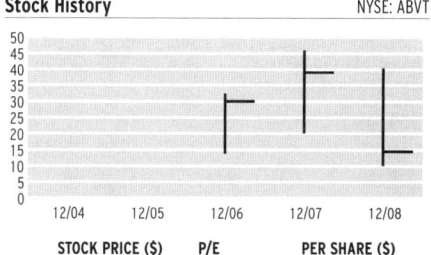

	STOCK PRICE ($) FY Close	P/E High/Low		PER SHARE ($) Earnings	Dividends	Book Value
12/08	14.50	23	6	1.73	—	11.75
12/07	39.00	81	36	0.56	—	9.25
12/06	30.00	16	7	1.97	—	9.01
Annual Growth	(30.5%)	—	—	(6.3%)	—	14.2%

Accuray Incorporated

Accuray's CyberKnife radiosurgery system zaps solid tumors with precisely aimed, high-dose radiation. The system, approved for use in the US, the EU, and several Asian countries, improves upon older radiosurgery systems that have limited mobility and are mostly used to treat brain tumors. Doctors can use CyberKnife to treat tumors anywhere in the body; the system tracks and adjusts for movement in real time, allowing for patient and tumor movement. Procedures with CyberKnife require no anesthesia and can be performed on an outpatient basis. More than 170 of the systems have been installed in hospitals around the world, over 100 of them in the US.

Through a "shared ownership" program, hospitals can reduce their upfront expense to install a CyberKnife system. Once the system is in place, Accuray provides training and technical support, and receives a significant portion of the revenue from each procedure performed. Additional revenues come from service plans and sales of system upgrades.

Accuray employs a direct sales force in the US and uses a combination of its own sales personnel and distributors elsewhere.

The company went public in 2007, with an eye toward using the money for sales and marketing, research and development, and acquisitions. John Adler Jr., a neurosurgeon from Stanford University, founded the company in 1990.

EXECUTIVES

Chairman: Wayne Wu, age 47
President, CEO, and Director: Euan S. Thomson, age 46, $2,521,156 total compensation
SVP and Chief Marketing Officer: Eric P. Lindquist, age 50, $1,126,965 total compensation
SVP Finance: Holly R. Grey, age 36, $416,242 total compensation
SVP, General Counsel, and Secretary: Darren J. Milliken, age 39
SVP and CFO: Derek A. Bertocci, age 56, $317,425 total compensation

SVP and COO: Chris A. Raanes, age 45, $1,109,959 total compensation
SVP Human Resources: Theresa L. Dadone, age 39
General Manager, Japan: Juki Hozumi
Auditors: Grant Thornton LLP

LOCATIONS

HQ: Accuray Incorporated
 1310 Chesapeake Terrace, Sunnyvale, CA 94089
Phone: 408-716-4600   **Fax:** 408-716-4601
Web: www.accuray.com

2009 Sales

	$ mil.	% of total
Americas	171.6	74
Europe	30.9	13
Asia (excluding Japan)	19.8	8
Japan	11.3	5
Total	**233.6**	**100**

PRODUCTS/OPERATIONS

2009 Sales

	$ mil.	% of total
Products	159.3	68
Services	66.3	28
Shared ownership programs	3.7	2
Other	4.3	2
Total	**233.6**	**100**

COMPETITORS

Best Medical International
Integra LifeSciences
Siemens Healthcare
TomoTherapy
Varian Medical Systems

HISTORICAL FINANCIALS

Company Type: Public

Income Statement

FYE: June 30

	REVENUE ($ mil.)	NET INCOME ($ mil.)	NET PROFIT MARGIN	EMPLOYEES
6/09	233.6	0.6	0.3%	458
6/08	210.4	5.4	2.6%	504
6/07	140.5	(6.5)	—	449
6/06	52.9	(33.7)	—	386
6/05	22.4	(25.2)	—	364
Annual Growth	**79.7%**	**—**	**—**	**5.9%**

2009 Year-End Financials

Debt ratio: —
Return on equity: 0.4%
Cash ($ mil.): 36.8
Current ratio: 1.71
Long-term debt ($ mil.): —
No. of shares (mil.): 57.4
Dividends
 Yield: 0.0%
 Payout: —
Market value ($ mil.): 381.2
R&D as % of sales: —
Advertising as % of sales: —

Stock History

NASDAQ (GM): ARAY

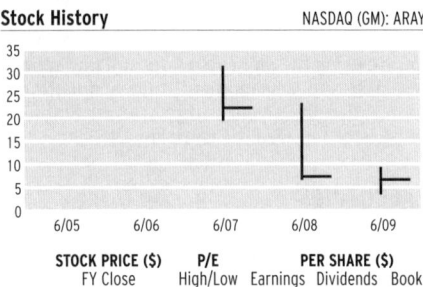

	STOCK PRICE ($) FY Close	P/E High/Low		PER SHARE ($) Earnings	Dividends	Book Value
6/09	6.64	908	370	0.01	0.00	2.68
6/08	7.29	255	76	0.09	0.00	2.28
6/07	22.17	—	—	(0.18)	0.00	2.19
Annual Growth	**(45.3%)**	**—**	**—**	**—**	**—**	**10.8%**

Acme Packet

Acme Packet brings networks together. The company makes communications equipment designed to ensure that advanced network services span multiple IP networks. Acme's family of Net-Net session border controllers (SBCs) are used to connect networks operated by service providers and enterprise customers. SBCs handle interactive services including Voice over Internet Protocol. Acme Packet also provides multiservice security gateways and session routing proxies. The company markets directly and through distribution partnerships with vendors including Ericsson and Sonus Networks. It counts Charter Communications, China Unicom, and Telstra among its customers.

SBCs are typically deployed at the borders between IP networks, such as where the networks of two service providers meet or at the intersection of a service provider's network and its business, residential, and mobile customers. SBCs integrate the control of signaling messages and media flows, complementing the functionality and effectiveness of routers, softswitches, and firewalls that reside within the network.

The company acquired Covergence, a developer of software-based SBCs, for about $23 million in 2009. The purchase extends Acme's product line to address the enterprise market, as Covergence's offerings are targeted toward small offices and remote sites with as few as 20 employees.

Acme Packet markets its products worldwide. The company, which generated roughly half of its revenues outside of the US and Canada in 2008, maintains sales offices in Japan, Spain, and the UK. Menlo Ventures owns about a quarter of the company.

EXECUTIVES

President, CEO, and Director: Andrew (Andy) Ory, age 42, $449,550 total compensation
CTO and Director: Patrick J. MeLampy, age 51, $362,113 total compensation
CFO and Treasurer: Peter J. Minihane, age 60, $130,391 total compensation
Chief Software Architect: Bob Penfield
VP Professional Services: Erin Medeiros, age 35
VP Marketing and Product Management: Seamus Hourihan, age 56, $248,184 total compensation
VP Product Management: Kevin Klett
VP Sales and Business Development: Dino Di Palma, age 42, $374,913 total compensation
VP Manufacturing Operations: John F. Shields, age 45
Auditors: Ernst & Young LLP

LOCATIONS

HQ: Acme Packet, Inc.
 71 3rd Ave., Burlington, MA 01803
Phone: 781-328-4400   **Fax:** 781-425-5077
Web: www.acmepacket.com

2008 Sales

	$ mil.	% of total
US & Canada	59.5	51
Other countries	56.9	49
Total	**116.4**	**100**

PRODUCTS/OPERATIONS

2008 Sales

	$ mil.	% of total
Products	91.3	78
Services	25.1	22
Total	**116.4**	**100**

COMPETITORS

AudioCodes
Cisco Systems
Ditech
Edgewater Networks
Ericsson
GENBAND
Juniper Networks
Sonus Networks

HISTORICAL FINANCIALS

Company Type: Public

Income Statement

FYE: December 31

	REVENUE ($ mil.)	NET INCOME ($ mil.)	NET PROFIT MARGIN	EMPLOYEES
12/08	116.4	11.6	10.0%	381
12/07	113.1	19.6	17.3%	322
12/06	84.1	28.9	34.4%	247
12/05	36.1	0.0	—	231
12/04	16.0	(7.0)	—	226
Annual Growth	**64.2%**	**—**	**—**	**13.9%**

2008 Year-End Financials

Debt ratio: —
Return on equity: 7.5%
Cash ($ mil.): 125.7
Current ratio: 6.33
Long-term debt ($ mil.): —
No. of shares (mil.): 58.2
Dividends
 Yield: 0.0%
 Payout: 0.0%
Market value ($ mil.): 306.4
R&D as % of sales: —
Advertising as % of sales: —

Stock History

NASDAQ (GM): APKT

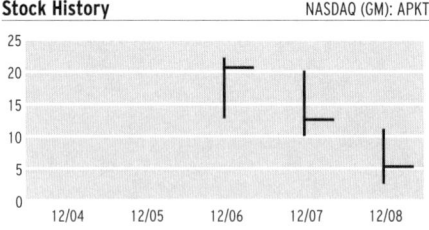

	STOCK PRICE ($) FY Close	P/E High/Low		PER SHARE ($) Earnings	Dividends	Book Value
12/08	5.26	61	16	0.18	0.00	2.52
12/07	12.59	66	34	0.30	0.00	2.80
12/06	20.64	44	26	0.50	0.00	2.25
Annual Growth	**(49.5%)**	**—**	**—**	**(40.0%)**	**—**	**5.9%**

Addus HomeCare

When caregivers need a little respite, Addus is there. Addus HomeCare provides home health care and related services such as rehabilitation and disease management. The company offers long-term home care for the elderly, which primarily includes in-home support services such as bathing, dressing, medication assistance, and other social activities. Additional offerings include short-term skilled home nursing and therapy (for patients recovering from a health condition) and adult day care. Addus serves more than 20,000 patients from around 120 offices in 16 states. Investment firm Eos Capital Partners owns a controlling stake in Addus HomeCare, which completed an IPO in 2009.

Addus HomeCare conducted its public share offering in October 2009 after announcing plans to go public earlier that year. Proceeds from the

IPO are being used to pay down debt and other expenses related to a 2006 transition in which Eos took control of Addus. Through that 2006 transaction, Addus HomeCare was created by Eos Capital as a holding company for the acquired operations of Addus HealthCare, which was founded in 1979 and is now the company's main operating subsidiary. Following the IPO, Eos Capital's stake in Addus HomeCare was reduced from nearly 80% to less than 40%.

Addus strives to provide a diverse line of services so that it can serve clients over a long timeframe as their conditions and needs change. The company employs home health aides, nurses, medical social workers, and physical, occupational, and speech therapists to meet its clients' various needs. It operates primarily in the western and midwestern US, with its largest markets in California, Illinois, Nevada, and Washington State. Addus receives about 75% of its revenues from home assistance services reimbursed by state and government elder care programs. It also relies on Medicare, commercial insurance companies, individuals, and other private payers.

Addus pursues expansion by acquiring smaller home health providers in existing as well as new markets. It also plans to grow by widening its service offerings and by opening new offices.

EXECUTIVES

Chairman, President, and CEO, Addus Holdings; President and CEO, Addus HealthCare:
Mark S. Heaney, age 53, $554,575 total compensation
VP Integrated Services: Donna McNally
VP Human Resources, Addus HealthCare:
Paul Diamond, age 54, $209,740 total compensation
VP Finance, Addus HealthCare: David W. Stasiewicz, $221,686 total compensation
VP Home Health Services, Addus HealthCare:
Sharon Rudden, age 49, $205,537 total compensation
VP Home and Community Services, Addus HealthCare:
Darby Anderson, age 43, $258,347 total compensation
VP, CFO, and Secretary, Addus Holdings and Addus HealthCare: Francis J. (Frank) Leonard, age 53, $150,748 total compensation
Director, Information Technology: Roger Ness
Corporate Director, Clinical Services: Emily Huebner
Director: Mark L. First, age 44
Auditors: BDO Seidman, LLP

LOCATIONS

HQ: Addus HomeCare Corporation
2401 S. Plum Grove Rd., Palatine, IL 60067
Phone: 847-303-5300 **Fax:** 847-303-5376
Web: www.addus.com

PRODUCTS/OPERATIONS

2008 Sales

	$ mil.	% of total
Home & community	189.0	80
Home health	47.3	20
Total	**236.3**	**100**

COMPETITORS

Active Day	Guardian Home Care
Almost Family	Holdings
Amedisys	Home Instead
American HomePatient	Lincare Holdings
Apria Healthcare	Manor Care
Arcadia Resources	National Home Health
Gentiva	Personal-Touch Home Care
Girling Health Care	Star Multi Care

HISTORICAL FINANCIALS
Company Type: Public

Income Statement
FYE: December 31

	REVENUE ($ mil.)	NET INCOME ($ mil.)	NET PROFIT MARGIN	EMPLOYEES
12/08	236.3	4.0	1.7%	12,137
12/07	194.6	0.2	0.1%	10,797
12/06	178.2	5.2	2.9%	9,440
Annual Growth	15.2%	(12.3%)	—	13.4%

2008 Year-End Financials

Debt ratio: (1,766.1%)
Return on equity: —
Cash ($ mil.): 6.1
Current ratio: 1.81
Long-term debt ($ mil.): 56.1

Net Income History
NASDAQ (GM): ADUS

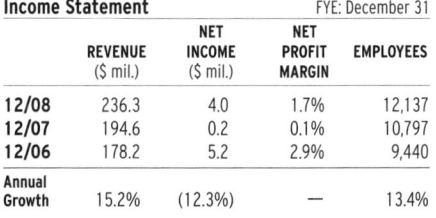

Advanced Battery Technologies

Advanced Battery Technologies, through its operating subsidiary ZQ Power-Tech, hopes to ride the rising wave of electric and hybrid-electric vehicle sales all the way to the bank. The company produces rechargeable polymer lithium-ion batteries used in cars, buses, cell phones, digital cameras, and other modern gadgets. Its batteries can be as thin as one-tenth of an inch or as large as 500 pounds (for commuter buses). ZQ makes lamps used on miners' helmets but most of its products are sold to OEMs for use in their finished goods. Customers for vehicle battery components include Aiyingsi, ZAP, and Beijing Guoqiang Global Technology Development Co. Chairman and CEO Zhiguo Fu formed the company in 2002.

The company is looking to expand its battery production capabilities; in September 2009 the company signed a letter of intent to acquire a leading battery manufacturing company located in Shenzhen, China. Earlier in the year the company acquired fellow Chinese firm Wuxi Angell Autocycle, an electric vehicle maker. It is also expanding its production capacity and expecting a 165% increase by 2010.

Mr. Fu, who pays for the company's New York office out of his own pocket, owns about 16% of Advanced Battery Technologies, a holding company consisting solely of Cashtech Investment, which is itself a holding company consisting

solely of Heilongjiang ZhongQiang Power-Tech, aka ZQ Power-Tech.

ZQ leases its 72,000-sq.-ft. production facility from the Chinese government rent-free as long as it continues manufacturing at the site.

EXECUTIVES

Chairman and CEO: Zhiguo Fu, age 58
CFO: Sharon Tang, age 49
Media Contact: Rita Lai
Sales Manager: Renkun Shao
Auditors: Bagell, Josephs, Levine & Company, LLC

LOCATIONS

HQ: Advanced Battery Technologies, Inc.
21 W. 39th St., Ste. 2A, New York, NY 10018
Phone: 212-391-2752 **Fax:** 212-391-2751
Web: www.abat.com.cn

COMPETITORS

China BAK
Ener1
Hitachi Maxell
Johnson Controls Power Solutions
SAFT
Ultralife
Unitech Battery
Valence Technology

HISTORICAL FINANCIALS
Company Type: Public

Income Statement
FYE: December 31

	REVENUE ($ mil.)	NET INCOME ($ mil.)	NET PROFIT MARGIN	EMPLOYEES
12/08	45.2	16.1	35.6%	909
12/07	31.9	10.2	32.0%	1,262
12/06	16.3	6.0	36.8%	1,264
12/05	4.2	(0.2)	—	1,621
12/04	1.2	(2.3)	—	362
Annual Growth	147.7%	—	—	25.9%

2008 Year-End Financials

Debt ratio: 0.0%
Return on equity: 28.5%
Cash ($ mil.): 32.7
Current ratio: 39.53
Long-term debt ($ mil.): 0.0
No. of shares (mil.): 66.9
Dividends
Yield: 0.0%
Payout: —
Market value ($ mil.): 178.0
R&D as % of sales: —
Advertising as % of sales: —

Stock History
NASDAQ (CM): ABAT

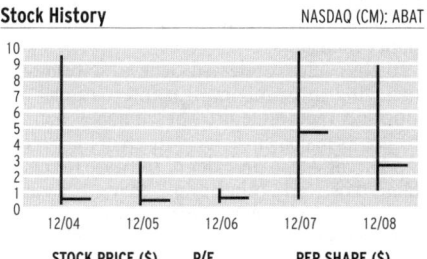

	STOCK PRICE ($) FY Close	P/E High/Low		PER SHARE ($) Earnings	Dividends	Book Value
12/08	2.66	28	4	0.31	0.00	1.14
12/07	4.70	44	3	0.22	0.00	0.55
12/06	0.63	9	3	0.13	0.00	0.32
12/05	0.48	—	—	(0.01)	0.00	0.14
12/04	0.56	—	—	(0.23)	0.00	0.08
Annual Growth	47.6%		—	—	—	92.1%

Advent Software

Advent Software manages investments from beginning to end. A provider of enterprise investment management software for investment advisors, banks, and corporations, Advent offers applications for managing everything from client relationships to trade order executions. The company's products are used for managing portfolio accounting, trading and order execution, hedge and venture fund allocation, securities clients, reconciliation, and other functions. Advent also offers services such as consulting, support, maintenance, systems integration, and installation.

The firm's Second Street Securities subsidiary provides SEC-registered broker/dealer services.

In October 2008 the company acquired Tamale Software for about $28 million; the purchase expands Advent's front office software applications and helps it establish a presence in the research management solutions niche market. Tamale Software provided about 1,700 investment professionals at hedge funds, endowments, private equity firms, and asset management firms with applications to manage their workflow and research process.

In 2009 Advent sold its MicroEdge subsidiary to Vista Equity Partners for about $30 million in cash. The deal enables Advent to focus on its core market of serving investment management industry clients.

HISTORY

Stephanie DiMarco was a financial analyst at a small investment bank when she sought to computerize the firm's back-office operations. The IBM PC soon came out, and DiMarco foresaw a promising market; she started Advent in 1985 with programmer Steve Strand. The following year the company sold its first product, Professional Portfolio, designed to help smaller investment firms with accounting and record keeping.

Sales grew to more than $4 million by 1990. The company introduced Axys, the first Windows-based portfolio management system software, in 1993. That year DiMarco bought out Strand. Advent went public in 1995. The next year the company bought Data Exchange, a maker of portfolio and trade order software designed for large regional broker/dealers and money managers.

In 1997 Advent released Geneva, software for managing investments with international accounting requirements. The company bought the grants management operations of Blackbund and MicroEdge, a provider of software for charitable trusts and other grant-giving organizations, in 1998. New product releases that year included Advent Office, a suite of applications for automating investment management.

In 1999 DiMarco handed over the CEO post to president Peter Caswell; DiMarco remained chairman. The company expanded into the UK in 2000 when it opened a London office.

In 2001 the company continued to expand its offerings, branching out into not-for-profit software products through its purchase of privately held NPO Solutions. The next year Advent added wealth management software to its product line

through its purchase of privately held Kinexus for about $68 million, and it acquired portfolio management software provider Techfi for about $23 million.

As part of a larger restructuring designed to reduce costs and refocus on core markets, Caswell resigned as president and CEO in 2003. DiMarco resumed the CEO position and handed over the chairman title to director John Scully.

EXECUTIVES

Chairman: John H. Scully, age 64
CEO and Director: Stephanie G. DiMarco, age 51, $1,514,062 total compensation
President: Peter F. (Pete) Hess, age 39, $1,003,628 total compensation
EVP and CTO: Lily S. Chang, age 60, $832,892 total compensation
SVP and CFO: James S. (Jim) Cox, age 37
SVP Human Resources: John P. Brennan, age 53, $689,889 total compensation
SVP and General Manager, Tamale: Mark Rice
SVP and General Manager, Investment Management: Anthony Sperling
SVP and General Manager, Europe, Middle East, and Africa: Håkan Valberg
Co-Head Global Accounts and SVP and General Manager, Product Development, Client Services, and Support: Todd Gottula
Co-Head Global Accounts and SVP and General Manager, Sales and Marketing: Chris Momsen
VP Product Marketing: Chris Flynn
President, MicroEdge: Susan Harmon
Director Product Marketing: Michele Holton
Senior Director Investor Relations: Heidi Flaherty
Auditors: PricewaterhouseCoopers LLP

LOCATIONS

HQ: Advent Software, Inc.
600 Townsend St., San Francisco, CA 94103
Phone: 415-543-7696   **Fax:** 415-556-0607
Web: www.advent.com

2008 Sales

	% of total
US	86
Other countries	14
Total	**100**

PRODUCTS/OPERATIONS

2008 Sales

	% of total
Term license, maintenance & other recurring	79
Perpetual license fees	9
Professional services & other	12
Total	**100**

Selected Software and Services

Advent Office
Advent Browser Reporting line (Internet-based investment tracking)
Advent Warehouse (data warehouse)
Advent Partner (partnership allocation for hedge funds)
Axys (portfolio accounting and management)
Moxy (trading and order management)
MyAdvent (browser-based portal for Advent Office)
Qube (client contact and management)
Rex (online transaction reconciliation)
WealthLine (Internet-based communications with investors)

Data and data integration services
Advent Corporate Actions (corporate action notification and processing)
Advent Custodial Data (custodial relationship management)
Advent Market Data (transaction-based subscription service for pricing and corporate actions data)
Advent Wealth Service (outsourced data management for high net worth advisors and managers)
Global portfolio accounting
Geneva (global portfolio accounting system)
MicroEdge
FIMS (not-for-profit management)
FoundationPower (information management for not-for-profits)
GIFTS (grants management system)
Outsourced services
Advent BackOffice Service (outsourced daily reconciliation and portfolio reporting service)
AdvisorMart (online, hosted reporting and portfolio management)

COMPETITORS

Algorithmics
Charles River Systems
DST Systems
Eze Castle
Fidessa
Fiserv
Linedata
Misys
SS&C
SunGard

HISTORICAL FINANCIALS

Company Type: Public

Income Statement

FYE: December 31

	REVENUE ($ mil.)	NET INCOME ($ mil.)	NET PROFIT MARGIN	EMPLOYEES
12/08	264.8	18.9	7.1%	1,068
12/07	215.3	12.6	5.9%	946
12/06	184.1	82.6	44.9%	824
12/05	168.7	14.1	8.4%	736
12/04	150.0	(16.2)	—	752
Annual Growth	**15.3%**	**—**	**—**	**9.2%**

2008 Year-End Financials

Debt ratio: 12.8%
Return on equity: 10.1%
Cash ($ mil.): 48.4
Current ratio: 0.74
Long-term debt ($ mil.): 25.0
No. of shares (mil.): 25.7
Dividends
Yield: —
Payout: —
Market value ($ mil.): 512.7
R&D as % of sales: —
Advertising as % of sales: —

Stock History

NASDAQ (GS): ADVS

	STOCK PRICE ($) FY Close	P/E High/Low		PER SHARE ($) Earnings	Dividends	Book Value
12/08	19.97	81	26	0.68	—	7.63
12/07	54.10	129	72	0.45	—	7.01
12/06	35.29	14	10	2.70	—	8.17
12/05	28.94	75	37	0.44	—	9.43
12/04	20.48	—	—	(0.49)	—	10.35
Annual Growth	**(0.6%)**	**—**	**—**	**—**	**—**	**(7.3%)**

The Advisory Board Company

Here's where a hospital might go for a second opinion. The Advisory Board Company specializes in providing best practices consulting to member-clients in the health care industry, including more than 2,800 hospitals, pharmaceutical companies, insurance firms, and medical device manufacturers in the US. The Advisory Board offers more than 40 programs in areas such as strategy, operations, and management. Members buy annual subscriptions to one or more programs and participate in the firm's research efforts. Programs typically include best practices research studies, seminars, customized reports, and decision-support tools. The company was founded in 1979 as the Research Council of Washington.

The company has counted among its members such industry leaders as The Cleveland Clinic, Johns Hopkins Hospital, Massachusetts General Hospital, and Johnson & Johnson.

The Advisory Board hopes to grow not only by adding members, particularly from outside the US, but also by selling additional services to existing members. It also plans to continue to add to its list of programs. Since 2000, it has added 35 programs to its list of offerings, and it plans to launch about three to four new programs each year.

To carry out its growth agenda, The Advisory Board hired a new chief executive in late 2008. Former EVP Robert Musslewhite, who worked in several sales and product development roles, was tapped to replace Frank Williams as CEO, who retired in September 2008. (Williams stayed on as executive chairman.) At the same time, former COO David Felsenthal was promoted to president.

The program-membership business model distinguishes The Advisory Board from many of its competitors — consulting firms that are hired on a job-by-job basis. Benefits for The Advisory Board include the ability to spread program costs over a growing membership base and the opportunity to involve members in identifying issues and conducting research.

Advisory Board spinoff The Corporate Executive Board operates on a similar membership business model, serving companies in a variety of industries. A noncompetition agreement between the companies that expired in January 2007 barred The Corporate Executive Board from seeking clients in the health care industry and prevented The Advisory Board from seeking clients outside the health care industry; subsequently, the companies agreed to collaborate on several projects and to continue not competing in core business areas.

EXECUTIVES

Executive Chairman: Frank J. Williams, age 42,
  $2,792,866 total compensation
CEO and Director: Robert W. Musslewhite, age 39,
  $1,319,530 total compensation
President: David L. Felsenthal, age 38,
  $1,281,820 total compensation
CFO and Treasurer: Michael T. Kirshbaum, age 32,
  $587,550 total compensation
Chief Research Officer: Scott M. Fassbach, age 49,
  $866,546 total compensation

EVP: Scott A. Schirmeier, age 40
EVP: Richard A. Schwartz, age 43,
  $482,040 total compensation
General Counsel and Corporate Secretary:
  Evan R. Farber, age 36
Auditors: Ernst & Young LLP

LOCATIONS

HQ: The Advisory Board Company
  2445 M St., NW, Washington, DC 20037
Phone: 202-266-5600   **Fax:** 202-266-5700
Web: www.advisoryboardcompany.com

PRODUCTS/OPERATIONS

Selected Products and Services

Best practices installation and support
Business intelligence and analytics
Clinical research
Daily briefings and news
Executive education
Executive watches
Leadership development
Online advisory resources
Strategy and operations research
Workforce performance

COMPETITORS

Accenture	Deloitte Consulting
Booz Allen	IMS Health
Boston Consulting	McKinsey & Company
Conference Board	Towers Perrin

HISTORICAL FINANCIALS

Company Type: Public

Income Statement

FYE: March 31

	REVENUE ($ mil.)	NET INCOME ($ mil.)	NET PROFIT MARGIN	EMPLOYEES
3/09	230.4	21.5	9.3%	1,021
3/08	219.0	32.1	14.7%	910
3/07	189.8	27.4	14.4%	855
3/06	165.0	25.6	15.5%	768
3/05	141.6	23.3	16.5%	681
Annual Growth	12.9%	(2.0%)	—	10.7%

2009 Year-End Financials

Debt ratio: —
Return on equity: 19.4%
Cash ($ mil.): 23.7
Current ratio: 0.81
Long-term debt ($ mil.): —
No. of shares (mil.): 15.5
Dividends
  Yield: 0.0%
  Payout: —
Market value ($ mil.): 257.5
R&D as % of sales: —
Advertising as % of sales: —

Stock History

NASDAQ (GS): ABCO

	STOCK PRICE ($) FY Close	P/E High/Low	PER SHARE ($) Earnings	Dividends	Book Value
3/09	16.58	42 10	1.30	0.00	6.37
3/08	54.94	40 27	1.72	0.00	7.89
3/07	50.62	42 32	1.41	0.00	8.92
3/06	55.77	44 31	1.29	0.00	9.48
3/05	43.70	37 24	1.22	0.00	9.36
Annual Growth	(21.5%)	— —	1.6%	—	(9.2%)

Advocat Inc.

Spelling errors notwithstanding, Advocat strives to be an advocate for the elderly through its nursing homes and assisted-living facilities, most of which are located in the southeastern and southwestern US. The company operates some 50 nursing homes and assisted-living centers with a total of some 5,800 beds. Advocat, which focuses on rural areas, offers a range of health care services including skilled nursing, recreational therapy, and social services, as well as nutritional support, respiratory treatments, rehabilitative therapy, and other specialized ancillary services.

Payments from Medicare and Medicaid account for about 85% of the company's total revenues.

Advocat has facilities in Alabama, Arkansas, Florida, Kentucky, Ohio, Tennessee, Texas, and West Virginia. The company is divesting its assisted living operations to focus on its nursing homes. It is also expanding its nursing home operations through purchases, leases, and developments; Advocat acquired seven skilled nursing facilities in Texas in 2007 from Senior Management Services of America.

EXECUTIVES

Chairman: Wallace E. Olson, age 62
President, CEO and Director: William R. Council III,
  age 47, $726,951 total compensation
EVP, CFO, and Secretary: L. Glynn Riddle Jr., age 49,
  $351,905 total compensation
SVP Nursing Home Operations:
  Raymond L. (Ray) Tyler Jr., age 58,
  $471,287 total compensation
VP Business Development: David White, age 32
Auditors: BDO Seidman, LLP

LOCATIONS

HQ: Advocat Inc.
  1621 Galleria Blvd., Brentwood, TN 37027
Phone: 615-771-7575   **Fax:** 615-771-7409
Web: www.irinfo.com/avc

PRODUCTS/OPERATIONS

2008 Sales

	$ mil.	% of total
Medicaid	154	53
Medicare	91	32
Private pay & other	44	15
Total	**289**	**100**

Selected Subsidiaries

Advocat Ancillary Services, Inc.
Advocat Distribution Services, Inc.
Advocat Finance, Inc.
Diversicare Assisted Living Services, Inc.
Diversicare Assisted Living Services NC, LLC
Diversicare Leasing Corp.
Diversicare Management Services Co.

COMPETITORS

Capital Senior Living
Extendicare REIT
Genesis HealthCare
Golden Horizons
Life Care Centers
Manor Care
National HealthCare
SavaSeniorCare
Skilled Healthcare Group
Sun Healthcare

HISTORICAL FINANCIALS
Company Type: Public

Income Statement				FYE: December 31
	REVENUE ($ mil.)	NET INCOME ($ mil.)	NET PROFIT MARGIN	EMPLOYEES
12/08	288.8	5.7	2.0%	5,809
12/07	245.1	9.4	3.8%	5,638
12/06	216.8	21.9	10.1%	4,716
12/05	203.7	25.3	12.4%	4,682
12/04	202.8	2.8	1.4%	4,961
Annual Growth	9.2%	19.4%	—	4.0%

2008 Year-End Financials

Debt ratio: 171.9%
Return on equity: 37.6%
Cash ($ mil.): 7.6
Current ratio: 1.39
Long-term debt ($ mil.): 30.2
No. of shares (mil.): 5.7

Dividends
  Yield: —
  Payout: —
Market value ($ mil.): 16.9
R&D as % of sales: —
Advertising as % of sales: —

Stock History
NASDAQ (CM): AVCA

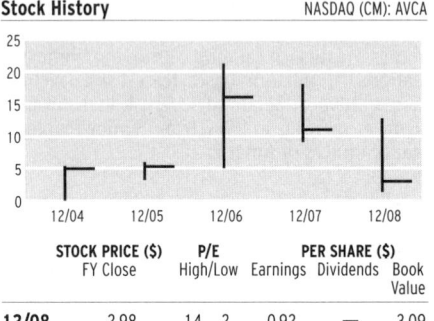

	STOCK PRICE ($) FY Close	P/E High/Low		PER SHARE ($) Earnings	Dividends	Book Value
12/08	2.98	14	2	0.92	—	3.09
12/07	11.02	12	6	1.48	—	2.24
12/06	16.07	6	2	3.35	—	0.68
12/05	5.27	1	1	3.88	—	(2.97)
12/04	4.95	12	1	0.42	—	(7.37)
Annual Growth	(11.9%)	—	—	21.7%	—	—

AeroCentury Corp.

With a high-flyin' inventory, AeroCentury leases used turboprop aircraft and engines to regional airlines and other commercial customers. The company often buys equipment from an airline, then leases it back to the seller, usually for a term of three to five years. AeroCentury also buys assets already under lease. The company only makes a purchase when it has a customer committed to a lease. Typically, lessees are responsible for any maintenance costs. Aero-Century owns about 30 aircraft, mainly de Havilland and Fokker models. The majority of the company's lease revenues come from airlines headquartered outside the US.

The company was formed by consolidating the aircraft equipment leasing and management partnerships JetFleet Aircraft and JetFleet Aircraft II. AeroCentury is managed by JetFleet Management, which in turn is overseen by AeroCentury officers.

High oil prices have actually been helping AeroCentury. Turboprop aircraft are more fuel efficient than jets, so demand for their use on shorter routes has increased.

Chairman and president Neal Crispin and SVP Toni Perazzo each own 21% of AeroCentury.

EXECUTIVES

Chairman and President: Neal D. Crispin, age 64, $210,001 total compensation
SVP, CFO, Secretary, and Director: Toni M. Perazzo, age 63, $206,500 total compensation
SVP: John S. Myers, age 63
VP Aircraft Remarketing: Steven H. Wallace, age 63
VP Maintenance: Jack Humphreys, age 61
VP Aircraft Acquisitions: Byron Hurey, age 61
VP and Controller: Glenn Roberts, age 44
VP Finance: Harold M. Lyons, age 50
VP Corporate Development: Brian J. Ginna, age 40
General Counsel: Christopher B. Tigno, age 47
Auditors: BDO Seidman, LLP

LOCATIONS

HQ: AeroCentury Corp.
    1440 Chapin Ave., Ste. 310, Burlingame, CA 94010
Phone: 650-340-1888   **Fax:** 650-696-3929
Web: www.aerocentury.com

COMPETITORS

AAR Corp.
AIG
Aviation Capital Group
Boeing Capital
Bombardier
CIT Group
EADS
GE Commercial Aviation Services
ILFC
Jetscape
Saab AB
Willis Lease

HISTORICAL FINANCIALS
Company Type: Public

Income Statement				FYE: December 31
	REVENUE ($ mil.)	NET INCOME ($ mil.)	NET PROFIT MARGIN	EMPLOYEES
12/08	31.8	3.3	10.4%	0
12/07	23.8	3.8	16.0%	0
12/06	18.3	0.8	4.4%	0
12/05	13.5	0.2	1.5%	0
12/04	10.9	0.3	2.8%	0
Annual Growth	30.7%	82.1%	—	—

2008 Year-End Financials

Debt ratio: —
Return on equity: 9.9%
Cash ($ mil.): 2.2
Current ratio: 0.09
Long-term debt ($ mil.): —
No. of shares (mil.): 1.5

Dividends
  Yield: 0.0%
  Payout: —
Market value ($ mil.): 14.2
R&D as % of sales: —
Advertising as % of sales: —

Stock History
NYSE Alternext: ACY

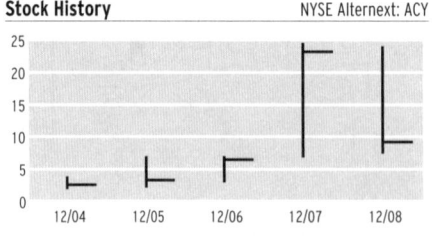

	STOCK PRICE ($) FY Close	P/E High/Low		PER SHARE ($) Earnings	Dividends	Book Value
12/08	9.20	11	4	2.08	0.00	22.57
12/07	23.20	10	3	2.36	0.00	20.83
12/06	6.46	13	6	0.53	0.00	13.19
12/05	3.29	52	18	0.13	0.00	12.31
12/04	2.57	21	12	0.17	0.00	12.18
Annual Growth	37.6%	—	—	87.0%	—	16.7%

AeroVironment, Inc.

AeroVironment (AV) gives soldiers a birds-eye view of their mission. The company designs and manufactures a line of small unmanned aircraft systems (UAS) for the Department of Defense. Small enough for one-man transport and launch, and operable through a hand-held control, more than 10,000 AV UAS have provided intelligence, surveillance, and reconnaissance for small tactical units. Through its Efficient Energy Systems unit, AV produces PosiCharge fast-charge systems for industrial equipment batteries and electric vehicles (EV) as well as EV testing systems used by auto, defense, and utility markets. Adding to its efficient solutions, AV makes green energy systems, like small wind turbines, for commercial buildings.

The company has evolved from a concentration on researching and developing unmanned aircraft systems and efficient energy systems to making and selling them. Strong demand by the US military for AV's spy drones continues to drive the company's growth and account for more than 60% of sales. The UASs are the search tool of choice by soldiers tracking international terrorists. Facing down a field of competition, AV picked up four US defense contracts in 2009 for the mini-UASs. However, in order to reduce its exposure to congressional funding, AV is angling to add militaries from allied nations and nonmilitary industries in the US to its roster of customers. To this end, the company is introducing upgraded applications such as petrochemical infrastructure monitoring and border surveillance.

More customers are also netted as AV continues to spotlight the advantages of its PosiCharge products; they help recharge vehicle batteries 16 times faster than traditional methods, and improve productivity and safety by eliminating frequent and laborious battery changes. In 2009 AV piggybacked on a partnership between the District of Columbia and Nissan to launch an electric car sharing program for city employees. The agreement includes setting up numerous charging stations for the fleet. Existing fans of the company's PosiCharge lineup include Ford, IKEA, and SYSCO.

Chairman and CEO Timothy Conver owns more than 10% of AV. He took the reins in 1993 from aeronautical inventor and company founder Paul MacCready.

EXECUTIVES

Chairman, President, and CEO: Timothy E. Conver, age 65, $941,073 total compensation
EVP and General Manager, Unmanned Aircraft Systems: John F. Grabowsky, age 62, $540,377 total compensation
SVP and General Manager, Efficient Energy Systems: Michael Bissonette, age 52, $474,401 total compensation
SVP Administration: Cathleen Cline, age 50, $316,696 total compensation
VP Finance, CFO, and Secretary: Stephen C. Wright, age 52, $533,889 total compensation
Auditors: Ernst & Young LLP

LOCATIONS

HQ: AeroVironment, Inc.
181 W. Huntington Dr., Ste. 202
Monrovia, CA 91016
Phone: 626-357-9983   **Fax:** 626-359-9628
Web: www.avinc.com

PRODUCTS/OPERATIONS

Selected Unmanned Aircraft Systems

	Wingspan (ft.)	Weight (lbs.)	Range (mi.)	Flight Time (min.)
Raven	4.5	4.2	6	90
Dragon Eye	3.8	5.9	3	60
Wasp III	2.4	1.0	5	45
Puma	8.5	12.5	6	240

2009 Sales

	$ mil.	% of total
UAS	211.4	85
Efficient Energy Systems	36.3	15
Total	**247.7**	**100**

COMPETITORS

AAI Corporation
Aker ASA
Aurora Flight Sciences
Boeing
Dassault Aviation
Edison International
Elbit Systems
General Atomics
Honeywell Aerospace
L-3 Communications
Lockheed Martin
Northrop Grumman

HISTORICAL FINANCIALS

Company Type: Public

Income Statement   FYE: April 30

	REVENUE ($ mil.)	NET INCOME ($ mil.)	NET PROFIT MARGIN	EMPLOYEES
4/09	247.7	24.2	9.8%	658
4/08	215.7	21.4	9.9%	543
4/07	173.7	20.7	11.9%	495
4/06	139.4	11.2	8.0%	447
4/05	105.2	14.7	14.0%	447
Annual Growth	**23.9%**	**13.3%**	**—**	**10.1%**

2009 Year-End Financials

Debt ratio: —   Dividends
Return on equity: 12.8%   Yield: —
Cash ($ mil.): 116.5   Payout: —
Current ratio: 5.73   Market value ($ mil.): 509.5
Long-term debt ($ mil.): —   R&D as % of sales: —
No. of shares (mil.): 21.5   Advertising as % of sales: —

Stock History   NASDAQ (GM): AVAV

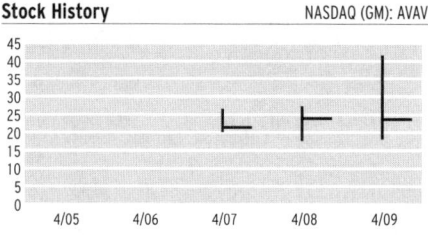

	STOCK PRICE ($) FY Close	P/E High/Low	PER SHARE ($) Earnings	Dividends	Book Value
4/09	23.66	37 17	1.11	—	9.63
4/08	23.91	27 18	1.00	—	7.88
4/07	21.40	21 17	1.22	—	6.33
Annual Growth	**5.1%**	**— —**	**(4.6%)**	**—**	**23.3%**

AGA Medical Holdings

AGA Medical Holdings heals broken hearts. The company specializes in making medical devices for treating structural heart defects and vascular diseases. Its AMPLATZER occlusion devices use minimally invasive small catheters, which physicians can retrieve and position without the need for multiple devices or repetition of procedures. Approved for use in both Europe and the US, the company sells its devices in more than 100 countries through its own sales force and direct distributors. Its primary customers are pediatric cardiologists, radiologists, and vascular surgeons. Dr. Kurt Amplatz and director Franck Gougeon established AGA Medical Holdings in 1995.

AGA Medical Holdings originally planned to go public in 2008 but held off until 2009 to finally complete its IPO. It intends to use the funds raised to pay down debt.

The company is focused on expanding its product portfolio by developing new products, as well as designing new applications and product enhancements. It is conducting clinical trials to measure the use of its devices to treat both stroke and migraines. It manufactures the majority of its own products at its headquarters in Minnesota.

To carry its newly approved products into more regions, AGA Medical Holdings plans to grow its direct sales force in Europe and the US.

Director Gougeon holds 20% of the company's stock; private equity firm Welsh, Carson, Anderson & Stowe holds 50% of the company and two seats on the board of directors.

EXECUTIVES

Chairman: Tommy G. Thompson, age 67
President and CEO: John R. Barr, age 52
CFO: Brigid A. Makes, age 53
General Counsel: Ronald E. Lund, age 74
VP Worldwide Sales and Marketing: Jack A. Darby
Deputy General Counsel and Chief Compliance Officer: Peter V. Rother
Research and Development Consultant: Kurt Amplatz, age 85
Auditors: Ernst & Young LLP

LOCATIONS

HQ: AGA Medical Holdings, Inc.
5050 Nathan Lane North, Plymouth, MN 55442
Phone: 763-513-9227   **Fax:** 763-513-9226
Web: www.amplatzer.com

2008 Sales

	$ mil.	% of total
US	68.0	41
Europe	64.5	39
Other	34.4	20
Total	**166.9**	**100**

COMPETITORS

Boston Scientific
Cook Incorporated
NMT Medical
St. Jude Medical
W.L. Gore

HISTORICAL FINANCIALS

Company Type: Public

Income Statement   FYE: December 31

	REVENUE ($ mil.)	NET INCOME ($ mil.)	NET PROFIT MARGIN	EMPLOYEES
12/08	166.9	9.1	5.5%	470
12/07	147.3	6.1	4.1%	335
12/06	127.5	12.6	9.9%	—
12/05	98.1	(48.8)	—	—
Annual Growth	**19.4%**	**—**	**—**	**40.3%**

2008 Year-End Financials

Debt ratio: —   Current ratio: 1.78
Return on equity: —   Long-term debt ($ mil.): 256.6
Cash ($ mil.): 22.8

Net Income History   NASDAQ (GM): AGAM

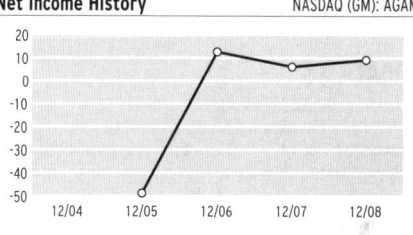

Air Methods

Air Methods flies to the rescue for people needing intensive medical care. With a fleet of about 320 medically equipped aircraft, mainly helicopters, the company provides emergency medical air transportation services throughout the US. The company's community-based division, which accounts for most of Air Methods' sales, provides transportation and in-flight medical care from its own bases in more than 20 states. Its hospital-based division contracts with hospitals in more than 30 states to transport critically ill patients to trauma centers or tertiary care facilities; under the hospital-based model, the hospitals themselves provide in-flight medical personnel.

Flight services account for nearly all of the company's sales. Air Methods also offers aircraft maintenance services and, through its products division, designs, services, and installs medical and other specialized interiors in aircraft owned by third parties, including commercial and government clients both in the US and abroad.

The company expanded significantly in 2007 by acquiring Pennsylvania-based FSS Airholdings and its CJ Systems Aviation Group, a provider of medical air transport services. The purchase added more that 100 helicopters and fixed-wing aircraft to the company's fleet and strengthened its presence in the eastern US.

To maintain its growth trajectory, Air Methods is integrating the CJ Systems operations and adding new aircraft to its fleet. In addition, the company sees room for growth in its products division.

Director Ralph Bernstein owns about 10% of Air Methods.

EXECUTIVES

Chairman: George W. Belsey, age 69
CEO and Director: Aaron D. Todd, age 47, $691,892 total compensation
COO: Paul H. Tate, age 58, $814,200 total compensation
CFO, Secretary, and Treasurer: Trent J. Carman, age 48, $395,850 total compensation
SVP Hospital-Based Services and Air Medical Services: Michael D. (Mike) Allen, age 46, $356,932 total compensation
SVP Community-Based Services: David L. Dolstein, age 60, $405,195 total compensation
Chief Accounting Officer and Controller: Sharon J. Keck, age 42, $267,707 total compensation
VP Products Division: Arthur Torwirt
VP Human Resources: Jackie Forker
New VP Products Division: Tom Curtis
Director Operations: Bill Salus
Director Product Development: Mike Knap
Director Marketing: Michael J. Slattery
Auditors: KPMG LLP

LOCATIONS

HQ: Air Methods Corporation
7301 S. Peoria, Englewood, CO 80112
Phone: 303-792-7400   **Fax:** 303-790-0499
Web: www.airmethods.com

PRODUCTS/OPERATIONS

2008 Sales

	$ mil.	% of total
Flight operations		
Community-based services	297.4	59
Hospital-based services	187.9	38
Products	13.5	3
Total	**498.8**	**100**

Selected Subsidiaries

Rocky Mountain Holdings, LLC (RMH)
FSS Airholdings, Inc. (FSS)
Mercy Air Service, Inc. (Mercy Air)
LifeNet, Inc. (LifeNet)

COMPETITORS

Acadian Ambulance Service, Inc.
Bristow Group Inc
CHC Helicopter
Evergreen Holdings
PHI, Inc.

HISTORICAL FINANCIALS

Company Type: Public

Income Statement
FYE: December 31

	REVENUE ($ mil.)	NET INCOME ($ mil.)	NET PROFIT MARGIN	EMPLOYEES
12/08	498.8	19.3	3.9%	2,976
12/07	396.3	27.5	6.9%	3,133
12/06	319.5	17.2	5.4%	2,155
12/05	337.0	11.8	3.5%	1,961
12/04	273.1	3.2	1.2%	1,833
Annual Growth	**16.3%**	**56.7%**	**—**	**12.9%**

2008 Year-End Financials

Debt ratio: 53.5%
Return on equity: 12.8%
Cash ($ mil.): 13.1
Current ratio: 2.26
Long-term debt ($ mil.): 85.9
No. of shares (mil.): 12.4

Dividends
  Yield: 0.0%
  Payout: —
Market value ($ mil.): 198.1
R&D as % of sales: —
Advertising as % of sales: —

	STOCK PRICE ($) FY Close	P/E High/Low		PER SHARE ($) Earnings	Dividends	Book Value
12/08	15.99	33	9	1.54	0.00	12.95
12/07	49.67	27	10	2.20	0.00	11.46
12/06	27.92	22	12	1.40	0.00	8.66
12/05	17.30	18	6	1.02	0.00	6.96
12/04	8.60	9	6	1.05	0.00	5.90
Annual Growth	**16.8%**	**—**	**—**	**10.0%**	**—**	**21.7%**

Air T, Inc.

So FedEx can deliver for you, Air T flies for FedEx. Air T owns two overnight air cargo subsidiaries — Mountain Air Cargo and CSA Air — which operate under contracts with the express delivery giant. Mountain Air Cargo flies mainly in the southeastern US, the Caribbean, and South America; CSA Air operates primarily in the upper Midwest. The carriers' combined fleet consists of about 90 turboprop aircraft, nearly all of which are leased from FedEx. Air cargo operations account for about half of Air T's sales. The company's other businesses — Global Ground Support and Global Aviation Services — make de-icing and scissor-lift equipment used at airports and provide related maintenance services.

Global Ground Support's top customer is the US Air Force, which buys de-icing equipment from the company; other clients have included the US Navy and various airports and airlines. Air T's ground equipment business, the company's fastest-growing segment, was augmented by the launch of the Global Aviation Services business in 2007.

Although FedEx is the sole customer of Air T's air cargo units, Air T is not barred from hauling freight for other clients. For the time being, however, Air T is working to maintain its share of feeder carrier business from FedEx, which has been a customer since 1980.

Chairman and CEO Walter Clark controls a 6% stake in Air T.

EXECUTIVES

Chairman and CEO: Walter Clark, age 52, $488,033 total compensation
EVP and Director; President, Mountain Air Cargo; CEO, CSA Air; EVP, Mountain Aircraft Services: William H. Simpson, age 61, $643,436 total compensation
VP Finance, CFO, Secretary, Treasurer, and Director: John Parry, age 51, $322,163 total compensation
Auditors: Dixon Hughes PLLC

LOCATIONS

HQ: Air T, Inc.
3524 Airport Rd., Maiden, NC 28650
Phone: 828-464-8741   **Fax:** 828-465-5281
Web: www.airt.net/home.html

PRODUCTS/OPERATIONS

2009 Sales

	$ mil.	% of total
Overnight air cargo		
FedEx	43	47
Ground equipment		
Military	21	23
Commercial		
US	12	13
Other countries	7	8
Ground support services	8	9
Total	**91**	**100**

COMPETITORS

Air Cargo Carriers
AirNet
Alpine Air
Ameriflight
Arrow Air
Evergreen Holdings
FMC
Goodrich Corp.
Grand Aire
Ram Air Freight

HISTORICAL FINANCIALS

Company Type: Public

Income Statement
FYE: March 31

	REVENUE ($ mil.)	NET INCOME ($ mil.)	NET PROFIT MARGIN	EMPLOYEES
3/09	90.7	4.4	4.9%	467
3/08	78.4	3.4	4.3%	460
3/07	67.3	2.5	3.7%	392
3/06	79.5	2.1	2.6%	390
3/05	70.0	2.1	3.0%	414
Annual Growth	**6.7%**	**20.3%**	**—**	**3.1%**

2009 Year-End Financials

Debt ratio: 0.1%
Return on equity: 22.3%
Cash ($ mil.): 6.9
Current ratio: 3.34
Long-term debt ($ mil.): 0.0
No. of shares (mil.): 2.4

Dividends
  Yield: 5.2%
  Payout: 16.6%
Market value ($ mil.): 13.9
R&D as % of sales: —
Advertising as % of sales: —

	STOCK PRICE ($) FY Close	P/E High/Low		PER SHARE ($) Earnings	Dividends	Book Value
3/09	5.72	7	3	1.81	0.30	8.97
3/08	9.61	9	5	1.40	0.25	7.31
3/07	7.99	13	8	0.94	0.25	6.37
3/06	11.31	26	12	0.77	0.25	5.98
3/05	17.31	46	6	0.78	0.20	5.40
Annual Growth	**(24.2%)**	**—**	**—**	**23.4%**	**10.7%**	**13.5%**

Aircastle Limited

Not to be confused with the inflatable palaces that parents rent for kids' birthday parties, Aircastle Limited is an aircraft leasing concern. The company owns a lineup of utility jet aircraft that it adds to, leases, and sells to passenger and cargo markets. Aircastle touts a portfolio of 130-plus aircraft, which are leased to about 60 different businesses. Lessees of Aircastle's aircraft maintain the planes, as well as pay operating and insurance expenses. The company's leases are managed from offices in Ireland, Singapore, and the US. Aircastle also invests in industry-related assets, such as financing vehicles secured by commercial aircraft. Its three largest customers are US Airways, Martinair, and Emirates.

The company's strategy for growth has long been underpinned by a drive to acquire a diversified lineup of commercial aircraft and related assets. In addition, Aircastle has looked to plow back a portion of its revenue into assets and investment securities. However, with tight credit and tough economic times on the horizon, the company began down-shifting its investments in late 2007. Recognizing the high costs faced by its customers to update and expand their airline fleets, Aircastle has gained ground by pushing its terms for outsourced aircraft ownership. The move has helped Aircastle realign its lineup and pay down debt.

The company has stayed the course on an earlier 2007 deal for 32 aircraft from Guggenheim Aviation Investment Fund. The acquisition was completed in 2008. The company also had agreed in 2007 to acquire 15 new freighter aircraft from Airbus SAS and engines for the aircraft from Rolls-Royce PLC and Pratt & Whitney. The purchase was later reduced to 12 aircraft, with a delivery start date deferred until 2009. The arrival of the new fleet has been accompanied by a home makeover; Aircastle successfully refinanced its warehouse facility in 2008 with $1 billion in long term debt.

Chairman Wesley Edens, through Fortress Investment Group, controls about 40% of Aircastle.

EXECUTIVES

Chairman: Wesley R. (Wes) Edens, age 47
Deputy Chairman: Joseph P. Adams Jr., age 52
CEO: Ron Wainshal, age 44,
  $2,072,836 total compensation
COO, Secretary, and General Counsel: David Walton, age 48
CFO: Michael J. Inglese, age 44,
  $1,891,028 total compensation
EVP Technical: Joseph Schreiner, age 52,
  $947,836 total compensation
EVP Marketing: Peter Chang
Chief Technology Officer: Jonathan Lang, age 39
Chief Investment Officer: Michael Platt, age 49,
  $1,484,597 total compensation
Investor Relations: Julia Hallisey
Chief Accounting Officer: Aaron Dahlke, age 40
Auditors: Ernst & Young LLP

LOCATIONS

HQ: Aircastle Limited
  300 First Stamford Pl., 5th Fl., Stamford, CT 06902
Phone: 203-504-1020   **Fax:** 203-504-1021
Web: www.aircastle.com

2008 Lease Rental Revenue

	% of total
Europe	46
Asia	24
North America	13
Middle East & Africa	10
Latin America	7
Total	**100**

PRODUCTS/OPERATIONS

2008 Sales

	$ mil.	% of total
Lease rentals	578.5	99
Interest income	3.2	1
Other	0.9	—
Total	**582.6**	**100**

COMPETITORS

AerCap
Aviation Capital Group
Boeing Capital
CIT Group
GE Commercial Aviation Services
ILFC
Royal Bank of Scotland

HISTORICAL FINANCIALS

Company Type: Public

Income Statement				FYE: December 31
	REVENUE ($ mil.)	NET INCOME ($ mil.)	NET PROFIT MARGIN	EMPLOYEES
12/08	582.6	115.3	19.8%	76
12/07	381.1	127.3	33.4%	69
12/06	189.3	51.2	27.0%	45
12/05	36.0	0.2	0.6%	29
12/04	0.1	(1.5)	—	—
Annual Growth	**773.7%**	**—**	**—**	**37.9%**

2008 Year-End Financials

Debt ratio: 242.8%
Return on equity: 9.6%
Cash ($ mil.): 80.9
Current ratio: 4.09
Long-term debt ($ mil.): 2,700.6
No. of shares (mil.): 79.2
Dividends
  Yield: 10.5%
  Payout: 33.8%
Market value ($ mil.): 378.7
R&D as % of sales: —
Advertising as % of sales: —

Stock History

NYSE: AYR

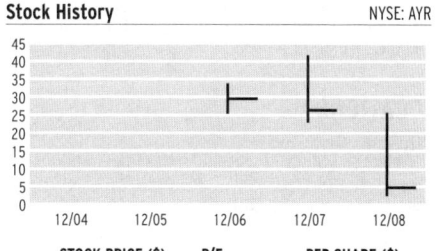

	STOCK PRICE ($) FY Close	P/E High/Low		PER SHARE ($) Earnings	Dividends	Book Value
12/08	4.78	17	2	1.48	0.50	14.04
12/07	26.33	22	12	1.89	2.45	16.34
12/06	29.50	30	23	1.11	0.63	8.04
Annual Growth	**(59.7%)**	**—**	**—**	**15.5%**	**(10.9%)**	**32.1%**

Akamai Technologies

Akamai Technologies offers an accelerated course on Internet delivery. The company's technology enables companies and government agencies to deliver Web content and applications, such as ads, business transaction tools, streaming video, and Web sites. Through its network of some 30,000 servers in about 70 countries, Akamai analyzes and manages Web traffic, transmitting content from the server geographically closest to the end user. The company's customers include Airbus, Apple, Best Buy, FedEx, Microsoft, MTV Networks, Sony Ericsson Mobile Communications, the US Department of Defense, the US Department of Labor, and Victoria's Secret.

The company offers audio and video streaming services, business intelligence and content targeting applications, and tools to avoid network congestion during periodic spikes in Web traffic. Akamai's Web Application Accelerator service speeds up applications using compression, connection optimization, dynamic caching, and routing technologies. The service is tailored for such online applications as airline reservation systems, course planning tools, customer order processing, and human resources.

Akamai has used acquisitions to expand its technology and grow its customer base. Early in 2007 the company acquired application delivery service provider Netli. In 2008 the company purchased acerno, a provider of online shopping and purchasing data.

EXECUTIVES

Executive Chairman of the Board: George H. Conrades, age 71
President, CEO, and Director: Paul L. Sagan, age 51,
  $4,596,969 total compensation
CFO: J. Donald (J. D.) Sherman, age 44,
  $2,156,046 total compensation
EVP Global Sales, Services, and Marketing:
  Robert W. (Bob) Hughes, age 42,
  $2,207,835 total compensation
EVP Products: Chris Schoettle, age 45
SVP and CTO: Michael M. (Mike) Afergan
SVP Engineering: Harald Prokop
SVP Networks and Operations: Robert Blumofe
SVP Human Resources: Debra Canner,
  $238,999 total compensation
SVP and General Counsel: Melanie Haratunian, age 49,
  $1,302,010 total compensation
VP and Chief Development Officer: Robert Wood
Chief Scientist and Director:
  F. Thomson (Tom) Leighton, age 52
President, Akamai Foundation: Wendy Ravech
Director, Corporate Communications and Media Relations: Jeff Young
Chief Strategist, eCommerce: Pedro Santos
Chief Security Architect: Andy Ellis
Investor Relations Manager: Noelle Faris
Auditors: PricewaterhouseCoopers LLP

LOCATIONS

HQ: Akamai Technologies, Inc.
  8 Cambridge Center, Cambridge, MA 02142
Phone: 617-444-3000   **Fax:** 617-444-3001
Web: www.akamai.com

2008 Sales

	% of total
US	75
Europe	18
Other regions	7
Total	**100**

COMPETITORS

DG FastChannel
Eyeblaster
EyeWonder
Level 3 Communications

Limelight
Mirror Image Internet
NaviSite

HISTORICAL FINANCIALS

Company Type: Public

Income Statement

FYE: December 31

	REVENUE ($ mil.)	NET INCOME ($ mil.)	NET PROFIT MARGIN	EMPLOYEES
12/08	790.9	145.1	18.3%	1,500
12/07	636.4	101.0	15.9%	1,300
12/06	428.7	57.4	13.4%	1,058
12/05	283.1	328.0	115.9%	784
12/04	210.0	34.4	16.4%	605
Annual Growth	39.3%	43.3%	—	25.5%

2008 Year-End Financials

Debt ratio: 12.7%
Return on equity: 9.9%
Cash ($ mil.): 156.1
Current ratio: 5.00
Long-term debt ($ mil.): 199.9
No. of shares (mil.): 171.3

Dividends
  Yield: —
  Payout: —
Market value ($ mil.): 2,584.6
R&D as % of sales: —
Advertising as % of sales: —

Stock History

NASDAQ (GS): AKAM

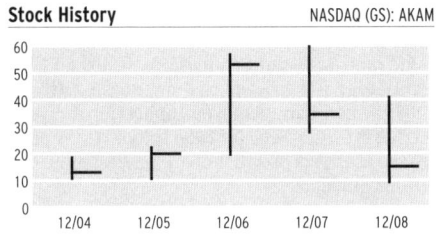

	STOCK PRICE ($) FY Close	P/E High/Low		PER SHARE ($) Earnings	Dividends	Book Value
12/08	15.09	52	12	0.79	—	9.16
12/07	34.60	107	50	0.56	—	7.93
12/06	53.12	167	58	0.34	—	5.57
12/05	19.93	11	5	2.11	—	3.64
12/04	13.03	74	43	0.25	—	(0.74)
Annual Growth	3.7%	—	—	33.3%	—	—

Alamo Group

Remember the Alamo Group for tractor-mounted mowing equipment (rotary, flail, and sickle-bar). The company's Alamo Industrial and Tiger hydraulically powered tractor-mounted mowers are primarily sold to government entities. Its Rhino and M&W subsidiaries sell rotary cutters and other equipment to farmers and ranchers for pasture maintenance. The McConnel, Bomford, and S.M.A. units sell hydraulic boom-mounted hedge and grass cutters. Reaching across the Atlantic, Alamo acquired Rivard Developpement, a France-based vacuum truck maker, for €15 million in 2008. The company makes about 60% of its sales in the US.

Alamo Group has as many challenges as opportunities. The company's operations may be negatively affected by general economic conditions, pricing and availability of raw materials,

government budgets, changes in government policies, interest rates, and tighter credit, not to mention the more specific threats of changes in farm incomes, droughts and floods, animal disease outbreaks and infestations of crop pests, worldwide demand for farm products, and limits on agricultural imports. Whew!

Alamo Group was founded in 1969 by chairman and former CEO Donald Douglass. The agricultural equipment manufacturer produces and assembles products in about a dozen major plants worldwide.

In 2005 Alamo Group's European subsidiary, Alamo Group (EUR), acquired UK-based Spearhead Machinery, a company that makes truck-mounted agricultural equipment.

In December of that same year Alamo Group announced that it would be consolidating its operations by closing its Holton, Kansas, manufacturing plant (agricultural equipment). In 2006 the company acquired the Gradall line of excavators from JLG Industries for $39.4 million. Later that year Alamo Group further expanded its product line when it purchased the vacuum truck and sweeper businesses of Clean Earth Environmental LLC and Clean Earth Kentucky LLC for about $8.9 million.

The company expanded its Schwarze sweeper division in 2006 with the acquisition of Nite-Hawk Sweepers.

Alamo further expanded its product line when it purchased Henke Manufacturing, a snow removal attachment company, in 2007.

Capital Southwest Venture Corporation owns about 28% of Alamo Group.

EXECUTIVES

Chairman: Donald J. Douglass, age 77
President, CEO, and Director:
  Ronald A. (Ron) Robinson, age 56,
  $839,074 total compensation
EVP and CFO: Dan E. Malone, age 48,
  $317,122 total compensation
VP and General Counsel: Donald C. Duncan, age 57,
  $223,363 total compensation
VP; Managing Director, Alamo Group, Europe:
  Geoffrey Davies, age 61, $412,512 total compensation
VP and Corporate Controller: Richard J. Wehrle, age 52,
  $212,206 total compensation
VP Administration, Secretary, and Treasurer:
  Robert H. George, age 62, $215,514 total compensation
Auditors: KPMG LLP

LOCATIONS

HQ: Alamo Group Inc.
  1627 E. Walnut St., Seguin, TX 78155
Phone: 830-379-1480   **Fax:** 830-372-9683
Web: www.alamo-group.com

2008 Sales

	$ mil.	% of total
North America		
US	331.7	60
Canada	22.2	4
Mexico	2.2	—
Europe		
France	99.7	18
UK	44.3	8
Australia	11.2	2
Other regions	45.8	8
Total	557.1	100

PRODUCTS/OPERATIONS

2008 Sales

	$ mil.	% of total
Industrial	254.8	46
Agricultural	120.2	21
European	182.1	33
Total	557.1	100

Selected Brands

Alamo Industrial (hydraulically-powered, tractor-mounted mowers)
Bomford (hydraulic, boom-mounted hedge and hedgerow cutters, industrial grass mowers, and agricultural seed bed preparation cultivators)
Gradall (excavators)
McConnel (hydraulic, boom-mounted hedge and grass cutters)
Rhino (tractor-mounted equipment, including rotary cutters, finishing mowers, flail mowers and disc mowers; posthole diggers, scraper blades and replacement parts)
Schulte (mechanical rotary mowers, snow blowers, and rock removal equipment)
Schwarze (air, mechanical broom, and regenerative air sweepers)
Tiger (heavy-duty, tractor-mounted mowing and vegetation maintenance equipment and replacement parts)

COMPETITORS

AGCO
Art's-Way
CNH Global
Deere
Elgin Sweeper Company
MTD Products

R.P.M. Tech
Scag Power Equipment
Tennant
Toro Company
TYMCO

HISTORICAL FINANCIALS

Company Type: Public

Income Statement

FYE: December 31

	REVENUE ($ mil.)	NET INCOME ($ mil.)	NET PROFIT MARGIN	EMPLOYEES
12/08	557.1	11.0	2.0%	2,460
12/07	504.4	12.4	2.5%	2,347
12/06	456.5	11.5	2.5%	2,215
12/05	368.1	11.3	3.1%	1,862
12/04	342.2	13.4	3.9%	1,914
Annual Growth	13.0%	(4.8%)	—	6.5%

2008 Year-End Financials

Debt ratio: 54.2%
Return on equity: 5.7%
Cash ($ mil.): 4.5
Current ratio: 3.10
Long-term debt ($ mil.): 99.9
No. of shares (mil.): 11.7

Dividends
  Yield: 1.2%
  Payout: 16.2%
Market value ($ mil.): 175.6
R&D as % of sales: —
Advertising as % of sales: —

Stock History

NYSE: ALG

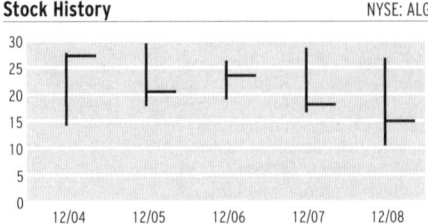

	STOCK PRICE ($) FY Close	P/E High/Low		PER SHARE ($) Earnings	Dividends	Book Value
12/08	14.95	24	10	1.11	0.18	15.69
12/07	18.12	23	14	1.24	0.24	16.91
12/06	23.46	22	17	1.16	0.24	15.47
12/05	20.50	26	16	1.14	0.24	13.92
12/04	27.16	20	11	1.36	0.24	13.69
Annual Growth	(13.9%)	—	—	(5.0%)	(6.9%)	3.5%

Albany Molecular Research

Albany Molecular Research, doing business as AMRI, pushes drug development efforts along from start to finish. The company provides contract research and manufacturing services to pharmaceutical and biotechnology firms. The company's services run the gamut — from compound screening and other drug discovery services to the contract manufacturing of drugs and drug ingredients for clinical trials and commercial sale. In addition to its work for other drug companies, AMRI conducts some of its own research, with the goal of licensing its compounds to other firms for further development. The company has R&D locations and manufacturing plants in North America, Europe, and Asia.

Responding to customer demand for lower-cost manufacturing, the company has been expanding in India particularly, buying several manufacturing plants there in 2007 and 2008. It is also expanding its research facilities in India, Hungary, and Singapore, as well as in the US. The company consolidated some facilities in 2009 to improve efficiencies following its previous growth efforts.

Albany Molecular Research in 2007 rebranded itself as AMRI, though it did not change its legal name. The change was meant, in part, to reflect AMRI's efforts to become a global contract organization. In addition to expanding its geographical footprint, the company is working to increase its comprehensive service contracts, which allow it to bring a drug from early discovery stages to commercialization.

Contract research and manufacturing customers in the US account for more than half of the company's total revenues. AMRI's largest contract services customer is GE Healthcare Medical Diagnostics, for which the company makes a raw ingredient for one of GE's diagnostic imaging agents. The GE contract accounts for about 15% of AMRI's sales.

The company's proprietary research efforts focus on oncology, obesity, gastroenterology, and nervous system ailments. AMRI intends to find development partners for the compounds once they are far enough advanced. AMRI has licensed some patents related to its central nervous system program to Bristol-Myers Squibb.

Historically, more than a quarter of AMRI's revenues were from royalties paid for its proprietary drug compound fexofenadine HCl, the key ingredient in Sanofi-Aventis' antihistamine Allegra. However, since generic versions of fexofenadine HCl hit the market in 2006 and 2007, its royalty revenues have shrunk to a little over 10% of annual sales. The popular allergy drug is also under assault from other over-the-counter remedies.

Chairman and CEO Thomas D'Ambra co-founded the company and, with his family, holds about 25% of its stock.

EXECUTIVES

Chairman, President, and CEO: Thomas E. D'Ambra, age 54, $3,470,444 total compensation
SVP Sales, Marketing, and Business Development: W. Steven (Steve) Jennings, age 58, $473,741 total compensation
SVP Administration, CFO, and Treasurer: Mark T. Frost, age 46, $639,985 total compensation
SVP Chemistry: Michael P. Trova, age 48

VP Human Resources: Brian D. Russell
VP, Pharmaceutical Development and Manufacturing: Jonathan D. Evans, age 38
VP Discovery Research and Development: Bruce J. Sargent
VP Science and Technology: Harold Meckler, age 52
VP Chemical Development and Small Scale cGMP Manufacturing: Michael D. Ironside
VP Pharmaceutical Development and Manufacturing: Steven R. Hagen, age 48, $384,892 total compensation
Director Chemistry, European Operations: Gergely Makara
Managing Director, European Operations: Philip William Small
Auditors: KPMG LLP

LOCATIONS

HQ: Albany Molecular Research, Inc.
21 Corporate Cir., Albany, NY 12212
Phone: 518-464-0279   **Fax:** 518-464-0289
Web: www.albmolecular.com

2008 Contract Revenues

	% of total
US	69
Europe	20
Other countries	11
Total	**100**

PRODUCTS/OPERATIONS

2008 Sales

	$ mil.	% of total
Contract revenues		
Discovery/development/small-scale manufacturing	114.0	50
Large-scale manufacturing	81.5	36
Royalties	28.3	12
Milestone payments	5.5	2
Total	**229.3**	**100**

COMPETITORS

Array BioPharma
Charles River Laboratories
Commonwealth Biotechnologies
Covance
Evotec
Kendle
MDS
PAREXEL
Pharmaceutical Product Development
Quintiles Transnational
Symyx Technologies
Synteract

HISTORICAL FINANCIALS

Company Type: Public

Income Statement

FYE: December 31

	REVENUE ($ mil.)	NET INCOME ($ mil.)	NET PROFIT MARGIN	EMPLOYEES
12/08	229.3	20.6	9.0%	1,357
12/07	192.5	8.9	4.6%	1,226
12/06	179.8	2.2	1.2%	1,015
12/05	183.9	16.3	8.9%	847
12/04	169.5	(11.7)	—	805
Annual Growth	**7.8%**	**—**	**—**	**13.9%**

2008 Year-End Financials

Debt ratio: 4.1%
Return on equity: 6.2%
Cash ($ mil.): 60.4
Current ratio: 5.16
Long-term debt ($ mil.): 13.5
No. of shares (mil.): 31.6
Dividends
  Yield: —
  Payout: —
Market value ($ mil.): 308.2
R&D as % of sales: —
Advertising as % of sales: —

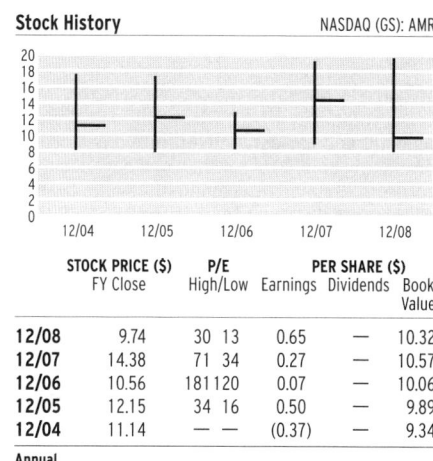

Stock History   NASDAQ (GS): AMRI

	STOCK PRICE ($) FY Close	P/E High/Low	PER SHARE ($) Earnings	Dividends	Book Value
12/08	9.74	30 13	0.65	—	10.32
12/07	14.38	71 34	0.27	—	10.57
12/06	10.56	181 120	0.07	—	10.06
12/05	12.15	34 16	0.50	—	9.89
12/04	11.14	— —	(0.37)	—	9.34
Annual Growth	**(3.3%)**	**— —**	**—**	**—**	**2.5%**

Alexion Pharmaceuticals

Alexion Pharmaceuticals can't suppress its enthusiasm for treating immune functions gone awry. The firm develops drugs that inhibit certain immune system functions that cause autoimmune disorders, cancers, and other diseases. The company's first marketed antibody product, Soliris, has won approval in the US, Canada, and the European Union for the treatment of a rare genetic blood disorder known as paroxysmal nocturnal hemoglobinuria (PNH). Alexion is developing the same antibody (eculizumab) used in Soliris as a potential treatment for other autoimmune and inflammatory conditions. The company has additional development programs for cancer-fighting antibodies.

Soliris is the first drug approved for the treatment of paroxysmal nocturnal hemoglobinuria (PNH), a rare disorder in which the death of red blood cells can bring on bouts of severe anemia, as well as blood clotting and organ damage. The drug is taken by relatively few and at a hefty cost: more than $400,000 per patient per year.

Soliris originally received approval in the EU and the US in 2007, and revenues for the company have since skyrocketed. Alexion is working to expand Soliris' sales into new markets: The drug gained approvals in Switzerland and Canada in 2008 and 2009, respectively, and the company is pursuing regulatory approval in Australia and Japan as well. The company believes the drug might be useful in treating additional conditions, including other rare blood disorders, transplant rejection, and severe asthma.

In early 2007 the company stopped development on pexelizumab, an anti-inflammation candidate it was working on with Procter &

Gamble, after getting disappointing results from a late-stage clinical trial.

The company relies on contract manufacturers (such as Lonza) to make Soliris, but in 2006 it bought a former Dow Chemical manufacturing plant and has converted it into one suitable for making biopharmaceuticals. It began manufacturing certain trial candidates at the facility in 2007, and it intends to use the plant for its future eculizumab manufacturing needs.

EXECUTIVES

Chairman: Max E. Link, age 68
CEO, Secretary, Treasurer, and Director: Leonard Bell, age 51, $3,939,351 total compensation
EVP and Head of Research and Clinical Development: Stephen P. Squinto, age 52, $1,516,625 total compensation
SVP and Chief Scientific Officer: Russell P. Rother, age 48
SVP and President, Alexion Europe SAS: Patrice Coissac, age 60
SVP Manufacturing and Technical Services: M. Stacy Hooks, age 41
SVP and General Counsel: Thomas I. H. Dubin, age 46, $1,427,293 total compensation
SVP and CFO: Vikas Sinha, age 45, $2,072,933 total compensation
SVP Strategic Development and Global Regulatory Affairs: Claude Nicaise
SVP and Chief Medical Officer: Camille L. Bedrosian, age 55
SVP Commercial Operations, Americas: David L. Hallal, age 43
VP Human Resources: Glenn R. Melrose, age 53
VP Finance and Assistant Secretary: Barry P. Luke, age 51
Controller and Chief Accounting Officer: Scott Phillips, age 32
Senior Director Corporate Communications: Irving Adler
Auditors: PricewaterhouseCoopers LLP

LOCATIONS

HQ: Alexion Pharmaceuticals, Inc.
352 Knotter Dr., Cheshire, CT 06410
Phone: 203-272-2596   **Fax:** 203-271-8198
Web: www.alexionpharm.com

2008 Sales

	$ mil.	% of total
Europe	143.7	55
US	113.2	44
Other regions & countries	2.2	1
Total	**259.1**	**100**

PRODUCTS/OPERATIONS

2008 Sales

	$ mil.	% of total
Product sales	259.0	100
Contract research revenue	0.1	—
Total	**259.1**	**100**

Selected Products

Approved
  Soliris (eculizumab, paroxysmal nocturnal hemoglobinuria)
In development
  CD200 monoclonal antibody (chronic lymphocytic leukemia, multiple myeloma)
  Intravenous eculizumab (atypical hemolytic uremic syndrome, myasthenia gravis, multifocal motor neuropathy, transplant rejection)
  New formulation eculizumab (asthma)

COMPETITORS

Abbott Labs
Amgen
Archemix
AstraZeneca
Baxter International
Celldex Therapeutics
ChemoCentryx
CSL Behring
Dyax
Genentech
GlaxoSmithKline
Medarex
Millennium Pharmaceuticals
MorphoSys
Neurogen
Novo Nordisk
Pfizer
Pharming
Sanofi-Aventis U.S
XOMA

HISTORICAL FINANCIALS

Company Type: Public

Income Statement

FYE: December 31

	REVENUE ($ mil.)	NET INCOME ($ mil.)	NET PROFIT MARGIN	EMPLOYEES
12/08	259.1	33.1	12.8%	504
12/07	72.0	(92.3)	—	434
12/06*	1.6	(131.5)	—	296
7/05	1.1	(108.8)	—	241
7/04	4.6	(74.1)	—	204
Annual Growth	**174.0%**	**—**	**—**	**25.4%**

*Fiscal year change

2008 Year-End Financials

Debt ratio: 57.3%
Return on equity: 19.0%
Cash ($ mil.): 138.0
Current ratio: 3.28
Long-term debt ($ mil.): 141.4
No. of shares (mil.): 88.6
Dividends
  Yield: —
  Payout: —
Market value ($ mil.): 3,205.2
R&D as % of sales: —
Advertising as % of sales: —

Stock History

NASDAQ (GM): ALXN

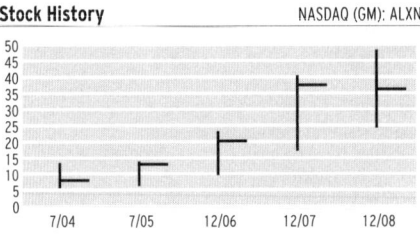

	STOCK PRICE ($) FY Close	P/E High/Low		PER SHARE ($) Earnings	Dividends	Book Value
12/08	36.19	123	63	0.39	—	2.79
12/07	37.51	—	—	(1.27)	—	1.15
12/06*	20.19	—	—	(2.08)	—	1.41
7/05	13.02	—	—	(1.95)	—	0.76
7/04	7.96	—	—	(1.72)	—	1.95
Annual Growth	**46.0%**	**—**	**—**	**—**	**—**	**9.4%**

*Fiscal year change

Align Technology

Brace-face begone! Align Technology produces and sells the Invisalign System, which corrects malocclusion, or crooked teeth. Instead of using metal or ceramic mounts that are cemented on the teeth and connected by wires (traditional braces), the system involves using an array of clear and removable dental Aligners to move a patient's teeth into a desired tooth alignment. The company markets its products to orthodontists and dentists worldwide. Align also provides training for practitioners to model treatment schemes using its Internet-based application called ClinCheck, which simulates tooth movement and suggests the appropriate Aligner.

Align Technology manufactures its products in the US, Costa Rica, and Mexico. Products are sold in the Americas, Europe, and the Asia/Pacific region, primarily through the company's direct sales force, but also through distributors in areas of Latin America and the Asia/Pacific.

The company continues to expand its Invisalign System and develop new products. It is targeting general practice dentists as a primary channel since general dentists have larger patient populations than orthodontists, who traditionally treat malocclusion.

In 2008 Align Technology launched its Invisalign Teen and Invisalign ClinAssist variations, adding to the existing Full Invisalign and Invisalign Express treatment options. The company hopes its teen-targeted launch will help it penetrate the orthodontic market, while its ClinAssist option provides enhanced monitoring tools to general practitioners.

EXECUTIVES

Chairman: C. Raymond Larkin Jr., age 60
President, CEO, and Director: Thomas M. Prescott, age 53, $2,331,754 total compensation
SVP Business Operations: Len M. Hedge, age 51, $1,247,166 total compensation
VP Finance and CFO: Kenneth B. (Ken) Arola, age 53, $968,245 total compensation
VP Operations: Emory M. Wright, age 39, $863,223 total compensation
VP Corporate and Legal Affairs, General Counsel, and Secretary: Roger E. George, age 43, $862,321 total compensation
VP Marketing and Chief Marketing Officer: Sheila Tan
VP Research and Development and Information Technology: Dana C. Cambra, age 51
VP International: Gil Laks, age 43
VP North American Sales: Dan S. Ellis, age 57
Investor Relations: Shirley Stacy
Auditors: PricewaterhouseCoopers LLP

LOCATIONS

HQ: Align Technology, Inc.
881 Martin Ave., Santa Clara, CA 95050
Phone: 408-470-1000   **Fax:** 408-470-1010
Web: www.aligntech.com

2008 Sales

	$ mil.	% of total
North America	230	76
Europe	62	20
Other international	12	4
Total	**304**	**100**

PRODUCTS/OPERATIONS

2008 Sales

	$ mil.	% of total
Invisalign	292	96
Other	12	4
Total	**304**	**100**

COMPETITORS

3M
Ceradyne
DENTSPLY
Henry Schein
National Dentex
Patterson Companies
Sybron Dental
Young Innovations

HISTORICAL FINANCIALS

Company Type: Public

Income Statement FYE: December 31

	REVENUE ($ mil.)	NET INCOME ($ mil.)	NET PROFIT MARGIN	EMPLOYEES
12/08	304.0	80.0	26.3%	1,394
12/07	284.3	35.7	12.6%	1,307
12/06	206.4	(35.0)	—	1,253
12/05	207.1	1.4	0.7%	1,097
12/04	172.8	8.8	5.1%	969
Annual Growth	**15.2%**	**73.6%**	**—**	**9.5%**

2008 Year-End Financials

Debt ratio: —
Return on equity: 42.1%
Cash ($ mil.): 87.1
Current ratio: 2.94
Long-term debt ($ mil.): —
No. of shares (mil.): 74.5
Dividends
  Yield: —
  Payout: —
Market value ($ mil.): 651.5
R&D as % of sales: —
Advertising as % of sales: —

Stock History NASDAQ (GM): ALGN

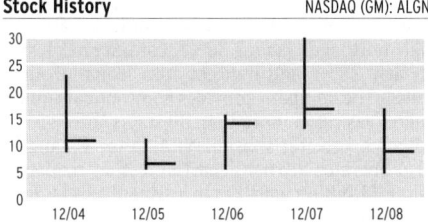

	STOCK PRICE ($) FY Close	P/E High/Low		PER SHARE ($) Earnings	Dividends	Book Value
12/08	8.75	14	4	1.18	—	2.93
12/07	16.68	59	26	0.50	—	2.16
12/06	13.97	—	—	(0.55)	—	1.12
12/05	6.47	544	282	0.02	—	1.25
12/04	10.75	163	63	0.14	—	1.15
Annual Growth	**(5.0%)**	**—**	**—**	**70.4%**	**—**	**26.4%**

Alkermes, Inc.

Alkermes, which is Arabic for "magic potion," is working some biotech alchemy. The firm uses its proprietary drug-delivery systems to make fragile biotech compounds that require less frequent dosing or provide more targeted delivery. Focusing on widespread diseases like diabetes, central nervous system disorders, and addiction, it has a couple of drugs on the market that use its injectable extended-release technology, which lets patients take a drug once or twice a month, rather than once or twice a day. One such drug is Risperdal Consta, a long-acting version of Janssen's schizophrenia medication Risperdal. Another is Vivitrol, a treatment for alcohol dependence that the company markets itself.

Alkermes had been working with Eli Lilly on an inhaled insulin; however, Lilly discontinued development in early 2008, following the high-profile exits from the inhalable insulin market of Pfizer and Novo Nordisk. Alkermes' product, which had conquered some of the problems faced by others, was in the later stages of clinical development but Lilly didn't want to risk taking a product to market if there was no market for it.

Shortly after the project was canceled, Alkermes moved to fend off financial ramifications by announcing an 18% workforce reduction and the shuttering of an AIR Insulin manufacturing plant in Massachusetts.

It continues to target diabetes, however, with Exenatide LAR, a long-acting injectable version of Amylin Pharmaceuticals' diabetes drug Byetta, that is in the late stages of clinical trials. Eli Lilly is also a development partner on Exenatide. Compounds at earlier stages of development include an inhalable treatment for chronic obstructive pulmonary disease (with Indevus), as well as orally administered medications for addiction.

Alkermes' development partner for Risperdal Consta, Janssen, has worldwide marketing rights to the drug. Alkermes manufactures the drug and receives royalties on sales. Cephalon, which had been its marketing partner for Vivitrol, pulled out in 2008 and Alkermes took on the job itself.

The company is led by CEO Richard Pops, who also serves as chairman. Pops replaced former CEO David Broecker when he resigned in 2009.

HISTORY

Floyd Bloom, Alexander Rich, Paul Schimmel, and Michael Wall founded Alkermes in 1987. The company targeted the development of diagnostic and therapeutic agents for central nervous system diseases. It went public in 1991.

The next year Alkermes created a separate partnership to fund development of Cereport technology, and in the mid-1990s it branched out into other types of delivery systems and forged alliances with major drug companies to adapt its technologies to their products.

In the late 1990s Alkermes began collaborations with Johnson & Johnson to develop erythropoietin blood booster Procrit with ProLease and with Genentech to develop Nutropin Depot, a sustained-release formulation of Genentech's human growth hormone.

In 1999, Alkermes bought AIR (Advanced Inhalation Research), its pulmonary drug delivery unit. In 2004 the company ceased making its first FDA-approved product, Nutropin Depot.

LOCATIONS

HQ: Alkermes, Inc.
88 Sidney St., Cambridge, MA 02139
Phone: 617-494-0171   **Fax:** 617-494-9263
Web: www.alkermes.com

PRODUCTS/OPERATIONS

2009 Sales

	$ mil.	% of total
Collaborative profits (Cephalon buyout)	130.2	40
Manufacturing	116.8	36
Collaborative R&D agreements	42.1	13
Royalties (Risperdal Consta)	33.2	10
Product sales	4.5	1
Total	**326.8**	**100**

Selected Products

Marketed
  Risperdal Consta (long-acting Risperdal for schizophrenia, with Janssen)
  Vivitrol (extended-release naltrexone for alcohol dependence)

In development
  ALKS 27 (inhalable treatment for chronic obstructive pulmonary disease, with Indevus Pharmaceuticals)
  ALKS 29 (oral medication for alcohol dependence)
  ALKS 33 (oral treatment for opioid addiction)
  Exenatide LAR (long-acting exenatide for type 2 diabetes, with Amylin Pharmaceuticals & Eli Lilly)

COMPETITORS

Biovail	Johnson & Johnson
Bristol-Myers Squibb	Nektar Therapeutics
Covidien	NPS Pharmaceuticals
DURECT	Odyssey Thera
Eli Lilly	Penwest Pharmaceuticals
Emisphere	Pfizer
Forest Labs	SkyePharma
IntelliPharmaCeutics	Tyco

HISTORICAL FINANCIALS

Company Type: Public

Income Statement FYE: March 31

	REVENUE ($ mil.)	NET INCOME ($ mil.)	NET PROFIT MARGIN	EMPLOYEES
3/09	326.8	130.5	39.9%	570
3/08	240.7	167.0	69.4%	610
3/07	240.0	9.4	3.9%	830
3/06	166.6	3.8	2.3%	760
3/05	76.1	(73.9)	—	528
Annual Growth	**44.0%**	**—**	**—**	**1.9%**

2009 Year-End Financials

Debt ratio: 11.5%
Return on equity: 35.3%
Cash ($ mil.): 86.9
Current ratio: 5.45
Long-term debt ($ mil.): 50.2
No. of shares (mil.): 94.8

Dividends
Yield: 0.0%
Payout: —
Market value ($ mil.): 1,149.5
R&D as % of sales: —
Advertising as % of sales: —

Stock History

NASDAQ (GS): ALKS

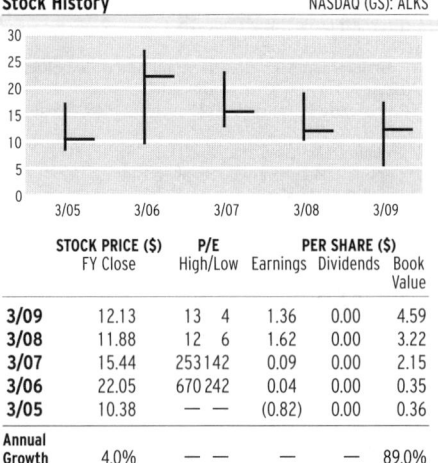

	STOCK PRICE ($) FY Close	P/E High/Low		PER SHARE ($) Earnings	Dividends	Book Value
3/09	12.13	13	4	1.36	0.00	4.59
3/08	11.88	12	6	1.62	0.00	3.22
3/07	15.44	253	142	0.09	0.00	2.15
3/06	22.05	670	242	0.04	0.00	0.35
3/05	10.38	—	—	(0.82)	0.00	0.36
Annual Growth	4.0%	—	—	—	—	89.0%

Allegiant Travel

Allegiant Travel pledges to serve the vacation needs of residents of more than 55 small US cities in more than 30 states. Through Allegiant Air, the company provides nonstop service to tourist destinations such as Las Vegas and Orlando, Florida, from places such as Cedar Rapids, Iowa; Fargo, North Dakota; and Toledo, Ohio. It maintains a fleet of about 45 MD-80 series aircraft. Besides scheduled service, Allegiant Air offers charter flights for casino operators Harrah's, MGM MIRAGE, and Wynn Resorts, in addition to other customers. Sister company Allegiant Vacations works with partners to allow customers to book hotel rooms and rental cars with their airline tickets.

The company hopes to thrive by sticking to what it believes to be an underserved niche: Allegiant Air is the only provider of nonstop service to its chosen destinations from most of the markets where it operates. Allegiant Travel has identified about 100 small cities in the US and Canada as candidates for its services. It also plans to expand its list of leisure destinations. In addition to Las Vegas and Orlando, Allegiant Travel offers service to Phoenix and to two other Florida markets, Fort Lauderdale and Tampa/St. Petersburg.

Allegiant Travel believes the diversity of its revenue mix will help ensure the company's success. The long-term, fixed-fee contract with Harrah's is a useful supplement to its scheduled airline service. Besides the fees it collects when customers arrange lodging and ground transportation via the Allegiant Air Web site, the company charges for ancillary services such as advance seat assignments and in-flight food and beverages.

In an effort to control aircraft-related costs, Allegiant Travel has chosen to fly planes from the venerable MD-80 series, which are readily available second-hand. The aircraft, formerly an industry mainstay, cost less than new planes would, and using a single type of plane makes

maintenance simpler and thus less expensive. On the downside, MD-80s are less fuel-efficient than newer aircraft. Sticking with this strategy, in late 2009 Allegiant Travel inked a deal to purchase 18 MD-80 aircraft from Scandinavian airline SAS. Allegiant Travel plans to place the majority of these planes into service by the end of 2011.

Just as the company's aircraft have been tested, so has Allegiant Travel's management team. This isn't the first go-round in the airline industry for CEO Maurice Gallagher and director Robert Priddy, who helped found low-fare carrier ValuJet (now AirTran). Gallagher owns 21% of Allegiant Travel. Private equity firm ComVest, represented on the company's board by Priddy, owns 8%.

The original Allegiant Air was founded in 1997. That company filed for Chapter 11 bankruptcy protection in 2000 and emerged from its reorganization in 2002 under new ownership and management, led by Gallagher. Allegiant Travel, which was formed in 2005 as a holding company for Allegiant Air and Allegiant Vacations, went public in 2006.

EXECUTIVES

Chairman and CEO: Maurice J. (Maury) Gallagher Jr., age 59, $123,011 total compensation
President and CFO: Andrew C. Levy, age 39, $732,836 total compensation
VP Flight Operations: James R. (Jim) Carr
Principal Accounting Officer: Scott Sheldon, age 31, $274,176 total compensation
Director Corporate Communications: Tyri Squyres
Auditors: Ernst & Young LLP

LOCATIONS

HQ: Allegiant Travel Company
3301 N. Buffalo Dr., Ste. B-9, Las Vegas, NV 89129
Phone: 702-851-7300   **Fax:** 702-256-7209
Web: www.allegiantair.com

PRODUCTS/OPERATIONS

2008 Sales

	$ mil.	% of total
Scheduled service	331.0	66
Ancillary	114.6	23
Fixed-fee contract	52.5	10
Other	5.9	1
Total	**504.0**	**100**

COMPETITORS

AirTran Holdings	Midwest Air
AMR Corp.	Northwest Airlines
Continental Airlines	Southwest Airlines
Delta Air Lines	UAL
Frontier Airlines	US Airways
JetBlue	

HISTORICAL FINANCIALS

Company Type: Public

Income Statement

FYE: December 31

	REVENUE ($ mil.)	NET INCOME ($ mil.)	NET PROFIT MARGIN	EMPLOYEES
12/08	504.0	35.4	7.0%	1,567
12/07	360.6	31.5	8.7%	1,363
12/06	243.4	8.7	3.6%	1,046
12/05	132.5	7.3	5.5%	596
12/04	90.4	9.1	10.1%	970
Annual Growth	53.7%	40.4%	—	12.7%

2008 Year-End Financials

Debt ratio: 16.8%
Return on equity: 15.9%
Cash ($ mil.): 97.2
Current ratio: 1.64
Long-term debt ($ mil.): 39.4
No. of shares (mil.): 19.9

Dividends
Yield: 0.0%
Payout: —
Market value ($ mil.): 964.6
R&D as % of sales: —
Advertising as % of sales: —

Stock History

NASDAQ (GM): ALGT

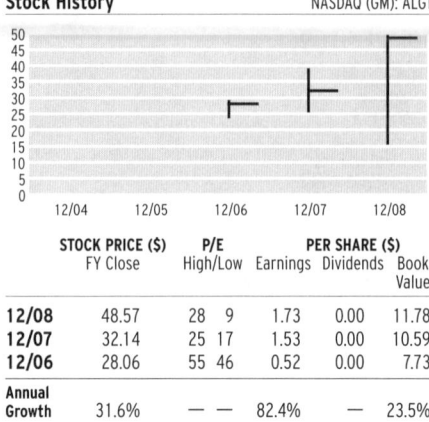

	STOCK PRICE ($) FY Close	P/E High/Low		PER SHARE ($) Earnings	Dividends	Book Value
12/08	48.57	28	9	1.73	0.00	11.78
12/07	32.14	25	17	1.53	0.00	10.59
12/06	28.06	55	46	0.52	0.00	7.73
Annual Growth	31.6%	—	—	82.4%	—	23.5%

Alliance Financial

Alliance Financial Corporation is the holding company for Alliance Bank, which operates about 30 branches in central New York state. Targeting individuals and small to midsized businesses, Alliance offers such retail banking products as checking and savings accounts, IRAs, and CDs. Its loan and lease portfolio mainly contains residential mortgages (about 30%), commercial loans (nearly 25%), and indirect auto loans (around 20%). The company provides commercial equipment leasing in more than 30 states through its Alliance Leasing subsidiary. Alliance Financial also operates a trust department that manages some $1 billion worth of investment assets.

Alliance Financial bought smaller area bank Bridge Street Financial for approximately $55 million in 2006. The acquisition also brought in insurance brokerage Ladd's Agency.

EXECUTIVES

Chairman and CEO; President and CEO, Alliance Bank: Jack H. Webb, age 56, $693,687 total compensation
EVP; EVP Commercial Banking Sales and Service and Trust and Investment Services, Alliance Bank; CEO Alliance Leasing: John H. Watt Jr., age 50, $321,744 total compensation
EVP and Senior Loan Officer, Credit Management and Administration, Alliance Bank: James W. Getman, age 56, $245,730 total compensation
CFO and Treasurer; VP and CFO, Alliance Bank: J. Daniel Mohr, age 43, $255,716 total compensation
SVP Commercial Banking and Cortland Market Executive, Alliance Bank: John A. Mason
SVP Marketing and Investor Relations, Alliance Bank: Joseph M. (Joe) Russo
SVP Human Resources, Alliance Bank: Colleen K. Lefeve

SVP and CIO, Alliance Bank: Mark A. Baker
SVP Retail Banking Sales and Service, Alliance Bank: Steven G. Cacchio, $229,788 total compensation
SVP Risk Management, Alliance Bank: Claudia J. Tavernese
SVP and Senior Credit Officer, Alliance Bank: Kathy L. Davis
SVP and Director Alliance Investment Management, Alliance Bank: Kenneth J. Entenmann

LOCATIONS

HQ: Alliance Financial Corporation
120 Madison St., Tower 2, 18th Fl.
Syracuse, NY 13202
Phone: 315-475-2100   **Fax:** 315-475-4421
Web: www.alliancebankna.com

PRODUCTS/OPERATIONS

Selected Subsidiaries

Alliance Bank, N.A.
  Alliance Leasing, Inc.
  Alliance Preferred Funding Corp.
Ladd's Agency, Inc.

COMPETITORS

Bank of America
Citizens Financial Group
Community Bank System
First Niagara Financial
HSBC USA
JPMorgan Chase
KeyCorp
M&T Bank
Oneida Financial

HISTORICAL FINANCIALS

Company Type: Public

Income Statement

FYE: December 31

	ASSETS ($ mil.)	NET INCOME ($ mil.)	INCOME AS % OF ASSETS	EMPLOYEES
12/08	1,367.4	10.4	0.8%	334
12/07	1,307.3	9.5	0.7%	335
12/06	1,273.0	7.3	0.6%	324
12/05	980.4	7.5	0.8%	269
12/04	893.9	7.3	0.8%	298
Annual Growth	11.2%	9.3%	—	2.9%

2008 Year-End Financials

Equity as % of assets: 8.6%
Return on assets: 0.8%
Return on equity: 8.9%
Long-term debt ($ mil.): 189.6
No. of shares (mil.): 4.6
Market value ($ mil.): 109.6
Dividends
  Yield: 4.2%
  Payout: 44.6%
Sales ($ mil.): 58.1
R&D as % of sales: —
Advertising as % of sales: —

Stock History

NASDAQ (GM): ALNC

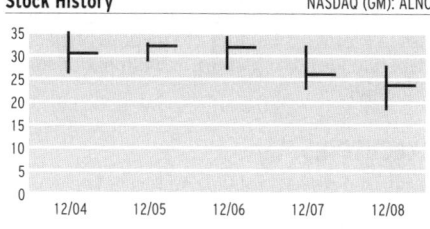

	STOCK PRICE ($) FY Close	P/E High/Low		PER SHARE ($) Earnings	Dividends	Book Value
12/08	23.70	12	8	2.24	1.00	31.24
12/07	26.00	16	12	1.98	0.90	24.99
12/06	31.86	18	15	1.88	0.88	23.68
12/05	32.09	16	14	2.05	0.84	15.04
12/04	30.50	17	13	2.00	0.84	14.90
Annual Growth	(6.1%)	—	—	2.9%	4.5%	20.3%

Allion Healthcare

Allion Healthcare is a specialty drug distributor focusing on patients with HIV, AIDS, and other chronic conditions. Through subsidiaries MOMS Pharmacy and Biomed America, the company fills prescriptions at more than 15 distribution centers and delivers them to patients, doctors' offices, and clinics nationwide. Allion also provides ancillary drugs and nutritional supplies, and it offers consulting and drug packaging services (such as pre-filled pill boxes) to help patients stick with their medication regimens. Most of Allion's customers rely on Medicaid or state programs such as the AIDS Drug Assistance Program to pay for their prescriptions. Allion was taken private by H.I.G. Capital in early 2010.

Investment firm H.I.G. acquired Allion in a $278 million deal, making the company a private entity. The acquisition, a cash-for-stock transaction that also included the assumption of about $79 million in debt, allowed Allion to deliver value to its shareholders.

To expand its specialty pharmacy operations into the home infusion market for chronically ill patients, Allion acquired Biomed America for $99 million in April 2008. Biomed America now makes up the company's specialty infusion segment. The acquisition added six pharmacy distribution centers and expanded the company's service offerings to include products for patients with hemophilia, respiratory syncytial virus (RSV), and other chronic conditions.

Allion's specialty HIV/AIDS business (MOMS Pharmacy) has remained its largest segment, accounting for 80% of sales in 2008. The division's operations are concentrated in the New York and California markets, as well as other areas where large populations of HIV/AIDS patients are located. Allion has expanded the MOMS Pharmacy business through acquisitions of regional or local specialty pharmacies in new or existing markets, as well as by increasing its patient load at existing facilities.

EXECUTIVES

Chairman, President, and CEO: Michael P. Moran, age 49, $542,500 total compensation
SVP and CFO: Russell J. (Russ) Fichera, age 56, $352,466 total compensation
VP Oris Health and HIV Sales: Anthony D. Luna, age 40, $313,290 total compensation
VP Pharmacy Operations: Robert E. Fleckenstein, age 56, $284,584 total compensation
Director Finance, Secretary, and Treasurer: Stephen A. Maggio, age 59, $206,266 total compensation
Auditors: BDO Seidman, LLP

LOCATIONS

HQ: Allion Healthcare, Inc.
1660 Walt Whitman Rd., Ste. 105
Melville, NY 11747
Phone: 631-547-6520   **Fax:** 631-249-5865
Web: www.allionhealthcare.com

2008 Specialty HIV Sales

	% of total
California	66
New York	31
Washington	2
Florida	1
Total	**100**

PRODUCTS/OPERATIONS

2008 Sales

	$ mil.	% of total
Specialty HIV	277.0	81
Specialty Infusion	63.7	19
Total	**340.7**	**100**

COMPETITORS

BioScrip
Cardinal Health
Caremark Pharmacy Services
Catalyst Health Solutions
Express Scripts
McKesson
Medco Health
Rite Aid
Walgreen
WellPoint

HISTORICAL FINANCIALS

Company Type: Private

Income Statement

FYE: December 31

	REVENUE ($ mil.)	NET INCOME ($ mil.)	NET PROFIT MARGIN	EMPLOYEES
12/08	340.7	7.5	2.2%	293
12/07	246.7	3.3	1.3%	226
12/06	209.5	3.2	1.5%	222
12/05	123.1	0.4	0.3%	170
12/04	64.6	(2.7)	—	140
Annual Growth	51.5%	—	—	20.3%

2008 Year-End Financials

Debt ratio: 31.7%
Return on equity: 5.4%
Cash ($ mil.): 18.4
Current ratio: 2.54
Long-term debt ($ mil.): 53.7

Net Income History

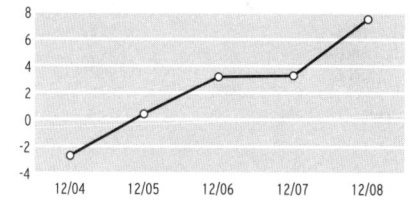

Allscripts-Misys Healthcare Solutions

Jokes about doctors' handwriting may go the way of house calls thanks to Allscripts-Misys Healthcare Solutions. The company, which does business as Allscripts, provides prescription management software and services that let doctors enter prescription information over computer networks, including tools that give doctors access (via desktop or wireless handheld devices) to patient drug history, drug interactions, and generic alternatives. Other services include electronic document imaging and scanning and physician feedback services. In 2008 Allscripts merged with Misys Healthcare (a division of Misys) to create Allscripts-Misys Healthcare Solutions.

Allscripts-Misys is focusing on its core business of providing information and connectivity products to physicians and hospitals. As part of that push, the company in 2009 sold its Medication Services business to A-S Medication Solutions for $26 million, and sold its Physicians Interactive business unit in 2008 to a fund managed by Perseus, L.L.C.

EXECUTIVES

Chairman: J. Michael (Mike) Lawrie, age 56
COO: Eileen J. McPartland, age 54
CEO and Director: Glen E. Tullman, age 50, $4,824,439 total compensation
President: Lee A. Shapiro, age 54, $2,823,276 total compensation
President, Government Sector: R. L. (Vem) Davenport, $1,548,337 total compensation
President, Strategic Accounts: Laurie A. S. McGraw, age 46, $1,379,785 total compensation
President, Sales: Jeff Surges, age 43
CFO: William J. (Bill) Davis, age 41, $2,413,572 total compensation
Chief Marketing Officer: Dan Michelson
EVP Human Resources: Diane Adams
SVP and General Counsel: Brian D. Vandenberg, age 47
SVP Product Development: Faisal Mushtaq
VP Investor Relations: Seth Frank
Auditors: PricewaterhouseCoopers LLP

LOCATIONS

HQ: Allscripts-Misys Healthcare Solutions, Inc.
222 Merchandise Mart Plaza, Ste. 2024
Chicago, IL 60654
Phone: 866-358-6869   **Fax:** 312-506-1201
Web: www.allscripts.com

PRODUCTS/OPERATIONS

2009 Sales

	$ mil.	% of total
Software & services		
System sales	98.5	18
Professional services	51.8	9
Maintenance	196.2	36
Transaction processing & other	187.5	34
Prepackaged medications	14.4	3
Total	**548.4**	**100**

Selected Products

AIC — Electronic document imaging and scanning solutions
TouchWorks — Electronic medical record and clinical information solutions

COMPETITORS

BioScrip
Cardinal Health
Caremark Pharmacy
Cerner
Eclipsys
McKesson
ProxyMed
TriZetto
WebMD Health

HISTORICAL FINANCIALS

Company Type: Public

Income Statement
FYE: May 31

	REVENUE ($ mil.)	NET INCOME ($ mil.)	NET PROFIT MARGIN	EMPLOYEES
5/09	548.4	26.0	4.7%	2,569
5/08*	383.8	25.4	6.6%	1,500
12/07	281.9	20.6	7.3%	1,155
12/06	228.0	11.9	5.2%	914
12/05	120.6	9.7	8.0%	386
Annual Growth	**46.0%**	**28.0%**	**—**	**60.6%**

*Fiscal year change

2009 Year-End Financials

Debt ratio: 9.1%
Return on equity: 6.4%
Cash ($ mil.): 71.2
Current ratio: 1.59
Long-term debt ($ mil.): 63.7
No. of shares (mil.): 146.0
Dividends
  Yield: —
  Payout: —
Market value ($ mil.): 1,884.5
R&D as % of sales: —
Advertising as % of sales: —

Stock History   NASDAQ (GS): MDRX

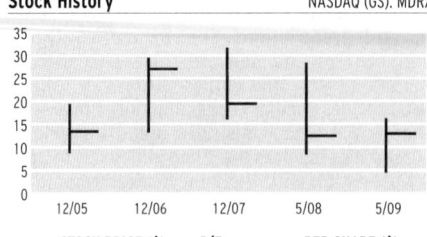

	STOCK PRICE ($) FY Close	P/E High/Low		PER SHARE ($) Earnings	Dividends	Book Value
5/09	12.91	76	22	0.21	—	4.80
5/08*	12.43	156	48	0.18	—	0.76
12/07	19.42	90	46	0.35	—	2.33
12/06	26.99	133	61	0.22	—	2.17
12/05	13.40	83	39	0.23	—	0.67
Annual Growth	**(0.9%)**	—	—	**(2.2%)**	—	**63.3%**

*Fiscal year change

Almost Family

If you live in California and you're worried about Mom's failing faculties back in Florida, you could call Almost Family. With its home health nursing services, Almost Family offers senior citizens in 11 states (including Florida) an alternative to spending their days in nursing homes. The company operates through two segments: Its visiting nurse unit provides skilled nursing care under the Caretenders and Mederi-Caretenders names, while its personal care segment (operating under the Almost Family banner) offers custodial care, such as housekeeping, meal preparation, and medication management. The company has about 70 skilled nursing and 20 personal care branch locations.

Payments from Medicare account for about 90% of revenue in the company's visiting nurse segment, making Almost Family sensitive to any changes in Medicare reimbursement policies. The company relies on its personal care segment, which depends far less on Medicare payments, to diversify its sources of revenue with income from private insurance, private pay, and Medicaid.

However, skilled nursing brings in most of the money for the company, and Almost Family is focused on growing that part of the business, in part, by acquiring other home nursing agencies. In 2008 the company acquired more than 10 visiting nurse branch locations, adding to its market presence in Florida, Connecticut, and Ohio, as well as marking its entry into the New Jersey and Pennsylvania skilled nursing markets.

That same year the company also acquired Patient Care for $45 million gaining eight facilities in the Northeast. Later in 2008 it purchased two home health agencies previously run by Fairfield

Medical Center in Columbus, Ohio, and Hardin Memorial Hospital in southern Kentucky.

Almost Family continued its run of acquisitions in 2009 when it agreed to buy the assets of Central Florida Health Alliance's home health agencies.

HISTORY

Almost Family was founded in 1976 as National Health Industries, a Louisville, Kentucky-based home health care company. After William Yarmuth became president in 1981, he expanded the company into such service areas as home infusion and home medical equipment.

The company became Caretenders Health in 1985, and in 1991 it merged with Senior Service Corporation, a small, public adult day care services company. The company further expanded the range of services it offered to the elderly through its home health care operations. It established beachheads in new geographic markets by opening home health offices (or buying them), and then adding day care centers. It also bought some existing care centers.

The company grew energetically following its decision to specialize in elder care. It made three acquisitions in 1997 and surpassed that feat by closing on four acquisitions in little over a month in early 1998. The company lost one of its revenue streams that year: Two home health agencies in the Louisville area that had been managed by Caretenders were sold by their owner, Columbia/HCA (now HCA). Caretenders sued Columbia/HCA for breach of contract and in 1999 won a $1.5 million settlement.

That year the company also sharpened its focus by selling its product operations (including infusion therapy, respiratory, and medical equipment) to Lincare Holdings, but decided not to discontinue its visiting nurses services.

In 2000 the company changed its name to Almost Family to underscore its focus on adult day care. The following year it bought back the 23% stake that rehabilitation titan HEALTHSOUTH had maintained in the company.

Almost Family acquired one adult day care center per year during 1999, 2000, and 2001. In July of 2002 the company announced it had completed the acquisition of Medlink of Ohio, a provider of home health care services that operated in Cleveland and Akron, Ohio.

To expand its visiting nurse segment, Almost Family acquired two home health agencies in 2005: Florida Palliative Home Care and Bradenton Florida Home Health. Also in 2005, the company sold its adult day care division to Active Services for $15 million.

In 2006 it acquired several home health agencies in Florida, including 21 locations owned by Mederi in Florida, Missouri, and Illinois for some $20 million.

EXECUTIVES

Chairman, President, and CEO: William B. Yarmuth, age 56, $1,083,295 total compensation
SVP Administration: P. Todd Lyles, age 47, $447,216 total compensation
SVP VN Florida Region: Phillis D. Montville, age 61
SVP Operations, VN North Region: Anne T. Liechty, age 57, $357,459 total compensation
SVP and CFO: C. Steven (Steve) Guenthner, age 48, $554,928 total compensation
SVP Sales and Clinical Programs: Cathy S. Newhouse, $307,493 total compensation

VP and General Counsel: Jerry Perchik
VP and Chief Accounting Officer: John Walker, age 51
VP Human Resources: Mark Sutton
VP Reimbursement: Cathy Pedigo
VP Group Living Facilities: Michael Moses
VP Operations: Carla Hengst
VP Operations, VN Northeast Operations: Ray Rasa
VP Operations, VN NE Florida Region: Nancy Ralston
VP Operations, VN North Region: Susan Long
VP Operations, VN Florida Region: Vicki Suplizio
VP Operations, PC Operations: David Pruitt, age 46
VP Marketing, VN NE Florida Region: James Spriggs
Auditors: Ernst & Young LLP

LOCATIONS

HQ: Almost Family, Inc.
9510 Ormsby Station Rd., Ste. 300
Louisville, KY 40223
Phone: 502-891-1000   **Fax:** 502-891-8067
Web: www.almostfamily.com

2008 Branch Locations

	Visiting nurses	Personal care
Florida	37	7
Kentucky	11	4
Ohio	7	4
Connecticut	4	6
New Jersey	3	—
Illinois	3	—
Missouri	2	—
Alabama	2	1
Massachusetts	2	1
Pennsylvania	1	—
Indiana	2	—
Total	**74**	**23**

PRODUCTS/OPERATIONS

2008 Sales

	$ mil.	% of total
Visiting nurses	173	81
Personal care	40	19
Total	**213**	**100**

2008 Sales

	% of total
Medicare	63
Medicaid & other government programs	24
Insurance & private pay	13
Total	**100**

COMPETITORS

Amedisys
Apria Healthcare
Gentiva
Girling Health Care
Home Instead
LHC Group
Lincare Holdings
Manor Care
National HealthCare
National Home Health

HISTORICAL FINANCIALS

Company Type: Public

Income Statement

FYE: December 31

	REVENUE ($ mil.)	NET INCOME ($ mil.)	NET PROFIT MARGIN	EMPLOYEES
12/08	212.6	16.3	7.7%	5,700
12/07	132.1	7.6	5.8%	4,800
12/06	91.8	4.2	4.6%	4,000
12/05	75.6	7.9	10.4%	3,200
12/04	86.8	1.2	1.4%	3,600
Annual Growth	**25.1%**	**92.0%**	**—**	**12.2%**

2008 Year-End Financials

Debt ratio: 28.7%	Dividends
Return on equity: 25.1%	Yield: —
Cash ($ mil.): 1.3	Payout: —
Current ratio: 1.17	Market value ($ mil.): 411.4
Long-term debt ($ mil.): 27.2	R&D as % of sales: —
No. of shares (mil.): 9.1	Advertising as % of sales: —

Stock History

NASDAQ (CM): AFAM

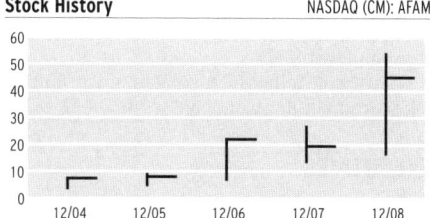

	STOCK PRICE ($) FY Close	P/E High/Low		PER SHARE ($) Earnings	Dividends	Book Value
12/08	44.98	25	8	2.16	—	10.36
12/07	19.43	20	10	1.36	—	3.81
12/06	21.91	27	9	0.80	—	3.03
12/05	8.00	6	3	1.51	—	2.20
12/04	7.36	32	16	0.23	—	1.48
Annual Growth	**57.2%**	**—**	**—**	**75.1%**	**—**	**62.6%**

Altra Holdings

Altra Holdings brings things to a stop. The company, through its principal subsidiary Altra Industrial Motion, designs, makes, and markets mechanical power transmission and motion control products under several brand names including Warner Electric and Boston Gear. The company's industrial clutches and brakes, gear drives, couplings, and bearings are used in such assemblies as elevator braking systems and wheelchairs. Altra sells directly and through distributors to industrial equipment makers in material handling, mining, and transportation. Leveling the cyclical impact of any one industry, it also taps into energy, food processing, medical, and turf and garden. About 70% of its sales are from North America.

Formed in the 2004 merger of Colfax's Power Transmission Group with Kilian Manufacturing, Altra's core business has added to its product portfolio and expanded its geographic reach through several acquisitions. Underpinning its choices has been a recognition that the bigger the company, and the more dominant its presence, the more revenue it can generate.

The assets of All Power Transmission Manufacturing were acquired late in 2007 for $7.2 million. All Power — a longtime supplier of Altra — muscles in specialty universal joints and driveline equipment. Earlier in the year Altra acquired TB Wood's, a manufacturer of electronic and mechanical industrial power transmission products, for around $93 million. The company sees the acquisition as leveraging its product portfolio. In an effort to focus on its electro-mechanical power transmission business, TB Wood's adjustable-speed drives business (Electronics Division) fell by the wayside for $29 million to Vacon.

A $5 million deal for Bear Linear (now known as Warner Linear) scored the manufacturing assets for linear actuators (electromechanical power transmission devices for moving loads in

off-highway and industrial applications). The acquisition is a strategic expansion into the motion control market.

Altra acquired Hay Hall Holdings, a UK manufacturer of clutch brakes and couplings, in 2006 for about $49 million. The acquisition added five main businesses with strong brand names including Inertia Dynamics, Matrix International, and Twiflex. These businesses diversified the company's revenue base and, when consolidated with Altra's Formsprag Clutch, Stieber Clutch, Warner Electric, and Wichita Clutch, made the company one of the largest individual manufacturers of industrial clutches and brakes in the world.

EXECUTIVES

Chairman: Michael L. Hurt, age 64,
$2,246,482 total compensation
President, CEO, and Director: Carl R. Christenson,
age 50, $866,944 total compensation
VP and CFO: Christian Storch, age 49,
$876,950 total compensation
VP Global Sales: Gerald Ferris, age 60,
$428,290 total compensation
VP Marketing and Business Development:
Craig Schuele, age 46, $348,734 total compensation
VP and General Manager Engineered Couplings:
Mark Klossner
VP and General Manager, Boston Gear, Formsprag, Steiber and Huco Business Units: Edward Novotny,
age 56
VP Human Resources: Chet Shubert, age 52
VP Finance and Controller: Todd B. Patriacca, age 39
VP Legal and Human Resources, General Counsel, and Secretary: Glenn E. Deegan, age 42
Auditors: Deloitte & Touche LLP

LOCATIONS

HQ: Altra Holdings, Inc.
300 Granite St., Ste. 201, Braintree, MA 02184
Phone: 781-917-0600   **Fax:** 781-843-0709
Web: www.altramotion.com

2008 Sales

	$ mil.	% of total
North America	451.2	71
Europe	29.6	5
Asia & other regions	154.5	24
Total	**635.3**	**100**

PRODUCTS/OPERATIONS

Selected Products

Electromagnetic Clutches and Brakes
Flexible Couplings
Gearing
Heavy Duty Clutches and Brakes
Linear Products
Overrunning Clutches

Selected Brands

Ameridrives Couplings
Bibby Transmission
Boston Gear
Delroyd Worm Gear
Formsprag Clutch
Huco Dynatork
Industrial Clutch
Inertia Dynamics
Kilian Manufacturing
Marland Clutch
Matrix International
Nuttall Gear
Saftek Friction
Stieber Clutch
TB Wood's Inc.
Twiflex Limited
Warner Electric
Warner Linear
Wichita Clutch

COMPETITORS

ABB	Hitachi
Baldor Electric	Regal Beloit
Danaher	Rexnord
Emerson Electric	Siemens AG
GE	

HISTORICAL FINANCIALS

Company Type: Public

Income Statement
FYE: December 31

	REVENUE ($ mil.)	NET INCOME ($ mil.)	NET PROFIT MARGIN	EMPLOYEES
12/08	635.3	6.5	1.0%	3,164
12/07	584.4	11.5	2.0%	3,455
12/06	462.3	8.9	1.9%	2,500
12/05	363.5	2.5	0.7%	2,745
12/04	303.7	1.0	0.3%	—
Annual Growth	20.3%	59.7%	—	4.8%

2008 Year-End Financials

Debt ratio: 200.3%
Return on equity: 4.7%
Cash ($ mil.): 52.1
Current ratio: 2.99
Long-term debt ($ mil.): 258.1
No. of shares (mil.): 26.6

Dividends
 Yield: 0.0%
 Payout: —
Market value ($ mil.): 210.6
R&D as % of sales: —
Advertising as % of sales: —

Stock History
NASDAQ (GM): AIMC

	STOCK PRICE ($) FY Close	P/E High/Low		PER SHARE ($) Earnings	Dividends	Book Value
12/08	7.91	75	20	0.25	0.00	4.84
12/07	16.63	40	29	0.47	0.00	5.50
12/06	14.05	32	29	0.46	0.00	2.98
Annual Growth	(25.0%)	—	—	(26.3%)	—	27.4%

AMCOL International

AMCOL International is nothing if not diverse, with operations in minerals, environmental services, oilfield services, and transportation. Its minerals segment is a global supplier of bentonite products used in cat litter, laundry detergent, metal casting, paper manufacturing, and as a plastic additive. Its environmental segment provides building materials and construction services to concrete waterproofing, drilling, flood control, and site remediation projects. AMCOL's oilfield services unit offers water treatment and well testing to the oil and gas industry. The company's transportation business provides long-haul trucking and freight brokerage services to AMCOL units and third parties in the US and Canada.

The Americas account for the majority of the company's sales. AMCOL also operates in Asia, Australia, Europe, and Africa.

In 2009 the company agreed to buy a minority stake in a South African chromite mine; it also has an option to buy up most of the rest of the mine after two years. Should AMCOL fulfill its option clause, the total price it would pay for the potential 74% stake in the mine would be about $25 million. The purchase will give AMCOL the opportunity to further build its position as a supplier of chrome sand to the metal casting industry.

A trust controlled by members of the founding Weaver family owns about a third of AMCOL.

EXECUTIVES

Chairman: John Hughes, age 67
President, CEO, and Director:
Lawrence E. (Larry) Washow, age 56,
$1,472,217 total compensation
COO: Ryan F. McKendrick, age 57,
$893,207 total compensation
SVP and CFO: Donald W. Pearson, age 47,
$259,689 total compensation
VP Environmental; President, Colloid Environmental Technologies (CETCO): Bob Trauger
VP; President, American Colloid: Gary D. Morrison,
$389,935 total compensation
VP and CIO: Lloyd F. Love, age 58
VP; President, Oilfield Services Company, Colloid Environmental Technologies (CETCO):
Michael (Mike) Johnson, age 51
President, Global Minerals: Gary L. Castagna, age 48,
$601,403 total compensation
Auditors: Ernst & Young LLP

LOCATIONS

HQ: AMCOL International Corporation
 2870 Forbs Ave., Hoffman Estates, IL 60192
Phone: 847-851-1500
Web: www.amcol.com

2008 Sales

	% of total
Americas	68
Europe, Middle East & Africa	23
Asia/Pacific	9
Total	**100**

PRODUCTS/OPERATIONS

2008 Sales

	$ mil.	% of total
Minerals	429.0	49
Environmental	278.7	32
Oilfield services	133.6	15
Transportation	63.9	4
Adjustments	(21.6)	—
Total	**883.6**	**100**

Selected Operations

American Colloid Company (bentonite and bentonite-related products)
Ameri-Co Carriers, Inc. (long-haul trucking)
Ameri-Co Logistics, Inc. (freight brokerage)
Colloid Environmental Technologies Company (CETCO; products and services related to soil sealing/lining, groundwater monitoring, wastewater treatment, and construction waterproofing/coating agents)
Nanocor, Inc. (chemically modified clays used as additives for plastics)
Volclay International Corp. (bentonite and bentonite-related products)

COMPETITORS

Albemarle	Süd-Chemie
Halliburton	Schneider National
International Specialty Products	Smith International
M-I SWACO	SunOpta
Oil-Dri	Unimin

HISTORICAL FINANCIALS

Company Type: Public

Income Statement
FYE: December 31

	REVENUE ($ mil.)	NET INCOME ($ mil.)	NET PROFIT MARGIN	EMPLOYEES
12/08	883.6	25.3	2.9%	2,388
12/07	744.3	56.7	7.6%	2,017
12/06	611.6	50.2	8.2%	1,759
12/05	535.9	41.0	7.7%	15,742
12/04	459.1	31.6	6.9%	1,427
Annual Growth	17.8%	(5.4%)	—	13.7%

2008 Year-End Financials

Debt ratio: 78.7%
Return on equity: 7.5%
Cash ($ mil.): 19.4
Current ratio: 3.42
Long-term debt ($ mil.): 256.8
No. of shares (mil.): 30.7

Dividends
 Yield: 3.2%
 Payout: 82.9%
Market value ($ mil.): 642.5
R&D as % of sales: —
Advertising as % of sales: —

Stock History
NYSE: ACO

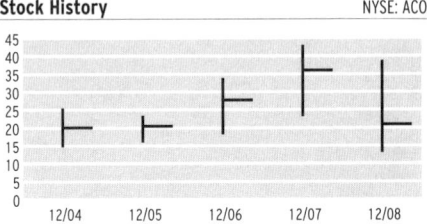

	STOCK PRICE ($) FY Close	P/E High/Low		PER SHARE ($) Earnings	Dividends	Book Value
12/08	20.95	47	16	0.82	0.68	10.64
12/07	36.03	23	13	1.83	0.60	11.49
12/06	27.74	21	11	1.62	0.49	9.61
12/05	20.52	17	12	1.33	0.38	8.11
12/04	20.09	24	15	1.03	0.32	7.24
Annual Growth	1.1%	—	—	(5.5%)	20.7%	10.1%

Ameriana Bancorp

Ameriana Bancorp may sound merry, but it takes business seriously. It's the parent of Ameriana Bank, which has about a dozen offices in central Indiana. The bank offers standard deposit products, including checking, savings, and money market accounts; CDs; and IRAs. It focuses on real estate lending: Residential mortgages account for about half of its loan portfolio, and commercial real estate loans represent about 30%. The company sells auto, home, life, health, and business coverage through its Ameriana Insurance Agency subsidiary. Another unit, Ameriana Investment Management, provides brokerage and investment services through an agreement with LPL Financial.

EXECUTIVES

President, CEO, and Director, Ameriana Bancorp and Ameriana Bank and Trust: Jerome J. (Jerry) Gassen, age 59, $300,626 total compensation
EVP and COO, Ameriana Bancorp and Ameriana Bank and Trust: Timothy G. Clark, age 58, $194,725 total compensation
SVP, Treasurer, and CFO, Ameriana Bancorp and Ameriana Bank and Trust: John J. Letter, age 64, $140,134 total compensation

SVP and Chief Credit Officer, Ameriana Bank and
  Trust: Matthew (Matt) Branstetter, age 42
SVP and Chief Commercial Lending Officer, Ameriana
  Bank and Trust: James A. Freeman, age 60
SVP Retail Banking and Chief Marketing Officer,
  Ameriana Bank and Trust: Deborah C. Robinson
SVP Mortgage Banking, Ameriana Bank and Trust:
  Janice L. Brehm
SVP and CIO, Ameriana Bank and Trust:
  Deborah A. Bell, age 56
SVP Loan Review, Ameriana Bank and Trust:
  Ronald M. Holloway, age 59
SVP and Agency Manager, Ameriana Insurance:
  M. Todd Thalls
SVP Investor Relations and Secretary, Ameriana
  Bancorp and Ameriana Bank and Trust:
  Nancy A. Rogers, age 66
SVP Commercial Lending, Ameriana Bank and Trust:
  Jan F. Wright, age 65
Auditors: BKD, LLP

LOCATIONS

HQ: Ameriana Bancorp
  2118 Bundy Ave., New Castle, IN 47362
Phone: 765-529-2230   Fax: 765-529-2232
Web: www.ameriana.com

COMPETITORS

Fifth Third
Huntington Bancshares
JPMorgan Chase
KeyCorp
MainSource Financial
Old National Bancorp
STAR Financial Group
U.S. Bancorp

HISTORICAL FINANCIALS

Company Type: Public

Income Statement				FYE: December 31
	ASSETS ($ mil.)	NET INCOME ($ mil.)	INCOME AS % OF ASSETS	EMPLOYEES
12/08	463.5	0.7	0.2%	171
12/07	426.8	1.2	0.3%	171
12/06	437.2	(1.0)	—	177
12/05	449.4	2.1	0.5%	171
12/04	428.6	1.4	0.3%	171
Annual Growth	2.0%	(15.9%)	—	0.0%

2008 Year-End Financials

Equity as % of assets: 7.3%
Return on assets: 0.2%
Return on equity: 2.1%
Long-term debt ($ mil.): 97.7
No. of shares (mil.): 3.0
Market value ($ mil.): 16.7
Dividends
  Yield: 2.9%
  Payout: 64.0%
Sales ($ mil.): 15.6
R&D as % of sales: —
Advertising as % of sales: —

Stock History

NASDAQ (GM): ASBI

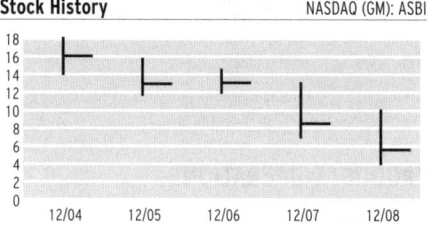

	STOCK PRICE ($) FY Close	P/E High/Low		PER SHARE ($) Earnings	Dividends	Book Value
12/08	5.58	40	16	0.25	0.16	11.30
12/07	8.50	33	18	0.39	0.16	11.26
12/06	13.07	—	—	(0.31)	0.52	11.08
12/05	12.95	24	18	0.65	0.64	11.93
12/04	16.04	40	31	0.45	0.64	12.93
Annual Growth	(23.2%)	—	—	(13.7%)	(29.3%)	(3.3%)

American CareSource

American CareSource mends the connection
between medical plan sponsors and supplemental health care providers. Operating through its
Ancillary Care Services subsidiary, the company
negotiates contracts with more than 2,500
providers of supplemental health care (i.e., rehabilitation, hospice, laboratory, infusion, and
other services); in turn, the company offers insurance companies and other health benefit administrators access to a vast network of
reduced-cost supplemental care services. American CareSource's clients include preferred
provider organizations (PPOs), health maintenance organizations (HMOs), third-party administrators, and self-insured employers. The
company's roots go back to the mid-1990s.

American CareSource has historically relied
on a few large clients for most of its revenue;
however, it has recently been attempting to expand into new US markets, mainly through the
addition of new clients and through expansion of
its services with existing clients.

EXECUTIVES

Chairman: David A. George, age 53
President, CEO, and Director: David S. Boone, age 48,
CFO: Steven J. (Steve) Armond, age 40,
  $430,820 total compensation
CIO: Rost A. Ginevich, age 45,
  $231,339 total compensation
SVP Sales and Marketing: James T. Robinson, age 49
$534,379 total compensation
VP Client Development: Kurt Fullmer, age 47,
  $327,500 total compensation
VP Network Development: M. Cornelia Outten, age 49,
  $325,881 total compensation
Controller and Principal Accounting Officer:
  Matthew D. Thompson, age 37
Auditors: McGladrey & Pullen, LLP

LOCATIONS

HQ: American CareSource Holdings, Inc.
  5429 LBJ Freeway, Ste. 850, Dallas, TX 75240
Phone: 972-308-6830   Fax: 972-980-2560
Web: www.anci-care.com

PRODUCTS/OPERATIONS

Selected Services

Bone growth stimulation
Chiropractic services
Diagnostic imaging/radiology
Dialysis services
Durable medical equipment
Home health services
Home infusion therapy
Hospice services
Laboratory services
Orthotics and prosthetics
Outpatient therapy/rehabilitation
Pain management
Pharmacy (infusion)
Physical therapy
Respiratory services
Sleep studies
Sub-acute and skilled nursing facilities
Surgical centers

COMPETITORS

Aetna
Blue Cross
CIGNA
Preferred Network Access
United Healthcare Insurance

HISTORICAL FINANCIALS

Company Type: Public

Income Statement				FYE: December 31
	REVENUE ($ mil.)	NET INCOME ($ mil.)	NET PROFIT MARGIN	EMPLOYEES
12/08	58.3	3.6	6.2%	59
12/07	23.5	(0.8)	—	38
12/06	11.4	(1.3)	—	33
12/05	4.4	(2.4)	—	38
12/04	6.0	(2.8)	—	31
Annual Growth	76.6%	—	—	17.5%

2008 Year-End Financials

Debt ratio: 0.0%
Return on equity: 27.8%
Cash ($ mil.): 10.6
Current ratio: 1.86
Long-term debt ($ mil.): 0.0
No. of shares (mil.): 15.4
Dividends
  Yield: 0.0%
  Payout: —
Market value ($ mil.): 108.8
R&D as % of sales: —
Advertising as % of sales: —

Stock History

NASDAQ (CM): ANCI

	STOCK PRICE ($) FY Close	P/E High/Low		PER SHARE ($) Earnings	Dividends	Book Value
12/08	7.05	45	11	0.21	0.00	1.00
12/07	3.20	—	—	(0.06)	0.00	0.67
12/06	1.85	—	—	(0.09)	0.00	0.69
12/05	5.47	—	—	(0.19)	0.00	0.15
Annual Growth	8.8%	—	—	—	—	36.5%

American Dental Partners

Helping dentists focus on drilling (and not
billing) is the mission of American Dental Partners. The company provides management and
support services for the growing group practice
segment of the dental care industry. Through
long-term service agreements, the company manages about 25 general and specialty dental practice groups operating some 250 dental facilities in
18 states, mainly in the eastern and midwestern
US. Its services include planning and budgeting,
facilities development and management, scheduling, training, recruiting, economic analysis, financial reporting, and quality assurance.

The dental hygienists and non-clinical staff of
the affiliated practices are generally the employees of American Dental Partners, but dentists
are employed by (or contract with) the practice
itself. One exception to this rule is Arizona Tooth
Doctor for Kids: The company owns an 85%
stake in the practice group and employs all of the
affiliated dentists.

American Dental Partners knows that its own
success depends largely on the success of its practices. It looks to grow patient revenue from each

affiliated group by 8-10% a year by assisting with organizational planning; recruiting, training, and retaining qualified personnel; investing in facilities and information systems; implementing quality assurance programs; and putting in place competent local management teams.

Additionally, the company grows by adding service agreements with new group practices and acquiring companies that broaden its service offerings. American Dental formed a new affiliation with the Advanced Dental Specialists group practice in Wisconsin (2008) and expanded into Florida with an affiliation struck with Christie Dental Practice Group (2009).

American Dental acquired group practice management firm Metropolitan Dental Holdings for $95 million in 2007. Through the purchase, American Dental took over an affiliation agreement with Metro Dentalcare, a dental group with about 35 offices in the Minneapolis and St. Paul (Twin Cities) area.

Late in 2007 American Dental Partners settled a lawsuit with former Twin Cities-based dental practice partner PDG (Park Dental). A jury in Minnesota had previously found American Dental liable for breaching a service agreement with PDG, but the companies later reached a settlement agreement in which American Dental Partners transferred management of most of the affiliated practices (and rights to the Park Dental name) back to PDG.

EXECUTIVES

Chairman, President, and CEO: Gregory A. Serrao, age 46, $748,806 total compensation
EVP and COO: Michael J. Vaughan, age 55, $474,179 total compensation
EVP, CFO, and Treasurer: Breht T. Feigh, age 42, $438,361 total compensation
SVP and Chief Professional Officer: Jesley C. Ruff, age 54
SVP Regional Operations: Michael J. Kenneally, age 48
VP and Chief Accounting Officer: Mark W. Vargo, age 57, $209,031 total compensation
VP Planning and Investment: Ian H. Brock, age 39
VP Information Services: Robert A. Duncan, age 61
Director Regional Operations: William P. Koffler
Auditors: PricewaterhouseCoopers LLP

LOCATIONS

HQ: American Dental Partners, Inc.
  401 Edgewater Place, Ste. 430, Wakefield, MA 01880
Phone: 781-224-0880   **Fax:** 781-224-4216
Web: www.amdpi.com

Selected Dental Groups

1st Advantage Dental — New England (Malta, NY)
1st Advantage Dental — New York (Malta, NY)
Advanced Dental Specialists (Milwaukee, WI)
American Family Dentistry (Germantown, TN)
Arizona's Tooth Doctor for Kids (Phoenix, AZ)
Associated Dental Care Providers (Chandler, AZ)
Assure Dental (Roseville, MN)
Carus Dental (Austin, TX)
Chestnut Hills Dental (Pittsburgh)
Cumberland Dental (Gadsden, AL)
Deerwood Orthodontics (Franklin, WI)
Dental Arts Center (Reston, VA)
Forward Dental (Milwaukee, WI)
Greater Maryland Dental Partners (Clarksville, MD)
Lakeside Dental Care (Metarie, LA)
Metro Dentalcare (Richfield, MN)
Oklahoma Dental Group (Oklahoma City)
Orthodontic Care Specialists (Apple Valley, MN)
Premier Dental Partners (St. Louis)
Redwood Dental Group (Madison Heights, MI)
Riverside Dental Group (Riverside, CA)
Sacramento Oral Surgery (Sacramento, CA)
University Dental Associates (Charlotte, NC)
Valley Dental Group (Roseville, MN)
Western New York Dental Group (Williamsville, NY)

PRODUCTS/OPERATIONS

2008 Sales

	$ mil.	% of total
Reimbursement of expenses	189.5	65
Business service fees	56.0	19
Patient revenue, professional services, lab fees & other	45.6	16
Total	**291.1**	**100**

2008 Sales by Payor

	% of total
PPO & dental referral plans	70
Fee-for-service	19
Capitated managed care plans	11
Total	**100**

COMPETITORS

Birner Dental
Coast Dental Services
Delta Dental Plans
Dental Health Alliance
InterDent
OrthoSynetics
Pacific Dental Services, Inc.
Smile Brands
Western Dental Services

HISTORICAL FINANCIALS

Company Type: Public

Income Statement

FYE: December 31

	REVENUE ($ mil.)	NET INCOME ($ mil.)	NET PROFIT MARGIN	EMPLOYEES
12/08	291.1	30.1	10.3%	2,531
12/07	278.8	(7.7)	—	3,418
12/06	217.9	11.1	5.1%	2,347
12/05	196.9	10.3	5.2%	2,197
12/04	178.6	8.5	4.8%	1,725
Annual Growth	**13.0%**	**37.2%**	**—**	**10.1%**

2008 Year-End Financials

Debt ratio: 89.7%
Return on equity: 23.0%
Cash ($ mil.): 6.6
Current ratio: 1.44
Long-term debt ($ mil.): 131.4
No. of shares (mil.): 15.7

Dividends
  Yield: —
  Payout: —
Market value ($ mil.): 108.8
R&D as % of sales: —
Advertising as % of sales: —

Stock History

NASDAQ (GS): ADPI

	STOCK PRICE ($) FY Close	P/E High/Low		PER SHARE ($) Earnings	Dividends	Book Value
12/08	6.94	6	3	2.29	—	9.34
12/07	10.03	—	—	(0.61)	—	7.33
12/06	18.89	24	13	0.86	—	7.42
12/05	18.08	29	15	0.81	—	6.50
12/04	12.64	19	10	0.71	—	5.56
Annual Growth	**(13.9%)**	**—**	**—**	**34.0%**	**—**	**13.8%**

American Ecology

American Ecology and its US Ecology subsidiary help keep a lid on hazardous waste, industrial waste, and low-level radioactive waste. The company handles hazardous and nonhazardous waste at sites in Texas, Nevada, and Idaho, and it operates a low-level radioactive waste facility in Washington state. In 2007 Honeywell International and the US Army Corps of Engineers accounted for 41% and 6% of sales, respectively. Other customers include nuclear plants, steel mills, petrochemical facilities, and academic and medical institutions. American Ecology retains interests in several nonoperating waste-disposal facilities.

The company pursues a value-added strategy of aggressively bidding bundled transportation and disposal services, which allows it to be competitive in winning multiple project contracts.

To extend the geographic reach of its hazardous waste facility in Robstown, Texas, the company built a new rail transfer system nearby; this allowed American Ecology to compete for clean-up projects throughout the eastern US. In 2007 this plant expanded its laboratory capabilities to include the analysis of organic chemical compounds.

The company sold its low-level radioactive waste processing facility in Oak Ridge, Tennessee, in 2004.

EXECUTIVES

Chairman: Stephen A. Romano, age 55, $616,041 total compensation
President, CEO, and COO: James R. (Jim) Baumgardner, age 47
VP and CFO: Jeffrey R. (Jeff) Feeler, age 40, $312,875 total compensation
VP and Controller: Eric Gerratt, age 40
VP Operations: Simon G. Bell, age 39, $303,088 total compensation
VP Sales and Marketing: Steven D. (Steve) Welling, age 51, $543,835 total compensation
VP and CIO: John M. Cooper, age 55, $265,201 total compensation
VP and Director Occupational Health and Safety: Terry Andrew Geis
Director Sales and Marketing: Chad Hyslop
Director Transportation: Chuck Overman
Director Environmental Affairs: Richard O'Hara
Director Human Resources: Betsy Sterk
Auditors: Moss Adams, LLP

LOCATIONS

HQ: American Ecology Corporation
  300 E. Mallard Dr., Ste. 300, Boise, ID 83706
Phone: 208-331-8400   **Fax:** 208-331-7900
Web: www.americanecology.com

American Ecology has disposal facilities in Idaho, Nevada, Texas, and Washington.

PRODUCTS/OPERATIONS

Selected Subsidiaries

Texas Ecologists, inc.
US Ecology, Inc.
US Ecology Idaho, Inc.
US Ecology Nevada, Inc.
US Ecology Texas, L.P.
US Ecology Washington, Inc.

COMPETITORS

Clean Harbors	Stericycle
EnergySolutions	Valhi
Heritage Environmental	Veolia ES Technical
Perma-Fix Environmental	Solutions
Safety-Kleen	Waste Management
Shaw Group	

HISTORICAL FINANCIALS

Company Type: Public

Income Statement — FYE: December 31

	REVENUE ($ mil.)	NET INCOME ($ mil.)	NET PROFIT MARGIN	EMPLOYEES
12/08	175.8	21.5	12.2%	253
12/07	165.5	19.4	11.7%	238
12/06	116.8	15.9	13.6%	226
12/05	79.4	15.4	19.4%	214
12/04	54.2	23.4	43.2%	178
Annual Growth	34.2%	(2.1%)	—	9.2%

2008 Year-End Financials

Debt ratio: 0.0%	Dividends
Return on equity: 24.6%	Yield: 2.4%
Cash ($ mil.): 18.5	Payout: 40.7%
Current ratio: 3.08	Market value ($ mil.): 370.3
Long-term debt ($ mil.): 0.0	R&D as % of sales: —
No. of shares (mil.): 18.3	Advertising as % of sales: —

Stock History — NASDAQ (GS): ECOL

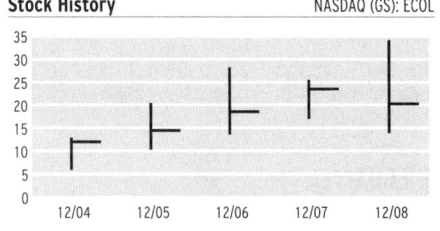

	STOCK PRICE ($) FY Close	P/E High/Low		PER SHARE ($) Earnings	Dividends	Book Value
12/08	20.23	29	12	1.18	0.48	5.02
12/07	23.48	24	16	1.06	0.60	4.54
12/06	18.51	32	16	0.87	0.45	4.01
12/05	14.43	23	12	0.86	0.45	3.49
12/04	11.97	10	5	1.32	0.25	2.82
Annual Growth	14.0%	—	—	(2.8%)	17.7%	15.5%

American Italian Pasta

American Italian Pasta Company (AIPC) uses its noodle in many different ways. The company is the largest maker of dry pasta in North America, offering some 300 different pasta shapes (and 3,700 SKUs), everything from angel hair to ziti. Its consumer brands, such as Golden Grain, Heartland, and Mrs. Grass, are staples in supermarkets throughout the US, as well as overseas. The Kansas City, Missouri-based company's private-label customers include most major US grocers and club stores. It also serves the food ingredient sector, supplying companies with pasta products for use in food manufacturing.

During 2009 AIPC focused on increasing the number of its private-label customers in the general market, as well as increasing proprietary-brand customers in those core markets where the brands were already strongest. It was a successful strategy — 2009 saw revenue growth in the pasta maker's private-label and proprietary-brand products.

The company's foodservice operations saw changes as well. The foodservice sector, including restaurants, has experienced a fall-off in business as a result of the recessionary conditions in the economy (i.e., fewer people went out to eat). As a result, AIPC saw a decrease in its revenue for its foodservice business, as restaurants, etc., ordered fewer AIPC pasta products.

Overall, AIPC continues to focus on its historical business lines (branded, private-label, foodservice, and industrial products), as well as on new product innovation. Keenly aware that pasta is among the first foods eliminated in many diets, AIPC has added low-carbohydrate pastas to its offerings.

Wal-Mart accounted for 25% of American Pasta's sales in 2009.

The company operates four pasta plants, one each in Arizona, Missouri, South Carolina, and Italy. The investment firm FMR owns about 16% of AIPC.

EXECUTIVES

Chairman: William R. Patterson, age 67
President, CEO, and Director: John P. (Jack) Kelly, age 57
EVP and CFO: Paul R. Geist, age 46
EVP and COO: Walter N. George, age 53
EVP and General Counsel: Robert W. (Bob) Schuller, age 48
SVP Retail Sales: Thomas J. (Tom) Branich
SVP International: Patrick D. Regan
SVP Retail Sales: Michael J. (Mike) Kaczynski
VP and CIO: Steven A. Tesdahl
VP Customer Marketing: Daniel M. Rennell
VP Operations: Tim E. Lethcoe
VP Sales and Operations Planning: Kevin A. Hall
VP Information Systems: Chrystal L. Johnson
VP Finance, Sales, and Marketing: Teri S. Runnebaum
VP and Corporate Controller: Douglas W. Fleming
VP Technical Services: George Michael (Mike) Willhoite
VP Quality, Research and Development: Jayne S. Hoover
President, Italy: Francesco (Frank) Bonfanti
Auditors: Ernst & Young LLP

LOCATIONS

HQ: American Italian Pasta Company
4100 N. Mulberry Dr., Ste. 200
Kansas City, MO 64116
Phone: 816-584-5000   **Fax:** 816-584-5100
Web: www.aipc.com

2009 Sales

	% of total
North America	93
Rest of the world	7
Total	**100**

PRODUCTS/OPERATIONS

2009 Sales

	$ mil.	% of total
Retail	495.6	79
Institutional	132.6	21
Total	**628.2**	**100**

Selected Brands

Consumer
  Anthony's
  Golden Grain
  Heartland
  Luxury
  Martha Gooch
  Mrs. Grass
  Mueller's
  Pennsylvania Dutch
  R & F
  Ronco
Foodservice
  Heartland
  Montalcino
  Pasta Chef
  R&F

COMPETITORS

Annie's, Inc.
Barilla
Campbell Soup
Cento
Colavita
Dakota Growers
De Cecco
Eden Foods
Faribault Foods
Hain Celestial
Manischewitz Food Products
Marzetti
Nestlé
New World Pasta
NORPAC
Rossi Pasta

HISTORICAL FINANCIALS

Company Type: Public

Income Statement — FYE: Friday nearest September 30

	REVENUE ($ mil.)	NET INCOME ($ mil.)	NET PROFIT MARGIN	EMPLOYEES
9/09	628.2	88.3	14.1%	675
9/08	569.2	19.1	3.4%	665
9/07	398.1	5.3	1.3%	651
9/06	367.0	(30.4)	—	620
9/05	364.2	(100.2)	—	604
Annual Growth	14.6%	—	—	2.8%

2009 Year-End Financials

Debt ratio: 33.9%	Dividends
Return on equity: 34.4%	Yield: 0.0%
Cash ($ mil.): 31.0	Payout: —
Current ratio: 2.61	Market value ($ mil.): 572.3
Long-term debt ($ mil.): 104.1	R&D as % of sales: —
No. of shares (mil.): 21.1	Advertising as % of sales: —

Stock History — NASDAQ (GM): AIPC

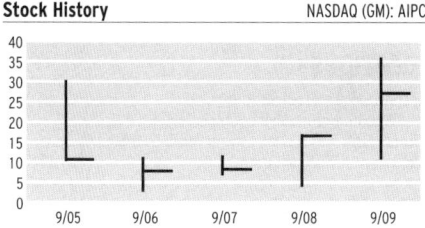

	STOCK PRICE ($) FY Close	P/E High/Low		PER SHARE ($) Earnings	Dividends	Book Value
9/09	27.18	9	3	4.10	0.00	14.60
9/08	16.60	17	4	0.99	0.00	9.78
9/07	8.23	41	25	0.28	0.00	8.17
9/06	7.78	—	—	(1.65)	0.00	7.62
9/05	10.66	—	—	(5.49)	0.56	8.84
Annual Growth	26.4%	—	—	—	—	13.4%

American Medical Alert

It's like having a guardian angel hovering above, but without the wings. American Medical Alert Corp. provides health care communication and monitoring services. The company's Health Safety and Monitoring Services (HSMS) unit markets remote patient monitoring systems, including personal emergency response systems, health management and medication management systems, and safety monitoring systems. Its Telephony Based Communication Services (TBCS) unit provides telephone answering services and operates clinical trial recruitment call centers. Products are sold to consumers and health care facilities such as home care, hospice, pharmacy, managed care, and other health care organizations.

American Medical Alert operates about 10 call centers in the Northeast, as well as in Illinois, Maryland, and New Mexico, that support both its emergency response systems and its telephone-answering operations. It also has a deal with Walgreen Co. to provide its personal emergency response systems under the Walgreen brand.

In 2008 American Medical Alert began distributing the Intel Health Guide, a personal health system that allows clinicians to monitor and manage patients remotely. Also that year the company revamped its PhoneScreen offering, which recruits patients for clinical trials, by integrating it within its call center and IT infrastructure, and launched MedSmart, a medication management, reporting, and reminder system.

Chairman Howard Siegel owns more than 10% of the company; director Gregory Fortunoff owns nearly 10%.

EXECUTIVES

Chairman, Senior Advisor and Director:
 Howard M. Siegel, age 76, $226,359 total compensation
President, CEO, and Director: Jack Rhian, age 55,
 $353,688 total compensation
CFO; COO, HSMS Division: Richard Rallo, age 45,
 $230,773 total compensation
EVP and Director: Frederic S. Siegel, age 40,
 $287,803 total compensation
SVP Marketing and Program Development:
 Randi M. Baldwin, age 41, $156,955 total compensation
VP MD On Call and Capitol Medical Bureau:
 Louis Shapiro
VP Field Operations and Secretary: John Rogers, age 63
Director Management Information Systems:
 Kirk Amico
Auditors: Margolin, Winer & Evens LLP

LOCATIONS

HQ: American Medical Alert Corp.
 3265 Lawson Blvd., Oceanside, NY 11572
Phone: 516-536-5850   **Fax:** 516-536-5276
Web: www.amacalert.com

PRODUCTS/OPERATIONS

2008 Sales

	$ mil.	% of total
HSMS	19.6	51
TBCS	19.0	49
Total	**38.6**	**100**

HISTORICAL FINANCIALS
Company Type: Public

Income Statement   FYE: December 31

	REVENUE ($ mil.)	NET INCOME ($ mil.)	NET PROFIT MARGIN	EMPLOYEES
12/08	38.6	1.4	3.6%	528
12/07	35.6	1.5	4.2%	580
12/06	30.8	1.3	4.2%	531
12/05	22.4	0.9	4.0%	389
12/04	19.1	0.4	2.1%	328
Annual Growth	**19.2%**	**36.8%**	**—**	**12.6%**

2008 Year-End Financials

Debt ratio: 11.0%
Return on equity: 5.7%
Cash ($ mil.): 2.5
Current ratio: 2.41
Long-term debt ($ mil.): 2.8
No. of shares (mil.): 9.5

Dividends
 Yield: 0.0%
 Payout: —
Market value ($ mil.): 45.8
R&D as % of sales: —
Advertising as % of sales: —

Stock History   NASDAQ (CM): AMAC

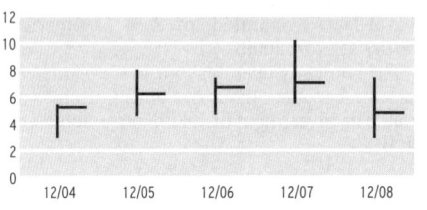

	STOCK PRICE ($) FY Close	P/E High/Low		PER SHARE ($) Earnings	Dividends	Book Value
12/08	4.80	49	20	0.15	0.00	2.68
12/07	7.03	63	35	0.16	0.00	2.48
12/06	6.69	56	37	0.13	0.00	2.24
12/05	6.20	79	47	0.10	0.00	1.93
12/04	5.22	107	60	0.05	0.00	1.60
Annual Growth	**(2.1%)**	**—**	**—**	**31.6%**	**—**	**13.7%**

American Medical Systems

American Medical Systems (AMS) aims to make life better for millions of patients afflicted with pelvic disorders. A leading maker of urological devices, AMS makes erectile dysfunction products such as inflatable penile implants, as well as urinary incontinence devices for men and women. Its other products treat such conditions as menorrhagia (excessive uterine bleeding), enlarged prostate, and fecal incontinence. AMS has around 60 international distributors in addition to a direct sales force of nearly 500 employees. Marketing efforts target urologists, gynecologists, colorectal surgeons, and other specialty physicians.

Though most people don't want to talk or even think about the products AMS sells, it appears plenty of people need them. In 2008 the company passed the $500 million revenue mark through its three primary business lines: men's health, women's health, and its treatments for enlarged prostates.

The prostate treatment line — named BPH Therapy after the condition called benign prostatic hyperplasia — was borne out of AMS's 2006 acquisition of Laserscope and its GreenLight laser. AMS formed the line, which includes both the laser and an in-office treatment called TherMatrx, in 2008 after divesting Laserscope's aesthetics business to IRIDEX.

AMS's growth strategy is centered around acquisitions and new product development. Along with the Laserscope buy, AMS has in recent years acquired BioControl Medical, an Israeli company focused on developing medical devices for the application of electrical stimulation technology, and Solarant Medical, which specializes in incontinence treatments for women.

Most of AMS's development activity occurs at its Arizona, California, and Minnesota facilities, but it also works with research hospitals and universities in the US and abroad. AMS has seen its greatest success with the MiniArc Single Incision Sling (for female incontinence) and the InhibiZone-coated AMS 800, an artificial urinary sphincter. AMS has two products in the pipeline awaiting FDA approval. The Topas sling device to treat fecal incontinence is in clinical trials. The Continuum, a device used to hold tissue together during and after prostate cancer surgery, entered trials in 2009.

After buying up Ovion's transcervical sterilization technology in 2005, AMS decided to sell the patents to Conceptus for $23 million in 2009. Conceptus had been paying royalties on the non-incisional permanent birth-control method and the purchase gave it clearer ownership of the technology.

EXECUTIVES

President, CEO, and Director:
 Anthony P. (Tony) Bihl III, age 53,
 $1,608,955 total compensation
EVP and CFO: Mark A. Heggestad, age 50,
 $827,614 total compensation
SVP and General Manager, Women's Health:
 John F. Nealon, age 46, $706,399 total compensation
SVP and General Manager, BPH Therapy Business:
 Joe W. Martin, age 56
SVP Human Resources: Janet L. Dick, age 52
SVP Global Operations: R. Scott Etlinger, age 48,
 $638,075 total compensation
SVP Compliance, Quality, and Legal:
 Lawrence W. Getlin, age 63
VP Research and Technology: Daniel R. Mans
VP and General Manager, Asia/Pacific and Latin America Region: Michael E. Ryan, age 49
VP and General Manager, Men's Health:
 Whitney D. Erickson, age 43,
 $784,683 total compensation
VP and General Manager, Europe, Middle East, and Africa Region: Francois Georgelin, age 43
Director Information Technology: Michael J. Casey
Treasurer: John D. Armbruster
Secretary: Thomas A. Letscher
Auditors: Ernst & Young LLP

LOCATIONS

HQ: American Medical Systems Holdings, Inc.
 10700 Bren Rd. West, Minnetonka, MN 55343
Phone: 952-930-6000   **Fax:** 952-930-6373
Web: www.americanmedicalsystems.com

2008 Sales

	$ mil.	% of total
US	355.6	71
Other countries	146.0	29
Total	**501.6**	**100**

PRODUCTS/OPERATIONS

2008 Sales

	$ mil.	% of total
Men's health	219.2	44
Women's health	166.1	33
BPH line	116.3	23
Total	**501.6**	**100**

COMPETITORS

Bard
Boston Scientific
Celsion
Coloplast
HealthTronics
Hologic
Johnson & Johnson
Lumenis
Medtronic
Urologix
Uroplasty

HISTORICAL FINANCIALS

Company Type: Public

Income Statement — FYE: December 31

	REVENUE ($ mil.)	NET INCOME ($ mil.)	NET PROFIT MARGIN	EMPLOYEES
12/08	501.6	42.6	8.5%	1,205
12/07	463.9	12.9	2.8%	1,239
12/06	358.3	(49.3)	—	1,095
12/05	262.6	39.3	15.0%	720
12/04	208.8	(3.1)	—	627
Annual Growth	24.5%	—	—	17.7%

2008 Year-End Financials

Debt ratio: 147.2%
Return on equity: 11.9%
Cash ($ mil.): 11.6
Current ratio: 3.07
Long-term debt ($ mil.): 567.7
No. of shares (mil.): 74.4
Dividends
  Yield: —
  Payout: —
Market value ($ mil.): 669.2
R&D as % of sales: —
Advertising as % of sales: —

Stock History — NASDAQ (GS): AMMD

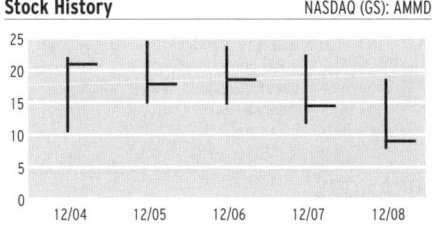

	STOCK PRICE ($) FY Close	P/E High/Low	PER SHARE ($) Earnings	Dividends	Book Value
12/08	8.99	32 14	0.58	—	5.18
12/07	14.46	123 66	0.18	—	4.41
12/06	18.52	— —	(0.70)	—	3.78
12/05	17.83	44 27	0.55	—	4.07
12/04	20.91	— —	(0.05)	—	3.35
Annual Growth	(19.0%)	— —	—	—	11.5%

American Pacific

American Pacific knows how to have a blast. The company's products launch rockets, propel missiles, deploy airbags, and suppress fires. Its largest unit also makes active pharmaceutical ingredients. American Pacific's specialty chemicals include ammonium perchlorate (AP), a rocket fuel oxidizer; sodium azide, an airbag deployment chemical also used in pharmaceuticals; and Halotron, an ozone-friendly fire suppressant. The company also makes commercial packaged explosives, aerospace propulsion equipment for satellites, and environmental protection products.

American Pacific relies heavily on a few customers, with its five largest accounting for more than two-thirds of sales; Alliant Techsystems accounts for 15%. Other AP customers include commercial satellite launchers and contractors participating in NASA and Department of Defense programs.

The company is the only commercial producer of ammonium perchlorate in the US. Specialty chemicals used to account for nearly 80% of American Pacific's sales, with perchlorate chemicals alone accounting for about half.

Its Ampac ISP unit is an in-space propulsion (ISP) business, and pharmaceutical ingredient manufacturer Ampac Fine Chemicals (AFC) is American Pacific's largest segment. The company acquired AFC in 2005, when it was called Aerojet. Its sales now account for more than half of the company's total figure.

International sales have risen at the company in the past few years, rising from less than 20% of total sales in 2006 to more than half in 2008.

EXECUTIVES

Chairman: John R. Gibson, age 73
President, CEO, and Director: Joseph (Joe) Carleone, age 62
VP and CTO: Jeffrey M. Gibson
VP Engineering: Dirk Venderink
VP Ampac-ISP Operations: Robert Huebner, age 56
VP, CFO, and Treasurer: Dana M. Kelley, age 47
VP Administration and Secretary: Linda G. Ferguson, age 67
Administrator Investor Relations: Deanna Riccardi
President, Ampac Fine Chemicals: Aslam Malik, age 50
Auditors: Deloitte & Touche LLP

LOCATIONS

HQ: American Pacific Corporation
3883 Howard Hughes Pkwy., Ste. 700
Las Vegas, NV 89169
Phone: 702-735-2200   **Fax:** 702-735-4876
Web: www.apfc.com

PRODUCTS/OPERATIONS

2009 Sales

	% of total
Fine chemicals	48
Specialty chemicals	32
Aerospace equipment	17
Other	3
Total	**100**

Selected Products

Fine chemicals (pharmaceutical ingredients; Ampac Fine Chemicals)
Specialty chemicals
  Ammonium perchlorate (oxidizing agent for solid fuel rockets; Western Electrochemical)
  Commercial explosives (Energetic Systems, 50%)
  Halotron (fire extinguisher; Halotron)
  Sodium azide (airbag chemical; American Azide Corporation)
Aerospace equipment (propulsion systems, thrusters, and propellant tanks; Ampac-ISP)
Other operations
  Environmental protection equipment (Pepcon Systems)
  ChlorMaster system (disinfects wastewater, brine, and sea water)
  OdorMaster system (controls noxious odors)
  Real estate development (Ampac Development)

COMPETITORS

APi Group
Arch Chemicals
Austin Chemical
Cambrex
Daicel Chemical
DuPont
Evonik Degussa Corporation
GenCorp
Nippon Kayaku
Orica
SNPE

HISTORICAL FINANCIALS

Company Type: Public

Income Statement — FYE: September 30

	REVENUE ($ mil.)	NET INCOME ($ mil.)	NET PROFIT MARGIN	EMPLOYEES
9/08	203.1	9.0	4.4%	530
9/07	183.9	5.0	2.7%	487
9/06	141.9	(3.9)	—	485
9/05	83.3	(11.2)	—	254
9/04	59.5	0.4	0.7%	200
Annual Growth	35.9%	117.8%	—	27.6%

2008 Year-End Financials

Debt ratio: 168.0%
Return on equity: 11.3%
Cash ($ mil.): 26.9
Current ratio: 3.67
Long-term debt ($ mil.): 139.4
No. of shares (mil.): 7.5
Dividends
  Yield: 0.0%
  Payout: —
Market value ($ mil.): 98.0
R&D as % of sales: —
Advertising as % of sales: —

Stock History — NASDAQ (GM): APFC

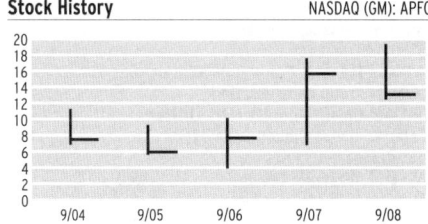

	STOCK PRICE ($) FY Close	P/E High/Low	PER SHARE ($) Earnings	Dividends	Book Value
9/08	13.06	16 11	1.18	0.00	11.05
9/07	15.62	26 10	0.67	0.00	10.09
9/06	7.66	— —	(0.53)	0.00	9.58
9/05	5.92	— —	(1.33)	0.00	9.95
9/04	7.47	— —	(0.05)	0.42	11.30
Annual Growth	15.0%	— —	—	—	(0.5%)

American Public Education

American Public Education promotes military intelligence. The company offers online postsecondary education to those in the military and other public servants such as police officers or firefighters Its American Military University and American Public University make up the American Public University System, which offers more than 70 degree programs and nearly as many certificate programs in such disciplines as business administration, criminal justice, intelligence, technology, liberal arts, and homeland security. Enrollment in the online university consists of more than 42,000 part-time students from all 50 states and about 100 foreign countries. More than 80% of students serve in the US military or are veterans.

American Public Education's nationally and regionally accredited online education system offers associate's, bachelor's and master's degrees. It is specifically geared toward adult students who are on-call for rapid response missions or extended deployment. It has an open enrollment system, accepting all applicants with a high school diploma or equivalent. For those with limited financial resources, tuition assistance programs offered by the US Department of Defense constitute more than two-thirds of the company's annual revenues.

American Public Education is ramping up its outreach efforts, focusing on retention of students in its core military market, while marketing the availability of federal student aid grants and low-cost loans to the public service and civilian markets. It is also expanding the number and type of degrees offered.

The company was founded in 1991 as American Military University by a retired Marine Corps major. It went public in 2007 and used the proceeds to pay stockholders more than $93 million.

EXECUTIVES
Chairman: Phillip A. (Phil) Clough, age 48
President, CEO, and Director: Wallace E. Boston Jr., age 55, $1,229,940 total compensation
EVP, CFO, and Assistant Treasurer: Harry T. Wilkins, age 53, $810,475 total compensation
EVP Programs and Marketing: Carol S. Gilbert, age 51, $388,688 total compensation
EVP and Provost: Frank B. McCluskey, age 61, $391,316 total compensation
SVP and Chief Administrative Officer: Peter W. (Pete) Gibbons, age 57
SVP Finance: Lisa Kessler
SVP and Academic Dean: Karan H. Powell
VP Military Programs: James M. Sweizer
VP Academic Services: Phillip A. McNair
VP Student Services and University Registrar: Lyn M. Geer
Auditors: McGladrey & Pullen, LLP

LOCATIONS
HQ: American Public Education, Inc.
111 W. Congress St., Charles Town, WV 25414
Phone: 304-724-3700   **Fax:** 304-724-3780
Web: www.apus.edu

PRODUCTS/OPERATIONS
Selected Degree Programs
Accounting
Business Administration
Communication
Computer Applications
Counter Terrorism
Criminal Justice
Database Application
Early Childhood Development
Emergency and Disaster Management
English
Environmental Services
Explosive Ordnance Disposal
Fire Science
General Studies
History
Homeland Security
Hospitality
Information Technology
Intelligence Studies
Legal Studies
Management
Marketing
Middle Eastern Studies
Military History
Paralegal Studies
Personnel Administration
Philosophy
Psychology
Public Health
Real Estate Studies
Religion
Space Studies
Transportation and Logistics Management
Weapons of Mass Destruction Preparedness
Web Publishing

HISTORICAL FINANCIALS
Company Type: Public

Income Statement
FYE: December 31

	REVENUE ($ mil.)	NET INCOME ($ mil.)	NET PROFIT MARGIN	EMPLOYEES
12/08	107.1	16.2	15.1%	1,180
12/07	69.1	8.8	12.7%	910
12/06	40.0	1.8	4.5%	798
12/05	28.2	1.1	3.9%	660
12/04	23.1	2.3	10.0%	—
Annual Growth	46.7%	62.9%	—	21.4%

2008 Year-End Financials
Debt ratio: —
Return on equity: 37.2%
Cash ($ mil.): 47.7
Current ratio: 2.68
Long-term debt ($ mil.): —
No. of shares (mil.): 18.2
Dividends
  Yield: 0.0%
  Payout: —
Market value ($ mil.): 677.3
R&D as % of sales: —
Advertising as % of sales: —

Stock History
NASDAQ (GM): APEI

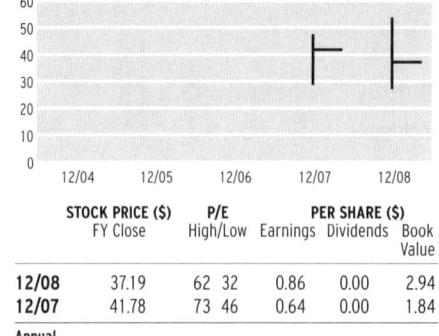

	STOCK PRICE ($) FY Close	P/E High/Low	Earnings	PER SHARE ($) Dividends	Book Value
12/08	37.19	62 32	0.86	0.00	2.94
12/07	41.78	73 46	0.64	0.00	1.84
Annual Growth	(11.0%)	— —	34.4%	—	59.6%

American Railcar Industries

American Railcar Industries doesn't make the little engine that could, but it does make the cars that make up the train. The company is a North American manufacturer of railcars and railcar components and a provider of maintenance and fleet management services to freight shippers, railcar leasing companies, and railroads. Types of railcars it produces include covered hopper cars for grains, cement, and other dry bulk and tank cars for liquid and gas commodities. The company also makes industrial products for both the rail and non-rail industries with operations in steel and aluminum casting, machining, stamping, welding, and fabrication.

Billionaire financier and American Railcar Industries chairman Carl Icahn controls the company with a 54% stake.

Icahn also controls railcar lessors ACF Industries and American Railcar Leasing; the latter accounts for about 25% of the company's annual revenues. Lessor CIT Group is American Railcar Industries' largest customer, accounting for nearly half of its annual revenues.

The company sells and markets its railcars and specialty components directly to customers, through product catalogs, and through its Web site.

EVP/COO James Cowan was promoted to president and CEO in 2009, following the resignation of James Unger. Cowan joined American Railcar Industries in 2005, after serving as president and COO of Maverick Tube.

EXECUTIVES
Chairman: Carl C. Icahn, age 73
President and CEO: James A. (Jim) Cowan, age 51, $688,406 total compensation
SVP Sales, Marketing and Services: Alan C. Lullman, age 54, $471,248 total compensation
SVP, CFO, and Treasurer: Dale C. Davies, age 57, $249,367 total compensation
Auditors: Grant Thornton LLP

LOCATIONS
HQ: American Railcar Industries, Inc.
100 Clark St., St. Charles, MO 63301
Phone: 636-940-6000   **Fax:** 636-940-6030
Web: www.americanrailcar.com

PRODUCTS/OPERATIONS
2008 Sales

	$ mil.	% of total
Manufacturing operations	757.5	94
Railcar services	51.3	6
Total	808.8	100

Selected Subsidiaries
American Railcar Mauritius I
American Railcar Mauritius II
ARI Component Venture, LLC
ARI Longtrain, Inc.
Castings, LLC

COMPETITORS
FreightCar America
Greenbrier Companies
Greenbrier Rail Services
Miner Enterprises
Trinity Industries
Union Tank Car

HISTORICAL FINANCIALS

Company Type: Public

Income Statement

FYE: December 31

	REVENUE ($ mil.)	NET INCOME ($ mil.)	NET PROFIT MARGIN	EMPLOYEES
12/08	808.8	31.4	3.9%	2,353
12/07	698.1	37.3	5.3%	2,238
12/06	646.1	35.8	5.5%	2,575
12/05	608.2	28.0	4.6%	2,425
12/04	355.1	15.2	4.3%	2,372
Annual Growth	22.8%	19.9%	—	(0.2%)

2008 Year-End Financials

Debt ratio: 87.4%
Return on equity: 10.4%
Cash ($ mil.): 291.8
Current ratio: 6.14
Long-term debt ($ mil.): 275.0
No. of shares (mil.): 21.3

Dividends
  Yield: 1.1%
  Payout: 8.2%
Market value ($ mil.): 224.3
R&D as % of sales: —
Advertising as % of sales: —

Stock History

NASDAQ (GS): ARII

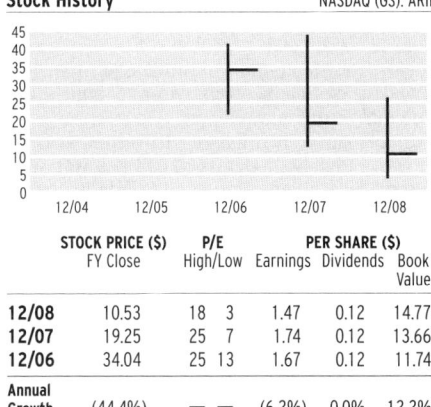

	STOCK PRICE ($) FY Close	P/E High/Low		PER SHARE ($) Earnings	Dividends	Book Value
12/08	10.53	18	3	1.47	0.12	14.77
12/07	19.25	25	7	1.74	0.12	13.66
12/06	34.04	25	13	1.67	0.12	11.74
Annual Growth	(44.4%)	—	—	(6.2%)	0.0%	12.2%

American Science and Engineering

You can't hide from American Science and Engineering (AS&E). The company makes X-ray detection systems for inspection and security applications at airports, border protection sites, shipping ports, and special events. Unlike ordinary X-rays, AS&E's backscatter technology detects organic materials such as illegal drugs, plastic explosives, and plastic weapons; its Z Backscatter three-sided X-ray system is built into a delivery van for remote detection. AS&E also makes scanning equipment for detecting contraband on persons, in aircraft, vehicles, and in luggage and packages. Customers include the Department of Homeland Security. About 55% of sales are to the US government and its contractors.

The company's Z Backscatter, along with its Flying Spot technology, takes X-ray images using a substantially lower radiation dose than other systems. Its SmartCheck personnel X-ray screening is equipped with additional software to protect the privacy of persons being screened, while still detecting both organic and inorganic threats. Its breakthrough OmniView Gantry systems are the only relocatable inspection systems which provide high-energy, multiple X-ray

views, and are used to inspect dense cargo. AS&E's Gemini parcel screening systems were used at the 2008 Beijing Olympics. AS&E and the US Nuclear Regulatory Commission intend to enter a one-year contract for support and maintenance services.

The US Department of Defense has bought AS&E's MobileSearch X-ray inspection systems and Z Backscatter Vans (ZBV) with radioactive threat detection technology for use at domestic military bases to guard against the threat of nuclear devices and dirty bombs. The company has ruggedized its Forwardscatter module for military deployment, and developed and prototyped its ZBV Military Trailer for war zone detection. It has also deployed a miniaturized Z Backscatter module on a robotic platform for use in high-threat environments.

While customers located in the US account for a little over 60% of sales, the biggest new client contracts are coming from foreign government entities, primarily Western Europe, the Middle East, and Africa. AS&E experienced a 9% increase in revenues overall in 2008, but its international revenues demonstrated an increase of over 40%. Hong Kong Customs, UK Customs, and the Royal Thai Police number among AS&E's international clients.

The company has focused on making its business more versatile by adding several proprietary technological products and targeting international markets that are showing growth promise. In 2008 its Cargo revenues made a 150% leap year-on-year, and its Parcel revenues racked up over a 100% increase, while its Z Backscatter systems saw a decrease of 40%. Additionally, the company is capturing new customers; approximately 60% of contracts in 2008 were from new clients.

American Science and Engineering, a Massachusetts corporation, was formed in 1958. It began as a developer of scientific instruments for NASA.

EXECUTIVES

Chairman: Denis R. Brown, age 71
President, CEO, and Director: Anthony R. Fabiano, age 56, $3,097,000 total compensation
SVP Science and Technology: Joseph Callerame, age 59, $645,000 total compensation
SVP Human Resources: George M. Peterman, age 61
SVP Operations: Robert Cline, age 48
SVP Worldwide Marketing and Sales:
  Robert G. (Bob) Postle, age 55, $743,000 total compensation
SVP, CFO and Treasurer: Kenneth J. (Ken) Galaznik, age 58, $937,000 total compensation
SVP Product Management and Engineering:
  Kenneth A. Breur, age 54, $605,000 total compensation
SVP Strategic Planning: Paul H. Grazewski, age 53
SVP, General Counsel, and Clerk: Patricia A. Gray, age 55
Auditors: Vitale, Caturano & Company, Ltd.

LOCATIONS

HQ: American Science and Engineering, Inc.
  829 Middlesex Tpke., Billerica, MA 01821
Phone: 978-262-8700   **Fax:** 978-262-8804
Web: www.as-e.com

2009 Sales by Region

	% of total
Middle East & Africa	85
Pacific Rim	7
Europe	8
Total	100

2009 Sales

	$ mil.	% of total
US	138.3	63
Other countries	80.1	37
Total	218.4	100

PRODUCTS/OPERATIONS

2009 Sales

	$ mil.	% of total
Product sales & contract revenue	142.9	65
Service revenue	75.5	35
Total	218.4	100

Selected Security Products

CargoSearch Inspection Systems
Contract Research and Development (CRAD)
ParcelSearch Inspection Systems
Personnel Inspection (personnel screening system)
Z Backscatter Inspection Systems
  Z Backscatter Portal (drive-through inspection system for scanning vehicles)
  Z Backscatter Van (screening system built into commercial delivery van)

COMPETITORS

Ahura	OSI Systems
Analogic	Ranger Security Detectors
Anritsu	Rapiscan Systems
GE Security	Smiths Detection
ICTS International	Syagen
Image Scan Holdings	X-Ray Industries

HISTORICAL FINANCIALS

Company Type: Public

Income Statement

FYE: Friday nearest March 31

	REVENUE ($ mil.)	NET INCOME ($ mil.)	NET PROFIT MARGIN	EMPLOYEES
3/09	218.4	28.4	13.0%	375
3/08	166.7	17.5	10.5%	346
3/07	153.2	24.6	16.1%	299
3/06	163.6	29.8	18.2%	288
3/05	88.3	11.2	12.7%	286
Annual Growth	25.4%	26.2%	—	7.0%

2009 Year-End Financials

Debt ratio: 4.6%
Return on equity: 16.3%
Cash ($ mil.): 105.4
Current ratio: 3.31
Long-term debt ($ mil.): 8.4
No. of shares (mil.): 8.9

Dividends
  Yield: 1.4%
  Payout: 25.2%
Market value ($ mil.): 496.1
R&D as % of sales: —
Advertising as % of sales: —

Stock History

NASDAQ (GS): ASEI

	STOCK PRICE ($) FY Close	P/E High/Low		PER SHARE ($) Earnings	Dividends	Book Value
3/09	55.80	26	13	3.18	0.80	20.48
3/08	54.57	39	25	1.87	0.60	18.68
3/07	52.67	39	15	2.38	0.00	18.86
3/06	93.40	29	11	3.27	0.00	14.64
3/05	44.71	38	10	1.31	0.00	6.93
Annual Growth	5.7%	—	—	24.8%	—	31.1%

American Vanguard

American Vanguard Corporation (AMVAC) bugs bugs, roots out weeds, and helps people take care of their person. The company makes specialty chemicals designed to protect the health of animals, crops, and people. Products made by its AMVAC Chemical subsidiary include pesticides, plant-growth regulators, herbicides, and soil fumigants. Its GemChem subsidiary distributes the company's chemicals nationally to the cosmetic, nutritional, and pharmaceutical industries. American Vanguard also has marketing subsidiaries in the UK, Switzerland, and Mexico. Collectively, co-chairmen Herbert Kraft and Glenn Wintemute and CEO Eric Wintemute own almost a quarter of American Vanguard.

The company's SmartBox delivery system allows for controlled and regular dissemination of crop protection products. AMVAC pairs the SmartBox system with its own insecticides as well as with products of Bayer CropScience and Syngenta Crop Protection (through licensing agreements). This allows AMVAC to offer farmers multiple crop protection options, thereby not allowing insects to develop resistance to any one pesticide.

In 2005 and 2006 AMVAC enhanced its marketing opportunities in the EU by opening new offices in Switzerland and the UK. Since 2006, the company's sales outside the US have more than doubled. It has made a number of small purchases of insecticide and fungicide product lines since then as well, from the likes of Syngenta, BASF, and Chemtura. It kept up with these small, bolt-on acquisitions in 2008, when it acquired another couple of insecticide lines from Valent Corporation and Aceto and a formulating and packaging facility in Idaho from Bayer CropScience.

EXECUTIVES

Co-Chairman: Glenn A. Wintemute, age 84
Co-Chairman: Herbert A. Kraft, age 85
President, CEO, and Director; President and CEO, AMVAC Chemical: Eric G. Wintemute, age 53, $883,150 total compensation
VP and CFO: David T. Johnson, age 52, $330,700 total compensation
VP, General Counsel, and Secretary: Timothy J. (Tim) Donnelly, age 49
Chief Administrative Officer, Treasurer, and Assistant Secretary: James A. (Jim) Barry, age 58, $328,642 total compensation
Human Resources Manager: Teresa Chavez
Director Investor Relations: William A. Kuser
President, GemChem: Robert F. (Bob) Gilbane, age 58
EVP and COO, AMVAC Chemical: Trevor Thorley, age 52
SVP and Director Business Development, AMVAC Chemical: Glen D. Johnson, age 54, $456,740 total compensation
VP and Director Technology, AMVAC Chemical: William A. (Bill) Feiler
VP and Director Manufacturing, AMVAC Chemical: Douglas (Doug) Ashmore, age 62, $384,561 total compensation
Director Marketing, AMVAC Chemical: Ted Ramirez
Auditors: BDO Seidman, LLP

LOCATIONS

HQ: American Vanguard Corporation
4695 MacArthur Ct., Newport Beach, CA 92660
Phone: 949-260-1200   **Fax:** 949-260-1201
Web: www.american-vanguard.com

2008 Sales

	$ mil.	% of total
US	196.2	83
Other countries	41.3	17
Total	**237.5**	**100**

PRODUCTS/OPERATIONS

2008 Sales

	$ mil.	% of total
Crop	193.2	81
Non-crop	44.3	19
Total	**237.5**	**100**

Selected Subsidiaries

2110 Davie Corporation (real estate investment)
Agroservicios Amvac, SA de CV (Mexico)
American Vanguard Corporation of Imperial Valley (90%)
AMVAC Ag-Chem
AMVAC Chemical Corporation (manufacturing)
AMVAC Chemical UK Ltd. (distribution)
Calhart Corporation
Environmental Mediation, Inc. (environmental consulting)
GemChem, Inc. (distribution)
Manufacturers Mirror & Glass Co., Inc.
Quimica Amvac de Mexico S.A. de C.V. (marketing)
Todagco (80%)

COMPETITORS

Aceto	FMC
Bayer CropScience	KMG Chemicals
Dow AgroSciences	Nippon Soda
DuPont Agriculture	

HISTORICAL FINANCIALS

Company Type: Public

Income Statement   FYE: December 31

	REVENUE ($ mil.)	NET INCOME ($ mil.)	NET PROFIT MARGIN	EMPLOYEES
12/08	237.5	20.0	8.4%	320
12/07	216.7	18.7	8.6%	309
12/06	193.8	15.4	7.9%	285
12/05	189.8	19.0	10.0%	300
12/04	150.9	14.5	9.6%	229
Annual Growth	**12.0%**	**8.4%**	**—**	**8.7%**

2008 Year-End Financials

Debt ratio: 48.9%
Return on equity: 13.5%
Cash ($ mil.): 1.2
Current ratio: 2.99
Long-term debt ($ mil.): 76.3
No. of shares (mil.): 27.2
Dividends
Yield: 0.4%
Payout: 6.8%
Market value ($ mil.): 317.7
R&D as % of sales: —
Advertising as % of sales: —

Stock History   NYSE: AVD

	STOCK PRICE ($) FY Close	P/E High/Low		PER SHARE ($) Earnings	Dividends	Book Value
12/08	11.70	25	10	0.73	0.05	5.74
12/07	17.35	30	17	0.68	0.07	5.15
12/06	15.90	49	23	0.57	0.08	4.45
12/05	17.63	28	16	0.74	0.06	3.04
12/04	13.79	27	15	0.57	0.05	2.36
Annual Growth	**(4.0%)**	**—**	**—**	**6.4%**	**0.0%**	**25.0%**

America's Car-Mart

No Credit? Bad Credit? No problem. America's Car-Mart targets car buyers with poor or limited credit histories. Car-Mart's subsidiaries operate 90 used-car dealerships in more than half a dozen states, primarily in smaller urban and rural markets throughout the south-central region of the US. The dealerships focus on selling basic, affordable transportation (average selling price about $8,700). The company is expanding primarily in Alabama, Oklahoma, and Missouri. While its traditional business plan has focused on cities of 20,000 to 50,000 in population, the company has begun opening dealerships in more populous cities, including Tulsa, Oklahoma. America's Car-Mart was founded in 1981 as the Crown Group.

Traditionally, America's Car-Mart has expanded in existing and contiguous markets. However, it has put the brakes on growth in recent years, with no plans to open any new locations in fiscal 2009.

Most customers take advantage of financing that the company offers through subsidiary Colonial Auto Finance.

Chairman Tilman Falgout III retired as CEO of the company in October 2008 and was succeeded by William Henderson. Falgout owns about 8% of the company.

EXECUTIVES

Chairman and General Counsel: Tilman J. (Skip) Falgout III, age 60, $541,165 total compensation
Vice Chairman, President, and CEO: William H. (Hank) Henderson, age 46, $1,339,433 total compensation
COO: Eddie L. Hight, age 46, $830,327 total compensation
VP Finance, CFO and Secretary: Jeffrey A. Williams, age 47, $524,557 total compensation
Auditors: Grant Thornton LLP

LOCATIONS

HQ: America's Car-Mart, Inc.
802 SE Plaza Ave., Ste. 200, Bentonville, AR 72712
Phone: 479-464-9944   **Fax:** 479-273-7556
Web: www.car-mart.com

2009 Stores

	No.
Arkansas	36
Oklahoma	17
Texas	13
Missouri	11
Kentucky	9
Alabama	5
Indiana	1
Tennessee	1
Total	**93**

PRODUCTS/OPERATIONS

2009 Sales

	$ mil.	% of total
Sales	273	91
Interest income & other	26	9
Total	**299**	**100**

Selected Subsidiaries

America's Car-Mart, Inc.
Colonial Auto Finance, Inc.
Colonial Underwriting, Inc.
Texas Car-Mart, Inc.

COMPETITORS

Ancira	CarMax
Asbury Automotive	DriveTime Automotive
AutoNation	Group 1 Automotive
Carbiz	Sonic Automotive

HISTORICAL FINANCIALS

Company Type: Public

Income Statement

FYE: April 30

	REVENUE ($ mil.)	NET INCOME ($ mil.)	NET PROFIT MARGIN	EMPLOYEES
4/09	299.0	17.9	6.0%	915
4/08	274.6	15.0	5.5%	840
4/07	240.3	4.2	1.7%	800
4/06	234.2	16.7	7.1%	779
4/05	204.8	18.0	8.8%	715
Annual Growth	9.9%	(0.1%)	—	6.4%

2009 Year-End Financials

Debt ratio: 19.0%	Dividends
Return on equity: 12.2%	Yield: —
Cash ($ mil.): 0.2	Payout: —
Current ratio: 8.18	Market value ($ mil.): 190.3
Long-term debt ($ mil.): 29.8	R&D as % of sales: —
No. of shares (mil.): 11.7	Advertising as % of sales: —

Stock History

NASDAQ (GS): CRMT

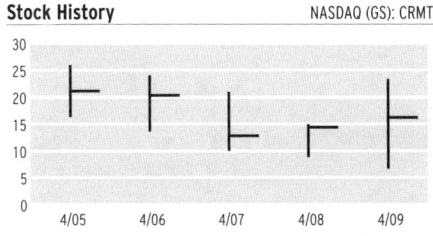

	STOCK PRICE ($) FY Close	P/E High/Low		PER SHARE ($) Earnings	Dividends	Book Value
4/09	16.22	15	5	1.52	—	13.38
4/08	14.39	12	7	1.26	—	11.70
4/07	12.82	59	29	0.35	—	10.55
4/06	20.33	17	10	1.39	—	10.16
4/05	21.14	17	11	1.49	—	8.80
Annual Growth	(6.4%)	—	—	0.5%	—	11.0%

Ameron International

Hardly a gearhead, Ameron is more interested in fluid transmission, not transmission fluid. The company designs, makes, and markets fiberglass-composite pipes for transmitting oil, chemicals, corrosive liquids, and other specialty materials. Ameron also makes and sells concrete and steel pipe used for water transmission and wind towers to developers, contractors, and government agencies in the western US. Additionally, the company supplies ready-mix concrete and aggregates, box culverts, and dune sand for construction projects in Hawaii; it also manufactures concrete and steel poles for lighting and traffic signals.

Ameron has minority-owned joint ventures in Saudi Arabia that produce concrete pipe and glass and epoxy pipe fittings. The company partners with Tokyo Steel and Mitsui & Company in joint ownership of TAMCO, a California steel minimill, which makes steel reinforcing bars (rebar) for the construction industry in the western US; Ameron's stake in the venture is 50%.

The US accounts for more than two-thirds of Ameron's total sales, though the company is also active elsewhere in North and South America, Western Europe, Asia, and the Middle East.

Ameron's largest operating segment had been its protective coatings and finishes unit, which brought in about a third of sales but had not grown as much as the company had hoped. Ameron in 2006 sold the segment to PPG for $115 million and turned its focus to its infrastructure and water transmission operations. In 2009 the company sold its pressurized gas systems business to electronics manufacturer AMETEK. Ameron has also diversified into new markets, such as supplying wind towers to the wind-energy market.

Institutional investors Invesco, Tontine Capital, and T. Rowe Price each own about 10% of the company. The estate of Taro Iketani, which also owns 16% of Tokyo Steel, owns 7%.

HISTORY

Ameron International was founded in 1907, and it merged with another company in 1929 to form American Concrete Pipe Co. The enterprise diversified into construction products in 1942 and became known as American Pipe and Construction Co.

By the 1960s American Pipe and Construction Co. had further diversified into protective coatings, ready-mix concrete, and resin piping. The company shortened its name to Ameron, Inc., in 1970, and over the next 20 years, it grew to have a worldwide presence.

Ameron adopted its current name in 1996 to reflect its international focus. That year the company bought Imperial Chemical's Devoe marine coatings unit in a move that helped it become one of the nation's leading providers of marine and offshore coatings. In a similar move, it bought the maintenance-coatings unit of Valspar Corporation in 1997, significantly increasing its product finishes business.

Bargain-basement gasoline prices and Asia's economic crisis hurt results in 1998, but the acquisition of Croda Coatings later in the year enabled the company to post a sales gain. The same year Ameron sold its 50% ownership in Gifford-Hill-American (concrete pipe). In 1999 the company established Bonstrand Ltd. (fiberglass pipe), a joint venture company in Kuwait. Bonstrand began operations in 2000. In 2001 Ameron International's Performance Coatings and Finishes unit inked a deal with Duron, the third-largest paint manufacturer in the US, to distribute Ameron's products using Duron's company stores.

In 2002 Ameron announced it would become PPG Industries' distributor of its PITT-CHAR XP fire protective coatings, primarily used in fireproofing off-shore oil rigs. The company sold its 25% stake of Amercoat Mexicana in 2003. In 2006 Ameron sold its protective coatings and finishes business to PPG.

EXECUTIVES

Chairman, President, and CEO: James S. Marlen, age 67, $7,526,796 total compensation
SVP Technology: Ralph S. (Rocky) Friedrich, age 62, $488,834 total compensation
SVP Finance and Administration and CFO:
  Gary Wagner, age 58, $2,095,946 total compensation
SVP, Secretary, and General Counsel:
  Stephen E. (Steve) Johnson, age 55

SVP Corporate Development and Treasurer:
  James R. (Jim) McLaughlin, age 61, $936,068 total compensation
VP and Controller: Daniel J. Emmett, age 48
VP; Group President, Fiberglass-Composite Pipe; Division President, Fiberglass-Composite Pipe Americas: Mark J. Nowak, age 55, $797,037 total compensation
VP Human Resources: Terrence P. (Terry) O'Shea, age 63
VP Operations Compliance: Christine Stanley, age 51
VP Operations Maui, Hawaii Division, Infrastructure Products Group: Eric Yoshizawa
VP and Controller: James L. Balas
VP Operations, Fiberglass-Composite Pipe Group: David B. Jones
VP Operations Oahu, Hawaii Division, Infrastructure Products Group: George N. West
Group President, Water Transmission Group: Richard I. Mueller
President, Pole Products Division: John Szabo
President, Hawaii Division, Infrastructure Products Group: Wade Wakayama
Auditors: PricewaterhouseCoopers LLP

LOCATIONS

HQ: Ameron International Corporation
  245 S. Los Robles Ave., Pasadena, CA 91101
Phone: 626-683-4000   **Fax:** 626-683-4060
Web: www.ameron.com

Ameron International operates manufacturing facilities in Brazil, Colombia, Malaysia, Mexico, the Netherlands, Singapore, and the US. It also has joint ventures in Egypt, Saudi Arabia, and the US.

2008 Sales

	$ mil.	% of total
US	459.8	69
Asia	135.1	20
Europe	35.7	5
Other	37.9	6
Elmininations	(1.0)	—
Total	**667.5**	**100**

PRODUCTS/OPERATIONS

2008 Sales

	$ mil.	% of total
Fiberglass-Composite Pipe	274.1	41
Water Transmission	215.3	32
Infrastructure Products	179.1	27
Eliminations	(1.0)	—
Total	**667.5**	**100**

Selected Products

Box culverts
Concrete and steel poles for street lights and traffic signals
Concrete pipe
Crushed and sized basaltic aggregates
Dune sand
Filament-wound and molded-fiberglass pipe and fittings
Ready-mix concrete
Reinforced concrete pipe
Steel pipe

COMPETITORS

Berg Steel Pipe
Cascade Steel
CSR Limited
Dalmine
Denali
Lafarge North America
SSAB North America
Valmont Industries

HISTORICAL FINANCIALS
Company Type: Public

Income Statement				FYE: November 30
	REVENUE ($ mil.)	NET INCOME ($ mil.)	NET PROFIT MARGIN	EMPLOYEES
11/08	667.5	58.6	8.8%	2,800
11/07	631.0	67.2	10.6%	2,600
11/06	549.2	52.2	9.5%	2,500
11/05	704.6	32.6	4.6%	3,000
11/04	605.9	13.5	2.2%	2,800
Annual Growth	2.5%	44.3%	—	0.0%

2008 Year-End Financials
Debt ratio: 7.5%
Return on equity: 12.7%
Cash ($ mil.): 143.6
Current ratio: 2.87
Long-term debt ($ mil.): 36.0
No. of shares (mil.): 9.2

Dividends
Yield: 2.1%
Payout: 18.0%
Market value ($ mil.): 496.5
R&D as % of sales: —
Advertising as % of sales: —

Stock History
NYSE: AMN

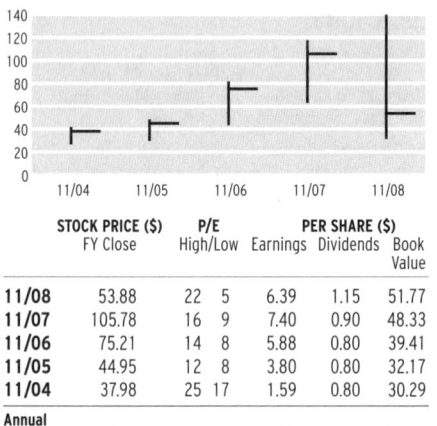

	STOCK PRICE ($) FY Close	P/E High/Low		PER SHARE ($) Earnings	Dividends	Book Value
11/08	53.88	22	5	6.39	1.15	51.77
11/07	105.78	16	9	7.40	0.90	48.33
11/06	75.21	14	8	5.88	0.80	39.41
11/05	44.95	12	8	3.80	0.80	32.17
11/04	37.98	25	17	1.59	0.80	30.29
Annual Growth	9.1%	—	—	41.6%	9.5%	14.3%

Ampco-Pittsburgh Corporation

All amped up to make some financial noise, Ampco-Pittsburgh manufactures a variety of heavy metal products. Operations straddle two arenas. Its forged and cast steel rolls units, Union Electric Steel and Davy Roll Co., make hardened-steel rolls for steel and aluminum manufacturers. Its air and liquid processing segment comprises three companies: Buffalo Pumps, offering centrifugal pumps for refrigeration, marine defense, and power generation industries; Aerofin, driving finned-tube heat-exchange coils for construction and utility applications; and Buffalo Air Handling, supplying custom air-handling systems used in commercial, industrial, and institutional buildings.

The weakened economy has slowed Ampco-Pittsburgh's progress. The company's forged and cast rolls business has pushed back by reaching for a larger role in the global market for forged roll production. Foreign sales account for about 65% of this segment's sales, with two customers collectively contributing over 20%. Although the weakened economy in 2008-09 slashed manufacturers' production, prompting delayed deliveries, the overall shortfall in sources for forged hardened steel roll-makers is presenting opportunities. A Union Electric Steel subsidiary scored a 49% share in a joint venture set-up with Maanshan Iron & Steel Co. Ltd. to make backup rolling-mill rolls in China during 2010. Davey Roll is financing a cast roll-maker in China, too.

The company's air and liquid processing business has withstood damage from the economic downturn. However, this segment continues to face exposure to reduced construction in industrial and institutional markets. The power generation industry and the US Navy are relied on to drive sales of commercial pumps.

The Louis Berkman Investment Company holds about a 15% stake in the company. Louis Berkman, founder and chairman emeritus of Ampco-Pittsburgh, is a Louis Berkman Investment Company officer, director, and shareholder. Ampco-Pittsburgh president and CEO, and son-in-law of Berkman, Robert A. Paul also serves as president and director of Louis Berkman Investment.

EXECUTIVES
Chairman and CEO: Robert A. Paul, age 72, $1,117,835 total compensation
SVP and Secretary: Rose Hoover, age 54, $482,147 total compensation
VP, Treasurer, and Controller:
Marliss D. (Dee Ann) Johnson, age 45, $348,689 total compensation
VP Industrial Relations and Senior Counsel:
Robert F. Schultz, age 62
President Air and Liquid Processing:
Terrence W. Kenny, age 50, $469,683 total compensation
Chairman, President, and CEO, Forged and Cast Rolls; President, Union Electric Steel: Robert G. Carothers
Director Pension and Risk Management:
Linda Sismondo
Auditors: Deloitte & Touche LLP

LOCATIONS
HQ: Ampco-Pittsburgh Corporation
600 Grant St., Ste. 4600, Pittsburgh, PA 15219
Phone: 412-456-4400 **Fax:** 412-456-4404
Web: www.ampcopgh.com

2008 Sales
	$ mil.	% of total
US	145.0	37
Other countries	249.5	63
Total	394.5	100

PRODUCTS/OPERATIONS
2008 Sales
	$ mil.	% of total
Forged & cast rolls	282.9	72
Air & liquid processing		
Heat exchange coils	41.3	10
Air handling systems	37.7	10
Centrifugal pumps	32.6	8
Total	394.5	100

Selected Operations
Forged and Cast Rolls
The Davy Roll Company Limited
Union Electric Steel Corporation

Air and Liquid Processing
Aerofin Corporation
Buffalo Air Handling Company
Buffalo Pumps, Inc.

COMPETITORS
Cardo
Colfax
Connell LP
Gorman-Rupp
Roper Industries

HISTORICAL FINANCIALS
Company Type: Public

Income Statement				FYE: December 31
	REVENUE ($ mil.)	NET INCOME ($ mil.)	NET PROFIT MARGIN	EMPLOYEES
12/08	394.5	12.6	3.2%	1,306
12/07	346.8	39.2	11.3%	1,323
12/06	301.8	16.6	5.5%	1,324
12/05	247.0	15.0	6.1%	1,234
12/04	202.9	(2.6)	—	1,252
Annual Growth	18.1%	—	—	1.1%

2008 Year-End Financials
Debt ratio: —
Return on equity: 7.6%
Cash ($ mil.): 81.6
Current ratio: 2.59
Long-term debt ($ mil.): —
No. of shares (mil.): 10.2

Dividends
Yield: 4.0%
Payout: 70.2%
Market value ($ mil.): 221.9
R&D as % of sales: —
Advertising as % of sales: —

Stock History
NYSE: AP

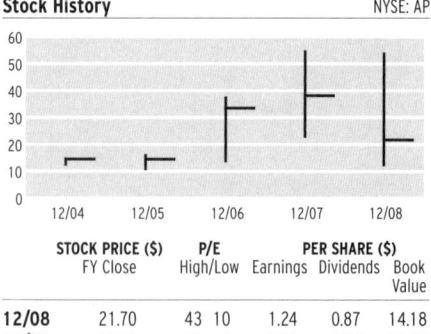

	STOCK PRICE ($) FY Close	P/E High/Low		PER SHARE ($) Earnings	Dividends	Book Value
12/08	21.70	43	10	1.24	0.87	14.18
12/07	38.13	14	6	3.88	0.55	18.36
12/06	33.48	22	8	1.67	0.40	13.71
12/05	14.51	10	7	1.53	0.40	13.82
12/04	14.60	—	—	(0.27)	0.40	12.57
Annual Growth	10.4%	—	—	—	21.4%	3.1%

AmSurg Corp.

AmSurg serves only certain cuts, but it's not a pricey steakhouse — the company operates specialty ambulatory surgery centers that focus on a narrow range of high-volume, low-risk procedures. Specialties include gastroenterology (colonoscopy and endoscopy), orthopedics (knee scopes and carpal tunnel repair), and ophthalmology (cataracts and laser eye surgery). AmSurg promotes its centers, which are each affiliated with a physicians practice group, to patients and doctors, as well as managed care organizations and employers. AmSurg owns a majority interest in more than 190 outpatient centers in 32 states and the District of Columbia. It also has three centers under development.

AmSurg steadily grows its number of surgery centers through small acquisitions, mostly of centers that already have minority physician ownership, or by developing new facilities in partnership

with physician groups. AmSurg plans to acquire about 15 new centers in 2009.

The company primarily targets single-specialty facilities because they generally involve high-volume, lower risk, outpatient procedures. Of those, about 90% specialize in gastroenterology or ophthalmology because those specialties have a greater concentration of older patients which represent a high-growth demographic. AmSurg derives about 35% of its revenues from Medicare and other government programs.

However, when the Centers for Medicare & Medicaid Services revised the payment system in 2008 for services provided in centers like the ones operated by AmSurg, the company saw a big reduction in reimbursement rates for gastroenterology procedures (which comprise about 80% of the procedures performed at the surgery centers).

In 2008 the publicly traded company sold three surgery centers, closed three surgery centers, and placed one more up for sale because of limited growth opportunities at those locations.

EXECUTIVES

Chairman: Thomas G. (Tom) Cigarran, age 67
President, CEO, and Director: Christopher A. Holden, age 45, $1,456,609 total compensation
EVP and Chief Development Officer: David L. Manning, age 61, $890,495 total compensation
EVP, CFO, Secretary, and Director: Claire M. Gulmi, age 56, $741,115 total compensation
SVP Finance and Chief Accounting Officer: Kevin D. Eastridge, age 44
SVP Operations: Billie A. Payne, $429,188 total compensation
SVP Corporate Services and Chief Compliance Officer: Phillip Clendenin, age 45
Auditors: Deloitte & Touche LLP

LOCATIONS

HQ: AmSurg Corp.
20 Burton Hills Blvd., Ste. 500, Nashville, TN 37215
Phone: 615-665-1283   **Fax:** 615-665-0755
Web: www.amsurg.com

2008 Selected Locations

	No. of centers
Florida	31
California	18
Maryland	15
Tennessee	12
Ohio	11
Texas	11
Arizona	10
Pennsylvania	8
New Jersey	7
Louisiana	6
North Carolina	6
Kansas	5
South Carolina	5
Washington	5
Kentucky	4
Missouri	4
Arkansas	3
Colorado	3
Delaware	3
Indiana	3
Michigan	3
Minnesota	3
Nevada	3
Oklahoma	3
Utah	2
Other states	9
Total	**193**

COMPETITORS

Dynacq Healthcare	Symbion
HCA	Tenet Healthcare
LCA	TLC Vision
NovaMed	United Surgical Partners
PainCare Holdings	Universal Health Services

HISTORICAL FINANCIALS
Company Type: Public

Income Statement   FYE: December 31

	REVENUE ($ mil.)	NET INCOME ($ mil.)	NET PROFIT MARGIN	EMPLOYEES
12/08	600.7	47.0	7.8%	2,460
12/07	531.1	44.2	8.3%	2,150
12/06	464.6	37.7	8.1%	2,000
12/05	391.8	35.2	9.0%	1,705
12/04	334.3	39.7	11.9%	1,480
Annual Growth	**15.8%**	**4.3%**	**—**	**13.5%**

2008 Year-End Financials

Debt ratio: 57.7%	Dividends
Return on equity: 10.8%	Yield: 0.0%
Cash ($ mil.): 31.5	Payout: —
Current ratio: 3.35	Market value ($ mil.): 715.9
Long-term debt ($ mil.): 265.8	R&D as % of sales: —
No. of shares (mil.): 30.7	Advertising as % of sales: —

Stock History   NASDAQ (GS): AMSG

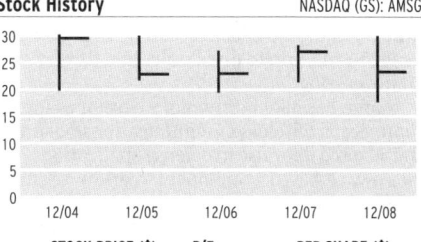

	STOCK PRICE ($) FY Close	P/E High/Low		PER SHARE ($) Earnings	Dividends	Book Value
12/08	23.34	20	12	1.47	0.00	15.01
12/07	27.06	20	15	1.42	0.00	13.41
12/06	23.00	22	16	1.24	0.00	11.19
12/05	22.86	25	19	1.17	0.00	9.61
12/04	29.54	23	15	1.30	0.00	8.29
Annual Growth	**(5.7%)**	**—**	**—**	**3.1%**	**—**	**16.0%**

AmTrust Financial

Catering specifically to small businesses (with an average of six employees), AmTrust Financial Services offers specialty and commercial property/casualty insurance, workers' compensation, and extended service and warranty coverage of consumer and commercial goods. The company's seven subsidiaries, which operate in the US, Bermuda, Ireland, and England, underwrite insurance policies that are then distributed through brokers, agents, and claims administrators. Its customers include restaurants, retail stores, physicians' offices, auto and consumer electronics manufacturers, and nonprofit organizations. AmTrust has announced plans to acquire GMAC's US consumer property/casualty insurance operations.

That acquisition will bounce AmTrust into the consumer market and broaden its distribution network of independent agents.

AmTrust's premium revenue has been fairly evenly split between its three segments. While its workers' compensation and property/casualty business is limited to the US, its specialty risk and extended warranty coverage is split neatly between the US and Europe.

The company has been able to expand its product offerings and geographic reach through acquisitions of smaller competitors, including Princeton Insurance Company in the Northeast; The Covenant Group, Inc. in the South; Associated Industries Insurance Company, Inc. in Florida; Muirfield Underwriters, Ltd. in the Midwest; and IGI Group, Ltd. in the UK. The company acquired the renewal rights to Unitrin's Business Insurance unit in 2008.

In 2009 AmTrust expanded its online workers' compensation offering by snapping up CyberComp from Swiss Re. CyberComp focuses on small to midsized employers in about 25 states. The digital platform allows agents to enter data, get quotes, and issue policies online.

AmTrust was established in 1998, when it was acquired from Wang Laboratories. Chairman Michael Karfunkel holds 30% of AmTrust, his brother George Karfunkel holds 30%, and his son-in-law CEO Barry Zyskind holds 10%.

The company had been in a struggle with unrelated AmTrust Bank over the use of the name "AmTrust"; the bank went out of business in 2009. AmTrust Financial Services is also unrelated to AmTrust Financial Corp., the former parent of AmTrust Bank.

EXECUTIVES

Chairman: Michael Karfunkel, age 67
President, CEO, and Director: Barry D. Zyskind, age 38, $2,233,649 total compensation
COO: Michael J. Saxon, age 51, $1,235,476 total compensation
CFO: Ronald E. Pipoly Jr., age 43, $1,108,823 total compensation
CIO: Christopher M. Longo, age 36, $987,560 total compensation
VP Investor Relations: Hilly Gross
General Counsel and Secretary: Stephen B. Ungar
President, AmTrust International Insurance Ltd and AmTrust International Underwriters Ltd: Max G. Caviet, age 56, $1,115,063 total compensation
Investor Relations: Ellen Taylor
Auditors: BDO Seidman, LLP

LOCATIONS

HQ: AmTrust Financial Services, Inc.
59 Maiden Ln., 6th Fl., New York, NY 10038
Phone: 212-220-7120   **Fax:** 212-220-7130
Web: www.amtrustgroup.com

PRODUCTS/OPERATIONS

2008 Revenues

	% of total
Net earned premium	77
Ceding commission — primarily related party	20
Commission & fee income	1
Net investment income	2
Total	**100**

Selected Subsidiaries

AmTrust International Insurance Ltd. (reinsurance, Bermuda)
AmTrust International Underwriters Limited (specialty risk and extended warranty coverage, EU)
Associated Industries Insurance Company, Inc. (workers' compensation)
IGI Insurance Company, Ltd. (specialty risk and extended warranty coverage, EU)
Rochdale Insurance Company (specialty property/casualty, specialty risk and extended warranty, workers' compensation)
Technology Insurance Company, Inc. (specialty property/casualty, specialty risk and extended warranty, workers' compensation)
Wesco Insurance Company (specialty property/casualty, specialty risk and extended warranty, workers' compensation)

COMPETITORS

AIG
Allianz Insurance
Amica Mutual
Bankers Financial
Berkshire Hathaway
Chubb Corp
FCCI
The Hartford
Liberty Mutual
National Indemnity Company
Travelers Companies

HISTORICAL FINANCIALS

Company Type: Public

Income Statement

FYE: December 31

	ASSETS ($ mil.)	NET INCOME ($ mil.)	INCOME AS % OF ASSETS	EMPLOYEES
12/08	3,143.9	82.9	2.6%	900
12/07	2,322.8	90.1	3.9%	625
12/06	1,185.4	48.9	4.1%	325
12/05	612.9	37.6	6.1%	286
12/04	497.5	14.1	2.8%	—
Annual Growth	58.6%	55.7%	—	46.5%

2008 Year-End Financials

Equity as % of assets: —
Return on assets: 3.0%
Return on equity: —
Long-term debt ($ mil.): 157.0
No. of shares (mil.): 59.3
Market value ($ mil.): 687.9
Dividends
  Yield: 1.6%
  Payout: 13.1%
Sales ($ mil.): 576.4
R&D as % of sales: —
Advertising as % of sales: —

Stock History

NASDAQ (GM): AFSI

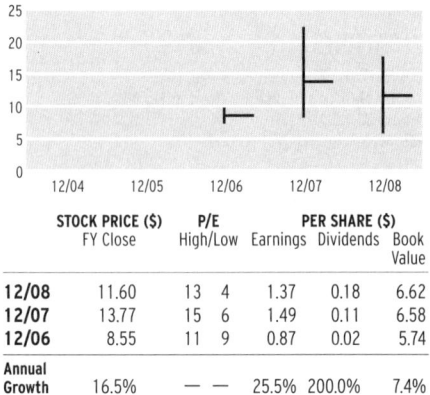

	STOCK PRICE ($) FY Close	P/E High/Low		PER SHARE ($) Earnings	Dividends	Book Value
12/08	11.60	13	4	1.37	0.18	6.62
12/07	13.77	15	6	1.49	0.11	6.58
12/06	8.55	11	9	0.87	0.02	5.74
Annual Growth	16.5%	—	—	25.5%	200.0%	7.4%

Anaren, Inc.

Anaren is hot for wireless. The company makes microwave and radio-frequency (RF) components, assemblies, and subsystems used in signal processing devices for defense, satellite, and wireless communications applications. Its products include the Xinger line of surface mount passive microwave components, RF power amplifiers, ferrite devices, signal splitters, and backplanes that are incorporated into amplifiers, receivers, and cellular base station gear. Other products range from RF measurement devices to beamformers (used to locate fixed beams from antennas) and switch matrices (used to route RF signals). The company counts Lockheed Martin, Nokia Siemens, Northrup Grumman, and Raytheon among its customers.

Anaren also custom builds subassemblies and components for satellite and military applications. The company has manufacturing locations in the US and in China. As it shifts its focus to defense related applications, the company is investing in facilities that produce more complex subassemblies such as multi-layer ceramic circuits. The company sells its standard components, such as its Xinger line of surface mount components, through distributors including Avnet, Richardson Electronics, and E.G. Components, in addition to direct sales and through an online catalog.

Anaren has taken technology developed for its commercial wireless communications business and adapted it for use in defense applications. Its microwave-based components can be used in radar systems, jamming systems, surveillance systems, and smart munitions. The company has also expanded the breadth and complexity of its product lines designed for defense applications through acquisitions. In 2008 the company bought M.S. Kennedy Corp. (MSK), a supplier of analog and mixed-signal hybrid circuits for military/aerospace applications, for $28 million. Later that year Anaren acquired Unicircuit, a manufacturer of printed circuit boards for aerospace and military customers, for almost $22 million. Both acquisitions added additional manufacturing capabilities.

In order to keep costs low, Anaren has continued to expand its manufacturing facility in Suzhou, China, moving more of its labor intensive and high volume manufacturing operations from the US to China. It is also sourcing more of its raw materials at a lower price from suppliers in the region.

EXECUTIVES

Chairman, President, and CEO: Lawrence A. Sala, age 46, $1,346,384 total compensation
Vice Chairman and CTO: Carl W. Gerst Jr., age 72, $1,159,585 total compensation
SVP, CFO, and Treasurer: George A. Blanton, age 48, $335,380 total compensation
SVP Technology: Gert R. Thygesen, age 54
SVP Human Resources: Amy B. Tewksbury, age 45
SVP Business Development: Timothy P. Ross, age 50, $511,643 total compensation
SVP and General Manager: Mark P. Burdick, age 51, $464,796 total compensation
VP Accounting: Joseph E. Porcello, age 57
Secretary and General Counsel: David M. Ferrara, age 54
Manager Marketing Communications: John Hoeschele
Auditors: KPMG LLP

LOCATIONS

HQ: Anaren, Inc.
  6635 Kirkville Rd., East Syracuse, NY 13057
Phone: 315-432-8909   **Fax:** 315-432-9121
Web: www.anaren.com

2009 Sales

	$ mil.	% of total
Americas		
US	104.2	63
Other countries	2.6	2
Asia/Pacific	37.4	22
Europe	15.7	9
Other regions	7.0	4
Total	**166.9**	**100**

PRODUCTS/OPERATIONS

2009 Sales

	$ mil.	% of total
Space & defense	98.3	59
Wireless	68.6	41
Total	**166.9**	**100**

Selected Products

Space and Defense
  Defense radar countermeasure subsystems
  Passive beamformers (determine number, size, and quality of antenna beams)
  Radar feed networks
  Switch matrices (route radio-frequency signals)
Wireless Communications
  Custom radio-frequency (RF) backplane assemblies
  Custom splitting and combining products
  Ferrite components
  Hybrid matrix assemblies
  Power splitting and combining networks (AdrenaLine)
  Resistive components
    Attenuators
    Power terminations
    Resistors
  Surface mount components (Xinger)

COMPETITORS

Aeroflex
American Technical Ceramics
Brush Engineered Materials
Cobham
Cohu
COM DEV
EMS Technologies
Endwave
Filtronic
Herley Farmingdale
International Rectifier
ISCO International
Merrimac Industries
Mini-Circuits
NGK INSULATORS
ORBIT/FR
Radiall
STC Microwave Systems
TTM Technologies
Tyco Electronics
Wireless Telecom

HISTORICAL FINANCIALS

Company Type: Public

Income Statement

FYE: June 30

	REVENUE ($ mil.)	NET INCOME ($ mil.)	NET PROFIT MARGIN	EMPLOYEES
6/09	166.9	9.9	5.9%	1,060
6/08	131.3	9.2	7.0%	930
6/07	129.0	15.3	11.9%	871
6/06	105.5	12.2	11.6%	708
6/05	94.5	7.4	7.8%	587
Annual Growth	15.3%	7.5%	—	15.9%

2009 Year-End Financials

Debt ratio: 24.9%
Return on equity: 6.4%
Cash ($ mil.): 49.9
Current ratio: 5.12
Long-term debt ($ mil.): 40.0
No. of shares (mil.): 14.9
Dividends
  Yield: —
  Payout: —
Market value ($ mil.): 263.9
R&D as % of sales: —
Advertising as % of sales: —

Stock History

NASDAQ (GM): ANEN

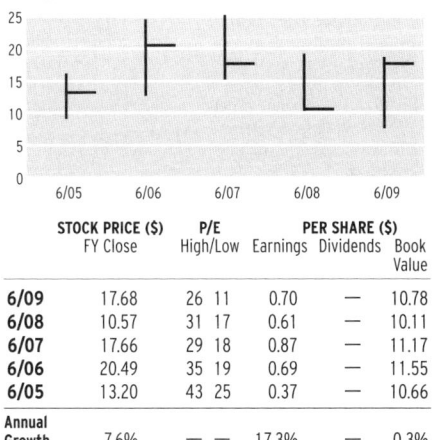

	STOCK PRICE ($) FY Close	P/E High/Low		PER SHARE ($) Earnings	Dividends	Book Value
6/09	17.68	26	11	0.70	—	10.78
6/08	10.57	31	17	0.61	—	10.11
6/07	17.66	29	18	0.87	—	11.17
6/06	20.49	35	19	0.69	—	11.55
6/05	13.20	43	25	0.37	—	10.66
Annual Growth	7.6%	—	—	17.3%	—	0.3%

Ancestry.com Inc.

Got the urge to know your roots? Ancestry.com helps people discover, research, and share family histories, and create family trees. Users can search through a variety of documents, photographs, maps, and newspapers on the company's Web site. In addition to user generated content, the site's information comes from the digitized archives of publicly available US and UK census records and other government documents, historical societies, religious institutions, and private collectors of historical content. The company also provides family history desktop software, Family Tree Maker. Most of Ancestry.com's revenues come from subscription fees.

Nearly 1 million paying subscribers access Ancestry.com's offerings, which include 11 million family trees containing more than 1 billion profiles. The company is using proceeds from its IPO in order to pay down debt and expand through acquisitions and investments. Its strategy for growth includes improving marketing efforts for increased brand awareness, adding new content, and growing internationally. In addition, it plans to focus on improving its product through providing a bigger outlet for social networking and other activities that encourage collaboration.

The company has taken steps towards achieving these goals. Its recently launched Member Connect service lets members who are researching common ancestors communicate with one another. Ancestry.com launched Mundia.com, a global, multilanguage family-history networking product, later in 2009. In 2008 the company launched Chinese family history Web site jiapu.com. It has also been broadening its content by digitizing more historical records, and in 2008 the company added more census, military, and immigration records, as well as Jewish and African-American family history records.

The company was founded in 1983. It filed an IPO in 2009. Private equity firm Spectrum Equity Investors and its affiliates own more than half of Ancestry.com.

EXECUTIVES

President, CEO, and Director:
  Timothy P. (Tim) Sullivan, age 46
CFO: Howard Hochhauser, age 38
SVP Strategy and Corporate Development:
  David H. Rinn
SVP Operations: Christopher Tracy, age 41
SVP and General Manager, International: Josh Hanna, age 37
SVP and CTO: Michael (Mike) Wolfgramm, age 42
SVP and General Manager, Family History:
  Andrew Wait, age 47
VP Community Relations: Loretto Dennis (Lou) Szucs
VP Development, Ancestry.com: Jonathan Young
VP Legal: David Farnsworth
VP International Legal and Content: Ruth Daniels
VP Product, Ancestry.com: Eric Shoup
General Counsel and Corporate Secretary:
  William Stern, age 45
Public Relations Director: Mike Ward
Auditors: Ernst & Young LLP

LOCATIONS

HQ: Ancestry.com Inc.
  360 W. 4800 North, Provo, UT 84604
Phone: 801-705-7000   **Fax:** 801-705-7001
Web: corporate.ancestry.com

PRODUCTS/OPERATIONS

2008 Sales

	$ mil.	% of total
Subscriptions	181.4	92
Product & other	16.2	8
Total	**197.6**	**100**

Selected Sources

Birth, marriage, and death records
Census records
Court, land, and probate records
Immigration records
Military records
Newspapers

HISTORICAL FINANCIALS

Company Type: Public

Income Statement

FYE: December 31

	REVENUE ($ mil.)	NET INCOME ($ mil.)	NET PROFIT MARGIN	EMPLOYEES
12/08	197.6	2.4	1.2%	670
12/07	166.4	6.5	3.9%	—
12/06	150.6	8.1	5.4%	—
Annual Growth	14.5%	(45.6%)	—	—

2008 Year-End Financials

Debt ratio: 50.8%
Return on equity: —
Cash ($ mil.): 40.1
Current ratio: 0.59
Long-term debt ($ mil.): 111.5

Net Income History

NASDAQ (GS): ACOM

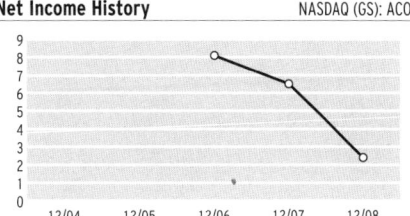

AngioDynamics, Inc.

AngioDynamics gets your blood flowing, and flowing easier if need be. The company makes medical devices for the treatment of peripheral vascular disease (PVD, where arteries or veins in the arms or legs become blocked or restricted by plaque), including catheters for use in angiography and angioplasty procedures to treat PVD. Other interventional products made by AngioDynamics include laser venous systems to treat varicose veins, vascular access products for drug delivery, kidney dialysis catheters, and abscess drainage products. The company also offers tools and systems for minimally-invasive oncological treatments. AngioDynamics' sales force markets products to doctors in the US and internationally.

The company has been growing via acquisitions over the last few years, expanding its market footprint as well as operations overseas. Though the US remains its largest market, international sales have steadily grown to account for more than 10% of sales. To reflect its increasing diversity, in 2009 the company reorganized its operations into three divisions: Peripheral Vascular (vascular and angiographic), Access (dialysis and port products), and Oncology/Surgery.

The oncology division includes cancer treatment technologies added through the 2007 acquisition of oncology device maker RITA Medical Systems for $220 million. The deal gave AngioDynamics a line of medical devices and systems for treating cancer, including radiofrequency ablation (RFA), resectioning (Habib), and embolizing (LC Beads) products. The company then spent $25 million to acquire Oncobionics in 2008, adding another technology for cancer tissue ablation known as irreversible electroporation (IRE). The company began marketing IRE products in 2009.

Also in 2008 the company acquired Diomed Holdings for $11 million in cash. The two companies had been engaged in a patent dispute over its varicose vein laser treatment system. Diomed had filed for bankruptcy protection early that year. The acquisition included Diomed's UK operations and allowed AngioDynamics to expand its sales force in the US and internationally.

In 2009 AngioDynamics shifted its acquisition strategy toward smaller operations when it paid about $2 million to buy the renal therapy product line of FlowMedica. The purchase included the Benephit kidney drug delivery systems.

AngioDynamics was spun off from former parent company E-Z-EM in late 2004. The companies agreed not to compete during AngioDynamics' first couple of years as a public company. E-Z-EM was acquired by health care firm Bracco in 2008.

EXECUTIVES

Chairman: Vincent Bucci, age 54
President, CEO, and Director: Jan Keltjens, age 52,
  $386,572 total compensation
EVP, CFO, and Treasurer: D. Joseph (Joe) Gersuk,
  age 59, $593,452 total compensation
SVP and General Manager, International:
  Stephen McGill
SVP Advanced Research: William M. Appling, age 46
SVP Operations: Harold C. Mapes, age 49,
  $445,972 total compensation
SVP; General Manager, Peripheral Vascular:
  Shawn P. McCarthy, age 40
SVP; General Manager, Access Division:
  Robert M. Rossell, age 53, $446,266 total compensation

VP and Corporate Controller: Wayne McDougall, age 46
VP Regulatory, Quality and Clinical Affairs:
  Michael S. Sharp, age 60
Director Marketing Communications: John Mousaw
Auditors: PricewaterhouseCoopers LLP

LOCATIONS

HQ: AngioDynamics, Inc.
  603 Queensbury Ave., Queensbury, NY 12804
Phone: 518-798-1215   **Fax:** 518-798-3625
Web: www.angiodynamics.com

2009 Sales

	$ mil.	% of total
US	173.4	89
Other countries	21.7	11
Total	**195.1**	**100**

PRODUCTS/OPERATIONS

2009 Sales

	$ mil.	% of total
Peripheral vascular	83.5	43
Access	66.8	34
Oncology/surgery	44.8	23
Total	**195.1**	**100**

COMPETITORS

Bard	ev3
BioSphere Medical	Navilyst Medical
Boston Scientific	Radionics
Cook Incorporated	Smiths Group
Cordis	Teleflex
Covidien	Vascular Solutions

HISTORICAL FINANCIALS

Company Type: Public

Income Statement				FYE: Saturday nearest May 31
	REVENUE ($ mil.)	NET INCOME ($ mil.)	NET PROFIT MARGIN	EMPLOYEES
5/09	195.1	9.9	5.1%	715
5/08	166.5	10.9	6.5%	566
5/07	112.2	(9.1)	—	530
5/06	78.5	6.9	8.8%	306
5/05	60.3	4.5	7.5%	252
Annual Growth	**34.1%**	**21.8%**	**—**	**29.8%**

2009 Year-End Financials

Debt ratio: 1.8%
Return on equity: 2.7%
Cash ($ mil.): 27.9
Current ratio: 5.00
Long-term debt ($ mil.): 6.8
No. of shares (mil.): 24.6

Dividends
  Yield: —
  Payout: —
Market value ($ mil.): 302.0
R&D as % of sales: —
Advertising as % of sales: —

Stock History

NASDAQ (GS): ANGO

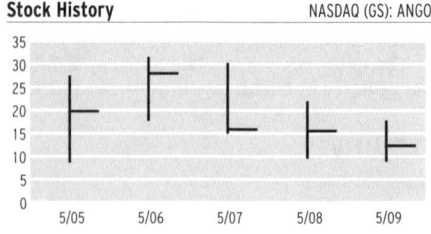

	STOCK PRICE ($) FY Close	P/E High/Low		PER SHARE ($) Earnings	Dividends	Book Value
5/09	12.30	43	22	0.41	—	15.16
5/08	15.49	48	22	0.45	—	14.49
5/07	15.85	—	—	(0.49)	—	13.68
5/06	28.00	59	34	0.53	—	5.03
5/05	19.77	74	24	0.37	—	2.00
Annual Growth	**(11.2%)**	**—**	**—**	**2.6%**	**—**	**65.9%**

Anika Therapeutics

Anika Therapeutics is roosterrific. The company uses hyaluronic acid (HA), a natural polymer extracted from rooster combs and other sources, to make products that treat bone, cartilage, and soft tissue. Anika's OrthoVisc treats osteoarthritis of the knee and is available in the US and overseas. DePuy Mitek sells the product in the US. A unit of Boehringer Ingelheim sells Anika's osteoarthritis treatment for racehorses, Hyvisc. Bausch & Lomb sells two of the company's products that maintain eye shape and protect tissue during eye surgery. Other products include surgical anti-adhesives and aesthetic dermatology products.

Anika's first ELEVESS product for facial wrinkles and scars has been approved in the US, Canada, Europe, and other regions. Additional ELEVESS products are in development.

Anika is also developing more osteoarthritis and joint health treatments. The company received Canadian approval for its next-generation osteoarthritis treatment Monovisc in 2009; the drug was launched in the EU the previous year.

Later that year Anika bought Fidia Farmaceutici Biopolymers, an Italian producer of HA-based products in a number of therapeutic areas including the regeneration of connective and structural tissues damaged by injuries, aging, or degenerative diseases.

The $17 million buy includes research and development and cell culture laboratories, as well as commercial and manufacturing operations in Italy. Anika also receives FAB's patented technology for modifying HA to produce fibers, films, and textile biomaterials for medical device applications. FAB's modified HA technology is also commercialized in a range of orthopedic, otolaryngology, and urogynecology products.

Bausch & Lomb and Depuy Mitek are Anika's largest customers, each accounting for more than 35% of product sales.

EXECUTIVES

President, CEO, and Director: Charles H. Sherwood, age 62, $1,039,214 total compensation
COO: Frank J. Luppino, age 40
CFO: Kevin W. Quinlan, age 59, $537,872 total compensation
CTO: Andrew J. Carter, age 53, $492,012 total compensation
VP Human Resources: William J. Mrachek, age 65, $373,055 total compensation
VP Regulatory and Clinical Affairs: Irina B. Kulinets, age 54, $348,098 total compensation
VP Operations: Randall W. (Randy) Wilhoite, age 44
Auditors: PricewaterhouseCoopers LLP

LOCATIONS

HQ: Anika Therapeutics, Inc.
  32 Wiggins Ave., Bedford, MA 01730
Phone: 781-457-9000   **Fax:** 781-305-9720
Web: www.anikatherapeutics.com

PRODUCTS/OPERATIONS

Selected Products

Approved
  Amvisc (eye surgery product, sold by Bausch & Lomb)
  Amvisc Plus (eye surgery product, sold by Bausch & Lomb)
  ELEVESS (aesthetic dermatology products)
  Hyvisc (equine osteoarthritis treatment, distributed by Boehringer Ingelheim)
  INCERT (post-surgical adhesion prevention product)
  OrthoVisc (human osteoarthritis treatment, marketed by DePuy Mitek)
  ShellGel (ophthalmic product, sold by Cytosol Ophthalmics)
  STAARVISC II (ophthalmic product, sold by STAAR Surgical)
In Development
  Cingal (osteoarthritis/joint health treatment)
  Monovisc (osteoarthritis/joint health treatment)

COMPETITORS

Allergan
BioMS Medical
Fibrocell Science
Genzyme Biosurgery
Lifecore Biomedical
Medicis Pharmaceutical
OrthoLogic
Pfizer
Protein Polymer Technologies
Solta Medical
Stellar Pharmaceuticals

HISTORICAL FINANCIALS

Company Type: Public

Income Statement				FYE: December 31
	REVENUE ($ mil.)	NET INCOME ($ mil.)	NET PROFIT MARGIN	EMPLOYEES
12/08	35.8	3.6	10.1%	84
12/07	30.8	6.0	19.5%	82
12/06	26.8	4.6	17.2%	64
12/05	29.8	5.9	19.8%	65
12/04	26.5	11.2	42.3%	61
Annual Growth	**7.8%**	**(24.7%)**	**—**	**8.3%**

2008 Year-End Financials

Debt ratio: 23.7%
Return on equity: 6.2%
Cash ($ mil.): 43.2
Current ratio: 6.18
Long-term debt ($ mil.): 14.4
No. of shares (mil.): 11.4

Dividends
  Yield: —
  Payout: —
Market value ($ mil.): 34.8
R&D as % of sales: —
Advertising as % of sales: —

Stock History

NASDAQ (GS): ANIK

	STOCK PRICE ($) FY Close	P/E High/Low		PER SHARE ($) Earnings	Dividends	Book Value
12/08	3.04	46	9	0.32	—	5.31
12/07	14.55	42	23	0.53	—	4.81
12/06	13.27	37	23	0.41	—	3.98
12/05	11.69	33	15	0.52	—	3.31
12/04	9.15	18	7	0.98	—	2.65
Annual Growth	**(24.1%)**	**—**	**—**	**(24.4%)**	**—**	**18.9%**

ANSYS, Inc.

ANSYS helps designers and engineers around the world really visualize their ideas. With the company's software, developers and engineers can see a simulation of their design concept on their desktop computer before a prototype is built. The computerized models are analyzed for their response to combinations of such physical variables as stress, pressure, impact, temperature, and velocity. Ranging from small consulting firms to multinational industrial firms, the company's customers come from a broad range of industries and have included Boeing, Cummins, and Motorola. ANSYS sells its products directly and through channel partners worldwide.

The company utilizes distribution partners in more than 40 countries. It generated about two-thirds of its revenues outside the US in 2008, with Japan and Germany leading among its international markets. Indirect sales accounted for about 30% of ANSYS' total revenues in 2008.

ANSYS purchased competitor Ansoft for $832 million in cash and stock in 2008. Ansoft specializes in electromagnetics, circuit, and system simulation. The acquisition expanded ANSYS' simulation expertise, moving it into the design of communication systems, radar systems, satellites, and mobile phones.

EXECUTIVES

Chairman: Peter J. Smith, age 64
President, CEO, and Director:
James E. (Jim) Cashman III, age 55,
$2,206,141 total compensation
CFO: Maria T. Shields, age 44,
$813,629 total compensation
VP; General Manager, Fluids Business Unit:
Hasan Ferit Boysan, age 60
VP Human Resources: Elaine Keim
VP Central Business Unit: Brian C. Drew, age 51,
$678,754 total compensation
VP Industry Marketing Aerospace and Turbomachinery:
Brad Hutchinson
VP, General Counsel, and Secretary: Sheila S. DiNardo,
age 48, $621,228 total compensation
VP Mechanical Business Unit: Joseph S. (Joe) Solecki
VP Sales and Support: Joseph C. (Joe) Fairbanks Jr.,
age 54, $904,909 total compensation
VP Marketing: J. Christopher (Chris) Reid, age 54
VP and General Manager, Electronics Business Unit:
Shane Emswiler
Treasurer and Investor Relations: Annette N. Arribas,
age 42
Auditors: Deloitte & Touche LLP

LOCATIONS

HQ: ANSYS, Inc.
275 Technology Dr., Canonsburg, PA 15317
Phone: 724-746-3304 **Fax:** 724-514-9494
Web: www.ansys.com

2008 Sales

	$ mil.	% of total
US	151.7	32
Europe		
Germany	68.4	14
Other countries	127.2	27
Japan	67.0	14
Canada	8.0	2
Other regions	56.0	11
Total	**478.3**	**100**

PRODUCTS/OPERATIONS

2008 Sales

	$ mil.	% of total
Software licenses		
Lease licenses	177.4	37
Perpetual licenses	140.7	30
Maintenance	135.8	28
Service	24.4	5
Total	**478.3**	**100**

COMPETITORS

Altair Engineering
Autodesk
Bentley Systems
Cadence Design
Cimatron
Dassault
Delcam
FARO Technologies
Kubotek USA
MathWorks
Mentor Graphics
Moldflow
MSC.Software
Parametric Technology
Siemens PLM Software
SIMULIA
SofTech
SolidWorks
think3
Vero Software
Z Corp.

HISTORICAL FINANCIALS

Company Type: Public

Income Statement

FYE: December 31

	REVENUE ($ mil.)	NET INCOME ($ mil.)	NET PROFIT MARGIN	EMPLOYEES
12/08	478.3	111.7	23.4%	1,750
12/07	385.3	82.4	21.4%	1,400
12/06	263.6	14.2	5.4%	1,400
12/05	158.0	43.9	27.8%	600
12/04	134.5	34.6	25.7%	550
Annual Growth	**37.3%**	**34.0%**	**—**	**33.6%**

2008 Year-End Financials

Debt ratio: 21.1%
Return on equity: 12.2%
Cash ($ mil.): 228.2
Current ratio: 1.48
Long-term debt ($ mil.): 249.8
No. of shares (mil.): 88.7
Dividends
Yield: —
Payout: —
Market value ($ mil.): 2,473.9
R&D as % of sales: —
Advertising as % of sales: —

Stock History

NASDAQ (GS): ANSS

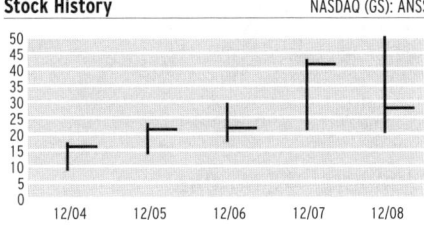

	STOCK PRICE ($) FY Close	P/E High/Low		PER SHARE ($) Earnings	Dividends	Book Value
12/08	27.89	39	16	1.29	—	13.34
12/07	41.46	42	21	1.02	—	7.23
12/06	21.75	157	97	0.19	—	6.03
12/05	21.34	35	22	0.65	—	2.54
12/04	16.03	32	17	0.52	—	1.98
Annual Growth	**14.8%**	**—**	**—**	**25.5%**	**—**	**61.1%**

Appliance Recycling Centers of America

Appliance Recycling Centers of America (ARCA) retrieves, recycles, repairs, and resells household appliances. The company collects used appliances and reconditions them for resale at about 15 ApplianceSmart retail stores in Georgia, Minnesota, Ohio, and Texas. ARCA also sells "special-buy appliances" — returned, exchanged, or discontinued units, "scratch-and-dent" units, and factory overruns from manufacturers (mainly GE, Frigidaire, and Whirlpool). Additionally, the company collects fees for appliance disposal, sells scrap metal and reclaimed chlorofluorocarbons (CFCs) from processed appliances, and recycles household appliances for energy conservation programs of electric utilities.

Appliance Recycling Centers of America (ARCA) doesn't plan to expand its used/refurbished appliance business, mainly due to the abundance of "special-buy appliances."

The company's focus is on opening large showroom outlet stores in heavily trafficked areas. In 2004 the company opened a 58,800-sq.-ft. ApplianceSmart factory outlet superstore in Saint Paul, Minnesota, and other factory outlets in San Antonio, Texas, and Smyrna, Georgia. ARCA opened a processing and recycling facility in Austin, Texas. The company opened two new outlet stores in Atlanta in 2006. It opened a store in Columbus, Ohio, and closed its Los Angeles location in 2007.

The company is pursuing utility customers to partner with on energy efficiency programs. The programs encourage residents to replace their energy inefficient appliances with newer, more efficient ones.

ARCA owns a 60% stake in McAllen, Texas-based North America Appliance Company LLC, a retailer of special-buy appliances.

Chairman and CEO Edward Cameron owns about 7% of ARCA. Perkins Capital Management owns 13% while Medallion Capital holds another 11% stake.

EXECUTIVES

Chairman, President, and CEO:
Edward R. (Jack) Cameron, age 69,
$443,259 total compensation
EVP, CFO, and Recycling Operations:
Peter P. Hausback, age 49, $249,255 total compensation
VP Recycling Systems: Jeffrey M. (Jeff) Brown, age 55
VP and General Manager, ARCA California:
Jeffrey L. Woloz, age 57
VP Retail Operations: Bradley S. (Brad) Bremer, age 40
VP Resource Efficiency Programs: Bruce J. Wall, age 54
VP Business Development and Environmental Affairs:
Rachel L. Holmes, age 45
Managing Director, ARCA Canada Inc:
Joseph M. (Joe) Berta, age 43
Corporate Controller: Jeffrey A. Cammerrer, age 38
Secretary: Denis E. Grande
Auditors: Virchow, Krause & Company, LLP

LOCATIONS

HQ: Appliance Recycling Centers of America, Inc.
7400 Excelsior Blvd., Minneapolis, MN 55426
Phone: 952-930-9000 **Fax:** 952-930-1800
Web: www.arcainc.com

2008 Sales

	% of total
Retail	68
Recycling	27
By-product	5
Total	**100**

Selected Merchandise

Compactors
Cooktops
Dehumidifiers
Dishwashers
Dryers
Freezers
Microwaves
Range hoods
Ranges
Refrigerators
Room air conditioners
Washers

COMPETITORS

Best Buy
GE Consumer & Industrial
Goodman Manufacturing
Home Depot
Lowe's
Philip Services
Sears

HISTORICAL FINANCIALS

Company Type: Public

Income Statement — FYE: Saturday nearest December 31

	REVENUE ($ mil.)	NET INCOME ($ mil.)	NET PROFIT MARGIN	EMPLOYEES
12/08	111.0	0.4	0.4%	429
12/07	100.8	2.5	2.5%	411
12/06	77.8	(1.4)	—	30
12/05	74.9	(0.9)	—	294
12/04	52.8	(1.3)	—	300
Annual Growth	**20.4%**	**—**	**—**	**9.4%**

2008 Year-End Financials

Debt ratio: —
Return on equity: 5.2%
Cash ($ mil.): 3.5
Current ratio: 1.24
Long-term debt ($ mil.): —
No. of shares (mil.): 4.6
Dividends
  Yield: —
  Payout: —
Market value ($ mil.): 13.5
R&D as % of sales: —
Advertising as % of sales: —

Stock History — NASDAQ (CM): ARCI

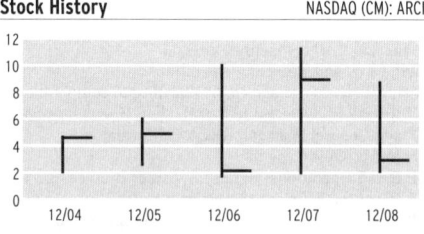

	STOCK PRICE ($) FY Close	P/E High/Low		PER SHARE ($) Earnings	Dividends	Book Value
12/08	2.95	109	26	0.08	—	1.75
12/07	8.95	20	4	0.57	—	1.59
12/06	2.15	—	—	(0.33)	—	0.90
12/05	4.90	—	—	(0.22)	—	1.18
12/04	4.60	—	—	(0.48)	—	1.32
Annual Growth	**(10.5%)**	**—**	**—**	**—**	**—**	**7.1%**

Approach Resources

Approach Resources takes a different approach to natural gas and oil exploration, development, and production. Specializing in finding and exploiting unconventional reservoirs, the company operates primarily in West Texas' Ozona Northeast field. It also has operations in western Kentucky, and northern New Mexico. The company's unconventional designation results from a focus on developing natural gas reserves in tight gas sands and shale areas, necessitating a reliance on advanced completion, fracturing and drilling techniques. In 2008 Approach Resources reported proved reserves of 193.7 billion cu. ft. of oil equivalent, with a reserve life index of about 19 years. Yorktown Energy Partners controls the company.

A "growth-through-the-drillbit" company, all of the company's proved reserves and production have so far been limited to its West Texas operations and consist primarily of natural gas. The company has one key customer, Ozona Pipeline Energy Company, that accounts for 86% of sales.

The company has a non-operating interest in a property in British Columbia.

EXECUTIVES

Chairman: Bryan H. Lawrence, age 67
President, CEO, and Director: J. Ross Craft, age 53, $686,028 total compensation
EVP Land: Ralph P. Manoushagian, age 58, $318,003 total compensation
EVP, CFO and Treasurer: Steven P. Smart, age 55, $474,703 total compensation
EVP and General Counsel: J. Curtis Henderson, age 47, $833,673 total compensation

LOCATIONS

HQ: Approach Resources Inc.
  1 Ridgmar Centre, 6500 West Fwy., Ste. 800
  Fort Worth, TX 76116
Phone: 817-989-9000   **Fax:** 817-989-9001
Web: www.approachresources.com

Areas of Operation

West Texas
  Ozona Northeast field (Wolfcamp, Canyon Sands, Strawn, and Ellenburger)
  Cinco Terry project (Wolfcamp, Canyon Sands, and Ellenburger)
East Texas
  (Cotton Valley Sands, Bossier, and Cotton Valley Lime)
Southwestern Kentucky
  Boomerang prospect (New Albany Shale)
Northern New Mexico
  El Vado East prospect (Mancos Shale)
Northeastern British Columbia
  Montney Tight Gas (Doig Shale)

PRODUCTS/OPERATIONS

2008 Sales

	$ mil.	% of total
Gas	59	74
Oil	16	20
NGLs	5	6
Total	**80**	**100**

COMPETITORS

Anadarko Petroleum
Chesapeake Energy
Parallel Petroleum
Quicksilver Resources
RAM Energy

HISTORICAL FINANCIALS

Company Type: Public

Income Statement — FYE: December 31

	REVENUE ($ mil.)	NET INCOME ($ mil.)	NET PROFIT MARGIN	EMPLOYEES
12/08	79.9	23.4	29.3%	36
12/07	39.1	2.7	6.9%	25
12/06	46.7	21.2	45.4%	19
12/05	43.3	12.1	27.9%	19
12/04	5.7	(0.3)	—	—
Annual Growth	**93.5%**	**—**	**—**	**23.7%**

2008 Year-End Financials

Debt ratio: 19.5%
Return on equity: 11.0%
Cash ($ mil.): 4.1
Current ratio: 1.13
Long-term debt ($ mil.): 43.5
No. of shares (mil.): 20.7
Dividends
  Yield: —
  Payout: —
Market value ($ mil.): 151.6
R&D as % of sales: —
Advertising as % of sales: —

Stock History — NASDAQ (GM): AREX

	STOCK PRICE ($) FY Close	P/E High/Low		PER SHARE ($) Earnings	Dividends	Book Value
12/08	7.31	27	5	1.12	—	10.79
12/07	12.86	57	49	0.24	—	9.64
Annual Growth	**(43.2%)**	**—**	**—**	**366.7%**	**—**	**12.0%**

ArcSight, Inc.

ArcSight keeps a watchful eye on business risk. The company provides security and compliance management products used to identify, prioritize, and respond to corporate policy violations and cyber attacks. Its software and appliances handle such functions as compliance automation, event collection and management, identity monitoring, and log management. The company also provides consulting, implementation, maintenance, support, and training services. ArcSight markets to the aerospace and defense, energy and utilities, financial services, food production, health care, insurance, media, retail, technology, and telecom sectors.

The company primarily sells its products directly, but it also utilizes a network of resellers and systems integrators, particularly in the government sector. ArcSight counts more than 20 major US government agencies among its customers.

ArcSight's growth strategy includes broadening its customer base beyond large enterprises to include more midsized companies. In 2009 the company launched its ArcSight Express appliance, which it designed for midsized businesses with limited network security resources. The company is also looking to expand its geographic reach. Roughly 30% of its sales were to customers outside the US in fiscal 2009.

EXECUTIVES

President, CEO, and Director: Thomas (Tom) Reilly, age 48
EVP Research and Development and CTO: Hugh S. Njemanze, age 53, $618,801 total compensation
CFO: Stewart Grierson, age 44, $536,477 total compensation
CIO: Anya Yudin-Baehrle
SVP Worldwide Field Operations: Kevin P. Mosher, age 53, $624,967 total compensation
SVP Marketing: Reed T. Henry, age 45, $595,970 total compensation
SVP Business Development: Jeffrey A. (Jeff) Scheel, age 48
SVP Services and Support: Joni Kahn, age 54
VP Human Resources: Gail Boddy
VP Worldwide Channel Sales: Matt Hynes
VP Engineering: Haiyan Song
VP Customer Support: Laura Tom
VP, General Counsel, and Secretary: Trâm T. Phi, age 39
VP Professional Services: Raymond (Ray) Patterson Jr.
Auditors: Ernst & Young LLP

LOCATIONS

HQ: ArcSight, Inc.
5 Results Way, Cupertino, CA 95014
Phone: 408-864-2600   **Fax:** 408-342-1615
Web: www.arcsight.com

2009 Sales

	$ mil.	% of total
Americas		
US	99.7	73
Other countries	10.2	8
Europe, Middle East & Africa	19.4	14
Asia/Pacific	6.9	5
Total	**136.2**	**100**

PRODUCTS/OPERATIONS

2009 Sales

	$ mil.	% of total
Products	80.6	59
Maintenance	38.5	28
Services	17.1	13
Total	**136.2**	**100**

COMPETITORS

CA, Inc.
Cisco Systems
EMC
Hewlett-Packard
IBM
Intellitactics
Novell
SenSage
Symantec

HISTORICAL FINANCIALS

Company Type: Public

Income Statement

FYE: April 30

	REVENUE ($ mil.)	NET INCOME ($ mil.)	NET PROFIT MARGIN	EMPLOYEES
4/09	136.2	9.9	7.3%	400
4/08	101.5	(2.0)	—	335
4/07	69.8	(0.3)	—	287
4/06	39.4	(16.7)	—	308
4/05	32.8	(2.8)	—	—
Annual Growth	42.7%	—	—	9.1%

2009 Year-End Financials

Debt ratio: —
Return on equity: 15.1%
Cash ($ mil.): 90.5
Current ratio: 2.38
Long-term debt ($ mil.): —
No. of shares (mil.): 33.7
Dividends
  Yield: —
  Payout: —
Market value ($ mil.): 508.9
R&D as % of sales: —
Advertising as % of sales: —

Stock History

NASDAQ (GM): ARST

	STOCK PRICE ($) FY Close	P/E High/Low		PER SHARE ($) Earnings	Dividends	Book Value
4/09	15.10	54	14	0.30	—	2.27
4/08	7.69	—	—	(0.08)	—	1.63
Annual Growth	96.4%	—	—	—	—	40.0%

Arena Resources

Independent energy company Arena Resources battles with the big boys in the arena of oil and gas exploration and production. The company operates in Kansas, New Mexico, Oklahoma, and Texas, and has proved reserves of 55.4 million barrels of oil equivalent. Its assets in Oklahoma and Texas account for the bulk of the company's proved reserves. About 30% of its reserves depend upon secondary recovery techniques to make productive. Arena Resources had an average daily production of 5,565 barrels of oil equivalent in 2007. That year Navajo Refining and DCP Midstream accounted for most of the company's oil and gas sales.

Arena Resources was founded in 2000. The exploration and production independent drilled its first successful well (in Oklahoma) in 2001. It expanded its operations that year by acquiring assets in Texas. In 2005 the company acquired the Parrish Lease located in Andrews County, Texas, for a price of $1.2 million. The deal added 945,000 barrels of oil equivalent to Arena Resources' proved reserves.

In 2007 the company acquired two oil and gas properties in Texas for $49 million. In 2008 it added 1.2 million of estimated proved reserves through the acquisition of a New Mexico property for $10.3 million.

EXECUTIVES

Chairman: Lloyd T. (Tim) Rochford, age 63
President and CEO: Phillip (Phil) Terry, age 60, $1,242,451 total compensation
VP, CFO, Secretary, and Treasurer: William Randall (Randy) Broaddrick, age 32, $487,876 total compensation
VP Geology and Exploration: Patric R. McConn
VP Land Department: Thomas W. Wahl, $482,913 total compensation

---

VP Investor Relations: William (Bill) Parsons, age 61
VP Operations: David D. Ricks, age 49, $627,726 total compensation
Manager Reservoir Engineering and Acquisitions: W. Craig Gaines, $395,203 total compensation
Auditors: Hansen, Barnett & Maxwell

LOCATIONS

HQ: Arena Resources, Inc.
6555 S. Lewis, Tulsa, OK 74136
Phone: 918-747-6060   **Fax:** 918-747-7620
Web: www.arenaresourcesinc.com

PRODUCTS/OPERATIONS

2008 Oil and Gas Sales

	% of total
Navajo Refining	83
DCP Midstream	8
ConocoPhillips & other	9
Total	**100**

COMPETITORS

Anadarko Petroleum
Apache
Cabot Oil & Gas
Chesapeake Energy
Key Energy
Pioneer Natural Resources

HISTORICAL FINANCIALS

Company Type: Public

Income Statement

FYE: December 31

	REVENUE ($ mil.)	NET INCOME ($ mil.)	NET PROFIT MARGIN	EMPLOYEES
12/08	208.9	83.6	40.0%	71
12/07	100.1	34.4	34.4%	86
12/06	59.8	23.3	39.0%	52
12/05	25.8	9.5	36.8%	22
12/04	8.5	2.6	30.6%	10
Annual Growth	122.7%	138.1%	—	63.2%

2008 Year-End Financials

Debt ratio: 0.0%
Return on equity: 22.6%
Cash ($ mil.): 58.5
Current ratio: 4.52
Long-term debt ($ mil.): 0.0
No. of shares (mil.): 38.4
Dividends
  Yield: 0.0%
  Payout: —
Market value ($ mil.): 1,079.3
R&D as % of sales: —
Advertising as % of sales: —

Stock History

NYSE: ARD

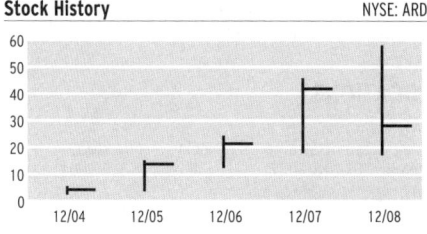

	STOCK PRICE ($) FY Close	P/E High/Low		PER SHARE ($) Earnings	Dividends	Book Value
12/08	28.09	26	8	2.20	0.00	12.55
12/07	41.71	44	18	1.02	0.00	6.71
12/06	21.35	31	17	0.77	0.00	3.12
12/05	13.80	39	11	0.38	0.00	1.53
12/04	4.25	34	19	0.15	0.00	0.54
Annual Growth	60.3%	—	—	95.7%	—	119.9%

Argan, Inc.

Argan makes sure its customers stay all juiced up. Its Gemma Power Systems division designs and builds power plants including traditional and alternate fuel plants. Argan's Southern Maryland Cable (SMC) unit provides inside premise wiring and also performs splicing and underground and aerial telecom infrastructure construction services to carriers, government entities, service providers, and electric utilities. SMC's three largest customers are Southern Maryland Electrical Cooperative, Verizon, and now HP Enterprise Services. The holding company's Vitarich Laboratories subsidiary makes and distributes private-label dietary supplements and other nutraceuticals and personal health-care products.

As the power generation and energy industries continue their move into biofuels and other alternative energy sources, Argan has moved along with them. Its largest Gemma Power customers include Altra Biofuels Nebraska, Renewable Bio-Fuels Port Neches, Green Earth Fuels of Houston, and the Connecticut Municipal Electrical Energy Cooperative.

Argan acquired Gemma Power Systems, which provides engineering and construction services to the alternative fuel industry, in 2006 for more than $30 million. In 2009 the company announced plans to acquire United American Steel Constructors (Unamsco) and its National Steel Constructors and Peterson Beckner Industries subsidiaries for some $50 million. In addition to construction, the companies also focus on reducing emissions at coal-fired power plants.

William Griffin and Joe Canino, both vice-chairmen of Gemma Power Systems, own around 14% and 12%, respectively. Director Daniel Levinson owns another 12%.

EXECUTIVES

Chairman, President, and CEO: Rainer H. Bosselmann, age 65, $632,559 total compensation
SVP, CFO, and Secretary: Arthur F. Trudel Jr., age 57, $608,279 total compensation
President, Gemma Power Systems: Eric Whitehouse
Vice Chairman and CEO, Gemma Power Systems: William F. (Bill) Griffin Jr., age 54, $1,680,000 total compensation
Auditors: Grant Thornton LLP

LOCATIONS

HQ: Argan, Inc.
1 Church St., Ste. 201, Rockville, MD 20850
Phone: 301-315-0027   **Fax:** 301-315-0064
Web: www.arganinc.com

PRODUCTS/OPERATIONS

2009 Sales

	$ mil.	% of total
Power industry services	202	91
Nutritional products	10	5
Telecommunications infrastructure services	9	4
Total	**221**	**100**

COMPETITORS

4Life Research	Quanta Services
EMCOR	Shaw Group
Fluor	SNC-Lavalin
Foster Wheeler	USANA Health Sciences
GNC	Washington Division
Integrated Electrical	

HISTORICAL FINANCIALS

Company Type: Public

Income Statement

FYE: January 31

	REVENUE ($ mil.)	NET INCOME ($ mil.)	NET PROFIT MARGIN	EMPLOYEES
1/09	220.9	10.0	4.5%	524
1/08	206.8	(3.2)	—	424
1/07	68.9	(0.1)	—	525
1/06	28.5	(9.5)	—	204
1/05	14.5	(2.6)	—	164
Annual Growth	97.6%	—	—	33.7%

2009 Year-End Financials

Debt ratio: 2.3%
Return on equity: 16.5%
Cash ($ mil.): 74.7
Current ratio: 1.99
Long-term debt ($ mil.): 1.8
No. of shares (mil.): 13.6
Dividends
  Yield: —
  Payout: —
Market value ($ mil.): 152.7
R&D as % of sales: —
Advertising as % of sales: —

Stock History

NYSE Alternext: AGX

	STOCK PRICE ($) FY Close	P/E High/Low	PER SHARE ($) Earnings	Dividends	Book Value
1/09	11.24	24 11	0.78	—	5.82
1/08	11.34	— —	(0.29)	—	3.08
1/07	6.20	— —	(0.02)	—	3.28
1/06	2.35	— —	(2.76)	—	0.86
1/05	5.65	— —	(1.20)	—	1.21
Annual Growth	18.8%	— —	—	—	48.1%

Art's-Way Manufacturing

Sinatra did it his way, but farmers are able to do it Art's way since 1956. Art's-Way Manufacturing makes an assortment of machinery under its own label and private labels. The company's equipment includes custom animal-feed processing machines, high-bulk mixing wagons, mowers and stalk shredders, and equipment for harvesting sugar beets and potatoes. Its private-label customers include CNH Global, for which the company makes feed-processing products, service parts, and tillage equipment. Equipment dealers throughout the US sell Art's-Way products. Steel truck bodies are manufactured under the Cherokee Truck Bodies name. Chairman J. Ward McConnell Jr. owns roughly 40% of the company.

Private-label manufacturing accounts for 13% of Art's-Way Manufacturing's sales; CNH Global accounts for about 8% of total sales. Art's-Way has signed an exclusive agreement to market moldboard plows and service parts to CNH customers. Additionally, the company has purchased the assets of OBECO Incorporated, a steel truck body manufacturer; the company's name has since been changed to Cherokee Truck Bodies.

In recent years, Art's-Way Manufacturing has been growing through acquisitions. It bought Vessel Systems of Dubuque, Iowa, creating Art's-Way Vessels. The company acquired the hay and forage product lines of Miller Pro from Miller St. Nazianz, Inc. The Miller Pro product lines have annual sales of about $8 million, including a substantial portion in supplying spare parts. Art's-Way is moving production of the Miller Pro product lines to Armstrong, Iowa, from St. Nazianz, Wisconsin.

EXECUTIVES

Chairman: J. Ward McConnell Jr., age 77
Vice Chairman: Marc H. McConnell, age 30
President and CEO: Carrie L. Majeski, age 33, $186,320 total compensation
Director Finance: Amber J. Murra
General Manager, Art's-Way Vessels: Patrick M. (Pat) O'Neill
Manager Information Services: Kent C. Kollasch
Manager Sales, Art's-Way Scientific: Dan Palmer
Manager Production, Art's-Way Scientific: John Fuelling
Manager Sales: Kevin R. Zahrt
Manager Manufacturing: Gene L. Tonne
Manager Purchasing: Donald R. Leach
Manager Engineering: Thomas W. Spisak
Auditors: Eide Bailly LLP

LOCATIONS

HQ: Art's-Way Manufacturing Co., Inc.
5556 Hwy. 9, Armstrong, IA 50514
Phone: 712-864-3131   **Fax:** 712-864-3154
Web: www.artsway-mfg.com

PRODUCTS/OPERATIONS

Selected Products

Animal-feed processing equipment
Grain wagons
High-bulk mixing wagons
Land-maintenance equipment
Mowers
Plows
Seed-bed preparation equipment
Stalk shredders
Steel truck bodies
Sugar beet and potato harvesting equipment
Tillage equipment

COMPETITORS

AGCO
Alamo Group
Caterpillar
Deere
Gencor Industries
Scag Power Equipment

HISTORICAL FINANCIALS
Company Type: Public

Income Statement
FYE: November 30

	REVENUE ($ mil.)	NET INCOME ($ mil.)	NET PROFIT MARGIN	EMPLOYEES
11/08	32.0	1.8	5.6%	129
11/07	25.5	2.2	8.6%	107
11/06	19.9	0.9	4.5%	102
11/05	14.6	1.0	6.8%	116
11/04	12.8	1.4	10.9%	109
Annual Growth	25.7%	6.5%	—	4.3%

2008 Year-End Financials

Debt ratio: 50.6%	Dividends
Return on equity: 16.2%	Yield: 0.0%
Cash ($ mil.): 0.1	Payout: —
Current ratio: 2.29	Market value ($ mil.): 16.3
Long-term debt ($ mil.): 6.1	R&D as % of sales: —
No. of shares (mil.): 4.0	Advertising as % of sales: —

Stock History
NASDAQ (CM): ARTW

	STOCK PRICE ($) FY Close	P/E High/Low		PER SHARE ($) Earnings	Dividends	Book Value
11/08	4.08	43	6	0.46	0.00	3.01
11/07	11.80	24	5	0.56	0.05	2.54
11/06	3.18	20	10	0.23	0.03	2.02
11/05	2.42	23	9	0.25	0.03	1.80
11/04	3.05	10	6	0.36	0.00	1.55
Annual Growth	7.5%	—	—	6.3%	—	18.0%

Astec Industries

"On the Road Again" isn't just a Willie Nelson song to Astec Industries, it's a way of life. The company, and its 14 manufacturing subsidiaries, makes equipment for every phase of road building, utility, and other construction projects. Its products include aggregate crushers, pavers, and portable hot-mix asphalt plants. Its auger-boring, impact-crusher, trenching, directional-drilling, and heat-transfer equipment is used in the construction, demolition, mining, recycling, and oil and gas industries. Founded in 1972, Astec also sells replacement parts. Customers are both government and private clients, including asphalt road paving contractors, utility and pipeline contractors, and mine and quarry operators.

Astec's manufacturing companies are divided into four segments: the Asphalt Group; the Aggregate and Mining Group (representing nearly 40% of sales); the Mobile Asphalt Paving Group; and the Underground Group. Companies under the Astec umbrella include Heatec, Roadtec, Telsmith, Kolberg, Breaker Technology, and American Augers.

Astec Industries, which plans to grow in international markets, generates about a third of its revenue through sales abroad. In late 2009 the company purchased Ontario-based Industrial Mechanical & Integration (IMI). The acquisition brings expertise in machinery for processing wood rounds into finished pellets, used in heating. Demand, current in Europe, for manufacturing the renewable fuel is anticipated to spread, along with the adoption of green energy standards, and surge in fossil fuel prices. Reaching around the world, Astec formed Astec Australia in 2008 through an acquisition of most of the assets of Q-Pave. Considerably expanding product distribution, the division sells, services, and provides parts support for the Astec lineup.

At home the company has been growing through acquisitions. In 2007 it expanded its offerings through the purchase of Peterson, a manufacturer of horizontal grinders, blower trucks, and whole-tree pulpwood chippers. The following year Astec acquired Dillman Equipment, a Wisconsin-based manufacturer of asphalt plant equipment. The acquisition gave Astec a third asphalt plant manufacturing facility.

Astec expects demand for its equipment to increase as more infrastructure and roadbuilding projects receive funding. Some funding is expected to come by way of the new American Recovery and Reinvestment Act, which includes some $27.5 billion for highway and bridge construction projects.

Chairman J. Don Brock owns about 12% of Astec Industries.

EXECUTIVES

Chairman, President, and CEO: J. Don Brock, age 70, $1,456,420 total compensation
Group VP, Mobile Asphalt Paving and Underground: Thomas R. Campbell, age 59, $509,534 total compensation
Group VP Asphalt and Director: W. Norman Smith, age 69, $530,707 total compensation
VP, CFO, and Treasurer: Fred McKamy Hall, age 66, $402,189 total compensation
VP Research and Development: Robert G. Stafford, age 70
President, Heatec, Inc.: Richard J. Dorris, age 48
President, Roadtec: Jeffery L. Richmond Sr., age 53
President, Astec, Inc.: Benjamin G. Brock, age 38
President, Kolberg-Pioneer, Inc.: Joseph P. Vig, age 59, $404,910 total compensation
Director Investor Relations and Secretary: Stephen C. (Steve) Anderson, age 45
Corporate Controller: David C. Silvious, age 41
Auditors: Ernst & Young LLP

LOCATIONS

HQ: Astec Industries, Inc.
1725 Shepherd Rd., Chattanooga, TN 37421
Phone: 423-899-5898   **Fax:** 423-899-4456
Web: www.astecindustries.com

2008 Sales

	$ mil.	% of total
US	621.0	63
Canada	77.2	8
Africa	63.3	7
Europe	39.2	4
South America	36.5	4
Asia	33.2	3
Middle East	28.8	3
Central America	26.7	3
Australia	26.1	3
Southeast Asia	11.7	1
West Indies	4.8	—
Other regions	5.2	1
Total	973.7	100

PRODUCTS/OPERATIONS

2008 Sales

	$ mil.	% of total
Aggregate & Mining Group	350.3	36
Asphalt Group	257.3	26
Mobile Asphalt Paving Group	150.7	16
Underground Group	135.2	14
Others	80.2	8
Total	973.7	100

Selected Products

Aggregate and Mining Group
  Cone crushers
  Conveyors
  Feeders
  Impact crushers
  Recycle plants
  Vibrating screens
Asphalt Group
  Heaters
  Hot mix asphalt plants
  Mixers
  Storage tanks
Mobile Asphalt Paving Group
  Material transfer vehicles (Shuttle Buggy)
  Milling machines
  Wheel and track asphalt pavers
Underground Group
  Auger boring machines
  Trenchers
  Underground directional drills

COMPETITORS

Caterpillar
Charles Machine Works
CMI Terex
Con Forms
Dynapac
Gencor Industries
Ingersoll-Rand
Lennox
Metso
Paul Mueller
Powerscreen
Regal Beloit
Rogers Group
Sandvik
Terex
Vapor Power
Vermeer Manufacturing Co.

HISTORICAL FINANCIALS
Company Type: Public

Income Statement
FYE: December 31

	REVENUE ($ mil.)	NET INCOME ($ mil.)	NET PROFIT MARGIN	EMPLOYEES
12/08	973.7	63.1	6.5%	1,135
12/07	869.0	56.8	6.5%	991
12/06	710.6	39.6	5.6%	875
12/05	616.1	28.1	4.6%	826
12/04	504.6	20.2	4.0%	781
Annual Growth	17.9%	32.9%	—	9.8%

2008 Year-End Financials

Debt ratio: —	Dividends
Return on equity: 15.5%	Yield: 0.0%
Cash ($ mil.): 9.7	Payout: —
Current ratio: 2.75	Market value ($ mil.): 706.5
Long-term debt ($ mil.): —	R&D as % of sales: —
No. of shares (mil.): 22.5	Advertising as % of sales: —

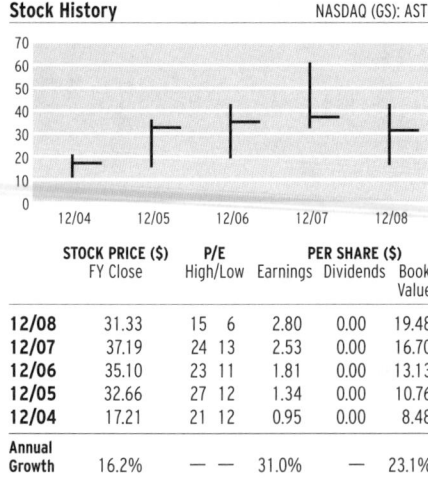

	STOCK PRICE ($) FY Close	P/E High/Low		PER SHARE ($) Earnings	Dividends	Book Value
12/08	31.33	15	6	2.80	0.00	19.48
12/07	37.19	24	13	2.53	0.00	16.70
12/06	35.10	23	11	1.81	0.00	13.13
12/05	32.66	27	12	1.34	0.00	10.76
12/04	17.21	21	12	0.95	0.00	8.48
Annual Growth	16.2%	—	—	31.0%	—	23.1%

Astronics Corporation

Is it a UFO? Is it a shooting star? No, it's Astronics! Astronics Corporation makes external and internal lighting systems, as well as power generation and distribution technology, for commercial, general aviation, and military defense aircraft. Products include cabin emergency lighting systems (escape path markers and exit locators), cockpit lighting systems (avionics keyboards, ambient light sensors, annunciator panels, and electronic dimmers), and formation lighting systems (external lights). Astronics operates three wholly owned subsidiaries including Astronics Advanced Electronic Systems Corp. (AES), Astronics Luminescent Systems Inc. (LSI), and Astronics DME Corporation (DME).

AES provides electronics for military and commercial aerospace applications; branded products include EmPower, CorePower, and ArcSafe. LSI engineers and manufactures products such as interior and exterior aerospace lighting systems, and installed or retrofitted night vision products including keyboards and edge lit panels. Customers include Airbus, Boeing, Embraer, Lockheed Martin, Rockwell Collins, and Thales, to name a few. AES and LSI also offer repair facilities and aircraft servicing.

Astronics acquired DME Corporation in early 2009. The company stands to make a substantial increase in product offerings, sales, and headcount through the acquisition. The subsidiary makes weapons and communications test equipment, training and simulation devices, and aviation safety products, as well as providing contractor logistics management, support, and training. This segment's customers include the US Marine Corps, leading defense contractors, and the Federal Aviation Administration, among others. The deal gives Astronics a stronger foothold in the defense industry and is intended to provide balance to its core lighting systems business. The company forecasts that DME will contribute approximately $75 million in 2009 sales.

Almost 25% of the company's revenue is generated by sales to Panasonic Avionics. The company's 2008 profits were negatively impacted by

the light jet supplier Eclipse Aerospace's (formerly Eclipse Aviation) bankruptcy and subsequent liquidation. Astronics revised its 4Q08 results to take a bigger write-off on its business; the company earned almost 80 cents per diluted share. Even so, the company recognized an overall increase of 36% in sales showing positive results for all its markets.

The aerospace industry, however, is not exempt from the effects of the worldwide financial crisis. The business jet market took the hardest hit in 2009, but all major aircraft manufacturers have been affected. Though the commercial transport and military markets have maintained their positions fairly well, Astronics expected flatter results in 2009. The company still plans to develop new technologies and aircraft programs for each of its markets. The company's products and technologies are used in the F-35 Joint Strike Fighter, the Cessna Mustang, Learjet 85, and the Boeing 787, to name a few.

Chairman Kevin Keane owns a 25% equity stake in Class B stock of Astronics Corporation. President and CEO Peter Gundermann owns 5% of the company's Class B stock.

HISTORY

Founded in 1968, Astronics was originally involved in electroluminescent products until it began to diversify into the packaging and printing industries. The company acquired MOD-PAC, a maker of paperboard packaging, in 1972, and Krepe-Kraft, a specialized printing company, in 1987.

In 1995 Astronics bought Loctite Luminescent Systems and integrated it with E-L FlexKey Technologies, which specialized in components used in the aerospace and military electronics industries. Later renamed Luminescent Systems, the division was awarded two high-dollar Canadian contracts the following year. One contract was for cockpit lighting systems for Bombardier's long-range business jets; the other was for ruggedized keyboards for the control room of a Canadian nuclear power plant.

The US Air Force awarded Astronics a contract to manufacture night-vision lighting for the F-16 aircraft in 1998. The next year the company was awarded an additional contract that almost doubled the number of units it would provide for F-16s. Astronics' aerospace and electronics segment doubled its manufacturing capabilities with the addition of two new facilities.

Astronics further enhanced its ability to fulfill its F-16 contract with the acquisition of Canada-based CRL Technologies (lighted keyboards) in 2000. Also that year the company acquired illuminated indicators for use in aircraft cockpits from Aerospace Avionics. In late 2001 the company was awarded a contract from the US government to provide lighted control panels for the Bradley M2A3 infantry fighting vehicle. The following year Astronics received a contract from the US Air Force valued at up to $30 million to develop spare parts for the F-16.

Astronics discontinued its electroluminescent lamp business in 2002 and spun off MOD-PAC in 2003.

Astronics entered the market for electrical power generation, control, and distribution systems for aircraft in 2005 by buying the assets of Airborne Electronics Systems from a unit of General Dynamics. Astronics paid $13 million for Airborne Electronics Systems, which had revenues of about $25 million in 2004.

EXECUTIVES

Chairman: Kevin T. Keane, age 76
President, CEO, and Director: Peter J. Gundermann, age 47
EVP, Advanced Electronics Systems: Mark Peabody
VP, CFO, Treasurer, and Secretary: David C. Burney, age 47
VP, Luminescent Systems: Richard C. (Rick) Miller
VP, Luminescent Systems: James S. (Jim) Kramer
VP, Luminescent Systems: Frank G. Johns III
Manager Human Resources: Jill Draper
Auditors: Ernst & Young LLP

LOCATIONS

HQ: Astronics Corporation
130 Commerce Way, East Aurora, NY 14052
Phone: 716-805-1599   **Fax:** 716-805-1286
Web: www.astronics.com

2008 Sales

	$ mil.	% of total
North America	147.9	85
Europe	13.8	8
Asia	10.2	6
South America	1.5	1
Other	0.3	—
Total	**173.7**	**100**

PRODUCTS/OPERATIONS

2008 Sales

	% of total
Cabin electronics	49
Cockpit lighting	25
Airframe power	13
Exterior lighting	7
Cabin lighting	5
Other	1
Total	**100**

2008 Sales by Customer

	% of total
Commercial transport	60
Business jet	20
Military	20
Total	**100**

Selected Products

Astronics Advanced Electronic Systems
  ArcSafe (wiring integrity tester)
  ControllersEmPower (in-seat power for personal
    computers)
  CorePower (aircraft electronic power distribution
    systems)
  Lighting control products
  Power supplies custom products
Astronics-Luminescent Systems
  Cabin lighting
  Cockpit lighting systems
  Exterior lighting
  Night vision modifications
DME Corporation
  Aircraft products
  Airfield lighting
  Manufacturing
  Satum marker buoy (DMB)
  Test systems
  Tower equipment
  Training and simulation

COMPETITORS

Ducommun
Goodrich Corp.
Honeywell Aerospace
Indel
Ultra Electronics

HISTORICAL FINANCIALS
Company Type: Public

Income Statement
FYE: December 31

	REVENUE ($ mil.)	NET INCOME ($ mil.)	NET PROFIT MARGIN	EMPLOYEES
12/08	173.7	8.4	4.8%	989
12/07	158.2	15.4	9.7%	967
12/06	110.8	5.7	5.1%	787
12/05	75.4	2.7	3.6%	700
12/04	34.7	(0.7)	—	424
Annual Growth	49.6%	—	—	23.6%

2008 Year-End Financials
Debt ratio: 23.2%
Return on equity: 15.6%
Cash ($ mil.): 3.0
Current ratio: 2.85
Long-term debt ($ mil.): 13.5
No. of shares (mil.): 10.8

Dividends
Yield: 0.0%
Payout: —
Market value ($ mil.): 95.9
R&D as % of sales: —
Advertising as % of sales: —

Stock History
NASDAQ (GM): ATRO

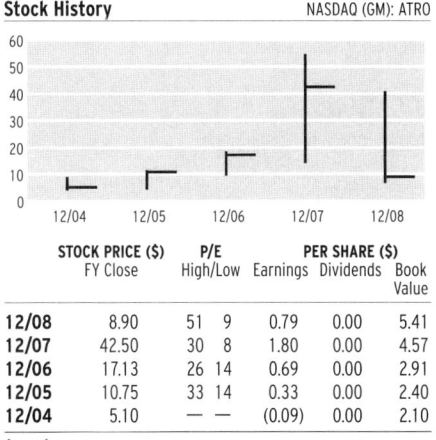

	STOCK PRICE ($) FY Close	P/E High/Low		PER SHARE ($) Earnings	Dividends	Book Value
12/08	8.90	51	9	0.79	0.00	5.41
12/07	42.50	30	8	1.80	0.00	4.57
12/06	17.13	26	14	0.69	0.00	2.91
12/05	10.75	33	14	0.33	0.00	2.40
12/04	5.10	—	—	(0.09)	0.00	2.10
Annual Growth	14.9%	—	—	—	—	26.6%

athenahealth, Inc.

athenahealth knows that managing physician practices can result in a splitting headache, especially when patients are late paying bills. The company provides health care organizations with Web-based software and services (athenaCollector) that streamline practice management, workflow routing, revenue management, patient information management, billing and collection, and other health care management tasks. athenahealth also offers a clinical cycle management service (athenaClinicals) that automates and manages medical record-related functions for physician practices.

More than 12,000 medical providers (including more than 9,000 physicians) use the company's services, with clients spanning more than 30 states and 50 medical specialties.

athenahealth's strategy includes expanding its athenaClinicals client base and maintaining and expanding its payer rules database, which increases the likelihood that client transactions are successfully executed and take the least amount of time possible to resolve.

In 2008 the company completed its first major acquisition, purchasing Crest Line Technologies, a provider of automated appointment reminder

technology. In 2009 athenahealth bought Anodyne Health Partners, a provider of on-demand business intelligence software for health care providers. athenahealth will incorporate Anodyne's reporting and business intelligence capabilities into its broader product lines.

EXECUTIVES
Chairman, President, and CEO: Jonathan S. Bush, age 39, $1,094,075 total compensation
EVP and COO: David E. (Dave) Robinson, age 65
SVP and CFO: Timothy M. (Tim) Adams, age 50
SVP People and Process: Leslie Locke, age 37
SVP Business Development and Government Affairs: Nancy G. Brown, age 48, $610,816 total compensation
SVP Sales: Robert M. Hueber, age 54, $617,134 total compensation
SVP and Chief Marketing Officer: Robert L. (Rob) Cosinuke, age 48, $1,229,211 total compensation
VP, General Counsel, and Secretary: Daniel H. Orenstein
Chief Accounting Officer, Treasurer, and Principal Accounting Officer: Dawn Griffiths, age 42
Director: William Winkenwerder Jr.
Auditors: Deloitte & Touche LLP

LOCATIONS
HQ: athenahealth, Inc.
311 Arsenal St., Watertown, MA 02472
Phone: 617-402-1000 **Fax:** 617-402-1099
Web: www.athenahealth.com

PRODUCTS/OPERATIONS
2008 Sales

	$ mil.	% of total
Business services	131.9	94
Implementation & other	7.7	6
Total	**139.6**	**100**

Selected Software
athenaClinicals (medical record management)
athenaCollector (claims management)

COMPETITORS
Allscripts
CBIZ
GE Healthcare
McKesson
Quality Systems
Sage Group
Siemens Healthcare

HISTORICAL FINANCIALS
Company Type: Public

Income Statement
FYE: December 31

	REVENUE ($ mil.)	NET INCOME ($ mil.)	NET PROFIT MARGIN	EMPLOYEES
12/08	139.6	28.9	20.7%	824
12/07	100.8	(3.5)	—	380
12/06	75.8	(8.9)	—	564
12/05	53.5	(11.4)	—	564
12/04	38.9	(3.6)	—	—
Annual Growth	37.6%	—	—	13.5%

2008 Year-End Financials
Debt ratio: 7.2%
Return on equity: 30.2%
Cash ($ mil.): 28.9
Current ratio: 4.16
Long-term debt ($ mil.): 8.4
No. of shares (mil.): 33.7

Dividends
Yield: —
Payout: —
Market value ($ mil.): 1,267.4
R&D as % of sales: —
Advertising as % of sales: —

Stock History
NASDAQ (GM): ATHN

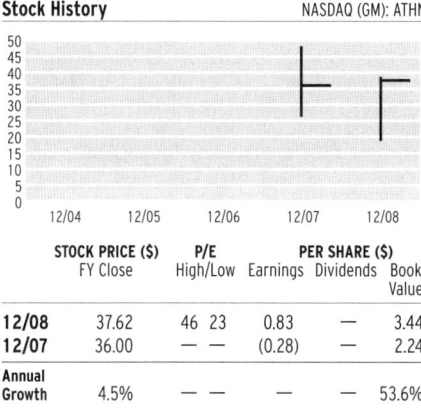

	STOCK PRICE ($) FY Close	P/E High/Low		PER SHARE ($) Earnings	Dividends	Book Value
12/08	37.62	46	23	0.83	—	3.44
12/07	36.00	—	—	(0.28)	—	2.24
Annual Growth	4.5%	—	—	—	—	53.6%

Atheros Communications

Atheros Communications builds high-speed connections right through the ether. Its radio-frequency transceiver chipsets combine features such as a radio, power amplifier, low-noise amplifier, and a media access control (MAC) processor onto just two or three chips, eliminating the need for bulkier components in wireless networking equipment. The company's customers include Apple, Dell, Fujitsu, Hewlett-Packard, Hon Hai Precision Industry (19% of sales), IBM, Microsoft, QUALCOMM, Sony, and Toshiba. The fabless semiconductor company was started by faculty members from Stanford and Berkeley. Nearly all of Atheros' sales are to customers in Asia, principally in Taiwan and China.

Among the company's challenges in 2009 were the global recession and the resulting downturn in semiconductor industry sales, largely driven by lower sales for consumer electronics, PCs, and wireless handsets. Atheros plans to expand its product portfolio and to push the upgrades through its established customer base. To this end, in December 2009 the company acquired Intellon Corp. for about $244 million in cash and stock. Intellon offers capabilities in designing chips for high-speed network connections through power lines, a complement to Atheros' expertise in chips for wireless communications equipment.

Prior to the recession, rival chip makers scrambled to add GPS and related location capabilities to their lineup. Demand was fueled by suppliers of navigation devices, as well as manufacturers of mobile handsets and other portable electronics. Late in 2007 Atheros acquired u-Nav Microelectronics, a developer of Global Positioning System (GPS) chipsets and software for mobile location-based products and services. In 2006 the company acquired ZyDAS Technology, a Taiwan-based designer of chips for wireless networks used in embedded, mobile, and PC applications. Also that year Atheros acquired ASUSTeK Computer subsidiary Attansic Technology, a developer of networking semiconductors.

Atheros contracts out manufacturing of its chips to such silicon foundries as Taiwan Semiconductor, Semiconductor Manufacturing International, Chartered Semiconductor Manufacturing, Tower Semiconductor, and United Microelectronics. Packaging and testing chores are done for the company by Amkor Technology, ASAT, Siliconware Precision Industries, and STATS ChipPAC, among others.

EXECUTIVES

Chairman: John L. Hennessy, age 56
President, CEO, and Director: Craig H. Barratt, age 46, $2,020,406 total compensation
CTO: William J. (Bill) McFarland
VP Corporate Development, CFO, and Secretary: Jack R. Lazar, age 43, $1,043,029 total compensation
VP Worldwide Sales: Gary L. Szilagyi, age 40, $1,044,860 total compensation
VP and General Manager, Wireless Networking Business Unit: Ben D. Naskar, age 54, $1,498,455 total compensation
VP and Chief Accounting Officer: David D. (Dave) Torre, age 52
VP Software Engineering: Kenneth P. (Ken) McKeithan
VP Engineering: Richard G. (Rick) Bahr, age 55
VP, General Counsel, and Assistant Secretary: Adam H. Tachner, age 42, $663,456 total compensation
VP Operations: Hing C. Chu, age 57
VP Software Development: Charles Marker
VP Marketing and Alliances: Reynette Au
VP Global Human Resources: Sharon Thompson
Senior Manager Corporate Communications: Dakota Lee
Director Investor Relations: David H. Allen
Auditors: Deloitte & Touche LLP

LOCATIONS

HQ: Atheros Communications, Inc.
5480 Great America Pkwy., Santa Clara, CA 95054
Phone: 408-773-5200 **Fax:** 408-773-9940
Web: www.atheros.com

Atheros Communications has operations in China, Hong Kong, India, Japan, South Korea, Taiwan, and the US.

2008 Sales

	% of total
Taiwan	41
China	29
Hong Kong	10
US	1
Other countries	19
Total	**100**

COMPETITORS

Bandspeed
Broadcom
Conexant Systems
CSR plc
Freescale Semiconductor
Intel
Intellon
Intersil
Marvell Technology
MediaTek
Metalink
Motia
National Semiconductor
QUALCOMM
RF Micro Devices
Texas Instruments
Toshiba Semiconductor

HISTORICAL FINANCIALS
Company Type: Public

Income Statement — FYE: December 31

	REVENUE ($ mil.)	NET INCOME ($ mil.)	NET PROFIT MARGIN	EMPLOYEES
12/08	472.4	18.9	4.0%	1,079
12/07	417.0	40.0	9.6%	878
12/06	301.7	18.7	6.2%	660
12/05	183.5	16.7	9.1%	327
12/04	169.6	10.8	6.4%	260
Annual Growth	**29.2%**	**15.0%**	**—**	**42.7%**

2008 Year-End Financials

Debt ratio: —
Return on equity: 4.3%
Cash ($ mil.): 114.5
Current ratio: 4.56
Long-term debt ($ mil.): —
No. of shares (mil.): 62.4
Dividends
Yield: 0.0%
Payout: —
Market value ($ mil.): 893.5
R&D as % of sales: —
Advertising as % of sales: —

Stock History — NASDAQ (GS): ATHR

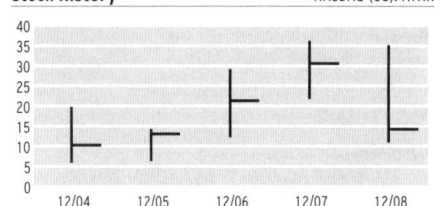

	STOCK PRICE ($) FY Close	P/E High/Low	PER SHARE ($) Earnings	Dividends	Book Value
12/08	14.31	116 38	0.30	0.00	7.55
12/07	30.54	53 33	0.67	0.00	6.43
12/06	21.32	85 37	0.34	0.00	4.50
12/05	13.00	45 21	0.31	0.00	3.15
12/04	10.25	93 30	0.21	0.00	2.77
Annual Growth	**8.7%**	**— —**	**9.3%**	**—**	**28.5%**

Atlantic Tele-Network

Atlantic Tele-Network (ATN) is making connections from the rain forests of Guyana to the maple groves of Vermont. ATN owns 80% of incumbent carrier Guyana Telephone & Telegraph (GT&T), which operates more than 130,000 fixed access telephone lines and has about 330,000 cellular subscribers. In the US, ATN provides wholesale wireless voice and data roaming services to local and national communications carriers through subsidiary Commnet. The company offers these international long distance services mainly in five states in the Southwest and Midwest regions, largely through partnerships with US-based carriers AT&T and Verizon Communications.

ATN's other holdings include Choice Communications, which provides Internet access and wireless cable television services in the US Virgin Islands. Through its other subsidiaries, ATN provides communcations services in the state of Vermont (SoVerNet) and in Bermuda (BDC).

ATN bought wireless assets in six states from Verizon Wireless as that company shed overlapping operations acquired in its purchase of Alltel earlier that year in order to meet anti-trust

regulatory compliance. The $200 million acquisition expanded ATN's subscriber base by about 800,000 in mostly rural areas.

Chairman Cornelius Prior owns 37% of ATN.

EXECUTIVES

Chairman; Chairman, Guyana Telephone and Telegraph: Cornelius B. Prior Jr., age 75
President, CEO, and Director: Michael T. Prior, age 44, $1,097,097 total compensation
CFO and Treasurer: Justin D. Benincasa, age 47, $568,497 total compensation
Chief Accounting Officer: Andrew S. Fienberg, age 41, $255,881 total compensation
SVP Corporate Development: William F. (Bill) Kreisher, age 46, $471,909 total compensation
VP, General Counsel, and Secretary: Douglas J. Minster, age 48
VP Financial Analysis and Planning: John P. Audet, age 51, $260,812 total compensation
CEO, Guyana Telephone and Telegraph: Sonita Jagan, age 42
CEO, Atlantic Wireless Communications: Frank A. O'Mara, age 42
Auditors: PricewaterhouseCoopers LLP

LOCATIONS

HQ: Atlantic Tele-Network, Inc.
10 Derby Sq., Salem, MA 01970
Phone: 978-619-1300 **Fax:** 978-744-3951
Web: www.atni.com

PRODUCTS/OPERATIONS

2008 Sales

	% of total
Wireless	51
Local telephone & data	24
International long distance	23
Other services	2
Total	**100**

Selected Services

Local telephone access
National and international interconnections
Public phones
Wireless communications

Selected Subsidiaries and Affiliates

Bermuda Digital Communications, Ltd. (Cellular One, 43%, competitive PCS and cellular services)
Choice Communications, LLC (ISP and wireless TV provider, US Virgin Islands)
Commnet Wireless, LLC (wireless roaming provider)
Guyana Telephone and Telegraph Company Limited (GT&T, 80%, local and long-distance phone services)
SoVerNet, Inc. (96%, facilities-based voice and data services)

COMPETITORS

AT&T Mobility
Cellco
Sprint Nextel
Verizon

HISTORICAL FINANCIALS
Company Type: Public

Income Statement — FYE: December 31

	REVENUE ($ mil.)	NET INCOME ($ mil.)	NET PROFIT MARGIN	EMPLOYEES
12/08	207.3	34.8	16.8%	864
12/07	186.7	37.9	20.3%	823
12/06	155.4	23.5	15.1%	852
12/05	102.3	13.6	13.3%	853
12/04	84.0	12.1	14.4%	700
Annual Growth	**25.3%**	**30.2%**	**—**	**5.4%**

2008 Year-End Financials

Debt ratio: 32.0%
Return on equity: 15.9%
Cash ($ mil.): 79.7
Current ratio: 2.74
Long-term debt ($ mil.): 73.3
No. of shares (mil.): 15.2

Dividends
  Yield: 2.6%
  Payout: 29.8%
Market value ($ mil.): 404.5
R&D as % of sales: —
Advertising as % of sales: —

Stock History

NASDAQ (GM): ATNI

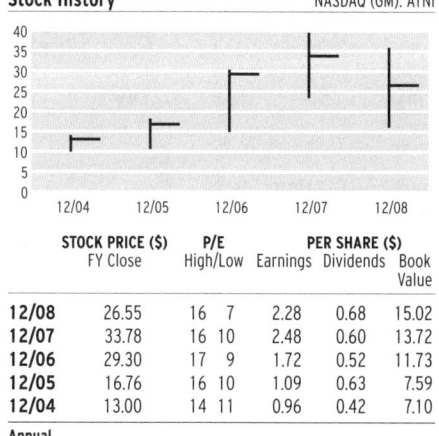

	STOCK PRICE ($) FY Close	P/E High/Low		PER SHARE ($) Earnings	Dividends	Book Value
12/08	26.55	16	7	2.28	0.68	15.02
12/07	33.78	16	10	2.48	0.60	13.72
12/06	29.30	17	9	1.72	0.52	11.73
12/05	16.76	16	10	1.09	0.63	7.59
12/04	13.00	14	11	0.96	0.42	7.10
Annual Growth	19.5%	—	—	24.1%	12.8%	20.6%

ATP Oil & Gas

ATP Oil & Gas looks for its revenues where others have shelved their operations. The company's strategy is to exploit continental shelf assets that are being sold by larger oil companies searching for higher returns in deeper waters. It explores and develops natural gas and oil properties primarily on the outer continental shelf of the Gulf of Mexico (where it has interests in 76 offshore blocks, 40 platforms, and 127 wells) and in the Southern Gas Basin of the UK's North Sea. Its proved reserves total 715.6 billion cu. ft. of natural gas equivalent; natural gas makes up the bulk of the reserves. Founder Paul Bulmahn owns about 19% of ATP Oil & Gas.

To raise cash, in 2008 the company sold a part of its producing and undeveloped properties in the UK North Sea to EDF Production UK for $430 million. In 2009 it sold oil and natural gas pipelines that service the Gomez Hub in the deepwater Gulf of Mexico to Offshore Infrastructure Partners for $78 million.

ATP Oil & Gas was founded in Texas in 1991. In 1995 ATP pioneered the use of offshore horizontal drilling in the Gulf of Mexico at its South Timbalier 30 block. In 2005 the company acquired the Rowan-Midland mobile offshore drilling unit from an operating subsidiary of Rowan Companies.

EXECUTIVES

Chairman and CEO: T. Paul Bulmahn, age 65, $6,940,329 total compensation
President: Leland E. Tate, age 62, $2,187,201 total compensation
COO: George R. Morris, age 54, $1,132,586 total compensation
CFO and Treasurer: Albert L. Reese Jr., age 60, $956,352 total compensation
Chief Accounting Officer: Keith R. Godwin, age 42, $929,998 total compensation

Chief Communications Officer and Secretary: Isabel M. Plume, age 49
SVP International and General Counsel: John E. Tschirhart, age 59
VP and Controller: Scott D. Heflin
VP Business Development: Timothy P. McGinty
VP Production Operations: Mickey W. Shaw
VP Projects: Robert M. Shivers III
VP Engineering: G. Ross Frazer
VP Administration: Pauline van der Sman-Archer
VP Finance: Brian C. Nelson
Auditors: Deloitte & Touche LLP

LOCATIONS

HQ: ATP Oil & Gas Corporation
  4600 Post Oak Place, Ste. 200, Houston, TX 77027
Phone: 713-622-3311   **Fax:** 713-622-5101
Web: www.atpog.com

2008 Sales

	$ mil.	% of total
Gulf of Mexico	521.4	84
North Sea	96.6	16
Total	**618.0**	**100**

COMPETITORS

Apache	McMoRan Exploration
BP	Meridian Resource
Comstock Resources	Murphy Oil
Devon Energy	Newfield Exploration
Eni	Petsec Energy
Forest Oil	Royal Dutch Shell

HISTORICAL FINANCIALS

Company Type: Public

Income Statement

FYE: December 31

	REVENUE ($ mil.)	NET INCOME ($ mil.)	NET PROFIT MARGIN	EMPLOYEES
12/08	618.0	121.7	19.7%	63
12/07	607.9	48.6	8.0%	64
12/06	419.8	(39.3)	—	59
12/05	146.7	(2.7)	—	48
12/04	116.1	1.4	1.2%	50
Annual Growth	51.9%	205.3%	—	5.9%

2008 Year-End Financials

Debt ratio: 428.7%
Return on equity: 38.9%
Cash ($ mil.): 215.0
Current ratio: 1.11
Long-term debt ($ mil.): 1,356.1
No. of shares (mil.): 50.6

Dividends
  Yield: —
  Payout: —
Market value ($ mil.): 295.9
R&D as % of sales: —
Advertising as % of sales: —

Stock History

NASDAQ (GS): ATPG

	STOCK PRICE ($) FY Close	P/E High/Low		PER SHARE ($) Earnings	Dividends	Book Value
12/08	5.85	15	1	3.39	—	6.25
12/07	50.54	37	23	1.55	—	6.13
12/06	39.57	—	—	(1.33)	—	0.71
12/05	37.01	—	—	(0.43)	—	4.30
12/04	18.59	383	94	0.05	—	1.13
Annual Growth	(25.1%)	—	—	187.0%	—	53.4%

Atwood Oceanics

Atwood Oceanics is at work in oceans all over the world. An offshore oil and gas drilling contractor, the firm owns nine drilling rigs, including four semisubmersible rigs, three jack-ups, one submersible, and one semisubmersible tender assist vessel (which places drilling equipment on permanent platforms). Its rigs operate in the Gulf of Mexico, offshore Southeast Asia, offshore Africa, offshore India, offshore Australia, and in the Mediterranean. In fiscal 2009 some 97% of Atwood Oceanics' sales came from its international operations; the company had contracts with 13 different customers.

In 2009 Atwood Oceanics had five rigs engaged in contract drilling in the waters around Africa, three in southeast Asia, and one in the Gulf of Mexico.

The company is committed to upgrading its fleet to keep pace with the increasing demand for global offshore exploration. Its ninth rig, the ultra premium jack-up rig ATWOOD AURORA was completed by Keppel AmFELS in Brownsville, Texas, and delivered to the company in late 2008. During 2008 Atwood Oceanics contracted Jurong Shipyard Pte. Ltd. to build two semisubmersible drilling units, due to become operational in 2011 and 2012.

In late 2009 industry veteran Robert Saltiel replaced John Irwin as Atwood Oceanics' president and CEO.

Fellow drilling contractor Helmerich & Payne owns 12% of Atwood Oceanics. Its CEO, Hans Helmerich, serves as the chairman of Atwood Oceanics.

EXECUTIVES

Chairman: Hans Helmerich, age 51
President, CEO, and Director: Robert J. (Rob) Saltiel, age 46
SVP, CFO, Secretary, and Director: James M. (Jim) Holland, age 64, $774,040 total compensation
SVP Operations: Alan Quintero, age 46, $751,550 total compensation
SVP Administration and Marketing: Glen P. Kelley, age 61, $900,170 total compensation
VP Technical Services: Barry M. Smith, age 50
VP Administrative Services: Randal F. Presley, age 58
VP and Controller: Michael A. (Mike) Campbell, age 40
VP Operations: Ronald L. (Ronnie) Hall, age 57, $551,810 total compensation
General Counsel: Rodney Mallams
Manager, Human Resources: James E. Gillenwater
Auditors: PricewaterhouseCoopers LLP

LOCATIONS

HQ: Atwood Oceanics, Inc.
  15835 Park Ten Place Dr., Houston, TX 77084
Phone: 281-749-7800   **Fax:** 281-492-7871
Web: www.atwd.com

PRODUCTS/OPERATIONS

2009 Sales

	% of total
Noble Energy Mediterranean	26
Woodside Energy	20
Sarawak Shell	14
Other customers	40
Total	**100**

COMPETITORS

Diamond Offshore	Parker Drilling
ENSCO	Pride International
Nabors Industries	Saipem
Noble	Schlumberger
Oceaneering International	Transocean

HISTORICAL FINANCIALS
Company Type: Public

Income Statement
FYE: September 30

	REVENUE ($ mil.)	NET INCOME ($ mil.)	NET PROFIT MARGIN	EMPLOYEES
9/09	586.5	250.7	42.7%	1,000
9/08	526.6	215.4	40.9%	1,200
9/07	403.0	139.0	34.5%	900
9/06	276.6	86.1	31.1%	1,100
9/05	176.2	26.0	14.8%	1,100
Annual Growth	35.1%	76.2%	—	(2.4%)

2009 Year-End Financials

Debt ratio: 24.9%
Return on equity: 25.8%
Cash ($ mil.): 100.3
Current ratio: 2.70
Long-term debt ($ mil.): 275.0
No. of shares (mil.): 64.3

Dividends
  Yield: —
  Payout: —
Market value ($ mil.): 2,266.5
R&D as % of sales: —
Advertising as % of sales: —

Stock History
NYSE: ATW

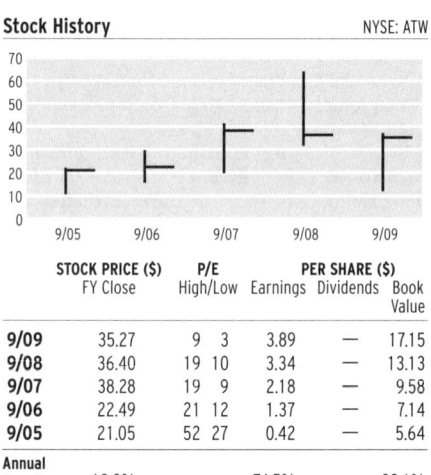

	STOCK PRICE ($) FY Close	P/E High	P/E Low	Earnings	Dividends	Book Value
9/09	35.27	9	3	3.89	—	17.15
9/08	36.40	19	10	3.34	—	13.13
9/07	38.28	19	9	2.18	—	9.58
9/06	22.49	21	12	1.37	—	7.14
9/05	21.05	52	27	0.42	—	5.64
Annual Growth	13.8%	—	—	74.5%	—	32.1%

AZZ incorporated

When companies need to power up or get that "zinc-ing" feeling, they give AZZ incorporated a buzz. AZZ has two business segments: electrical and industrial products, and galvanizing services. Through subsidiaries, AZZ makes electrical power distribution systems, industrial lighting, switchgear, motor control centers, bus duct systems, and tubular goods. Industrial, petrochemical, and power-generation and -transmission industries use the company's products. To protect steel from environmental corrosion, galvanizing services dip steel products into baths of molten zinc. The process is vital for steel fabricators who serve highway construction, electrical utility, transportation, and water-treatment industries.

AZZ is unswerving in its focus on growth through tapping a larger share of the power and galvanizing markets and through expanding its product offerings. To this end, in 2009 it acquired almost all of the assets of Pilot Galvanizing and Bristol Galvanizing, both in West Virginia.

In 2008 AZZ inked an asset purchase agreement with AAA Industries. The assets include AAA's six galvanizing plants dotting Illinois, Indiana, Minnesota, and Oklahoma. The addition broadens AZZ's geographical footprint in galvanizing services and fits well with its 2006 acquisition of Witt Industries. The Witt deal scored the assets of three galvanizing plants in Indiana and Ohio.

Giving a boost to its electrical and industrial products business, AZZ also acquired Canada-based Blenkhorn and Sawle in 2008. Blenkhorn and Sawle supply electrical equipment, which AZZ intends to use in further developing its portfolio of products. The addition also opens the door to markets in Canada.

EXECUTIVES

Chairman: H. Kirk Downey, age 66
President, CEO, and Director: David H. Dingus, age 61, $1,451,822 total compensation
SVP Finance, CFO, Secretary, and Director: Dana L. Perry, age 60, $575,272 total compensation
SVP Operations, Electrical Products: John V. Petro, age 63, $522,719 total compensation
VP Galvanizing Southern Operations: Bryan Stovall
VP Human Resources: Francis D. Quinn, age 43
VP Electrical and Industrial Products: John Petitto
VP Galvanizing Northern Operations: John Lincoln, age 47
VP and Corporate Controller: Richard W. Butler, age 43
VP Business and Manufacturing Systems: James C. (Jim) Stricklen, age 60
VP Business Development: Ashok E. Kolady, age 35
VP Operations, Galvanizing Services Segment: Tim E. Pendley, age 47, $475,783 total compensation
VP Sales, Electrical Products: Clement H. Watson, age 62, $381,918 total compensation
VP Electrical and Industrial Products: Bill Estes, age 44
Auditors: BDO Seidman, LLP

LOCATIONS

HQ: AZZ incorporated
  1300 S. University Dr., University Centre 1, Ste. 200
  Fort Worth, TX 76107
Phone: 817-810-0095   **Fax:** 817-336-5354
Web: www.azzincorporated.com

PRODUCTS/OPERATIONS

2009 Sales

	$ mil.	% of total
Electrical & industrial products	225.8	55
Galvanizing services	186.6	45
Total	**412.4**	**100**

COMPETITORS

ABB
Chamberlin
Earle M. Jorgensen
Eaton
Energy Focus
Friedman Industries
GE
Gewiss
Jarden
JJI Lighting
Legrand
LSI Industries
North American Galvanizing & Coatings
Philips Lighting North America
Powell Industries
SPX

HISTORICAL FINANCIALS
Company Type: Public

Income Statement
FYE: Last day in February

	REVENUE ($ mil.)	NET INCOME ($ mil.)	NET PROFIT MARGIN	EMPLOYEES
2/09	412.4	42.2	10.2%	1,722
2/08	320.2	27.7	8.7%	1,422
2/07	260.3	21.7	8.3%	1,301
2/06	187.2	7.8	4.2%	1,019
2/05	152.4	4.8	3.1%	965
Annual Growth	28.3%	72.2%	—	15.6%

2009 Year-End Financials

Debt ratio: 53.4%
Return on equity: 25.3%
Cash ($ mil.): 47.6
Current ratio: 3.12
Long-term debt ($ mil.): 100.0
No. of shares (mil.): 12.3

Dividends
  Yield: 0.0%
  Payout: —
Market value ($ mil.): 249.0
R&D as % of sales: —
Advertising as % of sales: —

Stock History
NYSE: AZZ

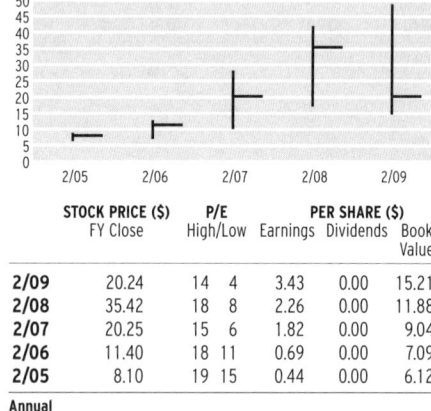

	STOCK PRICE ($) FY Close	P/E High	P/E Low	Earnings	Dividends	Book Value
2/09	20.24	14	4	3.43	0.00	15.21
2/08	35.42	18	8	2.26	0.00	11.88
2/07	20.25	15	6	1.82	0.00	9.04
2/06	11.40	18	11	0.69	0.00	7.09
2/05	8.10	19	15	0.44	0.00	6.12
Annual Growth	25.7%	—	—	67.1%	—	25.5%

Badger Meter

Badger Meter does not measure the frequency of the appearance of a certain nocturnal carnivorous mammal. Instead, it provides water utilities and industrial customers with instruments that measure and control the flow of liquids. Badger, which was established in 1905, makes meters, valves, flow tubes, and other measurement devices for original equipment manufacturers, water and wastewater utilities, and companies in the pharmaceutical, chemical, concrete, and food and beverage industries. Its utility meters come with manual or automatic reading technology systems. Badger also makes a handheld device that dispenses and monitors oil and other fluids for the automotive market.

The company manufactures its products at facilities located around the globe, including two in the US (Oklahoma and Wisconsin). It also operates facilities in the Czech Republic, Germany, and Mexico. It maintains a global network to distribute its products to customers around the world.

The firm has been working with Israel-based Miltel Communications to develop an advanced metering infrastructure technology that water utility companies can use to read meters. In 2008 Badger Meter acquired the technology from Miltel. Badger Meter hopes the technology will provide a foundation for future growth opportunities.

EXECUTIVES

Chairman, President, and CEO: Richard A. Meeusen, age 54, $1,020,316 total compensation
SVP Finance, CFO, and Treasurer: Richard E. Johnson, age 54, $616,667 total compensation
SVP Administration and Director: Ronald H. Dix, age 64, $642,115 total compensation
VP Engineering: Gregory M. Gomez, age 44
VP Manufacturing: Raymond G. Serdynski, age 52
VP, General Counsel, and Secretary:
William R.A. Bergum, age 44
VP International Operations: Horst E. Gras, age 53, $612,422 total compensation
VP Sales and Marketing: Dennis J. Webb, age 61, $493,605 total compensation
VP and Corporate Controller: Beverly L. P. Smiley, age 59
VP Business Development: Daniel D. Zandron, age 60
Public Relations: Joan C. Zimmer
Auditors: Ernst & Young LLP

LOCATIONS

HQ: Badger Meter, Inc.
4545 W. Brown Deer Rd., Milwaukee, WI 53223
Phone: 414-355-0400   **Fax:** 414-371-5956
Web: www.badgermeter.com

2008 Sales

	$ mil.	% of total
US	246.9	88
Europe	11.5	4
Mexico	9.6	3
Other regions	11.6	5
Total	**279.6**	**100**

PRODUCTS/OPERATIONS

Selected Products

Industrial
Chemical dispenser systems
Concrete batch meters
Electromagnetic meters
Lubrication meters (for automobiles)
Oscillating piston meters
Oval gear transmitters
Utility
Disc and compound water meters
Instrumentation systems
Reclaimed water meters
Transmitter registers
Turbo meters

COMPETITORS

Dwyer Instruments
Elster American Meter
Invensys
Itron
Jordan Company
K-Tron
Liquid Controls, LLC
Mesa Laboratories
Roper Industries
Schlumberger
Siemens Water Technologies
SpiraxSarco
Teledyne Isco
Thermo Fisher Scientific

HISTORICAL FINANCIALS

Company Type: Public

Income Statement

FYE: December 31

	REVENUE ($ mil.)	NET INCOME ($ mil.)	NET PROFIT MARGIN	EMPLOYEES
12/08	279.6	25.1	9.0%	1,224
12/07	234.8	16.5	7.0%	1,132
12/06	229.8	7.5	3.3%	1,113
12/05	216.7	13.3	6.1%	1,052
12/04	205.0	9.6	4.7%	1,073
Annual Growth	**8.1%**	**27.2%**	**—**	**3.3%**

2008 Year-End Financials

Debt ratio: 5.0%
Return on equity: 24.7%
Cash ($ mil.): 6.2
Current ratio: 1.70
Long-term debt ($ mil.): 5.5
No. of shares (mil.): 14.9
Dividends
Yield: 1.4%
Payout: 23.7%
Market value ($ mil.): 433.8
R&D as % of sales: —
Advertising as % of sales: —

Stock History

NYSE: BMI

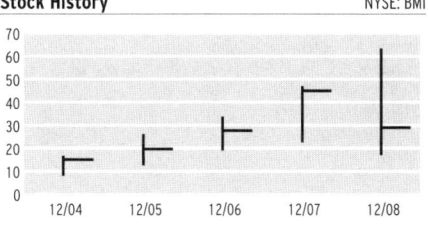

	STOCK PRICE ($) FY Close	P/E High/Low		PER SHARE ($) Earnings	Dividends	Book Value
12/08	29.02	37	10	1.69	0.40	7.43
12/07	44.95	41	20	1.13	0.34	6.15
12/06	27.70	64	38	0.52	0.31	4.80
12/05	19.62	27	14	0.94	0.29	4.91
12/04	14.98	23	12	0.71	0.28	4.29
Annual Growth	**18.0%**	**—**	**—**	**24.2%**	**9.3%**	**14.7%**

Balchem Corporation

Believe Balchem when they say they have it covered. The company has developed a technology that covers or encapsulates ingredients used in food and animal health products; the encapsulation improves nutritional value and shelf life and allows for controlled time release. Balchem also distributes specialty gases such as ethylene oxide (used to sterilize medical instruments), propylene oxide (used to reduce bacteria in spice treating and chemical processing), and methyl chloride. The company's unencapsulated-feed-ingredients segment supplies the nutrient choline chloride to poultry and swine farmers. Reashure, an encapsulated choline product, increases milk production in dairy cows.

Balchem's unencapsulated feed ingredients segment, also referred to as BCP Ingredients, got a whole lot bigger in 2007 when the company acquired two choline-related businesses. The first was in Italy from Akzo Nobel, and the other deal was for a company called Chinook Global Limited, whose operations were integrated into Balchem's business. Those deals nearly tripled the size of BCP Ingredients, making it Balchem's largest unit.

HISTORY

Herbert Weiss, Leslie Balassa, three ex-officers of the Alcolac company, and a group of Baltimore-based investors founded Balchem in 1967 in New York City. The company focused on the development of encapsulated specialty ingredients (the coating of individual particles that allow precise control of nutrient delivery). Initially, Balchem developed food ingredients used in meat processing, flavor enhancement, and dough leavening, as well as in nutritional supplements. In 1971 the company won its first big order: encapsulating the ingredients in pudding mix for General Foods. Balchem later applied the same technology to foaming agents for plastics, aquaculture supplements, and animal feeds. It also developed a line of specialty gases.

In 1994 Balchem boosted its gas business with the purchase of AlliedSignal's sterilant gas business (used to sterilize medical devices). Weiss retired as CEO in 1996 and was succeeded by EVP Raymond Reber. Reber left the company a few months later, and chemical industry veteran Dino Rossi replaced him. The next year Balchem developed a rumen-protected choline chloride for the animal nutrition market.

Balchem restructured its operations in 1998 away from aquaculture and towards animal nutrition and other growth markets. After successful university and field trials, the company introduced Reashure, its encapsulated choline product for dairy cows.

In 2000 Balchem was granted a patent for its technology that increases milk production in dairy cows. In 2001 the company acquired the choline and encapsulated product lines of DCV, Inc., and its DuCoa L.P. affiliate, which contributed to the company's increase in net sales by about 30% in 2002. In 2002 sales continued to build as the encapsulated/nutritional products segment introduced several new products and product applications for the enhancement of shelf-life and fortification of products in certain markets of the food industry.

EXECUTIVES

President, CEO, and Director: Dino A. Rossi, age 54, $837,963 total compensation
CFO, Treasurer, and Assistant Secretary:
Francis J. (Frank) Fitzpatrick, age 48, $459,897 total compensation
VP Research and Development: Paul H. Richardson, age 39, $368,258 total compensation
VP and General Manager, ARC Specialty Products:
David R. Ludwig, age 51, $462,459 total compensation
Auditors: McGladrey & Pullen, LLP

LOCATIONS

HQ: Balchem Corporation
52 Sunrise Park Rd., New Hampton, NY 10958
Phone: 845-326-5600   **Fax:** 845-326-5742
Web: www.balchem.com

2008 Sales

	% of total
US	63
Other countries	37
Total	**100**

PRODUCTS/OPERATIONS

2008 Sales

	% of total
Animal nutrition & health	70
Specialty products	15
Food, pharma & nutrition	15
Total	**100**

Selected Products

BCP Ingredients
  Choline chloride (essential nutrient for animal health)
  Choline chloride derivatives
Encapsulated/Nutritional Products
  Food, Pharma & Human Nutrition Products
    Bakeshure (leavening agents, dough conditioners, fortifiers, acidifiers, and antimicrobials)
    Confecshure (acidulants for flavor)
    Flavorshure (taste and flavor masking)
    Meatshure (acidifiers, antioxidants, and flavors)
    Vitashure (vitamins, nutraceuticals, and botanicals)
  Animal Nutrition & Health Products
    Niashure
      Niacine (prevents niacin degradation)
      Urea (regulates nitrogen/carbohydrates ratio in proteins)
    Reashure (rumen-stable choline for dairy cows)
Specialty Products
  Ethylene oxide (sterilant gas for the health care industry)
  Methyl chloride (specialty herbicides)
  Propylene oxide (bacteria reduction in spices)

COMPETITORS

BioDelivery Sciences
Clariant
Coating Place
IGENE

Mitsubishi Chemical
Nutrition 21
Praxair

HISTORICAL FINANCIALS

Company Type: Public

Income Statement

FYE: December 31

	REVENUE ($ mil.)	NET INCOME ($ mil.)	NET PROFIT MARGIN	EMPLOYEES
12/08	232.1	19.0	8.2%	332
12/07	176.2	16.1	9.1%	320
12/06	100.9	12.3	12.2%	230
12/05	83.1	11.0	13.2%	200
12/04	67.4	8.0	11.9%	200
Annual Growth	36.2%	24.1%	—	13.5%

2008 Year-End Financials

Debt ratio: 5.8%
Return on equity: 18.3%
Cash ($ mil.): 3.4
Current ratio: 2.15
Long-term debt ($ mil.): 6.7
No. of shares (mil.): 18.7

Dividends
  Yield: 0.4%
  Payout: 11.0%
Market value ($ mil.): 464.7
R&D as % of sales: —
Advertising as % of sales: —

Stock History

NASDAQ (GS): BCPC

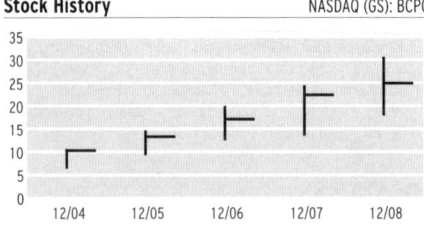

	STOCK PRICE ($) FY Close	P/E High/Low		PER SHARE ($) Earnings	Dividends	Book Value
12/08	24.91	30	18	1.00	0.11	6.14
12/07	22.38	28	16	0.87	0.11	4.99
12/06	17.12	29	19	0.67	0.06	4.04
12/05	13.25	24	16	0.61	0.04	3.27
12/04	10.28	23	15	0.46	0.03	2.69
Annual Growth	24.8%	—	—	21.4%	38.4%	22.9%

BancTrust Financial

BancTrust Financial makes its sweet home in Alabama, but also spends a little time in the Florida panhandle. It is the holding company for two banks that operate as BankTrust throughout southern Alabama and neighboring parts of Florida. Through more than 50 branch offices, the banks offer such deposit products as CDs and checking, savings, and retirement accounts. The company's lending activities include mortgages (more than 40% of its loan portfolio), construction loans (nearly 30%), and commercial, agricultural, and consumer loans. Subsidiaries offer insurance, trust, and investment services. BancTrust Financial bought fellow Alabama bank holding company The Peoples BancTrust Company in 2007.

EXECUTIVES

Chairman: J. Stephen Nelson, age 71
President, CEO and Director; Chairman and CEO, Mobile Bank: W. Bibb Lamar Jr., age 65, $480,789 total compensation
EVP; President and CEO, Florida Bank; EVP, Mobile Bank: Michael D. Fitzhugh, age 60, $245,182 total compensation
EVP: Fred W. Taul
EVP BancTrust: Edward T. Livingston, age 62, $216,992 total compensation
EVP, CFO, and Secretary; EVP and Cashier, Mobile Bank: F. Michael Johnson, age 63, $257,308 total compensation
EVP; COO BankTrust: Andrew C. Bearden Jr., age 62
SVP Auditor: Mark E. McVay
SVP and Senior Loan Officer; EVP, Mobile Bank: Bruce C. Finley Jr., age 60, $236,912 total compensation
SVP BankTrust, Accounting: Mark Thompson
SVP Human Resources: J. Dianne Hollingsworth
VP Marketing and Communications: Rebecca (Becky) Minto
VP Finance, Corporate Governance and Investor Relations: Leigh G. Thompson
Auditors: KPMG LLP

LOCATIONS

HQ: BancTrust Financial Group, Inc.
  100 St. Joseph St., Mobile, AL 36602
Phone: 251-431-7800   **Fax:** 251-431-7851
Web: www.banctrustfinancialgroupinc.com

COMPETITORS

Ameris
Compass Bancshares
Regions Financial
SunTrust
Whitney Holding

HISTORICAL FINANCIALS

Company Type: Public

Income Statement

FYE: December 31

	ASSETS ($ mil.)	NET INCOME ($ mil.)	INCOME AS % OF ASSETS	EMPLOYEES
12/08	2,088.2	1.3	0.1%	621
12/07	2,240.1	6.2	0.3%	686
12/06	1,353.4	13.3	1.0%	419
12/05	1,305.5	15.1	1.2%	396
12/04	1,191.2	11.3	0.9%	380
Annual Growth	15.1%	(41.8%)	—	13.1%

2008 Year-End Financials

Equity as % of assets: 11.6%
Return on assets: 0.1%
Return on equity: 0.5%
Long-term debt ($ mil.): 113.4
No. of shares (mil.): 17.6
Market value ($ mil.): 260.3

Dividends
  Yield: 3.5%
  Payout: 866.7%
Sales ($ mil.): 83.9
R&D as % of sales: —
Advertising as % of sales: —

Stock History

NASDAQ (GS): BTFG

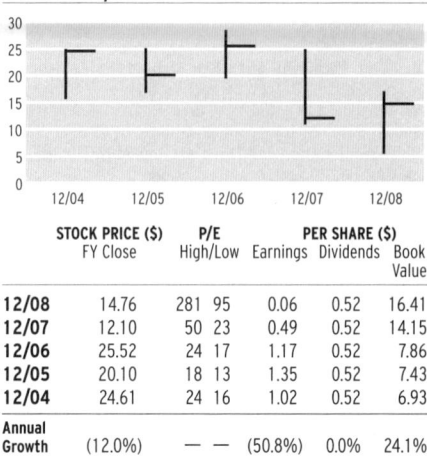

	STOCK PRICE ($) FY Close	P/E High/Low		PER SHARE ($) Earnings	Dividends	Book Value
12/08	14.76	281	95	0.06	0.52	16.41
12/07	12.10	50	23	0.49	0.52	14.15
12/06	25.52	24	17	1.17	0.52	7.86
12/05	20.10	18	13	1.35	0.52	7.43
12/04	24.61	24	16	1.02	0.52	6.93
Annual Growth	(12.0%)	—	—	(50.8%)	0.0%	24.1%

Bank of the Ozarks

Bank of the Ozarks is the holding company for the bank of the same name, which has around 65 branches in Arkansas. It also has about five locations in Texas and a loan production office in North Carolina. Serving individuals and small to midsized businesses, the bank offers traditional deposit and loan services, in addition to trust services, retirement planning, cash management, and equipment leasing. Mutual funds, annuities, insurance, and other investment products and services are available through a third-party provider. Construction and land development loans make up the largest portion of Bank of the Ozarks' loan portfolio, followed by commercial real estate loans and residential mortgages.

Bank of the Ozarks' expansion strategy had centered on opening new branches in smaller communities in Arkansas. But after tasting success in larger markets like Little Rock and Fort Smith, the company is targeting Bentonville (home of Wal-Mart's headquarters) and Hot Springs, Arkansas; Texarkana (which straddles the Arkansas and Texas border); and Frisco, Texas, (a suburb of Dallas) for further growth.

Chairman and CEO George Gleason owns more than 20% of the company; institutional investors FMR and Neuberger Berman own about 10% apiece.

EXECUTIVES

Chairman and CEO, Bank of the Ozarks, Inc. and Bank of the Ozarks: George G. Gleason, age 55, $912,336 total compensation
Vice Chairman, President, and COO, Bank of the Ozarks, Inc. and Bank of the Ozarks: Mark Ross, age 53, $331,995 total compensation
CFO and Chief Accounting Officer, Bank of the Ozarks, Inc. and Bank of the Ozarks: Paul Moore, age 62, $257,421 total compensation
CIO: Ron Kuykendall
EVP Human Resources: Diane Hilburn
EVP Controller: Greg McKinney, $247,279 total compensation
EVP, Bank of the Ozarks, Inc. and Bank of the Ozarks: Dan Rolett, age 46
President, Trust Division, Bank of the Ozarks: Rex Kyle, age 52, $226,988 total compensation
President, Mortgage Division, Bank of the Ozarks: Gene Holman, age 61
President, Leasing Division, Bank of the Ozarks: Scott Hastings, age 51
Auditors: Ernst & Young LLP

LOCATIONS

HQ: Bank of the Ozarks, Inc.
12615 Chenal Pkwy., Little Rock, AR 72231
Phone: 501-978-2265 **Fax:** 501-978-2350
Web: www.bankozarks.com

PRODUCTS/OPERATIONS

2008 Gross Revenues

	$ mil.	% of total
Interest		
Loans & leases	141.7	69
Investment securities & other	41.3	20
Noninterest		
Service charges on deposit accounts	12.0	6
Bank-owned life insurance	4.1	2
Other	7.2	3
Adjustments	(3.9)	—
Total	**202.4**	**100**

COMPETITORS

Arvest Bank
BancorpSouth
BOK Financial
First Federal Bancshares of Arkansas
Home BancShares
IBERIABANK
Regions Financial
Simmons First

HISTORICAL FINANCIALS

Company Type: Public

Income Statement				FYE: December 31
	ASSETS ($ mil.)	NET INCOME ($ mil.)	INCOME AS % OF ASSETS	EMPLOYEES
12/08	3,233.3	34.7	1.1%	705
12/07	2,710.9	31.7	1.2%	689
12/06	2,529.4	31.7	1.3%	699
12/05	2,134.9	31.5	1.5%	629
12/04	1,726.8	25.9	1.5%	561
Annual Growth	**17.0%**	**7.6%**	**—**	**5.9%**

2008 Year-End Financials

Equity as % of assets: 7.8%
Return on assets: 1.2%
Return on equity: 15.7%
Long-term debt ($ mil.): 489.9
No. of shares (mil.): 16.9
Market value ($ mil.): 500.5
Dividends
Yield: 1.7%
Payout: 24.5%
Sales ($ mil.): 118.1
R&D as % of sales: —
Advertising as % of sales: —

Stock History NASDAQ (GS): OZRK

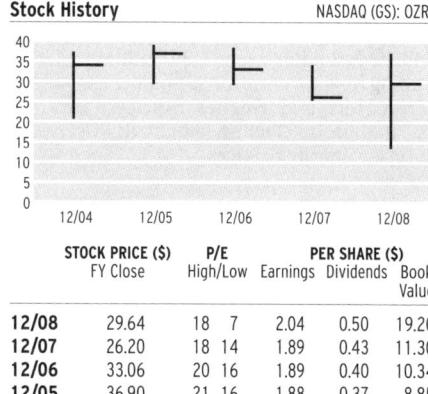

	STOCK PRICE ($) FY Close	P/E High/Low		PER SHARE ($) Earnings	Dividends	Book Value
12/08	29.64	18	7	2.04	0.50	19.20
12/07	26.20	18	14	1.89	0.43	11.30
12/06	33.06	20	16	1.89	0.40	10.34
12/05	36.90	21	16	1.88	0.37	8.85
12/04	34.03	24	13	1.56	0.30	7.19
Annual Growth	**(3.4%)**	**—**	**—**	**6.9%**	**13.6%**	**27.8%**

Bare Escentuals

When it comes to keeping its customers looking naturally pretty, Bare Escentuals has a mineral interest. The company, which rolled out its bareMinerals makeup brand in 1976 along with its first retail shop, develops, markets, and sells natural cosmetics, skin care, and body care items. Brand names include bareMinerals, Buxom, md formulations, RareMinerals, and its namesake line. Bare Escentuals sells its products in the US through about 100 company-owned shops, 800 beauty product retailers, and 1,500 spas and salons. It also boasts distributors in Canada, Japan, and the UK, among other European countries. Japanese cosmetics company Shiseido agreed in January 2010 to acquire Bare Escentuals for $1.7 billion.

As part of the deal, Bare Escentuals will have greater access to the Asian cosmetics market, where Shiseido is a leader. Shiseido had been looking for a way to extend its reach into US cosmetics, as well. The agreement will make Bare Escentuals a separate division under Shiseido and will retain the company's CEO Leslie Blodgett.

Bare Escentuals, before the Shiseido deal, extended its reach abroad by acquiring European cosmetics distributor Cosmeceuticals Ltd. and renamed the company Bare Escentuals UK in 2007. Mirroring its US program, Bare Escentuals has built its international business through its relationship with retailer Sephora and other department stores, about 2,000 UK spas and salons, as well as infomercials and home-shopping TV channels.

To strengthen its domestic foothold, Bare Escentuals plans to continue fueling its media-driven marketing campaign. Sales deriving from infomercials, home-shopping shows, and the Internet accounted for about 30% of sales in 2008. On the retail store front, Bare Escentuals also plans to boost its number of company-owned brick-and-mortar boutiques.

Besides brick-and-mortar distribution outlets, the company also peddles its products via television airwaves (on QVC and major cable networks) and the Internet. Its primary shopping Web sites are www.bareminerals.com and www.mdformulations.com.

Berkshire Partners LLC and JH MDB Investors own a majority stake in the firm. The cosmetics maker raised about $370 million in its initial public offering. It used the net proceeds to repay its debt valued at more than $230 million. Formerly STB Beauty, the company changed its name to Bare Escentuals in 2006.

EXECUTIVES

Chairman: Ross M. Jones, age 44
CEO and Director: Leslie A. Blodgett, age 46, $2,817,066 total compensation
EVP, COO, and CFO: Myles B. McCormick, age 37, $999,896 total compensation
VP, Controller, and Principal Accounting Officer: Kevin Bradshaw, age 51
Auditors: Ernst & Young LLP

LOCATIONS

HQ: Bare Escentuals, Inc.
71 Stevenson St., 22nd Fl.
San Francisco, CA 94105
Phone: 415-489-5000 **Fax:** 877-963-3329
Web: www.bareescentuals.com

2008 Sales

	$ mil.	% of total
US	489.0	88
Other countries	67.2	12
Total	**556.2**	**100**

PRODUCTS/OPERATIONS

2008 Sales

	$ mil.	% of total
Retail	320.0	58
Direct to consumer	170.3	30
Other	65.9	12
Total	**556.2**	**100**

COMPETITORS

Amway Global
Avon
BeautiControl
Beauty Brands
BeneFit Cosmetics
Borlind of Germany, Inc.
CA Botana
Canderm Pharma
Clarins
Clinique Laboratories
CVS Caremark
Del Laboratories
drugstore.com
Elizabeth Arden Inc
Estée Lauder Cosmetics
The Forever Group
Fresh Inc.
Guthy-Renker
Ideal Shopping Direct
L'Oréal
Mary Kay
Nu Skin
Ortho Dermatologics
Procter & Gamble
PureBeauty
QVC
Revlon
Rite Aid
Sally Beauty
Ulta
Vertical Branding
Walgreen
Whole Foods

HISTORICAL FINANCIALS

Company Type: Public

Income Statement
FYE: Sunday nearest December 31

	REVENUE ($ mil.)	NET INCOME ($ mil.)	NET PROFIT MARGIN	EMPLOYEES
12/08	556.2	98.0	17.6%	2,779
12/07	511.0	88.1	17.2%	1,571
12/06	394.5	50.2	12.7%	863
12/05	259.3	23.9	9.2%	576
12/04	141.8	4.0	2.8%	706
Annual Growth	40.7%	122.5%	—	40.9%

2008 Year-End Financials

Debt ratio: —
Return on equity: —
Cash ($ mil.): 48.0
Current ratio: 3.56
Long-term debt ($ mil.): 223.8
No. of shares (mil.): 92.0

Dividends
Yield: —
Payout: —
Market value ($ mil.): 481.3
R&D as % of sales: —
Advertising as % of sales: —

Stock History
NASDAQ (GS): BARE

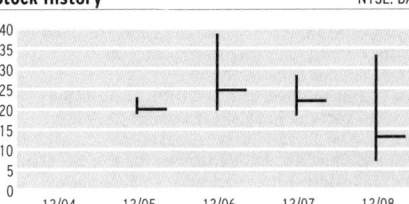

	STOCK PRICE ($) FY Close	P/E High/Low		PER SHARE ($) Earnings	Dividends	Book Value
12/08	5.23	28	3	1.05	—	(0.00)
12/07	24.25	45	20	0.95	—	(1.14)
12/06	31.07	54	41	0.65	—	(2.48)
Annual Growth	(59.0%)	—	—	27.1%	—	—

Basic Energy Services

Oil and gas producers turn to Basic Energy Services for the fundamentals. The company provides well site services with its fleet of well-servicing rigs (at more than 410, the third-largest in the US behind Key Energy Services and Nabors Industries), 820 fluid service trucks, and related equipment. These services include acidizing, cementing, fluid handling, fracturing, well construction, well maintenance, and workover. Basic Energy Services serves about 2,000 producers operating in Louisiana, New Mexico, Oklahoma, and Texas. It also has a contract drilling operation. Investment firm DLJ Merchant Banking Partners III, L.P., owns 44.4% of the company.

In 2008 Basic Energy Services agreed to be acquired by drilling contractor Grey Wolf, but Grey Wolf shareholders rejected the deal; Grey Wolf was subsequently acquired by Precision Drilling Trust.

The company has grown through complementary acquisitions in its core geographic and business markets. In 2007 the company acquired two barge-mounted workover rigs and related equipment from Parker Drilling for $26 million. That

year Basic Energy Services also acquired pressure pumping equipment operator JetStar Consolidated Holdings for $120 million, Sledge Drilling Holding Corp. for $51 million, and Steve Carter, Inc. and Hughes Services, Inc. for $20 million. In 2008 it bought fluid services company Azurite Services.

EXECUTIVES

Chairman: Steven A. Webster, age 56
President, CEO, and Director:
Kenneth V. (Ken) Huseman, age 57,
$1,719,321 total compensation
SVP, CFO, Treasurer, and Secretary: Alan Krenek,
age 54, $833,295 total compensation
SVP Operations Support: Charles W. (Charlie) Swift,
age 61, $603,523 total compensation
SVP Rig and Truck Operations:
Thomas Monroe (Roe) Patterson, age 35,
$581,295 total compensation
Group VP Completion and Remedial Services:
James F. Newman, age 44
VP Human Resources: James E. Tyner, age 59,
$422,071 total compensation
VP Risk Management: Mark D. Rankin, age 56
VP Contract Drilling: David W. Sledge, age 52
Auditors: KPMG LLP

LOCATIONS

HQ: Basic Energy Services, Inc.
500 W. Illinios, Ste. 800, Midland, TX 79701
Phone: 432-620-5500   **Fax:** 432-620-5501
Web: www.basicenergyservices.com

PRODUCTS/OPERATIONS

2008 Sales

	$ mil.	% of total
Well servicing	343.1	34
Fluid services	315.8	32
Completion & remedial services	304.3	30
Contract drilling	41.7	4
Total	**1,004.9**	**100**

COMPETITORS

BJ Services
Halliburton
Key Energy
Nabors Industries
Pride International
Schlumberger
Weatherford International

HISTORICAL FINANCIALS

Company Type: Public

Income Statement
FYE: December 31

	REVENUE ($ mil.)	NET INCOME ($ mil.)	NET PROFIT MARGIN	EMPLOYEES
12/08	1,004.9	68.2	6.8%	5,000
12/07	877.2	87.7	10.0%	4,500
12/06	730.1	98.8	13.5%	4,000
12/05	459.8	44.8	9.7%	3,280
12/04	311.5	12.9	4.1%	3,200
Annual Growth	34.0%	51.6%	—	11.8%

2008 Year-End Financials

Debt ratio: 76.3%
Return on equity: 12.2%
Cash ($ mil.): 111.1
Current ratio: 3.17
Long-term debt ($ mil.): 454.3
No. of shares (mil.): 40.7

Dividends
Yield: 0.0%
Payout: —
Market value ($ mil.): 530.6
R&D as % of sales: —
Advertising as % of sales: —

Stock History
NYSE: BAS

	STOCK PRICE ($) FY Close	P/E High/Low		PER SHARE ($) Earnings	Dividends	Book Value
12/08	13.04	20	4	1.64	0.00	14.62
12/07	21.95	13	9	2.13	0.00	12.90
12/06	24.65	15	8	2.56	0.00	9.32
12/05	19.95	17	14	1.35	0.00	6.36
Annual Growth	(13.2%)	—	—	40.6%	—	48.7%

Beneficial Mutual Bancorp

You would expect something beneficial from the city of brotherly love. Beneficial Mutual Bancorp is the holding company for Beneficial Bank, which serves the greater Philadelphia area and southern New Jersey through about 70 branches. Founded in 1853 as Beneficial Mutual Savings Bank, the bank provides traditional deposit products such as checking, savings, and money market accounts; IRAs; and CDs. Commercial real estate loans account for approximately a third of the company's loan portfolio; residential mortgages are more than 20%. Home equity, business, and consumer loans help round out its lending activities.

The company sells insurance and offers investment advisory services through subsidiaries Beneficial Insurance Services and Beneficial Advisors.

Beneficial Mutual was busy in 2007. The company went public in conjunction with its acquisition of bank holding company FMS Financial, which cemented its presence in southern New Jersey. It also augmented its insurance business with the acquisition of property/casualty and professional liability insurance brokerage CLA Agency.

Mutual holding company Beneficial Savings Bank MHC owns approximately 55% of Beneficial Mutual Bancorp.

EXECUTIVES

Chairman, President, and CEO: Gerard P. Cuddy,
age 49, $760,064 total compensation
EVP Advisory Services: Robert J. Bush, age 51,
$455,763 total compensation
EVP Retail Banking: Denise Kassekert, age 58,
$312,859 total compensation
EVP and Chief Lending Officer: Andrew J. Miller,
age 54, $534,334 total compensation
EVP and CFO: Joseph F. Conners, age 52,
$508,155 total compensation
VP and Manager, Customer Contact: James J. Fecca
VP and Regional Officer, Community Banking Division:
Brian C. Miller
Auditors: Deloitte & Touche LLP

LOCATIONS

HQ: Beneficial Mutual Bancorp, Inc.
510 Walnut St., 19th Fl., Philadelphia, PA 19106
Phone: 215-864-6000   **Fax:** 215-864-6177
Web: www.thebeneficial.com

PRODUCTS/OPERATIONS

2008 Gross Revenues

	$ mil.	% of total
Interest		
Loans, including fees	132.6	60
Taxable investment securities	58.1	26
Other	2.2	1
Noninterest		
Insurance commissions	10.1	5
Services charges & other	16.7	8
Total	**219.7**	**100**

COMPETITORS

Bank of America
Citizens Financial Group
First Chester County
Firstrust Savings Bank
National Penn Bancshares
PNC Financial
Prudential Bancorp
Republic First Bank
TD Bank USA

HISTORICAL FINANCIALS

Company Type: Public

Income Statement				FYE: December 31
	ASSETS ($ mil.)	NET INCOME ($ mil.)	INCOME AS % OF ASSETS	EMPLOYEES
12/08	4,002.1	16.5	0.4%	970
12/07	3,557.8	(1.5)	—	912
12/06	1,188.1	5.3	0.4%	577
12/05	2,392.4	13.2	0.6%	577
Annual Growth	18.7%	7.7%	—	18.9%

2008 Year-End Financials

Equity as % of assets: 15.3%   Dividends
Return on assets: 0.4%   Yield: 0.0%
Return on equity: 2.7%   Payout: —
Long-term debt ($ mil.): 203.6   Sales ($ mil.): 137.6
No. of shares (mil.): 81.9   R&D as % of sales: —
Market value ($ mil.): 920.9   Advertising as % of sales: —

Stock History

NASDAQ (GS): BNCL

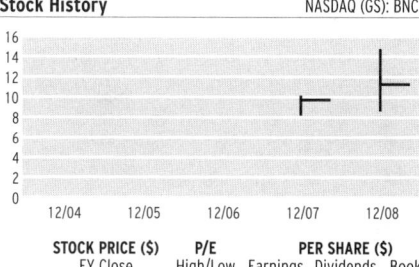

	STOCK PRICE ($) FY Close	P/E High/Low	Earnings	PER SHARE ($) Dividends	Book Value
12/08	11.25	70 42	0.21	0.00	7.46
12/07	9.72	— —	(0.03)	0.00	7.57
Annual Growth	15.7%	— —	—	—	(1.5%)

Berkshire Hills Bancorp

Berkshire Hills Bancorp is the holding company for Berkshire Bank, which serves individuals and small businesses through about 40 branches in western Massachusetts, eastern New York, and southern Vermont. Established in 1846, the bank provides an array of deposit products such as savings, checking, and money market accounts; CDs; and IRAs. It also offers credit cards, insurance, investments, private banking, and wealth management services. Berkshire Hills Bancorp also owns Berkshire Bank Municipal Bank, which collects deposits from municipalities and other government entities in New York.

Residential mortgages and commercial mortgages each make up approximately 35% of the Berkshire Hills Bancorp's loan portfolio, which also includes consumer loans (about 20%) and business loans.

The company expanded its presence in western Massachusetts with its 2005 purchase of Woronoco Bancorp. In 2007 it bought Factory Point Bancorp, the holding company for Factory Point National Bank of Manchester Center. The deal gave Berkshire Hills Bancorp its first seven branches in southern Vermont. The company is eyeing expansion into neighboring Connecticut as well.

In 2009 the company arranged to acquire smaller Massachusetts bank CNB Financial, but its $19.5 million offer was topped by United Financial Bancorp following a bidding war.

EXECUTIVES

Chairman: Lawrence A. (Larry) Bossidy, age 73
President, CEO, and Director, Berkshire Hills Bancorp and Berkshire Bank: Michael P. Daly, age 47, $1,044,751 total compensation
EVP, CFO, Treasurer, and Secretary: Kevin P. Riley, age 49, $443,639 total compensation
EVP and Chief Risk Officer: Shepard D. Rainie
EVP Integrated Services, Berkshire Hills Bancorp and Berkshire Hills Bank: David B. (Dave) Farrell, age 53
EVP: Michael J. (Mike) Oleksak, age 50
SVP Retail Banking: Sean A. Gray
SVP Wealth Management and Trust: Thomas W. Barney
SVP Human Resources: Linda A. Johnston
SVP Commercial Lending: Michael J. Ferry
President and CEO, Berkshire Insurance Group: John S. Millet, age 44
Auditors: Wolf & Company, P.C.

LOCATIONS

HQ: Berkshire Hills Bancorp, Inc.
24 North St., Pittsfield, MA 01201
Phone: 413-443-5601   **Fax:** 413-443-3587
Web: www.berkshirebank.com

PRODUCTS/OPERATIONS

2008 Gross Revenues

	$ mil.	% of total
Interest		
Loans	120.6	73
Securities	12.5	8
Other	0.2	—
Noninterest		
Insurance commissions & fees	13.6	8
Deposit service fees	9.8	6
Wealth management fees	5.7	3
Other	2.4	1
Total	**164.8**	**100**

COMPETITORS

Bank of America
Citizens Financial Group
Hudson City Bancorp
Legacy Bancorp
Pathfinder Bancorp
TD Bank USA

HISTORICAL FINANCIALS

Company Type: Public

Income Statement				FYE: December 31
	ASSETS ($ mil.)	NET INCOME ($ mil.)	INCOME AS % OF ASSETS	EMPLOYEES
12/08	2,666.7	22.2	0.8%	610
12/07	2,513.4	13.5	0.5%	560
12/06	2,149.6	11.3	0.5%	522
12/05	2,035.6	8.2	0.4%	399
12/04	1,310.1	11.5	0.9%	241
Annual Growth	19.4%	17.9%	—	26.1%

2008 Year-End Financials

Equity as % of assets: 13.9%   Dividends
Return on assets: 0.9%   Yield: 1.6%
Return on equity: 6.4%   Payout: 23.3%
Long-term debt ($ mil.): 351.4   Sales ($ mil.): 107.3
No. of shares (mil.): 13.9   R&D as % of sales: —
Market value ($ mil.): 430.0   Advertising as % of sales: —

Stock History

NASDAQ (GS): BHLB

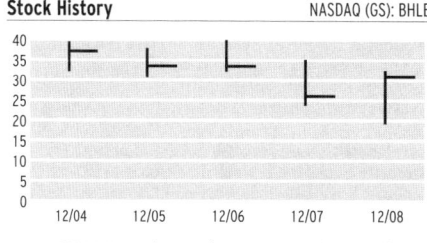

	STOCK PRICE ($) FY Close	P/E High/Low	Earnings	PER SHARE ($) Dividends	Book Value
12/08	30.86	16 9	2.06	0.48	29.31
12/07	26.00	24 17	1.44	0.58	23.46
12/06	33.46	31 25	1.29	0.56	18.53
12/05	33.50	34 28	1.10	0.52	17.66
12/04	37.15	20 16	2.01	0.48	9.45
Annual Growth	(4.5%)	— —	0.6%	0.0%	32.7%

Berry Petroleum

It may be small fruit in the giant petroleum industry, but Berry Petroleum delivers the juice. The company buys properties with heavy crude oil reserves for exploitation and sale to refining companies. Berry Petroleum's core properties are in California (Kern, Los Angeles, and Ventura counties), Colorado, and Utah. In 2008 it reported proved reserves of 225 million barrels of oil equivalent. The company squeezes the most from its Californian heavy oil assets by using thermal recovery: Steam is injected into heavy crude oil reserves to reduce oil viscosity and allow it to flow to the surface. Berry Petroleum also owns three gas-fired cogeneration facilities.

The company is pursuing a growth strategy of developing light and medium oil assets outside of California.

In a move to geographically diversify, in 2008 Berry Petroleum acquired interests in gas-producing properties in East Texas from private sellers for about $670 million. To pay down debt, in 2009 it sold its mature, non-core assets in the Denver-Julesburg basin for $154 million.

In 2010 in a further expansion, Berry Petroleum agreed to buy assets in West Texas' Wolfberry trend for $126 million. The deal adds reserves of about 11.2 million barrels of oil equivalent.

In 2006 Berry Petroleum acquired a 50% stake in some natural gas assets in the Piceance Basin of western Colorado from a private concern for $150 million. To raise cash, in 2007 the company sold its non-core West Montalvo assets, near Ventura, California, for $63 million.

EXECUTIVES

Chairman: Martin H. Young Jr., age 56
President, CEO, and Director: Robert F. Heinemann, age 55, $5,063,256 total compensation
EVP and COO: Michael Duginski, age 42, $1,386,612 total compensation
EVP and CFO: David D. Wolf, age 38, $1,019,259 total compensation
SVP California Production and Assistant Secretary: George T. (Tim) Crawford, age 48
Chief Geoscientist: Bruce S. Kelso, age 53, $694,964 total compensation
VP Rocky Mountain Production: Daniel G. (Dan) Anderson, age 46, $762,669 total compensation
VP Human Resources: Walter B. Ayers, age 65
VP and Controller: Shawn M. Canaday, age 33, $480,508 total compensation
Treasurer and Assistant Secretary: Steven B. Wilson, age 45
Investor Relations Specialist: Todd A. Crabtree
Corporate Secretary: Kenneth A. Olson, age 53
Auditors: PricewaterhouseCoopers LLP

LOCATIONS

HQ: Berry Petroleum Company
1999 Broadway, Ste. 3700, Denver, CO 80202
Phone: 303-999-4400
Web: www.bry.com

PRODUCTS/OPERATIONS

2008 Sales

	$ mil.	% of total
Oil & gas	698.0	87
Electricity	63.5	8
Other	40.0	5
Total	**801.5**	**100**

COMPETITORS

Aera Energy
Chevron
Ellora
EXCO Resources
Royal Dutch Shell
Royale Energy
Samson Oil
SandRidge Energy
TARC
Vulcan Energy

HISTORICAL FINANCIALS

Company Type: Public

Income Statement

FYE: December 31

	REVENUE ($ mil.)	NET INCOME ($ mil.)	NET PROFIT MARGIN	EMPLOYEES
12/08	801.5	133.5	16.7%	303
12/07	583.5	129.9	22.3%	263
12/06	486.3	107.9	22.2%	243
12/05	406.7	112.4	27.6%	209
12/04	274.9	69.2	25.2%	157
Annual Growth	**30.7%**	**17.9%**	**—**	**17.9%**

2008 Year-End Financials

Debt ratio: 136.8%
Return on equity: 20.7%
Cash ($ mil.): 0.2
Current ratio: 0.73
Long-term debt ($ mil.): 1,131.8
No. of shares (mil.): 44.7
Dividends
Yield: 4.0%
Payout: 10.2%
Market value ($ mil.): 337.6
R&D as % of sales: —
Advertising as % of sales: —

Stock History

NYSE: BRY

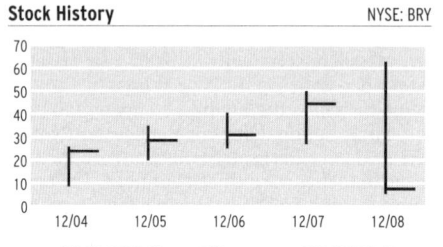

	STOCK PRICE ($) FY Close	P/E High/Low		Earnings	PER SHARE ($) Dividends	Book Value
12/08	7.56	21	2	2.94	0.30	18.53
12/07	44.45	17	10	2.89	0.30	10.30
12/06	31.01	17	11	2.41	0.28	9.58
12/05	28.60	14	8	2.50	0.25	7.48
12/04	23.85	16	6	1.54	0.23	5.89
Annual Growth	**(25.0%)**	**—**	**—**	**17.5%**	**6.9%**	**33.2%**

Bidz.com, Inc.

Bidz.com combines the markdowns of a dollar store, the format of an auction house, and the convenience of the Internet to bring sparkling deals to shoppers. The company buys closeout merchandise and sells it using a live-auction format, with no reserve prices and $1 opening bids, even on items that might retail for more than $20,000. It mostly sells jewelry, including gold, platinum, and silver items set with diamonds, and other precious and semi-precious stones, but visitors will also find deals on electronics and collectibles such as art and antiques, coins, and sports cards. In 2008 the company introduced foreign language versions of its auction site and launched Buyz.com, a fixed-price e-commerce site.

The global economic downturn has raised the stakes for Bidz.com. The company saw its profits plummet about 65% during the 2008 holiday selling season. It also cut about 30% of its full-time staff in anticipation of a challenging economic climate. To shore up business in 2009, the company focused on its online consumer

segment and opportunities arising from jewelry businesses exiting the market. To that end, in September 2009 it acquired the intellectual property and customer data from now-defunct Whitehall Jewelers at a bankruptcy auction.

The company is also under investigation by the SEC regarding its inventory accounting practices, among other matters.

In a bid to broaden its presence, the company expanded into English-speaking international markets, including Australia and New Zealand. In 2008 Bidz.com unveiled Spanish, Arabic, and German language versions of its auction site. About 24% of Bidz.com's sales come from outside the US.

Bidz.com purchased about 12% of its merchandise from jewelry liquidator LA Jewelers in 2007, making that company one of Bidz.com's largest suppliers. It also purchased about $24 million in finished jewelry at a bankruptcy auction held in 2008 for LID Ltd., a top maker of diamond jewelry.

The Internet auctioneer sought to raise funds through an initial public offering filed in March 2006. After reducing the size of the offering to 3 million shares from 6.2 million shares and a tepid reception from investors, the company postponed the IPO indefinitely.

Chairman and CEO David Zinberg and his sister, VP Marina Zinberg, together own about 60% of the company's stock.

EXECUTIVES

Chairman and CEO: David Zinberg, age 51, $433,434 total compensation
President and CTO: Leon Kuperman, age 35, $424,414 total compensation
COO: Claudia Y. Liu, age 49, $524,448 total compensation
CFO, Secretary, Treasurer, and Director: Lawrence Y. Kong, age 48, $743,663 total compensation
VP and Executive Secretary: Marina Zinberg
Chief Compliance Officer: Larry E. Russell, age 57
Controller: Jessica Kao, age 32
Customer Service Manager: Jorge L. Gonzalez
Auctions Manager: Vilius Zukauskas
Auditors: Stonefield Josephson, Inc.

LOCATIONS

HQ: Bidz.com, Inc.
3562 Eastham Dr., Culver City, CA 90232
Phone: 310-280-7373   **Fax:** 310-280-7375
Web: www.bidz.com

2008 Sales

	$ mil.	% of total
US	157.7	76
International	49.7	24
Total	**207.4**	**100**

COMPETITORS

Blue Nile, Inc.
Costco Wholesale
eBay
Enable Holdings
Finlay Enterprises
HSN
J. C. Penney
Overstock.com
QVC
Reeds Jewelers
Target
Walmart.com
Zale

HISTORICAL FINANCIALS

Company Type: Public

Income Statement

FYE: December 31

	REVENUE ($ mil.)	NET INCOME ($ mil.)	NET PROFIT MARGIN	EMPLOYEES
12/08	207.4	14.4	6.9%	165
12/07	187.1	18.1	9.7%	240
12/06	131.8	5.4	4.1%	198
12/05	90.6	2.6	2.9%	170
12/04	65.3	0.8	1.2%	175
Annual Growth	33.5%	106.0%	—	(1.5%)

2008 Year-End Financials

Debt ratio: —
Return on equity: 42.7%
Cash ($ mil.): 4.5
Current ratio: 3.41
Long-term debt ($ mil.): —
No. of shares (mil.): 22.1

Dividends
  Yield: 0.0%
  Payout: —
Market value ($ mil.): 101.7
R&D as % of sales: —
Advertising as % of sales: —

Stock History

NASDAQ (CM): BIDZ

	STOCK PRICE ($) FY Close	P/E High/Low		PER SHARE ($) Earnings	Dividends	Book Value
12/08	4.60	24	4	0.57	0.00	1.57
12/07	8.97	33	7	0.69	0.00	1.48
Annual Growth	(48.7%)	—	—	(17.4%)	—	6.5%

Bill Barrett Corporation

Bill Barrett Corp. (named after a veteran oil industry wildcatter) is hoping for a Rocky Mountain high as it digs down deep for oil and gas. The company focuses its exploration and development activities in the Wind River, Uinta, Piceance, Powder River, Big Horn, and Paradox Basins and the Montana Overthrusts. Bill Barrett holds about 1.2 million net undeveloped leasehold acres. Some 90% of the company's properties are unconventional resources, such as coal bed methane and shale gas. In 2008 the oil and gas firm had working interests in 950 drilling locations and had estimated net proved reserves of 818.3 billion cu. ft. of natural gas equivalent. It also directly operates 97% of its net production.

Bill Barrett pursues a growth strategy of focusing on developing and exploiting natural gas fields in the Rockies. It has developed a large inventory of 3,100 development locations in its core areas (Uinta, Piceance, Powder River, and Wind River Basins) and (since its founding) has drilled more than 1,772 gross wells at a success rate of 98%.

In 2009 the company paid $60 million to acquire a 90% stake in 40,300 undeveloped leasehold acres in Cottonwood Gulch, in the Piceance Basin of western Colorado. The company anticipates that the purchase will add more than 2 trillion cu. ft. of natural gas equivalent to its probable and possible reserves.

Bill Barrett was established in 2002 by former managers of Barrett Resources (which was acquired by The Williams Companies in 2001). The company went public in 2004.

In 2007, in order to raise cash for core property investments, the company sold its oil and gas properties in the Williston Basin for $81.4 million.

EXECUTIVES

Chairman and CEO: Fredrick J. (Fred) Barrett, age 48, $1,959,411 total compensation
President, COO, and Director: Joseph N. (Joe) Jaggers, age 55, $2,239,696 total compensation
CFO and Treasurer: Bob Howard, age 54, $1,452,563 total compensation
EVP, General Counsel, and Secretary: Francis B. Barron, age 47, $1,088,412 total compensation
EVP Exploration: Kurt M. Reinecke, age 50
SVP Operations: R. Scot Woodall, age 47, $975,818 total compensation
SVP Geophysics: Wilfred R. (Roy) Roux, age 51
SVP Government and Regulatory Affairs: Duane J. Zavadil, age 49
SVP Land: Huntington T. Walker, age 53
SVP Rockies Exploration: Terry R. Barrett, age 49
VP Information Systems: Kevin M. Finnegan, age 49
VP Accounting: David R. Macosko, age 47
VP Finance: William M. Crawford, age 47
Director Investor Relations: Jennifer Martin
Auditors: Deloitte & Touche LLP

LOCATIONS

HQ: Bill Barrett Corporation
1099 18th St., Ste. 2300, Denver, CO 80202
Phone: 303-293-9100   **Fax:** 303-291-0420
Web: www.billbarrettcorp.com

PRODUCTS/OPERATIONS

2008 Sales

	% of total
EnCana Oil & Gas	17
Sempra Energy Trading	17
Other customers	66
Total	**100**

2008 Sales

	$ mil.	% of total
Oil & gas production	605.9	98
Commodity derivative gain	7.9	1
Other	4.1	1
Total	**617.9**	**100**

COMPETITORS

Abraxas Petroleum
Delta Petroleum
Double Eagle Petroleum
EnCana Oil & Gas (USA) Inc.
Occidental Petroleum
Teton Energy

HISTORICAL FINANCIALS

Company Type: Public

Income Statement

FYE: December 31

	REVENUE ($ mil.)	NET INCOME ($ mil.)	NET PROFIT MARGIN	EMPLOYEES
12/08	617.9	107.6	17.4%	274
12/07	390.3	26.8	6.9%	252
12/06	375.3	62.0	16.5%	216
12/05	288.8	23.8	8.2%	190
12/04	170.0	(5.3)	—	150
Annual Growth	38.1%	—	—	16.3%

2008 Year-End Financials

Debt ratio: 39.2%
Return on equity: 11.6%
Cash ($ mil.): 43.1
Current ratio: 1.39
Long-term debt ($ mil.): 426.5
No. of shares (mil.): 45.5

Dividends
  Yield: 0.0%
  Payout: —
Market value ($ mil.): 961.0
R&D as % of sales: —
Advertising as % of sales: —

Stock History

NYSE: BBG

	STOCK PRICE ($) FY Close	P/E High/Low		PER SHARE ($) Earnings	Dividends	Book Value
12/08	21.13	28	6	2.39	0.00	23.92
12/07	41.87	82	41	0.60	0.00	17.01
12/06	27.21	29	16	1.40	0.00	16.63
12/05	38.61	77	47	0.55	0.00	13.87
12/04	31.99	—	—	(15.40)	0.00	13.63
Annual Growth	(9.8%)	—	—	—	—	15.1%

BioClinica, Inc.

BioClinica (formerly Bio-Imaging Technologies) helps drug developers keep track of their X-rays, MRIs, and other forms of medical imaging collected during clinical drug and medical device trials. The company provides medical imaging support services including image processing and analysis, digitizing, archival services, and database maintenance. Its proprietary software systems, including Bio/ImageBase, let clients and regulatory officials electronically review images and related data. The company's eClinical Services division provides electronic data capture for large drug developers. BioClinica serves clients primarily in the US and Europe; its European operations are based in the Netherlands.

BioClinica primarily serves companies conducting Phase I-IV clinical trials on drugs treatments for cancer, cardiovascular disease, central nervous system disorders, and musculoskeletal disease — therapeutic areas that generally require greater use of medical imaging. The company also works with clients that are developing new diagnostic imaging agents.

In 2007 BioClinica expanded its European operations through the acquisition of France-based

Theralys, including its proprietary imaging processing software and imaging services specializing in CNS and neurovascular disorders. Then, in 2008 it acquired privately held Phoenix Data Systems, a provider of electronic data capture services and online clinical data management products to drug and medical device companies. Phoenix Data Systems formed the core of BioClinica's eClinical Services business.

BioClinica sold its CapMed division (personal health records management software), to Metavante in 2009. The sale freed up the company's attention to focus on its medical image management and electronic data capture services. The company then changed its name from Bio-Imaging Technologies to BioClinica to reflect the expansion of its services.

Briefly in 2009 BioClinica agreed to acquire clinical trial software provider etrials Worldwide, but the deal was canceled after etrials received a higher offer from Merge Healthcare. The acquisition would have expanded the firm's product offerings for drug and medical equipment trial clients.

Later that year the company bought Tourtellotte, a software support company for the pharmaceutical industry, for about $2 million. Tourtellotte's software allows biopharmaceutical companies to simulate the clinical trial process to increase efficiency by viewing possible roadblocks ahead of time.

Covance, a leading contract research organization (CRO), owns about 15% of BioClinica.

EXECUTIVES

Chairman: David E. Nowicki, age 57
President, CEO, and Director: Mark L. Weinstein, age 56, $734,869 total compensation
EVP; President, eClinical Division: Peter S. Benton, age 44
EVP; President, Bioimaging Services: David A. Pitler, age 54, $444,854 total compensation
EVP Finance and Administration, CFO, and Secretary: Ted I. Kaminer, age 50, $507,631 total compensation
SVP and Managing Director, European Headquarters: John Blank
SVP Medical Affairs: Colin G. Miller, age 48, $381,215 total compensation
SVP Global Business Development: Mark Endres
VP Finance: Ivan Joseph
VP Clinical Operations and Medical Director: Andrea M. Perrone
VP Business Development and Clinical Affairs, US: Igor Grachev
VP and Corporate Controller: Maria Kraus
VP Client Services: Dawn Flitcraft
VP Technical Services: Andrew (Andy) Reiter, age 54
VP Marketing: Jim Dorsey
Director Human Resources: Carmella Miller
Auditors: PricewaterhouseCoopers LLP

LOCATIONS

HQ: BioClinica, Inc.
826 Newtown-Yardley Rd., Newtown, PA 18940
Phone: 267-757-3000 **Fax:** 267-757-3010
Web: www.bioclinica.com

PRODUCTS/OPERATIONS

2008 Revenues

	$ mil.	% of total
Service revenues	56.2	81
Reimbursement revenues	12.9	19
Total	**69.1**	**100**

COMPETITORS

DATATRAK International
eResearchTechnology
Kendle
PAREXEL
Pharmaceutical Product Development
Synarc

HISTORICAL FINANCIALS

Company Type: Public

Income Statement

FYE: December 31

	REVENUE ($ mil.)	NET INCOME ($ mil.)	NET PROFIT MARGIN	EMPLOYEES
12/08	69.1	2.8	4.1%	474
12/07	47.9	2.3	4.8%	337
12/06	40.5	1.0	2.5%	283
12/05	30.5	(2.5)	—	264
12/04	29.7	0.9	3.0%	269
Annual Growth	**23.5%**	**32.8%**	**—**	**15.2%**

2008 Year-End Financials

Debt ratio: 0.1%
Return on equity: 8.4%
Cash ($ mil.): 14.3
Current ratio: 1.33
Long-term debt ($ mil.): 0.1
No. of shares (mil.): 14.4
Dividends
Yield: 0.0%
Payout: —
Market value ($ mil.): 52.7
R&D as % of sales: —
Advertising as % of sales: —

Stock History

NASDAQ (GM): BIOC

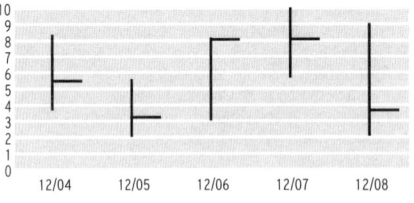

	STOCK PRICE ($) FY Close	P/E High/Low		PER SHARE ($) Earnings	Dividends	Book Value
12/08	3.66	47	11	0.19	0.00	3.02
12/07	8.08	55	32	0.18	0.00	1.63
12/06	8.06	101	39	0.08	0.00	1.31
12/05	3.23	—	—	(0.23)	0.00	1.19
12/04	5.48	104	47	0.08	0.00	1.36
Annual Growth	**(9.6%)**	**—**	**—**	**24.1%**	**—**	**22.1%**

BioMarin Pharmaceutical

BioMarin Pharmaceuticals works to raise orphan drugs up right. The company has developed three FDA-approved drugs that qualify for orphan drug status, a financial incentive that encourages companies to create drugs for rare diseases by giving the compounds a period of market exclusivity. BioMarin's Aldurazyme (co-developed with Genzyme) treats the life-threatening inherited condition MPS I, caused by a rare enzyme deficiency. Its drug Naglazyme is approved in the US and Europe to treat another rare genetic disease called MPS VI.

BioMarin's drug Kuvan is the only drug approved to treat phenylketonuria (PKU), an enzyme deficiency which prevents patients from metabolizing certain proteins.

BioMarin developed and sells Aldurazyme through a joint venture with Genzyme. Under the agreement, BioMarin manufactures the drug, and Genzyme markets it worldwide. BioMarin uses its own sales force to market Naglazyme in the US, Europe, and other international markets. It also markets Kuvan in the US where it was approved in 2007; Merck Serono markets the drug in Europe.

Since a relatively small number of people have the diseases treated by BioMarin's products, it sells mainly to specialty pharmacies and hospitals, rather than to large wholesalers like McKesson. In markets where it doesn't have its own sales force, BioMarin sells through distributors.

The company has several investigational drugs in its pipeline, including a second PKU treatment (dubbed PEG-PAL). Merck Serono is the company's development partner for PEG-PAL, which is designed for PKU patients who don't respond to Kuvan. Other BioMarin drug candidates in clinical and preclinical development include possible treatments for cardiovascular disease and genetic conditions.

To expand its pipeline, in 2009 BioMarin swapped $7.5 million for stock in La Jolla Pharmaceutical to obtain the rights to develop and commercialize its lupus drug candidate Riquent. However, shortly after the ink dried on the deal, a late-stage trial of the drug showed poor results and was halted. BioMarin sold its 15% ownership of La Jolla and walked away a bit poorer. The company had better results with a deal it struck with drug developer Summit Corporation. What began as a 2008 licensing agreement turned into a complete asset purchase in 2009 of Summit's drug candidate in development to treat Duchenne muscular dystrophy.

Like all drug development companies, BioMarin has a constant need for capital infusion and is wondering how it will rustle up enough during difficult economic times.

EXECUTIVES

Chairman: Pierre Lapalme, age 68
CEO and Director: Jean-Jacques (J.J.) Bienaimé, age 55, $4,999,668 total compensation
SVP and Chief Medical Officer: Henry J. (Hank) Fuchs, age 51
SVP and CFO: Jeffrey H. (Jeff) Cooper, age 53, $1,113,390 total compensation
SVP Global Commercial Operations: Stephen J. (Steve) Aselage, age 58, $1,372,719 total compensation
SVP Technical Operations: Robert A. Baffi, age 54, $1,265,190 total compensation
VP Human Resources: Mark Wood, age 43
VP Intellectual Property: Luisa Bigornia
VP Global Marketing: Lewis P. Chapman
VP Research: Gordon Vehar
VP Regulatory and Government Affairs: Amy Waterhouse
VP Sales and Marketing Operations: Jeff Ajer, age 47
VP Technology and CIO: Eduardo E. Von Pervieux
VP Business and Corporate Development: Joshua A. Grass
VP, General Counsel, and Secretary: G. Eric Davis, age 38
VP and Controller: Brian Mueller
Senior Manager Investor Relations: Eugenia Shen
Auditors: KPMG LLP

LOCATIONS

HQ: BioMarin Pharmaceutical Inc.
105 Digital Dr., Novato, CA 94949
Phone: 415-506-6700   **Fax:** 415-382-7889
Web: www.biomarinpharm.com

2008 Sales

	% of total
US	56
Europe	25
Latin America	10
Other	9
Total	**100**

PRODUCTS/OPERATIONS

2008 Sales

	$ mil.	% of total
Product sales		
Naglazyme	132.7	45
Aldurazyme	72.5	24
Kuvan	46.7	16
Collaborative agreements	38.9	13
Royalties & licensing fees	5.7	2
Total	**296.5**	**100**

Selected Products

Approved
  Aldurazyme (MPS I)
  Kuvan (phenylketonuria, or PKU)
  Naglazyme (MPS VI)

In Development
  6R-BH4 (hypertension)
  GALNS (MPS IVA)
  PEG-PAL (phenylketonuria)

COMPETITORS

Aldagen
Amicus Therapeutics
Applied Genetic Technologies
Enzon
Metagenics
Shire

HISTORICAL FINANCIALS

Company Type: Public

Income Statement

FYE: December 31

	REVENUE ($ mil.)	NET INCOME ($ mil.)	NET PROFIT MARGIN	EMPLOYEES
12/08	296.5	30.8	10.4%	649
12/07	121.6	(15.8)	—	525
12/06	84.2	(28.5)	—	410
12/05	25.7	(74.3)	—	314
12/04	18.6	(187.4)	—	359
Annual Growth	**99.8%**	**—**	**—**	**16.0%**

2008 Year-End Financials

Debt ratio: 179.7%
Return on equity: 13.3%
Cash ($ mil.): 222.9
Current ratio: 5.67
Long-term debt ($ mil.): 497.1
No. of shares (mil.): 100.7
Dividends
  Yield: 0.0%
  Payout: —
Market value ($ mil.): 1,793.0
R&D as % of sales: —
Advertising as % of sales: —

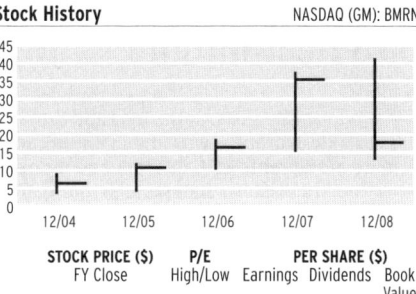

Stock History				NASDAQ (GM): BMRN

	STOCK PRICE ($) FY Close	P/E High/Low		PER SHARE ($) Earnings	Dividends	Book Value
12/08	17.80	141	46	0.29	0.00	2.75
12/07	35.40	—	—	(0.16)	0.00	1.86
12/06	16.39	—	—	(0.34)	0.00	1.17
12/05	10.78	—	—	(1.08)	0.00	(0.77)
12/04	6.39	—	—	(2.91)	0.00	(0.67)
Annual Growth	**29.2%**	**—**	**—**	**—**	**—**	**—**

Bio-Reference Laboratories

Bio-Reference Laboratories has tested positive as the lab of choice for many in the Northeast. Primarily serving the greater New York Metropolitan Area, the company offers routine clinical tests, including Pap smears, pregnancy tests, cholesterol checks, and blood cell counts. Through its GenPath business unit, it also performs more sophisticated "esoteric" testing such as cancer pathology and molecular diagnostics. It gets most of its orders (about 4.1 million per year) from doctors' offices, collecting specimens at draw stations scattered throughout its primary service area in the New York area. Bio-Reference Laboratories also has facilities in Connecticut, Delaware, Maryland, New Jersey, and Pennsylvania.

The company's laboratory service in the New York Metro area is its core business, but it has expanded its geographic reach through acquisitions, particularly in the area of specialty testing. In 2006, for instance, it bought Diagnostic Pathology Services, a Maryland-based anatomic pathology lab serving the mid-Atlantic states.

Its key acquisition that year, however, was its purchase of GeneDx, which specializes in diagnosing rare genetic disorders using DNA sequencing technology. GeneDx serves customers both in the US and abroad. In 2007 it launched its GenomeDx service, a full-genome test used to diagnose, among other things, developmental disorders such as mental retardation.

The company's specialty testing operations have been growing at a faster clip than its core routine testing business, but routine lab tests still account for half of the company's sales.

Doctors can place orders for lab tests and get test results using the company's proprietary CareEvolve online portal. Outside of its customer relationships with doctors' offices, Bio-Reference Laboratories serves government agencies and large employers (for substance abuse testing, for instance) and prison systems in the northeastern US.

Another Bio-Reference unit, PSIMedica, makes health informatics software that combines information from health care claims, lab results, and other sources and markets it to managed care organizations. Its CareEvolve subsidiary markets the company's online connectivity software to other laboratories. However, revenues from PSIMedica and CareEvolve have been negligible as a percentage of the company's overall sales.

Founder, chairman, and CEO Marc Grodman owns more than 10% of the company.

HISTORY

Marc Grodman founded Med-Mobile in 1981, offering mobile medical examination services. In 1987 it opened a clinical laboratory in New Jersey. The purchase of Cytology and Pathology Associates, a small, specialized lab, followed in 1988. Demand for tests rose, leading the company to relocate all operations to a modern lab near New York City. It renamed itself Bio-Reference Laboratories in 1989 and went public in 1993.

The company moved into specialty testing to compensate for the industry-wide drop in reimbursement rates that hit its general labs, acquiring GenCare Biomedical Research (cancer testing, 1995), Oncodec Labs (gene mutations, 1995), and SmithKline Beecham's renal dialysis testing business (1996). Late in 1996 the firm sued SmithKline Beecham, accusing it of fraud regarding the purchase.

In 1997 the company sold part of its GenCare oncology laboratory services division to IMPATH. To build its regional presence, the company acquired Medilabs from Long Term Care in 1998. The next year it ventured into new frontiers, opening and acquiring Web sites for online ventures and buying the Right Body Foods health foods business. In 2000 Bio-Reference Laboratories expanded its Internet presence (including a business-to-business Web portal for health care professionals, CareEvolve.com) and re-entered the oncology market, resuming full service testing to physicians and institutions.

EXECUTIVES

Chairman, President, and CEO: Marc D. Grodman, age 58
EVP, COO, and Director: Howard Dubinett, age 58
SVP, CFO, Chief Accounting Officer, and Director: Sam Singer Sr., age 66
SVP: Azmy Awad
SVP and Director Operations: Warren Erdmann
SVP: Scott Fein
SVP Sales and Marketing: Charles T. Todd Jr., age 59
VP and Chief Medical Officer: James Weisberger, age 54
VP Genpath: Maryanne Amato
VP Accounts Receivable: Sally Howlett
VP Financial Operations: Nicholas Papazicos
VP and Director Operations: Nick Cetani
CIO; President, PsiMedica: Richard L. Faherty, age 63
President, CareEvolve: Cory Fishkin
Co-President and Scientific Director, GeneDx: John Compton, age 62
President and Clinical Director, GeneDX: Sherri Bale
Investor Relations Coordinator: Tara Mackay
Auditors: Moore Stephens, P.C.

LOCATIONS

HQ: Bio-Reference Laboratories, Inc.
481 Edward H. Ross Dr., Elmwood Park, NJ 07407
Phone: 201-791-2600   **Fax:** 201-791-1941
Web: www.bioreference.com

PRODUCTS/OPERATIONS

2008 Sales

	% of total
Routine testing	50
Esoteric testing	50
Total	**100**

Selected Products and Services

Routine testing
- Blood cell counts
- Cholesterol levels
- HIV tests
- Pap smears
- Pregnancy tests
- Substance abuse tests
- Urinalysis

Esoteric testing
- Endocrinology
- Genetics
- Immunology
- Microbiology
- Oncology
- Serology
- Toxicology

Other
- CareEvolve (physician-based connectivity portal for clinical laboratories)
- PSIMedica Clinical Knowledge Management System (health informatics software)

COMPETITORS

American Bio Medica	LabCorp
Athena Diagnostics	MEDTOX Laboratories
Genzyme Genetics	Quest Diagnostics
Kroll Background	

HISTORICAL FINANCIALS

Company Type: Public

Income Statement
FYE: October 31

	REVENUE ($ mil.)	NET INCOME ($ mil.)	NET PROFIT MARGIN	EMPLOYEES
10/08	301.1	15.6	5.2%	1,907
10/07	250.4	14.0	5.6%	1,648
10/06	193.1	11.3	5.9%	1,551
10/05	163.9	7.6	4.6%	1,276
10/04	136.2	8.5	6.2%	1,156
Annual Growth	**21.9%**	**16.4%**	**—**	**13.3%**

2008 Year-End Financials

Debt ratio: 8.6%
Return on equity: 16.7%
Cash ($ mil.): 12.7
Current ratio: 1.96
Long-term debt ($ mil.): 8.8
No. of shares (mil.): 13.8

Dividends
  Yield: 0.0%
  Payout: —
Market value ($ mil.): 340.0
R&D as % of sales: —
Advertising as % of sales: —

Stock History
NASDAQ (GS): BRLI

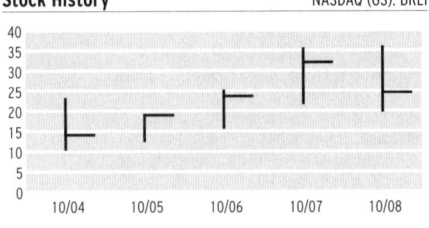

	STOCK PRICE ($) FY Close	P/E High/Low		PER SHARE ($) Earnings	Dividends	Book Value
10/08	24.59	32	18	1.12	0.00	7.34
10/07	32.08	35	22	1.01	0.00	6.17
10/06	23.63	29	19	0.85	0.00	4.97
10/05	18.96	33	22	0.58	0.00	3.67
10/04	14.07	34	16	0.67	0.00	2.94
Annual Growth	**15.0%**	**—**	**—**	**13.7%**	**—**	**25.7%**

BJ's Restaurants

The Windy City inspires the food and drink at BJ's. BJ's Restaurants owns and operates more than 80 restaurants in California and a dozen other mostly Western states under the names BJ's Restaurant & Brewhouse, BJ's Restaurant & Brewery, and BJ's Pizza & Grill. The casual-dining eateries offer Chicago-style pizza, salads, sandwiches, pasta, and the company's own handcrafted beers. Its dozen Restaurant & Brewery locations, which feature an onsite microbrewery, help supply beer to the rest of the chain. Holding company The Jacmar Companies owns more than 15% of the company.

BJ's has aggressively expanded its restaurant chain the past few years, opening 15 new restaurants during 2008, up from about a dozen locations the year previous. It is focused on making its Restaurant & Brewhouse format its flagship concept. The economic recession, though, has hurt sales at many of its restaurants, especially those in California and Arizona where the housing market has been especially hard hit.

In addition to being a major shareholder, Jacmar Companies owns restaurant supply business Jacmar Foodservice Distribution, a major supplier of BJ's locations. It also owns family pizza chain Shakey's USA.

EXECUTIVES

Chairman, President, and CEO:
  Gerald W. (Jerry) Deitchle, age 58, $742,326 total compensation
EVP, CFO, and Secretary: Gregory S. (Greg) Levin, age 42, $590,488 total compensation
EVP and Chief Restaurant Operations Officer:
  Wayne L. Jones, age 50
EVP and Chief Development Officer:
  Gregory S. (Greg) Lynds, age 48, $510,883 total compensation
Chief Marketing Officer: Matthew W. (Matt) Hood
Chief Supply Chain Officer: John D. Allegretto, age 46, $461,101 total compensation
SVP Brewing Operations: Alexander M. (Alex) Puchner, age 48
SVP Restaurant Operations: Lon F. Ledwith, age 52
VP Information Services: Brian Pearson
VP Operational Support and Restaurant Openings:
  Nanette McWhertor
VP Accounting and Controller: Rana G. Schirmer
VP Restaurant Facilities: Donald M. (Don) Gardner Jr.
VP Culinary Development: Raymond G. (Ray) Martin
President, BJ's Restaurants Foundation:
  Robert (Rob) DeLiema
Director Corporate Relations: Dianne Scott
Auditors: Ernst & Young LLP

LOCATIONS

HQ: BJ's Restaurants, Inc.
  7755 Center Ave., Ste. 300
  Huntington Beach, CA 92647
Phone: 714-500-2400
Web: www.bjsbrewhouse.com

2008 Locations

	No.
California	44
Texas	13
Arizona	5
Florida	4
Colorado	3
Nevada	2
Ohio	2
Oklahoma	2
Oregon	2
Washington	2
Indiana	1
Kentucky	1
Louisiana	1
Total	**82**

COMPETITORS

Applebee's
Brinker
California Pizza Kitchen
Carlson Restaurants
Darden
Elephant Bar
Gordon Biersch
Jerry's Famous Deli
Johnny Rockets
OSI Restaurant Partners
Pat & Oscars
Rock Bottom Restaurants
Round Table Pizza
Ruby Tuesday
Uno Restaurants

HISTORICAL FINANCIALS

Company Type: Public

Income Statement
FYE: Tuesday nearest December 31

	REVENUE ($ mil.)	NET INCOME ($ mil.)	NET PROFIT MARGIN	EMPLOYEES
12/08	374.1	10.3	2.8%	9,200
12/07	316.1	11.7	3.7%	8,610
12/06	238.9	9.8	4.1%	6,546
12/05	178.2	8.4	4.7%	5,424
12/04	129.0	6.3	4.9%	4,003
Annual Growth	**30.5%**	**13.1%**	**—**	**23.1%**

2008 Year-End Financials

Debt ratio: 4.1%
Return on equity: 4.5%
Cash ($ mil.): 8.9
Current ratio: 0.65
Long-term debt ($ mil.): 9.5
No. of shares (mil.): 26.8

Dividends
  Yield: 0.0%
  Payout: —
Market value ($ mil.): 288.4
R&D as % of sales: —
Advertising as % of sales: —

Stock History
NASDAQ (GS): BJRI

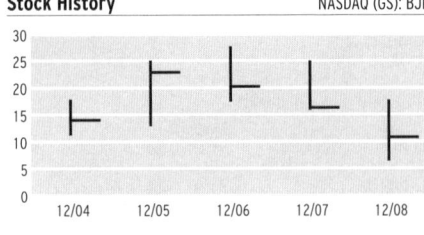

	STOCK PRICE ($) FY Close	P/E High/Low		PER SHARE ($) Earnings	Dividends	Book Value
12/08	10.77	45	17	0.39	0.00	8.68
12/07	16.26	56	37	0.44	0.00	8.24
12/06	20.21	67	43	0.41	0.00	7.58
12/05	22.86	69	36	0.36	0.00	4.85
12/04	14.00	59	38	0.30	0.00	2.94
Annual Growth	**(6.3%)**	**—**	**—**	**6.8%**	**—**	**31.0%**

Black Hills Corporation

Black Hills is alive with the sound of energy. Its Black Hills Power utility unit distributes electricity to 69,000 customers in Montana, South Dakota, and Wyoming, while its Cheyenne Light Fuel & Power unit serves 39,800 electric customers and 33,300 natural gas customers in the greater Cheyenne area. Its Black Hills Energy segment serves 524,000 natural gas customers in Colorado, Iowa, Kansas, and Nebraska, and 93,300 electricity customers in Colorado. Black Hills' power plants produce more than 1,000 MW a year. The company's wholesale segment is engaged in coal mining, power generation, oil and gas production (185.4 billion cu. ft. of natural gas reserves in 2008), and energy marketing.

In 2008 Black Hills greatly expanded its utility business, acquiring Aquila's electric and gas utility operations in Colorado, Kansas, Nebraska, and Iowa for $940 million.

Over the past few years Black Hills has divested a number of other businesses in order to focus on beefing up its core energy distribution and transmission operations. In 2008 it sold seven independent power production gas-fired plants (with a total capacity of 974 MW) for $840 million to affiliates of Hastings Funds Management Ltd and IIF BH Investment LLC in order to raise funds for its Aquila purchase. The deal came on the heels of several other disposals of non-core assets by Black Hills. This included the sale of its broadband communications business (Black Hills FiberCom, with 26,000 regional customers) in 2005. In 2006 Black Hills sold its Black Hills Energy Resources oil marketing unit to a subsidiary of Sunoco Logistics Partners for $41 million.

EXECUTIVES

Chairman, President, and CEO: David R. Emery, age 46, $1,709,354 total compensation
President and COO, Non-regulated Energy: Thomas M. (Tom) Ohlmacher, age 57, $846,025 total compensation
President and COO, Utilities: Linden R. (Linn) Evans, age 46, $639,976 total compensation
EVP and CFO: Anthony S. Cleberg, age 56, $225,670 total compensation
SVP, General Counsel, and Chief Compliance Officer: Steven J. Helmers, age 52, $561,609 total compensation
SVP and CIO: Scott A. Buchholz, age 47
SVP Communications and Investor Relations: Lynnette K. Wilson, age 49
SVP Human Resources: Robert A. (Bob) Myers, age 51
VP Governance and Secretary: Roxann R. Basham, age 47
VP, Natural Gas Utilities: Steve Pella
VP, Electric Utilities: Stuart Wevik
VP Strategic Planning and Development: Richard W. Kinzley, age 43
VP Customer Service, Utilities: Randy Winkleman
VP and Controller: Jeffrey B. Berzina
VP Supply Chain: Perry S. Krush, age 49
VP, Treasurer, and Chief Risk Officer: Garner M. Anderson, age 46
VP Regulatory and Governmental Affairs: Kyle D. White, age 49
Director Investor Relations: Jason Ketchum
Auditors: Deloitte & Touche LLP

LOCATIONS

HQ: Black Hills Corporation
625 9th St., Rapid City, SD 57701
Phone: 605-721-1700   **Fax:** 605-721-2599
Web: www.blackhillscorp.com

PRODUCTS/OPERATIONS

2008 Sales

	$ mil.	% of total
Utilities		
Electric utility	472.2	47
Electric & gas utility	277.1	27
Non-regulated energy		
Oil & gas	106.3	11
Energy marketing	59.3	6
Power generation	38.0	4
Coal mining	31.8	3
Corporate & other	21.1	2
Total	**1,005.8**	**100**

COMPETITORS

Alliant Energy
Basin Electric Power
Bonneville Power
BP
Chevron
Dominion Resources
Dynegy
Energy West
Exxon Mobil
IDACORP
MDU Resources
Noble Energy
Otter Tail
Questar
Samson Oil
Southern Company
Vulcan Energy
Xcel Energy

HISTORICAL FINANCIALS

Company Type: Public

Income Statement

FYE: December 31

	REVENUE ($ mil.)	NET INCOME ($ mil.)	NET PROFIT MARGIN	EMPLOYEES
12/08	1,005.8	105.1	10.4%	2,122
12/07	695.9	98.8	14.2%	998
12/06	656.9	81.0	12.3%	819
12/05	1,391.6	33.4	2.4%	803
12/04	1,121.7	58.0	5.2%	926
Annual Growth	**(2.7%)**	**16.0%**	**—**	**23.0%**

2008 Year-End Financials

Debt ratio: 47.7%
Return on equity: 10.4%
Cash ($ mil.): 168.5
Current ratio: 0.64
Long-term debt ($ mil.): 501.3
No. of shares (mil.): 38.9
Dividends
  Yield: 5.2%
  Payout: 50.9%
Market value ($ mil.): 1,047.8
R&D as % of sales: —
Advertising as % of sales: —

Stock History

NYSE: BKH

	STOCK PRICE ($) FY Close	P/E High/Low	PER SHARE ($) Earnings	Dividends	Book Value
12/08	26.96	16 8	2.75	1.40	27.03
12/07	44.10	17 13	2.64	1.37	24.95
12/06	36.94	16 13	2.42	1.32	20.33
12/05	34.61	45 29	1.00	1.28	19.01
12/04	30.68	18 15	1.76	1.24	18.93
Annual Growth	**(3.2%)**	**— —**	**11.8%**	**3.1%**	**9.3%**

Blackbaud, Inc.

Blackbaud's customers aren't in it for the cash, but that doesn't mean they can't use some financial help. Blackbaud provides financial, fundraising, and administrative software for not-for-profit organizations and educational institutions. Its software includes The Raiser's Edge for fundraising management, The Financial Edge for accounting, and The Education Edge for managing school admissions, registration, and billing. Blackbaud has about 22,000 customers in 55 countries, including colleges, environmental groups, health and human services providers, churches, and animal welfare groups.

The company's strategy includes expanding its international operations; Blackbaud currently has international offices in Canada, the UK, and Australia.

Blackbaud acquired eTapestry, a software-as-a-service provider focused on fundraising tools for the nonprofit sector, for about $25 million in 2007, as well as Target Software. The following year it purchased chief competitor Kintera for $46 million in cash.

EXECUTIVES

President, CEO, and Director: Marc E. Chardon, age 53, $2,551,006 total compensation
SVP, CFO, Treasurer, and Assistant Secretary: Timothy V. (Tim) Williams, age 60, $813,642 total compensation
SVP and President, Target Software Division: Lee W. Gartley, age 45
SVP Products and Services: Charles T. (Charlie) Cumbaa, age 56, $774,542 total compensation
SVP Customer Support: Gerard J. (Jerry) Zink, age 45, $699,300 total compensation
SVP, Controller, Assistant Treasurer, and Assistant Secretary: Heidi H. Strenck, age 39
SVP and CEO, Kintera Division: Richard N. (Rich) LaBarbera, age 60
SVP Human Resources: John J. Mistretta, age 53
SVP Sales and Marketing and Chief Commercial Officer: Kevin W. Mooney, age 51
SVP Products: Louis J. (Lou) Attanasi, age 47, $712,800 total compensation
VP, General Counsel, and Corporate Secretary: Andrew L. (Andy) Howell, age 42
Chief Scientist: Charles L. (Chuck) Longfield, age 52
Public Relations Manager: Melanie Mathos
Director Corporate Relations and Philanthropy: Rachel Hutchisson
Auditors: PricewaterhouseCoopers LLP

LOCATIONS

HQ: Blackbaud, Inc.
2000 Daniel Island Dr., Charleston, SC 29492
Phone: 843-216-6200   **Fax:** 843-216-6100
Web: www.blackbaud.com

PRODUCTS/OPERATIONS

2008 Sales

	$ mil.	% of total
Maintenance	107.3	35
Services	100.8	33
Subscriptions	49.7	17
License fees	36.0	12
Other	8.7	3
Total	**302.5**	**100**

Selected Products

Accounting software
The Financial Edge (nonprofit accounting software)

Analytical services
ProspectPoint (custom modeling service)
WealthPoint (wealth identification and information service)

Business intelligence software
The Information Edge (business intelligence software for not-for-profits)

Education administration software
Admissions Office
Education Administration (school administration suite)
The Education Edge (admissions, registrar, business office, and development office software)
Registrar's Office
School Store Manager
Student Billing

Fundraising management software
MatchFinder (database of corporate gift-matching program information)
NetSolutions (online application for organizing fundraising and volunteers)
The Raiser's Edge (fundraising management system)

COMPETITORS

Acorn Systems	MicroEdge
Advanced Solutions	Microsoft
Auctionpay	Oracle
Convio	Sage Software
Intuit	SunGard

HISTORICAL FINANCIALS

Company Type: Public

Income Statement

FYE: December 31

	REVENUE ($ mil.)	NET INCOME ($ mil.)	NET PROFIT MARGIN	EMPLOYEES
12/08	302.5	29.9	9.9%	1,977
12/07	257.0	31.7	12.3%	1,655
12/06	192.0	30.5	15.9%	1,165
12/05	166.3	33.3	20.0%	1,014
12/04	138.7	12.6	9.1%	880
Annual Growth	21.5%	24.1%	—	22.4%

2008 Year-End Financials

Debt ratio: 1.6%	Dividends
Return on equity: 29.4%	Yield: 3.0%
Cash ($ mil.): 16.4	Payout: 58.8%
Current ratio: 0.49	Market value ($ mil.): 596.2
Long-term debt ($ mil.): 1.5	R&D as % of sales: —
No. of shares (mil.): 44.2	Advertising as % of sales: —

Stock History

NASDAQ (GS): BLKB

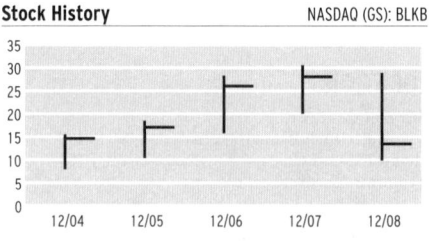

	STOCK PRICE ($) FY Close	P/E High/Low		PER SHARE ($) Earnings	Dividends	Book Value
12/08	13.50	42	15	0.68	0.40	2.05
12/07	28.04	43	29	0.71	0.34	2.56
12/06	26.00	41	24	0.68	0.28	2.20
12/05	17.08	25	15	0.72	0.20	1.50
12/04	14.64	56	31	0.27	0.00	2.03
Annual Growth	(2.0%)	—	—	26.0%	—	0.2%

Blackboard Inc.

Chalk up Blackboard's success to the Internet. Blackboard develops software that enables schools to create Internet-based learning programs and communities. The company's software connects teachers, students, parents, and administrators via the Web, enabling Internet-based assignments, class Web sites, and online collaboration with classmates. The software also assists instructors with course administration and includes a content management system for creating and managing digital course content. Blackboard's software includes transaction, community, and payment management tools that enable students to use their college IDs for meal plans, event access, and tuition payments.

The company expanded its product lines and customer base in 2008-2009 with two major acquisitions: ANGEL Learning and The NTI Group.

Its Blackboard Connect product line (which is used for the rapid dissemination of critical information via voice and text devices) stemmed from the purchase of NTI, which itself was renamed Blackboard Connect Inc. after the acquisition.

Postsecondary schools are Blackboard's primary market, and the company continues to focus on increasing its penetration of this market. While the company derives most of its sales from customers in the US, Blackboard is also targeting international colleges and universities as a market for further growth.

Blackboard has clients in more than 60 countries, and in addition to its core base of postsecondary education clients, the company counts K-12 schools, government agencies, educational publishers, and commercial education providers among its customers.

Most of Blackboard's sales come from local installations of its software for its clients, but the company also offers its software as hosted, Internet-based applications.

EXECUTIVES

Chairman: Matthew L. Pittinsky, age 37
President, CEO, and Director: Michael L. Chasen, age 38, $3,137,809 total compensation
CFO and Treasurer: Michael J. Beach, age 38, $1,412,055 total compensation
Chief Business Officer, Chief Legal Officer, and Secretary: Matthew H. Small, age 36, $1,317,958 total compensation
SVP Client Success: Craig Chanoff
SVP Product Development: Jessica Finnefrock
SVP Treasury and Corporate Affairs: Michael Stanton
SVP Finance: John Kinzer
VP Finance and Accounting: Jonathan R. Walsh, age 36, $516,217 total compensation
President, Blackboard Learn Higher Education: C. Russ Carlson
President, Blackboard Learn International: Juan Lucca
President, Blackboard Learn Professional Education: Timothy L. (Tim) Hill
President, Blackboard Learn K-12: Jessie Woolley-Wilson, age 44
President and COO, Blackboard Learn: Judy Verses
President and COO, Blackboard Transact: David Marr
President and COO, Blackboard Connect: Thomas Motter
Director Public Relations: Matthew Maurer
Auditors: Ernst & Young LLP

LOCATIONS

HQ: Blackboard Inc.
1899 L St. NW, 11th Fl., Washington, DC 20036
Phone: 202-463-4860 **Fax:** 202-463-4863
Web: www.blackboard.com

2008 Sales

	$ mil.	% of total
US	251.2	80
Other countries	60.9	20
Total	**312.1**	**100**

PRODUCTS/OPERATIONS

2008 Sales

	$ mil.	% of total
Products	283.3	91
Professional services	28.8	9
Total	**312.1**	**100**

COMPETITORS

Arel Communications and Software
ARTEL
The CBORD Group
Datatel
Diebold
eCollege.com
Jenzabar
Microsoft
Morrison Consulting
Pearson Education
SunGard Higher Education

HISTORICAL FINANCIALS

Company Type: Public

Income Statement

FYE: December 31

	REVENUE ($ mil.)	NET INCOME ($ mil.)	NET PROFIT MARGIN	EMPLOYEES
12/08	312.1	2.8	0.9%	1,087
12/07	239.4	12.9	5.4%	890
12/06	183.1	(10.7)	—	765
12/05	135.7	41.9	30.9%	549
12/04	111.4	10.0	9.0%	481
Annual Growth	29.4%	(27.3%)	—	22.6%

2008 Year-End Financials

Debt ratio: 60.7%	Dividends
Return on equity: 1.2%	Yield: 0.0%
Cash ($ mil.): 141.7	Payout: —
Current ratio: 1.21	Market value ($ mil.): 853.7
Long-term debt ($ mil.): 163.2	R&D as % of sales: —
No. of shares (mil.): 32.5	Advertising as % of sales: —

Stock History

NASDAQ (GS): BBBB

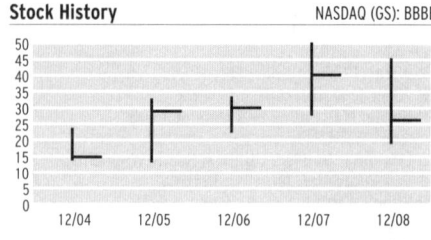

	STOCK PRICE ($) FY Close	P/E High/Low		PER SHARE ($) Earnings	Dividends	Book Value
12/08	26.23	500	215	0.09	0.00	8.25
12/07	40.25	116	65	0.43	0.00	5.67
12/06	30.04	—	—	(0.39)	0.00	4.31
12/05	28.98	22	9	1.47	0.00	4.00
12/04	14.81	111	67	0.21	0.00	2.12
Annual Growth	15.4%	—	—	(19.1%)	—	40.4%

BNC Bancorp

BNC Bancorp knows the ABCs of the financial world. The firm is the holding company for Bank of North Carolina, which has about a dozen bank branches and loan offices in central and northeastern portions of the state. The bank offers community-oriented services to local business and retail customers, providing checking, savings, and money market accounts, credit cards, and CDs. Its loan portfolio is mainly composed of residential and commercial mortgages and construction loans. Bank of North Carolina also offers insurance, retirement planning, and other investment products and services. BNC Bancorp acquired Greensboro, North Carolina-based SterlingSouth Bank & Trust in late 2006.

EXECUTIVES

Chairman of the Board: Thomas R. Sloan, age 64
Chairman Emeritus: W. Groome Fulton Jr., age 70
President, CEO, and Director; President and CEO, Bank of North Carolina: W. Swope Montgomery Jr., age 60, $638,607 total compensation
EVP and CFO BNC and Bank of North Carolina: David B. Spencer, age 46, $365,600 total compensation
EVP, COO, and Director; EVP and COO, Bank of North Carolina: Richard D. Callicutt II, age 50, $401,545 total compensation
SVP and City Executive, Lexington, Bank of North Carolina: William H. McMurray III, $267,655 total compensation
SVP, Bank of North Carolina: Thomas N. Nelson, $235,571 total compensation
Secretary and Director: Richard F. Wood, age 65
Auditors: Cherry, Bekaert & Holland, LLP

LOCATIONS

HQ: BNC Bancorp
831 Julian Ave., Thomasville, NC 27360
Phone: 336-476-9200 **Fax:** 336-476-5818
Web: www.bankofnc.com

PRODUCTS/OPERATIONS

2008 Gross Revenues

	$ mil.	% of total
Interest		
Loans, including fees	64.8	85
Debt securities	5.7	7
Other	0.5	1
Noninterest		
Service charges	3.0	4
Mortgage fees	0.8	1
Other	1.8	2
Total	**76.6**	**100**

COMPETITORS

Bank of America
Bank of the Carolinas
BB&T
Carolina Bank
First Bancorp (NC)
First Citizens BancShares
FNB United
NewBridge Bancorp
Piedmont Federal
RBC Bank
Southern Community Financial
Wells Fargo

HISTORICAL FINANCIALS

Company Type: Public

Income Statement

FYE: December 31

	ASSETS ($ mil.)	NET INCOME ($ mil.)	INCOME AS % OF ASSETS	EMPLOYEES
12/08	1,572.9	4.0	0.3%	222
12/07	1,130.1	7.4	0.7%	223
12/06	951.7	6.2	0.7%	193
12/05	594.5	4.5	0.8%	142
12/04	497.5	3.8	0.8%	126
Annual Growth	**33.3%**	**1.3%**	**—**	**15.2%**

2008 Year-End Financials

Equity as % of assets: 5.7%
Return on assets: 0.3%
Return on equity: 4.6%
Long-term debt ($ mil.): 105.7
No. of shares (mil.): 7.3
Market value ($ mil.): 55.1
Dividends
  Yield: 2.7%
  Payout: 38.5%
Sales ($ mil.): 39.3
R&D as % of sales: —
Advertising as % of sales: —

Stock History

NASDAQ (CM): BNCN

	STOCK PRICE ($) FY Close	P/E High/Low		PER SHARE ($) Earnings	Dividends	Book Value
12/08	7.51	33	13	0.52	0.20	16.44
12/07	16.91	20	15	1.05	0.18	11.77
12/06	18.58	20	16	0.95	0.15	9.88
12/05	16.86	20	14	0.88	0.12	4.51
12/04	13.09	18	15	0.75	0.10	3.96
Annual Growth	**(13.0%)**	**—**	**—**	**(8.7%)**	**18.9%**	**42.8%**

Boardwalk Pipeline

Boardwalk Pipeline Partners is in the business of interstate transportation, gathering, and storage of natural gas, and operates three subsidiaries — Texas Gas Transmission, Gulf South Pipeline Company, and Gulf Crossing Pipeline Company — with a combined 14,200 miles of pipeline in 11 states. Texas Gas operates in Arkansas, Illinois, Indiana, Kentucky, Louisiana, Mississippi, Ohio, Tennessee, and Texas. Gulf South operates in Alabama, Florida, Louisiana, Mississippi, and Texas. Customers include local gas distribution companies, local governments, other interstate and intrastate pipeline companies, industrial users, and electric power generators. Boardwalk Pipeline Partners is owned by Loews Corporation.

In 2008 the company's pipeline systems shipped about 1.7 trillion cu. ft. of natural gas. Its eleven natural gas storage facilities in four states reported an aggregate gas capacity of 160 billion cu. ft.

Boardwalk Pipeline Partners' strategy is to expand its pipeline and storage assets organically and by making acquisitions that complement its existing portfolio.

Expanding its interstate pipeline operations, in 2009 the company opened the Gulf Crossing Pipeline (350 miles of 42-inch pipeline) which originates near Sherman, Texas, and supplies gas from the Barnett Shale and Caney Woodford Shale plays to end users in the Midwest, Northeast, and Southeast.

EXECUTIVES

Chairman, Boardwalk GP, LLC: Arthur L. Rebell, age 68
CEO and Director, Boardwalk GP, LLC: Rolf A. Gafvert, age 55
COO, Boardwalk GP LLC: Brian A. Cody, age 52
SVP, CFO, and Treasurer: Jamie L. Buskill, age 44
SVP, General Counsel, and Secretary: Michael E. McMahon, age 54
VP, Controller, and Chief Accounting Officer: Steven Barkauskas
Director Investor Relations: Allison McLean
Auditors: Deloitte & Touche LLP

LOCATIONS

HQ: Boardwalk Pipeline Partners, LP
9 Greenway Plaza, Ste. 2800, Houston, TX 77046
Phone: 713-479-8000
Web: www.boardwalkpipelines.com

PRODUCTS/OPERATIONS

2008 Sales

	$ mil.	% of total
Gas transportation	698.2	89
Gas storage	51.5	7
Parking & lending	16.3	2
Other	18.8	2
Total	**784.8**	**100**

COMPETITORS

Columbia Gulf Transmission
El Paso
Energy Future
Florida Gas Transmission
Southwest Gas
Williams Gas Pipeline

HISTORICAL FINANCIALS

Company Type: Public

Income Statement

FYE: December 31

	REVENUE ($ mil.)	NET INCOME ($ mil.)	NET PROFIT MARGIN	EMPLOYEES
12/08	784.8	294.0	37.5%	1,128
12/07	643.3	220.7	34.3%	1,084
12/06	607.6	197.6	32.5%	1,150
12/05	560.5	100.9	18.0%	1,100
12/04	263.6	48.8	18.5%	—
Annual Growth	**31.4%**	**56.7%**	**—**	**0.8%**

2008 Year-End Financials

Debt ratio: —
Return on equity: —
Cash ($ mil.): 137.7
Current ratio: 1.04
Long-term debt ($ mil.): 2,889.4
No. of shares (mil.): 192.6
Dividends
  Yield: 10.5%
  Payout: 103.9%
Market value ($ mil.): 3,424.2
R&D as % of sales: —
Advertising as % of sales: —

Stock History

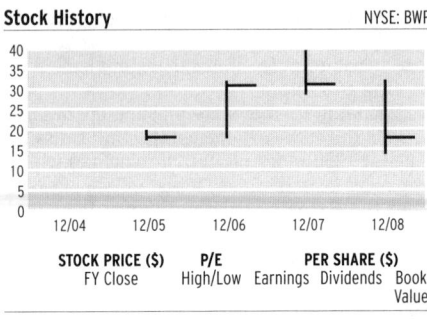

	STOCK PRICE ($) FY Close	P/E High/Low		PER SHARE ($) Earnings	Dividends	Book Value
12/08	17.78	18	8	1.80	1.87	—
12/07	31.10	21	15	1.91	1.74	9.36
12/06	30.82	17	10	1.85	1.32	6.61
12/05	17.98	—	—	—	0.00	5.13
Annual Growth	(0.4%)	—	—	(1.4%)	—	18.2%

BofI Holding

BofI Holding owns Bank of Internet USA, a savings bank that operates online in all 50 states. The bank offers checking, savings, and money market accounts, CDs, and ATM and check cards. Multifamily real estate loans account for nearly two-thirds of the company's loan portfolio, although the bank only offers them in selected states; it also acquires them on the secondary market. Offered nationwide, single-family residential mortgages make up nearly 30% of its loan portfolio. Bank of Internet USA also issues home equity, automobile, and recreational vehicle loans. Officers and directors own more than 30% of BofI Holding's stock.

EXECUTIVES

Chairman: Theodore C. (Ted) Allrich, age 63
President and CEO: Gregory Garrabrants, age 38
SVP and CFO: Andrew J. Micheletti, age 50
VP and CTO, Bank of Internet USA:
Michael J. (Mike) Berengolts, age 37
VP Internet Development: Barbara Fronek
Auditors: Crowe Horwath LLP Grand Rapids

LOCATIONS

HQ: BofI Holding, Inc.
12777 High Bluff Dr., Ste. 100
San Diego, CA 92130
Phone: 858-350-6200   **Fax:** 858-350-0443
Web: www.bofiholding.com

PRODUCTS/OPERATIONS

2009 Gross Revenues

	$ mil.	% of total
Interest		
Loans, including fees	41.8	52
Investments	36.0	45
Noninterest		
Total realized gain (loss) on sale of securities	(5.1)	—
Total unrealized loss on securities	(3.5)	—
Mortgage banking & other	1.9	3
Total	**71.1**	**100**

COMPETITORS

Allstate Bank	ING DIRECT
Bank of America	ISN Bank
Citigroup	UnionBanCal
E*TRADE Bank	WebFinancial
First IB	

HISTORICAL FINANCIALS

Company Type: Public

Income Statement

FYE: June 30

	ASSETS ($ mil.)	NET INCOME ($ mil.)	INCOME AS % OF ASSETS	EMPLOYEES
6/09	1,302.2	6.5	0.5%	57
6/08	1,194.2	4.2	0.4%	44
6/07	947.2	3.0	0.3%	40
6/06	737.8	2.9	0.4%	26
6/05	609.5	2.5	0.4%	26
Annual Growth	20.9%	27.0%	—	21.7%

2009 Year-End Financials

Equity as % of assets: 6.1%
Return on assets: 0.5%
Return on equity: 8.5%
Long-term debt ($ mil.): 263.0
No. of shares (mil.): 8.2
Market value ($ mil.): 49.7
Dividends
 Yield: 0.0%
 Payout: —
Sales ($ mil.): 29.7
R&D as % of sales: —
Advertising as % of sales: —

Stock History

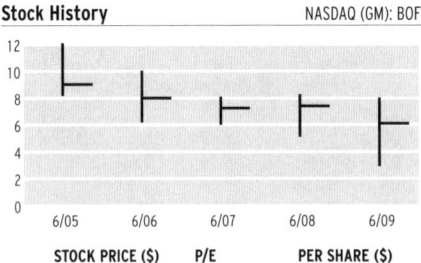

	STOCK PRICE ($) FY Close	P/E High/Low		PER SHARE ($) Earnings	Dividends	Book Value
6/09	6.09	10	4	0.78	0.00	10.89
6/08	7.39	18	11	0.46	0.00	10.18
6/07	7.24	22	17	0.36	0.00	8.91
6/06	7.99	29	18	0.34	0.00	8.60
6/05	9.04	30	21	0.40	0.00	8.41
Annual Growth	(9.4%)	—	—	18.2%	—	6.7%

Boston Beer

A half-pint compared to megabrewers like Anheuser-Bush InBev, The Boston Beer Company holds the distinction of being America's largest microbrewer. It produces some 30 seasonal and year-round varieties of craft-brewed beers at its Cincinnati and Boston breweries. Annually, it sells almost 2 million barrels of lager (such as its flagship Samuel Adams Boston Lager), ales (other Samuel Adams brands), HardCore brand cider, and Twisted Tea malt beverages. The company distributes its brews primarily in the US, but they are also sold in Canada, the Caribbean, Europe, Israel, and the Pacific Rim countries. Chairman C. James Koch owns some 32% of the company; investment firm Neuberger Berman owns about 12%.

In order to keep adventurous drinkers brand-loyal, Boston Beer offers new brews and discon-

tinues others. Along with Sam Adams Light, the company also offers Extreme Beers, including Utopia, a limited-release $100-a-bottle brew that is 25% alcohol. Its seasonal brews include Summer Ale, Octoberfest, and Old Fezziwig.

In addition to production at its breweries in Boston and Cincinnati, the company contracts out production to brewers, among them MillerCoors and High Falls Brewing. Boston Beer products are distributed through independent distributors and are available at pubs, restaurants, stadiums, grocery chains, package stores, and other retail outlets.

In 2007 the company announced a brewing agreement with City Brewing to brew some of City's Latrobe brand beer. In order to add to its brewing capacity for its Samuel Adams brand, in 2008 Boston Beer acquired Pennsylvania Brewery from Diageo North America for $55 million.

Chairman C. James Koch owns approximately 33% of the company; investment firm Barclay's Global Investors owns about 10%.

HISTORY

Management consultant James Koch started The Boston Beer Company with his former secretary, Rhonda Kallman, in 1983. With Koch's $100,000 in life savings plus $300,000 raised from family and friends, the company contracted with Pittsburgh Brewing to make beer using Koch's great-great-grandfather's recipe. (Louis Koch had brewed beer in Germany before opening a St. Louis brewery in 1860.)

Koch and Kallman launched their premium beer in Boston in 1985, and four years later Boston Beer contracted with Blitz-Weinhard Brewing in Oregon to make beer for distribution in the western US.

The company's rise to the top of the small hop-meister heap was driven by Koch's earnest radio spots and by the quality of the product. Boston Beer went public in 1995 while the craft-brewing sector was booming, but by 1997 the market stopped growing, soggy with competing brands.

Using recipes gleaned from a home-brewing contest, the company briefly brewed the Long-Shot line of beers in 1996. The next year Boston Beer moved into the fledgling alcoholic cider market with HardCore Cider, and it purchased a small-batch brewery in Koch's hometown of Cincinnati. In 1998 Boston Beer expanded distribution to Japan and Australia, while 1999 saw the introduction of Millennium Ale.

In 2000 Boston Beer launched BoDean's Twisted Tea, a malt-and-tea-based beverage. In 2001 president Martin Roper was named CEO, succeeding Koch, who remains chairman.

In 2002 Boston Beer began selling its first light beer, Sam Adams Light, in most of its top US markets. The following year the company broke records with its 25% alcohol Utopia brew, and a year later introduced Chocolate Bock. These joined Millennium and Triple Bock under the heading Extreme Beers. Limited edition Samuel Adams Chocolate Bock, which uses Scharffen Berger Chocolate, was introduced in 2004.

EXECUTIVES

Chairman: C. James (Jim) Koch, age 59,
$490,812 total compensation
President, CEO, and Director: Martin F. Roper, age 46,
$2,753,253 total compensation
CFO and Treasurer: William F. Urich, age 52,
$739,141 total compensation
VP Operations: Thomas W. Lance, age 55,
$804,141 total compensation

VP Sales: John C. Geist, age 48,
$579,280 total compensation
VP Brewing: David A. Grinnell, age 51
VP Brand Development: Robert H. Hall, age 48,
$626,255 total compensation
General Counsel: Frederick H. Grein Jr.
Director Information Technology: Frank Wiggins
Director Human Resources: Amy Waryas
Shareholder Relations Manager: Helen Bornemann
Corporate Controller: Matthew Murphy
Auditors: Ernst & Young LLP

LOCATIONS

HQ: The Boston Beer Company, Inc.
1 Design Center, Ste. 850, Boston, MA 02110
Phone: 617-368-5000   **Fax:** 617-368-5500
Web: www.bostonbeer.com

PRODUCTS/OPERATIONS

Selected Brands

Brewmaster's collection
Samuel Adams Black Lager
Samuel Adams Boston Ale
Samuel Adams Brown Ale
Samuel Adams Cherry Wheat
Samuel Adams Cream Stout
Samuel Adams Hefeweizen
Samuel Adams Honey Porter
Samuel Adams Pale Ale

Flagship beers
Samuel Adams Boston Lager
Sam Adams Light

Hard cider
HardCore Crisp Hard Cider

Limited-edition beers
Samuel Adams Chocolate Bock
Samuel Adams Imperial Pilsner
Samuel Adams Triple Bock
Samuel Adams Utopias

Flavored malt beverages
Twisted Tea Half Hard Iced Tea & Half Hard Lemonade
Twisted Tea Hard Iced Tea
Twisted Tea Light
Twisted Tea Peach Hard Iced Tea
Twisted Tea Raspberry Hard Iced Tea

Seasonal beers
Samuel Adams Double Bock
Samuel Adams Octoberfest
Samuel Adams Summer Ale
Samuel Adams White Ale
Samuel Adams Winter Lager

COMPETITORS

Anchor Brewing	Massachusetts Bay Brewing
Anheuser-Busch InBev	Michigan Brewing
Asahi Breweries	MillerCoors
Bacardi	New Belgium Brewing
Carlsberg	Pabst
Craft Brewers Alliance	Pyramid Breweries
Diageo	Rheingold
Grupo Modelo	Rogue Ales
Heineken USA	Shipyard Brewing
High Falls Brewing	Sierra Nevada
Kirin Brewery of America	Sprecher
Lancaster Brewing Co.	Stoudt's Brewing
Lion Brewery	Victory Brewing
Magic Hat Brewing	Weyerbacher Brewing

HISTORICAL FINANCIALS
Company Type: Public

Income Statement
FYE: Last Saturday in December

	REVENUE ($ mil.)	NET INCOME ($ mil.)	NET PROFIT MARGIN	EMPLOYEES
12/08	398.4	8.1	2.0%	775
12/07	341.6	22.5	6.6%	500
12/06	285.4	18.2	6.4%	433
12/05	238.3	15.6	6.5%	390
12/04	217.2	12.5	5.8%	370
Annual Growth	16.4%	(10.3%)	—	20.3%

2008 Year-End Financials

Debt ratio: —
Return on equity: 5.9%
Cash ($ mil.): 9.1
Current ratio: 1.03
Long-term debt ($ mil.): —
No. of shares (mil.): 14.3

Dividends
Yield: 0.0%
Payout: —
Market value ($ mil.): 404.8
R&D as % of sales: —
Advertising as % of sales: —

Stock History
NYSE: SAM

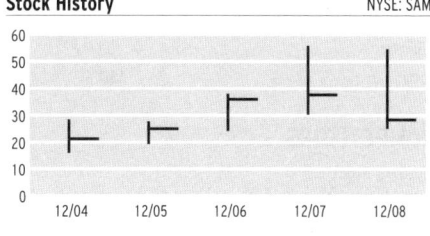

	STOCK PRICE ($) FY Close	P/E High/Low	PER SHARE ($) Earnings	Dividends	Book Value
12/08	28.40	97 46	0.56	0.00	9.82
12/07	37.65	36 20	1.53	0.00	9.37
12/06	35.98	30 19	1.27	0.00	7.62
12/05	25.00	25 19	1.07	0.00	6.03
12/04	21.27	33 19	0.86	0.00	5.50
Annual Growth	7.5%	— —	(10.2%)	—	15.6%

BreitBurn Energy Partners

Oil and gas futures burn brightly for BreitBurn Energy Partners, one of California's largest independent exploration and production companies. With assets in Antrim Shale (Michigan), the Los Angeles Basin, the Wind River and Big Horn Basins (both in Wyoming), the Sunniland Trend (Florida), the New Albany Shale (Indiana and Kentucky), and the Permian Basin (West Texas), in 2008 the company reported estimated proved reserves of 103.6 million barrels of oil equivalent (78% of which were located in Michigan). In 2008 Canada's Provident Energy Trust sold its 96% stake in BreitBurn Energy Partners to Metalmark Capital, Greenhill Capital Partners, and BreitBurn managers for $305 million.

BreitBurn Energy Partners is pursuing a strategy of acquiring long-lived assets with relatively low-risk exploitation and development opportunities. The company is investing heavily in its high-potential Antrim Shale assets in Michigan, and drilled 116 wells there in 2008.

In 2007 the company acquired Quicksilver Resources (which had oil and gas properties and facilities in Michigan, Indiana, and Kentucky) for $750 million.

BreitBurn Energy Partners' predecessor was founded in 1998 by Randall Breitenbach and Halbert Washburn. Breitenbach and Washburn serve as co-CEOs of BreitBurn Energy Partners' general partner, BreitBurn GP LLC.

EXECUTIVES

Chairman and Co-CEO: Halbert S. (Hal) Washburn, age 47
Co-CEO and Director: Randall H. (Randy) Breitenbach, age 48
COO: Mark L. Pease, age 52
EVP and CFO: James G. Jackson, age 44
EVP and General Counsel: Gregory C. Brown, age 57
SVP Production Operations and Western Division: Chris E. Williamson, age 51
VP Geosciences and Eastern Division: Dwayne T. Stewart, age 38
VP Business Development: W. Jackson Washburn, age 46
VP Eastern Region: David D. Baker, age 36
Controller: Lawrence C. Smith, age 55
Treasurer: Bruce D. McFarland, age 52
Auditors: PricewaterhouseCoopers LLP

LOCATIONS

HQ: BreitBurn Energy Partners L.P.
515 S. Flower St., Ste. 4800, Los Angeles, CA 90071
Phone: 213-225-5900   **Fax:** 213-225-5916
Web: www.breitburn.com

PRODUCTS/OPERATIONS

2008 Sales

	$ mil.	% of total
Oil, natural gas & NGLs	467.4	58
Gains on derivatives	332.1	42
Other	2.9	—
Total	**802.4**	**100**

COMPETITORS

Aera Energy
Atlas Energy Resources
Aurora Oil & Gas
Berry Petroleum
Bill Barrett
Chevron
DTE
Windsor Energy Resources

HISTORICAL FINANCIALS
Company Type: Public

Income Statement
FYE: December 31

	REVENUE ($ mil.)	NET INCOME ($ mil.)	NET PROFIT MARGIN	EMPLOYEES
12/08	802.4	378.2	47.1%	395
12/07	75.0	(60.4)	—	335
12/06	133.0	49.3	37.1%	150
12/05	101.9	39.0	38.3%	146
12/04	31.6	9.7	30.7%	—
Annual Growth	124.5%	149.9%	—	39.3%

2008 Year-End Financials

Debt ratio: —
Return on equity: —
Cash ($ mil.): 2.5
Current ratio: 1.76
Long-term debt ($ mil.): 736.0
No. of shares (mil.): 52.8

Dividends
Yield: 21.8%
Payout: 24.5%
Market value ($ mil.): 372.1
R&D as % of sales: —
Advertising as % of sales: —

Stock History

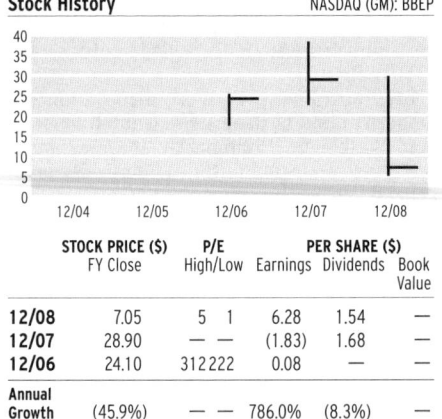

NASDAQ (GM): BBEP

	STOCK PRICE ($) FY Close	P/E High/Low	PER SHARE ($) Earnings	PER SHARE ($) Dividends	PER SHARE ($) Book Value
12/08	7.05	5 1	6.28	1.54	—
12/07	28.90	— —	(1.83)	1.68	—
12/06	24.10	312 222	0.08	—	—
Annual Growth	(45.9%)	— —	786.0%	(8.3%)	—

Bridge Bancorp

Bridge Bancorp wants you to cross over to its subsidiary The Bridgehampton National Bank, which operates more than a dozen locations in eastern Long Island, New York. Founded in 1910, the bank offers traditional deposit services to area individuals, small businesses, and municipalities, including checking, savings, and money market accounts, and CDs. Deposits are invested primarily in mortgages, which account for some 80% of the bank's loan portfolio. Title insurance services are available through bank subsidiary Bridge Abstract; wealth management services include financial planning, estate administration, and trustee services.

The bank opened three new branches in 2007 and continues to expand its geographic footprint westward.

Individual investor Patrick Malloy is the only single beneficial owner of Bridge Bancorp with about a 5% stake; a group of 11 officers and board members owns approximately 8%.

EXECUTIVES

Chairperson, Bridge Bancorp and Bridgehampton National Bank: Marcia Z. Hefter, age 65
Vice Chairperson: Dennis A. Suskind, age 66
President, CEO, and Director: Kevin M. O'Connor, age 46, $428,123 total compensation
SEVP, CFO, Chief Administrative Officer, Secretary, and Director: Howard H. Nolan, age 48, $425,549 total compensation
SVP and Chief Lending Officer, Bridgehampton National Bank: Kevin L. Santacroce, $316,784 total compensation
SVP and Director of Human Resources: Deborah McGrory
SVP and Corporate Secretary; VP and Director Marketing, Bridgehampton National Bank: Sandra K. Novick
SVP and CIO, Bridgehampton National Bank: Thomas H. Simson
VP and Director Risk Management, Bridgehampton National Bank: Maureen P. Mougios
VP and Senior Lending Officer, North Fork Market Area, Bridgehampton National Bank: Peter M. (Pete) Coleman
VP and Director of Internal Audit, Bridgehampton National Bank: Diane Murray

VP and Manager, Bridge Abstract: Steven Bodziner
VP and Chief Administration, Bridgehampton National Bank: John R. Blasi
VP and Commercial Lending Officer, Bridgehampton National Bank: Kimberly Cioch

LOCATIONS

HQ: Bridge Bancorp, Inc.
 2200 Montauk Hwy., Bridgehampton, NY 11932
Phone: 631-537-1000   **Fax:** 631-537-1835
Web: www.bridgenb.com

PRODUCTS/OPERATIONS

2008 Gross Revenues

	$ mil.	% of total
Interest		
Loans	28.0	61
Mortgage-backed securities	8.4	19
Other	3.2	7
Noninterest		
Service charges on deposit accounts	3.1	7
Other customer services fees	1.8	4
Title fees	1.1	2
Other	0.1	—
Total	**45.7**	**100**

COMPETITORS

Bank of America
Bank of New York Mellon
JPMorgan Chase
Smithtown Bancorp
State Bancorp
Suffolk Bancorp

HISTORICAL FINANCIALS

Company Type: Public

Income Statement

FYE: December 31

	ASSETS ($ mil.)	NET INCOME ($ mil.)	INCOME AS % OF ASSETS	EMPLOYEES
12/08	839.1	8.8	1.0%	175
12/07	607.4	8.3	1.4%	157
12/06	573.6	8.2	1.4%	123
12/05	533.4	9.6	1.8%	120
12/04	547.2	10.4	1.9%	115
Annual Growth	11.3%	(4.1%)	—	11.1%

2008 Year-End Financials

Equity as % of assets: —
Return on assets: 1.2%
Return on equity: —
Long-term debt ($ mil.): 30.0
No. of shares (mil.): 6.2
Market value ($ mil.): 115.3
Dividends
 Yield: 5.0%
 Payout: 64.3%
Sales ($ mil.): 36.2
R&D as % of sales: —
Advertising as % of sales: —

Stock History

NASDAQ (GS): BDGE

	STOCK PRICE ($) FY Close	P/E High/Low	PER SHARE ($) Earnings	PER SHARE ($) Dividends	PER SHARE ($) Book Value
12/08	18.50	17 12	1.43	0.92	9.01
12/07	24.30	19 17	1.36	0.92	8.20
12/06	24.00	20 17	1.33	0.92	7.31
12/05	24.70	22 16	1.53	0.91	7.49
12/04	30.60	21 14	1.64	0.72	7.58
Annual Growth	(11.8%)	— —	(3.4%)	6.3%	4.4%

Bridgepoint Education

Bridgepoint Education invites students from all walks to cross on over to the educated side. The for-profit company offers associate's, bachelor's, master's, and doctoral programs at its Ashford University (Iowa) and University of the Rockies (Colorado) campuses and online. Academic disciplines include business, education, psychology, and health services. Most of the company's campus-based revenues are derived from federal financial aid. More than 95% of Bridgeport Education's 42,000-plus registered students are enrolled exclusively online; the schools have a 29-to-1 student/faculty ratio. Hoping to take advantage of the growing market for online and nontraditional schools, the company went public in 2009.

Much like a community college, Bridgepoint appeals to students who might find tuition costs, credit transfer, or work schedules to be barriers to traditional universities. The company is also seeking to increase its student base by offering programs for corporate employees and military personnel. Both universities work with employers offering education reimbursement programs, and Ashford University has a grant program offering a 30% tuition discount to General Motors, Chrysler, and Ford employees seeking undergraduate degrees. In addition, Ashford University offers educational opportunities to active-duty personnel in US armed forces branches (US Army, Marine Corps, Navy, Air Force, Coast Guard) with special tuition rates, waived fees, and free books and shipping costs. Nearly 20% of students are with the military.

The IPO filing came on the heels of the public offerings of education companies China Distance Education Holdings and Grand Canyon Education. Bridgepoint will use its raised funds to pay investors and for general corporate purposes. Principal investor Warburg Pincus retained ownership of more than half of Bridgepoint's shares after the IPO.

Ashford University was founded in 1918 as Mount St. Clare College by the Sisters of St. Francis. It became The Franciscan University in 2002 and was purchased in 2005 by Bridgepoint, which changed the university's name. In 2007 Bridgepoint acquired University of the Rockies (formerly Colorado School of Professional Psychology), which offers graduate degrees in psychology.

EXECUTIVES

CEO and Director: Andrew S. Clark, age 44
SVP and CFO: Daniel J. (Dan) Devine, age 45
CTO: Rick Gessner
SVP and Chief Admissions Officer: Christopher L. (Chris) Spohn, age 49
SVP and General Counsel: Diane Thompson, age 54
SVP and Chief Information Officer: Thomas (Tom) Ashbrook, age 45
SVP and Chief Academic Officer: Jane McAuliffe, age 43
SVP and Chief Administrative Officer: Rodney T. (Rocky) Sheng, age 43
SVP and Chief Marketing Officer: Ross Woodard, age 44
SVP, Corporate Development: Wayne Clugston
SVP, Human Resources: Charlene Dackerman, age 49
VP and President, University of the Rockies: Charlita Shelton
VP, University Services: Sheri Jones
VP and Senior Corporate Attorney: Robert Wernli Jr.
VP, Corporate Communications: Diane Salucci
VP and Controller: Brandon Pope
Auditors: PricewaterhouseCoopers LLP

LOCATIONS

HQ: Bridgepoint Education, Inc.
13500 Evening Creek Dr. North, Ste. 600
San Diego, CA 92128
Phone: 858-668-2586   **Fax:** 858-408-2903
Web: www.bridgepointeducation.com

PRODUCTS/OPERATIONS

2008 Student Enrollment

	No.	% of total
Online	29,786	98
Campus-based	761	2
Total	**30,547**	**100**

2008 Enrollment by Degree Type

	No.	% of total
Bachelor's	25,563	84
Associate's	2,554	8
Master's	2,174	7
Doctoral	60	—
Other	196	1
Total	**30,547**	**100**

Selected Programs

Associate of Arts
 Business
Bachelor of Arts
 Accounting
 Communication Studies
 Computer Graphic Design
 Elementary Education
 Health Care Administration
 Social and Criminal Justice
 Social Science
 Sociology
Bachelor of Science
 Biology
 Clinical Cytotechnology
 Health Science Administration
Bachelor of Applied Science
 Accounting Core
 Computer Graphic Design Core
Doctorate
 Psychology
  Clinical Psychology
  Non-Profit Management
Master of Arts
 Organizational Management
 Psychology
  Executive Coaching
  Organizational Leadership
Master of Business Administration

COMPETITORS

American Public Education
Apollo Group
Capella Education
Corinthian Colleges
DeVry
Grand Canyon Education
Lincoln Educational Services
Strayer Education

HISTORICAL FINANCIALS

Company Type: Public

Income Statement

FYE: December 31

	REVENUE ($ mil.)	NET INCOME ($ mil.)	NET PROFIT MARGIN	EMPLOYEES
12/08	218.3	26.4	12.1%	1,200
12/07	85.7	3.3	3.9%	2,800
12/06	28.6	(5.2)	—	—
12/05	8.0	(8.0)	—	—
Annual Growth	**201.1%**	**—**	**—**	**(57.1%)**

2008 Year-End Financials

Debt ratio: 7.7%
Return on equity: —
Cash ($ mil.): 56.5
Current ratio: 1.08
Long-term debt ($ mil.): 0.5

Net Income History

NYSE: BPI

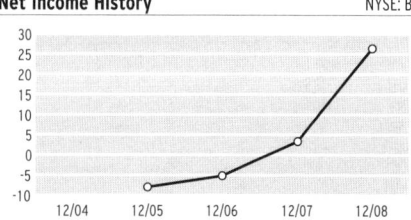

Broadway Financial

This company won't quit 'til it's a star! Broadway Financial is the holding company for Broadway Federal Bank, a savings and loan which serves the low- and moderate-income minority neighborhoods of central and south-central Los Angeles and nearby Inglewood. Through about a half-dozen branches and loan offices, the bank primarily originates multi-family (about 40% of its loan portfolio) and commercial real estate loans (another 40%). These loans are secured primarily by multi-family dwellings and properties used for business and religious purposes. Deposit products include CDs and savings, checking, money market, and NOW accounts.

Cathay General Bancorp, First Financial Fund, and CEO Paul Hudson are all beneficial owners of Broadway Financial stock, with an approximate 12%, 7%, and 5% share, respectively.

EXECUTIVES

Chairman and CEO, Broadway Financial and Broadway Federal Bank: Paul C. Hudson, age 60, $365,871 total compensation
President and COO: Wayne-Kent A. Bradshaw, age 62
SVP and CFO, Broadway Financial and Broadway Federal Bank: Sam Sarpong, age 48, $247,238 total compensation
SVP and Chief Loan Officer: Wilbur A. McKesson Jr., age 55, $236,841 total compensation
First VP and Director Internal Audit: Emmanuel Boateng
First VP Controller: Mildred Cayton
VP and Director Wealth Management: Wayne Standback
VP and Senior Credit Officer: Godwin Segbefia
VP and Training Manager: Robin Kynard
VP and Chief Credit Officer: Susan Mackey
Network Administrator, Information Technology: Greg Demus
Chief Funding Officer: Anita Reed
Human Resources: Kim Johnson
Corporate Secretary: Daniele Johnson
Public Relations: Karen E. Hudson

LOCATIONS

HQ: Broadway Financial Corporation
4800 Wilshire Blvd., Los Angeles, CA 90010
Phone: 323-634-1700   **Fax:** 323-634-1717
Web: www.broadwayfederalbank.com

PRODUCTS/OPERATIONS

2008 Gross Revenues

	$ mil.	% of total
Interest		
Loans receivable	23.7	87
Mortgage-backed securities	1.4	5
Other	0.4	2
Noninterest		
Service charges	1.2	4
Other	0.5	2
Adjustments	(0.3)	—
Total	**26.9**	**100**

COMPETITORS

Bank of America
Cathay General Bancorp
City National
Comerica
East West Bancorp
Nara Bancorp
UnionBanCal
Wilshire Bancorp

HISTORICAL FINANCIALS

Company Type: Public

Income Statement

FYE: December 31

	ASSETS ($ mil.)	NET INCOME ($ mil.)	INCOME AS % OF ASSETS	EMPLOYEES
12/08	407.9	2.3	0.6%	91
12/07	356.8	1.5	0.4%	84
12/06	301.0	1.7	0.6%	72
12/05	292.3	1.7	0.6%	56
12/04	276.5	1.7	0.6%	69
Annual Growth	**10.2%**	**7.8%**	**—**	**7.2%**

2008 Year-End Financials

Equity as % of assets: 5.8%
Return on assets: 0.6%
Return on equity: 10.1%
Long-term debt ($ mil.): 80.0
No. of shares (mil.): 1.7
Market value ($ mil.): 6.7
Dividends
 Yield: 3.9%
 Payout: 12.7%
Sales ($ mil.): 15.7
R&D as % of sales: —
Advertising as % of sales: —

Stock History

NASDAQ (CM): BYFC

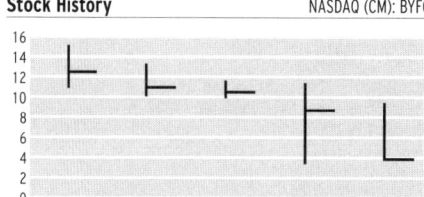

	STOCK PRICE ($) FY Close	P/E High/Low		Earnings	PER SHARE ($) Dividends	Book Value
12/08	3.84	8	3	1.18	0.15	18.75
12/07	8.69	15	5	0.74	0.20	12.65
12/06	10.50	13	11	0.90	0.20	11.49
12/05	10.95	13	10	1.00	0.20	9.62
12/04	12.49	15	11	0.99	0.19	8.66
Annual Growth	**(25.5%)**	**—**	**—**	**4.5%**	**(5.7%)**	**21.3%**

Brooklyn Federal Bancorp

Brooklyn Federal Bancorp won't sell you a bridge, but it might loan you money to build one yourself. It's the holding company for Brooklyn Federal Savings Bank, which has been operating since 1887. As one might expect, the thrift operates in the New York City area, with two branches in Brooklyn and two on Long Island. It provides traditional deposit and loan services to area individuals and businesses and focuses on real estate lending: Commercial mortgages make up more than 40% of the company's loan portfolio, which also includes one- to four-family home mortgages (more than 30%), multifamily residential loans (about 15%), and construction loans.

Brooklyn Federal Bancorp has been writing more commercial mortgages and construction loans. Those loans represented about a quarter of the company's loan book in 2001 but were up to nearly 50% by 2007.

Mutual holding company BFS Bancorp owns about 70% of Brooklyn Federal Bancorp.

EXECUTIVES

President and CEO: Richard A. Kielty, age 62
SVP and Chief Lending Officer: Marc Leno
SVP and Loan Servicing Officer: Marilyn Alberici
VP and CFO: Ralph Walther
VP and Residential Mortgage Officer: Edward Bolmarcich
VP and Retail Banking Officer: Salvatore Gargaro
VP and Retail Banking Administrator: Rosemary Demeo
Assistant VP and Loan Servicing Manager: Natalya Khandros
Assistant VP and Assistant Financial Officer: Joseph Raucci
Assistant VP and Commercial Loan Officer: Richard Maher
Assistant VP and Assistant Controller: Erica Minott
Auditors: Beard Miller Company LLP

LOCATIONS

HQ: Brooklyn Federal Bancorp, Inc.
81 Court St., Brooklyn, NY 11201
Phone: 718-855-8500   **Fax:** 718-858-5174
Web: www.brooklynbank.com

PRODUCTS/OPERATIONS

2009 Gross Revenues

	$ mil.	% of total
Interest		
First mortgage & other loans	30.1	83
Mortgage-backed securities	3.7	10
Other securities & interest-earning assets	0.3	1
Noninterest		
Banking fees & service charges	1.4	4
Net gain on sale of loans held for sale	0.3	1
Net loss on OTTI securities	(2.9)	—
Other	0.5	1
Total	**33.4**	**100**

COMPETITORS

Apple Bank	Emigrant Bank
Astoria Financial	First of Long Island
Bank of America	JPMorgan Chase
Berkshire Bancorp	New York Community
Bridge Bancorp	Bancorp
Citibank	Ridgewood Savings Bank
Dime Community	State Bancorp
Bancshares	

HISTORICAL FINANCIALS

Company Type: Public

Income Statement

FYE: September 30

	ASSETS ($ mil.)	NET INCOME ($ mil.)	INCOME AS % OF ASSETS	EMPLOYEES
9/09	521.4	1.3	0.2%	104
9/08	483.8	5.6	1.2%	103
9/07	390.4	3.8	1.0%	94
9/06	408.0	4.6	1.1%	91
9/05	340.9	3.8	1.1%	59
Annual Growth	**11.2%**	**(23.5%)**	**—**	**15.2%**

2009 Year-End Financials

Equity as % of assets: 15.7%
Return on assets: 0.3%
Return on equity: 1.5%
Long-term debt ($ mil.): —
No. of shares (mil.): 12.9
Market value ($ mil.): 157.3
Dividends
  Yield: 3.3%
  Payout: 400.0%
Sales ($ mil.): 23.6
R&D as % of sales: —
Advertising as % of sales: —

Stock History

NASDAQ (GM): BFSB

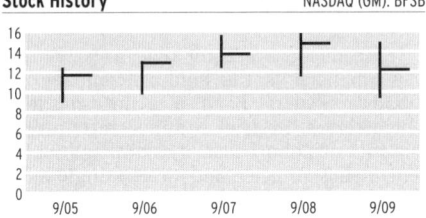

	STOCK PRICE ($) FY Close	P/E High/Low		PER SHARE ($) Earnings	Dividends	Book Value
9/09	12.20	148	95	0.10	0.40	6.35
9/08	14.79	36	27	0.43	0.29	6.70
9/07	13.75	53	43	0.29	0.10	6.61
9/06	12.90	37	28	0.35	—	6.20
9/05	11.69	82	61	0.15	—	5.83
Annual Growth	**1.1%**	**—**	**—**	**(9.6%)**	**100.0%**	**2.1%**

Bruker Corporation

Bruker (formerly Bruker BioSciences) is the parent company of a handful of operating subsidiaries working in the life sciences research field. The company sells X-ray analysis products from the Bruker AXS portfolio and Bruker Daltonics' life science tools based on mass spectrometry for customers such as pharmaceutical companies, biotechs, academic institutions, and government agencies. Bruker Optics develops tools based on molecular spectroscopy, and Bruker BioSpin makes research equipment using magnetic resonance technology. Advanced Supercon makes the superconducting wires used in magnetic resonance imaging (MRI) and other magnet applications, and superconducting devices used in motors and generators.

The company has coalesced out of several entities owned by the Bruker-controlling Laukien family. In 2008 Bruker purchased Bruker Biospin, another life sciences company privately owned by the Laukiens. It acquired the company, which makes life science and research systems using magnetic resonance technology, in a cash and stock deal worth more than $900 million. Following the close of the acquisition, Bruker dropped the "BioSciences" from its name.

Also in 2008 the company formed Advanced Supercon (ASCI), a subsidiary comprising six Laukien-owned, Bruker-titled entities. ASCI produces low temperature superconductors (LTS) and high temperature superconductor (HTS) wires at factories in Germany and Scotland; sales and administrative offices are in the US.

After the 2009 acquisition of ACCEL Research Instruments, Bruker reorganized itself once again, establishing two new business segments. The Bruker Scientific Instruments segment comprises four divisions: Bruker AXS, Bruker BioSpin, Bruker Daltonics, and Bruker Optics. The new Bruker Energy & SuperCon Technologies (BEST) combines the ACCEL business and the superconductor and the Advanced Supercon business.

Through the acquisitions and startups, the company hopes to leverage the Bruker brand name, diversify its product line, and strengthen its global distribution capabilities. It also hopes the various iterations will produce cross-selling opportunities among the various Bruker customer bases.

CEO Frank Laukien owns about 23% of Bruker. His brothers, SVP Dirk Laukien and Jörg Laukien (COO Europe), own about 13% each.

EXECUTIVES

Chairman, President, and CEO: Frank H. Laukien, age 49, $1,080,864 total compensation
COO: William J. (Bill) Knight, age 60, $613,482 total compensation
CFO and Chief Accounting Officer: Brian P. Monahan, age 37, $343,392 total compensation
Co-President, BioSpin Division: Bernd Gewiese
President, Bruker Optics and Managing Director, Bruker GmbH: Urban Faeh
Co-President, BioSpin Division: Werner Maas
Treasurer and Director Investor Relations: Stacey Desrochers
COO Europe and Director: Jörg C. Laukien, age 55
SVP and CFO, Advanced Supercon: Thomas M. (Tom) Rosa
SVP Marketing and IT and Director; President, Bruker Optics: Dirk D. Laukien, age 44, $765,697 total compensation
Secretary and Director: Richard M. Stein, age 57
Auditors: Ernst & Young LLP

LOCATIONS

HQ: Bruker Corporation
40 Manning Rd., Billerica, MA 01821
Phone: 978-663-3660   **Fax:** 978-667-5993
Web: www.bruker-biosciences.com

2008 Sales

	$ mil.	% of total
Europe	691.1	62
North America	264.3	25
Asia/Pacific	125.1	11
Other regions	26.6	2
Total	**1,107.1**	**100**

PRODUCTS/OPERATIONS

2008 Sales

	$ mil	% of total
Product	974.9	88
Service	126.9	12
Other	5.3	—
Total	**1,107.1**	**100**

2008 Sales

	$ mil	% of total
BioScience	633.2	57
BioSpin	528.0	48
Adjustments	(54.1)	—
Total	**1,107.1**	**100**

COMPETITORS

Agilent Technologies	Renishaw
AMETEK	Shimadzu
GE Healthcare	Smiths Detection
Hitachi Medical Systems	Spectris
JEOL	Thermo Fisher Scientific
Oxford Instruments	Varian
PerkinElmer	Waters Corp.

HISTORICAL FINANCIALS

Company Type: Public

Income Statement
FYE: December 31

	REVENUE ($ mil.)	NET INCOME ($ mil.)	NET PROFIT MARGIN	EMPLOYEES
12/08	1,107.1	64.9	5.9%	4,400
12/07	547.6	31.5	5.8%	2,212
12/06	435.8	18.5	4.2%	3,542
12/05	297.6	3.6	1.2%	2,549
12/04	284.4	(7.8)	—	1,270
Annual Growth	40.5%	—	—	36.4%

2008 Year-End Financials

Debt ratio: 58.8%
Return on equity: 22.8%
Cash ($ mil.): 166.2
Current ratio: 1.58
Long-term debt ($ mil.): 182.8
No. of shares (mil.): 164.2
Dividends
　Yield: 0.0%
　Payout: —
Market value ($ mil.): 663.3
R&D as % of sales: —
Advertising as % of sales: —

Stock History
NASDAQ (GM): BRKR

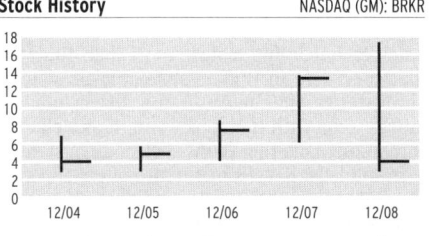

	STOCK PRICE ($) FY Close	P/E High/Low		PER SHARE ($) Earnings	Dividends	Book Value
12/08	4.04	44	8	0.39	0.00	1.89
12/07	13.30	45	21	0.30	0.00	1.58
12/06	7.51	47	24	0.18	0.00	1.17
12/05	4.86	140	77	0.04	0.00	1.27
12/04	4.03	—	—	(0.09)	0.00	1.32
Annual Growth	0.1%	—	—	—	—	9.4%

Bsquare Corporation

Bsquare is hip to intelligent computing devices (ICDs) and smart devices, including Internet appliances, handheld computers, TV set-top boxes, and gaming consoles. With Bsquare's engineering and development services and software, equipment makers can integrate Microsoft's Windows operating systems into their products. Its consumer software enables handheld PCs to perform such tasks as faxing and printing. Bsquare also resells products from assorted vendors, including Adobe Systems and Microsoft, which provides the majority of the company's revenues.

The company's customers have included Arima Communications, Hand Held Products, Micros Systems, Motorola, and Qualcomm.

In 2008 Bsquare purchased the intellectual property and assets of TestQuest, a provider of test automation and management tools for mobile and embedded devices. The purchase expanded Bsquare's product line and added new customers such as the United States Postal Service, T-Mobile International, Kyocera, Telefónica Móviles, and Siemens. It also bolstered the company's presence in China and India, furthering BSQUARE's goal of growing its international sales.

While the company's offerings are largely centered around the Windows Embedded and Windows Mobile operating systems, Bsquare is also exploring products based on non-Microsoft operating systems such as Google Android.

EXECUTIVES

Chairman: Elliott H. (Ren) Jurgensen Jr., age 64
President, CEO, and Director: Brian T. Crowley, age 49, $442,228 total compensation
VP Finance, CFO, Secretary, and Treasurer: Scott C. Mahan, age 45, $313,996 total compensation
VP Professional Engineering Services: Carey E. Butler, age 55
VP Products: Rajesh Khera, age 39
VP Sales and Marketing: Larry C. Stapleton, age 46, $370,390 total compensation
Country Manager, Japan: Kiyonori Takahashi
Marketing Manager: Molly Allen
Auditors: Moss Adams, LLP

LOCATIONS

HQ: Bsquare Corporation
　110 110th Ave. NE, Ste. 200, Bellevue, WA 98004
Phone: 425-519-5900　　**Fax:** 425-519-5999
Web: www.bsquare.com

2008 Sales

	$ mil.	% of total
North America	60.6	92
Asia	4.6	7
Other regions	0.6	1
Total	**65.8**	**100**

PRODUCTS/OPERATIONS

2008 Sales

	$ mil.	% of total
Third-party software	35.4	54
Services	27.2	41
Proprietary software	3.2	5
Total	**65.8**	**100**

COMPETITORS

Arrow Electronics
Avnet
Intrinsyc Software
Motorola, Inc.
Nokia
Palm, Inc.
Wind River Systems
Wipro Technologies

HISTORICAL FINANCIALS

Company Type: Public

Income Statement
FYE: December 31

	REVENUE ($ mil.)	NET INCOME ($ mil.)	NET PROFIT MARGIN	EMPLOYEES
12/08	65.8	2.0	3.0%	232
12/07	59.4	2.8	4.7%	175
12/06	49.8	(0.5)	—	170
12/05	42.9	(1.3)	—	155
12/04	38.9	(7.1)	—	110
Annual Growth	14.0%	—	—	20.5%

2008 Year-End Financials

Debt ratio: —
Return on equity: 11.3%
Cash ($ mil.): 7.7
Current ratio: 2.25
Long-term debt ($ mil.): —
No. of shares (mil.): 10.1
Dividends
　Yield: 0.0%
　Payout: —
Market value ($ mil.): 23.9
R&D as % of sales: —
Advertising as % of sales: —

Stock History
NASDAQ (GM): BSQR

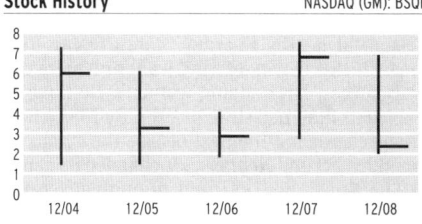

	STOCK PRICE ($) FY Close	P/E High/Low		PER SHARE ($) Earnings	Dividends	Book Value
12/08	2.36	36	11	0.19	0.00	1.87
12/07	6.79	28	10	0.27	0.00	1.63
12/06	2.85	—	—	(0.05)	0.00	1.19
12/05	3.24	—	—	(0.14)	0.00	1.13
12/04	5.96	—	—	(0.76)	0.00	1.26
Annual Growth	(20.7%)	—	—	—	—	10.4%

The Buckle, Inc.

The Buckle has done away with the notion that midwestern kids wear only overalls. With about 390 mostly mall-based stores in 40 states, The Buckle sells fashion-conscious 12- to 24-year-olds the clothes they've just got to have. The company retails a variety of clothing items, including mid- to higher-priced casual apparel (pants, tops, and outerwear), shoes, and accessories. Its products portfolio boasts such brands as Lucky Brand Dungarees, Hurley, Roxy, Silver, Billabong, Fossil, and Ed Hardy. The Buckle operates under the names Buckle and The Buckle; it also has an online store. Born and raised in Nebraska, it has expanded into the South and West.

Denim, which accounted for about 40% of 2008 sales, is popular with its customers. Unlike competitors Gap and Abercrombie & Fitch, the teen retailer relies heavily on brand-name clothing, which generated some 70% of sales in 2008; the rest comes from private labels. Brand names are big among its youthful target audience, which tends to be fickle and chases after the "it" brands of the moment.

The Buckle has moved "down market" to appeal to the younger set — children ages 8 to 15 — with apparel that can only be purchased online.

The chain, which has added about 165 stores during the past 10 years, plans to open about 20 new locations in 2009. The Buckle is opening stores in existing markets and adding new stores in New York and New Jersey.

Chairman Daniel Hirschfeld, the founder's son, owns about 37% of The Buckle's shares.

HISTORY

David Hirschfeld and a partner, Ivan Mills, founded Mills Clothing in Kearney, Nebraska, in 1948 with a single men's clothing store. Hirschfeld's son Daniel worked as a clerk there, took over the business in the mid-1960s, and bought a second store, The Brass Buckle, in 1967.

Catering to students (like future CEO Dennis Nelson) at nearby Kearney State College, The Brass Buckle began offering jeans and more casual clothes, later adding women's clothing; it opened its first mall store in 1977. By 1981 it had 17 stores. During the next decade the company expanded beyond Nebraska. It changed its name to The Buckle in 1991 and promoted Nelson, who started as a part-time clerk in 1970, to president. The company had 89 stores in 13 states when it went public in 1992.

The Buckle continued to stretch in the 1990s, opening scores of stores — including locations in the West and Southeast — and introducing its Primo frequent-shopper card. Nelson became CEO in 1997. The following year, as Generation Y flexed its spending power, the retailer expanded its distribution center in Kearney, enabling it to handle another 250 stores. The Buckle opened about 30 stores and moved into six new states during fiscal 2000, and another two dozen new stores and two new states in 2001.

The company in 2002 kicked off a multiyear expansion plan that includes locating new stores in high-traffic shopping malls. During the period of 2003 (when The Buckle boasted 307 stores) to 2008 (when it operated 371), the retailer has slowly increased its presence in malls through its organic growth.

EXECUTIVES

Chairman: Daniel J. Hirschfeld, age 67
President, CEO, and Director: Dennis H. Nelson, age 59, $8,664,342 total compensation
VP Women's Merchandising: Patricia K. Whisler, age 52, $1,797,549 total compensation
VP Men's Merchandising: Robert M. (Bob) Carlberg, age 46
VP Finance, CFO, Treasurer, and Director: Karen B. Rhoads, age 50, $1,742,932 total compensation
VP Sales: Kari G. Smith, age 45, $1,771,086 total compensation
VP Leasing: Brett P. Milkie, age 49, $1,788,470 total compensation
Secretary and General Counsel: Kyle L. Hanson, age 44
Auditors: Deloitte & Touche LLP

LOCATIONS

HQ: The Buckle, Inc.
2407 W. 24th St., Kearney, NE 68845
Phone: 308-236-8491   **Fax:** 308-236-4493
Web: www.buckle.com

2009 Stores

	No.
Texas	42
California	18
Iowa	18
Michigan	18
Florida	17
Kansas	17
Ohio	17
Illinois	16
Indiana	14
Nebraska	13
Colorado	13
Oklahoma	13
Wisconsin	13
Minnesota	12
Missouri	12
Washington	12
Tennessee	11
Utah	11
Arizona	9
Louisiana	9
North Carolina	8
Pennsylvania	8
Alabama	7
Arkansas	6
Idaho	6
Kentucky	5
Mississippi	5
Montana	5
Georgia	5
Other states	31
Total	**391**

PRODUCTS/OPERATIONS

2009 Sales

	% of total
Denims	41
Tops (including sweaters)	39
Accessories	8
Footwear	5
Sportswear/fashions	5
Outerwear	2
Total	**100**

COMPETITORS

Abercrombie & Fitch	The Gap
Aéropostale	Hot Topic
American Eagle Outfitters	J. C. Penney
Benetton	J. Crew
Bon-Ton Stores	Macy's
Casual Male Retail Group	Maurices
Deb Shops	Pacific Sunwear
dELiA*s	Saks
Dillard's	Urban Outfitters
Eddie Bauer llc	Wet Seal
Forever 21	

HISTORICAL FINANCIALS

Company Type: Public

Income Statement

FYE: Saturday nearest January 31

	REVENUE ($ mil.)	NET INCOME ($ mil.)	NET PROFIT MARGIN	EMPLOYEES
1/09	792.0	104.4	13.2%	8,225
1/08	619.9	75.2	12.1%	6,700
1/07	530.1	55.7	10.5%	6,100
1/06	501.1	51.9	10.4%	6,100
1/05	470.9	43.2	9.2%	6,100
Annual Growth	**13.9%**	**24.7%**	**—**	**7.8%**

2009 Year-End Financials

Debt ratio: —	Dividends
Return on equity: 30.9%	Yield: 3.5%
Cash ($ mil.): 162.5	Payout: 32.6%
Current ratio: 3.21	Market value ($ mil.): 979.1
Long-term debt ($ mil.): —	R&D as % of sales: —
No. of shares (mil.): 46.3	Advertising as % of sales: —

Stock History

NYSE: BKE

	STOCK PRICE ($) FY Close	P/E High/Low		PER SHARE ($) Earnings	Dividends	Book Value
1/09	21.15	20	6	2.24	0.73	7.28
1/08	27.73	18	12	1.63	0.60	7.31
1/07	22.39	20	12	1.24	0.37	6.19
1/06	15.67	18	12	1.13	0.27	6.48
1/05	12.72	16	13	0.86	0.20	7.19
Annual Growth	**13.6%**	**—**	**—**	**27.0%**	**38.2%**	**0.3%**

Buffalo Wild Wings

Hot sauce fuels the flight of this restaurateur. Buffalo Wild Wings (BWW) operates a chain of more than 600 Buffalo Wild Wings Grill & Bar quick-casual dining spots in more than 40 states that specialize in Buffalo-style chicken wings. The eateries offer more than a dozen dipping sauces to go with their spicy wings, as well as a complement of other items such as chicken tenders and legs. BWW's menu also offers appetizers, burgers, tacos, salads, and desserts, along with beer, wine, and other beverages. The company owns and operates nearly 200 of the restaurants, while the rest are operated by franchisees.

The company has been expanding rapidly since its 2003 IPO, opening more than 60 new locations during 2008 on top of 60 openings the previous year. It also purchased nine of its franchised restaurants in the Las Vegas area for $23 million in 2008. BWW is aiming to reach about 1,000 locations by 2013, with plans calling for corporate-owned restaurants to make up about 40% of the portfolio.

Jim Disbrow and Scott Lowery opened the first Buffalo Wild Wings restaurant on the campus of Ohio State University in Columbus in 1982. (Legend has it that they started the eatery because they craved the style of chicken wings they had eaten in Buffalo, New York.) Originally called Buffalo Wild Wings & Weck (a reference to the Kimmelweck brand rolls used for sandwiches), the chain became known as BW3 for short. Rapid expansion and financial mismanagement pushed Buffalo Wild Wings to the brink of bankruptcy by the mid-1990s. Sally Smith became CEO in 1996 and helped retool the chain's branding strategy to appeal more to families and non-students.

EXECUTIVES

Chairman: James M. Damian, age 58
President, CEO, and Director: Sally J. Smith, age 52, $1,708,491 total compensation
EVP, CFO, and Treasurer: Mary J. Twinem, age 49, $1,073,343 total compensation
EVP, General Counsel, and Secretary: James M. Schmidt, age 50, $835,170 total compensation

SVP Marketing and Brand Development:
Kathleen M. (Kathy) Benning, age 47,
$653,715 total compensation
SVP Franchise and Development: Mounir N. Sawda,
age 52
SVP Operations: Judith A. (Judy) Shoulak, age 50,
$729,154 total compensation
SVP Human Resources: Linda G. Traylor, age 58
Auditors: KPMG LLP

LOCATIONS

HQ: Buffalo Wild Wings, Inc.
5500 Wayzata Blvd., Ste. 1600
Minneapolis, MN 55416
Phone: 952-593-9943   **Fax:** 952-593-9787
Web: www.buffalowildwings.com

2008 Locations

	No.
Ohio	86
Texas	61
Illinois	42
Indiana	39
Michigan	35
Minnesota	22
Missouri	22
Virginia	19
Wisconsin	19
Florida	18
Arizona	15
Kentucky	14
New York	13
North Carolina	13
Colorado	12
Tennessee	11
Alabama	10
Iowa	10
Nevada	10
Louisiana	8
Oklahoma	8
Georgia	7
Kansas	7
Nebraska	7
West Virginia	6
California	5
Delaware	5
Mississippi	5
North Dakota	5
Pennsylvania	5
Other states	21
Total	**560**

2008 Locations

	No.
Franchised	363
Company-owned	197
Total	**560**

PRODUCTS/OPERATIONS

2008 Sales

	$ mil.	% of total
Restaurants	379.7	90
Franchising	42.7	10
Total	**422.4**	**100**

COMPETITORS

Applebee's
Brinker
Carlson Restaurants
Damon's
Darden
Dave & Buster's
Family Sports Concepts
Fox & Hound Restaurant
Hooters
Houlihan's
Rock Bottom Restaurants
Ruby Tuesday
Wingstop
Zaxby's

HISTORICAL FINANCIALS
Company Type: Public

Income Statement			FYE: Last Sunday in December	
	REVENUE ($ mil.)	NET INCOME ($ mil.)	NET PROFIT MARGIN	EMPLOYEES
12/08	422.4	24.4	5.8%	12,000
12/07	329.7	19.7	6.0%	9,564
12/06	278.2	16.3	5.9%	7,482
12/05	209.7	8.9	4.2%	6,125
12/04	171.0	7.2	4.2%	4,532
Annual Growth	**25.4%**	**35.7%**	**—**	**27.6%**

2008 Year-End Financials

Debt ratio: —
Return on equity: 15.6%
Cash ($ mil.): 8.3
Current ratio: 1.50
Long-term debt ($ mil.): —
No. of shares (mil.): 18.0
Dividends
  Yield: 0.0%
  Payout: —
Market value ($ mil.): 462.4
R&D as % of sales: —
Advertising as % of sales: —

Stock History

NASDAQ (GS): BWLD

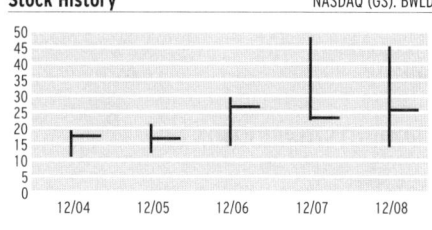

	STOCK PRICE ($) FY Close	P/E High/Low	PER SHARE ($) Earnings	Dividends	Book Value
12/08	25.65	33 11	1.36	0.00	9.52
12/07	23.22	43 21	1.10	0.00	7.86
12/06	26.60	32 16	0.93	0.00	6.45
12/05	16.60	41 25	0.51	0.00	5.37
12/04	17.41	45 27	0.42	0.00	4.75
Annual Growth	**10.2%**	**— —**	**34.1%**	**—**	**19.0%**

Cabot Oil & Gas

Like a cog on a gear in a well-oiled machine, Cabot Oil & Gas (ticker symbol: COG) has engaged in the oil industry very efficiently. Cabot explores for and produces natural gas and oil, and it sells gas to industrial customers, local utilities, and gas marketers. It has estimated proved reserves of 1.9 trillion cu. ft. of natural gas equivalent. Major areas of operation include Appalachia, the Anadarko Basin (Kansas, Oklahoma, and Texas), the Rocky Mountains (Wyoming), and the Texas and Louisiana Gulf Coast. The company also has reserves. In 2008 it was operating almost 4,700 net wells and had more than 183,630 net acres of undeveloped assets.

In 2008 the company announced successes from its drilling program at County Line and Hinton sites (in Texas) and at Moxa Arch (in Wyoming). It also acquired east Texas properties from Enduring Resources, LLC, Mustang Drilling, Inc. and Minden Gathering Services, LLC.

In order to focus on its core US regions, in 2009 Cabot Oil & Gas sold its operations in Canada (reserves of about 40 billion cu. ft. of natural gas equivalent in Alberta and British Columbia) to a private Canadian company.

EXECUTIVES

Chairman, President, and CEO: Dan O. Dinges, age 56,
$4,496,943 total compensation
SVP and COO: Michael B. Walen, age 61,
$2,510,582 total compensation
VP, Controller, and Treasurer: Henry C. (Chuck) Smyth,
age 63
VP Human Resources: Abraham D. Garza, age 63
VP Information Services and Operational Accounting:
Robert G. Drake, age 62
VP and CFO: Scott C. Schroeder, age 47,
$1,861,498 total compensation
VP Land and General Counsel: J. Scott Arnold, age 56,
$1,387,407 total compensation
VP, Managing Counsel, and Corporate Secretary:
Lisa A. Machesney, age 54
VP Marketing: Jeffrey W. Hutton, age 54,
$1,012,149 total compensation
Auditors: PricewaterhouseCoopers LLP

LOCATIONS

HQ: Cabot Oil & Gas Corporation
1200 Enclave Pkwy., Houston, TX 77077
Phone: 281-589-4600   **Fax:** 281-589-4828
Web: www.cabotog.com

2008 Proved Reserves

	% of total
East	45
Gulf Coast	29
Rocky Mountains	14
Midcontinent	10
Canada	2
Total	**100**

PRODUCTS/OPERATIONS

2008 Sales

	$ mil.	% of total
Natural gas production	758.8	80
Brokered natural gas	114.2	12
Crude oil & condensate	69.7	8
Other	3.1	—
Total	**945.8**	**100**

COMPETITORS

Anadarko Petroleum
Atlas Energy
Belden & Blake
Black Hills
BP
Brigham Exploration
Chevron
CREDO Petroleum
Dominion Resources
EQT Corporation
Exxon Mobil
Key Energy
Petroleum Development
Range Resources
Royal Dutch Shell

HISTORICAL FINANCIALS
Company Type: Public

Income Statement			FYE: December 31	
	REVENUE ($ mil.)	NET INCOME ($ mil.)	NET PROFIT MARGIN	EMPLOYEES
12/08	945.8	211.3	22.3%	560
12/07	732.2	167.4	22.9%	404
12/06	762.0	321.2	42.2%	374
12/05	682.8	148.4	21.7%	354
12/04	530.4	88.4	16.7%	346
Annual Growth	**15.6%**	**24.3%**	**—**	**12.8%**

2008 Year-End Financials

Debt ratio: 46.4%
Return on equity: 14.8%
Cash ($ mil.): 28.1
Current ratio: 1.22
Long-term debt ($ mil.): 831.1
No. of shares (mil.): 103.7

Dividends
  Yield: 0.5%
  Payout: 5.8%
Market value ($ mil.): 2,695.0
R&D as % of sales: —
Advertising as % of sales: —

Stock History
NYSE: COG

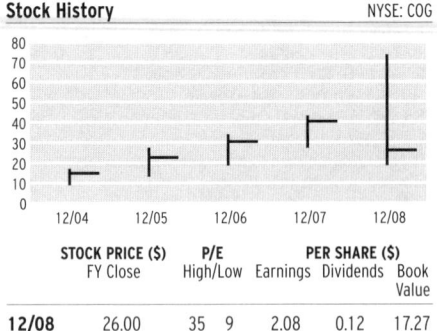

	STOCK PRICE ($) FY Close	P/E High/Low		PER SHARE ($) Earnings	Dividends	Book Value
12/08	26.00	35	9	2.08	0.12	17.27
12/07	40.37	25	16	1.71	0.11	10.33
12/06	30.33	10	6	3.26	0.08	9.12
12/05	22.55	18	9	1.50	0.07	5.79
12/04	14.75	18	11	0.90	0.05	4.40
Annual Growth	15.2%	—	—	23.3%	24.5%	40.8%

Cal Dive International

Cal Dive International may or may not be California dreaming, but its waking hours are spent beneath the waters of the world's oceans. The subsea contractor operates a fleet of 24 surface and saturation diving support vessels, six shallow water pipelay vessels, one dedicated pipebury barge, one combination pipelay/derrick barge, and two derrick barges. It installs and maintains offshore platforms, pipelines, and production systems on the Outer Continental Shelf of the Gulf of Mexico, as well as in offshore markets in the Middle East, Southeast Asia, and Trinidad. Cal Dive also provides shallow water diving services and performs salvage operations on abandoned fields. Helix Energy Solutions owns 25% of Cal-Dive.

The subsea contractor has a proven track record of executing acquisitions that complement its fleet and enhance its service capabilities. Expanding geographically, in 2006 Cal Dive purchased Singapore-based Fraser Diving, whose assets included 21 diving systems (six portable saturation and 15 surface). Fraser Diving operated primarily in Australia, the Middle East, and Southeast Asia. In 2007 Cal Dive acquired Horizon Offshore in a $650 million deal that added nine vessels to its fleet.

Cal Dive was formerly a division of Helix Energy Solutions before that company spun it off in 2006. Helix owned a majority stake until a secondary offering in 2009 brought its share to the current 25%.

EXECUTIVES

Chairman: Owen E. Kratz, age 54
President, CEO, and Director: Quinn J. Hébert, age 46, $2,093,714 total compensation
EVP and COO: Scott T. Naughton, age 55, $1,161,545 total compensation
EVP, CFO, and Treasurer: Bruce P. Koch, age 50

EVP, General Counsel, and Secretary: Lisa Manget Buchanan, age 49, $732,369 total compensation
EVP Eastern Hemisphere: G. Kregg Lunsford, age 41, $785,802 total compensation
SVP Sales and Marketing Western Hemisphere: Christopher W. Landry
SVP International Business Development Eastern Hemisphere: Michael Ambrose
SVP Pipelay Western Hemisphere: Steven J. Brazda
VP Personnel and Administration: Travis Trahan
VP Projects and Operations, Eastern Hemisphere: Jon Minshall
Director Human Resources: Rebecca G. Gottsegen
Auditors: Ernst & Young LLP

LOCATIONS

HQ: Cal Dive International, Inc.
  2500 CityWest Blvd., Ste. 2200, Houston, TX 77042
Phone: 713-361-2600   **Fax:** 713-361-2690
Web: www.caldive.com

2008 Sales

	$ mil.	% of total
US	606.0	71
Other countries	250.9	29
Total	**856.9**	**100**

PRODUCTS/OPERATIONS

2008 Sales

	% of total
GDF Suez	14
Helix Energy Solutions	13
Chevron	11
Other customers	62
Total	**100**

COMPETITORS

Global Industries
Halliburton
J. Ray McDermott
Oceaneering International
Parker Drilling
Pride International
Saipem
Subsea 7
Technip
TETRA Technologies
Tidewater Inc.

HISTORICAL FINANCIALS

Company Type: Public

Income Statement
FYE: December 31

	REVENUE ($ mil.)	NET INCOME ($ mil.)	NET PROFIT MARGIN	EMPLOYEES
12/08	856.9	109.5	12.8%	2,000
12/07	623.6	105.6	16.9%	2,000
12/06	509.9	119.4	23.4%	1,300
12/05	224.3	37.7	16.8%	1,200
12/04	125.8	7.7	6.1%	1,200
Annual Growth	61.6%	94.2%	—	13.6%

2008 Year-End Financials

Debt ratio: 33.7%
Return on equity: 16.9%
Cash ($ mil.): 60.6
Current ratio: 1.52
Long-term debt ($ mil.): 237.7
No. of shares (mil.): 93.0

Dividends
  Yield: 0.0%
  Payout: —
Market value ($ mil.): 605.2
R&D as % of sales: —
Advertising as % of sales: —

Stock History
NYSE: DVR

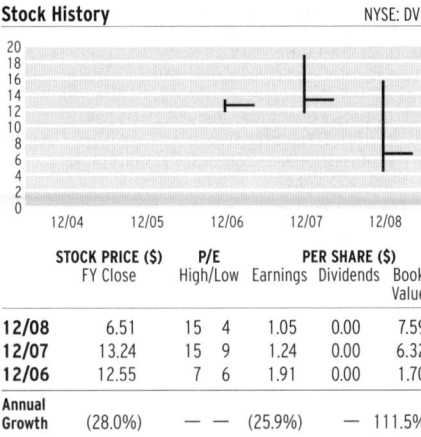

	STOCK PRICE ($) FY Close	P/E High/Low		PER SHARE ($) Earnings	Dividends	Book Value
12/08	6.51	15	4	1.05	0.00	7.59
12/07	13.24	15	9	1.24	0.00	6.32
12/06	12.55	7	6	1.91	0.00	1.70
Annual Growth	(28.0%)	—	—	(25.9%)	—	111.5%

Calavo Growers

The avocado growers of Calavo Growers might not be a cooperative anymore, but they're still friendly folks. Calavo (the name is a combination of "California" and "avocado") began as a growers' marketing cooperative founded in 1924 in order to transform the exotic hobby crop, avocados, into a culinary staple. And the avocado has become, if not a staple, a regular in US supermarket shopping carts. Calavo procures and processes avocados, tomatoes, and other fresh fruits grown mainly in California, Chile, and Mexico. The products are then distributed to the retail food outlets and foodservice operators throughout the world.

More than 2,300 growers deliver their crops to Calavo for processing. Its ProRipeVIP system ripens the fruit to each customer's specifications. In addition to whole avocados, the company manufactures avocado pulp, guacamole, and frozen peeled avocado halves.

In 2007 the company expanded its US operations to include ripening facilities in New Jersey and Texas. Widening its selection of produce, that year it also added tomatoes to its produce offerings, inking a marketing and distribution agreement with Mexican grower, Agricola Belher.

In an effort to further diversify its offerings, later that year the company struck a deal with Maui Land & Pineapple, to sell, market, and distribute the Hawaiian grower's *Maui Gold* fresh pineapples throughout the continental US and Canada. In addition to pineapples, the agreement, broadened Calavo's perishable food products to include tomatoes, mushrooms, onions, and coconuts.

That year also saw the company agree to market and distribute Calavo-branded fresh mushrooms in conjunction with Canadian grower, Farmers' Fresh Mushrooms.

In 2008 the company continued its expansion, this time with papaya businesses in Hawaii, when it acquired tropical-product packing and processing operations owned by CEO Lee Cole. Calavo purchased Hawaiian Sweet and Hawaii Pride for between $10 million and $14 million cash, depending on earnout payments. Later that same year it purchased Hawaiian Sweet and Hawaiian Pride, two Hawaiian tropical fruit packers, for $3.5 million in cash.

EXECUTIVES

Chairman, President, and CEO: Lecil E. (Lee) Cole, age 70
COO, CFO, and Corporate Secretary: Arthur J. (Art) Bruno, age 59
VP Sales and Operations: Alan C. (Al) Ahmer, age 60
VP Fresh Operations: Michael A. (Mike) Browne, age 51
VP Calavo de Mexico Operations: Dionisio Ortiz
VP Fresh Marketing and Sales: Robert J. (Rob) Wedin, age 60
Director Strategic Development: Michael (Mike) Lippold
Director Corporate Marketing: Robin Osterhues
Director Human Resources: Patricia (Pat) Vorhies
Director Fresh Sales: Mike Angelo
Director Grower Relations: Bob Coleman
Auditors: Ernst & Young LLP

LOCATIONS

HQ: Calavo Growers, Inc.
1141-A Cummings Rd., Santa Paula, CA 93060
Phone: 805-525-1245   **Fax:** 805-921-3223
Web: www.calavo.com

PRODUCTS/OPERATIONS

2008 Sales

	$ mil.	% of total
Fresh products	315.7	87
Processed products	45.8	13
Total	**361.5**	**100**

2008 Sales

	% of total
Fresh products	
Imported avocados	40
California avocados	31
Tomatoes	6
Pineapples	5
Papayas	1
Other	1
Processed products	
Foodservice	12
Retail & club stores	4
Total	**100**

COMPETITORS

Agromar
Appleton Produce
BC Hot House Foods
Chiquita Brands
Coast Citrus Distributors
Del Monte Foods
Dole Food
Eastern Fresh Growers, Inc.
Eurofresh
Fresh Del Monte Produce
FreshPoint
Gentile Bros.
Gills Onions
Giumarra Companies
Index Fresh
Interfresh
JR Simplot
Monterey Mushrooms
The Mushroom Company
Oakshire Mushroom Farm
Oceanside Produce
Pacific Tomato Growers
Pinos Produce
Six L's Packing Company
Sylvan
Tanimura & Antle
VSP Products

HISTORICAL FINANCIALS

Company Type: Public

Income Statement

FYE: October 31

	REVENUE ($ mil.)	NET INCOME ($ mil.)	NET PROFIT MARGIN	EMPLOYEES
10/08	361.5	7.7	2.1%	876
10/07	303.0	7.3	2.4%	830
10/06	273.9	5.8	2.1%	750
10/05	258.8	3.3	1.3%	701
10/04	274.2	6.2	2.3%	674
Annual Growth	**7.2%**	**5.6%**	**—**	**6.8%**

2008 Year-End Financials

Debt ratio: 38.7%
Return on equity: 11.0%
Cash ($ mil.): 1.5
Current ratio: 1.39
Long-term debt ($ mil.): 25.4
No. of shares (mil.): 14.5
Dividends
Yield: 3.4%
Payout: 66.0%
Market value ($ mil.): 147.2
R&D as % of sales: —
Advertising as % of sales: —

Stock History

NASDAQ (GM): CVGW

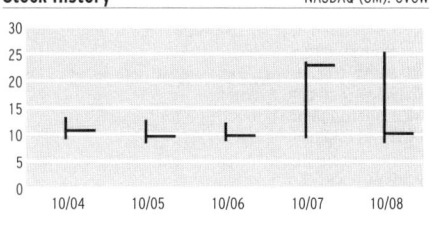

	STOCK PRICE ($) FY Close	P/E High/Low		PER SHARE ($) Earnings	Dividends	Book Value
10/08	10.15	47	16	0.53	0.35	4.52
10/07	22.91	46	19	0.51	0.32	5.10
10/06	9.75	30	22	0.40	0.32	4.06
10/05	9.62	52	36	0.24	0.30	4.46
10/04	10.70	28	20	0.46	0.25	3.03
Annual Growth	**(1.3%)**	**—**	**—**	**3.6%**	**8.8%**	**10.5%**

Calgon Carbon

With pure intentions, Calgon Carbon makes activated carbons and purification systems and offers purification, separation, and concentration services to the industrial process and environmental markets. The company provides activated, impregnated, and acid-washed carbons (about 130 million pounds annually) for use in applications such as food processing, wastewater treatment, and emissions control. Calgon Carbon also sells equipment that uses activated carbon and ion exchange resins for the purification of products in the chemical, food, and pharmaceutical industries. The company's consumer products include charcoal and carbon cloth.

Calgon Carbon operates in a geographically diverse array of markets, and almost half of the company's sales come from outside the US. It's strategy is to maintain its global coverage while developing or acquiring products and services that complement its existing portfolio.

In 2008 Calgon Carbon was awarded a contract by Huntsman Textile Effects (Qingdao) Co. Ltd. to supply activated carbon adsorption equipment for wastewater treatment activities in China as well as to provide reactivation services.

In 2009 its contracts included a $25 million award for removing mercury from US Midwest power plants, and a multimillion-dollar award for drinking water treatment in South Korea.

The company also divests businesses that no longer fit its business plan. In 2006 Calgon Carbon sold its Bodenfelde, Germany-based premium charcoal and derivatives business to local management and a German investor group. The unit made charcoal for consumer use and sold liquids that were recovered during charcoal production.

EXECUTIVES

Chairman, President, and CEO: John S. Stanik, age 55, $1,832,974 total compensation
SVP and CFO: Leroy M. Ball, age 40, $686,105 total compensation
SVP Americas: Robert P. O'Brien, age 59, $625,248 total compensation
SVP Europe and Asia: C. H. S. (Kees) Majoor, age 60, $879,721 total compensation
VP UV and Corporate Business Development: James A. (Jim) Sullivan, age 45
VP, General Counsel, and Secretary: Dennis M. Sheedy, age 62, $506,838 total compensation
VP Investor Relations, Communications, and Human Resources: Gail A. Gerono, age 58
Auditors: Deloitte & Touche LLP

LOCATIONS

HQ: Calgon Carbon Corporation
400 Calgon Carbon Dr., Pittsburgh, PA 15205
Phone: 412-787-6700   **Fax:** 412-787-4511
Web: www.calgoncarbon.com

2008 Sales

	$ mil.	% of total
US	218.6	55
UK	25.9	6
Canada	17.7	4
Germany	17.1	4
France	16.6	4
Belgium	10.9	3
Japan	10.7	3
Other	82.8	21
Total	**400.3**	**100**

PRODUCTS/OPERATIONS

2008 Sales

	$ mil.	% of total
Activated carbon & service	342.3	85
Equipment	47.3	12
Consumer	10.7	3
Total	**400.3**	**100**

Selected Subsidiaries and Operating Units

Advanced Separation Technologies Inc.
Calgon Carbon Asia (Singapore)
Calgon Carbon Canada, Inc.
Calgon Carbon (Tianjin) Co., Ltd. (China)
Charcoal Cloth (International) Ltd. (UK)
Chemviron Carbon Ltd. (UK)
Datong Carbon Corporation (China)
Solarchem Environmental Systems Inc.
Sutcliffe Speakman Ltd. (UK)

COMPETITORS

CUNO
MeadWestvaco
Met-Pro
Norit
Trojan Technologies
WEDECO

HISTORICAL FINANCIALS

Company Type: Public

Income Statement

FYE: December 31

	REVENUE ($ mil.)	NET INCOME ($ mil.)	NET PROFIT MARGIN	EMPLOYEES
12/08	400.3	38.4	9.6%	943
12/07	351.1	15.3	4.4%	868
12/06	316.1	(7.8)	—	847
12/05	290.8	(7.4)	—	972
12/04	336.6	5.9	1.8%	1,150
Annual Growth	4.4%	59.7%	—	(4.8%)

2008 Year-End Financials

Debt ratio: 0.0%
Return on equity: 18.1%
Cash ($ mil.): 16.8
Current ratio: 3.03
Long-term debt ($ mil.): 0.0
No. of shares (mil.): 56.0

Dividends
  Yield: 0.0%
  Payout: —
Market value ($ mil.): 859.7
R&D as % of sales: —
Advertising as % of sales: —

Stock History

NYSE: CCC

	STOCK PRICE ($) FY Close	P/E High/Low	Earnings	PER SHARE ($) Dividends	Book Value
12/08	15.36	32 13	0.72	0.00	4.52
12/07	15.89	55 18	0.31	0.00	3.08
12/06	6.20	— —	(0.20)	0.00	2.64
12/05	5.69	— —	(0.19)	0.09	2.69
12/04	9.08	65 35	0.15	0.12	3.00
Annual Growth	14.0%	— —	48.0%	—	10.8%

California Pizza Kitchen

California Pizza Kitchen (CPK) puts a West Coast twist on an old favorite. The company operates a chain of more than 250 casual-dining restaurants in more than 30 states and 10 other countries offering pizzas with a variety of unique topping combinations, including duck, barbecued chicken, and grilled shrimp. It also serves Neapolitan pizzas from Italy, as well as American-style pies. CPK rounds out its menu with pastas, soups, salads, and desserts. The company owns more than 200 of its locations, while the rest are franchised. In addition to its full-service establishments, CPK has about 20 quick-service kiosk locations. The company also markets a line of frozen pizzas through Kraft Foods.

CPK has become a leader in the casual dining business thanks to its attention to food quality and unique menu choices. The economic recession, however, has hurt sales as consumers rein in spending on such things as eating out. In response, the company has scaled back its expansion plans, opening just a handful of new restaurants during 2008, down from about 30 locations the year previous.

More than half of CPK's franchised locations are California Pizza Kitchen ASAP quick-service units, operated by HMSHost in such non-traditional locations as airports, travel plazas, and office buildings. CPK is also developing a new restaurant concept called LA Food Show Grill & Bar.

Founders and co-chairmen Larry Flax and Rick Rosenfield each control nearly 10% of CPK.

EXECUTIVES

Co-Chairman, Co-President, and Co-CEO: Larry S. Flax, age 66, $2,337,423 total compensation
Co-Chairman, Co-President, and Co-CEO: Richard L. (Rick) Rosenfield, age 63, $2,272,887 total compensation
EVP, COO, and CFO: Susan M. Collyns, age 42, $1,028,308 total compensation
SVP Marketing and Public Relations and Chief Communications Officer: Sarah Goldsmith Grover, age 44, $455,891 total compensation
SVP Corporate Finance, Controller, and Chief Accounting Officer: Todd Slayton
SVP ASAP Operations: Rudy Sugueti, age 43, $539,557 total compensation
SVP Construction: Thomas P. (Tom) Beck, age 62, $457,943 total compensation
Director IT: Brian Krakower
Auditors: Ernst & Young LLP

LOCATIONS

HQ: California Pizza Kitchen, Inc.
  6053 W. Century Blvd., 11th Fl.
  Los Angeles, CA 90045
Phone: 310-342-5000   **Fax:** 310-342-4640
Web: www.cpk.com

2008 Locations

	No.
US	
California	88
Florida	15
Illinois	11
Texas	10
Arizona	7
Missouri	7
New York	7
Colorado	6
Michigan	6
North Carolina	6
Virginia	6
Georgia	5
Hawaii	5
Massachusetts	5
Maryland	4
Minnesota	4
Nevada	4
Connecticut	3
New Jersey	3
Ohio	3
Pennsylvania	3
Utah	3
Washington	3
Alabama	2
Oregon	2
Kansas	1
Kentucky	1
Louisiana	1
Nebraska	1
New Mexico	1
Tennessee	1
Washington, DC	1
Wisconsin	1
International	27
Total	**253**

2008 Locations

	No.
Company-owned	205
Franchised & licensed	48
Total	**253**

PRODUCTS/OPERATIONS

2008 Sales

	$ mil.	% of total
Restaurants	665.6	98
Food products	6.6	1
Franchising	4.9	1
Total	**677.1**	**100**

COMPETITORS

Applebee's
BJ's Restaurants
Brinker
Bubba Gump Shrimp
BUCA
Cheesecake Factory
Darden
Johnny Rockets
Noodles & Company
OSI Restaurant Partners
Panera Bread
P.F. Chang's
Pizza Hut
Red Robin
Round Table Pizza
Sbarro
Uno Restaurants
Wolfgang Puck

HISTORICAL FINANCIALS

Company Type: Public

Income Statement

FYE: Sunday nearest December 31

	REVENUE ($ mil.)	NET INCOME ($ mil.)	NET PROFIT MARGIN	EMPLOYEES
12/08	677.1	8.7	1.3%	15,100
12/07	632.9	14.8	2.3%	14,800
12/06	554.6	21.0	3.8%	13,900
12/05	479.6	19.5	4.1%	12,900
12/04	422.5	17.8	4.2%	10,200
Annual Growth	12.5%	(16.4%)	—	10.3%

2008 Year-End Financials

Debt ratio: 42.4%
Return on equity: 4.4%
Cash ($ mil.): 14.4
Current ratio: 0.47
Long-term debt ($ mil.): 74.0
No. of shares (mil.): 24.1

Dividends
  Yield: 0.0%
  Payout: —
Market value ($ mil.): 258.9
R&D as % of sales: —
Advertising as % of sales: —

Stock History

NASDAQ (GS): CPKI

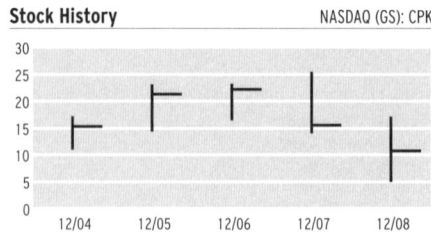

	STOCK PRICE ($) FY Close	P/E High/Low	Earnings	PER SHARE ($) Dividends	Book Value
12/08	10.72	50 15	0.34	0.00	7.23
12/07	15.57	50 29	0.50	0.00	9.03
12/06	22.21	33 24	0.71	0.00	8.63
12/05	21.31	35 22	0.66	0.00	8.17
12/04	15.33	28 18	0.61	0.00	6.92
Annual Growth	(8.6%)	— —	(13.6%)	—	1.1%

California Water Service

A big fish in California's water industry pond, California Water Service Group is in the swim in three other states, as well. The company's main subsidiary, regulated utility California Water Service Company (Cal Water), keeps water flowing in for 460,000 customers in California. California Water Service Group's other water utility subsidiaries include Washington Water (15,800 customers), New Mexico Water (7,600 water and wastewater customers), and Hawaii Water (3,700 customers). The company's CWS Utility Services unit contracts to provide water system operation, meter reading, and billing services. All told, California Water Service Group provides services to about 2 million people.

About 95% of the company's multistate water utility's operations are regulated by state utilities commissions.

The company's growth strategy includes geographic expansion through the acquisition of water and wastewater systems. Since 1999, California Water Service Group has established businesses in three new states (Washington, New Mexico, and Hawaii). Beefing up its Hawaiian operations (which were established in 2003), in 2007 Hawaii Water formed HWS Utility Services LLC, which then began non-regulated operations in 2008. Later that year it acquired Waikoloa Resort Utilities, Waikoloa Water Company, and Waikoloa Sanitary Sewer Company, boosting its regulated customer count in Hawaii from 1,500 to more than 3,700.

EXECUTIVES

Chairman, California Water Service Group and Subsidiaries: Robert W. Foy, age 72
President, CEO, and Director, California Water Service Group and Subsidiaries: Peter C. Nelson, age 61
VP, CFO, and Treasurer: Martin A. (Marty) Kropelnicki, age 42
VP Operations: Robert R. Guzzetta, age 51
VP Regulatory Matters and Corporate Relations: Thomas F. Smegal III
VP Customer Service and Information Systems: Paul G. Ekstrom, age 57
VP Human Resources: Christine L. McFarlane, age 62
VP Corporate Development: Francis S. Ferraro, age 57
VP Engineering and Water Quality: Michael J. Rossi, age 55
President, Washington Water Service: Michael P. Ireland, age 55
Corporate Secretary: Lynne P. McGhee, age 44
Corporate Counsel: John S. Tootle
Director Corporate Communications: Shannon C. Dean
Auditors: KPMG LLP

LOCATIONS

HQ: California Water Service Group
1720 N. 1st St., San Jose, CA 95112
Phone: 408-367-8200   **Fax:** 408-367-8430
Web: www.calwatergroup.com

PRODUCTS/OPERATIONS

2008 Sales

	$ mil.	% of total
Residential	271.9	66
Business	71.6	18
Public authorities	20.8	5
Industrial	18.0	4
Other	28.0	7
Total	**410.3**	**100**

Selected Subsidiaries

California Water Service Company
CWS Utility Services
Hawaii Water Service Company, Inc.
HWS Utility Services LLC
New Mexico Water Service Company
Washington Water Service Company

COMPETITORS

American States Water
American Water
Consolidated Water
Los Angeles Water and Power
Siemens Water Technologies
SJW
Southwest Water
United Water Inc.

HISTORICAL FINANCIALS

Company Type: Public

Income Statement

FYE: December 31

	REVENUE ($ mil.)	NET INCOME ($ mil.)	NET PROFIT MARGIN	EMPLOYEES
12/08	410.3	39.8	9.7%	929
12/07	367.1	31.2	8.5%	891
12/06	334.7	25.6	7.6%	869
12/05	320.7	27.2	8.5%	840
12/04	315.6	26.0	8.2%	837
Annual Growth	**6.8%**	**11.2%**	**—**	**2.6%**

2008 Year-End Financials

Debt ratio: 71.3%	Dividends
Return on equity: 10.1%	Yield: 2.5%
Cash ($ mil.): 13.9	Payout: 61.6%
Current ratio: 0.65	Market value ($ mil.): 963.2
Long-term debt ($ mil.): 287.5	R&D as % of sales: —
No. of shares (mil.): 20.7	Advertising as % of sales: —

Stock History

NYSE: CWT

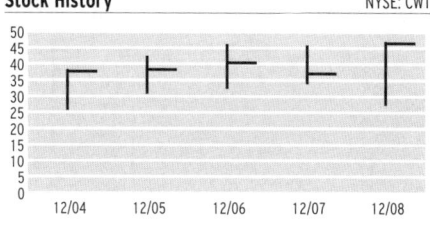

	STOCK PRICE ($) FY Close	P/E High/Low	PER SHARE ($) Earnings	Dividends	Book Value
12/08	46.43	25 15	1.90	1.17	19.42
12/07	37.02	30 23	1.50	1.16	18.76
12/06	40.40	34 24	1.34	1.15	18.40
12/05	38.23	29 21	1.47	1.14	14.34
12/04	37.65	26 18	1.46	1.13	14.03
Annual Growth	**5.4%**	**— —**	**6.8%**	**0.9%**	**8.5%**

Cal-Maine Foods

Which comes first, the chicken or the egg? At Cal-Maine Foods, it's the egg, and the company's 27 million laying hens can attest to that. It is one of the largest fresh shell egg producers in the US. Cal-Maine sells its eggs to US food retailers. It produces value-added specialty eggs (organic, Omega-3 enhanced, free range) that it sells under the Egg-Land's Best and Farmhouse labels. The company controls all aspects of the business, from hatching chicks, making feed, housing hens, and distributing eggs. Its operations include two breeding facilities, two hatcheries, five distribution centers, 19 feed mills, 37 shell-egg production operations, 26 pullet-growing facilities, and 31 processing and packing sites.

Most of the eggs Cal-Maine sells are produced at its own facilities; the rest are produced by contractors who use Cal-Maine flocks and feed. The company's long-term strategy is to grow through acquisitions. The company says it has completed 16 acquisitions since 1989.

Recent acquisitions include Cal-Maine's buyout of Pier 44's interest in Green Forest in 2007. It also completed another acquisition in 2007 — the purchase of the shell-egg division of George's Inc., for which it paid $11 million in cash. In 2009 it acquired the Zephyr Egg Company; Tampa Farm Service (including its specialty-egg brand 4-Grain Eggs), as well as Tampa Farms' interest in American Egg Products and the Egg-land's Best franchise for southern Florida. The Tampa Farm and Eggland's Best acquisitions have allowed Cal-Maine to better serve its growing Florida customer base.

The company has operations in Alabama, Arkansas, Florida, Georgia, Kansas, Kentucky, Louisiana, Mississippi, New Mexico, North and South Carolina, Ohio, Tennessee, Texas, and Utah. Its customer base is located primarily in the southwestern, southeastern, midwestern, and mid-Atlantic regions of the US.

In fiscal 2009 Cal-Maine sold 778 million dozen shell eggs. Together, Wal-Mart and Sam's Club accounted for 33% of the company's 2009 sales.

Founder, chairman, and CEO Fred Adams Jr. and his immediate family control about 54% of the company's voting power.

HISTORY

One can side with the chicken or the egg in the which-came-first argument, but it was Fred Adams Jr. who came first at Cal-Maine. A former salesman with pet food giant Ralston Purina (now Nestlé Purina PetCare), Adams founded a poultry and egg business in Mendenhall, Mississippi, in 1957. He focused exclusively on egg sales in 1960 and merged his company in 1969 with Maine Egg Farms and Dairy Fresh Foods in California to form Cal-Maine Foods.

Cal-Maine cracked new markets through internal growth and the acquisition of rival egg firms. The company acquired Egg City (Arkansas, 1989), Sunny Fresh Foods (Arkansas, 1990), Sunnyside Eggs (North Carolina, 1991), Wayne Detling Farms (Ohio, 1994), A&G Farms (Kentucky, 1995), and Sunbest Farms (Arkansas, 1996). After going public in 1996, Cal-Maine bought two Georgia firms: Southern Empire Egg Farm (1997) and J&S Farms (1998).

In 1998 the company sold off its egg products division, which provided food makers with egg whites and yolks and accounted for 4% of sales.

In 1999 Cal-Maine bought two egg producers and processors: Kentucky-based Hudson Brothers and Texas-based Smith Farms. Declining supplies in the cyclical egg market and increasing demand in late 2000 raised the company out of the loss column for the first time in 18 months. In late 2001 Cal-Maine's board of directors voted to explore the possibility of the company becoming privately held but abandoned the idea because of a sagging egg market. Industry-wide overproduction helped to drive down egg prices, pecking away at the company's profits in 2002.

In 2003 Cal-Maine's board of directors voted to take the company private. However, as demand for eggs shot up, so did Cal-Maine stock prices, and shareholders were unconvinced such a move would benefit them. Faced with shareholder lawsuits, in November of that year the board voted to terminate the proposal to take the company private.

After years of oversupply and weak prices, starting in 2003 the entire egg industry enjoyed a boost from the popular protein-heavy Atkins diet. Cal-Maine's sales jumped as people chose hard-boiled eggs as snacks. However, by 2004 its popularity had peaked, leaving the market (and Cal-Maine) with an egg glut and plunging sales. In 2005 the company acquired egg supplier Hillandale Farms.

In 2006 the company formed a 50-50 joint venture (Green Forest Foods) with Pier 44 Properties to lease and operate Green Forest Egg's production assets, which included about 1 million laying hens at facilities located in Arkansas.

EXECUTIVES

Chairman and CEO: Fred R. Adams Jr., age 77, $848,137 total compensation
Vice Chairman: Richard K. Looper, age 82
President, COO, and Director: Adolphus B. (Dolph) Baker, age 52, $1,073,211 total compensation
VP, CFO, Secretary, Treasurer, and Director: Timothy A. Dawson, age 55, $1,014,994 total compensation
VP Feed Mill Division: Joe M. Wyatt, age 70, $750,734 total compensation
VP Operations: Bob L. (Bobby) Scott, $554,642 total compensation
VP Operations and Production: Jack B. Self, age 81
VP Egg Products: James Hull
VP Egg Sales: Matthew Arrowsmith
VP Sales: Kyle Morris
VP Sales: Charles J. (Jeff) Hardin
VP and Controller: Charles F. Collins, age 65
Director Human Resources: Alan Holland
General Counsel: James Neeld III
Auditors: Ernst & Young LLP

LOCATIONS

HQ: Cal-Maine Foods, Inc.
3320 Woodrow Wilson Ave., Jackson, MS 39209
Phone: 601-948-6813   **Fax:** 601-969-0905
Web: www.calmainefoods.com

PRODUCTS/OPERATIONS

Selected Brands
4-Grain
Cal-Maine
Egg-Land's Best (licensed from Egg-Land's Best, Inc.)
Farmhouse
Rio Grande
Sunny Meadows
Sunups

Selected Subsidiaries
American Egg Products, Inc. (99.5%)
Benton County Foods, LLC
Cal-Maine Farms, Inc.
Hillandale, LLC (100%)
South Texas Protein, LLC (43%)
Tampa Farms, LLC
Texas Egg Products, LLC (37%)
Zephyr Egg, LLC

COMPETITORS
Cargill Kitchen Solutions
Chino Valley Ranchers
ConAgra
Cooper Farms
Crystal Farms
Egg Innovations
Golden Oval Eggs
Hickman's Family Farms
Ise America
Lincoln Poultry
Luberski
Michael Foods Egg Products
Michael Foods, Inc.
Moark
National Food
Norco Ranch
Rose Acre Farms
Wilson Farms

HISTORICAL FINANCIALS
Company Type: Public

Income Statement

	REVENUE ($ mil.)	NET INCOME ($ mil.)	NET PROFIT MARGIN	EMPLOYEES
5/09	928.8	79.5	8.6%	2,100
5/08	915.9	151.9	16.6%	1,800
5/07	598.1	36.7	6.1%	1,600
5/06	477.6	(1.0)	—	1,650
5/05	375.3	(10.4)	—	1,400
Annual Growth	25.4%	—	—	10.7%

FYE: Saturday nearest May 31

2009 Year-End Financials
Debt ratio: 34.9%
Return on equity: 26.2%
Cash ($ mil.): 66.9
Current ratio: 2.33
Long-term debt ($ mil.): 116.0
No. of shares (mil.): 23.8
Dividends
Yield: 6.1%
Payout: 44.6%
Market value ($ mil.): 580.2
R&D as % of sales: —
Advertising as % of sales: —

Stock History
NASDAQ (GM): CALM

	STOCK PRICE ($) FY Close	P/E High	P/E Low	PER SHARE ($) Earnings	PER SHARE ($) Dividends	PER SHARE ($) Book Value
5/09	24.37	15	5	3.34	1.49	13.95
5/08	31.20	6	2	6.40	0.83	11.58
5/07	13.35	9	4	1.55	0.05	6.54
5/06	7.00	—	—	(0.04)	0.05	5.03
5/05	6.49	—	—	(0.43)	0.05	5.12
Annual Growth	39.2%	—	—	—	133.6%	28.5%

Capella Education

At Capella Education, the line to receive your sheepskin is *online*. The fast-growing company operates Capella University, an online university that offers more than 20 undergraduate and graduate degree programs. More than 26,000 students are enrolled in the school, which employs more than 1,000 faculty members (most of which are part-time employees, typically teaching one to three courses per semester). Capella's typical student is a working adult. Nearly half are pursuing master's degrees; more than a third are doctoral candidates. Some three-quarters of the company's revenues are derived from federal student financial aid programs.

Capella Education has grown its revenue and enrollment through the expansion of its program offerings. It also establishes working relationships with corporations, the military, and other entities, offering professional development for those organizations' workforce. The growing acceptance of online education has undoubtedly helped business as well.

Capella's founder, Stephen Shank, stepped down as CEO in 2009 but remained chairman. Kevin Gilligan, the former CEO of United Subcontractors, filled the executive post. Shank owns some 12% of Capella Education; institutional investors hold nearly an additional 20%.

EXECUTIVES

Chairman; Chancellor, Capella University: Stephen G. (Steve) Shank, age 66, $913,067 total compensation
CEO and Director: J. Kevin Gilligan, age 54
SVP and CFO: Lois M. Martin, age 46, $778,152 total compensation
SVP; President, Capella University: Christopher (Chris) Cassirer, age 44
SVP Human Resources: Sally B. Chial, age 48, $490,359 total compensation
SVP Operations and CIO: Scott M. Henkel, age 54
SVP Strategy and Business Development: Kyle M. Carpenter
VP, General Counsel, and Secretary: Gregory W. (Greg) Thom, age 52
VP Differentiation Strategy: Reed A. Watson, age 51, $546,094 total compensation
Director Public Relations: Irene Silber
Director Investor Relations: Heide Erickson
Vice Chairman, External University Initiatives and President Emeritus, Capella University: Michael J. (Mike) Offerman, age 62, $533,529 total compensation
Auditors: Ernst & Young LLP

LOCATIONS

HQ: Capella Education Company
225 S. 6th St., 9th Fl., Minneapolis, MN 55402
Phone: 612-339-8650   **Fax:** 612-977-5060
Web: www.capellaeducation.com

PRODUCTS/OPERATIONS

Selected Academic Programs
Bachelor of Science in Business
Bachelor of Science in Information Technology
Bachelor of Science in Public Safety
Doctor of Philosophy in Counselor Education and Supervision
Doctor of Philosophy in Education
Doctor of Philosophy in Human Services
Doctor of Philosophy in Information Technology
Doctor of Philosophy in Organization and Management
Doctor of Philosophy in Public Safety
Doctor of Philosophy in Psychology

Doctor of Psychology
Master of Business Administration
Master of Science in Education
Master of Science in Human Resource Management
Master of Science in Human Services
Master of Science in Information Technology
Master of Science in Organizational Development
Master of Science in Psychology
Master of Science in Public Health
Master of Science in Public Safety

2008 Students by Program

	No.	% of total
Master's	12,388	46
Doctoral	9,723	36
Bachelor's	4,635	17
Other	137	1
Total	**26,883**	**100**

COMPETITORS

Apollo Group
Cardean Learning Group
The College Network
Corinthian Colleges
DeVry
eCollege.com
Jones Knowledge
Kaplan
Laureate Education
Strayer Education

HISTORICAL FINANCIALS
Company Type: Public

Income Statement

	REVENUE ($ mil.)	NET INCOME ($ mil.)	NET PROFIT MARGIN	EMPLOYEES
12/08	272.3	28.8	10.6%	1,140
12/07	226.2	22.8	10.1%	2,207
12/06	179.9	13.4	7.4%	1,787
12/05	149.2	10.3	6.9%	1,649
12/04	117.7	18.8	16.0%	1,372
Annual Growth	**23.3%**	**11.3%**	**—**	**(4.5%)**

FYE: December 31

2008 Year-End Financials
Debt ratio: —
Return on equity: 19.3%
Cash ($ mil.): 31.2
Current ratio: 4.68
Long-term debt ($ mil.): —
No. of shares (mil.): 16.7
Dividends
 Yield: 0.0%
 Payout: —
Market value ($ mil.): 981.3
R&D as % of sales: —
Advertising as % of sales: —

Stock History
NASDAQ (GM): CPLA

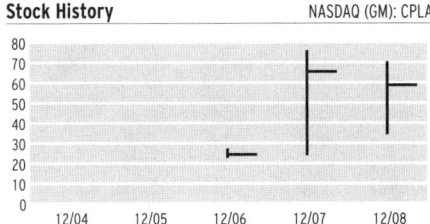

	STOCK PRICE ($) FY Close	P/E High/Low	Earnings	Dividends	Book Value
12/08	58.76	42 21	1.66	0.00	8.43
12/07	65.46	57 18	1.33	0.00	9.39
12/06	24.25	25 22	1.06	0.00	5.61
Annual Growth	**55.7%**	**— —**	**25.1%**	**—**	**22.6%**

Capital Senior Living

Capital Senior Living wants to capitalize on the growing numbers of seniors in the US. The company owns or manages about 65 senior residential properties in more than 20 states scattered across the country. Formed to consolidate the operations of several partnerships that previously owned its facilities, the company provides independent living, assisted living, and skilled nursing services. Capital Senior Living also operates a home health care agency that manages the health care needs of residents at one of its communities. Specialized care units for treatment of Alzheimer's patients are also available. Private pay sources comprise about 95% of the company's revenue.

Capital Senior Living has grown partly through acquisitions and the development of new communities. In 2006 the company formed a joint venture with GE Healthcare Financial Services to acquire five senior communities.

Late in 2007 the company entered a deal to acquire about 30 leases on senior living communities from Hearthstone Senior Services. However, it terminated the agreement early the next year.

In addition, Capital Senior Living works to grow revenue at its existing facilities through rate hikes and increasing occupancy rates. It is also converting some of its units from independent living to more expensive assisted-living or dementia care units, which offer higher levels of care to residents.

Chairman James Stroud owns about 10% of the company.

EXECUTIVES

CEO and Director: Lawrence A. Cohen, age 55, $747,142 total compensation
President, COO, and Director: Keith N. Johannessen, age 52, $510,476 total compensation
EVP and CFO: Ralph A. Beattie, age 59, $427,977 total compensation
VP Finance: Gloria M. Holland, age 41
VP Development: Glen H. Campbell, age 64
VP National Marketing: Rob L. Goodpaster, age 56
VP Operations: David W. Beathard Sr., age 62
VP, General Counsel, and Secretary: David R. Brickman, age 50, $275,417 total compensation
Director Information Technology: Marty Kangiser
Director Human Resources: Colleen Landino
Property Controller: Robert F. Hollister, age 54
Corporate Controller: Jerry D. Lee, age 49
Auditors: Ernst & Young LLP

LOCATIONS

HQ: Capital Senior Living Corporation
 14160 Dallas Pkwy., Ste. 300, Dallas, TX 75254
Phone: 972-770-5600   **Fax:** 972-770-5666
Web: www.capitalsenior.com

PRODUCTS/OPERATIONS

2008 Sales

	% of total
Resident & health care	89
Community reimbursement	8
Affiliated management services	3
Total	**100**

COMPETITORS

Assisted Living Concepts
Atria Senior Living Group
BPM Senior Living
Brookdale Senior Living
Emeritus Corporation
Five Star Quality Care
Golden Horizons
Life Care Centers
Sunrise Senior Living

HISTORICAL FINANCIALS
Company Type: Public

Income Statement

	REVENUE ($ mil.)	NET INCOME ($ mil.)	NET PROFIT MARGIN	EMPLOYEES
12/08	193.3	3.7	1.9%	3,871
12/07	189.1	4.4	2.3%	3,711
12/06	159.1	(2.6)	—	3,681
12/05	105.2	(5.4)	—	2,867
12/04	93.3	(6.8)	—	2,795
Annual Growth	**20.0%**	**—**	**—**	**8.5%**

FYE: December 31

2008 Year-End Financials
Debt ratio: 114.4%
Return on equity: 2.4%
Cash ($ mil.): 25.9
Current ratio: 1.39
Long-term debt ($ mil.): 177.5
No. of shares (mil.): 27.2
Dividends
 Yield: 0.0%
 Payout: —
Market value ($ mil.): 81.2
R&D as % of sales: —
Advertising as % of sales: —

Stock History
NYSE: CSU

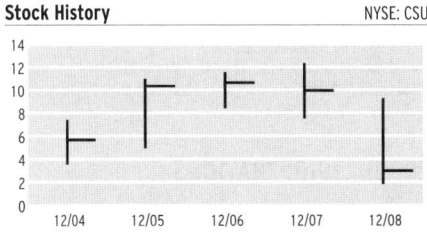

	STOCK PRICE ($) FY Close	P/E High/Low	Earnings	Dividends	Book Value
12/08	2.98	65 14	0.14	0.00	5.70
12/07	9.93	76 48	0.16	0.00	5.51
12/06	10.64	— —	(0.10)	0.00	5.29
12/05	10.34	— —	(0.21)	0.00	5.34
12/04	5.66	— —	(0.27)	0.00	5.49
Annual Growth	**(14.8%)**	**— —**	**—**	**—**	**0.9%**

Capitol Federal Financial

Dorothy and Toto may not be in Kansas anymore, but Capitol Federal Financial is. The holding company owns Capitol Federal Savings Bank, a thrift that serves metropolitan areas throughout the Sunflower State, including Kansas City, Emporia, Lawrence, Manhattan, Salina, Topeka, and Wichita. It has about 40 branches serving consumers and commercial customers by offering loans, CDs, and money market, checking, and savings accounts. The thrift mainly originates one- to four-family home mortgages (about 95% of its loan portfolio), but it also writes consumer, construction, and other real estate loans.

Its Capitol Agency Insurance affiliate sells life, liability, and property/casualty coverage. Capitol Federal Savings also offers investments through an agreement with CMIC Financial Services.

About 70% of Capitol Federal Financial's stock is held by a mutual holding company, Capitol Federal Savings Bank MHC.

EXECUTIVES

Chairman Emeritus: John C. (Jack) Dicus, age 75
Chairman, President, CEO, and Director, Capitol Federal Financial and Capitol Federal Savings Bank: John B. Dicus, age 48
EVP, CFO, and Treasurer, Capitol Federal Financial and Capitol Federal Savings Bank: Kent G. Townsend, age 47
EVP and Chief Lending Officer, Capitol Federal Savings Bank; President, Capitol Funds and Capitol Federal Mortgage Reinsurance Company: Morris J. (Jack) Huey III, age 59
EVP Retail Operations, Capitol Federal Savings Bank: Richard J. (Joe) Aleshire, age 60
EVP Corporate Services, Capitol Federal Savings Bank: Larry K. Brubaker, age 61
First VP, Principal Accounting Officer, and Reporting Director, Capitol Federal Financial and Capitol Federal Savings Bank: Tara D. Van Houweling, age 35
Investor Relations Officer: Jim Wempe
Auditors: Deloitte & Touche LLP

LOCATIONS

HQ: Capitol Federal Financial
700 S. Kansas Ave., Topeka, KS 66603
Phone: 785-235-1341   **Fax:** 785-231-6264
Web: www.capfed.com

PRODUCTS/OPERATIONS

2009 Gross Revenues

	$ mil.	% of total
Interest		
Loans receivable	305.8	69
Mortgage-related securities	97.9	21
Investment securities	5.5	1
Other	3.5	1
Noninterest		
Retail fees & charges	18.0	4
Insurance commissions	2.5	1
Loan fees	2.3	1
Other	5.9	2
Total	**441.4**	**100**

COMPETITORS

Bank of America
Commerce Bancshares
First Federal of Olathe
Landmark Bancorp
UMB Financial
U.S. Bancorp

HISTORICAL FINANCIALS

Company Type: Public

Income Statement				FYE: September 30
	ASSETS ($ mil.)	NET INCOME ($ mil.)	INCOME AS % OF ASSETS	EMPLOYEES
9/09	8,403.7	66.3	0.8%	749
9/08	8,055.2	51.0	0.6%	740
9/07	7,675.9	32.3	0.4%	758
9/06	8,199.1	48.1	0.6%	738
9/05	8,409.7	65.1	0.8%	761
Annual Growth	(0.0%)	0.5%	—	(0.4%)

2009 Year-End Financials

Equity as % of assets: 11.2%
Return on assets: 0.8%
Return on equity: 7.3%
Long-term debt ($ mil.): 3,106.2
No. of shares (mil.): 74.1
Market value ($ mil.): 2,439.4

Dividends
Yield: 6.1%
Payout: 219.8%
Sales ($ mil.): 205.2
R&D as % of sales: —
Advertising as % of sales: —

Stock History

NASDAQ (GS): CFFN

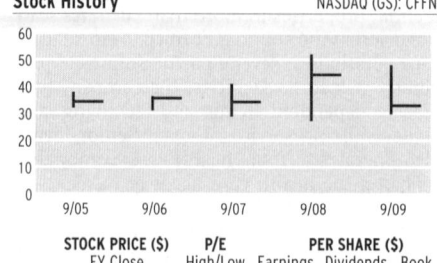

	STOCK PRICE ($) FY Close	P/E High/Low	PER SHARE ($) Earnings	Dividends	Book Value
9/09	32.92	52 33	0.91	2.00	12.70
9/08	44.33	74 39	0.70	2.00	11.76
9/07	34.20	92 66	0.44	2.00	11.71
9/06	35.56	54 48	0.66	2.00	11.65
9/05	34.22	42 37	0.89	2.00	11.67
Annual Growth	(1.0%)	— —	0.6%	0.0%	2.1%

CARBO Ceramics

CARBO Ceramics' proppants (tiny alumina-based ceramic beads) are a welcome release for natural gas and oil well operators. To increase well production, operators often pump fluids down wells at high pressure to create fractures in the hydrocarbon-bearing rock formation (hydraulic fracturing). Proppants are suspended in the fluid to fill the channels and "prop" up the fissures so that natural gas and oil may flow to the surface. The company's products compete against sand-based proppants. CARBO Ceramics also operates related software, consulting services, and geotechnical monitoring businesses. Chairman William Morris owns about 14% of CARBO Ceramics.

CARBO Ceramics' three top customers — BJ Services, Schlumberger, and Halliburton — together accounted for 72% of sales in 2008.

The company's ceramic proppants are made from alumina-bearing ores (including clay, bauxite, bauxitic clay, and kaolin). The main deposits of these ores in the US are in Arkansas, Alabama, and Georgia; other economically viable deposits are found in Australia, Brazil, China, Gabon, India, Jamaica, Russia, and Surinam.

In 2008 CARBO Ceramics sold a portion of its assets (primarily its fracture and reservoir diagnostics business) to Halliburton for $137 million in order to raise cash. The next year, adding a complementary business, it bought the assets of BBL Falcon, a spill prevention and containment products maker. The services allows CARBO Ceramics to both gain new customers and to give environmental support to its existing customers' well-site operations.

EXECUTIVES

Chairman: William C. Morris, age 71
President, CEO, and Director: Gary A. Kolstad, age 51, $1,557,805 total compensation
VP and CFO: Ernesto Bautista III, age 38
VP Software: Neill Northington
VP Consulting: Mike Shade
VP Marketing and Sales: David G. Gallagher, age 51, $730,048 total compensation
VP Operations: Mark L. Edmunds, age 54, $606,203 total compensation
Chief Compliance Officer, General Counsel, and Corporate Secretary: R. Sean Elliott, age 36, $417,918 total compensation
Development Engineer: Peter Van Dyke
Director Marketing Communications: Steve Bell
Director Sales and Marketing, North America: Mark McGill
Auditors: Ernst & Young LLP

LOCATIONS

HQ: CARBO Ceramics Inc.
6565 MacArthur Blvd., Ste. 1050, Irving, TX 75039
Phone: 972-401-0090   **Fax:** 972-401-0705
Web: www.carboceramics.com

2008 Sales

	$ mil.	% of total
US	273.8	71
Canada	42.2	11
Other countries	71.8	18
Total	**387.8**	**100**

PRODUCTS/OPERATIONS

Selected Products

High-strength, sintered bauxite proppants (CarboHSP)
Intermediate-strength proppants (CarboPROP)
Lightweight ceramic proppants (CarboECONOPROP)
Lightweight, intermediate-strength proppants (CarboLITE)

COMPETITORS

BJ Services
Core Laboratories
Saint-Gobain
Schlumberger
Unimin

HISTORICAL FINANCIALS

Company Type: Public

Income Statement				FYE: December 31
	REVENUE ($ mil.)	NET INCOME ($ mil.)	NET PROFIT MARGIN	EMPLOYEES
12/08	387.8	110.3	28.4%	648
12/07	340.4	53.9	15.8%	759
12/06	312.1	54.3	17.4%	630
12/05	252.7	46.6	18.4%	530
12/04	223.1	41.7	18.7%	426
Annual Growth	14.8%	27.5%	—	11.1%

2008 Year-End Financials

Debt ratio: —
Return on equity: 26.5%
Cash ($ mil.): 154.8
Current ratio: 3.53
Long-term debt ($ mil.): —
No. of shares (mil.): 23.1

Dividends
Yield: 1.7%
Payout: 13.7%
Market value ($ mil.): 819.2
R&D as % of sales: —
Advertising as % of sales: —

Stock History

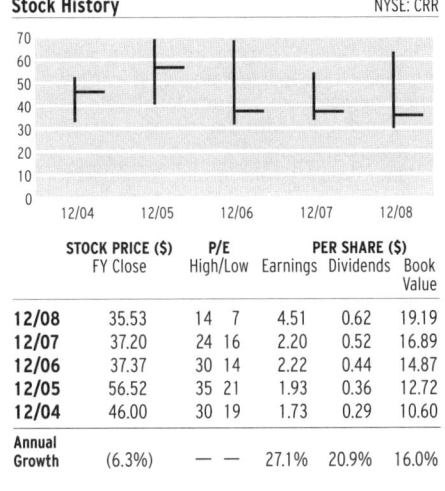

NYSE: CRR

	STOCK PRICE ($) FY Close	P/E High/Low		PER SHARE ($) Earnings	Dividends	Book Value
12/08	35.53	14	7	4.51	0.62	19.19
12/07	37.20	24	16	2.20	0.52	16.89
12/06	37.37	30	14	2.22	0.44	14.87
12/05	56.52	35	21	1.93	0.36	12.72
12/04	46.00	30	19	1.73	0.29	10.60
Annual Growth	(6.3%)	—	—	27.1%	20.9%	16.0%

CardioNet, Inc.

CardioNet wants to be as close as your next heartbeat. The company provides real-time outpatient cardiac monitoring services for ambulatory (mobile) patients. Aiming to improve on existing monitoring technologies by providing continuous heartbeat monitoring with up to 21 days of data, the CardioNet System provides doctors with a more complete picture of heart functions when diagnosing and monitoring arrhythmias (abnormal heart rhythms). The system relies on two-way wireless communication — providing mobility for the patient and remote adjustment for physicians. CardioNet also sells traditional cardiac event and Holter monitors, which rely on digital or taped data transmissions.

The CardioNet System is marketed directly to doctors and patients throughout the US and has been used with about 185,000 patients. The company's Mobile Cardiac Outpatient Telemetry services rely on the system's FDA-approved monitoring equipment, wireless transmission network, proprietary software, and a 24-hour monitoring center.

CardioNet's products and services are primarily reimbursed by Medicare (about one-third of revenues) and other insurance and managed care companies, and the company is working to expand its reimbursement contracts. The company also hopes to expand its products' uses beyond arrhythmia monitoring into fields such as disease management, inpatient care, and clinical trials monitoring.

The company conducted some restructuring efforts during 2008 in order to reduce operating costs, including the consolidation of some administrative and sales functions. The reorganization was also part of CardioNet's efforts to integrate PDSHeart, which was acquired in 2007 for about $52 million and significantly expanded the company's service offerings and geographic presence; it also more than doubled the size of CardioNet's sales force. The acquisition of PDSHeart added Holter, event, and pacemaker monitoring services, and allows CardioNet new cross-selling avenues, as well as the capability to provide one-stop-shopping opportunities in the cardiac monitoring field.

To gain more wireless technology and add clinical research services to its offerings, CardioNet in 2009 agreed to pay $14 million to acquire Biotel, but later cancelled the deal saying Biotel failed to meet the agreement terms. Biotel then disputed the claim by filing a lawsuit against CardioNet.

In 2007 CardioNet completed an IPO. Proceeds from the public offering were used to pay off debt, fund the PDSHeart transaction, build up inventory of CardioNet systems, and develop improved versions of the product.

EXECUTIVES

Chairman, President, and CEO: Randy H. Thurman, age 59
CFO: Martin P. (Marty) Galvan, age 57, $643,489 total compensation
SVP Business Operations: John F. Imperato, age 51, $609,560 total compensation
SVP Sales and Marketing: Matthew (Matt) Margolies
SVP Reimbursement Serivices, Regulatory, and Compliance: Philip G. Leone, age 44
SVP Clinical Operations: Anna McNamara, age 61, $464,923 total compensation
VP Information Technology: Curt Baldwin
VP Human Resources: George Hrenko, age 46
VP Marketing: Andy Broadway
VP Finance: Heather Getz
VP Research and Development: Charles M. Gropper, age 51
Media Relations: Derek Lucchese
Auditors: Ernst & Young LLP

LOCATIONS

HQ: CardioNet, Inc.
227 Washington St., Ste. 300
Conshohocken, PA 19428
Phone: 610-729-7000 **Fax:** 610-828-8048
Web: www.cardionet.com

PRODUCTS/OPERATIONS

2008 Sales

	$ mil.	% of total
Patient revenues	119.8	99
Other	0.7	1
Total	**120.5**	**100**

COMPETITORS

Biotel	LifeWatch
Cardiac Science	Philips Healthcare
Diagnostic Health	Spacelabs Healthcare
eResearchTechnology	United Therapeutics
GE Healthcare	Welch Allyn
Heart Tronics	

HISTORICAL FINANCIALS

Company Type: Public

Income Statement				FYE: December 31
	REVENUE ($ mil.)	NET INCOME ($ mil.)	NET PROFIT MARGIN	EMPLOYEES
12/08	120.5	9.2	7.6%	756
12/07	73.0	(8.7)	—	604
12/06	33.9	(7.6)	—	509
12/05	30.9	(11.5)	—	—
12/04	22.2	(20.9)	—	—
Annual Growth	52.6%	—	—	21.9%

2008 Year-End Financials

Debt ratio: 0.0%
Return on equity: 26.4%
Cash ($ mil.): 58.2
Current ratio: 6.73
Long-term debt ($ mil.): 0.0
No. of shares (mil.): 23.9

Dividends
Yield: 0.0%
Payout: —
Market value ($ mil.): 588.4
R&D as % of sales: —
Advertising as % of sales: —

Stock History

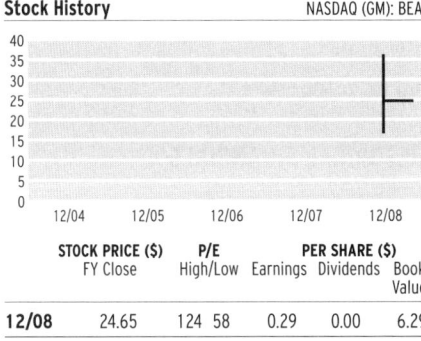

NASDAQ (GM): BEAT

	STOCK PRICE ($) FY Close	P/E High/Low		PER SHARE ($) Earnings	Dividends	Book Value
12/08	24.65	124	58	0.29	0.00	6.29

Carolina Bank Holdings

Carolina Bank Holdings owns Carolina Bank, which serves individuals and small to midsized businesses through some 10 branches in northern portions of North Carolina. The community-oriented financial institution offers standard services such as checking and savings accounts, money market and individual retirement accounts, CDs, ATM and debit cards, and online banking and bill payment. Loans secured by commercial properties account for about 40% of the company's portfolio, followed by residential mortgages, construction and land development loans, commercial and industrial loans, and consumer loans.

In 2007 Carolina Bank formed a wholesale mortgage division that originates residential home loans through third-party brokers and banks, then sells them into the secondary market.

EXECUTIVES

Chairman: John D. (Jay) Cornet, age 62
Vice Chairman: Gary N. Brown, age 64
President, CEO, and Director; President and CEO, Carolina Bank: Robert T. Braswell, age 57, $491,052 total compensation
EVP and Senior Loan Officer, Carolina Bank: Gunnar N. R. Fromen, age 60, $313,586 total compensation
EVP and Chief Credit Officer, Carolina Bank: Daniel D. Hornfeck, age 41, $147,802 total compensation
Treasurer and Secretary; EVP, CFO, and Secretary, Carolina Bank: T. Allen Liles, age 56, $254,626 total compensation
SVP, Carolina Bank: W. Keith Strickland
SVP, Carolina Bank: H. Dean Sexton
SVP, Carolina Bank: F. Virginia Grimes
SVP, Carolina Bank: Gerald W. Church
SVP, Carolina Bank: Linwood A. (Chip) Harris
SVP, Carolina Bank: W. McDuffy (Duffy) Johnson
SVP, Carolina Bank: Paul L. Kennedy
VP, Human Resources and Accounting Officer, Carolina Bank: Angela J. Nowlin
President, Carolina Bank Wholesale Mortgage and SVP, Carolina Bank: Phillip B. Carmac, age 55, $334,191 total compensation
Auditors: Cherry, Bekaert & Holland, LLP

LOCATIONS

HQ: Carolina Bank Holdings, Inc.
101 N. Spring St., Greensboro, NC 27401
Phone: 336-288-1898 **Fax:** 336-286-5553
Web: www.carolinabank.com

COMPETITORS

AF Financial
BB&T
First Citizens BancShares
FNB United
RBC Bank

HISTORICAL FINANCIALS

Company Type: Public

Income Statement

	ASSETS ($ mil.)	NET INCOME ($ mil.)	INCOME AS % OF ASSETS	EMPLOYEES
				FYE: December 31
12/08	616.6	2.2	0.4%	119
12/07	500.1	3.0	0.6%	89
12/06	411.6	2.8	0.7%	72
12/05	365.2	2.0	0.5%	59
12/04	311.5	1.6	0.5%	51
Annual Growth	18.6%	8.3%	—	23.6%

2008 Year-End Financials

Equity as % of assets: 5.1%
Return on assets: 0.4%
Return on equity: 7.2%
Long-term debt ($ mil.): 76.1
No. of shares (mil.): 3.4
Market value ($ mil.): 20.8

Dividends
Yield: 0.0%
Payout: —
Sales ($ mil.): 19.3
R&D as % of sales: —
Advertising as % of sales: —

Stock History

NASDAQ (CM): CLBH

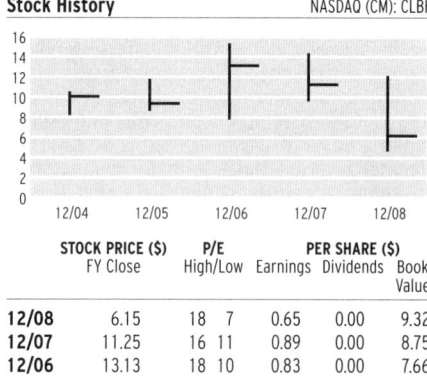

	STOCK PRICE ($) FY Close	P/E High/Low		PER SHARE ($) Earnings	Dividends	Book Value
12/08	6.15	18	7	0.65	0.00	9.32
12/07	11.25	16	11	0.89	0.00	8.75
12/06	13.13	18	10	0.83	0.00	7.66
12/05	9.38	19	14	0.61	0.00	6.73
12/04	10.07	21	17	0.49	0.00	6.24
Annual Growth	(11.6%)	—	—	7.3%	—	10.6%

Cash America

If cash is king, then Cash America International is king of pawns. Ruling over a kingdom of some 500 locations in 22 states, and another 112 stores in Mexico, it's one of the largest providers of secured, non-recourse loans (known as pawn loans) in North America. It operates through Cash America Pawn and SuperPawn shops; customers collateralize high-interest loans with jewelry, electronics, and other items. Stores may sell unredeemed merchandise. Cash America also offers cash advances, check cashing, and money orders and transfers through stores operating as Cashland Financial Services and Cash America Payday Advance. Check cashing services are offered through about 130 owned and franchised Mr. Payroll stores.

The company continues to expand through the acquisition of established pawnshops and cash advance facilities within Cash America's current geographic scope. The company expanded its horizons in 2006 with the purchase of Chicago-based Check Giant, a company that makes short-term advances via the Internet using the name CashNetUSA. Today, the company has an Internet lending presence in more than 30 states.

After selling its UK retail operations in 2004, the company made a return visit in 2007 with plans to offer cash advances there through an online platform.

In 2008 the company established a presence in Mexico, where it bought a majority interest in a 112-store chain of pawnshops for some $91 million. Prenda Facíl, with shops located throughout central Mexico, is regarded as the second-largest privately owned pawn company in the country. The new shops provide Cash America with a significant lending platform in Mexico — a market where growth is predicted.

Also that year three states in which Cash America operates — Ohio, Pennsylvania, and Minnesota — lowered the maximum interest rate that can be charged on loans. Cash America altered its operations in Ohio and is evaluating the result. In Pennsylvania, Cash America sued the state's banking department over the regulatory changes. And in Minnesota, a trade group's challenge to the change forced the state to reverse its ruling.

Cash America and other pawn shop operations were one of the few industries to see a sizeable increase in revenues in 2008. Recession-battered consumers used pawn loans to keep the mortgage paid and put gas in their tanks. Cash America's revenues topped the $1 billion mark for the first time in company history.

About one-third of Cash America's loans are not redeemed and the collateral is sold. However, the company isn't built on selling pawned merchandise alone. It charges up to 300% interest on the loans it makes.

HISTORY

When Jack Daugherty was a student, he hocked his guitar to finance dates. In 1970, after quitting school, he opened a pawnshop that was so successful he used the proceeds to invest in oil. When oil took a downturn, he returned to the pawn business, incorporating Cash America in 1984; it went public in 1987.

Cash America bought UK-based Harvey & Thompson Ltd. in 1992; two years later, the company acquired Sweden's Svensk Pantbelåning.

Operational problems, including a failed retail venture, caused a brief downturn in 1995, but Cash America refocused on its core business and recovered in 1996. As part of a low-cost expansion program, the next year the firm introduced a Cash America franchise plan to independent pawnshop owners.

Over the next two years, Cash America expanded further in Texas and Utah. In 1998 Mr. Payroll rolled out automated check-cashing machines that identified customers by their facial features; it formed an alliance with Crestar to supplement the bank's Virginia supermarket branches with the machines. Also that year the company launched its Rent-A-Tire subsidiary in Texas.

In 1999 Cash America expanded its automated check cashing business, participating in InnoVentry, a joint venture with Wells Fargo (InnoVentry ceased operations in 2001). In 2000 Cash America got lots of publicity (presumably unwanted) when its nine-story headquarters in downtown Fort Worth was slammed by a tornado; the building was later renovated.

In an attempt to focus on lending activities, subsidiary Rent-A-Tire was sold off in 2002. The following year Cash America doubled its cash advance operations with the purchase of Cashland Financial Services.

With a desire to concentrate on US operations, Cash America sold off its operations in Sweden and the UK in 2004, while at the same time expanding its presence in Southern California with the purchase of UrgentMoney and GoldX.

EXECUTIVES

Chairman: Jack R. Daugherty, age 61
President, CEO, and Director: Daniel R. (Dan) Feehan, age 58, $2,230,606 total compensation
EVP, General Counsel, and Secretary: J. Curtis Linscott, age 43
EVP and CFO: Thomas A. Bessant Jr., age 50, $866,915 total compensation
President, Internet Services: Timothy J. Ho, age 29
President and COO, Retail Services: Dennis J. Weese, age 45, $561,360 total compensation
Auditors: PricewaterhouseCoopers LLP

LOCATIONS

HQ: Cash America International, Inc.
1600 W. 7th St., Fort Worth, TX 76102
Phone: 817-335-1100   **Fax:** 817-570-1225
Web: www.cashamerica.com

2008 Locations

	No.
US	
Texas	199
Florida	69
Nevada	26
Tennessee	22
Louisiana	20
Georgia	17
Missouri	17
Oklahoma	15
Indiana	13
Illinois	13
Arizona	11
Kentucky	10
North Carolina	10
Alabama	9
Utah	7
Ohio	6
South Carolina	6
Alaska	5
Colorado	5
Washington	5
California	1
Mexico	112
Total	**598**

PRODUCTS/OPERATIONS

2008 Sales

	$ mil.	% of total
Sale of merchandise	465.7	45
Cash advance fees	364.6	35
Finance & service charges	185.0	18
Check cashing royalties & fees	15.5	2
Total	**1,030.8**	**100**

COMPETITORS

ACE Cash Express
Advance America
Cash Converters
DGSE Companies
Dollar Financial
EZCORP
First Cash Financial Services
Winmark
World Acceptance
Xponential

HISTORICAL FINANCIALS
Company Type: Public

Income Statement
FYE: December 31

	ASSETS ($ mil.)	NET INCOME ($ mil.)	INCOME AS % OF ASSETS	EMPLOYEES
12/08	1,186.5	81.1	6.8%	5,587
12/07	904.6	79.3	8.8%	5,501
12/06	776.2	60.9	7.8%	5,152
12/05	598.6	45.0	7.5%	4,565
12/04	555.2	56.8	10.2%	4,279
Annual Growth	20.9%	9.3%	—	6.9%

2008 Year-End Financials
Equity as % of assets: 48.5%
Return on assets: 7.8%
Return on equity: 15.1%
Long-term debt ($ mil.): 422.3
No. of shares (mil.): 29.3
Market value ($ mil.): 801.4
Dividends
 Yield: 0.5%
 Payout: 5.2%
Sales ($ mil.): 1,030.8
R&D as % of sales: —
Advertising as % of sales: —

Stock History
NYSE: CSH

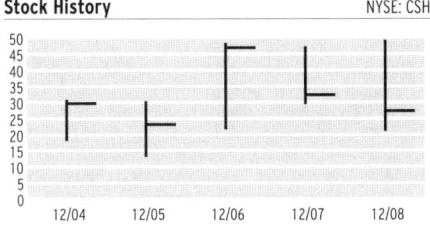

	STOCK PRICE ($) FY Close	P/E High/Low		PER SHARE ($) Earnings	Dividends	Book Value
12/08	27.35	18	8	2.70	0.14	19.62
12/07	32.30	18	11	2.61	0.14	16.95
12/06	46.90	24	11	2.00	0.10	15.04
12/05	23.19	20	9	1.49	0.10	12.79
12/04	29.73	16	10	1.92	0.07	11.40
Annual Growth	(2.1%)	—	—	8.9%	18.9%	14.6%

Cavium Networks

Cavium Networks can help keep networks secure without hiding them in a cave somewhere. The company designs specialized microprocessors used in secure network transmissions, based on processor technology developed by ARM and MIPS Technologies. Cavium's customers include such heavy hitters as Cisco Systems, F5 Networks, Fujitsu, Nokia, Samsung Electronics, Sumitomo, and ZTE. Manufacturing is contracted out to Fujitsu Microelectronics, Taiwan Semiconductor Manufacturing, and United Microelectronics. Distributors handle around one-third of sales. Customers in the US provide about half of Cavium's sales.

Cavium Networks has a limited number of customers; its top five clients account for more than half of sales. The company's operating results tend to fluctuate, due to economic and market conditions. Cavium went into the red in late 2008, as the semiconductor industry in particular and the electronics market in general experienced an extended downturn due to the global recession. Since the company outsources its manufacturing and logistics functions, it relies on a number of third parties to carry out those duties.

Looking to enter the embedded Linux software market, in 2009 Cavium bought MontaVista Software for about $50 million. MontaVista develops Linux-based operating systems that are embedded into electronics that operate automobiles, electronics, and communications products.

In 2008 the company acquired assets belonging to Taiwan-based Star Semiconductor for about $9 million in cash. The deal gave Cavium Networks a system-on-a-chip (SoC) and a software design team with broadband and network connectivity experience. Later that year Cavium acquired W&W Communications, a developer of video processors, for about $19 million. As many PC users grow accustomed to watching video material on the Internet, video codecs will increase in sales volume. W&W's PureVu processor line became a Cavium product family.

Cavium Networks acquired the assets of Menlo Logic in 2006, adding embedded enterprise security software to its product portfolio. The company gained software developers in California and India through the acquisition.

The company used proceeds from its 2007 IPO to repay a $4 million loan from SVB Financial Group (formerly Silicon Valley Bank) and Gold Hill Ventures 03 LP. Cavium also used the money for working capital and other general corporate purposes, including potential acquisitions and investments.

EXECUTIVES
Chairman, President, and CEO: Syed B. Ali, age 51, $678,191 total compensation
VP Software and CTO: Muhammad R. Hussain, age 36
VP IC Engineering: Anil K. Jain, age 53, $357,891 total compensation
VP Operations: Syed A. Zaheer, age 40
VP Sales and Field Applications: Andrew J. (Andy) Rava, age 50
VP and General Manager, Networking and Communications Division: Rajiv Khemani, age 42, $547,503 total compensation
VP Finance and Administration, CFO, and Secretary: Arthur D. (Art) Chadwick, age 53, $324,228 total compensation
VP and General Manager, Broadband and Consumer Division: Sandeep S. Vij, age 43, $570,811 total compensation
Senior Director Corporate and Business Development: Amer Haider
Marketing Communications Manager: Angel Atondo
Auditors: PricewaterhouseCoopers LLP

LOCATIONS
HQ: Cavium Networks, Inc.
 805 E. Middlefield Rd., Mountain View, CA 94043
Phone: 650-623-7000   **Fax:** 650-625-9751
Web: www.caviumnetworks.com

Cavium Networks has offices in China, India, Spain, Taiwan, and the US.

2008 Sales

	$ mil.	% of total
US	44.8	52
Japan	11.6	13
Taiwan	11.5	13
China	6.2	7
Other countries	12.5	15
Total	**86.6**	**100**

PRODUCTS/OPERATIONS

Selected Products
Accelerator boards
ECONA ARM-based processors
Embedded processors
Intelligent network adapters
NITROX security macro processors
OCTEON MIPS64 processors
PureVu video processors

COMPETITORS
Applied Micro Circuits
Broadcom
Certicom
Elliptic Technologies
Exar
Freescale Semiconductor
Ikanos
Intel
Marvell Technology
NetLogic Microsystems
PMC-Sierra
SafeNet

HISTORICAL FINANCIALS
Company Type: Public

Income Statement
FYE: December 31

	REVENUE ($ mil.)	NET INCOME ($ mil.)	NET PROFIT MARGIN	EMPLOYEES
12/08	86.6	1.5	1.7%	347
12/07	54.2	2.2	4.1%	202
12/06	34.2	(9.0)	—	157
12/05	19.4	(11.6)	—	125
12/04	7.4	(11.7)	—	—
Annual Growth	85.0%	—	—	40.5%

2008 Year-End Financials
Debt ratio: 1.6%
Return on equity: 1.2%
Cash ($ mil.): 77.0
Current ratio: 5.67
Long-term debt ($ mil.): 2.1
No. of shares (mil.): 41.7
Dividends
 Yield: 0.0%
 Payout: —
Market value ($ mil.): 438.0
R&D as % of sales: —
Advertising as % of sales: —

Stock History
NASDAQ (GM): CAVM

	STOCK PRICE ($) FY Close	P/E High/Low	PER SHARE ($) Earnings	Dividends	Book Value
12/08	10.51	665 205	0.04	0.00	3.09
12/07	23.02	509 235	0.07	0.00	2.80
Annual Growth	(54.3%)	— —	(42.9%)	—	10.0%

Cbeyond, Inc.

Cbeyond isn't looking past the millions of small businesses in the US to find customers. A telecommunications company, Cbeyond uses Voice over Internet Protocol (VoIP) technologies to provide local and long-distance services and broadband Internet access to small businesses. It offers its services over its own private IP network. The company's other offerings include mobile voice and data services, as well as file sharing and backup services. It targets businesses in large metropolitan areas, including Atlanta, Denver, Houston, Chicago, and Los Angeles. Typical customers include legal firms, physicians' offices, real estate companies, and accounting firms. Cbeyond was founded in 1991 by CEO James Geiger.

The company's primary means of growth revolves around its small business-centric approach. It attempts to sidestep stiff competition from incumbent carriers (who frequently target large businesses and residential customers) by focusing on the traditionally underserved small-business market. Cbeyond intends to maintain its focus on this core group of customers, and it will continue to expand in its existing geographical markets and move into new areas as well.

EXECUTIVES

Chairman, President, and CEO: James F. (Jim) Geiger, age 50, $2,249,384 total compensation
COO: Richard J. Batelaan, age 43
EVP and CFO: J. Robert (Bob) Fugate, age 48, $1,066,605 total compensation
CTO: Christopher C. (Chris) Gatch, age 36
CIO: Joseph A. (Joe) Oesterling, age 41, $846,272 total compensation
Chief People Officer: Robert R. (Bob) Morrice, age 60, $902,818 total compensation
Chief Administrative Officer: William H. Weber
Chief Customer Officer: N. Brent Cobb, age 39
Chief Marketing Officer: Brooks A. Robinson, age 37, $846,694 total compensation
VP Sales: Cleveland A. Lewis
VP Marketing: Mary N. Ford
VP Finance and Treasurer: Kurt J. Abkemeier, age 39
VP and Chief Accounting Officer: Henry C. Lyon, age 44
VP Operations Support Systems: Minaz Vastani
VP Customer Experience: Terry S. Trout, age 49
VP Human Resources: Joan L. Tolliver
VP Customer Service Operations: Ashish Bisaria
VP Marketing: Stephen P. Zimba
Auditors: Ernst & Young LLP

LOCATIONS

HQ: Cbeyond, Inc.
   320 Interstate North Pkwy., Ste. 500
   Atlanta, GA 30339
Phone: 678-424-2400   **Fax:** 678-424-2500
Web: www.cbeyond.net

2008 Sales

	% of total
Atlanta	23
Dallas	20
Denver	20
Houston	13
Chicago	10
Los Angeles	7
San Diego	3
Detroit	2
San Francisco Bay Area	1
Other cities	1
Total	**100**

PRODUCTS/OPERATIONS

Selected Services
Broadband Internet access
Calling cards
Conference calling
E-mail
Local voice access
Long-distance voice
Toll-free
Virtual private network (VPN)
Voicemail
Web hosting

COMPETITORS

8x8
AT&T
Cablevision Systems
Comcast
Covad Communications Group
Cox Communications
Deltathree
DSL.net
Integra Telecom
ITC^DeltaCom
NuVox
One Communications
Qwest Communications
Time Warner Cable
tw telecom
U.S. TelePacific
Verizon
Vonage
XO Holdings

HISTORICAL FINANCIALS
Company Type: Public

Income Statement
FYE: December 31

	REVENUE ($ mil.)	NET INCOME ($ mil.)	NET PROFIT MARGIN	EMPLOYEES
12/08	349.7	3.7	1.1%	1,493
12/07	280.0	21.5	7.7%	1,187
12/06	213.9	7.8	3.6%	905
12/05	159.1	(4.8)	—	707
12/04	113.3	(18.5)	—	586
Annual Growth	**32.5%**	—	—	**26.3%**

2008 Year-End Financials

Debt ratio: —
Return on equity: 2.7%
Cash ($ mil.): 37.0
Current ratio: 1.30
Long-term debt ($ mil.): —
No. of shares (mil.): 29.0
Dividends
   Yield: 0.0%
   Payout: —
Market value ($ mil.): 462.8
R&D as % of sales: —
Advertising as % of sales: —

Stock History
NASDAQ (GM): CBEY

	STOCK PRICE ($) FY Close	P/E High/Low	PER SHARE ($) Earnings	Dividends	Book Value
12/08	15.98	330 68	0.12	0.00	4.96
12/07	38.99	65 37	0.72	0.00	4.40
12/06	30.59	128 35	0.27	0.00	3.15
12/05	10.30	— —	(1.16)	0.00	2.58
Annual Growth	**15.8%**	— —	—	—	—

Century Bancorp

Century Bancorp is the holding company for Century Bank and Trust, which serves Boston and surrounding northeastern Massachusetts from about 20 branch locations. The bank offers standard deposit products, including checking, savings, and money market accounts; CDs; and IRAs. Some 45% of the bank's loan portfolio is dedicated to commercial real estate. It also writes residential mortgages (25%), construction and development loans, business loans, and home equity loans. The company provides cash management and transaction processing services to municipalities; subsidiary Century Financial Services offers investment and brokerage services. Chairman Marshall Sloane controls the company.

EXECUTIVES

Founder and Chairman, Century Bancorp and Century Bank: Marshall M. Sloane, age 82
President, CEO, and Director: Barry R. Sloane, age 54, $1,203,085 total compensation
CFO and Treasurer: William P. Hornby, age 42, $207,707 total compensation
EVP and Head of Lending, Century Bank and Trust: David B. Woonton, age 53, $484,110 total compensation
EVP Retail, Cash Management, Operations, and Marketing, Century Bank and Trust: Paul A. Evangelista, age 45, $409,774 total compensation
EVP and Head of Institutional Services, Century Bank and Trust: Brian J. Feeney, age 48, $248,563 total compensation
Auditors: KPMG LLP

LOCATIONS

HQ: Century Bancorp, Inc.
   400 Mystic Ave., Medford, MA 02155
Phone: 781-391-4000   **Fax:** 781-393-4071
Web: www.century-bank.com

COMPETITORS

Boston Private
Brookline Bancorp
Cambridge Financial
Capital Crossing
Central Bancorp
Citizens Financial Group
Eastern Bank
Middlesex Savings
Sovereign Bank

HISTORICAL FINANCIALS
Company Type: Public

Income Statement
FYE: December 31

	ASSETS ($ mil.)	NET INCOME ($ mil.)	INCOME AS % OF ASSETS	EMPLOYEES
12/08	1,801.6	9.0	0.5%	380
12/07	1,680.3	7.9	0.5%	373
12/06	1,644.3	4.7	0.3%	373
12/05	1,728.8	6.9	0.4%	391
12/04	1,833.7	8.9	0.5%	289
Annual Growth	**(0.4%)**	**0.3%**	—	**7.1%**

2008 Year-End Financials

Equity as % of assets: 6.7%
Return on assets: 0.5%
Return on equity: 7.5%
Long-term debt ($ mil.): 274.6
No. of shares (mil.): 5.5
Market value ($ mil.): 87.1
Dividends
   Yield: 3.0%
   Payout: 29.4%
Sales ($ mil.): 58.8
R&D as % of sales: —
Advertising as % of sales: —

NASDAQ (GM): CNBKA

	STOCK PRICE ($) FY Close	P/E High/Low		PER SHARE ($) Earnings	Dividends	Book Value
12/08	15.75	14	7	1.63	0.48	21.79
12/07	20.17	20	14	1.42	0.48	21.48
12/06	27.30	36	29	0.84	0.48	19.32
12/05	29.27	28	21	1.24	0.48	18.66
12/04	29.50	23	18	1.60	0.48	18.95
Annual Growth	(14.5%)	—	—	0.5%	0.0%	3.6%

CEVA, Inc.

CEVA has a fever for semiconductor design. CEVA specializes in technology — both integrated circuit and software designs — used in cell phones, handheld computers, MP3 players, and other wireless devices. It licenses its semiconductor intellectual property (SIP) designs to such industry heavyweights as Broadcom, Fujitsu, Hitachi, National Semiconductor, Sony, and Texas Instruments. The company derives nearly 90% of its sales from technology licensing and royalties, with the remainder coming from design and consulting services, along with maintenance and support fees from licensees. CEVA's SIP is shipped in more than 300 million devices a year.

CEVA operates in a highly competitive sector of the semiconductor industry, with some of its rivals offering better business terms to certain customers. The company has a limited number of customers; its top five clients account for more than three-quarters of royalty revenues. CEVA is looking for future growth through licensing arrangements with system OEMs and with small to midsized semiconductor companies. The company also wants to diversify its geographic reach, since it gets more than half of revenues from Europe and the Middle East region.

The revenue mix is shifting from primarily licensing to more of royalties. CEVA signed 30 new license agreements in 2008, compared with 36 the year before and 38 in 2006. Gartner, the market research firm, estimated the company's share of the licensable digital signal processor (DSP) market at 61% for 2008. DSPs are widely used in wireless handsets and other portable electronics.

The company took the name ParthusCeva after Ireland's Parthus Technologies combined its operations with the Ceva unit of DSP Group; the combined company later changed its name to CEVA.

HISTORY

Brian Long and Peter McManamon founded Silicon Systems in 1993. Long's background included a stint at AT&T and 17 years with Digital Equipment; McManamon co-founded a large-screen projector company. Silicon Systems was aided early on by seed capital from Enterprise Ireland, a government-run development agency, plus its first customer, STMicroelectronics. Long took advantage of his previous contact with the Switzerland-based semiconductor giant to secure early contracts.

Over the next five years, Silicon Systems honed its design skills in a number of technologies, performing contract work for STMicroelectronics and other chip manufacturers. During this period the company retained ownership and licensing rights to its intellectual property, which incorporated expertise in digital, analog, and mixed-signal chips, as well as in software design.

Silicon Systems narrowed its focus in 1998, deciding to concentrate on technology for mobile devices. That year Goldman Sachs invested in the company, trading $16 million for a 23% stake (reduced to 19% after Parthus' public offering, and subsequently divested).

In 2000 Silicon Systems changed its name to Parthus Technologies and acquired the Global Positioning System (GPS) division of electronics maker Symmetricom. Later that year the company went public, listing on both the Nasdaq and the London Stock Exchange in what was at that time the largest technology float by an Irish company. The offering made the reticent Long (he was often accused of being too modest about the company's achievements) one of the richest men in Ireland.

Parthus secured a number of major contracts in 2000, including licensing deals for its NavStream GPS with ARM Holdings, and for processor design for wireless devices (InfoStream) with Motorola and Psion. The next year the company bought privately held Chicory Systems (technology for speeding up mobile Internet applications) in a cash and stock deal valued at about $41 million.

In 2002 the company combined its operations with Ceva, the IP licensing arm of DSP Group, to form a new company called ParthusCeva. Parthus president Kevin Fielding became CEO of the combined company. Fielding stepped down in 2003; Long became interim CEO for a few months until industry veteran Chet Silvestri succeeded him as president and CEO. That same year the company changed its name from ParthusCeva to CEVA. Silvestri added the post of chairman in 2004.

Silvestri resigned as chairman and CEO the following year, leaving CEVA's board altogether. Co-founder Peter McManamon replaced him as chairman and EVP/GM Gideon Wertheizer was promoted to CEO.

In 2006 the company sold its Global Positioning System (GPS) technology and associated products to GloNav, a fabless semiconductor startup, in return for an equity stake of about 20% in the firm. GloNav also licensed the CEVA-TeakLite digital signal processor core for the development of its GPS chipsets. At the end of 2007, however, NXP acquired GloNav, and CEVA divested its 20% stake.

EXECUTIVES

Chairman: Peter McManamon, age 60
CEO: Gideon Wertheizer, age 52,
$912,651 total compensation
CFO: Yaniv Arieli, age 40, $542,035 total compensation
CTO: Erez Bar-Niv
EVP Worldwide Sales: Issachar Ohana, age 43,
$563,249 total compensation
VP Corporate Marketing: Eran Briman
VP Strategic Accounts and Partners: Eyal Ben-Avraham
VP Operations: Aviv Malinovitch

VP Research and Development: Menachem Stern
Director Marketing: Richard Kingston
Director Product Marketing Communications Division:
Paddy McWilliams
Auditors: Ernst & Young

LOCATIONS

HQ: CEVA, Inc.
2033 Gateway Place, Ste. 150, San Jose, CA 95110
Phone: 408-514-2900   **Fax:** 408-514-2995
Web: www.ceva-dsp.com

2008 Sales

	$ mil.	% of total
Europe & Middle East		
Sweden	8.0	20
Switzerland	5.9	15
Other countries	8.4	20
Asia/Pacific		
Japan	5.1	13
Other countries	7.7	19
US	5.3	13
Total	**40.4**	**100**

PRODUCTS/OPERATIONS

2008 Sales

	$ mil.	% of total
Licensing	21.7	54
Royalties	14.3	35
Other	4.4	11
Total	**40.4**	**100**

COMPETITORS

Analog Devices
ARC International plc
ARM Holdings
AXEON
Fairchild Semiconductor
Freescale Semiconductor
Fujitsu Microelectronics
Gennum
Imagination Technologies
Infineon Technologies
MIPS Technologies
NXP
Patriot Scientific
Renesas Technology
Silicon Image
Synopsys
Tensilica
Texas Instruments
VeriSilicon
Virage Logic
Zoran

HISTORICAL FINANCIALS

Company Type: Public

Income Statement				FYE: December 31
	REVENUE ($ mil.)	NET INCOME ($ mil.)	NET PROFIT MARGIN	EMPLOYEES
12/08	40.4	8.6	21.3%	187
12/07	33.2	1.3	3.9%	192
12/06	32.5	(0.1)	—	196
12/05	35.6	(2.3)	—	209
12/04	37.7	1.6	4.2%	227
Annual Growth	1.7%	52.3%	—	(4.7%)

2008 Year-End Financials

Debt ratio: —
Return on equity: 7.3%
Cash ($ mil.): 52.8
Current ratio: 7.91
Long-term debt ($ mil.): —
No. of shares (mil.): 19.9

Dividends
  Yield: 0.0%
  Payout: —
Market value ($ mil.): 139.6
R&D as % of sales: —
Advertising as % of sales: —

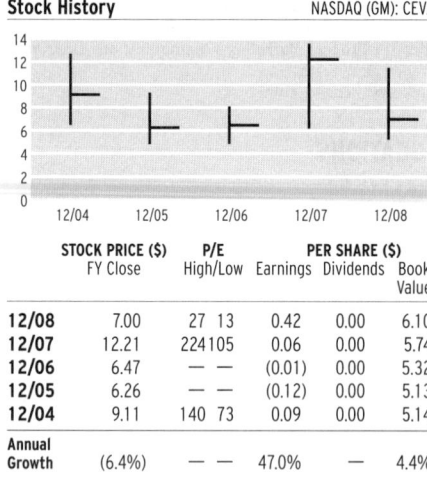

	STOCK PRICE ($) FY Close	P/E High/Low	PER SHARE ($) Earnings	Dividends	Book Value
12/08	7.00	27 13	0.42	0.00	6.10
12/07	12.21	224105	0.06	0.00	5.74
12/06	6.47	— —	(0.01)	0.00	5.32
12/05	6.26	— —	(0.12)	0.00	5.13
12/04	9.11	140 73	0.09	0.00	5.14
Annual Growth	(6.4%)	— —	47.0%	—	4.4%

Chart Industries

They're just chillin' at Chart Industries. The company designs equipment for low-temperature uses, including cryogenic systems that can operate at temperatures near absolute zero. Chart's vessels are used to process, liquefy, store, and transport gases, which are marketed to petrochemical and natural gas processors, producers of industrial gas, satellite testing companies, and restaurants and convenience stores. The company also performs engineered bulk gas installations and makes specialty liquid nitrogen end-use equipment used in the hydrocarbon processing and industrial gas industries. Chart's products are sold worldwide; the US accounts for about three-quarters of sales.

To streamline operations, Chart Industries reorganized its subsidiaries into three business segments: Energy & Chemicals (E&C), Distribution & Storage (D&S), and BioMedical. Though the segments deal with different equipment and end-users, they are related in their use of heat transfer and low temperature storage processes. The E&C and D&S segments make products used in energy-related (62% of sales) and general industrial applications. The BioMedical segment supplies cryogenic equipment for storing biological material and oxygen, which is used primarily in the medical, biological research, and animal breeding industries.

The E&C segment is focused on equipment and systems for the energy and chemicals markets, such as cold boxes and heat exchangers, process systems, and LNG (liquid natural gas) vacuum insulated pipe. Customers for this area include ExxonMobil, ConocoPhillips, and Samsung.

D&S supplies cryogenic equipment to global bulk and packaged industrial gas markets, as well as bulk fountain syrup and liquid CO2 containers used for beverage carbonation in restaurants and convenience stores. The D&S segment has benefited from an increase in orders since the 2008 acquisition of German-based Flow Instruments & Engineering (Flow). Flow manufactures cryogenic flow meter systems, gas distribution equipment, and provides calibration services.

BioMedical provides products and systems based on cryogenics, but with a focus on respiratory therapy and biological users of liquids and gases. It also manufactures MRI components, which are marketed to customers like General Electric. Late in 2009 Chart Industries acquired Covidien's oxygen therapy business, including its Companion and HELiOS brands. The purchase adds a worldwide sales and service organization, along with liquid oxygen therapy product offerings, to the BioMedical segment's CAIRE respiratory therapy business. CAIRE sells primarily to the home health care market.

The company is continually adjusting base prices and surcharges for its atmospheric and CO2 bulk tanks due to escalating costs in carbon steel plate, chromium, iron, nickel, and other materials. The rising prices of petroleum-based fuels are also affecting Chart's freight transportation costs. The company is adjusting its surcharge schedules on a monthly basis as a result.

Neuberger Berman owns about 10% of Chart Industries. AXA Assurances and Wentworth, Hauser & Violich each have an equity stake of around 5%.

HISTORY

In 1986 Arthur Holmes teamed up with his brother Charles to purchase ALTEC International, a struggling maker of brazed aluminum heat exchangers that dated to 1949. The brothers turned ALTEC around and used it to acquire undervalued companies. From 1986 to 1991, they purchased storage and transportation equipment for liquefied gases and high-pressure cryogenic equipment, including Greenville Tube Corporation (stainless steel tubing, 1987); Process Engineering, Inc. (cryogenic tanks, 1990); and Process Systems International (cold boxes, 1991). The Holmes brothers finally established a public holding company in 1992, and named it Chart Industries (for CHarles and ARThur).

The company ran into trouble over the next few years trying to make its acquisitions profitable. Chart restructured its most troubled unit, Process Engineering, Inc., in 1994. It bought cryogenic vacuum pumps maker CVI to build systems for NASA. In 1995 the company began supplying vacuum equipment for the Laser Interferometer Gravitational-Wave Observatory project, a research program searching for cosmic gravitational waves.

In 1997 Chart bought Cryenco Sciences, which makes cryogenic road trailers. The next year the company acquired the Industrial Heat Exchanger division of UK-based IMI Marston (IMI sold the Marston aerospace business in 1999). In a move intended to increase foreign sales, Chart in 1999 bought MVE Holding, a cryogenic storage and transportation company with facilities in the US and Europe, for $240 million in cash. The company also expanded its cryogenic equipment repair services across the US with the purchase of Northcoast Cryogenics.

Chart signed an agreement in 2000 to build and maintain a new liquid natural gas fueling station for Waste Management. The new refueling station will be the world's largest, capable of refueling 120 trucks per four hours. In March 2002 the company announced it would place surcharges on its bulk storage tanks to offset the tariffs set by the US government on imported steel products, which would increase manufacturing costs.

In 2003 the NYSE suspended trading of the company's shares after the company fell below

continued listing standards and fell into bankruptcy protection. Later that year, Chart Industries came out of bankruptcy protection with a new board membership and senior management. Chairman Arthur Holmes also resigned his post in 2003, but continued as a board member until 2005.

Chart Industries filed for another IPO in 2006, applying to list on the Big Board once more. The company had to settle for a Nasdaq listing, but completed its IPO in mid-2006.

Also in 2006 the company acquired Cooler Service Company of Tulsa, Oklahoma, for nearly $16 million, net of cash. Cooler Service makes custom air-cooled heat exchangers for hydrocarbon, petrochemical, and industrial gas processing and power generation. The firm became part of the Energy & Chemicals segment.

In mid-2007 First Reserve sold its 48% equity stake in Chart Industries through a secondary offering, receiving approximately $263 million.

EXECUTIVES

Chairman, President, and CEO: Samuel F. Thomas, age 57, $1,748,598 total compensation
EVP and CFO: Michael F. Biehl, age 53, $803,357 total compensation
VP, General Counsel, and Secretary: Matthew J. Klaben, age 39, $592,129 total compensation
VP Human Resources: Mark H. Ludwig
VP Corporate Development and Treasurer: James H. (Jim) Hoppel Jr., age 44, $460,598 total compensation
Chief Accounting Officer and Controller: Kenneth J. (Ken) Webster, age 46, $319,262 total compensation
Chairman and Managing Director, Chart Ferox: Hans Lonsain, age 54
President, Chart Asia: Eric M. Rottier
President, Distribution and Storage Group: Thomas M. (Tom) Carey
President, Biomedical Group: Steven T. (Steve) Shaw
President, Energy and Chemicals Group: Michael T. Bright
Auditors: Ernst & Young LLP

LOCATIONS

HQ: Chart Industries, Inc.
1 Infinity Corporate Centre Dr., Ste. 300
Garfield Heights, OH 44125
Phone: 440-753-1490   **Fax:** 440-753-1491
Web: www.chart-ind.com

2008 Sales

	$ mil.	% of total
US	539.3	73
Czech Republic	113.8	15
Other countries	91.3	12
Total	**744.4**	**100**

PRODUCTS/OPERATIONS

2008 Sales

	$ mil.	% of total
Distribution & Storage		
Cryogenic bulk storage systems	164.2	22
Cryogenic packaged gas systems & beverage liquid systems	123.7	17
Cryogenic services	29.0	4
Cryogenic systems & components	19.1	3
Energy & Chemicals		
Heat exchangers	197.9	26
Cold boxes & liquid natural gas vacuum-insulated pipe	114.6	15
BioMedical		
Medical products & biological storage systems	83.9	11
MRI components & other	12.0	2
Total	**744.4**	**100**

Selected Products

Cold boxes (reduce the temperature of gas mixtures to liquefy and separate them)
Cryogenic components (pumps, valves, vacuum-jacketed piping systems, and specialty components)
Cryogenic storage tanks (tanks, trailers, intermodal containers, and railcars)
Heat exchangers (facilitate cooling and liquefaction of air or hydrocarbons)
Space simulation systems (satellite and spacecraft testing)
Thermal vacuum systems (aerospace and research applications)
Vacuum insulated bulk liquid CO_2 containers (beverage carbonation)

COMPETITORS

Air Products
Cobham
Covidien
Flowserve
Graham Corp.
Ingersoll-Rand
Kobe Steel
L'Air Liquide
The Linde Group
Matrix Service
Nordon et Compagnie
Praxair
QualMark
Reliance Steel
Senior plc
Sumitomo Metal Industries

HISTORICAL FINANCIALS
Company Type: Public

Income Statement
FYE: December 31

	REVENUE ($ mil.)	NET INCOME ($ mil.)	NET PROFIT MARGIN	EMPLOYEES
12/08	744.4	78.9	10.6%	2,945
12/07	666.4	44.2	6.6%	2,751
12/06	537.5	26.9	5.0%	2,703
12/05	403.1	8.4	2.1%	2,556
12/04	305.6	22.6	7.4%	—
Annual Growth	24.9%	36.7%	—	4.8%

2008 Year-End Financials

Debt ratio: 60.2%
Return on equity: 21.6%
Cash ($ mil.): 122.2
Current ratio: 2.09
Long-term debt ($ mil.): 243.2
No. of shares (mil.): 28.5
Dividends
  Yield: 0.0%
  Payout: —
Market value ($ mil.): 302.7
R&D as % of sales: —
Advertising as % of sales: —

Stock History
NASDAQ (GS): GTLS

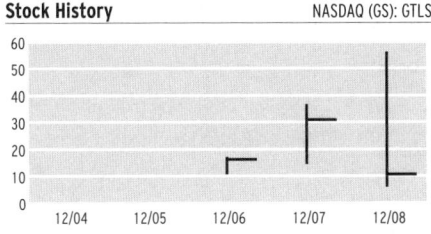

	STOCK PRICE ($) FY Close	P/E High/Low		PER SHARE ($) Earnings	Dividends	Book Value
12/08	10.63	20	2	2.72	0.00	14.18
12/07	30.90	22	9	1.61	0.00	11.52
12/06	16.21	10	7	1.65	0.00	7.72
Annual Growth	(19.0%)	—	—	28.4%	—	35.6%

Chesapeake Utilities

Chesapeake Utilities gasses up the Chesapeake Bay, and then some. The company, through its subsidiaries, serves about 34,100 retail propane customers in Delaware, Florida, Maryland, and Virginia. Another subsidiary, Xeron, sells propane at wholesale to distributors, industrial users, and resellers throughout the US. Chesapeake's three natural gas distribution divisions serve 62,900 customers. Chesapeake's interstate pipeline company, Eastern Shore Natural Gas, transmits gas to its parent and other utilities. Through BravePoint, the company also offers data services, consulting, and software development. Other operations include real estate investment.

Chesapeake Utilities' business strategy is to grow its core energy businesses while exploring strategic acquisitions to diversify its portfolio. In 2009 the company acquired Florida Public Utilities Company in a move that raised its customer base to about 200,000.

The company was founded in 1859 as the Dover Gas Light Company. It became Chesapeake Utilities Corporation in 1947. During 2003, Chesapeake began to exit the water services business, selling six of its seven dealerships. The company sold the remaining water dealership in 2004.

EXECUTIVES

Chairman: Ralph J. Adkins, age 66
President, CEO, and Director; President and CEO, Florida Public Utilities: John R. Schimkaitis, age 61, $978,931 total compensation
EVP and COO: Michael P. (Mike) McMasters, age 51, $604,713 total compensation
SVP, CFO, Corporate Secretary, and Treasurer: Beth W. Cooper, age 42, $338,186 total compensation
SVP; President, Eastern Shore Natural Gas: Stephen C. (Steve) Thompson, age 48, $518,205 total compensation
VP; President, PESCO: Joseph (Joe) Cummiskey, age 38
VP: Thomas A. (Tom) Geoffroy
VP, Eastern Shore Natural Gas: Elaine B. Bittner, age 40
Communications Manager: Sydney H. Davis
Controller: Matthew M. Kim
President and COO, BravePoint: John R. Harlow, age 54
President and COO, Sharp Energy: S. Robert (Bob) Zola, age 58, $258,965 total compensation
President and COO, Xeron: David E. (Dave) Snyder, age 62
Investor Relations Administrator: Heidi W. Watkins
Auditors: PricewaterhouseCoopers LLP

LOCATIONS

HQ: Chesapeake Utilities Corporation
  909 Silver Lake Blvd., Dover, DE 19904
Phone: 302-734-6799   **Fax:** 302-734-6750
Web: www.chpk.com

PRODUCTS/OPERATIONS

2008 Sales

	% of total
Natural gas	91
Propane	6
Advanced information services	2
Other & eliminations	1
Total	**100**

Selected Subsidiaries

Central Florida Gas Company (natural gas distribution)
Chesapeake Service Company
  BravePoint (formerly United Systems, Inc., information technology)
  Chesapeake Investment Company (real estate investments)
  Eastern Shore Real Estate, Inc. (office building leases)
  Skipjack, Inc. (office building leases)
Eastern Shore Natural Gas Company (transmission)
Sharp Energy, Inc. (propane distribution)
  Sharpgas, Inc.
  Tri-County Gas Co., Incorporated
Sharp Water, Inc.
Xeron, Inc. (propane marketing)

COMPETITORS

Allegheny Energy
Constellation Energy Group
Delmarva Power
Energy Transfer
Ferrellgas Partners
Florida Public Utilities
FPL Group
JEA
New Jersey Resources
Suburban Propane
UGI

HISTORICAL FINANCIALS
Company Type: Public

Income Statement
FYE: December 31

	REVENUE ($ mil.)	NET INCOME ($ mil.)	NET PROFIT MARGIN	EMPLOYEES
12/08	291.4	13.6	4.7%	448
12/07	258.3	13.2	5.1%	445
12/06	231.2	10.5	4.5%	437
12/05	229.6	10.5	4.6%	423
12/04	178.0	9.4	5.3%	426
Annual Growth	13.1%	9.7%	—	1.3%

2008 Year-End Financials

Debt ratio: 70.2%
Return on equity: 11.2%
Cash ($ mil.): 1.6
Current ratio: 0.91
Long-term debt ($ mil.): 86.4
No. of shares (mil.): 6.9
Dividends
  Yield: 3.8%
  Payout: 61.1%
Market value ($ mil.): 217.2
R&D as % of sales: —
Advertising as % of sales: —

Stock History
NYSE: CPK

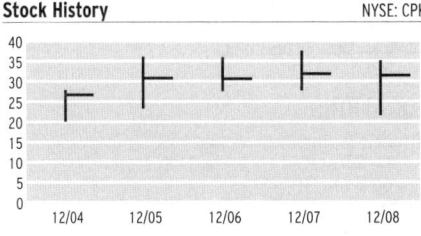

	STOCK PRICE ($) FY Close	P/E High/Low		PER SHARE ($) Earnings	Dividends	Book Value
12/08	31.48	18	11	1.98	1.21	17.84
12/07	31.85	19	14	1.94	1.17	17.33
12/06	30.65	21	16	1.72	1.15	16.11
12/05	30.80	20	13	1.77	1.13	12.28
12/04	26.70	17	13	1.62	1.12	11.30
Annual Growth	4.2%	—	—	5.1%	2.0%	12.1%

Chindex International

Chindex International is good at being a go-between. The company provides Western makers of medical equipment and supplies with access to Chinese markets. Its Medical Products division distributes capital medical equipment — such as diagnostic imaging and robotic surgery systems — and other medical products to hospitals in China and Hong Kong. A second division (Healthcare Services) operates United Family Healthcare, a growing network of private hospitals and satellite medical clinics in Shanghai and Beijing. The division's two 50-bed hospitals cater to the expatriate community and to affluent Chinese customers.

Both of Chindex's United Family hospitals are joint ventures with Chinese entities, though Chindex takes a majority of the net profits in both cases. The company intends to expand its Healthcare Services division by building facilities in other Chinese cities and in its existing markets of Beijing and Shanghai. It is also trying to get management contracts for hospitals owned by third parties.

In 2006 Chindex decided to close down its money-losing retail pharmacy division.

EXECUTIVES

Chairman: A. Kenneth Nilsson, age 77
President, CEO, and Director: Roberta Lipson, age 55, $998,923 total compensation
Senior Advisor to the CEO: Anne Marie Moncure, age 54, $770,644 total compensation
EVP, CFO, Treasurer, and Director: Lawrence Pemble, age 53, $814,511 total compensation
EVP, Secretary, and Director: Elyse Beth Silverberg, age 53, $873,866 total compensation
SVP, China Administration: Walter Stryker
VP Information Technology Services: Daniel Fulton
VP and Chief Financial Officer, United Family Hospitals: Ming Wong
VP Medical Diagnostic and Imaging Products: Wai Ho Leung
VP Finance, Chief Accounting Officer, and Controller: Robert C. Low, age 55, $120,380 total compensation
VP Technical Service, Medical Products Division: Pin Qing Zhang
VP Finance and Controller, China: Walter Xue
VP US Operations: Judy Zakreski
Auditors: BDO Seidman, LLP

LOCATIONS

HQ: Chindex International, Inc.
4340 East West Hwy., Ste. 1100
Bethesda, MD 20814
Phone: 301-215-7777 **Fax:** 301-215-7719
Web: www.chindex.com

PRODUCTS/OPERATIONS

2009 Sales

	$ mil.	% of total
Medical Products Division	92.1	54
Healthcare Services Division	79.3	46
Total	**171.4**	**100**

COMPETITORS

GE Healthcare
Philips Electronics
Toshiba

HISTORICAL FINANCIALS
Company Type: Public

Income Statement
FYE: March 31

	REVENUE ($ mil.)	NET INCOME ($ mil.)	NET PROFIT MARGIN	EMPLOYEES
3/09	171.4	5.0	2.9%	1,276
3/08	130.1	3.7	2.8%	1,181
3/07	105.9	2.7	2.5%	1,007
3/06	90.8	(2.9)	—	950
3/05	100.8	(5.7)	—	1,003
Annual Growth	**14.2%**	**—**		**6.2%**

2009 Year-End Financials

Debt ratio: 24.6%
Return on equity: 5.4%
Cash ($ mil.): 20.3
Current ratio: 3.29
Long-term debt ($ mil.): 23.7
No. of shares (mil.): 14.8
Dividends
  Yield: 0.0%
  Payout: —
Market value ($ mil.): 73.4
R&D as % of sales: —
Advertising as % of sales: —

Stock History
NASDAQ (GM): CHDX

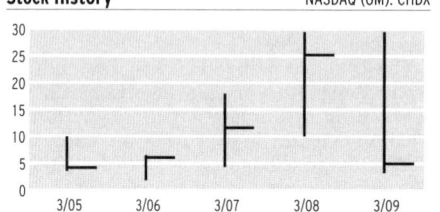

	STOCK PRICE ($) FY Close	P/E High/Low		PER SHARE ($) Earnings	Dividends	Book Value
3/09	4.97	94	11	0.31	0.00	6.53
3/08	25.17	108	38	0.27	0.00	5.92
3/07	11.65	74	19	0.24	0.00	1.89
3/06	6.04	—	—	(0.29)	0.00	1.53
3/05	4.12	—	—	(0.71)	0.00	1.69
Annual Growth	**4.8%**	**—**	**—**		**—**	**40.2%**

Citi Trends

Citi Trends hopes to transport its customers to Trend City as quickly as possible. The fast-growing urban fashion apparel and accessory chain operates about 355 stores in more than 20 US states focusing primarily on the African-American market. Its brand-name and private-label offerings — which include hip-hop jeans and oversized T-shirts; men's, women's, and children's clothing; shoes; housewares; and accessories — are sold at 30%-70% less than department and specialty stores' regular prices. Founded in 1946 as Allied Department Stores, the company changed its name to Citi Trends after it was acquired by former parent Hampshire Equity Partners.

Since its IPO in the mid 2000s, the chain has been adding stores and entering new markets — most recently Philadelphia and Kansas City — at a rapid pace. Indeed, Citi Trends has added more than 150 stores since fiscal 2005, including about 40 stores in fiscal 2009, despite the sour retail climate. In the coming year, another 45 new stores are planned. However, while the number of stores and sales have been increasing, same-store-sales growth (the best measure

---

of a retailer's health) was flat in fiscal 2009 and has been declining since 2006.

To boost store sales, the retailer has been tinkering with its merchandise mix, reducing inventory, and focusing on current fashion trends and brands. National brands account for about 47% of sales, with lesser known and the company's proprietary brands — Diva Blue, Red Ape, and Lil Miss Hollywood — making up the remainder. The chain hired a new chief merchandising officer in 2008 to lead its remerchandising efforts.

The firm promoted David Alexander to CEO following the retirement of R. Edward Anderson in April 2009. Before moving into the chief executive's suite, Alexander, a 30-year retail veteran, served as president and COO of Citi Trends. Anderson remains with the company as its chairman.

Following the 2005 initial public offering, former owner Hampshire Equity Partners sold off its remaining shares in the company during the course of 2006 and 2007.

EXECUTIVES

Executive Chairman: R. Edward (Ed) Anderson, age 59, $1,305,284 total compensation
President, CEO, and Director: R. David Alexander, age 52
EVP and Chief Merchandising Officer: Elizabeth R. Feher, age 48, $656,521 total compensation
SVP and CFO: Bruce D. Smith, age 50, $475,851 total compensation
SVP Human Resources: Ivy D. Council, age 52, $396,191 total compensation
SVP Store Operations: James A. Dunn, age 52, $390,089 total compensation
Auditors: KPMG LLP

LOCATIONS

HQ: Citi Trends, Inc.
104 Coleman Boulevard, Savannah, GA 31408
Phone: 912-236-1561 **Fax:** 912-443-3663
Web: www.cititrends.com

2009 Stores

	No.
Georgia	52
South Carolina	39
North Carolina	34
Texas	37
Florida	30
Louisiana	29
Alabama	25
Mississippi	22
Virginia	16
Tennessee	13
Ohio	13
Arkansas	7
Michigan	11
Indiana	7
Maryland	5
Kentucky	3
Missouri	4
Illinois	4
Pennsylvania	2
Oklahoma	2
Kansas	1
Wisconsin	1
Total	**357**

PRODUCTS/OPERATIONS

2009 Sales

	% of total
Women's	35
Children's	29
Men's	22
Accessories	12
Home decor	2
Total	**100**

COMPETITORS

Burlington Coat Factory
Dollar General
DOTS
Family Dollar Stores
Kmart
Rainbow Apparel
Ross Stores
TJX Companies
Wal-Mart

HISTORICAL FINANCIALS

Company Type: Public

Income Statement				FYE: Saturday nearest January 31
	REVENUE ($ mil.)	NET INCOME ($ mil.)	NET PROFIT MARGIN	EMPLOYEES
1/09	488.2	17.4	3.6%	4,000
1/08	437.5	14.2	3.2%	3,500
1/07	381.9	21.4	5.6%	3,000
1/06	289.8	14.2	4.9%	2,800
1/05	203.4	7.3	3.6%	1,800
Annual Growth	24.5%	24.3%	—	22.1%

2009 Year-End Financials

Debt ratio: 0.0%
Return on equity: 11.7%
Cash ($ mil.): 33.5
Current ratio: 1.81
Long-term debt ($ mil.): 0.0
No. of shares (mil.): 14.7

Dividends
  Yield: —
  Payout: —
Market value ($ mil.): 140.0
R&D as % of sales: —
Advertising as % of sales: —

Stock History

NASDAQ (GS): CTRN

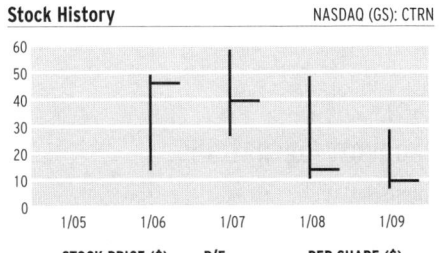

	STOCK PRICE ($) FY Close	P/E High/Low		PER SHARE ($) Earnings	Dividends	Book Value
1/09	9.53	23	6	1.22	—	10.77
1/08	13.67	48	11	1.00	—	9.40
1/07	39.41	38	18	1.51	—	8.05
1/06	46.00	45	13	1.08	—	5.70
Annual Growth	(40.8%)	—	—	16.2%	—	60.6%

CKX, Inc.

CKX is ready to sing "Viva Las Vegas," but any performance will be critiqued by *American Idol*'s Simon Cowell. The company controls 85% of Elvis Presley Enterprises, which manages the King's estate and licenses his likeness, songs, and name, and operates tours of Graceland. CKX also owns 19 Entertainment, the firm responsible for the *American Idol* TV show, and has a "long-term agreement" with *Idol* creator Simon Fuller. As such, it owns the rights to the *IDOLS* brand, which appears in more than 100 countries around the world. Additionally, CKX has an 80% stake in the name, image, likeness, and intellectual property of Muhammad Ali. Entertainment impresario Robert Sillerman owns about 30% of the company.

CKX also owns Morra, Brezner, Steinberg & Tenenbaum Entertainment (MBST), a talent agency that represents several big-name stars, including Robin Williams and Billy Crystal. In other dealings with major personalities, through an exclusive arrangement that runs through the end of 2011, 19 Entertainment has an interest in product merchandising related to projects from soccer superstar David Beckham and his posh wife Victoria. Overall, CKX does business across multiple revenue streams, including music and television, licensing and merchandising, artist management, themed attractions, and touring/live events.

19 Entertainment is active in content creation through partnership with other media firms. FremantleMedia is 19 Entertainment's television production and distribution partner for *IDOLS* programming, and Sony Music is the record label partner of *IDOLS* artists. In addition to its *IDOLS* shows, 19 Entertainment co-produces other TV programs, such as *So You Think You Can Dance* (which airs on the FOX network) and *Little Britain USA* (HBO). Revenue from FOX, FremantleMedia, and Sony Music accounts for 25%, 5%, and 7%, respectively, of CKX's revenue. (Sony Music also distributes recordings from Elvis Presley.)

Sillerman leads a group called 19X, which includes Fuller and members of management, that in 2008 offered to acquire CKX for more than $1 billion. Citing turmoil in the financial sector, 19X later called off its $12-a-share bid for CKX. The proposal came just three years after Sillerman acquired control of the company, then known as Sports Entertainment Enterprises, to use it as a vehicle for acquiring entertainment properties. (Sillerman previously founded radio station operator SFX Broadcasting and its concert promoting subsidiary SFX Entertainment, both of which were subsumed by radio giant Clear Channel. Sports Entertainment Enterprises previously owned Las Vegas' All-American SportPark.)

CKX built its portfolio of assets through a number of acquisitions. It purchased an 80% stake in Muhammad Ali Enterprises for $50 million in cash in 2006. The previous year the company acquired 19 Entertainment for $156 million in cash and stock.

EXECUTIVES

Chairman and CEO: Robert F. X. Sillerman, age 61, $1,961,742 total compensation
COO: Mitchell J. Slater, age 48, $1,081,670 total compensation
SEVP, Director Legal and Governmental Affairs, and Director: Howard J. Tytel, age 63, $1,081,670 total compensation
EVP, CFO, Treasurer, and Director: Thomas P. Benson, age 47, $801,064 total compensation
EVP, Chief Corporate Development Officer, and Secretary: Kraig G. Fox
Director; CEO, 19 Entertainment: Simon R. Fuller, age 49, $4,253,268 total compensation
CEO, Elvis Presley Enterprises: Jack Soden
President, 19 Entertainment: Robert Dodds
President Commercial, 19 Entertainment: Janet Scardino, age 49
Auditors: Deloitte & Touche LLC

LOCATIONS

HQ: CKX, Inc.
650 Madison Ave., New York, NY 10022
Phone: 212-838-3100   **Fax:** 212-872-1473
Web: ir.ckx.com

PRODUCTS/OPERATIONS

2008 Sales

	$ mil.	% of total
19 Entertainment	223.5	78
Presley business		
Graceland operations	36.7	13
Royalties & licensing	18.2	6
Ali business	4.0	1
MBST & other	5.7	2
Total	**288.1**	**100**

Selected Operations

19 Entertainment
  American Idol
  So You Think You Can Dance
Ali Business
MBST
Presley Business
  Graceland Operations
  Royalties and Licensing

COMPETITORS

Brillstein
CAA
Gaylord Entertainment
Gersh Agency
Herschend Entertainment
IMG
Sony/ATV
United Talent

HISTORICAL FINANCIALS

Company Type: Public

Income Statement				FYE: December 31
	REVENUE ($ mil.)	NET INCOME ($ mil.)	NET PROFIT MARGIN	EMPLOYEES
12/08	288.1	19.0	6.6%	629
12/07	266.8	12.1	4.5%	619
12/06	210.2	9.2	4.4%	564
12/05	120.6	(7.5)	—	487
12/04	0.0	(0.1)	—	499
Annual Growth	—	—	—	6.0%

2008 Year-End Financials

Debt ratio: 47.3%
Return on equity: 7.9%
Cash ($ mil.): 101.9
Current ratio: 1.96
Long-term debt ($ mil.): 101.4
No. of shares (mil.): 93.0

Dividends
  Yield: —
  Payout: —
Market value ($ mil.): 341.5
R&D as % of sales: —
Advertising as % of sales: —

Stock History

NASDAQ (GS): CKXE

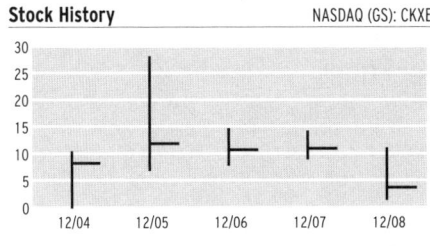

	STOCK PRICE ($) FY Close	P/E High/Low		PER SHARE ($) Earnings	Dividends	Book Value
12/08	3.67	60	9	0.18	—	2.55
12/07	10.91	127	83	0.11	—	3.11
12/06	10.66	180	100	0.08	—	3.99
12/05	11.82	—	—	(0.35)	—	3.48
12/04	8.18	—	—	(0.03)	—	(0.00)
Annual Growth	(18.2%)	—	—	—	—	—

Clayton Williams Energy

Former Texas gubernatorial candidate Clayton Williams once devoted his energy to politics. Now he's devoted to the independent oil and gas firm that he founded. Clayton Williams Energy explores for oil and gas deposits primarily in Louisiana, New Mexico, and Texas and exploits those resources. In 2007 the company reported proved reserves of 290.8 billion cu. ft. of natural gas equivalent. Most of those reserves are in the Permian Basin and in East Texas. It also operates 94 miles of gas pipeline and processing plants in Texas and Mississippi. Williams is CEO, and he and his family control 47% of the firm.

The company's strategy of aggressive exploration and complementary development drilling activities is shaped primarily by Clayton Williams himself (50 years of experience in the oil industry).

In 2004 and 2005 Clayton Williams Energy boosted its reserves with the acquisition of Southwest Royalties and a property in Ward County.

The company announced plans in 2007 to participate in the drilling of a 12,000-foot exploratory well, the Lamb #1 in the Overthrust prospect in Sanpete County, Utah.

It sold two 2,000-horsepower drilling rigs in 2008 to help pay down debt.

EXECUTIVES

Chairman, President, and CEO: Clayton W. Williams, age 78, $726,737 total compensation
EVP, COO, and Director: L. Paul Latham, age 58, $878,976 total compensation
SVP Finance, CFO, Secretary, Treasurer, and Director: Mel G. Riggs, age 55, $799,341 total compensation
VP Accounting: Michael L. Pollard, age 60, $425,953 total compensation
VP and General Counsel: T. Mark Tisdale, age 53
VP Land: Gregory S. Welborn, age 36
VP Acquisitions and New Ventures: Patrick C. Reesby, age 57, $1,298,551 total compensation
VP Gas Gathering and Marketing: Robert C. Lyon, age 73
Executive Assistant: Kay Hardin
Director Human Resources: LuAnn Bolding
Director Investor Relations: Patti Hollums
Auditors: KPMG LLP

LOCATIONS

HQ: Clayton Williams Energy, Inc.
6 Desta Dr., Ste. 3000, Midland, TX 79705
Phone: 432-682-6324   **Fax:** 432-688-3247
Web: www.claytonwilliams.com

PRODUCTS/OPERATIONS

2008 Sales

	% of total
Oil & gas	82
Drilling rig services	8
Natural gas services	2
Other (gain on sales of property & equipment)	8
Total	**100**

COMPETITORS

Anadarko Petroleum	Exxon Mobil
Chevron	Pioneer Natural Resources
EOG	XTO Energy

HISTORICAL FINANCIALS

Company Type: Public

Income Statement

FYE: December 31

	REVENUE ($ mil.)	NET INCOME ($ mil.)	NET PROFIT MARGIN	EMPLOYEES
12/08	565.5	140.5	24.8%	202
12/07	393.9	6.0	1.5%	186
12/06	266.0	17.8	6.7%	180
12/05	283.6	0.3	0.1%	174
12/04	206.3	(14.0)	—	173
Annual Growth	**28.7%**	**—**	**—**	**4.0%**

2008 Year-End Financials

Debt ratio: 110.3%
Return on equity: 59.1%
Cash ($ mil.): 41.2
Current ratio: 1.02
Long-term debt ($ mil.): 347.2
No. of shares (mil.): 12.1
Dividends
  Yield: —
  Payout: —
Market value ($ mil.): 551.8
R&D as % of sales: —
Advertising as % of sales: —

Stock History

NASDAQ (GM): CWEI

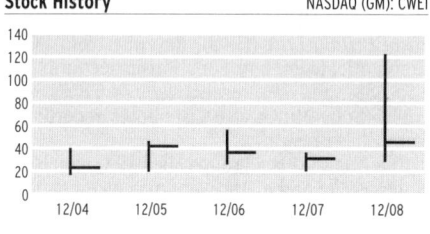

	STOCK PRICE ($) FY Close	P/E High/Low		PER SHARE ($) Earnings	Dividends	Book Value
12/08	45.44	10	3	11.67	—	25.91
12/07	31.16	68	41	0.52	—	13.24
12/06	36.31	35	17	1.58	—	11.94
12/05	41.74	2,248	1,031	0.02	—	9.91
12/04	22.90	—	—	(1.37)	—	9.68
Annual Growth	**18.7%**	**—**	**—**	**—**	**—**	**27.9%**

Clean Harbors

One of North America's leading hazardous-waste management companies, Clean Harbors does more than its name suggests. Clean Harbors' technical services, which account for most of the company's sales, encompass the collection, transportation, treatment, and disposal of hazardous waste, including chemical and laboratory waste but not nuclear waste. The company's 100 service locations include nine landfills, six incineration locations, and six wastewater treatment centers. Among Clean Harbors' more than 47,000 customers are commercial and industrial companies, educational and research organizations, and health care providers. Alan McKim, the company's chairman and CEO, controls 12% of Clean Harbors.

Clean Harbors is working to increase the efficiency of its waste-handling facilities and to expand its industrial maintenance business. The company is also pursuing acquisitions that complement its existing operations.

In 2008 Clean Harbors acquired two solvent recycling facilities in Hebron, Ohio, and Chicago from Safety-Kleen. It also purchased Universal Environmental, an environmental services company based near San Francisco.

In 2009 Clean Harbors acquired Eveready Income Fund, a Canadian firm that provided industrial maintenance and production, lodging, and exploration services to the oil and gas, chemical, pulp and paper, and other industries, for $387 million.

EXECUTIVES

Chairman, President, and CEO: Alan S. McKim, age 54, $625,552 total compensation
EVP Sales and Services, Clean Harbors Environmental Services: David M. Parry, age 43, $584,989 total compensation
EVP and CFO: James M. Rutledge, age 56, $810,321 total compensation
EVP Corporate Sales and Business Development, Clean Harbors Environmental Services: Deirdre J. Evens, age 45
EVP Disposal Services, Clean Harbors Environmental Services: Eric W. Gerstenberg, age 40, $592,634 total compensation
SVP and General Counsel: Michael R. McDonald, age 43
SVP and CIO, Clean Harbors Environmental Services: Michael J. Twohig, age 46
SVP Sales, Line of Business, Clean Harbors Environmental Services: Jerry E. Correll, age 59
VP, Corporate Controller, and Principal Accounting Officer: John R. Beals, age 54
Secretary: C. Michael Malm
President, Clean Harbors Development: William J. (Bill) Geary, age 61
Auditors: Deloitte & Touche LLP

LOCATIONS

HQ: Clean Harbors, Inc.
42 Longwater Dr., Norwell, MA 02061
Phone: 781-792-5000   **Fax:** 781-792-5900
Web: www.cleanharbors.com

PRODUCTS/OPERATIONS

2008 Sales

	$ mil.	% of total
Technical services	712.3	69
Site services	320.6	31
Adjustments	(2.2)	—
Total	**1,030.7**	**100**

COMPETITORS

Heritage Environmental Services
Philip Services
Siemens Water Technologies
SUEZ Environnement
Veolia ES Technical Solutions
Waste Management

HISTORICAL FINANCIALS

Company Type: Public

Income Statement

FYE: December 31

	REVENUE ($ mil.)	NET INCOME ($ mil.)	NET PROFIT MARGIN	EMPLOYEES
12/08	1,030.7	57.5	5.6%	4,804
12/07	946.9	44.0	4.6%	4,769
12/06	829.8	46.4	5.6%	4,574
12/05	711.2	25.6	3.6%	3,900
12/04	643.2	2.6	0.4%	3,792
Annual Growth	**12.5%**	**116.9%**	**—**	**6.1%**

2008 Year-End Financials

Debt ratio: 12.4%
Return on equity: 18.2%
Cash ($ mil.): 249.5
Current ratio: 2.70
Long-term debt ($ mil.): 53.2
No. of shares (mil.): 26.2
Dividends
  Yield: 0.0%
  Payout: —
Market value ($ mil.): 1,663.4
R&D as % of sales: —
Advertising as % of sales: —

Stock History

NYSE: CLH

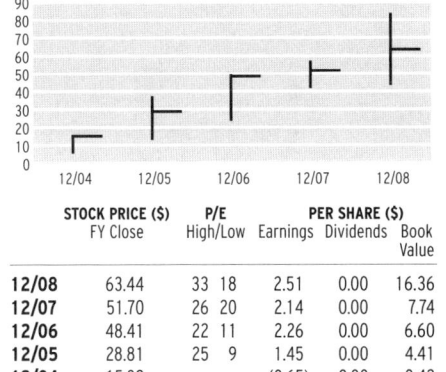

	STOCK PRICE ($) FY Close	P/E High/Low		PER SHARE ($) Earnings	Dividends	Book Value
12/08	63.44	33	18	2.51	0.00	16.36
12/07	51.70	26	20	2.14	0.00	7.74
12/06	48.41	22	11	2.26	0.00	6.60
12/05	28.81	25	9	1.45	0.00	4.41
12/04	15.09	—	—	(0.65)	0.00	0.42
Annual Growth	43.2%	—	—	—	—	149.7%

Clearfield, Inc.

Clearfield provides fiber optic cable and related optical networking equipment. Products include fiber distribution panels and cable management systems, optical components (couplers, multiplexers, and splitters), and copper and fiber-optic cable assemblies. It sells directly to telecom service providers and OEMs. Formerly called APA Enterprises, the company merged its operations with those of its primary subsidiary, APA Cables & Networks (APACN), and changed its name to Clearfield in 2008. Previously the company also operated an optronics unit, but it exited that business in 2007.

Operating in a sector with large competitors that target the dominant telecom carriers, Clearfield has its eye on small, independent telephone companies. Its customers include CenturyTel, Hickory Tech, and SureWest.

EXECUTIVES

Chairman: Ronald G. (Ron) Roth, age 63
President, CEO, and Director: Cheri Beranek Podzimek, age 46
COO: Johnny Hill
CFO and Secretary: Bruce G. Blackey
VP Sales: Bob Poorman
Auditors: Grant Thornton LLP

LOCATIONS

HQ: Clearfield, Inc.
5480 Nathan Ln. North, Ste. 120
Plymouth, MN 55442
Phone: 763-476-6866 **Fax:** 763-475-8457
Web: www.clearfieldconnection.com

PRODUCTS/OPERATIONS

COMPETITORS

ADC Telecommunications
Alcatel-Lucent
American Furukawa
Corning Cable Systems
Telect
Tyco Electronics

HISTORICAL FINANCIALS
Company Type: Public

Income Statement
FYE: September 30

	REVENUE ($ mil.)	NET INCOME ($ mil.)	NET PROFIT MARGIN	EMPLOYEES
9/09	24.9	3.8	15.3%	113
9/08	23.5	1.5	6.4%	112
9/07*	10.3	(1.3)	—	107
3/07	18.4	(2.1)	—	133
3/06	15.7	(3.3)	—	128
Annual Growth	12.2%	—	—	(3.1%)

*Fiscal year change

2009 Year-End Financials

Debt ratio: 0.0%
Return on equity: 24.2%
Cash ($ mil.): 4.7
Current ratio: 4.37
Long-term debt ($ mil.): 0.0
No. of shares (mil.): 12.0
Dividends
  Yield: —
  Payout: —
Market value ($ mil.): 53.3
R&D as % of sales: —
Advertising as % of sales: —

Stock History
NASDAQ (GM): CLFD

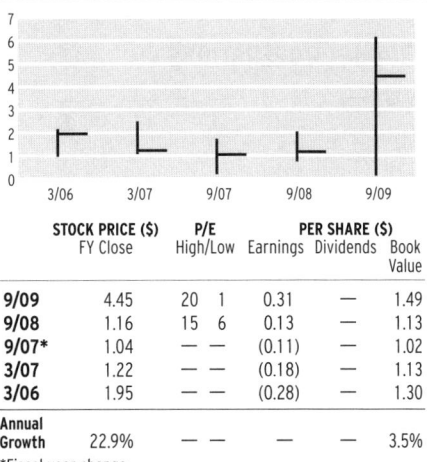

	STOCK PRICE ($) FY Close	P/E High/Low		PER SHARE ($) Earnings	Dividends	Book Value
9/09	4.45	20	1	0.31	—	1.49
9/08	1.16	15	6	0.13	—	1.13
9/07*	1.04	—	—	(0.11)	—	1.02
3/07	1.22	—	—	(0.18)	—	1.13
3/06	1.95	—	—	(0.28)	—	1.30
Annual Growth	22.9%	—	—	—	—	3.5%

*Fiscal year change

CNX Gas

CNX Gas may sound like a product for riot control, but it is in fact a company that produces a more innocuous, but valuable, commodity. A part of CONSOL Energy, CNX Gas is one of the most productive coalbed methane gas (CBM) producers in the US. Through its properties in the Appalachian Basin (primarily in Pennsylvania, Tennessee, Virginia, and West Virginia), CNX Gas is responsible for producing about 58.3 billion cu. ft. of gas per year. In 2007 the company had 1.3 trillion cu. ft. of proved reserves. That year it acquired 1 million acres of coalbed methane properties from Peabody Energy for $66.5 million. CONSOL owns 82% of the company.

In 2007 CNX Gas also attained the rights to CONSOL Energy's CBM properties in northern and central Appalachia, as well as the Illinois Basin; the properties represent an estimated 4.5 billion tons of coal reserves.

EXECUTIVES

Chairman and CEO: J. Brett Harvey, age 58
President and COO: Nicholas J. DeIuliis, age 40
EVP and CFO: William J. Lyons, age 60
EVP Business Advancement and Support Services: Robert P. King, age 56
EVP, Secretary, and General Counsel: Stephen W. Johnson, age 50
EVP Energy Sales and Transportation Services: Robert F. Pusateri, age 58
EVP Corporate Affairs, Chief Legal Officer, and Secretary: P. Jerome Richey, age 59
SVP Established Business Units: J. Michael Onifer, age 53
SVP Emerging Business Units: Randall M. Albert, age 52
VP Business Development: Robert Belesky
VP Land Resources: William (Gill) Gillenwater
VP Investor Relations: Daniel J. (Dan) Zajdel
VP Marketing: Roland J. Campanelli
Director Human Resources: Kurt Salvatori
Manager Public Relations: Laural Ziemba
Auditors: Ernst & Young LLP

LOCATIONS

HQ: CNX Gas Corporation
CNX Center, 1000 CONSOL Energy Dr.
Canonsburg, PA 15317
Phone: 724-485-4000
Web: www.cnxgas.com

PRODUCTS/OPERATIONS

2008 Sales

	% of total
Outside sales	86
Royalty interest gas sales	10
Related party sales	1
Purchased gas sales	1
Other	2
Total	**100**

COMPETITORS

Quicksilver Resources
Range Resources
Sharpe Resources
Southwestern Energy

HISTORICAL FINANCIALS
Company Type: Public

Income Statement
FYE: December 31

	REVENUE ($ mil.)	NET INCOME ($ mil.)	NET PROFIT MARGIN	EMPLOYEES
12/08	789.4	239.1	30.3%	373
12/07	477.3	135.7	28.4%	281
12/06	513.9	159.9	31.1%	192
12/05	613.4	102.2	16.7%	134
12/04	397.5	80.8	20.3%	124
Annual Growth	18.7%	31.2%	—	31.7%

2008 Year-End Financials

Debt ratio: 5.4%
Return on equity: 19.9%
Cash ($ mil.): 1.9
Current ratio: 0.89
Long-term debt ($ mil.): 74.7
No. of shares (mil.): 151.0
Dividends
  Yield: —
  Payout: —
Market value ($ mil.): 4,121.9
R&D as % of sales: —
Advertising as % of sales: —

Stock History

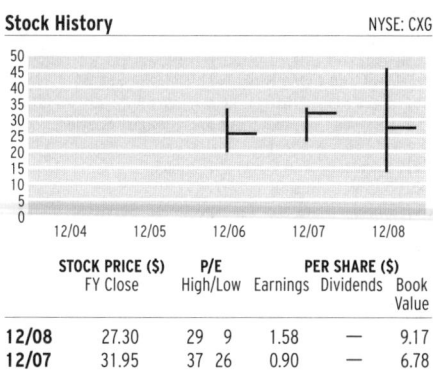

NYSE: CXG

	STOCK PRICE ($) FY Close	P/E High/Low		PER SHARE ($) Earnings	Dividends	Book Value
12/08	27.30	29	9	1.58	—	9.17
12/07	31.95	37	26	0.90	—	6.78
12/06	25.50	31	19	1.06	—	5.83
Annual Growth	**3.5%**	**—**	**—**	**22.1%**	**—**	**25.4%**

Cogent Communications

Cogent Communications Group offers a compelling sales pitch: data at the speed of light. The company operates a fiber-optic IP network that serves customers in North America and Europe. It offers dedicated Internet access to businesses through Ethernet connections linking its facilities directly to customers' office buildings. The company's customers include financial services companies, universities, and law firms. Cogent also sells access to its network and provides colocation and modem management services to ISPs, hosting companies, and other big bandwidth users.

The company generates most of its revenues from customers connected directly to its network (on-net customers); clients served through other carriers' facilities (off-net customers) accounted for 16% of Cogent's revenues in 2008. Customers outside North America accounted for about 20% of it sales.

Cogent does business in 135 metropolitan markets with operations that serve more than 950 multitenant office buildings. Its growth strategy is focused on expanding its on-net customers, and Cogent has expanded its sales force to address a broader range of clients. The company is also seeking acquisitions as a means to expand its customer base and utilize unused capacity on its network.

EXECUTIVES

Chairman and CEO: David (Dave) Schaeffer, age 52, $9,716,664 total compensation
CFO and Treasurer: Thaddeus G. (Tad) Weed, age 48, $1,049,162 total compensation
VP Global Sales and Chief Revenue Officer: Jeffrey (Jeff) Karnes, age 37, $933,150 total compensation
VP, General Counsel, Chief Legal Officer, and Assistant Secretary: Robert N. Beury Jr., age 55, $891,681 total compensation

VP Real Estate: Guy Banks
VP Product Management and EU Sales: Lori Brown
VP Provisioning and Carrier Services: Lee Livingston
VP IP Engineering: Mark A. Schleifer, age 40
VP Optical Transport Engineering and CTO: R. Brad Kummer, age 60
VP Field Engineering, Construction, and Network Operations: Timothy G. (Tim) O'Neill, age 53
Director EU Marketing and Sales: Vincent Teissier, age 38
Manager Marketing Communications: Travis Wachter
Secretary: Ried R. Zulager
Auditors: Ernst & Young LLP

LOCATIONS

HQ: Cogent Communications Group, Inc.
1015 31st St. NW, Washington, DC 20007
Phone: 202-295-4200   **Fax:** 202-295-9061
Web: www.cogentco.com

2008 Sales

	$ mil.	% of total
North America	167.3	78
Europe	48.2	22
Total	**215.5**	**100**

PRODUCTS/OPERATIONS

2008 Sales

	$ mil.	% of total
On-net	176.0	82
Off-net	34.6	16
Other	4.9	2
Total	**215.5**	**100**

COMPETITORS

AboveNet
AT&T
Covad Communications Group
EarthLink
Everest Interlink Broadband
FiberNet Telecom
Level 3 Communications
Verio
Verizon
Wave2Wave
XO Holdings

HISTORICAL FINANCIALS

Company Type: Public

Income Statement

FYE: December 31

	REVENUE ($ mil.)	NET INCOME ($ mil.)	NET PROFIT MARGIN	EMPLOYEES
12/08	215.5	26.8	12.4%	531
12/07	185.7	(31.0)	—	431
12/06	149.1	(53.8)	—	377
12/05	135.2	(67.5)	—	340
12/04	91.3	(89.7)	—	297
Annual Growth	**23.9%**	**—**	**—**	**15.6%**

2008 Year-End Financials

Debt ratio: 154.2%
Return on equity: 20.5%
Cash ($ mil.): 71.3
Current ratio: 2.98
Long-term debt ($ mil.): 188.6
No. of shares (mil.): 44.6

Dividends
  Yield: —
  Payout: —
Market value ($ mil.): 291.1
R&D as % of sales: —
Advertising as % of sales: —

Stock History

NASDAQ (GM): CCOI

	STOCK PRICE ($) FY Close	P/E High/Low		PER SHARE ($) Earnings	Dividends	Book Value
12/08	6.53	39	6	0.59	—	2.74
12/07	23.71	—	—	(0.65)	—	3.11
12/06	16.22	—	—	(1.16)	—	4.84
12/05	5.49	—	—	(1.96)	—	4.96
12/04	21.60	—	—	(175.03)	—	4.77
Annual Growth	**(25.8%)**	**—**	**—**	**—**	**—**	**(12.9%)**

Cogent, Inc.

Cogent knows the power of good security. The company provides Automated Fingerprint Identification Systems (AFIS) that governments, law enforcement agencies, and other organizations use to capture, analyze, and compare fingerprints. Cogent's offerings include proprietary fingerprint biometrics software, hardware, and professional services such as consulting, implementation, and systems integration. The US Department of Homeland Security is a major customer. Cogent has offices in Austria, Canada, China, Taiwan, the UK, and the US. Chairman, president, and CEO Ming Hsieh controls more than 55% of the company.

The US Department of Homeland Security accounted for more than half of sales in 2008. Cogent expects revenues to increase in 2009 due to contracts with customers including the State of Maryland, Northrop Grumman, the US Bureau of Census, and the County of Los Angeles. Internationally, it has contracts with the Egyptian government and various programs in Europe. In addition, Cogent was awarded a contract to provide a palm and fingerprint identification system to the Belgium National Police, as well as a contract to provide biometric collection services to U.K. Post Office Limited.

The company expanded its offerings with the purchase of the Security Solutions Division of MAXIMUS for $5 million in 2008. The division is a provider of security systems integration services. The previous year Cogent settled its lawsuit with Northrop Grumman for $25 million. Cogent initiated the lawsuit alleging misappropriation of Cogent's AFIS technology. Northrop Grumann also agreed to pay Cogent $15 million for a non-exclusive license to use automated fingerprint technology and agreed to enter into a five year research and development agreement with Cogent.

EXECUTIVES

Chairman, President, and CEO: Ming Hsieh, age 53, $395,207 total compensation
CFO: Paul Kim, age 41, $621,518 total compensation
EVP Operations: Michael Hollowich, age 62, $337,720 total compensation

EVP Federal and State Systems: James Jasinski, age 59, $524,114 total compensation
VP Systems Integration: Jian (James) Xie
VP International: Wally Briefs
VP Commercial Systems: Bruno Lassus
Director Commercial Business: Christopher Crump
Manager Marketing: Teresa Wu
Auditors: Deloitte & Touche LLP

LOCATIONS

HQ: Cogent, Inc.
 209 Fair Oaks Ave., South Pasadena, CA 91030
Phone: 626-799-8090   **Fax:** 626-799-8996
Web: www.cogentsystems.com

2008 Sales

	$ mil.	% of total
Americas	107.7	86
Europe	6.6	5
Asia	1.4	1
Other regions	10.0	8
Total	**125.7**	**100**

PRODUCTS/OPERATIONS

2008 Sales

	$ mil.	% of total
Products	90.8	72
Maintenance & services	34.9	28
Total	**125.7**	**100**

Selected Applications

Access conrol
Identification card programs
Law enforcement scanners
Mobile identification checks
 Ports of entry and exit
 Public events
 Roadside vehicle checks

COMPETITORS

AuthenTec
Digimarc
ImageWare Systems
L-1 Identity Solutions
NEC
Northrop Grumman
SAFRAN

HISTORICAL FINANCIALS

Company Type: Public

Income Statement				FYE: December 31
	REVENUE ($ mil.)	NET INCOME ($ mil.)	NET PROFIT MARGIN	EMPLOYEES
12/08	125.7	45.2	36.0%	365
12/07	105.8	28.6	27.0%	260
12/06	101.7	29.7	29.2%	195
12/05	159.9	65.3	40.8%	164
12/04	87.7	42.6	48.6%	137
Annual Growth	**9.4%**	**1.5%**	**—**	**27.8%**

2008 Year-End Financials

Debt ratio: —
Return on equity: 8.8%
Cash ($ mil.): 34.9
Current ratio: 5.18
Long-term debt ($ mil.): —
No. of shares (mil.): 89.7
Dividends
 Yield: 0.0%
 Payout: —
Market value ($ mil.): 1,217.8
R&D as % of sales: —
Advertising as % of sales: —

HOOVER'S HANDBOOK OF EMERGING COMPANIES 2010

Stock History

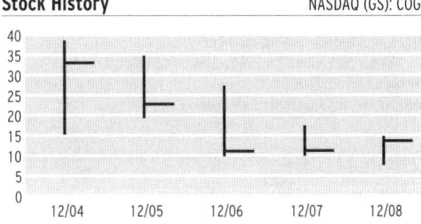

	STOCK PRICE ($) FY Close	P/E High/Low		PER SHARE ($) Earnings	Dividends	Book Value
12/08	13.57	29	16	0.50	0.00	5.79
12/07	11.15	57	34	0.30	0.00	5.69
12/06	11.01	87	33	0.31	0.00	5.47
12/05	22.68	50	28	0.69	0.00	5.11
12/04	33.00	68	28	0.56	0.00	2.47
Annual Growth	**(19.9%)**	**—**	**—**	**(2.8%)**	**—**	**23.7%**

Coinstar, Inc.

There's big money in spare change, and Coinstar has turned the previously underutilized "fourth wall" area between the cash registers and the door in grocery stores into a profit center. Coinstar's core business is its more than 18,400 coin-counting machines in the US, Canada, and the UK, and some 159,000 entertainment services (skill-crane, bulk vending, and kiddie ride) machines across the US and Mexico. Coinstar also operates more than 23,000 point-of-sale terminals in the US and the UK, and offers money transfer services at 38,000 locations. In 2008 Coinstar added some 14,000 self-service DVD rental machines to its repertoire.

Coinstar operates in Canada, Latin America, the UK, and the US. Its coin-counting units are located mainly in supermarkets (such as Kroger and SUPERVALU); the entertainment services machines can be found in more than 27,000 retail locations, including Wal-Mart and Kmart stores.

Coinstar's machines charge transaction fees (of which retail partners receive a portion) and transmit information to the company daily, reducing downtime by alerting field service staff when collection or maintenance is necessary. Since inception, its coin-counting machines have counted and processed more than 395 billion coins worth nearly $22 billion.

Over the past several years, Coinstar has transitioned from a one-product company — offering just coin-counting services — to a business with a variety of products and services through several key acquisitions. Its 2008 acquisition of DVD rental kiosk owner Redbox Automated Retail (previously co-owned by a McDonald's Corporation subsidiary) and a stake in Video Vending New York (dba DVDXpress) gave Coinstar a toehold into the self-service movie rental business.

Coinstar added coin-operated amusement equipment such as plush toy "grabbers," kiddie rides, and video games to its arsenal through the 2004 acquisition of American Coin Merchandising (now Coinstar Entertainment Services), which does business as SugarLoaf. It also bought Amusement Factory, a vending machine company based in California with machines in some 14,000 stores across the country.

Continuing its investment streak, Coinstar bought Travelex Holdings' Travelex Money Transfer business for $27 million in cash (presumably not in change). Travelex Money Transfer operates in some 140 countries. In 2008 it acquired GroupEx Financial Corporation, a provider of electronic money transfer services between the US and Latin America.

One of the company's added services allows customers to change their coins for retailer gift cards or eCertificates. Partners include Starbucks, Amazon.com, Apple iTunes, and Clinton Cards, the UK's #1 greeting card retailer. In a move designed to provide greater access to drugstore customers, Coinstar bought CellCards of Illinois, which offers a set of prepaid products, including wireless, long-distance, and MasterCard cards, in addition to bill payment capabilities for public services such as utilities.

EXECUTIVES

Chairman: Deborah L. Bevier, age 58
CEO and Director: Paul D. Davis, age 52,
 $777,485 total compensation
President and COO: Gregg A. Kaplan, age 39
Interim CFO: James A. Blanda, age 66
Chief People Officer: Dora Summers-Ewing, age 52
Chief Accounting Officer and Controller:
 Richard C. (Rich) Deck, age 39
Chief Customer Officer: James C. (Jim) Blakely, age 53,
 $864,350 total compensation
SVP Technology and Money Transfer:
 Stephen J. (Steve) Verleye, age 50
VP, General Counsel, and Corporate Secretary:
 Donald R. (Don) Rench, age 42,
 $546,748 total compensation
VP New Ventures: Peter D. Rowan, age 42
VP Manufacturing and Supply Chain: Carl Poteete
VP Marketing: Gretchen J. Marks, age 48
VP Information Technology: Christiane M. Liebe
President Coin and E-Payment Services:
 Michael J. (Mike) Skinner, age 55
President, Redbox: J. Mitchell (Mitch) Lowe, age 56
Director Public Relations: Marci Maule
Auditors: KPMG LLP

LOCATIONS

HQ: Coinstar, Inc.
 1800 114th Ave. SE, Bellevue, WA 98004
Phone: 425-943-8000   **Fax:** 425-637-0045
Web: www.coinstar.com

2008 Sales

	$ mil.	% of total
North America	844.2	93
International	67.7	7
Total	**911.9**	**100**

PRODUCTS/OPERATIONS

2008 Sales

	$ mil.	% of total
DVD services	388.5	43
Coin revenue	261.3	29
Entertainment revenue	150.2	16
Money transfer services	87.4	9
E-payment services	24.5	3
Total	**911.9**	**100**

COMPETITORS

Blockbuster Inc.
Cash Systems
Cash Technologies
Cummins-American
Dollar Financial
Global Payment Technologies
Netflix
Safeway
Western Union

HISTORICAL FINANCIALS

Company Type: Public

Income Statement

FYE: December 31

	REVENUE ($ mil.)	NET INCOME ($ mil.)	NET PROFIT MARGIN	EMPLOYEES
12/08	911.9	14.1	1.5%	1,700
12/07	546.3	(22.3)	—	1,900
12/06	534.4	18.6	3.5%	1,900
12/05	459.7	22.3	4.9%	2,000
12/04	307.1	20.4	6.6%	1,694
Annual Growth	31.3%	(8.8%)	—	0.1%

2008 Year-End Financials

Debt ratio: 99.8%
Return on equity: 4.5%
Cash ($ mil.): 192.0
Current ratio: 0.96
Long-term debt ($ mil.): 319.5
No. of shares (mil.): 31.1

Dividends
  Yield: —
  Payout: —
Market value ($ mil.): 606.1
R&D as % of sales: —
Advertising as % of sales: —

Stock History

NASDAQ (GS): CSTR

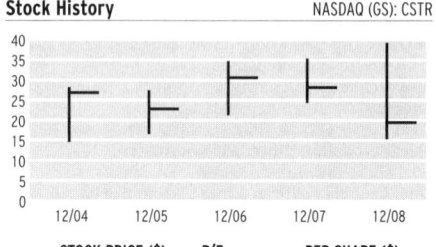

	STOCK PRICE ($) FY Close	P/E High/Low		Earnings	PER SHARE ($) Dividends	Book Value
12/08	19.51	78	31	0.50	—	10.30
12/07	28.15	—	—	(0.80)	—	9.82
12/06	30.57	52	33	0.66	—	10.34
12/05	22.83	32	20	0.86	—	9.47
12/04	26.83	30	16	0.93	—	7.28
Annual Growth	(7.7%)	—	—	(14.4%)	—	9.1%

Colonial Bankshares

Community banking is a revolutionary idea for Colonial Bankshares. The holding company owns Colonial Bank, a regional thrift serving southern New Jersey from six locations. The bank offers checking and savings accounts, bank cards, loans, and brokerage services. It uses funds from deposits to originate primarily real estate loans, with one- to four-family mortgages accounting for nearly 50% of its loan portfolio. It also writes construction, business, home equity, and consumer loans, as well as loans for other types of real estate. Mutual holding company Colonial Bankshares MHC owns about 55% of Colonial Bankshares; it owned 100% before the company's 2005 public stock offering.

EXECUTIVES

Chairman: Albert A. Fralinger Jr., age 77
President, CEO, and Director: Edward J. Geletka, age 48, $291,810 total compensation
EVP and Operations Officer: William F. Whelan, age 57, $163,759 total compensation
EVP and CFO: L. Joseph Stella III, age 52, $183,776 total compensation
SVP and Chief Credit Officer: Richard W. Dapp, age 56

LOCATIONS

HQ: Colonial Bankshares, Inc.
  2745 S. Delsea Dr., Vineland, NJ 08360
Phone: 856-205-0058
Web: www.colonialbankfsb.com

COMPETITORS

1st Colonial Bancorp
Bank of America
Cape Bancorp
Hudson City Bancorp
Parke Bancorp
Sun Bancorp (NJ)
TD Bank USA

HISTORICAL FINANCIALS

Company Type: Public

Income Statement

FYE: December 31

	ASSETS ($ mil.)	NET INCOME ($ mil.)	INCOME AS % OF ASSETS	EMPLOYEES
12/08	530.6	1.3	0.2%	104
12/07	457.9	1.2	0.3%	92
12/06	383.6	1.6	0.4%	83
12/05	336.9	1.8	0.5%	75
12/04	291.0	1.8	0.6%	77
Annual Growth	16.2%	(7.8%)	—	7.8%

2008 Year-End Financials

Equity as % of assets: 7.7%
Return on assets: 0.3%
Return on equity: 3.3%
Long-term debt ($ mil.): 28.2
No. of shares (mil.): 4.4
Market value ($ mil.): 34.7

Dividends
  Yield: 0.0%
  Payout: —
Sales ($ mil.): 12.1
R&D as % of sales: —
Advertising as % of sales: —

Stock History

NASDAQ (GM): COBK

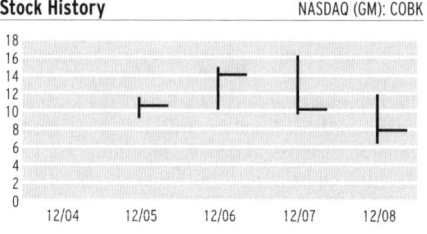

	STOCK PRICE ($) FY Close	P/E High/Low		Earnings	PER SHARE ($) Dividends	Book Value
12/08	7.85	38	21	0.31	0.00	9.19
12/07	10.15	55	34	0.29	0.00	8.82
12/06	14.06	40	28	0.37	0.00	8.29
12/05	10.55	57	47	0.20	0.00	8.11
Annual Growth	(9.4%)	—	—	15.7%	—	24.6%

Command Security

At its customers' command are the security guards employed by Command Security. The company's guard services division provides security guards for commercial, governmental, and institutional clients. However, most of Command Security's business (more than half of sales) comes from its aviation services division. Although passenger screening services have been taken over by the US government, Command Security personnel are called upon for support services such as baggage-related security duties, document verification, and skycap and wheelchair escort services, in addition to

general security tasks. Delta Air Lines, the company's largest customer, accounts for about 15% of sales.

In addition to its aviation and guard services operations, Command Security provides support services for other security companies and for law enforcement agencies. The company operates from more than 40 offices in nearly 20 states throughout the US.

The years 2008 and 2009 were marked by acquisitions of security services businesses in Florida and Maryland (Expert Security Services, Eagle International Group, and International Security & Safety Group), and expanded services at Los Angeles International Airport in California and JFK and LaGuardia airports in New York. However, these gains were offset by lost revenues at seven airports due to a change in government policy that requires the TSA to provide certain document verification services that Command Security formerly provided.

Edward Fleury was appointed CEO of the company in 2008.

EXECUTIVES

Chairman: Peter T. Kikis, age 87
CEO and Director: Edward S. Fleury, age 67, $176,925 total compensation
COO and Director: Martin C. Blake Jr., age 56, $336,290 total compensation
President, CFO, and Director: Barry I. Regenstein, age 52, $355,500 total compensation
VP Administration: Debra M. Miller
VP Sales and Marketing: Lynda B. Blake
VP Corporate; Regional VP, West Region: Marc W. Brown, age 54, $175,656 total compensation
VP Human Resources and Training: Robert Sagginario
Regional VP, New England: John C. Reed, age 45, $130,635 total compensation
Regional VP, Mid-Atlantic: William A. Vigna, age 48, $136,163 total compensation
Regional VP, Aviation Services, West Region: Sunia A. Williams
Regional VP, Aviation Safeguards, West Region: Joseph Conlon, age 49, $118,627 total compensation
Manager Information Technology: Brett Henderson
Auditors: D'Arcangelo & Co., LLP

LOCATIONS

HQ: Command Security Corporation
  1133 Route 55, Ste. D, LaGrangeville, NY 12540
Phone: 845-454-3703   **Fax:** 845-454-0075
Web: www.commandsecurity.com

PRODUCTS/OPERATIONS

2009 Sales

	$ mil.	% of total
Aviation Services	73.8	56
Security Services	60.0	44
Total	**130.8**	**100**

Selected Services

Access control
Aircraft security
Baggage handlers
Skycaps
Uniformed security officers for cargo security areas
Uniformed security officers for industrial, commercial, and residential property
Wheelchair escorts

COMPETITORS

AlliedBarton Security
Guardsmark
ICTS International
Kastle Systems
Kroll
Wackenhut

HISTORICAL FINANCIALS

Company Type: Public

Income Statement

FYE: March 31

	REVENUE ($ mil.)	NET INCOME ($ mil.)	NET PROFIT MARGIN	EMPLOYEES
3/09	130.8	1.3	1.0%	6,000
3/08	119.4	2.5	2.1%	4,500
3/07	93.8	1.2	1.3%	3,650
3/06	85.2	(0.1)	—	3,400
3/05	79.7	(0.4)	—	3,300
Annual Growth	13.2%	—	—	16.1%

2009 Year-End Financials

Debt ratio: 0.7%
Return on equity: 9.3%
Cash ($ mil.): 0.2
Current ratio: 1.38
Long-term debt ($ mil.): 0.1
No. of shares (mil.): 10.9

Dividends
  Yield: 0.0%
  Payout: —
Market value ($ mil.): 35.1
R&D as % of sales: —
Advertising as % of sales: —

Stock History

NYSE Alternext: MOC

	STOCK PRICE ($) FY Close	P/E High/Low	PER SHARE ($) Earnings	Dividends	Book Value
3/09	3.23	37 20	0.11	0.00	1.35
3/08	4.10	20 12	0.22	0.00	1.23
3/07	3.20	28 18	0.12	0.00	0.84
3/06	2.85	— —	(0.01)	0.00	0.70
3/05	2.02	— —	(0.06)	0.00	0.41
Annual Growth	12.5%	— —	—	—	35.2%

CommVault Systems

CommVault Systems wants to have a lock on data management. The company provides software that customers use to store and manage enterprise data. Its Simpana software suite handles such tasks as resource management, backup, archiving, data replication, disaster recovery, and search. The company's customers come from industries including manufacturing, financial services, health care, and transportation, as well as from the public sector. CommVault's strategic partners include systems integrators and professional services firms, distributors and resellers, and technology providers. It counts Dell and Hitachi Data Systems (HDS) among its key strategic partners.

CommVault markets its products worldwide. More than a third of the its revenues were generated outside of the US in fiscal 2009. The company counts Crutchfield, Meridian Health, SPSS, and Welch's among its end-use customers.

The company competes against a number of much larger companies, many of which offer complete data storage hardware and software systems. CommVault has identified partnerships

as an essential component of its sales strategy. Though it sells directly to some customers, the majority of the company's revenues come from sales through resellers, OEMs, and systems integrators. OEMs such as Dell and HDS resell CommVault's products or integrate them into their own offerings. Dell accounted for about a quarter of CommVault's revenues in fiscal 2009.

The company was founded as an independent segment of Bell Laboratories in 1988; senior management (backed in part by funding from Sprout Group) purchased the company's assets from Lucent Technologies in 1996.

EXECUTIVES

Chairman, President, and CEO:
N. Robert (Bob) Hammer, age 67, $1,681,857 total compensation
EVP, COO, and Director: Alan G. (Al) Bunte, age 55, $1,269,040 total compensation
Chief Evangelist and Microsoft Relationship:
Randy DeMeno
SVP Product Development: Anand Prahlad, age 42
VP and CFO: Louis F. (Lou) Miceli, age 60, $785,093 total compensation
VP, EMEA & ASEAN: Steven Rose, age 52, $1,014,519 total compensation
VP Sales, Americas: Ron Miiller, age 43, $880,921 total compensation
VP Product and Segment Marketing: Michael Marchi
VP Operations: Allen Shoemaker
VP Finance and Chief Accounting Officer:
Brian Carolan
VP Sales Engineering: Robert Kaloustian
VP, General Counsel, and Secretary:
Warren H. Mondschein
VP Product Management: Brian Brockway
VP Marketing and Business Development:
David (Dave) West, age 44
VP Sales Operations: Brian D. McAteer
VP Human Resources: William (Bill) Beattie
Director Investor Relations: Michael Picariello
Media Relations: Dani Kenison
Auditors: Ernst & Young LLP

LOCATIONS

HQ: CommVault Systems, Inc.
2 Crescent Place, Oceanport, NJ 07757
Phone: 732-870-4000   **Fax:** 732-870-4525
Web: www.commvault.com

2009 Sales

	$ mil.	% of total
US	143.0	61
Other countries	91.5	39
Total	**234.5**	**100**

PRODUCTS/OPERATIONS

2009 Sales

	$ mil.	% of total
Software	121.7	52
Services	112.8	48
Total	**234.5**	**100**

COMPETITORS

CA, Inc.
Data Domain
EMC
Hewlett-Packard
IBM Software
NetApp
Symantec

HISTORICAL FINANCIALS

Company Type: Public

Income Statement

FYE: March 31

	REVENUE ($ mil.)	NET INCOME ($ mil.)	NET PROFIT MARGIN	EMPLOYEES
3/09	234.5	12.3	5.2%	1,070
3/08	198.3	20.8	10.5%	866
3/07	151.1	61.4	40.6%	727
3/06	109.5	5.1	4.7%	176
3/05	82.6	0.5	0.6%	642
Annual Growth	29.8%	122.7%	—	13.6%

2009 Year-End Financials

Debt ratio: —
Return on equity: 11.1%
Cash ($ mil.): 105.2
Current ratio: 2.04
Long-term debt ($ mil.): —
No. of shares (mil.): 42.1

Dividends
  Yield: 0.0%
  Payout: —
Market value ($ mil.): 462.0
R&D as % of sales: —
Advertising as % of sales: —

Stock History

NASDAQ (GM): CVLT

	STOCK PRICE ($) FY Close	P/E High/Low	PER SHARE ($) Earnings	Dividends	Book Value
3/09	10.97	67 26	0.28	0.00	2.64
3/08	12.40	50 27	0.46	0.00	2.60
3/07	16.20	— —	(1.35)	0.00	1.86
Annual Growth	(17.7%)	— —	—	—	19.2%

Compass Minerals

Salt is Compass Minerals' true north. The company is one of the largest salt producers in North America. Its salt products include rock, evaporated, and solar salt and are used for applications such as water softening, road deicing, and food preparation. Highway deicing salt — generally sold to state, province, or municipal governments — accounts for almost half of its annual sales. Compass Minerals operates through subsidiaries North American Salt, Great Salt Lake Minerals (a top producer of the crop nutrient sulfate of potash), Sifto Canada, and Salt Union (based in the UK). It has seven manufacturing facilities and two salt mines in Canada, the UK, and the US.

EXECUTIVES

Chairman, President, and CEO: Angelo C. Brisimitzakis, age 51, $2,675,165 total compensation
VP Engineering: Larry Schulte
VP and CIO: Jerry Smith
VP Strategic Development: David J. Goadby, age 54, $828,706 total compensation
VP, CFO, Secretary, and Treasurer:
Rodney L. (Rod) Underdown, age 42, $816,785 total compensation

VP and General Manager, Consumer and Industrial Business: Gerald (Jerry) Bucan, age 45, $541,799 total compensation
VP Human Resources: Victoria Heider
Director Environment, Health, and Safety: James Wolf
VP Manufacturing and Engineering: Jack Leunig
VP Supply Chain and Technology: Dennis Bergeson
VP and General Manager, Great Salt Lake Minerals and Compass Minerals UK: Ronald Bryan, age 57, $838,584 total compensation
VP and General Manager, North American Highway: Keith E. Clark, age 53, $828,706 total compensation
Director Investor Relations and Corporate Communications: Peggy Landon
Auditors: Ernst & Young LLP

LOCATIONS

HQ: Compass Minerals International, Inc.
9900 W. 109th St., Ste. 600
Overland Park, KS 66210
Phone: 913-344-9200   **Fax:** 913-338-7932
Web: www.compassminerals.com

2008 Sales

	$ mil.	% of total
US	844.5	72
Canada	245.5	21
UK	56.0	5
Other countries	21.7	2
Total	**1,167.7**	**100**

PRODUCTS/OPERATIONS

2008 Sales

	$ mil.	% of total
Salt	923.3	79
Specialty Fertilizers	232.9	20
Corporate	11.5	1
Total	**1,167.7**	**100**

Selected Subsidiaries

Compass Minerals Group, Inc.
  Compass Minerals (Europe) Limited
    Compass Minerals (UK) Limited
    Salt Union Ltd. (UK)
  GSL Corporation
    Great Salt Lake Minerals (sulfate of potash)
  NAMSCO Inc.
    Carey Salt Company
    North American Salt Company
    Sifto Canada Corp.

COMPETITORS

Akzo Nobel
Cargill
Ercros
Innophos
K+S
PotashCorp
Tata Chemicals
United Salt

HISTORICAL FINANCIALS

Company Type: Public

Income Statement				FYE: December 31
	REVENUE ($ mil.)	NET INCOME ($ mil.)	NET PROFIT MARGIN	EMPLOYEES
12/08	1,167.7	159.5	13.7%	1,743
12/07	857.3	80.0	9.3%	1,588
12/06	660.7	55.0	8.3%	1,557
12/05	742.3	30.9	4.2%	1,506
12/04	695.1	49.8	7.2%	1,541
Annual Growth	**13.8%**	**33.8%**	**—**	**3.1%**

2008 Year-End Financials

Debt ratio: 762.2%
Return on equity: 532.6%
Cash ($ mil.): 34.6
Current ratio: 1.81
Long-term debt ($ mil.): 491.6
No. of shares (mil.): 32.6
Dividends
  Yield: 2.3%
  Payout: 27.9%
Market value ($ mil.): 1,911.9
R&D as % of sales: —
Advertising as % of sales: —

Stock History

NYSE: CMP

	STOCK PRICE ($) FY Close	P/E High/Low		PER SHARE ($) Earnings	Dividends	Book Value
12/08	58.66	18	7	4.81	1.34	1.98
12/07	41.00	18	12	2.43	1.28	(0.14)
12/06	31.56	21	13	1.69	1.22	(2.00)
12/05	24.54	28	22	0.97	1.10	(2.43)
12/04	24.23	16	9	1.57	0.94	(2.71)
Annual Growth	**24.7%**	**—**	**—**	**32.3%**	**9.3%**	**—**

comScore, Inc.

comScore knows the score when it comes to measuring online audience behavior. The company provides data, analysis, and consultancy to some 1,100 clients looking to fortify their marketing, sales, and trading initiatives. Its global panel of more than 2 million Internet users measures and tracks consumer behaviors, demographics, and advertising responsiveness for clients in such industries as travel, pharmaceuticals, finance, and telecommunications. Branded products include comScore Media Metrix suite of Web site and online advertising network measurement tools, and comScore Marketing Solutions products, which provide custom research and analysis. Clients include AT&T, Verizon, and Viacom.

The majority of the company's revenue (83% in 2008) comes from the fees it charges for its subscription-based services. The remaining percentage comes from its custom research services. In 2008, Microsoft accounted for 12% of its revenue.

comScore's plan for growth involves broadening its international scope. Its European panel's presence is mostly in the UK, and the company plans to expand its consumer research and analysis to additional European clients as well as other global clients looking to conduct audience research in Europe.

In 2008 comScore strengthened its position in measuring cell phone usage — especially mobile Internet browsing — with the $46 million acquisition of M:Metrics.

Investment firm Accel Partners, represented on comScore's board of directors by Bruce Golden, owns 21% of the company.

EXECUTIVES

Chairman: Gian M. Fulgoni, age 61, $867,764 total compensation
President, CEO, and Director: Magid M. Abraham, age 50, $1,060,386 total compensation
COO: Gregory T. (Greg) Dale, age 39, $421,145 total compensation
CFO: Kenneth (Ken) Tarpey
General Counsel and Chief Privacy Officer: Christiana L. Lin, age 39, $390,352 total compensation
Chief Product Officer: Eric Bosco
EVP Asia/Pacific Region: Will Hodgman
EVP Advertising Solutions: Lynn Bolger
EVP and Head Human Capital: John M. Green, age 57
EVP Media Metrix, North America, Europe, Latin America: Jack Flanagan
EVP Product Managment: Linda Boland Abraham
SVP Mobile Products: Mark Donovan
SVP: Serge Matta
President Media Metrix, comScore Canada: Brent Bernie
Search Evangelist and Product Management: Eli Goodman
Auditors: Ernst & Young LLP

LOCATIONS

HQ: comScore, Inc.
11465 Sunset Hills Rd., Ste. 200, Reston, VA 20190
Phone: 703-438-2000   **Fax:** 703-438-2051
Web: www.comscore.com

2008 Sales

	$ mil.	% of total
US	100.9	86
Canada	5.8	5
UK & other	10.7	9
Total	**117.4**	**100**

COMPETITORS

Arbitron
DoubleClick
Dynamic Logic
Google
Harris Interactive
Hitwise
IMS Health
Ipsos
The Nielsen Company
Nielsen Media Research
Nielsen Mobile
Omniture
TNS Custom
ValueClick
WebTrends
WPP

HISTORICAL FINANCIALS

Company Type: Public

Income Statement				FYE: December 31
	REVENUE ($ mil.)	NET INCOME ($ mil.)	NET PROFIT MARGIN	EMPLOYEES
12/08	117.4	25.2	21.5%	581
12/07	87.2	19.3	22.1%	452
12/06	66.3	5.7	8.6%	377
12/05	50.3	(4.0)	—	377
12/04	34.9	(3.2)	—	—
Annual Growth	**35.4%**	**—**	**—**	**15.5%**

2008 Year-End Financials

Debt ratio: 0.0%
Return on equity: 21.2%
Cash ($ mil.): 34.3
Current ratio: 2.08
Long-term debt ($ mil.): 0.0
No. of shares (mil.): 30.3
Dividends
  Yield: 0.0%
  Payout: —
Market value ($ mil.): 386.1
R&D as % of sales: —
Advertising as % of sales: —

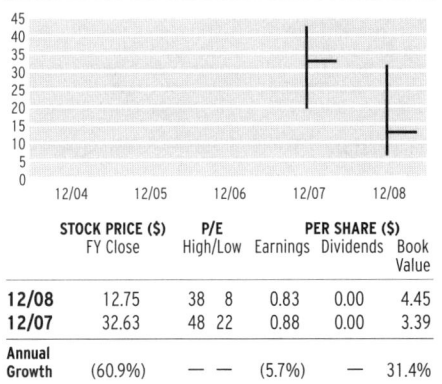

	STOCK PRICE ($) FY Close	P/E High/Low		PER SHARE ($) Earnings	Dividends	Book Value
12/08	12.75	38	8	0.83	0.00	4.45
12/07	32.63	48	22	0.88	0.00	3.39
Annual Growth	(60.9%)	—	—	(5.7%)	—	31.4%

Comtech Telecommunications

Comtech means contact. Through its subsidiaries, Comtech Telecommunications operates in three divisions: telecommunications transmission, mobile data communications, and RF microwave amplifiers. The company makes equipment used largely by the US government and related defense contractors. Other customers include satellite systems integrators, communications service providers, and oil companies. Its transmission equipment includes modems, frequency converters, high-power amplifiers, very-small-aperture terminal (VSAT) satellite transceivers and antennas, and microwave radios.

Comtech makes radio-frequency signal amplifiers used to enable wireless instrumentation and medical systems and provides satellite-based messaging services and location tracking.

The company's government segment, which serves branches of the military including the US Army, accounted for 56% of the company's revenues in fiscal 2009. Comtech's wireless and satellite products have been incorporated into military logistics and battlefield control systems and several combat vehicles including tanks and helicopters.

Comtech's acquisition activities since 2005 have served to round out its product lines. It bought logistics software developer Insite in 2006 and Digicast, a maker of digital video broadcasting equipment, the following year. In 2008 Comtech acquired competitor Radyne for about $224 million. It also purchased network backhaul assets from Verso Technologies for about $3.9 million.

EXECUTIVES

Chairman, President, and CEO: Fred V. Kornberg, age 73, $4,815,998 total compensation
SVP Operations: Frank W. Otto, age 60
SVP; President, Comtech Mobile Datacom: Daniel S. Wood, age 51, $972,896 total compensation
SVP; President, Comtech EF Data: Robert L. McCollum, age 60, $1,373,825 total compensation
SVP Strategy and Business Development: Jerome V. Kapelus, age 44, $817,959 total compensation

SVP and CFO: Michael D. Porcelain, age 40, $1,143,524 total compensation
SVP; President, Comtech PST: Larry Konopelko, age 56
SVP; President, Comtech Systems: Richard L. Burt, age 68
VP Finance: Nancy Stallone
President, Comtech Memotec: Yves Hupé
President, Comtech Xicom Technology: John Branscum
President, Comtech AeroAstro: Paul Lithgow
President, Comtech AHA: William Thomson
Controller: Michael A. Bondi
Auditors: KPMG LLP

LOCATIONS

HQ: Comtech Telecommunications Corp.
68 S. Service Rd., Ste. 230, Melville, NY 11747
Phone: 631-962-7000   **Fax:** 631-962-7001
Web: www.comtechtel.com

2009 Sales

	% of total
US	
Government	56
Commercial	12
Other countries	32
Total	**100**

PRODUCTS/OPERATIONS

2009 Sales

	$ mil.	% of total
Telecommunications transmission	254.3	43
Mobile data communications	177.0	30
RF microwave amplifiers	155.1	27
Total	**586.4**	**100**

Selected Products

Mobile data communications services
   Location tracking
   Two-way messaging
Telecommunications transmission equipment
   Error-correction and compression chips
   Over-the-horizon microwave communications products
   Satellite earth station equipment (modems, frequency converters, amplifiers, transceivers)
Radio-frequency microwave amplifiers

COMPETITORS

e2v
EMS Technologies
Ericsson
General Dynamics
Harmonic
Harris Corp.
Herley Industries
iDirect Technologies
Northrop Grumman
QUALCOMM
Raytheon
Surrey Satellite Technology
ViaSat

HISTORICAL FINANCIALS

Company Type: Public

Income Statement   FYE: July 31

	REVENUE ($ mil.)	NET INCOME ($ mil.)	NET PROFIT MARGIN	EMPLOYEES
7/09	586.4	49.6	8.5%	1,607
7/08	531.6	76.4	14.4%	1,350
7/07	445.7	65.2	14.6%	1,230
7/06	391.5	45.3	11.6%	1,228
7/05	307.9	36.7	11.9%	1,090
Annual Growth	17.5%	7.8%	—	10.2%

2009 Year-End Financials

Debt ratio: 31.8%	Dividends
Return on equity: 9.3%	Yield: —
Cash ($ mil.): 485.5	Payout: —
Current ratio: 7.45	Market value ($ mil.): 900.1
Long-term debt ($ mil.): 200.0	R&D as % of sales: —
No. of shares (mil.): 28.2	Advertising as % of sales: —

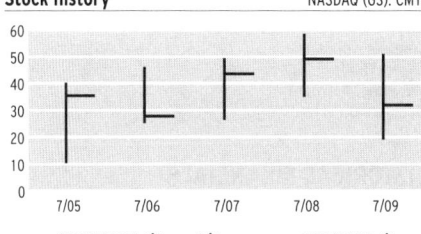

	STOCK PRICE ($) FY Close	P/E High/Low		PER SHARE ($) Earnings	Dividends	Book Value
7/09	31.87	29	11	1.73	—	22.28
7/08	49.13	21	13	2.76	—	15.68
7/07	43.47	20	11	2.42	—	12.24
7/06	27.76	27	15	1.72	—	9.00
7/05	35.35	28	8	1.42	—	6.96
Annual Growth	(2.6%)	—	—	5.1%	—	33.7%

Concho Resources

Concho Resources explores and develops properties, located primarily in the Permian Basin region of eastern New Mexico and West Texas, for the production of oil and gas. It also owns properties in North Dakota and Arkansas. More than half of the company's 550 billion cu. ft. in proved reserves is made up of crude oil, while the rest consists of natural gas. Concho Resources gets two-thirds of its sales from crude oil. Two customers, energy marketers Navajo Refining Company (60% of 2007 sales) and DCP Midstream (23%), account for a great majority of Concho's sales. The company has more than 85 producing wells in operation.

The company has been focused on expanding its holdings through medium-sized acquisitions. To boost its Permian Basin holdings, in 2008 Concho Resources spent $585 million to buy Henry Petroleum. In 2010 the company acquired two properties in the Permian Basin for $225 million.

EXECUTIVES

Chairman and CEO: Timothy A. Leach, age 50, $2,188,166 total compensation
VP, CFO, and Treasurer: Darin G. Holderness, age 45, $383,291 total compensation
VP, General Counsel, and Secretary: C. William Giraud
VP Engineering and Operations: E. Joseph Wright, age 50, $982,601 total compensation
VP Business Development and Capital Markets: Jack F. Harper, age 38, $1,171,896 total compensation
VP Exploration and Land: Matthew G. Hyde
Manager Investor Relations: Toffee McAlister
Auditors: Grant Thornton LLP

LOCATIONS

HQ: Concho Resources Inc.
550 W. Texas Ave., Ste. 100, Midland, TX 79701
Phone: 432-683-7443   **Fax:** 432-683-7441
Web: www.conchoresources.com

2008 Sales

	$ mil.	% of total
Oil	391.0	73
Natural gas	142.8	27
Total	**533.8**	**100**

COMPETITORS

Chevron
ConocoPhillips
Exxon Mobil
Marathon Petroleum
Occidental Petroleum

HISTORICAL FINANCIALS

Company Type: Public

Income Statement
FYE: December 31

	REVENUE ($ mil.)	NET INCOME ($ mil.)	NET PROFIT MARGIN	EMPLOYEES
12/08	533.8	—	—	245
12/07	294.3	—	—	113
12/06	198.3	—	—	80
12/05	54.9	—	—	80
12/04	3.6	—	—	—
Annual Growth	**249.0%**	**—**	**—**	**45.2%**

Revenue History
NYSE: CXO

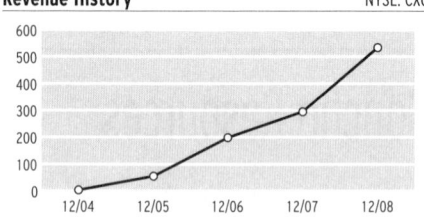

Concur Technologies

Concur Technologies can help you make sure that all of your expense reports are in perfect harmony with budgeting and accounting. The company offers corporate expense management software that enables businesses to automate and streamline the process for submitting and approving employee expense reports. Concur's software features Web-based modules for tracking, submitting, and processing reports for travel and entertainment costs, as well as applications to track employee requests for vendor payments. Concur licenses its software directly to companies and offers its applications by subscription through application service providers.

In 2006 Concur acquired corporate travel software company Outtask. The following year the company purchased H-G Holdings, which primarily operated through its subsidiary Gelco Information Network.

In 2008 the company announced a strategic partnership with American Express to provide its products and services to American Express clients; as part of the deal American Express also purchased a 13% equity stake in Concur.

Concur has strategically expanded its international operations, which now account for about 11% of sales.

EXECUTIVES

Chairman and CEO: S. Steven (Steve) Singh, age 47
President, COO, and Director: Rajeev Singh, age 40
EVP Client Development: Robert Cavanaugh, age 40
EVP Sales and Business Development:
Michael L. Eberhard, age 43
EVP Research and Development: Tom DePasquale, age 48
EVP Worldwide Marketing: Michael W. Hilton, age 44
SVP Information Services: Michael Bowden
Chief Legal Officer and Corporate Secretary:
Kyle R. Sugamele, age 46
Senior Manager Marketing Communications, US:
Hubie Sturtevant
Investor Relations Contact: John Torrey
Auditors: Grant Thornton LLP

LOCATIONS

HQ: Concur Technologies, Inc.
18400 NE Union Hill Rd., Redmond, WA 98052
Phone: 425-702-8808   **Fax:** 425-702-8828
Web: www.concur.com

2009 Sales

	$ mil.	% of total
US	222.5	90
Europe	14.5	6
Other	10.6	4
Total	**247.6**	**100**

PRODUCTS/OPERATIONS

2009 Sales

	$ mil.	% of total
Subscription	239.2	97
Consulting & other	8.4	3
Total	**247.6**	**100**

Selected Services
Consulting
Customer support
Training

Selected Software
Concur Compliance Solution (fraud detection)
Concur Expense (travel and entertainment expense management)
Concur Imaging Service (electronic capture, storage, and archive of receipts and invoices)
Concur Payment (employee request for vendor payment)
Concur Travel Integration (travel procurement and expense management)

COMPETITORS

American Express
Ariba
Bank of America
Compuware
IBM
OneMind Connect
Oracle
SAP

HISTORICAL FINANCIALS

Company Type: Public

Income Statement
FYE: September 30

	REVENUE ($ mil.)	NET INCOME ($ mil.)	NET PROFIT MARGIN	EMPLOYEES
9/09	247.6	25.7	10.4%	1,100
9/08	215.5	17.2	8.0%	932
9/07	129.1	8.2	6.4%	575
9/06	97.1	34.2	35.2%	500
9/05	71.8	5.4	7.5%	395
Annual Growth	**36.3%**	**47.7%**	**—**	**29.2%**

2009 Year-End Financials

Debt ratio: 0.0%	Dividends
Return on equity: 4.9%	Yield: —
Cash ($ mil.): 119.2	Payout: —
Current ratio: 2.84	Market value ($ mil.): 1,949.7
Long-term debt ($ mil.): 0.2	R&D as % of sales: —
No. of shares (mil.): 49.0	Advertising as % of sales: —

Stock History
NASDAQ (GM): CNQR

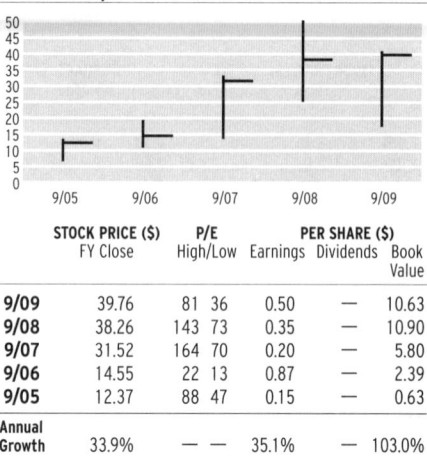

	STOCK PRICE ($) FY Close	P/E High/Low		PER SHARE ($) Earnings	Dividends	Book Value
9/09	39.76	81	36	0.50	—	10.63
9/08	38.26	143	73	0.35	—	10.90
9/07	31.52	164	70	0.20	—	5.80
9/06	14.55	22	13	0.87	—	2.39
9/05	12.37	88	47	0.15	—	0.63
Annual Growth	**33.9%**	**—**	**—**	**35.1%**	**—**	**103.0%**

Connecticut Water Service

A splash from Connecticut Water Service (CWS) might have helped Mark Twain's Yankee wake up from King Arthur's court. CWS's subsidiary Connecticut Water Company, through its three operating divisions — Connecticut Water, Crystal, and Unionville — serves more than 86,000 residential, commercial, and industrial customers in 54 Connecticut towns. The nonoperating holding company's subsidiaries gather water from wells and reservoirs and produce 49 million gallons daily. They also offer fire protection and other water-related services. CWS's growth strategy is based on acquisitions.

Founded in 1956, the utility's water infrastructure consists of 28 noncontiguous water systems in Connecticut and one system in Massachusetts, totaling about 1,400 miles of water main and reservoir storage capacity of 7 billion gallons.

In 2008 CWS acquired the Eastern Operations of Birmingham Utilities, which serves more than 2,300 customers, and in 2009 it acquired Ellington Acres Company, a regulated water utility company that provides water service to 750 customers.

EXECUTIVES

Chairman, President, and CEO: Eric W. Thornburg, age 49, $644,597 total compensation
VP Human Resources: Kristen A. Johnson, age 42
VP Finance, CFO, and Treasurer: David C. Benoit, age 52, $399,494 total compensation
VP Operations and Engineering: Terrance P. O'Neill, age 54, $344,996 total compensation
VP Administration and Government Affairs:
Maureen P. Westbrook, age 50, $350,564 total compensation
VP Business Development: Thomas R. Marston, age 56, $395,211 total compensation

Corporate Secretary: Daniel J. Meaney, age 48
Controller and Principal Accounting Officer; Controller and Principal Accounting Officer, Connecticut Water Company: Nicholas A. Rinaldi, age 56
Director Rates and Forecasting and Assistant Treasurer: Peter J. Bancroft, age 58
Corporate Secretary and Assistant to the President: Michele G. DiAcri, age 63
Auditors: PricewaterhouseCoopers LLP

LOCATIONS

HQ: Connecticut Water Service, Inc.
93 W. Main St., Clinton, CT 06413
Phone: 860-669-8636   Fax: 860-669-5579
Web: www.ctwater.com

PRODUCTS/OPERATIONS

2008 Sales

	$ mil.	% of total
Residential	38.0	62
Fire protection	10.6	17
Commercial	7.2	12
Public authority	2.0	3
Industrial	1.8	3
Other	1.7	3
Total	**61.3**	**100**

COMPETITORS

American Water
Aquarion
Pennichuck
United Water Inc.
Veolia Water North America

HISTORICAL FINANCIALS

Company Type: Public

Income Statement   FYE: December 31

	REVENUE ($ mil.)	NET INCOME ($ mil.)	NET PROFIT MARGIN	EMPLOYEES
12/08	61.3	9.4	15.3%	226
12/07	59.0	8.8	14.9%	206
12/06	46.9	7.0	14.9%	200
12/05	47.5	10.3	21.7%	191
12/04	48.5	9.4	19.4%	193
Annual Growth	6.0%	0.0%	—	4.0%

2008 Year-End Financials

Debt ratio: 89.1%
Return on equity: 9.2%
Cash ($ mil.): 0.7
Current ratio: 0.83
Long-term debt ($ mil.): 92.2
No. of shares (mil.): 8.5
Dividends
Yield: 3.7%
Payout: 79.3%
Market value ($ mil.): 201.7
R&D as % of sales: —
Advertising as % of sales: —

Stock History   NASDAQ (GS): CTWS

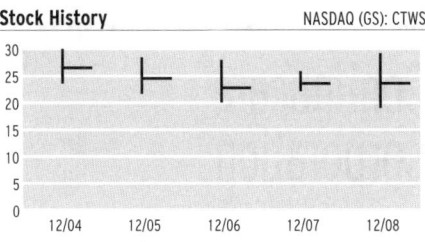

	STOCK PRICE ($) FY Close	P/E High/Low	Earnings	PER SHARE ($) Dividends	Book Value
12/08	23.61	26 17	1.11	0.88	12.11
12/07	23.57	24 21	1.05	0.87	11.72
12/06	22.75	33 24	0.84	0.86	11.32
12/05	24.51	22 17	1.26	0.85	11.11
12/04	26.49	26 21	1.16	0.83	10.39
Annual Growth	(2.8%)	— —	(1.1%)	1.5%	3.9%

Consolidated Communications

Consolidated Communications is just what its name implies. The company encompasses operations based in Illinois, Pennsylvania, and Texas, providing voice and data telecommunications to business and residential customers. It operates rural local-exchange carriers that offer local access and long distance, Internet access, business phone systems, and related services through more than 280,000 local access lines and nearly 83,000 digital subscriber lines (DSL) in service. The company also offers directory publishing and carrier services. Operating subsidiaries include Illinois Consolidated Telephone Company (ICTC), Consolidated Communications of Fort Bend Company, and Consolidated Communications of Texas Company.

The company's Illinois phone operations consist of 35 incumbent local exchanges serving primarily small towns and rural areas of Coles, Christian, Montgomery, Effingham, and Shelby counties in the central part of the state. It has about 74,000 local access lines in service and serves residential and small business customers.

In Texas, the company operates 21 local exchanges serving business and residential customers in the eastern communities of Lufkin, Conroe, and Katy. Once a subsidiary of Texas-based utility TXU Corp. (now Energy Future Holdings), the business was acquired in 2004 by Consolidated Communications in a deal valued at $524 million in cash and $3 million in assumed debt.

The company moved into the Pennsylvania market with the acquisition of North Pittsburgh in 2007. Its serves portions of Allegheny, Armstrong, Butler, and Westmorland counties in the western region of the state.

Chairman Richard Lumpkin owns 19% of the company. His great-grandfather, Iverson A. Lumpkin, founded the company (then called Mattoon Telephone Company) in 1894.

EXECUTIVES

Chairman: Richard A. (Dick) Lumpkin, age 75
President, CEO, and Director: Robert J. (Bob) Currey, age 64, $1,582,690 total compensation
SVP, Secretary, and President, Enterprise Operations: Steven J. (Steve) Shirar, age 51, $504,352 total compensation
SVP and CFO: Steven L. (Steve) Childers, age 54, $470,020 total compensation
SVP and President, Illinois Telephone Operations: Joseph R. (Joe) Dively, age 50, $476,475 total compensation
SVP and President, Texas Telephone Operations: C. Robert (Bob) Udell Jr., age 44, $576,867 total compensation
VP Market Response: Rick Hall
CIO: Christopher A. (Chris) Young, age 54
Director Investor Relations: Matthew Smith
Treasurer and Secretary: David Doedtman
Corporate Communications: Laura ZuHone
Auditors: Ernst & Young LLP

LOCATIONS

HQ: Consolidated Communications Holdings, Inc.
121 S. 17th St., Mattoon, IL 61938
Phone: 217-235-3311   Fax: 217-258-7883
Web: www.consolidated.com

PRODUCTS/OPERATIONS

2008 Sales

	$ mil.	% of total
Telephone operations	378.0	90
Other	40.4	10
Total	**418.4**	**100**

COMPETITORS

AT&T
Comcast
Mediacom
Qwest Communications
Sprint Nextel
Suddenlink
Time Warner Cable
Verizon

HISTORICAL FINANCIALS

Company Type: Public

Income Statement   FYE: December 31

	REVENUE ($ mil.)	NET INCOME ($ mil.)	NET PROFIT MARGIN	EMPLOYEES
12/08	418.4	5.3	1.3%	1,315
12/07	329.2	11.4	3.5%	1,081
12/06	320.8	13.3	4.1%	1,123
12/05	321.4	(14.7)	—	1,229
12/04	269.6	(1.1)	—	—
Annual Growth	11.6%	—	—	2.3%

2008 Year-End Financials

Debt ratio: 1,255.8%
Return on equity: 4.7%
Cash ($ mil.): 15.5
Current ratio: 1.10
Long-term debt ($ mil.): 880.3
No. of shares (mil.): 29.6
Dividends
Yield: 13.0%
Payout: 369.0%
Market value ($ mil.): 352.1
R&D as % of sales: —
Advertising as % of sales: —

Stock History   NASDAQ (CM): CNSL

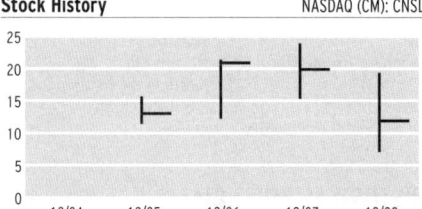

	STOCK PRICE ($) FY Close	P/E High/Low	Earnings	PER SHARE ($) Dividends	Book Value
12/08	11.88	46 17	0.42	1.55	2.36
12/07	19.90	54 35	0.44	1.55	5.24
12/06	20.90	45 26	0.47	1.55	3.88
12/05	12.99	— —	(0.83)	0.41	6.72
Annual Growth	(2.9%)	— —	—	—	—

Contango Oil & Gas

It takes two to tango but several more to make Contango, a successful independent oil and natural gas company. Contango Oil & Gas (named after a term used by oil and gas traders to describe anticipated rising prices in the futures market) explores for and acquires oil and gas properties in the Gulf of Mexico and in the Arkansas Fayetteville Shale. Contango, which holds proved reserves of about 369 billion cu. ft. of natural gas equivalent, has strategic exploration alliances with Juneau Exploration, Alta Resources, and others. CEO Kenneth Peak owns 15% of Contango.

The company is focused on oil and gas exploration. It occasionally sells assets in order to reinvest in its core business. For example, in 2004 it sold its South Texas natural gas and oil assets to Edge Petroleum for $50 million. It sold its 10% stake in a limited partnership (formed to develop an LNG receiving terminal in Freeport, Texas) in 2008.

EXECUTIVES

Chairman, President, CEO, CFO, and Secretary: Kenneth R. Peak, age 63
President and COO, Contango Oil & Gas, Contango Resources, and Contango Operators: Marc Duncan, age 57
SVP and Controller: Lesia Bautina, age 39
VP, Treasurer, and Secretary: Sergio Castro, age 40
Auditors: Grant Thornton LLP

LOCATIONS

HQ: Contango Oil & Gas Company
3700 Buffalo Speedway, Ste. 960
Houston, TX 77098
Phone: 713-960-1901   **Fax:** 713-960-1065
Web: contango.com

Contango Oil & Gas operates in Arkansas and in the Gulf of Mexico.

COMPETITORS

BP
Brigham Exploration
Chevron
Devon Energy
Exxon Mobil
Marathon Oil
Murphy Oil
Newfield Exploration
Royal Dutch Shell

HISTORICAL FINANCIALS

Company Type: Public

Income Statement

	REVENUE ($ mil.)	NET INCOME ($ mil.)	NET PROFIT MARGIN	EMPLOYEES
6/09	190.7	55.9	29.3%	7
6/08	116.5	256.9	220.5%	6
6/07	18.7	(2.7)	—	6
6/06	0.9	(0.2)	—	6
6/05	4.3	12.4	288.4%	6
Annual Growth	158.1%	45.7%	—	3.9%

2009 Year-End Financials

Debt ratio: 0.0%
Return on equity: 16.2%
Cash ($ mil.): 44.4
Current ratio: 1.81
Long-term debt ($ mil.): 0.0
No. of shares (mil.): 15.8

Dividends
　Yield: 0.0%
　Payout: —
Market value ($ mil.): 672.6
R&D as % of sales: —
Advertising as % of sales: —

	STOCK PRICE ($) FY Close	P/E High/Low		Earnings	PER SHARE ($) Dividends	Book Value
6/09	42.49	28	9	3.35	0.00	22.07
6/08	93.04	6	2	14.88	0.00	21.60
6/07	36.28	—	—	(0.21)	0.00	5.74
6/06	14.14	—	—	(0.05)	0.00	3.95
6/05	9.20	11	6	0.92	0.00	3.22
Annual Growth	46.6%	—	—	38.1%	—	61.8%

Continental Resources

The continental resources that Continental Resources searches for are oil and natural gas assets beneath the North American continent, in the Rocky Mountain, Mid-Continent, and Gulf Coast regions. The independent oil and gas exploration and production company has added reserves of 121.7 million barrels of oil equivalent through internal growth (aka "growing through the drill bit") between early 2004 and the end of 2008. In 2008 Continental Resources reported estimated proved reserves of 159.3 million barrels of oil equivalent. It holds more than 1.5 million net acres of leasehold properties.

The company focuses its exploration activities on oil rather than natural gas, in large new or developing plays, where horizontal drilling, advanced fracture stimulation, and enhanced recovery technologies enable Continental Resources to economically develop and produce reserves from unconventional formations.

In 2008 the company added 36,000 acres to its holdings in North Dakota, boosting its acreage position in the lucrative Bakken shale play in North Dakota and Montana to 577,000 net acres.

EXECUTIVES

Chairman and CEO: Harold G. Hamm, age 63
President and COO: Jeffrey B. (Jeff) Hume, age 57
SVP Exploration: Jack H. Stark, age 54
SVP Land: Tom E. Luttrell, age 51
SVP Resource Development: Gene R. Carlson, age 55
VP Public Affairs: Brian K. Engel
VP Investor Relations: J. Warren Henry
VP, CFO, and Treasurer: John D. Hart, age 41
President, Eastern Division: Richard H. Straeter, age 50
Secretary: Don Fischbach
Auditors: Grant Thornton LLP

LOCATIONS

HQ: Continental Resources, Inc.
302 N. Independence, Enid, OK 73702
Phone: 580-233-8955   **Fax:** 580-548-5253
Web: www.contres.com

PRODUCTS/OPERATIONS

2008 Sales

	$ mil.	% of total
Oil & gas	875.2	90
Oil & gas sales to affiliates	64.7	7
Service operations	28.6	3
Adjustments	(8.0)	—
Total	**960.5**	**100**

COMPETITORS

Abraxas Petroleum
Anadarko Petroleum
Chesapeake Energy
EOG

HISTORICAL FINANCIALS

Company Type: Public

Income Statement　　　　FYE: December 31

	REVENUE ($ mil.)	NET INCOME ($ mil.)	NET PROFIT MARGIN	EMPLOYEES
12/08	960.5	321.0	33.4%	394
12/07	582.2	28.6	4.9%	332
12/06	483.7	253.1	52.3%	299
12/05	375.8	194.3	51.7%	286
Annual Growth	36.7%	18.2%	—	11.3%

2008 Year-End Financials

Debt ratio: 39.7%
Return on equity: 40.8%
Cash ($ mil.): 5.2
Current ratio: 0.69
Long-term debt ($ mil.): 376.4
No. of shares (mil.): 169.9

Dividends
　Yield: 0.0%
　Payout: —
Market value ($ mil.): 3,517.7
R&D as % of sales: —
Advertising as % of sales: —

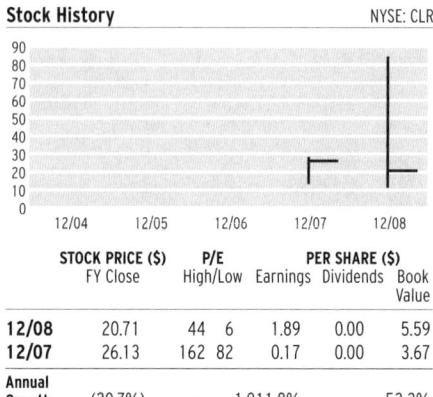

	STOCK PRICE ($) FY Close	P/E High/Low		Earnings	PER SHARE ($) Dividends	Book Value
12/08	20.71	44	6	1.89	0.00	5.59
12/07	26.13	162	82	0.17	0.00	3.67
Annual Growth	(20.7%)	—	—1,011.8%	—	52.2%

Continucare Corporation

Continucare keeps on caring for South and Central Florida's Medicare recipients. The company provides primary care medical services through a network of around 20 centers in Broward, Miami-Dade, and Hillsborough counties. It also provides practice management services to about 25 independent doctors' practices affiliated with Humana. A majority of the patients who seek care at Continucare clinics and practices are members of Medicare Advantage health plans; virtually all of the company's revenue comes from managed care contracts with

HMOs operated by Humana, Vista Healthplan of South Florida, and Wellcare.

In 2008 Continucare opened a handful of walk-in clinics, called ValuClinics, in pharmacies in Florida. The venture was short-lived: By September it had closed those clinics and instead focused on offering walk-in services at existing medical centers. The move is part of the company's plan to expand its services, increase patient volume, and expand geographically.

In 2009 Continucare switched gears again and acquired Professional Sleep Diagnostics, which operates about 13 centers in six states (South Carolina, North Carolina, West Virginia, Virginia, Colorado, Ohio) for about $2 million. Continucare will operate the sleep diagnostic centers under a newly created subsidiary called Seredor Corp. The company made the purchase to diversify its revenue base and establish itself in a new market.

Later that year the company expanded its sleep diagnostic business further with the purchase of Sleep Disorder Solutions, which operates centers in Miami and Pembroke Pines, Florida. The purchase marked Continucare's entry into the Florida sleep diagnostic market.

Continucare provides medical services to around 40,000 patients, most of them through capitated arrangements in which participating health plans pay a set monthly fee (usually a percentage of premiums) for each member. Humana accounts for a majority of revenue.

The company also serves participants in Medicaid health plans, though to a much lesser extent than its Medicare customer base. Director Philip Frost owns nearly 45% of Continucare.

EXECUTIVES

Chairman, President, and CEO:
Richard C. Pfenniger Jr., age 53, $896,386 total compensation
Vice Chairman: Luis Cruz, age 48
EVP: Jose M. Garcia
EVP Operations: Gemma Rosello, age 53, $550,261 total compensation
SVP Center Operations: Sadita Bustamante
SVP Marketing and Business Development:
Luis H. Izquierdo, age 54, $409,769 total compensation
SVP Finance, CFO, Treasurer, and Secretary:
Fernando L. Fernandez, age 48, $463,630 total compensation
VP Support Services: Holly Lopez
VP IPA and Special Projects: Dora Rodriguez-Duran
President, Seredor: David Neel
Medical Director: Sonia Michael
Auditors: Ernst & Young LLP

LOCATIONS

HQ: Continucare Corporation
7200 Corporate Center Dr., Ste. 600
Miami, FL 33126
Phone: 305-500-2000   **Fax:** 305-500-2080
Web: www.continucare.com

COMPETITORS

Baptist Health South Florida
Broward Health
HCA
MetCare
Mount Sinai Medical Center of Florida
Public Health Trust
South Broward Hospital District
Tenet Healthcare

HISTORICAL FINANCIALS

Company Type: Public

Income Statement

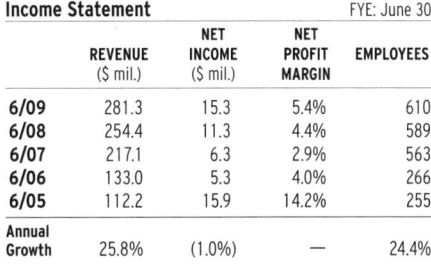

	REVENUE ($ mil.)	NET INCOME ($ mil.)	NET PROFIT MARGIN	EMPLOYEES
6/09	281.3	15.3	5.4%	610
6/08	254.4	11.3	4.4%	589
6/07	217.1	6.3	2.9%	563
6/06	133.0	5.3	4.0%	266
6/05	112.2	15.9	14.2%	255
Annual Growth	25.8%	(1.0%)	—	24.4%

FYE: June 30

2009 Year-End Financials

Debt ratio: —
Return on equity: 14.1%
Cash ($ mil.): 13.9
Current ratio: 4.81
Long-term debt ($ mil.): —
No. of shares (mil.): 59.5
Dividends
Yield: 0.0%
Payout: —
Market value ($ mil.): 138.6
R&D as % of sales: —
Advertising as % of sales: —

Stock History

NYSE Alternext: CNU

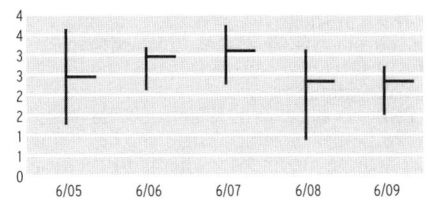

6/05	6/06	6/07	6/08	6/09

	STOCK PRICE ($) FY Close	P/E High/Low		Earnings	PER SHARE ($) Dividends	Book Value
6/09	2.33	11	6	0.24	0.00	1.87
6/08	2.33	19	6	0.16	0.00	1.77
6/07	3.09	37	23	0.10	0.00	1.75
6/06	2.95	32	22	0.10	0.00	0.62
6/05	2.45	12	4	0.31	0.00	0.51
Annual Growth	(1.2%)	—	—	(6.2%)	—	38.4%

Cornerstone Therapeutics

Cornerstone Therapeutics (formerly Critical Therapeutics) wants to help clear things up for the allergic, the asthmatic, the congested, and the inflamed. The drug company is focused on developing and commercializing therapeutic products to prevent and treat acute inflammation and other respiratory ailments. Its marketed products include AlleRx, Balacet, Deconsal, Spectracef, and Zyflo CR. Cornerstone Therapeutics was formed by the 2008 merger of Critical Therapeutics and privately held respiratory therapy firm Cornerstone BioPharma. Italian drugmaker Chiesi Farmaceutici owns a majority stake in the company.

Cornerstone Therapeutics announced a $70 million strategic transaction agreement with Chiesi in 2009. The Italian firm gained a 51% share in Cornerstone, while Cornerstone received the rights to market Chiesi's respiratory distress treatment, Curosurf, in the US market. The deal strengthened Cornerstone's finances, as well as broadened its product offerings and customer segments.

The former Critical Therapeutics had announced in late 2007 that it was exploring strategic alternatives to increase shareholder value, such as a possible asset sale, merger, or other transaction. In early 2008 the company announced its plan to merge with respiratory drug maker Cornerstone BioPharma. Cornerstone's drugs included antibiotic Spectracef and AlleRx for allergic rhinitis. Prior to the merger Critical Therapeutics cut about 20% of its workforce in an effort to conserve cash.

Critical Therapeutics brought two drugs in development to the deal, while Cornerstone already had drugs on the market. Following the merger, Cornerstone shareholders held 70% of the combined company, while Critical Therapeutics' owners held 30%.

Renamed Cornerstone Therapeutics, the company is less likely to pursue development of drug candidates, and instead will probably place its energies into commercializing products ready for market. Candidates already in its pipeline may be licensed out to other developers.

In mid-2009 the company agreed to acquire North American and select European marketing rights to bronchitis and pneumonia antibiotic Factive from Oscient Pharmaceuticals for $5 million.

The company acquired worldwide rights from Abbott Laboratories for Zyflo, an immediate-release zileuton that has FDA approval to treat chronic asthma. Zyflo CR, which is marketed through the firm's direct sales force and marketing partner Dey, received FDA approval in 2007, and the company launched the product that year.

Cornerstone Therapeutics' pipeline includes an injectable version of zileuton. Additional products under development target inflammatory ailments associated with trauma, burns, and chronic ailments such as Crohn's disease. The company is collaborating with MedImmune on the development of HMGB1 inhibitors for the treatment of inflammatory diseases including rheumatoid arthritis and sepsis.

EXECUTIVES

Chairman, President, and CEO: Craig A. Collard, age 43
EVP Finance, CFO, and Treasurer: David Price, age 46
EVP Manufacturing and Trade: Steven M. Lutz, age 42
EVP, General Counsel, and Secretary:
Andrew K. W. Powell, age 51
VP Scientific Affairs: Alan T. Roberts
VP Sales and Marketing: Joshua B. Franklin, age 39
Auditors: Deloitte & Touche LLP

LOCATIONS

HQ: Cornerstone Therapeutics, Inc.
1255 Crescent Green Dr., Ste. 250, Cary, NC 27518
Phone: 919-678-6611   **Fax:** 866-443-3092
Web: www.crtx.com

PRODUCTS/OPERATIONS

2008 Sales

	$ mil.	% of total
Product sales	63.2	97
Royalty agreements	1.7	3
Total	**64.9**	**100**

COMPETITORS

Abbott Labs	Genentech
Amgen	GlaxoSmithKline
AstraZeneca	Johnson & Johnson
Biogen Idec	Merck
Boehringer Ingelheim	Novartis Pharmaceuticals
Bristol-Myers Squibb	Pfizer
Eli Lilly	

HISTORICAL FINANCIALS
Company Type: Public

Income Statement
FYE: December 31

	REVENUE ($ mil.)	NET INCOME ($ mil.)	NET PROFIT MARGIN	EMPLOYEES
12/08	64.9	9.0	13.9%	107
12/07	12.9	(37.0)	—	80
12/06	13.1	(48.8)	—	61
12/05	6.2	(47.1)	—	175
12/04	4.4	(33.3)	—	66
Annual Growth	96.0%	—	—	12.8%

2008 Year-End Financials
Debt ratio: 0.0%
Return on equity: 38.7%
Cash ($ mil.): 9.3
Current ratio: 1.09
Long-term debt ($ mil.): 0.0
No. of shares (mil.): 25.1
Dividends
  Yield: 0.0%
  Payout: —
Market value ($ mil.): 66.6
R&D as % of sales: —
Advertising as % of sales: —

Stock History
NASDAQ (CM): CRTX

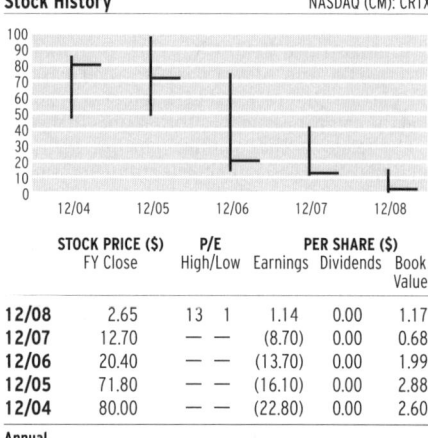

	STOCK PRICE ($) FY Close	P/E High/Low		PER SHARE ($) Earnings	Dividends	Book Value
12/08	2.65	13	1	1.14	0.00	1.17
12/07	12.70	—	—	(8.70)	0.00	0.68
12/06	20.40	—	—	(13.70)	0.00	1.99
12/05	71.80	—	—	(16.10)	0.00	2.88
12/04	80.00	—	—	(22.80)	0.00	2.60
Annual Growth	(57.3%)	—	—	—	—	(18.1%)

Corporate Executive Board

Don't fear the competition; learn from them. So says The Corporate Executive Board Company (CEB), a provider of business research and analysis services to more than 5,000 companies worldwide. Its 40-plus program areas cover "best practices" in such areas as finance, human resources, information technology, operations, and sales and marketing. Unlike consulting firms, which engage with one client at a time, CEB operates on a membership-based business model. Members subscribe to one or more of the company's programs and participate in the research and analysis, thus sharing expertise with

others. Besides reports on best practices, CEB offers seminars, customized research briefs, and decision-support tools.

With many of the firm's corporate customers cutting costs because of the recession, CEB announced in early 2009 that it would reduce its workforce by 15%, and shed or change about 10 of its then 52 programs.

CEB's health relies on adding more clients to its network and persuading existing clients to subscribe to more research programs — which may prove difficult with the economic slowdown. In prior years, CEB has maintained a client renewal rate of about 90% per year. However, that rate dropped to 84% in 2008, the first time it had dipped below 90% since at least the year 2004.

Despite the economic downturn, CEB bought TowerGroup from MasterCard in October 2009, deepening its financial services offerings, especially in technology, and sales and marketing. Terms of the deal were not disclosed.

Before the decline in the economy, CEB acquired ITtoolbox, an online professional networking provider, for $59 million in mid-2007. The buyout gave CEB access to more than 1 million of ITtoolbox's users in the IT and professional community.

CEB was spun off in 1999 from The Advisory Board Company, which offers similar research and analysis services for clients in the health care industry. A noncompete agreement that prevented CEB from seeking health care clients and kept The Advisory Board from operating outside that industry expired in January 2007; subsequently, the companies agreed to collaborate on selected projects and to continue not competing in core businesses.

EXECUTIVES

Chairman and CEO: Thomas L. Monahan III, age 42, $3,177,078 total compensation
CFO: Richard S. Lindahl, age 45
Chief Human Resources Officer: Melody L. Jones, age 49, $1,374,109 total compensation
Managing Director, Financial Planning and Analysis: Joyce Liu, age 40, $403,644 total compensation
General Manager: Glenn P. Tobin, age 47, $1,603,176 total compensation
Media and Public Relations: Joni Renick
Investor Relations: Lisa Herold
Auditors: Ernst & Young LLP

LOCATIONS

HQ: The Corporate Executive Board Company
  1919 N. Lynn St., Arlington, VA 22209
Phone: 571-303-3000   **Fax:** 571-303-5014
Web: www.executiveboard.com

2008 Sales

	$ mil.	% of total
US	382.7	68
Europe	98.8	18
Other regions	76.9	14
Total	**558.4**	**100**

PRODUCTS/OPERATIONS

Selected Practice Areas
Communications
Financial services
General management
Human resources
Information technology
Legal and compliance
Operations and procurement
Sales and marketing
Strategy and research and development

COMPETITORS

Accenture
BearingPoint
Booz Allen
Boston Consulting
Conference Board
McKinsey & Company

HISTORICAL FINANCIALS
Company Type: Public

Income Statement
FYE: December 31

	REVENUE ($ mil.)	NET INCOME ($ mil.)	NET PROFIT MARGIN	EMPLOYEES
12/08	558.4	50.8	9.1%	2,430
12/07	532.7	80.6	15.1%	2,440
12/06	460.6	79.2	17.2%	2,279
12/05	362.2	75.1	20.7%	1,865
12/04	280.7	53.7	19.1%	1,448
Annual Growth	18.8%	(1.4%)	—	13.8%

2008 Year-End Financials
Debt ratio: —
Return on equity: 105.7%
Cash ($ mil.): 16.2
Current ratio: 0.54
Long-term debt ($ mil.): —
No. of shares (mil.): 34.1
Dividends
  Yield: 8.0%
  Payout: 118.9%
Market value ($ mil.): 753.1
R&D as % of sales: —
Advertising as % of sales: —

Stock History
NASDAQ (GS): EXBD

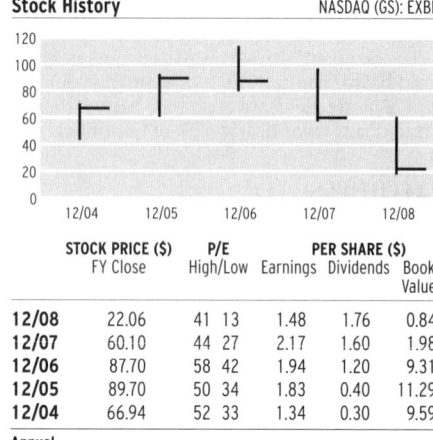

	STOCK PRICE ($) FY Close	P/E High/Low		PER SHARE ($) Earnings	Dividends	Book Value
12/08	22.06	41	13	1.48	1.76	0.84
12/07	60.10	44	27	2.17	1.60	1.98
12/06	87.70	58	42	1.94	1.20	9.31
12/05	89.70	50	34	1.83	0.40	11.29
12/04	66.94	52	33	1.34	0.30	9.59
Annual Growth	(24.2%)	—	—	2.5%	55.6%	(45.6%)

CPI Aerostructures

To build an aircraft, some assembly is required, and that's where CPI Aerostructures comes in. CPI Aero makes structural aircraft subassemblies for the US Air Force and other US military customers. Primary military products include skin panels, flight control surfaces, leading edges, wing tips, engine components, cowl doors, and nacelle and inlet assemblies for military aircraft such as the A-10 Warthog, C-5 Galaxy, C-130 Hercules, E-3 Sentry AWACs jet, and T-38 Talon. CPI Aero also makes aprons and engine mounts for commercial aircraft such as business jets.

Government contracts account for nearly all of CPI Aero's sales, and the company hopes to grow by concentrating its efforts on that market segment rather than on its commercial business.

Most of the company's contracts are valued at less than $200,000, but the company is in the midst of a $61 million contract for the T-38 training jet and a $215 million contract for the C-5 cargo plane. Combined, both contracts accounted for nearly half of CPI Aero's 2007 sales.

Chairman Eric Rosenfeld, through investment firm Crescendo Partners, controls about 18% of CPI Aero.

EXECUTIVES

Non-Executive Chairman: Eric S. Rosenfeld, age 51
President, CEO, and Director: Edward J. Fred, age 50, $541,309 total compensation
COO: Douglas J. McCrosson, age 46
CFO and Secretary: Vincent (Vince) Palazzolo, age 45, $342,654 total compensation
Auditors: J.H. Cohn LLP

LOCATIONS

HQ: CPI Aerostructures, Inc.
60 Heartland Blvd., Edgewood, NY 11717
Phone: 631-586-5200 **Fax:** 631-586-5814
Web: www.cpiaero.com

PRODUCTS/OPERATIONS

Selected Products

Cowl doors
Engine components
Flight control surfaces
Inlet assemblies
Leading edges
Nacelle assemblies
Skin panels
Wing tips

COMPETITORS

Boeing
Lockheed Martin
NORDAM
Northrop Grumman
Vought Aircraft

HISTORICAL FINANCIALS

Company Type: Public

Income Statement

FYE: December 31

	REVENUE ($ mil.)	NET INCOME ($ mil.)	NET PROFIT MARGIN	EMPLOYEES
12/08	35.6	2.6	7.3%	85
12/07	28.0	1.9	6.8%	65
12/06	17.9	(1.3)	—	61
12/05	25.5	1.5	5.9%	72
12/04	30.3	6.9	22.8%	67
Annual Growth	4.1%	(21.7%)	—	6.1%

2008 Year-End Financials

Debt ratio: 7.1%
Return on equity: 8.2%
Cash ($ mil.): 0.4
Current ratio: 6.25
Long-term debt ($ mil.): 2.4
No. of shares (mil.): 6.0
Dividends
 Yield: 0.0%
 Payout: —
Market value ($ mil.): 33.0
R&D as % of sales: —
Advertising as % of sales: —

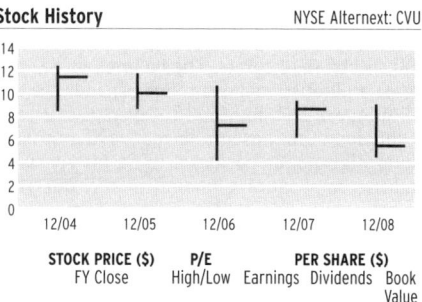

Credit Acceptance Corporation

In the world of Credit Acceptance Corporation (CAC), to purchase a car is not an impossible dream for problem borrowers — just an expensive reality. Working with more than 3,000 independent and franchised automobile dealers in the US, CAC provides capital for auto loans to people with substandard credit. The company also provides other services to dealers, including payment servicing, receivables management, marketing, and service contracts. It originates more than 1.7 million loans per year; Texas is the company's largest market. Founder and chairman Donald Foss owns more than 60% of Credit Acceptance.

In 2008 the company agreed to pay some 15,000 Missouri customers to settle a class action lawsuit. The lawsuit, filed more than a decade ago, alleged that Credit Acceptance overcharged customers for fees and interest on their loans. As part of the settlement, Credit Acceptance said it would write off $39 million in outstanding accounts and distribute another $13 million to customers.

HISTORY

Donald Foss was a used-car dealer in Detroit, where, to make sales, he sometimes financed cars out of his own pocket. As Foss's chain of dealerships grew, so did his financing business. In 1972 he established it as a separate company, and 20 years later took it public.

For most of its history CAC stood alone in the field of subprime auto lending, but stagnating salaries made it a competitive growth business in the early 1990s. At mid-decade, the company entered Canada and the UK to tap similar markets there. In 1996 CAC acquired Montana Investment Group, a credit reporting service.

Even as rising consumer debt and bad credit continued to pump buyers into CAC's loan pipeline, the economic boom of the mid-1990s paradoxically made used cars less desirable. The soft used-car market squeezed several of CAC's

competitors out of business; a staggering default rate — nearing 40% — also pressured CAC, whose auditors insisted it increase reserves to cover losses. The subsequent earnings dive spurred a shareholder lawsuit accusing CAC of hiding its poor fiscal health. Although bad loans had damaged its bottom line, the company adopted more stringent lending policies to reduce risk. Consumers filed class-action suits alleging unethical practices in 1998, but many claims were dismissed.

To pay off debt acquired through bad loans, CAC sold Montana Investment Group in 1999. In 2000 it launched CAC Leasing, to further offset losses from a decrease in subprime lending, but in 2002 the company exited that line, deciding the lending field was more profitable. CAC stopped originating new loans in the UK and Canada in 2003.

In 2005 the SEC investigated CAC's accounting methods, specifically related to its loan portfolio, and the company restated portions of its past financial results.

EXECUTIVES

Chairman: Donald A. Foss, age 64, $476,250 total compensation
CEO and Director: Brett A. Roberts, age 42, $3,776,263 total compensation
President: Steven M. Jones, age 45, $1,214,991 total compensation
CFO: Kenneth S. Booth, age 41, $556,050 total compensation
CIO: Michael P. Miotto, age 48, $462,063 total compensation
Chief Legal Officer and Corporate Secretary: Charles A. Pearce, age 44
SVP Loan Servicing: Michael W. Knoblauch, age 45
Treasurer: Douglas W. Busk, age 48
Auditors: Grant Thornton LLP

LOCATIONS

HQ: Credit Acceptance Corporation
25505 W. Twelve Mile Rd., Ste. 3000
Southfield, MI 48034
Phone: 248-353-2700 **Fax:** 248-827-8553
Web: www.creditacceptance.com

PRODUCTS/OPERATIONS

2008 Sales

	$ mil.	% of total
Finance charges	286.8	92
Premiums earned	4.0	1
Other income		
Marketing	4.2	1
Remarketing charges	4.0	1
Dealer support	2.4	1
Interest	2.0	1
Dealer enrollment fees	1.9	1
Other	6.9	2
Total	**312.2**	**100**

Selected Subsidiaries

Arlington Investment Company
Auto Funding America, Inc.
Auto Lease Services, LLC
AutoNet Finance Company.com, Inc.
Buyers Vehicle Protection Plan, Inc.
CAC Leasing, Inc.
CAC Reinsurance, Ltd.
Credit Acceptance Motors, Inc.
Credit Acceptance Wholesale Buyers Club, Inc.
Vehicle Remarketing Services, Inc.
VSC Re Company

COMPETITORS

American Honda Finance	GMAC
AmeriCredit	Mercedes-Benz Credit
Bank of America	Toyota Motor Credit
Capital One Auto Finance	Union Acceptance
Daimler Financial	Volkswagen Financial
First Investors Financial	Volvo Car Finance
Ford Motor Credit	Wells Fargo Auto Finance

HISTORICAL FINANCIALS

Company Type: Public

Income Statement

FYE: December 31

	ASSETS ($ mil.)	NET INCOME ($ mil.)	INCOME AS % OF ASSETS	EMPLOYEES
12/08	1,139.4	67.2	5.9%	1,048
12/07	942.2	54.9	5.8%	971
12/06	725.2	58.6	8.1%	788
12/05	619.4	72.6	11.7%	777
12/04	591.3	57.3	9.7%	757
Annual Growth	17.8%	4.1%	—	8.5%

2008 Year-End Financials

Equity as % of assets: 29.6%
Return on assets: 6.5%
Return on equity: 22.3%
Long-term debt ($ mil.): 580.4
No. of shares (mil.): 31.0
Market value ($ mil.): 424.5

Dividends
  Yield: 0.0%
  Payout: —
Sales ($ mil.): 312.2
R&D as % of sales: —
Advertising as % of sales: —

Stock History

NASDAQ (GM): CACC

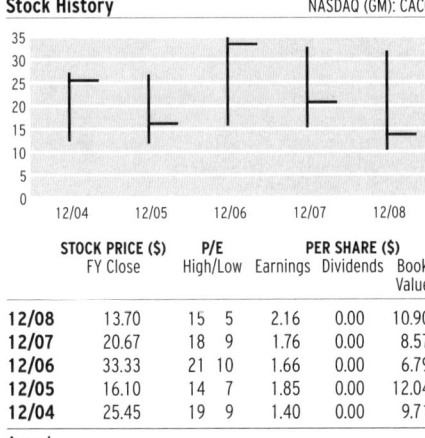

	STOCK PRICE ($) FY Close	P/E High/Low		PER SHARE ($) Earnings	Dividends	Book Value
12/08	13.70	15	5	2.16	0.00	10.90
12/07	20.67	18	9	1.76	0.00	8.57
12/06	33.33	21	10	1.66	0.00	6.79
12/05	16.10	14	7	1.85	0.00	12.04
12/04	25.45	19	9	1.40	0.00	9.71
Annual Growth	(14.3%)	—	—	11.5%	—	2.9%

Cree, Inc.

Cree has its name in lights. Its blue, green, and near-ultraviolet light-emitting diodes (LEDs) — made from silicon carbide (SiC) and gallium nitride (GaN) — are used in products such as dashboard lights, architectural light fixtures, market tickers, and video screens, including the giant screen in New York City's Times Square. Cree also sells SiC wafers, which work better at higher temperatures and voltages than standard silicon devices, and SiC and GaN materials. Its power and radio-frequency (RF) products include Schottky diodes and transistors. Leading customers include Seoul Semiconductor, Arrow Electronics, and Sumitomo. Cree sells products globally, but Asia accounts for more than two-thirds of sales.

Cree created the first blue LED, which, when combined with red and yellow LEDs, creates a full spectrum of colors. The technology has become an industry standard and expands the applications of LED lighting. To leverage this core technology, Cree has introduced the XLamp family of high-power packaged LEDs for specialty lighting applications, hoping to stay one step ahead of the competition. Cree's XLamp products have a wide array of residential and commercial uses, including appliance lighting and reading lamps, as well as backlighting for large flat-panel and retail displays.

The trends towards increased energy-efficient and environmental lighting, and the growing number of standard lighting products that use LEDs have helped Cree weather a challenging economic environment better than many in the electronics industry. The company has combined external acquisitions and internal R&D to broaden its offerings — and increase its sales and market reach — into LED lighting fixtures, power switching, and RF products.

On the acquisition side, Cree bought LED Lighting Fixtures in 2008 for about $77 million; the acquisition added lighting fixtures such as down lights and luminaires that use Cree's XLamp LEDs. Neal Hunter, CEO of LED Lighting Fixtures and a co-founder of Cree, rejoined Cree through the acquisition of his firm, which was renamed Cree LED Lighting Solutions. Hunter serves as president of the subsidiary.

In 2007 Cree acquired Hong Kong-based COTCO Luminant Device for about $200 million; the COTCO acquisition gave Cree the ability to offer more value-added products by providing a broader range of LED components, access to a lower cost manufacturing facility, and established sales channels in the fast growing China market.

Cree has also been successful in inking big deals. In 2009 the Department of Defense announced it would be installing Cree luminaires in the Pentagon as part of a major renovation. The first ecofriendly McDonald's in North Carolina uses Cree downlights, bulbs, and other products for more than 97% of its lighting.

HISTORY

Cree started at North Carolina State University, where brothers Eric and Neal Hunter and Calvin Carter researched silicon carbide (SiC) applications, in part with US government funding. In 1987 the trio founded Cree Research to continue their research. The company shipped its first-to-market blue light-emitting diode (LED) in 1991, and went public in 1993.

In 1995 the company began developing blue lasers — a project that continued for years to follow — via a 1999 pact with Microvision. Also that year Cree and Siemens formed a development and manufacturing agreement for blue and green LEDs. In 1997 Cree began supplying SiC crystals to gemstone manufacturer C3.

Cree in 1998 signed or extended pacts with Kansai Electric Power, Siemens, and Asea Brown Boveri (now ABB Ltd.). The next year the company shortened its name to Cree, Inc., and released its first radio-frequency transistor.

In 2000 Cree acquired semiconductor R&D boutique Nitres for $233 million and, to close out the year, purchased the UltraRF division of Spectrian (a maker of linear power amplifiers) for $113.5 million. (It later renamed the unit Cree Microwave.)

In 2004 Cree acquired the gallium nitride substrate and epitaxy assets of Advanced Technology Materials, a subsidiary of ATMI, for about $10 million, boosting its materials business and IP portfolio.

Co-founder Neal Hunter, who served as CEO of Cree from 1994 to 2001, resigned as chairman in 2005 after a decade in that post, and left the company's board of directors. Charles Swoboda, who had succeeded Hunter as CEO in 2001, succeeded him as chairman, as well.

Cree phased out its silicon-based RF and microwave semiconductor business in 2005, citing losses by its Cree Microwave subsidiary. The company refocused on its wide-bandgap RF and microwave devices fabricated on SiC and GaN substrates. In 2006 the company opened a new engineering and production facility in Research Triangle Park, measuring 230,000 sq. ft., for making SiC and GaN devices.

That same year Cree acquired INTRINSIC Semiconductor for around $46 million, including $43.6 million in cash. INTRINSIC Semiconductor made low-defect-density SiC substrates, enabling high-power semiconductor devices and lower-cost LEDs.

EXECUTIVES

Chairman, President, and CEO: Charles M. (Chuck) Swoboda, age 42, $2,301,703 total compensation
EVP and COO: Stephen D. Kelley, age 47, $1,024,698 total compensation
EVP Finance, CFO, and Treasurer: John T. Kurtzweil, age 53, $1,078,834 total compensation
SVP Sales: Robert (Bob) Pollock, age 55
VP and General Manager Power and RF: Cengiz Balkas
VP Market Development, Cree LED Lighting: Gary Trott
VP Corporate Marketing: Greg Merritt
CTO, Advanced Devices and Director: John W. Palmour, age 48, $682,795 total compensation
Secretary: Adam H. Broome
Corporate Communications: Michelle Murray
President, Cree LED Lighting: Neal Hunter, age 47
Director Marketing, LED Components: Paul Thieken
Director Investor Relations: Raiford Garrabrant
Director RF and Microwave Products: Jim Milligan
Director Business Development, Solid State Lighting: Mark McClear
Auditors: Ernst & Young LLP

LOCATIONS

HQ: Cree, Inc.
  4600 Silicon Dr., Durham, NC 27703
Phone: 919-313-5300   **Fax:** 919-313-5558
Web: www.cree.com

2009 Sales

	% of total
Asia/Pacific	
Hong Kong & China	38
South Korea	15
Japan	9
Malaysia	3
Taiwan	3
US	20
Europe	10
Other regions	2
Total	**100**

PRODUCTS/OPERATIONS

2009 Sales

	$ mil.	% of total
LED products	494.4	87
Power & RF products	26.6	5
Materials products	21.9	4
Contracts	18.8	3
Upfront licensing fees	5.6	1
Total	**567.3**	**100**

Selected Products

Blue and green light-emitting diodes (LEDs; used in displays and indicators)
High-power packaged LEDs (XLamp)
LED light fixtures (architectural lay-in, bulbs, downlights, housings, narrow beam spotlight)
Silicon carbide (SiC) products
  Crystals (used in manufacturing man-made gemstones)
  Radio-frequency and microwave transistors (used in communications applications)
  Rectifiers
  Wafers (used in research programs)

COMPETITORS

Advanced Photonix	Optek Technology
Avago Technologies	OSRAM SYLVANIA
Eudyna Devices	Panasonic Corp
Hitachi	Philips Solid-State
II-VI	Lighting
Infineon Technologies	Planar Systems
Kopin	RF Micro Devices
LG Electronics	Rubicon Technology
Lighting Science Group	Sanken Electric
Lumileds Lighting	Sony
MEMC Electronic Materials	Toyoda Gosei
NEC	TriQuint
Nichia	Zhejiang BOE Display
Nitronex	

HISTORICAL FINANCIALS

Company Type: Public

Income Statement

FYE: Last Sunday in June

	REVENUE ($ mil.)	NET INCOME ($ mil.)	NET PROFIT MARGIN	EMPLOYEES
6/09	567.3	30.3	5.3%	3,172
6/08	493.3	33.4	6.8%	3,168
6/07	394.1	57.3	14.5%	2,578
6/06	423.0	76.7	18.1%	1,364
6/05	389.1	91.1	23.4%	1,322
Annual Growth	9.9%	(24.1%)	—	24.5%

2009 Year-End Financials

Debt ratio: —
Return on equity: 2.6%
Cash ($ mil.): 290.2
Current ratio: 4.89
Long-term debt ($ mil.): —
No. of shares (mil.): 103.6

Dividends
  Yield: 0.0%
  Payout: —
Market value ($ mil.): 3,046.8
R&D as % of sales: —
Advertising as % of sales: —

Stock History

NASDAQ (GS): CREE

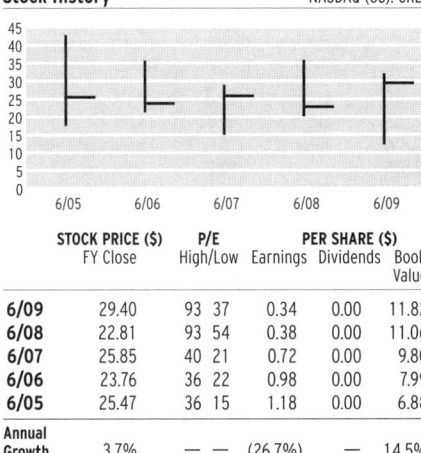

	STOCK PRICE ($) FY Close	P/E High/Low	PER SHARE ($) Earnings	Dividends	Book Value
6/09	29.40	93 37	0.34	0.00	11.82
6/08	22.81	93 54	0.38	0.00	11.06
6/07	25.85	40 21	0.72	0.00	9.80
6/06	23.76	36 22	0.98	0.00	7.99
6/05	25.47	36 15	1.18	0.00	6.88
Annual Growth	3.7%	— —	(26.7%)	—	14.5%

CryoLife, Inc.

CryoLife preserves lives, as well as the cardiovascular tissues that keep life going. The company takes human heart valves and blood vessels from deceased volunteer donors, processes them, and stores them in liquid nitrogen freezers (a process called *cryopreservation*). It then ships them to surgeons nationwide, who implant them during cardiac and vascular repair procedures. For some preserved tissue, the company uses its proprietary SynerGraft technology, which reduces the presence of donor cells and makes the tissue more compatible with the recipient. CryoLife also develops implantable biomaterials, including BioGlue, an adhesive used to seal internal surgical wounds.

Children with heart defects make up the company's largest end-user market for its preserved tissue, since human heart valves last longer and come in smaller sizes than either mechanical or pig heart valves (two other common treatment options). The company also sells a pig heart valve product, but only in European markets.

CryoLife sharpened its focus on cardiovascular products by ridding itself of a business devoted to cryopreserving tendons and cartilage used in orthopedic procedures. As part of its strategy to zero in on cardiovascular products, CryoLife decided to phase out its orthopedic operations. The company made a deal with fellow human tissue processor RTI Biologics, under which CryoLife transferred its orthopedic tissue business to RTI in return for that company's cardiovascular and vascular processing arrangements.

It is also expanding its cardiovascular market offerings through physician education efforts, the expansion of its network of donating tissue and organ procurement organizations, and the development of new products and technologies.

At the center of the company's product development efforts is its SynerGraft decellularization technology. The technology, which not only disinfects donated tissue but also removes some donor cells, aims to reduce the risk that a recipient's body will reject the implanted tissue. In 2008 CryoLife won FDA approval for the CryoValve SG pulmonary heart valve, its first human heart valve using the SynerGraft process. The following year the company received approval for a second SynerGraft product, the CryoPatch human cardiac patch material.

CryoLife is also focused on developing the market for BioGlue and creating similar products using its underlying Protein Hydrogel Technology. To that end, it is working on BioFoam, a treatment for severe bleeding, and BioDisc, used for spinal repair. Additionally, CryoLife has expanded its product line through acquisition and distribution deals: It acquired US distribution rights to MAST BioSurgery's CardioWrap product, which is used in cardiac reconstruction; and in 2008 it partnered with Trophic Solutions to develop better technologies for cold storage of internal organs such as kidneys.

That same year the company entered into an agreement with development firm Medafor to distribute Medafor's clotting agent, HemoStase, in the US, the UK, Germany, and Canada. After sales of the product proved successful, in early 2010 CryoLife made an unsolicited proposal to acquire Medafor.

HISTORY

When the University of Alabama began using cryopreserved heart valves instead of the mechanical ones he sold, Roy Holloway saw an opportunity. In 1984 he teamed with Steven Anderson, a former marketing executive at pacemaker manufacturer Intermedics (now Guidant) to offer cryopreservation services to hospitals and medical examiners' offices.

CryoLife initially met resistance to its cryopreserved valves (harvested from hearts unsuitable for transplanting). But as word of the valves' superiority spread, CryoLife began to grow. (Cryopreserved human valves do not fail, like mechanical ones, or calcify, like pig valves.)

CryoLife went public in 1993. In 1995 it bought the rights to the synergraft technology. The next year it bought United Cryopreservation Foundation, expanding its line of body parts.

In 1997 CryoLife started selling BioGlue in Europe. It also diversified into surgical instruments with the purchase of Ideas for Medicine (IFM). The next year CryoLife sold IFM's product line to Horizon Medical Products (HMP). But HMP's failure to fulfill a supply contract that was part of the deal forced CryoLife to take a charge in 1999. In 2000 CryoLife was hit by publicity surrounding press reports highlighting the profits derived from the "sale" of body parts harvested along with major organs from volunteer donors. The next year it formed AuraZyme Pharmaceuticals to develop light-activated drug delivery systems.

The year 2002 was a tough one for CryoLife, as questions from the FDA about the safety of CryoLife's human tissue and heart valves put the company on the defensive. Following the 2001 death of a patient who received a CryoLife implant as well as an inspection of the company's facilities, the FDA issued a recall of some of CryoLife's already distributed products, saying it couldn't guarantee that the tissue wasn't contaminated. Several years of legal troubles and financial losses followed. The company has since laid to rest the lawsuits related to the recall, including a class action suit that it settled in 2005 by agreeing to pay $23 million. It returned to profitability in 2006.

EXECUTIVES

Chairman, President, and CEO: Steven G. Anderson, age 70, $1,549,746 total compensation
EVP, COO, and CFO: D. Ashley Lee, age 44, $980,271 total compensation
SVP Sales and Marketing: Gerald B. (Gerry) Seery, age 52, $577,677 total compensation
SVP Research and Development: Albert E. Heacox, age 58, $570,844 total compensation
VP Regulatory Affairs and Quality Assurance: David M. Fronk, age 45, $478,939 total compensation
VP Clinical Research: Scott B. Capps, age 42
VP Laboratory Operations: Timothy M. Neja, age 43
VP International Sales and Marketing: Richard C. Gridley, age 38
VP; General Manager, CryoLife Europa: David N. Hollinworth
VP Medical Relations and Education: William F. Northrup
VP US Sales and Marketing: Bruce G. Anderson, age 43
Secretary: Suzanne K. Gabbert
Chief Accounting Officer: Amy D. Horton, age 39
General Counsel: Jeff Burris
Auditors: Deloitte & Touche LLP

LOCATIONS

HQ: CryoLife, Inc.
1655 Roberts Blvd., NW, Kennesaw, GA 30144
Phone: 770-419-3355   **Fax:** 770-426-0031
Web: www.cryolife.com

2008 Sales

	% of total
US	85
International	15
Total	**100**

PRODUCTS/OPERATIONS

2008 Sales

	% of total
Human tissue preservation services	51
Products (BioGlue, other medical devices)	48
Other	1
Total	**100**

Selected Products

CryoValve SG (pulmonary human heart valve)
ProPatch (surgical mesh for tissue repair)
CryoPatch SG (pulmonary artery branch patch)
CryoPatch SG (pulmonary artery trunk patch)
CryoPatch SG (pulmonary hemiartery)
CardioWrap (postsurgical healing)
BioGlue (surgical adhesive)
HemoStase (absorbable hemostatic particles)

COMPETITORS

ATS Medical
Bard
Baxter International
Covidien
Edwards Lifesciences
Ethicon
Haemacure
Johnson & Johnson
LifeCell
Medtronic
Osteotech
Pfizer
RTI Biologics
St. Jude Medical
Synovis Life Technologies

HISTORICAL FINANCIALS

Company Type: Public

Income Statement

FYE: December 31

	REVENUE ($ mil.)	NET INCOME ($ mil.)	NET PROFIT MARGIN	EMPLOYEES
12/08	105.1	32.9	31.3%	435
12/07	94.8	7.0	7.4%	405
12/06	81.3	(0.6)	—	388
12/05	69.3	(20.3)	—	363
12/04	62.4	(18.7)	—	349
Annual Growth	13.9%	—	—	5.7%

2008 Year-End Financials

Debt ratio: 0.3%
Return on equity: 40.6%
Cash ($ mil.): 17.2
Current ratio: 3.83
Long-term debt ($ mil.): 0.3
No. of shares (mil.): 28.5
Dividends
  Yield: 0.0%
  Payout: —
Market value ($ mil.): 276.4
R&D as % of sales: —
Advertising as % of sales: —

Stock History   NYSE: CRY

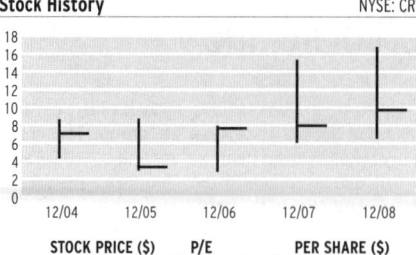

	STOCK PRICE ($) FY Close	P/E High/Low		PER SHARE ($) Earnings	Dividends	Book Value
12/08	9.71	14	6	1.16	0.00	3.49
12/07	7.95	58	24	0.26	0.00	2.20
12/06	7.65	—	—	(0.02)	0.00	1.83
12/05	3.34	—	—	(0.85)	0.00	1.78
12/04	7.07	—	—	(0.81)	0.00	1.74
Annual Growth	8.3%	—	—	—	—	18.9%

CSG Systems International

CSRs love CSG. CSG Systems International makes life a little easier for customer service representatives (CSRs) with its customer care and billing software and services. Designed for clients who handle a high volume of transactions, the company offers outsourced transaction processing and customer service systems that are used to establish customer accounts, process orders, manage and mail monthly statements, perform marketing analysis, and other functions. The company serves primarily North American cable TV, direct broadcast satellite, online services, and telecom companies. CSG's clients include Time Warner and Comcast.

Comcast was responsible for more than 25% of the company's sales in 2008. Time Warner and the company's other key clients, DISH Network and Charter Communications, together accounted for about 40% of the company's sales that same year. (Charter filed for Chapter 11 bankruptcy in 2009; it represented the smallest sales percentage [8%] of CSG's key clients.)

The company intends to expand its customer base by extending its offerings to other industries, including financial services, utilities, health care, and home security companies. Other growth strategies include a focus on evolving its technologies alongside the technology needs of its core industries.

CSG sometimes uses acquisition as a means of expanding its business. In 2008 the company agreed to purchase Quaero, a marketing services provider with expertise in customer strategy, analytics, and marketing performance management. The move expanded CSG's product line by incorporating customer intelligence applications, as well as expanding CSG's presence in new industries. The company traces its roots back to the early 1980s.

EXECUTIVES

Chairman: Bernard W. (Bernie) Reznicek, age 72
President, CEO, and Director: Peter E. Kalan, age 49, $1,975,177 total compensation
EVP and COO: Robert M. (Mike) Scott, age 58, $1,665,157 total compensation
EVP and CFO: Randy R. Wiese, age 49, $1,275,663 total compensation
EVP, General Counsel, Corporate Secretary, and Chief Administrative Officer: Joseph T. (Joe) Ruble, age 48, $1,011,772 total compensation
EVP Operations, Delivery, and CIO: Bret C. Griess
SVP Product Management: Dwayne Ruffin
SVP and General Manager, Quaero: Naras Eechambadi
SVP Strategic Business Units: Jay McCracken
SVP and General Manager, Prairie Interactive Messaging: Tom Nichting
SVP Business and New Market Development: Jerry Baker
SVP and General Manager, Output Solutions: Pam Sellenrick
VP Investor Relations: Elizabeth A. (Liz) Bauer
VP Corporate Communications: Karen Eckmann
VP Human Resources: Suzanne Broski
Auditors: KPMG LLP

LOCATIONS

HQ: CSG Systems International, Inc.
9555 Maroon Cir., Englewood, CO 80112
Phone: 303-200-2000   **Fax:** 303-804-4965
Web: www.csgsystems.com

PRODUCTS/OPERATIONS

2008 Sales

	% of total
Processing & related services	93
Software, maintenance & services	7
Total	**100**

COMPETITORS

ADC Telecommunications
Amdocs
Convergys
DST Systems
Oracle
Telcordia

HISTORICAL FINANCIALS

Company Type: Public

Income Statement

FYE: December 31

	REVENUE ($ mil.)	NET INCOME ($ mil.)	NET PROFIT MARGIN	EMPLOYEES
12/08	472.1	61.8	13.1%	2,066
12/07	419.3	60.8	14.5%	1,877
12/06	383.1	59.8	15.6%	1,685
12/05	377.3	53.2	14.1%	1,540
12/04	529.7	47.2	8.9%	2,549
Annual Growth	(2.8%)	7.0%	—	(5.1%)

2008 Year-End Financials

Debt ratio: 137.2%
Return on equity: 53.2%
Cash ($ mil.): 83.9
Current ratio: 2.79
Long-term debt ($ mil.): 205.4
No. of shares (mil.): 35.1
Dividends
  Yield: 0.0%
  Payout: —
Market value ($ mil.): 613.7
R&D as % of sales: —
Advertising as % of sales: —

Stock History

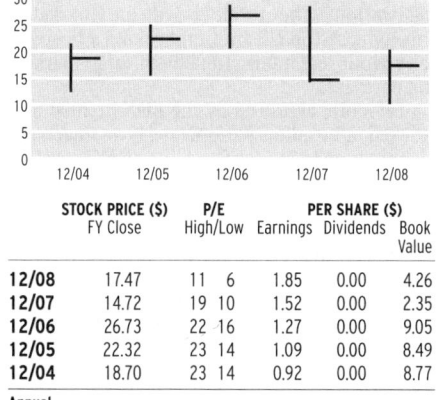

	STOCK PRICE ($) FY Close	P/E High/Low	Earnings	PER SHARE ($) Dividends	Book Value
12/08	17.47	11 6	1.85	0.00	4.26
12/07	14.72	19 10	1.52	0.00	2.35
12/06	26.73	22 16	1.27	0.00	9.05
12/05	22.32	23 14	1.09	0.00	8.49
12/04	18.70	23 14	0.92	0.00	8.77
Annual Growth	(1.7%)	— —	19.1%	—	(16.5%)

CTI Industries

Ballooning profits would be most welcome at CTI Industries Corporation. The company's metalized and latex balloons are decorated with messages and cartoon characters, such as Garfield and Miss Spider. It sells balloons and novelty inflatable items to distributors, retailers, grocers, and florists. CTI Industries also makes wrapping and custom film for commercial and industrial uses such as food packaging (candy wrappers) and dunnage bags (inflatable pouches used as cushioning during shipping). Its top three customers account for about 50% of sales.

Chairman John Schwan and EVP Stephen Merrick each own approximately 27% of CTI. John's brother, president Howard Schwan, owns another 10% of the company.

The company's largest customers are Dollar Tree (balloons, 20% of sales), Rapak L.L.C. (films, 20%), and Illinois Tool Works (pouches, 10%).

The company's latex balloons are made in Mexico by subsidiary Flexo Universal.

EXECUTIVES

Chairman: John H. Schwan, age 65, $144,133 total compensation
President and Director: Howard W. Schwan, age 54, $226,124 total compensation
CFO: Stephen M. Merrick, age 67, $109,028 total compensation
VP Sales: Steven Frank, age 48
VP Marketing: Samuel (Sam) Komar, age 52, $149,382 total compensation
VP Finance and Administration:
Timothy (Tim) Patterson, age 47, $137,350 total compensation
Manager Human Resources: Mary Allen Dammyer
National Sales Manager, Balloons and Novelties: Rick Migal
Lamination Sales Manager: Rick Sherman
Auditors: Blackman Kallick Bartelstein, LLP

LOCATIONS

HQ: CTI Industries Corporation
22160 N. Pepper Rd., Barrington, IL 60010
Phone: 847-382-1000   **Fax:** 847-382-1219
Web: www.ctiindustries.com

2008 Sales

	$ mil.	% of total
US	34.7	77
Mexico	7.5	17
UK	2.8	6
Total	**45.0**	**100**

PRODUCTS/OPERATIONS

2008 Sales

	% of total
Metalized balloons	40
Pouches	24
Films	18
Latex balloons	17
Helium & other	1
Total	**100**

Selected Products

Mylar (Metalized) Balloons
Balloon Jamz (large balloons attached to a speaker)
Card-B-Loons (air-filled balloons on sticks)
Miniloons (small balloons on sticks)
Minishapes (small shaped balloons on sticks)
Shape-A-Loons (shaped balloons)
Superloons (round and heart-shaped helium-filled balloons)
Ultraloons (large helium-filled balloons)
Commercial Films and Containers
Bags (including Simply Smart food storage bags)
Custom film products
Packaging films
Pouches
Latex Balloons
Partyloons (standard balloons)
Toy balloon products (punch balls, water bombs, animal twisties)

COMPETITORS

American Greetings
Amscan
Conver
CSS Industries
Litco
Sigma Plastics
Tredegar
US Balloon Manufacturing

HISTORICAL FINANCIALS

Company Type: Public

Income Statement

FYE: December 31

	REVENUE ($ mil.)	NET INCOME ($ mil.)	NET PROFIT MARGIN	EMPLOYEES
12/08	45.0	1.2	2.7%	330
12/07	36.5	0.1	0.3%	84
12/06	35.4	1.9	5.4%	89
12/05	29.2	(0.3)	—	280
12/04	37.2	(2.5)	—	293
Annual Growth	4.9%	—	—	3.0%

2008 Year-End Financials

Debt ratio: 77.8%
Return on equity: 16.8%
Cash ($ mil.): 0.2
Current ratio: 1.09
Long-term debt ($ mil.): 6.0
No. of shares (mil.): 2.7
Dividends
  Yield: 0.0%
  Payout: —
Market value ($ mil.): 5.7
R&D as % of sales: —
Advertising as % of sales: —

Stock History

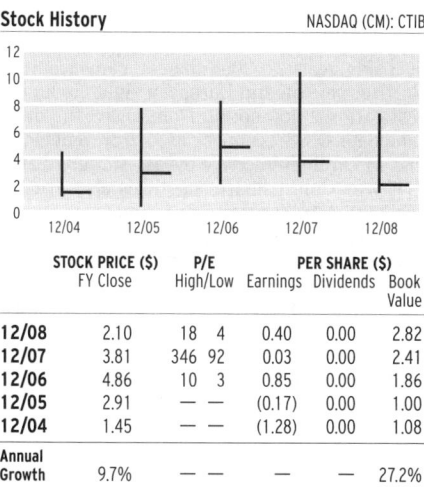

	STOCK PRICE ($) FY Close	P/E High/Low	Earnings	PER SHARE ($) Dividends	Book Value
12/08	2.10	18 4	0.40	0.00	2.82
12/07	3.81	346 92	0.03	0.00	2.41
12/06	4.86	10 3	0.85	0.00	1.86
12/05	2.91	— —	(0.17)	0.00	1.00
12/04	1.45	— —	(1.28)	0.00	1.08
Annual Growth	9.7%	— —	—	—	27.2%

Cubist Pharmaceuticals

Fighting infection is a modern art form at Cubist Pharmaceuticals. The company is developing antimicrobial agents that aim to treat drug-resistant infections typically found in hospitals and other health care institutions. Its flagship product Cubicin is an intravenous antibiotic that is FDA-approved to fight staph infections of the skin and blood; it has also received regulatory approval in Europe and a handful of non-European countries to treat certain kinds of infections. Cubist markets the drug in the US using its own sales force. It has agreements with numerous other firms to develop and market the drug internationally; its partners include Novartis for Europe, Merck for Japan, and AstraZeneca for China.

With Cubicin as its main source of revenue (the drug has received regulatory approval in nearly 60 countries and is being marketed in about 25) Cubist Pharmaceuticals is vulnerable to changes in the market for the drug, including the introduction of new competitors and changes in reimbursement policies. The company is also completely dependent on third-party manufacturers to produce Cubicin, and as such is vulnerable to changes in supply and pricing from those manufacturers.

Still, the drug has been a success, and the company continues to expand its promotional efforts behind it. But it is also increasing its spending on R&D, working on pushing investigational products through its pipeline to accompany Cubicin.

To further expand its pipeline, while keeping focused on killing hospital-acquired infections, the company has announced it intends to spend $92.5 million to buy up privately held Calixa Therapeutics. Calixa will bring its lead drug candidate, CXA-201, an intravenous antibiotic, in clinical trials for the treatment of specific Gram-negative bacterial infections.

Cubist Pharmaceuticals is working to expand the number of approved indications for Cubicin, but also has several other drugs in development, including one for treating *C. difficile* bacterial infections (CDAD) and one for an IV antibiotic therapy for multidrug-resistant infections.

Along with developing drugs, the company is expanding its pipeline through acquisitions and licensing deals. In 2008 the company acquired North American and European rights to an investigational compound from Dyax; the drug candidate, DX-88, could be used to prevent blood loss in cardiopulmonary bypass surgery. Later that year Cubist Pharmaceuticals also made a deal with AstraZeneca to co-promote that company's Merrem IV antibiotic in the US.

The following year the company entered into a collaboration agreement with Alnylam Pharmaceuticals to develop and market Alnylam's RNA interference (RNAi), a potential therapy for respiratory infections.

The company's top customers are drug wholesalers Cardinal Health, AmerisourceBergen, and McKesson, which collectively account for about 80% of sales.

EXECUTIVES

President, CEO, and Director:
Michael W. (Mike) Bonney, age 50,
$1,905,064 total compensation
EVP and COO: Robert J. Perez, age 44,
$1,187,316 total compensation
SVP Discovery and Non-Clinical Development, and Chief Scientific Officer: Steven C. Gilman, age 56, $654,393 total compensation
SVP and CFO: David W. J. McGirr, age 54,
$923,301 total compensation
SVP Technical Operations: Lindon M. Fellows, age 57, $675,343 total compensation
SVP Commercial Operations: Gregory (Greg) Stea, age 51
SVP, General Counsel, and Secretary: Tamara L. Joseph, age 46
SVP Scientific Affairs: Barry I. Eisenstein, age 60
SVP Clinical Development and Chief Medical Officer:
Santosh J. Vetticaden, age 49
CIO: Anthony S. (Tony) Murabito
VP Human Resources: Maureen H. Powers
VP, Chief Intellectual Property Counsel, and Head Litigation: Timothy J. Douros
VP Finance and Treasurer: Mary C. Stack
Senior Director Corporate Communications:
Eileen McIntyre
Auditors: PricewaterhouseCoopers LLP

LOCATIONS

HQ: Cubist Pharmaceuticals, Inc.
65 Hayden Ave., Lexington, MA 02421
Phone: 781-860-8660   **Fax:** 781-240-0256
Web: www.cubist.com

PRODUCTS/OPERATIONS

2008 Sales

	$ mil.	% of total
US products	415.7	96
International products	7.4	2
Service	9.4	2
Other	2.1	—
Total	**433.6**	**100**

COMPETITORS

Abbott Labs	NovaBay
Achillion	Ortho-McNeil
Actavis	Paratek
Astellas Pharma	Pfizer
Eli Lilly	Ranbaxy Laboratories
GlaxoSmithKline	Sandoz International
Inhibitex	Sanofi-Aventis
Ironwood	Shionogi & Co.
Johnson & Johnson	Teva Pharmaceuticals
King Pharmaceuticals	Theravance
Mylan	Watson Pharmaceuticals

HISTORICAL FINANCIALS

Company Type: Public

Income Statement

FYE: December 31

	REVENUE ($ mil.)	NET INCOME ($ mil.)	NET PROFIT MARGIN	EMPLOYEES
12/08	433.6	169.8	39.2%	554
12/07	294.6	48.1	16.3%	489
12/06	194.7	(0.4)	—	410
12/05	120.6	(31.9)	—	369
12/04	68.1	(76.5)	—	300
Annual Growth	**58.8%**	**—**	**—**	**16.6%**

2008 Year-End Financials

Debt ratio: 96.2%
Return on equity: 82.7%
Cash ($ mil.): 409.0
Current ratio: 6.54
Long-term debt ($ mil.): 300.0
No. of shares (mil.): 57.9
Dividends
  Yield: 0.0%
  Payout: —
Market value ($ mil.): 1,400.0
R&D as % of sales: —
Advertising as % of sales: —

Stock History

NASDAQ (GS): CBST

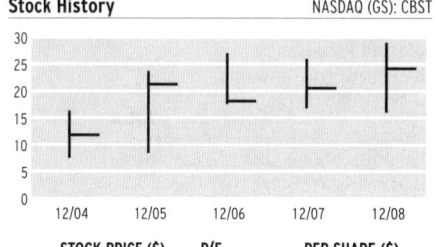

	STOCK PRICE ($) FY Close	P/E High/Low		PER SHARE ($) Earnings	Dividends	Book Value
12/08	24.16	11	6	2.56	0.00	5.38
12/07	20.51	31	20	0.83	0.00	1.70
12/06	18.11	—	—	(0.01)	0.00	0.70
12/05	21.24	—	—	(0.60)	0.00	0.29
12/04	11.83	—	—	(1.86)	0.00	0.36
Annual Growth	**19.5%**	—	—	**—**	**—**	**96.7%**

Cumberland Pharmaceuticals

Cumberland Pharmaceuticals wants to make your search for the right drugs less cumbersome. The specialty pharmaceutical company focuses on acquiring, developing, and commercializing branded prescription drugs. Targeting the hospital acute care and gastroenterology segments, Cumberland's FDA-approved drugs include Acetadote for the treatment of acetaminophen poisoning; Kristalose, a prescription strength laxative; and Caldolor (neé Amelior), the first injectable dosage form of ibuprofen. The company also has several projects in early-stage development. Acetadote and Kristalose are marketed through Cumberland's own hospital and gastroenterology sales forces. The company went public in an IPO in mid-2009.

Cumberland's August 2009 public offering was based on a May 2007 filing. It intends to use proceeds from its public offering to fund potential acquisitions, drug development programs, and sales force expansion efforts, including the commercial launch of Caldolor, which was approved by the FDA earlier in 2009.

Caldolor is designed as an alternative pain and fever treatment for patients unable to ingest oral medication. The product will be marketed throughout the US by Cumberland's hospital sales group and internationally through marketing partners.

Acetadote, approved by the FDA in 2004 and stocked in hospitals nationwide, is an injectable formulation of N-acetylcysteine (NAC) used to prevent or lessen potential liver damage resulting from acetaminophen overdose.

Prescription laxative Kristalose is a dry powder crystalline formulation of lactulose developed for the treatment of acute and chronic constipation. Cumberland acquired rights to market Kristalose in the US in 2006 when it signed a licensing agreement with Inalco S.p.A. of Italy and its US division, Inalco Biochemicals. Cumberland previously co-promoted Kristalose through an agreement with the product's former owner, Bertek Pharmaceuticals.

The company's early-stage product candidates, which include a treatment for fluid buildup in cancer patients' lungs and an anti-infective for treating fungal infections in patients with weakened immune systems, are developed by its majority-owned subsidiary Cumberland Emerging Technologies (CET).

EXECUTIVES

Chairman and CEO: A. J. Kazimi, age 51
SVP and Medical Director: Gordon R. Bernard, age 57
SVP Commercial Development and Director:
Martin E. Cearnal, age 64
SVP and Corporate Secretary: Jean W. Marstiller, age 59
VP and CFO: David L. Lowrance, age 41
VP Sales and Marketing: J. William Hix, age 61
VP Operations: Leo Pavliv, age 48
Senior Manager Regulatory Affairs: Amy Dix Rock, age 38
Senior Director National Accounts and Corporate Compliance Officer: James L. Herman, age 54
Director Business Development: Elizabeth G. Gerken, age 40
Director Medical Affairs: Arthur P. (Art) Wheeler, age 52
Product Director: Barry L. Lee, age 51
Auditors: KPMG LLP

LOCATIONS

HQ: Cumberland Pharmaceuticals Inc.
2525 West End Ave., Ste. 950, Nashville, TN 37203
Phone: 615-255-0068   **Fax:** 615-255-0094
Web: www.cumberlandpharma.com

COMPETITORS

Ben Venue	Roxane Laboratories
Cadence Pharmaceuticals	SkyePharma
Hospira	Sucampo
Javelin Pharmaceuticals	Takeda Pharmaceutical
Merck	

HISTORICAL FINANCIALS

Company Type: Public

Income Statement

FYE: December 31

	REVENUE ($ mil.)	NET INCOME ($ mil.)	NET PROFIT MARGIN	EMPLOYEES
12/08	35.1	4.8	13.7%	53
12/07	28.1	4.0	14.2%	43
12/06	17.8	4.4	24.7%	33
12/05	10.7	2.0	18.7%	—
12/04	12.0	0.6	5.0%	—
Annual Growth	**30.8%**	**68.2%**	**—**	**26.7%**

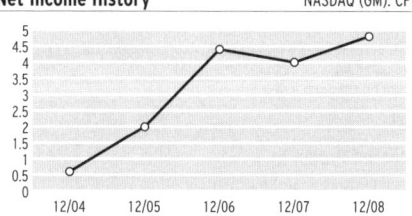
Cyanotech Corporation

Cyanotech transforms the scum of the earth into health products. The majority of the company's sales come from Spirulina Pacifica, a nutritional supplement made from tiny blue-green vegetable algae and sold as powder, flakes, and tablets. The firm also produces BioAstin, an astaxanthin-based dietary supplement full of antioxidants. Cyanotech produces the microalgae used in its product lines at a 90-acre production facility on the Kona Coast of Hawaii. It sells them primarily to health food and dietary supplement makers. In order to focus on its nutritional supplement business, the company has discontinued some other product lines, including NatuRose, an algae-based pigmentation used to color farm-raised fish. Cyanotech has also halted production of phycobiliproteins, which are used as fluorescent markers in biotechnology research.

International sales account for about half of Cyanotech's revenues, with Japan and the Netherlands serving as the company's primary international markets. Spirulina International, a Netherlands-based distributor, accounts for about 10% of sales.

Japan's aquaculture industry had been a major market for the company's NatuRose product. But overall sales of NatuRose had decreased as the product was competing with cheaper synthetic astaxanthin products. The company had been looking to diversify its customer base for NatuRose to include more European markets and poultry feed producers, who could use the product to enhance pigmentation in chicken egg yolks.

However, in 2008 Cyanotech decided to forfeit the animal feed market altogether and focus on its first priority — increasing sales for BioAstin.

Director Michael Davis controls about 17% of the company.

EXECUTIVES

Chairman: Gregg W. Robertson, age 75
President, CEO, and Director: Andrew H. Jacobson, age 48, $407,489 total compensation
EVP, Chief Scientific Officer, and Director: Gerald R. (Gerry) Cysewski, age 60, $135,225 total compensation
VP Sales and Marketing: Robert J. (Bob) Capelli, age 49, $141,000 total compensation
VP Operations: Glenn D. Jensen, age 51, $102,225 total compensation
VP Finance and Administration, CFO, Secretary, and Treasurer: Deanna Spooner, age 57, $117,854 total compensation
Auditors: KPMG LLP

LOCATIONS

HQ: Cyanotech Corporation
　73-4460 Queen Kaahumanu Hwy., Ste. 102
　Kailua-Kona, HI 96740
Phone: 808-326-1353　　**Fax:** 808-329-4533
Web: www.cyanotech.com

2009 Sales

	$ mil.	% of total
US	7.4	53
Germany	2.0	14
The Netherlands	1.4	11
Japan	0.3	2
Other countries	2.8	20
Total	**13.9**	**100**

PRODUCTS/OPERATIONS

2009 Sales

	$ mil.	% of total
Natural astaxanthin products (BioAstin)	7.1	51
Spirulina products	6.7	48
Other products	0.1	1
Total	**13.9**	**100**

COMPETITORS

ADM
Advanced BioNutrition
AMS Health Sciences
DIC Corporation
DSM
Martek Biosciences
Mera
NBTY
Simplexity Health

HISTORICAL FINANCIALS

Company Type: Public

Income Statement   FYE: March 31

	REVENUE ($ mil.)	NET INCOME ($ mil.)	NET PROFIT MARGIN	EMPLOYEES
3/09	13.9	1.1	7.9%	66
3/08	11.4	(1.1)	—	53
3/07	9.7	(7.4)	—	64
3/06	11.1	(0.3)	—	62
3/05	11.4	0.5	4.4%	64
Annual Growth	**5.1%**	**21.8%**	**—**	**0.8%**

2009 Year-End Financials

Debt ratio: 11.7%   Dividends
Return on equity: 15.5%   　Yield: —
Cash ($ mil.): 1.0   　Payout: —
Current ratio: 2.85   Market value ($ mil.): 10.6
Long-term debt ($ mil.): 0.9   R&D as % of sales: —
No. of shares (mil.): 5.2   Advertising as % of sales: —

Stock History   NASDAQ (CM): CYAN

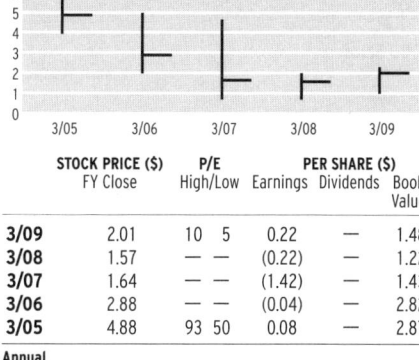

	STOCK PRICE ($) FY Close	P/E High/Low		PER SHARE ($) Earnings	Dividends	Book Value
3/09	2.01	10	5	0.22	—	1.48
3/08	1.57	—	—	(0.22)	—	1.22
3/07	1.64	—	—	(1.42)	—	1.43
3/06	2.88	—	—	(0.04)	—	2.82
3/05	4.88	93	50	0.08	—	2.87
Annual Growth	**(19.9%)**	**—**	**—**	**28.8%**	**—**	**(15.3%)**

CyberSource Corporation

When it comes to moving money through cyberspace, CyberSource could be the place to start. The company provides electronic payment systems and software to merchants that accept point-of-sale, phone, and Web-based payments. Its systems enable credit card and electronic check processing, as well as reoccurring bill payments. The company also offers security-based services such as online and credit card fraud screening, as well as software that assists merchants with tax payment processes and regulatory compliance. CyberSource designs products for small businesses and midsized to large corporations, including those in the airline, retail, media, and telecom industries. The company was founded in 1994.

CyberSource's customers include such large firms as British Airways, H&R Block, Home Depot, and Starbucks. More than 90% of the company's revenue comes from its US customers.

In addition to its software and systems, it offers payment processing services to customers through partnerships with payment processors. All in all, the company processes about 2 billion transactions per year.

Michael Walsh, CyberSource's SVP of worldwide sales for five years, was promoted to president and CEO of the company in 2010, succeeding founder William McKiernan, who remained executive chairman of CyberSource.

CyberSource operates offices in the US, the UK, Japan, and Singapore.

EXECUTIVES

Chairman: William S. (Bill) McKiernan, age 53, $1,174,401 total compensation
President and CEO: Michael A. Walsh, age 41, $765,087 total compensation
EVP Product Development and CTO: Robert J. Ford, age 60, $655,625 total compensation
SVP Finance and CFO: Steven D. Pellizzer, age 40, $706,106 total compensation
VP Customer Support: Patricia A. (Trish) Martin, age 48
VP Product Management: Kirsten Fry-Sanchez, age 50
VP Marketing: Perry S. Dembner, age 49
VP, General Counsel, and Secretary: David J. Kim, age 42
VP Worldwide Operations: George Barby, age 54
VP Human Resources: Gregory T. (Greg) Pappas, age 46
Director Corporate Communications: Bruce Frymire
Director Investor Relations: Katrina Rymill
Auditors: Ernst & Young LLP

LOCATIONS

HQ: CyberSource Corporation
　1295 Charleston Rd., Mountain View, CA 94043
Phone: 650-965-6000　　**Fax:** 650-625-9145
Web: www.cybersource.com

PRODUCTS/OPERATIONS

Selected Products

Authorize.net (electronic payment software and service targeted to small and midsized merchants)
CyberSource Advanced (electronic payment software and service for medium to large-sized companies)
CyberSource Tax Service (tax payment and regulatory compliance software)

Transaction Services and Software

Address information standardization and validation
Credit card authorization
Electronic payment
Export control
Fraud prediction and detection
Gift certificate and promotional coupon issuance and
  redemption
Payment services implementation and integration
Payment systems management (CyberSource Payment
  Manager)
Reporting systems development and integration
Risk management operation assessment
Sales and use tax calculation

COMPETITORS

Bottomline Technologies
Chase Paymentech Solutions
Digital River
Fair Isaac
First Data
GSI Commerce
IBM
InfoSpace
Microsoft
Retail Decisions
Royal Bank of Scotland
SAS Institute
SPSS
Sterling Commerce
Total System Services
VeriSign

HISTORICAL FINANCIALS

Company Type: Public

Income Statement
FYE: December 31

	REVENUE ($ mil.)	NET INCOME ($ mil.)	NET PROFIT MARGIN	EMPLOYEES
12/08	229.0	10.7	4.7%	614
12/07	117.0	2.4	2.1%	496
12/06	70.3	14.4	20.5%	247
12/05	50.5	9.2	18.2%	185
12/04	36.7	4.5	12.3%	43
Annual Growth	58.0%	24.2%	—	94.4%

2008 Year-End Financials

Debt ratio: —
Return on equity: 2.1%
Cash ($ mil.): 73.3
Current ratio: 2.73
Long-term debt ($ mil.): —
No. of shares (mil.): 70.0

Dividends
Yield: 0.0%
Payout: —
Market value ($ mil.): 839.1
R&D as % of sales: —
Advertising as % of sales: —

Stock History
NASDAQ (GM): CYBS

	STOCK PRICE ($) FY Close	P/E High/Low		PER SHARE ($) Earnings	Dividends	Book Value
12/08	11.99	136	40	0.15	0.00	7.40
12/07	17.77	327	181	0.06	0.00	7.19
12/06	11.02	33	16	0.39	0.00	1.12
12/05	6.60	31	18	0.26	0.00	0.81
12/04	7.15	78	33	0.12	0.00	0.68
Annual Growth	13.8%	—	—	5.7%	—	81.7%

Cynosure, Inc.

Beauty may be skin deep, but that's just deep enough for Cynosure to help. The company makes laser and pulsed-light devices used to perform noninvasive aesthetic procedures to remove hair, treat varicose veins, remove tattoos, and reduce the appearance of birthmarks, freckles, and cellulite. Folks who want to go deeper can opt for its minimally invasive procedures to remove unwanted fat using lasers. Cynosure's systems are marketed under such names as Apogee, Cynergy, and Smartlipo. Its customers include doctors and health spas served by distributors in more than 60 countries.

Cynosure uses an in-house sales force to represent its products in North America, China, Japan, and parts of Europe. Elsewhere it sells through local independent distributors. Beyond just targeting dermatologists and plastic surgeons, the company is pitching its products to primary care physicians, gynecologists, and other doctors who might offer such services to patients.

New product development is key to the company's growth. The company introduced its Accolade system, which uses lasers to remove pigmented skin and tattoos, in 2008. It also launched next-generation versions of two products: the Smartlipo MPX workstation for fat removal and the Affirm CO2 workstation for wrinkle treatment.

Italian laser maker El.En. controls more than 20% of the company's voting shares and manufactures several of the company's products. El.En. spun off its majority interest in Cynosure in a public offering in 2005.

EXECUTIVES

Chairman, President, and CEO: Michael R. Davin, age 51, $2,230,387 total compensation
EVP Operations: David Mackie, age 47
EVP, CFO, and Treasurer: Timothy W. Baker, age 48, $1,083,663 total compensation
EVP Sales: Douglas J. Delaney, age 42, $1,080,568 total compensation
EVP International Sales: Kenji Shimizu, age 56
SVP International Sales: William T. (Bill) Kelley
CTO: Rafael Sierra, age 59
VP International Distribution, Asia/Pacific Region: Stephen Lim
VP Global Marketing: H. Travis Lee
VP Business Development: Paul B. Cardarelli, age 42
VP International Distribution: John F. Lenihan, age 53
Auditors: Ernst & Young LLP

LOCATIONS

HQ: Cynosure, Inc.
  5 Carlisle Rd., Westford, MA 01886
Phone: 978-256-4200   **Fax:** 978-256-6556
Web: www.cynosurelaser.com

2008 Sales

	$ mil.	% of total
US	85.7	61
Europe	27.7	20
Asia/Pacific	16.3	12
Other	10.0	7
Total	139.7	100

PRODUCTS/OPERATIONS

2008 Sales

	$ mil.	% of total
Product sales		
North America	85.2	61
Other regions	38.0	27
Parts, accessories & service sales	14.8	11
Original equipment manufacturer sales & revenue sharing	1.7	1
Total	139.7	100

Selected Products

Accolade (tattoo and pigmented lesion removal)
Affirm (skin tightening and texture treatment)
Apogee Elite (hair removal)
Cynergy (treatment of vascular lesions)
SmartCool (cooling system used during treatments)
Smartlipo (removal of unwanted fat)
TriActive LaserDermology (temporary cellulite
  appearance reduction)

COMPETITORS

Allergan
Alma Lasers
Candela Corporation
Cutera
Dynatronics
Galderma Laboratories
IRIDEX
Lumenis
MedSurge Advances
Palomar Medical
PhotoMedex
Solta Medical
Syneron

HISTORICAL FINANCIALS

Company Type: Public

Income Statement
FYE: December 31

	REVENUE ($ mil.)	NET INCOME ($ mil.)	NET PROFIT MARGIN	EMPLOYEES
12/08	139.7	10.2	7.3%	288
12/07	124.3	14.5	11.7%	295
12/06	78.4	(0.6)	—	213
12/05	56.3	4.2	7.5%	184
12/04	41.6	5.3	12.7%	178
Annual Growth	35.4%	17.8%	—	12.8%

2008 Year-End Financials

Debt ratio: 0.3%
Return on equity: 7.8%
Cash ($ mil.): 49.3
Current ratio: 4.48
Long-term debt ($ mil.): 0.4
No. of shares (mil.): 12.7

Dividends
Yield: 0.0%
Payout: —
Market value ($ mil.): 116.4
R&D as % of sales: —
Advertising as % of sales: —

Stock History
NASDAQ (GM): CYNO

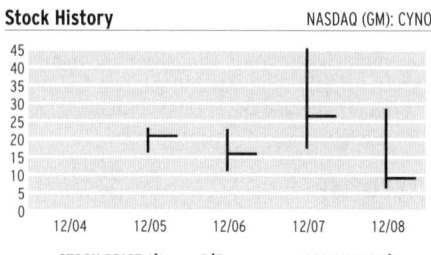

	STOCK PRICE ($) FY Close	P/E High/Low		PER SHARE ($) Earnings	Dividends	Book Value
12/08	9.13	35	8	0.80	0.00	11.01
12/07	26.46	39	15	1.15	0.00	9.48
12/06	15.83	—	—	(0.06)	0.00	6.74
12/05	20.86	42	31	0.54	0.00	6.52
Annual Growth	(24.1%)	—	—	(3.4%)	—	76.0%

Daily Journal Corporation

Legal matters dominate the news in these papers. Daily Journal Corporation is a leading newspaper publisher with more than a dozen papers serving markets primarily in California. Its flagship papers include the *Los Angeles Daily Journal* and the *San Francisco Daily Journal*, which offer in-depth coverage of legal cases and court matters in addition to general interest news. The company also publishes legal affairs magazine *California Lawyer*, operates subscription-based access to court case and real estate information, and publishes a legal directory for California. Chairman Charles Munger (who also serves as vice chairman of Berkshire Hathaway) and Ira Marshall control 40% of the company.

The company's top two papers in Los Angeles and San Francisco boast a combined 11,500 subscribers and account for about 30% of revenue. In addition to its publishing business, Daily Journal Corporation owns Sustain Technologies, a software maker that specializes in products for justice agencies and other law organizations.

EXECUTIVES

Chairman: Charles T. (Charlie) Munger, age 85
Vice Chairman: J. P. Guerin, age 80
President, CEO, CFO, Treasurer, Assistant Secretary, and Director: Gerald L. Salzman, age 70
Secretary: Michelle Stephens
Auditors: Ernst & Young LLP

LOCATIONS

HQ: Daily Journal Corporation
915 E. 1st St., Los Angeles, CA 90012
Phone: 213-229-5300   **Fax:** 213-229-5481
Web: www.dailyjournal.com

PRODUCTS/OPERATIONS

2009 Sales

	$ mil.	% of total
Advertising	23.6	59
Circulation	7.8	19
Information systems & services	4.9	12
Advertising services & other	4.1	10
Total	**40.4**	**100**

Selected Publications

Business Journal (Riverside, CA)
California Real Estate Journal (Los Angeles)
Daily Commerce (Los Angeles)
The Daily Recorder (Sacramento, CA)
The Inter-City Express (Oakland, CA)
Los Angeles Daily Journal
Orange County Reporter (Santa Ana, CA)
The Record Reporter (Phoenix)
San Diego Commerce
San Francisco Daily Journal
San Jose Post-Record (California)
Sonoma County Herald-Recorder (Santa Rosa, CA)

COMPETITORS

Bureau of National Affairs
Freedom Communications
Hearst Newspapers
Legal Directories Publishing
LexisNexis
SF Newspaper Co.
Thomson West
Tribune Company

HISTORICAL FINANCIALS

Company Type: Public

Income Statement

FYE: September 30

	REVENUE ($ mil.)	NET INCOME ($ mil.)	NET PROFIT MARGIN	EMPLOYEES
9/09	40.4	8.0	19.8%	225
9/08	40.6	7.1	17.5%	240
9/07	35.1	5.3	15.1%	255
9/06	32.4	2.4	7.4%	275
9/05	34.3	4.3	12.5%	275
Annual Growth	**4.2%**	**16.8%**	**—**	**(4.9%)**

2009 Year-End Financials

Debt ratio: —	Dividends
Return on equity: 18.9%	Yield: —
Cash ($ mil.): 1.4	Payout: —
Current ratio: 2.90	Market value ($ mil.): 83.9
Long-term debt ($ mil.): —	R&D as % of sales: —
No. of shares (mil.): 1.4	Advertising as % of sales: —

Stock History

NASDAQ (GM): DJCO

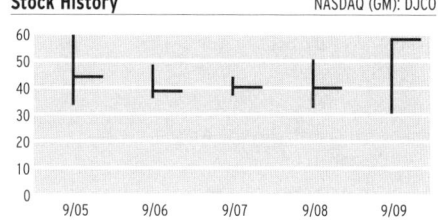

	STOCK PRICE ($) FY Close	P/E High/Low		PER SHARE ($) Earnings	Dividends	Book Value
9/09	57.98	10	5	5.70	—	38.23
9/08	39.90	10	7	4.90	—	20.39
9/07	40.14	12	10	3.66	—	15.40
9/06	38.67	29	22	1.68	—	11.73
9/05	43.98	20	12	2.95	—	10.05
Annual Growth	**7.2%**	**—**	**—**	**17.9%**	**—**	**39.7%**

Daktronics, Inc.

Daktronics always knows the score. The company designs and manufactures electronic display systems. Its products include scoreboards, game timers, shot clocks, and animation displays for sports facilities; advertising and information displays for businesses; and electronic messaging displays used by transportation departments for motorist alerts. Other applications include airport information, securities trading, and outdoor advertising signs. Daktronics converted many of its products to light-emitting diode (LED) technology, which is brighter than other light sources and uses less electricity. The company makes most of its sales in the US.

In 2007 the company reorganized into five business units — Commercial, Small Sports Venues (later called Schools & Theatres), Live Events, Transportation, and International. Each focused business unit is led by a company VP. Daktronics sees the organizational structure allowing each business unit to draw on corporate resources for its specific market, while also providing flexibility and accountability. Live Events accounts for nearly half of the company's sales.

Daktronics' programmable signs display everything from a pitcher's statistics to road conditions

to the time and temperature. Its products also tally votes in legislative chambers and tout beer in Times Square. With its acquisition of UK-based European Timing Systems, Daktronics' signs also keep cricket and rugby scores in the UK.

The company's high-profile installations include two of the biggest scoreboards in the world — for the football stadiums of the Miami Dolphins and the University of Texas Longhorns. Daktronics installed video and scoreboard systems in the new Yankee Stadium, which opened in 2009. The company also won the scoring and video system work for Citi Field, the new home of the New York Mets, and has equipment installed in 26 of Major League Baseball's 30 ball parks. Daktronics will supply the scoring and display system for Target Field, the future home of the Minnesota Twins.

The company installed two of its HD-X LED video display systems and about 1,625 feet of its ProAd digital ribbon display in the refurbished Arrowhead Stadium for the Kansas City Chiefs. It provided the video display and 360-degree ribbon display for Lucas Oil Stadium, the home of the Indianapolis Colts. The company is installing four HD-X video displays in the Meadowlands Stadium, scheduled to open in 2010 as home of the New York Giants and the New York Jets, replacing Giants Stadium.

Because its products are becoming more affordable, Daktronics is selling more to midsized universities and the minor leagues. The company is also seeing an increase in sales to commercial customers, due in part to Daktronics' increased use of LEDs; the technology has become more popular since the mid-1990s because of its visual clarity and cost-efficiency.

Co-founder Aelred Kurtenbach (chairman) and his brother Frank (VP) together own about 9% of Daktronics.

HISTORY

Daktronics was founded in a garage in 1968 by engineering professors Aelred Kurtenbach and Duane Sander (who later became dean of engineering at South Dakota State University). The company name came from combining "Dakota" with "electronics." Two years later the company delivered its first product, a voting display system for the Utah legislature. Scoreboards were added to the product line in 1971; commercial displays in 1973. It introduced computerized controllers in the late 1970s.

The 1980 Winter Olympics in Lake Placid, New York, marked the first time the company provided scoreboards to the Olympic games. During the 1980s Daktronics began installing displays in major-league sports stadiums. In 1988 it bought auto-racing timing equipment maker Chondek. Daktronics continued to advance sign technology during the 1990s, acquiring technology for light-emitting diode (LED) displays. It went public in 1994.

The company supplied five displays and 24 digital clocks to Times Square locations in 1995. Daktronics also provided scoreboards to the 1996 Atlanta Summer Olympics. That year the blue LED, a tiny bulb used with green and red LEDs to produce color on large TV-like screens, was introduced. This allowed the company to add video to its scoreboards. In 1998 Daktronics installed systems in the Indianapolis Motor Speedway and sports venues in Cleveland, Seattle, and Phoenix.

The company's displays were featured at the 2000 Olympics in Sydney. In 2001 Daktronics

bought 80% of Servtrotech (a Canadian electronic display system maker) and Sportslink, Ltd. (a large screen video rental display company). James Morgan became CEO in 2001; Kurtenbach remained chairman.

In 2003 the company won a contract to provide digital advertising and information displays at the Hubert H. Humphrey Metrodome in Minneapolis. The following year Daktronics expanded its product line and geographic reach with the acquisition of UK-based European Timing Systems (scoreboards and timing systems for cricket, aquatics, and rugby), which was renamed Daktronics UK. Also in 2004 the company acquired the assets of Dodge Electronics, doing business as Dodge Systems, a supplier of audio systems for sports facilities.

In 2006 Daktronics acquired the assets of Hoffend & Sons for about $4 million. Hoffend was a manufacturer of hoist systems for sports and theatrical venues, and functioned as a supplier to Daktronics. The business became the Vortek division of Daktronics Hoist. The Louisiana Superdome, damaged by Hurricane Katrina, underwent renovation in 2006. The work included new scoreboards and displays from Daktronics, valued at nearly $6 million.

Daktronics expanded its manufacturing facilities in 2006, adding 110,000 sq. ft. of space to its main manufacturing facility in Brookings, South Dakota, and leasing a vacant plant in Sioux Falls with 120,000 sq. ft. of manufacturing space.

In 2007 the company acquired an existing plant in Redwood Falls, Minnesota, from Emerson Electric. Daktronics used the facility to manufacture its Galaxy line of electronic message displays. Moving Galaxy production to Minnesota freed up manufacturing space at the company's plant in Brookings.

At the same time the company began construction of a facility in Brookings for office and warehouse space, a $19 million project. Daktronics occupied its new headquarters and factory in 2007.

EXECUTIVES

Chairman: Aelred J. (Al) Kurtenbach, age 76, $175,161 total compensation
President, CEO, and Director: James B. (Jim) Morgan, age 63, $488,423 total compensation
CFO and Treasurer: William R. (Bill) Retterath, age 49, $314,370 total compensation
VP Commercial and Transportation Business Units: Bradley T. (Brad) Wiemann, age 47, $275,400 total compensation
VP Live Events and International Business Units: Reece A. Kurtenbach, age 45, $279,468 total compensation
VP Sales and Director: Frank J. Kurtenbach
VP Schools and Theatres Business Unit: Dan Bierschbach
VP Human Resources: Carla S. Gatzke, age 47
VP Manufacturing: Matt Kurtenbach
Commercial Development: Jim Vasgaard
Commercial Marketing: Dawn Waterman
Support Manager, Marketing and Sales: Mark Steinkamp
Auditors: Ernst & Young LLP

LOCATIONS

HQ: Daktronics, Inc.
201 Daktronics Dr., Brookings, SD 57006
Phone: 605-692-0200   **Fax:** 605-697-4700
Web: www.daktronics.com

Daktronics has manufacturing facilities in the US, with sales offices in Australia, Canada, China, France, Germany, the United Arab Emirates, the UK, and the US.

2009 Sales

	$ mil.	% of total
US	512.5	88
Other countries	69.4	12
Total	**581.9**	**100**

PRODUCTS/OPERATIONS

2009 Sales

	$ mil.	% of total
Live Events	269.6	46
Commercial	155.9	27
Schools & Theatres	66.4	11
International	55.7	10
Transportation	34.3	6
Total	**581.9**	**100**

Selected Applications and Brands

Business (text-based message displays)
  DataMaster
  DataTime
  DataTrac
  InfoNet
  Galaxy
Sports (indoor and outdoor scoreboards)
  All Sport
  DakStats
  OmniSport
Transportation (traffic direction and motorist information)
  Vanguard
Video (displays combining video, graphics, animation, and text)
  ProAd
  ProStar

COMPETITORS

Advance Display Technologies
Aristocrat Leisure
AutoComm
Barco
Colorado Time Systems
D3 LED
DRI Corp.
LSI Industries
Mitsubishi Electric
Opto Tech
Panasonic Corporation of North America
PolyVision
Samsung Electronics America
Screen Technology
Sony
Toyoda Gosei North America
Trans-Lux
Waytronx

HISTORICAL FINANCIALS

Company Type: Public

Income Statement			FYE: Saturday nearest April 30	
	REVENUE ($ mil.)	NET INCOME ($ mil.)	NET PROFIT MARGIN	EMPLOYEES
4/09	581.9	26.4	4.5%	3,500
4/08	499.7	26.2	5.2%	3,400
4/07	433.2	24.4	5.6%	3,200
4/06	309.4	21.0	6.8%	2,100
4/05	230.3	15.7	6.8%	1,630
Annual Growth	**26.1%**	**13.9%**	**—**	**21.1%**

2009 Year-End Financials

Debt ratio: 2.6%
Return on equity: 13.4%
Cash ($ mil.): 36.5
Current ratio: 2.02
Long-term debt ($ mil.): 5.6
No. of shares (mil.): 41.0
Dividends
  Yield: 1.0%
  Payout: 14.1%
Market value ($ mil.): 370.9
R&D as % of sales: —
Advertising as % of sales: —

Stock History

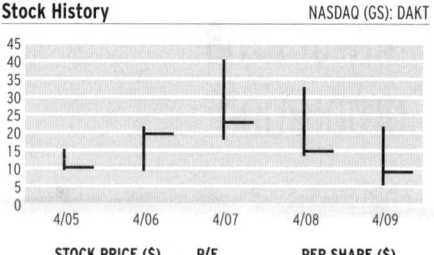

NASDAQ (GS): DAKT

	STOCK PRICE ($) FY Close	P/E High/Low		PER SHARE ($) Earnings	Dividends	Book Value
4/09	9.04	33	9	0.64	0.09	5.16
4/08	14.79	51	22	0.63	0.07	4.47
4/07	22.78	68	31	0.59	0.06	3.75
4/06	19.58	41	18	0.52	0.05	3.05
4/05	10.18	38	25	0.39	—	2.53
Annual Growth	**(2.9%)**	**—**	**—**	**13.2%**	**21.6%**	**19.5%**

Darling International

It's not the most darling of businesses — in fact it's messy and it's stinky — but Darling International, the largest independent rendering operation in the US, is willing to do it. The company collects and processes animal by-products and used cooking grease from approximately 116,000 restaurants, butcher shops, grocery stores, and independent meat and poultry processors throughout the US. Its rendering operations produce yellow grease, tallow, and meat, bone, and blood meal, which Darling sells in the US as well as internationally to makers of soap, rubber, pet and livestock feed, and chemicals.

For Darling, competition comes mostly from the obtaining of its raw materials. Large meat-packing companies usually handle their own rendering in-house. As the meat industry has consolidated, fewer independent meat and poultry processors are left from whom to collect scraps; however, Darling has seen growth in its restaurant-services division, although collecting spent grease from restaurants is also highly competitive. When it comes time to sell its commodity-grade products, Darling competes with vegetable-oil producers as well as other rendering operations.

The company operates a fleet of some 960 trucks and tractor-trailers for collection of its raw materials. The company has no foreign collection operations but does export its products to Asia, Mexico, North Africa, the Pacific Rim, and South America.

In 2009 Darling acquired Smyrna, Georgia-headquarted Boca Industries. Boca is a provider of grease-trap and oil-collection services to restaurants and other foodservice operators in Georgia and surrounding states. The purchase complements Darling's other oil collection business, API Recycling, which also serves Georgia and surrounding areas. Darling acquired API from American Proteins in 2008.

Darling's profits have suffered due to higher raw-material costs and rising fuel prices. However, the 2006 acquisition of one of its main competitors, rendering firm National By-Products,

for approximately $70 million cash and 20% of its outstanding common stock, helped increase the company's bottom line by increasing its capacity. The National acquisition brought Darling's processing-facility count up to 39 (as of 2009 it operated 43 sites).

EXECUTIVES

Chairman and CEO: Randall C. Stuewe, age 46, $3,150,904 total compensation
EVP Commodities: Mitchell (Mitch) Kilanowski, age 57
EVP Sales and Services: Robert H. Seemann, age 58
EVP and COO: Neil Katchen, age 63, $779,839 total compensation
EVP Finance and Administration: John O. Muse, age 60, $1,343,962 total compensation
EVP, General Counsel, and Secretary: John F. Sterling, age 45, $719,760 total compensation
VP International Commodities: Ernie DiLiberto
VP Information Services: Robert Hinerman
VP and Manager, National Accounts, Oil Collections Division: Bill Borrelli
VP Environmental Support: John Bohannon
Director Research Nutritional Services: C. Ross Hamilton
Treasurer: Brad Phillips
Auditors: KPMG LLP

LOCATIONS

HQ: Darling International Inc.
251 O'Connor Ridge Blvd., Ste. 300
Irving, TX 75038
Phone: 972-717-0300   **Fax:** 972-717-1588
Web: www.darlingii.com

2008 Sales

	$ mil.	% of total
US	675.3	84
Other countries	132.2	16
Total	**807.5**	**100**

PRODUCTS/OPERATIONS

2008 Sales

	$ mil.	% of total
Rendering	636.0	73
Restaurant service	232.5	27
Eliminations	(61.0)	—
Total	**807.5**	**100**

COMPETITORS

ADM
Ag Processing
Baker Commodities
Griffin Industries
Kenosha Beef
Maple Leaf Foods
North State Rendering Company
Prosper De Mulder
Restaurant Technologies
Sanimax
Tyson Foods
Valley Proteins

HISTORICAL FINANCIALS

Company Type: Public

Income Statement

FYE: Saturday nearest December 31

	REVENUE ($ mil.)	NET INCOME ($ mil.)	NET PROFIT MARGIN	EMPLOYEES
12/08	807.5	54.6	6.8%	1,870
12/07	645.3	45.5	7.1%	1,830
12/06	407.0	5.1	1.3%	1,830
12/05	308.9	7.7	2.5%	1,110
12/04	320.2	13.9	4.3%	1,150
Annual Growth	**26.0%**	**40.8%**	**—**	**12.9%**

2008 Year-End Financials

Debt ratio: 13.7%
Return on equity: 25.0%
Cash ($ mil.): 50.8
Current ratio: 1.95
Long-term debt ($ mil.): 32.5
No. of shares (mil.): 82.2
Dividends
  Yield: —
  Payout: —
Market value ($ mil.): 451.4
R&D as % of sales: —
Advertising as % of sales: —

Stock History   NYSE: DAR

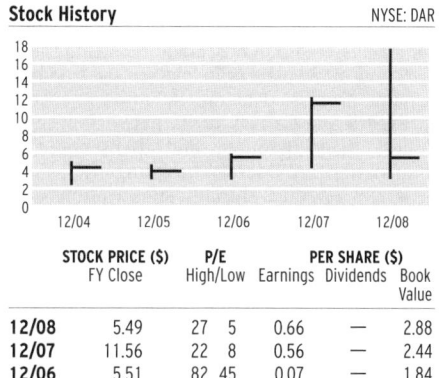

	STOCK PRICE ($) FY Close	P/E High/Low		PER SHARE ($) Earnings	Dividends	Book Value
12/08	5.49	27	5	0.66	—	2.88
12/07	11.56	22	8	0.56	—	2.44
12/06	5.51	82	45	0.07	—	1.84
12/05	3.97	38	27	0.12	—	0.90
12/04	4.36	22	12	0.22	—	0.82
Annual Growth	**5.9%**	**—**	**—**	**31.6%**	**—**	**37.0%**

Datalink Corporation

Datalink serves up storage system smorgasbords. The company builds and implements high-end, custom-designed data storage systems for large corporations. Datalink's storage systems include disk- and tape-based storage devices, storage networking components, and data management software. The company employs an open-system standard, building its offerings from products made by leading manufacturers such as Brocade Communications Systems, EMC, and Hitachi Data Systems. Datalink also provides support and maintenance services. Datalink markets its products directly to customers in the US.

The company has about 20 locations across the US, with the highest revenue concentration in the central region. It has designed systems for clients including AT&T, Harris Corporation, NAVTEQ, and St. Jude Medical.

Datalink continues to focus on growing its service expertise and geographic presence. It expanded its operations by acquiring systems integrator Midrange Computer Solutions for $14 million. The Midrange purchase extended Datalink's operations in the northeastern and midwestern regions, as well as in California. In 2009 the company bought the networking division of Minneapolis-based Cross Telecom for $2 million; the deal expanded Datalink's expertise in designing, implementing, and managing network storage and backup products. Late that year it acquired IT systems distributor and managed services provider Incentra for $8.8 million in cash. The deal expanded the company's presence in Chicago and the Northeast, as well as in several western states.

Chairman and former CEO Greg Meland owns about 20% of Datalink.

HISTORY

Founded in 1963 as Stan Clothier, Datalink was originally a manufacturers' representative for technology products and components. Its name change to Datalink in 1987 reflected the company's growing role as a distributor of data storage products. Datalink opened a Chicago office in 1989 and expanded beyond the Midwest in 1992 with an office in Seattle. Greg Meland, formerly the company's VP of sales, was named president and CEO in 1993.

In 1995, with the introduction of its DataCare program, the company began to reposition itself as a provider of information management services rather than strictly a value-added distributor. Two years later Datalink began offering its consulting services to customers in the information management industry.

In 1998 Datalink initiated an IPO, which it later withdrew. That year the company expanded throughout the US, opening offices in Massachusetts, New Jersey, and California and adding five offices in the Southeast US with the acquisition of Georgia-based rival Direct Connect Systems. Datalink successfully went public in 1999. Its expansion continued in 2000, with additional offices opening in North Carolina and Oregon. In 2001 the company moved its headquarters from Edina, Minnesota to Chanhassen, a Minneapolis suburb.

Datalink raised more than $5 million in a 2002 private placement of stock, with institutional investors buying the shares.

Charlie Westling, previously the company's VP of market development, was promoted to president and COO in 2003. He joined Datalink in 2001.

Meland was made chairman in 2005.

EXECUTIVES

Chairman: Greg R. Meland, age 55
President, CEO, and Director: Paul F. Lidsky, age 55
CTO: Scott D. Robinson, age 49
SVP Field Operations: Robert R. (Rob) Beyer, age 48, $667,200 total compensation
VP Finance and CFO: Gregory T. Barnum, age 54, $443,490 total compensation
VP Technical Services: Tom Sylvester
VP Human Resources: Mary E. West, age 60
Media Relations: Bob Connolly
Director Sales West Region: Mike Cannon
Director Sales North Central Region: Tim Rasmussen
Engineering Director Eastern Region: Kevin Campbell
Secretary: Jeffrey C. Robbins
Controller: Denise M. Westenfield
Investor Relations: Kim Payne
Auditors: McGladrey & Pullen, LLP

LOCATIONS

HQ: Datalink Corporation
8170 Upland Cir., Chanhassen, MN 55317
Phone: 952-944-3462   **Fax:** 952-944-7869
Web: www.datalink.com

PRODUCTS/OPERATIONS

2008 Sales

	$ mil.	% of total
Products	113.5	58
Services	82.1	42
Total	**195.6**	**100**

Selected Products and Suppliers

Disk storage
 Data Domain
 EMC
 Hitachi Data Systems
 IBM
 Network Appliance
 Sun Microsystems

Software
 APTARE
 Diligent Technologies
 EMC
 Symantec
 VMware

Storage networking
 Brocade Communications Systems
 Cisco Systems
 F5 Networks
 Riverbed Technology

Tape automation
 Quantum
 Spectra Logic
 Sun Microsystems

COMPETITORS

Cranel	IBM
Dell	InterVision Systems
Dot Hill	Midwave
EMC	NetApp
Forsythe Technology	Presidio, Inc.
Fujitsu	Qualstar
Hewlett-Packard	Sirius Computer Solutions
Hitachi Data Systems	Sun Microsystems

HISTORICAL FINANCIALS

Company Type: Public

Income Statement

FYE: December 31

	REVENUE ($ mil.)	NET INCOME ($ mil.)	NET PROFIT MARGIN	EMPLOYEES
12/08	195.6	3.4	1.7%	208
12/07	177.8	1.2	0.7%	199
12/06	146.0	8.5	5.8%	160
12/05	117.1	(2.9)	—	147
12/04	93.3	(3.1)	—	147
Annual Growth	20.3%	—	—	9.1%

2008 Year-End Financials

Debt ratio: —
Return on equity: 8.4%
Cash ($ mil.): 26.3
Current ratio: 1.25
Long-term debt ($ mil.): —
No. of shares (mil.): 12.9

Dividends
 Yield: —
 Payout: —
Market value ($ mil.): 41.4
R&D as % of sales: —
Advertising as % of sales: —

Stock History

NASDAQ (GM): DTLK

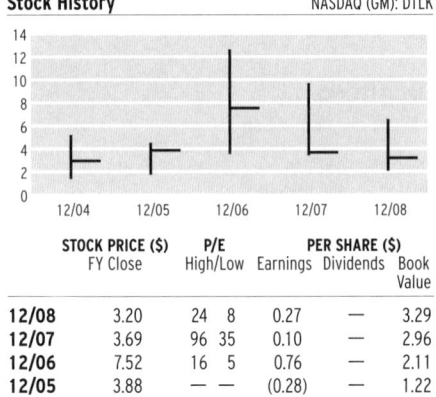

	STOCK PRICE ($) FY Close	P/E High/Low		PER SHARE ($) Earnings	Dividends	Book Value
12/08	3.20	24	8	0.27	—	3.29
12/07	3.69	96	35	0.10	—	2.96
12/06	7.52	16	5	0.76	—	2.11
12/05	3.88	—	—	(0.28)	—	1.22
12/04	2.94	—	—	(0.31)	—	1.43
Annual Growth	2.1%	—	—	—	—	23.1%

DealerTrack Holdings

DealerTrack Holdings helps car dealers play their cards right in the financing game. The company provides Web-based software that links automotive dealerships with banks, finance companies, credit unions, credit reporting agencies, and other players in the car sales and financing process. DealerTrack connects clients in the US and Canada to its network of auto dealers, financing sources, and other service and information providers. The company, which generates revenues through subscriptions and transaction-based fees, also offers tools that automate credit application processing, ensure document legal compliance, and execute electronic financing contracts.

The company saw its transaction services revenue drop in 2008, as turmoil in the credit market led to a decline in the number of lenders and a drop in auto sales. The company's growth strategy also includes shifting its sales emphasis from individual products to integrated offerings focused on four lines: dealer management systems (DMS), compliance, sales, and inventory management. DealerTrack continues to expand its customer network, targeting regional banks, credit unions, financing and insurance companies, and accessory providers.

DealerTrack has used acquisitions to grow its product line. In 2007 the company acquired Arkona, a provider of auto dealership management products and services. It also purchased Curomax, a provider of an Internet-based credit application and contract processing network in Canada. As part of a strategy to grow its inventory management product portfolio, DealerTrack acquired a suite of inventory management tools from JM Dealer Services, a division of JM Family Enterprises, early in 2009.

EXECUTIVES

Chairman, President, and CEO: Mark F. O'Neil, age 50, $2,373,049 total compensation
SVP, CFO, Chief Administrative Officer, and Treasurer: Eric D. Jacobs, age 43, $929,003 total compensation
SVP and CIO: Richard McLeer, age 45
SVP Sales, Marketing, and International: Rick G. Von Pusch, age 48
SVP Solutions and Services Group: Raj Sundaram, age 43, $974,832 total compensation
VP Lender Solutions; General Manager, DealerTrack ToolKit: Mark Brown, age 53
VP, Finance Solutions: Alan Lehmann, age 50
VP and General Counsel: Gary Papilsky
VP, Human Resources, DealerTrack, Inc.: Ana M. Herrera, age 53
VP, Aftermarket Network Solutions: Hugh Abernethy
Auditors: PricewaterhouseCoopers LLP

LOCATIONS

HQ: DealerTrack Holdings, Inc.
 1111 Marcus Ave., Ste. M04
 Lake Success, NY 11042
Phone: 516-734-3600   **Fax:** 516-734-3809
Web: www.dealertrack.com

PRODUCTS/OPERATIONS

2008 Sales

	$ mil.	% of total
Transaction services	132.4	55
Subscription services	94.7	39
Other	15.6	6
Total	**242.7**	**100**

COMPETITORS

ADP	Microsoft Dynamics
American Honda Finance	Reynolds and Reynolds
Compli	RouteOne

HISTORICAL FINANCIALS

Company Type: Public

Income Statement

FYE: December 31

	REVENUE ($ mil.)	NET INCOME ($ mil.)	NET PROFIT MARGIN	EMPLOYEES
12/08	242.7	1.7	0.7%	1,100
12/07	233.8	19.8	8.5%	1,000
12/06	173.3	19.3	11.1%	670
12/05	120.2	4.5	3.7%	539
12/04	70.0	11.3	16.1%	499
Annual Growth	36.5%	(37.7%)	—	21.8%

2008 Year-End Financials

Debt ratio: 0.3%
Return on equity: 0.4%
Cash ($ mil.): 155.5
Current ratio: 7.29
Long-term debt ($ mil.): 1.1
No. of shares (mil.): 40.4

Dividends
 Yield: 0.0%
 Payout: —
Market value ($ mil.): 480.6
R&D as % of sales: —
Advertising as % of sales: —

Stock History

NASDAQ (GM): TRAK

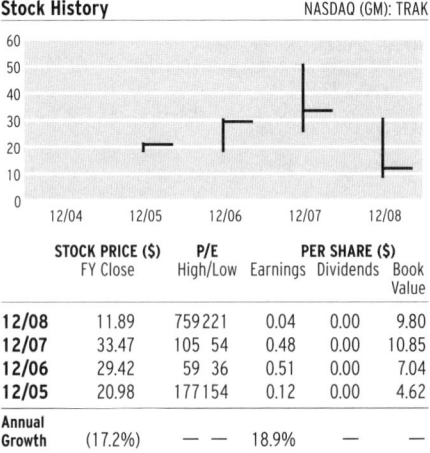

	STOCK PRICE ($) FY Close	P/E High/Low		PER SHARE ($) Earnings	Dividends	Book Value
12/08	11.89	759	221	0.04	0.00	9.80
12/07	33.47	105	54	0.48	0.00	10.85
12/06	29.42	59	36	0.51	0.00	7.04
12/05	20.98	177	154	0.12	0.00	4.62
Annual Growth	(17.2%)	—	—	18.9%	—	—

Deckers Outdoor

There's no business like shoe business for Deckers Outdoor. It makes and markets Teva sports sandals — a cross between a hiking boot and a flip-flop. They're used for walking, hiking, and rafting, among other pursuits. While imitations flood the market, the company distinguishes Teva from its numerous competitors by avoiding distribution in off-price outlets. Other product lines include Simple and TSUBO (casual footwear), as well as iconic UGG (sheepskin boots/shoes). Deckers Outdoor's products are made by independent contractors in Asia, Australia, and New Zealand. It sells them through 10 US retail stores, independent distributors, catalogs, the Internet, and two company-owned outlets in the UK.

With its Teva shoe business sliding from 18% of 2007's sales to 12% of its revenue in 2008, Deckers Outdoor worked to fill the gap. To this end, it bought the TSUBO shoe brand in mid-2008. TSUBO was founded by a British designer in 1998; the name means "pressure point" in

Japanese. The complementary footwear company boasts ergonomic sport and casual shoes, boots, sandals, and heels. They're sold in the US, primarily, but also in Canada, France, Australia, and Japan. In turn, TSUBO helped to generate about 1% of the company's sales in 2008.

Deckers Outdoor's flagship UGG brand hit the ground running in 2008. The brand's revenue rose significantly from 65% of 2007 sales to 70% in 2008. One of the company's top customers, Nordstrom, was responsible for a large portion of UGG sales in the US. The footwear firm's joint venture agreement with Stella International Holdings, inked in July 2008, was also key for the increase. The agreement has given the UGG brand a foothold in China, where Deckers Outdoor is opening retail stores and distributing its products as a wholesaler. Soon thereafter, the company opened its first UGG Australia-branded concept store in Beijing in November 2008.

The company's focus on its international business helped to soften the blow of the lingering recession in the US. Deckers Outdoor's international sales grew from 14% in 2007 to 16% of its overall revenue in 2008. The company logged most of its sales in Europe, with the balance coming from the Asia/Pacific region, Canada, and Latin America. To springboard from its successes and give it momentum for future growth, Deckers Outdoor in 2008 appointed brand managers in Europe for its UGG Australia, Teva, and Simple names. It opened a pair of UGG Australia retail stores in Europe, as well.

A continuing rise in UGG sales has extended debates over whether the name is generic or a trademark that could possibly be defended over international boundaries. Australian makers of the sheepskin boots, traditionally called uggs, contend that the name is generic, with the controversy akin to trying to protect the name "sneaker" as a trademark.

HISTORY

Douglas Otto and his former partner, Karl Lopker, founded Styled Steers in 1973. But the small, obscure maker of leather sandals gained prominence with a line of multicolored rubber sandals. Surfers in Hawaii called them "deckers," and the company soon adopted the name. In 1985 Deckers Outdoor licensed Teva from river guide Mark Thatcher, who invented the Teva strapping system for rafters to ensure sandals remained attached in turbulent waters. Teva sport sandals became a popular form of casual footwear, largely through word of mouth. The company is the exclusive licensee of Teva shoes, the design of which Thatcher has defended repeatedly against would-be copycats.

In 1994 Deckers Outdoor expanded the Teva line to include closed footwear. With the popularity of Teva sandals seemingly on the wane, the next year it diversified, acquiring rival shoe companies Alp Sport Sandals and UGG Holdings and expanding into the women's and children's markets. A glut of sports sandals depressed sales the following year, but with new products and new marketing, Teva sales increased in 1997.

That year, targeting international expansion, the company acquired German distribution rights to Simple shoes from Vision Warenhandels. Also in 1997 Deckers Outdoor sold its interest in Trukke Winter Sports Products to focus on its core lines.

Thatcher settled with Wal-Mart Stores in 1998 after suing the company over patent and copyright infringement. The firm exited the manufacturing business that year and turned production over to suppliers, mainly in China. In mid-1999 Deckers Outdoor renewed its license with Thatcher through 2011. Continuing to divest noncore operations, in 2000 the company sold its 50% interest in Heirlooms, the makers of the Picante line. The company also hired an ex-adidas exec to help increase Teva's global business (26% in 1999).

In 2000 Otto gave up the president in his title to Peter Benjamin, who was charged with rejuvenating and giving each brand more individualized marketing. In 2001 sales slumped nearly 20% due in part to the weak economy and a bankruptcy filing by one of Deckers Outdoor's largest customers, Track n' Trail. In late 2002 Peter Benjamin resigned as president so that he could return to focusing on sales to Asia.

The company purchased Teva's total assets from its inventor and trademarks and patents holder, Mark Thatcher, in November 2002.

In the second half of 2003 the UGG brand enjoyed unusually rapid growth in demand, helping to send Deckers Outdoor's sales up 22% for the year. In 2004 Deckers inked licensing agreements for the manufacture of UGG handbags and outerwear, as well as gloves, hats, and scarves. The same year the company signed a separate licensing deal with RMP Athletic Locker for the manufacture of Teva sportswear.

In April 2005 Angel Martinez, a former Reebok executive, was named president and CEO of the company. (Doug Otto retained his position as chairman of the board.) Martinez became chairman of the board in May 2008.

Continued acquisitions and joint ventures have enabled Deckers Outdoor to ride out the recession that began in 2008.

EXECUTIVES

Chairman, President, and CEO: Angel R. Martinez, age 53, $5,951,782 total compensation
COO: Zohar Ziv, age 56, $2,330,555 total compensation
CFO: Thomas A. George, age 54
SVP International: Colin G. Clark, age 46, $1,783,711 total compensation
SVP Supply Chain: Mark N. Fegley
VP Human Resources: Graciela Montgomery
VP Legal and Assistant Secretary: Stephanie E. S. Cucururllo
VP Consumer Direct: John A. Kalinich, age 41
President, TSUBO Brand: Ray Mosley
President, Teva Brand: Peter K. (Pete) Worley, age 48
President, Ugg and Simple Divisions: Constance X. (Connie) Rishwain, age 51, $2,105,661 total compensation
Director Global Marketing, Teva: Joel Heath
Auditors: KPMG LLP

LOCATIONS

HQ: Deckers Outdoor Corporation
495-A S. Fairview Ave., Goleta, CA 93117
Phone: 805-967-7611   **Fax:** 805-967-7862
Web: www.deckers.com

2008 Sales

	$ mil.	% of total
US	581.5	84
International	107.9	16
Total	**689.4**	**100**

PRODUCTS/OPERATIONS

2008 Sales

	$ mil.	% of total
UGG wholesale	483.8	70
Teva wholesale	80.9	12
eCommerce	68.8	10
Retail	38.4	5
Simple wholesale	13.9	2
TSUBO wholesale	3.6	1
Total	**689.4**	**100**

COMPETITORS

adidas	L.L. Bean
Birkenstock Distribution	NIKE
C&J Clark	North Face
Cole Haan	Patagonia, Inc.
Columbia Sportswear	Phoenix Footwear
Converse	PUMA AG
Crocs	Quiksilver
Diesel SpA	R. Griggs
Fila USA	Rocky Brands
Guess?	Skechers U.S.A.
Jimlar	Steven Madden
Keds	Timberland
Kenneth Cole	Vans
K-Swiss	Wolverine World Wide

HISTORICAL FINANCIALS

Company Type: Public

Income Statement

FYE: December 31

	REVENUE ($ mil.)	NET INCOME ($ mil.)	NET PROFIT MARGIN	EMPLOYEES
12/08	689.4	73.9	10.7%	780
12/07	448.9	66.4	14.8%	370
12/06	304.4	31.5	10.3%	276
12/05	264.8	31.8	12.0%	225
12/04	214.8	25.5	11.9%	187
Annual Growth	**33.8%**	**30.5%**	**—**	**42.9%**

2008 Year-End Financials

Debt ratio: —
Return on equity: 21.6%
Cash ($ mil.): 176.8
Current ratio: 4.34
Long-term debt ($ mil.): —
No. of shares (mil.): 12.8
Dividends
　Yield: —
　Payout: —
Market value ($ mil.): 1,026.3
R&D as % of sales: —
Advertising as % of sales: —

Stock History

NASDAQ (GS): DECK

	STOCK PRICE ($) FY Close	P/E High/Low		PER SHARE ($) Earnings	Dividends	Book Value
12/08	79.87	26	8	5.60	—	29.90
12/07	155.06	33	11	5.06	—	23.24
12/06	59.95	25	11	2.45	—	16.67
12/05	27.62	19	7	2.48	—	13.82
12/04	46.99	23	8	2.10	—	10.97
Annual Growth	**14.2%**	**—**	**—**	**27.8%**	**—**	**28.5%**

Deltek, Inc.

Deltek provides project management software designed to meet the needs of professional services firms and project-based businesses. Its applications handle expense reporting, HR administration, materials management, customer management, and sales force automation. Deltek integrates tools from partners such as Cognos and Microsoft with its own software, and it also provides consulting and implementation services. Deltek targets such industries as aerospace, construction, engineering, and information technology. It also serves government agencies and government contractors, an area of strength for Deltek where it holds a large market share. Donald and Kenneth deLaski (father and son) co-founded Deltek in 1983.

The company has said that it is taregting overseas markets for future growth, with an initial focus on English-speaking countries outside the US; currently only 5% of its sales are from international clients.

In a bid to make further inroads into the government contracting market, Deltek bought Reston, Virginia-based mySBX (an online networking community for government contractors) in late 2009. Customers including Lockheed Martin and Serco use mySBX to connect with subcontracting partners and drum up new business.

In September 2008 the company purchased PlanView's MPM software line and associated assets. Deltek has actively used acquisitions to flesh out its product line and grow its customer base, with past deals such as the purchases of Wind2 Software, WST Corporation, C/S Solutions, and Applied Integration Management Corporation.

EXECUTIVES

Chairman, President, and CEO: Kevin T. Parker, age 49, $1,772,059 total compensation
EVP, CFO, and Treasurer: Michael P. Corkery, age 47
EVP and Chief Marketing Officer:
William D. (Bill) Clark, age 49
EVP Worldwide Sales: Carolyn J. Parent, age 42, $929,327 total compensation
EVP Product Development: Eric J. Brehm, age 50
EVP Products and Strategy: Richard P. (Rick) Lowrey, age 49, $920,242 total compensation
EVP Professional Services:
Richard M. (Rick) Lowenstein, age 46, $884,208 total compensation
EVP Global Services: Jim Dellamore
CIO: Deb Fitzgerald
SVP Global Support: Garland T. Hall, age 48
SVP Human Resources: Holly C. Kortright, age 42
SVP, General Counsel, and Secretary:
David R. Schwiesow, age 58
VP Investor Relations: Dave Spille
Director Public and Analyst Relations: Patrick Smith
Auditors: Deloitte & Touche LLP

LOCATIONS

HQ: Deltek, Inc.
13880 Dulles Corner Ln., Herndon, VA 20171
Phone: 703-734-8606   **Fax:** 703-734-1146
Web: www.deltek.com

2008 Sales

	% of total
US	95
Other countries	5
Total	**100**

PRODUCTS/OPERATIONS

2008 Sales

	$ mil.	% of total
Maintenance & support services	115.7	40
Consulting services	91.6	31
Software license fees	77.4	27
Other	4.7	2
Total	**289.4**	**100**

Selected Products

Deltek Costpoint (ERP software for large organizations)
Deltek Enterprise Project Management Solutions (project management suite)
Deltek GCS Premier (project accounting for federal contractors)
Deltek Vision (Web-based suite automation for professional services firms)

COMPETITORS

Artemis International Solutions
CA, Inc.
Lawson Software
Microsoft Dynamics
Oracle
SAP
Ultimate Software

HISTORICAL FINANCIALS

Company Type: Public

Income Statement

FYE: December 31

	REVENUE ($ mil.)	NET INCOME ($ mil.)	NET PROFIT MARGIN	EMPLOYEES
12/08	289.4	23.5	8.1%	1,240
12/07	278.2	22.5	8.1%	1,255
12/06	228.3	15.3	6.7%	1,041
12/05	153.0	8.7	5.7%	1,212
12/04	121.2	27.9	23.0%	—
Annual Growth	**24.3%**	**(4.2%)**	**—**	**0.8%**

2008 Year-End Financials

Debt ratio: —
Return on equity: —
Cash ($ mil.): 35.8
Current ratio: 1.58
Long-term debt ($ mil.): 182.7
No. of shares (mil.): 66.0
Dividends
Yield: —
Payout: —
Market value ($ mil.): 306.0
R&D as % of sales: —
Advertising as % of sales: —

Stock History

NASDAQ (GS): PROJ

	STOCK PRICE ($) FY Close	P/E High/Low		PER SHARE ($) Earnings	Dividends	Book Value
12/08	4.64	29	6	0.53	—	(0.82)
12/07	15.23	34	25	0.54	—	(1.31)
Annual Growth	**(69.5%)**	**—**	**—**	**(1.9%)**	**—**	**—**

DG FastChannel

Commercials don't signify bathroom breaks for DG FastChannel (formerly Digital Generation Systems, which did business as DG Systems). The company provides digital distribution services for advertisers, agencies, newspaper publishers, and TV and radio broadcasters. Ad agencies and other content providers route their clients' audio and video spots to radio and TV stations and other traditional media outlets through DG FastChannel's nationwide digital distribution network. Electronic transmissions are made across the Internet and via satellite. Chairman and CEO Scott Ginsburg owns about 15% of the company, which became DG FastChannel in 2006 after purchasing competitor FastChannel Network for $37.5 million.

The company's digital network connects more than 5,000 advertisers and advertising agencies with more than 4,000 cable and TV network broadcast outlets, approximately 10,000 radio stations, and more than 6,500 print publications across the US and Canada. While content distribution accounts for most of DG FastChannel's business, the company also provides online business intelligence offerings and a searchable database of television advertisements; post-production services; digital asset management tools for archiving and collaboration; and media intelligence offerings, such as broadcast verification.

In 2009 the company announced plans to develop a system for high definition syndicated content and news. Called the HD Digital Media Gateway (DMG), it is being built in partnership with Dell, and is scheduled for launch in 2010. The previous year DG FastChannel expanded its distribution, post-production, and customer service operations with the acquisition of the Vyvx advertising business from Level 3 Communications for $129 million. Later that year DG FastChannel purchased digital advertising firm Enliven Marketing Technologies Corporation for some $71 million in stock. The acquisition enhanced the company's digital media services, ad distribution, Internet marketing, and online and mobile advertising capabilities. Included in the deal was Enliven's Springbox subsidiary, an interactive, digital Web marketing firm.

The company also made several acquisitions in 2007, including the purchase of the advertising distribution operations of multimedia firm Point.360 for about $34 million. DG FastChannel additionally acquired Pathfire, a distributor of syndicated programming such as *Jeopardy*, *Friends*, and *The Oprah Winfrey Show*, for nearly $30 million. It next acquired automotive advertising provider GTN for $11.5 million (at the same time it sold GTN's post-production operations for $3 million).

EXECUTIVES

Chairman and CEO: Scott K. Ginsburg, age 56, $1,572,492 total compensation
President and COO: Neil H. Nguyen, age 35, $638,509 total compensation
CFO and Director: Omar A. Choucair, age 47, $643,558 total compensation
CTO: Gregory M. (Greg) Smith

EVP, Unicast and Pathfire: Derek Smith
SVP SourceEcreative: Pamela (Pam) Maythenyi, age 53,
 $270,862 total compensation
Co-President, Springbox: Adam Moore
Co-President, Springbox: Dan Isaacs
Public Relations: Aisling Garvey
Investor Relations: Bryan Armstrong
Managing Director, Europe: Richard Kidd
Auditors: Ernst & Young LLP

LOCATIONS

HQ: DG FastChannel, Inc.
 750 W. John Carpenter Fwy., Ste. 700
 Irving, TX 75039
Phone: 972-581-2000   **Fax:** 972-581-2001
Web: www.dgfastchannel.com

PRODUCTS/OPERATIONS

2008 Sales

	$ mil.	% of total
Audio & video content distribution	148.9	95
Other	8.2	5
Total	**157.1**	**100**

Selected Services

A/V production
Audio delivery
Conversion
Digital distribution
Duplication
Media asset management
Music distribution
Syndicated program distribution
Sweeps
Video delivery

COMPETITORS

Akamai
EDnet
Eyeblaster
EyeWonder
Google
Limelight
Medialink
Radiance Technologies

HISTORICAL FINANCIALS

Company Type: Public

Income Statement

FYE: December 31

	REVENUE ($ mil.)	NET INCOME ($ mil.)	NET PROFIT MARGIN	EMPLOYEES
12/08	157.1	15.1	9.6%	770
12/07	97.7	10.4	10.6%	552
12/06	68.7	(0.6)	—	376
12/05	58.4	(1.1)	—	317
12/04	62.4	3.2	5.1%	403
Annual Growth	26.0%	47.4%	—	17.6%

2008 Year-End Financials

Debt ratio: 57.5%
Return on equity: 6.5%
Cash ($ mil.): 17.2
Current ratio: 1.49
Long-term debt ($ mil.): 155.0
No. of shares (mil.): 23.9
Dividends
 Yield: 0.0%
 Payout: —
Market value ($ mil.): 297.9
R&D as % of sales: —
Advertising as % of sales: —

Stock History   NASDAQ (GM): DGIT

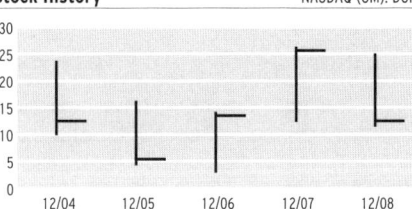

	STOCK PRICE ($) FY Close	P/E High/Low		PER SHARE ($) Earnings	Dividends	Book Value
12/08	12.48	31	15	0.79	0.00	11.29
12/07	25.64	43	21	0.61	0.00	8.05
12/06	13.48	—	—	(0.06)	0.00	5.94
12/05	5.40	—	—	(0.10)	0.00	3.36
12/04	12.50	59	25	0.40	0.00	3.33
Annual Growth	(0.0%)	—	—	18.5%	—	35.7%

Dialysis Corporation

Dialysis Corporation of America (DCA) operates about 35 outpatient dialysis clinics in more than half a dozen US states, providing life-sustaining services to patients with chronic kidney failure (also known as end-stage renal disease). The company also provides inpatient dialysis through contracts with about a dozen hospitals, all of them in markets where it has outpatient facilities; and, through its dialysis clinics, DCA provides training and support to patients who use peritoneal dialysis at home. Many of the company's clinics are owned jointly with local nephrologists; others are wholly owned by DCA.

The company is continuing to grow both through the acquisition of existing centers (two in 2007) and the establishment of new centers. Additionally, it is looking to negotiate more contracts with hospitals and to add patients at its existing outpatient clinics.

Medicare reimbursements account for about half of the company's revenue.

EXECUTIVES

Chairman: Thomas K. Langbein, age 63
President, CEO, and Director: Stephen W. Everett,
 age 52, $374,189 total compensation
VP Finance and CFO: Andrew J. Jeanneret, age 44,
 $274,705 total compensation
VP and Treasurer: Daniel R. Ouzts, age 62,
 $193,530 total compensation
VP Operations: Thomas P. Carey, age 55,
 $268,472 total compensation
VP Clinical Services and Compliance Officer:
Joanne Zimmerman, age 54,
 $217,228 total compensation
Auditors: MSPC

LOCATIONS

HQ: Dialysis Corporation of America
 1302 Concourse Dr., Ste. 204
 Linthicum, MD 21090
Phone: 410-694-0500   **Fax:** 410-694-0596
Web: www.dialysiscorporation.com

Dialysis Corporation of America has operations in Georgia, Maryland, New Jersey, Ohio, Pennsylvania, South Carolina, and Virginia.

PRODUCTS/OPERATIONS

2008 Sales

	$ mil.	% of total
Medical services	85.7	99
Product sales	1.1	1
Total	**86.8**	**100**

COMPETITORS

Baxter International
DaVita
Dialysis Clinic Inc
DSI
FMCNA
Fresenius Medical Care
Renal Advantage

HISTORICAL FINANCIALS

Company Type: Public

Income Statement

FYE: December 31

	REVENUE ($ mil.)	NET INCOME ($ mil.)	NET PROFIT MARGIN	EMPLOYEES
12/08	86.8	2.8	3.2%	550
12/07	74.5	3.1	4.2%	653
12/06	62.5	3.0	4.8%	601
12/05	45.4	1.9	4.2%	493
12/04	41.0	2.2	5.4%	402
Annual Growth	20.6%	6.2%	—	8.2%

2008 Year-End Financials

Debt ratio: 40.5%
Return on equity: 8.3%
Cash ($ mil.): 6.5
Current ratio: 2.36
Long-term debt ($ mil.): 14.3
No. of shares (mil.): 9.6
Dividends
 Yield: 0.0%
 Payout: —
Market value ($ mil.): 67.2
R&D as % of sales: —
Advertising as % of sales: —

Stock History   NASDAQ (GM): DCAI

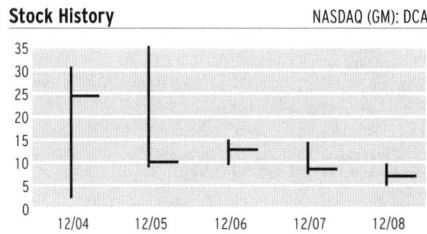

	STOCK PRICE ($) FY Close	P/E High/Low		PER SHARE ($) Earnings	Dividends	Book Value
12/08	7.00	32	17	0.30	0.00	3.67
12/07	8.50	44	24	0.32	0.00	3.33
12/06	12.71	46	30	0.32	0.00	3.03
12/05	10.03	175	46	0.20	0.00	2.67
12/04	24.43	122	10	0.25	0.00	1.39
Annual Growth	(26.8%)	—	—	4.7%	—	27.5%

Diamond Hill Investment

Diamond Hill Investment Group takes a shine to investing. Operating through flagship subsidiary Diamond Hill Capital Management, the firm oversees approximately $5 billion in assets, most of it invested in mutual funds. Serving institutional and individual clients, the company administers several mutual funds and sells them mainly through independent investment advisors, broker-dealers, financial planners, investment consultants, and third-party marketing firms. It also manages separate accounts and hedge funds.

In 2008 the company said that it will establish a brokerage subsidiary that will offer statutory underwriting services to its own funds and to other mid-market funds.

President and CEO Ric Dillon owns about 7% of the company.

EXECUTIVES

President, CEO and Director; Chief Investment Officer, Diamond Hill Capital Management, Inc.: Roderick H. (Ric) Dillon Jr., age 52, $2,467,600 total compensation
CFO, Secretary and Treasurer; President, Diamond Hill Funds: James F. (Jim) Laird Jr., age 52, $744,000 total compensation
Managing Director, Planning and Operations: Randall J. Demyan
Managing Director, Strategic Income, Diamond Hill Investments: Kent K. Rinker, age 58
Chairman, Diamond Hill Funds: Thomas E. (Tom) Line
Managing Director, Equities, Diamond Hill Capital Management: Charles S. (Chuck) Bath, age 54
Portfolio Manager, Strategic Income: William P. Zox
Portfolio Manager, Equities; Portfolio Manager, Diamond Hill Small-Mid Cap Fund: Christopher A. (Chris) Welch
Coporate Controller and Chief Compliance Officer, Diamond Hills Funds: Gary R. Young
Auditors: Plante & Moran, PLLC

LOCATIONS

HQ: Diamond Hill Investment Group, Inc.
325 John H. McConnell Blvd., Ste. 200
Columbus, OH 43215
Phone: 614-255-3333   **Fax:** 614-255-3363
Web: www.diamond-hill.com

PRODUCTS/OPERATIONS

2008 Sales

	$ mil.	% of total
Investment advisory	40.5	86
Mutual fund administration	6.1	13
Performance incentive	0.4	1
Total	**47.0**	**100**

COMPETITORS

AllianceBernstein	GAMCO Investors
American Century	Janus Capital
Calamos Asset Management	Legg Mason
	MFS
Cohen & Steers	Putnam
Columbia Management	Raymond James Financial
Davis Advisers	Sanders Morris Harris
Duncan-Hurst	T. Rowe Price
Edward Jones	The Vanguard Group
FMR	Waddell & Reed
Franklin Resources	

HISTORICAL FINANCIALS

Company Type: Public

Income Statement   FYE: December 31

	ASSETS ($ mil.)	NET INCOME ($ mil.)	INCOME AS % OF ASSETS	EMPLOYEES
12/08	44.5	3.3	7.4%	57
12/07	53.3	9.9	18.6%	42
12/06	37.2	8.1	21.8%	32
12/05	12.7	3.7	29.1%	21
12/04	4.0	(0.2)	—	19
Annual Growth	**82.6%**	**—**	**—**	**31.6%**

2008 Year-End Financials

Equity as % of assets: 68.0%	Dividends
Return on assets: 6.7%	Yield: 0.0%
Return on equity: 9.5%	Payout: —
Long-term debt ($ mil.): —	Sales ($ mil.): 47.0
No. of shares (mil.): 2.6	R&D as % of sales: —
Market value ($ mil.): 170.1	Advertising as % of sales: —

Stock History   NASDAQ (GM): DHIL

	STOCK PRICE ($) FY Close	P/E High/Low		PER SHARE ($) Earnings	Dividends	Book Value
12/08	65.00	74	34	1.36	0.00	11.55
12/07	73.10	26	16	4.39	0.00	15.02
12/06	83.73	25	8	3.63	0.00	7.83
12/05	31.30	21	8	1.83	0.00	4.15
12/04	16.75	—	—	(0.11)	0.00	1.36
Annual Growth	**40.4%**	**—**	**—**	**—**	**—**	**70.7%**

Dice Holdings

Dice Holdings rolls along with Web sites devoted to employee recruiting and career development. Through its flagship, Dice.com, it provides job postings and career-related resources for technology professionals in the US. Dice also operates ClearanceJobs.com, for people with US government security clearances; eFinancialCareers.com, aimed at the financial services industry; AllHealthcareJobs.com, targeting health care workers; and JobsintheMoney.com, for accounting and finance professionals. It also puts on job fairs. Most of the company's revenue comes from employers, who pay to post job listings and view resumes. Investment firms General Atlantic and Quadrangle Group own a controlling stake in Dice Holdings.

The economic downturn that started in 2008 has driven hits on Dice Holdings' Web sites up with unemployment reaching the highest rates in decades, but the same factors have hurt the company as fewer employers are paying to post job notices. To control costs, Dice Holdings cut its own staff by about 10% in November 2008.

The company's future plans for growth including developing career Web sites tailored for new industry niches and new geographic areas, as well as by gaining customers for its existing offerings. It also is working to build its brands, particularly Dice and eFinancialCareers. In June 2009 Dice Holdings branched out into the burgeoning health care industry job search market with the purchase of AllHealthcareJobs.com for $2.8 million.

In order to focus on its core job search Web sites, Dice Holdings in 2007 terminated its MeasureUp.com business, an online provider of technology certification test preparation products and services. In 2008 the company completed its exit from a joint venture in India, CyberMediaDice Careers, that operated a career Web site for technology professionals.

Career-oriented Web sites are a relatively new business, but in Internet terms, Dice.com is ancient — the online job listing service got its start in 1991. The service has gone through several corporate incarnations over the years; it was acquired by General Atlantic and Quadrangle in 2005 after its previous owner filed for bankruptcy protection in 2003. The investment firms took the company public in 2007.

EXECUTIVES

Chairman, President, and CEO: Scot W. Melland, age 46, $2,795,184 total compensation
SVP North America: Thomas M. Silver, age 49, $1,137,313 total compensation
SVP Finance and CFO: Michael P. Durney, age 46, $1,282,490 total compensation
VP Business and Legal Affairs, General Counsel, and Secretary: Brian P. Campbell, age 44, $526,343 total compensation
VP Sales Operations: Kent E. Thompson
VP Technology: Paul C. Melde, age 48
VP Treasury and Strategic Planning: Constance E. Melrose, age 55
CEO, eFinancialCareers; Managing Director, Dice International: John P. R. Benson, age 47, $582,845 total compensation
Director Investor Relations and Corporate Communications: Jennifer Bewley
Auditors: Deloitte & Touche LLP

LOCATIONS

HQ: Dice Holdings, Inc.
1040 Avenue of the Americas, 16th Fl.
New York, NY 10018
Phone: 212-725-6550   **Fax:** 212-725-6559
Web: www.diceholdingsinc.com

PRODUCTS/OPERATIONS

2008 Sales

	$ mil.	% of total
DCS Online	107.3	69
eFinancialCareers	37.2	24
Other	10.5	7
Total	**155.0**	**100**

Selected Operating Units

DCS Online
  Dice.com (recruiting and career development Web site for technology and engineering professionals in the US)
  ClearanceJobs.com (recruiting and career development Web site for professionals with active US government security clearances)
eFinancialCareers
  eFinancialCareers.com (UK, global recruiting and career development Web sites for capital markets and financial services professionals)
Other
  AllHealthcareJobs.com (recruiting Web site for health care professionals)
  JobsintheMoney.com (recruiting and career development Web site for accounting and finance professionals in the US)
  Targeted Job Fairs (producer and host of career fairs and open houses for technology and security-cleared candidates in the US)

COMPETITORS

CareerBuilder
craigslist
Google
HotJobs
LinkedIn
Monster.com
News Corp. Digital Media

HISTORICAL FINANCIALS

Company Type: Public

Income Statement
FYE: December 31

	REVENUE ($ mil.)	NET INCOME ($ mil.)	NET PROFIT MARGIN	EMPLOYEES
12/08	155.0	15.4	9.9%	283
12/07	142.4	15.5	10.9%	308
12/06	83.7	6.8	8.1%	329
12/05	17.0	(1.7)	—	202
Annual Growth	108.9%	—	—	11.9%

2008 Year-End Financials

Debt ratio: 65.2%
Return on equity: 12.6%
Cash ($ mil.): 55.1
Current ratio: 1.43
Long-term debt ($ mil.): 80.5
No. of shares (mil.): 62.5
Dividends
  Yield: —
  Payout: —
Market value ($ mil.): 254.9
R&D as % of sales: —
Advertising as % of sales: —

Stock History
NYSE: DHX

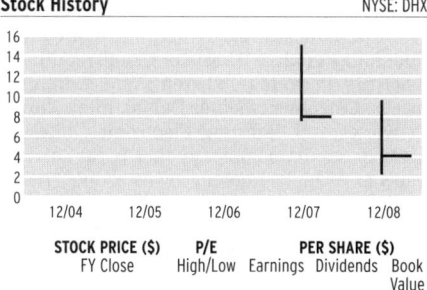

	STOCK PRICE ($) FY Close	P/E High/Low	PER SHARE ($) Earnings	Dividends	Book Value
12/08	4.08	40 10	0.24	—	1.98
12/07	7.99	— —	(3.26)	—	1.93
Annual Growth	(48.9%)	— —	—	—	2.4%

Digital Ally

Digital video systems manufacturer Digital Ally is an ally to police and other law enforcement that want more than a paper record of their traffic stops. Targeted to city, state, and commercial law enforcement agencies, the company designs and manufactures specialized digital video cameras, including a rear-view mirror with a built-in digital video camera (used to capture video from inside police vehicles), as well as a portable digital video flashlight, which can be used to record routine traffic stops, sobriety tests, and other law enforcement/civilian interactions. The company also offers a version of their video camera that can be worn on law enforcement officers' uniforms. Digital Ally was formed in 2004.

Although it has built its business by targeting agencies in the US market, Digital Ally has recently begun selling its products to international law enforcement agencies. The company is also growing its business by expanding its core product offerings; in early 2009, it began marketing a weatherproof digital video system for installation on police motorcycles.

Additionally, Digital Ally intends to move beyond the law enforcement market by designing video camera systems that can be installed in various products manufactured by third-party companies. Through partnerships with these companies, Digital Ally hopes to design systems for products like stun guns, sports-related speed measuring devices (i.e., devices that measure baseball or tennis ball speed), and recording systems for medical procedures (used to record surgical procedures for legal or education purposes).

EXECUTIVES

Chairman, President, and CEO: Stanton E. Ross, age 47, $1,002,396 total compensation
CFO, Secretary, and Treasurer: Thomas J. Heckman, $338,357 total compensation
VP Operations: Edward E. Smith
VP Sales and Marketing: Kenneth L. (Ken) McCoy, age 60, $471,780 total compensation
VP Strategic Development: Michael Caulfield
VP Engineering and Product Developemente: Robert Haler, $459,448 total compensation
VP Engineering: Steven Phillips
Director Sales and Marketing: Darrin McCoy
Manager Sales, International: Jeff Oost
Auditors: McGladrey & Pullen, LLP

LOCATIONS

HQ: Digital Ally, Inc.
  7311 West 130th St., Ste. 170,
  Overland Park, KS 66213
Phone: 913-814-7774   **Fax:** 913-814-7775
Web: www.digitalallyinc.com

HISTORICAL FINANCIALS

Company Type: Public

Income Statement
FYE: December 31

	REVENUE ($ mil.)	NET INCOME ($ mil.)	NET PROFIT MARGIN	EMPLOYEES
12/08	32.6	3.4	10.4%	117
12/07	19.4	4.5	23.2%	72
12/06	4.1	(3.4)	—	37
Annual Growth	182.0%	—	—	77.8%

2008 Year-End Financials

Debt ratio: —
Return on equity: 25.9%
Cash ($ mil.): 1.2
Current ratio: 4.55
Long-term debt ($ mil.): —
No. of shares (mil.): 15.8
Dividends
  Yield: —
  Payout: —
Market value ($ mil.): 48.8
R&D as % of sales: —
Advertising as % of sales: —

Stock History
NASDAQ (CM): DGLY

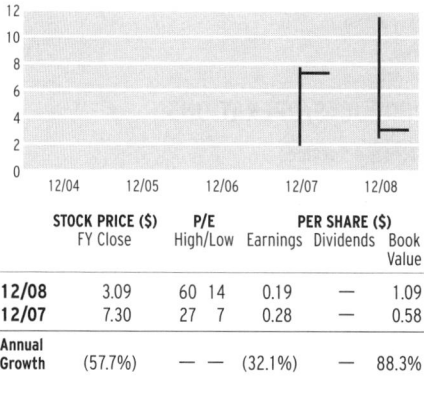

	STOCK PRICE ($) FY Close	P/E High/Low	PER SHARE ($) Earnings	Dividends	Book Value
12/08	3.09	60 14	0.19	—	1.09
12/07	7.30	27 7	0.28	—	0.58
Annual Growth	(57.7%)	— —	(32.1%)	—	88.3%

Digital River

Digital River helps keep the e-commerce flowing. The company provides technology and services that enable its clients to sell their products on the Web without building an e-commerce platform from the ground up. Using its own proprietary server technology, Digital River offers Web development and hosting, transaction processing, fulfillment, and fraud screening services to more than 40,000 customers operating online retail and distribution businesses. It also provides its customers with Web traffic data that allows them to better market their online presence. Security software client Symantec accounted for 24% of total sales in 2008. Digital River has been growing through a steady stream of acquisitions.

In 2007, Digital River fortified its e-commerce offerings when it acquired Netgiro Systems AB, an online payment services provider based in Sweden. The year before, Digital River bought MindVision, a software provider specializing in installation programs.

Most of Digital River's business comes from software publishers and online software retailers, but it is trying to build up more business with manufacturers and distributors of physical goods.

Digital River was established in 1994 and began offering online stores for its clients in 1996.

EXECUTIVES

CEO and Director: Joel A. Ronning, $3,202,641 total compensation
CFO: Thomas M. Donnelly, $1,886,238 total compensation
VP and General Counsel: Kevin L. Crudden, age 53, $596,622 total compensation
VP Investor Relations: Ed Merritt
VP Global Client Development Consumer Electronics: Don Peterson
Director Public Relations: Gerri Dyrek
Auditors: Ernst & Young LLP

LOCATIONS

HQ: Digital River, Inc.
 9625 W. 76th St., Ste. 150, Eden Prairie, MN 55344
Phone: 952-253-1234   **Fax:** 952-253-8497
Web: www.digitalriver.com

2008 Sales

	% of total
US	58
International	42
Total	**100**

PRODUCTS/OPERATIONS

Selected Services

Customer service
Digital and physical fulfillment
Fraud detection
Merchandising and marketing
Transaction processing
Web commerce hosting

COMPETITORS

Accenture	IBM
Amazon.com	INTERSHOP
Ariba	Microsoft
Art Technology Group	NaviSite
BroadVision	Oracle
CyberSource	SAP
DoubleClick	Sterling Commerce
eBay	USinternetworking
GSI Commerce	ValueClick
HP Enterprise Services	

HISTORICAL FINANCIALS

Company Type: Public

Income Statement

FYE: December 31

	REVENUE ($ mil.)	NET INCOME ($ mil.)	NET PROFIT MARGIN	EMPLOYEES
12/08	394.2	63.6	16.1%	1,335
12/07	349.3	70.8	20.3%	1,265
12/06	307.6	60.8	19.8%	1,086
12/05	220.4	54.3	24.6%	948
12/04	154.1	35.3	22.9%	727
Annual Growth	**26.5%**	**15.9%**	**—**	**16.4%**

2008 Year-End Financials

Debt ratio: 1.5%
Return on equity: 10.0%
Cash ($ mil.): 490.3
Current ratio: 1.36
Long-term debt ($ mil.): 8.8
No. of shares (mil.): 38.6

Dividends
 Yield: 0.0%
 Payout: —
Market value ($ mil.): 958.4
R&D as % of sales: —
Advertising as % of sales: —

Stock History

NASDAQ (GS): DRIV

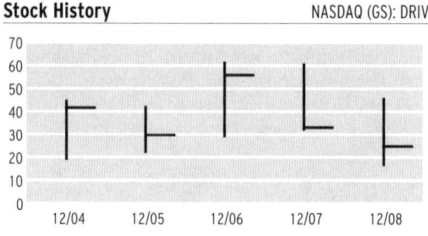

	STOCK PRICE ($) FY Close	P/E High/Low		PER SHARE ($) Earnings	Dividends	Book Value
12/08	24.80	29	11	1.55	0.00	15.58
12/07	33.07	38	20	1.58	0.00	17.50
12/06	55.79	44	21	1.40	0.00	15.62
12/05	29.74	31	16	1.36	0.00	7.90
12/04	41.61	46	20	0.96	0.00	4.99
Annual Growth	**(12.1%)**	**—**	**—**	**12.7%**	**—**	**32.9%**

DigitalGlobe, Inc.

DigitalGlobe has its eye on you. The company provides satellite imagery that is used for a variety of applications, including mapping, urban planning, oil exploration, land management, and disaster assessment. DigitalGlobe's products include standard images, panchromatic images, multispectral images, and color infrared images, as well as mosaics and digital elevation models. The company's customers come from fields such as agriculture, civil government, oil and gas exploration, and military intelligence. DigitalGlobe's images and services are incorporated into popular mapping applications such as Google Maps and Microsoft Virtual Earth, as well as into GPS systems from Garmin and Nokia.

The company in 2009 completed an IPO in order to raise funds for satellite construction and to pay down debt.

While the company serves a variety of commercial clients, its top client is the National Geospatial-Intelligence Agency (nearly 75% of sales), which buys images for use by US government agencies for defense, intelligence, and foreign policy applications.

DigitalGlobe's acquisition of GlobeXplorer from Stewart REI Group signaled the company's expansion of its digital Earth imagery and products. GlobeXplorer provided geographic data integration and publishing services.

The company owns and operates two imagery satellites. Its most recent launch — of World-View-2 in late 2009 — roughly doubled Digital-Globe's image collection capability.

Morgan Stanley owns 32% of the company.

EXECUTIVES

Chairman, President, and CEO: Jill D. Smith, age 50, $1,626,482 total compensation
EVP, CFO, and Treasurer: Yancey L. Spruill, age 41, $667,040 total compensation
EVP and CTO: Walter S. Scott, age 51, $559,203 total compensation
SVP and COO: S. Scott Smith, age 50, $637,944 total compensation
SVP, Secretary, and General Counsel: J. Alison Alfers, age 42, $777,672 total compensation
SVP and CIO: Scott M. Hicar
SVP Commercial: Rafay Khan
SVP and General Manager, Defense and Intelligence: Jeffrey S. (Jeff) Kerridge, age 47
VP Government Relations: Dawn Sienicki
Principal Scientist: Kumar Navulur
Auditors: PricewaterhouseCoopers LLP

LOCATIONS

HQ: DigitalGlobe, Inc.
 1601 Dry Creek Dr., Ste. 260, Longmont, CO 80503
Phone: 303-684-4000   **Fax:** 303-682-3848
Web: www.digitalglobe.com

2008 Sales

	$ mil.	% of total
US	228.0	83
Other countries	47.2	17
Total	**275.2**	**100**

PRODUCTS/OPERATIONS

2008 Sales by Market

	% of total
Defense & intelligence	83
Commercial	17
Total	**100**

COMPETITORS

GeoEye
Google
Microsoft
Orbital Sciences
Trimble Navigation

HISTORICAL FINANCIALS

Company Type: Public

Income Statement

FYE: December 31

	REVENUE ($ mil.)	NET INCOME ($ mil.)	NET PROFIT MARGIN	EMPLOYEES
12/08	275.2	53.8	19.5%	464
12/07	151.7	95.8	63.2%	410
12/06	106.8	9.2	8.6%	—
12/05	65.4	(28.7)	—	—
Annual Growth	**61.4%**	**—**	**—**	**13.2%**

2008 Year-End Financials

Debt ratio: 68.3%
Return on equity: 14.4%
Cash ($ mil.): 60.8
Current ratio: 2.54
Long-term debt ($ mil.): 274.6

Net Income History

NYSE: DGI

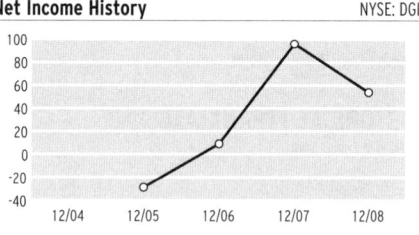

Diodes Incorporated

Diodes Incorporated knows how important it is to be discrete in business. The company manufactures discrete semiconductors — fixed-function devices that are much less complex than integrated circuits. Diodes' products are used by makers of automotive, computing, consumer electronics, and telecommunications gear. The company makes hundreds of products (including diodes, transistors, and rectifiers) that vary in voltage, current, and switching speeds. Customers include Delphi, Intel, Nortel Networks, and Samsung Electronics. Lite-On Semiconductor, a company that is part of Taiwan's Lite-On Technology, owns about 20% of Diodes. Lite-On Semiconductor is also Diodes' biggest customer and its biggest supplier.

Diodes draws about two-thirds of its sales from customers in Asia, where it has significant manufacturing operations.

Global economic weakness has hurt many of the company's customers, especially those in the automotive industry and consumer electronics. Even without crushing recessions, the semiconductor industry is highly cyclical, as sales of computers and telecom equipment wax and wane on a regular basis. Diodes is under continuous pressure from customers and competitors to reduce the prices of its products, which can result in lower sales and profits for the company. Customers require Diodes to submit its products to an expensive and lengthy qualification

process, including reliability testing, without any guarantee of sales.

The company expanded its market reach by focusing on higher-margin, proprietary product lines, such as high-density arrays and ultraminiature switching diodes used in mobile applications.

In 2008 Diodes acquired a UK-based competitor, Zetex, for about $176 million in cash. Zetex specialized in discrete components and analog integrated circuits for power management and signal processing. Diodes was attracted to buying the company for its strong European presence and its focus on automotive and industrial applications, among other factors.

In 2006 Diodes acquired Anachip, a fabless semiconductor firm in Taiwan, for about $30 million in cash. Anachip developed power management chips, analog integrated circuits used in such products as brushless DC motor fans, LCD monitors and TVs, modems, portable DVD players, and power supplies.

Later that year the company acquired APD Semiconductor, another fabless firm, based in the US with operations in Taiwan. APD developed discrete semiconductors. The purchase price was about $8 million.

Diodes transferred its analog wafer probe and final test operations from Taiwan to China. The move affected about 40 employees in Hsinchu, Taiwan, where product design, R&D, sales, marketing, administration, and support service employees will continue to operate.

EXECUTIVES

Chairman: Raymond Soong, age 67
Vice Chairman: C. H. Chen, age 66
President, CEO, and Director: Keh-Shew Lu, age 62, $3,458,936 total compensation
CFO, Secretary, and Treasurer: Richard D. White, age 61, $689,099 total compensation
SVP Sales and Marketing: Mark A. King, age 50, $920,183 total compensation
SVP Operations: Joseph Liu, age 67, $1,016,801 total compensation
SVP Business Development: Hans Rohrer, age 60
VP Finance and Investor Relations: Carl C. Wertz, age 54, $627,376 total compensation
VP Product Development: Francis Tang, age 55
VP Corporate Administration: Edmund (Ed) Tang, age 61
VP Packaging Operations: T.J. Lee, age 60
VP Worldwide Analog Products: Julie Holland, age 47
Europe President and VP, Europe Sales and Marketing: Colin Greene, age 53
Auditors: Moss Adams, LLP

LOCATIONS

HQ: Diodes Incorporated
15660 Dallas Pkwy., Ste. 850, Dallas, TX 75248
Phone: 972-385-2810
Web: www.diodes.com

Diodes has facilities in China, France, Hong Kong, Taiwan, and the US.

2008 Sales

	$ mil.	% of total
Asia/Pacific		
China	130.0	30
Taiwan	118.6	27
South Korea	21.9	5
Singapore	14.9	4
US	85.9	20
Europe		
Germany	17.0	4
UK	12.8	3
Other regions	31.7	7
Total	**432.8**	**100**

PRODUCTS/OPERATIONS

Selected Products

Diodes
  Schottky diodes
  Switching diodes
  Zener diodes
High-density arrays
Metal oxide semiconductor field-effect transistors (MOSFETs)
Rectifiers
  Bridge rectifiers
  Schottky rectifiers
  Standard, fast, superfast, and ultrafast recovery rectifiers
Transient voltage suppressors
  Thyristor surge protection devices
  Zener transient-voltage suppressors
Transistors
  Bipolar transistors
  Darlington transistors
  Prebiased transistors

COMPETITORS

Advanced Photonix
BCD Semiconductor
Fairchild Semiconductor
Infineon Technologies
International Rectifier
IXYS
Microsemi
NXP
ON Semiconductor
ROHM
Sanken Electric
Shindengen Electric
Siliconix
STMicroelectronics
Toshiba Semiconductor
Vishay Intertechnology

HISTORICAL FINANCIALS

Company Type: Public

Income Statement

FYE: December 31

	REVENUE ($ mil.)	NET INCOME ($ mil.)	NET PROFIT MARGIN	EMPLOYEES
12/08	432.8	39.0	9.0%	3,067
12/07	401.2	59.7	14.9%	2,612
12/06	343.3	48.1	14.0%	2,268
12/05	214.8	33.3	15.5%	1,621
12/04	185.7	25.6	13.8%	1,370
Annual Growth	**23.6%**	**11.1%**	**—**	**22.3%**

2008 Year-End Financials

Debt ratio: 108.1%
Return on equity: 10.5%
Cash ($ mil.): 103.5
Current ratio: 3.41
Long-term debt ($ mil.): 402.5
No. of shares (mil.): 43.6
Dividends
  Yield: —
  Payout: —
Market value ($ mil.): 264.4
R&D as % of sales: —
Advertising as % of sales: —

Stock History

NASDAQ (GS): DIOD

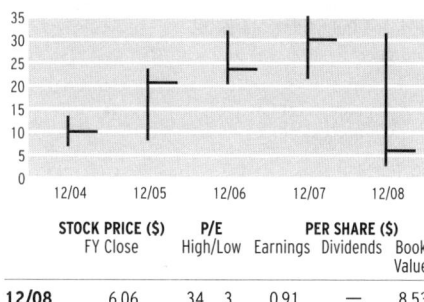

	STOCK PRICE ($) FY Close	P/E High	P/E Low	PER SHARE ($) Earnings	PER SHARE ($) Dividends	PER SHARE ($) Book Value
12/08	6.06	34	3	0.91	—	8.53
12/07	30.07	25	16	1.41	—	8.47
12/06	23.65	27	18	1.16	—	6.74
12/05	20.70	27	10	0.86	—	5.17
12/04	10.06	18	10	0.73	—	2.57
Annual Growth	**(11.9%)**	**—**	**—**	**5.7%**	**—**	**35.0%**

DivX, Inc.

FX from DVDs benefit from DivX, a digital media format for content playback, creation, and distribution. The company introduced a video compression-decompression (or codec) software library that has been downloaded more than 250 million times. It has built on the success of this technology by distributing the DivX software through its own Web site, and through licenses with consumer video hardware original equipment manufacturers (OEMs) such as LG Electronics, Samsung, and Philips. CEO Kevin Hell and former executives Darrius Thompson, Joe Bezdek, Tay Nguyen, and Gej Vashisht-Rota founded DivX in 2000.

In 2009 DivX acquired AnySource Media, the creator of an Internet Television streaming platform, for some $7.5 million. The service allows users to directly connect their TV to content and services on the Internet, enabling hundreds of virtual on-demand channels.

Yahoo! accounts for nearly 20% of DivX's sales; LG Electronics accounts for some 10%.

The company's Stage6 was an online service that had allowed users to publish and download video content; however Universal Music Group (UMG) and other firms claimed copyright infringement, and in 2008 DivX shut down Stage6. It is currently involved in litigation with UMG, which is seeking monetary damages.

EXECUTIVES

CEO: Kevin C. Hell, age 44, $2,715,904 total compensation
EVP Operations and CFO: Dan L. Halvorson, age 44, $1,713,807 total compensation
EVP Business and Legal Affairs: David J. Richter, age 40, $1,076,357 total compensation
SVP Products: Patrice Lagrange
VP Operations: Michael Floyd
VP Investor Relations and Compliance: Karen Fisher
VP Engineering: Jim Reesman
VP Product Management: Kanaan Jemili
VP Finance and Treasurer: Trevor Renfield
Senior Manager, Intellectual Property: Kimberly Johnson
General Manager, Greater China and South APAC: Samson S. Lee
Director Corporate Communications: Tom Huntington
General Counsel: Johnny Chen
Auditors: Ernst & Young LLP

LOCATIONS

HQ: DivX, Inc.
4780 Eastgate Mall, San Diego, CA 92121
Phone: 858-882-0600   **Fax:** 858-882-0601
Web: www.divx.com

2008 Sales

	$ mil.	% of total
Asia	58.0	62
North America	24.4	26
Europe	11.3	12
Other regions	0.2	—
Total	**93.9**	**100**

PRODUCTS/OPERATIONS

Selected Technologies

Digital rights management
DivX file format
DivX media format
DivX video compression technology

COMPETITORS

Adobe Systems	NDS Group
Amazon.com	Netflix
Apple Inc.	News Corp.
CinemaNow	On2 Technologies
ContentGuard	RealNetworks
Dolby	Sony
Google	Yahoo!
Intertrust Technologies	YouTube
Microsoft	

HISTORICAL FINANCIALS

Company Type: Public

Income Statement				FYE: December 31
	REVENUE ($ mil.)	NET INCOME ($ mil.)	NET PROFIT MARGIN	EMPLOYEES
12/08	93.9	10.0	10.6%	301
12/07	84.9	9.2	10.8%	389
12/06	59.3	16.4	27.7%	108
12/05	33.0	2.3	7.0%	189
12/04	16.4	(4.3)	—	216
Annual Growth	54.7%	—	—	8.6%

2008 Year-End Financials

Debt ratio: —
Return on equity: 5.7%
Cash ($ mil.): 43.4
Current ratio: 8.51
Long-term debt ($ mil.): —
No. of shares (mil.): 32.7

Dividends
  Yield: —
  Payout: —
Market value ($ mil.): 171.1
R&D as % of sales: —
Advertising as % of sales: —

Stock History NASDAQ (GM): DIVX

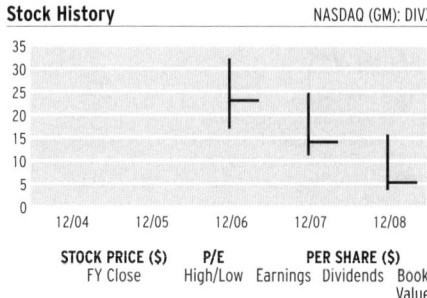

	STOCK PRICE ($) FY Close	P/E High/Low	PER SHARE ($) Earnings	Dividends	Book Value
12/08	5.23	51 13	0.30	—	5.32
12/07	14.00	94 44	0.26	—	5.36
12/06	23.07	52 28	0.61	—	4.61
Annual Growth	(52.4%)	— —	(29.9%)	—	7.4%

Dolan Media

Helping law firms is a big part of the process for this publisher. Dolan Media is a diversified legal services provider with a significant interest in local business news publishing. Through subsidiaries American Processing Company and Counsel Press, the company offers outsourced services aimed at processing residential mortgage defaults and related appeals, evictions, and foreclosures. Dolan also publishes more than 40 daily and weekly newspapers serving mostly markets on the East Coast and in the Midwest. Its portfolio includes *The Daily Record* (Baltimore), *Massachusetts Lawyers Weekly*, and *New Orleans*

CityBusiness. In addition, Dolan Media operates a number of news Web sites in conjunction with its papers.

Expanding its product offerings for the legal profession, in 2009 the company acquired an 85% interest in DiscoverReady, an outsourced discovery-management provider. DiscoverReady's customers include top US law firms, major banks and Wall Street firms, and *FORTUNE* 500 corporations. It comes under the purview of Dolan's professional services division.

The company's financial and legal services units experienced a boost in business during 2008 due to the credit crisis and recession that led to an explosion of mortgage defaults. It also purchased mortgage default processing firm National Default Exchange that year. Professional services account for more than 50% of sales.

Meanwhile, Dolan's publishing operations have been boosted by such acquisitions as *The Mecklenburg Times* (Charlotte, NC) in 2008. The papers generate most of their revenue through advertising, subscriptions, and fees for publishing public notices.

Founder Jim Dolan, a former journalist turned investment banker, started the business in 1992 by acquiring the Minneapolis newspaper *Finance and Commerce* with backing from private equity firm Cherry Tree Investments. Dolan Media expanded through additional newspaper acquisitions. Its focus on law periodicals led the company to target acquisitions of legal services business. Dolan Media later went public through an IPO in 2007 to help fund its growth and acquisitions strategy.

EXECUTIVES

Chairman, President, and CEO: James P. (Jim) Dolan, age 60, $987,480 total compensation
EVP and COO: Scott J. Pollei, age 49, $477,880 total compensation
EVP Business Information: Mark W. C. Stodder, age 50, $474,187 total compensation
VP, CFO, and Secretary: Vicki J. Duncomb, age 53
President, American Processing: David A. Trott, age 49, $479,128 total compensation
Director Investor Relations: Haug Scharnowski
Auditors: McGladrey & Pullen, LLP

LOCATIONS

HQ: Dolan Media Company
  1200 Baker Bldg., 706 2nd Ave. South, Ste. 1200
  Minneapolis, MN 55402
Phone: 612-317-9420   **Fax:** 612-317-9434
Web: www.dolanmedia.com

Selected Publishing Markets

Baltimore
Boise, ID
Boston
Charlotte, NC
Colorado Springs
Columbia, SC
Detroit
Jackson, MS
Kansas City
Milwaukee
Minneapolis
New Orleans
Oklahoma City
Phoenix
Portland, OR
Providence, RI
Raleigh, NC
Richmond, VA
Rochester, NY
St. Louis

PRODUCTS/OPERATIONS

2008 Sales

	$ mil.	% of total
Professional services	99.5	52
Publishing & business information	90.4	48
Total	**189.9**	**100**

COMPETITORS

American City Business Journals
Crain Communications
Daily Journal
The Detroit News
First American
Gannett
GateHouse Media
Herald Media
Journal Communications
Lee Enterprises
Lender Processing Services
McClatchy Company
Media General
MediaNews
New York Times
News & Record
Star Tribune
Times-World
Tribune Company

HISTORICAL FINANCIALS

Company Type: Public

Income Statement				FYE: December 31
	REVENUE ($ mil.)	NET INCOME ($ mil.)	NET PROFIT MARGIN	EMPLOYEES
12/08	189.9	14.3	7.5%	1,812
12/07	152.0	(54.0)	—	1,237
12/06	111.6	(14.0)	—	1,177
12/05	77.9	(7.5)	—	574
12/04	51.7	(1.3)	—	—
Annual Growth	38.4%	—	—	46.7%

2008 Year-End Financials

Debt ratio: 64.5%
Return on equity: 8.1%
Cash ($ mil.): 2.5
Current ratio: 0.81
Long-term debt ($ mil.): 143.4
No. of shares (mil.): 30.1

Dividends
  Yield: 0.0%
  Payout: —
Market value ($ mil.): 198.2
R&D as % of sales: —
Advertising as % of sales: —

Stock History NYSE: DM

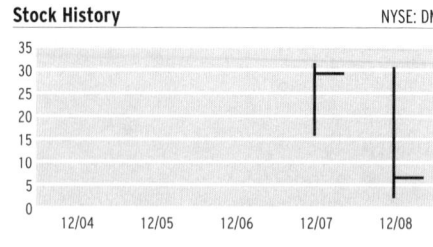

	STOCK PRICE ($) FY Close	P/E High/Low	PER SHARE ($) Earnings	Dividends	Book Value
12/08	6.59	57 5	0.53	0.00	7.39
12/07	29.17	— —	(3.41)	0.00	4.29
Annual Growth	(77.4%)	— —	—	—	72.2%

Dolby Laboratories

Talk about having a sound business model. Dolby Laboratories is the market leader in developing sound processing and noise reduction systems for use in professional and consumer audio and video equipment. Though it does make some of its own products, Dolby mostly licenses its technology to other manufacturers. (Licensing accounts for more than 80% of revenue.) The firm has about 1,600 patents and more than 960 trademarks worldwide. In film, the Dolby Digital format has become the de facto audio standard; its systems equip movie screens around the globe. The company has expanded into digital audio compression. American engineer and physicist Ray Dolby and his family own the company.

The more than 40-year-old company has managed to remain a technological ruler. The global transition to digital broadcast, the upgrade to high-definition (HD) technology, the increase in popularity of 3-D cinema, and the advancement in online and mobile delivery has helped Dolby's business. The company is the leading maker of the digital sound technology built into DVD and CD players, surround-sound theater systems, and HD TV sets. Its system records the sounds of nearly every movie, professional music performance, and radio and TV broadcast in the world. About two-thirds of the company's sales come from outside the US.

Dolby's largest customer group comes from the personal computer market; in 2009 personal computing clients were responsible for some 35% of licensing revenues. Software giant Microsoft, a Dolby licensee, includes Dolby technologies in several versions of its Vista and Windows 7 operating systems, and accounts for about 10% of the company's revenue. Other major market segments served include broadcasting and consumer electronics, each of which accounts for some 25% of Dolby's licensing revenues. In addition to licensing, the company earns revenues from cinema and broadcast equipment sales and services.

In 2009 the company had a good year despite the down economy, primarily due to the proliferation of all things digital. Its revenues grew as a result of an increase in sales of TV set top boxes in the US and digital TV sets in Europe and Asia that incorporate Dolby's technology, as well as an increase in digital cinema products. At the end of 2009 movie-goers flocked to see *Avatar* at theaters equipped with Dolby 3D. Also that year, the company continued to expand its offerings with the launch of Dolby Mobile. The product is designed to enhance the audio quality of media delivered on mobile devices. In addition, in 2009 longtime Dolby executive Bill Jasper retired as president and CEO of the company. Jasper remains on the board of directors, and Kevin Yeaman, former CFO, replaced him as head of the company.

Ray Dolby founded the firm in London in 1965 and moved it to San Francisco in 1977. He controls 91% of the company's voting power.

EXECUTIVES

Chairman: Peter Gotcher, age 50
President and CEO: Kevin J. Yeaman, age 43, $2,077,610 total compensation
EVP and CFO: Murray J. Demo, age 48, $639,569 total compensation
EVP Products and Technologies:
 Michael J. (Mike) Rockwell, age 42, $1,152,804 total compensation
EVP Sales and Marketing: Ramzi Haidamus, age 45
SVP and CIO: George Lin
SVP Sales: J. Stuart Mitchell
SVP Human Resources: Andrew Dahlkemper
SVP and CTO: Craig Todd
SVP Research: Steven E. (Steve) Forshay, age 53
SVP Marketing: Robin Selden
SVP Corporate Development: Eric Cohen
Investor Relations: Alex Hughes
Auditors: KPMG LLP

LOCATIONS

HQ: Dolby Laboratories, Inc.
 100 Potrero Ave., San Francisco, CA 94103
Phone: 415-558-0200   **Fax:** 415-863-1373
Web: www.dolby.com

2009 Sales

	$ mil.	% of total
US	467.2	35
Other countries	252.3	65
Total	**719.5**	**100**

2009 Sales

	% of total
Asia	
Japan	21
Taiwan	11
South Korea	8
China	6
US	35
Europe	17
Other regions	2
Total	**100**

PRODUCTS/OPERATIONS

2009 Sales

	$ mil.	% of total
Technology licensing	594.7	83
Product sales	96.0	13
Production services	28.8	4
Total	**719.5**	**100**

Selected Dolby Technologies

Advanced Audio Coding (AAC, audio compression technology)
Dolby 3D (3-D image delivery)
Dolby AC-2 (digital audio processing for satellite and digital audio storage)
Dolby Digital (digital sound for film soundtracks and DVDs)
Dolby Digital Surround EX (expanded surround sound for theaters)
Dolby E (eight-channel digital sound systems)
Dolby Headphone (audio processing for headphone applications)
Dolby Mobile (digital audio processing for mobile devices)
Dolby SR (spectral recording, used in professional audio equipment)
Dolby Surround (four-channel sound for home theaters)

COMPETITORS

Ascent Media	QSound Labs
DivX	RealNetworks
DTS	Sony
Eastman Kodak	SRS Labs
Microsoft	THOMSON
NEC	THX

HISTORICAL FINANCIALS
Company Type: Public

Income Statement
FYE: Last Friday in September

	REVENUE ($ mil.)	NET INCOME ($ mil.)	NET PROFIT MARGIN	EMPLOYEES
9/09	719.5	243.0	33.8%	1,135
9/08	640.2	199.5	31.2%	1,153
9/07	482.0	142.8	29.6%	976
9/06	391.5	89.5	22.9%	864
9/05	328.0	52.3	15.9%	825
Annual Growth	**21.7%**	**46.8%**	**—**	**8.3%**

2009 Year-End Financials

Debt ratio: 0.4%
Return on equity: 20.3%
Cash ($ mil.): 451.7
Current ratio: 5.75
Long-term debt ($ mil.): 5.8
No. of shares (mil.): 114.0

Dividends
 Yield: —
 Payout: —
Market value ($ mil.): 4,354.6
R&D as % of sales: —
Advertising as % of sales: —

Stock History
NYSE: DLB

	STOCK PRICE ($) FY Close	P/E High/Low	Earnings	PER SHARE ($) Dividends	Book Value
9/09	38.19	20 12	2.11	—	11.76
9/08	35.19	31 19	1.74	—	9.20
9/07	34.82	30 15	1.26	—	6.99
9/06	19.85	30 18	0.80	—	5.21
9/05	16.00	51 29	0.50	—	4.04
Annual Growth	**24.3%**	**— —**	**43.3%**	**—**	**30.6%**

Double Eagle Petroleum

It's double or nothing for Double Eagle Petroleum (formerly Double Eagle Petroleum and Mining), which gambles on hitting pay dirt as it explores for and produces oil and gas in the Rocky Mountains of Utah and Wyoming. Double Eagle owns interests in 888 producing wells, and natural gas accounts for more than 95% of the oil and gas independent's production and reserves. The company has proved reserves of more than 413,000 barrels of oil and 71.3 billion cu. ft. of natural gas, and leases acreage in seven states. Double Eagle sells its oil and gas on the spot market.

In 2007 Double Eagle had working interests in 473,724 gross (263,745 net) developed and undeveloped acres.

The company pursues a strategy of growing reserves and production through the development of existing properties, selectively moving into new exploration projects, and complementary acquisitions.

In 2009 Double Eagle acquired fellow explorer Petrosearch Energy.

EXECUTIVES

Chairman, President, and CEO: Richard D. (Dick) Dole,
age 64, $598,308 total compensation
CFO: Kurtis S. Hooley, age 44,
$451,728 total compensation
SVP Exploration and New Ventures:
D. Steven Degenfelder, age 52,
$402,742 total compensation
VP Eastern Washakie Midstream: Aubrey Harper,
age 58, $240,346 total compensation
VP Operations: Robert F. Reiner, age 61,
$345,499 total compensation
VP and Controller: Ashley Jenkins
Investor Relations: John Campbell
Secretary: Carol A. Osborne, age 57
Auditors: Hein & Associates LLP

LOCATIONS

HQ: Double Eagle Petroleum Co.
1675 Broadway, Ste. 2200, Denver, CO 80202
Phone: 303-794-8445   **Fax:** 303-794-8451
Web: www.dble.us

Double Eagle Petroleum explores for oil and gas in the
Christmas Meadows area in northeastern Utah, the
Green River Basin in southwestern Wyoming, the
Powder River Basin in northeastern Wyoming, the
Washakie Basin in south central Wyoming, and the Wind
River Basin in central Wyoming.

PRODUCTS/OPERATIONS

2008 Sales

	$ mil.	% of total
Oil & gas	39.2	79
Price risk management	5.3	11
Transportation & gathering	4.8	10
Other	0.3	—
Total	**49.6**	**100**

2008 Sales

	% of total
Gas	95
Oil	5
Total	**100**

COMPETITORS

Abraxas Petroleum
BP
Delta Petroleum
Devon Energy
Exxon Mobil
Noble Energy
Samson Oil
Stone Energy
Swift Energy

HISTORICAL FINANCIALS

Company Type: Public

Income Statement

FYE: December 31

	REVENUE ($ mil.)	NET INCOME ($ mil.)	NET PROFIT MARGIN	EMPLOYEES
12/08	49.6	10.4	21.0%	26
12/07	17.2	(13.4)	—	15
12/06	19.0	2.1	11.1%	17
12/05	20.5	4.0	19.5%	14
12/04	13.3	4.0	30.1%	3
Annual Growth	**39.0%**	**27.0%**	**—**	**71.6%**

2008 Year-End Financials

Debt ratio: 46.8%
Return on equity: 24.9%
Cash ($ mil.): 0.0
Current ratio: 0.86
Long-term debt ($ mil.): 25.7
No. of shares (mil.): 11.0
Dividends
  Yield: —
  Payout: —
Market value ($ mil.): 77.5
R&D as % of sales: —
Advertising as % of sales: —

Stock History

NASDAQ (GS): DBLE

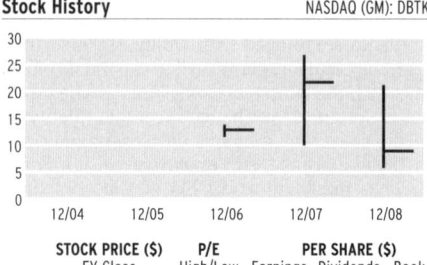

	STOCK PRICE ($) FY Close	P/E High/Low		PER SHARE ($) Earnings	Dividends	Book Value
12/08	7.02	27	6	0.73	—	4.97
12/07	15.76	—	—	(1.47)	—	2.59
12/06	24.55	123	58	0.24	—	2.99
12/05	20.40	55	34	0.46	—	2.70
12/04	19.31	43	25	0.47	—	2.26
Annual Growth	**(22.4%)**	**—**	**—**	**11.6%**	**—**	**21.8%**

Double-Take Software

Double-Take Software helps companies take a
second look at their data protection. The company provides data-replication-and-storage software designed to help businesses protect and
manage data assets. Its core Double-Take product line features data backup and disaster recovery software for a variety of systems; the
company also offers professional services such
as consulting, implementation, and support.
Double-Take's customers come from fields such
as education, financial and legal services, government, health care, manufacturing, retail, and
telecommunications. The company sells its
products through resellers, server makers such
as Dell and Hewlett-Packard (HP), and distributors like Bell Microproducts and Tech Data.

The company's growth strategy includes plans
to broaden its distribution network in its current
markets and move into new international markets through direct sales channels and by leveraging its relationship with HP. Double-Take is
also focusing on expanding its product offerings.

About 14% of the company's shares are owned
and managed by affiliates of ABS Capital Partners;
one of ABS Capital Partners' general partners,
Ashoke (Bobby) Goswami, sits on Double-Take's
board of directors.

EXECUTIVES

Chairman, President, and CEO: Dean F. Goodermote,
age 55, $1,033,814 total compensation
CTO: David J. Demlow, age 41
VP and CFO: S. Craig Huke, age 47,
$410,384 total compensation
VP Engineering: Robert L. (Rob) Beeler, age 43,
$342,552 total compensation
VP Professional Services and Support:
Michael (Mike) Lesh, age 64
VP Sales and Marketing: Daniel M. (Dan) Jones, age 41,
$566,259 total compensation
VP International: Jo Murciano, age 57,
$668,424 total compensation
UK Sales Director: Ian Masters
Director Business Development: Christian Tate
Auditors: Eisner LLP

LOCATIONS

HQ: Double-Take Software, Inc.
257 Turnpike Rd., Ste. 210
Southborough, MA 01772
Phone: 508-229-8483   **Fax:** 508-229-0866
Web: www.doubletake.com

2008 Sales

	% of total
The Americas	64
Europe, Middle East, & Africa	31
Asia/Pacific	5
Total	**100**

PRODUCTS/OPERATIONS

2008 Sales

	% of total
Software licenses	55
Maintenance & professional services	45
Total	**100**

COMPETITORS

CA, Inc.
CommVault
DataCore
EMC
FalconStor
Hitachi Data Systems
IBM
Microsoft
Symantec

HISTORICAL FINANCIALS

Company Type: Public

Income Statement

FYE: December 31

	REVENUE ($ mil.)	NET INCOME ($ mil.)	NET PROFIT MARGIN	EMPLOYEES
12/08	96.3	17.6	18.3%	392
12/07	82.8	20.1	24.3%	354
12/06	60.8	(0.6)	—	301
12/05	40.7	(11.8)	—	296
12/04	29.8	(8.0)	—	—
Annual Growth	**34.1%**	**—**	**—**	**9.8%**

2008 Year-End Financials

Debt ratio: 0.0%
Return on equity: 20.8%
Cash ($ mil.): 40.7
Current ratio: 3.09
Long-term debt ($ mil.): 0.0
No. of shares (mil.): 22.1
Dividends
  Yield: 0.0%
  Payout: —
Market value ($ mil.): 198.0
R&D as % of sales: —
Advertising as % of sales: —

Stock History

NASDAQ (GM): DBTK

	STOCK PRICE ($) FY Close	P/E High/Low		PER SHARE ($) Earnings	Dividends	Book Value
12/08	8.97	28	8	0.76	0.00	4.23
12/07	21.72	31	12	0.87	0.00	3.42
12/06	12.88	—	—	(0.13)	0.00	2.05
Annual Growth	**(16.5%)**	**—**	**—**	**—**	**—**	**43.7%**

Dril-Quip, Inc.

Dril-Quip equips the folks with the drills — the oil and gas industry. Its products include drilling and production riser systems, subsea and surface wellheads and production trees, mudline hanger systems, and specialty connectors and pipe. Dril-Quip's offshore rig equipment includes drilling and completion riser systems, wellhead connectors and diverters. The company, which specializes in deep-water or severe-condition equipment, also provides installation, reconditioning, and tool-rental services. Dril-Quip has major manufacturing plants in Brazil, Singapore, the UK, and the US.

The company's global manufacturing and servicing locations allows it to have short supply lines and delivery times for its clients in far-flung oil and gas fields worldwide. Dril-Quip's top 15 customers account for 45% of total revenues. Non-US business accounts for 69% of total sales.

In 2006 Dril-Quip installed its first subsea control system, a "signal on power" multiplex system that controls both a satellite subsea tree and subsea manifold.

In 2008 co-chairmen and co-founders Larry Reimert, Gary Smith (who died in 1999), and Mike Walker owned 7%, 8%, and 11% of the company, respectively.

EXECUTIVES

Co-Chairman and Co-CEO: Larry E. Reimert, age 61, $1,484,230 total compensation
Co-Chairman and Co-CEO: J. Mike Walker, age 66, $1,484,230 total compensation
VP Finance and CFO: Jerry M. Brooks, age 58, $456,766 total compensation
Auditors: BDO Seidman, LLP

LOCATIONS

HQ: Dril-Quip, Inc.
13550 Hempstead Hwy., Houston, TX 77040
Phone: 713-939-7711 **Fax:** 713-939-8063
Web: www.dril-quip.com

2008 Sales

	$ mil.	% of total
Western Hemisphere	332.3	54
Eastern Hemisphere	190.8	31
Asia/Pacific	93.7	15
Adjustments	(74.0)	—
Total	**542.8**	**100**

PRODUCTS/OPERATIONS

2008 Sales

	$ mil.	% of total
Products	453.3	84
Services	89.5	16
Total	**542.8**	**100**

Selected Products and Services

Product Group
 Diverters
 Drilling riser systems
 Mudline hanger systems
 Platform production trees
 Platform wellheads
 Production risers
 Specialty connectors
 Subsea production trees
 Subsea wellheads
 Surface wellheads
 Wellhead connectors
 Valves
 Well systems

Service Group
 Field installation
 Reconditioning
 Rental

COMPETITORS

ABB	FMC
Aker Solutions	Global Power Equipment
Cameron International	McDermott

HISTORICAL FINANCIALS

Company Type: Public

Income Statement

FYE: December 31

	REVENUE ($ mil.)	NET INCOME ($ mil.)	NET PROFIT MARGIN	EMPLOYEES
12/08	542.8	105.6	19.5%	2,051
12/07	495.6	107.9	21.8%	1,890
12/06	442.7	86.9	19.6%	1,709
12/05	340.8	32.6	9.6%	1,514
12/04	221.6	12.5	5.6%	1,289
Annual Growth	**25.1%**	**70.5%**	**—**	**12.3%**

2008 Year-End Financials

Debt ratio: 0.2%
Return on equity: 18.3%
Cash ($ mil.): 96.0
Current ratio: 4.52
Long-term debt ($ mil.): 0.9
No. of shares (mil.): 39.4

Dividends
 Yield: —
 Payout: —
Market value ($ mil.): 808.9
R&D as % of sales: —
Advertising as % of sales: —

Stock History

NYSE: DRQ

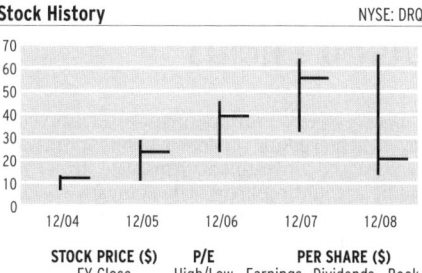

	STOCK PRICE ($) FY Close	P/E High/Low		Earnings	PER SHARE ($) Dividends	Book Value
12/08	20.51	25	5	2.62	—	14.18
12/07	55.66	24	12	2.63	—	15.02
12/06	39.16	21	11	2.15	—	11.85
12/05	23.60	31	13	0.90	—	8.35
12/04	12.13	35	20	0.36	—	5.49
Annual Growth	**14.0%**	**—**	**—**	**64.2%**	**—**	**26.8%**

Ducommun Incorporated

Plans are always up in the air at Ducommun (rhymes with "uncommon"). The company makes aerostructures and electromechanical components for commercial and military aircraft, as well as missile and space programs. Ducommun AeroStructures manufactures structures and assemblies such as aircraft wing spoilers and helicopter blades using shaped aluminum, composites, and titanium. Ducommun Technologies makes electromechanical components such as switch assemblies, actuators, gyroscopes, keyboard panels, and avionics racks. Its

Miltec subsidiary designs missile and aerospace systems. Products destined for military applications account for more than half of sales. Aircraft giant Boeing represents about 30% of sales.

Other major customers include Raytheon and the US government (about 10% of sales). Sales to Ducommun's top customers reflect a mix of military, commercial, and space-related business.

In late 2008 Ducommun paid more than $46 million in cash and notes to acquire privately held DynaBil Industries, Inc., of Coxsackie, New York. DynaBil broadens Ducommun's product line by making titanium and aluminum structural components and assemblies for commercial and military aerospace applications. The firm became part of Ducommun AeroStructures.

The company has manufacturing facilities in Alabama, Arizona, California, Kansas, Mississippi, and New York. It also makes its components in Mexico and Thailand.

In January 2010 Joseph Berenato resigned as CEO but remained chairman. Tony Reardon, who had served as president and COO since 2008, was named to replace Berenato. Reardon previously led the company's AeroStructures subsidiary, and has more than 25 years of experience in the aviation industry.

HISTORY

Swiss immigrant Charles Ducommun walked from Arkansas to California to take part in the California Gold Rush in 1849. He soon started a small watch-repair shop and then expanded his business to include general supplies. In the early 1900s the firm moved into the metals business as Ducommun Hardware Company and started making parts for California's aviation industry. The firm profited from increased demand during both World Wars, and by the 1960s Ducommun had expanded into the electronics industry. It sold its metals business in 1981 and used the proceeds to buy aerospace companies.

The semiconductor business went bust in the early 1980s, hurting Ducommun's sales. In 1986 the *Challenger* space shuttle explosion also took its toll on the company as the government scaled back on the space program. In 1987 Ducommun sold its electronics companies to Arrow Electronics, the world's leading electronics distributor.

In 1988 the company began cutting costs and restructuring and by 1990 had made a small profit. In 1994 Ducommun began to remake itself as an aerospace component supplier. It bought Brice (aircraft seating, 1994), 3dbm (telecommunications, 1995), and MechTronics (radar enclosures, 1996). A revived aerospace industry took off in 1997, fueling Ducommun's growth. Focusing on the aerospace industry, the company sold 3dbm to COM DEV International (1998) and bought Jordan Industries' titanium components unit (1999).

In 2001 Ducommun announced the creation of Ducommun AeroStructures, a combination of three of its subsidiaries (AHF-Ducommun Incorporated, Aerochem, Inc., and Parsons Precision Products, Inc.), in an effort to reduce costs. Later in the year the company combined Ducommun AeroStructures with Composite Structures LLC. Ducommun sold Brice Manufacturing Company, its airline seating manufacturer, in 2002. The next year Ducommun acquired DBP Microwave, a maker of radio frequency and microwave switches, and incorporated those operations into its Technologies sector.

Ducommun went on a buying spree in 2006, spending roughly $66 million to acquire three

new operations. Those were Miltec, which provides missiles and aerospace systems; WiseWave, a maker of microwave and millimeter-wave products; and CMP Display Systems, a light-emitting diode (LED) edge-lit panel manufacturer. All three acquisitions were incorporated into Ducommun Technologies as part of an effort to bolster sales for that segment, which served primarily military customers.

EXECUTIVES

Chairman: Joseph C. Berenato, age 62, $1,927,776 total compensation
President, CEO, COO and Director: Anthony (Tony) J. Reardon, age 58, $1,192,398 total compensation
VP and CFO: Joseph P. (Joe) Bellino, age 58, $170,337 total compensation
VP, General Counsel, and Secretary: James S. Heiser, age 52, $747,361 total compensation
VP and Controller: Samuel D. Williams, age 60, $522,960 total compensation
VP and Treasurer: Donald C. DeVore, age 47
VP Human Resources: Rosalie F. Rogers, age 47
VP Intenal Audit: Kathryn M. Andrus, age 41
President, Miltec: James (Mike) Stanfield
Auditors: PricewaterhouseCoopers LLP

LOCATIONS

HQ: Ducommun Incorporated
23301 Wilmington Ave., Carson, CA 90745
Phone: 310-513-7280   **Fax:** 310-513-7279
Web: www.ducommun.com

PRODUCTS/OPERATIONS

2008 Sales

	$ mil.	% of total
AeroStructures	251.2	62
Technologies	152.6	38
Total	**403.8**	**100**

COMPETITORS

AIM Group
Barnes Group
BBT Thermotechnik
BE Aerospace
C&D Zodiac
CPI Aerostructures
DeCrane
Esterline
GE
Goodrich Corp.
Hunting
Kreisler Manufacturing
L-3 Avionics
LMI Aerospace
Magellan Aerospace
Orbit International
Panasonic Corp
Smiths Group
Vought Aircraft

HISTORICAL FINANCIALS

Company Type: Public

Income Statement

				FYE: December 31
	REVENUE ($ mil.)	NET INCOME ($ mil.)	NET PROFIT MARGIN	EMPLOYEES
12/08	403.8	13.1	3.2%	2,048
12/07	367.3	19.6	5.3%	1,865
12/06	319.0	14.3	4.5%	1,740
12/05	249.7	16.0	6.4%	1,353
12/04	224.9	11.2	5.0%	1,337
Annual Growth	15.8%	4.0%	—	11.2%

2008 Year-End Financials

Debt ratio: 12.6%
Return on equity: 6.0%
Cash ($ mil.): 3.5
Current ratio: 1.78
Long-term debt ($ mil.): 28.3
No. of shares (mil.): 10.5
Dividends
  Yield: 0.9%
  Payout: 12.2%
Market value ($ mil.): 174.5
R&D as % of sales: —
Advertising as % of sales: —

Stock History

NYSE: DCO

	STOCK PRICE ($) FY Close	P/E High/Low		PER SHARE ($) Earnings	Dividends	Book Value
12/08	16.70	29	10	1.23	0.15	21.48
12/07	38.00	23	11	1.88	0.00	20.48
12/06	22.88	19	12	1.39	0.00	17.90
12/05	21.36	14	10	1.57	0.00	16.06
12/04	20.85	23	17	1.10	0.00	14.50
Annual Growth	(5.4%)	—	—	2.8%	—	10.3%

Duff & Phelps

Duff & Phelps provides financial advisory and investment banking services to public and private corporations, investment firms, law firms, and public accounting firms. The company specializes in offering fairness opinions regarding financial reporting, tax valuations, real estate and other asset valuations, and dispute resolution. Its investment banking services include mergers and acquisitions advice, financial restructurings, private placements of shares, or other transactions. Its Chanin Capital Partners unit provides similar services to smaller firms. Duff & Phelps has about 24 offices worldwide. Duff & Phelps went public in 2007.

Duff & Phelps formed an operational risk due diligence practice in 2009 that will provide investors with an independent assessment of their hedge fund manager's operating policies and procedures. The practice will assist pension plans, endowments, family offices, and fund of funds to assess the operational risks associated with their alternative investments.

Duff & Phelps made a number of acquisitions in 2008 to bolster its tax and litigation practice. It acquired Kane Reece Associates, which provides valuation and management consulting for the media, communications, and other industries. It also acquired Lumin Expert Group, a Houston-based business specializing in intellectual property and expert testimony; World Tax Service US, an advisory firm focused on international and domestic tax services; and litigation and support services consulting firm Dubinsky and Company.

Vestar Capital Partners and Lovell Minnick Equity Partners own about 20% and 15%, respectively, of the company. Duff & Phelps Corporation is unrelated to Duff & Phelps Investment Management, which is owned by The Phoenix Companies.

EXECUTIVES

Chairman and CEO: Noah Gottdiener, age 52, $4,628,411 total compensation
President and Director: Gerard (Gerry) Creagh, age 50, $5,103,945 total compensation
EVP and COO: Brett A. Marschke, age 46, $2,374,306 total compensation
EVP and CFO: Jacob L. Silverman, age 37, $2,472,740 total compensation
EVP, General Counsel, and Secretary: Edward S. Forman, age 40, $1,684,558 total compensation
Managing Director and Head, Investment Banking: Steve Burt
Auditors: Grant Thornton LLP

LOCATIONS

HQ: Duff & Phelps Corporation
55 E. 52nd. St., Fl. 31, New York, NY 10055
Phone: 212-871-2000
Web: www.duffandphelps.com

2008 Sales

	% of total
US	90
Europe	9
Asia	1
Total	**100**

PRODUCTS/OPERATIONS

2008 Sales

	$ mil.	% of total
Financial advisory	309.7	79
Investment banking	71.8	18
Reimbursable expenses	10.5	3
Total	**392.0**	**100**

COMPETITORS

Accenture
Citigroup Global Markets
Deloitte
Ernst & Young Global
Goldman Sachs
Grant Thornton International
H&R Block
KPMG
Merrill Lynch
Morgan Stanley
PricewaterhouseCoopers
RBC Wealth Management
UBS Financial Services

HISTORICAL FINANCIALS

Company Type: Public

Income Statement

				FYE: December 31
	REVENUE ($ mil.)	NET INCOME ($ mil.)	NET PROFIT MARGIN	EMPLOYEES
12/08	392.0	5.2	1.3%	1,236
12/07	353.9	0.5	0.1%	1,070
12/06	259.3	10.5	4.0%	870
12/05	78.2	(12.5)	—	—
12/04	30.5	1.8	5.9%	—
Annual Growth	89.3%	30.4%	—	19.2%

2008 Year-End Financials

Debt ratio: 42.1%
Return on equity: 6.1%
Cash ($ mil.): 81.4
Current ratio: 2.59
Long-term debt ($ mil.): 42.2
No. of shares (mil.): 40.2
Dividends
  Yield: —
  Payout: —
Market value ($ mil.): 769.2
R&D as % of sales: —
Advertising as % of sales: —

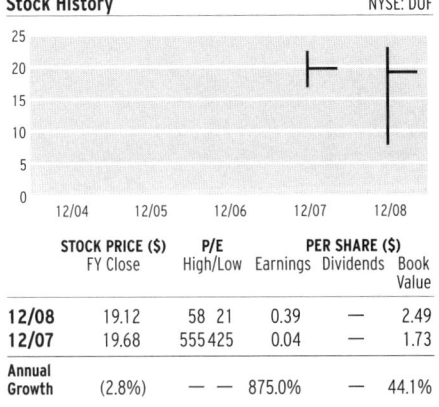

Stock History

NYSE: DUF

	STOCK PRICE ($) FY Close	P/E High/Low		PER SHARE ($) Earnings	Dividends	Book Value
12/08	19.12	58 21		0.39	—	2.49
12/07	19.68	555 425		0.04	—	1.73
Annual Growth	(2.8%)	— —		875.0%	—	44.1%

DuPont Fabros Technology

DuPont Fabros Technology owns, develops, operates, and manages wholesale data centers — the facilities that house, power, and cool computer servers for such technology companies as Facebook, Google, Microsoft, and Yahoo! The company establishes its rental rates based on the amount of power reserved for tenant use and the square footage they occupy. As a wholesale provider the company targets clients with high power requirements and a preference for long-term licenses.

DuPont Fabros Technology developed its wholesale data centers to compete with more traditional colocation models in which managed services are bundled with power and cooling. Wholesale customers typically install and maintain their own servers.

The company's largest clients, Microsoft and Yahoo!, account for 70% of its annualized rent.

EXECUTIVES

Chairman: Lammot J. du Pont, age 42,
$258,841 total compensation
President, CEO, and Director: Hossein Fateh, age 41,
$258,841 total compensation
EVP, CFO, and Treasurer: Mark L. Wetzel, age 50,
$335,710 total compensation
SVP Sales and Leasing: M. Lee Kestler Jr., age 45
SVP Finance and Acquisitions: Maria Kenny, age 42
SVP Construction: Robert J. Berlinsky, age 49
SVP Operations: Scott A. Davis, age 49
General Counsel and Secretary:
Richard A. (Rick) Montfort Jr., age 48,
$365,029 total compensation
Investor Relations: Victoria (Vicki) Baker
Human Resources: Kathy Murphy
Auditors: Ernst & Young LLP

LOCATIONS

HQ: DuPont Fabros Technology, Inc.
1212 New York Ave. NW, Ste. 900
Washington, DC 20005
Phone: 202-728-0044   **Fax:** 202-728-0220
Web: www.dft.com

COMPETITORS

AT&T
Digital Realty
Equinix
Internap Network Services
Rackspace
SAVVIS
Verizon

HISTORICAL FINANCIALS

Company Type: Public

Income Statement

FYE: December 31

	REVENUE ($ mil.)	NET INCOME ($ mil.)	NET PROFIT MARGIN	EMPLOYEES
12/08	173.7	19.1	11.0%	67
12/07	61.3	(100.9)	—	52
12/06	54.8	0.8	1.5%	50
Annual Growth	78.0%	388.6%	—	15.8%

2008 Year-End Financials

Debt ratio: —
Return on equity: 3.4%
Cash ($ mil.): 53.5
Current ratio: 0.20
Long-term debt ($ mil.): —
No. of shares (mil.): 42.0
Dividends
  Yield: 18.1%
  Payout: 70.4%
Market value ($ mil.): 86.9
R&D as % of sales: —
Advertising as % of sales: —

Stock History

NYSE: DFT

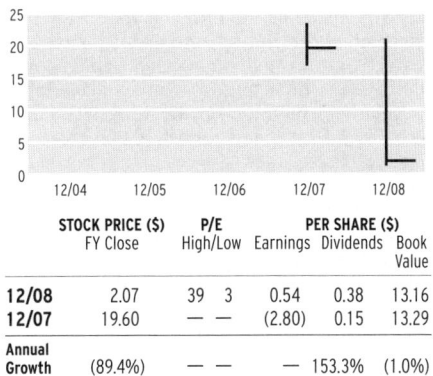

	STOCK PRICE ($) FY Close	P/E High/Low		PER SHARE ($) Earnings	Dividends	Book Value
12/08	2.07	39 3		0.54	0.38	13.16
12/07	19.60	— —		(2.80)	0.15	13.29
Annual Growth	(89.4%)	— —		—	153.3%	(1.0%)

DXP Enterprises

DXP Enterprises is well-equipped to meet its customers' needs. The company distributes maintenance, repair, and operating (MRO) equipment and products, primarily to the oil and gas, petrochemical, and wood products industries. It also distributes centrifugal pumps, rotary gear pumps, plunger pumps, and other fluid-handling equipment as well as bearings and power transmission equipment, general mill (cutting tools) and safety supplies, and electrical products (wire conduit). DXP's MRO unit also provides system design, fabrication, and repair services. DXP's electrical contractor division sells a range of electrical products including wire conduit, wiring devices, electrical fittings and boxes, and tools.

DXP tends to grow strategically by acquiring niche companies that enhance its existing businesses, which enables the company to quickly integrate the products and reap the resulting benefits and profits.

From 2006-2009 DXP completed nine acquisitions, ranging in value from $2.2 million to $106 million. Major purchases included buying industrial products distributor Precision Industries, Inc., and paying $65 million to buy PFI, a distributor of fasteners, rivets, and clamps.

Unlike many of its smaller competitors, DXP operates as a first-tier distributor, getting its products directly from manufacturers, which typically allows it to offer very competitive pricing on the goods it distributes.

Chairman, CEO, and president David Little owns about 14% of DXP Enterprises; SVP David Vinson holds around 22% of the company.

EXECUTIVES

Chairman, President, and CEO: David R. Little, age 57,
$1,480,146 total compensation
SVP Service Centers: Gregory Oliver, age 49,
$427,336 total compensation
SVP Finance, CFO, and Secretary: Mac McConnell,
age 55, $495,838 total compensation
SVP Strategic Initiatives and Director:
Charles R. (Chuck) Strader, age 58
SVP Innovative Pumping Solutions: David C. Vinson,
age 58, $450,925 total compensation
VP Information Technology: Suzhanna Dahle, age 58
Auditors: Hein & Associates LLP

LOCATIONS

HQ: DXP Enterprises, Inc.
7272 Pinemont, Houston, TX 77040
Phone: 713-996-4700   **Fax:** 713-996-4701
Web: www.dxpe.com

PRODUCTS/OPERATIONS

Maintenance, Repair, and Operating (MRO)
Equipment and Products
Fluid handling equipment
  Air-operated diaphragm pumps
  Centrifugal pumps
  Piston pumps
  Plunger pumps
  Rotary gear pumps
General mill and safety supplies
  Abrasives
  Coatings and lubricants
  Cutting tools
  Eye and face protection products
  Fasteners
  First aid products
  Hand tools
  Hazardous material handling products
  Instrumentation and respiratory protection products
  Janitorial products
  Pneumatic tools
  Protection products
  Tapes and adhesive products
  Welding equipment
Hoses
  Expansion joints
  Hydraulic hoses
  Industrial fittings
  Stainless steel hoses
  Teflon hoses
Power Transmission Equipment
  Brakes
  Chain drives
  Clutches
  Conveyors
  Flexible coupling drives
  Gears
  Speed reducers
  Sprockets

Electrical Contractor Products

Batteries
Electrical fittings and boxes
Fans and fuses
Heaters
Lamps
Lighting
Lugs
Signaling devices
Switch gear
Tape
Tools
Wire conduit
Wire nuts
Wiring devices

COMPETITORS

Applied Industrial Technologies
Dillon Supply
DoALL
Graco
HWC
Industrial Distribution Group
MSC Industrial Direct
MSC/J&L Metalworking
Production Tool Supply
Roper Industries
R.S. Hughes

HISTORICAL FINANCIALS

Company Type: Public

Income Statement

FYE: December 31

	REVENUE ($ mil.)	NET INCOME ($ mil.)	NET PROFIT MARGIN	EMPLOYEES
12/08	736.9	25.9	3.5%	1,874
12/07	444.5	17.3	3.9%	1,603
12/06	279.8	11.8	4.2%	763
12/05	185.4	5.4	2.9%	519
12/04	160.6	2.8	1.7%	448
Annual Growth	46.4%	74.4%	—	43.0%

2008 Year-End Financials

Debt ratio: 118.8%
Return on equity: 22.4%
Cash ($ mil.): 5.7
Current ratio: 2.25
Long-term debt ($ mil.): 154.6
No. of shares (mil.): 12.9

Dividends
  Yield: 0.0%
  Payout: —
Market value ($ mil.): 189.0
R&D as % of sales: —
Advertising as % of sales: —

Stock History

NASDAQ (GS): DXPE

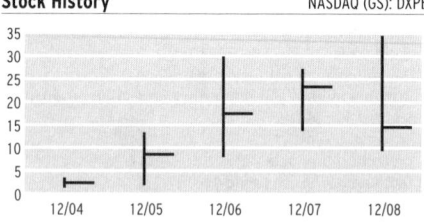

	STOCK PRICE ($) FY Close	P/E High/Low		PER SHARE ($) Earnings	Dividends	Book Value
12/08	14.61	18	5	1.89	0.00	10.06
12/07	23.34	20	10	1.36	0.00	7.85
12/06	17.52	28	8	1.04	0.00	2.76
12/05	8.60	28	5	0.47	0.00	1.51
12/04	2.40	13	7	0.25	0.00	1.00
Annual Growth	57.1%	—	—	65.8%	—	78.3%

Dynamic Materials

Dynamic Materials Corporation (DMC) has an explosive personality when it comes to working with metal. Formerly Explosive Fabricators, the company uses explosives to metallurgically bond, or "clad," metal plates; the process usually joins a corrosion-resistant alloy with carbon steel, metals that do not bond easily. Its clad metal plates are central to making heavy-duty pressure vessels and heat exchangers used in industries from alternative energy to shipbuilding. In addition to explosive metalworking, DMC produces and sells oilfield components used to knock open oil and gas wells. Its subsidiary, AMK Welding, machines and welds parts for commercial and military aircraft engines and power-generation turbines.

DMC strives for a global presence in targeting energy and process industries that require high-strength, corrosion-resistant metals for new construction of large industrial equipment and materials, and facility maintenance. DMC's reach is driven through manufacturing plants in Pennsylvania, Germany, France, and Sweden, and a worldwide network of sales professionals.

Acquisitions of complementary businesses are enhancing the breadth and depth of DMC's operations, too. In October 2009 the company acquired Canada-based LRI Oil Tools (LRI), a producer of perforating equipment for oil and gas exploration and production applications. DMC values the acquisition for its geographic and market expansion opportunities. The deal includes $650,000 and almost 10,000 shares of DMC restricted stock.

In 2007 DMC boosted its explosives business operation with the purchase of Germany-based DYNAenergetics. The addition reinforces DMC's lineup of clad metal plates and hooked an assortment of explosives-related oil field products. Leveraging the capabilities of its new oil field products, DMC is broadening its international oil and gas industry services by offering to design and manufacture custom-ordered products for third-party end-users. The deal for DYNAenergetics topped an earlier acquisition. DMC picked up Nobelclad, a French maker of explosion-welded clad offerings, in 2001.

EXECUTIVES

Chairman: Dean K. Allen, age 74
President, CEO, and Director: Yvon Pierre Cariou, age 64, $2,038,384 total compensation
SVP, CFO, and Secretary: Richard A. (Rick) Santa, age 58, $1,083,464 total compensation
SVP Customers and Technology; VP Sales and Marketing, Clad Metal Group: John G. Banker, age 63, $1,128,211 total compensation
Director; CEO, DYNAenergetics; President, Oilfield Products Division: Rolf Rospek, age 51
Controller: Don Rittenhouse
Auditors: Ernst & Young LLP

LOCATIONS

HQ: Dynamic Materials Corporation
  5405 Spine Rd., Boulder, CO 80301
Phone: 303-665-5700   **Fax:** 303-604-1897
Web: www.dynamicmaterials.com

2008 Sales

	$ mil.	% of total
US	82.0	35
Germany	24.5	10
South Korea	12.9	6
Canada	11.7	5
Australia	11.3	5
France	10.5	4
Italy	9.5	4
China	8.2	4
India	7.2	3
Spain	7.2	3
Netherlands	4.1	2
Russia	3.6	2
South Africa	3.4	1
Belgium	3.3	1
UK	3.2	1
Romania	2.6	1
Kazakhstan	2.4	1
Mexico	2.4	1
Malaysia	1.9	1
Switzerland	1.9	1
Norway	1.7	1
Brazil	1.6	1
Sweden	1.4	1
Other countries	14.1	6
Total	**232.6**	**100**

PRODUCTS/OPERATIONS

2008 Sales

	$ mil.	% of total
Explosive Metalworking	195.0	84
Oilfield Products	27.8	12
AMK Welding	9.8	4
Total	**232.6**	**100**

COMPETITORS

Alliant Techsystems
American Commerce Solutions
AMETEK
Asahi Kasei
Eagle-Picher
Engineered Materials Solutions
Halliburton
HITCO Carbon Composites
Japan Steel Works
Kaiser Aluminum
Schlumberger
Technical Materials

HISTORICAL FINANCIALS

Company Type: Public

Income Statement

FYE: December 31

	REVENUE ($ mil.)	NET INCOME ($ mil.)	NET PROFIT MARGIN	EMPLOYEES
12/08	232.6	24.1	10.4%	408
12/07	165.2	24.6	14.9%	446
12/06	113.5	20.8	18.3%	230
12/05	79.3	10.4	13.1%	181
12/04	54.2	2.8	5.2%	163
Annual Growth	43.9%	71.3%	—	25.8%

2008 Year-End Financials

Debt ratio: 39.3%
Return on equity: 22.2%
Cash ($ mil.): 14.4
Current ratio: 2.00
Long-term debt ($ mil.): 46.5
No. of shares (mil.): 12.9

Dividends
  Yield: 0.0%
  Payout: —
Market value ($ mil.): 248.8
R&D as % of sales: —
Advertising as % of sales: —

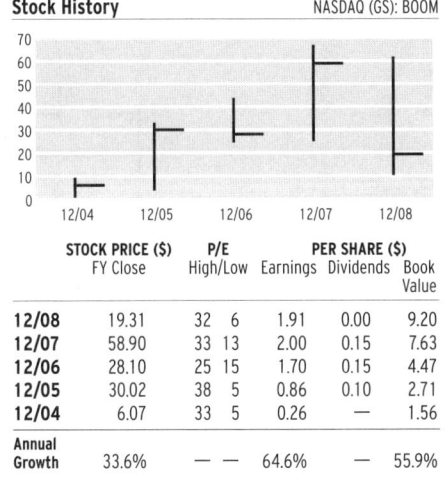

	12/04	12/05	12/06	12/07	12/08

	STOCK PRICE ($) FY Close	P/E High/Low		PER SHARE ($) Earnings	Dividends	Book Value
12/08	19.31	32	6	1.91	0.00	9.20
12/07	58.90	33	13	2.00	0.15	7.63
12/06	28.10	25	15	1.70	0.15	4.47
12/05	30.02	38	5	0.86	0.10	2.71
12/04	6.07	33	5	0.26	—	1.56
Annual Growth	33.6%	—	—	64.6%	—	55.9%

Eagle Bancorp

For those nest eggs that need a little help hatching, holding company Eagle Bancorp would recommend its community-oriented EagleBank subsidiary. The bank serves businesses and individuals through about 15 branches in Washington, DC, and its suburbs. Deposit products include checking, savings, and money market accounts; certificates of deposit; and IRAs. Commercial, residential, and construction real estate loans combined represent 70% of its loan portfolio, which also includes business (it has significant expertise as a Small Business Administration lender), consumer, and home equity loans.

In 2008 Eagle Bancorp acquired Fidelity & Trust Financial Corporation along with its Fidelity & Trust Bank subsidiary. The $13 million deal added six branches in Maryland, Northern Virginia, and Washington, DC, to its network.

A group of about a dozen officers and directors owns approximately 20% of Eagle Bancorp, led by president, CEO, and director Ronald Paul who controls 7%.

EXECUTIVES

Chairman, President, and CEO; Chairman and CEO, EagleBank: Ronald D. (Ron) Paul, age 54, $489,388 total compensation
Vice Chairman: Robert P. Pincus, age 62
EVP and COO: Michael T. (Mike) Flynn, age 62
EVP and CFO; EVP and CFO, EagleBank:
James H. Langmead, age 61, $314,758 total compensation
EVP and COO, EagleBank: Susan G. Riel, age 60, $315,857 total compensation
EVP and Chief Lending Officer, EagleBank:
Martha Foulon-Tonat, age 54, $304,482 total compensation
EVP and Chief Administrative Lending Officer:
Robert R. Hoffmann

EVP and Chief Credit Officer: Janice L. Williams
EVP and Senior Operating Officer: Kim Ray
EVP and Controller: Diane M. Begg
SVP and Director Marketing: J. Mercedes Alvarez
SVP and Chief Risk Officer: Cynthia A. Pehl
President, Montgomery County Division EagleBank:
Thomas D. Murphy, age 62, $303,294 total compensation
President, Eagle Commercial Ventures:
Richard D. Corrigan
President, EagleBank, Washington, DC and Virginia:
Barry C. Watkins
Auditors: Stegman & Company

LOCATIONS

HQ: Eagle Bancorp, Inc.
7815 Woodmont Ave., Bethesda, MD 20814
Phone: 301-986-1800   **Fax:** 301-986-8529
Web: www.eaglebankmd.com

PRODUCTS/OPERATIONS

2008 Gross Revenues

	$ mil.	% of total
Interest		
Loans	59.9	86
Securities	5.5	8
Other	0.3	—
Noninterest		
Service charges on deposits	2.4	3
Gain on sale of loans	0.4	1
Other	1.5	2
Total	**70.0**	**100**

Selected Subsidiaries

Bethesda Leasing LLC
EagleBank
Eagle Land Title Company, LLC
Eagle Commercial Ventures, LLC
Woodmont Holdings, Inc.

COMPETITORS

Bank of America
BB&T
Chevy Chase Bank
SunTrust

HISTORICAL FINANCIALS

Company Type: Public

Income Statement

	ASSETS ($ mil.)	NET INCOME ($ mil.)	INCOME AS % OF ASSETS	EMPLOYEES	FYE: December 31
12/08	1,496.8	7.4	0.5%	235	
12/07	846.4	7.7	0.9%	173	
12/06	773.5	8.0	1.0%	171	
12/05	672.3	7.5	1.1%	145	
12/04	553.5	5.1	0.9%	124	
Annual Growth	28.2%	9.8%	—	17.3%	

2008 Year-End Financials

Equity as % of assets: 7.1%
Return on assets: 0.6%
Return on equity: 7.9%
Long-term debt ($ mil.): 62.2
No. of shares (mil.): 19.5
Market value ($ mil.): 112.2
Dividends
  Yield: 1.9%
  Payout: 17.7%
Sales ($ mil.): 46.3
R&D as % of sales: —
Advertising as % of sales: —

	12/04	12/05	12/06	12/07	12/08

	STOCK PRICE ($) FY Close	P/E High/Low		PER SHARE ($) Earnings	Dividends	Book Value
12/08	5.75	21	9	0.62	0.11	7.30
12/07	11.00	22	14	0.71	0.22	4.16
12/06	15.82	26	20	0.74	0.21	3.74
12/05	16.19	25	15	0.70	0.20	3.33
12/04	11.03	24	19	0.48	—	3.00
Annual Growth	(15.0%)	—	—	6.6%	(18.1%)	24.9%

Eagle Bulk Shipping

Some eagles soar through the skies, but Eagle Bulk Shipping rides the waves. The company owns a fleet of about 20 Handymax dry bulk carriers that it charters to customers, typically on one- to three-year contracts. Most of its vessels are classified as Supramaxes — large Handymaxes, essentially. The Supramaxes range in capacity from 50,000 to 60,000 deadweight tons (DWT) and feature on-board cranes for cargo loading and unloading. Overall, the company's fleet has a carrying capacity of more than 1.1 million DWT. Cargo carried by charterers of Eagle Bulk Shipping's vessels includes cement, coal, fertilizer, grain, and iron ore.

To grow, Eagle Bulk Shipping is moving to more than double its fleet. In mid-2007, the company agreed to acquire 26 new Supramax vessels for $1.1 billion from Greece-based Kyrini Shipping. (Eagle Bulk Shipping has since amended its order to 24 vessels.) That transaction and other pending deals for new buildings will give Eagle Bulk Shipping a fleet of about 50 vessels. The newly constructed vessels are scheduled to be delivered by 2012.

EXECUTIVES

Chairman and CEO: Sophocles N. Zoullas, age 43, $20,741,976 total compensation
COO, Eagle Shipping International (USA):
Claude G. Thouret Jr.
CFO and Secretary: Alan S. Ginsberg, age 50, $1,942,679 total compensation
Auditors: Ernst & Young LLP

LOCATIONS

HQ: Eagle Bulk Shipping Inc.
477 Madison Ave., Ste. 1405, New York, NY 10022
Phone: 212-785-2500   **Fax:** 212-785-3311
Web: www.eagleships.com

COMPETITORS

A.P. Møller - Mærsk
DryShips Inc.
Excel Maritime Carriers
Genco Shipping
Hanjin Shipping
Kawasaki Kisen
Mitsui O.S.K. Lines
Overseas Shipholding
Pacific Basin Shipping
Star Bulk

HISTORICAL FINANCIALS

Company Type: Public

Income Statement

FYE: December 31

	REVENUE ($ mil.)	NET INCOME ($ mil.)	NET PROFIT MARGIN	EMPLOYEES
12/08	185.4	61.6	33.2%	495
12/07	124.8	52.2	41.8%	387
12/06	104.6	33.8	32.3%	339
12/05*	56.1	6.7	11.9%	295
3/05	0.0	(0.8)	—	4
Annual Growth	—	—	—	233.5%

*Fiscal year change

2008 Year-End Financials

Debt ratio: 167.5%
Return on equity: 12.5%
Cash ($ mil.): 9.2
Current ratio: 0.79
Long-term debt ($ mil.): 789.6
No. of shares (mil.): 62.1

Dividends
Yield: 29.3%
Payout: 152.7%
Market value ($ mil.): 423.2
R&D as % of sales: —
Advertising as % of sales: —

Stock History

NASDAQ (GS): EGLE

	STOCK PRICE ($) FY Close	P/E High/Low		PER SHARE ($) Earnings	Dividends	Book Value
12/08	6.82	28	2	1.31	2.00	7.60
12/07	26.55	29	14	1.24	1.98	8.30
12/06	17.34	18	12	0.98	2.08	5.18
12/05	15.92	59	40	0.30	0.54	5.09
Annual Growth	(24.6%)	—	—	63.4%	54.7%	14.3%

Ebix, Inc.

Ebix (formerly Delphi Information Systems) sells insurance industry software products and professional services to property/casualty insurers, brokerages, and individuals in Asia, Australia, Europe, and North America. The company's Ebix.com Web site acts as an online auction house where buyers and carriers can exchange bids for auto, home, health, life, and other types of insurance, while paying Ebix a fee on each transaction. Its Ebix.one and e.global agency management software build upon its legacy products with added workflow and customer relationship management capabilities. UK insurer BRiT Insurance Holdings owns 25% of the firm.

In 2006 Ebix acquired insurance software developer and supplier Infinity Systems Consulting; later that year the company also purchased Finetre Corporation.

In 2008 the company acquired Telstra eBusiness Services for about $44 million. It also acquired Acclamation Systems, a developer of benefits and claim management software, for $22 million.

Also in 2008, Ebix made a $6.8 million bid to acquire online benefits administration service provider Healthaxis. Healthaxis, which had already agreed to be acquired by BPO Management Services, rejected the offer. Ebix then raised its bid to $9.9 million, to no avail.

EXECUTIVES

Chairman, President, and CEO: Robin Raina, age 43, $2,781,769 total compensation
CFO and Corporate Secretary: Robert (Bob) Kerris, age 55, $167,249 total compensation
SVP Agency Systems: Graham Prior
SVP Ebix Health: Jim Senge
SVP Infinity Carrier: Christine M. Denham
SVP, Infinity Carrier: Kathryn S. Cay
SVP EbixExchange: Dan Delity
VP System Development Group, Infinity Carrier: John L. Schmitt
Managing Director Ebix New Zealand: Anthony (Tony) Wisniewski
Managing Director Ebix Singapore: Andy Wakefield
Auditors: Habif, Arogeti, & Wynne, LLP

LOCATIONS

HQ: Ebix, Inc.
5 Concourse Pkwy., Ste. 3200, Atlanta, GA 30328
Phone: 678-281-2020 **Fax:** 678-281-2019
Web: www.ebix.com

COMPETITORS

Answer Financial
Applied Systems
BenefitMall
CCC Information
Computer Sciences Corp.
Cover-All
Crawford & Company
E*TRADE Bank
Healthaxis
InsWeb
Intuit
Life Quotes
SunGard

HISTORICAL FINANCIALS

Company Type: Public

Income Statement

FYE: December 31

	REVENUE ($ mil.)	NET INCOME ($ mil.)	NET PROFIT MARGIN	EMPLOYEES
12/08	74.8	27.3	36.5%	637
12/07	42.8	12.7	29.7%	391
12/06	29.3	6.0	20.5%	292
12/05	24.1	4.3	17.8%	229
12/04	20.0	2.2	11.0%	239
Annual Growth	39.1%	87.7%	—	27.8%

2008 Year-End Financials

Debt ratio: 21.8%
Return on equity: 41.9%
Cash ($ mil.): 9.5
Current ratio: 0.47
Long-term debt ($ mil.): 15.3
No. of shares (mil.): 11.3

Dividends
Yield: 0.0%
Payout: —
Market value ($ mil.): 270.5
R&D as % of sales: —
Advertising as % of sales: —

Stock History

NASDAQ (GM): EBIX

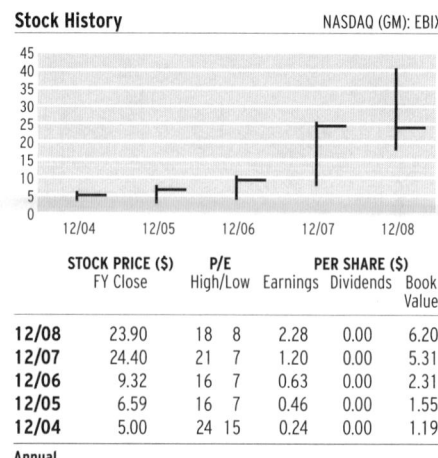

	STOCK PRICE ($) FY Close	P/E High/Low		PER SHARE ($) Earnings	Dividends	Book Value
12/08	23.90	18	8	2.28	0.00	6.20
12/07	24.40	21	7	1.20	0.00	5.31
12/06	9.32	16	7	0.63	0.00	2.31
12/05	6.59	16	7	0.46	0.00	1.55
12/04	5.00	24	15	0.24	0.00	1.19
Annual Growth	47.9%	—	—	75.6%	—	51.0%

Echo Global Logistics

By land, air, or sea, Echo Global Logistics can help you deliver the goods. The company provides a wide range of transportation services, including truckload, small parcel, domestic air, international, and expedited services. In order to facilitate the shipping process, the firm also offers assistance with logistics such as claims processing, rate negotiation, and shipment execution and tracking. In addition, its Evolved Transportation Manager (ETM) software analyzes clients' transportation needs and helps reduce costs, as well as manages all procedures in shipping. Established in 2005, Echo Global Logistics serves more than 4,600 customers in the manufacturing and consumer products industries, among others.

Echo Global Logistics expanded its reach in June 2009 by acquiring transportation brokerage firm Raytrans Distribution Services. Raytrans, which will become a division of Echo, specializes in flatbed, over-sized, auto-haul and other specialty dry van brokerage services.

Echo Global Logistics went public in late 2009. It intends to enter new geographic markets in the US and is considering expanding abroad. About 16,000 transportation providers make up its carrier network, which consists of small and midsized fleets, trucking companies, and single-truck owners.

A group of company executives, including directors Henry Weller, Eric Letkofsky, and Bradley Keywell, control more than half of Echo Global Logistics.

EXECUTIVES

Chairman: Samuel K. Skinner, age 71
CEO and Director: Douglas R. (Doug) Waggoner, age 50
COO: Orazio Buzza, age 36
CFO: David B. (Dave) Menzel, age 47
CTO: David C. Rowe, age 42
EVP, Sales: Vipon Sandhir, age 37
Auditors: Ernst & Young LLP

LOCATIONS

HQ: Echo Global Logistics, Inc.
    600 W. Chicago Ave., Ste. 725, Chicago, IL 60610
Phone: 800-354-7993   **Fax:** 888-796-4445
Web: www.echo.com

COMPETITORS

C.H. Robinson Worldwide
FedEx
J.B. Hunt
Ozburn-Hessey Logistics
Ryder System
Schneider Logistics
UPS

HISTORICAL FINANCIALS

Company Type: Public

Income Statement

FYE: December 31

	REVENUE ($ mil.)	NET INCOME ($ mil.)	NET PROFIT MARGIN	EMPLOYEES
12/08	202.8	2.9	1.4%	553
12/07	95.5	1.7	1.8%	245
12/06	33.2	(0.2)	—	—
12/05	7.3	(0.5)	—	—
Annual Growth	**202.9%**	—	—	**125.7%**

2008 Year-End Financials

Debt ratio: —
Return on equity: —
Cash ($ mil.): 1.9

Current ratio: 1.12
Long-term debt ($ mil.): 0.4

Net Income History

NASDAQ (GM): ECHO

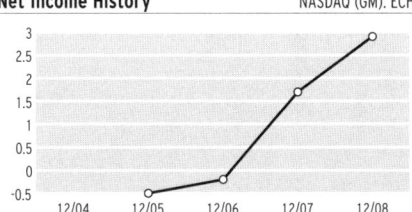

Ecology and Environment

Every day is Earth Day at environmental consulting and testing company Ecology and Environment. The company, which has completed 35,000 projects in 83 countries, provides engineering, permitting, and environmental support for all kinds of energy development, including offshore energy, power plants, pipelines, and renewables. Services include environmental impact assessments, air pollution control, wastewater analyses, and site-planning. It offers hazardous waste site evaluations and field assessments across the US and provides cleanups of Superfund sites and emergency response to hazardous waste spills for the EPA. The four founders of Ecology and Environment control about 64% of the company.

The company is pursuing the challenge of helping companies reduce carbon emissions as a major focus of its growth strategy. It provides

support and service for non-carbon energy projects (wind, solar, and hydropower), offers clean coal technology (carbon sequestration), and advises on energy efficiency strategies for buildings and transportation projects.

HISTORY

Gerhard Neumaier, Frank Silvestro, Gerald Strobel, and Ronald Frank worked together at Cornell Aeronautical Laboratory in the 1960s. With the number of environmental regulations passed during the late 1960s, the quartet knew an opportunity when they saw it. They founded Ecology and Environment in 1970. One of the company's first contracts, environmental work on the construction of the Alaskan pipeline, came in 1974. In the 1970s, with the environment on the front burner, the pollution control industry as a whole thrived, and in the 1980s investors discovered it. The company went public in 1987 to great enthusiasm.

The bubble burst in the early 1990s. Despite optimism after the Clinton-Gore electoral victory, Congress was resistant to heavy spending for environmental protection. The Environmental Protection Agency, its budget slashed, canceled a company contract in 1991. Over the next several years the company's sales and profits drizzled away like a slow oil leak. The company began searching for other sources of income, including shrimp farming and real estate. In the meantime, it continued pulling in government contracts from Umiat, Alaska, to Fort Worth, Texas.

In 1999 the company diversified into shrimp farming in Costa Rica and bought a controlling interest in a Chilean environmental services company. It also began examining opportunities for its services in the buildout of telecommunications operations worldwide.

The group expanded in the US with its 2000 purchase of Walsh Environmental Scientists and Engineers, a Boulder, Colorado-based environmental engineering consulting firm. At the end of 2000, the group won three Superfund contracts with the US Environmental Protection Agency to provide assistance to the EPA for hazardous waste spill response, removal, and prevention programs in the eastern and western US.

The company continued to diversify operations in 2001 when it acquired a fish farm in Jordan. However, its shrimp farming business in Costa Rica suffered that year because of a nationwide viral disease that forced the company to temporarily halt operations. After the Costa Rican shrimp farm suffered again from the white spot syndrome virus in 2002, the company cut down on the operations to reduce its losses in the aquaculture business.

Through Colorado-based subsidiary Walsh Environmental, Ecology and Environment expanded its operations in resource evaluation by acquiring a controlling interest in oil and minerals consulting firm Gustavson Associates in 2004.

The group had anticipated that more contracts would result from growing concerns — brought on by the September 11th terrorist attacks — about damage from biological or chemical weapons. For the EPA and other government agencies, it had been conducting counter-terrorism exercises, such as simulated "dirty bomb" and biological attacks. However, the Department of Defense cut its spending on environment-related projects not tied directly

to national defense, and in 2005 Ecology and Environment closed its Analytical Service Center facility, which handled the company's US laboratory operations.

In 2007 the company liquidated its interest in Frutas Marinas Del Mar, S.R.L., a discontinued shrimp farm operation in Costa Rica for $2.5 million.

EXECUTIVES

Chairman: Gerhard J. Neumaier, age 72
President and CEO: Kevin S. Neumaier, age 72
EVP Environmental Sustainability:
  Gerard A. Gallagher III
EVP and Director: Ronald L. Frank, age 71
EVP Technical Services and Director:
  Gerald A. Strobel Jr., age 69
EVP and Director: Frank B. Silvestro, age 72
SVP: Laurence M. Brickman, age 65
VP, CFO, and Treasurer: H. John Mye III, age 57
Auditors: Schneider Downs & Co., Inc.

LOCATIONS

HQ: Ecology and Environment, Inc.
    Buffalo Corporate Center, 368 Pleasant View Dr.
    Lancaster, NY 14086
Phone: 716-684-8060   **Fax:** 716-684-0844
Web: www.ene.com

PRODUCTS/OPERATIONS

Selected Services

Air, water, and groundwater monitoring and analytical
    laboratory services
Air-quality management and air toxics pollution control
Archeological and cultural resource studies
Carbon emission management and remission
Environmental audits
Environmental engineering
Environmental impact assessments
Environmental infrastructure planning
Feasibility studies for energy projects
Hazardous waste site evaluations
Industrial hygiene and occupational health studies
Noise-pollution evaluations
Terrestrial, aquatic, and marine surveys
Wastewater analyses
Water-pollution control

COMPETITORS

ATC Associates
Brown and Caldwell
CH2M HILL
Clean Harbors
GZA GeoEnvironmental
Malcolm Pirnie
Sevenson Environmental
TestAmerica
Tetra Tech
TRC Companies
Versar
Weston

HISTORICAL FINANCIALS

Company Type: Public

Income Statement

FYE: July 31

	REVENUE ($ mil.)	NET INCOME ($ mil.)	NET PROFIT MARGIN	EMPLOYEES
7/09	146.9	5.2	3.5%	1,100
7/08	110.5	1.8	1.6%	1,000
7/07	103.5	3.5	3.4%	870
7/06	81.8	2.6	3.2%	801
7/05	74.5	(1.6)	—	700
Annual Growth	**18.5%**	—	—	**12.0%**

2009 Year-End Financials

Debt ratio: 1.7%
Return on equity: 13.0%
Cash ($ mil.): 16.6
Current ratio: 2.18
Long-term debt ($ mil.): 0.7
No. of shares (mil.): 4.1

Dividends
Yield: 2.6%
Payout: 30.5%
Market value ($ mil.): 62.7
R&D as % of sales: —
Advertising as % of sales: —

Stock History

NASDAQ (GM): EEI

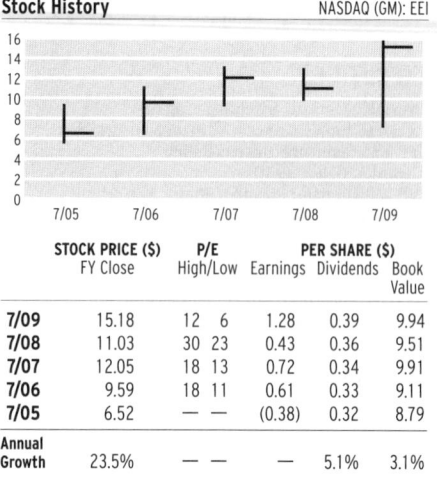

	STOCK PRICE ($) FY Close	P/E High/Low		PER SHARE ($) Earnings	Dividends	Book Value
7/09	15.18	12	6	1.28	0.39	9.94
7/08	11.03	30	23	0.43	0.36	9.51
7/07	12.05	18	13	0.72	0.34	9.91
7/06	9.59	18	11	0.61	0.33	9.11
7/05	6.52	—	—	(0.38)	0.32	8.79
Annual Growth	23.5%	—	—	—	5.1%	3.1%

eHealth, Inc.

eHealth brought e-commerce to the insurance business. Through its eHealthInsurance Services subsidiary, the company sells health insurance online to more than 600,000 individual, family, and small business members. The company is licensed to sell in all 50 states and Washington, DC, and it has partnerships with some 180 health insurance carriers. It offers more than 10,000 products online — including health, dental, and vision insurance products from the likes of Aetna, Humana, Kaiser Permanente, and Wellpoint, as well as more than 40 Blue Cross and Blue Shield licensees. The company was founded in 1997.

eHealth is trying to fill a gap in the health insurance brokerage business, left by large brokers who cater to large and mid-sized companies and local agents who sell to individuals and small businesses but offer plans from a limited number of carriers. eHealth's technology platform and nationwide presence allow customers to get online rate quotes and side-by-side plan comparisons from a much wider range of providers. The company's online applications are delivered electronically to insurance carriers' information systems, reducing the time it takes to process and enroll new members.

The company gets most of its revenue from commissions off sales of policies. A much smaller amount comes from advertising sponsorships on its Web site and licensing agreements with agents and carriers who use the company's e-commerce technology. The company launched its online advertising business in 2006.

eHealth is working to build greater brand awareness with consumers and drive more traffic to its Web site. The company has marketing partnerships with online financial services firms and medical information providers to help get potential customers to its site. By making more people aware of the company's offering and by providing more products from an ever-growing network of carriers, the company hopes to grow its membership.

Though the company operates a technology center in China, almost all its revenues come from the US. However, it has launched a pilot program in China to sell insurance online in select markets within the country.

EXECUTIVES

Chairman, President, and CEO: Gary L. Lauer, age 56, $981,040 total compensation
EVP Technology and CTO: Sheldon X. Wang, age 50, $595,977 total compensation
EVP Business and Corporate Development, Secretary, and General Counsel: Bruce A. Telkamp, age 42, $467,458 total compensation
Chief Marketing and Revenue Officer: Scott C. Sanborn, age 39
SVP and CFO: Stuart M. Huizinga, age 47, $393,810 total compensation
SVP Sales: Samuel C. (Sam) Gibbs III, age 52, $293,169 total compensation
SVP Carrier Relations: Robert S. Hurley, age 50
VP Public Policy and Government Affairs: John D. Desser
Director Public Relations: Brian Mast
Senior Media Consultant: Sande Drew
Auditors: Ernst & Young LLP

LOCATIONS

HQ: eHealth, Inc.
440 E. Middlefield Rd., Mountain View, CA 94043
Phone: 650-584-2700   **Fax:** 650-961-2153
Web: www.ehealthinsurance.com

PRODUCTS/OPERATIONS

2008 Sales

	$ mil.	% of total
Commissions	100.8	90
Sponsorships, licensing & other	10.9	10
Total	**111.7**	**100**

Selected Insurance Carriers

Aetna
Altius
Anthem Blue Cross and Blue Shield
Assurant Health
Bay Dental
Blue Cross of California
Blue Cross Blue Shield of Texas
CareFirst
CIGNA
ConnectiCare
Coventry Health Care
HCC Life Insurance Company
HealthAmerica
HealthNet
Humana
Kaiser Permanente
LifeWise Health Plans
Mountain State BlueCross BlueShield
Oxford Health Plans
PacifiCare
Regence Blue Cross BlueShield
Scott & White Health Plan
Total Dental Administrators Health Plan
Unicare
WellPath Select

COMPETITORS

Aflac
Answer Financial
Aon
BenefitMall
Bollinger, Inc.

Life Quotes
Marsh Inc.
Matrix Direct
Wells Fargo Insurance

HISTORICAL FINANCIALS

Company Type: Public

Income Statement

FYE: December 31

	REVENUE ($ mil.)	NET INCOME ($ mil.)	NET PROFIT MARGIN	EMPLOYEES
12/08	111.7	14.2	12.7%	482
12/07	87.8	31.6	36.0%	437
12/06	61.3	16.5	26.9%	357
12/05	41.8	(0.4)	—	292
12/04	30.2	(3.3)	—	320
Annual Growth	38.7%	—	—	10.8%

2008 Year-End Financials

Debt ratio: —
Return on equity: 9.8%
Cash ($ mil.): 94.1
Current ratio: 12.33
Long-term debt ($ mil.): —
No. of shares (mil.): 23.3

Dividends
Yield: 0.0%
Payout: —
Market value ($ mil.): 310.0
R&D as % of sales: —
Advertising as % of sales: —

Stock History

NASDAQ (GM): EHTH

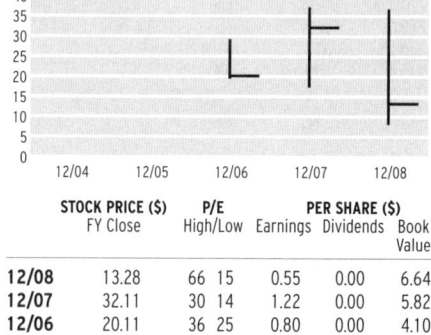

	STOCK PRICE ($) FY Close	P/E High/Low		PER SHARE ($) Earnings	Dividends	Book Value
12/08	13.28	66	15	0.55	0.00	6.64
12/07	32.11	30	14	1.22	0.00	5.82
12/06	20.11	36	25	0.80	0.00	4.10
Annual Growth	(18.7%)	—	—	(17.1%)	—	27.2%

El Paso Electric

El Paso Electric creates currents along the Rio Grande River. The utility transmits and distributes electricity to some 363,000 customers in West Texas and southern New Mexico. More than half of the company's sales come from its namesake city and nearby Las Cruces, New Mexico. The firm has more than 1,500 MW of nuclear and fossil-fueled generating capacity. El Paso Electric also purchases power from other utilities and marketers, and sells wholesale power in Texas and New Mexico, as well as in Mexico. Its largest customers include military installations, such as Fort Bliss in Texas and White Sands Missile Range and Holloman Air Force Base in New Mexico.

In 2008 about 42% of the company's energy sources came from nuclear power, and 24% from natural gas. El Paso Electric's Renewable Energy Program gives incentives to customers using power generated from renewable energy sources, such as geothermal, solar, and wind.

In 2008 the company appointed industry veteran David Stevens as CEO, replacing interim president and CEO J. Frank Bates.

EXECUTIVES

Chairman: Kenneth R. Heitz, age 61
CEO: David W. Stevens, $1,421,924 total compensation
President: J. Frank Bates, age 59,
$1,284,003 total compensation
SVP and COO: George A. Williams, age 47
SVP and General Counsel: Gary D. Sanders, age 51,
$517,876 total compensation
SVP and CFO: David G. Carpenter, age 54,
$423,265 total compensation
SVP Corporate Planning and Development:
Rocky Miracle
VP Transmission and Distribution: Hector R. Puente,
age 53, $564,994 total compensation
VP, Treasurer, and Chief Risk Officer: Steven P. Busser,
age 41
VP New Mexico Affairs: Robert C. Doyle, age 50
VP Public Affairs: Helen W. Knopp, age 67
VP System Operations and Planning: John A. Whitacre,
age 60
VP Power Generation: Andres (Andy) Ramirez, age 49
VP Customer Care: Kerry B. Lore, age 50
VP Legal and Chief Compliance Officer: Mary E. Kipp
Corporate Secretary: Guillermo Silva Jr., age 56
Senior Investor Relations Analyst: Rachelle Williams
Auditors: KPMG LLP

LOCATIONS

HQ: El Paso Electric Company
Stanton Tower, 100 N. Stanton, El Paso, TX 79901
Phone: 915-543-5711   **Fax:** 915-521-4787
Web: www.epelectric.com

PRODUCTS/OPERATIONS

2008 Sales

	$ mil.	% of total
Retail		
Residential	184.8	18
Small commercial & industrial	174.6	17
Public authorities	74.4	7
Large commercial & industrial	36.3	4
Fuel	309.7	30
Off-system sales	232.5	22
Wholesale	1.6	—
Other	25.0	2
Total	**1,038.9**	**100**

COMPETITORS

AEP
Atmos Energy
Avista
Brazos Electric
Cap Rock Energy
CenterPoint Energy
Edison International
El Paso
Energy Future
Entergy
Green Mountain Energy
LCRA
NV Energy
PNM Resources
Tri-State Generation and Transmission

HISTORICAL FINANCIALS

Company Type: Public

Income Statement

FYE: December 31

	REVENUE ($ mil.)	NET INCOME ($ mil.)	NET PROFIT MARGIN	EMPLOYEES
12/08	1,038.9	77.6	7.5%	1,000
12/07	877.4	74.8	8.5%	1,000
12/06	816.5	61.4	7.5%	1,000
12/05	803.9	36.6	4.6%	1,000
12/04	708.6	33.4	4.7%	1,000
Annual Growth	**10.0%**	**23.5%**	**—**	**0.0%**

2008 Year-End Financials

Debt ratio: 116.6%
Return on equity: 11.4%
Cash ($ mil.): 91.6
Current ratio: 1.97
Long-term debt ($ mil.): 809.7
No. of shares (mil.): 44.3
Dividends
 Yield: —
 Payout: —
Market value ($ mil.): 800.6
R&D as % of sales: —
Advertising as % of sales: —

Stock History

NYSE: EE

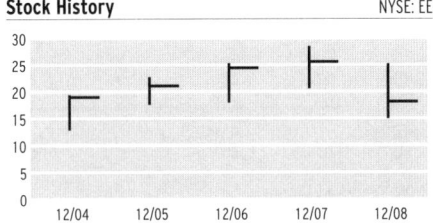

	STOCK PRICE ($) FY Close	P/E High/Low		PER SHARE ($) Earnings	Dividends	Book Value
12/08	18.09	14	9	1.73	—	15.69
12/07	25.57	17	13	1.63	—	15.06
12/06	24.37	18	13	1.40	—	13.10
12/05	21.04	30	24	0.74	—	12.57
12/04	18.94	26	18	0.73	—	12.02
Annual Growth	**(1.1%)**	**—**	**—**	**24.1%**	**—**	**6.9%**

El Paso Pipeline Partners

While El Paso Pipeline Partners might seem like the way El Paso gets great Mexican food across the border, it's actually a natural gas pipeline and storage company. The firm, which consists primarily of Wyoming Interstate Company (WIC) and partial interests in Colorado Interstate Gas Company (CIG) and Southern Natural Gas Company (SNG), has 12,500 miles of pipeline, and storage facilities totaling 89 billion cubic feet. Parent El Paso Corporation owns the remainder of CIG and SNG. El Paso Pipeline Partners' customers include local distribution companies, industrial users, electricity generators, and natural gas marketing and trading companies. El Paso Corporation controls about 74% of the company.

The partnership's strategy is to increase the efficiency of its pipelines while making complementary asset acquisitions from its parent and from third parties.

In 2008 the company acquired from El Paso Corporation an additional 30% general partner interest in CIG and an additional 15% general partner interest in SNG, boosting its overall ownership to 40% of CIG and 25% of SNG.

EXECUTIVES

Chairman: Ronald L. Kuehn Jr., age 73
President, CEO, and Director: James C. (Jim) Yardley, age 57
EVP and General Counsel: Robert W. Baker, age 52
SVP, CFO, and Director: John R. (J. R.) Sult, age 49
SVP: Daniel B. Martin, age 52
SVP: Norman G. Holmes, age 52
SVP: James J. Cleary, age 54
VP, Controller, and Principal Accounting Officer:
Rosa P. Jackson, age 56
Auditors: Ernst & Young LLP

LOCATIONS

HQ: El Paso Pipeline Partners, L.P.
1001 Louisiana St., Houston, TX 77002
Phone: 713-420-2600   **Fax:** 713-420-4417
Web: www.eppipelinepartners.com

COMPETITORS

ANR Pipeline
Bridgeline
Duncan Energy
Gulf South Pipeline
Southern Union
Tidelands Oil & Gas
Transcontinental Gas
 Pipe Line
U.S. Transmission

HISTORICAL FINANCIALS

Company Type: Public

Income Statement

FYE: December 31

	REVENUE ($ mil.)	NET INCOME ($ mil.)	NET PROFIT MARGIN	EMPLOYEES
12/08	141.1	114.5	81.1%	0
12/07	110.0	66.0	60.0%	0
12/06	97.0	65.0	67.0%	—
Annual Growth	**20.6%**	**32.7%**	**—**	**—**

2008 Year-End Financials

Debt ratio: —
Return on equity: —
Cash ($ mil.): 10.9
Current ratio: 2.90
Long-term debt ($ mil.): 777.3
No. of shares (mil.): 97.6
Dividends
 Yield: 6.5%
 Payout: 82.8%
Market value ($ mil.): 1,522.8
R&D as % of sales: —
Advertising as % of sales: —

Stock History

NYSE: EPB

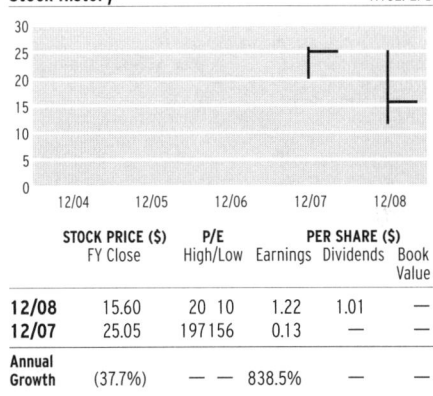

	STOCK PRICE ($) FY Close	P/E High/Low		PER SHARE ($) Earnings	Dividends	Book Value
12/08	15.60	20	10	1.22	1.01	—
12/07	25.05	197	156	0.13	—	—
Annual Growth	**(37.7%)**	**—**	**—**	**838.5%**	**—**	**—**

Empire District Electric

Empire District Electric (EDE) has the sovereign authority to light up its territory. The utility transmits and distributes electricity to a population base of more than 450,000 customers in southwestern Missouri and adjacent areas of Arkansas, Kansas, and Oklahoma. It also supplies water to three Missouri towns and natural gas throughout most of the state.

EDE's interests in fossil-fueled and hydroelectric power plants give it a generating capacity of 1,255 MW, with an expected increase to 1,410 MW by 2010; it also buys and sells power on the wholesale market. In addition, the company is pursuing nonregulated opportunities such as leasing capacity on its fiber-optic network. It also distributes automated meter reading equipment.

EDE's natural gas operations, acquired from Aquila in 2006, distribute natural gas through the The Empire District Gas Company to nearly 50 communities in northwest, north central, and west central Missouri, and to some 175 transportation customers.

The company has been boosting its generating capacity, including partial ownership in the Plum Point Energy Station in Arkansas, and through several wind farm contracts.

In 2007 EDE exited the Internet business, selling Fast Freedom, Inc., a service provider.

EXECUTIVES

Chairman: D. Randy Laney, age 54
President, CEO, and Director: William L. (Bill) Gipson, age 52, $928,271 total compensation
VP Energy Supply: Harold R. Colgin II, age 60
VP and COO, Gas: Ronald F. Gatz, age 59, $278,046 total compensation
VP and COO, Electric: Bradley P. Beecher, age 44, $397,188 total compensation
VP Finance and CFO: Gregory A. Knapp, age 58, $415,219 total compensation
VP Commercial Operations: Michael E. Palmer, age 53, $352,119 total compensation
VP Regulatory and General Services: Kelly S. Walters, age 44
Controller, Assistant Secretary, and Assistant Treasurer: Laurie A. Delano, age 54
Director Corporate Communications: Amy Bass
Secretary and Treasurer: Janet S. (Jan) Watson, age 57
Auditors: PricewaterhouseCoopers LLP

LOCATIONS

HQ: The Empire District Electric Company
602 Joplin St., Joplin, MO 64801
Phone: 417-625-5100   **Fax:** 417-625-5146
Web: www.empiredistrict.com

The Empire District Electric Company provides electricity in southwestern Missouri, as well as in smaller portions of northwestern Arkansas, southeastern Kansas, and northeastern Oklahoma. It also distributes water in three communities in Missouri and natural gas in about 45 communities in northwest, north central, and west central Missouri.

PRODUCTS/OPERATIONS

2008 Sales

	$ mil.	% of total
Electric	446.5	86
Gas	65.4	13
Non-regulated	4.5	1
Water	1.8	—
Total	**518.2**	**100**

Selected Subsidiaries

EDE Holdings, Inc. (nonregulated operations)
Empire District Industries, Inc. (fiber-optic services)
The Empire District Gas Company

COMPETITORS

AEP
Ameren
Associated Electric
Charter Communications
Entergy
Grand River Dam Authority
Great Plains Energy
Laclede Group
MidAmerican Energy
OGE Energy
Southern Union
Westar Energy
Western Farmers Electric
Xcel Energy

HISTORICAL FINANCIALS
Company Type: Public

Income Statement
FYE: December 31

	REVENUE ($ mil.)	NET INCOME ($ mil.)	NET PROFIT MARGIN	EMPLOYEES
12/08	518.2	39.7	7.7%	733
12/07	490.2	33.2	6.8%	733
12/06	413.5	39.3	9.5%	705
12/05	386.2	23.8	6.2%	851
12/04	325.5	21.8	6.7%	855
Annual Growth	**12.3%**	**16.2%**	**—**	**(3.8%)**

2008 Year-End Financials

Debt ratio: 115.6%
Return on equity: 7.4%
Cash ($ mil.): 2.8
Current ratio: 0.68
Long-term debt ($ mil.): 611.6
No. of shares (mil.): 34.5

Dividends
Yield: 7.3%
Payout: 109.4%
Market value ($ mil.): 607.1
R&D as % of sales: —
Advertising as % of sales: —

Stock History
NYSE: EDE

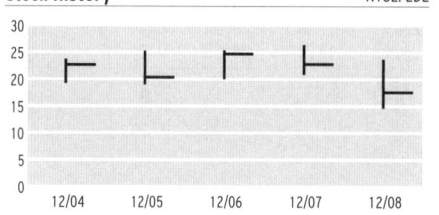

	STOCK PRICE ($) FY Close	P/E High/Low		PER SHARE ($) Earnings	Dividends	Book Value
12/08	17.60	20	13	1.17	1.28	15.33
12/07	22.78	24	19	1.09	1.28	15.63
12/06	24.69	18	15	1.39	1.28	13.59
12/05	20.33	27	21	0.92	1.28	11.41
12/04	22.68	27	23	0.86	1.28	10.99
Annual Growth	**(6.1%)**	**—**	**—**	**8.0%**	**0.0%**	**8.7%**

Empire Resources

When it comes to aluminum, Empire Resources is especially resourceful. The company distributes semifinished aluminum products, including sheet, foil, wire, plate, and coil. Products are sold primarily to manufacturers of appliances, automobiles, packaging, and housing materials. Empire Resources provides a variety of related services, including sourcing of aluminum products, storage and delivery, and handling foreign exchange transactions. Company president and CEO Nathan Kahn and CFO Sandra Kahn, who are husband and wife, own almost 40% of Empire Resources.

Empire Resources relies on a single supplier, Hulamin, for more than half of its products. However, Empire Resources has begun to make its own aluminum extrusions. As for customers, Ryerson is the company's largest, accounting for more than 10% of sales.

EXECUTIVES

Chairman: William Spier, age 74
President and CEO: Nathan Kahn, age 54
CFO: Sandra R. Kahn, age 51
VP Sales: Harvey Wrubel, age 55
Director Information Technology: Ross Toombs
Regional Managing Director, Australia/Asia:
Peter G. Howard, age 73
Sales Manager: Jeff Lowy
Sales Manager: Alan Papier
Senior Logistics Manager: Tom Lehr
Customer Service Manager: Ginette Raymond
Marketing Administrator: Jane Barnett
Human Resources: Deborah Waltuch
Investor Relations Contact: David Kronfeld
Auditors: Eisner LLP

LOCATIONS

HQ: Empire Resources, Inc.
1 Parker Plaza, Fort Lee, NJ 07024
Phone: 201-944-2200   **Fax:** 201-944-2226

PRODUCTS/OPERATIONS

Selected Aluminum Products

Circles
Coil/sheet
Foil
Plate
Profiles/extruded products
Treadplate

COMPETITORS

Alcoa
Commercial Metals
Rio Tinto Alcan

HISTORICAL FINANCIALS
Company Type: Public

Income Statement
FYE: December 31

	REVENUE ($ mil.)	NET INCOME ($ mil.)	NET PROFIT MARGIN	EMPLOYEES
12/08	429.0	3.9	0.9%	85
12/07	475.5	4.5	0.9%	80
12/06	426.0	8.7	2.0%	65
12/05	358.5	9.5	2.6%	50
12/04	212.6	4.8	2.3%	30
Annual Growth	**19.2%**	**(5.1%)**	**—**	**29.7%**

2008 Year-End Financials

Debt ratio: 6.1%
Return on equity: 12.4%
Cash ($ mil.): —

Current ratio: —
Long-term debt ($ mil.): 1.9

Net Income History
Pink Sheets: ERSO

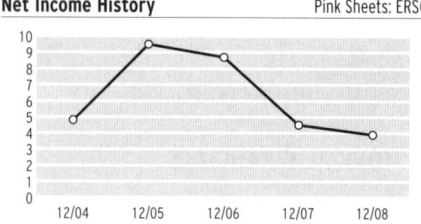

EMS Technologies

EMS Technologies' wireless systems can help you communicate, whether you're walking the warehouse floor or floating in space. The company's LXE unit makes handheld and vehicle-mounted computers used for logistics management. EMS also makes microwave-based communications hardware for defense contractors through its Defense & Space Systems unit. Its SATCOM division makes aeronautical satellite antennas and Earth station antennas and control terminals used for emergency management. The company's EMS Sky Connect business provides telephony and flight tracking services for aircraft over the Iridium Satellite network.

The company's largest division, LXE, accounted for more than 40% of its revenues in 2008. EMS has looked to international markets to fuel growth of its LXE business, and the company partnered with the European division of distributor ScanSource in 2009 to further its strategy. Overall EMS generates about 40% of its revenues outside the US. Most of its international operations are based in Europe.

Paul Domorski resigned as president, CEO, and a director in 2009, after leading the company for three years. EVP/COO Neilson Mackay, an EMS executive since 1993, was promoted to president and CEO, succeeding Domorski, and was elected to a seat on the company's board. Mackay has a stronger engineering background than Domorski.

EMS acquired Sky Connect for $15.5 million in 2008. It purchased Satamatics Global, a provider of satellite-based machine-to-machine (M2M) services, the following year. The Sky Connect and Satamatics acquisitions expanded the company's satellite communications division, which accounted for about a third of its revenues in 2008.

Prior to the purchase of Sky Connect, the company had significantly streamlined its operations. EMS divested its commercial space division, which had been a part of the Defense & Space Systems unit, in light of weak sales in that industry. The company discontinued operations of the division and sold the assets to Vancouver-based MacDonald, Dettwiler and Associates in 2005. In 2006 EMS sold its Satellite Networks unit — which made antennas, processors, and broadband gear — to Advantech Advanced Microwave Technologies. It also sold its wireless division, which sold base station antennas, to Andrew for $50 million.

EXECUTIVES

Chairman and Executive Director:
John B. (Jack) Mowell, age 73
President, CEO, and Director: Neilson A. (Neil) Mackay, age 68, $687,453 total compensation
SVP, CFO, and Treasurer: Gary B. Shell, age 54, $494,839 total compensation
SVP and Acting General Manager, LXE Inc.:
William H. (Bill) Roeder, age 54
VP Innovation and Strategy: Gary M. Hebb, age 47, $420,194 total compensation
VP and General Manager, EMS Defense and Space Systems: David A. Smith, age 57, $487,024 total compensation

VP Marketing and Information Management:
Perry D. Tanner, age 51
VP Programs, Defense and Sapce Systems:
Martin M. (Marty) Broadwell, age 52
VP Finance and Chief Accounting Officer:
David M. Sheffield, age 47
VP and General Counsel: Timothy C. Reis, age 51
COO, EMS Sky Connect: Wiley Loughran
Director Human Resources: Michael R. Robertson
Public Relations Manager: Halina Rydel
Auditors: KPMG LLP

LOCATIONS

HQ: EMS Technologies, Inc.
660 Engineering Dr., Norcross, GA 30092
Phone: 770-263-9200   **Fax:** 770-263-9207
Web: www.ems-t.com

2008 Sales

	$ mil.	% of total
US	202.5	60
UK	28.4	9
Other countries	104.1	31
Total	**335.0**	**100**

PRODUCTS/OPERATIONS

2008 Sales

	$ mil.	% of total
LXE	145.9	43
Satellite Communications	112.5	34
Defense & Space Systems	76.6	23
Total	**335.0**	**100**

Selected Operations

LXE
  Barcode scanners
  Handheld and vehicle-mounted computers
  Wireless access devices, antennas, and power supplies
Satellite Communications
  Satamatics
  SATCOM
    Aeronautical satellite antennas
    Emergency management products
      Geostationary satellite Earth station terminals
      Satellite antenna subsystems
    Mobile land satellite antennas
  Sky Connect
Defense & Space Systems
  Antenna systems
  Computer processor cards
  Demodulators
  Digital command and control processors and software
  Manufacturing and testing services
  Microwave amplifiers, oscillators, receivers, and transponders
  Motor drive amplifiers
  Optical star trackers
  Phase shift arrays
  Power converters
  Satellite broadband communications equipment
  Satellite tracking modulators
  Switches

COMPETITORS

BAE Systems Inc.
Boeing
DRS Technologies
Harris Corp.
Intermec
L-3 Communications
Lockheed Martin
Motorola, Inc.
Northrop Grumman
Psion Teklogix
QUALCOMM
Thrane & Thrane

HISTORICAL FINANCIALS

Company Type: Public

Income Statement

FYE: December 31

	REVENUE ($ mil.)	NET INCOME ($ mil.)	NET PROFIT MARGIN	EMPLOYEES
12/08	335.0	20.5	6.1%	1,200
12/07	287.9	18.7	6.5%	1,100
12/06	261.1	33.0	12.6%	900
12/05	310.0	(11.4)	—	1,300
12/04	260.4	0.2	0.1%	1,000
Annual Growth	**6.5%**	**218.2%**	**—**	**4.7%**

2008 Year-End Financials

Debt ratio: 3.8%
Return on equity: 8.4%
Cash ($ mil.): 87.0
Current ratio: 3.46
Long-term debt ($ mil.): 9.3
No. of shares (mil.): 15.3
Dividends
  Yield: —
  Payout: —
Market value ($ mil.): 395.1
R&D as % of sales: —
Advertising as % of sales: —

Stock History

NASDAQ (GS): ELMG

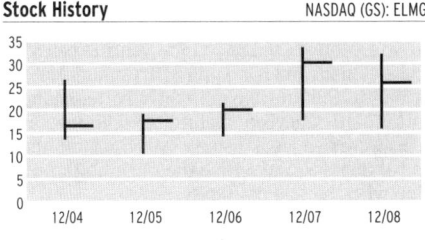

	STOCK PRICE ($) FY Close	P/E High/Low		PER SHARE ($) Earnings	Dividends	Book Value
12/08	25.87	24	12	1.31	—	15.90
12/07	30.24	27	15	1.21	—	16.18
12/06	20.03	9	6	2.25	—	13.95
12/05	17.70	—	—	(1.02)	—	7.44
12/04	16.62	1,316	692	0.02	—	8.25
Annual Growth	**11.7%**	**—**	**—**	**184.5%**	**—**	**17.8%**

Energy Conversion Devices

Energy Conversion Devices (ECD) gets a charge out of its technology. ECD makes storage products that generate and store power or store information electronically. Subsidiary United Solar Ovonic, which accounts for more than 95% of sales, makes flexible solar panels mainly for roofs, but also for telecom, lighting, and other uses. The Ovonic Materials Division licenses its optical memory storage technology to the likes of Sony and Toshiba. It also produces materials for use in NiMH and other batteries; Sanyo licenses its battery technology.

In 2009 ECD acquired its largest customer, Solar Integrated Technologies, a supplier of building-integrated photovoltaic roofing products, for about $16 million in cash and assumed debt. The company sees the acquisition as a way to transition from a manufacturing and sales organization to one that offers complete systems and services. The acquisition also improves its field engineering and technical capabilities in rooftop solar for customers in Europe and the US. Customers in France, Italy,

Germany, and Switzerland account for more than two-thirds of sales.

ECD has established manufacturing facilities in low cost regions, including Mexico and China. The company has slowed aggressive production and expansion plans to better align with current market conditions, and is consolidating some facilities and cutting jobs.

ECD works to develop cutting edge technologies, often with funding from government contracts and strategic alliances, and then seeks to commercialize them. Some of its projects include portable hydrogen canisters (currently being manufactured in pre-production quantities), metal hydride fuel cell stacks, and a technology to produce high-purity hydrogen at lower temperatures from multiple renewable sources (currently moving from laboratory to pilot production).

In 2009 ECD sold its Cobasys joint venture with Chevron, which makes NiMH and other rechargeable batteries to power items ranging from consumer electronics to electric vehicles, to SB LiMotive Co. Ltd., a joint venture between Robert Bosch and Samsung SDI. General Motors is tied to Cobasys for its hybrid battery supply until 2010. Chevron Technology Ventures and ECD were in a legal dispute over the joint funding of Cobasys, and settled their pending arbitration with the sale of Cobasys.

The company's Ovonyx joint venture is developing ECD's Ovonic Unified Memory technology for use in non-volatile memory semiconductors. The technology, also known as phase-change random-access memory, could provide a successor to the NAND flash memory devices commonly used in digital still cameras, MP3 music players, and other popular consumer electronics.

ECD also is developing thin-film devices that could be used in cognitive processors and neural networks, advanced forms of computing and networking that are years away from realization.

VP and director Iris Ovshinsky, a co-founder of the company, died in 2006 at the age of 79. Her husband and co-founder, Stan Ovshinsky, retired from ECD as an employee and a director one year later.

EXECUTIVES

President, CEO, and Director: Mark D. Morelli, age 46, $2,124,880 total compensation
EVP and Chief Human Resources Officer: Gary M. Glandon, age 50
EVP Photovoltaic Technology; Chairman, United Solar Ovonic: Subhendu Guha, age 67, $653,501 total compensation
EVP; SVP Operations, United Solar Ovonic: Joseph P. (Joe) Conroy, age 45, $696,185 total compensation
EVP and Chief Marketing Officer; President, Americas: Kenneth P. (Ken) Fox, age 56
EVP; President, Europe, Middle East, and Africa: Ted F. Amyuni, age 56
SVP, General Counsel, and Chief Administrative Officer: Jay B. Knoll, age 47, $787,394 total compensation
VP and CFO: Harry W. Zike, age 54, $597,973 total compensation
VP Human Resources and Administration: Arthur A. (Art) Rogers Jr., age 59
VP Systems Engineering: Tom Toner, age 50
VP Sales: Corby C. Whitaker, age 39
VP Investor Relations and Communications: Mark Trinske
Corporate Secretary: Ghazaleh Koefod
Auditors: Grant Thornton LLP

LOCATIONS

HQ: Energy Conversion Devices, Inc.
2956 Waterview Dr., Rochester Hills, MI 48309
Phone: 248-293-0440   **Fax:** 248-844-1214
Web: www.ovonic.com

2009 Sales

	$ mil.	% of total
US	82.6	26
France	69.3	22
Italy	66.8	21
Germany	60.3	19
Switzerland	16.7	5
South Korea	6.4	2
Japan	6.2	2
Hong Kong	3.4	1
China	0.4	—
Other countries	4.2	2
Total	**316.3**	**100**

PRODUCTS/OPERATIONS

2009 Sales

	$ mil.	% of total
United Solar Ovonic	302.8	96
Ovonic Materials	13.3	4
Corporate & other	0.2	—
Total	**316.3**	**100**

2009 Sales

	$ mil.	% of total
Product sales	295.0	93
Product development	13.4	4
Royalties	6.4	2
License & other revenues	1.5	1
Total	**316.3**	**100**

COMPETITORS

Acumentrics
Ballard Power
BP Solar
China Sunergy
Conergy
DayStar Technologies
Douglas Battery
First Solar
FuelCell Energy
Kyocera Solar
Mitsubishi Electric
MTI MicroFuel Cells
Plug Power
Q-Cells
Quantum Fuel Systems
SANYO
SCHOTT Solar
Sharp Corp.
SolarWorld
SunPower
Suntech Power
Toyota

HISTORICAL FINANCIALS

Company Type: Public

Income Statement

FYE: June 30

	REVENUE ($ mil.)	NET INCOME ($ mil.)	NET PROFIT MARGIN	EMPLOYEES
6/09	316.3	12.5	4.0%	1,800
6/08	255.9	3.9	1.5%	1,768
6/07	113.6	(25.2)	—	1,204
6/06	102.4	(18.6)	—	964
6/05	156.6	48.1	30.7%	746
Annual Growth	**19.2%**	**(28.6%)**	**—**	**24.6%**

2009 Year-End Financials

Debt ratio: 51.0%	Dividends
Return on equity: 1.9%	Yield: —
Cash ($ mil.): 56.4	Payout: —
Current ratio: 7.54	Market value ($ mil.): 647.3
Long-term debt ($ mil.): 337.7	R&D as % of sales: —
No. of shares (mil.): 45.7	Advertising as % of sales: —

Stock History

NASDAQ (GS): ENER

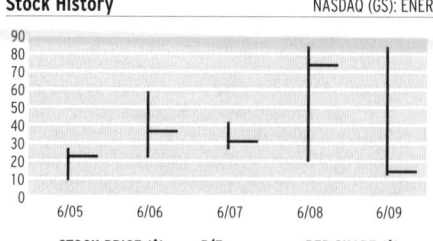

	STOCK PRICE ($) FY Close	P/E High/Low		PER SHARE ($) Earnings	Dividends	Book Value
6/09	14.15	287	44	0.29	—	14.47
6/08	73.64	926	227	0.09	—	14.03
6/07	30.82	—	—	(0.64)	—	11.49
6/06	36.43	—	—	(0.57)	—	11.74
6/05	22.38	15	6	1.70	—	3.40
Annual Growth	**(10.8%)**	**—**	**—**	**(35.7%)**	**—**	**43.6%**

Energy Recovery

Desalination makes seawater potable; Energy Recovery makes desalination practical. The company designs, develops, and manufactures energy recovery devices for use in sea water reverse osmosis (SWRO) desalination plants. The SWRO process is energy intensive, using high pressure to drive salt water through membranes to produce fresh water. The company's primary product, the PX Pressure Exchanger, helps recapture and recycle up to 98% of the energy available in the high-pressure reject stream, a by-product of the SWRO process. The PX can reduce the energy consumption of a desalination plant by up to 60% compared with a plant lacking an energy recovery device. Energy Recovery completed an IPO in mid-2008.

Primary customers for Energy Recovery (ERI) consist of international engineering, procurement, and construction firms (which serve large desalination plants) and OEMs for installation in hotels, power plants, and municipal facilities. The company's PX device has been installed in more than 300 desalination plants and specified in the designs for plants by more than 60 OEM or EPC firms worldwide. Acciona Water, Geida, and Doosan Heavy Industries account for 20%, 23%, and 13% of the company's revenues, respectively.

ERI continues to build on its desalination market share. In late 2009 the company acquired a 100% equity interest in Michigan-based Pump Engineering, a provider of centrifugal turbine technology for desalination systems. The acquisition broadens ERI's portfolio in brackish and seawater desalination as well as in promising sectors of natural gas and high pressure fluid processing.

The company sees China, Algeria, Australia, and India as growth markets in the desalination industry with the Middle East, North America, the Caribbean, and Europe representing maturing markets.

EXECUTIVES

Executive Chairman: Hans Peter (HP) Michelet, age 49
President and CEO: G.G. Pique, age 61
CFO: Thomas D. (Tom) Willardson, age 58
VP and General Manager, OEM: Hattie Wang
VP Service, Operations, and Maintenance Group:
William (Bill) Anderson
VP and General Manager, Large Projects Division:
Borja Blanco
VP Manufacturing: Terrill (Terry) Sandlin, age 60
VP Administration and Human Resources:
MariaElena Ross, age 59
VP Marketing: Audrey Bold
Chief Accounting Officer: Deno G. Bokas
Chief Accounting Officer and Corporate Controller:
Marilyn A. Lobel, age 55
Auditors: BDO Seidman, LLP

LOCATIONS

HQ: Energy Recovery, Inc.
1908 Doolittle Dr., San Leandro, CA 94577
Phone: 510-483-7370   **Fax:** 510-483-7371
Web: www.energyrecovery.com

2008 Sales

	$ mil.	% of total
US	3.5	7
Other countries	48.6	93
Total	**52.1**	**100**

COMPETITORS

GE Water and Process Technologies
Seprotech
Siemens Water Technologies

HISTORICAL FINANCIALS

Company Type: Public

Income Statement

FYE: December 31

	REVENUE ($ mil.)	NET INCOME ($ mil.)	NET PROFIT MARGIN	EMPLOYEES
12/08	52.1	8.7	16.7%	89
12/07	35.4	5.8	16.4%	67
12/06	20.1	2.4	12.0%	—
Annual Growth	61.0%	90.4%	—	32.8%

2008 Year-End Financials

Debt ratio: 0.4%
Return on equity: 13.7%
Cash ($ mil.): 79.3
Current ratio: 8.82
Long-term debt ($ mil.): 0.4
No. of shares (mil.): 50.2

Dividends
  Yield: 0.0%
  Payout: —
Market value ($ mil.): 380.3
R&D as % of sales: —
Advertising as % of sales: —

Stock History

NASDAQ (GM): ERII

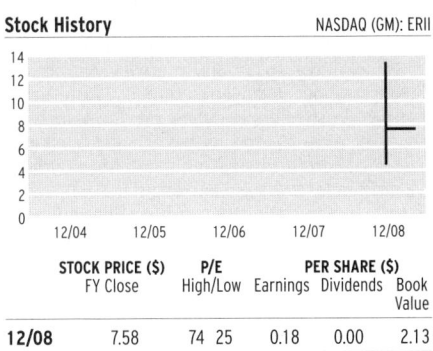

	STOCK PRICE ($) FY Close	P/E High/Low	PER SHARE ($) Earnings	Dividends	Book Value
12/08	7.58	74 25	0.18	0.00	2.13

ENGlobal Corporation

ENGlobal hopes to engineer its way into the hearts of energy companies throughout the world. The company provides engineering and systems services, procurement, construction management, inspection, and control system automation services to the pipeline and process divisions of major oil and gas companies. It also designs and installs control and instrumentation systems for energy companies. Subsidiary ENGlobal Land (formerly WRC Corporation) provides land management, environmental compliance, and other services. Other subsidiaries include ENGlobal Automation Group (EAG), which offers control system automation products, and Analyzer Technology, which provides online process analyzer systems.

The company has been focused on growing its engineering operations through geographical expansion and acquisitions. Over the course of several years it made many acquisitions including the 2006 purchase of WRC. In 2009 the company acquired Illinois-based PCI Management and Consulting Company (renamed ENGlobal Power Group), a provider of engineering, consultation, and management services for energy transmission projects. Through its growth efforts, the company has set up shop throughout Texas and Oklahoma. ENGlobal also has offices in Louisiana, Colorado, and Georgia, as well as in Canada and Costa Rica.

ENGlobal reorganized in 2007, focusing on four segments: engineering, construction, automation, and land. The move paid off with a profitable year. Operating profits increased in 2008, partly due to the amount of additional work generated by Hurricane Ike in the Gulf Coast region. Profitability continued into 2009, with 51% of the company's revenues coming from its engineering operations.

Founder and president William Coskey announced in early 2010 that he will resign as CEO of ENGlobal as soon as a replacement is named, but he will remain active with the company as board chairman. The ENGlobal board has initiated a search for CEO candidates, but has given no deadline to name a successor for Coskey.

Coskey controls around 33% of the firm; activist investor Jeffrey Gendell of Tontine Partners owns around 10%.

EXECUTIVES

Chairman, President, and CEO:
William A. (Bill) Coskey, age 57,
$368,014 total compensation
CFO and Treasurer: Robert W. (Bob) Raiford, age 64,
$406,465 total compensation
SVP Corporate Services: R. David Kelley,
$273,964 total compensation
SVP Business Development: J. Michael (Mike) Harrison
**VP Investor Relations, Chief Governance Officer, and
Corporate Secretary:** Natalie S. Hairston
VP Legal Affairs and Contracts: H. Paul Cohen
VP Quality Assurance/Quality Control: James D. Larkin
VP Project Controls: Kenneth P. Collins
Corporate Information Technology Manager:
Alex Schroeder

President, ENGlobal Engineering: David W. Smith
President, ENGlobal Construction Resources:
Ronald W. Winthrop
**President, ENGlobal Systems and ENGlobal
Automation Group:** Shelly D. Leedy
President Government and Infrastructure:
Michael M. (Mike) Patton, age 56,
$346,904 total compensation
President and COO, ENGlobal Land: Michael H. Lee
Corporate Human Resources Manager:
Robert J. Church
Auditors: Hein & Associates LLP

LOCATIONS

HQ: ENGlobal Corporation
654 N. Sam Houston Pkwy. East, Ste. 400
Houston, TX 77060
Phone: 281-878-1000   **Fax:** 281-878-1010
Web: www.englobal.com

PRODUCTS/OPERATIONS

2008 Sales

	$ mil.	% of total
Engineering	251.7	51
Construction	139.4	28
Automation	59.7	12
Land	42.5	9
Total	**493.3**	**100**

Selected Subsidiaries

ENGlobal ACE, LLC, Texas
ENGlobal Automation Group, Inc., Texas
ENGlobal Canada, ULC, Alberta, Canada
ENGlobal Construction Resources, Inc., Texas
ENGlobal Corporate Services, Inc., Texas
ENGlobal Engineering, Inc., Texas
ENGlobal Land, Inc. f/k/a WRC Corporation, Colorado
ENGlobal Systems, Inc., Texas
ENGlobal Technical Services, Inc., Texas
RPM Engineering, Inc. d/b/a ENGlobal Engineering,
  Inc., Louisiana
WRC Canada, Alberta, Canada

COMPETITORS

Austin Industries
Babcock Eagleton
Halliburton
Jacobs Engineering
Matrix Service
Mustang Engineering

HISTORICAL FINANCIALS

Company Type: Public

Income Statement

FYE: December 31

	REVENUE ($ mil.)	NET INCOME ($ mil.)	NET PROFIT MARGIN	EMPLOYEES
12/08	493.3	18.3	3.7%	2,302
12/07	363.2	12.5	3.4%	2,443
12/06	303.1	(3.5)	—	2,100
12/05	233.6	4.8	2.1%	1,724
12/04	148.9	2.4	1.6%	1,329
Annual Growth	34.9%	66.2%	—	14.7%

2008 Year-End Financials

Debt ratio: 31.1%
Return on equity: 27.6%
Cash ($ mil.): 1.0
Current ratio: 2.12
Long-term debt ($ mil.): 23.9
No. of shares (mil.): 27.4

Dividends
  Yield: 0.0%
  Payout: —
Market value ($ mil.): 88.9
R&D as % of sales: —
Advertising as % of sales: —

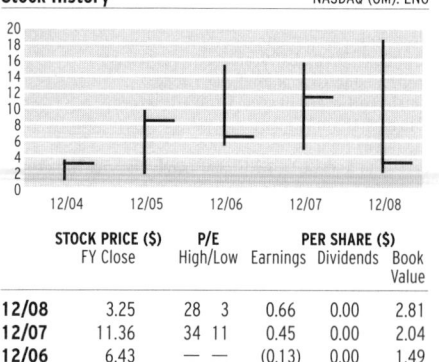

	STOCK PRICE ($) FY Close	P/E High/Low		PER SHARE ($)	
			Earnings	Dividends	Book Value
12/08	3.25	28	3	0.66	0.00	2.81
12/07	11.36	34	11	0.45	0.00	2.04
12/06	6.43	—	—	(0.13)	0.00	1.49
12/05	8.40	50	10	0.19	0.00	1.46
12/04	3.10	34	12	0.10	0.00	0.73
Annual Growth	1.2%	—	—	60.3%	—	39.9%

Ensign Group

The Ensign Group hangs its insignia at dozens of senior living facilities in the western US. Most of its facilities (which Ensign either owns or operates under lease agreements) are nursing homes, but it also operates a number of assisted-living facilities and has assisted-living wings at some of its nursing centers. The company has a decentralized operating structure, with its portfolio of homes organized into five regional operating companies, each with its own management team. In turn, each home operates under local, and largely independent, management. The Ensign Group went public in 2007.

The company has historically grown by snapping up underperforming nursing homes and turning them around, both in terms of operating performance and clinical quality. After a quiet period of integrating some acquired facilities, it restarted acquisition activity in 2006, acquiring 15 facilities in that year and in 2007. It is using proceeds from its 2007 IPO to fund more acquisitions, as well as to upgrade existing facilities and pay down debt, and for general corporate purposes.

In 2008 Ensign shifted a bit and began acquiring companies and facilities that weren't necessarily struggling or underperforming; it only picked up two facilities that year, both in Utah. In early 2009 it moved into Colorado as part of a plan to expand into other western states. It purchased four long-term care operations in the Denver area with a total of 265 beds. Ensign added to its Utah, Arizona, and Idaho holdings with additional acquisitions later in 2009.

In addition to acquiring new facilities and developing its leadership, the company strives to increase patient occupancy at its existing facilities, many of which were in bad shape at their time of acquisition. It does this by developing quality staff and clinical processes and through facility upgrades, as well as by adding services such as outpatient therapy services. It is also trying to attract more high-acuity patients, who require higher levels of medical and rehabilitative care and for whom the company is generally reimbursed at higher rates.

The company derives about three-fourths of its revenues from Medicaid and Medicare programs.

Ensign Group officers and directors collectively own around 60% of the company. Chairman Roy Christensen; his son, CEO Christopher Christensen; and director Charles Blalack each own about 15%.

EXECUTIVES

Chairman: Roy E. Christensen, age 76
President, CEO, and Director: Christopher R. Christensen, age 41, $986,658 total compensation
CFO: Suzanne D. Snapper
EVP: Gregory K. Stapley, age 50, $905,115 total compensation
VP Organizational Development: David M. Sedgewick, age 34
VP and General Counsel: Beverly B. Wittekind
President, Bandera Healthcare: Michael C. Dalton, age 34, $718,262 total compensation
President, The Flagstone Group: Covey Christensen, age 35, $718,262 total compensation
President, Touchstone Care: John P. Albrechtsen, age 32
President, Keystone Care: Barry R. Port, age 35
President, Northern Pioneer Healthcare: Cory R. Monette, age 40
Auditors: Deloitte & Touche LLP

LOCATIONS

HQ: The Ensign Group, Inc.
27101 Puerta Real, Ste. 450
Mission Viejo, CA 92691
Phone: 949-487-9500
Web: www.ensigngroup.net

2008 Facilities

	No.
California	31
Arizona	12
Texas	10
Utah	6
Washington	3
Idaho	1
Total	**63**

PRODUCTS/OPERATIONS

2008 Sales

	$ mil.	% of total
Medicaid	196.0	42
Medicare	154.9	33
Managed care	64.4	13
Private & other payors	54.1	12
Total	**469.4**	**100**

COMPETITORS

Amedisys
American Baptist Homes of the West
Apria Healthcare
Catholic Healthcare West
Extendicare REIT
Five Star Quality Care
Golden Horizons
Kindred Healthcare
Manor Care
Skilled Healthcare Group
Sun Healthcare
Sunrise Senior Living
Sutter Health
Tenet Healthcare

HISTORICAL FINANCIALS

Company Type: Public

Income Statement   FYE: December 31

	REVENUE ($ mil.)	NET INCOME ($ mil.)	NET PROFIT MARGIN	EMPLOYEES
12/08	469.4	27.5	5.9%	6,153
12/07	411.3	20.5	5.0%	5,603
12/06	358.6	22.5	6.3%	5,435
12/05	300.9	18.4	6.1%	5,506
12/04	244.5	11.1	4.5%	—
Annual Growth	17.7%	25.5%	—	3.8%

2008 Year-End Financials

Debt ratio: 38.1%
Return on equity: 19.3%
Cash ($ mil.): 41.3
Current ratio: 1.81
Long-term debt ($ mil.): 59.5
No. of shares (mil.): 20.6
Dividends
  Yield: 0.7%
  Payout: 9.0%
Market value ($ mil.): 345.4
R&D as % of sales: —
Advertising as % of sales: —

	STOCK PRICE ($) FY Close	P/E High/Low		PER SHARE ($)	
			Earnings	Dividends	Book Value
12/08	16.74	14	6	1.33	0.12	7.56
12/07	14.40	14	10	1.17	0.04	6.29
Annual Growth	16.2%	—	—	13.7%	200.0%	20.3%

Enterprise Financial Services

Enterprise Financial Services wants you to boldly bank where many have banked before. It's the holding company for Enterprise Bank & Trust, which primarily targets closely held businesses and their owners, but also serves individuals in the St. Louis and Kansas City metropolitan areas. Through about a dozen branches, Enterprise Bank & Trust offers standard products such as checking, savings, and money market accounts and CDs. Loans to businesses, including commercial mortgages and operating loans, make up most of the company's lending activities. The bank also originates consumer, construction, and residential mortgage loans.

Enterprise Financial Services provides wealth management services through its Millennium Brokerage subsidiary and Enterprise Bank & Trust's trust division. Accounting for about 10% of the company's revenues, wealth management offerings include financial planning and advisory, investment management, and trust services for businesses and individuals. Millennium Brokerage, acquired in full in late 2007, provides advisory and brokerage support for businesses nationwide from about 15 offices. Enterprise

Trust serves business owners and high-net-worth individuals and has some $1.7 billion in assets under administration.

In 2006 the company acquired Kansas City-based NorthStar Bancshares, which operated five branches in Missouri and Kansas. The following year it bought Clayco Banc Corporation (also based in Kansas City) and its Great American Bank subsidiary. (The company subsequently sold Great American Bank's bank charter, sold one of its two offices, and folded the other into Enterprise Bank & Trust.)

Enterprise Financial also plans to establish a state bank in Arizona in order to take advantage of the market growth in Phoenix. It opened a loan production office there in 2007.

EXECUTIVES

Chairman: James J. (Jim) Murphy Jr., age 65
President, CEO, and Director: Peter F. Benoist, age 61, $1,288,540 total compensation
EVP; Chairman, CEO, and Chief Credit Officer, Enterprise Bank & Trust: Stephen P. (Steve) Marsh, age 54, $662,452 total compensation
EVP and CFO: Frank H. Sanfilippo, age 46, $682,448 total compensation
SVP Marketing, Enterprise Bank & Trust: Jerry Mueller
SVP, Human Resources: Mark Murtha
SVP, Support Center Operations: Joseph (Joe) Feld
VP and Corporate Secretary: Karen Sher
President and CEO, Clayco Banc Corporation: Jeffrey (Jeff) Kiefer
President and CEO, Enterprise Trust: Paul L. Vogel
President, Kansas City North Region, Enterprise Bank & Trust: Angela Wasson-Hunt
President, Kansas City Region, Enterprise Bank & Trust: Linda M. Hanson, age 48, $619,285 total compensation
Chairman, Kansas City Region, Enterprise Bank & Trust: Jack L. Sutherland
Auditors: KPMG LLP

LOCATIONS

HQ: Enterprise Financial Services Corp
150 N. Meramec Ave., Clayton, MO 63105
Phone: 314-725-5500   **Fax:** 314-812-4025
Web: www.enterprisebank.com

Enterprise Bank & Trust has offices in Johnson County, Kansas; and in Clay, Jackson, Platte, St. Charles, and St. Louis counties in Missouri.

PRODUCTS/OPERATIONS

2008 Gross Revenues

	$ mil.	% of total
Interest		
Loans, including fees	112.4	79
Securities	4.8	3
Other	0.8	—
Noninterest		
Wealth management	10.8	8
Service charges on deposit accounts	4.4	3
Net gain on state tax credits	4.2	3
Gain on sale of branches/charter	3.4	2
Other	2.5	2
Total	**143.3**	**100**

COMPETITORS

Bank of America
Commerce Bancshares
First Clover Leaf Financial
Midwest BankCentre
Pulaski Financial
U.S. Bancorp

HISTORICAL FINANCIALS

Company Type: Public

Income Statement

FYE: December 31

	ASSETS ($ mil.)	NET INCOME ($ mil.)	INCOME AS % OF ASSETS	EMPLOYEES
12/08	2,270.2	4.4	0.2%	348
12/07	1,999.1	17.6	0.9%	364
12/06	1,535.6	15.5	1.0%	329
12/05	1,287.0	11.3	0.9%	261
12/04	1,060.0	8.2	0.8%	214
Annual Growth	**21.0%**	**(14.4%)**	**—**	**12.9%**

2008 Year-End Financials

Equity as % of assets: 8.2%
Return on assets: 0.2%
Return on equity: 2.4%
Long-term debt ($ mil.): 251.2
No. of shares (mil.): 12.8
Market value ($ mil.): 195.6
Dividends
Yield: 1.4%
Payout: 61.8%
Sales ($ mil.): 92.0
R&D as % of sales: —
Advertising as % of sales: —

Stock History

NASDAQ (GM): EFSC

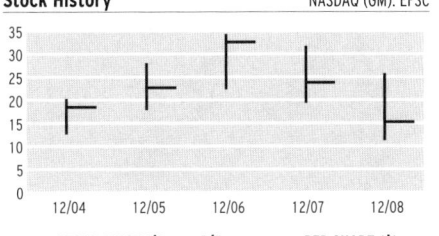

	STOCK PRICE ($) FY Close	P/E High/Low		Earnings	PER SHARE ($) Dividends	Book Value
12/08	15.24	75	34	0.34	0.21	16.97
12/07	23.81	22	14	1.40	0.21	13.49
12/06	32.58	25	17	1.36	0.18	10.36
12/05	22.68	26	17	1.05	0.14	7.22
12/04	18.50	24	16	0.82	—	5.67
Annual Growth	**(4.7%)**	**—**	**—**	**(19.8%)**	**14.5%**	**31.5%**

Enzo Biochem

For Enzo Biochem, antisense is perfectly sensible. The biotech company's Enzo Therapeutics subsidiary is developing antisense technology, a kind of gene therapy that switches off disease-causing genes, to fight such diseases as HIV, hepatitis, and Crohn's disease. This work is funded by two other subsidiaries. Enzo Clinical Labs provides diagnostic testing services in the New York City area. And Enzo Life Sciences makes reagents used by pharmaceutical and biotech companies, as well as academic institutions, in biomedical research. Enzo Biochem has collaborative partnerships with academic and research centers such as the University of Connecticut and the Hadassah University Hospital in Jerusalem.

The company's diagnostic testing operations bring in more than half of revenue. Enzo Clinical Labs operates a full-service reference lab, performing routine and esoteric (highly specialized) tests, in Farmingdale, New York, as well as about 20 specimen collection centers.

Product sales, as well as royalties and licensing fees, from Enzo Life Sciences account for the rest of the company's revenues. The Life Sciences unit manufactures some 5,000 chemical reagents used in a wide variety of biomedical research fields, including cancer research, immunology, gene expression, and DNA damage. It sells the products under such brand names as Enzo, Alexis, and Apotech.

The company has been steadily expanding its Life Sciences operations through acquisitions including Axxora Life Sciences (2007), a maker of biomedical research products, and Biomol (2008), a maker of research products focused on cellular biochemistry. In 2009 the company added Assay Designs, a private US maker of kits and reagents used to detect and measure small molecules. The acquisitions have helped Enzo expand its global sales and distribution of its life sciences products.

The money Enzo makes from its diagnostics and research product segments allows its third unit, Enzo Therapeutics, to continue development of a pipeline of drug candidates that is focused on infectious diseases and immune-mediated diseases, in which the immune system goes haywire. It is working on an antisense therapy for HIV and a potential treatment for uveitis (a kind of eye inflammation), both of which are in early clinical trials.

Its uveitis candidate, as well as other products targeting Crohn's disease and hepatitis B, use proprietary immune regulation technology that aims to control how a patient's body response to particular antigens, or foreign invaders.

Co-founders and brothers-in-law Barry Weiner and Elazar Rabbani, along with the latter's brother Shahram, own about 17% of Enzo; investor Morton Davis owns about 9%.

HISTORY

Chemist Elazar Rabbani and economist Barry Weiner founded Enzo Biochem in 1976 for biotechnology research and development. In 1980 it became the first biotechnology firm to go public. Two years later it got its first R&D contract; the venture with Johnson & Johnson subsidiary Ortho-Clinical Diagnostics failed and led to a $35 million settlement in Enzo's favor in 1994.

Enzo purchased its first clinical lab in 1985 and began offering testing services to the New York medical community. In 1987 the Research Foundation of the State University of New York granted the company exclusive rights to gene control technology for a wide range of therapeutic and agricultural uses.

In 1994 Enzo developed a DNA test for identifying hepatitis B, and the following year it signed an agreement with Cornell University to evaluate antisense technology for possible treatment of HIV. Lower reimbursement by Medicare and other insurers for diagnostic tests and a lease dispute with New York City contributed to a loss for 1996. In 1997 the company announced plans to begin the first human trials of its antisense HIV treatment. A federal judge invalidated two and upheld one of Enzo Biochem's patents in a 1998 dispute with Calgene, a division of what became Pharmacia (which itself is now part of Pfizer). In 1999 Enzo listed on the NYSE.

As the 21st century dawned, Enzo looked to prove its therapeutic development abilities. It began clinical studies of its immune modulation technology to graft vs. host disease, which can afflict bone marrow transplant patients. Trials were also launched for its hepatitis B, hepatitis C, and liver cancer drug candidates.

Product sales in 2003 were lower as drugmakers scaled back their R&D spending. Another contributing factor was Affymetrix: Before its

distributorship deal ended in late 2003, the company cut back orders, contributing to the dip in sales. Enzo Life Sciences in October 2003 sued Affymetrix for breach of contract, claiming its partner manufactured and sold some of Enzo Life Sciences' products without authorization.

EXECUTIVES

Chairman, CEO, and Secretary: Elazar Rabbani, age 66, $1,186,705 total compensation
President, CFO, Principal Accouting Officer, Treasurer, and Director: Barry W. Weiner, age 60, $980,720 total compensation
SVP Finance: Andrew R. Crescenzo, age 53, $323,129 total compensation
VP Scientific Affairs, Enzo Clinical Labs: Mohan Chellani
VP Corporate Development: David C. Goldberg, age 52
VP Business Development; COO, Enzo Life Sciences: Andrew P. Whiteley, age 51
VP Finance; SVP, Enzo Clinical Labs: Herbert B. Bass, age 61
President, Enzo Therapeutics: Christine T. Fischette, age 58
President, Enzo Life Sciences: Carl W. Balezentis, age 52, $348,732 total compensation
President, Enzo Clinical Labs: Kevin Krenitsky, age 43, $95,208 total compensation
Auditors: Ernst & Young LLP

LOCATIONS

HQ: Enzo Biochem, Inc.
527 Madison Ave., New York, NY 10022
Phone: 212-583-0100
Web: www.enzo.com

2009 Sales

	$ mil.	% of total
US	75.9	85
Switzerland	6.5	7
UK	2.5	3
Other countries	4.7	5
Total	**89.6**	**100**

PRODUCTS/OPERATIONS

2009 Revenue

	$ mil.	% of total
Product sales	40.6	45
Clinical laboratory services	39.6	44
Royalties & licensing fees	9.4	11
Total	**89.6**	**100**

Selected Products and Brands

Research reagents and kits
  Alexis
  Apotech
  Axxora
  Biomol
  Enzo
Therapeutics
  Alequel (Crohn's disease)
  Enzo-D58 (osteoporosis)
  HGTV43 gene medicine (HIV)
  Optiquel (autoimmune uveitis)
Clinical laboratory services
  Esoteric clinical tests
  Routine clinical tests

COMPETITORS

Abbott Labs	Johnson & Johnson
Affymetrix	LabCorp
AVI BioPharma	Life Technologies
BD Biosciences	Corporation
Beckman Coulter	Merck
Bio-Reference Labs	Millennium
Bristol-Myers Squibb	PerkinElmer
Gilead Sciences	Pfizer
Idera	Quest Diagnostics
Isis Pharmaceuticals	TECHNE

HISTORICAL FINANCIALS

Company Type: Public

Income Statement

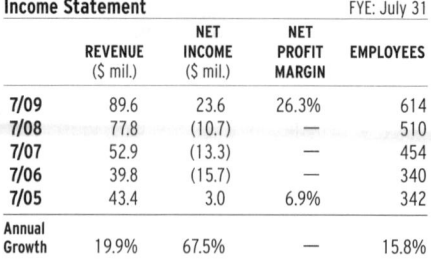

	REVENUE ($ mil.)	NET INCOME ($ mil.)	NET PROFIT MARGIN	EMPLOYEES
FYE: July 31				
7/09	89.6	23.6	26.3%	614
7/08	77.8	(10.7)	—	510
7/07	52.9	(13.3)	—	454
7/06	39.8	(15.7)	—	340
7/05	43.4	3.0	6.9%	342
Annual Growth	19.9%	67.5%		15.8%

2009 Year-End Financials

Debt ratio: —	Dividends
Return on equity: 18.5%	Yield: —
Cash ($ mil.): 6.9	Payout: —
Current ratio: 5.34	Market value ($ mil.): 193.1
Long-term debt ($ mil.): —	R&D as % of sales: —
No. of shares (mil.): 37.9	Advertising as % of sales: —

Stock History

NYSE: ENZ

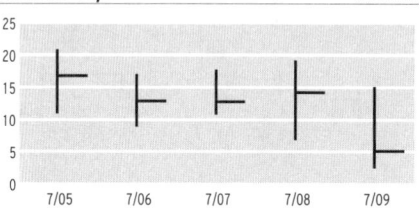

	STOCK PRICE ($) FY Close	P/E High/Low		PER SHARE ($) Earnings	Dividends	Book Value
7/09	5.10	24	4	0.63	—	3.08
7/08	14.21	—	—	(0.29)	—	3.65
7/07	12.78	—	—	(0.38)	—	3.75
7/06	12.89	—	—	(0.49)	—	2.52
7/05	16.78	230	124	0.09	—	2.86
Annual Growth	(25.8%)	—	—	62.7%	—	1.9%

Epicor Software

Epicor Software hopes the middle of the road proves paved with gold. The company provides enterprise resource planning software for mid-sized businesses. Epicor's software integrates back-office applications for manufacturing, distribution, and accounting with customer relationship management functions, including sales, marketing, and customer support. The company's software also includes collaborative applications that link employees, distributors, and suppliers, encompassing operations such as supply chain management, sourcing, and procurement. In October 2008 Elliott Associates (which holds a 10% stake in the company) made an unsolicited bid to acquire Epicor. Epicor's board of directors rejected the offer.

Epicor primarily targets midsized customers with annual sales between $10 million and $1 billion. The company's more than 20,000 clients come from industries such as manufacturing, distribution, financial services, and hospitality.

In February 2008 the company acquired NSB Retail Systems. The deal expanded Epicor's portfolio of products and services for large and midsized retailers and department stores.

HISTORY

Platinum Holdings was founded in 1984 by Gerald Blackie, former CEO of bankrupt software maker Heritage Computing, and former Heritage programmers Timothy McMullen and Kevin Riegelsberger. They introduced the Platinum line of financial accounting software in 1985. Platinum expanded by signing marketing agreements with Arthur Andersen in 1987 and IBM in 1989. In 1992 the company went public and changed its name to Platinum Software.

Two years later Platinum revealed that it had misstated its earnings by booking some sales before they had closed. The company paid $17 million to settle a class-action lawsuit and reorganized. (Blackie and two other ex-execs were later forced to repay hundreds of thousands of dollars in gains and bonuses.)

George Klaus was recruited as CEO in 1996 after twice turning down Platinum's board. The company quickly expanded into enterprise resource planning applications through acquisitions. The next year it bought customer relationship management software developer Clientele Software and manufacturing and distribution software provider FocusSoft. The moves helped Platinum to a profitable fiscal 1998, its first in six years. In late 1998 it bought larger rival DataWorks, cut 15% of its workforce, and changed its fiscal year to December.

The next year the company settled a trademark lawsuit, filed in 1997, with PLATINUM Technology, and Platinum changed its name to Epicor Software in 1999.

Amid declining sales in 2001 the company restructured, cutting jobs and selling its Impresa and Platinum for Windows product lines.

Epicor boosted its procurement and supply chain management offerings by acquiring certain assets of Clarus in 2002. In 2004 the company purchased Scala Business Solutions for about $45 million, as well as buying the assets of Platsoft and Strongline.

In late 2005 the company acquired CRS Retail Technology Group for about $123.5 million.

EXECUTIVES

Chairman, President, and CEO: L. George Klaus, age 68, $2,077,203 total compensation
EVP Finance and Administration and CFO: Michael Pietrini, age 39
EVP and General Manager, Epicor Retail: David Henning
EVP Worldwide Consulting: Lauri Klaus
SVP and General Counsel: John D. Ireland
SVP Finance and Principal Accounting Officer: Russell (Russ) Clark, age 40, $486,080 total compensation
SVP Worldwide Research and Development: Paul Farrell
SVP, Worldwide Support: Daniel (Dan) Whelan, age 41
SVP and Chief Marketing Officer: John Hiraoka
VP Information Systems: Rick Parrish
Director, Public Relations and Analyst Relations: Lisa A. Preuss
Senior Public Relations Specialist: Erin Stone
Auditors: McGladrey & Pullen, LLP

LOCATIONS

HQ: Epicor Software Corporation
18200 Von Karman Ave., Ste. 1000
Irvine, CA 92612
Phone: 949-585-4000   **Fax:** 949-585-4091
Web: www.epicor.com

2008 Sales

	$ mil.	% of total
US	336.0	69
Other countries	151.9	31
Total	**487.9**	**100**

PRODUCTS/OPERATIONS

2008 Sales

	$ mil.	% of total
Maintenance	192.3	39
Consulting	152.2	31
License fees	90.4	18
Hardware & other	53.0	12
Total	**487.9**	**100**

Selected Software

Enterprise resource management (Epicor Enterprise)

Selected Services

Consulting
Custom software development
Technical support
Training

COMPETITORS

Deltek	Microsoft
FrontRange Solutions	Oracle
HighJump	Pivotal Corp.
IFS AB	QAD
Infor Global	Sage Software
Lawson Software	SAP
Manhattan Associates	Unit 4 Agresso

HISTORICAL FINANCIALS

Company Type: Public

Income Statement				FYE: December 31
	REVENUE ($ mil.)	NET INCOME ($ mil.)	NET PROFIT MARGIN	EMPLOYEES
12/08	487.9	1.0	0.2%	2,645
12/07	429.8	41.3	9.6%	2,907
12/06	384.1	23.8	6.2%	2,178
12/05	289.4	52.0	18.0%	1,887
12/04	226.2	25.3	11.2%	1,409
Annual Growth	21.2%	(55.4%)	—	17.1%

2008 Year-End Financials

Debt ratio: 118.5%
Return on equity: 0.4%
Cash ($ mil.): 89.8
Current ratio: 1.24
Long-term debt ($ mil.): 315.3
No. of shares (mil.): 61.4
Dividends
  Yield: 0.0%
  Payout: —
Market value ($ mil.): 294.7
R&D as % of sales: —
Advertising as % of sales: —

Stock History

NASDAQ (GS): EPIC

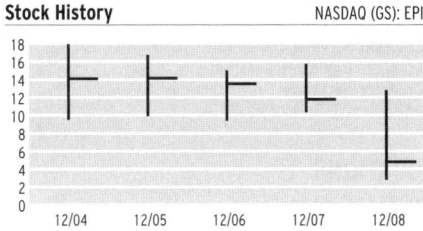

	STOCK PRICE ($) FY Close	P/E High/Low	PER SHARE ($) Earnings	Dividends	Book Value
12/08	4.80	632 146	0.02	0.00	4.33
12/07	11.78	22 15	0.71	0.00	4.28
12/06	13.51	35 23	0.42	0.00	3.40
12/05	14.13	18 11	0.92	0.00	2.78
12/04	14.09	38 21	0.47	0.00	1.64
Annual Growth	(23.6%)	— —	(54.6%)	—	27.4%

Equinix, Inc.

In the Internet game, Equinix is the neutral playing field. Founded in 1998, the company provides data and network hosting and colocation facilities (it calls them Internet Business Exchanges, or IBXs) where Internet service providers (ISPs), telecommunications carriers, and content providers can locate equipment and interconnect networks and operations. The company also offers colocation-related services that include providing clients with cabinets, operating space, and storage. Its clients have included such large firms as Apple, eBay, IBM, and Bank of America. Equinix operates dozens of IBXs in almost 20 major international markets, including Chicago, Hong Kong, Los Angeles, New York, and Tokyo.

In anticipation of a continued increase in demand for commercial data center services, Equinix is investing in its infrastructure in the US and Europe. The company spent $30 million in 2009 to acquire and equip an additional data center in Frankfurt and it announced a $100 million investment in its New York facilities. Also in 2009 Equinix said that it would acquire Tampa, Florida-based Switch and Data Facilities for $689 million in a move that will boost its number of data centers to 79.

EXECUTIVES

Chairman: Peter F. Van Camp, age 54
President, CEO, and Director:
  Stephen M. (Steve) Smith, age 53,
  $5,123,059 total compensation
COO: Sushil (Sam) Kapoor, age 63,
  $1,912,857 total compensation
CFO: Keith D. Taylor, age 48,
  $2,246,756 total compensation
CIO: Brian Lillie
CTO: David Pickut
Chief Development Officer: Mark Adams
SVP Global Human Resources: Keri Crask
SVP Global Real Estate: Howard B. Horowitz
General Counsel and Corporate Secretary:
  Brandi L. G. Morandi
Chief Technologist: Lane Patterson
Chief Marketing Officer: Jarrett Appleby, age 47
Chairman, Equinox Group Limited:
  Guy de Rohan Willner, $2,935,000 total compensation
President, Equinix U.S.: Peter T. Ferris, age 52,
  $1,976,808 total compensation
President, Equinix Asia/Pacific: Samuel Lee
President, Equinix Europe: Eric Schwartz, age 42,
  $2,005,912 total compensation
Senior Director Investor Relations: Jason Starr
Auditors: PricewaterhouseCoopers LLP

LOCATIONS

HQ: Equinix, Inc.
  301 Velocity Way, 5th Fl., Foster City, CA 94404
Phone: 650-513-7000   **Fax:** 650-513-7900
Web: www.equinix.com

2008 Sales

	% of total
United States	63
Europe	25
Asia/Pacific	12
Total	**100**

PRODUCTS/OPERATIONS

Selected Services

Central switching connections
Colocation-related equipment, operating space, and
  storage
Installation and maintenance of customer equipment
Power supply services
Private and shared cages

COMPETITORS

AboveNet
AT&T
COLT Telecom
Level 3 Communications
NTT
Qwest Communications
Rackspace
SAVVIS
SingTel
Switch and Data Facilities
Verio
Verizon

HISTORICAL FINANCIALS

Company Type: Public

Income Statement				FYE: December 31
	REVENUE ($ mil.)	NET INCOME ($ mil.)	NET PROFIT MARGIN	EMPLOYEES
12/08	704.7	131.5	18.7%	1,115
12/07	419.4	(5.2)	—	911
12/06	286.9	(6.8)	—	616
12/05	221.1	(42.6)	—	537
12/04	163.7	(68.6)	—	468
Annual Growth	44.0%	—	—	24.2%

2008 Year-End Financials

Debt ratio: 130.6%
Return on equity: 15.4%
Cash ($ mil.): 220.2
Current ratio: 1.31
Long-term debt ($ mil.): 1,165.5
No. of shares (mil.): 39.0
Dividends
  Yield: —
  Payout: —
Market value ($ mil.): 2,073.5
R&D as % of sales: —
Advertising as % of sales: —

Stock History

NASDAQ (GS): EQIX

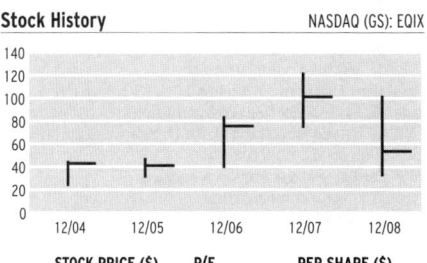

	STOCK PRICE ($) FY Close	P/E High/Low	PER SHARE ($) Earnings	Dividends	Book Value
12/08	53.19	31 10	3.31	—	22.90
12/07	101.07	— —	(0.16)	—	20.89
12/06	75.62	— —	(0.22)	—	9.11
12/05	40.76	— —	(1.78)	—	7.41
12/04	42.74	— —	(3.87)	—	7.02
Annual Growth	5.6%	— —	—	—	34.4%

eResearchTechnology

eResearchTechnology (eRT) e-cares about your e-clinical e-trial. The firm offers support services and software to help streamline the clinical trials process that drugs and medical devices must pass to earn regulatory approval. eRT's products automate all aspects of the process, from setup and data gathering to analysis and FDA application preparation. Customers include drugmakers, medical device firms, and contract research organizations (CROs). Flagship product EXPeRT ensures cardiac safety by collecting, processing, and interpreting electrocardiogram (ECG) data. eRT also provides site support including ECG equipment rentals and sales. The firm markets its products through a global sales force.

The company's cardiac safety services (primarily EXPeRT) account for a majority of sales. eRT has been able to issue the EXPeRT2, which adds features such as on-demand reporting, protocol-unique clinical alerts, use of standardized protocol templates, and enhanced query automation. Later that year the company launched its EXPeRT ePRO patient recorded outcomes product line.

eRT acquired Covance's centralized ECG business, which processes digital ECG results during clinical trials, for around $50 million. Under the terms of the deal, eRT will continue to provide the services to Covance's clients.

Novartis is eRT's largest client (accounting for about 23% of sales), but the company does business with some 235 customers, including most of the world's largest pharmaceutical firms. eResearchTechnology earns more than 20% of its revenues outside the US.

In mid-2009 the company sold its $6-million-a-year electronic data capture business to OmniComm Systems to focus on its cardiac safety and ePRO business lines.

EXECUTIVES

Chairman and Chief Scientific Officer:
Joel Morganroth, age 63,
$2,107,585 total compensation
President, CEO, and Director: Michael J. McKelvey,
age 56, $1,301,029 total compensation
EVP, CFO, and Secretary: Keith D. Schneck, age 53,
$252,995 total compensation
EVP Cardiac Safety: Amy Furlong, age 36,
$528,232 total compensation
EVP and Chief Development Officer:
Thomas P. (Tom) Devine, age 56
EVP and Chief Medical Officer: Jeffrey S. Litwin, age 51,
$604,765 total compensation
EVP Sales and Marketing: John M. Blakeley, age 41
SVP Americas Sales: George Tiger, age 49
SVP Strategic Marketing, Planning, and Partnerships:
Robert S. Brown, age 53
VP and Controller: Steven M. Eisenstein,
$278,645 total compensation
VP Human Resources: Valerie Mattern
Auditors: KPMG LLP

LOCATIONS

HQ: eResearchTechnology, Inc.
30 S. 17th St., Philadelphia, PA 19103
Phone: 215-972-0420   **Fax:** 215-972-0414
Web: www.ert.com

2008 Sales

	$ mil.	% of total
North America	105.6	79
Europe	27.5	21
Total	**133.1**	**100**

PRODUCTS/OPERATIONS

2008 Sales

	$ mil.	% of total
Services	99.3	75
Site support	30.6	23
Licenses	3.2	2
Total	**133.1**	**100**

Selected Products

eData Entry (data capture)
eData Management (trial data editing and management)
eResearch Network (trial management network
  infrastructure)
eSafety Net (adverse event management)
eStudy Conduct (trial setup and tracking)
EXPeRT Cardiac Safety (electrocardiogram analysis)
  Digital ECG Community
  EXPeRT Direct
  EXPeRT ECG Consulting
EXPeRT eClinical (clinical research platform)
  EXPeRT Adverse Event Reporting
  EXPeRT Data Capture
  EXPeRT Data Management
  EXPeRT eClinical Consulting
  EXPeRT Trial Management
EXPeRT ePRO (automated patient data collection)
EXPeRT Portal (research portal linking sponsors, CROs,
  doctors, and patients)

COMPETITORS

BioClinica
Biotel
CompuMed
Covance
DATATRAK International
Encorium
etrials Worldwide
LabVantage
Medifacts International
OmniComm
Perceptive Informatics
Phase Forward

HISTORICAL FINANCIALS

Company Type: Public

Income Statement

FYE: December 31

	REVENUE ($ mil.)	NET INCOME ($ mil.)	NET PROFIT MARGIN	EMPLOYEES
12/08	133.1	25.0	18.8%	415
12/07	98.7	15.3	15.5%	356
12/06	86.4	8.3	9.6%	341
12/05	86.8	15.4	17.7%	355
12/04	109.4	29.7	27.1%	353
Annual Growth	**5.0%**	**(4.2%)**	**—**	**4.1%**

2008 Year-End Financials

Debt ratio: 0.0%
Return on equity: 19.9%
Cash ($ mil.): 66.4
Current ratio: 3.80
Long-term debt ($ mil.): 0.0
No. of shares (mil.): 48.5
Dividends
  Yield: 0.0%
  Payout: —
Market value ($ mil.): 321.3
R&D as % of sales: —
Advertising as % of sales: —

Stock History

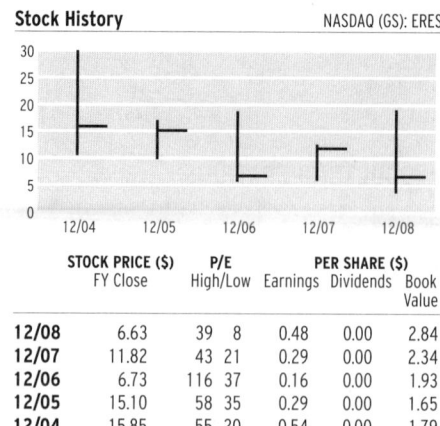

NASDAQ (GS): ERES

	STOCK PRICE ($) FY Close	P/E High/Low		PER SHARE ($) Earnings	Dividends	Book Value
12/08	6.63	39	8	0.48	0.00	2.84
12/07	11.82	43	21	0.29	0.00	2.34
12/06	6.73	116	37	0.16	0.00	1.93
12/05	15.10	58	35	0.29	0.00	1.65
12/04	15.85	55	20	0.54	0.00	1.79
Annual Growth	**(19.6%)**	**—**	**—**	**(2.9%)**	**—**	**12.2%**

ESSA Bancorp

ESSA Bancorp is the holding company for ESSA Bank & Trust, which offers deposits and loans to consumers and businesses in eastern Pennsylvania. One- to four-family residential mortgages dominate the bank's lending activities, representing more than 80% of its loan portfolio. Commercial real estate loans account for 10%, while home equity loans and lines of credit make up ESSA's other significant loan segments. In addition to its lending and deposit services, the bank also offers financial and investment services through a third-party firm. Founded in 1916, ESSA operates more than a dozen branches in Monroe and Northampton counties.

EXECUTIVES

Chairman: John E. Burrus, age 69
President, CEO, and Director: Gary S. Olson, age 54,
$401,485 total compensation
EVP and CFO: Allan A. Muto, age 48,
$337,053 total compensation
SVP, Lending Services Division: Robert S. Howes Jr.,
age 55
VP, Human Resources: Thomas J. Grayuski, age 47
VP, Commercial Lending: William J. Lewis
VP, Delivery Systems Division: Diane K. Reimer, age 52
VP, Branch Administration: Cathy J. Callahan
VP, Retail Services Division: V. Gail Warner, age 52,
$259,723 total compensation
Corporate Secretary: Suzie T. Farley
Auditors: S.R. Snodgrass, A.C.

LOCATIONS

HQ: ESSA Bancorp, Inc.
200 Palmer St., Stroudsburg, PA 18360
Phone: 570-421-0531   **Fax:** 570-476-6258
Web: www.essabank.com

COMPETITORS

First National Community Bancorp
Fulton Financial
Harleysville National
National Penn Bancshares
Norwood Financial
PNC Financial
Sovereign Bank

HISTORICAL FINANCIALS

Company Type: Public

Income Statement

FYE: September 30

	ASSETS ($ mil.)	NET INCOME ($ mil.)	INCOME AS % OF ASSETS	EMPLOYEES
9/09	1,042.1	6.6	0.6%	193
9/08	993.5	6.1	0.6%	184
9/07	910.4	(5.1)	—	185
9/06	725.8	4.0	0.6%	170
Annual Growth	**12.8%**	**18.2%**	**—**	**4.3%**

2009 Year-End Financials

Equity as % of assets: 17.8%
Return on assets: 0.6%
Return on equity: 3.4%
Long-term debt ($ mil.): 391.9
No. of shares (mil.): 14.6
Market value ($ mil.): 192.8
Dividends
Yield: 1.3%
Payout: 36.2%
Sales ($ mil.): 34.7
R&D as % of sales: —
Advertising as % of sales: —

Stock History

NASDAQ (GS): ESSA

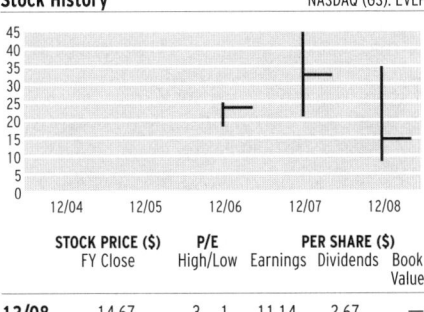

	STOCK PRICE ($) FY Close	P/E High/Low	PER SHARE ($) Earnings	Dividends	Book Value
9/09	13.21	30 23	0.47	0.17	12.71
9/08	13.90	37 25	0.38	0.08	13.71
9/07	11.15	— —	—	—	14.02
Annual Growth	**8.8%**	**— —**	**23.7%**	**112.5%**	**(4.8%**

EV Energy Partners

EV Energy Partners is a natural gas and oil exploration and production company, which operates in the Appalachian Basin, primarily in West Virginia and Ohio, as well as in Louisiana, Michigan, Oklahoma, and Texas. In 2007 EV Energy Partners reported estimated proved reserves of 250 billion cu. ft. of natural gas and 4.5 million barrels of oil. Its base in the Appalachian Basin puts EV Energy Partners in close proximity to the nation's major consuming markets, allowing for stronger pricing power. EV Energy Partners was formed in 2006 by Canadian energy industry investment group EnerVest, which owns 71% of EV Energy Partners' general partner.

EV Energy Partners' conservative growth strategy includes replacing and increasing reserves and production over the long term by pursuing acquisitions of long-lived oil or natural gas properties with low decline rates, predictable production profiles, and relatively low-risk drilling opportunities. It also retains control over the operation of a substantial portion of its production base.

The company acquired assets in Michigan in 2007. In 2008 EV Energy Partners acquired natural gas and oil properties in the San Juan Basin, Mid-Continent (Oklahoma, Texas Panhandle, and Kansas), Eastland County Texas, and West Virginia, for $173 million.

EXECUTIVES

Chairman and CEO: John B. Walker, age 63
President, COO, and Director; EVP and COO, EnerVest: Mark A. Houser, age 47
SVP and CFO: Michael E. (Mike) Mercer, age 50
SVP Acquisitions and Divestitures: Kathryn S. MacAskie, age 52
Controller: Frederick Dwyer, age 50
Auditors: Deloitte & Touche LLP

LOCATIONS

HQ: EV Energy Partners, L.P.
1001 Fannin St., Ste. 800, Houston, TX 77002
Phone: 713-651-1144 **Fax:** 713-651-1260
Web: www.evenergypartners.com

PRODUCTS/OPERATIONS

2008 Sales

	$ mil.	% of total
Natural gas & oil	192.8	93
Transportation & marketing	12.9	6
Gain on derivatives	1.6	1
Total	**207.3**	**100**

HISTORICAL FINANCIALS

Company Type: Public

Income Statement

FYE: December 31

	REVENUE ($ mil.)	NET INCOME ($ mil.)	NET PROFIT MARGIN	EMPLOYEES
12/08	207.3	225.5	108.8%	500
12/07	104.0	9.5	9.1%	465
12/06	47.9	3.3	6.9%	360
12/05	44.2	15.1	34.2%	332
12/04	30.1	8.4	27.9%	—
Annual Growth	**62.0%**	**127.6%**	**—**	**14.6%**

2008 Year-End Financials

Debt ratio: —
Return on equity: —
Cash ($ mil.): 41.6
Current ratio: 5.67
Long-term debt ($ mil.): 467.0
No. of shares (mil.): 20.4
Dividends
Yield: 18.2%
Payout: 24.0%
Market value ($ mil.): 298.9
R&D as % of sales: —
Advertising as % of sales: —

Stock History

NASDAQ (GS): EVEP

	STOCK PRICE ($) FY Close	P/E High/Low	PER SHARE ($) Earnings	Dividends	Book Value
12/08	14.67	3 1	11.14	2.67	—
12/07	32.50	60 29	0.74	1.92	—
12/06	23.44	57 43	0.43	0.00	—
Annual Growth	**(20.9%)**	**— —**	**409.0%**	**—**	**—**

Exactech, Inc.

Back off, lawman — Exactech's joints are medicinal. Hospitals, surgeons, and clinics worldwide use the company's knee and hip devices to replace joints weakened by injury or disease. Its Optetrak knee implants and AcuMatch hip implant system either partially or totally replace patients' damaged joints. It also markets Opteform and Optefil, bone allograft materials used to correct bone defects and damage. Exactech markets its products through independent dealers in the US and primarily through distributors in some 25 other countries. Chairman, president, and CEO William Petty and his family own about a third of Exactech, which was founded in 1985 by an orthopedic surgeon.

In addition to its orthopedic allograft products, Exactech distributes Regenaform and Regenafil allografting materials for the dental market. It distributes all of its allograft products through an agreement with RTI Biologics.

The company also has a licensing agreement with Italian manufacturer Tecres, through which it distributes its antibiotic-infused bone cement product, Cemex, in the US and Canada. Cemex is used by surgeons during joint replacement or repair procedures.

Exactech has expanded internationally by acquiring or setting up direct operations in some markets where it had formerly used distributorship agreements. In 2008 it acquired its French distributor, France Medica, and established its own direct distribution subsidiary in Japan.

Also in 2008 the company acquired Altiva, a spinal products company in which Exactech had previously held a minority stake. Altiva contributed a line of spinal fusion implants and instruments Exactech now sells through its Exactech Spine division.

Along with acquisitions, Exactech expands by growing its existing product lines. In 2008 the company introduced six new products in its knee and hip implant businesses. In 2009 the company planned rollouts of a new knee implant for its flagship Optetrak brand and an updated version of its Novation hip stem/Crown Cup acetabular systems.

EXECUTIVES

Chairman and CEO: William (Bill) Petty, age 66, $701,052 total compensation
President and Director: David W. Petty, age 43, $392,902 total compensation
CFO and Treasurer: Joel C. Phillips, age 41, $367,270 total compensation
EVP Research and Development: Gary J. Miller, age 61, $458,214 total compensation
SVP; General Manager, Biologics and Exactech Spine: Bruce Thompson, age 51, $432,600 total compensation
CTO; VP Biologics Research and Development: Steve Lin
VP Engineering and Development, Large Joints: Xavier Sarabia
VP Administration and Human Resources and Secretary: Betty B. Petty, age 66
VP Engineering and Development, Spine Systems: Raymond Cloutier
VP International Sales and Marketing: Daniel Berdat
VP Sales: Bob Purcell
Auditors: Deloitte & Touche LLP

LOCATIONS

HQ: Exactech, Inc.
2320 NW 66th Ct., Gainesville, FL 32653
Phone: 352-377-1140 **Fax:** 352-378-2617
Web: www.exac.com

2008 Sales

	$ mil.	% of total
US	112.5	70
Spain	10.0	6
Other countries	39.2	24
Total	**161.7**	**100**

PRODUCTS/OPERATIONS

2008 Sales

	$ mil.	% of total
Knee implants	72.6	45
Biologic & spine products	26.5	17
Hip implants	22.8	14
Extremity products	16.8	10
Other products	23.0	14
Total	**161.7**	**100**

COMPETITORS

Biomet
DePuy
DJO
Osteotech
Smith & Nephew
Stryker
Wright Medical Group
Zimmer Holdings

HISTORICAL FINANCIALS

Company Type: Public

Income Statement
FYE: December 31

	REVENUE ($ mil.)	NET INCOME ($ mil.)	NET PROFIT MARGIN	EMPLOYEES
12/08	161.7	11.1	6.9%	390
12/07	124.2	8.5	6.8%	265
12/06	102.4	7.8	7.6%	215
12/05	91.0	6.6	7.3%	214
12/04	81.8	7.3	8.9%	173
Annual Growth	**18.6%**	**11.0%**	**—**	**22.5%**

2008 Year-End Financials

Debt ratio: 18.4%
Return on equity: 10.6%
Cash ($ mil.): 3.3
Current ratio: 4.62
Long-term debt ($ mil.): 22.4
No. of shares (mil.): 12.8
Dividends
 Yield: 0.0%
 Payout: —
Market value ($ mil.): 215.6
R&D as % of sales: —
Advertising as % of sales: —

Stock History
NASDAQ (GM): EXAC

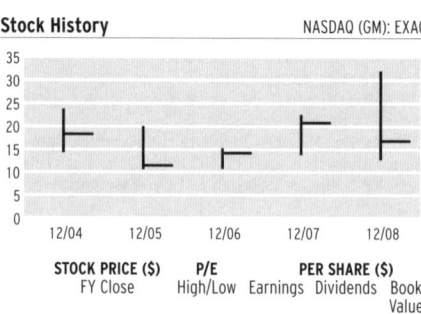

	STOCK PRICE ($) FY Close	P/E High/Low		PER SHARE ($) Earnings	Dividends	Book Value
12/08	16.84	36	15	0.87	0.00	9.50
12/07	20.75	31	20	0.72	0.00	6.85
12/06	14.23	22	16	0.67	0.00	6.01
12/05	11.44	35	19	0.57	0.00	5.29
12/04	18.29	37	23	0.63	0.00	4.67
Annual Growth	**(2.0%)**	**—**	**—**	**8.4%**	**—**	**19.4%**

ExlService Holdings

Have an extra-large task you'd rather not take on? Outsource it to ExlService Holdings. The company, known as EXL, offers business process outsourcing (BPO), research and analytics, and consulting services. EXL's BPO offerings, which generate most of its sales, include claims processing, collections, customer support, and finance and accounting. Customers come mainly from the banking, financial services, and insurance industries, but also from sectors such as utilities and telecommunications. Two UK-based customers, insurer Norwich Union and natural gas supplier Centrica, together account for about 35% of EXL's sales.

EXL markets and sells its services through offices in the US, the UK, and Singapore and operates from facilities in India and the Philippines. Business has been brisk for EXL and other BPO firms as the global economic downturn has caused many companies to cut costs and outsource operations.

The company hopes to grow primarily by selling more services to existing customers and by adding more Global 1,000 companies to its client list. In addition, EXL will continue to evaluate acquisition opportunities. EXL has been waiting for the right opportunity to make another acquisition since its last purchase. It expanded in 2006 by buying Inductis, a provider of consulting and data analysis services for companies in the financial services, insurance, and information services industries. EXL officials are looking at BPO firms in Eastern Europe or the US with capabilities in insurance, utilities, compliance, and risk management as acquisition targets. The company plans to spend $70 million-$75 million on acquisitions in 2009.

Adhering to this strategy, in July 2009 EXL acquired the back-office operations of Schneider Logistic's Czech Republic facility. The unit offers accounting and transaction processing services along with multilingual capabilities. The deal gives EXL an outpost to extend and diversify its outsourcing operations in Europe.

Affiliates of investment firm Oak Hill Capital Partners — represented on EXL's board by managing partner Steven Gruber, director Edward Dardani, executive chairman Vikram Talwar, and president and CEO Rohit Kapoor — control a 37% stake in the company.

EXECUTIVES

Chairman: Vikram Talwar, age 59,
 $1,676,154 total compensation
President, CEO, and Director: Rohit Kapoor, age 44,
 $1,708,560 total compensation
COO: Pavan Bagai, age 47
CFO: Vishal Chhibbar
VP and Chief Sales and Marketing Officer:
 Krishna Nacha, age 39, $551,165 total compensation
VP, Head of Transformation Services, and Managing Principal: Rembert de Villa, age 52,
 $510,762 total compensation
VP, General Counsel, and Secretary: Amit Shashank,
 age 39, $644,360 total compensation
VP and Global Head Human Resources: Amitabh Hajela,
 age 40
VP and Head Strategic Account Management, North America: Bruce Polsky
VP and Head Global Technology: Baljinder Singh
Head Investor Relations and Corporate Development:
 Jarrod Yahes
Auditors: Ernst & Young LLP

LOCATIONS

HQ: ExlService Holdings, Inc.
350 Park Ave., 10th Fl., New York, NY 10022
Phone: 212-277-7100 **Fax:** 212-277-7111
Web: www.exlservice.com

2008 Sales

	$ mil.	% of total
US	102.6	57
UK	77.8	43
India	0.7	—
Other countries	0.6	—
Total	**181.7**	**100**

PRODUCTS/OPERATIONS

2008 Sales

	$ mil.	% of total
Outsourcing services	138.8	76
Transformation services	42.9	24
Total	**181.7**	**100**

COMPETITORS

Accenture
Affiliated Computer Services
Genpact
HP Enterprise Services
IBM Global Services
Infosys
Tata Consultancy
Wipro
WNS (Holdings)

HISTORICAL FINANCIALS

Company Type: Public

Income Statement
FYE: December 31

	REVENUE ($ mil.)	NET INCOME ($ mil.)	NET PROFIT MARGIN	EMPLOYEES
12/08	181.7	18.9	10.4%	9,995
12/07	179.9	27.0	15.0%	10,000
12/06	121.8	13.4	11.0%	8,200
12/05	74.0	6.8	9.2%	7,300
12/04	60.5	5.4	8.9%	7,300
Annual Growth	**31.6%**	**36.8%**	**—**	**8.2%**

2008 Year-End Financials

Debt ratio: 0.1%
Return on equity: 10.9%
Cash ($ mil.): 112.2
Current ratio: 4.04
Long-term debt ($ mil.): 0.2
No. of shares (mil.): 29.0
Dividends
 Yield: 0.0%
 Payout: —
Market value ($ mil.): 248.2
R&D as % of sales: —
Advertising as % of sales: —

Stock History
NASDAQ (GS): EXLS

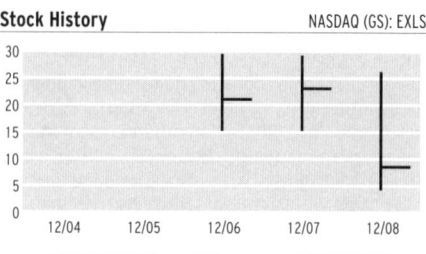

	STOCK PRICE ($) FY Close	P/E High/Low		PER SHARE ($) Earnings	Dividends	Book Value
12/08	8.57	53	9	0.49	0.00	5.92
12/07	23.08	31	17	0.93	0.00	6.01
12/06	21.04	50	27	0.58	0.00	4.39
Annual Growth	**(36.2%)**	**—**	**—**	**(8.1%)**	**—**	**16.1%**

Exponent, Inc.

Exponent has found success in failure. The science and engineering consulting firm specializes in analyzing and solving complex problems and preventing disasters and product failures. Exponent's 640 scientists, physicians, engineers, and business consultants assess environmental risks, regulatory issues, and workplace hazards for government agencies and clients from such industries as transportation, construction, and manufacturing. Established in 1967, its work has included analyzing such disasters as the Exxon Valdez oil spill and the bombing of the Murrah Federal Building in Oklahoma City. Exponent operates through more than 20 facilities in China, Germany, the UK, and the US.

Originally focused on product failure litigation, the company has used acquisitions to expand its range of expertise into prevention, as well as such fields as toxicology, epidemiology, and visual communications. Exponent is contributing to the US Army's efforts in Afghanistan and Iraq by developing technical solutions related to combat issues.

Helping companies comply with the European Union's new Registration, Evaluation, Authorisation and Restriction of Chemical Regulation gave Exponent's chemical registration and food safety unit a boost in 2008 and is expected to continue to be a growth area for the company.

EXECUTIVES

Chairman: Michael R. Gaulke, age 64, $2,166,057 total compensation
President, CEO, and Director: Paul R. Johnston, age 56, $1,315,894 total compensation
CFO and Corporate Secretary: Richard L. Schlenker Jr., age 44, $888,032 total compensation
CTO: Subbaiah V. Malladi, age 63
Group VP: Elizabeth L. Anderson, age 70, $1,143,238 total compensation
Group VP, Materials/Metallurgy, Mechanical Engineering, Electrical Engineering, and Thermal Sciences: Robert D. Caligiuri, age 58, $1,026,873 total compensation
Group VP and Principal Engineer: John E. Moalli, age 45
Group VP, Exponent Failure Analysis Associates and Principal Engineer: John D. Osteraas, age 56
Group VP: Paul D. Boehm, age 61
Corporate VP and Director, Health Sciences Center for Epidemiology, Biostatistics and Computational Biology: Suresh Moolgavkar
Corporate VP Human Resources: Gregory P. Klein
Auditors: KPMG LLP

LOCATIONS

HQ: Exponent, Inc.
149 Commonwealth Dr., Menlo Park, CA 94025
Phone: 650-326-9400   **Fax:** 650-326-8072
Web: www.exponent.com

2008 Sales

	$ mil.	% of total
US	213.4	93
Other countries	15.4	7
Total	**228.8**	**100**

PRODUCTS/OPERATIONS

2008 Sales

	$ mil.	% of total
Engineering services & other scientific	176.9	77
Environmental & health services	51.9	23
Total	**228.8**	**100**

Selected Practice Areas

Biomechanics
Buildings and structures
Civil engineering
Construction consulting
Data and risk analysis
Ecological and biological sciences
Electrical and semiconductors
Engineering management consulting
Environmental and earth sciences
Food and chemical research
Health and epidemiology
Health risk assessments
Human factors research
Industrial structures
Materials science
Mechanical engineering
Statistical and data sciences
Technology development
Thermal sciences
Vehicle analysis
Visual communications

COMPETITORS

Accenture	LECG
Bain & Company	McKinsey & Company
Battelle Memorial	National Technical Systems
BearingPoint	Norske Veritas
Booz Allen	PAREXEL
Boston Consulting	SGS
Bureau Veritas	Southwest Research
Computer Sciences Corp.	Institute
Day & Zimmermann	SRI International
Deloitte Consulting	Underwriters Labs
FTI Consulting	

HISTORICAL FINANCIALS

Company Type: Public

Income Statement

FYE: Friday nearest December 31

	REVENUE ($ mil.)	NET INCOME ($ mil.)	NET PROFIT MARGIN	EMPLOYEES
12/08	228.8	23.2	10.1%	937
12/07	205.1	20.3	9.9%	875
12/06	168.5	14.2	8.4%	835
12/05	155.2	14.2	9.1%	785
12/04	151.5	12.0	7.9%	743
Annual Growth	**10.9%**	**17.9%**	**—**	**6.0%**

2008 Year-End Financials

Debt ratio: —
Return on equity: 17.8%
Cash ($ mil.): 32.6
Current ratio: 2.70
Long-term debt ($ mil.): —
No. of shares (mil.): 13.8

Dividends
Yield: 0.0%
Payout: —
Market value ($ mil.): 414.0
R&D as % of sales: —
Advertising as % of sales: —

Stock History

NASDAQ (GS): EXPO

	STOCK PRICE ($) FY Close	P/E High/Low		PER SHARE ($) Earnings	Dividends	Book Value
12/08	30.08	26	16	1.47	0.00	9.31
12/07	27.04	25	14	1.25	0.00	9.59
12/06	18.66	23	17	0.83	0.00	9.03
12/05	14.19	20	14	0.81	0.00	9.68
12/04	13.74	21	15	0.70	0.00	8.50
Annual Growth	**21.6%**	**—**	**—**	**20.4%**	**—**	**2.3%**

EZCORP, Inc.

No mere pawn in the game, EZCORP is one of the largest operators of pawnshops in the US. In addition to collecting interest from loans it makes, EZCORP also sells second-hand jewelry, tools, electronics, sports equipment, and musical instruments through some 330 EZPAWN stores in 11 states and Mexico (under the Empeño Fácil banner); most are in Texas. Its inventory is built from items forfeited by customers who used them as collateral and then failed to repay small, short-term, high-interest loans. EZCORP also offers customers unsecured loans, commonly referred to as payday loans or payroll advances, through about 75 of its pawnshops, as well as more than 450 EZMONEY payday loan stores in about a dozen states.

EZCORP views its payday loan shops as its largest growth opportunity and opened about 170 such stores in 2007 and 2008. However, in 2005, EZMONEY stores in Texas (where a majority of them are located) ceased marketing payday loans and began providing fee-based advice and assistance to consumers in obtaining loans from an unaffiliated lender. About 350 of the company's payday loan stores and pawnshops now offer these credit services; EZCORP doesn't actually make or fund the loans, but typically earns a fee of 20% on each loan amount. If a borrower defaults on his or her loan, EZCORP pays the lender the principal and accrued interest, plus an insufficient funds fee. The company then attempts to collect these monies from the borrower.

EZCORP also sees its Mexico pawnshops as a growth area. It opened its first store there in 2006 and plans to open more.

In 2008 the company ran into legal problems and was forced to close 11 EZMONEY stores in Florida after the Florida Office of Financial Regulations filed action against EZCORP alleging that its stores violated state law. The action does not affect the company's pawn shops in the state. Also in 2008 EZCORP paid $600,000 in a settlement reached with the Texas Attorney General, who claimed that the company failed to adequately protect customer's private information. EZCORP disputed the claims.

The company continues to grow its EZPAWN stores, which have a retail ambience that dispels the industry's seedy image, and their services come at a price: an annual interest rate of up to 240%. About three in four borrowers redeem their property or renew or extend the terms of the loans, yet more than half of the company's revenues come from reselling merchandise.

At the end of 2008, EZCORP gained about 70 locations with the acquisition of Value Financial Services, which operates Value Pawn and Jewelry and Check Jewelry & Loan stores in Florida, Georgia, New Mexico, and Tennessee. Also that year, the company acquired 11 Pawn Plus and ASAP Pawn pawnshops in Las Vegas and Henderson, Nevada. The $35 million deal complemented EZCORP's existing four locations in Las Vegas, which is considered a good pawn market.

In 2007 EZCORP acquired 15 pawnshops in Colorado operating under the name Jumping Jack Cash. EZCORP also owns 30% stakes in international pawnshop operators Albemarle & Bond (UK) and Cash Converters (Australia).

HISTORY

Courtland Logue opened the first EZ Pawn in Austin, Texas, in 1974. By 1989 there were 16 U-Pawn-It and EZ Pawn stores. (All of them took the latter name in 1991.) Bankrolled by private investors, Logue began expanding nationally.

After going public in 1991, EZCORP tightened loan valuation standards, beefed up internal audit procedures to decrease shrinkage, set up a centralized jewelry center to refurbish forfeited collateral, and expanded retail sales.

In 1995 inventory reductions contributed to plummeting earnings. EZCORP closed 15 stores and combined 17 units with others; it also instituted a more restrictive lending policy to boost the number of repaid loans. Amid the turmoil, Logue was ousted as chairman and succeeded by Sterling Brinkley.

The company's first JewelryLand Outlet, a low-priced jewelry store, opened in Georgia in 1996. Four new EZ Pawns opened in 1997, and 1998 saw EZCORP go international, buying about 30% of Albemarle & Bond Holdings, a pawnshop operator in the UK.

EZCORP made headlines in 1998 and 1999 with its bid to keep small-caliber handguns off the streets; it gave guns from its stores to local police departments (although it continues to sell such "sporting long guns" as rifles and shotguns). As the booming US economy made it easier for the company's traditional clients to get mainstream credit, the company eyed expansion of its retail business, launching Web site EZPAWN.com.

In 2000 the company decided to shut down more than 50 underperforming stores. By year's end, almost 25 had been closed, and an additional 15 were closed in 2001.

EXECUTIVES

Chairman: Sterling B. Brinkley Jr., age 58
President, CEO, and Director: Joseph L. (Joe) Rotunda, age 62
EVP and COO: Paul Rothamel
CFO: Brad Wolfe
SVP Administration: Robert A. Kasenter, age 63
SVP EZPAWN Operations: Fred L. Fox, age 51
VP and CIO: Robert Jackson, age 54
VP EZMONEY: Michael Volpe, age 45
VP, Secretary, and General Counsel: Connie L. Kondik, age 45
VP Strategic Development: John R. Kissick, age 67
VP Property Management: James Rose, age 55
President, Signature Loans: Joe Borbely
President, Pawn Americas: Eric Fosse, age 46
Controller and Assistant Secretary: Daniel M. Chism, age 41
Auditors: BDO Seidman, LLP

LOCATIONS

HQ: EZCORP, Inc.
1901 Capital Pkwy., Austin, TX 78746
Phone: 512-314-3400   **Fax:** 512-314-3404
Web: www.ezcorp.com

PRODUCTS/OPERATIONS

2009 Sales

	$ mil.	% of total
Merchandise sales	323.6	54
Signature loan fees	133.3	22
Pawn service charges	130.2	22
Auto title loan fees	3.6	1
Other	6.8	1
Total	**597.5**	**100**

COMPETITORS

ACE Cash Express	DGSE Companies
Advance America	Dollar Financial
Cash America	First Cash Financial
Cash Plus	World Acceptance
Check Into Cash	Xponential

HISTORICAL FINANCIALS
Company Type: Public

Income Statement
FYE: September 30

	ASSETS ($ mil.)	NET INCOME ($ mil.)	INCOME AS % OF ASSETS	EMPLOYEES
9/09	492.5	68.5	13.9%	4,350
9/08	308.7	52.4	17.0%	3,300
9/07	251.2	37.9	15.1%	3,200
9/06	197.9	29.3	14.8%	3,100
9/05	165.4	14.8	8.9%	2,700
Annual Growth	**31.4%**	**46.7%**	**—**	**12.7%**

2009 Year-End Financials

Equity as % of assets: 84.4%	Dividends
Return on assets: 17.1%	Yield: 0.0%
Return on equity: 19.9%	Payout: —
Long-term debt ($ mil.): 25.0	Sales ($ mil.): 597.5
No. of shares (mil.): 48.7	R&D as % of sales: —
Market value ($ mil.): 665.4	Advertising as % of sales: —

Stock History
NASDAQ (GS): EZPW

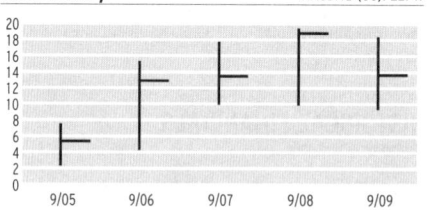

	STOCK PRICE ($) FY Close	P/E High	P/E Low	PER SHARE ($) Earnings	PER SHARE ($) Dividends	PER SHARE ($) Book Value
9/09	13.66	13	7	1.42	0.00	8.53
9/08	18.80	16	8	1.21	0.00	5.61
9/07	13.47	20	11	0.88	0.00	4.43
9/06	12.89	22	6	0.69	0.00	3.49
9/05	5.35	20	7	0.36	0.00	2.74
Annual Growth	**26.4%**	**—**	**—**	**40.9%**	**—**	**32.8%**

F5 Networks

F5 Networks wants to help your network take a load off. The company's products include application delivery controllers (ADC) and software that are used for network load balancing, availability assurance, and security assessment. The company also provides file virtualization, WAN optimization, and remote access products. It also offers services such as network monitoring, performance analysis, and training. F5 targets a variety of industries, including telecommunications, manufacturing, financial services, and e-commerce. The company counts Blue Cross and Blue Shield of Kansas, Microsoft, and Toshiba America among its customers. F5 Networks gets the majority of its sales in the Americas.

F5 sells primarily though distributors, systems integrators, and resellers, but it also maintains a direct sales force for major enterprise accounts. Distributing giants Avnet Technology Solutions and Ingram Micro together account for about a quarter of the company's sales.

F5 gets most of its product sales from its application delivery networking products. The company operates in a highly competitive market, bumping up against tech giants like Cisco Systems and EMC. F5 outsources the majority of its hardware manufacturing, with Flextronics International making the company's ADC product line and Sanmina-SCI producing the ARX line.

F5 purchased storage virtualization specialist Acopia Networks for $210 million in 2007. The company views storage virtualization as a natural complement to its traditional business. Its ADC products distribute Internet traffic over multiple servers, effectively making them act as one; the company's storage virtualization products similarly manage multiple storage devices.

EXECUTIVES

Chairman: Alan J. Higginson, age 62
President, CEO, and Director: John McAdam, age 58
SVP and General Counsel: Jeffrey A. (Jeff) Christianson, age 52
SVP and CFO: Andy Reinland, age 45
SVP Product Development and CTO: Karl D. Triebes, age 42
SVP Business Operations: Edward J. Eames, age 51
SVP and Chief Accounting Officer: John Rodriguez, age 49
SVP Marketing and Business Development: Dan Matte, age 43
SVP Worldwide Sales: Mark Anderson, age 47
VP Product Management and Marketing: Erik Giesa
Managing Director, Asia: Teong Eng Guan Petra
Managing Director Australia and New Zealand: Kurt Hansen
Auditors: PricewaterhouseCoopers LLP

LOCATIONS

HQ: F5 Networks, Inc.
401 Elliott Ave. West, Seattle, WA 98119
Phone: 206-272-5555   **Fax:** 206-272-5556
Web: www.f5.com

2009 Sales

	$ mil.	% of total
Americas	361.2	55
Europe, Middle East & Africa	150.8	23
Asia/Pacific		
Japan	56.8	9
Other countries	84.3	13
Total	**653.1**	**100**

PRODUCTS/OPERATIONS

2009 Sales

	$ mil.	% of total
Products	406.5	62
Services	246.6	38
Total	**653.1**	**100**

Selected Products

Application delivery controllers (BIG-IP)
File virtualization (ARX)
Management console (Enterprise Manager)
SSL/VPN access appliances (FirePass)
WAN optimization (WANJet)

COMPETITORS

Array Networks	Juniper Networks
Barracuda Networks	NetApp
Blue Coat	Nokia
Brocade Communications	Radware
Cisco Systems	Riverbed Technology
Citrix Systems	SonicWALL
EMC	Symantec
Extreme Networks	Zeus Technology
Fortinet	

HISTORICAL FINANCIALS

Company Type: Public

Income Statement

FYE: September 30

	REVENUE ($ mil.)	NET INCOME ($ mil.)	NET PROFIT MARGIN	EMPLOYEES
9/09	653.1	91.5	14.0%	1,646
9/08	650.2	74.3	11.4%	1,694
9/07	525.7	77.0	14.6%	1,582
9/06	394.0	66.0	16.8%	1,068
9/05	281.4	51.7	18.4%	792
Annual Growth	23.4%	15.3%	—	20.1%

2009 Year-End Financials

Debt ratio: —	Dividends
Return on equity: 12.1%	Yield: —
Cash ($ mil.): 110.8	Payout: —
Current ratio: 2.10	Market value ($ mil.): 3,141.5
Long-term debt ($ mil.): —	R&D as % of sales: —
No. of shares (mil.): 79.3	Advertising as % of sales: —

Stock History

NASDAQ (GS): FFIV

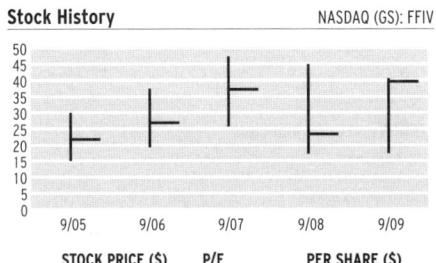

	9/05	9/06	9/07	9/08	9/09

	STOCK PRICE ($) FY Close	P/E High/Low	PER SHARE ($) Earnings	Dividends	Book Value
9/09	39.63	35 16	1.14	—	10.08
9/08	23.38	50 20	0.89	—	9.06
9/07	37.19	52 29	0.90	—	9.72
9/06	26.86	47 25	0.80	—	7.78
9/05	21.74	44 23	0.67	—	5.86
Annual Growth	16.2%	— —	14.2%	—	14.5%

FactSet Research Systems

Analysts, portfolio managers, and investment bankers know FactSet Research Systems has the scoop. The company offers global financial and economic information for investment analysis. FactSet complements its data with a variety of software for use in downloading and manipulating the data. (Its products can be fully integrated with Microsoft applications such as Excel and PowerPoint.) Among the company's applications are tools for presentations, data warehousing, portfolio analysis, and report writing.

Revenues are derived from month-to-month subscriptions to services, databases, and financial applications. More than 80% of revenue comes from investment managers; investment banking clients account for the rest.

More than 37,000 financial professionals from some 2,000 corporate clients use the company's services. FactSet managed to achieve growth in 2009 despite a weak economy. Its success is in part due to a focus on growing its proprietary content collection efforts, as well as investing in products and applications. In 2009 the company launched new data sets, including Debt Capital Structure (information on corporate financing activities), Global Private Equity & Venture Capital (a survey of private equity and venture capital firms), and FactSet People (a database of more than 500,000 executives). Also in 2009 it launched The New FactSet, which consolidates data and analytics that were previously spread across multiple applications onto one comprehensive interface.

In 2008 FactSet expanded its offerings with the acquisition of the Thomson Fundamentals business, which includes a global financial database with coverage of more than 43,000 companies. The company also purchased investment banking workflow tool DealMaven, reflecting its strategy of developing tools to make client workflows more efficient.

In addition, FactSet has been expanding globally in recent years. It opened an office in Manila in 2009, and in 2008 its India office opened. The previous year FactSet opened an office in Amsterdam. Additional international offices are located in France, Germany, Italy, Japan, Hong Kong, and Australia. Nearly a third of revenues come from outside the US.

HISTORY

Howard Wille and Charles Snyder founded FactSet in 1978. Both had previously worked for Wall Street investment firm Faulkner Dawkins & Sullivan (acquired by Shearson Hayden Stone in 1977). The company spent the 1980s building its client base and developing software that allowed clients to manipulate data on their own PCs.

FactSet opened an office in London in 1993 and one in Tokyo the next year. In 1994 the company added Morgan Stanley Capital International and EDGAR SEC filings to its database offerings. It added World Bank subsidiary International Finance Corp. in 1995 and the Russell U.S. Equity Profile report and Toyo Keizai, a Japanese company database, the next year. FactSet went public in 1996. Market Guide's information on US firms and ADRs (American depositary receipts) as well as the economic and financial databases of DRI/McGraw-Hill were added in 1997.

Snyder retired in 1999 but remained vice chairman. The following year Wille retired and Philip Hadley became chairman and CEO. The company made its first acquisition in 2000 when it bought Innovative Systems Techniques (Insyte), a maker of database management and decision support systems.

The company then began acquiring several content businesses. Its 2003 purchase of Mergerstat gave the company a database of global merger and acquisition and related information. In 2004 the company purchased JCF Group, a provider of broker estimates and other financial

data to institutional investors, and CallStreet, a provider of quarterly earnings call transcripts. The following year the company purchased TrueCourse, a provider of corporate competitive intelligence.

FactSet continued its acquisition spree with the 2005 purchase of Derivative Solutions (DSI), which offers fixed income analytics, portfolio management, and risk management services to financial institutions, and the 2006 purchase of AlphaMetrics, which provides institutional clients with software for capturing, measuring, and ranking financial information.

FactSet in 2007 released its ExcelConnect offering, which enables data and analytics to be compatible with Microsoft Excel. Also that year the company enhanced its wireless capabilities, giving users access to market, company, and portfolio information via PDAs and other wireless devices.

EXECUTIVES

Chairman and CEO: Philip A. Hadley, age 47, $1,146,811 total compensation
Vice Chairman: Charles J. Snyder, age 67
EVP and COO: Peter G. Walsh, age 43, $999,487 total compensation
EVP and Director Global Sales:
Michael D. Frankenfield, age 44, $947,171 total compensation
SVP and Chief Technology Officer: Jeff Young
SVP, Director Finance, and Principal Financial Officer: Maurizio Nicolelli
SVP and Director Content Operations: Mark J. Hale
SVP and Director Product Development: Research and Market Data: Goran Skoko
SVP and Director Product Development: Analytical Products: Christopher (Chris) Ellis
SVP and Director Investment Banking and Brokerage Services: Kieran M. Kennedy, age 44, $781,957 total compensation
SVP and Director Leadership Development: Laura C. Ruhe
SVP and Chief Content Officer: Townsend Thomas
SVP and Director International Operations: Scott L. Beyer
SVP General Counsel and Secretary: Rachel Stern
SVP and Director Software Engineering: Daniel Weinstein
Auditors: PricewaterhouseCoopers LLP

LOCATIONS

HQ: FactSet Research Systems Inc.
601 Merritt 7, Norwalk, CT 06851
Phone: 203-810-1000   **Fax:** 203-810-1001
Web: www.factset.com

2009 Sales

	$ mil.	% of total
US	423.9	68
Europe	156.6	25
Asia/Pacific	41.5	7
Total	622.0	100

PRODUCTS/OPERATIONS

Selected Applications

Company Analysis
Data Warehousing
Economic Analysis
Fixed Income Analysis
Pitchbook Building
Portfolio Analysis
Quantitative Analysis
Real-time Market Data

COMPETITORS

Bloomberg L.P.
Capital IQ
Data Transmission Network
Dow Jones
Hoover's, Inc.
IDD Information Services
Interactive Data
LexisNexis
MSCI
OneSource
Pearson plc
thinkorswim
Thomson Reuters
Track Data

HISTORICAL FINANCIALS

Company Type: Public

Income Statement

FYE: August 31

	REVENUE ($ mil.)	NET INCOME ($ mil.)	NET PROFIT MARGIN	EMPLOYEES
8/09	622.0	144.9	23.3%	2,962
8/08	575.5	125.0	21.7%	1,934
8/07	475.8	109.6	23.0%	1,653
8/06	387.4	82.9	21.4%	1,431
8/05	312.6	71.8	23.0%	1,226
Annual Growth	18.8%	19.2%	—	24.7%

2009 Year-End Financials

Debt ratio: —
Return on equity: 30.0%
Cash ($ mil.): 216.3
Current ratio: 3.01
Long-term debt ($ mil.): —
No. of shares (mil.): 47.3
Dividends
  Yield: 1.4%
  Payout: 25.6%
Market value ($ mil.): 2,603.6
R&D as % of sales: —
Advertising as % of sales: —

Stock History

NYSE: FDS

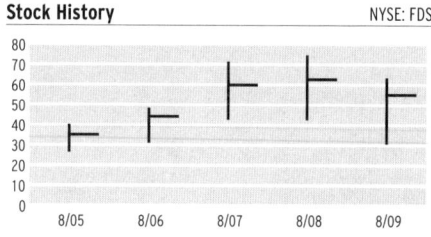

	STOCK PRICE ($) FY Close	P/E High/Low	PER SHARE ($) Earnings	Dividends	Book Value
8/09	55.04	21 10	2.97	0.76	10.59
8/08	62.71	30 17	2.50	0.60	9.84
8/07	59.93	33 20	2.14	0.36	8.65
8/06	44.10	29 19	1.64	0.22	7.58
8/05	35.00	28 19	1.43	0.20	5.67
Annual Growth	12.0%	— —	20.0%	39.6%	16.9%

FalconStor Software

FalconStor Software watches data like a hawk. The company provides network storage management software and related services. Its IPStor software is used to manage storage provisioning and virtualization, data availability, replication, and disaster recovery functions in disk-based systems. FalconStor also offers consulting, engineering, implementation, and maintenance services. Ranging from small and midsized businesses to large enterprises, the company's customers come from fields such as health care, financial services, education, and information technology. FalconStor sells predominantly through distributors, manufacturers, and resellers.

The company has partnerships with a wide range of storage product vendors. Its largest customers, EMC and Sun Microsystems, together accounted for about a third of its revenues in 2008.

FalconStor continues to upgrade its product line. The company introduced new products related to backup and recovery, data duplication, and virtualization in 2008.

The company markets its products worldwide. FalconStor generated about 40% of its revenues outside the US in 2008. The company has identified China and Japan as a growth opportunities, and it has formed partnerships with such companies as Acer, H3C Technologies, and SOFTBANK to further its expansion in Asia.

Chairman and CEO ReiJane Huai owns about 20% of the company.

EXECUTIVES

Chairman and CEO: ReiJane Huai, age 50, $310,000 total compensation
VP, CFO, and Treasurer: James Weber, age 38, $466,861 total compensation
VP Business Development: Bernard (Bernie) Wu, age 51, $555,129 total compensation
VP: Wayne Lam, age 45, $468,119 total compensation
VP Engineering and CTO: Wai Lam
Chief Strategy Officer: James P. McNiel, age 45
VP Technical Services and IPStor Development: Alan Chen
VP and Chief Technologist: Jimmy Wu
VP Worldwide Marketing: Alex Jiang
VP Data Protection: Prakash Babu
VP North American Sales: Wendy Petty
VP, General Counsel, and Secretary: Seth Horowitz
VP Technology: John Lallier
Investor Relations: Joanne Ferrara
Auditors: KPMG

LOCATIONS

HQ: FalconStor Software, Inc.
  2 Huntington Quadrangle, Ste. 2S01
  Melville, NY 11747
Phone: 631-777-5188   **Fax:** 631-501-7633
Web: www.falconstor.com

2008 Sales

	$ mil.	% of total
US	52.5	60
Asia	14.2	16
Other regions	20.3	24
Total	**87.0**	**100**

PRODUCTS/OPERATIONS

2008 Sales

	$ mil.	% of total
Software licenses	58.6	67
Maintenance	23.3	27
Software services & other	5.1	6
Total	**87.0**	**100**

COMPETITORS

Acronis
Atempo
CA, Inc.
DataCore
EMC
Hewlett-Packard
LeftHand Networks
Microsoft
NetApp
NovaStor
Symantec
Tivoli Software

HISTORICAL FINANCIALS

Company Type: Public

Income Statement

FYE: December 31

	REVENUE ($ mil.)	NET INCOME ($ mil.)	NET PROFIT MARGIN	EMPLOYEES
12/08	87.0	1.2	1.4%	505
12/07	77.4	12.7	16.4%	414
12/06	55.1	(3.4)	—	340
12/05	41.0	2.3	5.6%	279
12/04	28.7	(5.9)	—	217
Annual Growth	31.9%	—	—	23.5%

2008 Year-End Financials

Debt ratio: —
Return on equity: 1.6%
Cash ($ mil.): 22.4
Current ratio: 2.93
Long-term debt ($ mil.): —
No. of shares (mil.): 44.9
Dividends
  Yield: 0.0%
  Payout: —
Market value ($ mil.): 124.8
R&D as % of sales: —
Advertising as % of sales: —

Stock History

NASDAQ (GM): FALC

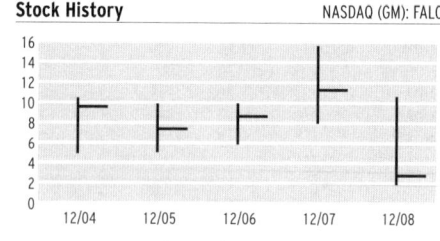

	STOCK PRICE ($) FY Close	P/E High/Low	PER SHARE ($) Earnings	Dividends	Book Value
12/08	2.78	525 101	0.02	0.00	1.45
12/07	11.26	65 34	0.24	0.00	1.95
12/06	8.65	— —	(0.07)	0.00	1.23
12/05	7.39	195 103	0.05	0.00	1.08
12/04	9.57	— —	(0.13)	0.00	1.03
Annual Growth	(26.6%)	— —	—	—	8.8%

FARO Technologies

FARO Technologies is putting the Arm on companies around the world — and they like it. With the touch of its mechanical arm, FARO's measuring systems can facilitate reverse engineering of an undocumented part or a competitor's product. The portable FaroArm, FARO Laser ScanArm, and FARO Gage are jointed devices that simulate the human arm's movement. Along with the FARO Laser Scanner LS, and Laser Tracker, inspections and measurements are integrated with companion CAM2, 3-D software. Aerospace, automotive, and heavy equipment companies such as Boeing, Caterpillar, General Motors, and Siemens use FARO Arm units in their factories. Customers located outside the Americas account for over 60% of sales.

FARO's computer-aided measurement hardware and software offer portability and a link to its computerized measurement processing system, thus providing speed and precision to its customers. Global competition has created a demand for higher quality products with shorter life cycles, which calls for more rapid design techniques and greater control of the manufacturing process. The company's use of reverse engineering discovers the technological principles of a device, object, or system through the analysis of its structure, function, and operation. Design decisions are garnered from the final product with minimal knowledge about the procedures involved in the original production.

The company's 2008 cash flow from operations decreased almost 40%, which caused the company to reduce its global workforce by 21% — the largest cuts coming from manufacturing and administrative functions. The company continues to believe that continued development and acquisition of new products is key to its future success. The field of CAM2 and 3-D measurement is expanding to involve new technologies and applications. In 2008 FARO acquired the global rights to technologies developed by Dimensional Photonics, which makes 3-D digital shape scanning systems.

FARO has more than 9,000 customers worldwide and manufactures from facilities located in Germany, Singapore, Switzerland, and the US. The company directs its sales to three main regions around the world: the Americas, Europe/Africa, and Asia/Pacific.

Co-founder and chairman Simon Raab owns a little over 5% of FARO Technologies.

EXECUTIVES

Chairman: Simon Raab, age 56
President, CEO, and Director: Jay W. Freeland, age 39, $627,752 total compensation
SVP and CFO: Keith S. Bair, age 53, $355,733 total compensation
SVP Engineering and CTO: James K. (Jim) West, age 56, $367,726 total compensation
SVP Human Resources: John E. Townsley, age 44, $370,842 total compensation
VP Business Development: Allen S. Sajedi, age 49
Director Engineering: Yuri Malinkevich
Director Laser Scanner Marketing and Product Management: Bernd-Dietmar Becker
Director Product Development: Ken Steffey
Global Public Relations Officer: Darin Sahler
Auditors: Grant Thornton LLP

LOCATIONS

HQ: FARO Technologies, Inc.
250 Technology Park, Lake Mary, FL 32746
Phone: 407-333-9911   **Fax:** 407-333-4181
Web: www.faro.com

2008 Sales

	$ mil.	% of total
Europe/Africa	93.6	44
Americas	78.3	37
Asia/Pacific	37.3	19
Total	**209.2**	**100**

PRODUCTS/OPERATIONS

Products

Computer-Aided Design (CAD)
  Articulated measuring devices
    FaroArm
    FARO Laser ScanArm
    FARO Gage
  Inspection (factory-level statistical process control and high-density surveying)
    FARO Laser Scanner LS
    FARO Laser Tracker
    CAM2 software (computer-aided measurement)

COMPETITORS

ANSYS	Hexagon AB
Autodesk	Leica Geosystems
Braintech	Parametric Technology
Cimatron	Perceptron
Dassault	Renishaw
Delcam	

HISTORICAL FINANCIALS

Company Type: Public

Income Statement

FYE: December 31

	REVENUE ($ mil.)	NET INCOME ($ mil.)	NET PROFIT MARGIN	EMPLOYEES
12/08	209.2	14.0	6.7%	959
12/07	191.6	18.1	9.4%	780
12/06	152.4	8.2	5.4%	641
12/05	125.6	8.2	6.5%	657
12/04	97.0	14.9	15.4%	453
Annual Growth	**21.2%**	**(1.5%)**	**—**	**20.6%**

2008 Year-End Financials

Debt ratio: 0.1%
Return on equity: 6.9%
Cash ($ mil.): 23.5
Current ratio: 5.20
Long-term debt ($ mil.): 0.3
No. of shares (mil.): 16.1
Dividends
  Yield: 0.0%
  Payout: —
Market value ($ mil.): 271.5
R&D as % of sales: —
Advertising as % of sales: —

Stock History

NASDAQ (GM): FARO

	STOCK PRICE ($) FY Close	P/E High/Low		PER SHARE ($) Earnings	Dividends	Book Value
12/08	16.86	44	13	0.83	0.00	13.18
12/07	27.18	44	21	1.15	0.00	12.08
12/06	24.04	44	21	0.56	0.00	6.90
12/05	20.00	56	29	0.57	0.00	6.14
12/04	31.18	33	16	1.06	0.00	5.54
Annual Growth	**(14.2%)**	**—**	**—**	**(5.9%)**	**—**	**24.2%**

FEI Company

FEI finds defects PDQ. The company makes structural process management systems that use ion beams to analyze and diagnose submicron structures in semiconductors, data storage components, and biological and industrial compounds. FEI makes focused ion beam and dual beam electron microscopes that analyze integrated circuits (ICs). It also makes scanning and transmission electron microscopes that detect defects in ICs and analyze biological specimens and materials. FEI is targeting applications in nanotechnology R&D, while still getting sales from semiconductor and data storage companies. Customers outside the US account for about two-thirds of sales.

Philips sold its entire stake in FEI through a public offering of the 8.4 million common shares it held in 2006. The Dutch giant, which has been divesting certain technology assets to focus on its consumer electronics products and medical systems, banked around $200 million from the share sale.

FEI went through a restructuring in 2005, including the closing of a facility in Peabody, Massachusetts. In 2006 the company consolidated several European sales offices into its facilities in the Netherlands. FEI realigned operations to focus on three areas in nanotechnology: nanobiology, nanoelectronics, and nanoresearch. Nanotech essentially means making things that have dimensions as small as 1 to 100 nanometers, with a nanometer being one-billionth of a meter or about one-80,000th the thickness of a human hair. Nanotech has applications in a variety of industries, from consumer products like clothing and golf balls to electronics and health care.

Vahé Sarkissian resigned as FEI's chairman, president, and CEO in 2006. Don Kania, previously the president and COO of rival Veeco Instruments, was named FEI's president and CEO later that year.

In 2003 the company expanded its offerings by purchasing the design-for-manufacturing software product lines of Electroglas. FEI turned this failure analysis and yield management software business into its Knights Technology subsidiary, which it sold in 2006 to Magma Design Automation, a supplier of semiconductor design software.

In 2005 FEI sold the assets of its secondary ion mass spectrometer product line for nearly $5 million.

FEI agreed in mid-2002 to be acquired by Veeco Instruments, but the deal fell through early in 2003. Rival Carl Zeiss SMT approached FEI about a possible acquisition of FEI by the German company in early 2006. After some talks, the two companies broke off the discussions without a deal.

The company was founded in 1971 as Field Emission Inc., referring to its use of field emission and ion technology. In 1997 FEI merged with Philips Electron Optics. Acquisitions include Micrion Corp. (1999), Atomika Instruments (2002), and Revise Inc. (2003).

EXECUTIVES

Chairman: Gerhard H. (Gerry) Parker, age 65
President, CEO, and Director: Don R. Kania, age 54, $2,607,008 total compensation
EVP and CFO: Raymond A. (Ray) Link, age 55, $693,120 total compensation
EVP Worldwide Sales and Service:
Benjamin Gek Lim Loh, age 44, $953,346 total compensation
EVP Marketing and Technology:
Robert H. J. (Rob) Fastenau, age 55, $686,264 total compensation
SVP, Worldwide Sales: John A. (Jack) Doherty, age 62
SVP, Human Resources: Jim D. Higgs, age 57
VP Research and Chief Technology Officer:
Michael R. Scheinfein
VP and CTO; General Manager, Beam Technology:
David H. Narum
VP, General Counsel, and Secretary:
Bradley J. (Brad) Thies, age 49, $396,618 total compensation
VP Worldwide Operations: Brian E. Pierson
VP Sales, North America: George D. Scholes
VP, Manufacturing: Jan Hulsmann
VP Finance and Controller: Stephen F. (Steve) Loughlin, age 58
Director Investor Relations: Fletcher C. Chamberlin
Auditors: Deloitte & Touche LLP

LOCATIONS

HQ: FEI Company
5350 NE Dawson Creek Dr., Hillsboro, OR 97124
Phone: 503-726-7500   **Fax:** 503-726-7509
Web: www.feicompany.com

FEI Company has manufacturing facilities in the Czech Republic, the Netherlands, and the US. The company also has sales and service offices in Austria, Belgium, China, Denmark, France, Germany, Hong Kong, Italy, Japan, the Netherlands, Norway, Singapore, Spain, Sweden, Switzerland, Taiwan, the UK, and the US.

2008 Sales

	$ mil.	% of total
Europe	251.3	42
North America	204.5	34
Asia/Pacific	143.4	24
Total	**599.2**	**100**

PRODUCTS/OPERATIONS

2008 Sales

	$ mil.	% of total
Products		
Research & industry	238.6	40
Electronics	152.1	25
Life sciences	70.8	12
Service & component sales	137.7	23
Total	**599.2**	**100**

Selected Products

Dual beam defect characterization workstations
Electron and ion emitters
Focusing columns
Focused ion beam (FIB) workstations
Scanning electron microscopes (SEMs) and environmental SEMs
Transmission electron microscopes (TEMs)

COMPETITORS

Applied Materials	Rudolph Technologies
Carl Zeiss	Seiko Instruments
Dainippon Screen	Spire Corp.
Denki Kagaku Kogyo	Tokyo Electron
Hitachi High-Technologies	TOPCON
JEOL	Veeco Instruments
KLA-Tencor	

HISTORICAL FINANCIALS

Company Type: Public

Income Statement

FYE: December 31

	REVENUE ($ mil.)	NET INCOME ($ mil.)	NET PROFIT MARGIN	EMPLOYEES
12/08	599.2	24.3	4.1%	1,830
12/07	592.5	58.3	9.8%	1,866
12/06	479.5	21.0	4.4%	1,683
12/05	427.2	(78.2)	—	1,674
12/04	465.7	16.6	3.6%	1,757
Annual Growth	**6.5%**	**10.0%**	**—**	**1.0%**

2008 Year-End Financials

Debt ratio: 22.2%
Return on equity: 4.8%
Cash ($ mil.): 146.5
Current ratio: 3.35
Long-term debt ($ mil.): 115.0
No. of shares (mil.): 37.7
Dividends
  Yield: 0.0%
  Payout: —
Market value ($ mil.): 710.7
R&D as % of sales: —
Advertising as % of sales: —

Stock History

NASDAQ (GM): FEIC

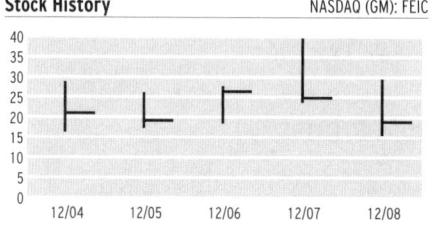

	STOCK PRICE ($) FY Close	P/E High/Low		PER SHARE ($) Earnings	Dividends	Book Value
12/08	18.86	48	26	0.61	0.00	13.77
12/07	24.83	29	18	1.36	0.00	12.93
12/06	26.37	52	35	0.53	0.00	9.29
12/05	19.17	—	—	(2.33)	0.00	7.76
12/04	21.00	68	40	0.42	0.00	10.07
Annual Growth	**(2.7%)**	**—**	**—**	**9.8%**	**—**	**8.1%**

First Business Financial Services

Business comes first at First Business Financial Services, which serves business customers through First Business Bank and First Business Bank - Milwaukee. The banks offer deposit products, cash management services, equipment leases, loans, and other products from a handful of offices in Madison and southeastern Wisconsin. About 40% of its loan portfolio is dedicated to commercial mortgages; business loans and leases add another 30%. Subsidiary First Business Capital specializes in asset-based lending. First Business Equipment Finance provides commercial equipment financing. First Business Trust & Investments offers investment management and retirement services.

Sam Jacobsen owns more than 10% of First Business Financial Services, which went public in 2005.

EXECUTIVES

Chairman: Jerome R. (Jerry) Smith, age 64
President, CEO, and Director: Corey A. Chambas, age 46, $452,694 total compensation
COO: Michael J. Losenegger, age 51, $274,097 total compensation
SVP, General Counsel, and Corporate Secretary:
Barbara M. Conley, age 55
SVP and CFO: James F. Ropella, age 49
President, Trust Division: Joan A. Burke, age 57
President and CEO, First Business Bank - Milwaukee:
David J. Vetta, age 54
President, CEO, and Director, First Business Capital:
Charles H. Batson, age 55, $313,846 total compensation
President and CEO, First Business Bank:
Mark J. Meloy, age 47
Auditors: KPMG LLP

LOCATIONS

HQ: First Business Financial Services, Inc.
401 Charmany Dr., Madison, WI 53719
Phone: 608-238-8008   **Fax:** 608-232-5920
Web: www.fbfinancial.net

PRODUCTS/OPERATIONS

2008 Gross Revenues

	$ mil.	% of total
Interest		
Loans & leases	55.0	85
Securities & other	4.8	7
Non-Interest		
Trust & investment services	2.0	3
Other	3.2	5
Total	**65.0**	**100**

COMPETITORS

AMCORE Financial
Anchor BanCorp
Associated Banc-Corp
Bank Mutual
Marshall & Ilsley
TCF Financial
U.S. Bancorp

HISTORICAL FINANCIALS

Company Type: Public

Income Statement

FYE: December 31

	ASSETS ($ mil.)	NET INCOME ($ mil.)	INCOME AS % OF ASSETS	EMPLOYEES
12/08	1,010.8	3.1	0.3%	152
12/07	918.4	3.3	0.4%	142
12/06	788.3	3.7	0.5%	242
12/05	669.2	4.8	0.7%	119
12/04	563.0	3.9	0.7%	—
Annual Growth	**15.8%**	**(5.6%)**	**—**	**8.5%**

2008 Year-End Financials

Equity as % of assets: 5.2%
Return on assets: 0.3%
Return on equity: 6.1%
Long-term debt ($ mil.): 104.8
No. of shares (mil.): 2.5
Market value ($ mil.): 33.0
Dividends
  Yield: 2.2%
  Payout: 21.9%
Sales ($ mil.): 31.4
R&D as % of sales: —
Advertising as % of sales: —

	STOCK PRICE ($) FY Close	P/E High/Low		PER SHARE ($) Earnings	Dividends	Book Value
12/08	13.00	16	10	1.28	0.28	20.87
12/07	17.50	17	13	1.32	0.26	19.12
12/06	22.83	17	14	1.50	0.24	18.02
12/05	23.70	15	12	1.93	0.06	16.48
Annual Growth	(18.1%)	—	—	(6.4%)	—	8.6%

First Capital Bancorp

Moolah, scratch, bread, chedda, bucks, dough, ducats, or skrilla — it all means business for First Capital Bank and its holding company, First Capital Bancorp. Founded in 1998, the bank provides general commercial banking services from more than six branches in the Richmond, Virginia, area. First Capital Bank offers the usual array of personal and business banking services including credit cards, IRAs, consumer and commercial loans, Internet banking services, and deposit accounts. It offers investment products in association with brokerage firm BI Investments. The company terminated its agreement to merge with Eastern Virginia Bankshares in 2009.

The companies mutually agreed to the cancellation, citing the unexpectedly long wait for regulatory approval.

Directors and executive officers collectively own about 25% of First Capital Bancorp.

EXECUTIVES

Chairman: Grant S. Grayson, age 56
Vice Chairman: Richard W. Wright, age 74
Managing Director and CEO: John M. Presley, age 48
EVP and Senior Credit Officer: K. Bradley Hildebrandt, $158,707 total compensation
SVP and COO: Katherine K. Wagner
SVP and Real Estate Lender: James E. Sedlar
SVP and CFO: William W. Ranson
SVP and Business Banking Team Leader: Ralph C. (Del) Ward Jr.
SVP and Operations Team Leader: Patty A. Cuccia
SVP and Retail Banking Team Leader: Barry P. Almond
SVP and Senior Lending Officer: William D. Bien Jr.
SVP and Private Client Group Team Leader: Richard C. McNeil
Director; President and CEO, First Capital Bank: Robert G. (Bob) Watts Jr., age 48, $203,192 total compensation
Auditors: Cherry, Bekaert & Holland, LLP

LOCATIONS

HQ: First Capital Bancorp, Inc.
 4222 Cox Rd., Ste. 200, Glen Allen, VA 23060
Phone: 804-273-1160   **Fax:** 804-527-0195
Web: www.1capitalbank.com

PRODUCTS/OPERATIONS

2008 Gross Revenues

	$ mil.	% of total
Interest Income		
Loans	22.2	89
Investments	1.5	6
Other	0.4	2
Noninterest		
Fees on deposits	0.2	1
Other	0.5	2
Total	**24.8**	**100**

COMPETITORS

Bank of America
Bank of Virginia
C&F Financial
Citigroup
Community Bankers Trust

HISTORICAL FINANCIALS

Company Type: Public

Income Statement				FYE: December 31
	ASSETS ($ mil.)	NET INCOME ($ mil.)	INCOME AS % OF ASSETS	EMPLOYEES
12/08	431.6	0.2	0.0%	77
12/07	351.9	1.7	0.5%	69
12/06	257.2	1.6	0.6%	62
12/05	209.5	1.3	0.6%	—
12/04	141.9	0.9	0.6%	32
Annual Growth	32.1%	(31.3%)	—	24.5%

2008 Year-End Financials

Equity as % of assets: 8.2%
Return on assets: 0.1%
Return on equity: 0.6%
Long-term debt ($ mil.): 57.2
No. of shares (mil.): 3.0
Market value ($ mil.): 19.1
Dividends
 Yield: —
 Payout: —
Sales ($ mil.): 11.8
R&D as % of sales: —
Advertising as % of sales: —

	STOCK PRICE ($) FY Close	P/E High/Low		PER SHARE ($) Earnings	Dividends	Book Value
12/08	6.43	238	96	0.06	—	11.92
12/07	11.55	28	15	0.71	—	11.73
12/06	17.95	28	20	0.83	—	5.27
Annual Growth	(40.1%)	—	—	(73.1%)	—	50.4%

First Clover Leaf Financial

First Clover Leaf Financial counts itself lucky to be in the banking business in the greater St. Louis area. The company (formerly First Federal Financial Services) is the holding company for three-branch First Clover Leaf Bank. Under its former name, the company in 2006 acquired Clover Leaf Financial and merged the acquisition's Clover Leaf Bank with First Federal Savings & Loan Association of Edwardsville to form First Clover Leaf Bank. The bank serves individuals and businesses in and around Edwardsville and Glen Carbon, offering such standard services as deposit accounts, credit cards, and loans, including real estate (about 85% of its total portfolio), business, and consumer loans.

EXECUTIVES

Chairman: Joseph (Joe) Helms, age 72
President, CEO and Director: Dennis M. Terry, age 62, $272,960 total compensation
EVP and COO: Bradley S. (Brad) Rench, age 50
SVP and CFO: Darlene F. (Dee) McDonald, age 46, $130,998 total compensation
SVP and Chief Lending Officer: Lisa M. Fowler, age 40, $162,048 total compensation
SVP Residential Lending and Director: Donald (Don) Engelke, age 46, $119,343 total compensation
VP, Retail Banking: Chad Abernathy
VP, Compliance Officer: Karen Kirkover
VP, Commercial Relationship Manager: Lynda L. Tite
Assistant VP, Business Development Officer: Shannon Bond
Corporate Secretary: Donna Brandmeyer
Loan Officer: Cathy Brandt
Operations Officer: Diana Kruckeberg
Loan Officer: Mary Kokorudz
Auditors: McGladrey & Pullen, LLP

LOCATIONS

HQ: First Clover Leaf Financial Corp.
 6814 Goshen Rd., Edwardsville, IL 62025
Phone: 618-656-6122
Web: www.cloverleafbank.com

PRODUCTS/OPERATIONS

2008 Gross Revenues

	$ mil.	% of total
Interest		
Loans	20.8	82
Securities	3.1	12
Other	0.8	3
Noninterest		
Deposit account service fees	0.2	1
Other	0.6	2
Total	**23.0**	**100**

COMPETITORS

Bank of America
Citizens Financial Group
Fifth Third
JPMorgan Chase
Midwest BankCentre
Northern Trust
Pulaski Financial
TCF Financial
U.S. Bancorp
Wells Fargo

HISTORICAL FINANCIALS
Company Type: Public

Income Statement
FYE: December 31

	ASSETS ($ mil.)	NET INCOME ($ mil.)	INCOME AS % OF ASSETS	EMPLOYEES
12/08	653.3	2.7	0.4%	85
12/07	413.3	2.4	0.6%	61
12/06	410.3	1.8	0.4%	52
12/05	140.2	1.9	1.4%	10
12/04	138.2	1.9	1.4%	10
Annual Growth	47.5%	9.2%	—	70.7%

2008 Year-End Financials
Equity as % of assets: 14.3%
Return on assets: 0.5%
Return on equity: 3.0%
Long-term debt ($ mil.): 53.9
No. of shares (mil.): 8.0
Market value ($ mil.): 54.9
Dividends
Yield: 3.5%
Payout: 72.7%
Sales ($ mil.): 13.1
R&D as % of sales: —
Advertising as % of sales: —

Stock History
NASDAQ (CM): FCLF

	STOCK PRICE ($) FY Close	P/E High/Low	PER SHARE ($) Earnings	Dividends	Book Value
12/08	6.86	32 18	0.33	0.24	11.70
12/07	10.15	44 37	0.27	0.24	11.07
12/06	11.50	90 44	0.23	0.36	11.65
12/05	13.25	31 26	0.49	0.37	4.71
12/04	14.60	30 22	0.51	0.07	4.57
Annual Growth	(17.2%)	— —	(10.3%)	36.1%	26.5%

First Mercury Financial

First Mercury Financial Corporation (FMFC) would like to take after its namesake, the Roman god of commerce and profit, by capitalizing on its expertise in niche insurance markets. Through its CoverX wholesale brokerage, the company underwrites general and professional liability policies for businesses, with a special focus on the security industry — private investigators, security guards, armored car units, and the like. It has also formed a special general liability unit that insures small to mid-sized builders, oil and gas contractors, and apartment building owners, among others.

FMFC operates in the excess and surplus lines (E&S) market, meaning that it provides niche insurance products for unique risks that are not covered by standard insurers; as a result, it operates on a non-admitted (or unlicensed) basis in the states where it does business. CoverX distributes its insurance products through a network of E&S wholesalers and some large retail agencies.

At one time, the company did not directly write most of the policies it sold through CoverX, but instead contracted with third-party insurers

to write the policies through fronting arrangements. Following an investment by Chicago-based private equity firm Glencoe Capital in 2004 (and an upgrade in its rating by A.M. Best), FMFC began writing its own policies. In doing so, the company is able to retain more of the premium revenue it generates through CoverX.

To facilitate CoverX's rapid growth, FMFC has opened regional offices in Atlanta, Boston, Chicago, Dallas, and Irvine, California. It is looking to continue its geographic expansion and to add additional niche products and specialty commercial lines to its offerings.

In addition to CoverX, FMFC has several other operating subsidiaries: First Mercury Insurance (which writes policies for CoverX), All Nation Insurance (which reinsures CoverX business), and American Risk Pooling Consultants (a third-party administrator for public-entity risk-sharing pools). Additionally, in 2008 the company acquired Arkansas-based American Management Corporation, an insurance services firm that specializes in marketing, underwriting, and servicing policies for petroleum marketers on behalf of several major insurance companies.

FMFC used the funds from its 2006 IPO to pay down debt; it also bought back most shares held by Glencoe, which previously had held a majority stake. Following the offering, Glencoe owned about 10% of FMFC, but in a secondary offering in 2007 it sold all its remaining shares in the company. FMFC founder and director Jerome Shaw owns 11% of the company; chairman and CEO Richard Smith owns 7%.

EXECUTIVES
Chairman, President, and CEO: Richard H. Smith, age 59, $3,628,570 total compensation
EVP, CFO, and Secretary: John A. Marazza, age 49, $1,246,499 total compensation
EVP and Chief Underwriting Officer: E. Edward (Ted) Camp, age 45
EVP: Jeffrey R. Wawok, age 33, $596,600 total compensation
Chief Claims Officer: Terrance A. Fleckenstein, $253,499 total compensation
VP Finance: Edward A. LaFramboise
Auditors: BDO Seidman, LLP

LOCATIONS
HQ: First Mercury Financial Corporation
29110 Inkster Rd., Ste. 100, Southfield, MI 48034
Phone: 248-358-4010 **Fax:** 248-358-2459
Web: www.firstmercury.com

PRODUCTS/OPERATIONS

2008 Sales

	$ mil.	% of total
Premiums	193.7	82
Investment income	21.6	9
Commissions & fees	21.0	9
Adjustments	(20.6)	—
Total	**215.7**	**100**

Selected Subsidiaries
All Nation Insurance Company
American Management Corporation
American Risk Pooling Consultants, Inc.
CoverX Corporation
First Mercury Insurance Company

COMPETITORS

Acadia Insurance	James River Group
ACE Limited	Lexington Insurance
Admiral Insurance	Markel
All Risks	OneBeacon
CNA Financial	ProCentury
The Hartford	RLI
HCC Insurance	Specialty Underwriters'
IFG Companies	Alliance

HISTORICAL FINANCIALS
Company Type: Public

Income Statement
FYE: December 31

	ASSETS ($ mil.)	NET INCOME ($ mil.)	INCOME AS % OF ASSETS	EMPLOYEES
12/08	943.7	40.8	4.3%	338
12/07	747.3	41.7	5.6%	195
12/06	512.9	21.9	4.3%	148
12/05	365.6	22.8	6.2%	136
12/04	254.0	17.7	7.0%	—
Annual Growth	38.8%	23.2%	—	35.5%

2008 Year-End Financials
Equity as % of assets: 27.7%
Return on assets: 4.8%
Return on equity: 16.6%
Long-term debt ($ mil.): 67.0
No. of shares (mil.): 17.2
Market value ($ mil.): 244.9
Dividends
Yield: —
Payout: —
Sales ($ mil.): 215.7
R&D as % of sales: —
Advertising as % of sales: —

Stock History
NYSE: FMR

	STOCK PRICE ($) FY Close	P/E High/Low	PER SHARE ($) Earnings	Dividends	Book Value
12/08	14.26	11 4	2.19	—	15.23
12/07	24.40	11 7	2.25	—	13.36
12/06	23.52	15 12	1.58	—	10.06
Annual Growth	(22.1%)	— —	17.7%	—	23.1%

FLIR Systems

You can run, but you cannot hide from FLIR Systems. The company's thermal imaging and obscurant-proof camera systems detect heat and radiation, thus allowing operators to see objects through fog, darkness, or smoke. FLIR's imaging products enhance vision for military and commercial applications, such as search and rescue, drug interdiction, border patrol, surveillance, navigation, and broadcast newsgathering. Industrial customers use FLIR's thermography products, which employ infrared cameras to measure temperatures from a distance, for equipment monitoring, process control, product development, and other applications. US government agencies collectively account for about half of FLIR's sales.

In 2008 it acquired a 69% stake in Cedip Infrared Systems, a French company that makes infrared cameras and stabilized gimbaled systems; Cedip broadens distribution to Asia. FLIR also purchased Ifara Technologias to provide it with in-house access to software.

Late in 2009 FLIR bought Directed Perception, a maker of pan-tilt motion control systems for commercial and military applications. The company, renamed FLIR Motion Control Systems, makes pan-tilt systems used in security, surveillance, robotic, marine, and instrumentation applications. The acquisition adds a key technology that will be integrated into FLIR's existing pan-tilt-zoom camera systems.

In 2009 the company launched a new line of commercial/industrial airborne inspection systems: the Kelvin 275, Corona 350, and Ultra 8000e. The Advanced Thermal Weapon Sight was developed by FLIR and uses Trijicon's expertise in weapon sights and FLIR's expertise in infrared imaging systems and sighting sensors. The company also signed a $13 million contract to provide its RECON III infrared cameras to Saudi Arabia, and has entered into contracts to provide products and systems to the Brazilian Navy and the Royal Australian Air Force ($13 million).

Government Systems is the largest division and is focused on government customers and markets for surveillance, force protection, drug interdiction, search and rescue, targeting, and border and maritime patrol. Products are specifically designed to meet military specifications.

Thermography products range from hand-held cameras to science cameras for imaging and temperature measurement. The primary component of thermal imaging systems is the infrared detector, which collects or absorbs infrared radiation (heat) and converts it into an electronic signal. Markets include predictive maintenance, R&D, manufacturing process control, building inspection, gas detection, and emerging thermography (health care, foodservice, veterinary science, automotive, and aircraft inspection).

Commercial Vision Systems deals with infrared imaging technology where the primary need is to see at night or in adverse conditions. Products are made for perimeter security, automotive night vision and pedestrian warning, watercraft, and law enforcement. Customers include Mine Safety Appliances (firefighting), Aerovironment (unmanned aerial vehicles), Northrop Grumman (military applications), and Hologic (circuit readout).

EXECUTIVES

Chairman, President, and CEO: Earl R. Lewis, age 66, $8,917,342 total compensation
EVP; President, Thermography Business: Arne Almerfors, age 64, $1,900,672 total compensation
SVP Finance and CFO: Stephen M. Bailey, age 61, $2,930,316 total compensation
SVP Corporate Strategy and Development: Anthony L. Trunzo, age 47
SVP, General Counsel, and Corporate Secretary: William W. Davis, age 53
VP, Human Resources: Paul T. Zaninovich
President, Commercial Vision Systems Division: Andrew C. Teich, age 49, $2,149,574 total compensation
President, Government Systems Division: William A. Sundermeier, age 46, $2,177,366 total compensation
Auditors: KPMG LLP

LOCATIONS

HQ: FLIR Systems, Inc.
27700A SW Parkway Ave., Wilsonville, OR 97070
Phone: 503-498-3547   **Fax:** 503-498-3904
Web: www.flir.com

2008 Sales

	$ mil.	% of total
US	669.2	62
Europe	239.5	22
Other regions	168.3	16
Total	**1,077.0**	**100**

PRODUCTS/OPERATIONS

2008 Sales

	$ mil.	% of total
Government Systems	569.1	53
Thermography	327.3	30
Commercial Vision Systems	180.6	17
Total	**1,077.0**	**100**

Selected Products

Government Systems
Fixed mounted infrared imaging systems for long-range and airborne military or law enforcement surveillance (ThermoVision Ranger lines)
Ground-based thermal imaging systems (ThermoVision 2000/3000 and ThermoVision Sentry lines)
Handheld infrared imaging systems (MilCAM)
Marine infrared imaging systems (BRITE Star and SeaFLIR)
Search and rescue thermal imaging systems (Star SAFIRE lines)
Thermography
Camera used for building inspection, electrical inspection, pest infestation control, and damage restoration (InfraCAM)
Industrial handheld and fixed thermal imaging systems (ThermaCAM lines)
Low-cost thermal imager (InfraScan)
Uncooled thermography cameras for process control (ThermoVision lines)
Commercial Vision Systems
Airborne multi-sensor imagers (Ultra 8000)
Camera systems for broadcast news and surveillance (UltraMedia lines)
Driver's vision enhancement devices for commercial, emergency, and military vehicles (ThermoVision PathfindIR)
Maritime navigation and security device (ThermoVision Mariner)

COMPETITORS

Axsys
BAE SYSTEMS
Boeing
CIC International
DRS Technologies
EMX
Fluke Corporation
ICx Technologies
Kollsman
L-3 Communications
Lockheed Martin
Mikron Infrared
MorphoTrak
NEC
Raytheon
SAFRAN
Thales

HISTORICAL FINANCIALS

Company Type: Public

Income Statement

FYE: December 31

	REVENUE ($ mil.)	NET INCOME ($ mil.)	NET PROFIT MARGIN	EMPLOYEES
12/08	1,077.0	203.7	18.9%	1,943
12/07	779.4	136.7	17.5%	1,743
12/06	575.0	100.9	17.5%	1,419
12/05	508.6	90.8	17.9%	1,320
12/04	482.7	71.5	14.8%	780
Annual Growth	**22.2%**	**29.9%**	**—**	**25.6%**

2008 Year-End Financials

Debt ratio: 22.7%
Return on equity: 27.8%
Cash ($ mil.): 289.4
Current ratio: 4.72
Long-term debt ($ mil.): 190.3
No. of shares (mil.): 151.8
Dividends
  Yield: —
  Payout: —
Market value ($ mil.): 4,656.7
R&D as % of sales: —
Advertising as % of sales: —

Stock History

NASDAQ (GS): FLIR

	STOCK PRICE ($) FY Close	P/E High/Low		PER SHARE ($) Earnings	Dividends	Book Value
12/08	30.68	36	19	1.28	—	5.53
12/07	31.30	41	17	0.89	—	4.11
12/06	15.91	26	16	0.66	—	2.63
12/05	11.16	31	18	0.58	—	2.43
12/04	15.95	35	19	0.47	—	2.06
Annual Growth	**17.8%**	**—**	**—**	**28.5%**	**—**	**28.0%**

Flushing Financial

Flush with cash? You could keep it at Flushing Financial. The holding company's Flushing Savings Bank operates about 15 branches in the Brooklyn, Manhattan, and Queens boroughs of New York City and in nearby Nassau County. Deposit products include CDs and checking, savings, passbook, money market, and NOW accounts. Multifamily residential and mixed-use real estate mortgage loans account for the majority of the bank's loan portfolio; other offerings include commercial mortgages and one- to four-family mortgages, construction loans, and SBA loans.

The bank has shifted its strategy from operating as a traditional thrift to a more commercial slant, focusing on such offerings as business lending and cash management services as well as commercial lending. The company formed

Flushing Commercial Bank in 2007 to accept municipal deposits and state funds.

Flushing Savings Bank has also expanded within its market area, both by opening new locations and through acquisitions, including its 2006 purchase of Brooklyn's Atlantic Liberty Financial. It also launched new Internet banking services in 2006.

Flushing Savings Bank offers services catering to the sizable populations of Asians and other ethnic groups in the bank's market.

EXECUTIVES

Chairman, Flushing Financial and Flushing Savings Bank: Gerard P. Tully Sr., age 81
President, CEO and Director, Flushing Financial and Flushing Savings Bank: John R. Buran, age 60
EVP, COO, and Secretary, Flushing Financial and Flushing Savings Bank: Maria A. Grasso, age 44
EVP, Treasurer, and CFO; EVP Finance Flushing Savings Bank: David W. Fry, age 59
EVP and Chief of Real Estate Lending, Flushing Financial and Flushing Savings Bank: Francis W. (Frank) Korzekwinski, age 47
SVP and Chief Internal Auditor: Robert G. (Bob) Kiraly, age 54
SVP and Chief Investment Officer: William J. (Jeff) Weichsel, age 60
SVP and Director Government Banking: Patricia Mezeul, age 49
SVP Commercial Real Estate Lending: Ronald Hartmann, age 53
SVP and Director Operations: Barbara A. Beckmann, age 50
SVP and Director Human Resources: Ruth E. Filiberto, age 50
SVP and CIO: Allen Brewer
Auditors: PricewaterhouseCoopers LLP

LOCATIONS

HQ: Flushing Financial Corporation
1979 Marcus Ave., Ste. E140
Lake Success, NY 11042
Phone: 718-961-5400
Web: www.flushingsavings.com

PRODUCTS/OPERATIONS

2008 Gross Revenues

	$ mil.	% of total
Interest		
Interest on loans & fees	190.0	85
Interest & dividends on securities	26.1	12
Other	0.6	—
Noninterest		
Loan fees	2.6	1
Banking fees	1.6	1
Other	2.7	1
Total	**223.6**	**100**

COMPETITORS

Apple Bank
Astoria Financial
Bank of America
Bank of New York Mellon
Citigroup
Dime Community Bancshares
First of Long Island
HSBC USA
JPMorgan Chase
Korea Exchange Bank
New York Community Bancorp
State Bancorp

HISTORICAL FINANCIALS

Company Type: Public

Income Statement

		NET	INCOME	
	ASSETS ($ mil.)	INCOME ($ mil.)	AS % OF ASSETS	EMPLOYEES
				FYE: December 31
12/08	3,949.5	22.3	0.6%	343
12/07	3,354.5	20.2	0.6%	269
12/06	2,836.5	21.6	0.8%	324
12/05	2,353.2	23.5	1.0%	264
12/04	2,058.0	22.6	1.1%	250
Annual Growth	**17.7%**	**(0.3%)**	**—**	**8.2%**

2008 Year-End Financials

Equity as % of assets: 7.6%
Return on assets: 0.6%
Return on equity: 8.3%
Long-term debt ($ mil.): 916.3
No. of shares (mil.): 31.1
Market value ($ mil.): 372.3
Dividends
Yield: 4.3%
Payout: 47.3%
Sales ($ mil.): 94.7
R&D as % of sales: —
Advertising as % of sales: —

Stock History

NASDAQ (GS): FFIC

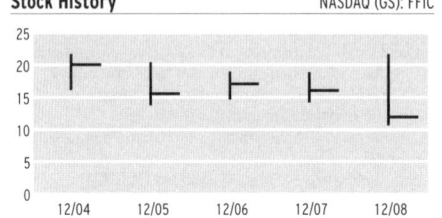

	STOCK PRICE ($) FY Close	P/E High/Low	PER SHARE ($) Earnings	Dividends	Book Value
12/08	11.96	20 10	1.10	0.52	9.69
12/07	16.05	18 14	1.02	0.48	7.51
12/06	17.07	16 13	1.14	0.44	7.02
12/05	15.57	15 11	1.31	0.40	5.67
12/04	20.06	17 13	1.25	0.35	5.16
Annual Growth	**(12.1%)**	**— —**	**(3.1%)**	**10.4%**	**17.0%**

F.N.B. Corporation

F.N.B. Corporation is the holding company for First National Bank of Pennsylvania, which operates more than 225 bank branches in Pennsylvania and northeastern Ohio. The company also has more than 50 consumer finance offices in those states and Tennessee, plus a handful of loan production offices in Florida. It operates in four segments, providing community banking, wealth management, insurance, and consumer finance products and services to retail clients and small businesses. Commercial loans make up about half of the company's loan portfolio. F.N.B. Corporation bought Pennsylvania-based banks Omega Financial and Iron and Glass Bancorp in 2008.

In 2009 former CEO Robert New unexpectedly stepped down after less than a year in the position. (The company's stock prices had fallen by some 75% in that time.) Former CEO Stephen Gurgovits resumed that position with the company, stepping down as chairman to conform to corporate governance policies.

F.N.B. Corporation, which moved its headquarters from Pennsylvania to Florida in 2001, spun off First National Bankshares of Florida at the start of 2004 and returned to the Pittsburgh

area. Next year, F.N.B. went back to Florida, opening loan offices in Orlando and Sarasota under the First National Bank banner.

The company is again rooted firmly in the Keystone State and bordering markets. Over the last few years the company has been expanding locally via acquisitions, including bank holding companies NSD Bancorp, Slippery Rock Financial, and North East Bancshares.

EXECUTIVES

Chairman: William B. Campbell, age 70
President and CEO; Chairman and CEO, First National Bank of Pennsylvania and FNB Capital: Stephen J. (Steve) Gurgovits, age 65, $2,073,002 total compensation
CFO and Controller: Vincent J. Calabrese, age 46, $299,487 total compensation
EVP and COO; Chief Administrative Officer, First National Bank of Pennsylvania: Brian F. Lilly, age 50, $581,344 total compensation
EVP and Chief Marketing Officer, First National Bank of Pennsylvania: Susan B. Bergen-Painter, age 39
EVP, First National Bank of Pennsylvania: Louice C. Lowrey, age 55, $330,215 total compensation
EVP Retail Banking, First National Bank of Pennsylvania: Jonathan W. Roberts
EVP and Senior Commercial Lending Officer, First National Bank of Pennsylvania: Frank Krieder
EVP and Chief Revenue Officer; President, First National Bank of Pennsylvania: Vincent J. (Vince) Delie Jr., age 44, $393,470 total compensation
EVP Small Business Lending, First National Bank of Pennsylvania: Peter J. Asimakopoulos
Chief Legal Officer; SVP, First National Bank: James G. Orie, age 50
SVP Human Resources, First National Bank of Pennsylvania: Bob Perrin
Investor Contact: Frank Milano
Corporate Secretary; SVP and Secretary, First National Bank: David B. Mogle, age 59
Auditors: Ernst & Young LLP

LOCATIONS

HQ: F.N.B. Corporation
1 F.N.B. Blvd., Hermitage, PA 16148
Phone: 724-981-6000   **Fax:** 724-983-4873
Web: www.fnbcorporation.com

PRODUCTS/OPERATIONS

2008 Gross Revenues

	$ mil.	% of total
Interest		
Loans, including fees	352.7	71
Securities, including dividends	57.1	11
Noninterest		
Service charges	54.7	11
Insurance commissions & fees	15.6	3
Trust services	12.1	2
Securities commissions & fees	8.1	2
Adjustments	(4.4)	—
Total	**495.9**	**100**

Selected Subsidiaries

First National Bank of Pennsylvania
First National Insurance Agency, Inc.
Regency Finance Company

COMPETITORS

AmeriServ Financial
Citizens Financial Group
Fifth Third
First Commonwealth Financial
Huntington Bancshares
Parkvale Financial
PNC Financial
S&T Bancorp
United Community Financial

HISTORICAL FINANCIALS

Company Type: Public

Income Statement

FYE: December 31

	ASSETS ($ mil.)	NET INCOME ($ mil.)	INCOME AS % OF ASSETS	EMPLOYEES
12/08	8,364.8	35.6	0.4%	2,497
12/07	6,088.0	69.7	1.1%	1,893
12/06	6,007.6	67.6	1.1%	1,844
12/05	5,590.3	55.3	1.0%	1,793
12/04	5,027.0	61.8	1.2%	1,516
Annual Growth	13.6%	(12.9%)	—	13.3%

2008 Year-End Financials

Equity as % of assets: 11.1%
Return on assets: 0.5%
Return on equity: 4.8%
Long-term debt ($ mil.): 695.6
No. of shares (mil.): 114.0
Market value ($ mil.): 1,504.7
Dividends
Yield: 7.3%
Payout: 218.2%
Sales ($ mil.): 337.9
R&D as % of sales: —
Advertising as % of sales: —

Stock History

NYSE: FNB

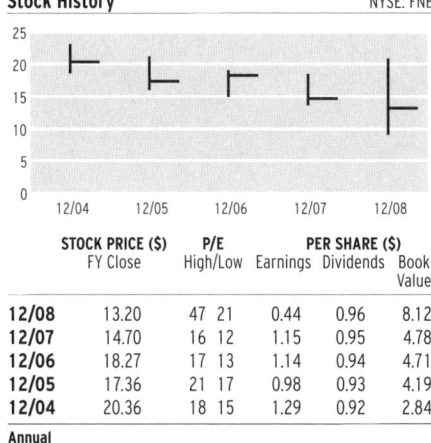

	STOCK PRICE ($) FY Close	P/E High/Low	PER SHARE ($) Earnings	PER SHARE ($) Dividends	PER SHARE ($) Book Value
12/08	13.20	47 21	0.44	0.96	8.12
12/07	14.70	16 12	1.15	0.95	4.78
12/06	18.27	17 13	1.14	0.94	4.71
12/05	17.36	21 17	0.98	0.93	4.19
12/04	20.36	18 15	1.29	0.92	2.84
Annual Growth	(10.3%)	— —	(23.6%)	1.1%	30.0%

Forrester Research

Can't see the tech forest for the trees? Maybe a Forrester ranger can guide you through the technological timber. One of the leading market research firms focused on the Internet and technology, Forrester Research supplies reports and briefs to more than 2,600 corporate clients, providing insight into market forces, industry trends, and consumer behavior. Forrester also offers custom research and consulting services to give its clients additional understanding of the technology market. In addition, the company produces a number of events where its clients can network with each other as well as with players in the technology industry.

Forrester makes its services available through annual contract subscriptions, which account for almost 65% of its revenue. Clients can acquire access to Forrester's RoleView service, giving them comprehensive access to its vast assortment of research offerings. The company

also offers advisory services (including consulting) for additional fees. It hopes to launch more value-added services leveraged from its core research, and in addition, it plans on augmenting its international presence.

In 2008, Forrester acquired JupiterResearch, a syndicated research firm specializing in online market forecasting, for about $23 million. The deal enhanced Forrester's product portfolio and client base as it subsequently folded Jupiter into its marketing and strategy client division.

Forrester has also taken advantage of cost cutting and redundancy measures. Along these lines, the company sold off its Ultimate Consumer Panel operations (credit card, financial statements, and transaction data analysis) to research panelist Lightspeed Online in October 2006. Going forward, Forrester plans to target a more broad and global focus on business information.

Chairman and CEO George Forrester Colony owns 34% of the company.

HISTORY

George Forrester Colony started Forrester Research (named after his grandmother) in 1983, initially offering a research service called Computing Strategy. New services followed at regular intervals, including advisories on networks (1986), software (1990), people and technology (1994), interactive technology (1996, the year it went public), and entertainment and technology (1997).

The company staked its claim in Europe in 1998, opening Amsterdam's Forrester European Research Center, which conducts research on the European market for high technology. The next year Forrester launched initiatives to deliver more of its products online, cut costs, and increase margins. Forrester furthered its reputation for candor with a 1999 report asserting that HDTV (high definition television) will fail to get off the ground as a viable commercial technology. That year it extended its reach into the UK when it bought Fletcher Research.

In 2000 Forrester Research formed Netquity, a joint venture with Information Resources, to deliver Internet-branding research. The following year the company partnered with firms such as NetRatings and Experian to launch new products and services. It also cut about 15% of its workforce (around 110 jobs) and sold online ad product InternetAdWatch in response to the poor economy. The company cut more jobs in 2002.

The following year, Forrester acquired rival market research firm Giga Information Group for about $62 million. Giga provided answers on day-to-day information technology issues, a complementary feature to Forrester's core industry-focused information.

EXECUTIVES

Chairman and CEO: George F. Colony, age 55, $458,635 total compensation
COO: Charles Rutstein, age 36, $646,418 total compensation
CFO and Treasurer: Michael A. Doyle, age 55, $570,844 total compensation
CIO and CTO: George M. Orlov, age 51
Chief Marketing Officer: Dwight Griesman, age 51
Chief Legal Officer and Secretary: Gail S. Mann, age 57
Chief People Officer: Elizabeth Lemons, age 52

Managing Director, Marketing and Strategy Client Group; Chief Europe, Middle East, and Africa Officer: Dennis van Lingen, age 44, $567,302 total compensation
Managing Director, Information Technology Client Group: Julie Meringer, age 40, $411,641 total compensation
Managing Director, Technology Industry Client Group: Mark R. Nemec, age 39
SVP Research, Europe, Middle East, and Africa: David Metcalfe
SVP: Merv Adrian
VP Corporate Communications: Karyl Levinson
Chief Accounting Officer: Scott Chouinard, age 40
Director Investor Relations: Phyllis Paparazzo
Auditors: BDO Seidman, LLP

LOCATIONS

HQ: Forrester Research, Inc.
400 Technology Sq., Cambridge, MA 02139
Phone: 617-613-6000   **Fax:** 617-613-5000
Web: www.forrester.com

2008 Sales

	$ mil.	% of total
US	173.0	72
Europe		
UK	14.3	6
Other countries	31.2	13
Canada	13.3	5
Other regions	9.1	4
Total	**240.9**	**100**

PRODUCTS/OPERATIONS

2008 Sales

	$ mil.	% of total
Research services	155.3	64
Advisory services & other	85.6	36
Total	**240.9**	**100**

Selected Products and Services

Research services
  RoleView
    Business strategy research (technology impact studies)
    Technology investments
    Customer Trends
Advisory services
  Consulting and customized research
Combined services
  Community events
    Forrester events
    Forrester Oval Programs
      Analyst Relations & Marketing Council
      Application Development Council
      The CIO Group
      Security & Risk Management Council
    Web site reviews
  Data services
    Business and consumer insight surveys
    Custom consumer research
    Direct consumer research

COMPETITORS

Aberdeen Group
AMR Research Inc
Datamonitor
Gartner
IDC
Ipsos
Millward Brown
The Nielsen Company
Penton Media
SYS-CON Media
TNS Custom
UBM Technology
WebMediaBrands
Yankee Group

Fortinet, Inc.

HISTORICAL FINANCIALS

Company Type: Public

Income Statement
FYE: December 31

	REVENUE ($ mil.)	NET INCOME ($ mil.)	NET PROFIT MARGIN	EMPLOYEES
12/08	240.9	29.2	12.1%	1,048
12/07	212.1	18.9	8.9%	903
12/06	181.5	17.8	9.8%	779
12/05	153.2	11.3	7.4%	693
12/04	138.5	4.1	3.0%	593
Annual Growth	14.8%	63.4%	—	15.3%

2008 Year-End Financials

Debt ratio: —
Return on equity: 10.1%
Cash ($ mil.): 129.5
Current ratio: 2.15
Long-term debt ($ mil.): —
No. of shares (mil.): 22.5

Dividends
Yield: 0.0%
Payout: —
Market value ($ mil.): 633.6
R&D as % of sales: —
Advertising as % of sales: —

Stock History
NASDAQ (GS): FORR

	STOCK PRICE ($) FY Close	P/E High/Low	PER SHARE ($) Earnings	Dividends	Book Value
12/08	28.21	29 16	1.24	0.00	13.51
12/07	28.02	39 25	0.80	0.00	12.24
12/06	27.11	42 23	0.77	0.00	10.90
12/05	18.75	42 26	0.52	0.00	8.85
12/04	17.94	109 70	0.18	0.00	8.90
Annual Growth	12.0%	— —	62.0%	—	11.0%

Fortinet, Inc.

Fortinet bravely tackles a host of security issues. The company develops and markets security appliances (sold under its FortiGate line) that integrate antivirus, firewall, content filtering, VPN, intrusion prevention systems (IPS), antispam, and traffic shaping to detect and eliminate computer viruses, worms, intrusions, and inappropriate Web content. Continuous updates against all new threats are delivered by Fortinet's FortiGuard subscription services to provide real-time network protection. The company also offers complementary products that include its FortiMail e-mail security system and FortiAnalyzer logging, reporting, and analysis systems. The company completed an IPO in 2009.

Fortinet will use the proceeds from the IPO for general corporate purposes, product development, and to pursue potential acquisitions. Past acquisitions included the purchase of the assets of IPLocks in 2008, a deal that expanded Fortinet's database security and compliance technologies.

Fortinet was founded in 2000 by CEO Ken Xie, who also founded leading firewall appliance provider NetScreen Technologies (which was acquired in 2004 by Juniper Networks). Xie holds an equity stake of more than 16% in the company, with venture capital firms Redpoint Ventures (about 12%) and Meritech Capital also holding minority stakes in Fortinet. VP and CTO Michael Xie, a co-founder of Fortinet and Ken Xie's younger brother, owns nearly 12% of the firm.

EXECUTIVES

Chairman: David D. H. Tsang, age 67
President, CEO, and Director: Ken Xie, age 46, $525,254 total compensation
VP and CFO: Kenneth A. (Ken) Goldman, age 60, $915,586 total compensation
VP Engineering, CTO, and Director: Michael Xie, age 40, $407,140 total compensation
VP and General Counsel: John Whittle, age 41, $378,858 total compensation
VP Corporate Communications: Michelle Spolver
VP Products: Anthony James
VP Channel Sales: Kendra Krause
VP Human Resources: Sherry Pulvers
VP, Asia/Pacific: Jens Andreassen
Auditors: Deloitte & Touche LLP

LOCATIONS

HQ: Fortinet, Inc.
1090 Kifer Rd., Sunnyvale, CA 94086
Phone: 408-235-7700   **Fax:** 408-235-7737
Web: www.fortinet.com

2008 Sales

	% of total
Europe, Middle East & Africa	38
US	36
Asia/Pacific	26
Total	**100**

PRODUCTS/OPERATIONS

2008 Sales

	$ mil.	% of total
Services	105.3	50
Product	94.6	45
Ratable products & services	11.9	5
Total	**211.8**	**100**

Selected Products

Network security appliances (FortiGate)
Security management (FortiManager)

COMPETITORS

Bivio Networks
Blue Coat
CA, Inc.
Check Point Software
Cisco Systems
Crossbeam
e-DMZ Security
eSoft
F5 Networks
Fortrex
Infoblox
Juniper Networks
McAfee
Microsoft
NetWolves
SonicWALL
SRA International
SteelCloud
Symantec
Trend Micro
VeriSign
WatchGuard Technologies

HISTORICAL FINANCIALS

Company Type: Public

Income Statement
FYE: December 31

	REVENUE ($ mil.)	NET INCOME ($ mil.)	NET PROFIT MARGIN	EMPLOYEES
12/08	211.8	7.4	3.5%	1,151
12/07	155.4	(21.8)	—	1,000
12/06	123.5	(5.3)	—	—
12/05	100.0	—	—	700
Annual Growth	28.4%	—	—	18.0%

2008 Year-End Financials

Debt ratio: —
Return on equity: —
Cash ($ mil.): 56.6

Current ratio: 1.23
Long-term debt ($ mil.): —

Net Income History
NASDAQ (GM): FTNT

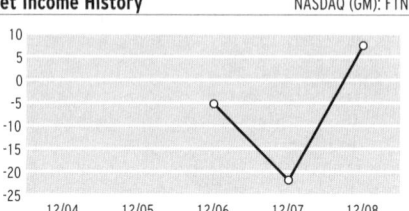

Forward Air

When it's time to haul freight, Forward Air never looks back. The company transports deferred airfreight — cargo that requires specific-time delivery but is less time-sensitive than airfreight. Forward Air typically receives freight that has been transported by plane, sends it to a sorting facility, then dispatches it by truck to a terminal near its destination. The company has about 2,300 trailers and 490 trailers and straight trucks in its fleet. It operates from about 85 terminals at or near airports in the US and Canada, including about a dozen regional hubs. Forward Air contracts with owner-operator truckers for cargo hauling. It also provides services such as warehousing and local pick-up and delivery.

The company markets its services to airfreight forwarders, air cargo carriers, and airlines, rather than directly to shippers. Although Forward Air does facilitate overnight delivery of freight, the company doesn't compete in the parcel delivery market, because it handles larger shipments.

Besides its expedited transportation business, the company offers pool distribution services through a second business segment, Forward Air Solutions. (Pool distribution involves combining goods from multiple shippers into loads headed to the same location.) Forward Air Solutions maintains about 20 terminals.

2008 was not kind to transportation companies as fuel prices skyrocketed to unprecedented heights followed by a plunge in demand brought on by the recession. Forward Air was hit hard in its core airport-to-airport services and responded by trimming its staff, freezing salaries, and scrutinizing costs. It's also put a hold on acquisitions, which has been a means of growth for the company in the past few years.

Forward Air Solutions was formed in 2007 when Forward Air bought key assets of pool distribution company USA Carriers. Retailers and

distributors are the main customers of Forward Air Solutions. Three more acquisitions in 2007 and 2008 — Black Hawk Freight; Pinch Holdings and a related company, AFTCO ENTERPRISES; and Service Express — have been folded into Forward Air and augment the company's pool distribution and expedited transportation businesses.

EXECUTIVES

Chairman, President, and CEO: Bruce A. Campbell, age 57, $1,751,279 total compensation
EVP and Chief Legal Counsel, and Secretary: Matthew J. Jewell, age 42, $713,118 total compensation
EVP Operations: Chris C. Ruble, age 46, $716,003 total compensation
SVP, CFO, and Treasurer: Rodney L. Bell, age 46, $733,715 total compensation
SVP Sales: Craig A. Drum, age 53, $604,141 total compensation
SVP and General Counsel: Michael L. Hance
VP and Chief Accounting Officer: Michael P. McLean, age 35
Assistant Corporate Secretary and Director Shareholder Services: Sandi Underwood
Auditors: Ernst & Young LLP

LOCATIONS

HQ: Forward Air Corporation
430 Airport Rd., Greeneville, TN 37745
Phone: 423-636-7000   **Fax:** 423-636-7279
Web: www.forwardair.com

PRODUCTS/OPERATIONS

2008 Sales

	$ mil.	% of total
Forward Air		
Airport-to-airport	334.9	71
Logistics	59.3	13
Other	25.1	5
Forward Air Solutions	55.1	11
Total	**474.4**	**100**

COMPETITORS

Alliance Air
CRST International
CRST Van Expedited
Daylight Transport
Express-1 Expedited Solutions
FedEx Freight
New Penn Motor Express
Old Dominion Freight
Panther Expedited Services
Schneider National
Towne Air Freight

HISTORICAL FINANCIALS

Company Type: Public

Income Statement

FYE: December 31

	REVENUE ($ mil.)	NET INCOME ($ mil.)	NET PROFIT MARGIN	EMPLOYEES
12/08	474.4	42.5	9.0%	2,021
12/07	392.7	44.9	11.4%	2,637
12/06	352.8	48.9	13.9%	1,225
12/05	320.9	44.9	14.0%	1,134
12/04	282.2	34.4	12.2%	1,008
Annual Growth	**13.9%**	**5.4%**	**—**	**19.0%**

2008 Year-End Financials

Debt ratio: 24.5%
Return on equity: 21.9%
Cash ($ mil.): 22.1
Current ratio: 3.50
Long-term debt ($ mil.): 53.0
No. of shares (mil.): 29.0
Dividends
  Yield: 1.2%
  Payout: 19.0%
Market value ($ mil.): 703.1
R&D as % of sales: —
Advertising as % of sales: —

Stock History

NASDAQ (GS): FWRD

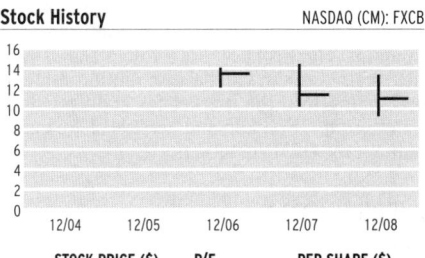

	STOCK PRICE ($) FY Close	P/E High/Low	PER SHARE ($) Earnings	Dividends	Book Value
12/08	24.27	27 12	1.47	0.28	7.47
12/07	31.17	28 18	1.50	0.28	5.93
12/06	28.93	28 19	1.55	0.28	6.39
12/05	36.65	29 16	1.39	0.24	6.17
12/04	29.80	30 18	1.05	0.00	6.25
Annual Growth	**(5.0%)**	**— —**	**8.8%**	**—**	**4.6%**

Fox Chase Bancorp

Fox Chase Bancorp is the holding company for Fox Chase Bank, which has served individuals and businesses in the Philadelphia area since 1867. The bank operates about a dozen offices in southeastern Pennsylvania and southern New Jersey; it offers standard products and services including checking and savings accounts, CDs, and money market accounts. Residential mortgages make up about half of the bank's loan portfolio; home equity loans add another 15%. Other offerings include commercial loans and automobile loans. Mutual holding company Fox Chase MHC owns 57% of Fox Chase Bancorp.

The company is increasingly focused on commercial lending. Commercial mortgages and business loans (which tend to carry a higher risk but provide higher yields than residential mortgages) make up a combined 25% of Fox Chase's lending portfolio.

EXECUTIVES

President, CEO, and Director; President and CEO, Fox Chase Bank and Fox Chase MHC: Thomas M. Petro, age 50, $514,314 total compensation
EVP and CFO: Roger Deacon, $220,770 total compensation
EVP and Senior Lending Officer: Michael Fitzgerald
EVP, COO, and Secretary: Jerry D. Holbrook, age 53, $361,686 total compensation
EVP and Chief Lending Officer, Fox Chase Bank: James V. Schermerhorn, age 65, $306,545 total compensation
EVP and Chief Payments Officer: Keiron G. (Kerry) Lynch, age 52, $240,699 total compensation
Auditors: KPMG LLP

LOCATIONS

HQ: Fox Chase Bancorp, Inc.
4390 Davisville Rd., Hatboro, PA 19040
Phone: 215-682-7400   **Fax:** 215-682-4147
Web: www.foxchasebank.com

PRODUCTS/OPERATIONS

2008 Gross Revenues

	$ mil.	% of total
Interest		
Loans, including fees	31.0	67
Mortgage-related securities	12.3	26
Other	2.5	5
Noninterest		
Service charges & other fees	0.7	1
Other	0.7	1
Total	**47.2**	**100**

COMPETITORS

Bank of America
Citizens Financial Group
DNB Financial
Harleysville National
M&T Bank
National Penn Bancshares
PNC Financial
Sovereign Bank
TD Bank USA

HISTORICAL FINANCIALS

Company Type: Public

Income Statement

FYE: December 31

	ASSETS ($ mil.)	NET INCOME ($ mil.)	INCOME AS % OF ASSETS	EMPLOYEES
12/08	931.3	1.2	0.1%	151
12/07	812.9	1.9	0.2%	153
12/06	757.0	3.6	0.5%	151
12/05	781.3	6.0	0.8%	145
Annual Growth	**6.0%**	**(41.5%)**	**—**	**1.4%**

2008 Year-End Financials

Equity as % of assets: 13.0%
Return on assets: 0.1%
Return on equity: 1.0%
Long-term debt ($ mil.): 199.0
No. of shares (mil.): 13.7
Market value ($ mil.): 150.3
Dividends
  Yield: 0.0%
  Payout: —
Sales ($ mil.): 23.2
R&D as % of sales: —
Advertising as % of sales: —

Stock History

NASDAQ (CM): FXCB

	STOCK PRICE ($) FY Close	P/E High/Low	PER SHARE ($) Earnings	Dividends	Book Value
12/08	11.00	147 104	0.09	0.00	8.87
12/07	11.40	102 74	0.14	0.00	8.95
12/06	13.50	100 87	0.14	0.00	9.19
Annual Growth	**(9.7%)**	**— —**	**(19.8%)**	**—**	**(1.8%)**

Franklin Electric

Franklin Electric would do Old Ben proud. The company keeps things flowing by making and distributing submersible and specialty electric motors, electronic drives and controls, and related items. Its fueling system products include electronic tank monitoring equipment, fittings, flexible piping, nozzles, and vapor recovery systems. Franklin Electric's products are used primarily by OEMs that incorporate them in underground petroleum pumping systems, sewage pumps, vacuum pumping systems, and freshwater pumping systems. The US makes up more than half of sales. Major customers include ITT Corp. and Pentair.

Other customers, such as independent distributors and repair shops, buy the company's products as replacement motors.

Franklin Electric enjoyed healthily growing sales in 2008, despite the recessionary environment. In 2009 the company may be challenged by lower demand for certain products due to fewer housing starts.

Franklin Electric is consolidating manufacturing operations in Europe and North America and expanding production in lower-cost regions. In 2007 the company laid off about 200 employees at its plant in Siloam Springs, Arkansas. Franklin Electric will continue to make submersible motors, pump motors, and motor components at the Siloam Springs plant.

Franklin Electric continues to expand into the pump business. In 2007 the company acquired Pump Brands (Pty) Limited, a pump supplier based in South Africa. Franklin also purchased Little Giant, previously a subsidiary of Tecumseh Products, for $121 million in stock. Little Giant makes pumps for commercial and consumer applications, including decorative fountains, HVAC, plumbing and wastewater, swimming pool and aquarium maintenance, and water gardening.

CAL Pump joined the Franklin family in 2009. Its products complement Little Giant's water gardening and other consumer applications. CAL also makes specialized lighting systems for water gardens. Vertical S.p.A., an Italian designer of pressed and welded stainless steel pumps and components, was another early 2009 snag for Franklin. The cash deal for a 75% stake in Vertical fuels Franklin's global distribution strategy by tapping into the market for stainless steel water pumps. Franklin and Vertical share many of the same OEM customers.

EXECUTIVES

Chairman and CEO: R. Scott Trumbull, age 60, $2,451,275 total compensation
SVP, Western Hemisphere Water Systems: Robert J. Stone, age 44, $749,498 total compensation
SVP, International and Fueling Systems: Gregg C. Sengstack, age 50, $835,674 total compensation
SVP; President, Europa Water Systems: Peter-Christian Maske III, age 58, $955,491 total compensation
VP, CFO, and Secretary: John J. Haines, age 45, $642,010 total compensation
VP; President, Water Transfer Systems: Thomas J. (Tom) Strupp, age 55, $594,837 total compensation
VP and Business Unit Manager, U.S. and Canada Water Systems: DeLancey W. (Dee) Davis, age 43
VP, North American Submersible Operations: Daniel J. (Dan) Crose, age 60

VP Human Resources: Gary D. Ward, age 53
VP, Office of the Chairman: Kirk M. Nevins, age 65
VP, Engineering and Electronic Technology: Thomas A. Miller, age 59
CEO, Industrias Schneider: Johann Heussinger
Auditors: Deloitte & Touche LLP

LOCATIONS

HQ: Franklin Electric Co., Inc.
400 E. Spring St., Bluffton, IN 46714
Phone: 260-824-2900　　**Fax:** 260-824-2909
Web: www.franklinelect.com

Franklin Electric has operations in Australia, Canada, China, the Czech Republic, Germany, Italy, Japan, Mexico, South Africa, Taiwan, and the US.

2008 Sales

	$ mil.	% of total
US	392.1	53
Other countries	353.5	47
Total	**745.6**	**100**

PRODUCTS/OPERATIONS

2008 Sales

	$ mil.	% of total
Water systems	557.0	75
Fueling systems	188.6	25
Total	**745.6**	**100**

Selected Products

Fuel pumping systems
Load control monitors
Motor leads and couplings
Submersible electric motors
Water pressure drives

COMPETITORS

A. O. Smith
American Manufacturing and Machine
Baldor Electric
Converteam
Dresser-Rand
Eaton
Emerson Electric
EXX
Hayward Industries
Interpump
Lincoln Electric
Magnetek
Regal Beloit
SPX
TECO-Westinghouse
WEG Electric Motors
Whittaker Controls

HISTORICAL FINANCIALS

Company Type: Public

Income Statement			FYE: Saturday nearest December 31	
	REVENUE ($ mil.)	NET INCOME ($ mil.)	NET PROFIT MARGIN	EMPLOYEES
12/08	745.6	44.1	5.9%	3,500
12/07	602.0	28.7	4.8%	3,200
12/06	557.9	57.4	10.3%	3,100
12/05	439.6	46.0	10.5%	2,800
12/04	404.3	38.1	9.4%	2,600
Annual Growth	**16.5%**	**3.7%**	**—**	**7.7%**

2008 Year-End Financials

Debt ratio: 53.2%
Return on equity: 12.1%
Cash ($ mil.): 46.9
Current ratio: 3.90
Long-term debt ($ mil.): 185.5
No. of shares (mil.): 23.1
Dividends
　Yield: 1.8%
　Payout: 26.3%
Market value ($ mil.): 649.5
R&D as % of sales: —
Advertising as % of sales: —

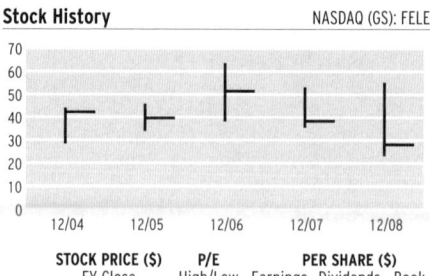

Stock History				NASDAQ (GS): FELE

	STOCK PRICE ($) FY Close	P/E High/Low		PER SHARE ($)	
			Earnings	Dividends	Book Value
12/08	28.11	29 13	1.90	0.50	15.10
12/07	38.27	43 30	1.22	0.47	16.38
12/06	51.39	26 16	2.44	0.43	14.97
12/05	39.54	23 17	1.98	0.38	11.58
12/04	42.26	26 18	1.65	0.31	10.14
Annual Growth	**(9.7%)**	**— —**	**3.6%**	**12.7%**	**10.5%**

FTI Consulting, Inc.

When someone has been cooking the books, FTI Consulting has a recipe for recovery. Established in 1982, the company is one of the leading providers of forensic accounting and litigation support services in the US. Its experts offer investigative services to companies confronted with problems such as fraud in order to assist them in their legal defense or pursuit of recoveries. FTI also provides consulting services related to corporate finance and restructuring, such as advice on mergers and acquisitions and performance improvement. Other consulting service areas include economics, strategic and financial communications, and technology. FTI's main clients are large business enterprises and major law firms.

FTI has diversified its service offerings and expanded its geographic reach through a number of acquisitions of niche-market firms. It entered the strategic and financial communications field in 2006 when it bought London-based Financial Dynamics for $260 million. (The acquired business changed its name to FD in 2007.) All in all, the company made seven acquisitions throughout 2007. That number increased to 16 in 2008.

FTI also made huge gains in the Asian market when it acquired Thompson Market Services Limited, a brand security and intellect property firm, in early 2008. Thompson operates across a network of about 20 cities in China. Shortly after, FTI obtained The Schonbraun McCann Group, a real estate and finance consultancy, for $125 million. Like the previous acquisition, the deal opened new channels for growth in Europe and Asia.

Outside the US, where the company has offices in about 30 cities, FTI and its subsidiaries maintain facilities in the Asia/Pacific region, Africa, Europe, Latin America, and the Middle East. US-based clients account for the vast majority of the company's sales, however.

EXECUTIVES

Chairman: Dennis J. Shaughnessy, age 62,
$3,685,321 total compensation
President, CEO, and Director: Jack B. Dunn IV, age 58,
$6,192,047 total compensation
CIO: Gregory (Greg) Wills
EVP and Chief Legal Officer: Eric B. Miller, age 49
VP and Chief Audit Officer: Curt A.H. Jeschke Jr.,
age 58
SVP, Controller, and Chief Accounting Officer:
Catherine M. Freeman, age 52
EVP and COO: Dominic (Dom) DiNapoli, age 54,
$3,320,913 total compensation
EVP and CFO: Jorge A. Celaya, age 43,
$1,424,813 total compensation
EVP and Chief Risk and Compliance Officer:
John A. MacColl, age 60
SVP and Chief Marketing Officer: Liz Nickles
VP Strategic Planning: Richard (Rich) Davis
VP and Treasurer: Ronald Reno
Auditors: KPMG LLP

LOCATIONS

HQ: FTI Consulting, Inc.
500 E. Pratt St., Ste. 1400, Baltimore, MD 21202
Phone: 410-951-4800 **Fax:** 410-224-8378
Web: www.fticonsulting.com

2008 Sales

	$ mil.	% of total
US	1,056.6	84
Other countries	236.5	16
Total	**1,293.1**	**100**

PRODUCTS/OPERATIONS

2008 Sales

	$ mil.	% of total
Corporate Finance/Restructuring	374.5	29
Forensic/Litigation	253.9	20
Strategic & Financial Communications	224.5	17
Technology	220.3	17
Economic	219.9	17
Total	**1,293.1**	**100**

Selected Services and Operating Units

Corporate Finance
Creditor and Lender Services
FTI Capital Advisors, LLC
FTI Palladium Partners (Interim Management)
Equity Sponsor Services
Transaction Advisory Services
Economic Consulting
FTI Helios
Lexecon
Network Industries Strategies
Forensic and Litigation Consulting
Dispute Advisory Services
Investigations and Forensic Accounting
Trial Services
Construction Solutions
Healthcare
Intellectual Property
Insurance
Strategic Communications
FD
Technology
Application Solutions
Technology Consulting
Technology Services

COMPETITORS

Accenture	HP Enterprise Services
Bain & Company	Huron Consulting
BearingPoint	IBM
Booz Allen	KPMG
Boston Consulting	LECG
Cornerstone Research	McKinsey & Company
CRA International	Navigant Consulting
Deloitte	ONSITE
Deloitte Consulting	PA Consulting
Ernst & Young Global	PricewaterhouseCoopers

HISTORICAL FINANCIALS

Company Type: Public

Income Statement

FYE: December 31

	REVENUE ($ mil.)	NET INCOME ($ mil.)	NET PROFIT MARGIN	EMPLOYEES
12/08	1,293.1	125.4	9.7%	3,378
12/07	1,001.3	92.1	9.2%	2,549
12/06	707.9	42.0	5.9%	2,079
12/05	539.5	56.4	10.5%	1,338
12/04	427.0	42.9	10.0%	1,035
Annual Growth	**31.9%**	**30.8%**	**—**	**34.4%**

2008 Year-End Financials

Debt ratio: 37.2%
Return on equity: 12.0%
Cash ($ mil.): 191.8
Current ratio: 1.30
Long-term debt ($ mil.): 418.6
No. of shares (mil.): 51.8
Dividends
　Yield: 0.0%
　Payout: —
Market value ($ mil.): 2,315.0
R&D as % of sales: —
Advertising as % of sales: —

Stock History

NYSE: FCN

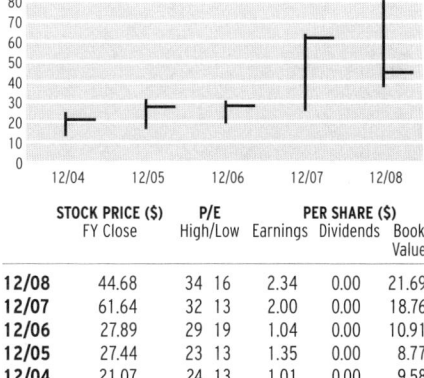

	STOCK PRICE ($) FY Close	P/E High/Low		PER SHARE ($) Earnings	Dividends	Book Value
12/08	44.68	34	16	2.34	0.00	21.69
12/07	61.64	32	13	2.00	0.00	18.76
12/06	27.89	29	19	1.04	0.00	10.91
12/05	27.44	23	13	1.35	0.00	8.77
12/04	21.07	24	13	1.01	0.00	9.58
Annual Growth	**20.7%**	**—**	**—**	**23.4%**	**—**	**22.7%**

Fuel Systems Solutions

Fuel Systems Solutions was green before green was hip. Operating through two primary subsidiaries, the holding company (formerly IMPCO Technologies, Inc.) manufactures and supplies equipment that allows internal combustion engines to run cleaner by using alternative fuels. Subsidiary IMPCO Technologies makes fuel systems that allow engines to burn gaseous fuels such as natural gas, propane, or biogas. IMPCO serves the heavy-duty, power generation, stationary power, and industrial markets. Italy-based BRC Gas Equipment subsidiary serves the transportation market by making fuel conversion systems for vehicles so they can meet

official government emission standards. Fuel Systems was formed in 1957 as IMPCO.

As Europe and the US implement more stringent fuel economy and emissions standards, logic dictates that Fuel Systems stands to capitalize with its mix of alternative fuel products and services. The company has experienced decent organic growth in Europe and is looking to expand and strengthen its global position in the alternative fuel industry.

The company acquired aftermarket conversion kit manufacturers, including Zavoli S.r.l. in 2007 and Argentina-based Distribuidora Shopping in early 2009. Conversion kits enable internal combustion engines to run on liquefied petroleum gas or compressed natural gas. Also in 2009 the company acquired the power systems (alternative fuel components and auxiliary power systems) business from Teleflex Incorporated for about $15 million. The acquisition strengthens the company in transportation and industrial markets, as well as gives it an entry into a new market segment. Earlier in the year the company purchased selected assets and technology of FuelMaker Corporation. The acquisition brings compressed natural gas technology and refueling products to Fuel Systems Solutions; the products will be integrated into its turn-key refueling equipment segment.

Fuel Systems Solutions also provides engineering and systems support to customers such as transit companies, delivery fleets, and automobile manufacturers. In 2009 IMPCO Technologies made significant headway in the US transportation market, specifically in automotive fleets, by signing a distribution agreement with CleanFUEL USA, a manufacturer of alternative fuel dispensing equipment. CleanFUEL will distribute and install IMPCO's Sequent system — dual propane and gasoline fuel system — to General Motors and Ford so that the auto companies can convert certain of their vehicles to run on propane.

There is a demand for gaseous fuel over liquid fuel among European consumers. Of the four largest natural gas-consumers in Europe (France, Germany, Italy, and the UK), all have launched incentives to encourage the use of gaseous fuel in vehicles and expect the replacement target to be 20% by 2020. Regions slated for rapid growth include Asia, the Middle East, and North Africa, as their respective economies increase along with personal vehicle ownership.

CEO Mariano Costamagna and his brother, Pier Antonio Costamagna, own about 21% of Fuel Systems Solutions.

HISTORY

In 1957 Herb Dills and Dick Babberstock founded tool and die company IMPCO. They invented a kit used by farmers to convert gasoline engines to propane engines. By the late 1980s IMPCO was the #1 alternative-fuels conversion-kit maker worldwide, but it was challenged by firms with more advanced technology. IMPCO planned to buy new technology from AirSensors, which had developed electronically regulated carburetion and fuel-injection systems. (AirSensors was founded in 1978 and went public in 1986.) Instead, in 1989 AirSensors bought privately held IMPCO, which was more than 20 times its size.

Saddled with heavy debt from the purchase, AirSensors struggled during the early 1990s. It posted a profit in 1993, in part because of the Energy Policy Act of 1992, which required 70%

of vehicles purchased by the US government to be low-polluting.

In 1995 AirSensors bought 51% of European alternative-fuels company Technisch Bureau Media (later IMPCO Technologies BV). The next year it acquired Garretson Equipment (conversion equipment for small engines) and Ateco Automotive (AirSensors' distributor in Australia). In 1997 the company began installing natural gas systems for GM models equipped with bi-fuel systems (work with gasoline or natural gas), and changed its name to IMPCO Technologies.

IMPCO helped train Chinese officials and auto experts in converting buses and taxis to natural gas in 1998. That year it bought the business of Thermo Power's Crusader Engines (propane- and natural-gas-powered industrial engines). In 1999 it bought the remainder of IMPCO Technologies BV.

In 2000 IMPCO formed an alliance with Alcoa's Thiokol unit for joint development of hydrogen fuel storage tanks for the emerging automotive fuel cell market. Later that year Hyundai selected IMPCO for the development of a hydrogen storage and fuel delivery system for Hyundai's prototype Santa Fe fuel-cell-powered SUV.

IMPCO spun off its Quantum Fuel Systems Technologies subsidiary in mid-2002.

IMPCO purchased a 50% stake in fellow alternative fuel system company BRC of Italy in 2003 and agreed to buy the other 50% the next year. BRC founder Mariano Costamagna became IMPCO's president and CEO in January 2005, and IMPCO took full ownership of BRC in March 2005.

The following year the company reorganized into a holding company structure, changing its name from IMPCO to Fuel Systems Solutions.

EXECUTIVES

CEO and Director; Managing Director, MTM:
Mariano Costamagna, age 58,
$632,052 total compensation
COO: Roberto Olivo, age 54,
$266,015 total compensation
President, CFO, and Secretary: Matthew Beale, age 42,
$262,633 total compensation
SVP Finance and Chief Accounting Officer:
Michael Helfand, age 49
Managing Director, IMPCO Technologies:
Richard Nielsen, age 53
Managing Director, BRC; Director Mechanical Engineering, MTM: Pier Antonio Costamagna, age 56,
$450,377 total compensation
Director Marketing, MTM: Marco Semandi, age 43
Auditors: BDO Seidman, LLP

LOCATIONS

HQ: Fuel Systems Solutions, Inc.
780 3rd Ave., 25th Fl., New York, NY 10017
Phone: 646-502-7170
Web: www.fuelsystemssolutions.com

2008 Sales

	$ mil.	% of total
Europe		
Italy	127.5	33
Other countries	135.8	36
Asia & Pacific Rim	57.5	15
North America	50.8	13
Latin America	11.1	3
Total	**382.7**	**100**

PRODUCTS/OPERATIONS

2008 Sales

	$ mil.	% of total
Transportation	302.7	80
Industrial	80.0	20
Total	**382.7**	**100**

2008 Sales

	$ mil.	% of total
BRC	291.3	76
IMPCO	91.4	24
Total	**382.7**	**100**

Selected Products and Services

Compressors
Design and systems integration
Electronic and controls
Engine-fuel delivery systems
Fuel metering
Fuel regulation
Fuel shut-off
Fuel systems
Gaseous-fueled internal combustion engines
Service parts and warranty support
Sub-system assembly
Testing and validation
Training and technical service

Selected Operating Units

BRC S.r.l (Italy)
Grupo IMPCO Mexicano
IMPCO Technologies, BV (The Netherlands)
IMPCO Technologies Japan KK
IMPCO Technologies, Pty. (Australia)

COMPETITORS

Aisan
Ballard Power
Continental AG
Delphi Automotive
Detroit Diesel
Plug Power
Robert Bosch
Teleflex
Visteon

HISTORICAL FINANCIALS

Company Type: Public

Income Statement

FYE: December 31

	REVENUE ($ mil.)	NET INCOME ($ mil.)	NET PROFIT MARGIN	EMPLOYEES
12/08	382.7	23.1	6.0%	1,448
12/07	265.3	5.9	2.2%	1,002
12/06	220.8	6.9	3.1%	845
12/05	174.5	(10.6)	—	694
12/04	118.3	(14.2)	—	721
Annual Growth	**34.1%**	**—**	**—**	**19.0%**

2008 Year-End Financials

Debt ratio: 3.2%
Return on equity: 16.0%
Cash ($ mil.): 26.5
Current ratio: 1.70
Long-term debt ($ mil.): 4.9
No. of shares (mil.): 17.6
Dividends
  Yield: 0.0%
  Payout: —
Market value ($ mil.): 576.1
R&D as % of sales: —
Advertising as % of sales: —

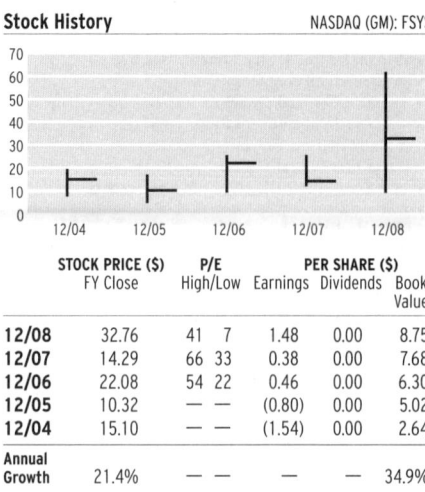

	STOCK PRICE ($) FY Close	P/E High	P/E Low	PER SHARE ($) Earnings	PER SHARE ($) Dividends	PER SHARE ($) Book Value
12/08	32.76	41	7	1.48	0.00	8.75
12/07	14.29	66	33	0.38	0.00	7.68
12/06	22.08	54	22	0.46	0.00	6.30
12/05	10.32	—	—	(0.80)	0.00	5.02
12/04	15.10	—	—	(1.54)	0.00	2.64
Annual Growth	**21.4%**	**—**	**—**	**—**	**—**	**34.9%**

Furmanite Corporation

Furmanite hopes its products stick. The specialty contractor provides on-site leak sealing, heat treating, and valve testing and repair primarily to the energy and power generation industries around the globe. Furmanite has 70 field offices on five continents. Formerly called Xanser, Furmanite spun off its oil pipeline operations and wholesale fuel marketing services businesses to focus on its technical services. Customers include petroleum refineries, chemical plants, steel mills, nuclear power stations, pulp and paper mills, and food processing plants. Subsidiary Xtria also provides information technology services through contracts with state and federal government agencies.

Furmanite specializes in sealing leaks in valves, pipes, and other flow-process systems often under emergency conditions involving exposure to high temperatures and pressures, potential contact with caustic or toxic materials, fire and explosion hazards, and environmental contamination. Furmanite has worked on fast-turnaround and custom engineering projects for such customers as Alcoa, GlaxoSmithKline, and PacifiCorp.

The company has seen significant revenue growth due to both organic overseas expansion into China and its 2005 acquisition of Flowserve's General Services Group (GSG), which added valve-repair and hot-tapping capabilities to its portfolio of services and effectively doubled the size of the business.

In 2008, Furmanite opened an office in West Africa to expand its service lines to customers in the region.

Franklin Resources owns 8% of Furmanite; bank investor Jeffrey Gendell owns 7%.

HISTORY

Kaneb Services, which became Xanser in 2001, was founded in 1953 as a pipeline company. It built its first pipeline between Kansas and Nebraska. As its pipeline advanced through the Midwest, Kaneb moved into offshore drilling, coal production, and banking. Profits sprung a leak during the Texas oil and banking bust, and new CEO John Barnes inherited $574 million in debt

when he came aboard in 1986. Barnes sold all of Kaneb's energy-related businesses except the pipeline company, restructured Kaneb's debt, and in 1989 took the pipeline public, forming Kaneb Pipeline Partners (KPP).

The company bought debt-laden Furmanite in 1991. Furmanite was founded in the 1920s by Clay Furman, who developed methods of sealing steam leaks.

In 1993 KPP bought Support Terminal Services, one of the largest US liquid-storage firms. KPP purchased 550 miles of pipeline from Wyco two years later, giving the company a presence in the Rocky Mountain area. That purchase and other terminal acquisitions in 1996 boosted Kaneb's sales.

Furmanite expanded internationally in 1997 with the acquisition of a longtime licensee serving Australia and New Zealand. In 1998 Furmanite teamed up with Yarway, a steam trap inspection unit of diversified manufacturer Tyco International, to offer service and repair to the hydrocarbon-processing industry. Also in 1998 the company diversified further through the acquisition of a products-marketing firm that offers wholesale fuel-marketing services in California, the Great Lakes region, and the Rockies.

In 1999 KPP acquired six storage terminals in the UK. Kaneb also moved into information technology in a big way by acquiring Ellsworth Associates, a major IT service provider to the US government. That year Kaneb won a multiyear, multimillion-dollar contract with the US Army to produce more than 2 million solid-state wearable medical data storage devices.

Kaneb's information services unit formed an alliance with Datakey in 2000 to make Datakey's smart cards for US government agencies. The next year the company integrated four information technology services units into a new subsidiary, Xtria.

Restructuring in 2001, the company spun off its stake in KPP and its fuel marketing operations to shareholders as Kaneb Services LLC. To reflect its shift in focus, Kaneb changed its name to Xanser that year. Also that year, subsidiary Furmanite Worldwide, along with BAE Systems, produced equipment for maintenance of Tornado fighter aircraft. In 2003 Xanser closed unprofitable operations in its Xtria subsidiary.

The company in 2006 then exited its health care-focused business (honoring existing contracts); these discontinued services included training and maintenance of digital radiology imaging systems.

EXECUTIVES

Chairman and CEO: Michael L. Rose, age 70, $426,369 total compensation
President and COO: Joseph E. (Joe) Milliron, age 54, $321,334 total compensation
Auditors: Grant Thornton LLP

LOCATIONS

HQ: Furmanite Corporation
    2435 N. Central Expwy., Richardson, TX 75080
Phone: 972-699-4000   **Fax:** 972-644-3524
Web: www.furmanite.com

2008 Sales

	$ mil.	% of total
US	147.0	46
Europe	141.7	44
Asia/Pacific	32.2	10
Total	**320.9**	**100**

PRODUCTS/OPERATIONS

2008 Sales

	$ mil.	% of total
Technical services		
Turnaround	174.3	55
Under pressure	103.6	32
Other	43.0	13
Total	**320.9**	**100**

Selected Subsidiaries and Affiliates

CMS: Corrision Monitoring Services AS
Furmanite America
Furmanite Equipment Leasing Company LLC (formerly Kaneb Equipment Leasing Company)
Furmanite GSG Limited
Furmanite International
Furmanite Limited (formerly Kaneb UK plc)
Furmanite Worldwide (formerly Kaneb International, Inc.)
Kaneb Financial Corporation (formerly Asset Based Lenders, Inc.)
Metaholding BV
Metalock BV
Specialty Industrial Services Sdn. Bhd.
Xtria LLC

COMPETITORS

Computer Sciences Corp.
Halliburton
ITT Corp.
T. D. Williamson
Team

HISTORICAL FINANCIALS

Company Type: Public

Income Statement

FYE: December 31

	REVENUE ($ mil.)	NET INCOME ($ mil.)	NET PROFIT MARGIN	EMPLOYEES
12/08	320.9	21.9	6.8%	1,925
12/07	290.3	12.5	4.3%	1,805
12/06	246.4	(3.4)	—	1,647
12/05	153.9	(4.3)	—	1,047
12/04	145.7	2.4	1.6%	1,050
Annual Growth	**21.8%**	**73.8%**	**—**	**16.4%**

2008 Year-End Financials

Debt ratio: 38.7%
Return on equity: 25.8%
Cash ($ mil.): 30.8
Current ratio: 2.91
Long-term debt ($ mil.): 35.4
No. of shares (mil.): 36.7

Dividends
    Yield: 0.0%
    Payout: —
Market value ($ mil.): 197.7
R&D as % of sales: —
Advertising as % of sales: —

Stock History

NYSE: FRM

	STOCK PRICE ($) FY Close	P/E High/Low		PER SHARE ($) Earnings	Dividends	Book Value
12/08	5.39	21	7	0.59	0.00	2.49
12/07	11.80	37	13	0.35	0.00	2.14
12/06	4.86	—	—	(0.10)	0.00	1.65
12/05	2.94	—	—	(0.13)	0.00	1.40
12/04	2.80	44	32	0.07	0.00	1.52
Annual Growth	**17.8%**	**—**	**—**	**70.4%**	**—**	**13.1%**

Genco Shipping & Trading

Marine transportation company Genco Shipping & Trading transports dry cargo in a wet environment. The company maintains a fleet of about 30 oceangoing dry bulk carriers, which it charters mainly on long-term contracts to shippers of bulk commodities and marine transportation companies. Its fleet has an overall capacity of about 2.4 million deadweight tons (DWT). Genco Shipping's vessels transport cargo such as coal, grain, iron ore, and steel products. About 90% of its vessels on time-charter contracts. Customers have included BHP Billiton, Cargill, Lauritzen Bulkers and NYK. Pacific Basin Chartering and Cargill make up about 10% of the company's revenues. Genco Shipping & Trading was founded in 2004.

Genco Shipping, which bought its first 15 vessels from a subsidiary of China National Cereals Oil and Foodstuffs Corp., plans to continue to expand its fleet through acquisitions. Once all the pending deals are done, the company will own about 35 vessels with an overall carrying capacity of some 3 million DWT.

In 2009 Genco Shipping formed Baltic Trading Limited, a new company focused on the dry bulk spot market. Genco Shipping is acting as Baltic's manager, providing strategic and administrative services and linking Baltic to other major marine transportation companies.

As with other players in the transportation industry, Genco Shipping felt the sting of the global financial downturn in 2008. To strengthen its liquidity, in November 2008 the company cancelled an agreement with a handful of companies to buy three Capesize and three Handysize newbuildings for $530 million. Genco Shipping took a $53.8 million hit in the lost deposit and interest. By the same token, the recession has caused the price of dry bulk ships to plunge to only $50 million compared to about $150 million in 2008, making it easier for companies like Genco Shipping to press on with plans to buy more vessels.

To tighten up its operational costs, in late 2008 Genco Shipping outsourced the technical management (such as routine maintenance and arranging for crews and supplies) of its fleet to Wallem Shipmanagement, Anglo-Eastern Group, and Barber International.

Chairman Peter Georgiopoulos, who is also the chairman and CEO of crude oil transporter General Maritime and the chairman of fuel supplier Aegean Marine Petroleum Network, owns 13% of Genco Shipping & Trading.

EXECUTIVES

Chairman: Peter C. Georgiopoulos, age 48, $1,372,360 total compensation
President: Robert Gerald Buchanan, age 60, $1,404,330 total compensation
CFO, Principal Accounting Officer, Secretary, and Treasurer: John C. Wobensmith, age 39, $2,998,427 total compensation
Auditors: Deloitte & Touche LLP

LOCATIONS

HQ: Genco Shipping & Trading Limited
    299 Park Ave., 20th Fl., New York, NY 10171
Phone: 646-443-8550   **Fax:** 646-443-8551
Web: gencoshipping.com

COMPETITORS

A.P. Møller — Mærsk	OceanFreight
DryShips Inc.	Overseas Shipholding
Eagle Bulk Shipping	Group
Excel Maritime Carriers	Pacific Basin Shipping
Hanjin Shipping	Paragon Shipping
Kawasaki Kisen	TBS International
Mitsui O.S.K. Lines	

HISTORICAL FINANCIALS

Company Type: Public

Income Statement

FYE: December 31

	REVENUE ($ mil.)	NET INCOME ($ mil.)	NET PROFIT MARGIN	EMPLOYEES
12/08	405.4	86.6	21.4%	701
12/07	185.4	106.8	57.6%	617
12/06	133.2	63.5	47.7%	475
12/05	116.9	54.5	46.6%	408
12/04	1.9	0.9	47.4%	—
Annual Growth	282.2%	213.2%	—	19.8%

2008 Year-End Financials

Debt ratio: 168.5%
Return on equity: 13.1%
Cash ($ mil.): 125.0
Current ratio: 4.66
Long-term debt ($ mil.): 1,173.3
No. of shares (mil.): 31.7

Dividends
Yield: 26.0%
Payout: 135.6%
Market value ($ mil.): 469.5
R&D as % of sales: —
Advertising as % of sales: —

Stock History

NYSE: GNK

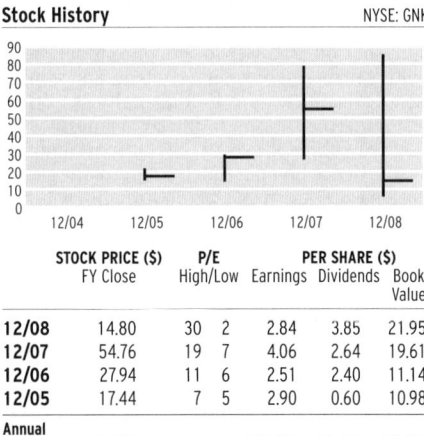

	STOCK PRICE ($) FY Close	P/E High/Low		PER SHARE ($) Earnings	Dividends	Book Value
12/08	14.80	30	2	2.84	3.85	21.95
12/07	54.76	19	7	4.06	2.64	19.61
12/06	27.94	11	6	2.51	2.40	11.14
12/05	17.44	7	5	2.90	0.60	10.98
Annual Growth	(5.3%)	—	—	152.4%	85.8%	75.5%

Gencor Industries

Gencor Industries loves the smell of asphalt in the morning. The company makes industrial process equipment, such as machinery that makes hot-mix asphalt and other highway construction materials. Gencor's products include asphalt plants, combustion systems (large burners that transform various fuels into usable energy), and fluid heat transfer systems under the Hy-Way and Beverley names. It also produces soil decontamination machines and combustion systems for dryers, kilns, boilers, and tank heaters. Gencor Industries makes most of its sales in the US.

The company sells used (or "pre-owned," as they like to say) equipment. Its customer support functions include a help desk, erection assistance and turnkey construction services, and training programs. To provide parts for its equipment, Gencor has two warehouses, in Florida and Iowa, and it also makes custom parts.

Chairman and CEO E. J. "Mike" Elliott owns about 13% of Gencor Industries; investor Harvey Houtkin holds around 27% of the company.

HISTORY

The company started out making combustion systems for paving contractors in the 1940s. It incorporated in Florida in 1960 as Mechtron Corporation. In 1969 it merged with Ohio-based General Combustion and Genco Manufacturing. E. J. "Mike" Elliott, chairman of General Combustion, was named president of the combined company, rechristened Mechtron International, in 1970. In 1987 it adopted its present name.

In the 1980s Gencor began beefing up its process machinery business, moving into thermal fluid heaters, industrial incinerators, and asphalt-making systems. Asphalt machinery accounted for 70% of sales, but the business suffered from cyclical swings. To smooth the ups and downs, in 1996 Gencor bought Ingersoll-Rand's food equipment division, a maker of pelleting, grinding, flaking, and filtration machines. The buy catapulted Gencor into a leading position in the food processing machinery field. In 1997 it made a series of acquisitions in South America, including Brazilian citrus processing equipment maker Gumaco.

In 1998 the company bought ACP Holdings, PLC (an asphalt production business with operations in the UK and Australia). It also acquired a 45% interest in Carbontronics and made machinery that company is using to produce synthetic fuel from coal waste. The firm suffered some serious setbacks that year: Bad weather damaged much of Brazil's orange crop, hurting results of Gencor's Gumaco subsidiary. The Asian financial crisis also slugged its Gencor ACP unit. Gencor ACP's chairman and CFO were both terminated after irregularities in accounting practices were discovered.

Gencor filed for Chapter 11 bankruptcy protection in 2000 and emerged from Chapter 11 at the end of 2001. The company sold its food processing machinery business for $52 million in 2001.

EXECUTIVES

Chairman and CEO: E. J. (Mike) Elliott
President and Director: Marc G. Elliott
CFO and Treasurer: L. Ray Adams, age 59
EVP: John E. Elliott
SVP Technology: David F. Brashears
SVP Sales and Marketing: Dennis Hunt
VP, Sales: William Dieli
Secretary: Jeanne M. Lyons
Auditors: Moore Stephens Lovelace, P.A.

LOCATIONS

HQ: Gencor Industries, Inc.
5201 N. Orange Blossom Trail, Orlando, FL 32810
Phone: 407-290-6000 **Fax:** 407-578-0577
Web: www.gencor.com

2008 Sales

	$ mil.	% of total
US	85.6	97
UK	2.7	3
Total	88.3	100

PRODUCTS/OPERATIONS

Selected Products

Asphalt plant equipment
  Cold feed bins
  Fabric filtration systems
  Hot-mix storage silos
  Plant components
Asphalt plants
  Batch plants
  Hot-mix asphalt plants
  Mobile shredders
  Trommel screens
Combustion systems and industrial incinerators (for use in rotary dryers, kilns, fume and liquid incinerators, boilers, and tank heaters)
Soil decontamination machinery
Fluid heat transfer systems (Hy-Way heat and Beverley lines of thermal fluid heat transfer systems and specialty storage tanks)

COMPETITORS

Art's-Way
Astec Industries
Cleaver-Brooks
CMI Terex
Coen Company
FMC
Forney Corporation
Gehl
Kemco Systems
Paul Mueller

HISTORICAL FINANCIALS

Company Type: Public

Income Statement

FYE: September 30

	REVENUE ($ mil.)	NET INCOME ($ mil.)	NET PROFIT MARGIN	EMPLOYEES
9/08	88.3	15.2	17.2%	461
9/07	75.3	18.5	24.6%	434
9/06	67.1	11.6	17.3%	346
9/05	48.1	31.3	65.1%	294
9/04	54.1	2.6	4.8%	299
Annual Growth	13.0%	55.5%	—	11.4%

2008 Year-End Financials

Debt ratio: 0.0%
Return on equity: 16.6%
Cash ($ mil.): 4.1
Current ratio: 8.97
Long-term debt ($ mil.): 0.0
No. of shares (mil.): 9.6

Dividends
Yield: 0.0%
Payout: —
Market value ($ mil.): 77.7
R&D as % of sales: —
Advertising as % of sales: —

Stock History

NASDAQ (GM): GENC

	STOCK PRICE ($) FY Close	P/E High/Low		PER SHARE ($) Earnings	Dividends	Book Value
9/08	8.08	21	5	1.59	0.00	10.30
9/07	9.90	7	5	1.91	0.00	8.72
9/06	9.25	9	5	1.17	0.00	6.56
9/05	8.15	3	2	3.29	0.00	5.35
9/04	8.75	32	8	0.27	0.00	1.59
Annual Growth	(2.0%)	—	—	55.8%	—	59.5%

Genesee & Wyoming

Genesee & Wyoming once relied on the salt of the earth — hauling salt on a 14-mile railroad for one customer. Now the company owns stakes in more than 60 short-line and regional freight railroads that operate over a total of about 10,700 miles of track, including about 6,800 miles of track owned and leased by the company and another 3,100 miles belonging to other railroads. Freight transported by Genesee & Wyoming railroads includes coal, forest products, and pulp and paper. Outside the US and Canada, the company has operations in Australia and the Netherlands and a minority stake in a railroad in Bolivia.

Like other freight moving companies, Genesee & Wyoming has been hit hard by the sharp drop in demand for cargo. To offset losses the company laid off about 230 employees (about 9% of its workforce) and parked about 65 locomotives (about 12% of its fleet).

Genesee & Wyoming, which has expanded over the years via acquisitions, hopes to continue to grow by buying railroads, not only in North America and Australia but also in markets such as South America and Europe. Potential acquisition opportunities include rail lines owned by industrial companies, branches of major railroad systems, and government-owned railways that are being privatized.

The company expanded into the Netherlands in 2008 by buying Rotterdam Rail Feeding, a provider of short-haul, "last-mile" rail services for major railroads that converge at the Port of Rotterdam, one of Europe's busiest.

Genesee & Wyoming added to its core US operations via three acquisitions in 2008. The largest, Ohio Central Railroad System (OCR), gave the company nine short-line railroads that operate over a network of about 445 miles of track in Ohio and Pennsylvania. Genesee & Wyoming paid about $234 million for OCR, which is expected to post sales of about $70 million in 2009. Other purchases included Mississippi-based CAGY Industries (parent of three short-line railroads in the southeastern US) for about $78 million, and Georgia Southwestern Railroad, for about $22 million.

Besides its railroad operations, Genesee & Wyoming provides freight car switching and related services for industrial companies that own railroad facilities. Chairman Mortimer Fuller, great-grandson of founder Edward L. Fuller, owns a 28% stake in Genesee & Wyoming.

EXECUTIVES

Chairman: Mortimer B. Fuller III, age 66, $2,328,974 total compensation
President, CEO, and Director: John C. Hellmann, age 38, $1,909,474 total compensation
COO: James W. Benz, age 60, $935,153 total compensation
CFO: Timothy J. Gallagher, age 46, $1,038,165 total compensation
Chief Accounting Officer and Global Controller: Christopher F. Liucci, age 40, $424,128 total compensation
General Counsel and Secretary: Allison M. Fergus, age 35, $576,563 total compensation
Chief Human Resources Officer: Matthew C. Brush
EVP Corporate Development: Mark W. Hastings

SVP Corporate Development and Treasurer: Matthew O. Walsh
SVP Illinois Region; President and General Manager, Illinois & Midland Railroad: Spencer D. White
SVP Canada Region; President, Genesee & Wyoming Canada: Mario Brault
Director Corporate Communications: Michael E. Williams
Auditors: PricewaterhouseCoopers LLP

LOCATIONS

HQ: Genesee & Wyoming Inc.
66 Field Point Rd., Greenwich, CT 06830
Phone: 203-629-3722   **Fax:** 203-661-4106
Web: www.gwrr.com

2008 Sales

	$ mil.	% of total
US	422.9	70
Australia	114.2	19
Canada	54.8	9
The Netherlands	10.1	2
Total	**602.0**	**100**

PRODUCTS/OPERATIONS

2008 Sales

	$ mil.	% of total
Freight		
Pulp & paper	72.4	12
Coal, coke & ores	71.6	12
Minerals & stone	45.1	8
Metals	42.1	7
Farm & food products	39.0	6
Lumber & forest products	33.2	6
Chemicals & plastics	32.5	5
Petroleum products	18.5	3
Autos & auto parts	6.7	1
Intermodal	0.5	—
Other	8.3	1
Non-freight		
Railcar switching	98.4	16
Fuel sales to third parties	36.5	6
Car hire & rental income	29.0	5
Demurrage & storage	20.9	4
Car repair services	7.8	1
Other	39.5	7
Total	**602.0**	**100**

COMPETITORS

Anacostia Rail Holdings
Burlington Northern Santa Fe
Canadian National Railway
Canadian Pacific Railway
CSX
Kansas City Southern
Montana Rail Link
Norfolk Southern
OmniTRAX
Pan Am Railways
Pioneer Railcorp
Providence and Worcester Railroad
RailAmerica
Union Pacific
Watco Companies

HISTORICAL FINANCIALS

Company Type: Public

Income Statement

FYE: December 31

	REVENUE ($ mil.)	NET INCOME ($ mil.)	NET PROFIT MARGIN	EMPLOYEES
12/08	602.0	72.2	12.0%	2,647
12/07	516.2	55.2	10.7%	2,307
12/06	478.8	134.0	28.0%	2,677
12/05	385.4	50.1	13.0%	3,513
12/04	303.8	37.1	12.2%	3,093
Annual Growth	**18.6%**	**18.1%**	**—**	**(3.8%)**

2008 Year-End Financials

Debt ratio: 112.0%
Return on equity: 15.9%
Cash ($ mil.): 31.7
Current ratio: 1.02
Long-term debt ($ mil.): 535.2
No. of shares (mil.): 41.0
Dividends
  Yield: —
  Payout: —
Market value ($ mil.): 1,250.2
R&D as % of sales: —
Advertising as % of sales: —

Stock History

NYSE: GWR

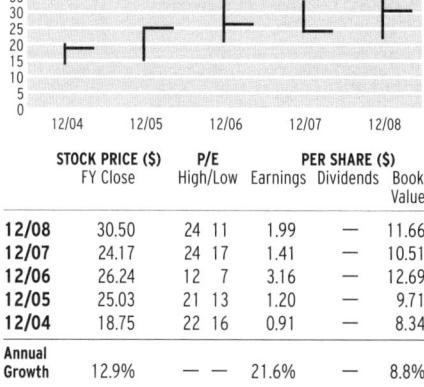

	STOCK PRICE ($) FY Close	P/E High/Low	PER SHARE ($) Earnings	Dividends	Book Value
12/08	30.50	24 11	1.99	—	11.66
12/07	24.17	24 17	1.41	—	10.51
12/06	26.24	12 7	3.16	—	12.69
12/05	25.03	21 13	1.20	—	9.71
12/04	18.75	22 16	0.91	—	8.34
Annual Growth	**12.9%**	**— —**	**21.6%**	**—**	**8.8%**

Genoptix, Inc.

Genoptix is promoting optimal cancer diagnostics. The biotechnology company is a specialized laboratory service provider founded in 1999. It analyzes blood and tissue samples in order to diagnose and monitor diseases such as leukemia, and markets those services to community-based hematologists and oncologists treating malignancies of the blood and bone marrow, as well as other types of cancer. Its key service offerings are COMPASS (short for Comprehensive Assessment) and CHART (a condition monitoring service). Genoptix was started by Dr. Tina Nova, who also co-founded San Diego-based life science companies Ligand Pharmaceuticals and Nanogen.

With the company's COMPASS service, customers authorize Genoptix's own specialized laboratory pathologists (dubbed hematopathologists) to analyze samples and determine whether additional diagnostic or treatment measures should be taken in each particular patient case; the hematopathologist then integrates the patient's individual history and most recent test results into a comprehensive, customized diagnostic report. Genoptix's CHART service, launched in 2007, compiles multiple COMPASS reports to track a patient's disease progression over time.

Genoptix uses a specialized direct sales force to promote its services to hematologists and oncologists across the US. The company plans to grow its market share in the laboratory services field by increasing headcount and adding infrastructure to handle new customers, as well as by expanding its service offering, partly by licensing or collaborating on new diagnostic tests and equipment. The company completed expansion efforts that doubled its California laboratory facility's capacity in 2008, but postponed plans to add another regional laboratory in 2009.

EXECUTIVES

Chairman: Andrew E. (Drew) Senyei, age 58
President, CEO, and Director: Tina S. Nova, age 55, $1,505,463 total compensation
CIO: Philippe J. Marchand, age 46
EVP and COO: Samuel D. Riccitelli, age 49, $976,812 total compensation
SVP, Sales and Marketing: Burt DeMill, age 49
SVP and CFO: Douglas A. Schuling, age 48, $724,778 total compensation
VP, Client Services: Mark S. Pitts, age 48
VP, General Counsel, and Secretary: Christian V. Kuhlen, age 36, $527,056 total compensation
VP, Human Resources: Cheri Caviness, age 61
VP, Cell Biology: Jeff M. Hall, age 53
VP, Applications and Molecular Laboratory: Jonathan Diver
VP, Reimbursement and Payor Markets: Walt Williams
VP, Business Development and Medical Affairs: Michael I. (Mike) Nerenberg, age 54
Laboratory Director and Senior Hematopathologist: Bashar Dabbas, age 50
Senior Director, Investor Relations: Marcy Graham
Auditors: Ernst & Young LLP

LOCATIONS

HQ: Genoptix, Inc.
  2110 Rutherford Rd., Carlsbad, CA 92008
Phone: 760-268-6200   **Fax:** 760-268-6201
Web: www.genoptix.com

PRODUCTS/OPERATIONS

Selected Services

Circulating Tumor Cells (CTC,tumor cell detection in blood samples)
Cytogenetics (detects chromosome abnormalities to assist in the prognosis of a malignancy)
Flow Cytometry (automated assessment of cellular surface characteristics to detect or measure leukemia/lymphoma)
Histopathology (or Morphology, microscopic blood or bone marrow evaluation)
Molecular (disease progression and therapy response monitoring through DNA and RNA analysis)

COMPETITORS

Associated Regional and University Pathologists
Bio-Reference Labs
Clarient
Genomic Health
Genzyme
LabCorp
Laboratory Sciences of Arizona
Mayo Clinic Rochester
Mid America Clinical Laboratories
NeoGenomics
Pathology Associates Medical Laboratories
Quest Diagnostics
Spectrum Laboratory Network

HISTORICAL FINANCIALS

Company Type: Public

Income Statement

FYE: December 31

	REVENUE ($ mil.)	NET INCOME ($ mil.)	NET PROFIT MARGIN	EMPLOYEES
12/08	116.2	31.4	27.0%	307
12/07	59.3	3.3	5.6%	155
12/06	24.0	(3.8)	—	113
12/05	5.2	(9.2)	—	120
12/04	0.7	(10.2)	—	—
Annual Growth	258.9%	—	—	36.8%

2008 Year-End Financials

Debt ratio: —
Return on equity: 28.2%
Cash ($ mil.): 38.1
Current ratio: 12.31
Long-term debt ($ mil.): —
No. of shares (mil.): 17.2
Dividends
  Yield: 0.0%
  Payout: —
Market value ($ mil.): 585.0
R&D as % of sales: —
Advertising as % of sales: —

Stock History

NASDAQ (GM): GXDX

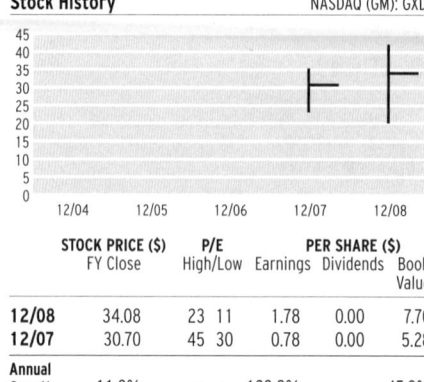

	STOCK PRICE ($) FY Close	P/E High/Low		Earnings	PER SHARE ($) Dividends	Book Value
12/08	34.08	23	11	1.78	0.00	7.70
12/07	30.70	45	30	0.78	0.00	5.28
Annual Growth	11.0%	—	—	128.2%	—	45.9%

Gen-Probe Incorporated

Gen-Probe knows the answer is flowing through your veins. The company is a leading provider of diagnostic tests and instruments to detect HIV, chlamydia, and other sexually transmitted diseases. Gen-Probe also makes diagnostics to detect a host of infectious, disease-causing bacteria and fungi, including those behind tuberculosis, strep throat and influenza. In addition, the company makes products that screen donated blood for these diseases. Gen-Probe's products are designed to provide results within hours, while traditional cultured tests can take days. Major blood suppliers, including The American Red Cross and America's Blood Centers, use its products to screen much of the US blood supply.

Major partner Novartis markets and distributes GenProbe's blood screening products worldwide and accounts for nearly half of the company's sales. In addition to GenProbe's HIV and Hepatitis C tests, the screening product line includes a test to detect West Nile Virus that Novartis' Chiron subsidiary developed in partnership with GenProbe.

The company handles its own clinical diagnostic product marketing in the US and Canada through a direct sales force, while it has agreements with other companies for international marketing. Primary customers for Gen-Probe's clinical diagnostic products, which account for about half of its revenues, include public health agencies, hospitals, and reference laboratories.

To expand its product and geographic range, in early 2009 the company spent $132 million to acquire UK-based Tepnel Life Sciences. Tepnel's operations, including its technology for identifying antigens used to help match transplant donors to patients, have been integrated into Gen-Probe's organization. The Tepnel acquisition also added molecular diagnostics and other types of genetic testing products.

That same year the company expanded its diagnostic capabilities once again with the purchase of Prodesse, a maker of clinical tests for influenza and other infectious diseases. Gen-Probe bought the privately held company for about $60 million in cash, but that number could increase to $85 million if Prodesse meets certain milestones over the next couple of years. Gen-Probe's sales force in North America and Europe started co-promoting Prodesse's products after the purchase.

Gen-Probe collaborated with others to develop non-clinical diagnostics to detect toxins in food and water. However, the company then decided to focus solely on human diagnostics. In 2009 the company spun off its industrial testing operations into a newly formed company, Roka Bioscience. Gen-Probe gave the new operations a handful of employees, and transferred its collaborations with GE Energy and Millipore to Roka. It held on to 20% of the new company and provided contract manufacturing services to Roka during the transition.

Gen-Probe was spun off from parent Chugai Pharmaceutical and went public in 2002. Chairman Henry Nordhoff served as its CEO from 1994 until his retirement in 2009. Company executive Carl Hull succeeded him.

EXECUTIVES

Chairman: Henry L. (Hank) Nordhoff, age 67, $4,052,126 total compensation
President and CEO: Carl W. Hull, age 51, $1,772,660 total compensation
EVP and Chief Scientist: Daniel L. Kacian, age 62, $1,435,493 total compensation
SVP Finance and CFO: Herm Rosenman, age 60, $1,074,138 total compensation
SVP, General Counsel, and Secretary: R. William Bowen, age 56, $1,178,509 total compensation
SVP Clinical, Regulatory, and Quality: Christina C. Yang, age 52
SVP Operations: Jorgine Ellerbrock, age 47
SVP Research and Development: Eric Lai, age 51
SVP Corporate Strategy: Eric Tardiff, age 39
SVP Human Resources: Diana De Walt, age 54
SVP Sales and Marketing: Stephen J. Kondor, age 53
VP and CIO: Brad Phillips
VP Investor Relations and Corporate Communications: Michael Watts
Auditors: Ernst & Young LLP

LOCATIONS

HQ: Gen-Probe Incorporated
  10210 Genetic Center Dr., San Diego, CA 92121
Phone: 858-410-8000   **Fax:** 858-410-8625
Web: www.gen-probe.com

2008 Sales

	$ mil.	% of total
North America	363.2	77
Other regions	109.5	23
Total	**472.7**	**100**

PRODUCTS/OPERATIONS

2008 Sales

	$ mil.	% of total
Products	429.2	91
Royalty & licensing	22.9	5
Collaborative research	20.6	4
Total	**472.7**	**100**

COMPETITORS

Abbott Labs	Inverness Medical
AutoGenomics	Luminex
Becton, Dickinson	Orchid Cellmark
bioMérieux	Ortho-Clinical Diagnostics
Cepheid	QIAGEN
Genzyme Diagnostics	Roche Holding
Hologic	Siemens Healthcare

HISTORICAL FINANCIALS

Company Type: Public

Income Statement

FYE: December 31

	REVENUE ($ mil.)	NET INCOME ($ mil.)	NET PROFIT MARGIN	EMPLOYEES
12/08	472.7	107.0	22.6%	1,037
12/07	403.0	86.1	21.4%	1,049
12/06	354.8	59.5	16.8%	925
12/05	306.0	60.1	19.6%	866
12/04	269.7	54.6	20.2%	809
Annual Growth	15.1%	18.3%	—	6.4%

2008 Year-End Financials

Debt ratio: —	Dividends
Return on equity: 13.8%	Yield: 0.0%
Cash ($ mil.): 60.1	Payout: —
Current ratio: 13.49	Market value ($ mil.): 2,102.9
Long-term debt ($ mil.): —	R&D as % of sales: —
No. of shares (mil.): 49.1	Advertising as % of sales: —

Stock History

NASDAQ (GS): GPRO

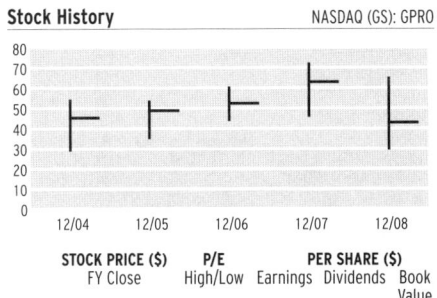

	STOCK PRICE ($) FY Close	P/E High/Low		Earnings	PER SHARE ($) Dividends	Book Value
12/08	42.84	33	15	1.95	0.00	16.58
12/07	62.93	45	29	1.58	0.00	15.04
12/06	52.37	54	40	1.12	0.00	11.62
12/05	48.79	46	31	1.15	0.00	9.11
12/04	45.21	51	28	1.06	0.00	7.35
Annual Growth	(1.3%)	—	—	16.5%	—	22.5%

GeoResources, Inc.

GeoResources has been expanding geographically to increase its oil and gas resources. The company, once a regional explorer in Montana and North Dakota only, has grown to incorporate exploration acreage in the Southwest and the Gulf Coast, as well as the Williston Basin. In 2009 GeoResources reported proved reserves of 141.4 billion cu. ft. of natural gas equivalent. That year it reported a portfolio of about 484,000 gross acres and 234,000 net acres. Its Southern Bay Energy unit operates out of Houston, while G3 Operating is based in Denver.

In a major expansion, in 2009 GeoResources made two oil and gas purchases. It acquired a 15% of 59 producing wells and 60,000 acres in the Bakken Shale trend of the Williston Basin for

$10 million. It also acquired 68 producing wells in the Giddings Field in Texas for $48 million.

Moving toward becoming a national oil and gas player, in 2007 the company acquired regional exploration firms Southern Bay Oil & Gas, L.P. and Chandler Energy, LLC, for $78 million. In 2008 subsidiary Catena Oil & Gas formed OKLA Energy Partners LP to buy producing oil and gas properties and undeveloped acreage across Oklahoma.

GeoResources once mined leonardite, an oxidized lignite coal, which it processed into a powder used primarily as a dispersant or thinner in drilling mud, but the company exited this business in 2007 to focus on oil and gas.

GeoResources was founded in 1958 and was originally engaged in uranium mining. It built its first leonardite processing plant in 1964, and moved into oil and gas exploration and production in 1969. GeoResources purchased an oil and gas drilling rig in 2001 and formed a subsidiary for drilling operations in 2002.

EXECUTIVES

President, CEO, and Director: Frank A. Lodzinski, age 60, $281,000 total compensation
EVP and Director; COO Northern Division: Collis P. Chandler III, age 40, $229,000 total compensation
EVP; COO Southern Division: Francis M. Mury, age 57, $245,250 total compensation
VP Business Development, Acquisitions, and Divestitures: Robert J. Anderson, age 46, $104,858 total compensation
VP and CFO: Howard E. Ehler, age 64, $202,800 total compensation
Secretary and Investor Relations: Cathy Kruse, age 53
Auditors: Grant Thornton LLP

LOCATIONS

HQ: GeoResources, Inc.
110 Cypress Station Dr., Ste. 220
Houston, TX 77090
Phone: 281-537-9920   **Fax:** 281-537-8324
Web: www.georesourcesinc.com

PRODUCTS/OPERATIONS

2008 Sales

	$ mil.	% of total
Oil & gas	85.3	90
Gain on sale of property & equipment	4.4	5
Partnership management fees	1.7	2
Property operating income	1.4	1
Partnership income	1.1	1
Other	0.7	1
Total	**94.6**	**100**

COMPETITORS

Abraxas Petroleum
Black Hills
BP
Brigham Exploration
Cabot Oil & Gas
Chevron
Devon Energy
Exxon Mobil
Forest Oil
Occidental Petroleum
Pioneer Natural Resources
Royal Dutch Shell

HISTORICAL FINANCIALS

Company Type: Public

Income Statement

FYE: December 31

	REVENUE ($ mil.)	NET INCOME ($ mil.)	NET PROFIT MARGIN	EMPLOYEES
12/08	94.6	13.5	14.3%	52
12/07	37.8	3.1	8.2%	61
12/06	8.9	1.7	19.1%	13
12/05	8.0	2.2	27.5%	13
12/04	6.8	1.1	16.2%	11
Annual Growth	93.1%	87.2%	—	47.5%

2008 Year-End Financials

Debt ratio: 28.4%	Dividends
Return on equity: 12.9%	Yield: 0.0%
Cash ($ mil.): 14.0	Payout: —
Current ratio: 1.31	Market value ($ mil.): 141.1
Long-term debt ($ mil.): 40.0	R&D as % of sales: —
No. of shares (mil.): 16.2	Advertising as % of sales: —

Stock History

NASDAQ (GM): GEOI

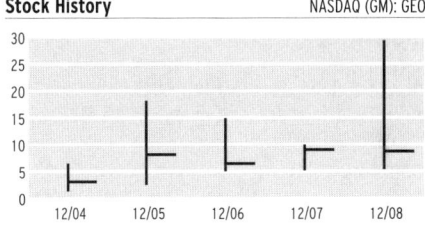

	STOCK PRICE ($) FY Close	P/E High/Low		Earnings	PER SHARE ($) Dividends	Book Value
12/08	8.69	34	7	0.86	0.00	8.68
12/07	9.00	39	22	0.25	0.00	4.19
12/06	6.42	33	12	0.45	0.00	0.69
12/05	8.11	32	5	0.57	0.00	0.58
12/04	3.06	21	5	0.30	0.00	0.44
Annual Growth	29.8%	—	—	30.1%	—	111.3%

GFI Group

A financial matchmaker, GFI Group is an inter-dealer hybrid brokerage that acts as an intermediary for more than 2,000 institutional clients such as banks, large corporations, insurance companies, and hedge funds. The firm deals primarily in over-the-counter derivatives, which tend to be less liquid and thus harder to trade than other assets. It also offers market data and analysis on credit, equity, commodity, and currency derivatives, and other financial instruments. Other products include foreign exchange options, freight, and energy derivatives including electric power, coal, and carbon emissions options. GFI has about 20 offices in North and South America, Europe, and Australasia.

Building its Americas operations, GFI opened an office in Alberta in 2007 and an office in Chile the following year. It also invested in Argentinian brokerage Premium Securities with the option to buy the rest of the company. GFI has also expanded into Dubai and Tel Aviv in recent years.

Jersey Partners, which is controlled by GFI chairman and CEO Michael Gooch, owns 43% of the company.

EXECUTIVES

Chairman and CEO: Michael A. (Mickey) Gooch, age 51, $2,187,440 total compensation
President and Director: Colin Heffron, age 47, $3,746,248 total compensation
COO: Ronald (Ron) Levi, age 47, $2,378,985 total compensation
CFO: James A. Peers, age 59, $991,057 total compensation
EVP Corporate Development: J. Christopher Giancarlo, age 50, $646,227 total compensation
SVP, Amerex Energy Services: Jeff Roberts
SVP Clearing, Data, Government Relations, Amerex Brokers: Mike Prokop
SVP Brokerage, Amerex Brokers: Scott Halperin
VP Public Relations: Patricia Gutierrez
General Counsel and Corporate Secretary: Scott Pintoff, age 39
Global Head, Development: Jerry Dobner
Global Human Resources Director: Sheena Griffiths
Public Relations Manager: Alan Bright
Investor Relations Manager: Chris Ann Casaburri
Auditors: Deloitte & Touche LLP

LOCATIONS

HQ: GFI Group Inc.
100 Wall St., New York, NY 10005
Phone: 212-968-4100   **Fax:** 212-968-4124
Web: www.gfigroup.com

2008 Sales

	$ mil.	% of total
EMEA brokerage	489.7	48
Americas brokerage	387.5	38
Asia brokerage	88.6	9
Other	49.7	5
Total	**1,015.5**	**100**

PRODUCTS/OPERATIONS

2008 Sales

	$ mil.	% of total
Brokerage		
Agency commissions	757.3	74
Principal transactions	206.7	20
Analytics & market data	51.2	5
Interest	8.6	1
Contracts	0.1	—
Adjustments	(8.4)	—
Total	**1,015.5**	**100**

COMPETITORS

ADM Investor Services
AIG Financial Products
BGC Partners
Cantor Fitzgerald
ICAP
Interactive Brokers
Newedge
Rosenthal Collins
Susquehanna International Group, LLP
Tullett Prebon
VIEL

HISTORICAL FINANCIALS

Company Type: Public

Income Statement

	REVENUE ($ mil.)	NET INCOME ($ mil.)	NET PROFIT MARGIN	EMPLOYEES
12/08	1,015.5	53.1	5.2%	1,740
12/07	970.5	94.9	9.8%	1,599
12/06	747.2	61.1	8.2%	1,438
12/05	533.6	48.1	9.0%	1,151
12/04	385.0	23.1	6.0%	868
Annual Growth	**27.4%**	**23.1%**	**—**	**19.0%**

2008 Year-End Financials

Debt ratio: 12.5%
Return on equity: 11.4%
Cash ($ mil.): 342.4
Current ratio: —
Long-term debt ($ mil.): 59.5
No. of shares (mil.): 118.4
Dividends
Yield: 7.2%
Payout: 56.8%
Market value ($ mil.): 419.3
R&D as % of sales: —
Advertising as % of sales: —

Stock History

NASDAQ (GS): GFIG

	STOCK PRICE ($) FY Close	P/E High/Low		PER SHARE ($) Earnings	Dividends	Book Value
12/08	3.54	52	6	0.44	0.25	4.03
12/07	23.93	32	17	0.80	0.00	3.82
12/06	15.56	32	21	0.52	0.00	2.79
12/05	11.86	30	13	0.44	0.00	2.01
Annual Growth	**(33.2%)**	**—**	**—**	**16.4%**	**—**	**72.9%**

Glacier Bancorp

Glacier Bancorp serves Big Sky Country. The company owns about a dozen community banks, including Glacier Bank, Western Security Bank, Big Sky Western Bank, Citizens State Bank, and 1st Bank. Together they serve individuals, small to midsized businesses, not-for-profits, and public entities in Montana, Idaho, Utah, Washington, Colorado, and Wyoming through about 100 branches. Glacier Bancorp offers traditional transaction and savings deposit products. Its lending activities consist mostly of commercial real estate loans (about 45% of the banks' portfolio) and residential mortgages (nearly 20%). Investment services are offered through Raymond James Financial.

The company is growing through selective acquisitions. To that end, it bought First National Bank of Morgan located in Morgan County, Utah, and Montana-based bank holding company Citizens Development in 2006. The following year it purchased North Side State Bank, then merged it into its 1st Bank subsidiary. In 2008 the company acquired the Bank of the San Juans in Durango, Colorado, marking its first entry into Colorado.

In 2009, Glacier Bancorp acquired First National Bank & Trust in Powell, Wyoming. The transaction makes Glacier's 11th bank acquisition since 2000 and its third in Wyoming.

EXECUTIVES

Chairman, Glacier Bancorp and Glacier Bank: Everit A. Sliter, age 70
President, CEO, and Director: Michael J. (Mick) Blodnick, age 56, $457,614 total compensation
EVP and Chief Administrative Officer: Don J. Chery, $268,808 total compensation
SVP Information Technology: Mark D. MacMillan
SVP and Controller: Donald B. McCarthy
SVP, CFO, and Treasurer: Ronald J. (Ron) Copher, age 52, $324,377 total compensation

SVP Human Resources: Robin S. Roush
SVP Operations: Marcia L. Johnson
SVP Credit Administration: Barry L. Johnston
SVP Internal Audit: Ryan T. Screnar
VP Information Technology: Glenn G. Nelson
Chairman, Mountain West Bank: Charles R. Nipp
Director; President, CEO, and Director, Mountain West Bank: Jon W. Hippler, age 64, $396,701 total compensation
Director; Vice Chairman, First Security Bank of Missoula: Allen J. Fetscher, age 63
Auditors: BKD, LLP

LOCATIONS

HQ: Glacier Bancorp, Inc.
49 Commons Loop, Kalispell, MT 59901
Phone: 406-756-4200
Web: www.glacierbancorp.com

2008 Bank Locations

	No.
Montana	50
Idaho	29
Wyoming	9
Utah	4
Washington	3
Colorado	3
Total	**98**

PRODUCTS/OPERATIONS

2008 Gross Revenues

	$ mil.	% of total
Interest		
Commercial loans	165.1	45
Real estate loans	51.2	14
Consumer & other loans	47.7	13
Securities & other	39.0	11
Noninterest		
Service charges & fees	41.6	12
Gain on sale of loans	14.8	4
Other	4.6	1
Total	**364.0**	**100**

COMPETITORS

BancWest
Eagle Bancorp
First Citizens Banc Corp
First Interstate
Sterling Financial (WA)
U.S. Bancorp

HISTORICAL FINANCIALS

Company Type: Public

Income Statement

FYE: December 31

	ASSETS ($ mil.)	NET INCOME ($ mil.)	INCOME AS % OF ASSETS	EMPLOYEES
12/08	5,554.0	65.7	1.2%	1,571
12/07	4,817.3	68.6	1.4%	1,480
12/06	4,467.7	61.1	1.4%	1,356
12/05	3,706.3	52.4	1.4%	1,125
12/04	3,010.7	44.6	1.5%	935
Annual Growth	**16.5%**	**10.2%**	**—**	**13.9%**

2008 Year-End Financials

Equity as % of assets: 12.2%
Return on assets: 1.3%
Return on equity: 10.9%
Long-term debt ($ mil.): 459.5
No. of shares (mil.): 61.6
Market value ($ mil.): 1,172.0
Dividends
Yield: 2.1%
Payout: 32.8%
Sales ($ mil.): 273.6
R&D as % of sales: —
Advertising as % of sales: —

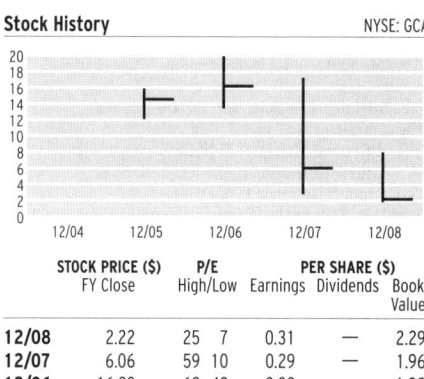

	STOCK PRICE ($) FY Close	P/E High/Low		PER SHARE ($) Earnings	Dividends	Book Value
12/08	19.02	34	11	1.19	0.39	10.99
12/07	18.74	20	14	1.28	0.62	8.58
12/06	24.44	21	15	1.21	0.33	7.40
12/05	20.03	20	13	1.09	0.40	5.41
12/04	18.15	20	13	0.95	0.45	4.38
Annual Growth	1.2%	—	—	5.8%	(3.5%)	25.8%

Global Cash Access

If you're losing your shirt at the casino tables Global Cash Access can get you more money on the spot. The company provides such services as ATM cash withdrawals, credit- and debit-card advances, and check guarantee to the gaming industry in the US, Asia, Canada, Latin America, South Africa, and Europe. Altogether the company provides services to more than 1,000 casinos including Harrah's and MGM Mirage. Global Cash Access also has developed cashless gaming systems including special ticket vouchers and systems that allow players to access funds without leaving their gaming machines. Other services include casino marketing and patron credit information through its QuikReports and CentralCredit database.

The company has decided to discontinue its Arriva Card, which was launched in 2006 to provide gamers with revolving credit. Arriva lost money in 2007; Global Cash Access hopes to insulate itself against riskier products and further loss. The company plans to focus instead on its core business of electronic payments.

Global Cash Access expanded its reach in 2008 by making acquisitions. The company purchased one of its top competitors, Certegy Gaming Services from Fidelity National Information Services for $25 million. It also bought Las Vegas-based Cash Systems for $33 million that year. The company gained about 120 new customers as a result. In mid-2009 the company announced plans to acquire kiosk manufacturer Western Money Systems. Global Cash Access has its sights set on further growth, especially overseas.

M&C International, owned by Global Cash Access co-chairman Karim Maskatiya and director Robert Cucinotta, holds around 13% each of the company; Summit Partners owns about 22%.

Financial services giant First Data sold its majority stake in Global Cash Access in 2004. First Data had agreed not to compete with Global Cash Access in Canada and the US until 2007, but that provision expired. In fact, president and CEO Scott Betts came to the company from First Data that year.

EXECUTIVES

President, CEO, Secretary, and Director: Scott H. Betts, age 55, $2,084,015 total compensation
EVP and CFO: George W. Gresham, age 42, $898,252 total compensation
EVP Sales: Stephen Lazarus, age 42, $636,455 total compensation
EVP Check Services and Central Credit: Kurt Sullivan, age 57, $673,087 total compensation
EVP and General Counsel: Kathryn S. Lever, age 41, $740,059 total compensation
EVP Business Development: Michael S. Dowty, age 41
EVP Technology and Development: Mari Ellis, age 55
VP Finance and Controller: Mark Labay, $675,627 total compensation
Auditors: Deloitte & Touche LLP

LOCATIONS

HQ: Global Cash Access Holdings, Inc.
3525 E. Post Rd., Ste. 120, Las Vegas, NV 89120
Phone: 702-855-3000   **Fax:** 866-672-4371
Web: www.globalcashaccess.com

PRODUCTS/OPERATIONS

2008 Sales

	$ mil.	% of total
Cash advance	326.5	49
ATM	289.1	43
Check services	42.4	6
Central Credit & other	13.6	2
Total	**671.6**	**100**

Selected Products and Services

Cash Access
  Casino Cash Plus 3-in-1 ATM
  QuikCash
  Check verification and warranty
  Money transfers
Information Services
  Central Credit
  QuikCash Plus Web
  QuikReports
  QuikMarketing
Cashless Gaming
  3-in1 Enabled Redemption Devices
  Powercash

COMPETITORS

Chase Paymentech Solutions
Comerica
First Data
Global Payments
Money Centers of America
U.S. Bancorp

HISTORICAL FINANCIALS

Company Type: Public

Income Statement

				FYE: December 31
	REVENUE ($ mil.)	NET INCOME ($ mil.)	NET PROFIT MARGIN	EMPLOYEES
12/08	671.6	23.6	3.5%	626
12/07	600.9	23.7	3.9%	354
12/06	548.1	26.6	4.9%	354
12/05	454.1	22.6	5.0%	279
12/04	403.0	254.6	63.2%	290
Annual Growth	13.6%	(44.8%)	—	21.2%

2008 Year-End Financials

Debt ratio: 165.2%   Dividends
Return on equity: 15.8%   Yield: —
Cash ($ mil.): 77.1   Payout: —
Current ratio: 1.20   Market value ($ mil.): 156.3
Long-term debt ($ mil.): 265.8   R&D as % of sales: —
No. of shares (mil.): 70.4   Advertising as % of sales: —

	STOCK PRICE ($) FY Close	P/E High/Low		PER SHARE ($) Earnings	Dividends	Book Value
12/08	2.22	25	7	0.31	—	2.29
12/07	6.06	59	10	0.29	—	1.96
12/06	16.23	62	42	0.32	—	1.88
12/05	14.59	52	41	0.30	—	1.34
Annual Growth	(46.6%)	—	—	(45.7%)	—	—

Global Defense Technology

Military intelligence is no joking matter to the folks at Global Defense Technology & Systems. The holding company operates mainly through subsidiary Global Strategies Group (North America). It provides software, system engineering, and technology development to help the Department of Defense, the CIA, Homeland Security, and other government agencies fight terrorism. Global Defense Technology's Technology and Intelligence Services (TIS) focuses on counterterrorism and communications systems, while its Force Mobility and Modernization Systems (FMMS) designs highly mobile computer systems to support military missions. The company, which filed its IPO in 2009, is part of British firm Global Strategies Group.

Global Defense Technology plans to use its $75 million in IPO proceeds to repay debt and for general corporate purposes. Its strategy includes expanding its current offerings to existing clients and going after more complex government contracts. About 80% of its revenue currently comes from contracts on which it is the prime contractor.

In 2009 the US Marines Corps awarded Global Defense Technology a $5 million troop sustainment contract. While the Marines had ordered from the company through indirect channels, this represents the first direct contract between the two organizations.

EXECUTIVES

Chairman: Vice Adm. Thomas R. Wilson, age 63
President, CEO, and Director: John F. Hillen III, age 43, $455,078 total compensation
EVP and CFO: James P. (Jim) Allen, age 60
EVP, Corporate Development and Director:
Ronald C. (Ron) Jones, age 50

SVP: Stephen Corey, age 46,
$881,315 total compensation
SVP, Contracts and Administration: Michael Weixel,
age 55
SVP, Business Development and Operations:
Kirk Herdman, age 45
VP and General Manager: Timothy Jones, age 46
VP, Business Operations: Shirley A. Place
VP, Human Resources: Lisa Broome
President, The Analysis Corp.: Alexander Drew, age 48
Media Relations: Lauren Peduzzi
Auditors: PricewaterhouseCoopers LLP

LOCATIONS

HQ: Global Defense Technology & Systems, Inc.
1501 Farm Credit Dr., Ste. 2300, McLean, VA 22102
Phone: 703-738-2840　　**Fax:** 703-883-4037
Web: www.globalgroup.us.com

PRODUCTS/OPERATIONS

2008 Sales

	$ mil.	% of total
FMMS	109.0	57
TIS	80.4	43
Total	**189.4**	**100**

2008 Sales

	% of total
DoD	74
Other US intelligence agencies	26
Total	**100**

COMPETITORS

AAR Corp.
BAE SYSTEMS
Boeing
CACI International
Finmeccanica
General Dynamics
ITT Corp.
L-3 Communications
Lockheed Martin
ManTech
Northrop Grumman
SAIC
SRA International

HISTORICAL FINANCIALS
Company Type: Public

Income Statement				FYE: December 31
	REVENUE ($ mil.)	NET INCOME ($ mil.)	NET PROFIT MARGIN	EMPLOYEES
12/08	189.4	1.1	0.6%	675
12/07	134.8	(4.1)	—	—
12/06	123.1	(0.8)	—	—
Annual Growth	**24.0%**	**—**	**—**	**—**

2008 Year-End Financials

Debt ratio: 40.8%　　Current ratio: 0.97
Return on equity: —　　Long-term debt ($ mil.): 17.6
Cash ($ mil.): 1.4

Net Income History　　NASDAQ (GM): GTEC

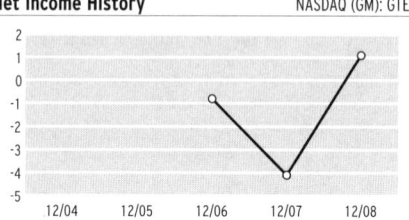

Goodrich Petroleum

From deep in the mystic Miocene sands and the good rich rocks of ancient Mother Earth, Goodrich Petroleum brings forth oil and gas. The independent exploration and production company delves into formations dating to the Miocene and Frio Age in southern Louisiana, where it has most of its proved reserves. The company also operates in the Cotton Valley trend in Texas and Louisiana, and it leases acreage in Michigan. Goodrich Petroleum owns interests in more than 300 active oil and gas wells and has estimated proved reserves of 357.8 billion cu. ft. of natural gas equivalent. Chairman Patrick Malloy owns 16% of the company; director Josiah Austin, 18%.

In a strategic move to boost its reserves and production, Goodrich Petroleum has launched a development drilling program in the Cotton Valley trend of East Texas and Northwest Louisiana.

In 2007 the company acquired drilling and development rights in 16,800 gross acres in the Angelina River play in Nacogdoches and Angelina counties in Texas, boosting its gross acreage in that area to 68,675 acres.

EXECUTIVES

Chairman: Patrick E. Malloy III, age 67
Vice Chairman and CEO: Walter G. (Gil) Goodrich, age 51, $1,562,589 total compensation
President, COO and Director: Robert C. Turnham Jr., age 52, $1,406,668 total compensation
EVP and CFO: David R. Looney, age 53, $1,359,515 total compensation
EVP: Mark E. Ferchau, age 55, $1,172,065 total compensation
SVP and Exploration Manager: Andrew W. Bagot
SVP Operations: Thomas S. (Tom) Nemec
SVP, General Counsel, and Corporate Secretary: Michael J. (Mike) Killelea, age 47
VP and Controller: Jan L. Schott, age 38
VP Land: James G. Marston III
Investor Relations: Kristie Buchanan
Auditors: KPMG LLP

LOCATIONS

HQ: Goodrich Petroleum Corporation
808 Travis St., Ste. 1320, Houston, TX 77002
Phone: 713-780-9494　　**Fax:** 713-780-9254
Web: www.goodrichpetroleum.com

PRODUCTS/OPERATIONS

2008 Sales

	% of total
Shell Energy	33
Louis Dreyfus Corporation	20
Crosstex Energy	9
Other	38
Total	**100**

COMPETITORS

Abraxas Petroleum
Anadarko Petroleum
Barnwell Industries
Black Hills
Cabot Oil & Gas
Dorchester Minerals
Pioneer Natural Resources
Range Resources

HISTORICAL FINANCIALS
Company Type: Public

Income Statement				FYE: December 31
	REVENUE ($ mil.)	NET INCOME ($ mil.)	NET PROFIT MARGIN	EMPLOYEES
12/08	216.1	136.2	63.0%	116
12/07	111.3	(45.0)	—	93
12/06	116.2	1.6	1.4%	84
12/05	68.3	(17.5)	—	64
12/04	47.3	18.5	39.1%	52
Annual Growth	**46.2%**	**64.7%**	**—**	**22.2%**

2008 Year-End Financials

Debt ratio: 38.6%　　　　　Dividends
Return on equity: 29.3%　　　Yield: 0.0%
Cash ($ mil.): 147.5　　　　　Payout: —
Current ratio: 1.93　　　　　Market value ($ mil.): 1,120.1
Long-term debt ($ mil.): 250.0　R&D as % of sales: —
No. of shares (mil.): 37.4　　Advertising as % of sales: —

Stock History　　　　　　　　NYSE: GDP

	STOCK PRICE ($)	P/E		PER SHARE ($)		
	FY Close	High/Low		Earnings	Dividends	Book Value
12/08	29.95	25	5	3.48	0.00	17.40
12/07	22.62	—	—	(1.76)	0.00	7.58
12/06	36.18	—	—	(0.24)	0.00	5.48
12/05	25.15	—	—	(0.78)	0.00	4.86
12/04	16.21	19	6	0.88	0.00	1.75
Annual Growth	**16.6%**	**—**	**—**	**41.0%**	**—**	**77.7%**

The Gorman-Rupp Company

Gorman-Rupp keeps pumping out pumps. The company, founded in 1933 by engineers J.C. Gorman and H.E. Rupp, makes a myriad of pumps and fluid controls used in construction, sewage treatment, petroleum refining, agriculture, and fire fighting, as well as for HVAC and military applications. Gorman-Rupp's pumps range in size from 1/4-inch (one gallon per minute) to 84-inch (500,000 gallons per minute). Smaller pumps are used for dispensing soft drinks and making ice cubes, while large pumps are central to refueling aircraft and boosting low water pressure in municipal fresh water markets. Gorman-Rupp sells its products through 1,000 distributors, OEM representatives, distributor catalogs, and direct sales.

Over the last decade, Gorman-Rupp has continued to grow by pursuing new routes to market its product lineup. The company has reached outside of North America by building distributor alliances and establishing plants and warehouses in Ireland and The Netherlands to serve customers in Europe, and Thailand to reach those in

Asia. Its European foothold deepened in 2007 when it acquired a controlling stake in Wavo Pompen, a Netherlands-based pump maker. The Dutch firm was renamed Gorman-Rupp Europe. Gorman-Rupp touts customers in over 100 countries, accounting for more than 30% of its sales. In the US, the company looks to gain a share of the water and wastewater infrastructure projects receiving Federal funding. (Capable of moving mountainous amounts of wastewater, the company's heavy-duty pumps are a respected brand among municipal treatment plants and 24/7 construction projects.)

Improving operations has been fundamental to the company's growth, too. In 2008 its Mansfield division took the second step in a $53 million manufacturing facility consolidation and expansion. The Mansfield division manufactures the company's lineup of pumps and wastewater pumping stations, enhanced by electrical control panels and customized fiberglass shields.

Gorman-Rupp's founding families collectively own more than a quarter of the company. Co-founder JC Gorman's son, James C. Gorman leads as chairman of Gorman-Rupp, and grandson Jeffrey S. Gorman serves as its president and CEO.

EXECUTIVES

Chairman: James C. Gorman, age 85
President, CEO, and Director: Jeffrey S. Gorman, age 57, $486,609 total compensation
CFO and Treasurer: Wayne L. Knabel, age 62
VP and CIO: William D. Danuloff, age 62, $233,251 total compensation
VP Human Resources: Lee A. Wilkins, age 55
VP and General Manager, Mansfield Division: Mark Kreinbihl, age 53
VP and General Manager, Canada: Gary W. Creeden, age 62
Corporate Counsel and Corporate Secretary: David P. (Dave) Emmens, age 61, $182,360 total compensation
President, Patterson Pump Company: Albert F. Huber, age 55
President and General Manager, American Machine and Tool: Keith Bearde, age 52
Managing Director, Gorman-Rupp Europe B.V.: Anton Rosier, age 60
Auditors: Ernst & Young LLP

LOCATIONS

HQ: The Gorman-Rupp Company
305 Bowman St., Mansfield, OH 44903
Phone: 419-755-1011   **Fax:** 419-755-1233
Web: www.gormanrupp.com

2008 Sales

	$ mil.	% of total
US	227.4	69
Other countries	103.2	31
Total	**330.6**	**100**

PRODUCTS/OPERATIONS

Selected Operations

American Machine & Tool Co. Inc. (self-priming centrifugal, standard centrifugal, diaphragm, engine-driven, priming assist, rotary drum, and piston drum pumps)
Gorman-Rupp Industries (bellows metering, centrifugal, magnetic drive, piston, peristaltic, gear, and oscillating pumps and valves)
The Gorman-Rupp International Company
Gorman-Rupp Mansfield Division (self-priming centrifugal, standard centrifugal, submersible, rotary gear, diaphragm, and utility pumps and packaged pump stations)

Gorman-Rupp of Canada Limited (self-priming centrifugal, standard centrifugal, submersible, rotary gear, diaphragm, and utility pumps and packaged pump stations)
Gorman-Rupp of Europe B.V. (self-priming centrifugal, standard centrifugal, submersible, rotary gear, diaphragm, and utility pumps and packaged pump stations)
Patterson Pump Company (horizontal split case, vertical in-line, end suction centrifugal, vertical turbine, sewage, multipurpose vertical turbine, axial, and mixed flow pumps)
Patterson Pump Ireland Limited

COMPETITORS

Ampco-Pittsburgh
Colfax
Flowserve
Goulds Pumps
Graco
Haskel
IDEX
Roper Industries
Weir Group

HISTORICAL FINANCIALS

Company Type: Public

Income Statement

FYE: December 31

	REVENUE ($ mil.)	NET INCOME ($ mil.)	NET PROFIT MARGIN	EMPLOYEES
12/08	330.6	27.2	8.2%	1,093
12/07	305.6	22.9	7.5%	1,065
12/06	270.9	19.1	7.1%	1,049
12/05	231.2	10.9	4.7%	1,021
12/04	203.6	9.3	4.6%	963
Annual Growth	**12.9%**	**30.8%**	**—**	**3.2%**

2008 Year-End Financials

Debt ratio: —
Return on equity: 17.7%
Cash ($ mil.): 23.8
Current ratio: 3.77
Long-term debt ($ mil.): —
No. of shares (mil.): 16.7
Dividends
Yield: 1.3%
Payout: 24.5%
Market value ($ mil.): 520.0
R&D as % of sales: —
Advertising as % of sales: —

Stock History

NYSE Alternext: GRC

	STOCK PRICE ($) FY Close	P/E High/Low		PER SHARE ($) Earnings	Dividends	Book Value
12/08	31.12	29	11	1.63	0.40	9.49
12/07	31.20	27	10	1.37	0.37	8.94
12/06	29.58	27	12	1.14	0.35	7.67
12/05	14.15	27	19	0.65	0.36	7.60
12/04	14.72	28	21	0.56	0.34	7.29
Annual Growth	**20.6%**	**—**	**—**	**30.6%**	**4.1%**	**6.8%**

GP Strategies

GP Strategies, through its General Physics subsidiary, offers a broad range of consulting, engineering, staffing, and training services. The company divides its offerings into four main business segments: manufacturing and business process outsourcing (BPO), which accounts for 45% of its total sales; process and government; energy (which offers engineering services to electric power utilities and clients in the power generation industry); and training and marketing (comprised primarily of its Sandy unit). General Physics has more than 500 clients, including auto manufacturers, electric utilities, government agencies and contractors, and technology companies.

US government agencies, led by the Department of the Army, account for about 18% of the company's sales; General Motors and its various affiliates, 20%.

GP Strategies plans to broaden General Physics' international business though acquisitions. In 2009 the company expanded its training offerings with the purchase of Option Six, which creates custom interactive online learning courses and tutorials. In 2008 it acquired two training and consulting companies in the UK and in 2009, it acquired Milsom Industrial Design, a UK firm that provides technical documentation and engineering design services to the aerospace industry. Besides the UK, potential areas for international expansion include India, China, Malaysia, and Singapore, and General Physics has established a foothold in each of those countries.

Also in 2008, the company enhanced its energy segment with the acquisition of Performance Consulting Services, an engineering and training firm catering to the power generation industry.

Over the years the training services business has been identified as a growth opportunity for General Physics, and in 2007 the company acquired Sandy Corporation, a consulting firm that specialized in sales training and support for customers in the automobile industry. Sandy had annual sales of about $60 million at the time.

EXECUTIVES

Chairman: Harvey P. Eisen, age 67
CEO and Director: Scott N. Greenberg, age 52, $477,863 total compensation
President; President and Director, General Physics: Douglas E. Sharp, age 51, $452,094 total compensation
EVP and CFO; EVP, General Physics: Sharon Esposito-Mayer, age 43, $354,911 total compensation
EVP Manufacturing; EVP, General Physics: Karl Baer, age 50, $380,442 total compensation
EVP; SVP, E-Business and Learning Solutions, General Physics: Donald R. (Don) Duquette, age 55, $362,472 total compensation
EVP; President and SVP, Sandy Corporation: Fredric H. (Fred) Strickland, age 65
SVP Process and Aerospace Group: Alan P. Tattersall, age 66
SVP, General Counsel, and Secretary, GP Strategies Corporation and General Physics: Kenneth L. Crawford, age 51
Investor Relations Contact: Ann M. Blank
Auditors: KPMG LLP

LOCATIONS

HQ: GP Strategies Corporation
6095 Marshalee Dr., Ste. 300, Elkridge, MD 21075
Phone: 410-379-3600 **Fax:** 410-540-5302
Web: www.gpstrategies.com

2008 Sales

	$ mil.	% of total
US	233.7	87
UK	26.5	10
Other countries	7.7	3
Total	**267.9**	**100**

PRODUCTS/OPERATIONS

2008 Sales

	$ mil.	% of total
Manufacturing & business process outsourcing	119.0	45
Sandy training & marketing	72.5	27
Process & government	54.4	20
Energy	22.0	8
Total	**267.9**	**100**

Selected Services

Manufacturing and business process outsourcing
  Business process and training outsourcing
  Consulting and technical services
  Curriculum design and development
  E-learning
  Staff augmentation
  System hosting, integration, and help desk support
  Training
Process, energy, and government
  Curriculum design and development
  Engineering consulting, design, and evaluation
    services
  Staff augmentation
  Training and technical services

COMPETITORS

Accenture
Arthur D Little
Bain & Company
Booz Allen
Boston Consulting
Deloitte Consulting
Harris Interactive
HP Enterprise Services
IBM
Infosys
J.D. Power
McKinsey & Company
Tata Consultancy
Wipro Technologies

HISTORICAL FINANCIALS

Company Type: Public

Income Statement				FYE: December 31
	REVENUE ($ mil.)	NET INCOME ($ mil.)	NET PROFIT MARGIN	EMPLOYEES
12/08	267.9	7.8	2.9%	1,777
12/07	248.4	9.7	3.9%	1,747
12/06	178.8	6.6	3.7%	1,205
12/05	175.6	7.2	4.1%	1,580
12/04	194.0	22.5	11.6%	1,449
Annual Growth	**8.4%**	**(23.3%)**	**—**	**5.2%**

2008 Year-End Financials

Debt ratio: —
Return on equity: 8.5%
Cash ($ mil.): 4.0
Current ratio: 1.58
Long-term debt ($ mil.): —
No. of shares (mil.): 15.7
Dividends
  Yield: 0.0%
  Payout: —
Market value ($ mil.): 70.7
R&D as % of sales: —
Advertising as % of sales: —

Stock History   NYSE: GPX

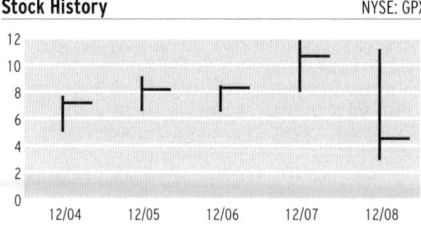

	STOCK PRICE ($) FY Close	P/E High/Low		PER SHARE ($) Earnings	Dividends	Book Value
12/08	4.51	24	6	0.47	0.00	5.92
12/07	10.65	21	14	0.56	0.00	5.77
12/06	8.30	21	16	0.40	0.00	5.09
12/05	8.16	24	17	0.38	0.00	6.02
12/04	7.15	6	4	1.23	0.00	5.85
Annual Growth	**(10.9%)**	**—**	**—**	**(21.4%)**	**—**	**0.3%**

Graham Corp.

You're not crackers if you know that Graham Corporation takes the biscuit when it comes to helping companies make beer, soap, and other products. The company makes vacuum systems, pumps, compressors, and heat exchangers designed to create vacuums, condense steam, or produce heat. Graham sells its equipment to manufacturers in the petroleum, plastics, chemicals, food processing, and other industries, where its gear is used in processes ranging from power generation to brewing beer and making soap. The company sells its products directly and through independent sales representatives worldwide.

Graham Corporation has seen demand for its products increase in recent years across the globe, largely due to oil and gas and other energy industries. In US and Western European markets an emphasis on fuel sources other than crude oil has led to the creation of new facilities utilizing products similar to the company's pumps, condensers, vacuums, and heat transfer products. Additionally, increased demand for consumer products in emerging markets has also led to a rise in manufacturing facilities. Graham has been attempting to address those markets through geographic expansion as well as increasing its production capacity.

Graham Corporation was founded in 1983 as the successor company to Graham Manufacturing Co., Inc., which was incorporated in 1936 under the leadership of Harold Graham.

EXECUTIVES

Chairman: Jerald D. Bidlack, age 74
President, CEO, and Director: James R. Lines, age 49, $529,618 total compensation
VP Finance and Administration and CFO: Jeffrey F. (Jeff) Glajch, $17,600 total compensation
VP Operations: Alan E. Smith, age 43, $257,597 total compensation
Controller and Chief Accounting Officer: Jennifer R. Condame, age 44, $181,659 total compensation
Corporate Secretary and Director: Cornelius S. Van Rees, age 81
Auditors: Deloitte & Touche LLP

LOCATIONS

HQ: Graham Corporation
20 Florence Ave., Batavia, NY 14020
Phone: 585-343-2216 **Fax:** 585-343-1097
Web: www.graham-mfg.com

2009 Sales

	% of total
North America	
US & Mexico	63
Canada	8
Asia & Africa	14
Middle East	8
South America	4
Western Europe	2
Australia & New Zealand	1
Total	**100**

PRODUCTS/OPERATIONS

2009 Sales

	% of total
Vacuum equipment	45
Heat transfer equipment	35
Other	20
Total	**100**

Selected Products

Helical coil exchangers
Liquid ring vacuum pumps and compressors
Plate and frame exchangers
Steam jet ejector vacuum systems
Surface condensers

COMPETITORS

Amsted
Connell LP
Cooper Industries
Dover Corp.
Haskel
IDEX
Ingersoll-Rand
Parker Hannifin HPD
Pfeiffer Vacuum
Weatherford International

HISTORICAL FINANCIALS

Company Type: Public

Income Statement				FYE: March 31
	REVENUE ($ mil.)	NET INCOME ($ mil.)	NET PROFIT MARGIN	EMPLOYEES
3/09	101.1	17.5	17.3%	270
3/08	86.4	15.0	17.4%	281
3/07	65.8	5.8	8.8%	265
3/06	55.2	3.6	6.5%	250
3/05	41.3	(2.9)	—	243
Annual Growth	**25.1%**	**—**	**—**	**2.7%**

2009 Year-End Financials

Debt ratio: 0.1%
Return on equity: 31.9%
Cash ($ mil.): 5.2
Current ratio: 3.14
Long-term debt ($ mil.): 0.0
No. of shares (mil.): 9.8
Dividends
  Yield: 0.7%
  Payout: 3.5%
Market value ($ mil.): 88.3
R&D as % of sales: —
Advertising as % of sales: —

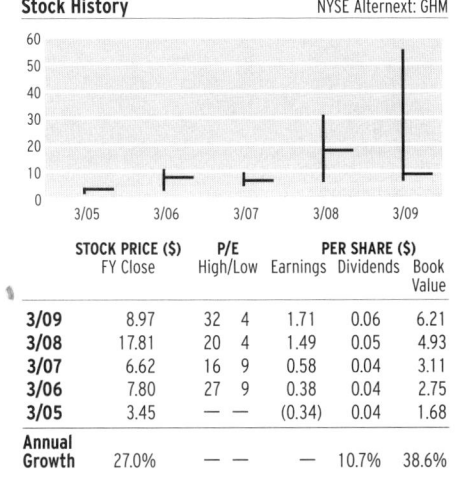

	STOCK PRICE ($) FY Close	P/E High/Low		PER SHARE ($) Earnings	Dividends	Book Value
3/09	8.97	32	4	1.71	0.06	6.21
3/08	17.81	20	4	1.49	0.05	4.93
3/07	6.62	16	9	0.58	0.04	3.11
3/06	7.80	27	9	0.38	0.04	2.75
3/05	3.45	—	—	(0.34)	0.04	1.68
Annual Growth	27.0%	—	—	—	10.7%	38.6%

Grand Canyon Education

Like its geological namesake, Grand Canyon Education (aka Grand Canyon University) wants to expand your horizons. The regionally accredited Christian institution offers online graduate and undergraduate programs in education, business, and health care through the Ken Blanchard College of Business, College of Education, College of Nursing and Health Sciences, and College of Humanities and Social Sciences. It also offers programs at its brick-and-mortar campus in Phoenix and onsite at the facilities of employers. Grand Canyon enrolls roughly 15,000 students annually; approximately 85% are enrolled in online programs, and more than half are pursuing master's degrees. The university filed to go public in 2008.

The company raised $126 million through its offering. It broke a four-month-long IPO drought in the US.

Annual enrollment at Grand Canyon University has grown nearly 50% each year since 2003. The school primarily focuses on recruiting and educating working adults, defined as students age 25 years or older who are pursuing a degree while employed.

Originally founded as Grand Canyon College, a private, non-profit college, in 1949, the university moved to its existing campus in Phoenix in 1951. In 2004 several of its stockholders acquired Grand Canyon University and converted it to a for-profit institution.

The company named Brian Mueller CEO in 2008. He replaces former CEO Brent Richardson, who was named executive chairman of the board of directors. Mueller is the former president of the Apollo Group.

EXECUTIVES

Executive Chairman: Brent D. Richardson, age 47, $345,038 total compensation
CEO and Director: Brian E. Mueller, age 55, $1,965,023 total compensation
CFO: Daniel E. Bachus, age 38, $254,667 total compensation
CIO: Michael S. Lacrosse, age 54, $372,724 total compensation
EVP: W. Stan Meyer, age 48, $282,365 total compensation
Provost and Chief Academic Officer: Kathy Player, age 46, $455,514 total compensation
General Counsel and Director: Christopher C. Richardson, age 37, $323,250 total compensation
Chief University Relations and Student Success Officer: Faith A. Weese
Auditors: Ernst & Young LLP

LOCATIONS

HQ: Grand Canyon Education, Inc.
3300 W. Camelback Rd., Phoenix, AZ 85017
Phone: 602-639-7500   **Fax:** 602-589-2717
Web: www.gcu.edu

COMPETITORS

Arizona State University
Azusa Pacific University
Baylor University
Capella Education
Northern Arizona University
University of Arizona

HISTORICAL FINANCIALS

Company Type: Public

Income Statement				FYE: December 31
	REVENUE ($ mil.)	NET INCOME ($ mil.)	NET PROFIT MARGIN	EMPLOYEES
12/08	161.3	6.7	4.2%	1,365
12/07	99.3	1.5	1.5%	702
12/06	72.1	0.6	—	—
Annual Growth	49.6%	234.2%	—	94.4%

2008 Year-End Financials

Debt ratio: 57.6%	Dividends
Return on equity: 31.0%	Yield: 0.0%
Cash ($ mil.): 35.2	Payout: —
Current ratio: 1.65	Market value ($ mil.): 856.6
Long-term debt ($ mil.): 30.8	R&D as % of sales: —
No. of shares (mil.): 45.6	Advertising as % of sales: —

Stock History   NASDAQ (GM): LOPE

	STOCK PRICE ($) FY Close	P/E High/Low		PER SHARE ($) Earnings	Dividends	Book Value
12/08	18.78	112	56	0.17	0.00	1.17

Great Lakes Dredge & Dock

Dig this: Great Lakes Dredge & Dock (GLDD) provides dredging services around the world. The company's services include beach improvement or renourishment, rock dredging, harbor excavation, land reclamation, demolition, and restoration of aquatic and wetland habitats. Among GLDD's projects are maintenance dredging at the Miami Harbor, nourishing San Diego beaches, and expanding Pier J in Long Beach, California. GLDD also owns an 85% stake in North American Site Developers, a commercial/industrial demolition firm. The company was founded in 1890 as the partnership of William A. Lydon & Fred C. Drews.

International operations account for about a quarter of GLDD's revenues. The company is increasingly focusing its efforts on the Middle East, where projects typically have a longer lifeline.

In 2007 Chicago-based private capital firm Madison Dearborn Partners sold GLDD to blank check company Aldabra Acquisition. Madison Dearborn still owns 25% of the company.

EXECUTIVES

President, CEO, and Director: Douglas B. (Doug) Mackie, age 57
EVP and COO: Richard M. Lowry, age 50
SVP and CFO: Deborah A. (Deb) Wensel, age 44
VP and Personnel Director Field Operations: David E. Simonelli, age 49
VP and Chief Estimator: John F. Karas, age 45
VP and Chief Contract Manager: Kyle D. Johnson, age 45
VP and Division Manager, Hydraulic: Bradley T. J. Hansen, age 53
VP and Division Manager, Hopper: William F. Pagendarm, age 57
VP and Division Manager, Clamshell: Steven F. O'Hara, age 52
VP and Special Projects Manager: J. Christopher Gillespie, age 46
Plant Equipment Manager and Chief Mechanical Engineer: Steven W. Becker, age 45
Controller and Assistant Secretary: Donald J. Luce, age 46

LOCATIONS

HQ: Great Lakes Dredge & Dock Corporation
2122 York Rd., Oak Brook, IL 60523
Phone: 630-574-3000   **Fax:** 630-574-2909
Web: www.gldd.com

COMPETITORS

A & L
Conti Enterprises
Costain
Penta-Ocean Construction
Royal BAM Group
Walsh Group
Weeks Marine
Willbros

HISTORICAL FINANCIALS

Company Type: Public

Income Statement				FYE: December 31
	REVENUE ($ mil.)	NET INCOME ($ mil.)	NET PROFIT MARGIN	EMPLOYEES
12/08	586.9	5.0	0.9%	317
12/07	515.8	7.1	1.4%	1,491
12/06	426.0	(6.0)	—	943
12/05	423.4	(14.6)	—	938
Annual Growth	11.5%	—	—	(30.3%)

2008 Year-End Financials

Debt ratio: 95.3%
Return on equity: 2.2%
Cash ($ mil.): 10.5
Current ratio: 1.68
Long-term debt ($ mil.): 216.5
No. of shares (mil.): 58.5

Dividends
  Yield: 0.8%
  Payout: 33.3%
Market value ($ mil.): 242.9
R&D as % of sales: —
Advertising as % of sales: —

Stock History

NASDAQ (GS): GLDD

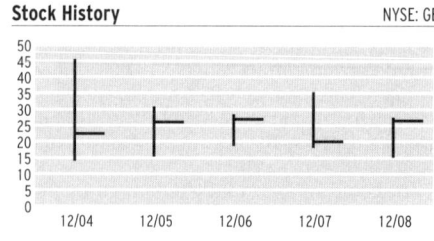

	STOCK PRICE ($) FY Close	P/E High/Low		PER SHARE ($) Earnings	Dividends	Book Value
12/08	4.15	91	29	0.09	0.03	3.88
12/07	8.72	73	44	0.14	—	3.90
12/06	6.45	—	—	(0.90)	—	2.20
12/05	5.29	—	—	(14.64)	—	(0.40)
Annual Growth	(7.8%)	—	—	—	—	—

Greatbatch, Inc.

Greatbatch likes to keep its business close to the heart. The company is a leading maker of batteries used in implantable medical devices such as pacemakers and implantable cardioverter defibrillators (ICDs). Other medical components include electrodes, capacitors, and feedthroughs (used to deliver electrical signals from an implantable medical device to an electrode). Greatbatch also makes batteries for demanding industrial applications, such as oil and gas exploration, and supplies power sources for the Space Shuttle. Boston Scientific, Medtronic, and St. Jude Medical are the company's top customers; together, they account for about 44% of sales. Greatbatch gets nearly half of its sales from US clients.

Greatbatch has aggressively used acquisitions to expand both its product lines and its research and development efforts. Its most recent acquisition was the early 2008 purchase of Precimed for about $125 million in cash. A Swiss-American firm, Precimed targets orthopedics OEMs with instrumentation for hip and knee replacement, trauma, and spinal treatments.

Past deals have included the 2007 purchase of Enpath Medical for about $102 million in cash. The acquisition was strategic, bringing in complementary products and services in cardiac rhythm management and neurostimulation; Enpath and Greatbatch also shared their top three customers in common.

In 2007 Greatbatch also acquired the assets of Emerteq Medical for $55 million in cash. Doing business as Quan Emerteq, the firm made single-use medical device products for the vascular, cardiac rhythm management, and neurostimulation markets.

EXECUTIVES

Chairman: William R. (Bill) Sanford, age 65
President, CEO, and Director: Thomas J. Hook, age 46, $2,321,234 total compensation
SVP and Business Leader, Cardiac and Neurology Group: Mauricio Arellano, age 42, $804,665 total compensation
SVP and CFO: Thomas J. Mazza, age 55, $925,746 total compensation
SVP Commercial Power Group: Susan M. Bratton, age 52, $831,748 total compensation
SVP and Business Leader Orthopedics Group: Susan H. Campbell, age 44, $779,922 total compensation
VP Human Resources: Barbara Davis, age 58
VP, General Counsel, and Secretary: Timothy G. McEvoy, age 51
VP Business Development: Richard M. Farrell, age 46
Corporate Controller and Treasurer: Marco F. Benedetti
Chief Audit Executive: Frank J. Forkl Jr.
Auditors: Deloitte & Touche LLP

LOCATIONS

HQ: Greatbatch, Inc.
10000 Wehrle Dr., Clarence, NY 14031
Phone: 716-759-5600   **Fax:** 716-759-5660
Web: www.greatbatch.com

2008 Sales

	$ mil.	% of total
US	267.0	49
Other countries	279.6	51
Total	**546.6**	**100**

PRODUCTS/OPERATIONS

2008 Sales

	$ mil.	% of total
CRM/Neuromodulation	278.3	50
Orthopedic	142.4	26
Electrochem	78.5	14
Vascular Access	47.4	10
Total	**546.6**	**100**

Selected Products

Implantable Medical Components (IMC)
  Batteries (for implantable medical devices)
  Capacitors (store energy generated by a battery before delivery to the heart)
  EMI filters (filter electromagnetic interference to limit undesirable response, malfunctioning, or degradation in the performance of electronic equipment)
  Feedthroughs (allow electrical signals to be brought from inside an implantable medical device to an electrode)
  Electrodes (deliver electric signal from the feedthrough to a body part undergoing stimulation)
  Enclosures and related components (cases and related parts for implantable medical devices)
Electrochem Commercial Power (ECP)
  Batteries and battery packs (batteries that function under high temperatures or despite exposure to shock and vibration)

COMPETITORS

Accellent
Angeion
AVX
Cardinal Health
Douglas Battery
Eagle-Picher
HEI
Heraeus Holding
Interstate Batteries
Laird Technologies
Medtronic
Micro Power Electronics
Morgan Crucible
National Manufacturing
Orchid Cellmark
SAFT
St. Jude Medical
Teleflex
Ultralife

HISTORICAL FINANCIALS

Company Type: Public

Income Statement				FYE: Friday nearest December 31
	REVENUE ($ mil.)	NET INCOME ($ mil.)	NET PROFIT MARGIN	EMPLOYEES
12/08	546.6	18.6	3.4%	3,283
12/07	318.7	15.1	4.7%	2,445
12/06	271.1	16.1	5.9%	1,835
12/05	241.1	10.1	4.2%	1,338
12/04	200.1	16.3	8.1%	1,225
Annual Growth	28.6%	3.4%	—	27.9%

2008 Year-End Financials

Debt ratio: 100.6%
Return on equity: 5.5%
Cash ($ mil.): 22.1
Current ratio: 2.52
Long-term debt ($ mil.): 352.9
No. of shares (mil.): 23.2

Dividends
  Yield: 0.0%
  Payout: —
Market value ($ mil.): 613.6
R&D as % of sales: —
Advertising as % of sales: —

Stock History

NYSE: GB

	STOCK PRICE ($) FY Close	P/E High/Low		PER SHARE ($) Earnings	Dividends	Book Value
12/08	26.46	33	19	0.81	0.00	15.12
12/07	19.99	52	28	0.67	0.00	13.91
12/06	26.92	38	26	0.73	0.00	12.92
12/05	26.01	66	34	0.46	0.00	11.58
12/04	22.42	60	19	0.75	0.00	11.05
Annual Growth	4.2%	—	—	1.9%	—	8.2%

Green Mountain Coffee Roasters

Green Mountain Coffee Roasters' business amounts to more than a hill of beans. The company offers about 180 varieties of coffee, cocoa, and tea, which it sells to wholesale customers including supermarkets, convenience stores, resorts, and office-delivery services. Among its customers are ExxonMobil's convenience stores and McDonald's restaurants. Green Mountain's coffee is also sold under the Newman's Own Organics brand, as well as its namesake Green Mountain Coffee and the Tully's label. The company also sells the Keurig single-cup brewing systems for office and home use. In late 2009 it agreed to acquire Diedrich Coffee.

The company moved into expansion mode in 2009. It acquired the brand and domestic wholesale business of Tully's Coffee for some $40 million. The deal added the well-known specialty coffee brand name to Green Mountain's offerings and expanded its presence on the West Coast. Tully's retail coffee shops continue to operate under license and supply agreements with Green Mountain. Its retail and international business remains an independent company, operating under the name of TC Global, owned by its existing shareholders and managed by its existing management team.

Later in 2009 Green Mountain opened its wallet again, this time to purchase Timothy's Coffees of the World for approximately $157 million. The deal gave Green Mountain a Canadian presence and a coffee-roasting facility in Toronto.

It closed out the year with a $245 million offer to buy Diedrich Coffee. The offer came after Peet's Coffee had earlier tried to acquire Diedrich for about $210 million. Immediately after Green Mountain announced its offer, Peet's countered with a raised bid of $265 million. Green Mountain matched the Peet's offer and subsequently upped its bid to $290 million; Diedrich's board recommended shareholders accept the offer.

Located in Irvine, California, Diedrich's brands include Coffee People, Diedrich Coffee, and Gloria Jean's Coffees. Its customers include office coffee service companies, restaurants, and specialty retailers. It also holds a license to produce K-Cups for the Keurig, which Green Mountain was already distributing for Diedrich.

Chairman and CEO Robert Stiller owns about 32% of Green Mountain.

HISTORY

In 1981 Robert Stiller had his first cup of Green Mountain coffee at a small Vermont coffee shop. He was so impressed, he bought the one-store company (using proceeds from the sale of E-Z Wider, the marijuana-rolling-paper business he co-founded in 1971). Stiller sought a wider market, and in 1984 he began generating word-of-mouth business by donating coffee to charities and civic groups and placing mail-order ads. By 1985 Green Mountain Coffee had four stores and was turning a profit.

Using direct-mail sales as a vanguard, Green Mountain continued its efforts to build a multi-channel distribution network. It was successful: Supermarkets began selling Green Mountain coffees, and institutions such as the Harvard Club began serving them. The company added retail locations in the late 1980s and early 1990s and went public in 1993. It had 12 stores by 1994, but earnings suffered as Green Mountain's expansion outpaced its sales growth.

The company began selling its products online in 1995, and Business Express Airlines began serving Green Mountain coffee on its flights in the US and Canada. Delta Air Lines' shuttle service followed suit the next year. Green Mountain signed a five-year agreement with Mobil Oil (later, ExxonMobil) in 1997 to provide coffee at its On The Run convenience stores.

Green Mountain inked a deal in 1998 with American Skiing Company to supply its nine US ski resorts, including Vermont's Killington and Sugarbush resorts. Also that year it expanded its organic coffee line, revamped its Web site, and began closing or selling its retail operations to concentrate on its wholesale business; all stores were closed by August 1999. Also in 1999 Green Mountain partnered with Keurig to offer one-cup brewing varieties of its coffees.

In 2000 the company agreed to supply coffee to more than 900 (up from nearly 500) ExxonMobil corporately owned convenience stores; as part of the deal, Green Mountain also became the recommended coffee to about 13,000 ExxonMobil dealer and franchise store locations. In mid-2001 Green Mountain purchased the Frontier Organic Coffee brand from Frontier Natural Products Co-op for about $2.4 million.

Green Mountain began selling coffee under the Newman's Own name in 2003. That year the company signed an agreement with Hain Celestial Group to sell a line of teas.

In 2004 the company expanded its Vermont manufacturing and distribution facility with a 52,000-sq.-ft. warehouse and packaging plant. The added space boosted Green Mountain's annual production capacity from 17 million pounds of coffee to 50 million pounds. Also in 2004 the company announced plans to sell Heifer Hope Blend, an organic coffee that generates income for Heifer Project International. The organization provides support and training for coffee farmers in Guatemala.

Green Mountain has pinned its growth hopes to the trend of "single-cup" brewers. The company had been a minority owner of single-cup brewing-system manufacturer Keurig since 2002. In 2006 Green Mountain acquired the remaining 65% of Keurig that it did not already own for $104 million.

In 2007, in conjunction with International Paper, it created an environmentally friendly coffee cup made of corn, natural paper, and water, which, unlike traditional paper cups, breaks down into organic matter after use. Green Mountain uses the new cup in all of its US outlets.

EXECUTIVES

Chairman: Robert P. (Bob) Stiller, age 65
President, CEO, and Director:
 Lawrence J. (Larry) Blanford, age 56,
 $1,763,784 total compensation
COO: R. Scott McCreary, age 50,
 $631,669 total compensation
VP, CFO, and Treasurer: Frances G. (Fran) Rathke,
 age 49, $646,244 total compensation
VP Human Resources and Organizational Development:
 Kathryn S. (Kathy) Brooks, age 54,
 $406,989 total compensation
VP Development: Stephen J. (Steve) Sabol, age 48,
 $334,042 total compensation
VP and CIO: James K. (Jim) Prevo, age 56
VP Corporate Social Responsibility:
 Michael (Mike) Dupee, age 41
VP, Corporate General Counsel, and Secretary:
 Howard Malovany, age 59
VP Environmental Affairs: Paul Comey, age 59
President, Keurig: Michelle V. Stacy, age 53
Director Creative: Rick Slade
Director Public Relations: Sandy Yusen
Auditors: PricewaterhouseCoopers LLP

LOCATIONS

HQ: Green Mountain Coffee Roasters, Inc.
 33 Coffee Ln., Waterbury, VT 05676
Phone: 802-244-5621   **Fax:** 802-244-5436
Web: www.greenmountaincoffee.com

PRODUCTS/OPERATIONS

2008 Sales

	% of total
Green Mountain coffee	56
Keurig	44
Total	**100**

COMPETITORS

Bucks County Coffee	Kraft Foods
Cafe Britt Coffee	Mars, Incorporated
Caribou Coffee	Nestlé
The Coffee Bean	Peet's Coffee & Tea
Community Coffee	Republic of Tea
Dunkin	Sara Lee
Farmer Bros.	Smucker
Fireside Coffee	Starbucks
Hawaii Coffee	Van Houtte

HISTORICAL FINANCIALS

Company Type: Public

Income Statement

FYE: Last Saturday in September

	REVENUE ($ mil.)	NET INCOME ($ mil.)	NET PROFIT MARGIN	EMPLOYEES
9/09	803.0	55.9	7.0%	1,517
9/08	500.3	22.3	4.5%	1,220
9/07	341.7	12.8	3.7%	995
9/06	225.3	8.4	3.7%	849
9/05	161.5	9.0	5.6%	676
Annual Growth	**49.3%**	**57.9%**	**—**	**22.4%**

2009 Year-End Financials

Debt ratio: 12.4%	Dividends
Return on equity: 15.3%	Yield: —
Cash ($ mil.): 241.8	Payout: —
Current ratio: 4.34	Market value ($ mil.): 3,223.6
Long-term debt ($ mil.): 73.0	R&D as % of sales: —
No. of shares (mil.): 43.7	Advertising as % of sales: —

Stock History

NASDAQ (GS): GMCR

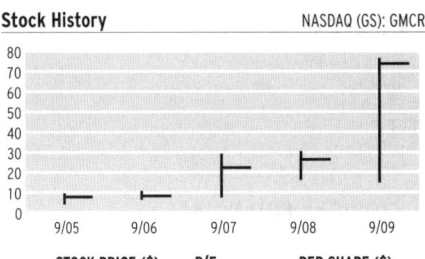

	STOCK PRICE ($) FY Close	P/E High/Low		PER SHARE ($) Earnings	Dividends	Book Value
9/09	73.84	55	11	1.39	—	13.52
9/08	26.23	51	29	0.58	—	3.20
9/07	22.13	83	23	0.35	—	2.27
9/06	8.18	42	29	0.24	—	1.72
9/05	7.73	34	18	0.26	—	1.38
Annual Growth	**75.8%**	**—**	**—**	**52.1%**	**—**	**76.8%**

Greene County Bancorp

This company helps put the "green" in Greene. Greene County Bancorp is the holding company for The Bank of Greene County, serving upstate New York's Catskill Mountains region from about 10 branches. Founded in 1889 as a building and loan association, the bank offers traditional retail products such as savings, NOW, checking, and money market accounts; IRAs; and CDs. Real estate loans make up nearly 85% of the bank's lending activities; it also writes business and consumer loans. Through affiliations with Fenimore Asset Management and Essex Corp., Greene County Bancorp offers investment products to existing customers. Subsidiary Greene County Commercial Bank is a state-chartered limited purpose commercial bank.

EXECUTIVES

Chairman: Martin C. Smith, age 64
President and CEO, Greene County Bancorp and The Bank of Greene County and Director:
Donald E. Gibson, age 44, $270,100 total compensation
EVP, COO, and CFO, Greene County Bancorp and The Bank of Greene County: Michelle M. Plummer, age 43, $242,000 total compensation
SVP and Chief Lending Officer, Greene County Bancorp and The Bank of Greene County: Stephen E. Nelson, age 42, $188,100 total compensation
CIO, The Bank of Greene County:
Gregory W. Spampinato
VP Commercial Lending, The Bank of Greene County:
Perry M. Lasher
VP and Mortgage Officer, The Bank of Greene County:
Trisha Lamb
VP and Mortgage Officer, The Bank of Greene County:
Charles McEntee
VP, Secretary, and Human Resources Director, The Bank of Greene County: Rebecca R. Main
VP Operations, The Bank of Greene County:
John Olivett
VP Municipal Banking and Commercial Sevices, The Bank of Greene County: Kresten M. Bjornsson
VP Investment Services, The Bank of Greene County:
Timothy J. Bartholomew
Auditors: Beard Miller Company LLP

LOCATIONS

HQ: Greene County Bancorp, Inc.
302 Main St., Catskill, NY 12414
Phone: 518-943-2600 **Fax:** 518-943-4431
Web: www.thebankofgreenecounty.com

COMPETITORS

First Niagara Financial
HSBC USA
KeyCorp
M&T Bank
TrustCo Bank Corp NY

HISTORICAL FINANCIALS

Company Type: Public

Income Statement

	ASSETS ($ mil.)	NET INCOME ($ mil.)	INCOME AS % OF ASSETS	EMPLOYEES
6/09	460.5	4.1	0.9%	124
6/08	379.6	2.7	0.7%	122
6/07	325.8	2.3	0.7%	118
6/06	307.6	2.2	0.7%	101
6/05	294.7	2.9	1.0%	106
Annual Growth	11.8%	9.0%	—	4.0%

FYE: June 30

2009 Year-End Financials

Equity as % of assets: 8.7%
Return on assets: 1.0%
Return on equity: 10.7%
Long-term debt ($ mil.): 19.0
No. of shares (mil.): 4.1
Market value ($ mil.): 59.6
Dividends
 Yield: 4.7%
 Payout: 68.7%
Sales ($ mil.): 21.8
R&D as % of sales: —
Advertising as % of sales: —

Stock History

NASDAQ (CM): GCBC

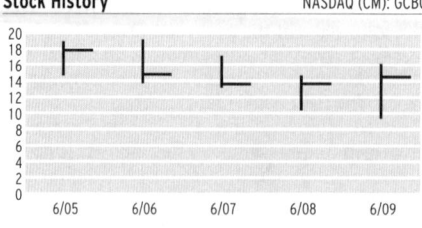

	STOCK PRICE ($) FY Close	P/E High/Low	PER SHARE ($) Earnings	Dividends	Book Value
6/09	14.50	16 10	0.99	0.68	9.80
6/08	13.65	22 16	0.65	0.70	8.83
6/07	13.60	31 25	0.54	0.48	8.62
6/06	14.80	35 26	0.54	0.45	8.18
6/05	17.81	27 21	0.70	0.43	7.97
Annual Growth	(5.0%)	— —	9.1%	12.1%	5.3%

GT Solar

GT Solar International is a beacon along the path of the solar power supply chain. The company manufactures equipment used in the production of silicon wafers, solar cells, and other products destined for use in solar power generation systems. Its key products include photovoltaic wafer fabrication machinery, silicon furnaces, and optical scanning systems. The company also provides solar module assembly services. GT Solar does most of its business in Asia, primarily in China. Top clients include such global solar products suppliers as BP Solar, LDK Solar (20% of sales), Schott Solar, SolarWorld, Suntech Power, and Yingli Green Energy.

The global economic crisis is having a negative effect on the solar power industry, slowing down that industry's explosive growth. The downturn in the global construction market reduced demand for solar panels being installed in new commercial and residential buildings. The global recession is expected to continue in the near term, which could affect GT Solar's business. The accompanying credit crisis weighs on the company, its customers, and its suppliers. Some customers failed to pay deposits on their contracts during fiscal 2009, and GT Solar terminated those contracts. The company has a limited number of customers. In early 2009 GT Solar had an order backlog of $1.2 billion, with three customers accounting for 60% of that total. Similarly, the company has a limited number of suppliers.

The solar photovoltaic (PV) energy business was worth $37 billion in 2008, according to the Solarbuzz research and consulting firm, with about $11 billion spent on capital expenditures in manufacturing crystalline silicon PV products and around $4 billion spent on expanding polysilicon production. Solarbuzz sees the global PV market growing to nearly $54 billion in 2013.

GT Solar is trying to tap that rapidly growing market, especially in China, which is rife with manufacturers producing polysilicon (the raw material that goes into making silicon wafers), solar-grade silicon wafers, solar cells, and solar modules (or panels). Chinese companies account for nearly two-thirds of sales, and the company has added facilities in Beijing and Shanghai as a result.

In 2007 GT Solar booked an order worth $171 million from China's Glory Silicon Energy Co., Ltd. The Chinese manufacturer will use GT Solar's DSS450 furnaces to produce solar-grade silicon wafers.

A year later GT Solar signed a contract with DC Chemical (now OCI Company) for polysilicon chemical vapor deposition reactors, valued at $173 million. Deliveries to the Korean chemical manufacturer began in 2009 and will continue through February 2012. OCI represents about 17% of GT Solar's sales.

GT Solar Holdings, which is controlled by GFI Energy Ventures and Oaktree Capital Management, owned nearly all of GT Solar International prior to the company's IPO. Following the 2008 offering, GT Solar Holdings owns about 78% of the company.

All proceeds from the IPO went to the principal shareholder, GT Solar Holdings.

EXECUTIVES

Chairman: J. Bradford Forth, age 44
President and CEO: Tom Gutierrez
VP and General Manager, Photovoltaic (PV) Equipment Divison: John (Rick) Tattersfield, age 46, $427,437 total compensation
VP Technology: Peter Bihuniak
VP Finance and Corporate Controller:
Richard E. Johnson, age 46
VP Human Resources: Brian Logue
VP Sales: Keith Matthei
VP and General Manager, Turnkey Division: Ron Jones
VP and General Manager, Polysilicon Division:
David W. Keck, age 44, $1,719,210 total compensation
VP Strategic Development: David C. Gray, age 43
VP and General Manager, Asia: Jeffrey J. Ford, age 53, $521,005 total compensation
VP, General Counsel, and Secretary: Hoil Kim, age 51
Investor Relations: Bob Blair
Auditors: Ernst & Young LLP

LOCATIONS

HQ: GT Solar International, Inc.
243 Daniel Webster Hwy., Merrimack, NH 03054
Phone: 603-883-5200 **Fax:** 603-595-6993
Web: www.gtsolar.com

2009 Sales

	$ mil.	% of total
Asia		
China	333.7	62
South Korea	109.5	20
Other countries	28.3	5
Europe	53.9	10
US	8.1	2
Other regions	7.5	1
Total	**541.0**	**100**

PRODUCTS/OPERATIONS

2009 Sales

	$ mil.	% of total
Photovoltaic business	443.9	82
Polysilicon business	97.1	18
Total	**541.0**	**100**

COMPETITORS

Advanced Metallurgical	Oerlikon
Amtech Systems	OTB Group
Applied Materials	Roth & Rau
BTU International	Spire Corp.
centrotherm	Sumitomo Electric
Dow Corning	Tokuyama
Ferrotec	ULVAC
Manz Automation	Veeco Instruments
MEMC Electronic Materials	Wacker Chemie
Mitsubishi Electric	

HISTORICAL FINANCIALS

Company Type: Public

Income Statement

FYE: March 31

	REVENUE ($ mil.)	NET INCOME ($ mil.)	NET PROFIT MARGIN	EMPLOYEES
3/09	541.0	88.0	16.3%	332
3/08	244.1	36.1	14.8%	305
Annual Growth	121.6%	143.8%	—	8.9%

2009 Year-End Financials

Debt ratio: —	Dividends
Return on equity: 101.4%	Yield: 0.0%
Cash ($ mil.): 107.1	Payout: —
Current ratio: 1.10	Market value ($ mil.): 952.9
Long-term debt ($ mil.): —	R&D as % of sales: —
No. of shares (mil.): 143.5	Advertising as % of sales: —

Stock History

NASDAQ (GS): SOLR

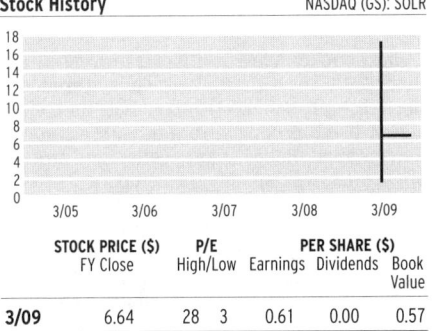

	STOCK PRICE ($) FY Close	P/E High/Low	PER SHARE ($) Earnings	Dividends	Book Value
3/09	6.64	28 3	0.61	0.00	0.57

GulfMark Offshore

GulfMark Offshore makes its mark on the high seas. The company offers support services for the construction, positioning, and operation of offshore oil and natural gas rigs and platforms. At the end of 2007 it owned, managed, or chartered 62 vessels in the North Sea (35 vessels), Southeast Asia (13), and offshore Brazil (4). Marine services include anchor handling; cargo, supply, and crew transportation; towing; and emergency services. Some of its ships conduct seismic data gathering and provide diving support. GulfMark Offshore serves both oil majors and smaller independents. In 2008 the company acquired Rigdon Marine, boosting GulfMark Offshore's fleet by 28 vessels.

GulfMark Offshore operates on a smaller scale in some of the world's other offshore oil patches, including India, the Gulf of Mexico, and West/South Africa.

EXECUTIVES

Chairman: David J. Butters, age 68
President, CEO, and Director: Bruce A. Streeter, age 60, $3,185,748 total compensation
EVP Operations: John E. (Gene) Leech, age 56, $1,575,550 total compensation
EVP, CFO, Treasurer, and Secretary: Quintin V. Kneen, age 44, $694,073 total compensation
VP, Controller, and Chief Accounting Officer: Samuel R. Rubio, age 50, $456,272 total compensation
VP Marketing: William L. (Billy) Guice IV
VP L.T. and CIO: Lee Johnson
VP International Operations: Darrel Plaisance
VP Internal Audit and Chief Compliance Officer: Anthony L. White
VP Business Development: Nathan T. Guice
VP Human Resources: David Darling
VP Operations, Americas: David Rossenwasser
VP Investor Relations and Treasurer: James A. (Jay) Harkness
Auditors: UHY LLP

LOCATIONS

HQ: GulfMark Offshore, Inc.
10111 Richmond Ave., Ste. 340, Houston, TX 77042
Phone: 713-963-9522   **Fax:** 713-963-9796
Web: www.gulfmark.com

GulfMark Offshore operates in the North Sea, off the coasts of Brazil, India, and Mexico, and in Southeast Asia, South and West Africa, and in the Mediterranean.

2008 Sales

	% of total
North Sea	55
Americas	26
Southeast Asia	19
Total	**100**

PRODUCTS/OPERATIONS

Selected Subsidiaries

Gulf Marine (Servicos Maritimos) do Brasil Limitada (Brazil)
GulfMark Norge AS (Norway)
GulfMark North Sea Ltd. (UK)
GulfMark Rederia (Norway)
Gulf Marine Far East PTE, Ltd. (Singapore)
Gulf Offshore Marine International, S. de R.L. (Panama)
GM Offshore, Inc.
Gulf Offshore Guernsey, Ltd. (UK)
Gulf Offshore N.S. Ltd. (UK)
S.E.A. Personnel Services Limited (UK)
Sea Truck (UK) Ltd.
Semaring Logistics (M) Sdn. Bhd. (Malaysia)

COMPETITORS

Acergy
Global Industries
SEACOR
Tidewater Inc.
Trico Marine

HISTORICAL FINANCIALS

Company Type: Public

Income Statement

FYE: December 31

	REVENUE ($ mil.)	NET INCOME ($ mil.)	NET PROFIT MARGIN	EMPLOYEES
12/08	411.7	195.5	47.5%	1,800
12/07	306.0	129.2	42.2%	1,300
12/06	250.9	89.7	35.8%	1,243
12/05	204.0	38.4	18.8%	1,212
12/04	139.3	2.7	1.9%	1,085
Annual Growth	31.1%	191.7%	—	13.5%

2008 Year-End Financials

Debt ratio: 54.2%	Dividends
Return on equity: 25.5%	Yield: 0.0%
Cash ($ mil.): 100.8	Payout: —
Current ratio: 2.84	Market value ($ mil.): 614.7
Long-term debt ($ mil.): 462.9	R&D as % of sales: —
No. of shares (mil.): 25.8	Advertising as % of sales: —

Stock History

NYSE: GLF

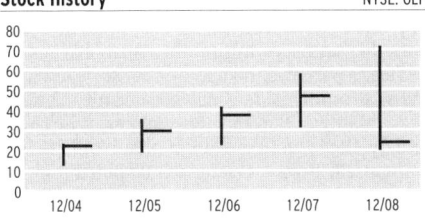

	STOCK PRICE ($) FY Close	P/E High/Low	PER SHARE ($) Earnings	Dividends	Book Value
12/08	23.79	9 3	7.56	0.00	33.08
12/07	46.79	13 7	4.29	0.00	26.17
12/06	37.41	10 5	4.28	0.00	20.95
12/05	29.62	19 11	1.86	0.00	12.39
12/04	22.27	— —	(0.23)	0.00	12.24
Annual Growth	1.7%	— —	—	—	28.2%

The Gymboree Corporation

Despite being more than a quarter-of-a-century old, The Gymboree Corporation is still a retail toddler, stumbling periodically, learning quickly, and growing fast. The company sells clothes and accessories for kids in the US, Canada, and Puerto Rico at about 615 Gymboree stores that carry colorful, fashionable playsuits and rompers for kids up to 12 years old. Gymboree also operates 115 Janie and Jack (better newborn and toddler apparel) and about 115 Gymboree Outlet stores and corresponding e-commerce sites. The firm also provides parent-child play programs (designed to enhance child development) at some 600 franchised and seven company-operated Gymboree Play & Music centers in the US and 30 other countries.

The company's Gymboree and Janie and Jack retail concepts span the price-range of children's clothing; Janie and Jack sell higher-priced apparel than Gymboree stores, and the Gymboree Outlet shops sell lower-priced clothing. A fourth retail concept — called Crazy 8 — debuted in August 2007 and offers discounted apparel at more than three dozen stores in sizes ranging from newborn up to size 14.

The company had a growth spurt in 2008 despite the ailing economy. The firm's lower-priced Crazy 8 format more than tripled in size, and the retailer added 50-plus new Gymboree and Gymboree Outlet locations, and another 20-odd Janie and Jack upscale shops. In 2009 another 75 new stores were planned, including 25 Crazy 8 locations. While net sales hit the billion-dollar mark in 2008 (up more than 8% vs. the prior year), same-store sales were flat. Retail sales account for 99% of the company's revenues, with its Play & Music business for parents and children contributing just 1%. The Play & Music business

also sells developmental toys, books, and music for young children.

The firm manages production of its apparel from design to manufacturing and outsources to about 120 firms (primarily in Asia).

HISTORY

Today's Gymboree is a far cry from the company begun by young mother Joan Barnes in 1976 as a parent-child play and sensory development program at a local community center. Franchising of Barnes' program began in 1979, and by 1984 the first foreign play program was franchised. Two years later a $300,000 initial investment by venture capitalists made The Gymboree Corporation a retail business as well. Though Barnes departed in 1990, the company continued to grow, going public in 1993.

Steady growth is a Gymboree priority, despite some falls and bumps. The company opened more than 70 new stores in 1995 and survived dismal holiday sales by slashing prices 50%. To prop up its overall profit margin, the following year it trimmed store inventories to reduce markdowns. This strategy caused same-store sales to slide, but Gymboree went ahead and opened 75 stores, including five in Canada, and saw gross profits rise. Also in 1996 it experimented with a short-lived catalog.

After the lessons of 1995 and 1996, Gymboree gradually began building up store inventories but buying less of each line and rotating collections faster. (Still, inventory surpluses resulted in markdowns, hurting profits in fiscal 1999.) CEO Nancy Pedot left the company in 1997 and was succeeded by Gary White. That year Gymboree opened stores in the UK and Ireland and launched an Internet sales site.

Gymboree launched Zutopia in 1999 and began adding more trendy lines in an attempt to broaden its customer base and deal with fewer markdowns. In 2000 Gymboree, staggering under falling sales, replaced some senior managers and installed chairman Stuart Moldaw as CEO. Lisa Harper was named CEO in 2001 while Moldaw remained chairman. The company sold Zutopia to fashion retailer Wet Seal in 2001. Mid-2002 Moldaw became chairman emeritus, and Harper added chairwoman to her existing title of CEO.

Janie and Jack, a new store concept, launched in October 2002. The stores offer newborn apparel, accessories, and gifts.

In April 2004 Gymboree launched its Janeville retail concept. Also that year the company closed all 23 of its stores in the UK and Ireland.

The retailer launched Gymboree Outlet, an outlet division for its namesake brand, in mid-2005. Matt McCauley was named president of the company in June and took over the position of CEO when Lisa Harper was made Chief Creative Officer in early 2006. When Harper retired as chairman and chief creative officer in July 2006, McCauley assumed the chairman's title as well.

In late 2006 Gymboree closed all 17 of its Janeville women's apparel stores (launched 2004), citing disappointing financial performance.

The company launched a fourth retail concept in August 2007 called Crazy 8 that sells newborn through size 14 apparel for boys and girls at price points about 30% lower than Gymboree stores.

EXECUTIVES

Chairman and CEO: Matthew K. (Matt) McCauley, age 36, $8,679,762 total compensation
President: Kip M. Garcia, age 58, $4,918,852 total compensation
COO, CFO, and Director: Blair W. Lambert, age 51, $4,005,637 total compensation
SVP Human Resources, Play and Music, and Secretary: Marina Armstrong, age 46, $4,048,592 total compensation
VP Finance: Jeffrey P. Harris, age 46
VP and Controller: Lynda G. Gustafson, age 44, $617,965 total compensation
Auditors: Deloitte & Touche LLP

LOCATIONS

HQ: The Gymboree Corporation
500 Howard St., San Francisco, CA 94105
Phone: 415-278-7000   **Fax:** 707-678-1315
Web: www.gymboree.com

2009 Stores

	No.
US	854
Canada	29
Puerto Rico	3
Total	**886**

PRODUCTS/OPERATIONS

2009 Stores

	No.
Gymboree	615
Gymboree Outlet	118
Janie & Jack	115
Crazy 8	38
Total	**886**

2009 Sales

	$ mil.	% of total
Retail stores	987.9	99
Play & Music	12.8	1
Total	**1,000.7**	**100**

COMPETITORS

The Children's Place
Dillard's
Discovery Toys
The Gap
Hanna Andersson
J. C. Penney
LeapFrog
Macy's
Sears
Target
Wal-Mart

HISTORICAL FINANCIALS

Company Type: Public

Income Statement			FYE: Sunday nearest January 31	
	REVENUE ($ mil.)	NET INCOME ($ mil.)	NET PROFIT MARGIN	EMPLOYEES
1/09	1,000.7	93.5	9.3%	11,500
1/08	920.8	80.3	8.7%	10,400
1/07	791.6	60.3	7.6%	9,500
1/06	678.5	34.5	5.1%	9,600
1/05	594.5	(2.2)	—	8,802
Annual Growth	**13.9%**	**—**	**—**	**6.9%**

2009 Year-End Financials

Debt ratio: —
Return on equity: 34.5%
Cash ($ mil.): 140.5
Current ratio: 2.58
Long-term debt ($ mil.): —
No. of shares (mil.): 30.0

Dividends
  Yield: —
  Payout: —
Market value ($ mil.): 734.3
R&D as % of sales: —
Advertising as % of sales: —

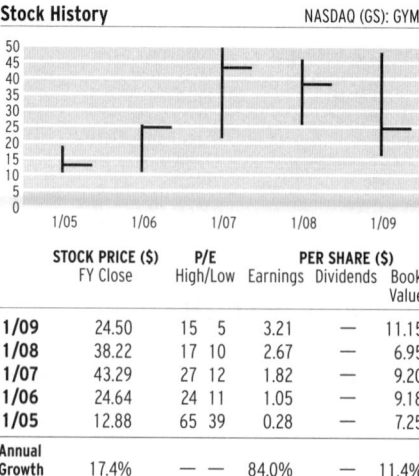

Stock History				NASDAQ (GS): GYMB

	STOCK PRICE ($) FY Close	P/E High/Low		PER SHARE ($) Earnings	Dividends	Book Value
1/09	24.50	15	5	3.21	—	11.15
1/08	38.22	17	10	2.67	—	6.95
1/07	43.29	27	12	1.82	—	9.20
1/06	24.64	24	11	1.05	—	9.18
1/05	12.88	65	39	0.28	—	7.25
Annual Growth	**17.4%**	**—**	**—**	**84.0%**	**—**	**11.4%**

Haemonetics Corporation

Haemonetics helps health care providers hold on to blood. The company develops and produces blood recovery systems that automate the collection of blood products from donors. Its donor systems allow blood banks to collect and process whole blood, taking only the components (such as plasma or red blood cells) that they might need. Haemonetics also makes systems that collect and re-infuse a patient's own blood during surgery; these surgical blood salvage systems are sold under the OrthoPAT, cardioPAT, and Cell Saver brand names by its patient division. Additionally, the company sells information management software and provides consulting services to blood banks and hospitals.

Haemonetics markets its products and services worldwide through a direct sales force and distributors. The company's primary markets are the US, Europe, and Japan, though it also maintains a direct sales presence in Canada and China. It uses distributors to sell its products in South America, the Middle East, and other markets. It has manufacturing facilities in the US and Scotland.

Collecting and banking blood is easier when hospitals and banks have good software to manage the process. Haemonetics built up its information management systems and services through acquisitions, eventually forming subsidiary Haemonetics Software Solutions. That business was further filled out with the 2009 acquisitions of Altivation Software and Neoteric Technology. Also in 2009 chairman and CEO Brad Nutter moved on to become just chairman of the company and former COO Brian Concannon took over the CEO role. The move was part of a multi-year succession plan.

HISTORY

Allan Latham founded Haemonetics in 1971. Its first product was a blood processing machine sold to blood banks and hospitals. The company went public in 1979. Early in the

1980s the company introduced the Cell Saver automated blood-salvage system. The product debuted at a time when the possibility of contracting HIV from blood transfusions had become a serious health concern, and by 1988 sales topped $90 million. The company was bought in 1983 and was passed around between several owners, including Baxter International, before going public again in 1991.

In 1996 the company formed key relationships with blood bank customers through which Haemonetics performed such management services as component collection, distribution, and donor recruitment; the move allowed the company to become more vertically integrated. The following year it acquired Santa Barbara, California-based Tri-Counties Blood Bank, which gave Haemonetics access to a distribution network of 24,000 annual units of red blood cells. A restructuring charge and discontinuation of some operations drained the company's bottom line in 1998.

The company's venture into blood bank operation was short-lived; by 1999 it exited that line when results didn't live up to expectations. The next year Haemonetics expanded its product line with its purchase of Transfusion Technologies. New devices included the Chairside Separator System, which separates donated blood into one unit of red blood cells and one unit of plasma.

In 2006 Haemonetics began broadening its product line to include software and consulting solutions, offering blood banks and hospitals ways to improve efficiencies and manage their blood supply, as well as providing equipment.

EXECUTIVES

Chairman: Brad Nutter, age 57, $3,074,444 total compensation
President, CEO, and Director: Brian Concannon, age 51, $1,173,228 total compensation
Chief Marketing Officer: Peter M. Allen, age 50, $938,287 total compensation
VP Business Development and CFO: Christopher J. (Chris) Lindop, age 51, $1,132,577 total compensation
VP Technical Operations: Robert B. (Bob) Ebbeling, $962,409 total compensation
VP Finance: Susan M. Hanlon
VP Research and Development: Jonathan White, age 50
VP Sales, North American Blood Bank: Mark Contardo
VP Human Resources: Joseph J. Forish
VP and Corporate Medical Doctor: Mark Popovsky
VP Corporate Affairs: Alicia R. (Lisa) Lopez
General Counsel: James O'Shaughnessy
President, Asia/Pacific: Remi Corlin
President, Haemonetics Japan: Keiko Hattori, age 57
President, Global Markets: Mikael Gordon, age 54
Director Investor Relations and Corporate Communications: Julie Fallon
Auditors: Ernst & Young LLP

LOCATIONS

HQ: Haemonetics Corporation
400 Wood Rd., Braintree, MA 02184
Phone: 781-848-7100   **Fax:** 781-356-3558
Web: www.haemonetics.com

2009 Sales

	$ mil.	% of total
International	318.9	53
US	279.0	47
Total	**597.9**	**100**

PRODUCTS/OPERATIONS

2009 Sales

	$ mil.	% of total
Disposables		
Donor		
Plasma	202.2	34
Blood bank	143.4	24
Red cell	49.5	8
Patient		
Surgical & diagnostic	87.6	15
OrthoPAT	35.4	6
Equipment	35.5	6
Software & services	44.3	7
Total	**597.9**	**100**

Selected Products

Donor products
  ACP (red blood cell collection and processing system)
  Cymbal (automated red blood cell collection system)
  MCS (automated platelet collection system)
  PCS (plasma collection system)

Patient products
  cardioPAT (heart surgery blood salvage system)
  Cell Saver (autologous blood recovery system)
  OrthoPAT (orthopedic blood salvage system)

Software and services
  Blood management assessment (for hospitals)
  Haemonetics Software Solutions (data management for blood and plasma collection centers)
  Six Sigma and LEAN manufacturing consulting (for blood banks)

COMPETITORS

CaridianBCT
Fresenius
Global Med
Medtronic
Sorin
Surgical Innovations
Terumo Medical Corporation

HISTORICAL FINANCIALS

Company Type: Public

Income Statement

FYE: Saturday nearest March 31

	REVENUE ($ mil.)	NET INCOME ($ mil.)	NET PROFIT MARGIN	EMPLOYEES
3/09	597.9	59.3	9.9%	2,016
3/08	516.4	52.0	10.1%	1,875
3/07	449.6	49.1	10.9%	1,826
3/06	419.7	69.1	16.5%	1,661
3/05	383.6	39.6	10.3%	1,546
Annual Growth	**11.7%**	**10.6%**	**—**	**6.9%**

2009 Year-End Financials

Debt ratio: 1.0%
Return on equity: 11.5%
Cash ($ mil.): 156.7
Current ratio: 4.12
Long-term debt ($ mil.): 5.3
No. of shares (mil.): 25.6
Dividends
  Yield: 0.0%
  Payout: —
Market value ($ mil.): 1,410.7
R&D as % of sales: —
Advertising as % of sales: —

Stock History

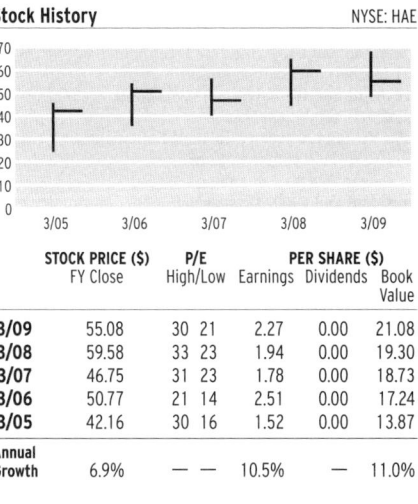

NYSE: HAE

	STOCK PRICE ($) FY Close	P/E High/Low	PER SHARE ($) Earnings	Dividends	Book Value
3/09	55.08	30 21	2.27	0.00	21.08
3/08	59.58	33 23	1.94	0.00	19.30
3/07	46.75	31 23	1.78	0.00	18.73
3/06	50.77	21 14	2.51	0.00	17.24
3/05	42.16	30 16	1.52	0.00	13.87
Annual Growth	**6.9%**	**— —**	**10.5%**	**—**	**11.0%**

Hallwood Group

What do a soldier's parachute and a Texas oil patch have in common? The Hallwood Group, a holding company with interests in both textiles and energy. Its Brookwood Companies subsidiary, which accounts for all of its revenue, develops and produces high-tech coated nylon fabric for the outdoors and sportswear industries. It is also a major supplier of specialty fabrics (including camouflage and waterproof items) to the US military, which is its largest customer. The Hallwood Group also owns less than a quarter of Hallwood Energy, which is involved in oil and gas exploration in Texas, Louisiana, and Arkansas.

One of the company's biggest challenges is the volatility of the US military business, on which its revenues are largely dependent. As a supplier of military apparel and textiles, The Hallwood Group attempts to gauge the federal government's changing specifications on certain products, so that it can supply a niche demand. Because of the unpredictable nature of this market, however, the company has experienced swinging sales margins. Analysts say that the US textile industry also is hampered by international competition and the rising costs of developing manufacturing technology.

Hallwood Energy and certain affiliates filed for Chapter 11 protection from creditors in 2009. The Hallwood Group did not seek bankruptcy protection and is a creditor of Hallwood Energy.

CEO Anthony Gumbiner owns about two-thirds of The Hallwood Group. Gumbiner proposed a liquidation of the company in mid-2007 that would include the sale of subsidiary Brookwood Companies Inc., with him purchasing the remaining interests in Hallwood Energy. The company's board established a special review committee, but it is unclear if or when such a transaction might be completed.

EXECUTIVES

Chairman and CEO: Anthony J. Gumbiner, age 64, $1,002,200 total compensation
President and COO: William L. Guzzetti, age 65, $325,643 total compensation
VP, CFO, and Secretary: Richard Kelley, age 49, $120,873 total compensation
Treasurer: Joseph T. Koenig
President and CEO, Brookwood: Amber M. Brookman, age 66, $1,368,744 total compensation
Auditors: Deloitte & Touche LLP

LOCATIONS

HQ: The Hallwood Group Incorporated
3710 Rawlins St., Ste. 1500, Dallas, TX 75219
Phone: 214-528-5588   **Fax:** 214-522-9254
Web: www.hallwood.com

COMPETITORS

Duro Industries
Noble Biomaterials
Polartec

HISTORICAL FINANCIALS
Company Type: Public

Income Statement
FYE: December 31

	REVENUE ($ mil.)	NET INCOME ($ mil.)	NET PROFIT MARGIN	EMPLOYEES
12/08	162.2	1.4	0.9%	460
12/07	132.5	(32.8)	—	467
12/06	112.2	(6.7)	—	447
12/05	134.6	26.3	19.5%	462
12/04	137.3	94.5	68.8%	514
Annual Growth	4.3%	(65.1%)	—	(2.7%)

2008 Year-End Financials

Debt ratio: 27.2%
Return on equity: 3.2%
Cash ($ mil.): 6.0
Current ratio: 2.71
Long-term debt ($ mil.): 10.4
No. of shares (mil.): 1.5

Dividends
 Yield: 0.0%
 Payout: —
Market value ($ mil.): 50.3
R&D as % of sales: —
Advertising as % of sales: —

Stock History
NYSE Alternext: HWG

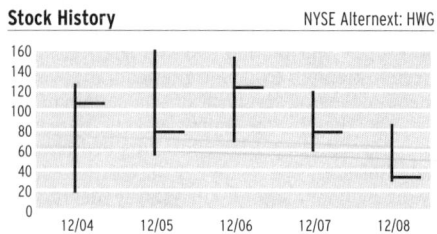

	STOCK PRICE ($) FY Close	P/E High/Low	Earnings	PER SHARE ($) Dividends	Book Value
12/08	33.00	92 33	0.92	0.00	25.09
12/07	78.00	— —	(21.61)	0.00	32.00
12/06	122.50	— —	(4.44)	0.00	53.74
12/05	77.88	9 3	17.47	0.00	57.99
12/04	106.50	2 0	63.55	0.00	81.66
Annual Growth	(25.4%)	— —	(65.3%)	—	(25.6%)

Hampden Bancorp

Despite its name, Hampden Bancorp's (the holding company for Hampden Bank) services extend beyond Massachusetts's Hampden County. Serving a handful of cities and towns in western Massachusetts, Hampden Bank offers savings and checking deposit services, as well as a variety of lending services, to its consumer and business customers. The bank's primary loan products include one- to four-family residential loans and commercial real estate loans, each of which make up about a third of the bank's total loan portfolio. Loans for construction, businesses, and consumers make up the rest. Hampden Bancorp operates through more than a half-dozen branches.

EXECUTIVES

Chairman: Stuart F. Young Jr., age 59
President, CEO, and Director: Thomas R. Burton, age 62, $665,544 total compensation
EVP Hampden Bancorp and Hampden Bank: Glenn S. Welch, age 47, $304,332 total compensation
SVP Hampden Bancorp and Hampden Bank; Division Executive IT and Operations: Sheryl L. Shinn
SVP Director Marketing, Hampden Bank: Richard L. DeBonis
SVP Hampden Bancorp and Hampden Bank; Division Executive Retail and Mortgage Lending: Robert J. Michel, age 57, $264,970 total compensation
SVP, CFO, and Treasurer, Hampden Bancorp and Hampden Bank; President, Hampden Bank Foundation: Robert A. Massey, age 58, $220,391 total compensation
SVP Hampden Bancorp and Hampden Bank; Division Executive Retail Banking and Financial Services: William D. Marsh III, age 59, $240,171 total compensation
VP Human Resources, Hampden Bank: Lynn Stevens Bunce
Secretary and Director: Richard J. Kos, age 56
Auditors: Wolf & Company, P.C.

LOCATIONS

HQ: Hampden Bancorp, Inc.
19 Harrison Ave., Springfield, MA 01103
Phone: 413-736-1812   **Fax:** 413-294-1099
Web: www.hampdenbank.com

COMPETITORS

Bank of America
Berkshire Hills Bancorp
Chicopee
Citizens Financial Group
Eastern Bank
Sovereign Bank
TD Bank USA
United Financial Bancorp

HISTORICAL FINANCIALS
Company Type: Public

Income Statement
FYE: June 30

	ASSETS ($ mil.)	NET INCOME ($ mil.)	INCOME AS % OF ASSETS	EMPLOYEES
6/09	567.7	0.3	0.1%	109
6/08	543.8	1.2	0.2%	105
6/07	523.9	(1.5)	—	107
6/06	468.8	1.0	0.2%	107
Annual Growth	6.6%	(33.1%)	—	0.6%

2009 Year-End Financials

Equity as % of assets: —
Return on assets: 0.1%
Return on equity: —
Long-term debt ($ mil.): 70.9
No. of shares (mil.): 7.3
Market value ($ mil.): 72.4

Dividends
 Yield: 1.2%
 Payout: 300.0%
Sales ($ mil.): 18.2
R&D as % of sales: —
Advertising as % of sales: —

Stock History
NASDAQ (GM): HBNK

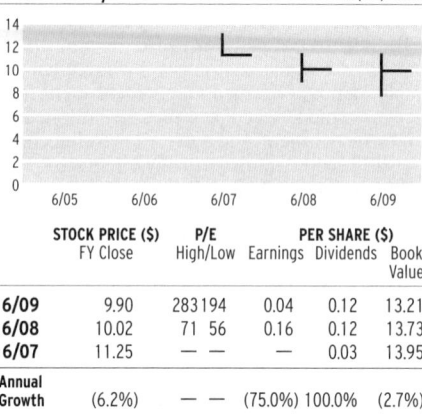

	STOCK PRICE ($) FY Close	P/E High/Low	Earnings	PER SHARE ($) Dividends	Book Value
6/09	9.90	283 194	0.04	0.12	13.21
6/08	10.02	71 56	0.16	0.12	13.73
6/07	11.25	— —		0.03	13.95
Annual Growth	(6.2%)	— —	(75.0%)	100.0%	(2.7%)

Hampton Roads Bankshares

Hampton Roads Bankshares is the holding company for the Bank of Hampton Roads and Shore Bank, which together have about 40 offices in southeastern Virginia and eastern Maryland. Gateway Bank & Trust, a division of Bank of Hampton Roads, has about 25 locations in Virginia and North Carolina. Serving area consumers and businesses, the banks offer standard services such as checking and savings accounts, CDs, retirement accounts, and loans. Through other affiliates, the banks also offer insurance, investment, and mortgage banking services. Hampton Roads Bankshares acquired Shore Financial and Gateway Financial Holdings in 2008.

Construction loans make up the largest portion of Hampton Roads Bankshares' loan portfolio (more than 33%), which is not surprising considering several company board members are also executives of construction firms. Commercial mortgages comprise about a quarter of the company's loan book, and residential mortgages and business loans are around 20% each.

EXECUTIVES

Chairman: Emil A. Viola, age 73
President, CEO, and Director; CEO, Bank of Hampton Roads: John A. B. (Andy) Davies, age 57
EVP, COO, and General Counsel: Douglas J. Glenn, age 42
EVP and CFO: Neal A. Petrovich, age 47
EVP and Chief Credit Risk Officer: Julie R. Anderson, age 50
EVP and Chief Operations Officer: Reneé R. McKinney, age 44
EVP and Investor Relations Officer and Secretary; EVP, Marketing Officer, and Secretary, Bank of Hampton Roads: Tiffany K. Glenn, age 39
EVP; President and CEO, Gateway Bank: David R. Twiddy, age 51

EVP Delmarva Operations; President and CEO, Shore Bank: Scott C. Harvard, age 54
Chief Credit Officer: Douglas D. (Doug) Wall
SVP and Treasurer: Mark D. Bedard
SVP and Chief Accounting Officer; CFO, Bank of Hampton Roads: Lorelle L. Fritsch, age 42, $213,475 total compensation
Auditors: KPMG LLP

LOCATIONS

HQ: Hampton Roads Bankshares, Inc.
999 Waterside Dr., Ste. 200, Norfolk, VA 23510
Phone: 757-217-1000   **Fax:** 757-217-3656
Web: www.bankofhamptonroads.com

PRODUCTS/OPERATIONS

2008 Gross Revenues

	$ mil.	% of total
Interest		
Loans, including fees	43.2	84
Investment securities	1.7	3
Other	0.3	1
Noninterest		
Service charges on deposit accounts	3.4	6
Other	3.1	6
Total	**51.7**	**100**

COMPETITORS

Bank of America	Monarch Financial
BB&T	Old Point Financial
Commonwealth Bankshares	SunTrust
Heritage Bankshares	TowneBank
	Xenith Bankshares

HISTORICAL FINANCIALS

Company Type: Public

Income Statement

	ASSETS ($ mil.)	NET INCOME ($ mil.)	INCOME AS % OF ASSETS	EMPLOYEES
12/08	3,085.7	7.2	0.2%	721
12/07	563.8	6.8	1.2%	182
12/06	476.3	6.0	1.3%	176
12/05	409.5	5.5	1.3%	175
12/04	345.0	4.1	1.2%	160
Annual Growth	**72.9%**	**15.1%**	**—**	**45.7%**

FYE: December 31

2008 Year-End Financials

Equity as % of assets: —
Return on assets: 0.4%
Return on equity: —
Long-term debt ($ mil.): 356.3
No. of shares (mil.): 21.9
Market value ($ mil.): 190.9
Dividends Yield: 5.0%
Payout: 74.6%
Sales ($ mil.): 33.2
R&D as % of sales: —
Advertising as % of sales: —

Stock History

NASDAQ (GS): HMPR

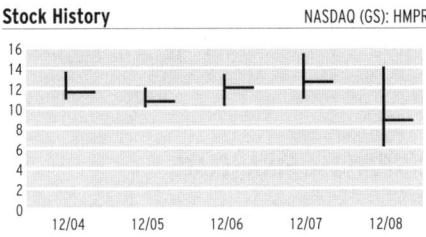

	STOCK PRICE ($) FY Close	P/E High/Low		PER SHARE ($) Earnings	Dividends	Book Value
12/08	8.73	24	11	0.59	0.44	15.77
12/07	12.56	23	17	0.65	0.11	3.37
12/06	12.00	20	16	0.65	0.00	3.21
12/05	10.65	18	15	0.66	0.00	2.25
12/04	11.60	27	22	0.50	0.00	1.99
Annual Growth	**(6.9%)**	**—**	**—**	**4.2%**	**—**	**67.7%**

H&E Equipment Services

Whether you're a he or a she, if you have a project that requires heavy lifting, H&E Equipment Services can help. The company sells and rents new and used equipment for construction, earthmoving, and material handling. H&E Equipment offers services such as planned maintenance, mobile service, repair, fleet management, and crane remanufacturing, as well as parts for aerial platform equipment and industrial lift trucks, among others. The company markets its products and services throughout the US and represents lift, crane, and truck manufacturers such as JLG, Bobcat, and Komatsu. President, CEO, and director John Engquist owns about 13% of the company.

H&E Equipment experienced a positive year in 2008, but the high became a low when first quarter 2009 results showed a substantial decline in company profits. About half of H&E's revenues are derived from the industrial sector (energy and mining) and 40% from non-residential construction, both of which have been negatively impacted by the economic crisis. Luckily for H&E Equipment, only about 10% of its revenues are derived from the residential construction sector which was hit the hardest. With an ailing economy, the company could not help but suffer from the inevitable negative-financial-result germ that infected its positive results. The company's solid presence along the Gulf Coast has been credited for fueling its revenues from equipment used for post-hurricane clean-up and hurricane protection work still to come. H&E Equipment is taking steps to recover its financial strength by reducing the size of its fleet, freezing staff salaries, and reducing its workforce by about 13%.

The company operates over 60 full-service facilities throughout the US. It made inroads into the mid-Atlantic region of the US when it acquired construction equipment distributor J.W. Burress for about $98 million in 2007. Burress shareholders can receive up to an additional $15 million over three years if Burress continues to sell, rent, and repair Hitachi equipment. Hitachi-related revenues represent more than one-quarter of the distributor's annual sales.

Its sales and rental activities are based on its four equipment categories, which include aerial platform equipment, cranes, earthmoving equipment, and industrial lift trucks. The company also offers insurance coverage plans for its equipment.

H&E Equipment was formed in 2002 through the merger of Head & Engquist (a subsidiary of Gulf Wide Industries) and ICM Equipment Company. Before their merger, the regional, integrated equipment service companies Head & Engquist (founded in 1961) and ICM Equipment Company (established in 1971) were operating in contiguous geographic markets.

EXECUTIVES

Chairman: Gary W. Bagley, age 62
President, CEO, and Director: John M. Engquist, age 55, $1,028,471 total compensation
EVP and COO: Bradley W. Barber, age 36, $858,552 total compensation
CFO and Secretary: Leslie S. Magee, age 40, $755,501 total compensation
VP Fleet Management: Louis St. Germain

VP Product Support: John D. Jones, age 51, $629,993 total compensation
VP Cranes and Earthmoving: William W. Fox, age 65, $332,507 total compensation
Auditors: BDO Seidman, LLP

LOCATIONS

HQ: H&E Equipment Services, Inc.
11100 Mead Rd., Ste. 200, Baton Rouge, LA 70816
Phone: 225-298-5200   **Fax:** 225-298-5377
Web: www.he-equipment.com

PRODUCTS/OPERATIONS

2008 Sales

	$ mil.	% of total
New equipment sales	374.1	35
Equipment rentals	295.4	28
Used equipment sales	160.8	15
Parts sales	118.3	11
Services revenues	70.1	6
Other	50.3	5
Total	**1,069.0**	**100**

Selected Products

Aerial lifts
Backhoes
Boom trucks
Compactors/rollers
Compressors
Concrete equipment and tools
Cranes
Crawler carriers and drills
Crushers and conveyors
Demolition tools
Dozers
Dump trucks
Excavators
Forestry equipment
Forklifts (telescopic)
Generators
Haul trucks
Heaters
Hoists/gantries
Industrial-personnel vehicles
Landscape equipment
Lighting
Material lifts
Motor graders
Pavers
Pumps
Rammers
Screeners
Sewer equipment
Skid loaders
Sweepers/scrubbers
Trailers
Water transporters (trailers, trucks, and wagons)
Welders
Wheel loaders

COMPETITORS

AMECO
Atlas Lift Truck Rentals
Berry Companies
Hertz
Holt CAT
ICON Capital
J. A. Riggs Tractor
NES Rentals
Park Corp.
Penhall International
RSC Equipment Rental
Sunbelt Rentals
United Rentals
Wacker Neuson

HISTORICAL FINANCIALS

Company Type: Public

Income Statement

FYE: December 31

	REVENUE ($ mil.)	NET INCOME ($ mil.)	NET PROFIT MARGIN	EMPLOYEES
12/08	1,069.0	43.3	4.1%	1,871
12/07	1,003.1	64.6	6.4%	2,095
12/06	804.4	32.7	4.1%	1,677
12/05	600.2	28.2	4.7%	1,448
12/04	478.2	(13.7)	—	1,318
Annual Growth	22.3%	—	—	9.2%

2008 Year-End Financials

Debt ratio: 87.6%
Return on equity: 15.0%
Cash ($ mil.): 11.3
Current ratio: 0.88
Long-term debt ($ mil.): 254.3
No. of shares (mil.): 34.9

Dividends
Yield: —
Payout: —
Market value ($ mil.): 269.1
R&D as % of sales: —
Advertising as % of sales: —

Stock History

NASDAQ (GS): HEES

	STOCK PRICE ($) FY Close	P/E High/Low		PER SHARE ($) Earnings	Dividends	Book Value
12/08	7.71	14	4	1.22	—	8.31
12/07	18.88	18	9	1.70	—	8.25
12/06	24.77	48	23	0.88	—	6.75
Annual Growth	(44.2%)	—	—	17.7%	—	11.0%

Hansen Natural

No matter the weather, Hansen Natural always has the energy to reach higher than the blue sky. Adding to its Blue Sky energy drink, the company has expanded its stable of "alternative" sodas, juices, and teas to include a variety of energy beverages, such as the popular Monster brand. Other products made by Hansen include fruit juice, smoothies, and dry juice mixes. The company sells its products to grocery chains, wholesale clubs, distributors, and foodservice operators mainly in the US and Canada. Through Branded Limited Partnership, Hansen chairman and CEO Rodney Sacks, and vice chairman and president Hilton Schlosberg own approximately 18% of the company.

Hansen does not directly make its own products; instead, it outsources the manufacturing and packaging to third-party bottlers and contract packers. Some of these third-party companies include Carolina Beer & Beverage, Lucerne Foods, Seven-Up/RC Bottling Company of Southern California, Nor-Cal Beverage, Dairy Farmers of America, Dr Pepper Bottling Co., and Olympic Food.

The "alternative" beverage industry has grown increasingly crowded with bottled water and juices from beverage giants such as Coca-Cola and PepsiCo. In order to compete, Hansen's product line includes "functional" drinks made by adding echinacea, ginseng, guarana, and other supplements to the beverages.

The company offers numerous lines of energy drinks (most with a mixture of caffeine, sweeteners, and vitamins), and the segment now pulls in more than 90% of the company's sales. Hansen's Lost Energy is a joint marketing initiative with surf board designer Lost International. Its Rumba Energy Juice is an all-juice product designed to replace both morning coffee and juice. The company has a distribution deal with Anheuser-Bush for its energy drinks. It also has an agreement with Cadbury Bebidas for the distribution of its Monster energy drinks in Mexico, as well as one with Pepsi Canada for distribution in that country.

In addition to the US, Mexico, and Canada, select Hansen's products are available in the Caribbean, Central and South America, Japan, Korea, Saudi Arabia, Hong Kong, South Africa, the UK, France, the Netherlands, Spain, Belgium, Luxembourg, Monaco, and Sweden.

Wal-Mart accounted for approximately 11% of Hansen's 2008 sales.

EXECUTIVES

Chairman and CEO: Rodney C. Sacks, age 59, $3,578,428 total compensation
Vice Chairman, COO, CFO, President, and Secretary: Hilton H. Schlosberg, age 56, $3,572,329 total compensation
VP Finance: Thomas J. Kelly, age 54, $338,073 total compensation
Human Resources Director: Linda Lopez
Assistant Secretary and Director: Benjamin M. Polk, age 58
President, Monster Beverage Company: Mark J. Hall, age 53, $2,286,299 total compensation
COO, Monster Beverage Company: Nick R. Gagliardi, age 52
Auditors: Deloitte & Touche LLP

LOCATIONS

HQ: Hansen Natural Corporation
550 Monica Circle, Ste. 201, Corona, CA 92880
Phone: 951-739-6200 **Fax:** 951-739-6220
Web: www.hansens.com

PRODUCTS/OPERATIONS

2008 Sales

	$ mil.	% of total
Energy drinks	939.7	91
Non-carbonated beverages	65.7	6
Carbonated beverages	28.4	3
Total	**1,033.8**	**100**

2008 Sales by Distribution Channel

	% of total
Full-service distributors	74
Club stores, drug chains & mass merchandisers	14
Retail grocery & specialty chains & wholesalers	8
Health food distributors	1
Other channels	3
Total	**100**

Selected Products and Brands

Bottled Water
  Vidration
Energy Drinks
  Assault
  Joker Mad Energy
  Lost Energy
  Monster Energy
  Monster Energy Heavy Metal
  Monster Energy Khaos
  Monster Energy M-80
  Monster Energy MIXXD
  Monster Hitman Energy Shooter
  RIPPER
  Rumba
  Samba
  Tango
Dry Juice Mixes
  Fizzit
Juices
  Apple
  Apple Grape
  Apple Strawberry
  Grape
  Juice Slam
  Junior Juice
  Organic Apple
  Pomegranate
  Smoothie
  White Grape
Soda
  Blue Sky
  Hansen's Natural and Diet
  Hansen's Natural Green Tea
  Hansen's Signature
Tea
  Iced Green
  Lychee Black
  Peach Tree
  Pomegranate Green

COMPETITORS

Caribou Coffee	Mott's
Celsius Holdings	Naked Juice
Chiquita Brands	National Beverage
Cinnabon	National Grape Cooperative
Clearly Canadian	Nestlé
Coca-Cola	Nestlé Waters
Coca-Cola North America	Ocean Spray
Cott	Odwalla
Cranberries Limited	PepsiCo
Del Monte Foods	Red Bull
Dole Food	Reed's
Dr Pepper Snapple Group	Smucker
Energy Brands	Snapple
Fuze Beverage	South Beach Beverage
Gatorade	Starbucks
Global Beverage	Sunny Delight
Godiva Chocolatier	Tree Top
Goya	Tropicana
Hobarama	Unilever
Hornell Brewing	Veryfine
Impulse Energy USA	Welch's
IZZE	Wet Planet Beverages
Jones Soda	XELR8
Kraft Foods	

HISTORICAL FINANCIALS

Company Type: Public

Income Statement

FYE: December 31

	REVENUE ($ mil.)	NET INCOME ($ mil.)	NET PROFIT MARGIN	EMPLOYEES
12/08	1,033.8	108.0	10.4%	1,270
12/07	904.5	149.4	16.5%	713
12/06	605.8	97.9	16.2%	748
12/05	348.9	62.8	18.0%	363
12/04	180.3	20.4	11.3%	293
Annual Growth	54.7%	51.7%	—	44.3%

2008 Year-End Financials

Debt ratio: —
Return on equity: 25.2%
Cash ($ mil.): 256.8
Current ratio: 3.00
Long-term debt ($ mil.): —
No. of shares (mil.): 89.1

Dividends
  Yield: 0.0%
  Payout: —
Market value ($ mil.): 2,987.2
R&D as % of sales: —
Advertising as % of sales: —

Stock History

NASDAQ (GS): HANS

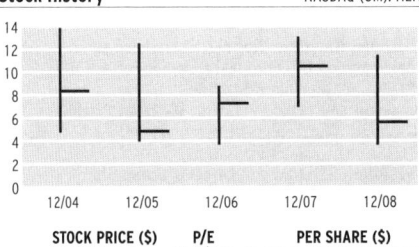

	STOCK PRICE ($) FY Close	P/E High/Low		PER SHARE ($) Earnings	Dividends	Book Value
12/08	33.53	41	18	1.11	0.00	4.90
12/07	44.29	45	22	1.51	0.00	4.74
12/06	33.68	53	20	0.99	0.00	2.53
12/05	19.70	34	6	0.65	0.00	1.41
12/04	4.55	21	4	0.22	0.00	0.66
Annual Growth	64.8%	—	—	49.9%	—	65.2%

Harmonic Inc.

Harmonic answers the demand for advanced television features. The company provides fiber-optic and wireless network transmission products used to enable video-on-demand services. Its video transmission equipment includes digital headend systems, digital signal encoders, and complete provider-to-subscriber delivery systems. Harmonic also supplies multiplexers, optical nodes, transmitters, optical amplifiers, and other broadband network access equipment. The company sells directly and through distributors and systems integrators, primarily to cable and satellite TV providers. Its customers include Cablevision, Charter Communications, Comcast, and Time Warner Cable.

Harmonic has used acquisitions to expand its product portfolio and marketing reach. The company purchased the video networking software business of Entone Technologies for $45 million in 2006. The Entone acquisition provided Harmonic with applications related to personalized services such as video-on-demand, targeted advertising insertion, and personal video recording (PVR). The following year it bought Rhozet, a developer of transcoding software, for $15.5 million. The Rhozet purchase brought technology that allows the creation of multi-format video for broadcast, Internet, and mobile device delivery. Increased sales of software products have helped improve Harmonic's margins.

Harmonic bought Israel-based Scopus Video Networks for about $51 million in 2009. The acquisition of Scopus, which did most of its business outside the Americas, was designed to bolster the company's presence in international markets, expand its distribution channels, and increase its research and development capabilities. Harmonic generated about 45% of its revenues outside the US in 2008.

EXECUTIVES

Chairman: Lewis (Lew) Solomon, age 75
President, CEO, and Director: Patrick J. Harshman, age 44, $1,583,499 total compensation
CFO: Robin N. Dickson, age 61, $861,807 total compensation
VP Research and Development: Neven Haltmeyer, age 44, $686,148 total compensation
VP Worldwide Sales and Service:
Matthew J. (Matt) Aden, age 53, $792,366 total compensation
VP Product Marketing, Solutions and Strategy:
Nimrod Ben-Natan, age 41, $660,109 total compensation
VP Asia Pacific Sales: Raymond Tse
VP North America Sales: Jim Marino
VP Sales and Service, Europe, Middle East, and Africa:
Ian Graham
VP Operations: Charles J. Bonasera, age 51
VP Human Resources: Peter E. (Pete) Hilliard
VP Corporate Development: Shahar Bar
VP Business Development and Marketing Communications: David Price
Director Marketing Communications: Sarah Lum
Auditors: PricewaterhouseCoopers LLP

LOCATIONS

HQ: Harmonic Inc.
549 Baltic Way, Sunnyvale, CA 94089
Phone: 408-542-2500   **Fax:** 408-542-2511
Web: www.harmonicinc.com

2008 Sales

	$ mil.	% of total
US	205.2	56
Other countries	159.8	44
Total	**365.0**	**100**

PRODUCTS/OPERATIONS

2008 Sales

	$ mil.	% of total
Edge & access	165.3	45
Video processing	137.4	38
Software, support & other	62.3	17
Total	**365.0**	**100**

COMPETITORS

ADC Telecommunications
Alcatel-Lucent
ARRIS
Aurora Networks
Blonder Tongue
Cisco Systems
Ericsson
Harris Corp.
JDS Uniphase
Motorola, Inc.
Nortel Networks
SAFRAN
TANDBERG Television
THOMSON
Tollgrade Communications

HISTORICAL FINANCIALS

Company Type: Public

Income Statement

FYE: December 31

	REVENUE ($ mil.)	NET INCOME ($ mil.)	NET PROFIT MARGIN	EMPLOYEES
12/08	365.0	64.0	17.5%	698
12/07	311.2	23.4	7.5%	658
12/06	247.7	1.0	0.4%	639
12/05	257.4	(5.7)	—	618
12/04	248.3	1.6	0.6%	590
Annual Growth	10.1%	151.5%	—	4.3%

2008 Year-End Financials

Debt ratio: —
Return on equity: 17.1%
Cash ($ mil.): 179.9
Current ratio: 4.94
Long-term debt ($ mil.): —
No. of shares (mil.): 96.1

Dividends
  Yield: 0.0%
  Payout: —
Market value ($ mil.): 539.2
R&D as % of sales: —
Advertising as % of sales: —

Stock History

NASDAQ (GM): HLIT

	STOCK PRICE ($) FY Close	P/E High/Low		PER SHARE ($) Earnings	Dividends	Book Value
12/08	5.61	17	6	0.67	0.00	4.31
12/07	10.48	46	25	0.28	0.00	3.48
12/06	7.27	867	379	0.01	0.00	1.51
12/05	4.85	—	—	(0.08)	0.00	1.18
12/04	8.34	688	243	0.02	0.00	1.15
Annual Growth	(9.4%)	—	—	140.6%	—	39.1%

Hawk Corporation

Whether you're flying an airplane or driving a tractor, Hawk wants to help you put a stop to it. The company's friction products segment manufactures components used in brakes, clutches, and transmissions for off-highway vehicles, motorcycles, and trucks, along with brake parts for commercial and general aircraft landing systems. In 2008 the company sold its performance racing division, which made racecar clutches, transmissions, and driveline systems, after the business failed to achieve a certain level of profitability. Hawk operates seven manufacturing facilities in four countries. The company gets more than half of its sales in the US.

Hawk's strategy is to focus on hard-to-produce specialty products with high margins, rather than products that are easy to mass-produce which compete primarily on price. It also is striving to build its aftermarket business.

The company plans to tighten up its worldwide manufacturing footprint so it can better serve global customers. To this end Hawk intends to expand operations in Asia, Australia, Europe, North America, and South America. It also hopes to continue efforts in research and development for improving current products, as well as designing new applications.

Just as 2006 was winding to a close, Hawk found a buyer for the precision components business in order to focus on its friction products and performance racing operations. Saw Mill Capital Partners agreed to pay about $94 million in cash and assumed debt. The sale was completed early in 2007.

The following year Hawk announced plans to sell its performance racing division, consisting of Quarter Master Industries and Tex Racing Enterprises. The move is part of Hawk's decision to focus on its friction products business. The company retained its Hawk Performance brake business following the divestitures.

Quarter Master Industries was sold to COMP Cams, based in Memphis, while Tex Racing Enterprises went to Leonard C. Long, a US manufacturer of motorsports components.

Founder Norman Harbert and CEO Ronald Weinberg together control about 30% of Hawk.

EXECUTIVES

Chairman Emeritus: Norman C. Harbert, age 75
Chairman and CEO: Ronald E. Weinberg, age 67, $2,699,342 total compensation
President and COO; President, Wellman Products Group: B. Christopher DiSantis, age 38, $1,731,031 total compensation
SVP Administration and Director Corporate Development: Joseph J. Levanduski, age 46, $853,454 total compensation
VP Finance and Treasurer: Thomas A. Gilbride, age 55, $619,918 total compensation
Secretary and Director: Byron S. Krantz, age 73
Interim Chief Accounting Officer and Corporate Controller: John T. Bronstrup
Auditors: Ernst & Young LLP

LOCATIONS

HQ: Hawk Corporation
200 Public Square, Ste. 1500, Cleveland, OH 44114
Phone: 216-861-3553   **Fax:** 216-861-4546
Web: www.hawkcorp.com

2008 Sales

	$ mil.	% of total
US	157.4	59
Italy	98.0	36
Other countries	14.2	5
Total	**269.6**	**100**

PRODUCTS/OPERATIONS

2008 Sales by Market

	% of total
Construction & mining	47
Aircraft & defense	20
Agriculture	15
Heavy truck	9
Performance friction	4
Specialty friction	4
Alternative energy	1
Total	**100**

COMPETITORS

BorgWarner
Dana Holding
GKN
Precision Castparts
Twin Disc
Wozniak Industries

HISTORICAL FINANCIALS

Company Type: Public

Income Statement

FYE: December 31

	REVENUE ($ mil.)	NET INCOME ($ mil.)	NET PROFIT MARGIN	EMPLOYEES
12/08	269.6	20.8	7.7%	1,110
12/07	228.7	17.3	7.6%	1,150
12/06	212.1	3.0	1.4%	1,115
12/05	265.4	(1.3)	—	1,800
12/04	241.2	1.1	0.5%	1,640
Annual Growth	**2.8%**	**108.5%**	**—**	**(9.3%)**

2008 Year-End Financials

Debt ratio: 112.5%
Return on equity: 28.7%
Cash ($ mil.): 62.5
Current ratio: 3.37
Long-term debt ($ mil.): 87.1
No. of shares (mil.): 8.1
Dividends
  Yield: —
  Payout: —
Market value ($ mil.): 133.8
R&D as % of sales: —
Advertising as % of sales: —

Stock History

NYSE Alternext: HWK

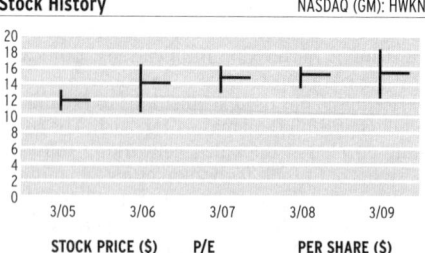

	STOCK PRICE ($) FY Close	P/E High	P/E Low	PER SHARE ($) Earnings	PER SHARE ($) Dividends	PER SHARE ($) Book Value
12/08	16.60	12	5	2.21	—	9.60
12/07	18.02	10	5	1.83	—	8.35
12/06	11.97	53	33	0.30	—	5.80
12/05	14.67	—	—	(0.17)	—	5.05
12/04	8.64	82	32	0.11	—	5.54
Annual Growth	**17.7%**	**—**	**—**	**111.7%**	—	**14.7%**

Hawkins, Inc.

Hawkins processes and distributes bulk specialty chemicals. Its industrial chemicals segment stores and distributes caustic soda, phosphoric acid, and aqua ammonia, among many others. The segment also makes bleach (sodium hypochlorite), repackages liquid chlorine, and custom blends other chemicals. Hawkins' water treatment group distributes products and equipment used to treat drinking water, municipal and industrial wastewater, and public swimming pools. It also distributes laboratory-grade chemicals for the pharmaceutical industry. Through its fleet of trucks and tankers, the company operates facilities and serves customers throughout the midwestern US.

In 2007 the company bought Trumark, a maker of antimicrobials used in food safety products, for $6 million. The move not only added new manufacturing and R&D capabilities, it also expands Hawkins' reach to the East Coast for the first time. Hawkins has retained the Trumark name for the business.

EXECUTIVES

Chairman: John S. (Jack) McKeon, age 64
CEO and Director: John R. Hawkins, age 57, $826,156 total compensation
VP, CFO, and Treasurer: Kathleen P. Pepski, age 54, $392,702 total compensation
VP Operations: Mark A. Beyer
VP, General Counsel, and Secretary: Richard G. (Rich) Erstad, age 45, $99,359 total compensation
VP Industrial Group: John R. Sevenich, age 51, $395,197 total compensation
VP Water Treatment Group: Keenan A. Paulson, age 59, $403,295 total compensation
Auditors: Deloitte & Touche LLP

LOCATIONS

HQ: Hawkins, Inc.
3100 E. Hennepin Ave., Minneapolis, MN 55413
Phone: 612-331-6910   **Fax:** 612-331-5304
Web: www.hawkinschemical.com

Hawkins operates about 20 warehouse facilities throughout the Midwest.

PRODUCTS/OPERATIONS

Selected Products

Industrial chemicals
Manufactured chemicals
Manufactured food ingredients
Specialty chemicals
Surface finishing chemicals
Water treatment and waste treatment products

COMPETITORS

Ashland Distribution
Brenntag North America
JCI Jones Chemicals
K.A. Steel Chemicals
Univar USA

HISTORICAL FINANCIALS

Company Type: Public

Income Statement

FYE: Sunday nearest March 31

	REVENUE ($ mil.)	NET INCOME ($ mil.)	NET PROFIT MARGIN	EMPLOYEES
3/09	284.4	23.8	8.4%	281
3/08	196.4	9.1	4.6%	265
3/07	160.4	8.1	5.0%	243
3/06	143.3	8.9	6.2%	235
3/05	115.3	8.1	7.0%	217
Annual Growth	**25.3%**	**30.9%**	**—**	**6.7%**

2009 Year-End Financials

Debt ratio: —
Return on equity: 25.2%
Cash ($ mil.): 29.5
Current ratio: 3.02
Long-term debt ($ mil.): —
No. of shares (mil.): 10.3
Dividends
  Yield: 3.4%
  Payout: 22.4%
Market value ($ mil.): 158.7
R&D as % of sales: —
Advertising as % of sales: —

Stock History

NASDAQ (GM): HWKN

	STOCK PRICE ($) FY Close	P/E High	P/E Low	PER SHARE ($) Earnings	PER SHARE ($) Dividends	PER SHARE ($) Book Value
3/09	15.43	8	5	2.32	0.52	10.09
3/08	15.23	18	15	0.89	0.48	8.27
3/07	14.76	20	16	0.79	0.44	7.78
3/06	14.07	19	12	0.87	0.40	7.40
3/05	11.91	16	14	0.79	0.36	7.02
Annual Growth	**6.7%**	**—**	**—**	**30.9%**	**9.6%**	**9.5%**

Health Grades

Health Grades (which does business as HealthGrades) takes the health care industry to school. The company offers report cards on hospitals, physicians, nursing homes, home health agencies, hospice programs, and other health care providers. It sells the quality and patient safety information to a number of constituencies, including consumers, health plans, employers, and liability insurance companies. Hospitals themselves represent its biggest customer base, however; providers can license HealthGrades' ratings and trademarks (its Distinguished Hospital Award, for instance) to use in their marketing campaigns. They also come to the company for quality improvement consulting.

HealthGrades' database has ratings and profiles on the US's more than 5,800 hospitals, as well as some 750,000 doctors and thousands of nursing homes and other health care providers.

Consumers can access certain basic information about these providers online for free but have to pay a fee for more in-depth profiles. In 2008 it announced it would also partner with Google to provide information on providers through the search giant's Google Health portal.

For employers and insurers, the company offers a wide array of information products (under the umbrella brand Health Management Suite). In addition to quality reports, HealthGrades offers medical cost calculators and disease management tools that an employer, for instance, could license and provide to its employees to help them make cost-effective health care decisions.

Doctors aren't left out of the HealthGrades business model. The company's Internet Patient Acquisition program lets doctors create and maintain online profiles that consumers can look at free of charge. In 2006 the company signed a multi-year deal with Tenet Healthcare to use the program to promote Tenet-affiliated physicians.

EXECUTIVES

Chairman, President, and CEO: Kerry R. Hicks, age 49, $768,716 total compensation
COO: Wes Crews, age 46
EVP: David G. Hicks, age 50, $317,937 total compensation
EVP and CFO: Allen Dodge, age 41, $310,719 total compensation
EVP and Chief Medical Officer: Samantha Collier
SVP Sponsorship and Advertising: Jan R. Rutherford Jr.
SVP: Michael (Mike) Shanks
SVP Information Technology: Mark Bartling
SVP Corporate Communications and Marketing: Scott Shapiro
SVP Provider Services: Tod Baker
SVP Operations: Bill Wosilius
Director Human Resources: Caroline Petty
Auditors: Grant Thornton LLP

LOCATIONS

HQ: Health Grades, Inc.
500 Golden Ridge Rd., Ste. 100, Golden, CO 80401
Phone: 303-716-0041   **Fax:** 303-716-1298
Web: www.healthgrades.com

PRODUCTS/OPERATIONS

2008 Sales

	% of total
Provider Services	74
Internet Business Group	21
Strategic Health Solutions	5
Total	**100**

Selected Products and Services

Provider Services
  Hospital marketing programs
    America's 50 Best Hospitals
    Distinguished Hospital Program for Patient Safety
    Strategic Quality Initiative
    Strategic Quality Partnership
  Quality improvement services
    Quality Assessment
    Quality Assessment and Implementation
    Quality Report for Hospital Professionals
Internet Business Group
  Healthcare Quality Reports for Consumers
  Internet Patient Acquisition program (marketing tools for physicians)
Strategic Health Solutions (for employers, benefit consultants, payors, and others)
  Decision Points (health care decision-making tools)
  Healthcare Quality Guides
  Health Management Suite (customized sets of quality data)
  Medical Cost Calculator

COMPETITORS

GE Healthcare	Premier, Inc.
Healthvision	Thomson Reuters
Ingenix	WebMD Health

HISTORICAL FINANCIALS

Company Type: Public

Income Statement

FYE: December 31

	REVENUE ($ mil.)	NET INCOME ($ mil.)	NET PROFIT MARGIN	EMPLOYEES
12/08	39.7	4.7	11.8%	184
12/07	36.2	6.7	18.5%	142
12/06	27.8	3.2	11.5%	123
12/05	20.8	4.1	19.7%	106
12/04	14.5	1.8	12.4%	67
Annual Growth	**28.6%**	**27.1%**	**—**	**28.7%**

2008 Year-End Financials

Debt ratio: 0.0%
Return on equity: 35.8%
Cash ($ mil.): 11.3
Current ratio: 0.91
Long-term debt ($ mil.): 0.0
No. of shares (mil.): 29.8
Dividends
  Yield: 0.0%
  Payout: —
Market value ($ mil.): 61.4
R&D as % of sales: —
Advertising as % of sales: —

Stock History

NASDAQ (CM): HGRD

	STOCK PRICE ($) FY Close	P/E High/Low		PER SHARE ($) Earnings	Dividends	Book Value
12/08	2.06	41	8	0.15	0.00	0.36
12/07	5.95	35	22	0.20	0.00	0.52
12/06	4.49	78	33	0.09	0.00	0.41
12/05	6.32	54	23	0.12	0.00	0.32
12/04	2.90	65	11	0.05	0.00	0.12
Annual Growth	**(8.2%)**	**—**	**—**	**31.6%**	**—**	**31.5%**

HealthStream, Inc.

HealthStream replenishes the well of knowledge for medical workers. The company offers Internet-based educational and training content for health care professionals. Courses train employees on new equipment, introduce new pharmaceuticals, provide continuing education credits, and disseminate regulatory information. The company's flagship HealthStream Learning Center has nearly 2 million subscribers. It generates sales from subscription fees based on the number of users and type of content provided. Clients include health care organizations, pharmaceutical companies, and medical device firms. The company also provides data management and research products through its HealthStream Research division.

HealthStream entered the research game when it acquired Data Management & Research (DMR) in 2005. Two years later the company added to its research capabilities when it acquired The Jackson Organization, Research Consultants (TJO) and it established the HealthStream Research business segment. HealthStream Research caters to patients, doctors, and others in the health care community by providing quality and satisfaction surveys, data analyses, and other research-based tools. The company continues to grow its HealthStream Research product by expanding its customer base of some 1,000 hospitals.

HealthStream was founded in 1990 and began its Internet-based services in 1999. CEO Robert Frist owns around 28% of HealthStream.

EXECUTIVES

Chairman, President, and CEO: Robert A. Frist Jr., age 42, $239,855 total compensation
EVP: Alfred E. Newman, age 60, $283,681 total compensation
SVP, General Counsel, and Compliance Officer: Kevin O'Hara, age 40, $223,902 total compensation
SVP and CFO: Gerard M. (Gerry) Hayden Jr., age 54, $148,140 total compensation
SVP and CTO: Jeffrey S. Doster, age 44, $144,671 total compensation
SVP and President HealthStream Research: J. Edward (Eddie) Pearson, age 46, $289,203 total compensation
Senior Director Communications, Research, and Investor Relations: Mollie Condra
Auditors: Ernst & Young LLP

LOCATIONS

HQ: HealthStream, Inc.
209 10th Ave. South, Ste. 450, Nashville, TN 37203
Phone: 615-301-3100   **Fax:** 615-301-3200
Web: www.healthstream.com

PRODUCTS/OPERATIONS

2008 Sales

	$ mil.	% of total
Learning	32.8	64
Research	18.8	36
Total	**51.6**	**100**

COMPETITORS

A.D.A.M.	NRC
AMA	Press Ganey
Cengage Learning	Reed Elsevier Group
EBSCO	Saba Software
Gallup	SumTotal
Medscape llc	

HISTORICAL FINANCIALS

Company Type: Public

Income Statement
FYE: December 31

	REVENUE ($ mil.)	NET INCOME ($ mil.)	NET PROFIT MARGIN	EMPLOYEES
12/08	51.6	2.9	5.6%	400
12/07	43.9	4.1	9.3%	420
12/06	31.8	2.5	7.9%	160
12/05	27.4	1.9	6.9%	160
12/04	20.1	(1.0)	—	146
Annual Growth	26.6%	—	—	28.7%

2008 Year-End Financials

Debt ratio: 0.9%
Return on equity: 8.0%
Cash ($ mil.): 4.1
Current ratio: 1.07
Long-term debt ($ mil.): 0.3
No. of shares (mil.): 21.6

Dividends
  Yield: —
  Payout: —
Market value ($ mil.): 50.3
R&D as % of sales: —
Advertising as % of sales: —

Stock History
NASDAQ (GM): HSTM

	STOCK PRICE ($) FY Close	P/E High/Low		PER SHARE ($) Earnings	Dividends	Book Value
12/08	2.33	27	14	0.13	—	1.70
12/07	3.50	26	14	0.18	—	1.66
12/06	3.95	47	21	0.11	—	1.37
12/05	2.33	45	21	0.09	—	1.20
12/04	2.68	—	—	(0.05)	—	1.01
Annual Growth	(3.4%)	—	—	—	—	14.0%

Healthways, Inc.

For health insurers, healthy plan members are cheap plan members; that's where Healthways comes in. The health services company provides disease management and wellness programs to managed care companies, self-insured employers, governments, and hospitals, with the ultimate goals of improving members' health and lowering health care costs. Its disease management programs help members manage chronic illnesses like diabetes and emphysema, making sure they keep up with treatment plans and maintain healthy behaviors. Healthways' wellness offerings, including its SilverSneakers program for seniors, encourage fitness and other good lifestyle choices.

The company provides services to more than 32 million people in all 50 states, Washington DC, and Puerto Rico through about a dozen service centers; it also provides services in some international markets. Its largest customers are health insurers CIGNA and Blue Cross and Blue Shield of Massachusetts, which account for 20% and 10% of total revenue, respectively.

Since healthy people require expensive health care services less often, Healthways' strategy consists of finding new and better ways of controlling health care costs by improving members' well-being. It has added services through partnerships with other health care companies, including collaborations with pharmacy benefits manager Medco and not-for-profit content provider Healthwise.

The company is also adding custom programs for targeted markets, such as its Senior Care Management (SCM) program which identifies and manages the care of high-risk Medicare Advantage members; the SCM program can be integrated with the SilverSneakers fitness program. In addition, Healthways added a behavioral health incentive program in 2009 through the acquisition of HealthHonors for $15 million.

Healthways set up shop overseas at the beginning of 2008, with a contract to provide disease management and wellness services to members of German health insurer Deutsche Angestellten Krankenkasse. That year it also entered the Brazil market via a partnership with Brazilian health services company Fleury. In 2009 the company established a presence in Australia when it entered into a wellness contract with insurer Hospitals Contribution Fund.

HISTORY

In 1981 Thomas Cigarran and Henry Herr (alumni of a company that's now part of HCA) joined with venture capitalist Martin Koldyke to found American Healthcorp to buy hospitals. The company diversified, entering the diabetes market in 1984 and arthritis care in 1987.

With profitability lagging, the company sold its hospitals to focus on niche care. In the same spirit, it de-emphasized arthritis care in 1990. The company went public in 1991.

After a brief foray into obesity treatment, the company in 1994 invested in AmSurg, a manager of ambulatory surgery centers. (AmSurg was spun off in 1997.)

By the late 1990s the company increasingly targeted HMOs. It signed its first contract with Principal Health Care (1996, ended in 1998 after Coventry Health Care bought the HMO). Contracts with such HMOs as John Deere Health Care and Health Options of Blue Cross & Blue Shield of Florida followed in 1998.

To standardize income, the company in 1998 converted all of its contracts from shared savings arrangements (in which the company's earnings were based on the payers' savings) to fee-based arrangements. In 1999 American Healthcorp began offering a cardiac health management program to its hospital and HMO clients; that year it changed its name to American Healthways to reflect its expanded product line.

American Healthways in 2000 signed a deal with Agilent Technologies to offer that company's home heart monitoring systems to its patients. It also launched MYHEALTHWAYS, a Web-based application, which offers disease-prevention plans to health plan members.

In 2001 American Healthways launched Comprehensive Care Enhancement Programs, under which all health plan members are screened and provided with any needed health care programs.

The company acquired Company StatusOne Health Systems in 2003 to expand its health management service offerings for high-risk populations. American Healthways changed its name to Healthways in early 2006.

In late 2006 the firm acquired preventive health services provider AXIA Health Management for more than $450 million. The acquisition added a host of wellness services, such as fitness and nutrition programs, to Healthways' service offering. Among them were the SilverSneakers program, as well as an online smoking cessation support group called QuitNet.

EXECUTIVES

Chairman: Thomas G. (Tom) Cigarran, age 67
CEO and Director: Ben R. Leedle Jr., age 49, $4,812,790 total compensation
President and COO: Stefen F. (Steve) Brueckner, age 60
EVP, CFO, and Secretary: Mary A. Chaput, age 59
EVP: Robert E. Stone, age 63, $939,575 total compensation
EVP and Chief Science Officer: James E. (Jim) Pope, age 56, $1,282,077 total compensation
EVP Operations Services: Robert L. Chaput, age 59
EVP Marketing and Strategy: Anne M. Wilkins, age 42
EVP: Mary D. Hunter, age 64
SVP, Outcomes Improvement and Chief Medical Officer: Dexter Shurney
SVP, Chief Accounting Officer, and Corporate Controller: Alfred Lumsdaine, age 44
SVP and Chief Communications Officer: Nicholas E. Dantona
SVP Human Resources and Organization Development: Christopher (Chris) Cigarran
SVP Marketing: Carol Murdock
President, International Business: Matthew E. Kelliher, age 54, $1,197,169 total compensation
Auditors: Ernst & Young LLP

LOCATIONS

HQ: Healthways, Inc.
  701 Cool Springs Blvd., Franklin, TN 37067
Phone: 615-614-4929
Web: www.healthways.com

PRODUCTS/OPERATIONS

Selected Products and Services

Disease management programs
  Asthma
  Back pain
  Cancer
  Chronic kidney disease/end-stage renal disease (CKD/ESRD)
  Chronic obstructive pulmonary disease (COPD)
  Coronary artery disease
  Depression
  Diabetes
  Heart failure
  Hepatitis C
  Obesity
  Osteoporosis
Forever Fit (wellness and fitness for older adults)
Gallup-Healthways Well-Being Index (collection and measurement of national health)
Healthways Center for Health Research (analytics)
Healthy Alignment (chiropractic conditioning program)
myhealthIQ (online health risk assessment)
Prime (fitness program for adults under 65 years of age)
QuitNet (smoking cessation program)
Senior Care Management (high-risk patient management)
SilverSneakers (fitness program for older adults)
StatusOne (care management program for members at high risk for hospitalization)
WholeHealth (alternative and complementary medicine and therapy program)

COMPETITORS

Accordant Health Services	Fresenius Medical Care
Accredo Health	Health Dialog
ActiveHealth Management	iMetrikus
APS Healthcare	Inverness Medical
CareGuide	Magellan Health
Comprehensive Care	OptumHealth
Express Scripts	SHPS

HISTORICAL FINANCIALS

Company Type: Public

Income Statement

FYE: December 31*

	REVENUE ($ mil.)	NET INCOME ($ mil.)	NET PROFIT MARGIN	EMPLOYEES
8/08	736.2	54.8	7.4%	3,500
8/07	615.6	45.1	7.3%	3,800
8/06	412.3	37.2	9.0%	2,855
8/05	312.5	33.1	10.6%	2,231
8/04	245.4	26.1	10.6%	1,875
Annual Growth	31.6%	20.4%	—	16.9%

*Fiscal year-end change

2008 Year-End Financials

Debt ratio: 97.5%
Return on equity: 15.3%
Cash ($ mil.): 35.2
Current ratio: 1.13
Long-term debt ($ mil.): 345.4
No. of shares (mil.): 33.8

Dividends
Yield: 0.0%
Payout: —
Market value ($ mil.): 643.9
R&D as % of sales: —
Advertising as % of sales: —

Stock History

NASDAQ (GS): HWAY

| | 8/04 | 8/05 | 8/06 | 8/07 | 8/08 |

	STOCK PRICE ($) FY Close	P/E High/Low		PER SHARE ($) Earnings	Dividends	Book Value
8/08	19.05	47	12	1.50	0.00	10.48
8/07	49.80	47	31	1.22	0.00	10.73
8/06	51.62	54	36	1.02	0.00	8.13
8/05	43.70	49	28	0.93	0.00	6.12
8/04	27.00	41	24	0.75	0.00	4.60
Annual Growth	(8.3%)	—	—	18.9%	—	22.9%

HEICO Corporation

Here's a HEICO haiku: HEICO companies/ Providing for jet engines/ In flight or on land. Through the subsidiaries that make up the company's Flight Support Group, HEICO manufactures parts for jet engines that can be substituted for original parts. Products include combustion chambers and compressor blades. Flight Support operations, which include repair and overhaul services, account for about three-quarters of HEICO's sales. Subsidiaries in HEICO's Electronic Technologies Group make a variety of electro-optical, electronic, and microwave products, primarily for military applications. The company gets around two-thirds of its sales from the US.

Despite its corporate name being similar to a certain well-known insurance company, HEICO doesn't have cavemen, a gecko, or any other animal, as its spokes-creature. But, moving to further diversify its product lineup, the company has netted the "pinger." In fall 2009 HEICO's Electronic Technologies Group purchased a maker of acoustic beacons, the Seacom division of Dukane Corp. Officially known as an Underwater Locator Beacon (ULB), the device deepens HEICO's reach into aircraft and marine markets, which are required by the US Federal Aviation Administration and European Aviation Safety Agency to install such equipment on flight data and cockpit voice recorders. HEICO is keeping the pinger-maker's management, and looks to reinforce the product's branding by renaming the division Dukane Seacom, Inc. The acquisition is also anticipated to complement HEICO's customer base in electronics and telecommunications, and to a lesser extent in industrial and medical markets. These customers account for a growing portion of the company's sales.

The deal was underpinned by a financial ramp up. In a year when many corporations found getting credit difficult, HEICO was able to increase its senior unsecured revolving credit facility in 2008 from $130 million to $300 million, with an upper limit of $500 million under certain circumstances. The company's lenders are J.P. Morgan Securities and SunTrust Robinson Humphrey.

Chairman, president, and CEO Laurans Mendelson and his family own about 17% of HEICO. Lufthansa holds a 20% stake in HEICO Aerospace (the umbrella company for the company's Flight Support Group).

HISTORY

Founded in 1957 as Heinicke Instruments to make laboratory products, the company moved into jet engine parts in 1974 with the acquisition of Jet Avion. The company changed its name to HEICO (a shortened version of its previous name) in 1985. After a faulty combustion chamber erupted in flames that year, the FAA ordered all combustion chambers on US jets to be inspected and, if necessary, replaced. HEICO's sales skyrocketed, but descended back to earth after airlines found they had overstocked.

By the early 1990s defense cutbacks and declining aircraft orders reduced business, and HEICO began to diversify. In 1991 it formed MediTek to acquire medical imaging facilities but then sold the company to U.S. Diagnostic for $24 million five years later. Lufthansa Technik AG, the service subsidiary of Deutsche Lufthansa, paid HEICO $26 million for a 20% stake in HEICO's flight support operations in 1997.

HEICO acquired jet engine parts companies McClain International and Rogers-Dierks in 1998. The next year the company added Radiant Power (back-up power supplies and battery packs for aerospace applications), Turbine Kinetics and AeroKinetics (replacement parts for aircraft engines), Santa Barbara Infrared (infrared and ground support equipment), and Thermal Structures (insulation products).

HEICO sold its Trilectron Industries ground support equipment subsidiary to Illinois Tool Works in 2000 in a deal worth about $64 million. The following year the company formed a joint venture with AMR (parent of American Airlines) to accelerate development of FAA-approved replacement parts. Also in 2001, HEICO bought Inertial Airline Services, Avitech Engineering Corp., and Aviation Facilities, Inc. In 2003 HEICO acquired Niacc Technology, an aircraft component repair and overhaul company.

The company added to its aerospace electronics operations with the acquisition of Connectronics, a maker of high-voltage wire and interconnection devices, in 2004.

In 2005 HEICO moved to expand its flight support business by buying a 51% stake in Seal Dynamics, a designer and distributor of hydraulic, pneumatic, mechanical, and electromechanical components for the commercial, regional, and general aviation markets.

In 2006 HEICO's Flight Support Group acquired Arger Enterprises, a subsidiary of Melrose PLC. Arger made and distributed aircraft parts, mainly for the commercial aviation market. Also in 2006, HEICO bought a controlling stake in Prime Air Parts, which dealt in spare parts for aircraft.

The following year HEICO's Electronic Technologies Group acquired EMD Technologies, a maker of high-voltage energy generators used in medical, industrial imaging, and baggage scanning systems.

A few years of careful acquisitions complemented by organic growth contributed to record sales and profits for HEICO in fiscal 2007. The company's Flight Support Group led the charge with a 38% increase in sales; Electronic Technologies was no slouch, with an 8% increase.

EXECUTIVES

Chairman and CEO: Laurans A. Mendelson, age 71, $2,674,790 total compensation
Co-President and Director; CEO, HEICO Aerospace Holdings: Eric A. Mendelson, age 44, $1,493,107 total compensation
Co-President and Director; President and CEO, HEICO Electronic Technologies: Victor H. Mendelson, age 42, $1,488,419 total compensation
EVP and CFO: Thomas S. Irwin, age 63, $1,542,059 total compensation
VP Corporate Development: William S. Harlow, age 61, $398,975 total compensation
General Counsel: Joseph W. Pallot, age 50
Auditors: Deloitte & Touche LLP

LOCATIONS

HQ: HEICO Corporation
3000 Taft St., Hollywood, FL 33021
Phone: 954-987-4000   **Fax:** 954-987-8228
Web: www.heico.com

2009 Sales

	$ mil.	% of total
US	367.7	68
Other countries	170.6	32
Total	538.3	100

PRODUCTS/OPERATIONS

2009 Sales

	$ mil.	% of total
Flight Support Group	395.4	73
Electronic Technologies Group	143.4	27
Adjustments	(0.5)	—
Total	538.3	100

Selected Subsidiaries and Affiliates

Flight Support
HEICO Aerospace Holdings Corp. (HEICO Aerospace, 80%)
  Aircraft Technology, Inc.
  Aviation Facilities, Inc.
  Future Aviation, Inc.
  HEICO Aerospace Corporation
  HEICO Aerospace Parts Corp.
  Jet Avion Corporation
  Jetseal, Inc.
  LPI Industries Corporation
  McClain International, Inc.
  Niacc-Avitech Technologies Inc.
  Northwings Accessories Corporation
  Rogers-Dierks, Inc.
  Thermal Structures, Inc.
  Turbine Kinetics, Inc.
Electronic Technologies
HEICO Electronic Technologies Corp.
  Analog Modules, Inc.
  Connectronics Corporation
  Leader Tech, Inc.
  Lumina Power, Inc.
  Radiant Power Corp.
  Santa Barbara Infrared, Inc.
  Sierra Microwave Technology, LLC

COMPETITORS

AAR Corp.
Barnes Group
BBA Aviation
CIC International
DeCrane
Doncasters
EMS Technologies
GE Aviation
Goodrich Corp.
Kellstrom Aerospace
Ladish Co.
LMI Aerospace
Mikron Infrared
Pratt & Whitney
Rolls-Royce
SIFCO
TIMCO Aviation
Triumph Group
Wyman-Gordon

HISTORICAL FINANCIALS

Company Type: Public

Income Statement			FYE: October 31
	REVENUE ($ mil.)	NET INCOME ($ mil.)	NET PROFIT MARGIN	EMPLOYEES
10/09	538.3	44.6	8.3%	2,100
10/08	582.3	48.5	8.3%	2,328
10/07	507.9	39.0	7.7%	2,185
10/06	392.2	31.9	8.1%	1,843
10/05	269.6	22.8	8.5%	1,556
Annual Growth	18.9%	18.3%	—	7.8%

2009 Year-End Financials

Debt ratio: 12.1%
Return on equity: 10.2%
Cash ($ mil.): 7.2
Current ratio: 3.72
Long-term debt ($ mil.): 55.2
No. of shares (mil.): 26.2
Dividends
  Yield: 0.3%
  Payout: 7.3%
Market value ($ mil.): 994.6
R&D as % of sales: —
Advertising as % of sales: —

Stock History

NYSE: HEI

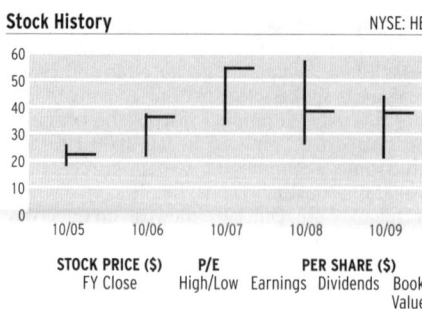

	STOCK PRICE ($) FY Close	P/E High/Low		PER SHARE ($) Earnings	Dividends	Book Value
10/09	38.03	27	13	1.65	0.12	17.51
10/08	38.47	32	15	1.78	0.10	15.97
10/07	54.44	38	23	1.45	0.08	14.21
10/06	36.28	31	18	1.20	0.08	12.13
10/05	22.17	29	21	0.87	0.05	10.46
Annual Growth	14.4%	—	—	17.4%	24.5%	13.7%

Henry Bros. Electronics

Security systems integrator Henry Bros. Electronics (formerly Diversified Security Solutions) designs, installs, and maintains closed-circuit television (CCTV) and access control systems. The company also installs system components such as CCTVs, intercoms, alarm monitors, video recorders, and card access controls. Henry Bros. Electronics markets its services to large and medium-sized businesses and to government agencies. Revenues from the government represent about 40% of the company's sales. New York, New Jersey, and California account for two-thirds of business.

Installation and maintenance of security systems accounts for most of Henry Bros. Electronics' revenue; the company also sells specialized wireless communications equipment used in mobile security applications.

The company, which was founded in 1952 as Henry Bros. Electronics but later sold, changed its name from Diversified Security Solutions to Henry Bros. Electronics in 2005.

Vice chairman Richard Rockwell owns about 35% of the company; chairman and CEO James Henry owns more than 20%.

EXECUTIVES

Chairman and CEO: James E. (Jim) Henry, age 54, $174,148 total compensation
Vice Chairman: Richard D. (Rick) Rockwell, age 53
President, COO, and Director: Brian L. Reach, age 53, $183,645 total compensation
CFO: John P. Hopkins, age 48, $206,879 total compensation
CTO: Emil J. Marone
Controller: Brian J. Smith, age 54, $112,258 total compensation

CIO and Chief Security Officer: Christopher D. (Chris) Peckham, age 43, $41,465 total compensation
VP Business Development: David (Dave) Fitzgerald, age 52
VP Human Resources: T. Robert (Bob) Hodgson
Director Operations, Airorlite: John A. Batsch
Director Business Development, DSSI: Bruce DeBon
Auditors: Amper, Politziner & Mattia, P.C.

LOCATIONS

HQ: Henry Bros. Electronics, Inc.
  17-01 Pollitt Dr., Fair Lawn, NJ 07410
Phone: 201-794-6500   **Fax:** 201-794-8341
Web: www.hbe-inc.com

COMPETITORS

ADT Security
Bosch
Checkpoint Systems
Extreme CCTV
GE Security
Honeywell International
MDI
Sentry Technology
Vicon Industries

HISTORICAL FINANCIALS

Company Type: Public

Income Statement			FYE: December 31
	REVENUE ($ mil.)	NET INCOME ($ mil.)	NET PROFIT MARGIN	EMPLOYEES
12/08	62.4	1.6	2.6%	246
12/07	57.9	(0.3)	—	205
12/06	42.1	(2.3)	—	198
12/05	42.2	1.1	2.6%	172
12/04	29.7	0.0	—	148
Annual Growth	20.4%	—	—	13.5%

2008 Year-End Financials

Debt ratio: 30.2%
Return on equity: 10.7%
Cash ($ mil.): 0.0
Current ratio: 1.91
Long-term debt ($ mil.): 4.9
No. of shares (mil.): 6.0
Dividends
  Yield: 0.0%
  Payout: —
Market value ($ mil.): 36.2
R&D as % of sales: —
Advertising as % of sales: —

Stock History

NASDAQ (CM): HBE

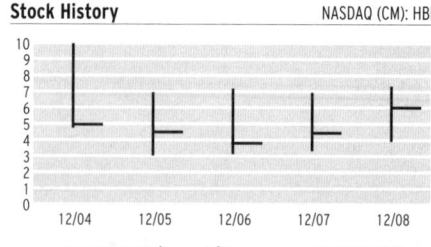

	STOCK PRICE ($) FY Close	P/E High/Low		PER SHARE ($) Earnings	Dividends	Book Value
12/08	6.00	28	15	0.26	0.00	2.66
12/07	4.43	—	—	(0.05)	0.00	2.31
12/06	3.79	—	—	(0.39)	0.00	2.32
12/05	4.48	36	16	0.19	0.00	2.66
12/04	4.95	990	481	0.01	0.00	2.44
Annual Growth	4.9%	—	—	125.8%	—	2.2%

Heritage Oaks Bancorp

Stash your acorns at Heritage Oaks Bancorp. It's the holding company for Heritage Oaks Bank, which serves retail customers, farmers, and small to midsized businesses in central California's San Luis Obispo and Santa Barbara counties. Through about a dozen offices, the bank offers standard products such as checking, savings, and money market accounts, CDs, IRAs, and credit cards. Commercial real estate loans account for more than 40% of its loan portfolio; business loans make up nearly 25%. Land loans are the third-largest segment of its portfolio. In 2007 Heritage Oaks Bancorp acquired Business First National Bank (now simply Business First), which operates as a division of Heritage Oaks Bank with two locations.

EXECUTIVES

Chairman, Heritage Oaks Bancorp and Heritage Oaks Bank: Michael J. Morris, age 63
Vice Chairman, Heritage Oaks Bancorp and Heritage Oaks Bank: Donald H. Campbell, age 67
President and CEO, Heritage Oaks Bancorp and Heritage Oaks Bank: Lawrence P. Ward, age 57, $599,976 total compensation
EVP Human Resources, Heritage Oaks Bancorp and Heritage Oaks Bank: Joni Watson, age 54
EVP and Southern Regional Manager, Heritage Oaks Bank: Mark W. Stasinis, age 58, $251,448 total compensation
EVP and Chief Lending Officer: Paul Tognazzini, age 59, $249,571 total compensation
EVP and CFO, Heritage Oaks Bancorp and Heritage Oaks Bank: Margaret A. Torres, age 58, $288,207 total compensation
EVP; President, Business First Bank: Joanne Funari, age 49, $228,648 total compensation
EVP, COO, and Chief Credit Officer, Heritage Oaks Bank: Ronald Oliveira, age 53
EVP and General Counsel: William (Bill) Raver, age 54
EVP Client Services, Heritage Oaks Bank: Craig Heyl, age 61
SVP Mortgage Department: Frederick J. Bond
Investor Relations: Tana L. Eade
Auditors: Vavrinek, Trine, Day & Co., LLP

LOCATIONS

HQ: Heritage Oaks Bancorp
545 12th St., Paso Robles, CA 93446
Phone: 805-239-5200   **Fax:** 805-238-6257
Web: www.heritageoaksbancorp.com

COMPETITORS

Bank of America
Bank of the West
Coast Bancorp
Mission Community Bancorp
Rabobank America
Santa Lucia Bancorp
Wells Fargo

HISTORICAL FINANCIALS

Company Type: Public

Income Statement

FYE: December 31

	ASSETS ($ mil.)	NET INCOME ($ mil.)	INCOME AS % OF ASSETS	EMPLOYEES
12/08	805.6	1.6	0.2%	223
12/07	745.6	6.9	0.9%	242
12/06	541.8	6.7	1.2%	212
12/05	488.5	6.6	1.4%	190
12/04	448.0	4.6	1.0%	170
Annual Growth	**15.8%**	**(23.2%)**	**—**	**7.0%**

2008 Year-End Financials

Equity as % of assets: 8.7%
Return on assets: 0.2%
Return on equity: 2.3%
Long-term debt ($ mil.): 23.4
No. of shares (mil.): 7.8
Market value ($ mil.): 39.0
Dividends
  Yield: 1.5%
  Payout: 38.1%
Sales ($ mil.): 43.8
R&D as % of sales: —
Advertising as % of sales: —

Stock History

NASDAQ (CM): HEOP

	STOCK PRICE ($) FY Close	P/E High/Low		PER SHARE ($) Earnings	Dividends	Book Value
12/08	5.02	60	22	0.21	0.08	9.03
12/07	12.00	19	13	0.95	0.30	8.95
12/06	16.37	23	15	0.96	0.15	6.38
12/05	19.52	23	13	0.96	0.00	5.78
12/04	12.58	19	14	0.68	0.00	4.80
Annual Growth	**(20.5%)**	**—**	**—**	**(25.5%)**	**—**	**17.1%**

HF Financial

Those in South Dakota who want their finances to go north might turn to HF Financial. It's the holding company for Home Federal Bank, which serves consumers and businesses through more than 30 branches in eastern and central South Dakota and a single branch in southwestern Minnesota. Deposit products include checking and savings accounts and CDs. Commercial mortgages and loans account for about 40% of HF Financial's loan portfolio. Residential, multifamily, and agricultural real estate loans account for another 30% of loans. Bank subsidiary Hometown Insurors sells insurance and annuities; Mid America Capital provides equipment financing. Home Federal Bank was founded in 1929.

EXECUTIVES

Chairman, President, and CEO; Chairman and CEO Home Federal Bank: Curtis L. Hage, age 64, $987,197 total compensation
Corporate EVP, CFO, and Treasurer: Darrel L. Posegate, age 52, $565,095 total compensation
SVP, CFO, and Treasurer, Home Federal Bank: Brent R. Olthoff, age 39, $207,892 total compensation
SVP Service and Support, Home Federal Bank: Natalie A. Sundvold, age 47
SVP Human Resources, Home Federal Bank: Mary F. Hitzemann, age 57
SVP Wealth Management, Home Federal Bank: Jon M. Gadberry, age 49, $258,781 total compensation
SVP Business Banking, Home Federal Bank: David A. Brown, age 49, $295,269 total compensation
SVP Retail Banking, Home Federal Bank: Michael Westberg, age 43
VP and Controller, Home Federal Bank: Bruce E. Hanson, age 46
Corporate Secretary: Pamela F. Russo
Auditors: Eide Bailly LLP

LOCATIONS

HQ: HF Financial Corp.
225 S. Main Ave., Sioux Falls, SD 57104
Phone: 605-333-7556   **Fax:** 605-333-7621
Web: www.homefederal.com

PRODUCTS/OPERATIONS

2009 Gross Revenues

	$ mil.	% of total
Interest		
Loans & leases receivable	49.5	67
Investment securities & interest-bearing deposits	11.2	15
Noninterest		
Fees on deposits	5.8	8
Loan servicing income	2.3	3
Net gain on sale of loans	1.9	3
Other	2.6	4
Total	**73.3**	**100**

COMPETITORS

Citigroup
First National of Nebraska
Great Western Bancorporation
Meta Financial Group
U.S. Bancorp

HISTORICAL FINANCIALS

Company Type: Public

Income Statement

FYE: June 30

	ASSETS ($ mil.)	NET INCOME ($ mil.)	INCOME AS % OF ASSETS	EMPLOYEES
6/09	1,176.8	7.8	0.7%	323
6/08	1,103.5	5.8	0.5%	307
6/07	1,001.5	5.4	0.5%	315
6/06	961.3	4.5	0.5%	312
6/05	897.9	5.2	0.6%	309
Annual Growth	**7.0%**	**10.7%**	**—**	**1.1%**

2009 Year-End Financials

Equity as % of assets: 5.8%
Return on assets: 0.7%
Return on equity: 11.7%
Long-term debt ($ mil.): 240.7
No. of shares (mil.): 4.0
Market value ($ mil.): 47.8
Dividends
  Yield: 3.8%
  Payout: 28.0%
Sales ($ mil.): 47.9
R&D as % of sales: —
Advertising as % of sales: —

	STOCK PRICE ($)	P/E		PER SHARE ($)		
	FY Close	High/Low	Earnings	Dividends	Book Value
6/09	11.82	10 6	1.61	0.45	16.98
6/08	16.30	13 10	1.45	0.43	15.88
6/07	17.52	14 12	1.33	0.42	15.40
6/06	17.10	17 14	1.13	0.41	13.86
6/05	19.86	19 10	1.29	0.40	13.26
Annual Growth	(12.2%)	— —	5.7%	3.0%	6.4%

Hiland Holdings

Hiland Holdings lets Hiland Partners do all the work. The company owns a 2% general partner interest in the natural gas gathering and processing company. Hiland Partners serves primarily the Mid-Continent and Rocky Mountain regions of the US. It maintains natural gas gathering systems, processing plants, treating facilities, and NGL fractionation facilities. Hiland Partners supplies natural gas and NGL products to transmission pipelines and various markets. Hiland Partners chairman Harold Hamm owns about 32% of Hiland Holdings and plans to take both companies private.

Hiland Partners emerged from a subsidiary of Continental Resources, to which it still provides compressed air and water for use in oil and gas secondary recovery operations. Continental Resources then sends its natural gas to Hiland Partners for processing.

Hiland Holdings provided funding for Hiland Partners' 2006 acquisition of natural gas gathering pipelines and other assets from Enogex in exchange for the partnership interests in Hiland Partners.

In 2009, in a move to consolidate his control, Hamm made an offer to acquire all of the shares of Hiland Partners and Hiland Holdings.

EXECUTIVES

Chairman: Harold G. Hamm, age 63
President, CEO, and Director: Joseph L. (Joe) Griffin, age 48, $660,690 total compensation
VP and COO: Kent Christopherson, age 51, $253,363 total compensation
VP Finance, CFO, Secretary, and Director: Matthew S. (Matt) Harrison, age 38, $499,900 total compensation
Director Information Technology: Jason Vann
Director Project Management: Mike Higgins
Director Engineering: Matthew Briscoe
Director Field Operations: Dwight VanDolah
Director Product Sales, Scheduling and Contract Administration: Mika Dick
Director Human Resources: Vanessa Gainer
Director Gas Supply, Arkoma Basin and Woodford Shale: Ron Hill, age 59
Business Development and Investor Relations: Derek Gipson
Auditors: Grant Thornton LLP

LOCATIONS

HQ: Hiland Holdings GP, LP
205 W. Maple, Ste. 1100, Enid, OK 73701
Phone: 580-242-6040 **Fax:** 580-548-5188
Web: www.hilandpartners.com

COMPETITORS

Atlas Energy
Belden & Blake
DCP Midstream Partners
Equitrans

HISTORICAL FINANCIALS

Company Type: Public

Income Statement

	REVENUE ($ mil.)	NET INCOME ($ mil.)	NET PROFIT MARGIN	EMPLOYEES
12/08	388.0	11.7	3.0%	121
12/07	278.0	5.2	1.9%	108
12/06	219.7	2.4	1.1%	95
12/05	166.6	0.9	0.5%	89
12/04	98.3	4.9	5.0%	—
Annual Growth	41.0%	24.3%	—	10.8%

2008 Year-End Financials

Debt ratio: —
Return on equity: —
Cash ($ mil.): 1.7
Current ratio: 1.04
Long-term debt ($ mil.): 256.5
No. of shares (mil.): 21.6

Dividends
Yield: 48.8%
Payout: 214.8%
Market value ($ mil.): 51.2
R&D as % of sales: —
Advertising as % of sales: —

	STOCK PRICE ($)	P/E		PER SHARE ($)		
	FY Close	High/Low	Earnings	Dividends	Book Value
12/08	2.37	54 4	0.54	1.16	—
12/07	27.35	176 94	0.24	0.87	1.02
12/06	28.90	327 208	0.09	0.00	1.90
Annual Growth	(71.4%)	— —	144.9%	—	(46.2%)

Hiland Partners

Hiland Partners is looking for the higher ground of increased profits. The company was formed through the combination of Hiland Partners LLC and Continental Gas, a former subsidiary of Continental Resources. Hiland provides natural gas gathering and processing services to customers in the Mid-Continent and Rocky Mountain regions of the US through 14 gas gathering systems with 2,024 miles of pipeline, five natural gas processing plants, seven natural gas treating facilities, and three NGL fractionation plants. It also provides air compression and water injection services for oil and gas recovery operations in North Dakota. Chair-

man Harold Hamm owns 61% of the company, but has made a bid for total ownership.

Hiland Partners has employed a strategy of pursuing construction and expansion projects and making complementary acquisitions of midstream assets in its operating areas.

In 2006 the company acquired more than 550 miles of natural gas gathering pipelines and other assets from Enogex Gas Gathering for $93 million.

The next year Hiland Partners completed the expansion of its Badlands (North Dakota) gathering system, the associated field gathering infrastructure, and processing plant.

In 2009, in a move to consolidate his control and take the company private, Hamm made an offer to acquire all of the shares of Hiland Partners and its general partner, Hiland Holdings GP, LP.

EXECUTIVES

Chairman, Hiland Partners GP, LLC: Harold G. Hamm, age 63
President, CEO, and Director, Hiland Partners GP, LLC: Joseph L. (Joe) Griffin, age 48, $646,190 total compensation
VP and COO, Hiland Partners and Hiland Holdings GP: Kent Christopherson, age 51, $253,363 total compensation
VP Finance and Business Development, CFO, Secretary, and Director: Matthew S. (Matt) Harrison, age 38, $449,532 total compensation
Auditors: Grant Thornton LLP

LOCATIONS

HQ: Hiland Partners, LP
205 W. Maple, Ste. 1100, Enid, OK 73701
Phone: 580-242-6040 **Fax:** 580-548-5188
Web: www.hilandpartners.com

PRODUCTS/OPERATIONS

2008 Sales

	% of total
Midstream operations	
Third parties	96
Affiliates	3
Compression services	1
Total	**100**

COMPETITORS

Atlas Energy
Belden & Blake
DCP Midstream Partners
Enogex
Equitrans

HISTORICAL FINANCIALS

Company Type: Public

Income Statement

	REVENUE ($ mil.)	NET INCOME ($ mil.)	NET PROFIT MARGIN	EMPLOYEES
12/08	388.0	20.4	5.3%	121
12/07	278.0	6.3	2.3%	108
12/06	219.7	14.7	6.7%	95
12/05	166.6	10.3	6.2%	67
12/04	98.3	4.9	5.0%	51
Annual Growth	41.0%	42.8%	—	24.1%

2008 Year-End Financials

Debt ratio: —
Return on equity: —
Cash ($ mil.): 1.2
Current ratio: 1.05
Long-term debt ($ mil.): 256.5
No. of shares (mil.): 9.4

Dividends
Yield: 65.6%
Payout: 227.7%
Market value ($ mil.): 48.0
R&D as % of sales: —
Advertising as % of sales: —

Stock History

NASDAQ (GS): HLND

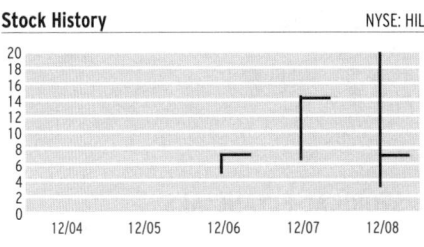

	STOCK PRICE ($) FY Close	P/E High/Low		PER SHARE ($) Earnings	Dividends	Book Value
12/08	5.13	35	2	1.48	3.37	—
12/07	50.55	92	27	0.67	2.91	—
12/06	54.70	42	27	1.36	2.65	—
12/05	36.81	35	21	1.32	1.20	—
Annual Growth	(48.2%)	—	—	3.9%	—	—

Hill International

Hill International, a leader in the construction advice business, is far from over the hill. The company offers project management and construction claims consulting services worldwide. It manages all aspects of the construction process, from pre-design through completion — even troubled project turnaround. Construction claims services include expert witness testimony and litigation support. The company provides its services for such clients as the Arizona Diamondbacks, Consolidated Edison, Kimpton Hotel & Restaurant Group, and Walt Disney. It also counts US government agencies and international governments among its clients. Hill International operates out of 80 offices in more than 30 countries.

In addition to the US, the company has operations in the Asia/Pacific region, Europe, and the Middle East/North Africa. It serves private, public, and government clients in a wide range of industries, including construction, environmental, high-tech, oil and gas, power, telecommunications, and transportation.

An integral part of its business strategy is to buy smaller competitors domestically and abroad. It acquired TRS Consultants in 2010. TRS provides civil engineering, program management, construction management, and information technology services in northern California. The previous year it acquired Boyken International, which operates in the South and the Caribbean.

Other deals have included the acquisitions of the West Coast-based KJM & Associates, UK-based firms John Shreeves Holdings and James R. Knowles (Holdings), Poland's Euromost Polska, a majority stake in Spanish firm Gerens Management, and London firm John Shreeves & Partners. In 2008 Hill International bought planning and project management services provider PCI Group, adding about a half-dozen offices in the western US.

Hill International has provided construction management services for projects such as the Comcast Center in Philadelphia and New York New York Hotel & Casino in Las Vegas. It is also taking on one of the world's largest and most ambitious retail outlet projects, the City of Arabia Mall development in Dubai.

Hill International went public in 2006 via a reverse acquisition of Arpeggio Acquisition, a special-purpose acquisition company. Upon completion of the deal, Arpeggio Acquisition changed its name to Hill International.

The family of chairman and CEO Irwin Richter and president and COO David Richter own about 32% of Hill International; Wells Fargo holds a 16% stake.

EXECUTIVES

Chairman and CEO: Irvin E. Richter, age 65, $1,889,504 total compensation
President, COO, and Director: David L. Richter, age 42, $1,436,148 total compensation
SVP and CFO: John Fanelli III, age 55, $343,429 total compensation
SVP and Chief Administrative Officer: Catherine H. (Cathy) Emma, age 50
SVP and CIO: Michael J. Petrisko, age 43
SVP and Director Transportation Group: James W. Palmer
SVP and Chief Accounting Officer: Ronald F. (Ron) Emma, age 58
SVP and General Counsel: William H. (Bill) Dengler Jr., age 43
SVP and Director Federal Buildings Group: Robert C. Hixon
VP Marketing and Corporate Communications: John P. Paolin
CEO, Hill TMG: Robert L. Houser
President, Construction Claims Group: Frederic Z. (Fred) Samelian, age 62, $695,175 total compensation
President, Project Management Group (Americas): Thomas J. (Tom) Spearing III, age 43
President, Project Management Group (International): Raouf S. Ghali, age 48, $868,425 total compensation
Auditors: Amper, Politziner & Mattia, P.C.

LOCATIONS

HQ: Hill International, Inc.
303 Lippincott Centre, Marlton, NJ 08053
Phone: 856-810-6200   **Fax:** 856-810-1309
Web: www.hillintl.com

2008 Sales

	$ mil.	% of total
Americas	118.5	31
Middle East	118.0	31
Europe	115.0	30
North Africa	21.6	6
Asia/Pacific	7.4	2
Total	**380.5**	**100**

PRODUCTS/OPERATIONS

2008 Sales

	$ mil.	% of total
Consulting fees	333.9	88
Reimbursable expenses	46.6	12
Total	**380.5**	**100**

Selected Services

Construction claims services
  Analysis and review
  Claims preparation
  Contract review and assessment
  Cost and damages assessment
  Delay and disruption analysis
  Expert witness testimony
  Litigation support
  Strategic advisory services
Project management services
  Construction management
  Estimating and cost management
  Management consulting
  Program management
  Project labor agreements
  Project management
  Project management oversight
  Staff augmentation
  Troubled project turnaround

COMPETITORS

Balfour Beatty
Bechtel
Fluor
Gilbane
GREYHAWK
Hunt Construction
Mtech Group
Parsons Brinckerhoff
Parsons Corporation
Skanska
Turner Corporation

HISTORICAL FINANCIALS

Company Type: Public

Income Statement

FYE: December 31

	REVENUE ($ mil.)	NET INCOME ($ mil.)	NET PROFIT MARGIN	EMPLOYEES
12/08	380.5	17.7	4.7%	2,342
12/07	290.3	14.1	4.9%	1,800
12/06	197.5	8.6	4.4%	1,426
Annual Growth	38.8%	43.5%	—	28.2%

2008 Year-End Financials

Debt ratio: 11.8%
Return on equity: 13.4%
Cash ($ mil.): 20.4
Current ratio: 2.00
Long-term debt ($ mil.): 16.0
No. of shares (mil.): 38.8

Dividends
Yield: 0.0%
Payout: —
Market value ($ mil.): 273.0
R&D as % of sales: —
Advertising as % of sales: —

Stock History

NYSE: HIL

	STOCK PRICE ($) FY Close	P/E High/Low		PER SHARE ($) Earnings	Dividends	Book Value
12/08	7.04	46	8	0.43	0.00	3.49
12/07	14.17	32	15	0.45	0.00	3.31
12/06	7.15	16	11	0.46	0.00	1.19
Annual Growth	(0.8%)	—	—	(3.3%)	—	71.6%

Hingham Institution for Savings

The Hingham Institution for Savings is a haven for wayward cash. The company has a handful of branches in Boston's south shore communities, operating in Boston, Cohasset, Hingham, Hull, Scituate, and South Weymouth, Massachusetts. Founded in 1834, the bank offers a wide variety of checking and savings products for individuals and businesses. Commercial mortgages make up about half of the bank's loan portfolio; residential mortgages represent about 40%. Hingham Institution for Savings also provides construction, business, and personal loans.

EXECUTIVES

President, CEO, and Director: Robert H. Gaughen Jr.
SVP and Treasurer: Deborah J. Jackson
VP Administration: William M. Donovan Jr.
VP Commercial Lending: William G. Bowers Jr.
VP Branch Operations: Thomas I. Chew
VP Commercial Lending: Shawn T. Sullivan
VP Commercial Lending: Peter R. Smollett
VP: Edward P. Zec
VP Retail Lending: Michael J. Sinclair
Auditors: Wolf & Company, P.C.

LOCATIONS

HQ: Hingham Institution for Savings
55 Main St., Hingham, MA 02043
Phone: 781-749-2200   **Fax:** 781-749-7835
Web: www.hinghamsavings.com

PRODUCTS/OPERATIONS

2008 Gross Revenues

	$ mil.	% of total
Interest		
Loans	39.5	88
Securities	2.3	5
Other	1.5	3
Noninterest		
Service charges on deposit accounts	0.9	2
Other	0.7	2
Total	**44.9**	**100**

COMPETITORS

Bank of America
Citizens Financial Group
Eastern Bank
Independent Bank (MA)
Sovereign Bank

HISTORICAL FINANCIALS

Company Type: Public

Income Statement			FYE: December 31	
	ASSETS ($ mil.)	NET INCOME ($ mil.)	INCOME AS % OF ASSETS	EMPLOYEES
12/08	806.2	6.3	0.8%	101
12/07	744.6	4.5	0.6%	—
12/06	691.7	4.6	0.7%	80
12/05	628.3	6.2	1.0%	81
12/04	547.1	5.8	1.1%	81
Annual Growth	**10.2%**	**2.1%**	**—**	**5.7%**

2008 Year-End Financials

Equity as % of assets: 7.4%	Dividends
Return on assets: 0.8%	Yield: 3.2%
Return on equity: 11.0%	Payout: 27.4%
Long-term debt ($ mil.): 215.0	Sales ($ mil.): 23.0
No. of shares (mil.): 2.1	R&D as % of sales: —
Market value ($ mil.): 53.2	Advertising as % of sales: —

Stock History

NASDAQ (GM): HIFS

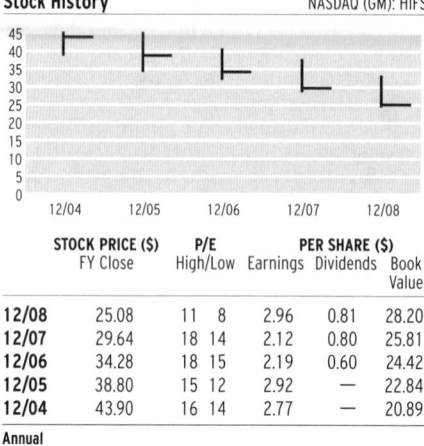

	STOCK PRICE ($) FY Close	P/E High/Low		PER SHARE ($) Earnings	Dividends	Book Value
12/08	25.08	11	8	2.96	0.81	28.20
12/07	29.64	18	14	2.12	0.80	25.81
12/06	34.28	18	15	2.19	0.60	24.42
12/05	38.80	15	12	2.92	—	22.84
12/04	43.90	16	14	2.77	—	20.89
Annual Growth	**(13.1%)**	**—**	**—**	**1.7%**	**16.2%**	**7.8%**

Hi-Tech Pharmacal

Hi-Tech Pharmacal combines imitation with innovation, making and distributing dozens of liquid and semi-solid prescription, over-the-counter, and nutritional products. The company primarily produces generic forms of prescription drugs, including off-brand versions of antibiotic Bactrim (made by Roche) and antihistamine Phenergan (a Pfizer drug, formerly of Wyeth), as well as prescription skin creams, mouthwashes, and pediatric multivitamins. Hi-Tech also makes branded over-the-counter products, including a line of products for diabetes patients and the Zostrix line of pain and arthritis medications. It has one branded prescription product, allergy medication Tanafed DMX.

Hi-Tech's expertise is with difficult to manufacture liquid and semi-solid products, including ophthalmic, otic, and inhaled pharmaceuticals. It provides contract manufacturing services to other drug firms needing this specialty.

Sales of generic drugs bring in most of Hi-Tech's revenue (more than 75%), and the company wants to speed up R&D and regulatory submissions in order to expand its core prescription drug line. Its generic product line is focused on oral solutions and suspensions, creams and ointments, and nasal sprays. In 2007 it acquired generic drug maker Midlothian Laboratories, gaining specialization in cough and cold products and prescription vitamins.

Hi-Tech sold the rights to another branded prescription drug, Naprelan, in 2007; it had previously acquired the pain medicine from Elan. However, branded drugs still are part of the company's future. The company has announced that it has agreed to purchase privately held ECR Pharmaceuticals for $5.1 million. ECR manufactures branded specialty prescription drugs (allergy, headache, dermatitis) and promotes them through an in-house force of sales representatives active in the mid-Atlantic and southern US.

The firm's Health Care Products division, which handles its branded OTC business, targets diabetes sufferers with such products as DiabetiSweet (sugar substitute), DiabetiDerm (moisturizing lotion), and DiabetiTrim (nutrition and weight loss drinks). It also makes topical pain cream Zostrix. It intends to continue developing new products for its niche diabetes market, possibly expanding into complementary areas such as podiatry.

Drug distributors and large drug retailers such as McKesson, Cardinal Health, and AmerisourceBergen are among the company's top customers.

The family of the company's founder Bernard Seltzer (who died in 2007) own about a quarter of the firm.

HISTORY

Reuben Seltzer started Hi-Tech Pharmacal's predecessor, Success Chemical, around 1930 in the back of his brother's drugstore in Brooklyn, New York. His son, Bernard, joined the company in the late 1940s and continued the business after his father died. The firm was acquired in 1967 by drug wholesaler Ketchum & Co. and adopted the name Ketchum Labs.

Seltzer and an associate bought the liquid and ointment division from Ketchum in 1981, creating Hi-Tech Pharmacal to make generic drugs. It went public in 1992 and started its Health Care Products division the next year to market hemorrhoid pads, cough remedies, and skin creams. In 1994 the company purchased Dr. Rose, Inc., a maker of generic over-the-counter and prescription suppositories, creams, and lotions.

In 1995 Hi-Tech Pharmacal introduced generic equivalents of constipation medications developed by what is now Sanofi-Aventis. In 1996 the company began marketing DiabetiSweet sugar substitute for diabetics and other people on special diets. That year the company opened a facility for making sterile ophthalmic and ear medication products. In 1996 and 1997 Hi-Tech Pharmacal won FDA approval for six new products, including a generic substitute for hairgrowth stimulant Rogaine. The next year it added a painkiller and pediatric antibiotic to its roster.

In 2000 Hi-Tech Pharmacal signed a co-marketing agreement with Diabetic.com, a Web site that targets the needs of individuals with diabetes. The company also launched its Kosher Care brand of products (cough, allergy, and pain treatments), aimed at the kosher consumer market. The following year the firm further bolstered its Internet presence with its acquisition of diabetic support site SweetThoughts.com.

EXECUTIVES

Chairman, President, CEO, Secretary, and Treasurer: David S. Seltzer, age 49, $603,000 total compensation
VP and CFO: William Peters, age 41, $384,000 total compensation
VP Operations: Eyal Mares, age 47
VP Sales and Marketing: Edwin A. Berrios, age 56
VP Information Systems: James P. Tracy, age 65
VP Pharmaceutical Operations, ECR Pharmaceuticals: Davis Caskey, age 61, $40,000 total compensation
VP and Controller: Margaret M. Santorufo, age 43
VP Corporate Development: Christopher LoSardo, age 43
Senior Director, Strategic Planning and Product Development and Director New Business Development: Tanya Akimova, age 55
Senior Director Science: Pudpong Poolsuk, age 65
Senior Director Research and Development: Polireddy Dondeti, age 44
Senior Director Quality Assurance: Jesse Kirsh, age 50

President, Health Care Products Division and Divisional VP, Sales: Gary M. April, age 52, $254,000 total compensation
President, Midlothian Laboratories Division: Bryce M. Harvey, age 53, $397,000 total compensation
Auditors: Eisner LLP

LOCATIONS

HQ: Hi-Tech Pharmacal Co., Inc.
369 Bayview Ave., Amityville, NY 11701
Phone: 631-789-8228　　**Fax:** 631-789-8429
Web: www.hitechpharm.com

PRODUCTS/OPERATIONS

2009 Sales

	% of total
Hi-Tech generics	82
Healthcare products	9
Midlothian Laboratories	6
ECR Pharmaceuticals	3
Total	**100**

Selected Products

Generic prescription drugs
　Acetaminophen & Codeine Phosphate oral solution
　　(Tylenol with codeine)
　Albuterol Sulfate Inhalation 0.5% solution (Proventil
　　inhalation)
　Albuterol Sulfate syrup (Ventolin syrup)
　Amantadine hydrochloride syrup (Symmetrel)
　Carbofed-DM syrup & drops (Rondec-DM)
　Chlorhexidine Gluconate oral rinse (Peridex)
　Cimetidine Hydrochloride oral solution (Tagamet)
　CP DEC Syrup (Rondec)
　Hydroxyzine hydrochloride syrup USP (Atarax)
　Lactulose Solution USP (Chronulac/Cephulac)
　Lidocaine 2% Solution USP (Xylocaine)
　Poly-Vitamin Drops with Iron & Fluoride (Poly-Vi-Flor
　　with Iron)
　Poly-Vitamin Drops with Fluoride (Poly-Vi-Flor)
　Promethazine HCI & Dextromethorphan Hbr Syrup
　　(Phenergan)
　Sulfamethoxazole and trimethoprim (Bactrim)
　Triple Tannate Pediatric Suspension (Rynatan)
　Tri-Vitamin Drops with Fluoride (Tri-Vi-Flor)
　Urea 40% cream, lotion, and gel
　Valproic Acid Syrup USP (Depakene)

Health Care Products Division
　Diabetic Tussin Allergy Relief Formula
　Diabetic Tussin Children's Formula
　Diabetic Tussin-Formula DM
　Diabetic Tussin-Formula EX
　DiabetiDerm Moisturizing Lotion for Severe Dry Skin
　DiabetiSweet
　DiabetiTrim
　Zostrix (pain relief)

Branded prescription drugs
　Tanafed DMX (cold/allergy)

COMPETITORS

Bayer AG
Bristol-Myers Squibb
Caraco Pharmaceutical
Forest Labs
GlaxoSmithKline
IMPAX Laboratories
Johnson & Johnson
K-V Pharmaceutical
Medicis Pharmaceutical
Merck
Mylan
Par Pharmaceutical Companies
Perrigo
Pfizer
Roche Holding
Sandoz International GmbH
Shionogi Pharma
Taro
Teva Pharmaceuticals USA
Watson Pharmaceuticals

HISTORICAL FINANCIALS

Company Type: Public

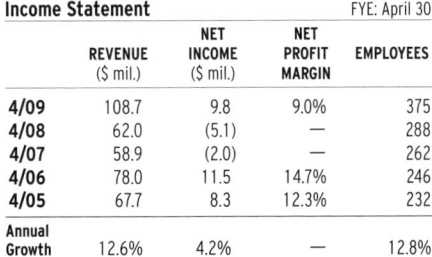

Income Statement

FYE: April 30

	REVENUE ($ mil.)	NET INCOME ($ mil.)	NET PROFIT MARGIN	EMPLOYEES
4/09	108.7	9.8	9.0%	375
4/08	62.0	(5.1)	—	288
4/07	58.9	(2.0)	—	262
4/06	78.0	11.5	14.7%	246
4/05	67.7	8.3	12.3%	232
Annual Growth	**12.6%**	**4.2%**	**—**	**12.8%**

2009 Year-End Financials

Debt ratio: 0.3%
Return on equity: 12.1%
Cash ($ mil.): 17.9
Current ratio: 3.82
Long-term debt ($ mil.): 0.2
No. of shares (mil.): 12.1
Dividends
　Yield: —
　Payout: —
Market value ($ mil.): 91.2
R&D as % of sales: —
Advertising as % of sales: —

Stock History

NASDAQ (GS): HITK

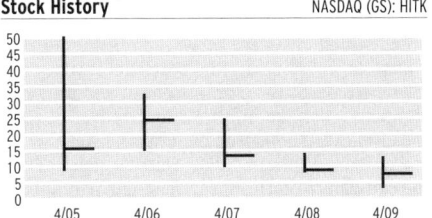

	STOCK PRICE ($) FY Close	P/E High/Low		PER SHARE ($) Earnings	Dividends	Book Value
4/09	7.55	15	4	0.84	—	7.15
4/08	8.75	—	—	(0.45)	—	6.22
4/07	13.24	—	—	(0.17)	—	6.87
4/06	24.41	38	18	0.85	—	7.32
4/05	15.57	78	14	0.64	—	5.77
Annual Growth	**(16.6%)**	**—**	**—**	**7.0%**	**—**	**5.5%**

Hittite Microwave

And lo, the Hittites did rise up out of their land, and they sacked Babylon. Actually, these Hittites rise up out of the Commonwealth of Massachusetts, and they're out to sell semiconductors. Hittite Microwave designs and develops microwave, millimeter-wave, and radio-frequency (RF) chips for aerospace, broadband, cellular, and military applications. In addition to amplifiers, frequency multipliers, mixers, modulators, switches, and other components, the company provides custom RF integrated circuits (ICs). Boeing and Motorola are among Hittite's hundreds of customers. The company gets more than half of its sales outside the US.

The global recession is posing drastic disruptions to the credit and financial markets, which affects Hittite, its customers, and its contractors and suppliers. The company doesn't see the uncertain economic conditions abating in 2009. Customer bookings are significantly down, and Hittite doesn't foresee revenue growth in the near term as a result. The company's 10 largest customers account for more than a third of sales. Hittite operates in a highly competitive segment of the semiconductor industry, which is notoriously cyclical.

Hittite Microwave is a fabless semiconductor company, which means that it contracts out the production of its chips to other companies, known as silicon foundries. Hittite's principal foundry contractors are Atmel, Cobham, Global Communication Semiconductors (GCS), IBM Microelectronics, Jazz Semiconductor, Taiwan Semiconductor Manufacturing, TriQuint Semiconductor, United Monolithic Semiconductors (UMS), and WIN Semiconductors. Hittite also competes with some of those companies with its microwave and RF ICs.

In 2007 the company licensed the Velocium line of monolithic microwave ICs and related intellectual property from Northrop Grumman Space Technology (now part of Northrop Grumman Aerospace Systems). Hittite assumed customer contracts from Northrop Grumman under the deal and became the worldwide supplier for the Velocium devices. The giant military contractor serves as a foundry contractor to Hittite in fabricating the products.

Hittite entered the electronic test and measurement market in 2008, debuting a line of signal generators. The microwave test instrument market is a natural extension for the company's technical expertise.

Founder Yalcin Ayasli owns about 28% of Hittite Microwave.

EXECUTIVES

Chairman, President, and CEO: Stephen G. Daly, age 43, $985,847 total compensation
CTO: Michael J. Koechlin, age 50
VP, CFO, and Treasurer: William W. Boecke, age 58, $545,400 total compensation
VP Operations: Brian J. Jablonski, age 50, $443,879 total compensation
VP: Norman G. Hildreth Jr., age 46, $546,986 total compensation
VP: Michael Olson, age 49, $348,205 total compensation
VP Hybrid Manufacturing: Everett N. Cole III
VP Global Operations: William D. Hannabach
VP Sales: Thomas D. H. Hwang
Manager MarCom (Marketing Communications): Beth McGreevy
Auditors: PricewaterhouseCoopers LLP

LOCATIONS

HQ: Hittite Microwave Corporation
20 Alpha Rd., Chelmsford, MA 01824
Phone: 978-250-3343　　**Fax:** 978-250-3373
Web: www.hittite.com

Hittite Microwave has facilities in Canada, China, Germany, Japan, South Korea, Sweden, Turkey, the UK, and the US.

2008 Sales

	$ mil.	% of total
US	73.4	41
China	34.3	19
Other countries	72.6	40
Total	**180.3**	**100**

PRODUCTS/OPERATIONS

Selected Products

Amplifiers
Attenuators
Frequency dividers and detectors
Frequency multipliers
Mixers and converters
Modulators
Oscillators
Sensors
Switches

COMPETITORS

Advanced Control Components	Merrimac Industries
ANADIGICS	NEC Electronics
Analog Devices	Peregrine Semiconductor
Avago Technologies	Powerwave Technologies
Cobham	RF Micro Devices
Endwave	RF Monolithics
Eudyna Devices	Rohde & Schwarz
L-3 Communications	Skyworks
Linear Technology	Tektronix
	TriQuint

HISTORICAL FINANCIALS
Company Type: Public

Income Statement				FYE: December 31
	REVENUE ($ mil.)	NET INCOME ($ mil.)	NET PROFIT MARGIN	EMPLOYEES
12/08	180.3	53.8	29.8%	332
12/07	156.4	51.2	32.7%	315
12/06	130.3	42.7	32.8%	267
12/05	80.7	20.1	24.9%	220
12/04	61.7	11.9	19.3%	186
Annual Growth	30.7%	45.8%	—	15.6%

2008 Year-End Financials
Debt ratio: 2.0%
Return on equity: 23.7%
Cash ($ mil.): 180.9
Current ratio: 17.58
Long-term debt ($ mil.): 4.7
No. of shares (mil.): 30.1
Dividends
  Yield: 0.0%
  Payout: —
Market value ($ mil.): 887.5
R&D as % of sales: —
Advertising as % of sales: —

Stock History
NASDAQ (GS): HITT

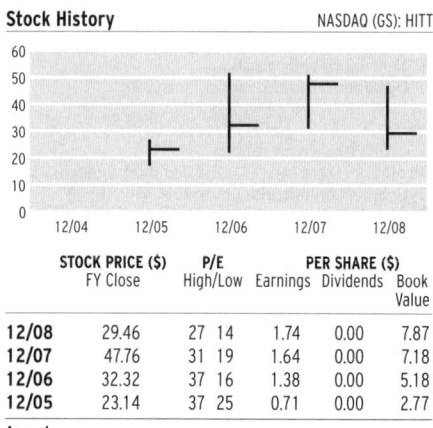

	STOCK PRICE ($) FY Close	P/E High/Low		PER SHARE ($) Earnings Dividends Book Value		
12/08	29.46	27	14	1.74	0.00	7.87
12/07	47.76	31	19	1.64	0.00	7.18
12/06	32.32	37	16	1.38	0.00	5.18
12/05	23.14	37	25	0.71	0.00	2.77
Annual Growth	8.4%	—	—	40.2%	—	77.8%

HMS Holdings

HMS Holdings makes sure government health providers are paying only as much as they have to. Through its Health Management Systems subsidiary, the company specializes in helping public programs (such as state Medicaid and child support agencies) identify and recover costs that should have been paid by a third party, or that were paid in error. It serves Medicaid programs in some 40 states, as well as Medicaid managed care plans, SCHIP programs, and veterans' health care facilities. Its Reimbursement Services Group subsidiary offers Medicare reimbursement services for hospitals. HMS Holdings has operations throughout the US.

HMS's largest clients are New York's Medicaid agency and the New Jersey Department of Human Services. Services provided by HMS include coordination of benefits, in which HMS works with other government agencies and private payors to make sure the right claim gets paid by the right program, and what it calls program integrity services, or the auditing of claims to find payments made in error.

The company is particularly focused on growing its program integrity business, which it expects will receive a boost from new federal mandates signed into law in 2006. In 2007 HMS bought Ohio-based Peer Review Systems (which does business as Permedion) to capitalize on these trends. Permedion brought 24 contracts in nine states, under which it reviews claims and predetermines the medical necessity of major medical procedures. The following year, HMS acquired Prudent Rx, which audits pharmacy providers and pharmacy claims.

Early in 2010 the company acquired Verify Solutions, a provider of dependent eligibility and other human resource services for group health plans, for $8 million (plus potential future performance payouts). The purchase widened the company's service offerings and moved it into the employer-sponsored benefits market.

President William Lucia was named CEO of the company in early 2009 after chairman Robert Holster stepped down from the position.

EXECUTIVES
Chairman: Robert M. Holster, age 63, $911,673 total compensation
CEO: William C. (Bill) Lucia, age 51, $883,457 total compensation
Chief Compliance Officer: Alexandra Holt
EVP Operations: Sean Curtin
EVP Government Markets: Maria Perrin
EVP Commercial Markets: Christina Dragonetti
SVP and CFO: Walter D. Hosp, age 51, $635,883 total compensation
VP Human Resources: John D. Schmid, age 61
Media Relations: Francesca Marraro
Investor Relations: Christine Rogers Saenz
Auditors: KPMG LLP

LOCATIONS
HQ: HMS Holdings Corp.
  401 Park Ave. South, New York, NY 10016
Phone: 212-857-5000   **Fax:** 212-857-5973
Web: www.hms.com

PRODUCTS/OPERATIONS

Selected Services
Coordination of benefits
Identification of third-party liability and recovery of payment
Program integrity services (identification and recovery of inappropriate payments)
SCHIP enrollment and compliance services

COMPETITORS
Affiliated Computer Services
Ernst & Young Global
McKesson
NCO
Perot Systems

HISTORICAL FINANCIALS
Company Type: Public

Income Statement				FYE: December 31
	REVENUE ($ mil.)	NET INCOME ($ mil.)	NET PROFIT MARGIN	EMPLOYEES
12/08	184.5	21.4	11.6%	922
12/07	146.7	15.0	10.2%	760
12/06	87.9	5.3	6.0%	578
12/05	60.0	8.0	13.3%	331
12/04	85.2	7.7	9.0%	516
Annual Growth	21.3%	29.1%	—	15.6%

2008 Year-End Financials
Debt ratio: 6.2%
Return on equity: 13.5%
Cash ($ mil.): 49.2
Current ratio: 3.43
Long-term debt ($ mil.): 11.0
No. of shares (mil.): 26.3
Dividends
  Yield: 0.0%
  Payout: —
Market value ($ mil.): 830.0
R&D as % of sales: —
Advertising as % of sales: —

Stock History
NASDAQ (GS): HMSY

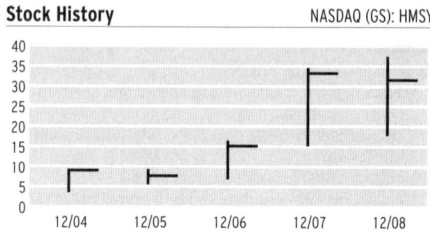

	STOCK PRICE ($) FY Close	P/E High/Low		PER SHARE ($) Earnings Dividends Book Value		
12/08	31.52	46	23	0.80	0.00	6.77
12/07	33.21	60	27	0.57	0.00	5.27
12/06	15.15	74	33	0.22	0.00	4.06
12/05	7.65	25	16	0.36	0.00	2.76
12/04	9.00	26	11	0.35	0.00	2.29
Annual Growth	36.8%	—	—	23.0%	—	31.1%

Holly Energy Partners

Holly Energy Partners is having a jolly good time piping petroleum. The company transports refined petroleum products and crude oil from Holly Corporation's Navajo refinery in New Mexico and Woods Cross refinery in Utah, and Alon USA's Big Spring refinery in Texas, to customers in the southwestern US. It operates 1,330 miles of refined petroleum pipelines (including 340 miles of leased pipelines), 11 distribution terminals, one jet fuel terminal, and two truck-loading facilities used to transport gasoline, diesel, and jet fuel. Holly Corporation, the parent of the company's general partner (Holly Logistics), holds a 46% stake in Holly Energy Partners.

Holly Energy Partners is integral to Holly Corporation's business growth. About 67% of the light refined products and crude oil from the Navajo refinery and 100% from the Woods Cross refinery are transported or stored in the infrastructure owned and operated by Holly Energy Partners. Furthering that relationship, in 2008 it acquired crude oil pipelines and tankage assets from Holly Corporation for $180 million. In 2009 it picked up the Roadrunner pipeline, a

65-mile pipeline connecting Holly's refining facilities in Lovington, New Mexico, to the terminus of a Centurion pipeline linking West Texas and Cushing, Oklahoma.

In 2005 Holly Energy Partners acquired more than 500 miles of pipelines and petroleum product terminals from Alon USA for $120 million. The company also acquired feedstock pipelines from Holly Corporation for $81.5 million.

EXECUTIVES

Chairman and CEO: Matthew P. (Matt) Clifton, age 57
President, Holly Energy Partners and Holly Logistic Services: David G. Blair, age 51, $744,232 total compensation
SVP and CFO: Bruce R. Shaw, age 42
VP Investor Relations, Holly Energy Partners and Holly Corporation: M. Neale Hickerson, age 57
VP and Treasurer: Stephen D. Wise
VP and Controller, Holly Logistic Services: Scott C. Surplus
VP Human Resources: Nancy F. Hartmann
VP Pipeline Operations: James G. Townsend, age 55
VP, Secretary, and General Counsel: W. John Glancy, age 67
Auditors: Ernst & Young LLP

LOCATIONS

HQ: Holly Energy Partners, L.P.
100 Crescent Ct., Ste. 1600, Dallas, TX 75201
Phone: 214-871-3555   **Fax:** 214-871-3560
Web: www.hollyenergy.com

PRODUCTS/OPERATIONS

2008 Sales

	$ mil.	% of total
Pipelines	103.3	88
Terminals & truck loading racks	14.8	12
Total	**118.1**	**100**

COMPETITORS

ExxonMobil Pipeline
Magellan Midstream
NuStar Energy
Shell Pipeline
Wolverine Pipe Line Company

HISTORICAL FINANCIALS

Company Type: Public

Income Statement

FYE: December 31

	REVENUE ($ mil.)	NET INCOME ($ mil.)	NET PROFIT MARGIN	EMPLOYEES
12/08	118.1	25.4	21.5%	121
12/07	102.7	36.3	35.3%	106
12/06	89.2	25.8	28.9%	89
12/05	80.1	26.1	32.6%	82
12/04	67.8	11.2	16.5%	73
Annual Growth	**14.9%**	**22.7%**	**—**	**13.5%**

2008 Year-End Financials

Debt ratio: —
Return on equity: —
Cash ($ mil.): 5.3
Current ratio: 0.35
Long-term debt ($ mil.): 355.8
No. of shares (mil.): 17.6

Dividends
Yield: 13.9%
Payout: 220.9%
Market value ($ mil.): 375.4
R&D as % of sales: —
Advertising as % of sales: —

Stock History

NYSE: HEP

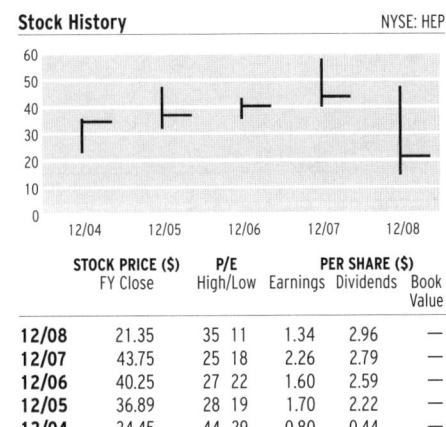

	STOCK PRICE ($) FY Close	P/E High/Low		PER SHARE ($) Earnings	Dividends	Book Value
12/08	21.35	35	11	1.34	2.96	—
12/07	43.75	25	18	2.26	2.79	—
12/06	40.25	27	22	1.60	2.59	—
12/05	36.89	28	19	1.70	2.22	—
12/04	34.45	44	29	0.80	0.44	—
Annual Growth	**(11.3%)**	**—**	**—**	**13.8%**	**61.0%**	

Home BancShares

At this Home, you don't have to stash your cash under the mattress. Instead, you can choose from a half-dozen bank subsidiaries in Arkansas and Florida. Home BancShares serves central and north central Arkansas through Bank of Mountain View, Centennial Bank, Community Bank, First State Bank, and Twin City Bank; it serves the Florida Keys and southwestern Florida through Marine Bank. With a combined network of some 50 branches, the banks offer checking, savings, NOW and money market accounts, and CDs. The banks focus on commercial real estate and development loans, which make up more than 60% of a lending portfolio that also includes residential mortgage, business, and other loans.

Non-bank subsidiaries provide bank customers with trust and title services and insurance products.

The company has grown through the addition of *de novo* branches, and continues to look for potential acquisitions in its geographical markets. It also buys established banks; its latest was the 2008 acquisition of Centennial Bank.

Chairman John Allison and his family own about 14% of Home BancShares; including his stake, executives and directors together own about 30% of the company.

EXECUTIVES

Chairman: John W. Allison, age 62, $824,985 total compensation
Vice Chairman: Robert H. Adcock Jr., age 60
CEO and Director: C. Randall (Randy) Sims, age 54, $524,073 total compensation
President, COO, and Director: Ron W. Strother, age 60, $390,705 total compensation
CFO and Treasurer: Randy E. Mayor, age 44, $561,323 total compensation

---

President, CEO, and Director, Centennial Bank: Chris S. Roberts, age 40
President, Centennial Bank: Teresa Condas
Regional President, Centennial Bank: Robert H. Padgett, age 50
President, CEO, and Director, Community Bank: Tracy M. French, age 47, $343,909 total compensation
President, CEO, and Director, Twin City Bank: Robert F. Birch Jr., age 59
CEO and Director, Bank of Mountain View: Michael L. (Mickey) Waddington, age 66
Director, Financial Reporting and Investor Relations: Brian S. Davis, age 43
Auditors: BKD, LLP

LOCATIONS

HQ: Home BancShares, Inc.
719 Harkrider, Conway, AR 72032
Phone: 501-328-4715   **Fax:** 501-328-4679
Web: www.homebancshares.com

Home BancShares has bank locations in the Arkansas counties of Faulkner, Lonoke, Pulaski, and Stone. It also has locations in Florida's Monroe County.

PRODUCTS/OPERATIONS

2008 Gross Revenues

	$ mil.	% of total
Interest		
Loans	127.8	73
Investment securities	17.5	10
Other	0.4	—
Noninterest		
Service charges on deposit accounts	13.7	8
Other service charges & fees	6.6	4
Mortgage banking	3.6	2
Increase in cash value of life insurance	2.1	1
Other	2.7	2
Total	**167.6**	**100**

COMPETITORS

Bank of America
Bank of Florida
Bank of the Ozarks
BB&T
First Federal Bancshares of Arkansas
Regions Financial
Simmons First
TIB Financial
U.S. Bancorp

HISTORICAL FINANCIALS

Company Type: Public

Income Statement

FYE: December 31

	ASSETS ($ mil.)	NET INCOME ($ mil.)	INCOME AS % OF ASSETS	EMPLOYEES
12/08	2,580.1	10.1	0.4%	594
12/07	2,291.6	20.4	0.9%	595
12/06	2,190.6	15.6	0.7%	562
12/05	1,911.5	10.9	0.6%	544
12/04	805.2	9.2	1.1%	567
Annual Growth	**33.8%**	**2.4%**	**—**	**1.2%**

2008 Year-End Financials

Equity as % of assets: 11.0%
Return on assets: 0.4%
Return on equity: 3.8%
Long-term debt ($ mil.): 330.5
No. of shares (mil.): 25.7
Market value ($ mil.): 692.2

Dividends
Yield: 0.8%
Payout: 44.0%
Sales ($ mil.): 114.8
R&D as % of sales: —
Advertising as % of sales: —

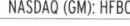

	STOCK PRICE ($)	P/E		PER SHARE ($)		
	FY Close	High/Low		Earnings	Dividends	Book Value
12/08	26.95	70	35	0.50	0.22	11.02
12/07	19.42	22	16	1.08	0.13	9.85
12/06	22.25	25	20	0.93	0.05	9.01
Annual Growth	10.1%	—	—	(26.7%)	109.8%	10.6%

HopFed Bancorp

HopFed Bancorp is the holding company for Heritage Bank (formerly Hopkinsville Federal Savings Bank), which started operations in 1879 as a building and loan association. The bank has about a dozen branches in southwestern Kentucky, with its market area extending into northwestern Tennessee. It offers standard products like checking, savings, money market, and NOW accounts, as well as CDs, IRAs, property/casualty insurance, and annuities. One- to four-family residential mortgages account for about 40% of its loan portfolio. To a lesser extent, Heritage Bank also writes multifamily residential, construction, commercial, and consumer loans. Directors and executives control 12% of the bank.

EXECUTIVES

President, CEO, and Director, HopFed Bancorp and Heritage Bank: John E. Peck, age 44, $341,954 total compensation
EVP and COO, Heritage Bank: Michael L. Woolfolk, age 55, $235,091 total compensation
SVP and Secretary; SVP Loan Administration, Heritage Bank: Boyd M. Clark, age 63, $151,600 total compensation
VP and Chief Credit Officer, HopFed Bancorp and Heritage Bank: Michael F. (Mike) Stalls, age 57, $193,877 total compensation
VP, CFO, and Treasurer, HopFed Bancorp and Heritage Bank: Billy C. Duvall, age 43, $169,458 total compensation
Market President, Calloway County: Jimmy D. Hicks
Market President, Cheatham County: Paige McVity
Market President, Marshall County: Paul Thurman
Market President, Montgomery and Houston County: Keith Bennett, age 47, $237,242 total compensation
Market President, Fulton County: Robert Burrow, age 54
Auditors: Rayburn, Betts & Bates, P.C.

LOCATIONS

HQ: HopFed Bancorp, Inc.
4155 Lafayette Rd., Hopkinsville, KY 42240
Phone: 270-885-1171   **Fax:** 270-889-0313
Web: www.bankwithheritage.com

COMPETITORS

Bank of America
BB&T
Fifth Third
Huntington Bancshares
U.S. Bancorp

HISTORICAL FINANCIALS

Company Type: Public

Income Statement   FYE: December 31

	ASSETS ($ mil.)	NET INCOME ($ mil.)	INCOME AS % OF ASSETS	EMPLOYEES
12/08	967.6	4.6	0.5%	233
12/07	808.4	4.1	0.5%	242
12/06	770.9	3.9	0.5%	217
12/05	639.6	4.1	0.6%	126
12/04	579.7	4.0	0.7%	133
Annual Growth	13.7%	3.6%	—	15.0%

2008 Year-End Financials

Equity as % of assets: 8.1%
Return on assets: 0.5%
Return on equity: 6.9%
Long-term debt ($ mil.): 140.3
No. of shares (mil.): 3.6
Market value ($ mil.): 35.9
Dividends
  Yield: 4.8%
  Payout: 37.8%
Sales ($ mil.): 31.4
R&D as % of sales: —
Advertising as % of sales: —

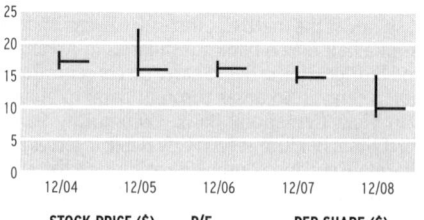

	STOCK PRICE ($)	P/E		PER SHARE ($)		
	FY Close	High/Low		Earnings	Dividends	Book Value
12/08	9.99	12	7	1.27	0.48	21.78
12/07	14.74	14	12	1.14	0.48	15.52
12/06	16.10	16	14	1.07	0.48	14.54
12/05	15.85	19	13	1.13	0.48	13.87
12/04	17.11	17	15	1.09	0.48	13.74
Annual Growth	(12.6%)	—	—	3.9%	0.0%	12.2%

Horizon Bancorp

Despite its name, Horizon Bancorp is on the up-and-up. It's the holding company for Horizon Bank, which serves northwest Indiana and southwest Michigan through about 20 branches. It provides local individuals and businesses such standard services as checking and savings accounts, IRAs, CDs, and credit cards. Commercial, financial, and agricultural loans make up the largest segment of Horizon's loan portfolio, which also includes mortgage warehouse loans (loans earmarked for sale into the secondary market), consumer installment loans, and residential mortgages. Through subsidiaries, the bank offers trust and investment management services, life and health insurance, property/casualty coverage, and annuities.

In 2009 Horizon announced plans to acquire the banking assets of American Trust & Savings

Bank in Whiting, Indiana. The deal will boost Horizon's assets and expand its market presence in northwest Indiana.

Wellington Management controls about 10% of Horizon Bancorp. Jeffrey Gendell's Tontine Financial Partners, Tontine Management, and Tontine Overseas Associates own about 9%. Tontine Management is an investment firm known for seeking out undervalued, well-managed financial stocks; this is one of its many holdings in banks and other financial institutions.

EXECUTIVES

Chairman: Robert C. Dabagia, age 70
CFO: Mark E. Secor, age 43, $180,596 total compensation
President, CEO, Chief Administrative Officer, and Director; Chairman and CEO, Horizon Bank: Craig M. Dwight, age 52, $486,146 total compensation
EVP; President and COO, Horizon Bank: Thomas H. Edwards, age 56, $249,081 total compensation
VP Marketing: Cindy Pavy
President, Elkhart County, Indiana, Horizon Bank: Christopher R. Wolfe
President, Porter County, Indiana, Horizon Bank: David G. Rose
President, Horizon Trust & Investment Management: Jeffry J. Trad
President, LaPorte County, Indiana, Horizon Bank: Steven C. Kring
President, Southwest Michigan, Horizon Bank: Donald E. (Don) Radde, age 56, $218,566 total compensation
President, North Central Indiana, Horizon Bank: Steven C. Watts, age 58
Secretary; EVP Mortgage Banking, Horizon Bank: James D. Neff, age 49, $329,023 total compensation
Investor Relations: Mary McColl
Auditors: BKD, LLP

LOCATIONS

HQ: Horizon Bancorp
515 Franklin Square, Michigan City, IN 46360
Phone: 219-879-0211   **Fax:** 219-874-9305
Web: www.accesshorizon.com

PRODUCTS/OPERATIONS

Selected Subsidiaries

Horizon Bank National Association
  Horizon Insurance Services, Inc.
  Horizon Investments, Inc.
  Horizon Trust & Investment Management, N.A.

COMPETITORS

1st Source Corporation	Farmers Mutual of NE
American United Mutual	Fifth Third
Bank of America	First Merchants
Brotherhood Mutual	Indiana Farmers Mutual

HISTORICAL FINANCIALS

Company Type: Public

Income Statement   FYE: December 31

	ASSETS ($ mil.)	NET INCOME ($ mil.)	INCOME AS % OF ASSETS	EMPLOYEES
12/08	1,306.9	9.0	0.7%	285
12/07	1,258.9	8.1	0.6%	265
12/06	1,222.4	7.5	0.6%	277
12/05	1,127.9	7.1	0.6%	283
12/04	913.8	6.9	0.8%	247
Annual Growth	9.4%	6.9%	—	3.6%

2008 Year-End Financials

Equity as % of assets: 6.1%
Return on assets: 0.7%
Return on equity: 12.0%
Long-term debt ($ mil.): 205.3
No. of shares (mil.): 3.3
Market value ($ mil.): 40.9

Dividends
  Yield: 5.3%
  Payout: 24.0%
Sales ($ mil.): 51.2
R&D as % of sales: —
Advertising as % of sales: —

Stock History NASDAQ (CM): HBNC

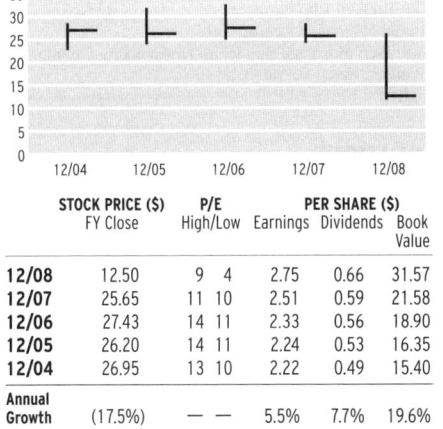

	STOCK PRICE ($) FY Close	P/E High/Low		PER SHARE ($) Earnings	Dividends	Book Value
12/08	12.50	9	4	2.75	0.66	31.57
12/07	25.65	11	10	2.51	0.59	21.58
12/06	27.43	14	11	2.33	0.56	18.90
12/05	26.20	14	11	2.24	0.53	16.35
12/04	26.95	13	10	2.22	0.49	15.40
Annual Growth	(17.5%)	—	—	5.5%	7.7%	19.6%

Hornbeck Offshore Services

At the beck and call of oil companies, Hornbeck Offshore Services provides marine transportation of oil field equipment and supplies and petroleum products. The company operates offshore supply vessels (OSVs) that support offshore oil and gas drilling and production in the deepwater regions of the Gulf of Mexico. The company's fleet of about 45 OSVs transports cargo such as pipe and drilling mud, as well as rig crew members. Hornbeck also operates oceangoing tug and tank barge units that transport crude and refined petroleum products in the Northeastern US, Great Lakes, and Puerto Rico as well as Mexico, Trinidad, Brazil, and Qatar. Its fleet includes about 15 tugs and 20 barges.

The company's OSVs, which were built beginning in 1997, were designed specifically to take advantage of the trend toward deepwater exploration in the Gulf of Mexico. Operations in US waters account for most of Hornbeck's sales, but the company also undertakes work in international offshore oil production areas. The vast majority of the company's vessels qualify to operate between US ports under the Jones Act, which requires vessels engaged in US coastwise trade to be built, owned, and crewed by US companies.

Due to a sharp drop in shipping demand caused by the global recession, in May 2009 Hornbeck sidelined five of its OSVs that operate in the Gulf of Mexico. A few months earlier, the company had laid up six tank barges and one tug that serve the same area. Hornbeck has been steadily expanding its fleet to include multi-purpose support vessels or MPSVs, which are designed to operate in deeper waters and have been less affected by the financial downturn. The company owns about five MPSVs.

Hornbeck also plans to grow by adding vessels to both its OSV fleet and its tug and tank barge fleet. It expanded significantly in 2007 when it bought 20 OSVs from Nabors Industries for about $186 million; in addition, it has about 15 vessels under construction, set to be delivered by 2010. Hornbeck also hopes to sell more services to existing customers, particularly to integrated oil and gas companies that can use OSVs in their exploration and production operations, and tug and tank barge units in their refining and marketing operations.

The William Herbert Hunt Trust Estate, represented on Hornbeck's board by Bruce Hunt, owns 8% of the company.

EXECUTIVES

Chairman, President, and CEO: Todd M. Hornbeck, age 40, $3,501,609 total compensation
EVP and COO: Carl G. Annessa, age 52, $1,696,760 total compensation
EVP and CFO: James O. Harp Jr., age 48, $1,701,133 total compensation
SVP and CIO: John S. Cook, age 39, $920,277 total compensation
SVP and General Counsel: Samuel A. Giberga, age 47, $1,011,185 total compensation
VP and General Manager, Tugs and Tank Barges: John Burns
VP and General Manager, HOS Operations: Andrew Bruzdzinski
VP and Chief Accounting Officer: Timothy P. McCarthy
Treasurer: Mark S. Myrtue
Auditors: Ernst & Young LLP

LOCATIONS

HQ: Hornbeck Offshore Services, Inc.
  103 Northpark Blvd., Ste. 300, Covington, LA 70433
Phone: 985-727-2000   **Fax:** 985-727-2006
Web: www.hornbeckoffshore.com

PRODUCTS/OPERATIONS

2008 Sales

	$ mil.	% of total
Offshore supply vessels		
US	262.2	61
Other countries	72.2	17
Tugs & tank barges		
US	88.2	20
Other countries	9.5	2
Total	**432.1**	**100**

COMPETITORS

Apex Oil
Chemoil
Colonial Pipeline
Crowley Maritime
GulfMark Offshore
Kinder Morgan
K-Sea Transportation
OSG America
Plantation Pipe Line
SEACOR
Siem Offshore
Tidewater Inc.
TMM
Trico Marine
U.S. Shipping

HISTORICAL FINANCIALS

Company Type: Public

Income Statement FYE: December 31

	REVENUE ($ mil.)	NET INCOME ($ mil.)	NET PROFIT MARGIN	EMPLOYEES
12/08	432.1	117.1	27.1%	1,113
12/07	339.0	94.8	28.0%	1,092
12/06	274.6	75.7	27.6%	742
12/05	182.6	37.4	20.5%	657
12/04	132.3	(2.5)	—	601
Annual Growth	34.4%	—	—	16.7%

2008 Year-End Financials

Debt ratio: 97.2%
Return on equity: 18.6%
Cash ($ mil.): 20.2
Current ratio: 1.97
Long-term debt ($ mil.): 674.6
No. of shares (mil.): 26.1

Dividends
  Yield: —
  Payout: —
Market value ($ mil.): 426.7
R&D as % of sales: —
Advertising as % of sales: —

Stock History NYSE: HOS

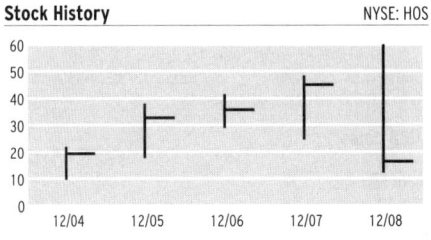

	STOCK PRICE ($) FY Close	P/E High/Low		PER SHARE ($) Earnings	Dividends	Book Value
12/08	16.34	14	3	4.33	—	26.59
12/07	44.95	13	7	3.58	—	21.53
12/06	35.70	15	11	2.76	—	17.42
12/05	32.70	23	11	1.64	—	16.45
12/04	19.30	—	—	(0.13)	—	7.00
Annual Growth	(4.1%)	—	—	—	—	39.6%

Houston American Energy

Houston-based, with North and South American properties, and energy focused, Houston American Energy explores for and produces oil and natural gas, primarily in Colombia, but also along the US Gulf Coast. In 2008 the company reported proved reserves of 18.8 million cu. ft. of natural gas and about 213,420 barrels of oil. Of its 5,360 gross acres of proved developed leasehold, about 30% is in Colombia. The bulk of the balance is in Louisiana and Texas, although the oil and gas independent also holds some acreage in Oklahoma. President and CEO John Terwilliger owns about 31% of Houston American Energy; director Orrie Tawes, 12%.

The company pursues a strategy of using advanced seismic techniques to more efficiently define prospects, and forms joint ventures and partnerships to spread the costs. It acts as a non-operating partner in the exploiting of its properties, relying on bigger and better financed exploration and production companies to conduct drilling operations through partnership deals.

Houston American Energy is putting its energy into exploiting its Colombian assets (15 wells drilled there in 2008, compared to one in the US), although given the political instability of Colombia in the past, the company's US assets act as a low-risk hedge to its South American activities.

In 2008 the company sold its stake in the Caracara Association Contract and related assets in Colombia for $11.5 million to free up cash to reinvest in its more productive Colombian prospects.

EXECUTIVES

Chairman, President, CEO, and Director:
John F. Terwilliger, age 61,
$1,736,772 total compensation
CFO: James J. (Jay) Jacobs, age 32,
$557,501 total compensation
Auditors: GBH CPAs, PC

LOCATIONS

HQ: Houston American Energy Corp.
801 Travis St., Ste. 2020, Houston, TX 77002
Phone: 713-222-6966   **Fax:** 713-222-6440
Web: www.houstonamericanenergy.com

2008 Sales

	$ mil.	% of total
South America	10.2	96
North America	0.4	4
Total	**10.6**	**100**

PRODUCTS/OPERATIONS

2008 Sales

	$ mil.	% of total
Oil	10.4	98
Gas	0.2	2
Total	**10.6**	**100**

COMPETITORS

Ecopetrol S.A.
Emerald Energy
Global Energy Development
HKN
Nexen
Pacific Rubiales
Petrobank Energy and Resources
Talisman Energy

HISTORICAL FINANCIALS

Company Type: Public

Income Statement

FYE: December 31

	REVENUE ($ mil.)	NET INCOME ($ mil.)	NET PROFIT MARGIN	EMPLOYEES
12/08	10.6	0.5	4.7%	3
12/07	5.0	0.5	10.0%	2
12/06	3.2	(0.5)	—	2
12/05	2.9	(0.5)	—	1
12/04	1.2	0.1	8.3%	1
Annual Growth	72.4%	49.5%	—	31.6%

2008 Year-End Financials

Debt ratio: —
Return on equity: 2.4%
Cash ($ mil.): 9.9
Current ratio: 8.62
Long-term debt ($ mil.): —
No. of shares (mil.): 28.0
Dividends
  Yield: 1.2%
  Payout: 200.0%
Market value ($ mil.): 94.6
R&D as % of sales: —
Advertising as % of sales: —

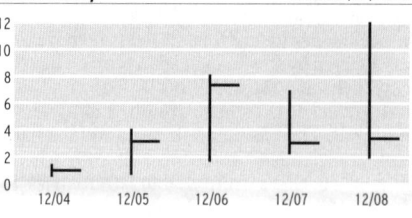

Stock History — NASDAQ (CM): HUSA

	STOCK PRICE ($) FY Close	P/E High/Low		PER SHARE ($) Earnings	Dividends	Book Value
12/08	3.38	599	101	0.02	0.04	0.75
12/07	3.05	345	115	0.02	0.00	0.72
12/06	7.36	—	—	(0.02)	0.00	0.69
12/05	3.15	—	—	(0.03)	0.00	0.03
12/04	0.98	135	60	0.01	0.00	0.04
Annual Growth	36.3%	—	—	18.9%	—	105.6%

Hudson City Bancorp

Hudson City Bancorp is the holding company for Hudson City Savings Bank. Founded in 1868, the bank has more than 125 branches in the New York City metropolitan area, including northern New Jersey, Long Island, and Fairfield County, Connecticut, as well as coastal portions of New Jersey and that state's Philadelphia suburbs. Serving middle- to high-income consumers, it originates and purchases high-quality first residential mortgages, which account for more than 98% of its loan portfolio. The bank gathers funds for its lending and investment activities by offering checking and savings accounts, CDs, and IRAs. In 2008 it began collecting deposits from customers nationwide through its online banking service.

Hudson City Savings also offers second mortgages and home equity lines of credit. It does not originate business loans or subprime mortgages. Subsidiary HC Value Broker Services sells life insurance products to bank customers.

In 2005 Hudson City Bancorp converted from a mutual holding company to a public stock company. The company bought Sound Federal Bancorp the following year. The acquisition gave Hudson City Savings entrée into the wealthy suburbs north of New York City, including Connecticut.

The bank has since focused on internal growth, hoping to take advantage of the turmoil in the industry. As most of its larger rivals have retrenched, Hudson City has grown both its loan volume and deposits. It is also expanding by opening new branches, adding about ten each year.

EXECUTIVES

Chairman, President, and CEO, Hudson City Bancorp and Hudson City Savings Bank:
Ronald E. Hermance Jr., age 61,
$10,590,630 total compensation
SEVP, COO, and Director, Hudson City Bancorp and Hudson City Savings Bank: Denis J. Salamone, age 56,
$4,909,286 total compensation
EVP and Chief Lending Officer, Hudson City Bancorp:
Thomas E. Laird, age 56,
$1,723,690 total compensation
EVP and CFO Hudson City Savings Bank:
James C. Kranz, age 60, $1,853,998 total compensation

SVP Information Services Hudson City Savings Bank:
Steven M. Schlesinger, age 53
SVP, Hudson City Bancorp and Hudson City Savings:
Ronald J. Butkovich, age 59,
$1,268,312 total compensation
SVP Hudson City Bancorp and Hudson City Savings:
James A. Klarer, age 56
SVP, Treasurer, and Secretary, Hudson City Bancorp and Hudson City Savings Bank: Veronica A. Olszewski, age 49
SVP Hudson City Bancorp and Hudson City Savings Bank: Michael B. Lee, age 59
SVP; SVP Mortgage Servicing, Hudson City Savings Bank: V. Barry Corridon, age 60
Auditors: KPMG LLP

LOCATIONS

HQ: Hudson City Bancorp, Inc.
W. 80 Century Rd., Paramus, NJ 07652
Phone: 201-967-1900   **Fax:** 201-967-0332
Web: www.hcsbonline.com

2008 Locations

	No.
New Jersey	93
New York	25
Connecticut	9
Total	**127**

PRODUCTS/OPERATIONS

2008 Gross Revenues

	$ mil.	% of total
Interest & dividend income		
First mortgage loans	1,523.5	57
Mortgage-backed securities held to maturity	497.9	19
Mortgage-backed securities available for sale	377.1	14
Investment securities available for sale	162.8	6
Other	91.9	4
Noninterest income		
Service charges & other	8.5	—
Total	**2,661.7**	**100**

Selected Subsidiaries

Hudson City Savings Bank
  HC Value Broker Services (life insurance brokerage)
  HudCiti Service Corporation
    Hudson City Preferred Funding Corp. (real estate investment trust)
    Sound REIT, Inc.

COMPETITORS

Bank of America
Camco Financial
Capital One
Citigroup
Citizens Financial Group
JPMorgan Chase
Pamrapo Bancorp
PNC Financial
TD Bank USA
Valley National Bancorp

HISTORICAL FINANCIALS

Company Type: Public

Income Statement

FYE: December 31

	ASSETS ($ mil.)	NET INCOME ($ mil.)	INCOME AS % OF ASSETS	EMPLOYEES
12/08	54,145.3	445.6	0.8%	1,496
12/07	44,424.0	295.9	0.7%	1,362
12/06	35,506.6	288.6	0.8%	1,319
12/05	28,075.4	276.1	1.0%	1,150
12/04	20,146.0	239.3	1.2%	1,115
Annual Growth	28.0%	16.8%	—	7.6%

2008 Year-End Financials

Equity as % of assets: 9.1%
Return on assets: 0.9%
Return on equity: 9.3%
Long-term debt ($ mil.): 15,125.0
No. of shares (mil.): 525.3
Market value ($ mil.): 8,384.0

Dividends
  Yield: 2.8%
  Payout: 50.0%
Sales ($ mil.): 950.5
R&D as % of sales: —
Advertising as % of sales: —

Stock History

NASDAQ (GS): HCBK

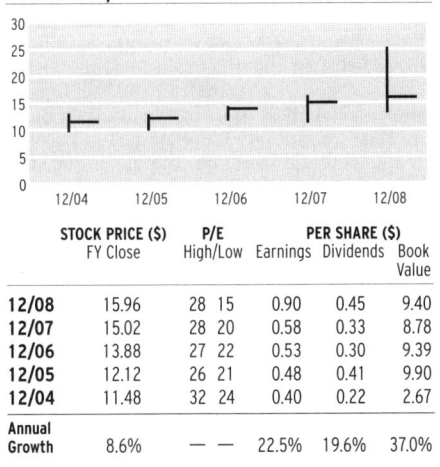

	STOCK PRICE ($) FY Close	P/E High/Low		PER SHARE ($) Earnings	Dividends	Book Value
12/08	15.96	28	15	0.90	0.45	9.40
12/07	15.02	28	20	0.58	0.33	8.78
12/06	13.88	27	22	0.53	0.30	9.39
12/05	12.12	26	21	0.48	0.41	9.90
12/04	11.48	32	24	0.40	0.22	2.67
Annual Growth	8.6%	—	—	22.5%	19.6%	37.0%

Hurco Companies

Hurco produces PC-based control systems and software and computerized machining tools designed to increase efficiencies in metal component production for the metalworking industry. Its products include computerized machine tools with integrated software and computer control systems that allow production floor operators to create programs for making new parts from a blueprint or an electronic design in order to begin production quickly. Products include vertical machining and turning centers for metal-cutting and metal-forming applications. Europe is Hurco's largest market, generating about two-thirds of sales.

The company continues to grow substantially, due to international demand, in spite of the worldwide recessionary conditions. Higher materials costs plagued Hurco in 2008 and new orders dropped off late in the year, leading the company to reduce expenses, but not headcount. Despite all the problems of the world economy, the company remains consistently profitable, with no outstanding debt and a healthy cash balance.

Hurco outsources manufacturing of all its machine systems and some of its computer controls. The company has distribution facilities in Los Angeles, Singapore, and Venlo, the Netherlands. Hurco sells to customers in the aerospace/military, automotive, computers/electronics, energy, medical equipment, and transportation industries in about 50 countries throughout North America, Europe, and Asia.

The company's brands include Ultimax and MAX software and computer control systems, VM and VMX vertical machining centers, Autobend computer control systems, and Advanced Velocity Control and Adaptive Surface Finish machining software.

EXECUTIVES

Chairman, President, and CEO: Michael Doar, age 54
VP, CFO, Secretary, and Treasurer: John G. Oblazney, age 41
General Manager, Hurco USA: Jim Kawaguchi
Manager Media Relations: Maggie Smith
Controller and Assistant Secretary: Sonja K. McClelland, age 38
Director Human Resources: Judy Summers
Auditors: Ernst & Young LLP

LOCATIONS

HQ: Hurco Companies, Inc.
  1 Technology Way, Indianapolis, IN 46268
Phone: 317-293-5309   **Fax:** 317-328-2811
Web: www.hurco.com

Hurco has operations in Canada, China, France, Germany, India, Italy, Poland, Singapore, Taiwan, the UK, and the US.

2008 Sales

	$ mil.	% of total
Europe		
Germany	82.0	37
UK	20.9	9
France	13.4	6
Other countries	46.5	21
North America	48.1	21
Asia	11.8	5
Other regions	1.3	1
Total	**224.0**	**100**

PRODUCTS/OPERATIONS

2008 Sales

	$ mil.	% of total
Computerized machine tools	199.2	89
Service parts	13.3	6
Service fees	5.8	3
Computer control systems & software	5.7	2
Total	**224.0**	**100**

Selected Products

Computerized Machine Tools
  Machining centers
  Metal-forming systems
  Milling machines
Other
  Control upgrades
  Hardware accessories
  Replacement parts
  Retrofit systems for metal-cutting and metal-forming machine applications
  Software

Selected Subsidiaries

Hurco BV (Netherlands)
Hurco Europe Limited (UK)
Hurco GmbH (Germany)
Hurco Manufacturing Ltd. (Taiwan)
Hurco Sarl (France)
Hurco (S. E. Asia) Pte Ltd. (Singapore)
Hurco Srl (Italy)

COMPETITORS

Cincinnati Automation
FANUC
Genesis Worldwide
Giddings & Lewis
GILDEMEISTER
Gleason Corp.
Haas Automation
Hardinge
IMTA
Mazak
Nicolás Correa
Okuma
Siemens AG
Thermwood
TRUMPF

HISTORICAL FINANCIALS

Company Type: Public

Income Statement

FYE: October 31

	REVENUE ($ mil.)	NET INCOME ($ mil.)	NET PROFIT MARGIN	EMPLOYEES
10/08	224.0	22.5	10.0%	430
10/07	188.0	20.9	11.1%	380
10/06	148.5	15.5	10.4%	320
10/05	125.5	16.4	13.1%	284
10/04	99.6	6.3	6.3%	250
Annual Growth	22.5%	37.5%	—	14.5%

2008 Year-End Financials

Debt ratio: —
Return on equity: 20.4%
Cash ($ mil.): 26.4
Current ratio: 2.96
Long-term debt ($ mil.): —
No. of shares (mil.): 6.4

Dividends
  Yield: 0.0%
  Payout: —
Market value ($ mil.): 144.9
R&D as % of sales: —
Advertising as % of sales: —

Stock History

NASDAQ (GS): HURC

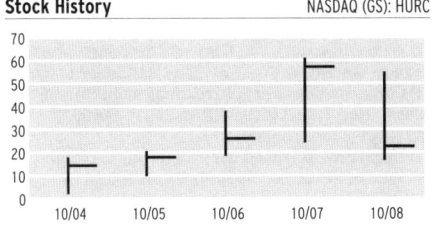

	STOCK PRICE ($) FY Close	P/E High/Low		PER SHARE ($) Earnings	Dividends	Book Value
10/08	22.50	16	5	3.49	0.00	19.17
10/07	57.10	19	8	3.24	0.00	15.15
10/06	26.06	15	8	2.42	0.00	11.70
10/05	17.83	8	4	2.60	0.00	9.15
10/04	14.33	17	2	1.04	0.00	5.97
Annual Growth	11.9%	—	—	35.3%	—	33.9%

Huron Consulting

Huron Consulting Group aims to help keep companies sailing smoothly, but the firm also will dredge through financial statements to address issues that cause businesses to sink. The firm provides a variety of financial consulting services to corporate clients that are in financial distress or involved in other legal and regulatory disputes. Its consultants offer forensic accounting and economic analysis expertise and often serve as expert witnesses. The firm's operational consulting services are delivered primarily to health care and education enterprises and to law firms. Huron Consulting operates from a network of about 20 offices, primarily in the US but also in Asia, Europe, and the Middle East.

The firm has grown both organically and via acquisitions, and it has signaled that it will continue to look for complementary businesses to acquire. Demand for its services has increased because of factors such as increased scrutiny of accounting practices by the SEC, Sarbanes-Oxley legislation, and an upswing in mergers and acquisitions.

Huron Consulting's own M&A activity in 2007 included the purchases of Wellspring Partners, a management consulting firm specializing in

hospitals and health systems; Callaway Partners, which specializes in finance- and accounting-related services; and project management and turnaround specialist Glass & Associates.

In 2008 Huron Consulting continued its acquisition streak when it bought Stockamp & Associates, another consulting firm specializing in assisting hospitals and health care facilities, to improve its overall financial and operational performance. Huron Consulting sees the health care sector as an emerging market and key for its strategic growth. The firm expanded its Middle East footprint with the 2009 acquisition of Nextmove, a Saudi Arabia-based health and education consulting firm.

EXECUTIVES

Chairman: George E. Massaro, age 61
CEO and Director: James H. (Jim) Roth
President and COO: David M. Shade, age 64
CFO and Treasurer: James K. Rojas
VP Healthcare Operational Consulting:
  Gordon J. Mountford
VP, General Counsel, and Corporate Secretary:
  Natalia Delgado, age 55, $714,201 total compensation
VP Corporate Consulting, Accounting and Financial Consulting: Daniel P. (Dan) Broadhurst, age 50, $1,570,449 total compensation
VP Healthcare Revenue Consulting: Paul Kohlheim
VP Human Resources: Mary M. Sawall, age 53, $548,535 total compensation
VP Legal Consulting: Shahzad Bashir
VP Health and Education Consulting: Robert E. Wilson
Auditors: PricewaterhouseCoopers LLP

LOCATIONS

HQ: Huron Consulting Group Inc.
  550 W. Van Buren St., Chicago, IL 60607
Phone: 312-583-8700   **Fax:** 312-583-8701
Web: www.huronconsultinggroup.com

PRODUCTS/OPERATIONS

2008 Revenues

	$ mil.	% of total
Health & education consulting	275.5	41
Accounting & financial consulting	134.0	20
Legal consulting	121.4	18
Corporate consulting	84.6	13
Reimbursable expenses	56.7	8
Total	**672.2**	**100**

Selected Services

Accounting and finance
Clinical research solutions and health care compliance
Corporate governance
Corporate tax solutions
Disputes
E-discovery
Government contracting
Health plans
Healthcare
Higher education
Investigations
Legal
Operations
Pharmaceutical and medical devices
Restructuring and turnaround
Stockamp
Strategy
Transactions
Utilities

COMPETITORS

Accenture	Ernst & Young Global
Bain & Company	FTI Consulting
BearingPoint	KPMG
Booz Allen	LECG
Boston Consulting	McKinsey & Company
CRA International	Navigant Consulting
Deloitte	PricewaterhouseCoopers

HISTORICAL FINANCIALS

Company Type: Public

Income Statement

FYE: December 31

	REVENUE ($ mil.)	NET INCOME ($ mil.)	NET PROFIT MARGIN	EMPLOYEES
12/08	672.2	40.7	6.1%	2,129
12/07	548.0	41.9	7.6%	1,600
12/06	321.9	26.7	8.3%	1,035
12/05	226.0	17.8	7.9%	773
12/04	173.9	9.9	5.7%	612
Annual Growth	**40.2%**	**42.4%**	**—**	**36.6%**

2008 Year-End Financials

Debt ratio: 87.8%
Return on equity: 16.2%
Cash ($ mil.): 14.1
Current ratio: 1.08
Long-term debt ($ mil.): 280.2
No. of shares (mil.): 21.3
Dividends
  Yield: 0.0%
  Payout: —
Market value ($ mil.): 1,220.6
R&D as % of sales: —
Advertising as % of sales: —

Stock History

NASDAQ (GS): HURN

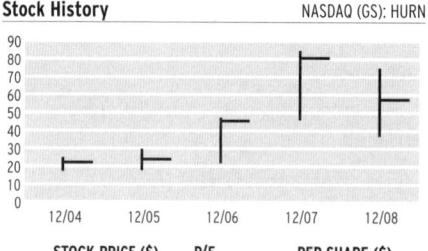

	STOCK PRICE ($) FY Close	P/E High/Low		PER SHARE ($) Earnings	Dividends	Book Value
12/08	57.27	35	18	2.13	0.00	14.97
12/07	80.63	36	20	2.32	0.00	8.62
12/06	45.34	30	15	1.54	0.00	5.47
12/05	23.99	28	18	1.05	0.00	3.54
12/04	22.20	34	25	0.72	0.00	2.31
Annual Growth	**26.7%**	**—**	**—**	**31.1%**	**—**	**59.5%**

IBERIABANK Corporation

IBERIABANK Corporation is a financial services holding company with some 150 locations, including nearly 90 bank branches and about 25 title insurance offices, almost all of them in Louisiana and Arkansas. It also has 35 mortgage loan offices in eight states. Its primary bank subsidiary, IBERIABANK, offers passbook and NOW accounts, CDs, and IRAs and uses funds from deposits mainly to make loans. Business operating loans and commercial mortgages make up approximately 60% of a portfolio that also includes consumer loans (about 25%) and residential mortgages (almost 15%). Expanding

headlong into Arkansas, IBERIABANK Corporation acquired Pulaski Investment Corporation and Pocahontas Bancorp in 2007.

Pocahontas Bancorp's First Community Bank of Jonesboro, Arkansas, operated about 20 branches and extended IBERIABANK's presence into northeast Arkansas. Pulaski Investment, the parent of Pulaski Bank & Trust, had about 50 offices in Arkansas. Not only did the latter purchase expand IBERIABANK geographically, it also added trust and title businesses.

These acquisitions were IBERIABANK Corporation's two largest in its history. Pulaski Bank and First Community Bank merged to become Pulaski Bank and Trust Company and in 2008 the bank opened nine new locations and expanded to northwest Arkansas after IBERIABANK acquired ANB Financial. The following year, Pulaski Bank and Trust changed its name to IBERIABANK to unify the company's brands.

IBERIABANK subsidiary Iberia Financial Services offers discount brokerage services through ProEquities, Inc. The bank sells insurance through IBERIABANK Insurance Services.

EXECUTIVES

Chairman: William H. Fenstermaker, age 60
Vice Chairman: E. Stewart Shea III, age 57
Vice Chairman and Manager, Brokerage, Trust and Wealth Management: Jefferson G. (Jeff) Parker, age 56
Vice Chairman and COO: Michael J. (Mike) Brown, age 52
President, CEO, and Director; President and CEO, IBERIABANK: Daryl G. Byrd, age 54, $1,403,916 total compensation
SEVP and CFO, IBERIABANK Corporation, IBERIABANK, Pulaski Bank and Trust Company, and First Community Bank: Anthony J. Restel, age 39, $420,900 total compensation
SEVP, IBERIABANK Corporation, IBERIABANK, Pulaski Bank and Trust Company, and First Community Bank: Michael A. Naquin, age 48, $645,513 total compensation
SEVP, Mergers and Acquisitions, Finance, and Investor Relations; Director, Financial Strategy and Mortgage: John R. Davis, age 48, $727,282 total compensation
EVP, Corporate Secretary, and Director, Corporate Operations: George J. Becker III, age 68
EVP and Director, Communications: Beth Ardoin
EVP and Chief Risk Officer: James B. Gburek
EVP and Internal Audit Manager: Lewis P. Rogers, age 56
EVP and Director, Enterprise Risk Management: Elise Latimer
Auditors: Ernst & Young LLP

LOCATIONS

HQ: IBERIABANK Corporation
  200 W. Congress St., Lafayette, LA 70501
Phone: 337-521-4012   **Fax:** 337-364-1171
Web: www.iberiabank.com

PRODUCTS/OPERATIONS

2008 Gross Revenues

	$ mil.	% of total
Interest		
Loans	213.7	60
Securities	42.4	12
Other	7.8	2
Noninterest		
Gain on sale of loans, net	25.3	7
Service charges on deposits	23.0	6
Title revenue	19.0	5
ATM/debit card fees	6.8	2
Broker commissions	5.5	2
Other	12.5	4
Total	**356.0**	**100**

Selected Subsidiaries

IBERIABANK
  Acadiana Holdings, LLC
  IBERIABANK Asset Management, Inc.
  IBERIABANK Insurance Services, LLC
    Pulaski Insurance Agency, Inc.
    Sun Realty, Inc.
  Iberia Financial Services, LLC
    Finesco, LLC
    Pulaski Financial Services, LLC
  Jefferson Insurance Corporation

Lenders Title Company
  Asset Exchange, Inc.
  United Title of Louisiana, Inc.

Pulaski Bank and Trust Company
  P.F. Services, Inc.
  Pulaski Mortgage Company

COMPETITORS

Capital One
GS Financial
Hancock Holding
Home Bank
JPMorgan Chase
Louisiana Bancorp
MidSouth Bancorp
Regions Financial
Teche Holding
Whitney Holding

HISTORICAL FINANCIALS

Company Type: Public

Income Statement

FYE: December 31

	ASSETS ($ mil.)	NET INCOME ($ mil.)	INCOME AS % OF ASSETS	EMPLOYEES
12/08	5,583.2	39.9	0.7%	1,356
12/07	4,917.0	41.3	0.8%	1,319
12/06	3,203.0	35.7	1.1%	754
12/05	2,852.6	22.0	0.8%	650
12/04	2,448.6	27.3	1.1%	628
Annual Growth	22.9%	10.0%	—	21.2%

2008 Year-End Financials

Equity as % of assets: 11.6%
Return on assets: 0.8%
Return on equity: 7.0%
Long-term debt ($ mil.): 568.5
No. of shares (mil.): 20.6
Market value ($ mil.): 991.0
Dividends
  Yield: 2.8%
  Payout: 44.7%
Sales ($ mil.): 229.6
R&D as % of sales: —
Advertising as % of sales: —

Stock History

NASDAQ (GS): IBKC

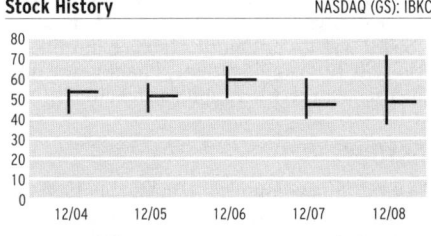

	STOCK PRICE ($) FY Close	P/E High/Low	PER SHARE ($) Earnings	Dividends	Book Value
12/08	48.00	23 12	3.04	1.36	35.56
12/07	46.75	18 12	3.27	1.34	24.12
12/06	59.05	18 14	3.57	1.22	15.48
12/05	51.01	25 19	2.24	1.00	12.77
12/04	53.09	18 14	3.01	0.85	10.66
Annual Growth	(2.5%)	— —	0.2%	12.5%	35.1%

Iconix Brand Group

Once a shoemaker, Iconix Brand Group has stepped it up as a licensing and brand management company. Its company-owned consumer and home brands are licensed to third parties that make and sell apparel, footwear, and a variety of other fashion and home products. Consumer brands in the Iconix stable include Badgley Mischka, Danskin, Mossimo, Mudd, and Rocawear; among the company's home brands are Cannon, Fieldcrest, and Waverly. Along with licensing the brands, Iconix markets and promotes them through its in-house advertising and public relations services.

Iconix expects to grow through its licensing agreements with Wal-Mart to sell Ocean Pacific, Danskin Now, and Starter apparel and accessories. The company also is looking to international markets to boost revenues as the US economy weakens. In 2008 Iconix formed joint ventures in China and Latin America to advance its brands.

Iconix collects brands the way some people collect shoes, making 15 acquisitions in the past five years. The company continues to evaluate potential purchases and hopes to one day grow to a collection of 25-30 brands. On its way to do just that, Iconix diversified beyond fashion and into home brands in 2007 by buying Official Pillowtex, a licensing company that held rights to the Cannon, Charisma, Fieldcrest, and Royal Velvet brands, for $231 million. (The Official Pillowtex brands were owned by Pillowtex Corp. before that company declared bankruptcy in 2003.)

In another move to broaden its offerings, in 2007 Iconix bought NIKE's Starter athletic apparel brand, the Danskin brand from Danskin, Inc., and Roc Apparel Group's Rocawear brand. In late 2008 Iconix acquired Waverly, a home furnishing brand, from NexCen Brands for $26 million. The Waverly acquisition opened up partnerships with retail giants such as Target, Lowe's, and J. C. Penney.

A year later, in late 2009, Iconix snatched up a 51% controlling interest in the brand portfolio of urban fashion firm Marc Ecko Enterprises. The firm manages such brands as Ecko Unlimited, Marc Ecko, the Rhino logo, and Zoo York. Iconix paid an overall purchase price of about $109 million for the brands.

Iconix, formerly a footwear company known as Candie's Inc., changed its name in 2005 to reflect a shift in focus from manufacturing to brand management. The company continues to keep a toe in the footwear business with the Candie's brand and through its subsidiary Bright Star, which oversees the design and arranges for the manufacturing and distribution of men's shoes sold under private labels, primarily by Wal-Mart.

Iconix owns 50% of Scion LLC, a joint venture with Shawn "Jay-Z" Carter. Scion bought the high-end urban apparel Artful Dodger brand in late 2007.

Iconix is led by chairman, president, and CEO Neil Cole, brother of fashion icon Kenneth Cole.

EXECUTIVES

Chairman, President, and CEO: Neil Cole, age 52, $8,997,489 total compensation
EVP and CFO: Warren Clamen, age 45, $516,633 total compensation
EVP and General Counsel: Andrew Tarshis, age 43, $533,296 total compensation
Chief Marketing Officer: Dari Marder
CEO, Marc Ecko Enterprises: Seth Gerszberg, age 35
Chief Creative Officer, Marc Ecko Enterprises: Marc Ecko, age 37
Auditors: BDO Seidman, LLP

LOCATIONS

HQ: Iconix Brand Group, Inc.
  1450 Broadway, 4th Fl., New York, NY 10018
Phone: 212-730-0030   **Fax:** 212-391-2057
Web: iconixbrand.com

2008 Sales

	$ mil.	% of total
US	195.9	90
Other countries	20.9	10
Total	**216.8**	**100**

PRODUCTS/OPERATIONS

2008 Sales

	$ mil.	% of total
Wholesale license	151.7	70
Direct-to-retail license	54.3	25
Other (commissions)	10.8	5
Total	**216.8**	**100**

Selected Brands

Consumer

Badgley Mischka	Mossimo
Bongo	Mudd
Candie's	Ocean Pacific
Danskin	Rampage
Joe Boxer	Rocawear
London Fog	Starter

Home

Cannon	Fieldcrest
Charisma	Royal Velvet

COMPETITORS

AnnTaylor	Kellwood
Billabong	Levi Strauss
Calvin Klein	Limited Brands
Cherokee Inc.	Liz Claiborne
Collective Licensing	L'Oréal
Diesel SpA	NIKE
The Gap	Pacific Sunwear
George Clothing	Pentland Group
Guess?	Polo Ralph Lauren
H&M	Quiksilver
Hanesbrands	R. Griggs
J. C. Penney	Vera Wang
Jaclyn	VF
Jones Apparel	Williamson-Dickie
Jordache Enterprises	

HISTORICAL FINANCIALS

Company Type: Public

Income Statement

FYE: December 31

	REVENUE ($ mil.)	NET INCOME ($ mil.)	NET PROFIT MARGIN	EMPLOYEES
12/08	216.8	70.2	32.4%	82
12/07	160.0	63.8	39.9%	94
12/06	80.7	32.5	40.3%	46
12/05	30.2	15.9	52.6%	39
12/04	69.0	0.2	0.3%	27
Annual Growth	33.1%	332.8%	—	32.0%

2008 Year-End Financials

Debt ratio: 96.9%
Return on equity: 12.3%
Cash ($ mil.): 66.4
Current ratio: 1.26
Long-term debt ($ mil.): 594.7
No. of shares (mil.): 71.4

Dividends
 Yield: 0.0%
 Payout: —
Market value ($ mil.): 698.4
R&D as % of sales: —
Advertising as % of sales: —

Stock History

NASDAQ (GS): ICON

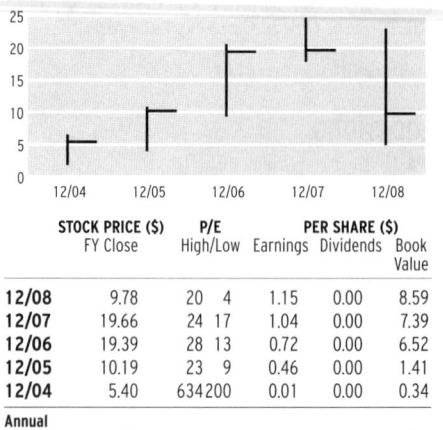

	STOCK PRICE ($) FY Close	P/E High/Low		PER SHARE ($) Earnings	Dividends	Book Value
12/08	9.78	20	4	1.15	0.00	8.59
12/07	19.66	24	17	1.04	0.00	7.39
12/06	19.39	28	13	0.72	0.00	6.52
12/05	10.19	23	9	0.46	0.00	1.41
12/04	5.40	634	200	0.01	0.00	0.34
Annual Growth	16.0%	—	—	227.5%	—	124.3%

Idera Pharmaceuticals

Idera Pharmaceuticals may try to manipulate you, but it's all for your own good. The biotech firm is developing DNA and RNA therapies that manipulate the immune system's response to disease. It is focused on Toll-Like Receptors (TLRs) — immune cell receptors that recognize and respond to viral and bacterial invaders. Some of Idera's drugs (such as treatments for infectious disease and cancer) mimic those invaders to stimulate an immune response; others (including treatments for autoimmune diseases) target TLRs to suppress the immune response. The company's lead candidate is a potential treatment for hepatitis C. Idera has partnered on some other programs with the likes of Merck & Co., Merck KGaA, and Novartis.

Idera is researching some compounds in-house, including its early-stage clinical program for hepatitis C, as well as preclinical programs in autoimmune disease and cancer. However, it has found collaborative partners for other programs, in order to take advantage of the funding and development capabilities of larger pharmaceutical firms. With Merck, Idera is developing adjuvants that boost the effectiveness of vaccines. And with Novartis it has been developing asthma and allergy therapies. In 2007 the company added Merck KGaA as a partner; the two companies are working on anti-cancer therapies.

Merck owns about 8% of Idera, and director Youssef El Zein holds 6%, primarily through investment firm Optima Life Sciences.

EXECUTIVES

Chairman: James B. Wyngaarden, age 84
Vice Chairman: Youssef El Zein, age 60
CEO, Chief Scientific Officer, and Director:
 Sudhir Agrawal, age 55, $1,577,248 total compensation
CFO and Treasurer: Louis J. (Lou) Arcudi III, age 49, $580,203 total compensation
VP Discovery: Ekambar R. Kandimalla
VP Intellectual Property and Contracts: Steven J. Ritter
VP Clinical Development: Alice S. Bexon, age 40, $466,504 total compensation
VP Corporate Development: Rahul Jasuja
VP Development Programs: Timothy M. Sullivan, age 54, $479,994 total compensation
Director Business Development and Alliance Management: David M. Lough
Controller: Frank Whalen
Manager Investor Relations and Corporate Communication: Kelly Luethje
Auditors: Ernst & Young LLP

LOCATIONS

HQ: Idera Pharmaceuticals, Inc.
 167 Sidney St., Cambridge, MA 02139
Phone: 617-679-5500   **Fax:** 617-679-5592
Web: www.iderapharma.com

COMPETITORS

Anadys Pharmaceuticals
Dynavax Technologies
GlaxoSmithKline
Hemispherx BioPharma
Intercell
Pfizer

HISTORICAL FINANCIALS

Company Type: Public

Income Statement

FYE: December 31

	REVENUE ($ mil.)	NET INCOME ($ mil.)	NET PROFIT MARGIN	EMPLOYEES
12/08	26.4	1.5	5.7%	37
12/07	8.0	(13.2)	—	38
12/06	2.4	(16.5)	—	33
12/05	2.5	(13.7)	—	27
12/04	0.9	(15.4)	—	24
Annual Growth	132.7%	—		11.4%

2008 Year-End Financials

Debt ratio: 0.1%
Return on equity: 10.0%
Cash ($ mil.): 45.2
Current ratio: 2.29
Long-term debt ($ mil.): 0.0
No. of shares (mil.): 23.5

Dividends
 Yield: —
 Payout: —
Market value ($ mil.): 180.3
R&D as % of sales: —
Advertising as % of sales: —

Stock History

NASDAQ (GM): IDRA

	STOCK PRICE ($) FY Close	P/E High/Low		PER SHARE ($) Earnings	Dividends	Book Value
12/08	7.68	260	93	0.06	—	0.94
12/07	13.10	—	—	(0.62)	—	0.33
12/06	5.39	—	—	(0.99)	—	0.52
12/05	4.88	—	—	(0.96)	—	(0.01)
12/04	3.84	—	—	(1.28)	—	0.54
Annual Growth	18.9%	—	—	—	—	14.8%

IDEXX Labs

If IDEXX Laboratories had been on the scene, Old Yeller might have had a happier ending. A leading animal health care company, IDEXX makes diagnostic testing kits and machines and drugs for pets and livestock. Veterinarians use the company's VetTest analyzers for blood and urine chemistry and its SNAP and PetChek in-office test kits to detect heartworms, feline leukemia, and other diseases. The company also provides veterinary lab testing services and practice management software. In addition, IDEXX makes diagnostic products to detect livestock and poultry diseases (such as swine or bird flu) and to test systems for contaminants in water and antibiotics in milk. The company serves customers in 75 countries.

The company distributes its products through its own marketing and sales force as well as via independent distributors and resellers. Foreign sales account for about a third of the company's revenue.

Products and services for companion animals (aka pets) account for about 80% of IDEXX's sales, and most of that revenue comes from diagnostic products and services, including analyzers, rapid test kits, and reference laboratory services. The company operates more than 50 laboratories, to which vets can send patient samples for analysis, in more than a dozen countries.

IDEXX's flagship diagnostic analyzer (the VetTest) has an installed base of about 30,000 systems; most of the product line's revenue comes from sales of consumables and test slides that are used with the systems. Johnson & Johnson subsidiary Ortho-Clinical Diagnostics supplies the slides and reagents used with VetTest and with a next-generation version of the analyzer called Catalyst Dx, which was launched in early 2008.

After companion animals, production animals (such as cows, pigs, and chickens) are the company's second-largest market. IDEXX's main product in its production animals segment is a test that detects bovine spongiform encephalopathy (BSE, or mad cow disease) post-mortem.

IDEXX's water testing segment produces tests to detect *E. coli*, *enterococci*, and *Cryptosporidia*, while its dairy testing unit produces a SNAP test for antibiotic residues in milk. It also sells human electrolyte, blood gases, and glucose analyzers to hospitals and clinics.

HISTORY

David Shaw founded IDEXX in 1984 as AgriTech Systems. An MBA who had specialized in agribusiness consulting, Shaw wanted to cut the costs and time involved in lab testing for diseases by producing kits that could be used on-site; an initial line of poultry disease tests proved successful. The company changed its name to IDEXX in 1988 and went public in 1991.

In 1994 IDEXX acquired AMIS International, a leading Japanese test lab for veterinarians. The next year the company opened offices in Spain and the Netherlands and introduced the SNAP test, which detects allergies in dogs.

In 1997 IDEXX acquired two software companies, Advanced Veterinary Systems and Professionals Software, and merged them to create IDEXX Informatics. That year the firm also bought Acumedia Manufacturers, a producer of more than 300 varieties of dehydrated culture

media. Looking to expand into animal drug development, the company bought animal health firm Blue Ridge Pharmaceuticals in 1998. In 2000 IDEXX sold Acumedia, as well as its food microbiology operations. It also launched VetConnect.com, which provides veterinary information and support and product sales.

In 2008 the company sold its veterinary pharmaceutical operations, which were miniscule, to focus on its core test kit and consumables business.

EXECUTIVES

Chairman, President, and CEO:
Jonathan W. (Jon) Ayers, age 52,
$2,697,621 total compensation
SVP and Chief Scientific Officer: William C. Wallen, age 65, $830,827 total compensation
Corporate VP Instrument Research and Development and Manufacturing: William E. Brown III, age 55
Corporate VP International Commercial Operations: Ali Naqui, age 55
Corporate VP Production Animal, Water, and Dairy: William B. Goodspeed, age 50
Corporate VP Companion Animal Group: Thomas J. Dupree, age 40, $623,489 total compensation
Corporate VP Rapid Assay and Digital Radiography: James F. Polewaczyk, age 45
Corporate VP and CFO: Merilee Raines, age 53, $777,737 total compensation
Corporate VP, General Counsel, and Secretary: Conan R. Deady, age 47, $673,442 total compensation
Corporate VP Worldwide Reference Laboratories Business: Johnny D. Powers, age 47
Corporate VP and General Manager Companion Animal Instrument and Consumables: Michael J. Williams, age 41
VP, Worldwide Operations: Irene Kerr, age 59
Business Communications Manager: Elisabeth L. Richards
Auditors: PricewaterhouseCoopers LLP

LOCATIONS

HQ: IDEXX Laboratories, Inc.
1 IDEXX Dr., Westbrook, ME 04092
Phone: 207-556-0300   **Fax:** 207-556-4346
Web: www.idexx.com

PRODUCTS/OPERATIONS

2008 Sales

	$ mil.	% of total
Companion animals		
Instruments & consumables	318.5	31
Lab & consulting services	288.2	28
Rapid assay products	146.9	14
Practice information management & digital radiography	61.3	6
Pharmaceuticals	19.1	3
Production animals	80.8	8
Water quality	74.5	7
Other	34.7	3
Total	**1,024.0**	**100**

Selected Products

Companion animals
  Catalyst Dx chemistry analyzer
  PetChek diagnostics
  LaserCyte hematology system
  SNAP 3Dx (Lyme disease, heartworm, and *Ehrlichia canis* test)
  SNAP Combo FIV Antibody/FeLV antigen test
  VetLyte electrolyte analyzer
Production animals
  Bovine spongiform encephalopathy diagnostic
  Bovine viral diarrhea diagnostic
  Swine influenza virus (H1N1 and H3N2)
  Swine reproductive and respiratory disease syndrome diagnostic
  Swine pseudorabies diagnostic

Water quality
  Colilert (*E. coli* detection)
  Colilert-18 (*E. coli* detection)
  Colisure (*E. coli* detection)
  Enterolert (*enterococci* detection)
  Filta-Max (giardia)
  Quanti-Cult (multiple testing in one sample)
Other
  OPTI human point-of-care analyzers
  SNAP beta-lactam test (detection of antibiotics in milk)

COMPETITORS

Abaxis
Abbott Labs
Bayer Animal Health
Eli Lilly
Heska
Instrumentation Laboratory Company
Merial
Neogen
PerkinElmer
Radiometer Medical
Roche Holding
Siemens Healthcare
Strategic Diagnostics
Synbiotics
Thermo Fisher Scientific
VCA Antech
Virbac Corporation

HISTORICAL FINANCIALS

Company Type: Public

Income Statement

FYE: December 31

	REVENUE ($ mil.)	NET INCOME ($ mil.)	NET PROFIT MARGIN	EMPLOYEES
12/08	1,024.0	116.2	11.3%	4,700
12/07	922.6	94.0	10.2%	4,700
12/06	739.1	93.7	12.7%	3,900
12/05	638.1	78.3	12.3%	3,300
12/04	549.2	78.3	14.3%	2,995
Annual Growth	**16.9%**	**10.4%**	—	**11.9%**

2008 Year-End Financials

Debt ratio: 1.2%
Return on equity: 26.5%
Cash ($ mil.): 78.9
Current ratio: 1.21
Long-term debt ($ mil.): 5.1
No. of shares (mil.): 58.6

Dividends
  Yield: —
  Payout: —
Market value ($ mil.): 2,114.0
R&D as % of sales: —
Advertising as % of sales: —

Stock History

NASDAQ (GS): IDXX

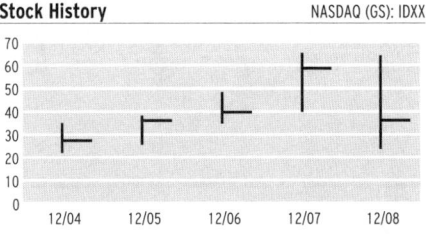

	STOCK PRICE ($) FY Close	P/E High/Low		PER SHARE ($) Earnings	Dividends	Book Value
12/08	36.08	34	13	1.87	—	7.48
12/07	58.63	44	28	1.46	—	7.48
12/06	39.65	34	25	1.42	—	7.00
12/05	35.99	33	23	1.15	—	6.30
12/04	27.30	31	21	1.10	—	6.79
Annual Growth	**7.2%**	—	—	**14.2%**	—	**2.5%**

IEC Electronics

IEC makes products you may never see. Most of IEC Electronics' sales come from the contract manufacturing of printed circuit boards. The company makes a mix of boards, including models that use surface-mount technology, pin-through-hole connections, and more advanced interconnection techniques. Like many contract electronics manufacturers, IEC also offers a variety of auxiliary services, including design and prototyping, materials procurement and management, engineering, testing, packaging, and distribution. Nearly all sales are to customers located in the US.

In 2009 IEC acquired contract manufacturer General Technology Corporation (GTC) from Crane Co. for a little over $14 million. GTC serves the military and defense sectors, a niche market in which IEC sees potential growth.

In 2008 the company acquired Val-U-Tech Corp., a privately held supplier of wire harness assemblies, for approximately $10 million in cash and stock. Val-U-Tech, with customers in the industrial, medical, and military markets, had annual revenues of about $11 million. The combined companies employed 360 people.

IEC started the 21st century practically pushing up daisies. It was struggling with a weak market for telecom equipment, dealing with fewer orders, and bidding farewell to major customer Motorola. The company resurrected itself over the next few years by streamlining its operations and paring its debt by more than a third; in addition, it gained new customers in industries such as alternative energy, gas monitoring equipment, and atomic clocks. Between 2005 and 2007 the company boosted its revenues by more than 80%; between 2005 and 2009 revenues increased by almost 30%.

Chairman, president, and CEO Barry Gilbert owns about 6% of IEC Electronics. Former director Michael Brudek and director James Rowe each hold around 5% of the company. Company insiders hold approximately 27% of IEC's equity.

HISTORY

General Dynamics veteran Roger Main and others founded IEC in 1966 to make components for handheld two-way radios and other electronic devices. IEC went public in 1967. It sold its radio business in 1979 in order to concentrate on contract electronics manufacturing. IEC began a partnership with Compaq in 1983 when the latter started building PCs. Main and other executives took IEC private in an LBO in 1988.

As Compaq's orders slowed during the recession of the early 1990s, IEC's profits fell. When Compaq rebounded, IEC did likewise. It acquired Texas-based Calidad Electronics in 1992, and went public again in 1993. In 1995 IEC expanded its production facilities and services, but component shortages and customer scheduling demands led to a drop in sales. After Main died in 1996, EVP Russell Stingel (Main's former General Dynamics co-worker) was named CEO. That year IEC's earnings slipped as computer equipment sales fell and the market for electronic components became saturated.

The company closed its money-losing Alabama plant in 1998, taking a restructuring charge that contributed to a loss for the year. In early 1999 IEC opened a manufacturing facility in Mexico. The following year IEC closed its operation in

Ireland and began to diversify its customer base, decreasing its dependence on PC makers and targeting the telecommunications equipment and industrial instrumentation markets. Also in 2000, turnaround specialist Thomas Lovelock succeeded Stingel as president and CEO; Stingel remained as chairman until 2001, when director W. Barry Gilbert took over the position.

As the economic downturn in the telecom equipment market resulted in fewer orders for IEC in 2001, the company responded with more restructuring, closing its Texas facility and transferring those operations to its plant in Mexico.

In 2002 the company laid off employees, and Lovelock resigned. (Gilbert became president and CEO, in addition to chairman.) Later that year, in response to continuing losses, the company sold the assets of its manufacturing plant in Mexico.

Sales continued to drop in 2004 and 2005, as IEC lost the business of two top customers. The company tried to make up the lost business by signing up many smaller customers. In 2006 IEC had around 25 customers and was able to reverse the sales decline. Its top five customers, however, accounted for around two-thirds of sales.

While IEC was able to stop a long decline in sales and return to profitability, its annual revenues in fiscal 2006 were less than one-tenth of what they were a decade earlier; its headcount, while rebounding from a low in 2005, was one-sixth that of 10 years before.

The company definitively reversed the decline in fiscal 2007, increasing revenues by 81% over the prior year, due to adding a number of new customers. IEC's five largest customers, however, account for about 60% of sales.

EXECUTIVES

Chairman, President, and CEO: W. Barry Gilbert, age 63
CTO: Ronald (Ron) Pratt
EVP Sales and Marketing: Jeffrey T. (Jeff) Schlarbaum, age 42
VP Operations: Donald S. (Don) Doody, age 40
VP Supply Chain: Stephanie A. Martin
VP and CFO: Michael (Mike) Schlehr, age 47
Secretary: Martin S. Weingarten
Director Human Resources: Tina DeVey
Director Business Development: Timothy S. (Tim) Fox
Assistant Secretary and Director: Justin L. Vigdor, age 79
Marketing Communications Specialist: Heather Keenan
Auditors: Rotenberg & Co. LLP

LOCATIONS

HQ: IEC Electronics Corp.
105 Norton St., Newark, NY 14513
Phone: 315-331-7742   **Fax:** 315-331-3547
Web: www.iec-electronics.com

PRODUCTS/OPERATIONS

Services

Complete systems building
Design services
Distribution
Engineering support for manufacturing
Final packaging
Material procurement and management
Printed circuit board assembly
Prototype assembly
Resources management
Statistical quality assurance
Testing

COMPETITORS

Ansen Corp.	Jabil
AsteelFlash	Merix
Benchmark Electronics	Nam Tai
Celestica	Nortech Systems
DDi Corp.	Plexus
Eltek	Sanmina-SCI
Entorian	SigmaTron
Flextronics	Suntron
Green St. Energy	SYNNEX
HEI	Wellex

HISTORICAL FINANCIALS

Company Type: Public

Income Statement

FYE: September 30

	REVENUE ($ mil.)	NET INCOME ($ mil.)	NET PROFIT MARGIN	EMPLOYEES
9/09	67.8	5.0	7.4%	368
9/08	51.1	10.5	20.5%	350
9/07	40.9	0.9	2.2%	229
9/06	22.6	0.2	0.9%	240
9/05	19.1	0.3	1.6%	118
Annual Growth	37.3%	102.1%	—	32.9%

2009 Year-End Financials

Debt ratio: 32.6%
Return on equity: 27.6%
Cash ($ mil.): 0.0
Current ratio: 2.50
Long-term debt ($ mil.): 6.6
No. of shares (mil.): 8.8
Dividends
  Yield: 0.0%
  Payout: —
Market value ($ mil.): 49.4
R&D as % of sales: —
Advertising as % of sales: —

Stock History

NYSE Alternext: IEC

	STOCK PRICE ($) FY Close	P/E High/Low		PER SHARE ($) Earnings	Dividends	Book Value
9/09	5.65	15	2	0.52	0.00	2.31
9/08	1.87	2	1	1.12	0.00	1.83
9/07	2.00	21	11	0.10	0.00	0.48
9/06	1.09	41	13	0.03	0.00	0.35
9/05	0.74	28	14	0.03	0.00	0.35
Annual Growth	66.2%	—	—	104.0%	—	60.9%

IHS Inc.

IHS Inc. (Information Handling Services Inc.) handles the hottest commodity around: information. A publisher of technical documents for clients in the energy, defense, aerospace, construction, electronics, and automotive industries, the company distributes its data in several electronic formats (Internet, intranet, extranet, CD-ROM). Products such as collections of technical specifications and standards, regulations, parts data, and design guides are sold through its four areas of information: Energy, Product Lifecycle, Security, and Environment. The company also offers economic-focused information and

analysis through its IHS Global Insight subsidiary. The Thyssen-Bornemisza family controls about 75% of IHS.

IHS's Energy segment is focused on information related to all aspects of oil and gas exploration, development, production, and transportation, while its Product Lifecycle segment provides information on all areas of a product's development, including conception, research, production, maintenance, and disposal. The Security segment focuses on topics such as defense, aerospace, and weapon systems, and the Environment segment provides data to help customers comply with environmental regulations and related issues.

The company specializes in delivering information to engineers, designers, technical professionals, senior managers, compliance officers, marketing executives, and strategic planners at both small and large businesses. IHS primarily earns revenue through subscription sales. The company does business in some 180 countries; international activities account for about half of IHS's sales.

IHS has been busy growing through acquisitions, having completed more than 20 purchases in the last three years. In 2008 the company expanded into the business of providing economic information and analysis with the purchase of consulting firm Global Insight, its largest acquisition to date, for about $165 million. IHS used the purchase to boost its research holdings; along these lines it formed IHS Insight, which includes subsidiaries Cambridge Energy Research Associates (a provider of analysis on energy markets, geopolitics, industry trends, and strategy), Jane's Information Group, a provider of information and analysis on global defense and security, and IHS Herold, a research firm specializing in the oil and gas sector, in addition to Global Insight.

Also in 2008 IHS added subsidiaries such as Dolphin Software (chemical data information and software) and Documental Solutions (market intelligence and analysis for the defense and aerospace industry) into the mix. In 2007 the company acquired EnvironMax, a provider of environmental management information systems, and coal research firm McCloskey Group, a provider of information on the international coal markets.

HISTORY

IHS Group traces its roots to Rogers Publishing, a company formed by Thomas Rogers in the 1940s to publish engineering magazine *Design News*. In the 1950s Rogers Publishing branched into automated information retrieval systems, choosing microfilm as a publishing medium for reference information.

In 1959 Richard O'Brien, an executive with Rogers Publishing, developed a product catalog database for aerospace engineers. Vendor Specs Microfilm File (VSMF), the flagship product, was produced on microfilm to conserve library space and was indexed to locate information quickly. When Cahners Publishing bought Rogers in 1961, the technical services division, which included catalog operations, was spun off as a separate company and named Information Handling Services (IHS).

An extended series of acquisitions helped to shape the company and bring it to the forefront of technical publishing. By the 1980s global giant TBG had become Information Handling Services' parent company and established the

foundation for further growth. IHS Group was formed in 1989 as the holding company for new subsidiaries as the company expanded into other markets, including regulatory information, and entered the international arena through a series of acquisitions.

Among the company's 1990s acquisitions were Beilstein Informationssysteme (Germany, 1994), Global Info Center Hong Kong (1994), Media Library (Japan, 1995), and Petroconsultants (Switzerland, 1996). The company branched into cyberspace in 1997 with the debut of its first Web-based products. Focusing on Web-based and electronic products, IHS Group ceased production of microfilm products the following year.

As IHS Group expanded into energy information, it acquired Petroleum Information/Dwights, PI (ERICO), IEDS, MAI Consultants, and QC Data Petroleum Services Division and its AccuMap Enerdata Division, forming IHS Energy in 1998 as a separate division of IHS Group to streamline energy information operations and services.

In 2000 IHS Group formed a joint venture with standards and quality service organization British Standards Institution (BSI) to distribute BSI's content. Additional acquisitions included the 2004 purchase of USA Information Systems, Intermat, and Cambridge Energy Research Associates (CERA), and the 2005 acquisition of American Technical Publishers.

IHS underwent a reorganization in 2005, which included 100 job cuts and two office closings in its Engineering segment; also that year the company began using the name IHS Inc. In 2006 IHS further reduced its headcount by 40 and sold certain IHS Energy assets.

Also in 2006 the company bought geoPLUS Corporation (software used by oil and gas companies to analyze data from oil and gas wells); Construction Research Communications Limited (products relating to the construction industry, ranging from environmental issues to fire safety); and Canadian Hydrodynamics Ltd (drillstem test information for the Western Canadian Sedimentary Basin).

Purchases in 2007 included Jane's Information Group, a provider of information and analysis on global defense and security; John S. Herold Inc., a research firm specializing in the oil and gas sector (now IHS Herold); EnvironMax, a provider of environmental management information systems; and McCloskey Group, a coal research firm.

EXECUTIVES

Chairman and CEO: Jerre L. Stead, age 65, $6,081,725 total compensation
President and COO: Jeffrey R. (Jeff) Tarr, age 46, $2,435,486 total compensation
EVP and CFO: Michael J. (Mike) Sullivan, age 44, $1,882,722 total compensation
EVP and Strategic Advisor; Chairman, CERA: Daniel Yergin, age 62, $3,352,471 total compensation
SVP and Chief Human Resources Officer: Jeffrey (Jeff) Sisson, age 52
SVP and Chief Customer Process Officer: Jane Okun, age 46
SVP and Chief Accounting Officer: Heather Matzke-Hamlin, age 41
SVP and CIO: H. John Oechsle, age 46
SVP Americas: Mark Rose
SVP Finance Planning and Analysis: Todd Hyatt
SVP Insight: Scott Key, age 50
SVP, Secretary, and General Counsel: Stephen (Steve) Green, age 57

SVP Critical Information: Gerald F. Chew, age 49
SVP Critical Information Development: Vicki P. Raeburn, age 59
SVP Acquisition Integration: Mark Kelly
SVP Product Lifecycle: Thomas (Tom) Littman
SVP Global Strategic Marketing and Corporate Development: Richard G. (Rich) Walker, age 45
VP Corporate Communications: Ed Mattix
Senior Director Investor Relations: Andy Schulz
President and COO, IHS Herold: Christine Juneau
President and COO, IHS CERA: Jonathan Gear
Auditors: Ernst & Young LLP

LOCATIONS

HQ: IHS Inc.
  15 Inverness Way East, Englewood, CO 80112
Phone: 303-790-0600   **Fax:** 303-754-3940
Web: www.ihs.com

2008 Sales

	$ mil.	% of total
Americas	520.9	62
Europe, Middle East & Africa	263.5	31
Asia/Pacific	59.6	7
Total	**844.0**	**100**

PRODUCTS/OPERATIONS

2008 Sales

	$ mil.	% of total
Energy	442.9	52
Product Lifecycle	290.6	34
Security	75.2	9
Environmental	22.5	3
Intersection	12.8	2
Total	**844.0**	**100**

Selected Information Offerings

Energy
  Exploration analysis
  Oil and gas well data
  Production data
  Reservoir data
Environment
  Climate change, greenhouse gas, and sustainability information
  Hazardous materials compliance
Product Lifecycle
  Catalog information
  Electronic components parts information
  Government parts information
  Regulatory data
  Specifications and standards
Security
  Defense forecasting
  Ports and terminals data
  Public safety handbooks and guides
  Terrorism and insurgency monitoring

COMPETITORS

Advanstar
Bonnierforetagen
Bureau of National Affairs
Crain Communications
Divestco
GlobalSpec
Hearst Corporation
i2 Technologies
IBC
Informa
International Data Group
John Wiley
McGraw-Hill
The Nielsen Company
Pearson plc
Penton Media
Reed Elsevier Group
Thomson Reuters
United Business Media
Wolters Kluwer

HISTORICAL FINANCIALS
Company Type: Public

Income Statement

FYE: November 30

	REVENUE ($ mil.)	NET INCOME ($ mil.)	NET PROFIT MARGIN	EMPLOYEES
11/08	844.0	99.0	11.7%	3,800
11/07	688.4	83.8	12.2%	3,000
11/06	550.8	56.3	10.2%	2,500
11/05	476.1	41.8	8.8%	265
11/04	394.0	61.3	15.6%	2,400
Annual Growth	**21.0%**	**12.7%**	**—**	**12.2%**

2008 Year-End Financials

Debt ratio: 0.0%
Return on equity: 12.1%
Cash ($ mil.): 31.0
Current ratio: 0.58
Long-term debt ($ mil.): 0.0
No. of shares (mil.): 63.2

Dividends
  Yield: —
  Payout: —
Market value ($ mil.): 2,295.3
R&D as % of sales: —
Advertising as % of sales: —

Stock History

NYSE: IHS

	STOCK PRICE ($) FY Close	P/E High/Low	PER SHARE ($) Earnings	Dividends	Book Value
11/08	36.29	46 19	1.57	—	12.67
11/07	70.14	51 25	1.39	—	13.30
11/06	37.05	38 17	0.99	—	8.94
11/05	19.26	26 22	0.75	—	7.54
Annual Growth	**23.5%**	**— —**	**9.1%**	**—**	**17.4%**

Illumina, Inc.

Illumina elucidates the human genome. The firm makes tools used by life sciences and drug researchers to isolate and analyze genes. Its systems include the machinery and the software used to sequence pieces of DNA and RNA, and the means to put them through large-scale testing of genetic variation and biological function. Its proprietary BeadArray technology uses microscopic glass beads which can carry samples through the array process. The tests allow medical researchers to determine what genetic combinations are associated with various diseases, enabling faster diagnosis, better drugs, and individualized treatment. Customers include pharma and biotech companies, research centers, and academic institutions.

For customers who don't want to buy its systems, Illumina also offers genome sequencing and genotyping array services.

Illumina has steadily augmented its offerings through acquisitions. The company bought up fellow genomics firm Solexa in a 2007 stock-for-stock deal. The acquisition added DNA sequencing (determining the order of DNA codes) and gene expression analysis technologies (studying when genes switch on or off) to Illumina's existing genotyping expertise, making it a kind of

one-stop-shop for genetic researchers. It also paid nearly $26 million to acquire sequencing technology developer Avantome in 2008.

Getting into the molecular diagnostics business has been a priority for Illumina. It gained its first toe-hold with the 2006 acquisition of CyVera, a maker of *in vitro* and molecular diagnostics. Following the acquisition of CyVera the company launched a new product, the BeadXpress System, based on CyVera's VeraCode technology. In time Illumina hopes to develop gene-based diagnostic tests — including tests related to heart disease, diabetes, and breast cancer — for use with the BeadXpress system.

The company was a leading participant in the International HapMap Project, a successor to the Human Genome Project that mapped genetic variations in an effort to improve understanding of the relationships between genetics and disease. Illumina received a $9.1 million grant from the National Institutes of Health for its work on the project, which was completed in 2005.

EXECUTIVES

Non-Executive Chairman: William H. (Bill) Rastetter, age 62
President, CEO, and Director: Jay T. Flatley, age 57, $5,115,085 total compensation
SVP Corporate Development and CFO: Christian O. Henry, age 41, $2,054,049 total compensation
SVP, General Counsel, and Secretary: Christian G. (Chris) Cabou, age 61, $1,885,805 total compensation
SVP and CTO: Mostafa Ronaghi, age 40
SVP Commercial Operations: Tristan B. Orpin, age 43, $1,653,475 total compensation
SVP and General Manager, Life Sciences: Joel McComb, age 44, $1,818,885 total compensation
SVP and General Manager, Diagnostics: Gregory F. (Greg) Heath, age 51
SVP Operations: Bill Bonnar
VP Business Development: Jorge Velarde
Associate Director Corporate Marketing: Philomena Walsh
Senior Director Investor Relations: Peter J. Fromen
Auditors: Ernst & Young LLP

LOCATIONS

HQ: Illumina, Inc.
9885 Towne Centre Dr., San Diego, CA 92121
Phone: 858-202-4500   **Fax:** 858-202-4545
Web: www.illumina.com

2008 Sales

	$ mil.	% of total
US	280.1	49
Asia/Pacific	72.7	13
UK	68.0	12
Other European countries	127.4	22
Other markets	25.0	4
Total	**573.2**	**100**

PRODUCTS/OPERATIONS

2008 Sales

	$ mil.	% of total
Products	532.4	93
Services & other	40.8	7
Total	**573.2**	**100**

Selected Products

BeadXpress Reader
Genome Analyzer II (gene sequencing system)
iScan System
iSelect Genotyping BeadChips

COMPETITORS

Affymetrix	Life Technologies
Agilent Technologies	Luminex
Beckman Coulter	Pacific Biosciences
Fluidigm	Roche Diagnostics
GE Healthcare	Sequenom

HISTORICAL FINANCIALS

Company Type: Public

Income Statement

FYE: December 31

	REVENUE ($ mil.)	NET INCOME ($ mil.)	NET PROFIT MARGIN	EMPLOYEES
12/08	573.2	50.5	8.8%	1,536
12/07	366.8	(278.4)	—	1,041
12/06	184.6	40.0	21.7%	596
12/05	73.5	(20.9)	—	375
12/04	50.6	(6.2)	—	278
Annual Growth	**83.5%**	**—**	**—**	**53.3%**

2008 Year-End Financials

Debt ratio: 0.0%
Return on equity: 8.0%
Cash ($ mil.): 327.0
Current ratio: 1.70
Long-term debt ($ mil.): 0.0
No. of shares (mil.): 125.1
Dividends
  Yield: 0.0%
  Payout: —
Market value ($ mil.): 3,258.7
R&D as % of sales: —
Advertising as % of sales: —

Stock History

NASDAQ (GM): ILMN

	STOCK PRICE ($) FY Close	P/E High/Low	PER SHARE ($) Earnings	PER SHARE ($) Dividends	PER SHARE ($) Book Value
12/08	26.05	126 50	0.38	0.00	6.78
12/07	29.63	— —	(2.57)	0.00	3.29
12/06	19.66	56 17	0.41	0.00	1.98
12/05	7.05	— —	(0.26)	0.00	0.58
12/04	4.74	— —	(0.09)	0.00	0.58
Annual Growth	**53.1%**	**— —**	**—**	**—**	**85.1%**

Image Sensing Systems

If you're stuck in traffic, you can't blame Image Sensing Systems (ISS). ISS's Autoscope vehicle detection system converts video images into digitized traffic data for traffic management. Unlike traditional embedded wire loop detectors, which are buried in the pavement, Autoscope enables wide-area detection using video cameras, a microprocessor, software, and a PC. The systems help users to design roads, manage traffic signals, and determine the environmental impact of gridlock. Royalty income from traffic management company Econolite Control Products accounts for nearly three-quarters of sales.

In late 2007 ISS bought selected assets from EIS Electronic Integrated Systems Inc. for nearly $11 million in cash and 147,202 shares of ISS common stock (valued at $2.5 million at the time of the transaction). The assets include EIS's

Remote Traffic Microwave Sensor (RTMS) radar product line. EIS had fiscal 2006 revenues of about $8 million.

AWM Investment/Special Situations Funds owns one-quarter of Image Sensing Systems; Nicusa Capital Partners holds about 9%. Founder and director Panos Michalopoulos has an equity stake of more than 8%.

EXECUTIVES

Chairman: James Murdakes, age 76
President, CEO, and Director: Kenneth R. (Ken) Aubrey, age 60, $411,983 total compensation
CFO and Treasurer: Gregory R. L. (Greg) Smith, age 42, $248,057 total compensation
VP Sales and Marketing: Kenneth S. Shain
General Manager, ISS Europe: Graham P. Heywood
Managing Director, Flow Traffic: Mats Johan Billow, age 46
Managing Director, ISS Canada: Dan Manor, age 64, $188,820 total compensation
Auditors: Grant Thornton LLP

LOCATIONS

HQ: Image Sensing Systems, Inc.
500 Spruce Tree Centre, 1600 University Ave. West
St. Paul, MN 55104
Phone: 651-603-7700   **Fax:** 651-305-6402
Web: www.imagesensing.com

2008 Sales

	% of total
North America	72
Europe	16
Asia/Pacific	12
Total	**100**

PRODUCTS/OPERATIONS

2008 Sales

	% of total
Autoscope	71
RTMS	29
Total	**100**

COMPETITORS

3M
Cognex
Econolite
Iteris, Inc.
Laser Technology
NEC
OMRON
Panasonic Electronic Devices
Quixote
Siemens AG
Sumitomo Electric

HISTORICAL FINANCIALS

Company Type: Public

Income Statement

FYE: December 31

	REVENUE ($ mil.)	NET INCOME ($ mil.)	NET PROFIT MARGIN	EMPLOYEES
12/08	26.5	5.0	18.9%	97
12/07	15.1	0.9	6.0%	80
12/06	13.1	3.1	23.7%	53
12/05	11.0	2.8	25.5%	49
12/04	10.8	2.7	25.0%	38
Annual Growth	**25.2%**	**16.7%**	**—**	**26.4%**

2008 Year-End Financials

Debt ratio: 9.6%
Return on equity: 19.3%
Cash ($ mil.): 10.3
Current ratio: 5.08
Long-term debt ($ mil.): 2.8
No. of shares (mil.): 4.0

Dividends
  Yield: 0.0%
  Payout: —
Market value ($ mil.): 25.4
R&D as % of sales: —
Advertising as % of sales: —

Stock History

NASDAQ (CM): ISNS

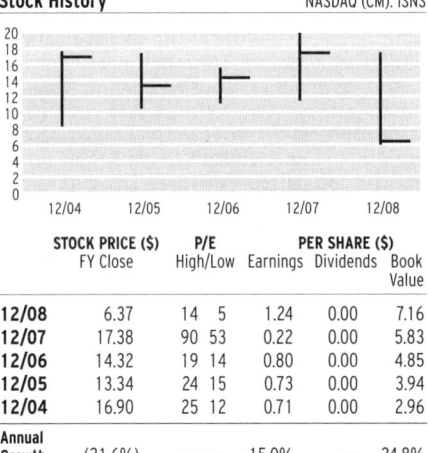

	STOCK PRICE ($) FY Close	P/E High/Low		PER SHARE ($) Earnings	Dividends	Book Value
12/08	6.37	14	5	1.24	0.00	7.16
12/07	17.38	90	53	0.22	0.00	5.83
12/06	14.32	19	14	0.80	0.00	4.85
12/05	13.34	24	15	0.73	0.00	3.94
12/04	16.90	25	12	0.71	0.00	2.96
Annual Growth	(21.6%)	—	—	15.0%	—	24.8%

Immucor, Inc.

Immucor makes sure you can feel good about getting a blood transfusion. The company makes automated analyzers and reagents used by blood banks, hospitals, and clinical laboratories to test blood prior to transfusions. Its Galileo and Galileo Echo systems use its Capture proprietary reagents to perform multiple routine blood tests, including blood type and group matching, antibody detection, and infectious disease screening. Its Capture Workstation is a semi-automated instrumentation system that the company markets to smaller laboratories or as a back-up system for the Galileo analyzers. Immucor sells its systems and reagent tests primarily in North America, Western Europe, and Japan.

In 2007 the company received FDA approval for its Galileo Echo system, which had previously won approval from European regulatory authorities. Galileo Echo is designed to appeal to small and midsized hospital customers, while the Galileo is designed for large hospitals, blood banks, and reference laboratories. The Galileo-branded systems replaced Immucor's legacy analyzers, ROSYS Plato and ABS2000. The company is also developing a next-generation version, the Galileo Neo system, that it hopes will replace the Galileo system for large customers beginning in 2010.

In 2008 the company broadened its product portfolio by acquiring BioArray Solutions, a maker of molecular diagnostic products, for $117 million. BioArray's BeadChip technology is used to analyze DNA in research settings, and Immucor is developing a system based on BioArray's technologies that will bring the company into the futuristic DNA blood typing market.

Immucor has consolidated its distribution operations and standardized its pricing mechanisms to become more competitive. It is also focused on expanding its installed base of systems in order to capitalize on the recurring revenue that comes from its proprietary Capture reagents. Immucor still gets about two-thirds of its revenues from the development and marketing of traditional reagents used in manual blood testing, but the company has shifted its focus, along with the rest of the industry, to providing more automated instrumentation systems and the reagents used with them.

In an effort to strengthen its foothold in Japan (one of its strategic markets), the company created a joint venture with its Japanese distributor, Kainos, and later acquired the company outright. It has also moved to direct sales in some other international markets, acquiring its UK distributor IBG Immucor in 2008 and terminating a distribution agreement with Bio-Rad Laboratories, which was distributing its products in France. The company's products are marketed through independent distributors in noncore regions.

Immucor operated a Houston facility making human collagen products under a contract with Inamed (acquired by Allergan) until 2008, when the company terminated that contract and discontinued operations at the Houston plant.

The firm's Norcross, Georgia, reagent manufacturing operations fell under FDA scrutiny in 2008 after an inspection revealed some deficiencies at the plant. The company is working to improve its processes and is performing upgrades on the facility's quality system.

EXECUTIVES

Chairman: Joseph E. Rosen, age 66
President, CEO, and Director:
  Gioacchino (Nino) De Chirico, age 56,
  $1,490,880 total compensation
SVP, Chief Scientific Officer, and Director:
  Ralph A. Eatz, age 65, $952,303 total compensation
VP and COO: Geoffrey S. (Geoff) Crouse, age 38
VP and CFO: Richard A. (Rick) Flynt,
  $548,296 total compensation
VP, General Counsel, and Secretary:
  Philip H. (Phil) Moise, age 59,
  $958,155 total compensation
VP Worldwide Quality System Compliance:
  Mitch Moheng
VP Internal Audit: David McKinlay
VP Research and Development: Lyle T. Sinor
VP Sales: Todd Bennett
VP Worldwide Logistics and European Operations:
  Daniel L. Ruckman
VP Worldwide Regulatory Affairs: J. Scott Webber
VP Worldwide Customer Solutions: Jim Kennedy
VP International: Jean-Jacques De Jaegher
VP Worldwide Human Resources: Wayne Guthrie
VP Marketing: Teresa Heflin
VP Worldwide Information Systems: David Campbell
VP Operations: Michael Pred
VP Worldwide Quality: Cindi Kisiel-Smith
VP International Finance: Patrick D. Waddy
Auditors: Grant Thornton LLP

LOCATIONS

HQ: Immucor, Inc.
  3130 Gateway Dr., Norcross, GA 30091
Phone: 770-441-2051   **Fax:** 770-441-3807
Web: www.immucor.com

2009 Sales

	$ mil.	% of total
North America		
US	237.8	72
Canada	14.2	4
Europe	70.8	21
Asia (Japan)	9.8	3
Adjustments	(32.1)	—
Total	**300.5**	**100**

PRODUCTS/OPERATIONS

2009 Sales

	$ mil.	% of total
Traditional reagents	199.3	66
Capture reagents	64.1	21
Instruments	34.7	12
Molecular immunohematology	2.4	1
Total	**300.5**	**100**

Selected Products

Instrument systems
  Capture Workstation (semi-automated blood screening system)
  Galileo (high-throughput blood screening system)
  Galileo Echo (automated blood screening system)
Reagents
  ABO Blood Grouping (blood group classification test)
  Antibody Potentiators (increase the sensitivity of antigen-antibody tests)
  Anti-human Globulin Serums (crossmatching and antibody detection)
  Capture -P, -R, -CMV, -S, -R Select (detection of various antibodies)
  Fetal Bleed Screen Kit (detects excessive fetal-maternal hemorrhage)
  Rare Serums (detects rare antigens)
  Reagent Red Blood Cells (detect and identify antibodies in blood)
  Rh Blood Typing (detect Rh antigens)

COMPETITORS

Abaxis
Abbott Labs
BD Biosciences
Beckman Coulter
Bio-Rad Labs
Biotest
Caliper Life Sciences
Grifols, Inc.
Innogenetics
MEDION
Olympus
Ortho-Clinical Diagnostics
R&D Systems
Roche Diagnostics
Siemens Healthcare Diagnostics
Thermo Fisher Scientific

HISTORICAL FINANCIALS

Company Type: Public

Income Statement

FYE: May 31

	REVENUE ($ mil.)	NET INCOME ($ mil.)	NET PROFIT MARGIN	EMPLOYEES
5/09	300.5	76.2	25.4%	729
5/08	261.2	71.5	27.4%	631
5/07	223.7	60.1	26.9%	610
5/06	183.5	39.8	21.7%	563
5/05	144.8	23.9	16.5%	526
Annual Growth	20.0%	33.6%	—	8.5%

2009 Year-End Financials

Debt ratio: —
Return on equity: 22.0%
Cash ($ mil.): 136.5
Current ratio: 4.68
Long-term debt ($ mil.): —
No. of shares (mil.): 69.9

Dividends
  Yield: —
  Payout: —
Market value ($ mil.): 1,051.5
R&D as % of sales: —
Advertising as % of sales: —

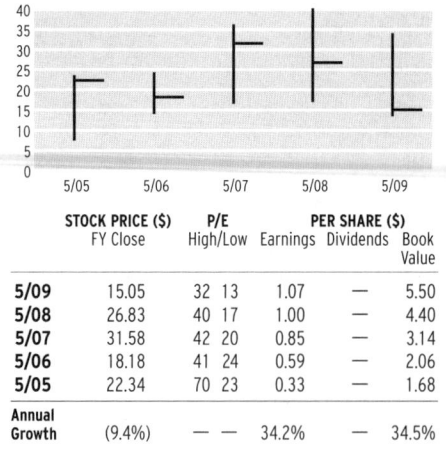

	STOCK PRICE ($) FY Close	P/E High/Low		PER SHARE ($) Earnings	Dividends	Book Value
5/09	15.05	32	13	1.07	—	5.50
5/08	26.83	40	17	1.00	—	4.40
5/07	31.58	42	20	0.85	—	3.14
5/06	18.18	41	24	0.59	—	2.06
5/05	22.34	70	23	0.33	—	1.68
Annual Growth	(9.4%)	—	—	34.2%	—	34.5%

Immunomedics, Inc.

Immunomedics is focused on developing humanized monoclonal antibodies (MAbs) to treat cancer and other serious diseases. Its lead product, epratuzumab, is in late-stage development for the treatment of lupus; biopharmaceutical firm UCB has licensed the drug for further applications in autoimmune diseases. Immunomedics is also conducting clinical trials for epratuzumab as an oncology treatment for non-Hodgkin's lymphoma and leukemia. The company has other drugs in clinical trials to treat various cancers, including veltuzumab (lymphoma) and milatuzumab (multiple myeloma).

The company also makes diagnostic imaging products; subsidiary IBC Pharmaceuticals develops radiotherapeutics for applications in oncology treatments.

Immunomedics is focusing less on its diagnostic imaging products, including imaging agent LeukoScan (approved in Europe), in order to focus on its drug therapies; it halted commercialization of CEA-Scan, which has US and EU approval as a colorectal cancer diagnostic.

In 2008 Immunomedics teamed up with Nycomed to develop and commercialize veltuzumab for non-cancer indications. UCB halted its late-stage epratuzumab trials for lupus in order to alter the protocols in 2007, but announced some positive results in 2008. That year milatuzumab received FDA orphan drug status for multiple myeloma. The designation gave Immunomedics seven years of exclusivity to market the drug before competing companies can step in.

Chairman David Goldenberg, who founded the company in 1982, owns approximately 11% of Immunomedics together with his wife, CEO Cynthia Sullivan.

EXECUTIVES

Chairman, Chief Strategic Officer, Chief Scientific Officer, and Chief Medical Officer: David M. Goldenberg, age 71, $1,463,362 total compensation
President, CEO, and Director: Cynthia L. Sullivan, age 54, $1,125,156 total compensation
SVP Finance and Business Development, and CFO: Gerard G. (Gerry) Gorman, age 58, $541,534 total compensation
Auditors: Ernst & Young LLP

LOCATIONS

HQ: Immunomedics, Inc.
300 American Rd., Morris Plains, NJ 07950
Phone: 973-605-8200   **Fax:** 973-605-8282
Web: www.immunomedics.com

COMPETITORS

Amgen	Human Genome Sciences
AstraZeneca	ImmunoGen
Bayer Schering Pharma	Ligand Pharmaceuticals
Biogen Idec	Medarex
Bristol-Myers Squibb	Millennium
Eli Lilly	Pharmaceuticals
Genentech	Oncolab
Genmab	PDL BioPharma
GlaxoSmithKline	Poniard Pharmaceuticals
Hoffmann-La Roche	

HISTORICAL FINANCIALS

Company Type: Public

Income Statement

FYE: June 30

	REVENUE ($ mil.)	NET INCOME ($ mil.)	NET PROFIT MARGIN	EMPLOYEES
6/09	30.0	2.3	7.7%	120
6/08	3.7	(22.9)	—	117
6/07	8.5	(16.7)	—	108
6/06	4.4	(28.8)	—	106
6/05	3.8	(26.8)	—	118
Annual Growth	67.6%	—	—	0.4%

2009 Year-End Financials

Debt ratio: —
Return on equity: 749.8%
Cash ($ mil.): 27.4
Current ratio: 0.60
Long-term debt ($ mil.): —
No. of shares (mil.): 75.2

Dividends
Yield: 0.0%
Payout: —
Market value ($ mil.): 191.1
R&D as % of sales: —
Advertising as % of sales: —

Stock History

NASDAQ (GM): IMMU

	STOCK PRICE ($) FY Close	P/E High/Low		PER SHARE ($) Earnings	Dividends	Book Value
6/09	2.54	95	28	0.03	0.00	0.03
6/08	2.13	—	—	(0.31)	0.00	(0.02)
6/07	4.16	—	—	(0.26)	0.00	0.27
6/06	2.64	—	—	(0.52)	0.00	(0.25)
6/05	1.71	—	—	(0.50)	0.00	(0.02)
Annual Growth	10.4%	—	—	—	—	—

IMPAX Laboratories

IMPAX Laboratories hopes that its combination of generic and branded pharmaceuticals will make an impact on its financial health. The company makes specialty generic pharmaceuticals, which it markets through its Global Pharmaceuticals division and through marketing alliances with other firms, including Teva. It concentrates on controlled-release versions of branded pharmaceuticals and niche pharmaceuticals that require difficult-to-obtain raw materials or specialized expertise. The company's branded pharmaceuticals business (called IMPAX Pharmaceuticals) is developing drugs that target Parkinson's disease, epilepsy, and other central nervous system disorders.

The company's Global Pharmaceuticals division sells its generic products to wholesalers, chain drug stores, and mail order pharmacies. IMPAX also works through strategic alliances; its deal with Teva, for instance, gives the generics giant US rights to some versions of its generic Claritin, Wellbutrin SR, and Prilosec products.

EXECUTIVES

Chairman: Robert L. (Bob) Burr, age 58
President, CEO, and Director: Larry Hsu, age 60, $1,710,094 total compensation
SVP Operations: Charles V. Hildenbrand, age 57, $736,309 total compensation
SVP Finance and CFO: Arthur A. Koch Jr., age 53, $919,338 total compensation
President, IMPAX Pharmaceuticals Division: Michael J. Nestor, age 56, $725,972 total compensation
President, Global Pharmaceuticals Division: Christopher Mengler, age 47
Chief Scientific Officer, IMPAX Pharmaceuticals: Suneel Gupta
Auditors: Grant Thornton LLP

LOCATIONS

HQ: Impax Laboratories, Inc.
30831 Huntwood Ave., Hayward, CA 94544
Phone: 510-476-2000   **Fax:** 510-471-3200
Web: www.impaxlabs.com

PRODUCTS/OPERATIONS

2008 Sales

	$ mil.	% of total
Global pharmaceuticals	197.2	94
Impax pharmaceuticals	12.9	6
Total	**210.1**	**100**

Selected Generic Products

Anagrelide hydrochloride (generic Agrylin, thrombocytosis)
Bupropion hydrochloride (generic Wellbutrin SR, depression)
Colestipol hydrochloride (generic Colestid, high cholesterol)
Dantrolene sodium (generic Dantrium, spasticity)
Metformin Hcl (generic Glucophage XR, diabetes)
Nadolol/Bendroflumethiazide (generic Corzide, hypertension)
Oxybutynin chloride (generic Ditropan XL, urinary incontinence, with Teva)
Oxycodone hydrochloride (generic OxyContin controlled release, pain)
Pilocarpine hydrochlorine (generic Salagen, dry mouth caused by radiation therapy)

COMPETITORS

Actavis	Par Pharmaceutical
Biovail	Ranbaxy Laboratories
Caraco Pharmaceutical	Sandoz International
Forest Labs	SkyePharma
King Pharmaceuticals	Synovics
K-V Pharmaceutical	Teva Pharmaceuticals
Mylan	Watson Pharmaceuticals

HISTORICAL FINANCIALS

Company Type: Public

Income Statement

FYE: December 31

	REVENUE ($ mil.)	NET INCOME ($ mil.)	NET PROFIT MARGIN	EMPLOYEES
12/08	210.1	18.7	8.9%	768

2008 Year-End Financials

Debt ratio: 3.8%
Return on equity: 16.6%
Cash ($ mil.): 69.3
Current ratio: 2.15
Long-term debt ($ mil.): 6.0
No. of shares (mil.): 61.9

Dividends
  Yield: 0.0%
  Payout: —
Market value ($ mil.): 550.1
R&D as % of sales: —
Advertising as % of sales: —

Stock History

NASDAQ (GM): IPXL

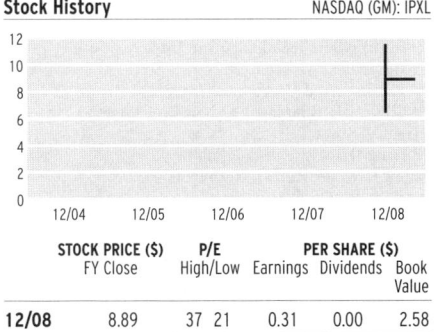

	STOCK PRICE ($) FY Close	P/E High/Low		PER SHARE ($) Earnings	Dividends	Book Value
12/08	8.89	37	21	0.31	0.00	2.58

Industrial Services of America

Industrial Services of America manages solid waste so its customers won't have to. Its Computerized Waste Systems (CWS) unit doesn't pick up trash but instead arranges waste disposal services for its commercial and industrial customers at 2,270 locations. CWS negotiates contracts with service providers and offers centralized billing and dispatching and invoice auditing services. Industrial Services of America's ISA Recycling unit handles ferrous and nonferrous metals and fiber products, and the company's Waste Equipment Sales & Service (WESSCO) unit sells, leases, and services waste handling and recycling equipment. Chairman and CEO Harry Kletter owns about 36% of the company; his wife, Roberta, owns 9%.

CWS offers its services throughout North America via a network of more than 6,500 vendors, including equipment manufacturing and maintenance companies, hauling companies, and recycling companies.

Industrial Services of America absorbed the loss of a major client (Home Depot) in 2005. The company maintains its growth strategy by increasing efficiencies and productivity in its core operations. However, it is open to possible acquisitions, strategic partnerships, mergers, and/or joint ventures that promise to enhance its overall profitability.

EXECUTIVES

Chairman and CEO: Harry Kletter, age 83, $793,272 total compensation
President, COO, and Director: Brian G. Donaghy, age 34, $332,400 total compensation
CFO and Treasurer: Alan L. Schroering, age 45
EVP Corporate Business Development: Nick Halaris
VP Recycling: James K. Wiseman, age 56, $177,852 total compensation
VP Alloys: Steve Jones, age 38
General Manager, Alloys: Jeff Valentine
Division Manager, WESSCO: Scott Necessary
Director, Human Resources: Marjorie Brian
Auditors: Mountjoy & Bressler, LLP

LOCATIONS

HQ: Industrial Services of America, Inc.
7100 Grade Ln., Louisville, KY 40232
Phone: 502-368-1661   **Fax:** 502-368-1440
Web: www.isa-inc.com

COMPETITORS

Aleris International
Avalon Holdings
Casella Waste Systems
Commercial Metals
David J. Joseph
OAKLEAF Waste Management
Philip Services
Republic Services
Rumpke
Smurfit-Stone Container
United Scrap Metal
Veolia Environmental Services North America
Waste Management
WM Recycle America

HISTORICAL FINANCIALS

Company Type: Public

Income Statement

FYE: December 31

	REVENUE ($ mil.)	NET INCOME ($ mil.)	NET PROFIT MARGIN	EMPLOYEES
12/08	100.0	1.5	1.5%	126
12/07	77.0	2.6	3.4%	139
12/06	62.1	2.2	3.5%	102
12/05	117.4	1.1	0.9%	103
12/04	139.6	1.5	1.1%	128
Annual Growth	(8.0%)	0.0%	—	(0.4%)

2008 Year-End Financials

Debt ratio: 69.1%
Return on equity: 12.3%
Cash ($ mil.): 1.1
Current ratio: 1.40
Long-term debt ($ mil.): 8.5
No. of shares (mil.): 4.3

Dividends
  Yield: 1.8%
  Payout: 23.3%
Market value ($ mil.): 23.4
R&D as % of sales: —
Advertising as % of sales: —

Stock History

NASDAQ (CM): IDSA

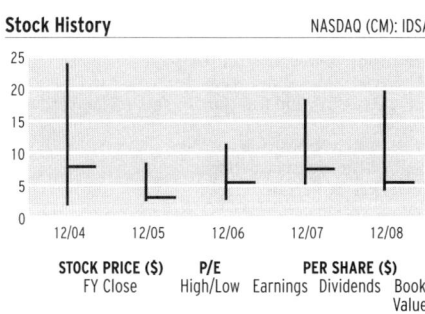

	STOCK PRICE ($) FY Close	P/E High/Low		PER SHARE ($) Earnings	Dividends	Book Value
12/08	5.45	45	10	0.43	0.10	2.88
12/07	7.53	26	8	0.71	0.10	2.80
12/06	5.45	18	5	0.61	0.00	2.27
12/05	3.10	27	9	0.31	0.00	1.74
12/04	7.87	57	5	0.42	0.10	1.38
Annual Growth	(8.8%)	—	—	0.6%	0.0%	20.2%

Infinera Corporation

To Infinera, and beyond! The buzz on this company is that it designs photonic integrated circuits (PICs) intended to replace much larger components within optical networks. It also offers networking equipment built around these chips. Infinera's chips are made from indium phosphide, a specialized compound semiconductor material that offers light-years faster performance than standard silicon. Customers include cable system operators, Internet service providers, and telecommunications carriers, such as Cox Communications, Deutsche Telekom, Global Crossing, Level 3 Communications (one-quarter of sales), Qwest Communications, and XO Communications. Infinera gets more than three-quarters of its sales in the US.

The company is diversifying and expanding its customer base, adding Internet content providers and operators of fiber-optic networks. Infinera also sees its Digital Optical Networking technology finding uses among educational, government, and research institutions. As "100-gig" (100 gigabits per second) optical networks become more common, the company believes its line cards can deliver not only that advanced level of data transmission, but the products can also scale up to increase its system capabilities from 400Gbps to 800Gbps.

Not only does Infinera design its own chips — it also manufactures them, using fabrication processes it developed. That's a rarity in the semiconductor and optical components industries, where most startups rely on contract manufacturers to make their parts. Infinera also developed a network operating system. The company continues to invest in its manufacturing capabilities.

In January 2010 company co-founder Jagdeep Singh stepped down as CEO, opting to focus on the long-term product strategy of the company as executive chairman. Singh was replaced by Tom Fallon, who joined the company in 2004 and had served as COO since 2006. Fallon has prior experience leading a business unit within Cisco.

EXECUTIVES

Chairman: Jagdeep Singh, age 42,
$1,555,911 total compensation
President, CEO, and Director: Thomas J. (Tom) Fallon,
age 48
CFO: Duston M. Williams, age 50,
$979,531 total compensation
CTO: Drew D. Perkins
Chief Legal Officer: Michael O. McCarthy III, age 44
Chief Marketing and Strategy Officer: David F. Welch,
age 48, $944,493 total compensation
VP Worldwide Sales: Scott Chandler, age 41,
$941,879 total compensation
**VP Worldwide Customer Service and Technical
Support:** Lonny Orona
VP Worldwide Sales: Ron Martin
VP Strategic Materials: Minoo Mortazavi
VP Systems Engineering: Dirk Corsus
VP PIC Development and Manufacturing:
Frederick A. (Fred) Kish Jr.
VP Human Resources: Paul M. Whitney
VP Strategic Sales: Howard Lukens
Director Communications: Jeff Ferry
Investor Relations: Bob Blair
President, Infinera Japan: Satoshi Fujita, age 65
Auditors: Ernst & Young LLP

LOCATIONS

HQ: Infinera Corporation
169 Java Dr., Sunnyvale, CA 94089
Phone: 408-572-5200   **Fax:** 408-572-5343
Web: www.infinera.com

Infinera has facilities in China, India, and the US.

2008 Sales

	$ mil.	% of total
US	412.6	79
Europe, Middle East & Africa	91.2	18
Asia/Pacific	15.4	3
Total	**519.2**	**100**

PRODUCTS/OPERATIONS

2008 Sales

	$ mil.	% of total
Product	306.8	59
Ratable product, support & services	193.7	37
Services	18.7	4
Total	**519.2**	**100**

Selected Products and Services

Products
 Infinera DTN (switched wavelength division
  multiplexing system)
 Infinera IQ Network Operating System
 Infinera Management Suite Software
 Infinera Optical Line Amplifier (bidirectional inline
  amplifier)
Services
 Deployment and professional services
 Technical support
 Training and documentation
 Warranty and maintenance

COMPETITORS

Alcatel-Lucent
Ciena
Cisco Systems
CyOptics
Ericsson
Fujitsu
Huawei Technologies
NEC
Nokia Siemens Networks
Nortel Networks
Oki Semiconductor
Opnext
PMC-Sierra
ZTE

HISTORICAL FINANCIALS

Company Type: Public

Income Statement

FYE: December 31

	REVENUE ($ mil.)	NET INCOME ($ mil.)	NET PROFIT MARGIN	EMPLOYEES
12/08	519.2	78.7	15.2%	937
12/07	245.9	(55.3)	—	711
12/06	58.2	(89.9)	—	605
12/05	4.1	(66.0)	—	617
12/04	0.6	(66.5)	—	—
Annual Growth	**442.4%**	**—**	**—**	**14.9%**

2008 Year-End Financials

Debt ratio: —
Return on equity: 22.5%
Cash ($ mil.): 166.8
Current ratio: 4.47
Long-term debt ($ mil.): —
No. of shares (mil.): 96.6
Dividends
 Yield: 0.0%
 Payout: —
Market value ($ mil.): 865.5
R&D as % of sales: —
Advertising as % of sales: —

Stock History

NASDAQ (GM): INFN

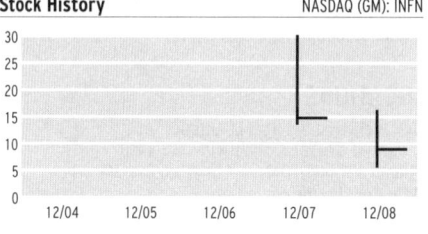

	STOCK PRICE ($) FY Close	P/E High/Low		PER SHARE ($) Earnings	Dividends	Book Value
12/08	8.96	20	7	0.81	0.00	4.20
12/07	14.84	—	—	(1.09)	0.00	3.05
Annual Growth	**(39.6%)**	**—**	**—**	**—**	**—**	**37.6%**

Infinity Pharmaceuticals

Infinity Pharmaceuticals acts on the endless possibilities for new cancer treatments. The firm develops small-molecule anti-cancer drugs for applications in many types of cancer therapy. Its most advanced candidate is retaspimycin, which is in clinical trials for gastrointestinal, lung, and prostate cancers. Other cancer drugs in the pipeline are in discovery or early development phases. Infinity Pharmaceuticals has licensing or collaborative development partnerships with companies such as Novartis, Amgen, and Johnson & Johnson Pharmaceutical Research & Development. In 2006 Infinity merged with Discovery Partners International (DPI) in a reverse merger that made Infinity a public company.

Infinity Pharmaceuticals had inked a multi-million dollar deal with biotech company MedImmune in 2006 to jointly develop its most advanced drug candidates (based on its hsp90 protein inhibitor technology) and share any future revenues on the drugs; however, the deal was canceled in 2008 after AstraZeneca acquired MedImmune. Infinity is seeking an international marketing partner for the program, but the company intends to retain US marketing rights for the products.

In 2007 lead candidate retaspimycin (also known as IPI-504), a drug in the hsp90 portfolio, was granted orphan drug status for the treatment of gastrointestinal stromal tumors (GIST). Orphan drug status assists developers of rare-disease treatments to optimize development and gives market exclusivity for seven years after market approval.

The company formed a partnership with Purdue Pharmaceutical and Mundipharma to develop and commercialize Infinity's discovery and early stage development programs in international markets. The company will receive $75 million plus additional potential credit and research funding while retaining US marketing rights to the candidates.

Partner Novartis owns a 7% stake in Infinity.

EXECUTIVES

CEO and Director: Adelene Q. Perkins, age 50,
$1,222,206 total compensation
**President, Research and Development and Chief
Scientific Officer:** Julian Adams, age 55,
$1,196,821 total compensation
VP and General Counsel: Gerald E. Quirk
VP Pharmaceutical Development: Michael S. Curtis
VP Corporate and Product Development:
Jeffrey K. Tong, age 32
VP Information Technology and Informatics:
John J. Keilty
VP Facilities and Operations: John McPherson
VP Clinical Development and Medical Affairs:
David S. Grayzel
VP Drug Discovery: Vito J. Palombella
Senior Director Human Resources:
Jeanette W. Kohlbrenner
VP Finance: Steven J. Kafka
**Senior Director, Controller, Assistant Treasurer, and
Principal Accounting Officer:** Christopher M. Lindblom
Senior Director, Product Development:
Margaret A. Reid
Senior Director, Cancer Biology: Christian C. Fritz
Corporate Communications: Monique Allaire
Auditors: KPMG LLP

LOCATIONS

HQ: Infinity Pharmaceuticals, Inc.
780 Memorial Dr., Cambridge, MA 02139
Phone: 617-453-1000   **Fax:** 617-453-1001
Web: www.ipi.com

COMPETITORS

Abbott Labs
Abraxis BioScience
Astex Therapeutics
AstraZeneca
Biogen Idec
Bristol-Myers Squibb
Curis
Genentech
GlaxoSmithKline
Hoffmann-La Roche
Novartis
Pfizer
Roche Holding
Sanofi-Aventis
Synta Pharmaceuticals
Vernalis plc

HISTORICAL FINANCIALS

Company Type: Public

Income Statement

FYE: December 31

	REVENUE ($ mil.)	NET INCOME ($ mil.)	NET PROFIT MARGIN	EMPLOYEES
12/08	83.4	23.7	28.4%	161
12/07	24.5	(16.9)	—	125
12/06	18.5	(28.4)	—	115
12/05	34.8	(16.5)	—	133
12/04	51.6	3.9	7.6%	191
Annual Growth	**12.8%**	**57.0%**	**—**	**(4.2%)**

2008 Year-End Financials

Debt ratio: 0.0%
Return on equity: 27.6%
Cash ($ mil.): 16.6
Current ratio: 8.52
Long-term debt ($ mil.): 0.0
No. of shares (mil.): 26.2

Dividends
Yield: 0.0%
Payout: —
Market value ($ mil.): 209.3
R&D as % of sales: —
Advertising as % of sales: —

Stock History

NASDAQ (GM): INFI

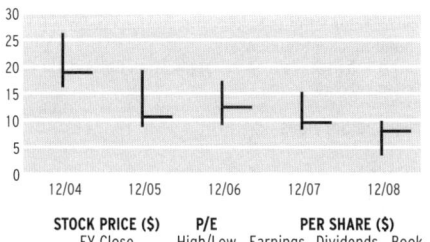

	STOCK PRICE ($) FY Close	P/E High/Low		PER SHARE ($) Earnings	Dividends	Book Value
12/08	7.99	8	3	1.14	0.00	4.59
12/07	9.55	—	—	(0.87)	0.00	1.95
12/06	12.41	—	—	(3.81)	0.00	2.38
12/05	10.60	—	—	(2.20)	0.00	3.63
12/04	18.84	43	27	0.60	0.00	4.14
Annual Growth	(19.3%)	—	—	17.4%	—	2.6%

infoGROUP Inc.

Making information available keeps this collective together. Formerly infoUSA, infoGROUP is a provider of business and consumer information and research services for direct marketing, sales prospecting, and business intelligence. Its Data Group has 12 databases with contact and credit information covering more than 15 million businesses. infoGROUP's Salesgenie.com subscription product provides access to its databases; the Data Group also includes Web-based information firm OneSource Information Services. The firm licenses its data to third parties through its Data Group. infoGROUP additionally includes a Services Group and a Marketing Research Group. Founder Vinod Gupta owns about 40% of the company.

The company's Services Group provides customer data management and brokerage services, e-mail marketing services, and catalog marketing services. It consists of holdings such as List Brokerage and List Management, Donnelley Marketing, Triplex (data processing services for high-profile political and non-profit organizations), and Yesmail. In 2008 infoGROUP added direct marketing firm Direct Media Millard to the division. The deal expanded its reach in list brokerage, list management, analytics, database marketing, and data processing services.

The company's acquisition of Opinion Research Corp. helped form its Marketing Research Group. The 2006 purchase of Opinion Research, a provider of market research services to business and government clients, cost infoGROUP about $134 million, including the assumption of debt. Opinion Research provides customer surveys, opinion polling, and other market research services for clients. infoGROUP then moved quickly to expand that business through the 2007 purchase of Guideline, a provider of custom business and market research and analysis, for approximately $42 million. In 2008 the company

combined Guideline and Opinion Research Corp. under a single management structure.

In order to meet customer demand for global information, in 2008 the company announced the addition of databases for China and India. It is compiling a database for the UK, and plans to add databases for Ireland, Australia, and New Zealand. Reflecting its strategy of global expansion, the company changed its name to infoGROUP from infoUSA in 2008.

infoGROUP is facing an SEC investigation related to securities trading and a shareholder lawsuit concerning Gupta's alleged misspending of company funds. The lawsuit alleges the company misspent millions, some of it on former President Bill Clinton and Secretary of State Hillary Rodham Clinton. (Gupta has been a major donor to the Democratic Party.) In response to the investigation, the company in 2008 separated the duties of chairman and CEO. Later that year, Gupta resigned from his executive position and former SITEL executive Bill Fairfield was named CEO. Gupta has also agreed to pay the company $9 million over the next five years.

HISTORY

Vinod Gupta and Glen Humphrey got started in the database business in 1972 with $100 and a stack of Yellow Pages. Through their company, American Business Information (ABI), the two compiled business listings into manufacturing directories and state business directories. ABI had every US Yellow Pages directory in its database by 1986. The company went public in 1992, the same year it formed a joint venture with conglomerate TRW to provide customers with marketing and credit information.

To expand its product line and distribution channels, ABI began acquiring related companies in 1993. Two years later it made its database available on America Online (later AOL), the Microsoft Network, and Bloomberg financial terminals. It launched its own Web site in 1996. During the next year ABI bought six more companies, including Database America for $100 million.

In a surprise move, the hands-on, entrepreneurial Gupta stepped back from his CEO duties in 1997 and appointed Scott Dahnke, a McKinsey consultant, as his replacement. The next year ABI failed in its bid to acquire consumer database company Metromail for $918 million (it was bought by UK-based Great Universal Stores). It later changed its name to infoUSA and launched VideoYellowPages.com, a Web site to provide pictures of businesses along with their yellow pages advertisement.

When infoUSA posted big losses, Dahnke was ousted in 1998 and Gupta came back as CEO. The company bought First Data's Donnelley Marketing division in 1999, and continued building online distribution units like listbazaar.com and businessCreditUSA.com. However, losses from the investments began piling up in 2000 and investors soured on ad-supported Internet sites. The company closed down and consolidated some of its online ventures in 2001 and cut some 500 people from its workforce. Previous CFO Stormy Dean found time to run for governor of Nebraska in 2002 (he lost the election and resigned from infoUSA the following year to pursue a political career full time).

infoUSA next began working to transform itself from a lists-and-labels company into a full-service information provider. After buying direct e-mail services company yesmail from CMGI in

2003, the company expanded its database holdings by acquiring business information provider OneSource Information Services for about $100 million. infoUSA also acquired list brokerage firm Edith Roman Associates in 2004.

Gupta made a $630 million bid to take the company private in 2005, but infoUSA's board rejected the offer. In 2006 it fought a hostile takeover attempt by shareholder Dolphin Partners.

Having expanded its databases to cover markets in Europe and Asia, the company changed its name to infoGROUP in 2008. After the company separated the duties of chairman and CEO, Gupta resigned from his executive position and Bill Fairfield was appointed the new CEO.

EXECUTIVES

Chairman: Roger S. Siboni, age 54
President, CEO, and Director: Bill L. Fairfield, age 62, $261,171 total compensation
EVP and CFO: Thomas (Tom) Oberdorf, age 51, $130,898 total compensation
EVP Business Conduct, General Counsel, and Secretary: Thomas J. McCusker, age 66
EVP and General Manager, Database Group Sales: Stormy L. Dean, age 51, $484,288 total compensation
SVP Corporate Relations: Lisa Olson
CIO: Thomas J. McAlister
Corporate Controller, Chief Accounting Officer, and CFO, Services Group: Alan Heckart
President, infoUSA Licensing: Jim DeRouchey
President, American Medical Information: Greg Hoye
President, infoGROUP Nonprofit: Gretchen Littlefield
President, Walter Karl: Robert FitzGerald
President, Opinion Research: Gerard J. Miodus, age 52
President, List Reseller Division: Joe Lemoine
President, Services Group: Edward C. (Ed) Mallin, age 58, $925,569 total compensation
President, Direct Media Millard: Larry May
President, Edith Roman Associates: Steve Roberts
President, Enterprise Sales Group: Rakesh Gupta
Director, Business Development: Barry Rubin
President, infoCANADA: Dan Cadieux
President and General Manager, Yesmail: Michael (Mike) Hilts
Director, External Communications: Kelly Loontjer
Auditors: KPMG LLP

LOCATIONS

HQ: infoGROUP Inc.
5711 S. 86th Circle, Omaha, NE 68127
Phone: 402-593-4500   **Fax:** 402-596-8902
Web: www.infogroup.com

PRODUCTS/OPERATIONS

2008 Sales

	$ mil.	% of total
Data	309.5	42
Market Research	265.5	36
Services	163.3	22
Total	**738.3**	**100**

Selected Operations

infoUSA Data Group
OneSource (Web-based business and financial information)
Salesgenie.com (Web-based database access)
MarketZone (customer relationship management platform)
infoUSA Marketing Research Group
Guideline (custom market research consulting and services)
Macro International (market research for government clients)
Northwest Research Group (market research services)
NWC Research (social and market research services)
Opinion Research (market research for business clients)

infoUSA Services Group
  Catalog Vision (catalog marketing)
  Direct Media (list brokerage and management
    services)
  List brokerage and list management services
    (customer data management)
  Triplex (data processing services)
  Yesmail (e-mail marketing)

COMPETITORS

Acxiom
CreditRiskMonitor.com
D&B
Data Warehouse
Equifax
Experian Americas
Forrester Research
Gartner
Harris Interactive
Harte-Hanks
InfoSpace
Maritz Research
Moody's
Reed Elsevier Group
USADATA
ZoomInfo

HISTORICAL FINANCIALS

Company Type: Public

Income Statement

FYE: December 31

	REVENUE ($ mil.)	NET INCOME ($ mil.)	NET PROFIT MARGIN	EMPLOYEES
12/08	738.3	4.8	0.7%	4,771
12/07	688.8	40.9	5.9%	4,815
12/06	434.9	33.3	7.7%	4,089
12/05	383.2	31.5	8.2%	2,695
12/04	344.9	17.8	5.2%	2,332
Annual Growth	21.0%	(27.9%)	—	19.6%

2008 Year-End Financials

Debt ratio: 119.6%
Return on equity: 1.9%
Cash ($ mil.): 4.8
Current ratio: 0.94
Long-term debt ($ mil.): 297.7
No. of shares (mil.): 57.5

Dividends
  Yield: 0.0%
  Payout: —
Market value ($ mil.): 272.7
R&D as % of sales: —
Advertising as % of sales: —

Stock History

NASDAQ (GS): IUSA

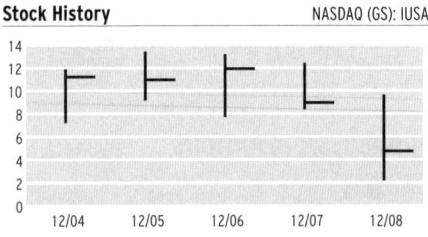

	STOCK PRICE ($) FY Close	P/E High/Low	PER SHARE ($) Earnings	Dividends	Book Value
12/08	4.74	119 29	0.08	0.00	4.33
12/07	8.93	17 12	0.73	0.25	4.67
12/06	11.91	22 13	0.60	0.00	4.07
12/05	10.93	23 16	0.58	0.20	3.44
12/04	11.19	36 22	0.33	—	2.98
Annual Growth	(19.3%)	— —	(29.8%)	—	9.8%

Informatica Corporation

Thinking about data? Think Informatica. The company provides enterprise data integration software that enables companies to access, integrate, and consolidate their data across a variety of systems and users. Informatica's PowerCenter platform consolidates, codes, and moves large data warehouses, and its PowerExchange software enables access to bulk or changed data. Other products include PowerAnalyzer, an application for improving data performance and efficiency, and SuperGlue, a metadata tool that creates data about data, integrating information from different databases to identify redundancies and analyze how the data is being used. Informatica's more than 3,400 customers include ABN AMRO, Avnet, and CVS.

Informatica is shifting its focus from data warehousing specifically to a broader enterprise data integration platform, which includes not only data warehousing, but also data migration, consolidation, management, and synchronization capabilities. The company is also increasing its focus on one of its key markets, the financial services industry, by developing versions of its software tailored to the needs of these customers.

Informatica has grown in part through acquisitions and partnerships, with the 2009 purchase of AddressDoctor adding global address validation technology to its product line, and the purchase of Applimation that same year expanding its information lifecycle management capabilities. The company also acquired Agent Logic, which provided technology to integrate alerting capabilities into business rules and event processing.

EXECUTIVES

Chairman, President, and CEO: Sohaib Abbasi, age 52, $2,511,317 total compensation
EVP, CFO, and Secretary: Earl E. Fry, age 50, $1,142,583 total compensation
EVP Worldwide Field Operations: Paul J. Hoffman, age 58, $1,111,055 total compensation
EVP and General Manager, Data Integration: Girish Pancha, age 44
SVP and CIO: Tony Young
SVP Asia Pacific: Graham Sowden
SVP Europe, Middle East, and Africa: John Poulter
SVP and CTO: James Markarian
SVP and General Manager, Data Quality: Ivan Chong
SVP Global Customer Support: Ansa Sekharan
VP Corporate Communications: Debbie Walery
Chief Marketing Officer: Chris Boorman
Senior Director, Investor Relations: Stephanie Wakefield
Auditors: Ernst & Young LLP

LOCATIONS

HQ: Informatica Corporation
  100 Cardinal Way, Redwood City, CA 94063
Phone: 650-385-5000   **Fax:** 650-385-5500
Web: www.informatica.com

2008 Sales

	$ mil.	% of total
US	297.1	65
Other countries	158.6	35
Total	**455.7**	**100**

PRODUCTS/OPERATIONS

2008 Sales

	$ mil.	% of total
Service	259.9	57
License	195.8	43
Total	**455.7**	**100**

Selected Software

PowerCenter (enterprise data integration platform for
  building data warehouses)
PowerExchange (data access application for bulk or
  changed data)

Selected Services

Configuration
Consulting
Implementation
Technical support

COMPETITORS

Cognos
Embarcadero Technologies
IBM
Microsoft
MicroStrategy
Oracle
SAP
SAS Institute

HISTORICAL FINANCIALS

Company Type: Public

Income Statement

FYE: December 31

	REVENUE ($ mil.)	NET INCOME ($ mil.)	NET PROFIT MARGIN	EMPLOYEES
12/08	455.7	56.0	12.3%	1,611
12/07	391.3	54.6	14.0%	1,365
12/06	324.6	36.2	11.2%	1,221
12/05	267.4	33.8	12.6%	1,010
12/04	219.7	(104.4)	—	837
Annual Growth	20.0%	—	—	17.8%

2008 Year-End Financials

Debt ratio: 67.9%
Return on equity: 16.8%
Cash ($ mil.): 179.9
Current ratio: 2.76
Long-term debt ($ mil.): 241.7
No. of shares (mil.): 89.5

Dividends
  Yield: —
  Payout: —
Market value ($ mil.): 1,228.1
R&D as % of sales: —
Advertising as % of sales: —

Stock History

NASDAQ (GS): INFA

	STOCK PRICE ($) FY Close	P/E High/Low	PER SHARE ($) Earnings	Dividends	Book Value
12/08	13.73	33 18	0.58	—	3.98
12/07	18.02	32 22	0.57	—	3.49
12/06	12.21	44 29	0.39	—	2.54
12/05	12.00	34 19	0.37	—	2.49
12/04	8.12	— —	(1.22)	—	2.19
Annual Growth	14.0%	— —	—	—	16.1%

InnerWorkings, Inc.

Printing procurement firm InnerWorkings has inserted itself into the process by which corporate customers get print jobs done. The company's proprietary software, PPM4, matches customers' jobs with printing companies' equipment and capacity. The InnerWorkings system submits a job to multiple printers, who then bid for the business. More than 7,000 suppliers participate in the company's network, which comprises 25 locations in the US and the UK. InnerWorkings' customers include companies in the advertising, consumer products, publishing, and retail industries.

InnerWorkings, which has largely grown through acquisitions, has slowed its expansion plans as its 2009 sales figures fell amid the economic downturn in the US. Although its customers slashed their spending on printing by about 25%, the company is hopeful that it can recapture the losses. To this end, InnerWorkings has inked agreements with about 20 new clients, including Bacardi and Movie Gallery, and is looking to add about $50 million in revenue in 2010. It also cut its non-sales workforce by about 15%, which is expected to save about $5 million annually.

Before its growth strategy was put on hold, InnerWorkings had focused on buying up complementary print management and fulfillment companies. In 2008 it completed five acquisitions, the most notable being New York-based Mikam Graphics, a management and procurement firm for printed and promotional products. InnerWorkings paid $13 million for Mikam Graphics and noted that it would pay out another $14 million if certain performance measures were met by 2011. Altogether, InnerWorkings dispensed about $40 million on acquisitions in 2008.

Its 2007 purchases included Chicago-based promotional products distributor Corporate Edge and Philadelphia-based Brown+Partners, which offers print management services. Fuel for the deals came from Innerworkings' 2006 initial public offering and a 2007 follow-on offering, which raised nearly $90 million in net proceeds.

Most of InnerWorkings' business comes from enterprise customers, for whom the company handles print jobs on a recurring basis. The company also takes work from customers on a transactional basis, one order at a time. It hopes to grow by turning transactional customers into enterprise customers.

The company saw new leadership step in at the beginning of 2009. President and COO Eric Belcher added CEO to his duties in January and joined the board as a director. He joined InnerWorkings in 2005 as EVP of operations. Former CEO Steven Zuccarini became the company's vice chairman.

In conjunction with InnerWorkings' IPO filing, founders Richard Heise and Eric Lefkofsky left the company's board, but they retain about 20% of the company. Affiliates of venture capital firm New Enterprise Associates, represented on InnerWorkings' board by Peter Barris, own about a 15% stake.

EXECUTIVES

Chairman: John R. Walter
Vice Chairman: Steven E. (Steve) Zuccarini, age 52, $959,302 total compensation
President, CEO, and Director: Eric D. Belcher, age 40, $1,347,106 total compensation
CFO and Secretary: Joseph M. Busky, age 41, $584,276 total compensation
EVP Sales: Ryan G. Irwin, age 42
SVP Supply Chain Management and Sales Operations: Jonathan M. Shean, age 36, $438,740 total compensation
CIO: Jan J. Sevcik, age 40
VP Technology: Neil P. Graver, age 38, $169,990 total compensation
VP Marketing: Kyle Berry
Mergers and Acquisitions: Chip Hodgkins
General Counsel and Human Resources: Todd Andrews
Auditors: Ernst & Young LLP

LOCATIONS

HQ: InnerWorkings, Inc.
    600 W. Chicago Ave., Ste. 850, Chicago, IL 60610
Phone: 312-642-3700   **Fax:** 312-642-3704
Web: www.iwprint.com

PRODUCTS/OPERATIONS

2008 Sales

	% of total
Enterprise clients	64
Transactional clients	36
Total	**100**

COMPETITORS

Cirqit
NewlineNoosh
Quad/Graphics
R.R. Donnelley
World Color Press

HISTORICAL FINANCIALS

Company Type: Public

Income Statement				FYE: December 31
	REVENUE ($ mil.)	NET INCOME ($ mil.)	NET PROFIT MARGIN	EMPLOYEES
12/08	419.0	16.0	3.8%	761
12/07	288.4	22.5	7.8%	567
12/06	160.5	6.9	4.3%	153
12/05	76.9	3.9	5.1%	154
12/04	38.9	1.8	4.6%	—
Annual Growth	**81.2%**	**72.7%**	**—**	**70.3%**

2008 Year-End Financials

Debt ratio: 0.1%
Return on equity: 11.4%
Cash ($ mil.): 4.0
Current ratio: 1.09
Long-term debt ($ mil.): 0.1
No. of shares (mil.): 45.6
Dividends
    Yield: 0.0%
    Payout: —
Market value ($ mil.): 298.8
R&D as % of sales: —
Advertising as % of sales: —

Stock History

NASDAQ (GM): INWK

	STOCK PRICE ($)	P/E		PER SHARE ($)		
	FY Close	High/Low		Earnings	Dividends	Book Value
12/08	6.55	51	15	0.32	0.00	2.93
12/07	17.26	42	24	0.45	0.00	3.23
12/06	15.96	88	46	0.21	0.00	1.79
Annual Growth	**(35.9%)**	**—**	**—**	**23.4%**	**—**	**28.1%**

Innodata Isogen

Innodata Isogen handles information inundation. The company provides content management and process outsourcing services to businesses and government agencies. It oversees abstracting and indexing, data capture and entry, research and analysis, and technical writing. Customers turn to Innodata Isogen to manage such tasks as digitizing paper documents into a more manageable electronic form. Innodata also provides consulting, technology integration and implementation services, and software and systems engineering. The company has ten offshore facilites located in India, Israel, the Philippines, and Sri Lanka.

The company serves clients involved in media and publishing, defense and aerospace, and technology. Its customers include Alcatel-Lucent, the Defense Intelligence Agency, EBSCO, Hamilton Sundstrand, Lockheed Martin, Nortel Networks, and Reed Elsevier.

EXECUTIVES

Chairman, President, and CEO: Jack S. Abuhoff, age 49, $697,641 total compensation
EVP and COO: Ashok K. Mishra, age 54, $345,672 total compensation
SVP Consulting Practice: Stephen Ryden-Lloyd
SVP and CFO: O'Neil Nalavadi
SVP Publishing Practice: Jan Palmen, age 54
SVP IT Services: Michael Abell
VP, Secretary, and General Counsel: Amy R. Agress, age 45
VP Technology: Klaas Brouwer, age 42
VP Marketing: Al Girardi, age 43
VP Corporate Development: Corey D. Luskin
Auditors: Grant Thornton LLP

LOCATIONS

HQ: Innodata Isogen, Inc.
    3 University Plaza, Hackensack, NJ 07601
Phone: 201-371-8000   **Fax:** 201-488-9099
Web: www.innodata-isogen.com

2008 Sales

	% of total
US	79
Netherlands	10
Other countries	11
Total	**100**

PRODUCTS/OPERATIONS

Selected Services

Abstracting
Application development
Consulting services
Content architecture services
Content creation and editorial services
Content enhancement
Cost benefit analysis
Data conversion services
Digital multimedia services
Digitization and imaging
Feasibility studies
Knowledge services
Metadata creation services
Project management
Specifications development
Systems design and integration
Taxonomy and controlled vocabulary development
XML services and training

COMPETITORS

Apex CoVantage
Aptara
Cenveo
Macmillan Publishers
Satyam
SPi Global Solutions

HISTORICAL FINANCIALS

Company Type: Public

Income Statement

FYE: December 31

	REVENUE ($ mil.)	NET INCOME ($ mil.)	NET PROFIT MARGIN	EMPLOYEES
12/08	75.0	7.6	10.1%	6,745
12/07	67.7	4.6	6.8%	7,768
12/06	41.0	(7.3)	—	5,476
12/05	42.1	(1.7)	—	6,087
12/04	53.9	7.9	14.7%	7,485
Annual Growth	8.6%	(1.0%)	—	(2.6%)

2008 Year-End Financials

Debt ratio: 5.5%
Return on equity: 28.5%
Cash ($ mil.): 13.9
Current ratio: 2.99
Long-term debt ($ mil.): 1.7
No. of shares (mil.): 25.4
Dividends
Yield: 0.0%
Payout: —
Market value ($ mil.): 63.4
R&D as % of sales: —
Advertising as % of sales: —

Stock History

NASDAQ (GM): INOD

	STOCK PRICE ($) FY Close	P/E High/Low		Earnings	PER SHARE ($) Dividends	Book Value
12/08	2.50	22	4	0.30	0.00	1.19
12/07	5.35	35	11	0.18	0.00	0.92
12/06	2.16	—	—	(0.30)	0.00	0.75
12/05	3.46	—	—	(0.07)	0.00	1.06
12/04	9.84	31	9	0.32	0.00	1.05
Annual Growth	(29.0%)	—	—	(1.6%)	—	3.1%

Innophos Holdings

Innophos Holdings adds a dash of its phosphate products to food, beverages, toothpaste, detergents, and ashphalt. Innophos manufactures specialty phosphates used in consumer products, pharmaceuticals, and industrial applications. The company was formed in 2004 when Bain Capital bought Rhodia's North American specialty phosphates business. Customers use the company's phosphates to improve the quality and performance of a broad range of products, from electronics and textiles to pharmaceuticals, water, and detergents. Innophos divides its business into three segments: specialty salts and specialty acids; purified phosphoric acid; and sodium tripolyphosphate.

Innophos ranks No. 1 in North America in specialty salts and specialty acids (ahead of ICL Performance Products) and purified phosphoric acid (ahead of PCS Phosphate). Though North America does account for more than three-quarters of its sales, Innophos sells globally.

Bain Capital took Innophos public in 2006. The private equity group paid down some of the company's debt and gave itself a healthy dividend with the proceeds from the offering. It now owns about 15% of Innophos.

EXECUTIVES

Chairman, CEO, President, and Director:
Randolph (Randy) Gress, age 53,
$2,264,643 total compensation
VP Research and Development: Russell Kemp, age 50
VP Supply Chain: Michael Lovrich, age 55
VP and CFO: Neil Salmon
VP Operations: Louis Calvarin, age 45,
$622,947 total compensation
VP Human Resources: Wilma Harris, age 63
VP Phosphates Business: Timothy Treinen, age 58
VP, General Counsel, and Corporate Secretary:
William Farran, age 59, $836,048 total compensation
VP Sales and Distribution: Joseph Golowski, age 47
VP Corporate Strategy and Worldwide Business Development: Mark Thurston, age 49
General Manager, Mexico Operations:
José Ramón González de Salceda, age 60,
$757,197 total compensation
Auditors: PricewaterhouseCoopers LLP

LOCATIONS

HQ: Innophos Holdings, Inc.
259 Prospect Plains Rd., Cranbury, NJ 08512
Phone: 609-495-2495   **Fax:** 609-860-0138
Web: www.innophos.com

2008 Sales

	$ mil.	% of total
US	451.1	48
Mexico	250.0	27
Canada	39.7	4
Other countries	194.0	21
Total	**934.8**	**100**

PRODUCTS/OPERATIONS

2008 Sales

	$ mil.	% of total
Specialty Salts & Specialty Acids	449.9	48
Purified Phosphoric Acid	251.7	27
STPP & other products	233.2	25
Total	**934.8**	**100**

Selected Products

Specialty Salts and Specialty Acids
  Salts
    Acid phosphates
    Aluminum phosphates
    Calcium phosphates
    Potassium phosphates
  Acids
    Phosbrites
    Phosphoric acids
Purified Phosphoric Acid
Sodium Tripolyphosphate (STPP)
  Granular
  Heavy
  Low
  Medium
  Powder

COMPETITORS

Compass Minerals
Hydrite
ICL Performance Products
Mexichem
PCS Phosphate

HISTORICAL FINANCIALS

Company Type: Public

Income Statement

FYE: December 31

	REVENUE ($ mil.)	NET INCOME ($ mil.)	NET PROFIT MARGIN	EMPLOYEES
12/08	934.8	207.2	22.2%	1,125
12/07	579.0	(5.5)	—	1,045
12/06	541.8	(7.9)	—	1,101
12/05	535.5	(11.7)	—	1,148
12/04	205.6	(0.8)	—	1,148
Annual Growth	46.0%	—	—	(0.5%)

2008 Year-End Financials

Debt ratio: 127.7%
Return on equity: 144.2%
Cash ($ mil.): 125.3
Current ratio: 2.72
Long-term debt ($ mil.): 309.9
No. of shares (mil.): 21.3
Dividends
Yield: 3.4%
Payout: 7.1%
Market value ($ mil.): 422.1
R&D as % of sales: —
Advertising as % of sales: —

Stock History

NASDAQ (GM): IPHS

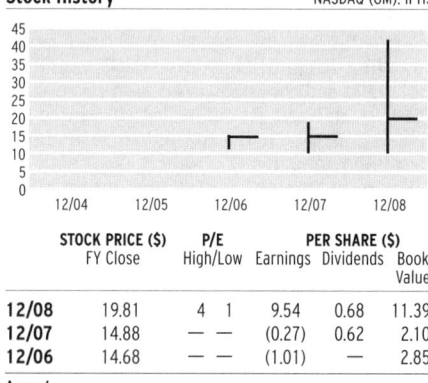

	STOCK PRICE ($) FY Close	P/E High/Low		Earnings	PER SHARE ($) Dividends	Book Value
12/08	19.81	4	1	9.54	0.68	11.39
12/07	14.88	—	—	(0.27)	0.62	2.10
12/06	14.68	—	—	(1.01)	—	2.85
Annual Growth	16.2%	—	—	—	9.7%	100.0%

Innovative Solutions

Pilots use products made by Innovative Solutions and Support (IS&S) to gauge their success. The company makes flight information computers, electronic displays, and monitoring systems that measure flight information such as airspeed, altitude, and engine and fuel data. IS&S's reduced vertical separation minimum (RVSM) products enable planes to fly closer together vertically; engine and fuel displays help the pilot track fuel and oil levels and other engine activities. IS&S uses flat-panel displays, which take up less cockpit space than conventional displays. The company gets nearly all of its sales in the US.

Since its business includes large contracts to small numbers of customers, the company typically derives most of its revenues from a handful of companies, including Bombardier, Raytheon, Northwest Airlines, Federal Express, Boeing, Lockheed Martin, and Rockwell Collins.

As worldwide air traffic increases, so will demand for IS&S's RVSM products, which allow for greater air traffic in high-traffic markets by decreasing the vertical separation between planes from about 2,000 feet to about 1,000 feet.

Chairman and CEO Geoffrey Hedrick owns about 22% of Innovative Solutions and Support.

EXECUTIVES

Chairman and CEO: Geoffrey S. M. Hedrick, age 67
President: Roman G. Ptakowski, age 61
CFO: John C. Long, age 44
VP Engineering: Shahram Askarpour
VP Operations: Robert M. Hyland
VP Quality: Brian Urbanski
Sales Manager International: Peter Robinson
Sales Manager: Fred Phelan
Director Military Marketing: Farhad Daghigh
Human Resources Generalist: Anita M. Broady
Auditors: Deloitte & Touche LLP

LOCATIONS

HQ: Innovative Solutions and Support, Inc.
720 Pennsylvania Dr., Exton, PA 19341
Phone: 610-646-9800   **Fax:** 610-646-0149
Web: www.innovative-ss.com

PRODUCTS/OPERATIONS

Selected Products

Air data systems
Cockpit display systems
Engine instruments
Fuel gauges

COMPETITORS

Aerosonic	Meggitt
GE Aviation	Rockwell Collins
Honeywell International	Smiths Group
Kollsman	Thales
L-3 Communications	

HISTORICAL FINANCIALS

Company Type: Public

Income Statement

FYE: September 30

	REVENUE ($ mil.)	NET INCOME ($ mil.)	NET PROFIT MARGIN	EMPLOYEES
9/09	36.7	5.0	13.6%	140
9/08	30.5	(7.9)	—	165
9/07	18.3	(8.8)	—	171
9/06	16.7	(2.9)	—	138
9/05	63.3	18.6	29.4%	153
Annual Growth	(12.7%)	(28.0%)	—	(2.2%)

2009 Year-End Financials

Debt ratio: 0.1%
Return on equity: 10.1%
Cash ($ mil.): 35.6
Current ratio: 11.71
Long-term debt ($ mil.): 0.0
No. of shares (mil.): 16.7

Dividends
Yield: —
Payout: —
Market value ($ mil.): 83.9
R&D as % of sales: —
Advertising as % of sales: —

Stock History

NASDAQ (GS): ISSC

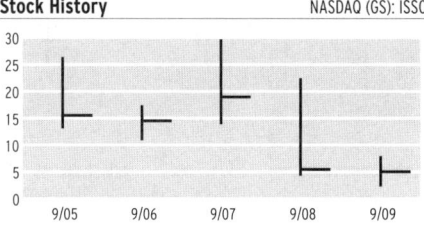

	STOCK PRICE ($) FY Close	P/E High/Low		PER SHARE ($) Earnings	Dividends	Book Value
9/09	5.01	25	8	0.30	—	3.13
9/08	5.45	—	—	(0.47)	—	2.80
9/07	18.97	—	—	(0.52)	—	4.22
9/06	14.53	—	—	(0.17)	—	4.67
9/05	15.53	26	13	1.02	—	5.84
Annual Growth	(24.6%)	—	—	(26.4%)	—	(14.5%)

Integra LifeSciences

Integra LifeSciences wants its products to be integral to the healing process. In fact, using its proprietary collagen matrix technology, the company makes biological implants for brain, spinal, and orthopedic surgeries that become part of a patient's body, helping it to generate new bone and tissue in place of what was damaged. In addition to its regenerative implants, grafts, and wound dressings, Integra LifeSciences makes surgical instruments, including ultrasonic surgical ablation systems and joint fixation devices, used primarily in neurosurgery and joint reconstruction. Integra LifeSciences sells products worldwide through several specialty sales forces and through distributors.

Integra's products are intended mainly for niche markets not targeted by larger medical device firms. Many of its orthopedic products, for instance, are designed for orthopedic reconstruction of the extremities such as the feet and ankles (rather than the hip and knee replacement products offered by the likes of Zimmer and DePuy). However, the company does reach those larger and more diverse markets through original equipment manufacturer deals with firms such as Medtronic and Zimmer.

Integra has several specialty sales forces that market its products directly in the US. Its Integra NeuroSciences unit targets neurosurgeons and intensive care doctors at hospitals and surgery centers. Its Integra Orthopedics businesses (Extremity Reconstruction, OrthoBiologics, and Spine) sell to orthopedic and spinal surgeons. The Integra Medical Instruments sales force markets the company's medical and surgical instruments (primarily under the Jarit, Luxtec, and Miltex brands) to hospitals and clinics. Integra also has direct sales representatives in Canada and several European and Asia/Pacific countries, and it utilizes independent distributors in certain markets.

To form the backbone of its newly formed Integra Spine unit, the company spent $75 million to purchase Theken Spine and two of its sister companies in 2008. The acquired spinal implant businesses make products including plates, screws, and trauma devices. Integra strengthened its posture in 2009 when it added the assets of Innovative Spinal Technologies, which it purchased for $9.25 million.

Other acquisitions have allowed the company to expand its product lines and geographic reach. It acquired the Omni-Tract line of surgical retractors in 2008, along with two distribution businesses in Australia and New Zealand to increase its direct sales efforts in the Asia/Pacific region. Integra had already established its acquisition pace in 2007 when it purchased California-based orthobiologics company IsoTis, then established its OrthoBiologics sales organization following the acquisition. The 2006 purchase of Radionics (now Integra Radionics) from Covidien added image-guided surgery systems to its NeuroSciences division. Integra also expands its product line through internal research and development efforts.

Chairman Richard Caruso owns nearly a quarter of the company. President and CEO Stuart Essig owns 7% of the business.

EXECUTIVES

Chairman: Richard E. Caruso, age 65
President, CEO, and Director: Stuart M. Essig, age 47,
$22,521,636 total compensation
CIO: Gabrielle Wolfson
Chief Scientific Officer: Simon J. Archibald
EVP and COO: Gerard S. Carlozzi, age 53,
$2,196,567 total compensation
EVP Finance and Administration, CFO, and Secretary:
John B. (Jack) Henneman III, age 47,
$2,326,694 total compensation
SVP Regulatory, Quality Assurance, and Clinical Affairs: Judith E. O'Grady, age 58,
$445,716 total compensation
SVP Global Operations: James A. Oti
SVP Finance: John Bostjancic
SVP Finance and Administration, Europe:
Wilma J. Davis
SVP, General Counsel, Human Resources and Secretary: Richard D. Gorelick
VP and Treasurer: Nora Brennan
VP Corporate and Controller: Jerry B. Corbin, age 50,
$313,278 total compensation
Manager Corporate Development and Investor Relations: Karen Mroz-Bremner
Manager Public Relations: Gianna Sabella
Auditors: PricewaterhouseCoopers LLP

LOCATIONS

HQ: Integra LifeSciences Holdings Corporation
311 Enterprise Dr., Plainsboro, NJ 08536
Phone: 609-275-0500   **Fax:** 609-275-5363
Web: www.integra-ls.com

2008 Sales

	$ mil.	% of total
US	494.5	76
Europe	98.8	15
Asia/Pacific	28.5	4
Other regions	32.8	5
Total	**654.6**	**100**

PRODUCTS/OPERATIONS

2008 Sales

	$ mil.	% of total
Integra NeuroSciences	256.9	39
Integra Orthopedics	217.9	33
Integra Medical Instruments	179.8	28
Total	**654.6**	**100**

Selected Products

NeuroSciences
  NeuroCritical Care
    External CSF drainage
    Neuromonitoring
  Neurosurgery
    Brain mapping
    Brain retraction systems
    Cranial closure
    Cranial stabilization
    Duraplasty
    Hydrocephalus management
    Neuronavigation
    Neurosurgical instruments
    Radiosurgery
    Stereotaxy
    Tissue ablation

Orthopedics
  Extremity Reconstruction
    Forefoot solutions
    Mid and hindfoot solutions
    Upper extremity solutions
    Wound dressings
  Orthobiologics (scaffolds, grafts, chips)
  Spine (screws, hooks, tethers, mesh, biologics)
Medical Instruments
  Miltex (surgical instruments including scissors,
    forceps, scopes)
  Pain Management (procedure trays and devices)
  Surgical (Darit instruments, Luxtec lights, Omni-
    Tract retractors)

COMPETITORS

Alphatec Spine
B. Braun Medical (UK)
Cardinal Health
Genzyme Biosurgery
Johnson & Johnson
LifeCell
Medtronic
NuVasive
Organogenesis
Orthofix
Orthovita
Osteotech
Smith & Nephew
Stryker
Synthes
Wright Medical Group
Zimmer Holdings

HISTORICAL FINANCIALS

Company Type: Public

Income Statement

FYE: December 31

	REVENUE ($ mil.)	NET INCOME ($ mil.)	NET PROFIT MARGIN	EMPLOYEES
12/08	654.6	34.9	5.3%	2,800
12/07	550.5	33.5	6.1%	2,500
12/06	419.3	29.4	7.0%	2,150
12/05	277.9	37.2	13.4%	1,180
12/04	229.8	17.2	7.5%	1,126
Annual Growth	29.9%	19.4%	—	25.6%

2008 Year-End Financials

Debt ratio: 139.9%
Return on equity: 11.4%
Cash ($ mil.): 183.5
Current ratio: 2.85
Long-term debt ($ mil.): 490.0
No. of shares (mil.): 28.5

Dividends
  Yield: 0.0%
  Payout: —
Market value ($ mil.): 1,013.1
R&D as % of sales: —
Advertising as % of sales: —

Stock History

NASDAQ (GS): IART

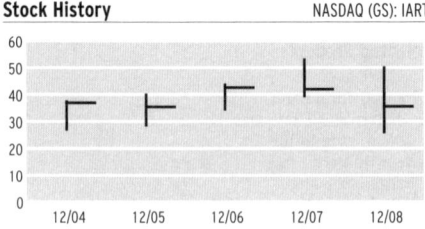

	STOCK PRICE ($) FY Close	P/E High/Low	PER SHARE ($) Earnings	Dividends	Book Value
12/08	35.57	41 21	1.22	0.00	12.30
12/07	41.93	47 35	1.13	0.00	9.14
12/06	42.59	45 36	0.97	0.00	10.40
12/05	35.46	35 25	1.15	0.00	10.18
12/04	36.93	68 49	0.55	0.00	10.81
Annual Growth	(0.9%)	— —	22.0%	—	3.3%

IntegraMed America

IntegraMed America provides fertile ground for the growth of reproductive services. The company provides a range of business, financial, and clinical services to a network of fertility clinics that span the US. Its network includes about 30 centers, located in major metropolitan areas, that provide in vitro fertilization (IVF), artificial insemination, and other reproductive assistance. IntegraMed offers those centers clinical support in the form of technical support through its ARTSworks practice management and electronic records information systems; accounting and human resource services; mail-order pharmacy services; and both traditional and online marketing and sales support.

The centers can also take advantage of IntegraMed's consumer offerings, such as patient financing options and its Shared Risk Refund program, which gives IVF patients a partial refund if the procedure fails. Additionally, the company offers medical malpractice coverage through its captive insurance company, Assisted Reproductive Technology Insurance Company (ARTIC).

IntegraMed offers two levels of participation to its center customers: Affiliate and Partner. Affiliated providers have access to the firm's information technology, marketing, financing, and consumer services and products. The company wants to expand its network of Affiliates to include centers in the top 100 metropolitan areas in the US and to sell those Affiliates more and higher-priced service packages.

It also wants to convert more of its long-standing Affiliates into Partners. When a center becomes a Partner, it generally sells IntegraMed its assets (facilities, equipment, and the like) and enters into a long-term management agreement, in which IntegraMed provides all the non-clinical personnel to run the center. Nearly ten centers in its network operate under Partner contracts.

In 2007 IntegraMed moved into a new area of medical facility management by acquiring Vein Clinics of America. The new Vein Clinics division provides administrative services to some 30 vein disorder treatment centers. IntegraMed believes the acquired business will provide a complementary high-growth market to its existing operations.

The company expanded its network of clinics to cover 13 states and made entry into the fertility markets in Idaho, Nevada, and Utah with the 2009 buy of Regents Management, which managed three fertility centers in the Western United States. The buy gave Integra the Nevada Center for Reproductive Medicine in Reno, NV; the Idaho Center for Reproductive Medicine in Boise, ID; and the Utah Fertility Center which will be located in Pleasant Grove, UT, outside Salt Lake City.

EXECUTIVES

Chairman: Gerardo Canet, age 64
President, CEO, and Director: Jay Higham, age 51,
  $658,078 total compensation
EVP and CFO: John W. Hlywak Jr., age 61,
  $430,461 total compensation
VP Information Systems: Vijay Reddy, age 43
VP Consumer Services: Pamela Schumann, age 43,
  $381,209 total compensation
VP Human Resources: Angela Gizinski, age 60
VP Marketing and Development: Scott Soifer, age 46
VP Corporate Secretary, and General Counsel:
  Claude E. White, age 60

President, Fertility Centers Division:
  Joseph J. Travia Jr., age 55,
  $452,459 total compensation
President, Vein Clinics Division:
  Daniel P. (Dan) Doman, age 47,
  $420,198 total compensation
Auditors: Amper, Politziner & Mattia, P.C.

LOCATIONS

HQ: IntegraMed America, Inc.
  2 Manhattanville Rd., Purchase, NY 10577
Phone: 914-253-8000   Fax: 914-253-8008
Web: www.integramed.com

PRODUCTS/OPERATIONS

2008 Sales

	% of total
Fertility centers	70
Vein clinics	20
Consumer services	10
Total	**100**

COMPETITORS

athenahealth
Johnson and Johnson Health Care Systems
McKesson
MEDNAX
Sheridan Healthcare
Sterling Healthcare

HISTORICAL FINANCIALS

Company Type: Public

Income Statement

FYE: December 31

	REVENUE ($ mil.)	NET INCOME ($ mil.)	NET PROFIT MARGIN	EMPLOYEES
12/08	197.4	3.5	1.8%	1,202
12/07	152.0	3.3	2.2%	1,182
12/06	126.4	3.2	2.5%	949
12/05	128.9	1.7	1.3%	881
12/04	107.7	1.2	1.1%	800
Annual Growth	16.4%	30.7%	—	10.7%

2008 Year-End Financials

Debt ratio: 37.2%
Return on equity: 7.1%
Cash ($ mil.): 28.3
Current ratio: 0.92
Long-term debt ($ mil.): 18.9
No. of shares (mil.): 8.8

Dividends
  Yield: —
  Payout: —
Market value ($ mil.): 59.3
R&D as % of sales: —
Advertising as % of sales: —

Stock History

NASDAQ (GM): INMD

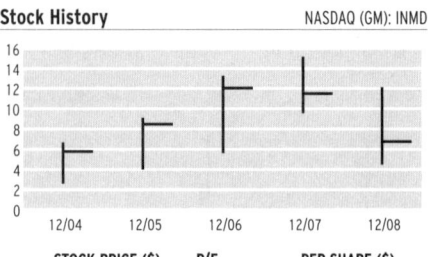

	STOCK PRICE ($) FY Close	P/E High/Low	PER SHARE ($) Earnings	Dividends	Book Value
12/08	6.75	30 11	0.40	—	5.78
12/07	11.50	39 25	0.39	—	5.52
12/06	12.04	34 15	0.39	—	4.65
12/05	8.47	41 19	0.22	—	4.19
12/04	5.76	41 17	0.16	—	3.88
Annual Growth	4.0%	— —	25.7%	—	10.4%

Inter Parfums

Would a perfumer by any other name smell as sweet? Inter Parfums certainly hopes not. Most of the fragrance developer and manufacturer's revenue is generated by sales of prestige fragrances, including Burberry, Christian Lacroix, Lanvin, Nickel, S.T. Dupont, Van Cleef & Arpels, Paul Smith, Quicksilver/Roxy, and Nickel. It also sells moderately priced perfumes, low-priced imitations of high-end perfumes, personal care products, and cosmetics, including Aziza eye makeup. The firm owns Lanvins Perfumes and the upscale men's skin care firm Nickel. Customers include department stores, mass merchandisers (Wal-Mart), and drugstore chains. The company's scents are sold in more than 120 countries.

The deep recession in the US took a toll on Inter Parfums' US sales in 2008 (down about 6%), but increases in Europe and the company's other markets led to a sales increase overall (up more than 14%).

Inter Parfums has grown by focusing on its prestige division, expanding existing product lines, and licensing or acquiring new fragrances. Burberry is company's largest brand, encompassing six fragrance families, accounting for about 56% of sales. To extend Burberry's reach, Inter Parfums plans to roll out a line of branded cosmetics in 2010. Overall, prestige brands have grown to account for 87% of the company's sales, up from 76% in 2003.

Inter Parfums signed an exclusive agreement with Gap Inc. in mid-2005 to design and manufacture personal care products under the Gap and Banana Republic brands. Inter Parfums is responsible for product development, production, packaging, and manufacturing, while Gap handles marketing and sales of the products. The deal marked Inter Parfums' entry into the specialty retail market. It has since inked similar deals with retailers New York & Company and Brooks Brothers in 2007 and bebe stores in 2008. In late 2008 Brooks Brothers New York debuted in the apparel retailer's US stores with international distribution following in the second half of 2009. Also in fall 2009, Brooks Brothers Black Fleece brand launched.

Still smelling sweet success in licensing, Inter Parfums signed an exclusive worldwide licensing deal in 2006 with sports manufacturer and retailer Quiksilver for a namesake and Roxy line of personal care products. As part of the deal, Inter Parfums develops and distributes Roxy fragrance, sun care, skin care, and related items, and Quiksilver sun care and other products through 2017. Inter Parfums is particularly interested in Quiksilver's outdoorsy, 15-year-old target audience. Quiksilver's strong presence in the US and its inroads into Western Europe and Australia bode well for Inter Parfums, as well.

Founders Jean Madar (CEO) and Philippe Benacin (vice chairman) jointly own more than 50% of the firm.

HISTORY

Jean Madar and Philippe Benacin founded Jean Philippe Fragrances in 1985 to make knock-off fragrances in the US, and took it public three years later. Jean Philippe bought fragrance and cosmetics rights from Jordache Enterprises in 1990. The next year it bought Inter Parfums S.A.,

a French affiliate Madar and Benacin founded in 1983. Jean Philippe took that subsidiary public in 1995.

The company aggressively expanded its markets and product line. In 1994 Inter Parfums S.A. acquired trademarks for a variety of fragrances from Parfums Molyneux and Parfums Weil, and Jean Philippe bought the worldwide trademark for Intimate and Chaz from Revlon. From Chesebrough-Pond's, Jean Philippe acquired rights that year to Cutex nail enamel and lipsticks (later relinquished) and Aziza eye makeup, which brought it greater access to mass-merchandise channels such as Wal-Mart.

A year later Jean Philippe launched Romantic Illusions, a collection of eight perfumes packed in cartons designed to look like romance novels. Sales declined in 1996 and 1997, partly due to increased US competition, economic turmoil in Russia, and lagging sales in Brazil. (The company closed its Brazilian subsidiary in 1998.) Also in 1998 Jean Philippe developed a line of medium-priced fragrances (not knockoffs).

The following year Jean Philippe decided to take the name of its primary sales vehicle, subsidiary Inter Parfums S.A., adding an Americanized "Inc." to the end. France's LVMH, which bottles Christian Dior and Givenchy perfumes, upped its stake in Inter Parfums to 20%.

Inter Parfums launched its Paul Smith line of fragrances in 2000 and announced plans for a new bath products line under the Burberry name. Two years later the company purchased certain mass-market fragrances and inventories of bankrupt and now defunct rival Tristar Corporation and also signed a license agreement with Diane Von Furstenberg to market her fragrance and beauty products.

In April 2004 Inter Parfums acquired a 67.5% interest in Nickel S.A., a men's skin care company with 1,700 outlets in France, Western Europe, and the US, as well as men's spas in Paris and New York. The acquisition cost Inter Parfums approximately $8.3 million in cash.

Inter Parfums replaced LVMH's YSL Beauté as the licensing contractor for Van Cleef & Arpels in 2006. Inter Parfums inked the deal to add a jewelry brand to its portfolio. Luxury goods maker LVMH licenses the Christian Lacroix line to Inter Parfums. The Parlux and LVMH deal to make a Celine-branded fragrance expired at the end of 2007.

EXECUTIVES

Chairman and CEO; Director General, Inter Parfums, S.A.: Jean Madar, age 48, $498,000 total compensation
Vice Chairman and President; President and CEO, Inter Parfums, S.A.: Philippe Benacin, age 50, $767,543 total compensation
EVP, CFO, and Director: Russell Greenberg, age 52, $553,214 total compensation
VP Distribution and Warehousing: Alex Canavan
VP Retail Sales: Michel Bes
VP Management Information Systems: Kiet T. Huynh
Northeast Regional Sales Manager: Lynn Konko
Westcoast Regional Sales Manager: Mike Hamerling
Controller and Secretary: Michelle Habert
Sales Administration: Jennifer Giachino
Director; EVP, CFO, and Director of Finance, Inter Parfums S.A.: Philippe Santi, age 47, $637,000 total compensation
Director, Luxury and Fashion Division, Inter Parfums, S.A.: Frederic Garcia-Pelayo, age 50, $637,136 total compensation
President, Inter Parfums USA, Specialty Retail Division: Henry B. (Andy) Clarke, age 48

Director, Parfums Burberry: Hugues de La Chevasnerie, age 40
Director, Operations, Inter Parfums S.A.: Axel Marot, age 35
Auditors: Mazars LLP

LOCATIONS

HQ: Inter Parfums, Inc.
551 5th Ave., Ste. 1500, New York, NY 10176
Phone: 212-983-2640   **Fax:** 212-983-4197
Web: www.interparfumsinc.com

2008 Sales

	$ mil.	% of total
Europe	204.1	46
North America	108.6	24
Central & South America	38.0	8
Middle East	39.2	9
Asia	53.0	12
Other	3.2	1
Total	**446.1**	**100**

PRODUCTS/OPERATIONS

2008 Sales

	% of total
Prestige fragrances	87
Specialty retail & mass-market fragrance & fragrance-related products	13
Total	**100**

Selected Brand Name and Licensed Fragrances and Cosmetics

Burberry
Christian Lacroix
Diane Von Furstenberg
Lanvin
Nickel
Paul Smith
S.T. Dupont

COMPETITORS

Abercrombie & Fitch
Avon
Body Shop
Borghese
Chanel
Clarins
Coty Inc.
Dana Classic Fragrances
Elizabeth Arden Inc
Estée Lauder
Limited Brands
L'Oréal
LVMH
Mary Kay
Parlux Fragrances
Procter & Gamble
Revlon
Shiseido
Unilever
Wella AG

HISTORICAL FINANCIALS

Company Type: Public

Income Statement				FYE: December 31
	REVENUE ($ mil.)	NET INCOME ($ mil.)	NET PROFIT MARGIN	EMPLOYEES
12/08	446.1	23.8	5.3%	245
12/07	389.6	23.8	6.1%	248
12/06	321.1	17.7	5.5%	235
12/05	273.5	15.3	5.6%	201
12/04	236.0	15.7	6.7%	144
Annual Growth	17.3%	11.0%	—	14.2%

2008 Year-End Financials

Debt ratio: 13.6%
Return on equity: 12.0%
Cash ($ mil.): 42.4
Current ratio: 2.34
Long-term debt ($ mil.): 27.7
No. of shares (mil.): 30.1

Dividends
  Yield: 1.7%
  Payout: 16.9%
Market value ($ mil.): 231.0
R&D as % of sales: —
Advertising as % of sales: —

Stock History

NASDAQ (GS): IPAR

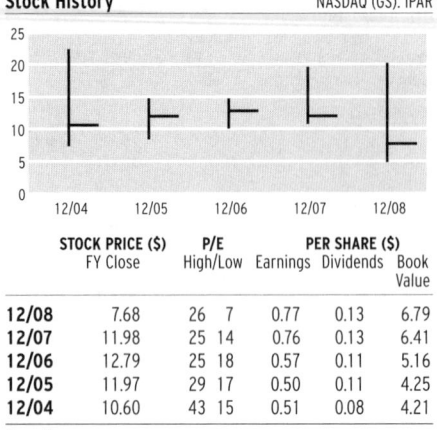

	STOCK PRICE ($) FY Close	P/E High/Low		PER SHARE ($) Earnings	Dividends	Book Value
12/08	7.68	26	7	0.77	0.13	6.79
12/07	11.98	25	14	0.76	0.13	6.41
12/06	12.79	25	18	0.57	0.11	5.16
12/05	11.97	29	17	0.50	0.11	4.25
12/04	10.60	43	15	0.51	0.08	4.21
Annual Growth	(7.7%)	—	—	10.8%	12.9%	12.7%

Interactive Data

Interactive Data Corporation has something vital to the information superhighway — the information. The company offers subscription services that provide financial market data, analytics, and related services to financial institutions, active traders, and individual investors. Interactive Data Corporation conducts business through two segments: Institutional Services and Active Trader Services. Products include Interactive Data Fixed Income Analytics (fixed-income portfolio analytics for institutions), Interactive Data Pricing and Reference Data (securities information for institutions), and eSignal (real-time market data for individuals). Pearson plc owns about 60% of the company.

The bulk of Interactive Data Corporation's business is derived from its institutional services, which account for more than 85% of sales. The core of its institutional operations is Interactive Data Pricing and Reference Data (formerly FT Interactive Data), the company's data content division that is responsible for collecting, editing, maintaining, and delivering securities data. Interactive Data Corporation is expanding globally; nearly 30% of sales come from outside the US.

The company is growing through acquisitions. In early 2010 Interactive Data purchased 7ticks, a provider of electronic trading networks and managed services, for some $30 million in cash. Adding 7ticks to its operations is part of Interactive Data's plan to enhance its trading technology offerings. In 2009 the company acquired the Online Financial Solutions (OFS) business of Dow Jones. Interactive Data made the purchase in order to grow its Web-based solutions business in North America, and placed the OFS assets into its U.S. Managed Solutions unit. Specifically, the deal boosts its Web capabilities in developing and hosting news, market data, research and advanced charting, portfolio management, and alerting.

The company expanded internationally when it purchased Kler's Financial Data Service, a provider of reference data to the Italian financial industry, for about $30 million in cash in 2008. It continued this strategy later that year when it acquired about 80% of NTT DATA Financial Corporation (NDF) for some ¥2.4 billion (or approximately $26 million). NDF gave Interactive Data a direct presence in Japan and expanded its business in the Asia/Pacific region.

The company appointed Raymond D'Arcy, former president of sales and marketing, to succeed Stuart Clark as president and CEO when Clark retired in 2009.

HISTORY

Data Broadcasting was formed in 1992 as the successor to the Financial News Network, a bankrupt financial cable TV network. Alan Hirschfield, former CEO of Twentieth Century Fox and Columbia Pictures, and Allan Tessler, experienced in restructuring businesses, were brought in; they sold many of Financial News' assets but held onto two information services, DBC West (stock data for private investors) and Shark Information Services (serving professional traders).

The company expanded its services and markets through key acquisitions. In 1994 it bought Computer Sports World (online sports data) and Capital Management Sciences (fixed-income data and analysis). The following year Data Broadcasting bought and merged with its chief rival (Broadcast International), bought a stake in Internet Financial Network (online distributor of SEC filings), and sold Shark. These transactions also hurt earnings in 1996.

Data Broadcasting acquired international news provider Federal News Service Group in 1997. It also put its InStore Satellite Network and CheckRite International business services divisions up for sale to focus on information services and fund future acquisitions. National Data Corporation, a provider of transaction processing services, bought CheckRite International in 1998; InStore Satellite was a tougher sell, but finally went to Muzak in 1999. Also that year MarketWatch.com, a financial news Web site operated by Data Broadcasting and CBS, went public (each company retained a 34% stake). (MarketWatch.com later changed its name to MarketWatch in 2004 and was sold to Dow Jones & Company in 2005.) Data Broadcasting later sold its AgCast business to closely held agricultural publisher The Farm Journal.

In 2000 UK media company Pearson took a 60% stake in Data Broadcasting in exchange for its global equities information business, Financial Times Asset Management. Former Pearson executives Stephen Hill and Stuart Clark took over as chairman and CEO, respectively. Data Broadcasting later sold its DBC Sports unit (including odds maker Las Vegas Sports Consultants) to former SportsLine.com subsidiary VegasInsider. Also that year Data Broadcasting acquired Thomson Financial's security data business (Muller Data Corporation).

In early 2001 Data Broadcasting sold its stake in MarketWatch.com to Pearson. It later changed its name to Interactive Data Corporation. The following year the company purchased Merrill Lynch's security data business (Merrill Lynch Securities Pricing Service). Interactive Data purchased McGraw Hill's S&P ComStock (now called Interactive Data Real-Time Services), a

provider of financial data, news, historical information, and software applications, for $115 million in cash, and added Hyperfeed Technologies' consolidated data feed business in 2003.

The following year Interactive Data acquired the assets of FutureSource, a provider of real-time futures and commodities data, and in 2005 it bought IS.Teledata, a provider of customized financial information portals and terminals. IS.Teledata was subsequently renamed Interactive Data Managed Solutions.

In a move to expand its revenue from consumer-oriented services, the company acquired online stock information provider Quote.com from search portal Lycos (owned by Korea's Daum Communication) for about $30 million in 2006. The acquired business, which includes investment community message board Raging Bull, operates as part of Interactive Data's eSignal division.

In 2007 the company grew when it acquired the market data division of Xcitek. The purchase added North American corporate actions information, such as reorganization, cost basis, and class action data, to its Interactive Data Pricing and Reference Data business.

Clark retired in 2009 and was replaced by Raymond D'Arcy, who had served in a variety of executive roles during his 29-year tenure with the company.

EXECUTIVES

Chairman: Rona A. Fairhead, age 47
President, CEO, and Director: Raymond L. D'Arcy, age 56, $1,059,952 total compensation
COO, Interactive Data Corp and Interactive Data Pricing and Reference Data: John L. King, age 58, $1,007,751 total compensation
EVP, General Counsel, and Corporate Secretary: Andrea H. Loew, age 51
CTO: Stephan Wolf, age 49
Chief Marketing Officer: Mary Ivaliotis
VP Finance, Interim CFO, and Chief Accounting Officer: Christine Sampson, age 56
VP and Chief Human Resources Officer: Lori B. Hannay, age 46
President, Institutional Business: Mark Hepsworth, age 49, $1,256,926 total compensation
President, Institutional Sales: Cort J. Williams, age 49
President, eSignal: Chuck Thompson
Managing Director, Interactive Data Asia/Pacific: James Farrer
Managing Director, Evaluations: Elizabeth (Liz) Duggan, age 44
Managing Director, Interactive Data Fixed Income Analytics: Keith Webster
Managing Director, International: Roger Sargeant, age 42
Director, Investor Relations: Andrew M. Kramer
Auditors: Ernst & Young LLP

LOCATIONS

HQ: Interactive Data Corporation
  32 Crosby Dr., Bedford, MA 01730
Phone: 781-687-8500   **Fax:** 781-687-8005
Web: www.interactivedata.com

2008 Sales

	$ mil.	% of total
US	529.6	71
Europe		
UK	85.7	11
Other countries	116.8	16
Asia/Pacific	18.4	2
Total	**750.5**	**100**

PRODUCTS/OPERATIONS

2008 Sales

	$ mil.	% of total
Institutional services		
Pricing & Reference Data Services	475.8	63
Real-Time Services	153.0	20
Fixed Income Analytics	32.8	5
Active trader services		
eSignal	88.9	12
Total	**750.5**	**100**

Selected Offerings

Desktop Solutions (market data and decision support tools)
Fixed Income Analytics (portfolio analysis software)
Pricing and Reference Data (global securities pricing)
Real-Time Services (global market data feed)

COMPETITORS

AOL	MSN
Bloomberg L.P.	PCQuote.com
Citigroup Global Markets	Reuters
CNN	S&P
Data Transmission Network	Telekurs
Dow Jones	TheStreet.com
FactSet	thinkorswim
Forbes	Track Data
Google	TradeStation
Motley Fool	Yahoo!

HISTORICAL FINANCIALS

Company Type: Public

Income Statement				FYE: December 31
	REVENUE ($ mil.)	NET INCOME ($ mil.)	NET PROFIT MARGIN	EMPLOYEES
12/08	750.5	142.6	19.0%	2,400
12/07	689.6	126.0	18.3%	2,304
12/06	612.4	93.4	15.3%	2,200
12/05	542.9	93.9	17.3%	2,100
12/04	484.6	80.3	16.6%	1,800
Annual Growth	11.6%	15.4%	—	7.5%

2008 Year-End Financials

Debt ratio: —
Return on equity: 14.8%
Cash ($ mil.): 154.2
Current ratio: 2.23
Long-term debt ($ mil.): —
No. of shares (mil.): 94.3
Dividends
 Yield: 2.4%
 Payout: 40.5%
Market value ($ mil.): 2,325.1
R&D as % of sales: —
Advertising as % of sales: —

Stock History

NYSE: IDC

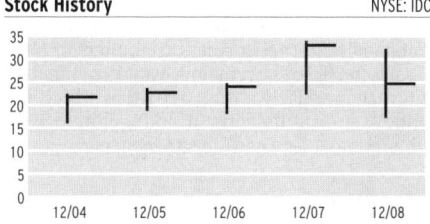

	STOCK PRICE ($) FY Close	P/E High/Low	PER SHARE ($) Earnings	Dividends	Book Value
12/08	24.66	22 12	1.48	0.60	10.18
12/07	33.01	26 17	1.30	0.50	10.22
12/06	24.04	25 19	0.98	0.00	9.67
12/05	22.71	24 19	0.98	0.00	9.07
12/04	21.74	26 19	0.84	0.00	9.10
Annual Growth	3.2%	— —	15.2%	—	2.9%

Interactive Intelligence

Interactive Intelligence knows that managing your communications is smart business. The company's software (which is available as a hosted application that customers subscribe to on a monthly basis) helps integrate a wide array of communication systems via VoIP technology, from phone calls, voice mail, and e-mail to faxes and Web-based communications. Its applications integrate with enterprise messaging platforms such as Microsoft's Exchange and Lotus Notes, and provide tools for connecting mobile workers to enterprise information systems. Interactive Intelligence also makes systems for call center operations.

Interactive Intelligence's products are available as both hosted applications and premise-based. The company markets its offerings as "Communication as a Service" or CaaS, a spin on the more recognizable Software as a Service (SaaS) business mode; Interactive Intelligence's customers pay a monthly subscription fee to access all the business communications offerings the company provides.

It sells its products through a network of more than 300 VARs, including Arvato (a division of Bertelsmann), AT&T, and Hitachi. The company's more than 2,000 customers have included Abbott Labs, AIG, Amway, and BMW.

The company markets its software-based products as a cost-efficient alternative to traditional business communication systems (which include PBX phone systems, automated call distributors, voice mail systems, and interactive voice response systems), which require significant working capital to purchase and maintain.

Founder and CEO Donald Brown owns about 27% of the business.

EXECUTIVES

Chairman, President, and CEO: Donald E. Brown, age 53, $694,914 total compensation
EVP Worldwide Sales: Gary R. Blough, age 53, $558,674 total compensation
SVP Worldwide Marketing: Joseph A. (Joe) Staples, age 49, $453,394 total compensation
Chief Scientist: Michael D. Gagle
VP Finance and Administration, CFO, Secretary, and Treasurer: Stephen R. (Steve) Head, age 55, $422,881 total compensation
VP Enterprise Sales, North America: Paul Weber
VP Business Development: William J. (Bill) Gildea III, age 42
VP Worldwide Customer Services: Pamela J. Hynes, age 47, $295,935 total compensation
Auditors: KPMG LLP

LOCATIONS

HQ: Interactive Intelligence, Inc.
 7601 Interactive Way, Indianapolis, IN 46278
Phone: 317-872-3000
Web: www.inin.com

PRODUCTS/OPERATIONS

2008 Sales

	$ mil.	% of total
Product	61.2	50
Services	60.2	50
Total	**121.4**	**100**

Selected Software

Automatic frequently asked question processing (e-FAQ)
Call center automation (Customer Interaction Center, Enterprise Interaction Center)
Call distribution (Interaction Director)
Call recording, storage, and management (Interaction Recorder)
Enterprise communication (Communité)
Outbound call management (Interaction Dialer)
Proxy server (Interaction SIP Proxy)
Wireless communication (Mobilité)
Speech-enabled voice response (Vocalité)

Selected Services

Education and certification
Project management
Systems engineering and customization
Technical support
Training

COMPETITORS

Alcatel-Lucent
Aspect Software
Avaya
Cisco Systems
Genesys Telecommunications
ShoreTel
Siemens AG

HISTORICAL FINANCIALS

Company Type: Public

Income Statement				FYE: December 31
	REVENUE ($ mil.)	NET INCOME ($ mil.)	NET PROFIT MARGIN	EMPLOYEES
12/08	121.4	4.3	3.5%	594
12/07	109.9	17.5	15.9%	595
12/06	83.2	10.2	12.3%	515
12/05	62.9	2.1	3.3%	390
12/04	55.1	1.0	1.8%	340
Annual Growth	21.8%	44.0%	—	15.0%

2008 Year-End Financials

Debt ratio: —
Return on equity: 9.0%
Cash ($ mil.): 34.7
Current ratio: 1.70
Long-term debt ($ mil.): —
No. of shares (mil.): 17.3
Dividends
 Yield: 0.0%
 Payout: —
Market value ($ mil.): 110.7
R&D as % of sales: —
Advertising as % of sales: —

Stock History

NASDAQ (GM): ININ

	STOCK PRICE ($) FY Close	P/E High/Low	PER SHARE ($) Earnings	Dividends	Book Value
12/08	6.41	100 24	0.23	0.00	2.73
12/07	26.35	33 15	0.91	0.00	2.81
12/06	22.45	40 8	0.56	0.00	1.41
12/05	5.10	60 28	0.13	0.00	0.45
12/04	4.50	111 51	0.06	0.00	0.29
Annual Growth	9.2%	— —	39.9%	—	75.0%

Intercontinental-Exchange

If there were money to be made in ice futures, IntercontinentalExchange (ICE) would probably trade that as well. The company provides an on-line marketplace for global commodity trading, primarily of electricity, natural gas, crude oil, refined petroleum products, precious metals, and weather and emission credits. It also owns the ICE Futures Europe, a leading European energy futures and options platform. ICE Data provides real-time, daily, and historical market data reports. In a major expansion the company acquired the New York Board of Trade (renamed ICE Futures US) for $1 billion in 2007.

ICE, which also offers real-time OTC clearing and credit and risk management services, was formed by a group of top financial and energy firms in 2000. The company is based in Atlanta and has regional offices in Calgary, Chicago, Houston, New York, and Singapore.

In 2006 ICE bought an 8% stake in India's National Commodity & Derivatives Exchange. The following year ICE acquired ChemConnect's US natural gas liquids (NGLs) and chemicals trading business, and the Winnipeg Commodity Exchange (renamed ICE Futures Canada) for C$40 million ($33 million). In 2008 the company bought financial services firm Creditex from Internet Capital Group for slightly more than $500 million, mostly in ICE stock.

EXECUTIVES

Chairman and CEO: Jeffrey C. Sprecher, age 54, $6,264,086 total compensation
President and COO: Charles A. (Chuck) Vice, age 45, $3,416,866 total compensation
SVP and CFO: Scott A. Hill, age 41, $1,798,707 total compensation
SVP and Chief Strategic Officer: David S. Goone, age 48, $2,837,117 total compensation
SVP and CTO: Edwin D. Marcial, age 41, $2,187,495 total compensation
SVP, General Counsel, and Secretary: Jonathan H. Short, age 43
VP and Corporate Controller: Dean S. Mathison
VP Investor Relations and Corporate Communications: Kelly L. Loeffler
President, Creditex: Sunil G. Hirani
President, YellowJacket: Jacob E. Pechenik
President, ICE Trust: Dirk J. Pruis
President and COO, ICE Clear US: Thomas J. (Tom) Hammond
President and COO, ICE Futures Canada: E. Bradley (Brad) Vannan
President and COO, ICE Futures Europe: David J. Peniket, age 43
President and COO, ICE Futures U.S.: Thomas W. Farley, age 33
President and COO, ICE Clear Europe: Paul Swann
Auditors: Ernst & Young LLP

LOCATIONS

HQ: IntercontinentalExchange, Inc.
2100 RiverEdge Pkwy., Ste. 500, Atlanta, GA 30328
Phone: 770-857-4700 **Fax:** 770-857-4755
Web: www.theice.com

2008 Sales

	$ mil.	% of total
US	565.0	69
EU & Canada	248.1	31
Total	**813.1**	**100**

PRODUCTS/OPERATIONS

2008 Sales

	$ mil.	% of total
OTC	396.4	49
Futures	362.2	44
Market data fees	54.5	7
Total	**813.1**	**100**

Founding Partners

BP p.l.c.
Deutsche Bank AG
The Goldman Sachs Group, Inc.
Morgan Stanley Dean Witter & Co.
Royal Dutch Shell plc
Société Générale
TOTAL S.A.

COMPETITORS

APX
Bloomberg L.P.
CHOICE! Energy
Enporion
ICAP
NYMEX Holdings
Reuters
Unitil

HISTORICAL FINANCIALS

Company Type: Public

Income Statement

FYE: December 31

	REVENUE ($ mil.)	NET INCOME ($ mil.)	NET PROFIT MARGIN	EMPLOYEES
12/08	813.1	301.0	37.0%	795
12/07	574.3	240.6	41.9%	506
12/06	313.8	143.3	45.7%	226
12/05	155.9	(20.9)	—	203
12/04	108.4	21.9	20.2%	91
Annual Growth	**65.5%**	**92.5%**	**—**	**71.9%**

2008 Year-End Financials

Debt ratio: 20.7%
Return on equity: 17.3%
Cash ($ mil.): 283.5
Current ratio: 1.02
Long-term debt ($ mil.): 415.5
No. of shares (mil.): 73.3
Dividends
Yield: 0.0%
Payout: —
Market value ($ mil.): 6,039.3
R&D as % of sales: —
Advertising as % of sales: —

Stock History

NYSE: ICE

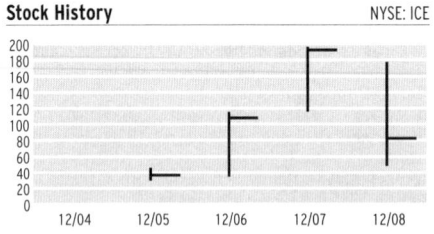

	STOCK PRICE ($) FY Close	P/E High/Low		PER SHARE ($) Earnings	Dividends	Book Value
12/08	82.44	42	12	4.17	0.00	27.39
12/07	192.50	57	35	3.39	0.00	20.16
12/06	107.90	47	15	2.40	0.00	6.20
12/05	36.35	—	—	(0.39)	0.00	3.18
Annual Growth	**31.4%**	**—**	**—**	**79.7%**	**—**	**97.4%**

Internet Brands

Internet Brands takes shopping from research to retail with a few clicks of a mouse. The company helps customers research and purchase big-ticket items, such as cars, real estate, and mortgages, and provides online travel and career services. Its more than 200 Web sites include those for homes and mortgages (Loan.com), automobiles (Autos.com, CarsDirect.com), and vacation rental properties (VacationHomes.com, BBOnline.com). The company offers financing and mortgages through various banks. More than 3,000 local car dealers have joined its nationwide network, and it has alliances with Penske Automotive Group (formerly United Auto Group). Founded as CarsDirect.com in 1998, Internet Brands went public in late 2007.

The Internet media and e-commerce company raised about $48 million in the November offering, which may be used to fund acquisitions or for general corporate purposes. To that end, in early 2008 Internet Brands purchased nine Web sites in the automotive and leisure categories and five more Web sites in April that includes FitDay.com and VetInfo.com.

The firm also aims to increase its advertiser base and international operations. Internet Brands got its start at e-commerce incubator Idealab, whose chairman and CEO William Gross controls more than two-thirds of Internet Brands' voting shares. Gross has been a director of Internet Brands since 1998.

After a quick start selling cars online, the firm changed its name to Internet Brands in 2005, to encompass its growing list of car and mortgage research and purchasing products. The fast-growing e-commerce firm's acquisitions since 2004 include the online community travel guides Wikitravel and World66. Other acquisitions include Jelsoft Enterprises, the developer of community bulletin board software vBulletin, and DoItYourself.com, a home improvement and home repair Web site.

Internet Brands also maintains Web sites for car, travel, and home improvement buffs (CorvetteForum.com, BrokerOutpost.com, and FlyerTalk.com), and career seekers (CVTips.com and GrooveJob.com). The company's Autodata Solutions business supplies licensed content and tech services to the auto industry. Overall, the company's Internet business accounted for 69% of sales in 2008. The remainder was generated by Internet Brands' licensing activities, which include licensing its content and technology to other companies and Web site owners.

EXECUTIVES

Chairman: Howard Lee Morgan, age 63
President, CEO, and Director: Robert N. (Bob) Brisco, age 47, $787,499 total compensation
COO: Lisa Morita, age 47, $405,429 total compensation
CFO: Scott A. Friedman, age 35, $169,651 total compensation
CTO: Joseph (Joe) Rosenblum, age 34
EVP Corporate Development and General Counsel: B. Lynn Walsh, age 52, $359,244 total compensation
Chief Marketing Officer: Charles E. (Chuck) Hoover, age 45, $282,327 total compensation
General Manager Home and Real Estate Division: Michael Dodge
General Manager Travel Division: John McGanty
President, Autodata Solutions Company: Gregory T. Perrier
Auditors: BDO Seidman, LLP

LOCATIONS

HQ: Internet Brands, Inc.
909 N. Sepulveda Blvd., 11th Fl.
El Segundo, CA 90245
Phone: 310-280-4000   **Fax:** 310-280-4868
Web: www.internetbrands.com

PRODUCTS/OPERATIONS

2008 Sales

	$ mil.	% of total
Consumer Internet	71.5	69
Licensing	32.5	31
Total	**104.0**	**100**

Selected Web Sites

Automotive
65SpeedOnline.com
Autos.com
CarsDirect.com
My350z.com
MyG37.com
NewCarTestDrive.com
ScoobyNet.com
ZDriver.com

Employment
CVTips.com
GrooveJob.com

Home and Home Improvement
Loan.com
LoanApp.com
RealEstateABC.com

Travel and Leisure
BBOnline.com
CruiseMates.com
FitDay.com
PuppyDogWeb.com
VacationHomes.com
VetInfo.com

COMPETITORS

AOL
Autobytel
AutoNation
AutoTrader
Brown Automotive
CarMax
Classified Ventures
ditech.com
E-LOAN
Expedia
Gillman Companies
GMAC
Google
Group 1 Automotive
Gunn Automotive
Hendrick Automotive
JM Family Enterprises
McCombs Enterprises
Monster Worldwide
MSN
Orbitz Worldwide
Penske Automotive Group
priceline.com
Sonic Automotive
Travelocity
Tree.com
Yahoo!

HISTORICAL FINANCIALS

Company Type: Public

Income Statement

FYE: December 31

	REVENUE ($ mil.)	NET INCOME ($ mil.)	NET PROFIT MARGIN	EMPLOYEES
12/08	104.0	11.6	11.2%	625
12/07	89.9	0.3	0.3%	613
12/06	84.8	38.8	45.8%	559
12/05	78.1	13.4	17.2%	559
12/04	61.1	9.3	15.2%	—
Annual Growth	**14.2%**	**5.7%**	**—**	**3.8%**

2008 Year-End Financials

Debt ratio: —
Return on equity: 3.3%
Cash ($ mil.): 43.6
Current ratio: 3.47
Long-term debt ($ mil.): —
No. of shares (mil.): 45.1

Dividends
Yield: —
Payout: —
Market value ($ mil.): 262.5
R&D as % of sales: —
Advertising as % of sales: —

Stock History

NASDAQ (GS): INET

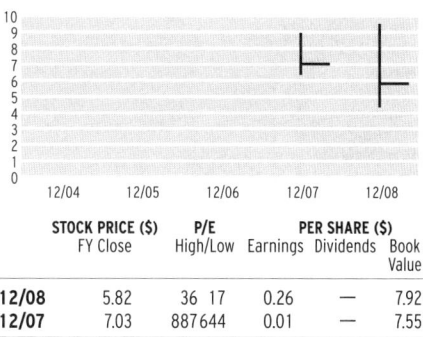

	STOCK PRICE ($) FY Close	P/E High/Low	Earnings	Dividends	Book Value
12/08	5.82	36 17	0.26	—	7.92
12/07	7.03	887 644	0.01	—	7.55
Annual Growth	**(17.2%)**	**—**	**—2,500.0%**	**—**	**4.9%**

Intrepid Potash

Hungry plants turn to Intrepid Potash for their food supply. The mining company produces two potassium-containing minerals, potash and langbeinite, that are essential nutrients in plant and crop fertilizer. Intrepid culls these minerals from five mines in New Mexico and Utah, where it also operates production facilities. Potash accounts for 90% of its sales. The company sells primarily within the US to the agricultural, industrial, and feed markets; PotashCorp sells Intrepid's potash outside North America. It supplies nearly 10% of US potash consumption annually and is the country's largest producer of the stuff. (The US imports a great majority of the potash it uses.)

Intrepid Potash went public in 2008, at which time it acquired all the assets and four main subsidiaries from former parent Intrepid Mining. It plans to sell these products overseas in emerging markets, such as Brazil, India, and China, where the demand for grain feed — and thus, fertilizer — has been growing steadily since the 1990s.

Chairman and CEO Robert Jornayvaz and COO Hugh Harvey together control about 45% of Intrepid Potash.

EXECUTIVES

Chairman and CEO: Robert P. Jornayvaz III, age 50
EVP Technology, CTO, and Director:
Hugh E. Harvey Jr., $964,178 total compensation
EVP, CFO, Treasurer, and Secretary:
David W. Honeyfield, age 42,
$862,333 total compensation
EVP Human Resources and Risk Management:
James N. Whyte, age 50, $1,246,697 total compensation
EVP and General Counsel: Martin D. Litt, age 44
SVP Sales and Marketing: Rufus L. Moore, age 59
VP and Controller: Rodney D. Gloss, age 52
VP Operations: John Mansanti, age 54
Auditors: KPMG LLP

LOCATIONS

HQ: Intrepid Potash, Inc.
700 17th St., Ste. 1700, Denver, CO 80202
Phone: 303-296-3006   **Fax:** 303-298-7502
Web: www.intrepidpotash.com

2008 Sales

	$ mil.	% of total
US	380.8	92
International	34.5	8
Total	**415.3**	**100**

COMPETITORS

Agrium
Arab Potash
CF Industries
Israel Chemicals
K+S
Mosaic Company
PotashCorp
SQM

HISTORICAL FINANCIALS

Company Type: Public

Income Statement

FYE: December 31

	REVENUE ($ mil.)	NET INCOME ($ mil.)	NET PROFIT MARGIN	EMPLOYEES
12/08	415.3	142.7	34.4%	776
12/07	213.5	29.7	13.9%	734
12/06	154.3	36.0	23.3%	710
12/05	153.0	34.5	22.5%	—
12/04	114.3	24.4	21.3%	—
Annual Growth	**38.1%**	**55.5%**	**—**	**4.5%**

2008 Year-End Financials

Debt ratio: 0.0%
Return on equity: 43.1%
Cash ($ mil.): 116.6
Current ratio: 5.09
Long-term debt ($ mil.): 0.0
No. of shares (mil.): 75.0

Dividends
Yield: 0.0%
Payout: —
Market value ($ mil.): 1,558.4
R&D as % of sales: —
Advertising as % of sales: —

Stock History

NYSE: IPI

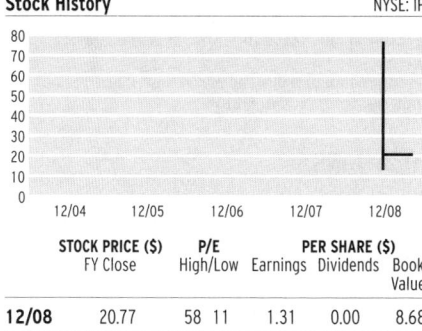

	STOCK PRICE ($) FY Close	P/E High/Low	Earnings	Dividends	Book Value
12/08	20.77	58 11	1.31	0.00	8.68

Intuitive Surgical

Intuitive Surgical is haptic to meet you. Employing haptics (the science of computer-aided touch sensitivity), the firm has developed the da Vinci Surgical System, a combination of software, hardware, and optics that allows doctors to perform robotically aided surgery from a remote console. The da Vinci system faithfully reproduces the doctor's hand movements in real time, with surgery performed by tiny electromechanical arms and instruments inserted in the patient's body through small openings. The company also makes instruments and accessories for use with its system. Intuitive sells its products in the Americas, Asia, Australia, and Europe through both a direct sales force and independent distributors.

The leading maker of surgical robots, Intuitive Surgical has seen strong growth as acceptance of less traumatic, minimally invasive surgical procedures has increased. The da Vinci systems (which cost a whopping $1.4 million) are primarily used in prostate-removal surgeries, but surgeons are increasingly using them for hysterectomies, removal of uterine fibroids, and other gynecological procedures. The company focuses its marketing efforts within these areas (urology and gynecology), as well as in the areas of cardiothoracic and general surgery, and it hopes to expand into additional surgical specialties.

The company has formed strategic alliances with a number of medical device businesses in the areas of product development, training, and marketing. Intuitive Surgical has such alliances with Gyrus, Olympus Corporation, and Ethicon Endo-Surgery, among others.

EXECUTIVES

Chairman and CEO: Lonnie M. Smith, age 65, $4,830,375 total compensation
President and COO: Gary S. Guthart, age 43, $3,592,948 total compensation
EVP Worldwide Sales and Marketing: Jerome J. (Jerry) McNamara, age 51, $2,945,299 total compensation
SVP and CFO: Marshall L. Mohr, age 53, $2,167,150 total compensation
SVP and General Counsel: Mark Meltzer, age 59, $2,339,426 total compensation
VP Customer Service: Colin Morales
VP Engineering: Sal Brogna
VP Product Development: Dave Rosa
VP Intellectual Property and Licensing: Frank D. Nguyen
VP Sales, US: Jim Alecxih
VP Finance: Benjamin B. (Ben) Gong
VP Human Resources: Heather Rider
VP Business Development: Aleks Cukic
VP Manufacturing: Augusto V. Castello
VP Clinical and Regulatory Affairs: Karen Uyesugi, age 53
VP International Sales and Marketing: Pierre Rivaux
Auditors: Ernst & Young LLP

LOCATIONS

HQ: Intuitive Surgical, Inc.
1266 Kifer Rd., Bldg. 101, Sunnyvale, CA 94086
Phone: 408-523-2100   **Fax:** 408-523-1390
Web: www.intuitivesurgical.com

2008 Sales

	$ mil.	% of total
US	679.7	78
Other countries	195.2	22
Total	**874.9**	**100**

PRODUCTS/OPERATIONS

2008 Sales

	$ mil.	% of total
Products		
Systems	455.3	52
Instruments & accessories	293.0	33
Services & training	126.6	15
Total	**874.9**	**100**

Selected Products

da Vinci Surgical System (surgeon's console, patient-side cart, and InSite 3-D visualization system)
Electrosurgical accessories
EndoWrist surgical instruments (scalpels, scissors, graspers)
Sterilization trays
Ultrasonic energy instruments
Vision equipment

COMPETITORS

Accuray
Bard
Boston Scientific
Curexo Technology
Hansen Medical
Hitachi
Integrated Surgical Systems
Maquet
Medtronic
MicroDexterity
Prosurgics
Stereotaxis
Terumo Medical Corporation
Toshiba

HISTORICAL FINANCIALS

Company Type: Public

Income Statement

				FYE: December 31
	REVENUE ($ mil.)	NET INCOME ($ mil.)	NET PROFIT MARGIN	EMPLOYEES
12/08	874.9	204.3	23.4%	1,049
12/07	600.8	144.5	24.1%	764
12/06	372.7	72.0	19.3%	563
12/05	227.3	94.1	41.4%	419
12/04	138.8	23.5	16.9%	321
Annual Growth	**58.4%**	**71.7%**	**—**	**34.5%**

2008 Year-End Financials

Debt ratio: —
Return on equity: 19.0%
Cash ($ mil.): 194.6
Current ratio: 4.28
Long-term debt ($ mil.): —
No. of shares (mil.): 38.2
Dividends
  Yield: —
  Payout: —
Market value ($ mil.): 4,849.7
R&D as % of sales: —
Advertising as % of sales: —

Stock History

NASDAQ (GS): ISRG

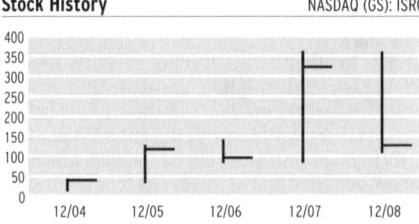

	STOCK PRICE ($) FY Close	P/E High/Low		PER SHARE ($) Earnings	Dividends	Book Value
12/08	126.99	70	22	5.12	—	33.17
12/07	323.00	97	23	3.70	—	23.27
12/06	95.90	74	45	1.89	—	15.44
12/05	117.27	50	14	2.51	—	11.59
12/04	40.02	61	23	0.67	—	8.25
Annual Growth	**33.5%**	**—**	**—**	**66.3%**	**—**	**41.6%**

Investment Technology Group

As its name implies, Investment Technology Group (ITG) combines technology with investing. The company provides automated equity trading products and services related to order management and execution management; it serves institutional investors and brokers throughout the trading process, from analysis before the trade to post-trading evaluation. Core products include its Portfolio System for Institutional Trading (POSIT) crossing system, which lets institutional clients confidentially trade shares and stock portfolios among themselves; ITG Algorithms; and ITG Logic, for risk management. The company is active in Asia, Australia, Canada, Europe, and the US.

ITG has filled in gaps in its service offerings primarily through acquisitions, including the 2006 buys of Macgregor (stock trade management technologies development) and Plexus Group (trading consulting services).

Additions to ITG's product mix include crossing opportunity scanner BLOCKalert, launched in 2006 through a joint venture with Merrill Lynch; broker-neutral trading system Radical; and the Channel ITG order management system.

ITG has been focusing on international growth, as well. Canada and Europe are among its primary target areas. Its strategy paid off in 2007 when its international operations totalled one-quarter of its sales. In 2008 it expanded its product offerings in the Asia/Pacific region with the launch of the Triton execution management system.

Jefferies Group spun off ITG in 1999.

EXECUTIVES

Chairman: Maureen O'Hara, age 56
President, CEO, and Director: Robert C. (Bob) Gasser, age 45, $4,026,989 total compensation
CFO: Howard C. Naphtali, age 55, $2,209,384 total compensation
General Counsel: Mats Goebels, age 42
Managing Director, US Sales and Trading: Christopher J. (Chris) Heckman, age 48, $2,098,629 total compensation
Managing Director: Ian Domowitz, age 57, $1,896,846 total compensation
Managing Director and Controller: Angelo Bulone, age 43
CEO, ITG Canada Corp.: Nicholas (Nick) Thadaney, age 40
CEO, ITG Europe: David Stevens, age 42
CEO, ITG Asia Pacific: Leon Christianakis
Auditors: KPMG LLP

LOCATIONS

HQ: Investment Technology Group, Inc.
380 Madison Ave., New York, NY 10017
Phone: 212-588-4000   **Fax:** 212-444-6295
Web: www.itginc.com

2008 Sales

	$ mil.	% of total
North America		
US	571.3	75
Canada	83.4	11
Europe	77.7	10
Asia/Other	30.6	4
Total	**763.0**	**100**

PRODUCTS/OPERATIONS

2008 Sales

	$ mil.	% of total
Commissions	654.9	86
Recurring revenue	88.0	12
Other	20.1	2
Total	**763.0**	**100**

COMPETITORS

Gelber Group
GSEC
Liquidnet
NASDAQ OMX
NexTrade
NYSE Euronext
TRADEBOOK

HISTORICAL FINANCIALS

Company Type: Public

Income Statement

FYE: December 31

	REVENUE ($ mil.)	NET INCOME ($ mil.)	NET PROFIT MARGIN	EMPLOYEES
12/08	763.0	114.6	15.0%	1,323
12/07	731.0	111.1	15.2%	1,060
12/06	599.5	97.9	16.3%	1,060
12/05	408.2	67.7	16.6%	714
12/04	334.5	41.0	12.3%	653
Annual Growth	**22.9%**	**29.3%**	**—**	**19.3%**

2008 Year-End Financials

Debt ratio: 12.0%
Return on equity: 15.4%
Cash ($ mil.): 353.0
Current ratio: 1.33
Long-term debt ($ mil.): 94.5
No. of shares (mil.): 43.7
Dividends
  Yield: 0.0%
  Payout: —
Market value ($ mil.): 993.2
R&D as % of sales: —
Advertising as % of sales: —

Stock History

NYSE: ITG

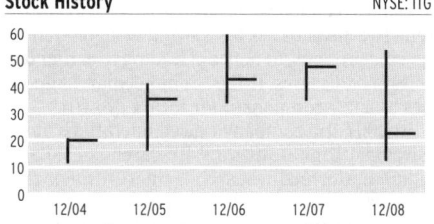

	STOCK PRICE ($) FY Close	P/E High/Low		Earnings	PER SHARE ($) Dividends	Book Value
12/08	22.72	20	5	2.61	0.00	18.01
12/07	47.59	20	14	2.48	0.00	16.11
12/06	42.88	27	16	2.21	0.00	13.91
12/05	35.44	26	10	1.60	0.00	10.58
12/04	20.00	21	12	0.96	0.00	8.48
Annual Growth	**3.2%**	**—**	**—**	**28.4%**	**—**	**20.7%**

IPC The Hospitalist Company

IPC The Hospitalist Company (IPC) is on the leading edge of the growing US trend toward hospitalist specialization. The staffing firm provides more than 500 hospitalists to more than 300 hospitals and other inpatient facilities. Hospitalists are health care providers (physicians, nurses, and physicians assistants) who oversee all of a patient's treatment from the beginning to the end of their stay. They answer questions and coordinate treatment programs to improve the quality of care and reduce the length of a patient's hospital stay. In addition to providing staff, the company offers training, information management services, and risk management services for its medical professionals and clients.

IPC has used part of its 2008 IPO funds to help pay off debt and acquire smaller regional hospitalist practice groups. In 2009 the company expanded into a new state territory when it acquired two hospitalist groups in New Jersey. Later that year it acquired practices in Connecticut and Rhode Island, expanding its presence into 21 states.

IPC intends to establish contracts with current hospitals and new inpatient facilities, as well as recruit and train additional hospitalists. Already the company manages more than 130 practice groups.

EXECUTIVES

Chairman, CEO, and Chief Medical Officer:
  Adam D. Singer, age 48, $1,141,438 total compensation
President, COO, and Director: R. Jeffrey Taylor, age 60, $632,555 total compensation
CFO and Secretary: Devra G. Shapiro, age 62, $528,843 total compensation
EVP and Chief Development Officer:
  Richard G. Russell, age 49, $458,852 total compensation
VP Physician Staffing: Timothy Lary
VP Health Services: Kathleen Loya
VP Legal Affairs: Perri Melnick
VP Information Systems: Mark C. Citron
VP Medical Affairs: Felix Aguirre
VP Finance and Corporate Controller:
  Fernando J. Sarria
VP Marketing and Development: Todd Kislak
VP Financial Analysis and Revenue Controls:
  Jamie S. Glazer
Auditors: Ernst & Young LLP

LOCATIONS

HQ: IPC The Hospitalist Company, Inc.
  4605 Lankershim Blvd., Ste. 617
  North Hollywood, CA 91602
Phone: 888-447-2362   **Fax:** 818-766-3999
Web: www.thehospitalistcompany.com

COMPETITORS

Cogent Healthcare
EmCare
Sterling Healthcare
Team Health

HISTORICAL FINANCIALS

Company Type: Public

Income Statement

FYE: December 31

	REVENUE ($ mil.)	NET INCOME ($ mil.)	NET PROFIT MARGIN	EMPLOYEES
12/08	251.2	13.6	5.4%	1,028
12/07	190.0	(0.9)	—	856
12/06	148.1	1.8	1.2%	757
12/05	110.9	4.6	4.1%	856
12/04	91.7	3.6	3.9%	—
Annual Growth	**28.7%**	**39.4%**	**—**	**6.3%**

2008 Year-End Financials

Debt ratio: 4.4%
Return on equity: 16.4%
Cash ($ mil.): 37.4
Current ratio: 3.93
Long-term debt ($ mil.): 5.4
No. of shares (mil.): 16.1
Dividends
  Yield: 0.0%
  Payout: —
Market value ($ mil.): 271.7
R&D as % of sales: —
Advertising as % of sales: —

Stock History

NASDAQ (GM): IPCM

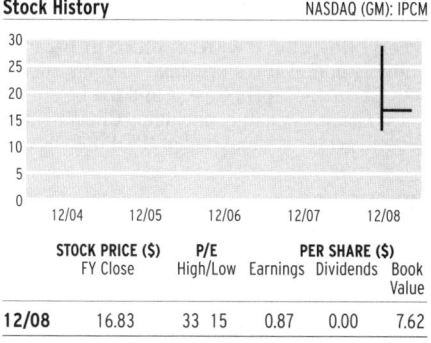

	STOCK PRICE ($) FY Close	P/E High/Low		Earnings	PER SHARE ($) Dividends	Book Value
12/08	16.83	33	15	0.87	0.00	7.62

IPG Photonics

IPG Photonics has its name in lights. The company makes fiber-optic signal amplifiers, fiber lasers, laser diodes, and pump lasers, which are primarily used in materials processing. Its fiber lasers also have applications in medicine and in telecommunications networks to enable voice and data transmission over optical lines, among other uses. IPG has shipped more than 40,000 units to hundreds of customers around the world. The company's customers include BAE SYSTEMS, Mitsubishi Heavy Industries, and Nippon Steel. IPG Photonics gets about three-quarters of its sales outside North America.

IPG Photonics primarily depends on capital expenditures by its customers in materials processing, which include the automotive, electronics, and photovoltaic solar power industries. The automotive and electronics industries are suffering through extended downturns due to economic uncertainty created by the global credit crisis and recession. It is not clear yet when these uncertain economic conditions will abate or recede. For all these concerns, IPG enjoyed healthy growth in sales and profits for 2008. The company also depends on wider acceptance and implementation of its fiber laser technology. IPG procures a variety of raw materials for its product manufacturing, such as diode packages and semiconductor wafers, and some of its suppliers are also competitors to the company.

Fiber lasers, which use semiconductor diodes as the light source to pump specialty optical fibers, are superior to conventional lasers in beam quality performance, lower total cost of ownership, ease of use, compact size and portability, and choice of wavelengths with precise control of the beam, according to IPG.

IPG Photonics raised about $100 million in private equity funding, with its investors including Apax Partners, Merrill Lynch, TA Associates, and Winston Partners. The company filed for an IPO in 2000 and withdrew the registration statement six months later. It filed for another IPO in 2006 and completed the offering by the end of the year.

The company used proceeds of its public offering to repurchase warrants, pay off debts, and for general corporate purposes, including working capital, expansion of manufacturing facilities, purchases of equipment, and expansion of applications development and services.

In 2007 IPG Photonics acquired its Chinese distributor, HM Laser, and established a subsidiary, IPG China, with an office in Beijing. China is one of IPG's principal markets, along with Germany, Japan, Russia, and the US.

The Gapontsev family (including CEO Valentin Gapontsev) owns about half of IPG Photonics.

EXECUTIVES

Chairman and CEO: Valentin P. Gapontsev, age 71, $619,083 total compensation
VP and CFO: Timothy P. V. Mammen, age 40, $416,706 total compensation
VP, General Counsel, and Secretary: Angelo P. Lopresti, age 46, $416,239 total compensation
VP Components: Alexander (Alex) Ovtchinnikov, age 48, $394,746 total compensation
VP Industrial Markets: William S. (Bill) Shiner, age 67
VP Telecommunications Products: George H. BuAbbud, age 54
VP Operations: Dennis P. Leonard Jr.
VP, Treasurer, and Controller: Paolo Sinni
Director Human Resources: Coral Barry
Director; Acting General Manager, NTO IRE-Polus: Igor Samartsev, age 47
Director Advanced Applications: Michael O'Connor
Director; Managing Director IPG Laser: Eugene Shcherbakov, age 61, $539,454 total compensation
Auditors: Deloitte & Touche LLP

LOCATIONS

HQ: IPG Photonics Corporation
50 Old Webster Rd., Oxford, MA 01540
Phone: 508-373-1100   **Fax:** 508-373-1103
Web: www.ipgphotonics.com

IPG Photonics has manufacturing operations in China, Germany, India, Italy, Russia, and the US, with sales offices in China, France, Germany, India, Japan, Russia, Singapore, South Korea, the UK, and the US.

2008 Sales

	$ mil.	% of total
Europe		
Germany	44.8	20
Other countries	49.3	21
Asia & Australia		
Japan	41.3	18
Other countries	36.3	16
North America	52.0	23
Other regions	5.4	2
Total	**229.1**	**100**

PRODUCTS/OPERATIONS

2008 Sales

	$ mil.	% of total
Materials processing	187.7	82
Advanced applications	24.7	11
Communications	12.9	5
Medical	3.8	2
Total	**229.1**	**100**

Selected Products

Broadband light sources
Continuous wave lasers
Diode laser systems
Erbium amplifiers
Fiber amplifiers
Fiber lasers
Fiber-coupled laser diodes
Praseodymium amplifiers
Pulsed fiber lasers
Raman pump lasers and amplifiers
Thulium lasers
Ytterbium lasers

COMPETITORS

Cisco Systems	Mitsubishi Materials
Coherent, Inc.	Newport Corp.
EMCORE	Oclaro
FANUC	Presstek
Furukawa Electric	ROFIN-SINAR
GSI Group	Swatch
Huawei Technologies	TRUMPF
JDS Uniphase	

HISTORICAL FINANCIALS

Company Type: Public

Income Statement

FYE: December 31

	REVENUE ($ mil.)	NET INCOME ($ mil.)	NET PROFIT MARGIN	EMPLOYEES
12/08	229.1	36.7	16.0%	1,420
12/07	188.7	29.9	15.8%	1,300
12/06	143.2	49.4	34.5%	1,040
12/05	96.4	7.4	7.7%	900
12/04	60.7	2.0	3.3%	—
Annual Growth	**39.4%**	**107.0%**	**—**	**16.4%**

2008 Year-End Financials

Debt ratio: 7.6%
Return on equity: 16.7%
Cash ($ mil.): 51.3
Current ratio: 3.69
Long-term debt ($ mil.): 18.0
No. of shares (mil.): 45.7

Dividends
Yield: 0.0%
Payout: —
Market value ($ mil.): 602.2
R&D as % of sales: —
Advertising as % of sales: —

Stock History

NASDAQ (GM): IPGP

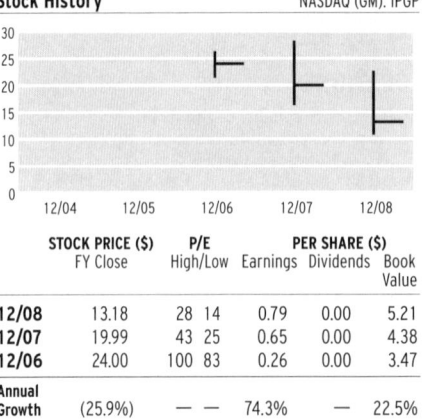

	STOCK PRICE ($) FY Close	P/E High/Low		PER SHARE ($) Earnings	Dividends	Book Value
12/08	13.18	28	14	0.79	0.00	5.21
12/07	19.99	43	25	0.65	0.00	4.38
12/06	24.00	100	83	0.26	0.00	3.47
Annual Growth	**(25.9%)**	**—**	**—**	**74.3%**	**—**	**22.5%**

IRIS International

IRIS International provides urinalysis technology to medical institutions around the globe. IRIS International's three divisions include Iris Diagnostics, which develops imaging systems used in urinalysis and microscopic analysis, as well as related consumables (reagents and test strips) and services. Its primary product is the iQ family of microscopy analyzers, which automate the steps of routine urinalysis. Iris Sample Processing makes a variety of other small instruments and laboratory supplies, including centrifuges. IRIS International sells its products through a direct sales force in the US; international sales are generally conducted through independent distributors.

IRIS International plans to grow through acquisitions and expand into new markets by increasing its international marketing efforts. In 2009 the company acquired its distribution operations in the UK and Germany from its European distributor, the Werfen Group, which will continue to represent IRIS International in nine other countries, including Spain, Italy, and Mexico. IRIS International made the buy to increase its direct sales presence internationally. The company generated about 30% of its revenue through international sales in 2007.

IRIS is also expanding its product portfolio through internal development; the company is working on an automated urine bacteria screening device as an alternative to urine cultures, and it plans to expand into other fluid-based diagnostics, such as hematology (blood analysis).

Acquisitions have included the purchase of Leucadia Technologies in 2006; Leucadia has been renamed IRIS Molecular Diagnostics. The division's technology allows IRIS to develop more sensitive tests based on molecular detection of specific proteins, in hopes of leading to earlier detection of diseases. IRIS sees molecular diagnostics as a key component for future growth.

In 2007 the company ceased operations at its Advanced Digital Imaging Research subsidiary, which performed research for government and corporate clients, after the unit lost its government grant funding due to new Small Business Administration guidelines.

EXECUTIVES

Chairman, President, and CEO: Cesar M. García, age 56, $1,078,373 total compensation
Corporate VP, CTO, and Director: Thomas H. Adams, age 66
VP, CFO, and Secretary: Peter L. Donato, age 39, $481,409 total compensation
VP; President, Iris Sample Processing Division: Thomas E. (Tom) Warekois, age 55, $556,277 total compensation
VP Operations: John U. Yi, age 48, $437,705 total compensation
VP Quality and Regulatory Affairs: David W. Gates
VP; President, Sample Processing Business Unit: Robert A. Mello, age 55, $457,392 total compensation
VP Sales and Marketing, Iris Sample Processing: Pamela Pasakarnis
VP Research and Development, Iris Diagnostics Business Unit: Lawrence J. Blecka
Auditors: BDO Seidman, LLP

LOCATIONS

HQ: IRIS International, Inc.
  9172 Eton Ave., Chatsworth, CA 91311
Phone: 818-709-1244   **Fax:** 818-700-9661
Web: www.proiris.com

PRODUCTS/OPERATIONS

2008 Sales

	% of total
IVD consumables & service	49
IVD instruments	37
Sample processing instruments & supplies	14
Total	**100**

COMPETITORS

Abbott Labs
BD Biosciences
Beckman Coulter
Biomerica
bioMérieux
Clarient
Gen-Probe
HORIBA
Hycor Biomedical
Nanosphere
Ortho-Clinical Diagnostics
Roche Diagnostics
Siemens Healthcare Diagnostics
SYSMEX
Thermo Fisher Scientific

HISTORICAL FINANCIALS

Company Type: Public

Income Statement — FYE: December 31

	REVENUE ($ mil.)	NET INCOME ($ mil.)	NET PROFIT MARGIN	EMPLOYEES
12/08	95.5	9.0	9.4%	318
12/07	84.3	7.5	8.9%	308
12/06	70.5	(0.2)	—	274
12/05	62.8	6.1	9.7%	236
12/04	43.7	2.3	5.3%	182
Annual Growth	**21.6%**	**40.6%**	**—**	**15.0%**

2008 Year-End Financials

Debt ratio: —
Return on equity: 11.9%
Cash ($ mil.): 24.4
Current ratio: 4.50
Long-term debt ($ mil.): —
No. of shares (mil.): 18.0

Dividends
  Yield: 0.0%
  Payout: —
Market value ($ mil.): 251.5
R&D as % of sales: —
Advertising as % of sales: —

Stock History

NASDAQ (GM): IRIS

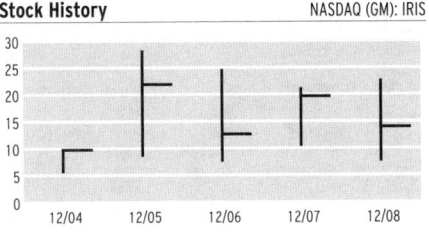

	STOCK PRICE ($) FY Close	P/E High/Low	PER SHARE ($) Earnings	PER SHARE ($) Dividends	PER SHARE ($) Book Value
12/08	13.94	47 16	0.48	0.00	4.21
12/07	19.62	52 26	0.40	0.00	4.15
12/06	12.61	— —	(0.01)	0.00	3.47
12/05	21.86	80 25	0.35	0.00	2.98
12/04	9.75	70 41	0.14	0.00	2.17
Annual Growth	**9.3%**	**— —**	**36.1%**	**—**	**18.0%**

iRobot Corporation

If you're a fan of the old Jetsons episodes, you'll probably appreciate iRobot. The company makes robots for all sorts of applications, from government and military to home appliances. Its Roomba FloorVac and Scooba are the first of their kind to automatically clean floors. iRobot also makes the Looj gutter-cleaning 'bot, the Seaglider unmanned underwater robot for use in oceans, and the PackBot, which performs battlefield reconnaissance and bomb disposal for the US Army. iRobot boasts offices in the US and Hong Kong and sells its products through retailers worldwide. The company was founded in 1990 by robot engineers from the Massachusetts Institute of Technology. iRobot acquired Nekton Research in 2008.

Purchasing Nekton, based in Raleigh-Durham, North Carolina, satisfies iRobot's push to expand its unmanned underwater segment of its business — a strategy that's still in place for 2009. Nekton specializes in making and marketing unmanned underwater robots for the Office of Naval Research, Naval Undersea Warfare Command, and other organizations. The deal has positioned iRobot as a leader in robot technology for both land and sea applications. The transaction involved a $10 million cash payment upfront and up to an additional $5 million for meeting certain business and financial milestones. iRobot and Nekton plan to pair their technology expertise to produce the Nekton Ranger prototype.

iRobot has been able to produce some of its tactical products and extend its reach in that segment through agreements with other companies. Its R-Gator, another unmanned ground vehicle model, is made through a partnership with Deere & Company. The company's alliance with The Boeing Company allows iRobot to develop products more quickly for its small unmanned ground vehicle (SUGV) items by using commercial off the shelf (COTS) components. For its autonomous vehicles, iRobot works with Advanced Scientific Concepts to integrate LADAR technology for navigation and mapping applications.

With its foothold in the robotic appliances niche, iRobot has boosted its consumer business by developing new products built on popular brand names. It has introduced several products, including the Roomba for Pets, Roomba Discovery for Pets, and the Dirt Dog Workshop Robot, which is designed to keep work spaces free of sawdust, small nails, and debris.

The company has sold more than 4 million home-care robots and some 2,200 PackBot tactical military robots, most of which were purchased by the US military for missions in Afghanistan and Iraq.

When Helen Greiner resigned as chairman in October 2008, CEO Colin Angle succeeded her while retaining his chief executive title. Greiner remained on the board.

EXECUTIVES

Chairman and CEO: Colin M. Angle, age 41, $642,757 total compensation
EVP, CFO, and Treasurer: John J. Leahy, age 50, $602,371 total compensation
SVP, Secretary, and General Counsel:
  Glen D. Weinstein, age 38, $525,974 total compensation
SVP Research and Development: Indrajit Purkayastha

VP Information Technology and CIO: Jay Leader
VP Financial Controls and Analysis: Alison Dean, age 44, $515,885 total compensation
VP Marketing Communications: Nancy Dussault Smith
VP Human Resources: Penny Outlaw
Investor Relations: Elise P. Caffrey
President and General Manager, Government and Industrial: Joseph W. (Joe) Dyer, age 62, $581,692 total compensation
President and General Manager, Home Robots:
  Jeffrey A. (Jeff) Beck, age 46
Auditors: PricewaterhouseCoopers LLP

LOCATIONS

HQ: iRobot Corporation
  8 Crosby Dr., Bedford, MA 01730
Phone: 781-430-3000   **Fax:** 781-430-3001
Web: www.irobot.com

PRODUCTS/OPERATIONS

2008 Sales

	$ mil.	% of total
Product	281.2	91
Contract	26.4	9
Total	**307.6**	**100**

2008 Sales

	$ mil.	% of total
Home robots	173.6	56
Government & industrial	134.0	44
Total	**307.6**	**100**

COMPETITORS

Allen-Vanguard Corporation
AM General
BAE SYSTEMS
BISSELL
Electrolux
GE Consumer & Industrial
General Dynamics
LG Electronics
Lockheed Martin
QinetiQ
REMOTEC UK
Samsung Electronics

HISTORICAL FINANCIALS

Company Type: Public

Income Statement — FYE: December 31

	REVENUE ($ mil.)	NET INCOME ($ mil.)	NET PROFIT MARGIN	EMPLOYEES
12/08	307.6	0.8	0.3%	479
12/07	249.1	9.1	3.7%	423
12/06	189.0	3.6	1.9%	371
12/05	142.0	1.6	1.1%	276
12/04	95.0	0.1	0.1%	214
Annual Growth	**34.1%**	**68.2%**	**—**	**22.3%**

2008 Year-End Financials

Debt ratio: —
Return on equity: 0.7%
Cash ($ mil.): 40.9
Current ratio: 3.13
Long-term debt ($ mil.): —
No. of shares (mil.): 25.0

Dividends
  Yield: 0.0%
  Payout: —
Market value ($ mil.): 226.0
R&D as % of sales: —
Advertising as % of sales: —

Stock History

| | 12/04 | 12/05 | 12/06 | 12/07 | 12/08 |

	STOCK PRICE ($) FY Close	P/E High/Low		PER SHARE ($) Earnings	Dividends	Book Value
12/08	9.03	747	239	0.03	0.00	4.78
12/07	18.08	67	35	0.36	0.00	4.40
12/06	18.06	271	115	0.14	0.00	3.79
12/05	33.33	339	239	0.11	0.00	3.50
Annual Growth	(35.3%)	—	—	31.6%	—	—

Isramco, Inc.

There may be milk and honey on the other side of the River Jordan, but to date, not much oil. Because of that, in 2007 Isramco sold to I.O.C Israel Oil Company the bulk of its Israel-based activities and assets including its stake in Isramco Oil & Gas. Focusing on growing its US operations, the company is engaged (through subsidiaries Jay Petroleum and Jay Management) in oil and gas exploration, primarily in Louisiana, Oklahoma, Texas, and Wyoming. In 2007 Isramco reported proved reserves of 50.3 billion cu. ft. of gas equivalent. Chairman and CEO Haim Tsuff owns 49.8% of Isramco.

In 2007 Isramco acquired oil and gas properties (including 650 oil and gas wells) in Texas and New Mexico from Five States Energy Company, L.L.C.

In 2008 the company continued to beef up its US assets with the acquisition of oil and gas properties in Texas, New Mexico, and Oklahoma (40 fields and 490 leases) from GFB Acquisition — I, L.P. and Trans Republic Resources, Ltd.

EXECUTIVES

Chairman and CEO: Haim Tsuff, age 52,
 $310,000 total compensation
President and Director: Jackob Maimon, age 53,
 $100,000 total compensation
CFO: Edy Francis, age 33
President, US Based Subsidiaries: Yossi Levy, age 56
Auditors: Malone & Bailey, PLLC

LOCATIONS

HQ: Isramco, Inc.
 2425 West Loop South, Ste. 810
 Houston, TX 77027
Phone: 713-621-5946   **Fax:** 713-621-3988

COMPETITORS

Anadarko Petroleum
Cabot Oil & Gas
Devon Energy
EOG
Samson Oil
XTO Energy

HISTORICAL FINANCIALS
Company Type: Public

Income Statement
FYE: December 31

	REVENUE ($ mil.)	NET INCOME ($ mil.)	NET PROFIT MARGIN	EMPLOYEES
12/08	52.2	3.2	6.1%	16
12/07	22.8	(6.4)	—	7
12/06	12.4	3.8	30.6%	13
12/05	7.7	(1.1)	—	13
12/04	8.9	0.0	—	8
Annual Growth	55.6%	—	—	18.9%

2008 Year-End Financials

Debt ratio: 493.5%
Return on equity: 12.7%
Cash ($ mil.): 3.1
Current ratio: 0.56
Long-term debt ($ mil.): 123.6
No. of shares (mil.): 2.7
Dividends
 Yield: —
 Payout: —
Market value ($ mil.): 84.9
R&D as % of sales: —
Advertising as % of sales: —

Stock History

| | 12/04 | 12/05 | 12/06 | 12/07 | 12/08 |

	STOCK PRICE ($) FY Close	P/E High/Low		PER SHARE ($) Earnings	Dividends	Book Value
12/08	31.25	50	16	1.19	—	9.21
12/07	47.47	—	—	(2.36)	—	9.37
12/06	29.35	22	9	1.41	—	12.78
12/05	15.07	—	—	(0.42)	—	10.48
12/04	5.24	—	—	0.00	—	11.23
Annual Growth	56.3%	—	—	—	—	(4.8%)

ITC Holdings Corp.

ITC Holdings owns and operates 2,800 miles of power transmission lines in southeastern Michigan (including Detroit and Ann Arbor). Through its subsidiaries, ITC Transmission, Michigan Electric Transmission Company (METC), and ITC Midwest LLC, ITC operates regulated, high-voltage transmission systems in Michigan's Lower Peninsula and portions of Illinois, Iowa, Minnesota, and Missouri serving a combined peak load in excess of 25,000 MW. ITC is a member of the Midwest ISO, a regional transmission organization. The company also as operates ITC Grid Development and ITC Great Plains, which invests in transmission infrastructure development in Kansas and the Great Plains region.

ITC is working on building a robust regional power infrastructure, using both renewable and traditional power resources. Through its Green Power Express unit ITC is looking to integrate wind and other renewable sources into ITC's future energy mix, as the company strives to meet state and federal demands for power generators to use cleaner energy. It is developing a network of 765 kV transmission facilities that will move up to 12,000 MW of renewable energy

(primarily wind-powered) to major load centers in the Midwest.

Building its traditional infrastructure, in 2006 ITC acquired METC for $865 million. The next year it acquired subsidiary Interstate Power and Light Company's transmission assets in Illinois, Iowa, and Minnesota for $783 million.

EXECUTIVES

Chairman, President, and CEO: Joseph L. Welch, age 61, $7,319,156 total compensation
EVP and Chief Business Officer: Linda H. Blair, age 40, $1,212,753 total compensation
EVP and COO: Jon E. Jipping, age 44, $1,187,162 total compensation
SVP, CFO, and Treasurer: Cameron M. Bready, age 37
SVP and General Counsel: Daniel J. Oginsky, age 36, $893,177 total compensation
VP Information Technology and Facilities and CIO: Denis DesRosiers
VP Energy Policy: Terry S. Harvill
VP Planning: Thomas W. Vitez
VP and General Counsel, Utility Operations: Christine Mason Soneral
VP Operations: Elizabeth A. Howell
VP Major Contracts and Special Projects: Joseph R. Dudak, age 60
VP Business Strategy: Gregory Ioanidis
Secretary: Wendy A. McIntyre
President, ITC Great Plains: Carl A. Huslig
Auditors: Deloitte & Touche LLP

LOCATIONS

HQ: ITC Holdings Corp.
 27175 Energy Way, Novi, MI 48377
Phone: 248-946-3000
Web: www.itc-holdings.com

PRODUCTS/OPERATIONS

2008 Sales

	$ mil.	% of total
Network	558.9	90
Point-to-point	23.4	4
Scheduling, control & dispatch	17.0	3
Regional cost sharing revenues	15.5	2
Other	3.1	1
Total	**617.9**	**100**

COMPETITORS

Detroit Edison
Midland Cogeneration Venture
Wolverine Power Supply

HISTORICAL FINANCIALS
Company Type: Public

Income Statement
FYE: December 31

	REVENUE ($ mil.)	NET INCOME ($ mil.)	NET PROFIT MARGIN	EMPLOYEES
12/08	617.9	109.2	17.7%	392
12/07	426.2	73.3	17.2%	302
12/06	223.6	33.2	14.8%	223
12/05	205.3	34.7	16.9%	137
12/04	126.4	2.6	2.1%	122
Annual Growth	48.7%	154.6%	—	33.9%

2008 Year-End Financials

Debt ratio: 242.0%
Return on equity: 14.6%
Cash ($ mil.): 58.1
Current ratio: 1.01
Long-term debt ($ mil.): 2,248.3
No. of shares (mil.): 50.8
Dividends
 Yield: 2.7%
 Payout: 54.3%
Market value ($ mil.): 2,217.4
R&D as % of sales: —
Advertising as % of sales: —

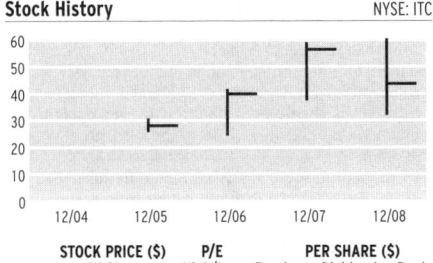

	STOCK PRICE ($)	P/E		PER SHARE ($)		
	FY Close	High/Low	Earnings	Dividends	Book Value	
12/08	43.68	27	15	2.19	1.19	18.30
12/07	56.42	35	23	1.68	1.13	11.09
12/06	39.90	45	27	0.92	1.08	10.48
12/05	28.09	29	25	1.06	0.52	5.19
Annual Growth	15.9%	—	—	128.7%	31.8%	47.4%

ITT Educational Services

To get a mortarboard from ITT, you may need to know a little something about motherboards. One of the largest US providers of technical education, ITT Educational Services offers mainly associate and bachelor degree programs to some 65,000 students at more than 105 ITT Technical Institutes in 37 states. The company has traditionally offered a range of technology-focused degrees in areas such as computer-aided design, engineering technology, and information technology. However, ITT Educational Services also offers degrees in business, criminal justice, design, and health sciences. Some programs are offered exclusively online, while others are offered through a combination of classroom and online instruction.

The company has benefited from funding cuts at state universities. The combination of rising tuition costs and class shortages at those institutions is making career college a more attractive option for postsecondary education. ITT is also benefitting from the poor economy, with many people who have lost jobs signing up to train for a new career.

In response to increasing enrollment rates, the company is expanding both the number and types of programs it offers. ITT opened eight new campuses in 2008, and plans to open another six or eight in 2009. ITT also plans to offer a broader range of both residence and online programs, and increase the number of campuses that offer bachelors degrees. ITT announced plans to acquire Daniel Webster College in New Hampshire in 2009. The four-year school is known for its aviation program.

A substantial majority of ITT Educational Services students work at least part-time during their programs of study. Most students pay a large portion of their tuition and expenses with funds received under various government-sponsored student financial aid programs, especially Title IV Programs. More than 60% of its revenues come from Title IV Program funds.

ITT Educational Services also gets revenue from student fees and the sale of computers and software.

Financial firm Columbia Wanger Asset Management own 12% of ITT Educational Services. Lazard Freres and Wellington Management each own about 10% of the company.

EXECUTIVES

Chairman and CEO: Kevin M. Modany, age 43, $4,154,987 total compensation
EVP and CFO: Daniel M. Fitzpatrick, age 50, $1,025,312 total compensation
EVP and President, ITT Technical Institute: Eugene W. Feichtner, age 54, $891,151 total compensation
EVP and President, ITT Online: June M. McCormack
EVP and Chief Marketing Officer: Glenn E. Tanner, age 62, $693,416 total compensation
EVP and CIO: Martin Van Buren, age 41
SVP, Secretary, and General Counsel: Clark D. Elwood, age 49, $956,118 total compensation
SVP, ITT Technical Institute Chief Academic Officer: P. Michael Linzmaier
SVP and Chief Compliance Officer: Jeffrey R. Cooper, age 58
SVP, ITT Technical Institute Operations: Barry S. Simich
SVP Business Development: David E. Catalano, age 43
SVP Human Resources: Nina F. Esbin, age 53
SVP, ITT Technical Institute Student Services: John W. Hawthorne
VP Marketing: Jill M. Minnick
VP Academic Affairs: Gary R. Carlson, age 62
VP, Treasurer, and Controller: Angela K. Knowlton
Director Recruitment: Thomas M. Montgomery
Director Public Relations: David Landau
Registrar: Tracy Terry
Auditors: PricewaterhouseCoopers LLP

LOCATIONS

HQ: ITT Educational Services, Inc.
13000 N. Meridian St., Carmel, IN 46032
Phone: 317-706-9200   **Fax:** 317-706-3040
Web: www.ittesi.com

PRODUCTS/OPERATIONS

Selected Schools and Programs

Business
  Business Accounting Technology
  Business Administration
  Technical Project Management
Criminal Justice
  Criminal Justice
  Criminal Justice — Cybersecurity
Computer Drafting and Design
  Construction Management
  Graphic Design
Electronics Technology
  Computer and Electronics Engineering Technology
  Electronics and Communications Engineering Technology
  Industrial Automation Engineering Technology
Health Science
  Health Information Technology
Information Technology
  Computer Network Systems
  Data Communication Systems Technology
  Information Systems Administration
  Information Systems Security
  Software Applications and Programming
  Software Engineering Technology
  Web Development

COMPETITORS

Apollo Group	Education Management
Career Education	Kaplan
Corinthian Colleges	SkillSoft
DeVry	Strayer Education

HISTORICAL FINANCIALS
Company Type: Public

Income Statement
FYE: December 31

	REVENUE ($ mil.)	NET INCOME ($ mil.)	NET PROFIT MARGIN	EMPLOYEES
12/08	1,015.3	203.0	20.0%	8,580
12/07	869.5	151.6	17.4%	7,200
12/06	757.8	118.5	15.6%	6,200
12/05	688.0	109.7	15.9%	6,000
12/04	617.8	75.3	12.2%	6,200
Annual Growth	13.2%	28.1%	—	8.5%

2008 Year-End Financials

Debt ratio: 79.9%
Return on equity: 157.1%
Cash ($ mil.): 226.3
Current ratio: 1.63
Long-term debt ($ mil.): 150.0
No. of shares (mil.): 36.9
Dividends
  Yield: 0.0%
  Payout: —
Market value ($ mil.): 3,509.0
R&D as % of sales: —
Advertising as % of sales: —

Stock History NYSE: ESI

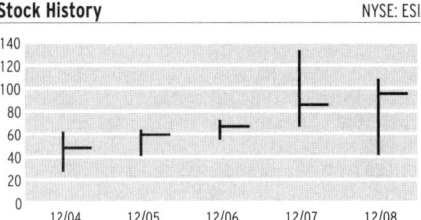

	STOCK PRICE ($)	P/E		PER SHARE ($)		
	FY Close	High/Low	Earnings	Dividends	Book Value	
12/08	94.98	21	8	5.17	0.00	5.08
12/07	85.27	36	18	3.71	0.00	1.91
12/06	66.37	26	20	2.72	0.00	2.81
12/05	59.11	27	18	2.33	0.00	8.35
12/04	47.55	38	17	1.61	0.00	6.36
Annual Growth	18.9%	—	—	33.9%	—	(5.5%)

j2 Global Communications

Checked your messages? Customers of j2 Global Communications can retrieve e-mail, faxes, and voicemail from a single phone line. Customers receive a private phone number that can handle unlimited incoming messages. The company operates primarily under the eFax, eVoice, Electric Mail, and Onebox brands, and claims more than 11 million phone numbers for customers located in nearly 50 countries worldwide, including major US cities and international business centers such as Frankfurt, London, and Tokyo. The company counts more than 1 million paid subscribers with the balance of phone lines going to advertising-supported free subscribers. j2 Global Communications gets most of its revenues in the US.

The company operates a global network based on both traditional phone infrastructure and Internet protocol (IP) technology. The network is leased from telecommunications carriers and from collocation providers in the US and abroad.

In 2007 j2 Global acquired messaging services firm YAC (as in "you're always connected") Limited. The company specializes in hosted messaging and communications services such as inbound call management, fax to e-mail, virtual numbers, audio conferencing, and personal numbers. j2 Global also bought the RapidFax business of EasyLink Services International.

Expansion through acquisitions continued into 2008 with the purchases of San Diego-based Phone People Holdings Corporation (toll-free calling services) and UK-based Mediaburst (digital faxing products and services). Late that year the company also purchased the assets of MailWise, a provider of hosted e-mail security services, as well as the fax and voice messaging assets of Mijanda, which offers digital fax and voice messaging applications.

HISTORY

What did rap music, East Berlin, and the dot-com crowds have in common? The answer was Jaye Muller. Born in the former East Germany, Muller moved to Paris at 17 to pursue a rap music career. During a 1994 UK concert tour, he became frustrated at missing too many faxes and phone messages. Conveniently enough, Muller had attended tech school and invented a virtual fax machine. He moved to New York to work on music, but it was the siren song of a universal inbox that haunted him. Finding software programmers in Australia to help develop a system, he launched the company in 1995 as JFAX Communications.

JFAX began offering voice and fax messages via e-mail in 1996 in Atlanta, London, and New York. The service soon caught on, and by the end of the year the company had phone numbers available in 15 cities. Muller snagged professional talent, hiring Motorola's Hemi Zucker as COO.

In 1997 the company introduced its outbound faxing service, and Muller brought in big investors, including Richard Ressler, who left his job at IT firm MAI Systems to become CEO. Shifting coasts, JFAX left New York for Los Angeles. The company penned a deal with QUALCOMM to offer JFAX through its Eudora e-mail client, and closed out the year serving 45 cities.

JFAX came of age in 1998 when it embarked on a three-year marketing agreement with America Online (now AOL), which promoted JFAX as its exclusive unified messaging service, while e-mail provider Critical Path, Internet portal Yahoo!, and ISP Prodigy Communications became strategic partners. Anxious to get back to his music, at least part time, Muller hired former AT&T executive Gary Hickox as president.

The company went public in 1999 and changed its name to JFAX.COM, and it launched free service in hopes of attracting customers that would upgrade to fee-based plans.

In 2000 JFAX.COM acquired Internet-based messaging provider SureTalk.Com for $9 million. SureTalk's Steven Hamerslag became president (Hickox left the company) and CEO (Ressler became chairman). Later the company changed its name again, this time to j2 Global Communications, and expanded by purchasing rival message services provider eFax.com. When

Hamerslag resigned at year's end, the board replaced him with a management team made up of the company's top executives.

The next year j2 Global was granted a US patent for its core technology. Also in 2001 the company announced an expansion of its network into Argentina, Chile, Colombia, and Mexico.

Expansion remained a big part of j2 Global Communications' scheme. The company increased its customer base with the acquisitions of rival messaging services providers SureTalk.com and eFax.com, and in 2004 it acquired British Columbia-based outsourced e-mail and messaging services provider The Electric Mail Company. That year the company also acquired the unified communications assets, branded Onebox, from Call Sciences. Its expansion plans in Europe got a boost with the company's acquisition in 2005 of UK-based messaging services provider Puma United Communications.

EXECUTIVES

Chairman: Richard S. Ressler, age 51
CEO: Nehemia (Hemi) Zucker, age 53, $572,320 total compensation
President: R. Scott Turicchi, age 46, $482,916 total compensation
CFO: Kathleen M. (Kathy) Griggs, age 55, $535,088 total compensation
EVP Corporate Strategy: Zohar Loshitzer, age 51
VP, General Counsel, and Secretary: Jeffrey D. (Jeff) Adelman, age 43, $287,026 total compensation
VP Sales: Thomas (Tom) Dolan
VP Product Development: Ken Truesdale
VP Global Web Marketing: Mike Pugh
VP Network Operations: Alan Alters
VP Marketing Services and Support: Ken Ford
VP Human Resources: Patty Brunton
VP Engineering: Vincent P. (Vince) Niedzielski
VP International: Tim McLean
Auditors: Singer Lewak Greenbaum & Goldstein LLP

LOCATIONS

HQ: j2 Global Communications, Inc.
6922 Hollywood Blvd., Ste. 500
Hollywood, CA 90028
Phone: 323-860-9200
Web: www.j2global.com

2008 Sales

	$ mil.	% of total
US	204.4	85
Other countries	37.1	15
Total	**241.5**	**100**

PRODUCTS/OPERATIONS

2008 Sales

	$ mil.	% of total
Direct inward dialing (DID) based	229.0	95
Non-DID-based	12.5	5
Total	**241.5**	**100**

Selected Products

eFax Broadcast (high-volume faxing service)
eFax Corporate (similar to eFax Plus and jConnect Premier but focused on enterprise users)
eFax Plus (unique phone number allows subscribers to receive inbound fax messages in their e-mail inbox and to send documents to any fax number directly from the subscriber's desktop)
eFaxFree (free, advertising-supported service similar to eFax Plus)

jBlast (high-volume faxing service)
jConnect Free (free, advertising-supported service similar to jConnect Premier)
jConnect Premier (unique phone number allows subscribers to receive inbound fax and voicemail messages in their e-mail inbox and to send documents to any fax number directly from the subscriber's desktop)
M4 Internet (outsourced service allows the subscriber to create and execute e-mail campaigns from their desktop)
Messenger Plus (desktop software program allows subscribers to view faxes and listen to voicemail messages received through j2 Global Communications' services)
Onebox (unified communications services suite)
PaperMaster Pro (application allows subscribers to automate the organizing, archiving, and retrieving of digital versions of documents and other file types)

COMPETITORS

Active Voice, LLC
CallWave
CommTouch Software
Critical Path
Deltathree
EasyLink
Notify Technology
Open Text
PPOL, Inc.
Premiere Global Services
Protus IP Solutions

HISTORICAL FINANCIALS

Company Type: Public

Income Statement

	REVENUE ($ mil.)	NET INCOME ($ mil.)	NET PROFIT MARGIN	EMPLOYEES
12/08	241.5	72.6	30.1%	400
12/07	220.7	68.5	31.0%	410
12/06	181.1	53.1	29.3%	341
12/05	143.9	51.3	35.6%	288
12/04	106.3	31.6	29.7%	202
Annual Growth	22.8%	23.1%	—	18.6%

FYE: December 31

2008 Year-End Financials

Debt ratio: —
Return on equity: 27.3%
Cash ($ mil.): 150.8
Current ratio: 5.39
Long-term debt ($ mil.): —
No. of shares (mil.): 45.2
Dividends
  Yield: 0.0%
  Payout: —
Market value ($ mil.): 905.1
R&D as % of sales: —
Advertising as % of sales: —

Stock History

NASDAQ (GS): JCOM

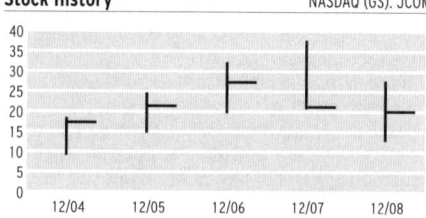

	STOCK PRICE ($) FY Close	P/E High/Low		PER SHARE ($) Earnings	Dividends	Book Value
12/08	20.04	17	8	1.58	0.00	5.53
12/07	21.17	28	16	1.35	0.00	6.26
12/06	27.25	31	19	1.04	0.00	5.64
12/05	21.37	24	15	1.00	0.00	4.51
12/04	17.25	29	15	0.63	0.00	3.10
Annual Growth	3.8%	—	—	25.8%	—	15.6%

Jacksonville Bancorp

Jacksonville Bancorp (unaffiliated with the Florida corporation of the same name) was formed in 2002 to be the holding company for Jacksonville Savings Bank, which serves consumers and businesses in western Illinois through more than five offices, including its Chapin State Bank, First Midwest Savings Bank, and Litchfield Community Savings divisions. The bank is mainly a real estate lender, with residential, commercial, and agricultural mortgages accounting for more than half of its loan portfolio. Subsidiary Financial Resources Group offers investment and trust services. Mutual holding company Jacksonville Bancorp, M.H.C. owns a majority of Jacksonville Bancorp's stock.

EXECUTIVES

Chairman: Andrew F. (Andy) Applebee, age 60, $106,020 total compensation
President, CEO, and Director; President and CEO, Financial Resources Group: Richard A. (Rich) Foss, age 59, $229,281 total compensation
CFO and Compliance Officer: Diana S. Tone, age 41
SVP Retail Banking: Laura A. Marks, age 51
SVP, Trust Officer, and Director: John C. Williams, age 60, $159,970 total compensation
VP Operations, Corporate Secretary, and Human Resources Officer: John D. Eilering, age 47
VP and Chief Lending Officer, Jacksonville Savings Bank: Chris A. Royal, age 53, $132,438 total compensation
VP Mortgage Banking, Jacksonville Savings Bank: Thomas A. (Tom) Luber, age 55
VP Lending, Jacksonville Savings Bank: Paul W. Miller
Auditors: BKD, LLP

LOCATIONS

HQ: Jacksonville Bancorp, Inc.
1211 W. Morton Ave., Jacksonville, IL 62650
Phone: 217-245-4111   **Fax:** 217-245-2010
Web: www.jacksonvillesavings.com

COMPETITORS

First Busey
Illini Corp.
JPMorgan Chase
Princeton National Bancorp
U.S. Bancorp

HISTORICAL FINANCIALS

Company Type: Public

Income Statement

	ASSETS ($ mil.)	NET INCOME ($ mil.)	INCOME AS % OF ASSETS	EMPLOYEES
12/08	288.3	1.5	0.5%	112
12/07	288.5	0.6	0.2%	118
12/06	267.4	0.9	0.3%	121
12/05	253.9	0.9	0.4%	98
12/04	253.3	0.9	0.4%	121
Annual Growth	3.3%	13.6%	—	(1.9%)

FYE: December 31

2008 Year-End Financials

Equity as % of assets: 8.4%
Return on assets: 0.5%
Return on equity: 6.4%
Long-term debt ($ mil.): 13.5
No. of shares (mil.): 1.9
Market value ($ mil.): 18.7
Dividends
Yield: 3.1%
Payout: 39.5%
Sales ($ mil.): 11.2
R&D as % of sales: —
Advertising as % of sales: —

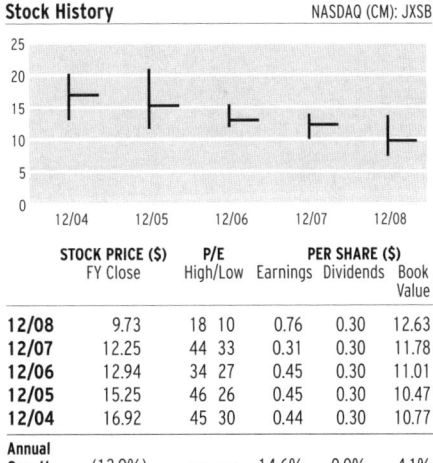

Stock History NASDAQ (CM): JXSB

	STOCK PRICE ($) FY Close	P/E High/Low		Earnings	PER SHARE ($) Dividends	Book Value
12/08	9.73	18	10	0.76	0.30	12.63
12/07	12.25	44	33	0.31	0.30	11.78
12/06	12.94	34	27	0.45	0.30	11.01
12/05	15.25	46	26	0.45	0.30	10.47
12/04	16.92	45	30	0.44	0.30	10.77
Annual Growth	(12.9%)	—	—	14.6%	0.0%	4.1%

JDA Software Group

JDA Software Group supplies the links in the supply chain. The company's supply and demand optimization (SDO) software helps retailers and other businesses manage supply and demand chains, as well as business processes ranging from planning and forecasting to e-commerce and store operations. The company also offers point-of-sale applications to handle back-office functions, including inventory management, receipts, and returns. Other products include analytic applications for decision support and collaborative tools for maintaining product and catalog information with partners, distributors, and suppliers. JDA boasts more than 5,800 customers, including Dr Pepper Snapple Group, Kraft Foods, and OfficeMax.

JDA's business is divided into three segments: Retail, Manufacturing and Distribution, and Services Industries. Its Retail segment, which generated more than half of its revenues in 2008, provides software that enables large retail chains to manage merchandise, supply chains, and inventory across their organizations, as well as tools that help manage point-of-sale, scheduling, and back-office functions at the level of individual stores. Manufacturing and Distribution serves auto makers, consumer goods manufacturers, oil and gas companies, technology providers, and aerospace and defense contractors. Services Industries caters to businesses involved in the hospitality, media, telecommunications, transportation, and travel segments.

JDA has pursued acquisitions as a means of growing its business and staying competitive in a consolidating market. It acquired rival Manugistics Group for about $213 million in cash in 2006. The purchase moved JDA beyond retail, expanding its offerings for consumer goods manufacturers and wholesale distributors, and creating its Services Industries segment. In 2008 the company agreed to acquire competitor i2 Technologies for $346 million in cash. JDA later requested a renegotiation of the purchase price, but i2 terminated the merger agreement. In November 2009 the two companies would once again return to the negotiating table, with i2 agreeing to be acquired for $434 million.

In 2009 the company expanded its presence into Germany and Eastern Europe after acquiring a 49% equity interest in Strategix Enterprise Technology's businesses in Germany and Poland.

The company markets its products worldwide. Customers outside the Americas accounted for about a third of JDA's revenues in 2008.

HISTORY

James Armstrong and Frederick Pakis founded JDA Software Group in 1985. The next year the company released MMS, a retail software package based on the IBM AS/400 platform. In 1994 JDA acquired DSS, an in-store system from JDA Canada (a software development company formed by Armstrong in 1978 and sold in 1987), and began developing open-platform products.

Armstrong and Pakis, who had served since the company's founding as CEO and president, respectively, passed the helm to COO Brent Lippman in 1997 and became co-chairmen. That year the company released an in-store Windows-based system (Win/DSS) and a data warehouse system (Retail IDEAS). It gained a warehouse automation and management system that year when it acquired LIOCS Corporation.

JDA in 1998 acquired the Arthur Retail business unit, a maker of retail decision support software, from financial analysis software specialist Comshare. The purchase helped cause losses at JDA for the year, and prompted the return of Pakis and Armstrong to the co-CEO and chairman posts in 1999. The two closed unprofitable locations and cut more than 50 employees before Pakis turned over full CEO duties to Armstrong.

In 2000 JDA purchased Sweden-based space management specialist Intactix. Pakis retired as co-chairman later that year. Growth in sales of the company's software licenses, coupled with increased international sales (especially in Asia) led the company back into the black for 2000. The next year JDA bought inventory management software maker E3 for about $50 million.

In 2003 Armstrong stepped down as CEO, but remained chairman. Hamish Brewer, who had served as the company's president since 2001, became CEO.

Also in 2003, the company acquired the assets of Engage, a provider of content management software for multi-channel marketing. The following year JDA bought the assets of integrated workforce management software maker Timera Retail Solutions for $13 million. The transaction adds Web-based labor management capabilities — such as scheduling and budgeting, time and attendance, and demand forecasting — to the JDA portfolio. Plans to acquire e-commerce technology provider QRS for $100 million in 2004 were terminated after two other suitors got into the game with more attractive takeover offers.

The company announced plans to cut staff and consolidate its product line in late 2004, when it launched PortfolioEnabled.

EXECUTIVES

Chairman: James D. Armstrong, age 58
President, CEO, and Director: Hamish N. Brewer, age 46, $1,326,332 total compensation
COO: Christopher J. Koziol, age 48, $821,429 total compensation
CIO: Mark Geninatti
EVP Services: Christopher J. (Chris) Moore, age 46, $664,842 total compensation
EVP and CFO: Peter S. (Pete) Hathaway, age 54
SVP and Chief Marketing Officer: Laurent F. (Larry) Ferrere II, age 49
SVP Consulting Services: Philip Boland, age 54

SVP Retail: Wayne J. Usie, age 42
SVP Human Resources: Brian P. Boylan, age 48
SVP, General Counsel, and Secretary:
  G. Michael Bridge, age 45
SVP Americas: Thomas (Tom) Dziersk, age 45,
  $928,129 total compensation
SVP Manufacturing and Wholesale Division:
  David J. Johnston, age 46
SVP Product Management and Development:
  David R. (Dave) King, age 64
VP Accounting, Finance, and Treasury: David Alberty
Director Marketing Communications: Karen Walker
Auditors: Deloitte & Touche LLP

LOCATIONS

HQ: JDA Software Group, Inc.
  14400 N. 87th St., Scottsdale, AZ 85260
Phone: 480-308-3000   **Fax:** 480-308-3001
Web: www.jda.com

2008 Sales

	$ mil.	% of total
Americas	269.3	69
Europe	87.6	22
Asia/Pacific	33.4	9
Total	**390.3**	**100**

PRODUCTS/OPERATIONS

2008 Sales

	$ mil.	% of total
Retail	210.6	54
Manufacturing & Distribution	159.3	41
Services Industries	20.4	5
Total	**390.3**	**100**

2008 Sales

	$ mil.	% of total
Products		
Maintenance	182.8	47
Software licenses	92.9	24
Services		
Consulting	104.1	27
Other	10.5	2
Total	**390.3**	**100**

COMPETITORS

Aldata
Alphameric
i2 Technologies
Information Resources
Kronos
Manhattan Associates
Micro Strategies
MICROS Systems
Oracle
Radiant Systems
RedPrairie
Retail Pro
Retalix
SAP
SAS Institute
Tomax
VeriFone

HISTORICAL FINANCIALS

Company Type: Public

Income Statement
FYE: December 31

	REVENUE ($ mil.)	NET INCOME ($ mil.)	NET PROFIT MARGIN	EMPLOYEES
12/08	390.3	3.1	0.8%	1,718
12/07	373.6	26.5	7.1%	1,596
12/06	277.5	(11.3)	—	1,701
12/05	215.8	7.0	3.2%	1,055
12/04	216.9	2.0	0.9%	1,156
Annual Growth	15.8%	11.6%	—	10.4%

2008 Year-End Financials

Debt ratio: 0.0%	Dividends
Return on equity: 0.9%	Yield: 0.0%
Cash ($ mil.): 32.7	Payout: —
Current ratio: 1.27	Market value ($ mil.): 453.2
Long-term debt ($ mil.): 0.0	R&D as % of sales: —
No. of shares (mil.): 34.5	Advertising as % of sales: —

Stock History
NASDAQ (GM): JDAS

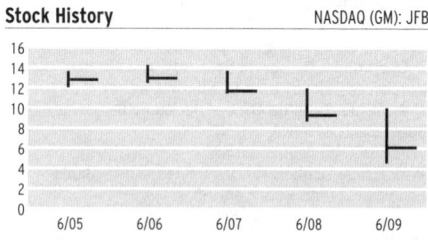

	STOCK PRICE ($) FY Close	P/E High/Low		Earnings	PER SHARE ($) Dividends	Book Value
12/08	13.13	233	112	0.09	0.00	9.89
12/07	20.46	34	18	0.76	0.00	9.73
12/06	13.77	—	—	(0.39)	0.00	8.41
12/05	17.01	71	41	0.24	0.00	8.17
12/04	13.62	261	136	0.07	0.00	8.00
Annual Growth	(0.9%)	—	—	6.5%	—	5.4%

Jefferson Bancshares

Here's a Tennessee bank that will definitely volunteer its services. Jefferson Bancshares is the holding company for Jefferson Federal Bank, which has about a dozen locations in eastern parts of the Volunteer State. Founded in 1963, the bank serves individuals and businesses in Hamblen, Knox, Sullivan, and Washington counties, offering standard services such as checking and savings accounts, CDs, and IRAs. Lending activities primarily consist of commercial real estate loans and one- to four-family residential mortgages, which together account for a majority of the company's loan portfolio. In 2008 Jefferson Bancshares acquired State of Franklin Bancshares, a community bank hurt by the national mortgage crisis.

EXECUTIVES

President, CEO, and Director; President and CEO, Jefferson Federal Bank: Anderson L. (Andy) Smith, age 61
CFO, Treasurer, and Corporate Secretary:
  Jane P. Hutton, age 50
EVP Retail Banking, Jefferson Federal Bank:
  Janet J. Ketner, age 56
SVP Jefferson Federal Bank: Douglas H. Rouse, age 56
VP and Senior Operations Officer, Jefferson Federal Bank: Eric S. McDaniel, age 38
President, Knoxville Region, Jefferson Federal Bank:
  Anthony J. (Tony) Carasso, age 50
President, Tri-Cities, Jefferson Federal Bank:
  Randal R. Greene
Auditors: Craine, Thompson & Jones, P.C.

LOCATIONS

HQ: Jefferson Bancshares, Inc.
  120 Evans Ave., Morristown, TN 37814
Phone: 423-586-8421   **Fax:** 423-587-2605
Web: www.jeffersonfederal.com

COMPETITORS

CFB Bancshares	Home Federal Bank (TN)
First Horizon	Regions Financial
First Security Group	SunTrust
Green Bankshares	Volunteer Bancorp

HISTORICAL FINANCIALS

Company Type: Public

Income Statement
FYE: June 30

	ASSETS ($ mil.)	NET INCOME ($ mil.)	INCOME AS % OF ASSETS	EMPLOYEES
6/09	662.7	2.6	0.4%	175
6/08	330.3	1.2	0.4%	91
6/07	339.7	1.7	0.5%	95
6/06	327.1	2.3	0.7%	101
6/05	295.0	3.5	1.2%	80
Annual Growth	22.4%	(7.2%)	—	21.6%

2009 Year-End Financials

Equity as % of assets: 12.0%	Dividends
Return on assets: 0.5%	Yield: 3.9%
Return on equity: 3.4%	Payout: 55.8%
Long-term debt ($ mil.): 97.2	Sales ($ mil.): 19.7
No. of shares (mil.): 6.7	R&D as % of sales: —
Market value ($ mil.): 40.8	Advertising as % of sales: —

Stock History
NASDAQ (GM): JFBI

	STOCK PRICE ($) FY Close	P/E High/Low		Earnings	PER SHARE ($) Dividends	Book Value
6/09	6.09	23	11	0.43	0.24	11.86
6/08	9.32	54	40	0.22	0.24	10.86
6/07	11.70	48	41	0.28	0.24	10.99
6/06	12.95	38	34	0.37	0.24	11.12
6/05	12.80	29	26	0.47	0.20	12.24
Annual Growth	(16.9%)	—	—	(2.2%)	4.7%	(0.8%)

Jos. A. Bank Clothiers

When casual Fridays put a wrinkle in the starched selling philosophy of Jos. A. Bank Clothiers, the company dressed down. Although it is still best known for making tailored clothing for the professional man, including suits, sport coats, dress shirts, and pants, it has added casual wear suitable for those dress-down Fridays and weekends. It also debuted the David Leadbetter line of golf wear. The company sells its Jos. A. Bank clothes and a few shoe brands through its catalogs, Web site, and some 460 company-owned or franchised stores in about 42 states and the District of Columbia. For corporate customers, it offers a credit card that provides users with discounts. Most stores house a tailoring shop.

Between 2002 and the end of 2008 the men's apparel chain added about 330 new stores. However, the downturn in the economy and lack of

available quality retail locations has the company reevaluating a previously stated plan to grow to 600 stores by the end of 2012. Still, Jos. A. Bank planned to add 10 to 15 stores in 2009, a sizable retreat from previous years. The retailer's about 135 lifestyle center stores (open-air environment shopping centers, which are reportedly growing more quickly than any other shopping center type) are proving to be the company's most successful.

To get men to shop in uncertain economic times, in March 2009 the retailer launched its "risk free" suit promotion, which promises to refund the price of a suit if the purchaser loses his job. (He also gets to keep the suit.)

The company shifted its executives in late 2008 as part of a planned succession. In December 2008 Robert Wildrick became chairman, Neal Black took the titles of CEO and director in addition to president, and Andrew Giordano took the role of chairman emeritus. Soon thereafter, the company appointed James Thorne, who joined the retailer in 1986, to head up Jos. A. Bank's merchandising function.

Jos. A Bank covers the bases with its "Three Levels of Luxury" strategy, ranging from the original Jos. A. Bank collection to the more upscale Signature collection to its exclusive Signature Gold collection.

Wellington Management Company owns about 15% of the company. The Bank of New York Mellon Corporation owns some 14%.

EXECUTIVES

Chairman Emeritus: Andrew A. Giordano, age 76
Chairman: Robert N. Wildrick, age 64,
  $4,339,738 total compensation
President, CEO, and Director: R. Neal Black, age 54,
  $1,043,743 total compensation
EVP, CFO, Principal Financial and Accounting Officer:
  David E. Ullman, age 51, $789,249 total compensation
EVP Merchandising and Chief Merchandising Officer:
  James W. (Jim) Thorne, age 49,
  $470,089 total compensation
EVP Store and Catalog Operations: Gary M. Merry,
  age 46
**EVP Human Resources, Real Estate, and Loss
  Prevention:** Robert B. Hensley, age 56,
  $1,067,954 total compensation
SVP Marketing: Jerry L. DeBoer, age 63
SVP, General Counsel and Secretary: Charles D. Frazer,
  age 48
VP Planning and Allocation: Robert R. Sears, age 52
VP Human Resources: Andrea Boling
VP and Controller Accounting: Catherine Dodson
Treasurer and Director Financial Planning:
  Todd Wemer
Auditors: Deloitte & Touche

LOCATIONS

HQ: Jos. A. Bank Clothiers, Inc.
  500 Hanover Pike, Hampstead, MD 21074
Phone: 410-239-2700   **Fax:** 410-239-5700
Web: www.josbank.com

2009 Stores

	No.
Texas	45
Florida	33
California	31
Illinois	28
Pennsylvania	25
New Jersey	24
Georgia	22
Virginia	21
Maryland	20
North Carolina	20
Ohio	19
New York	18
Massachusetts	13
Michigan	13
Connecticut	12
Tennessee	10
Alabama	9
Colorado	9
Indiana	9
South Carolina	9
Louisiana	6
Missouri	6
Wisconsin	6
Arizona	5
Minnesota	5
Arkansas	4
Kentucky	4
Oklahoma	4
District of Columbia	4
Iowa	3
Kansas	3
Nevada	3
Rhode Island	3
Washington	3
Other states	11
Total	**460**

PRODUCTS/OPERATIONS

2009 Sales

	$ mil.	% of total
Stores	623.1	89
Direct marketing	61.2	9
Other	11.6	2
Total	**695.9**	**100**

Selected Merchandise

Clothing accessories
Dress and casual shirts
Formal wear
Mufflers
Overcoats
Pajamas
Polos
Shoes
Shorts
Sport coats
Suits
Sweaters
Ties
Trousers
Underwear
Vests

COMPETITORS

Ashworth, Inc.
Astor & Black
Brooks Brothers
Dillard's
Lands' End
Macy's
Men's Wearhouse
Nordstrom
Phillips-Van Heusen
Polo Ralph Lauren

HISTORICAL FINANCIALS

Company Type: Public

Income Statement

FYE: Saturday nearest January 31

	REVENUE ($ mil.)	NET INCOME ($ mil.)	NET PROFIT MARGIN	EMPLOYEES
1/09	695.9	58.4	8.4%	4,040
1/08	604.0	50.2	8.3%	4,069
1/07	546.4	43.2	7.9%	3,375
1/06	464.6	35.3	7.6%	2,995
1/05	372.5	24.5	6.6%	2,350
Annual Growth	**16.9%**	**24.3%**	—	**14.5%**

2009 Year-End Financials

Debt ratio: 0.0%
Return on equity: 20.0%
Cash ($ mil.): 122.9
Current ratio: 3.21
Long-term debt ($ mil.): 0.0
No. of shares (mil.): 18.3
Dividends
  Yield: —
  Payout: —
Market value ($ mil.): 502.4
R&D as % of sales: —
Advertising as % of sales: —

Stock History

NASDAQ (GS): JOSB

	STOCK PRICE ($) FY Close	P/E High/Low		Earnings	PER SHARE ($) Dividends	Book Value
1/09	27.46	13	5	3.17	—	17.59
1/08	27.24	17	7	2.72	—	14.28
1/07	30.96	20	9	2.36	—	11.38
1/06	41.02	21	11	1.95	—	8.41
1/05	22.96	19	13	1.38	—	6.25
Annual Growth	**4.6%**	—	—	**23.1%**	—	**29.5%**

K12 Inc.

K12 isn't a missing element from the periodic table, but it could help your kids learn the periodic table. The "virtual public school" offers online educational programs for some 40,000 students in kindergarten through 12th grade. Products include online public schools (in 24 states and overseas), course material and product sales directly to parents, and individualized supplemental programs offered through traditional public schools. Web courses cover core subjects such as English, math, science, history and art.

K12 targets kids who underperform in public school or can't attend public school because of travel, disabilities, or because they are athletes or performers. CEO Ron Packard founded K12 in 2000.

K12's virtual public schools are online programs that adhere to the programs and policies of public entities such as public school districts, independent, non-profit charter school boards, and state education agencies. It offers the same coursework and curriculum as most school districts' "brick and mortar" campuses.

The company went public in 2007 and raised $108 million. The company used the IPO to grow

its operations, with enrollment going from 20,000 students in 2006 to more than 40,000 in 2009. K12 made expanding its customer base and product line a priority in order to decrease its reliance on large clients. In 2009 two of its major customers accounted for 30% of its revenues.

K12 started out offering programs for children in kindergarten through second grade. It has gradually expanded and now offers a self-paced high school program.

The company's first international academy was introduced in the United Arab Emirates in 2007. By 2008, the company had launched the K12 International Academy, a private school that enables K12 to deliver its learning system to students in more than 35 countries. The International Academy may represent the company's interest in testing the waters for further international expansion in addition to evaluating the demand for virtual private schools.

EXECUTIVES

Chairman: Andrew H. Tisch, age 59
CEO and Director: Ronald J. (Ron) Packard, age 46, $1,731,530 total compensation
EVP and Chief Marketing Officer: Celia Stokes, age 45, $532,604 total compensation
EVP School Services: George B. (Chip) Hughes Jr., age 50, $528,558 total compensation
EVP Worldwide Business Development: Bruce J. Davis, age 46, $496,078 total compensation
EVP Operations: John Olsen
SVP Public Affairs: Bryan W. Flood, age 42
SVP School Development: Peter G. Stewart, age 39
SVP Human Resources: Howard Allentoff, age 47
SVP Corporate Development: Janet Matricciani
SVP Systems and Technology: Ray Williams, age 46
SVP Product Development: Maria A. Szalay, age 42
SVP Finance and Investor Relations: Keith T. Haas
SVP Content and Curriculum: John Holdren
SVP, General Counsel, and Secretary: Howard D. Polsky, age 57
VP Public Relations: Jeff Kwitowski
Director: Nathaniel A. (Nate) Davis, age 55
Auditors: BDO Seidman, LLP

LOCATIONS

HQ: K12 Inc.
2300 Corporate Park Dr., Herndon, VA 20171
Phone: 703-483-7000   **Fax:** 703-483-7330
Web: www.k12.com

K12 Virtual Public Schools by State

Alaska	Minnesota
Arizona	New Jersey
Arkansas	Nevada
California	Ohio
Colorado	Oregon
District of Columbia	Pennsylvania
Florida	Texas
Hawaii	Utah
Georgia	Virginia
Idaho	Washington
Indiana	Wisconsin
Illinois	Wyoming
Kansas	

COMPETITORS

Apollo Group
Edison Learning
Houghton Mifflin Harcourt
Kaplan
McGraw-Hill
Pearson plc

HISTORICAL FINANCIALS

Company Type: Public

Income Statement

FYE: June 30

	REVENUE ($ mil.)	NET INCOME ($ mil.)	NET PROFIT MARGIN	EMPLOYEES
6/09	315.6	12.3	3.9%	993
6/08	226.2	33.8	14.9%	763
6/07	140.6	3.9	2.8%	636
6/06	116.9	(23.2)	—	558
6/05	85.3	(3.5)	—	—
Annual Growth	38.7%	—	—	21.2%

2009 Year-End Financials

Debt ratio: 6.1%
Return on equity: 7.4%
Cash ($ mil.): 49.5
Current ratio: 3.73
Long-term debt ($ mil.): 11.1
No. of shares (mil.): 29.5
Dividends
  Yield: 0.0%
  Payout: —
Market value ($ mil.): 636.3
R&D as % of sales: —
Advertising as % of sales: —

Stock History

NYSE Arca: LRN

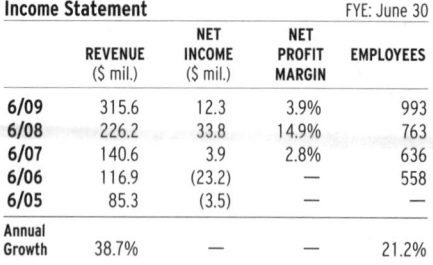

	STOCK PRICE ($) FY Close	P/E High/Low		PER SHARE ($) Earnings	Dividends	Book Value
6/09	21.55	70	28	0.42	0.00	6.17
6/08	21.51	27	15	1.10	0.00	5.09
Annual Growth	0.2%	—	—	(61.8%)	—	21.3%

Kaydon Corporation

Just about everything has a bearing on the business of Kaydon Corporation. The company custom designs, engineers, and manufactures bearings and bearing systems, slip rings, filtration products, and seals. Kaydon operates in three segments: friction and motion control products (anti-friction bearings, split roller bearings, and specialty balls), velocity control products (industrial shock absorbers and velocity controls), and sealing products (engine rings and shaft seals). Other products include metal alloys, machine tool components, presses, dies, and benders. These tap a diverse customer base — aerospace to defense and construction markets — for use in a range of robotics and material handling applications.

Kaydon has benefited from a diversified growth strategy driving critical performance products to the manufacturing industry. The company claims market dominance, or a significant share, in engineering and making bearing systems and components, linear deceleration products, gas filtration products, as well as aerospace seals and seal rings, and locomotive piston rings.

It has contributed to high profile projects such as the robotic arm used by the Phoenix Mars Lander. Scooping up samples of Martian soil, the arm's up-and-down, side-to-side, and back-and

forth motions relied on sets of thin-section bearings made by Kaydon. Proprietary products like these are custom engineered and consequently manufactured in-house, with subcontractors used for specialized services.

Kaydon sells its products through representatives in North America, Europe, and Asia, and a network of market niche distributors. Its largest end segments include automation and robotics, military, heavy equipment, and power generation. Wind energy sales (power generation) and medical businesses present the fastest growing opportunities. Several of the company's operating units sell to business units of General Electric, accounting for over 10% of total sales.

Acquisitions have impacted the company's development. In 2007 it scored Avon Bearings Corporation for $55 million. Avon designs and makes large-diameter turntable bearings. It also remanufactures bearings and sells replacement bearings. The purchase has boosted Kaydon's precision manufacturing capacity in the wind bearings market.

Leadership has also contributed to the company's operating performance. Former president and CEO Brian Campbell put in place several lean manufacturing and cost improvement initiatives. James O'Leary took the company reins in early 2007 from Campbell, who retired. O'Leary has continued these efforts and, as a result of the economic downturn in many of the company's customers, he has focused on an internal reorganization, curtailing staff, salary, and selected benefits.

HISTORY

The Kaydon Engineering Company was formed in 1941 to supply bearings for the war effort. Its product line grew to include difficult-to-make non-military products that required custom design and special engineering. Such challenging production jobs became the company's hallmark.

Acquisition specialist Glen Bailey bought the company in 1969. Over the next decade Bailey upgraded the company's plants, added specialty filtration products to its offerings, and included robotic and medical applications. In 1981 Bailey formed Bairnco as a holding company for his various businesses and prepared to spin them off. Kaydon's sales dropped in the early 1980s, but it was spun off anyway in 1984. New president Richard Shantz, like Bailey, began growing and diversifying through acquisitions. Acquired businesses included Koppers Company (1986, rings and seals), Spirolox (1987, retaining rings), and Electro-Tec (1989, slip rings). The company also went international, building a bearing plant in Mexico in 1988 and acquiring the UK's I.D.M. Electronics (1989, slip rings).

The acquisitions continued in the 1990s with another UK company, Cooper Bearings (1991, split bearings) and firms that made pulley and drive components and specialty balls. In 1995 Kaydon added large hydraulic cylinders and alloy steel castings to its product line with the acquisition of Seabee; the next year it bought two similar businesses, Victor Fluid Power and Benton Harbor Engineering. Kaydon pumped up its fluid power line in 1997 with the purchases of Great Bend Industries and Gold Star Manufacturing.

In 1998 Kaydon's board authorized the repurchase of 1.1 million shares of the company's stock, and the next year authorized the repurchase of an additional 4 million common shares. Also in 1999 President and CEO Brian Campbell

succeeded Lawrence Cawley as chairman. Later in the year the company picked up two acquisitions: Filterdyne Filtration Systems and Focal Technologies (fiber-optic electronic data and fluid transfer devices).

In 2000 Kaydon acquired the Tridan Group of companies which included Tridan International (air conditioning equipment), Indiana Precision (tooling for the plastic packaging industry), and Canfield Technologies (lead-free solder). Early the next year Kaydon added deceleration devices such as industrial shock absorbers and directional control valves to its product line with the $70 million acquisition of ACE Controls. On the last day of 2001 Kaydon sold its fluid power products division to a group of private investors.

In 2002 Kaydon sued Stephen Clough, Kaydon's former president and CEO, and six other former Kaydon employees for breach of contract and misappropriation of corporate secrets. The following year, the company completed its restructuring plan to strengthen its operating performance and manufacturing utilization in the Specialty Bearings Group, a unit of the Friction and Motion Controls Product segment.

In 2005 the company sold its Power and Data Transmission business to Moog Inc. for nearly $43 million.

EXECUTIVES

Chairman, President, and CEO: James O'Leary, age 46, $3,761,694 total compensation
SVP and CFO: Peter C. DeChants, age 57, $682,832 total compensation
SVP and Group President, Kaydon Custom Bearings, Sealings Products Operations, and Filtration Operations: John R. Emling, age 53, $972,543 total compensation
VP, General Counsel, and Secretary: Debra K. Crane, age 54
VP Human Resources: Anthony T. Behrman, age 46, $331,818 total compensation
VP Taxes: Dale E. Ulman, age 44
VP, Controller, Chief Accounting Officer: Donald I. Buzinkai, age 39
VP Information Technology and Operations Planning: John A. Madison, age 64
President, Canfield Technologies: Robert P. McIntire
President, Kaydon Ring and Seal: Christopher J. Armstrong
President, Purafil: James W. Mash
President, Kaydon Custom Filtration: Peter C. Scovic
President, Tridan International and Indiana Precision: Charles F. Holmes
President, Kaydon Industrial Bearings Division: L. Jeffrey Mazagol
President, ACE Controls: William J. Chorkey
Auditors: Ernst & Young LLP

LOCATIONS

HQ: Kaydon Corporation
315 E. Eisenhower Pkwy., Ste. 300
Ann Arbor, MI 48108
Phone: 734-747-7025   **Fax:** 734-747-6565
Web: www.kaydon.com

2008 Sales

	$ mil.	% of total
US	334.2	64
Germany	51.3	10
Other countries	136.9	26
Total	**522.4**	**100**

PRODUCTS/OPERATIONS

2008 Sales

	$ mil.	% of total
Friction control products	326.0	62
Velocity control products	69.6	13
Sealing products	45.0	9
Other products	81.8	16
Total	**522.4**	**100**

Selected Products

Industrial liquid filtration systems
Industrial shock absorbers
Metal castings
Sealing rings
Slip rings
Specialty balls
Split roller bearings

Selected Subsidiaries

ACE Controls, Inc.
ACE Stossdaempfer, GmbH (Germany)
ACE Japan, L.L.C.
Cooper Geteilte Rollenlager GmbH (Germany)
Cooper Roller Bearing Company Ltd.(UK)
Cooper Split Roller Bearing Corporation
Indiana Precision, Inc.
Kaydon Ring and Seal, Inc.
Kaydon S. de R.L. de C.V. (Mexico)

COMPETITORS

Applied Industrial Technologies	MINEBEA
Blount International	NN Inc.
Cascade Corp.	Northrop Grumman
Dover Corp.	Parker Hannifin
FAG Kugelfischer	PerkinElmer
General Bearing	SKF
Kaman	Timken

HISTORICAL FINANCIALS

Company Type: Public

Income Statement

FYE: December 31

	REVENUE ($ mil.)	NET INCOME ($ mil.)	NET PROFIT MARGIN	EMPLOYEES
12/08	522.4	67.1	12.8%	2,420
12/07	451.4	77.7	17.2%	2,125
12/06	403.9	69.5	17.2%	1,900
Annual Growth	**13.7%**	**(1.7%)**	**—**	**12.9%**

2008 Year-End Financials

Debt ratio: 0.0%
Return on equity: 12.1%
Cash ($ mil.): 233.0
Current ratio: 6.82
Long-term debt ($ mil.): 0.0
No. of shares (mil.): 33.2
Dividends
  Yield: 1.9%
  Payout: 30.6%
Market value ($ mil.): 1,141.3
R&D as % of sales: —
Advertising as % of sales: —

Stock History

NYSE: KDN

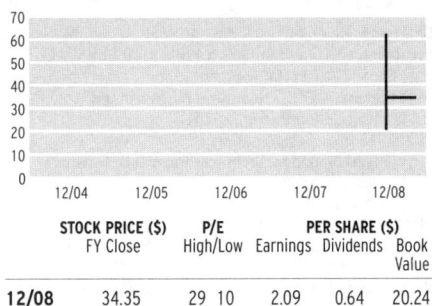

	STOCK PRICE ($) FY Close	P/E High/Low	PER SHARE ($) Earnings	PER SHARE ($) Dividends	PER SHARE ($) Book Value
12/08	34.35	29 10	2.09	0.64	20.24

Kendle International

When it comes to research and development, few can hold a candle to Kendle International. A leading contract research organization (CRO) for the biotechnology and pharmaceutical industries, the company provides services that facilitate Phase I through Phase IV clinical trials; those services include patient recruitment, clinical monitoring, statistical analysis, and consulting on regulatory issues. Additionally, Kendle's TrialWare software helps customers manage research and clinical trial data. The company has expertise in a range of therapeutic areas, including oncology, the central nervous system, cardiovascular disease, and inflammation. Kendle provides services in about 100 countries around the globe.

The company has clinical development locations in about 30 countries and has been working to expand its geographic footprint to accommodate clients seeking regulatory approval in multiple geographic markets or needing access to a large pool of patients. It's especially keen on expanding into high-growth regions such as Africa, the Asia/Pacific region, Eastern Europe, and Latin America. To further sales growth in Asia, in 2009 the firm opened new offices in Malaysia, Thailand, and the Philippines, as well as a second location in India. Revenues from low-cost trials conducted in the high-demand Latin American region increased by nearly 90% in 2008.

While Kendle organizes itself in two segments, most of its revenues come from its Late Stage business, which handles Phase II-IV clinical trials and provides regulatory, quality, and metrics services. The company is focused on expanding late-stage trial services as drug firms increasingly look to outsource expensive development processes. The company is also seeking more large trial contracts, which it defines as exceeding $10 million in value. Top global drugmaker Pfizer is one of Kendle's largest customers.

However, Kendle is also looking for opportunities to grow its Early Stage unit, which provides services related to preclinical research and Phase I trials and accounts for less than 10% of revenues. To that end the company acquired Canadian Phase I research firm DecisionLine Clinical Research, which specializes in testing central nervous system drugs for potential risk and abuse factors, in 2008.

Candace Kendle (CEO) and her husband, Christopher Bergen (COO), founded Kendle International in 1981 and together own about 5% of the company.

EXECUTIVES

Chairman and CEO: Candace Kendle, age 62, $771,241 total compensation
EVP, Chief Administrative Officer, and Director: Christopher C. (Chris) Bergen, age 58, $553,525 total compensation
SVP and COO: Stephen Cutler
SVP and CFO: Keith A. Cheesman, age 50
SVP and Chief Marketing Officer: Simon S. Higginbotham, age 48, $424,747 total compensation
SVP Global Clinical Development: Martha R. Feller, age 60
VP Global Clinical Development, Asia/Pacific: Ross J. Horsburgh
VP Commercial Operations: Patricia Williams
VP Global Late Phase: Patricia A. Steigerwald
VP Global Biometrics: Sylva H. Collins

VP Strategic Development and Corporate Treasurer:
Anthony L. (Tony) Forcellini, age 51
VP Global Human Resources: Karen L. Crone
VP, Chief Legal Officer, and Secretary: Jarrod Pontius
VP and CIO: Gary M. Wedig
VP Kendle Consulting: J. Michael Sprafka
Director Corporate Communications: Lori Dorer
Director Investor Relations: Michael K. (Mike) Lawson
Auditors: Deloitte & Touche LLP

LOCATIONS

HQ: Kendle International Inc.
1200 Carew Tower, 441 Vine St.
Cincinnati, OH 45202
Phone: 513-381-5550   **Fax:** 513-381-5870
Web: www.kendle.com

2008 Sales

	$ mil.	% of total
Net service revenues		
North America		
US	214.9	32
Other North American countries	14.4	2
Europe		
Germany	56.7	8
UK	42.3	6
Other European countries	90.6	13
Latin America	39.0	6
Asia	17.2	3
Reimbursable out-of-pocket revenues	203.5	30
Total	**678.6**	**100**

PRODUCTS/OPERATIONS

2008 Sales

	$ mil.	% of total
Late Stage	633.8	93
Early Stage	35.2	5
Support & other	9.6	2
Total	**678.6**	**100**

COMPETITORS

Albany Molecular Research	PAREXEL
Bilcare Limited	Pharmaceutical Product
Charles River Laboratories	Development
Covance	PharmaNet Development
ICON	PRA International
INC Research	Quintiles Transnational
inVentiv Health	Radiant Research
Life Sciences Research	ReSearch Pharmaceutical
MDS	Services
Medpace	WuXi PharmaTech

HISTORICAL FINANCIALS

Company Type: Public

Income Statement

FYE: December 31

	REVENUE ($ mil.)	NET INCOME ($ mil.)	NET PROFIT MARGIN	EMPLOYEES
12/08	678.6	29.4	4.3%	4,275
12/07	568.8	18.7	3.3%	3,325
12/06	373.9	8.5	2.3%	3,050
12/05	250.6	10.7	4.3%	1,900
12/04	215.9	3.6	1.7%	1,765
Annual Growth	**33.1%**	**69.0%**	**—**	**24.8%**

2008 Year-End Financials

Debt ratio: 108.1%
Return on equity: 18.0%
Cash ($ mil.): 35.2
Current ratio: 1.43
Long-term debt ($ mil.): 200.1
No. of shares (mil.): 14.9
Dividends
  Yield: 0.0%
  Payout: —
Market value ($ mil.): 382.8
R&D as % of sales: —
Advertising as % of sales: —

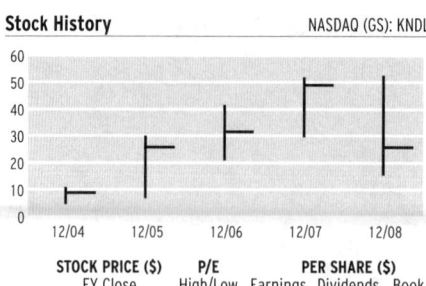

	STOCK PRICE ($) FY Close	P/E High/Low		PER SHARE ($) Earnings	Dividends	Book Value
12/08	25.72	27	8	1.96	0.00	12.44
12/07	48.92	41	24	1.26	0.00	9.51
12/06	31.45	71	37	0.58	0.00	9.42
12/05	25.74	39	10	0.76	0.00	8.23
12/04	8.80	38	19	0.27	0.00	6.91
Annual Growth	**30.8%**	**—**	**—**	**64.1%**	**—**	**15.9%**

Kewaunee Scientific

The nutty professor once wreaked havoc on furniture like that made by Kewaunee Scientific. The company makes furniture for laboratories, including wood and steel cabinets, fume hoods, and work surfaces. Its primary customers are labs (pharmaceutical, biotech, industrial, chemical, and commercial research), schools, and health care institutions. Kewaunee also makes technical workstations, workbenches, and computer enclosures for local area networking applications. The company's products are sold through VWR International, a school and lab products supplier (about 13% of sales), and through Kewaunee dealers.

Kewaunee Scientific has three foreign subsidiaries that aid in its international operations. Kewaunee Labway Asia Pte. Ltd. (51% owned) is a dealer for Kewaunee products in Singapore. Labway Scientific India Pvt. Ltd. deals the company's products in India, and Kewaunee Scientific Corporation India Pvt. Ltd. is concerned with the assembly of Kewaunee products.

Nearly 20% of the company's sales come internationally. Boosting international sales is a key component of Kewaunee's long-term strategy.

Director James Rhind and his wife own about 14% of capital stock in the company.

EXECUTIVES

Chairman: Eli Manchester Jr., age 78
President, CEO, and Director: William A. Shumaker, age 61, $521,620 total compensation
SVP Finance, CFO, Treasurer, and Secretary:
D. Michael (Mike) Parker, age 57, $308,358 total compensation
VP; General Manager, Technical Furniture Group:
K. Bain Black, age 63
VP Construction Services: David M. Rausch, age 51
VP Manufacturing: Keith D. Smith, age 40
VP Sales and Marketing, Laboratory Products Group:
Dana L. Dahlgren, age 53
VP International Operations: Sudhir K. (Steve) Vadehra, age 62, $252,908 total compensation
VP Engineering and Product Development:
Kurt P. Rindoks, age 51
Director Information Technology: Carl Roth
Auditors: Cherry, Bekaert & Holland, LLP

LOCATIONS

HQ: Kewaunee Scientific Corporation
2700 W. Front St., Statesville, NC 28677
Phone: 704-873-7202   **Fax:** 704-873-1275
Web: www.kewaunee.com

PRODUCTS/OPERATIONS

Selected Products

Laboratory furniture
  Cabinetry (steel, wood)
  Fume hoods
  Flexible systems
  Work surfaces
Technical furniture
  Computer enclosures
  Network storage systems
  Workbenches
  Workstations

COMPETITORS

Herman Miller
Kimball International
Wright Line

HISTORICAL FINANCIALS

Company Type: Public

Income Statement

FYE: April 30

	REVENUE ($ mil.)	NET INCOME ($ mil.)	NET PROFIT MARGIN	EMPLOYEES
4/09	104.0	4.2	4.0%	572
4/08	89.5	3.1	3.5%	569
4/07	81.4	1.5	1.8%	554
4/06	84.1	0.2	0.2%	566
4/05	73.5	(0.1)	—	484
Annual Growth	**9.1%**	**—**	**—**	**4.3%**

2009 Year-End Financials

Debt ratio: 0.7%
Return on equity: 15.6%
Cash ($ mil.): 3.6
Current ratio: 2.01
Long-term debt ($ mil.): 0.2
No. of shares (mil.): 2.6
Dividends
  Yield: 3.4%
  Payout: 19.3%
Market value ($ mil.): 24.1
R&D as % of sales: —
Advertising as % of sales: —

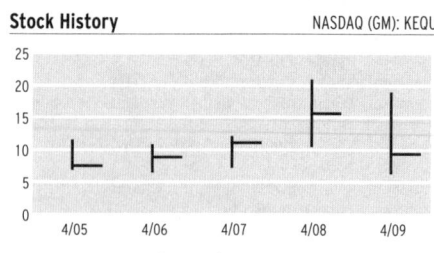

	STOCK PRICE ($) FY Close	P/E High/Low		PER SHARE ($) Earnings	Dividends	Book Value
4/09	9.38	11	4	1.66	0.32	10.49
4/08	15.60	17	9	1.23	0.28	10.49
4/07	11.07	19	12	0.62	0.28	9.36
4/06	8.85	133	83	0.08	0.28	9.94
4/05	7.51	—	—	(0.06)	0.28	10.12
Annual Growth	**5.7%**	**—**	**—**	**—**	**3.4%**	**0.9%**

Key Technology

When good french fries go bad, Key Technology comes to the rescue. The company makes food and material processing automation equipment. Its electro-optical automated inspection and sorting systems and product preparation systems can be used to evaluate fresh fruits and vegetables, beans, potato chips, and other snacks. Items can be sorted by color, size, and shape to identify defective or inconsistent products for removal. The company also makes conveyor and sorting systems for the tobacco, pharmaceutical, nutraceutical, and coffee industries. Key Technology gets about half of its sales outside the US.

In late 2008 the company purchased its headquarters building and primary manufacturing facility, which it had leased from the Port of Walla Walla since 1990, for about $6.5 million.

Key Technology posted record sales and earnings in 2007. Sales increased by nearly 27% over fiscal 2006. The company attributed its success to three key factors: increased global concern over the safety of food supplies, a worldwide shortage of cost-effective labor for the processing of food and pharmaceuticals, and Key's growth in the developing economies of Latin America and China. In a recessionary environment and amid uncertain economic conditions, the company was able to grow sales about 25% in fiscal 2008 to another new corporate record. More importantly, it maintained its consistent level of profitability. Sales in 2008 increased significantly for equipment handling potatoes and fresh-cut or processed fruits and vegetables.

The company sees a bright outlook as the drivers of its record year in 2007 are likely to remain at work for the foreseeable future. McCain Foods accounts for about 14% of Key Technology's sales, while Frito-Lay represents around 13%.

HISTORY

In 1948 vegetable farmer Claude Key set up Key Equipment Co. as a vegetable processing equipment company. He sold the firm to computer components maker Applied Magnetics in 1968.

In 1982 the company introduced its automated defect-removal system, a computer-aided monitoring and food processing conveyor system for selecting and removing defective french fries. A year later an investment group led by Madsen bought Key Equipment and renamed it Key Technology. A second automated system was launched in 1987, and the next year Key Technology introduced ColorSort, a system for sorting vegetables. The company went public in 1993 and debuted its AccuScan quality monitoring system that year.

Key Technology expanded its presence in Europe through the 1996 acquisition of Netherlands-based Superior B.V. (conveyor systems). That year the company diversified its offerings by purchasing a drug-inspection system product line from ONCOR. Key Technology also introduced its Tegra automated inspection system in 1996.

The company formed Key Technology Financial Services to offer financing with GE Capital in 1997. Key Technology stumbled a bit that year when problems in its Tegra systems prompted modifications. In 1998 the company developed new Tegra applications for processing coffee beans, tobacco, spinach, and cherries.

A plan to buy Allen Machinery's electronics division fell through in 2000, but Key Technology did buy Farmco (produce sorting equipment) and Advanced Machine Vision Corporation, which added machine vision companies SRC Vision (automated inspection and defect removal systems for food processing and industrial applications) and Ventek (inspection and process control systems for the plywood and wood panel industries). Key Technology later sold Ventek in 2001 to help pay down its more than $20 million in debt.

In 2002 Key Technology's gross profit margin increased when the company improved its parts and field service operations. The following year, Thomas Madsen, chairman and CEO, retired after serving as CEO since 1982. He remained chairman until 2007.

In 2004 Key Technology formed a company called InspX with Peco Controls to make X-ray inspection systems.

EXECUTIVES

Chairman: Charles H. (Chuck) Stonecipher, age 48
President, CEO, and Director: David M. Camp, age 59
CTO: Richard J. Hebel, age 58
SVP and CFO: John J. (Jack) Ehren, age 48
SVP Global Sales and Aftermarket: John C. Boutsikaris, age 61
VP Research and Development: James D. (Jim) Ruff, age 45
Corporate Controller and Principal Accounting Officer: James R. (Jim) Brausen, age 55
Secretary: Ronald L. Greenman
Managing Director, Key Technology BV: Saeed Tasbihgou, age 52
Manager Investor Relations: Cathy Burlingame
Auditors: Grant Thornton LLP

LOCATIONS

HQ: Key Technology, Inc.
150 Avery St., Walla Walla, WA 99362
Phone: 509-529-2161 **Fax:** 509-527-1331
Web: www.keyww.com

2008 Sales

	$ mil.	% of total
US	66.7	50
Other countries	67.4	50
Total	**134.1**	**100**

PRODUCTS/OPERATIONS

2008 Sales

	$ mil.	% of total
Process systems	56.6	42
Automated inspection systems	56.0	42
Parts & service	21.5	16
Total	**134.1**	**100**

Selected Divisions, Products, and Services

Automated inspection systems
  ADR system
  Optyx system
  Pharmaceutical inspection system
  ScanTrac X-ray system
  Tegra optical sorting system
  Tobacco sorter systems
Process systems
  Food pumping systems and belt conveyors
  Horizon vibratory conveyors
  Impulse electromagnetic conveyors
  Iso-Flo vibratory conveyors
  Preparation systems
Parts and Services/Contracts
  Customer training programs
  Diagnostic via Internet
  Engineering contracts
  Extended warranties

COMPETITORS

Barco	PAR Technology
Fives	PPT VISION
FMC	Summerlot Engineered
Heat and Control	Products
Körber	Toromont
K-Tron	

HISTORICAL FINANCIALS

Company Type: Public

Income Statement

FYE: September 30

	REVENUE ($ mil.)	NET INCOME ($ mil.)	NET PROFIT MARGIN	EMPLOYEES
9/08	134.1	7.5	5.6%	612
9/07	107.5	7.4	6.9%	532
9/06	84.8	(0.8)	—	486
9/05	80.3	2.7	3.4%	478
9/04	80.6	3.7	4.6%	470
Annual Growth	**13.6%**	**19.3%**	**—**	**6.8%**

2008 Year-End Financials

Debt ratio: —	Dividends
Return on equity: 13.5%	Yield: 0.0%
Cash ($ mil.): 36.3	Payout: —
Current ratio: 2.67	Market value ($ mil.): 118.6
Long-term debt ($ mil.): —	R&D as % of sales: —
No. of shares (mil.): 5.0	Advertising as % of sales: —

Stock History

NASDAQ (GM): KTEC

	STOCK PRICE ($) FY Close	P/E High/Low		PER SHARE ($) Earnings	Dividends	Book Value
9/08	23.70	29	16	1.35	0.00	12.06
9/07	30.10	23	8	1.37	0.00	10.07
9/06	12.78	—	—	(0.15)	0.00	8.24
9/05	14.20	29	16	0.52	0.00	8.08
9/04	11.25	27	15	0.71	0.00	7.20
Annual Growth	**20.5%**	**—**	**—**	**17.4%**	**—**	**13.8%**

KMG Chemicals

KMG Chemicals saves dead trees and kills weeds. The company makes and distributes wood preservatives and agricultural chemicals. Its wood preservatives are pentachlorophenol (penta), sodium penta, and creosote. KMG sells creosote and penta in the US, primarily to the railroad, construction, and utility industries. Sodium penta is sold in Latin America. The company makes herbicides used to protect cotton from weeds (Bueno) and to kill weeds along highways (Ansar), and its Rabon and Ravap pesticide lines keep pests from livestock and poultry. KMG also sells hydrochloric acid, a by-product of penta manufacturing, to the oil and steel industries. Chairman David Hatcher owns more than 60% of KMG.

The most common chemicals for wood preservation are chromated copper arsenate (CCA), creosote, and penta. CCA accounts for about 80% of the sales for wood preservation chemicals but is not produced by KMG.

In 2002 KMG bought an insecticide product line that sells tetrachlorvinphos under the Rabon brand name. It is used to protect livestock and poultry from flies and other pests. It bought an additional line of insecticides in 2004, called Ravap.

In 2005 the company acquired the penta assets of Occidental Chemical; OxyChem had gained the assets as part of its acquisition of Vulcan Chemicals earlier that year. This acquisition made KMG the sole distributor of penta for wood treatment purposes in the US. Two years later KMG made another acquisition, buying the high purity process chemicals business of Air Products & Chemicals for $75 million. The deal gave KMG access to another niche market, electronic chemicals (blends of acids and solvents) used in the manufacture of semiconductors.

KMG's largest customer (as well as a large supplier) is Koppers, which accounts for just under 10% of KMG's sales.

EXECUTIVES

Chairman: David L. Hatcher, age 66
President, CEO, COO, and Director: J. Neal Butler, age 57, $601,924 total compensation
VP Operations: Ernest C. (Ernie) Kremling II, age 45, $329,054 total compensation
VP and CFO: John V. Sobchak, age 49, $304,553 total compensation
VP Sales, KMB-Bernuth: Thomas H. (Tom) Mitchell, age 66
VP, General Counsel and Secretary: Roger C. Jackson, age 58, $256,076 total compensation
Auditors: UHY LLP

LOCATIONS

HQ: KMG Chemicals, Inc.
9555 W. Sam Houston Pkwy. South, Ste. 600
Houston, TX 77099
Phone: 713-600-3800   **Fax:** 713-600-3850
Web: www.kmgb.com

KMG Chemicals has facilities in Alabama, Kansas, Texas, and Mexico.

2009 Sales

	$ mil.	% of total
US	173.8	91
Other countries	16.9	9
Total	**190.7**	**100**

PRODUCTS/OPERATIONS

2009 Sales

	$ mil.	% of total
Wood treatment		
Creosote	67.8	35
Penta	26.2	14
Electronic chemicals	85.8	45
Animal health	10.9	6
Total	**190.7**	**100**

Selected Products

Creosote (wood preservative)
Hydrochloric acid (for use in the steel and oil well service industries)
Monosodium and disodium methanearsonic acids (MSMA, herbicide)
Pentachlorophenol (aka "penta," wood preservative)
Sodium pentachlorophenol (aka "sodium penta," wood preservative)
Tetrachlorvinphos (insecticide)

COMPETITORS

Arch Chemicals	Osmose
Koppers Holdings	Perstorp
Merichem	Rasa Industries
Monsanto Company	

HISTORICAL FINANCIALS

Company Type: Public

Income Statement

FYE: July 31

	REVENUE ($ mil.)	NET INCOME ($ mil.)	NET PROFIT MARGIN	EMPLOYEES
7/09	190.7	10.2	5.3%	272
7/08	154.4	5.4	3.5%	274
7/07	89.8	8.8	9.8%	118
7/06	71.0	3.8	5.4%	110
7/05	59.2	3.1	5.2%	93
Annual Growth	**34.0%**	**34.7%**	**—**	**30.8%**

2009 Year-End Financials

Debt ratio: 55.4%
Return on equity: 15.1%
Cash ($ mil.): 7.2
Current ratio: 1.96
Long-term debt ($ mil.): 39.3
No. of shares (mil.): 11.1
Dividends
Yield: 1.1%
Payout: 8.8%
Market value ($ mil.): 81.6
R&D as % of sales: —
Advertising as % of sales: —

Stock History

NASDAQ (GM): KMGB

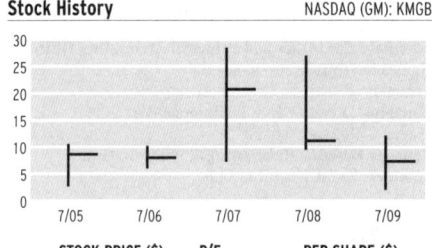

	STOCK PRICE ($) FY Close	P/E High	P/E Low	PER SHARE ($) Earnings	PER SHARE ($) Dividends	PER SHARE ($) Book Value
7/09	7.32	13	2	0.91	0.08	6.37
7/08	11.18	56	20	0.48	0.08	5.71
7/07	20.75	35	9	0.80	0.08	5.06
7/06	8.00	25	16	0.40	0.08	4.21
7/05	8.63	28	8	0.37	0.07	2.95
Annual Growth	**(4.0%)**	**—**	**—**	**25.2%**	**3.4%**	**21.2%**

The Knot

Here comes the bride, surfing online. Where is the groom? He's in a chat room. The Knot is a leading online publisher serving the wedding market sector with content and services through TheKnot.com. The site offers advice and information on topics from engagement to honeymoon, as well as wedding planning tools (budget planner, gown finder), chat rooms, a directory of local resources, and an online gift store. The company's WeddingChannel.com offers online registry services. Other products target newlyweds and pregnant women. In addition to online content, The Knot produces branded TV content and national and local magazines, as well as books on lifestyle topics (published by Random House and Chronicle Books).

The company has spend the last few years expanding beyond wedding-related content. Other brands from The Knot include *The Nest* maga-zine and TheNest.com for newlyweds; *Lilaguides*, which publishes local information guides for new parents; and PartySpot.com for party planning. In 2008 The Knot acquired The Bump Media, a publisher of local print guides for pregnancy, maternity, and baby resources. The company subsequently rebranded its TheNestBaby.com as TheBump.com.

In 2008 and 2009 the company added some 85 wedding sites focused on local markets such as Austin, Texas; Baltimore, Maryland; and Portland, Oregon. In further efforts to expand its brands focused on pregnancy and first-time parenting, in early 2009 the company acquired Breastfeeding.com. The site offers content such as breast-feeding advice, articles, and videos, as well as a directory of lactation consultants.

Comcast owns more than 15% of the company, while Macy's owns 11% and Time Warner has a 5% stake. (Macy's is also a major customer, accounting for approximately 10% of revenues.)

EXECUTIVES

Chairman, President, and CEO: David Liu, age 43, $906,962 total compensation
COO: Carol Koh Evans, age 37, $445,809 total compensation
CFO and Treasurer: John P. Mueller, age 46, $228,173 total compensation
Chief Content Officer: Carley Roney, age 40, $395,679 total compensation
EVP and Managing Director, Technology Group: Nic Di Iorio, age 49
SVP, General Counsel, and Secretary: Jeremy Lechtzin, age 35
VP and Executive Editor Print: Rebecca Dolgin
VP Executive Editor Online: Sally Jones
VP Business Integration: Rob Fassino
Editor, TheKnot.com: Anja Winikka
Fashion Editor, The Knot: Heather Levine
Deputy Editor, The Nest: Riann Smith
Auditors: Ernst & Young LLP

LOCATIONS

HQ: The Knot, Inc.
462 Broadway, 6th Fl., New York, NY 10013
Phone: 212-219-8555   **Fax:** 212-219-1929
Web: www.theknot.com

PRODUCTS/OPERATIONS

2008 Sales

	$ mil.	% of total
Online sponsorships & advertising	54.4	52
Merchandising	20.5	20
Registry	10.4	10
Publishing & other	18.6	18
Total	**103.9**	**100**

Selected Holdings

Breastfeeding.com
TheBump.com
GiftRegistryLocator.com
TheKnot.com
The Knot books
The Knot Book of Wedding Flowers
The Knot Book of Wedding Gowns
The Knot Bride's Journal
The Knot Guide for the Mother of the Bride
The Knot magazines
The Knot Local Weddings Magazines
The Knot Weddings Magazine
The Knot TV
Lilaguide.com
TheNest.com
The Nest magazine
PartySpot.com
PromSpot.com
WeddingChannel.com
WeddingTracker.com

COMPETITORS

About Group	Martha Stewart Living
AOL	Meredith Corporation
Condé Nast	WE: Women's
Fairchild Fashion Group	Entertainment
iVillage	Yahoo!

HISTORICAL FINANCIALS

Company Type: Public

Income Statement

FYE: December 31

	REVENUE ($ mil.)	NET INCOME ($ mil.)	NET PROFIT MARGIN	EMPLOYEES
12/08	103.9	4.1	3.9%	472
12/07	98.7	11.9	12.1%	451
12/06	72.7	23.4	32.2%	367
12/05	51.4	4.0	7.8%	260
12/04	41.4	1.3	3.1%	235
Annual Growth	25.9%	33.3%	—	19.0%

2008 Year-End Financials

Debt ratio: —
Return on equity: 2.1%
Cash ($ mil.): 61.5
Current ratio: 4.48
Long-term debt ($ mil.): —
No. of shares (mil.): 33.7

Dividends
  Yield: —
  Payout: —
Market value ($ mil.): 280.6
R&D as % of sales: —
Advertising as % of sales: —

Stock History

NASDAQ (GM): KNOT

	STOCK PRICE ($) FY Close	P/E High/Low	Earnings	PER SHARE ($) Dividends	Book Value
12/08	8.32	116 41	0.13	—	5.88
12/07	15.94	89 34	0.36	—	5.52
12/06	26.24	36 13	0.82	—	5.05
12/05	11.44	90 28	0.16	—	1.05
12/04	5.05	113 51	0.05	—	0.87
Annual Growth	13.3%	— —	27.0%	—	61.4%

Kopin Corporation

Kopin's semiconductor wafers are good at copin' with high speeds. The company makes specialized gallium arsenide (GaAs) wafers with heterojunction bipolar transistors engineered onto the surface vertically (horizontal is the industry norm). Companies such as Skyworks Solutions (26% of sales) use the specialized GaAs wafers — costlier than silicon but with higher performance — to make integrated circuits for wireless and fiber-optic gear that demands high speed or low power consumption. Kopin also makes tiny display devices used by Panasonic, Samsung Electronics, SANYO Electric (16% of sales), and Victor Company of Japan in digital camcorders. The company gets more than half of its sales in the Americas.

Kopin owns about 73% of South Korean GaAs optoelectronics maker Kowon Technology, a supplier to Kopin and Samsung.

Tocqueville Asset Management owns about 7% of Kopin; AWM Investment holds 7%.

EXECUTIVES

Chairman, President, and CEO: John C. C. Fan, age 65, $1,434,914 total compensation
CFO and Treasurer: Richard A. Sneider, age 49, $506,000 total compensation
EVP Display Operations: Bor-Yeu Tsaur, age 53, $700,293 total compensation
SVP, Gallium Arsenide Operations: Daily S. Hill, age 52, $411,810 total compensation
VP and CTO: Hong Choi, age 58, $391,570 total compensation
VP Government Programs and Special Projects: Michael J. Presz, age 55
VP Worldwide Display Operations: Steven A. Glaza
Golden-i Program Manager: Jeffrey Jacobsen
Director Display Marketing: Alan Richard
Director Human Resources: Joan Evans
Secretary and Director: David E. Brook, age 68
Auditors: Deloitte & Touche LLP

LOCATIONS

HQ: Kopin Corporation
  200 John Hancock Rd., Taunton, MA 02780
Phone: 508-824-6696   **Fax:** 508-824-6958
Web: www.kopin.com

Kopin has facilities in California and Massachusetts. Subsidiary Kowon Technology has operations in South Korea.

2008 Sales

	$ mil.	% of total
Americas	81.2	71
Asia/Pacific	33.6	29
Total	114.8	100

PRODUCTS/OPERATIONS

2008 Sales

	$ mil.	% of total
CyberDisplay	67.8	59
GaAs heterojunction bipolar transistor wafers	47.0	41
Total	114.8	100

Selected Products

Heterojunction bipolar transistor (HBT) wafers
Miniature displays (CyberDisplay)

COMPETITORS

Avago Technologies
Cree
eMagin
Epson
Fujitsu Microelectronics
Hitachi Cable
Hitachi Displays
IBM Microelectronics
IQE
Microvision
NEC
Nichia
RF Micro Devices
SANYO
Sharp Corp.
Soitec
Sony
Toshiba
Toyoda Gosei

HISTORICAL FINANCIALS

Company Type: Public

Income Statement

FYE: Last Saturday in December

	REVENUE ($ mil.)	NET INCOME ($ mil.)	NET PROFIT MARGIN	EMPLOYEES
12/08	114.8	2.6	2.3%	302
12/07	98.1	(6.6)	—	363
12/06	71.1	(2.1)	—	299
12/05	90.3	12.1	13.4%	317
12/04	87.3	(13.8)	—	379
Annual Growth	7.1%	—	—	(5.5%)

2008 Year-End Financials

Debt ratio: —
Return on equity: 1.9%
Cash ($ mil.): 57.9
Current ratio: 7.71
Long-term debt ($ mil.): —
No. of shares (mil.): 66.3

Dividends
  Yield: —
  Payout: —
Market value ($ mil.): 135.2
R&D as % of sales: —
Advertising as % of sales: —

Stock History

NASDAQ (GM): KOPN

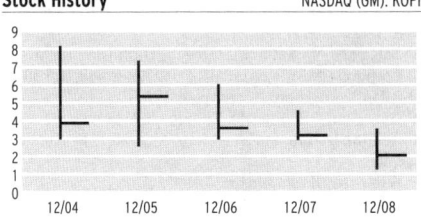

	STOCK PRICE ($) FY Close	P/E High/Low	Earnings	PER SHARE ($) Dividends	Book Value
12/08	2.04	86 33	0.04	—	2.09
12/07	3.16	— —	(0.10)	—	2.07
12/06	3.57	— —	(0.03)	—	2.13
12/05	5.35	43 15	0.17	—	2.21
12/04	3.87	— —	(0.20)	—	2.10
Annual Growth	(14.8%)	— —	—	—	(0.1%)

K-Sea Transportation

If you're transporting refined petroleum products, it's OK to go by K-Sea. K-Sea Transportation operates a fleet of about 75 tank barges and about 65 tugboats to propel them. Overall, the company's fleet has a carrying capacity of about 4.4 million barrels. K-Sea serves major oil companies, refiners, and oil traders, primarily along the east and west coasts of the US. About 80% of its business comes from one-year or longer contracts; major customers include BP, Chevron, ConocoPhillips, Exxon Mobil, and Tesoro. Investment funds managed by Jefferies Capital Partners, an affiliate of Jefferies Group, own K-Sea's general partner, which manages the company's operations.

Over the years the company has increased its fleet both by contracting to have new vessels built and by acquisitions, and it hopes to continue to pursue both strategies. K-Sea expanded its western operations in August 2007 when it acquired Seattle-based Sirius Maritime and Hawaii-based Smith Maritime for $205 million. The deal increased the carrying capacity of K-Sea's fleet by more than 20%.

While expanding its fleet, K-Sea hopes to maintain a mix of business tilted in favor of long-term contracts, or time charters, rather than voyage-by-voyage charters. Time charters tend to provide a more stable revenue stream.

Nearly all of K-Sea's vessels operate under the Jones Act, which restricts marine shipping between US ports to vessels built in the US and owned and operated by US companies.

Entities connected with Jefferies own about 27% of K-Sea, including a 1% general partner interest. Chairman James Dowling and director Brian Friedman represent Jefferies on the K-Sea board.

The company's general partner, K-Sea GP Holdings LP, filed for an IPO in March 2008, but the offering was withdrawn that October because of market conditions.

EXECUTIVES

Chairman: James J. Dowling, age 63
President, CEO, and Director: Timothy J. Casey, age 49
CFO: Terrence Gill, age 41
VP Sales and Marketing: Gregory J. Haslinsky, age 46
VP Corporate Development: Charles Kauffman, age 58
VP Atlantic Division: Christopher Palo
VP Operations: Thomas M. Sullivan, age 50
VP Administration and Secretary: Richard P. Falcinelli, age 48
VP Business Development: Carl Eklof Jr.
Information Systems Administrator: Chong Carl
President, Pacific Region: Gordon Smith, age 40
Director Human Resources: Dennis Luba
Special Assistant to President: Richard Heym
Auditors: PricewaterhouseCoopers LLP

LOCATIONS

HQ: K-Sea Transportation Partners L.P.
1 Tower Center Blvd., 17th Fl.
East Brunswick, NJ 08816
Phone: 732-339-6100   **Fax:** 732-339-6140
Web: www.k-sea.com

PRODUCTS/OPERATIONS

2009 Sales

	$ mil.	% of total
Voyage	310.4	94
Bareboat charter & other	20.1	6
Total	**330.5**	**100**

COMPETITORS

Apex Oil
Chemoil
Colonial Pipeline
Crowley Maritime
Hornbeck Offshore
Overseas Shipholding Group
Plantation Pipe Line
U.S. Shipping

HISTORICAL FINANCIALS

Company Type: Public

Income Statement

FYE: June 30

	REVENUE ($ mil.)	NET INCOME ($ mil.)	NET PROFIT MARGIN	EMPLOYEES
6/09	330.5	13.9	4.2%	992
6/08	326.3	25.7	7.9%	1,044
6/07	226.6	15.8	7.0%	925
6/06	182.8	5.9	3.2%	690
6/05	121.4	8.0	6.6%	490
Annual Growth	**28.5%**	**14.8%**	**—**	**19.3%**

2009 Year-End Financials

Debt ratio: —	Dividends
Return on equity: —	Yield: 15.7%
Cash ($ mil.): 1.8	Payout: 350.0%
Current ratio: 0.76	Market value ($ mil.): 375.1
Long-term debt ($ mil.): 366.2	R&D as % of sales: —
No. of shares (mil.): 19.1	Advertising as % of sales: —

Stock History

NYSE: KSP

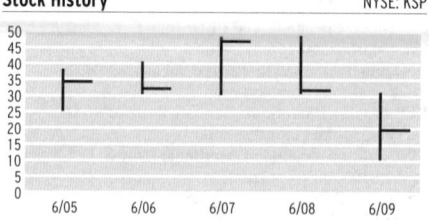

	STOCK PRICE ($) FY Close	P/E High/Low		PER SHARE ($) Earnings	Dividends	Book Value
6/09	19.61	35	12	0.88	3.08	—
6/08	31.77	25	16	1.95	2.92	—
6/07	46.96	31	20	1.55	2.60	—
6/06	32.15	67	52	0.60	2.32	—
6/05	34.25	40	27	0.95	2.14	—
Annual Growth	**(13.0%)**	**—**	**—**	**(1.9%)**	**9.5%**	**—**

K-Tron International

K-Tron International helps keep manufacturers well fed. Through its K-Tron Process Group subsidiary, the company makes feeders that let manufacturers control the flow of solid bulk and liquid materials during manufacturing processes by weight and volume. It also makes pneumatic conveying systems, including vacuum and pressure systems that precisely control the flow of ingredients used by the pharmaceutical, food, chemical, and plastics industries. Its companies make size reduction equipment, too, used to crush coal and wood products. Subsidiary K-Tron Electronics produces and tests electronic assemblies for K-Tron, as well as sells to regional producers. Casket maker Hillenbrand agreed to buy K-Tron in 2010.

Just out of the gate in 2010, Hillenbrand, which makes cremation products, plans to spend over $400 million in cash to purchase K-Tron International. K-Tron will become a subsidiary of Hillenbrand.

K-Tron's broad market reach stems from a wealth of capabilities, built through acquisition of complementing businesses. K-Tron designs and engineers, produces, peddles, and services all of its equipment. Its lineup is sold both on a stand-alone basis and as part of a larger system. Replacement parts are supplied, too. Despite the depth of operations, deteriorating markets across all industries have spurred K-Tron to downshift in 2009. The company shed employees at its offices in the US and Switzerland, and opted to freeze wages.

The move was a hard choice in light of the 20% increase in sales from 2007 to 2008. However, growth had been fueled by K-Tron's expansion of its pneumatic handling operations. It

---

bought Rader Companies in 2007 for about $16 million. A portfolio enhancement for K-Tron, Rader makes pneumatic conveying, storage, and screening systems, as well as bulk wood processing equipment for pulp, paper, and forest products industries.

K-Tron also picked up the assets of Wuxi Chenghao Machinery for its Process Group business. This addition promised to improve the company's share in the plastics markets, served by material conveyors, and bulk-handing equipment. But the plastics equipment business declined in 2008.

The Process Group had been boosted by an earlier score in 2006. K-Tron International acquired Premier Pneumatics, which makes pneumatic bulk-handling equipment. Following the acquisition, K-Tron even adopted the Premier brand for its pneumatic lineup.

The deal fell on the heels of picking up J.M.J. Industries to move its size reduction segment into new markets. J.M.J. makes crushing equipment for the coal industry. J.M.J was renamed Gundlach Equipment.

Chairman and CEO Edward Cloues owns nearly 10% of K-Tron. He has led the business since 1998, and is considered by Wall Street investors to have a talent for acquisitions.

EXECUTIVES

Chairman and CEO: Edward B. (Ed) Cloues II, age 61, $1,251,353 total compensation
SVP, CFO, and Treasurer: Robert E. Wisniewski, age 55
SVP Size Reduction Group; President and CEO, Pennsylvania Crusher: Donald W. Melchiorre, age 61, $548,686 total compensation
SVP Process Group; President and CEO, K-Tron America, Inc.: Kevin C. Bowen, age 58, $559,535 total compensation
SVP Corporate Development: Lukas Guenthardt, age 51, $487,339 total compensation
Director Corporate Accounting and Tax: Andrew T. Boyd, age 44
Secretary: Mary E. Vaccara
Auditors: Grant Thornton LLP

LOCATIONS

HQ: K-Tron International, Inc.
Rtes. 55 and 553, Pitman, NJ 08071
Phone: 856-589-0500   **Fax:** 856-589-8113
Web: www.ktron.com

2008 Sales

	$ mil.	% of total
Americas		
US	114.3	47
Canada	18.5	8
Other countries	26.5	11
EMEA/Asia		
Germany	12.1	5
UK	7.4	3
Netherlands	2.1	1
China	5.6	2
Italy	10.4	4
Other regions	46.1	19
Total	**243.0**	**100**

PRODUCTS/OPERATIONS

2008 Sales

	% of total
Equipment & parts	95
Services & freight	5
Total	**100**

Selected Products

Gravimetric feeding equipment (controls the flow of materials into a manufacturing process by mass or weight)
Pneumatic conveying equipment
Size reduction equipment (crushes coal for use in power plants and wood hogs for pulp, paper, and wood industries)
Volumetric feeders (control the flow of materials into a manufacturing process by volume)
Weigh belt feeders (move dry bulk material along a belt, continuously weighing the material)

COMPETITORS

Badger Meter
Cencorp
Clyde Process
Farrel
Heat and Control
Key Technology
Mesa Laboratories
Polysius

HISTORICAL FINANCIALS

Company Type: Public

Income Statement

FYE: Saturday nearest December 31

	REVENUE ($ mil.)	NET INCOME ($ mil.)	NET PROFIT MARGIN	EMPLOYEES
12/08	243.0	25.8	10.6%	727
12/07	201.7	21.3	10.6%	732
12/06	148.1	12.9	8.7%	625
12/05	118.9	7.3	6.1%	460
12/04	112.5	6.6	5.9%	467
Annual Growth	21.2%	40.6%	—	11.7%

2008 Year-End Financials

Debt ratio: 17.5%
Return on equity: 23.5%
Cash ($ mil.): 41.6
Current ratio: 2.45
Long-term debt ($ mil.): 22.0
No. of shares (mil.): 2.8
Dividends
  Yield: —
  Payout: —
Market value ($ mil.): 226.8
R&D as % of sales: —
Advertising as % of sales: —

Stock History

NASDAQ (GM): KTII

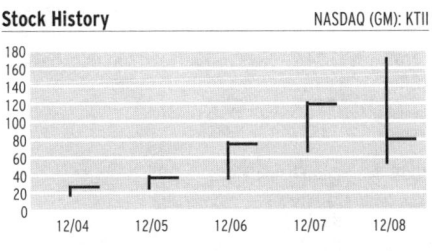

	STOCK PRICE ($) FY Close	P/E High/Low		PER SHARE ($) Earnings	Dividends	Book Value
12/08	79.90	19	6	9.03	—	44.41
12/07	119.25	16	9	7.49	—	33.10
12/06	74.67	17	8	4.59	—	23.03
12/05	37.10	14	9	2.68	—	17.44
12/04	26.55	11	7	2.53	—	16.05
Annual Growth	31.7%	—	—	37.4%	—	29.0%

Ladish Co.

Ladish got its start in 1905 when Herman Ladish bought a 1,500-pound steam hammer, and the company's been swinging ever since. Today the company designs and manufactures high-strength forged and cast metal components for aerospace and industrial markets. Jet engine parts, missile components, landing gear, helicopter rotors, and other aerospace products generate about 75% of the company's sales; general industrial components account for the remaining 25%. Aerospace industry giants Rolls-Royce (23%), United Technologies (15%), and General Electric (9%) together account for almost half of Ladish's sales. About 50% of its sales come from outside the US (the UK representing more than half of all foreign sales).

Even though Ladish reported a 60% jump in earnings in 2008, its engines were reversed the following year when the aerospace and industrial markets experienced a major stall. Ladish substantiated the trend by reporting its 2009 first quarter profits were down almost 80%. The company, which also sells its titanium and nickel-based alloy scrap, has been buffeted by the almost 14% drop in scrap exports. Ladish will stockpile its scrap in anticipation of higher titanium prices in the future.

The company is taking additional steps to control costs and improve its cash flow. Plans to invest up to $20 million to build a casting foundry in Mexico for the production of titanium components for the aerospace industry have been shelved temporarily. It reduced its workforce by 5%. Though Ladish was "cautious" in its outlook for 2009, demand for the company's helicopter components remains strong, and Ladish believes that airliner delivery will recover in 2010.

In 2008 Poland-based subsidiary ZKM Forging contracted with Goodrich Corporation to provide landing gear structural components for use on the new Gulfstream G650 business jet. This is a big step for Ladish in its desire to drive up ZKM's percentage of involvement in the aerospace business. Also in 2008 the company increased its aerospace scope by acquiring Aerex Manufacturing, a Connecticut-based precision manufacturing company. The acquisition of Chen-Tech Industries, which specializes in components for smaller jet engines, expands Ladish's technological capabilities, and adds the ability to make specialized nickel-based and titanium components.

EXECUTIVES

CEO and Director: Gary J. Vroman, age 49, $551,072 total compensation
VP Law, Finance; Secretary and Director:
  Wayne E. Larsen, age 54, $547,953 total compensation
VP Human Resources: Lawrence C. Hammond, age 61, $241,483 total compensation
VP Engineering: Gene E. Bunge, age 63
VP Materials Management: David L. Provan, age 59
President, Valley Machining: Robert C. Miller, age 58
President, Chen-Tech: Shannon J. S. Ko, age 66
President, Aerex: Armund N. Ek, age 74
President, Zaklad Kuznia Matrycowa: Jozef Burdzy, age 57
President, Stowe Machine: John Delaney, age 59
President, Pacific Cast Technologies, Inc.:
  Randy B. Turner, age 59, $303,511 total compensation
Auditors: Grant Thornton LLP

LOCATIONS

HQ: Ladish Co., Inc.
  5481 S. Packard Ave., Cudahy, WI 53110
Phone: 414-747-2611 **Fax:** 414-747-2963
Web: www.ladishco.com

PRODUCTS/OPERATIONS

2008 Sales

	$ mil.	% of total
Jet engine components	239	51
Aerospace components	124	26
General industrial components	107	23
Total	**470**	**100**

Selected Operating Units

Casting
  Pacific Cast Technologies
Forging
  Chen-Tech Industries
  Ladish Forging
  ZKM Forging
Machining
  Aerex
  Ladish Diecast Tooling
  Stowe Machine
  Valley Machining

COMPETITORS

Barnes Group
Goodrich Corp.
HEICO
Héroux-Devtek
Precision Castparts
Titanium Metals
Triumph Group
Unison Industries
Volvo Aero
Wyman-Gordon

HISTORICAL FINANCIALS

Company Type: Public

Income Statement

FYE: December 31

	REVENUE ($ mil.)	NET INCOME ($ mil.)	NET PROFIT MARGIN	EMPLOYEES
12/08	469.5	32.2	6.9%	1,380
12/07	424.6	32.3	7.6%	1,270
12/06	369.3	28.5	7.7%	1,200
12/05	266.8	13.7	5.1%	1,950
12/04	208.7	3.8	1.8%	1,075
Annual Growth	22.5%	70.6%	—	6.4%

2008 Year-End Financials

Debt ratio: 40.3%
Return on equity: 15.2%
Cash ($ mil.): 4.9
Current ratio: 2.52
Long-term debt ($ mil.): 90.0
No. of shares (mil.): 15.9
Dividends
  Yield: 0.0%
  Payout: —
Market value ($ mil.): 220.3
R&D as % of sales: —
Advertising as % of sales: —

Stock History

NASDAQ (GM): LDSH

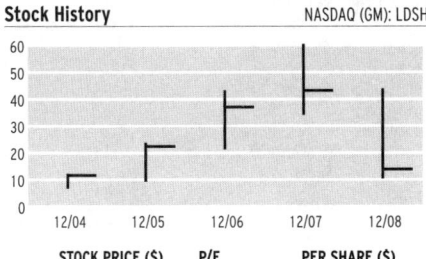

	STOCK PRICE ($) FY Close	P/E High/Low		PER SHARE ($) Earnings	Dividends	Book Value
12/08	13.85	20	5	2.15	0.00	14.05
12/07	43.19	27	16	2.22	0.00	12.67
12/06	37.08	21	11	2.00	0.00	9.60
12/05	22.35	24	10	0.98	0.00	7.39
12/04	11.60	42	26	0.28	0.00	7.70
Annual Growth	4.5%	—	—	66.5%	—	16.2%

Lakeland Bancorp

Lakeland Bancorp is shoring up in the Garden State. It's the holding company for Lakeland Bank, which serves northern New Jersey from about 50 branch offices. Targeting individuals and small to midsized businesses, the bank offers standard retail products such as checking and savings accounts, money market and NOW accounts, and CDs. It also offers financial planning and advisory services for consumers. The bank's lending activities primarily consist of commercial loans (about half of the company's loan portfolio) and residential mortgages (about a third of all loans). Its Lakeland Bank Equipment Leasing Division offers commercial equipment lease financing.

Company board members and executives collectively own 17% of Lakeland Bancorp.

EXECUTIVES

Chairman, Lakeland Bancorp and Lakeland Bank: John W. Fredericks, age 72
President, CEO, and Director; President and CEO, Lakeland Bank: Thomas J. Shara Jr., age 51, $442,540 total compensation
SEVP and COO: Robert A. Vandenbergh, age 57, $337,545 total compensation
EVP and Chief Retail Officer: Ronald E. (Ron) Schwarz, age 52
EVP and Chief Credit Officer: James R. Noonan, age 57
EVP Government and Business Services: Jeffrey J. Buonforte, age 57, $247,081 total compensation
EVP and Chief Operations Officer: Louis E. Luddecke, age 62, $247,539 total compensation
EVP, CFO, and Investor Relations: Joseph F. Hurley, age 58, $282,816 total compensation
EVP and Chief Lending Officer, Lakeland Bancorp and Lakeland Bank: David Yanagisawa
SVP Asset Based Lending: Thomas R. Keady
SVP and General Counsel: Timothy J. Matteson, age 39
SVP Leasing Division: Robert Ingram
SVP Bank Secrecy Act and Anti-Money Laundering, Lakeland Bank: Rasiel Kleiner
Secretary and Director: George H. Guptill Jr., age 70
Auditors: Grant Thornton LLP

LOCATIONS

HQ: Lakeland Bancorp, Inc.
250 Oak Ridge Rd., Oak Ridge, NJ 07438
Phone: 973-697-2000   **Fax:** 973-697-8385
Web: www.lakelandbank.com

PRODUCTS/OPERATIONS

2008 Gross Revenues

	$ mil.	% of total
Interest		
Loans & fees	127.4	79
Investment securities	13.7	8
Other	2.8	2
Noninterest		
Service charges on deposit accounts	11.1	7
Commissions & fees	3.4	2
Other	3.1	2
Total	**161.5**	**100**

COMPETITORS

Bank of America	Sovereign Bank
Bank of New York Mellon	Sussex Bancorp
Clifton Savings	TD Bank USA
Hudson City Bancorp	Valley National Bancorp
PNC Financial	Wachovia Corp

HISTORICAL FINANCIALS
Company Type: Public

Income Statement
FYE: December 31

	ASSETS ($ mil.)	NET INCOME ($ mil.)	INCOME AS % OF ASSETS	EMPLOYEES
12/08	2,642.6	15.2	0.6%	521
12/07	2,513.8	18.0	0.7%	540
12/06	2,263.6	17.0	0.8%	538
12/05	2,206.0	20.2	0.9%	548
12/04	2,141.0	16.5	0.8%	512
Annual Growth	5.4%	(2.0%)	—	0.4%

2008 Year-End Financials

Equity as % of assets: 8.4%
Return on assets: 0.6%
Return on equity: 7.0%
Long-term debt ($ mil.): 288.2
No. of shares (mil.): 23.8
Market value ($ mil.): 268.4
Dividends
Yield: 3.6%
Payout: 62.5%
Sales ($ mil.): 106.2
R&D as % of sales: —
Advertising as % of sales: —

Stock History
NASDAQ (GS): LBAI

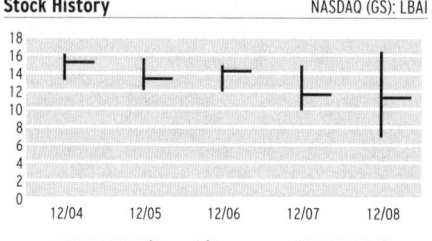

	STOCK PRICE ($) FY Close	P/E High/Low	PER SHARE ($) Earnings	Dividends	Book Value
12/08	11.26	25 11	0.64	0.40	9.27
12/07	11.59	19 13	0.77	0.29	8.88
12/06	14.19	20 16	0.73	0.37	8.37
12/05	13.33	18 14	0.85	0.35	8.05
12/04	15.16	21 17	0.77	0.35	8.16
Annual Growth	(7.2%)	— —	(4.5%)	3.4%	3.2%

Lakeland Financial

American dollars are preferred over Polish zloty in this Warsaw bank. Lakeland Financial is the holding company for Lake City Bank, which serves area business customers and individuals through more than 40 branches scattered across about a dozen northern Indiana counties.

Founded in 1872 in Warsaw, Indiana, the bank offers such standard retail services as checking and savings accounts, CDs, and money market accounts. Commercial loans, including agricultural loans and mortgages, make up about 80% of the bank's loan portfolio. Lake City Bank also offers investment products and services such as corporate and personal trust, brokerage, employee benefit plans, and estate planning.

EXECUTIVES

Chairman, President, and CEO, Lakeland Financial and Lake City Bank: Michael L. Kubacki, age 56, $732,257 total compensation
EVP, CFO, and Secretary, Lakeland Financial and Lake City Bank: David M. Findlay, age 46, $414,822 total compensation
EVP Retail, Lakeland Financial and Lake City Bank: Kevin L. Deardorff, age 48, $279,426 total compensation

EVP, Lakeland Financial and Lake City Bank: Charles D. Smith, age 65, $336,946 total compensation
SVP and Trust Officer, Lakeland Financial; Head, Wealth Advisory Group: James D. Westerfield, age 52, $228,370 total compensation
SVP, General Counsel, and Secretary, Lakeland Financial and Lake City Bank: Kristin Pruitt, age 37

LOCATIONS

HQ: Lakeland Financial Corporation
202 E. Center St., Warsaw, IN 46581
Phone: 574-267-6144   **Fax:** 574-267-6063
Web: www.lakecitybank.com

PRODUCTS/OPERATIONS

2008 Gross Revenues

	$ mil.	% of total
Interest		
Loans	99.6	72
Securities	18.6	13
Short-term investments	0.2	—
Noninterest		
Service charges on deposit accounts	8.6	6
Merchant card fees	3.5	3
Wealth advisory fees	3.3	2
Loan, insurance & service fees	2.8	2
Other	3.3	2
Total	**139.9**	**100**

COMPETITORS

1st Source Corporation
KeyCorp
Northeast Indiana Bancorp
PNC Financial

HISTORICAL FINANCIALS
Company Type: Public

Income Statement
FYE: December 31

	ASSETS ($ mil.)	NET INCOME ($ mil.)	INCOME AS % OF ASSETS	EMPLOYEES
12/08	2,377.4	19.7	0.8%	446
12/07	1,989.1	19.2	1.0%	447
12/06	1,836.7	18.7	1.0%	449
12/05	1,634.6	18.0	1.1%	434
12/04	1,453.1	14.5	1.0%	427
Annual Growth	13.1%	8.0%	—	1.1%

2008 Year-End Financials

Equity as % of assets: 6.3%
Return on assets: 0.9%
Return on equity: 13.3%
Long-term debt ($ mil.): 121.0
No. of shares (mil.): 12.4
Market value ($ mil.): 296.4
Dividends
Yield: 2.5%
Payout: 38.6%
Sales ($ mil.): 86.6
R&D as % of sales: —
Advertising as % of sales: —

Stock History
NASDAQ (GS): LKFN

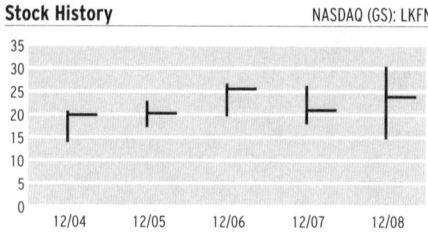

	STOCK PRICE ($) FY Close	P/E High/Low	PER SHARE ($) Earnings	Dividends	Book Value
12/08	23.82	19 9	1.58	0.61	12.05
12/07	20.90	17 12	1.55	0.55	11.76
12/06	25.53	17 13	1.51	0.38	10.46
12/05	20.19	15 12	1.46	0.46	9.11
12/04	19.85	17 12	1.20	0.42	8.18
Annual Growth	4.7%	— —	7.1%	9.8%	10.2%

Lannett Company

Lannett banks on the designation of "bio-equivalent" for its products. The firm manufactures and markets generic prescription drugs such as painkillers (including two versions of Novartis' migraine treatment Fiorinal), anticonvulsants for epileptics, and Digoxin for congestive heart failure (a version of Lanoxin). The company has also developed a generic version of Abbott Laboratories' Synthroid. While it manufactures some of its products, Jerome Stevens Pharmaceuticals manufactures a significant portion of Lannett's inventories. Lannett prefers to focus on products with few generic competitors. Chairman William Farber and his family own more than half of the company.

Formed in 1942, Lannett is one of the oldest generics manufacturers in the US. While the company manufacturers and/or distributes over 20 different generic drugs, four formulas account for more than 75% of its sales. Most of its products are sold as generics, but some receive private labeling with a customer's name.

Its customers include the big wholesale US pharmaceutical distributors as well as group purchasing organizations, chain drug stores, and other pharmaceutical companies. Its largest single customer, Walgreens, accounted for more than 35% of sales in 2007.

Lannett holds supply and development agreements with a handful of domestic and foreign companies, including Banner Pharmacaps. It also has agreements for new product formulation and development with other companies, but it intends to conduct its own manufacturing of any such products.

The company's 2007 acquisition of Cody Laboratories expanded its manufacturing capacity and it has been steadily beefing up its product development staff to bring more products through the FDA approval process.

EXECUTIVES

Chairman: William Farber, age 78
Vice Chairman: Ronald A. West, age 75
President, CEO, and Director: Arthur P. Bedrosian, age 64
CFO: Keith R. Ruck, age 48
EVP Cody Laboratories: Terence D. Vollrath, age 52
VP Operations: Stephen J. Kovary, age 52
VP Regulatory Affairs and Chief Compliance Officer: Ernest Sabo, age 62
VP Sales and Marketing: Kevin Smith, age 50
VP Logistics: William Schreck, age 61
Auditors: Grant Thornton LLP

LOCATIONS

HQ: Lannett Company, Inc.
9000 State Rd., Philadelphia, PA 19136
Phone: 215-333-9000   **Fax:** 215-333-9004
Web: www.lannett.com

PRODUCTS/OPERATIONS

Selected Products

Acetazolamide (Diamox, glaucoma)
Baclofen (Lioresal, muscle relaxant)
Butalbital (Fiorinal, migraines)
Dicyclomine (Bentyl, irritable bowel syndrome)
Digoxin (Lanoxin, congestive heart failure)
Hydromorphone (Dilaudid, pain management)
Oxycodone (Roxicodone, pain management)
Primidone (Mysoline, epilepsy)
Sulfamethoxazole (Bactrim, antibiotic)

COMPETITORS

Abbott Labs	Mylan
Actavis	Par Pharmaceutical
Caraco Pharmaceutical	Ranbaxy Laboratories
Forest Labs	Sandoz International
GlaxoSmithKline	Teva Pharmaceuticals
King Pharmaceuticals	Watson Pharmaceuticals

HISTORICAL FINANCIALS

Company Type: Public

Income Statement

FYE: June 30

	REVENUE ($ mil.)	NET INCOME ($ mil.)	NET PROFIT MARGIN	EMPLOYEES
6/09	119.0	6.5	5.5%	277
6/08	72.4	(2.3)	—	222
6/07	82.6	(6.9)	—	198
6/06	64.1	5.0	7.8%	—
6/05	44.9	(32.8)	—	172
Annual Growth	27.6%	—	—	12.7%

2009 Year-End Financials

Debt ratio: 9.9%
Return on equity: 8.9%
Cash ($ mil.): 25.8
Current ratio: 2.00
Long-term debt ($ mil.): 7.7
No. of shares (mil.): 24.7
Dividends
   Yield: —
   Payout: —
Market value ($ mil.): 169.2
R&D as % of sales: —
Advertising as % of sales: —

Stock History

NYSE Alternext: LCI

	STOCK PRICE ($) FY Close	P/E High/Low		Earnings	PER SHARE ($) Dividends	Book Value
6/09	6.85	29	6	0.27	—	3.14
6/08	3.90	—	—	(0.10)	—	2.80
6/07	6.09	—	—	(0.29)	—	2.84
6/06	5.69	40	18	0.21	—	3.07
6/05	5.22	—	—	(1.36)	—	2.80
Annual Growth	7.0%	—	—	—	—	2.9%

Layne Christensen

Layne Christensen cuts its way through the upper crust. The company provides drilling and construction services related to water, wastewater treatment, and mineral exploration. The company serves such clients as public and private water utilities, industrial companies, mining firms, and heavy civil construction contractors. It has operations throughout the Americas, as well as Africa, Australia, Europe, and Brazil. Layne Christensen's Water and Wastewater Infrastructure segment accounts for about two-thirds of company sales. Mineral exploration work accounts for most of the rest. The group has also entered the energy field, producing coal bed methane. The firm has some 80 sales and operations offices worldwide.

Layne Christensen's mineral exploration unit is primarily hired by mining companies to extract samples from sites before those companies invest more heavily in development. Its drilling operations are largely driven by the demand for underground base and precious mineral deposits that are used in automobiles, electronics, and other household and consumer items. There is a supply shortage, particularly in societies that are experiencing rapid industrialization, including Brazil, China, India, and Russia. As mineral resources in developed countries become depleted, mining companies are being forced to explore newer markets such as South America and Africa, where Layne Christensen is poised to meet that global demand.

The company also sees its energy unit as having great growth potential, given increased demand for cleaner-burning fuels. The company has working interests in developed and undeveloped Cherokee Basin properties in Kansas and Oklahoma, and may seek opportunities to acquire other unconventional natural gas properties for development.

As far as its water and wastewater segment, Layne Christensen hopes that its ability to bundle services — water well drilling, pump installation, and well rehabilitation — will help it achieve greater market share over companies that only offer single products and services. It plans to further penetrate the water infrastructure market, both organically and through acquisitions. The company intends to market its offerings beyond its core customer base, which are typically small to midsized plants, to larger customers in the power generation, pharmaceuticals, and food and beverage industries. Acquisitions of smaller regional companies, such as Denver-based Tierdael Construction Co., and Meadors Construction Company of Jacksonville, Florida, are widening its reach throughout the US. In 2009 it acquired Nashville-based W.L. Hailey & Company, one of the country's largest water infrastructure companies, for $15 million.

HISTORY

Layne Christensen was formed in 1882 as Layne Inc., a water well drilling equipment maker, by Mahlon Layne, a Kansas homesteader who had experimented with drilling techniques on his own land. During the early 20th century, Layne & Sons drilled water wells for individuals and small cities throughout Kansas. After WWII the company became a regional player. Reflecting its expansion into western states, Layne Inc. changed its name to Layne-Western in the 1960s.

In 1968 the company was acquired by Marley Holdings. Under new management, Layne-Western became an acquisition vehicle. Its most significant purchase in the 1970s was Singer, a major well-drilling and pump-repair business with operations across the western US. In 1991 Layne-Western began providing drilling services for mineral exploration in Mexico.

The next year Marley spun off the company as Layne, Inc. It expanded internationally, opening offices in Mexico and Thailand in 1995 and operating in Argentina, Bolivia, Canada, Chile, and Peru. Also that year Layne acquired Christensen Boyles, a top provider of drilling services for mining concerns. The firm changed its name to Layne Christensen in 1996.

Continuing its acquisition strategy, in 1997 the company acquired Stanley Mining Services, a top Australian and African mining concern, and in 1998 bought two African drilling firms,

Drillinti Africa and Afridrill. A year later it acquired Italian pump manufacturer Tecniwell and two Louisiana-based oil and gas service companies, Vibration Technologies and Toledo Oil and Gas Services.

The company created Layne Financial in 2000 to provide funding options for water supply and treatment system upgrade and development. In 2001 Layne Christensen sold manufacturing unit Christensen Products to Swedish industrial equipment maker Atlas Copco. Also that year Layne Water Development and Storage was created to provide risk-management and financial services for water resources and development companies.

In 2002 the group restructured its operations along its primary product lines. To enhance its position in the coalbed methane industry, Layne Christensen acquired oil and gas engineering and geological firm Mohajir Engineering in 2003.

The company sold two of its energy segment subsidiaries in 2004 — Toledo Oil and Gas Services and Layne Christensen Canada Limited. That year Layne Christensen strengthened its water resources presence on the West Coast by acquiring Beylik Drilling and Pump Service, a water drilling company in California, for about $14.7 million.

In 2005 the company purchased privately held Reynolds, a designer and builder of water and wastewater treatment plants, for $60 million and 2.2 million shares of stock. The deal added waste treatment and sewer rehabilitation capabilities to Layne Christensen's offerings. The company used the acquisition as impetus to combine its water resources and geoconstruction operations under one new segment, Water and Wastewater Infrastructure, which includes water system development, well and pump rehabilitation, water and wastewater treatment plant construction, sewer rehabilitation, and environmental assessment drilling.

Additional acquisitions have further bolstered the water and wastewater group; in 2007 the company acquired SolmeteX, whose products remove toxins from water, for $13.5 million in cash.

EXECUTIVES

Chairman: David A. B. Brown, age 66
President, CEO, and Director: Andrew B. Schmitt, age 61, $2,440,035 total compensation
EVP and Director: Jeffrey J. (Jeff) Reynolds, age 43
SVP and Division President, Mineral Exploration: Eric R. Despain, age 60, $793,588 total compensation
SVP, General Counsel, and Secretary: Steven F. Crooke, age 53, $869,836 total compensation
SVP Finance and Treasurer: Jerry W. Fanska, age 61, $1,080,067 total compensation
SVP and Division President, Water Resources: Gregory F. (Greg) Aluce, age 54, $664,222 total compensation
Manager Information Technology: Glenn Johnson
VP Human Resources: John Wright
Division President, Geoconstruction: Pier L. Iovino
Auditors: Deloitte & Touche LLP

LOCATIONS

HQ: Layne Christensen Company
1900 Shawnee Mission Pkwy.
Mission Woods, KS 66205
Phone: 913-362-0510   **Fax:** 913-362-0133
Web: www.laynechristensen.com

2009 Sales

	$ mil.	% of total
US	841.5	83
Africa/Australia	89.0	9
Mexico	37.8	4
Other regions	39.8	4
Total	**1,008.1**	**100**

PRODUCTS/OPERATIONS

2009 Sales

	$ mil.	% of total
Water infrastructure	767.0	76
Mineral exploration	188.9	19
Energy	46.4	4
Other	5.8	1
Total	**1,008.1**	**100**

COMPETITORS

Baker Hughes
Black & Veatch
Garney Holding
GeoTek Engineering & Testing Services
Insituform Technologies
Major Drilling Group
OCI
Parsons Corporation
STS Consultants

HISTORICAL FINANCIALS

Company Type: Public

Income Statement

FYE: January 31

	REVENUE ($ mil.)	NET INCOME ($ mil.)	NET PROFIT MARGIN	EMPLOYEES
1/09	1,008.1	26.5	2.6%	3,600
1/08	868.3	37.3	4.3%	4,300
1/07	722.8	26.3	3.6%	3,919
1/06	463.0	14.7	3.2%	3,551
1/05	343.5	9.8	2.9%	2,577
Annual Growth	**30.9%**	**28.2%**	**—**	**8.7%**

2009 Year-End Financials

Debt ratio: 5.8%
Return on equity: 6.0%
Cash ($ mil.): 67.2
Current ratio: 1.70
Long-term debt ($ mil.): 26.7
No. of shares (mil.): 19.4
Dividends
  Yield: —
  Payout: —
Market value ($ mil.): 306.7
R&D as % of sales: —
Advertising as % of sales: —

Stock History

NASDAQ (GS): LAYN

	STOCK PRICE ($) FY Close	P/E High/Low		PER SHARE ($) Earnings	Dividends	Book Value
1/09	15.78	43	8	1.37	—	23.47
1/08	36.90	27	14	2.20	—	21.79
1/07	35.03	22	15	1.68	—	10.55
1/06	30.11	29	14	1.05	—	8.83
1/05	18.50	27	17	0.75	—	5.39
Annual Growth	**(3.9%)**	**—**	**—**	**16.3%**	**—**	**44.5%**

L. B. Foster

L. B. Foster can help keep you on track whether you're riding the rails, or cruising the open road. The company manufactures new and relay rail and trackwork used in railroad and mass transit systems, as well as in industrial markets such as mining. L. B. Foster also supplies pipe coatings for oil and natural gas industries and pipe products for industrial, utility, and agricultural water wells. It taps federal, state, and local infrastructure markets, too, selling and renting steel sheet piling and earth wall systems necessary in highway and levee construction and repair. H-bearing piling is made to support bridges and high-rise buildings. US sales account for a majority of the company's operations.

New product launches helped to buffer the company from the economic downturn in 2008-09 and prepared it for projects fueled by federal stimulus funding. High on its agenda, the company aims to score work connected with funding for high-speed rails. The company has introduced insulated rail joints touting an improved service life, track components and fasteners to minimize slab track system noise and vibration, and a track electrification lineup offering improved energy efficiency. In 2008 L. B. Foster landed two transit projects in California for continuous welded rail. Looking for highway, road, and bridge construction funding, too, L. B. Foster has broadened its offerings with a pipe pile featuring material and transportation savings. Its lineup of precast concrete structures used in pre-fabricated utility buildings has also expanded.

Investment advisors Keely Asset Management Corp. and Keely Small Cap Fund collectively hold over a 20% stake in the company.

EXECUTIVES

Chairman: Lee B. Foster II, age 62, $508,130 total compensation
President, CEO, and Director: Stan L. Hasselbusch, age 61, $1,185,812 total compensation
SVP, CFO, and Treasurer: David J. Russo, age 50, $487,895 total compensation
SVP Operations and Manufacturing: John F. Kasel, age 44, $459,302 total compensation
SVP Construction Products: Donald L. (Don) Foster, age 53
SVP Rail Product Management: Samuel K. Fisher, age 56
VP and General Manager, CXT Concrete Products: Kevin R. Haugh, age 53, $476,034 total compensation
VP Tubular Products: Merry L. Brumbaugh, age 51
VP Rail Products Sales: Gregory W. Lippard, age 40
VP, General Counsel, and Secretary: David L. Voltz, age 56
VP Global Business Development: David Sauder
VP Human Resources: Brian Kelly, age 49
Controller: Linda K. Patterson, age 59
Auditors: Ernst & Young LLP

LOCATIONS

HQ: L. B. Foster Company
415 Holiday Dr., Pittsburgh, PA 15220
Phone: 412-928-3417   **Fax:** 412-928-7891
Web: www.lbfoster.com

PRODUCTS/OPERATIONS

2008 Sales

	$ mil.	% of total
Construction products	243.1	47
Rail products	234.7	46
Tubular products	34.8	7
Total	**512.6**	**100**

Selected Products

Rail
  Concrete ties
  Heavy and light rail
  Insulated rail joints
  Rail accessories
  Relay rail
Construction
  Fabricated highway products
  Precast concrete products
  Sheet and bearing piling
Tubular
  Column pipe
  Corrosion protection coatings
  Couplings
  Water well casing

COMPETITORS

ACF Industries
ALSTOM
Amsted
GATX
Greenbrier Rail Services
Trinity Industries
Westinghouse Air Brake

HISTORICAL FINANCIALS

Company Type: Public

Income Statement				FYE: December 31
	REVENUE ($ mil.)	NET INCOME ($ mil.)	NET PROFIT MARGIN	EMPLOYEES
12/08	512.6	27.7	5.4%	641
12/07	509.0	110.7	21.7%	655
12/06	389.8	13.5	3.5%	665
12/05	353.5	5.4	1.5%	641
12/04	297.9	1.5	0.5%	621
Annual Growth	**14.5%**	**107.3%**	**—**	**0.8%**

2008 Year-End Financials

Debt ratio: 10.0%
Return on equity: 12.8%
Cash ($ mil.): 115.1
Current ratio: 3.40
Long-term debt ($ mil.): 21.7
No. of shares (mil.): 10.2
Dividends
  Yield: 0.0%
  Payout: —
Market value ($ mil.): 317.9
R&D as % of sales: —
Advertising as % of sales: —

Stock History

NASDAQ (GS): FSTR

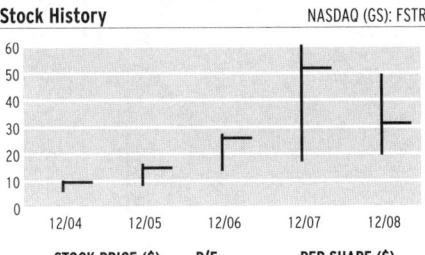

	STOCK PRICE ($) FY Close	P/E High/Low		PER SHARE ($) Earnings	Dividends	Book Value
12/08	31.28	19	8	2.57	0.00	21.41
12/07	51.73	6	2	10.09	0.00	21.04
12/06	25.91	22	11	1.25	0.00	9.65
12/05	14.87	31	16	0.52	0.00	7.87
12/04	9.52	69	46	0.14	0.00	7.26
Annual Growth	**34.6%**			**107.0%**	**—**	**31.1%**

Legacy Reserves

Legacy Reserves has its sights set on creating its very own prosperous legacy. The independent oil and gas company explores for oil and gas deposits in the Permian Basin of West Texas and southeast New Mexico and exploits those resources. In 2007 Legacy Reserves reported proved reserves of 32.1 million barrels of oil equivalent (74% oil and natural gas liquids; 87% proved developed). The company was formed in 2005 to own and operate the oil and natural gas properties that it acquired from the Moriah Group, the Brothers Group, and MBN Properties. These investors, along with the firm's directors and executive officers, own about 37% of Legacy Reserves.

In 2009 the company received a proposal from investment firm Apollo Management VII, LP to acquire control of Legacy Reserves.

Pursuing a strategy of growth through acquisitions, in 2006 the company boosted its reserves with the acquisition of 2.6 million barrels of oil equivalent (proved reserves), which it purchased in separate transactions from Larron Oil and Knight for approximately $36 million.

Legacy Reserves made 15 property acquisitions in 2007, and the next year the company bought Pantwist, LLC from Cano Petroleum for about $43 million. It also agreed to pay St. Mary Land & Exploration about $130 million for working interests in 13 oil fields in Wyoming.

EXECUTIVES

Chairman and CEO: Cary D. Brown, age 43, $550,366 total compensation
President, CFO, and Secretary:
Steven H. (Steve) Pruett, age 47, $499,588 total compensation
EVP Operations: Paul T. Horne, age 47, $439,197 total compensation
EVP Business Development and Land and Director:
Kyle A. McGraw, age 50, $420,464 total compensation
VP, Chief Accounting Officer, and Controller:
William M. Morris, age 56, $604,672 total compensation
Auditors: BDO Seidman, LLP

LOCATIONS

HQ: Legacy Reserves LP
303 W. Wall St., Ste. 1400, Midland, TX 79701
Phone: 432-689-5200   **Fax:** 432-689-5299
Web: www.legacylp.com

PRODUCTS/OPERATIONS

2008 Sales

	$ mil.	% of total
Oil	158.0	73
Gas	41.6	19
Natural gas liquids	15.8	8
Total	**215.4**	**100**

COMPETITORS

Carrizo Oil & Gas
Clayton Williams Energy
Eden Energy
Ellora
Glen Rose Petroleum
Occidental Permian
TBX Resources
TXCO Resources

HISTORICAL FINANCIALS

Company Type: Public

Income Statement				FYE: December 31
	REVENUE ($ mil.)	NET INCOME ($ mil.)	NET PROFIT MARGIN	EMPLOYEES
12/08	215.4	158.2	73.4%	98
12/07	112.2	(55.7)	—	58
12/06	69.1	4.4	6.4%	23
12/05	19.4	5.9	30.4%	24
12/04	14.3	9.2	64.3%	23
Annual Growth	**97.0%**	**103.6%**	**—**	**43.7%**

2008 Year-End Financials

Debt ratio: —
Return on equity: —
Cash ($ mil.): 2.5
Current ratio: 1.42
Long-term debt ($ mil.): 282.0
No. of shares (mil.): 34.9
Dividends
  Yield: 21.3%
  Payout: 38.3%
Market value ($ mil.): 324.8
R&D as % of sales: —
Advertising as % of sales: —

Stock History

NASDAQ (GS): LGCY

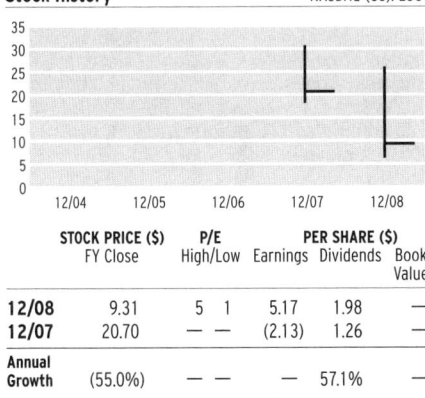

	STOCK PRICE ($) FY Close	P/E High/Low		PER SHARE ($) Earnings	Dividends	Book Value
12/08	9.31	5	1	5.17	1.98	—
12/07	20.70	—	—	(2.13)	1.26	—
Annual Growth	**(55.0%)**			**—**	**57.1%**	**—**

LHC Group

LHC Group operates care facilities and provides home health care services to rural markets in select US regions. The company's some 200 home health nursing agencies provide care to Medicare beneficiaries, offering such services as private duty nursing, physical therapy, and medically oriented social services. LHC also operates around a dozen hospices that provide palliative care for terminal patients, as well as several long-term, acute-care hospital facilities (mostly within host hospitals) that serve patients who no longer need intensive care but still require complex care in a hospital setting. The company also provides rehabilitation services.

Regulatory changes have made it less attractive to operate acute care hospitals within host hospitals, prompting the company to shift away from such facility-based services. Instead the company sees its future lying with acquisitions of additional home health care businesses in new geographic markets.

To that end, the company has made several small purchases of home health agencies, including the purchase of the Kentucky and Florida-based operations of Lifeline Home Health Care. To expand its reach in Tennessee, LHC purchased Extendicare of West Tennessee, which has four

home health agencies. Overall the company acquired more than 20 locations in 2007. The company also sold or shut down several hospital and pharmacy operations.

While LHC had not planned on making additional acquisitions in 2008, the habit was set and the company announced several purchase agreements that year, including one deal to acquire Home Care Solutions with eight operations in Tennessee and two in Virginia, and another deal to purchase HomeCall with 12 locations in Maryland. Late in 2008 LHC agreed to buy Washington-based Northwest Healthcare Alliance (dba Assured Home Health and Hospice); the deal was completed in early 2009, adding four home health care offices and five hospice locations.

The company has also beefed up its operations by forming multiple joint ventures, including one reached in 2008 with West Tennessee Healthcare to provide home health services. The following year it further expanded its home nursing operations by forming ventures with Southeast Alabama Medical Center, East Alabama Medical Center, Three Rivers Community Hospital (Oregon), and Woods Memorial Hospital (Tennessee).

Chairman, president, and CEO Keith Myers, who cofounded LHC Group in 1994, owns 17% of the company.

EXECUTIVES

Chairman, President, and CEO: Keith G. Myers, age 50, $836,708 total compensation
Special Advisor and Director: John L. Indest, age 57, $732,998 total compensation
SVP and COO: Donald D. (Don) Stelly, age 41, $491,741 total compensation
SVP, CFO, and Treasurer: Peter J. (Pete) Roman, age 58, $356,841 total compensation
SVP, Senior Counsel, Director Corporate Compliance, and Director Regulatory and Government Affairs: Richard A. MacMillan, age 57
SVP Corporate Development: Daryl J. Doise, age 52, $476,965 total compensation
SVP, General Counsel, and Director Mergers and Acquisitions: Peter C. November, age 39
CIO: Rajesh (Raj) Shetye
VP and Chief Administrative Officer: Marcus Macip
VP Investor Relations: Eric C. Elliott
VP Marketing: Blaine C. Williams
VP Finance: John Whitlock
Director Human Resources: Lolanda B. Brown
Auditors: KPMG LLP

LOCATIONS

HQ: LHC Group, Inc.
420 W. Pinhook Rd., Ste. A, Lafayette, LA 70503
Phone: 337-233-1307   **Fax:** 337-235-8037
Web: www.lhcgroup.com

PRODUCTS/OPERATIONS

2008 Sales

	$ mil.	% of total
Home-based services	326.0	85
Facility-based services	57.3	15
Total	**383.3**	**100**

COMPETITORS

Almost Family	Girling Health Care
Amedisys	Guardian Home Care
American HomePatient	Health First
Consulate Health Care	Home Instead
Critical Homecare Solutions	Kindred Healthcare
	Personal-Touch Home Care

HISTORICAL FINANCIALS

Company Type: Public

Income Statement

FYE: December 31

	REVENUE ($ mil.)	NET INCOME ($ mil.)	NET PROFIT MARGIN	EMPLOYEES
12/08	383.3	30.2	7.9%	5,376
12/07	298.0	19.6	6.6%	4,498
12/06	215.2	20.6	9.6%	3,959
12/05	162.5	10.1	6.2%	3,415
12/04	123.0	9.3	7.6%	2,554
Annual Growth	**32.9%**	**34.2%**	**—**	**20.5%**

2008 Year-End Financials

Debt ratio: 2.6%
Return on equity: 18.9%
Cash ($ mil.): 3.5
Current ratio: 1.65
Long-term debt ($ mil.): 4.5
No. of shares (mil.): 18.4
Dividends
  Yield: 0.0%
  Payout: —
Market value ($ mil.): 664.1
R&D as % of sales: —
Advertising as % of sales: —

Stock History

NASDAQ (GM): LHCG

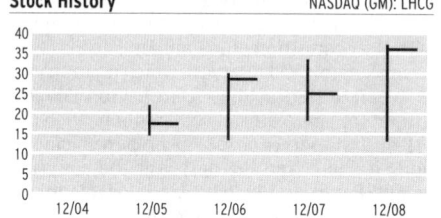

	STOCK PRICE ($) FY Close	P/E High/Low		PER SHARE ($) Earnings	Dividends	Book Value
12/08	36.00	22	8	1.69	0.00	9.59
12/07	24.98	30	17	1.11	0.00	7.77
12/06	28.51	23	11	1.27	0.00	6.61
12/05	17.43	37	25	0.59	0.00	4.25
Annual Growth	**27.4%**	**—**	**—**	**22.1%**	**—**	**81.3%**

Liberty Bancorp

Liberty Bancorp was formed in 2006 to be the holding company for BankLiberty (formerly Liberty Savings Bank), which operates ten branches in the Kansas City area. It offers traditional deposit services such as checking and savings accounts, CDs, and IRAs, in addition to newfangled offerings like Internet banking, bill payment, and cash management services. Construction loans, mainly to custom homebuilders, make up the largest part of the company's loan portfolio (more than 45%). It also offers business, residential and commercial real estate, and consumer loans.

Liberty Bancorp went public in 2006; Liberty Savings Bank changed its name to BankLiberty in conjunction with the stock offering. The bank plans to grow through acquisitions and by opening new branches in its market area.

In 2008 the company bought Farley State Bank, adding three branches in Missouri to BankLiberty's network.

EXECUTIVES

Chairman: Daniel G. O'Dell, age 55
President, CEO, and Director: Brent M. Giles, age 42
SVP and Chief Lending Officer: Mark E. Hecker, age 43

SVP and CFO; SVP and CFO, Liberty Savings Bank: Marc J. Weishaar, age 48
AVP and Branch Manager, Independence: Shawna Croucher
Branch Manager, Platte City: Diana Crockrill
Branch Manager, Plattsburg: Susan Tolle
Auditors: Michael Trokey & Company, P.C.

LOCATIONS

HQ: Liberty Bancorp, Inc.
16 W. Franklin St., Liberty, MO 64068
Phone: 816-781-4822   **Fax:** 816-781-6851
Web: www.libertysb.com

Liberty Bancorp has branches in Gladstone, Independence, Kansas City (2), Liberty, Platte City, and Plattsburg, Missouri.

PRODUCTS/OPERATIONS

2009 Gross Revenues

	$ mil.	% of total
Interest		
Loans receivable	18.3	82
Securities	1.7	8
Noninterest		
Deposit account service charges	1.3	6
Other	0.9	4
Total	**22.2**	**100**

COMPETITORS

Bank of America
Bank of the West
Commerce Bancshares
UMB Financial
U.S. Bancorp

HISTORICAL FINANCIALS

Company Type: Public

Income Statement

FYE: September 30

	ASSETS ($ mil.)	NET INCOME ($ mil.)	INCOME AS % OF ASSETS	EMPLOYEES
9/09	392.4	1.8	0.5%	111
9/08	336.2	1.9	0.6%	84
9/07	333.2	1.9	0.6%	74
9/06	287.6	1.5	0.5%	67
9/05	237.6	1.5	0.6%	74
Annual Growth	**13.4%**	**4.7%**	**—**	**10.7%**

2009 Year-End Financials

Equity as % of assets: 11.2%
Return on assets: 0.5%
Return on equity: 4.1%
Long-term debt ($ mil.): —
No. of shares (mil.): 3.6
Market value ($ mil.): 27.1
Dividends
  Yield: 1.3%
  Payout: 20.4%
Sales ($ mil.): 15.6
R&D as % of sales: —
Advertising as % of sales: —

Stock History

NASDAQ (CM): LBCP

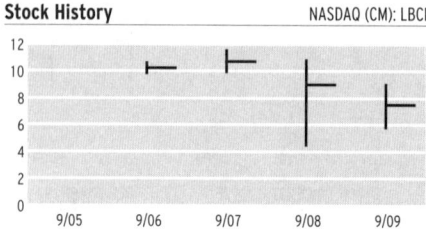

	STOCK PRICE ($) FY Close	P/E High/Low		PER SHARE ($) Earnings	Dividends	Book Value
9/09	7.51	18	12	0.49	0.10	12.11
9/08	9.00	23	10	0.47	0.10	12.18
9/07	10.71	27	24	0.42	0.10	13.89
9/06	10.23	34	32	0.31	0.03	13.55
Annual Growth	**(9.8%)**	**—**	**—**	**(18.9%)**	**49.4%**	**20.0%**

Life Partners Holdings

Life Partners Holdings, parent company of Life Partners, Inc., makes its bucks by helping its customers make a buck. The company facilitates viatical and life settlement transactions, in which an institution or wealthy investor purchases individual life insurance policies (at a discount) and becomes the beneficiary of those policies when they mature. Viatical settlements involve terminally ill policyholders with only a couple of years to live; life settlement transactions involve sellers with longer life expectancies. Life Partners makes its money from fees earned by facilitating viatical and life settlements.

Nearly all of the company's business is done through life settlement brokers.

Life Partners has been stepping up marketing efforts to institutional investors, which the company sees as key to its future growth. Since 2006 it has served as advisor and purchasing agent for a group of closed-end investment funds based in the Bahamas.

Chairman and CEO Brian Pardo owns just over 50% of the company.

EXECUTIVES

Chairman, President, and CEO; CEO, Life Partners, Inc.: Brian D. Pardo, age 67, $1,022,398 total compensation
CFO and Principal Accounting Officer: David M. Martin, age 51, $145,164 total compensation
Secretary, General Counsel, and Director; President, Life Partners, Inc.: R. Scott Peden, age 45, $557,503 total compensation
COO and CIO, Life Partners, Inc.: Mark Embry, age 53, $533,731 total compensation
VP Policy Administration, Life Partners, Inc.: Kurt D. Carr, age 40, $500,557 total compensation
VP Administration, Life Partners, Inc.: Deborah Carr, age 38, $463,702 total compensation
Auditors: Eide Bailly Llp Oklahoma City

LOCATIONS

HQ: Life Partners Holdings, Inc.
204 Woodhew, Waco, TX 76712
Phone: 254-751-7797   **Fax:** 254-751-1025
Web: www.lphi.net

COMPETITORS

Coventry First
Forum National Investments
Life Equity
Living Benefits
National Financial Partners

HISTORICAL FINANCIALS

Company Type: Public

Income Statement

FYE: February 28

	ASSETS ($ mil.)	NET INCOME ($ mil.)	INCOME AS % OF ASSETS	EMPLOYEES
2/09	52.4	27.2	51.9%	56
2/08	31.9	18.8	58.9%	40
2/07	16.6	3.4	20.5%	37
2/06	12.0	1.1	9.2%	37
2/05	10.3	2.7	26.2%	37
Annual Growth	50.2%	78.2%	—	10.9%

2009 Year-End Financials

Equity as % of assets: 84.0%
Return on assets: 64.5%
Return on equity: 81.4%
Long-term debt ($ mil.): 0.7
No. of shares (mil.): 14.9
Market value ($ mil.): 254.2
Dividends
Yield: 1.4%
Payout: 13.1%
Sales ($ mil.): 103.6
R&D as % of sales: —
Advertising as % of sales: —

Stock History

NASDAQ (GM): LPHI

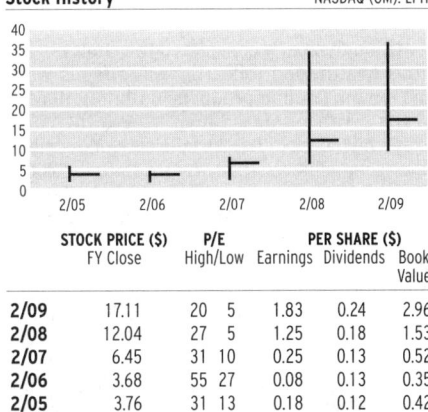

	STOCK PRICE ($) FY Close	P/E High/Low		PER SHARE ($) Earnings	Dividends	Book Value
2/09	17.11	20	5	1.83	0.24	2.96
2/08	12.04	27	5	1.25	0.18	1.53
2/07	6.45	31	10	0.25	0.13	0.52
2/06	3.68	55	27	0.08	0.13	0.35
2/05	3.76	31	13	0.18	0.12	0.42
Annual Growth	46.1%	—	—	78.6%	18.9%	62.8%

Life Time Fitness

Life Time Fitness wants to help you keep your New Year's resolutions. The company operates more than 80 exercise and recreation centers in about 15 states, including Illinois, Indiana, Michigan, Texas, and Virginia. Life Time Fitness facilities offer swimming pools, basketball and racquet courts, child care centers, spas, dining services, and climbing walls, in addition to some 400 pieces of exercise equipment. The company's members can access the facilities 24 hours a day, seven days a week. About 50 of the company's locations are larger than 100,000 sq. ft. and are designed to serve as an all-in-one sports and athletic club, professional fitness facility, family recreation center, and spa and resort.

In 2007 the company opened 10 locations. Life Time Fitness sold four health and wellness centers to Senior Housing Properties Trust for $100 million in 2008. Due to the economic recession, in 2008 the company introduced lower priced membership offerings and announced that it was reducing the number of planned new club openings in 2009 and 2010. As a result, Life Time eliminated some 100 corporate positions, mainly in its construction division.

The following year private equity firm Green Equity purchased a 9% stake in the company and announced plans to encourage Life Time to pursue options for enhancing shareholder value, including taking the company private, refinancing its debt, pursuing sale-leaseback transactions, and making acquisitions and divestitures. Chairman and CEO Bahram Akradi owns about 5% of Life Time Fitness.

EXECUTIVES

Chairman, President, and CEO: Bahram Akradi, age 47, $2,849,857 total compensation
EVP and CFO: Michael R. (Mike) Robinson, age 49, $876,288 total compensation
EVP: Mark L. Zaebst, age 49, $730,589 total compensation
EVP, General Counsel, and Secretary: Eric J. Buss, age 42, $682,010 total compensation
EVP and Chief Marketing Officer: Scott C. Lutz, age 50
SVP Operations: Jeff Zwiefel, age 46
VP Real Estate and Development: Dave DeCou
VP Corporate Business: John Reilly
VP Education: Pilar Gerasimo
VP and Corporate Controller: John Hugo
VP Management Information Services: Brent Zempel
VP Fitness and Nutrition Services: Mark Thom
VP Finance: Ken Cooper
Senior Director Corporate Communications: Jason Thunstrom
Auditors: Deloitte & Touche LLP

LOCATIONS

HQ: Life Time Fitness, Inc.
2902 Corporate Place, Chanhassen, MN 55317
Phone: 952-947-0000   **Fax:** 952-947-9137
Web: www.lifetimefitness.com

PRODUCTS/OPERATIONS

2008 Sales

	$ mil.	% of total
Membership dues	508.9	66
In-center revenue (trainers, sales of products, rentals)	218.2	28
Enrollment fees	26.6	4
Other	15.9	2
Total	**769.6**	**100**

Selected Amenities

Basketball courts
Cardiovascular training
Child care center
Free weights
Lap pool
Racquetball courts
Rock climbing
Saunas
Spa

Selected Services

Activities and events
  Cycling
  Pilates
  Swimming lessons
  Yoga
Locker and towel services
Massage therapy
Metabolic testing
Nutrition coaching
Personal training

COMPETITORS

24 Hour Fitness
Bally Total Fitness
Equinox Holdings
Gold's Gym
LA Fitness
The Sports Club
Town Sports International Holdings
Wellbridge
World Gym
YMCA

HISTORICAL FINANCIALS

Company Type: Public

Income Statement

	REVENUE ($ mil.)	NET INCOME ($ mil.)	NET PROFIT MARGIN	EMPLOYEES
12/08	769.6	71.8	9.3%	16,700
12/07	655.8	68.0	10.4%	15,000
12/06	511.9	50.6	9.9%	12,350
12/05	390.1	41.2	10.6%	9,500
12/04	312.0	25.3	8.1%	8,400
Annual Growth	25.3%	29.8%	—	18.7%

FYE: December 31

2008 Year-End Financials

Debt ratio: 107.6%
Return on equity: 11.7%
Cash ($ mil.): 10.8
Current ratio: 0.37
Long-term debt ($ mil.): 702.6
No. of shares (mil.): 41.4

Dividends
  Yield: 0.0%
  Payout: —
Market value ($ mil.): 536.0
R&D as % of sales: —
Advertising as % of sales: —

Stock History

NYSE: LTM

	STOCK PRICE ($) FY Close	P/E High/Low		PER SHARE ($) Earnings	Dividends	Book Value
12/08	12.95	26	4	1.83	0.00	15.77
12/07	49.68	37	26	1.78	0.00	13.83
12/06	48.51	39	27	1.37	0.00	9.48
12/05	38.09	36	21	1.13	0.00	7.44
12/04	25.88	31	23	0.87	0.00	6.06
Annual Growth	(15.9%)	—	—	20.4%	—	27.0%

Lifeway Foods

Kefir is not milk with a pedigree but it *is* cultured, and it's the lifeblood of Lifeway Foods. In addition to the yogurt-like dairy beverage called kefir, the company's products include Farmer's Cheese, Sweet Kiss (a sweetened cheese spread), and Soy-Treat, a soy-based kefir. A drinkable yogurt product is aimed at the Hispanic market under the brand name, La Fruta. Its Probugs offering, a flavored drink with live kefir cultures packaged in pouches, is aimed at children. A longtime staple in the dairy cases of health-food stores, Lifeway's products are available throughout the US, as well as internationally.

In 2008 the company broadened its operations to include product retailing, with the opening of its first kefir boutique cafe, Starfruit, located in Chicago. The company hopes to offer a healthier alternative to and take advantage of the popularity of similar frozen yogurt establishments. The following year it acquired the US's #2 kefir

maker, Philadelphia-based Fresh Made Dairy, for $14.5 million.

Chairman Ludmila Smolyansky and her family, including CEO Julie Smolyansky and CFO Edward Smolyansky, together own about 50% of the company; DS Waters owns about 21%.

HISTORY

Although mostly considered the choice of serious health-food folks, Lifeway's foods were and remain familiar products in Illinois, mainly in the greater Chicago area, where the company's own fleet of trucks take care of distribution. They achieved mainstream status in 2005, when they were introduced at Costco, Target, and Wal-Mart stores. Moving to non-US markets, they are also distributed in Canada (Ontario and Quebec provinces) and parts of Eastern Europe.

Lifeway acquired production facilities and a distribution center to better penetrate markets in the eastern US. It acquired Philadelphia-based cream cheese company Ilya's Farms in 2004 for about $575,000. In 2006 it bought kefir maker Helios for approximately $4 million in cash and stock. While no employees lost their jobs, production at Helios' Minnesota plant was transferred to Lifeway's Illinois site.

EXECUTIVES

Chairman: Ludmila Smolyansky, age 60, $248,476 total compensation
President, CEO, and Director: Julie Smolyansky, age 35, $329,376 total compensation
CFO, Chief Accounting Officer, and Controller; President and CEO Fresh Made Dairy: Edward P. (Ed) Smolyansky, age 29, $370,831 total compensation
VP Operations and Secretary: Valeriy (Val) Nikolenko, age 63, $145,086 total compensation
Auditors: Plante & Moran, PLLC

LOCATIONS

HQ: Lifeway Foods, Inc.
  6431 W. Oakton St., Morton Grove, IL 60053
Phone: 847-967-1010   **Fax:** 847-967-6558
Web: lifeway.net

PRODUCTS/OPERATIONS

Selected Products

Bambino (kefir-based cheese spread)
Basics Plus (enhanced kefir beverage)
Cream Cheese Gourmet (kefir-based cream cheese)
Elita (kefir-based cheese spread)
Golden Zesta (vegetable-based seasoning)
Helios Nutrition Organic Kefir (flavored kefir beverage)
It's Pudding (organic pudding)
Kefir (cultured milk beverage)
Kefir Starter (powdered mix)
Krestyanski Tworog (kefir-based cheese spread)
La Fruta (yogurt-based kefir)
La Fruta Cheese (kefir-based cheese)
Lassi (cultured beverage)
Lifeway's Farmer Cheese (kefir-based cheese)
Lifeway's Slim6 (low-fat kefir-based beverage)
Probugs (kefir-based beverage)
SoyTreat (soy-based kefir beverage)
Sweet Kiss (sweetened kefir-based cheese spread)
Tuscan (yogurt beverage)

Selected Subsidiaries

Fresh Made Dairy, Inc.
Helios Nutrition, Ltd.
LFI Enterprises, Inc.
Lifeway Foods Canada, LLC
Pride of Main Street Dairy, L.L.C.

COMPETITORS

Ben & Jerry's
Bruster's
Danone
Dean Foods
Dunkin
Freshëns
Galaxy Nutritional Foods
General Mills
KaleidoScoops

Kraft Foods
Odwalla
Organic Valley
Stonyfield Farm
Tofutti Brands
Vitasoy International
WhiteWave
YoCream

HISTORICAL FINANCIALS

Company Type: Public

Income Statement

	REVENUE ($ mil.)	NET INCOME ($ mil.)	NET PROFIT MARGIN	EMPLOYEES
12/08	44.5	1.9	4.3%	200
12/07	38.7	3.2	8.3%	120
12/06	27.7	2.9	10.5%	120
12/05	20.1	2.5	12.4%	86
12/04	16.3	2.1	12.9%	75
Annual Growth	28.5%	(2.5%)	—	27.8%

FYE: December 31

2008 Year-End Financials

Debt ratio: 11.8%
Return on equity: 7.3%
Cash ($ mil.): 0.3
Current ratio: 4.04
Long-term debt ($ mil.): 3.1
No. of shares (mil.): 16.8

Dividends
  Yield: —
  Payout: —
Market value ($ mil.): 150.6
R&D as % of sales: —
Advertising as % of sales: —

Stock History

NASDAQ (GM): LWAY

	STOCK PRICE ($) FY Close	P/E High/Low		PER SHARE ($) Earnings	Dividends	Book Value
12/08	8.98	141	49	0.11	—	1.57
12/07	11.83	109	45	0.19	—	1.54
12/06	9.35	64	30	0.17	—	1.41
12/05	6.22	61	24	0.15	—	1.19
12/04	4.57	118	27	0.12	—	1.07
Annual Growth	18.4%	—	—	(2.2%)	—	10.1%

LMI Aerospace

It don't mean a thing if it ain't got a wing. LMI Aerospace makes key airplane structures such as door and cockpit window frames, wing leading-edge skins, fuselage skins, and interior components. The Aerostructures segment fabricates, machines, finishes, and integrates more than 30,000 aluminum and specialty alloy components for commercial, corporate, and military aircraft. The Engineering Services segment (D3 Technologies) provides design, engineering, and program management services for aircraft. The Tempco Engineering unit serves the medical and semiconductor industries, as well as aircraft

manufacturers. Customers include Boeing, Gulfstream, and Sikorsky. CEO Ronald Saks owns about 17% of the company.

The volatility in the airline industry, compounded by military budget cuts and the Boeing strike, negatively impacted the company's commercial revenues. LMI made a move in 2009 to align its production to customer demand by reducing the number of employees in two plants by around 60 employees, representing approximately 6% of its Aerostructures segment workforce.

In 2009 LMI acquired 100% of Integrated Technologies (Intec) based in Everett, Washington. Intec provides materials testing, manufacturing, and design services for organic and metal composites and ceramics to the aerospace, defense and transportation industries. The acquisition of Intec supports the Aerostructures segment's trend toward the increased production of non-metallic products. In 2007 the company acquired D3 Technologies, a provider of engineering and design services to commercial and military aircraft, for $65 million.

The company has selected its strategic acquisitions with an eye toward expanding capabilities and technologies, rather than being product-focused. LMI believes the increased breadth of its technological capabilities will help it attract customers from a wider variety of industries. It wants to reduce its dependence on a select group of clients within a couple of industries. The company counts Bombardier, Spirit AeroSystems, and Vought among its customers.

EXECUTIVES

Chairman: Joseph Burstein, age 82
CEO and Director: Ronald S. (Ron) Saks, age 66, $385,884 total compensation
VP; President and CEO, D3 Technologies:
Ryan P. Bogan, age 35, $423,911 total compensation
VP, CFO, and Secretary: Lawrence E. (Ed) Dickinson, age 50, $295,142 total compensation
VP, Central Region: Robert T. (Bob) Grah, age 55, $326,899 total compensation
VP Human Resources and Organizational Development: Cindy Maness, age 58
CIO: Michael J. (Mike) Biffignani, age 54
Assistant Secretary and Director: Sanford S. Neuman, age 74
Director Program Management: Bruce Grimes
Auditors: BDO Seidman, LLP

LOCATIONS

HQ: LMI Aerospace, Inc.
411 Fountain Lakes Blvd., St. Charles, MO 63301
Phone: 636-946-6525 **Fax:** 636-949-1576
Web: www.lmiaerospace.com

PRODUCTS/OPERATIONS

2008 Sales

	$ mil.	% of total
Aerostructures	150.8	63
Engineering Services	89.9	37
Adjustments	(1.2)	—
Total	**239.5**	**100**

2008 Sales by Market

	% of total
Corporate & regional aircraft	35
Large commercial aircraft	36
Military	23
Technology	3
Other	3
Total	**100**

Selected Products

Auxiliary power units
Cockpit window-frame assemblies
Door components and assemblies and floorbeams
Fuselage skins and supports
Helicopter cabin and aft section components and assemblies
Interior component details
Landing-light lens assemblies
Leading-edge wing slats, flaps, and lens assemblies
Passenger and cargo door frames and supports
Structural sheet metal and extruded components
Thrust reversers and engine nacelles/cowlings
Wing panels and floor beams
Wing skins

Selected Services

Assembly
Distribution
Engineering services (design build)
Fabrication
Finishing
Kitting
Machining

COMPETITORS

AAR Corp.
Avcorp Industries
BE Aerospace
CPI Aerostructures
DeCrane
Ducommun
Goodrich Corp.
Magellan Aerospace
Synchronous Aerospace

HISTORICAL FINANCIALS

Company Type: Public

Income Statement

FYE: December 31

	REVENUE ($ mil.)	NET INCOME ($ mil.)	NET PROFIT MARGIN	EMPLOYEES
12/08	239.5	15.3	6.4%	1,350
12/07	168.5	13.2	7.8%	1,457
12/06	123.0	10.7	8.7%	916
12/05	101.1	5.2	5.1%	673
12/04	85.9	0.4	0.5%	662
Annual Growth	**29.2%**	**148.7%**	**—**	**19.5%**

2008 Year-End Financials

Debt ratio: 20.8%
Return on equity: 13.4%
Cash ($ mil.): 0.0
Current ratio: 3.99
Long-term debt ($ mil.): 25.5
No. of shares (mil.): 12.0
Dividends
Yield: 0.0%
Payout: —
Market value ($ mil.): 136.6
R&D as % of sales: —
Advertising as % of sales: —

Stock History

NASDAQ (GM): LMIA

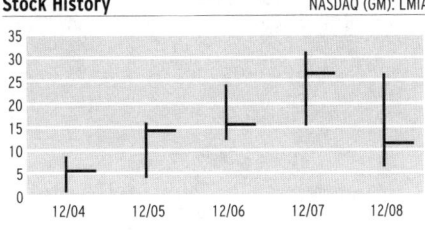

	STOCK PRICE ($) FY Close	P/E High	P/E Low	PER SHARE ($) Earnings	PER SHARE ($) Dividends	PER SHARE ($) Book Value
12/08	11.37	19	5	1.35	0.00	10.22
12/07	26.51	26	13	1.17	0.00	8.72
12/06	15.48	24	12	1.01	0.00	7.53
12/05	14.16	26	7	0.61	0.00	3.31
12/04	5.41	167	20	0.05	0.00	2.86
Annual Growth	**20.4%**	**—**	**—**	**128.0%**	**—**	**37.5%**

LoopNet, Inc.

Feeling out of the loop when it comes to commercial real estate? LoopNet provides information services to the commercial real estate market through its namesake Web site, LoopNet.com, an online marketplace that includes approximately 652,000 property listings. The company offers a free basic membership, as well as a subscription-based premium membership. LoopNet has about 3.2 million registered members and more than 77,000 premium members. The company also offers LoopLink, which helps real estate brokers integrate LoopNet listings into their own Web sites; BizBuySell, an online marketplace for operating businesses that are for sale; and commercial real estate network CityFeet.com.

Premium memberships cost about $65 per month. Such fees account for about 75% of LoopNet's business. In 2008 the company experienced the highest cancellation rate for premium memberships in its history, the result of an increase in membership prices, as well as the slowdown in the commercial real estate industry.

In 2008 the company expanded its offerings to include a software application and a Web site that covers an additional market (farmland). That year LoopNet purchased REApplications, a provider of brokerage operations software, for about $9 million, and LandAndFarm.com, an online marketplace for rural land, ranch, and agricultural property listings, for some $2 million.

The previous year LoopNet acquired online firm Cityfeet.com. The deal, worth about $15 million, added Cityfeet.com's online distribution network for commercial property listings to LoopNet's business. The Cityfeet Network distributes listings to content partners, such as Web sites of the *New York Times*, the *Boston Globe*, and the *Los Angeles Times*.

EXECUTIVES

Chairman and CEO: Richard J. (Rich) Boyle Jr., age 44, $926,992 total compensation
President and COO: Thomas Byrne, age 43
SVP Finance and Administration, CFO, and Secretary: Brent Stumme, age 48, $595,018 total compensation
SVP Corporate Development and Chief Strategy Officer: Jason Greenman, age 42, $556,170 total compensation
SVP Information Technology and CTO: Wayne Warthen, age 46, $492,230 total compensation
Public Relations: Cary Brazeman
Auditors: Ernst & Young LLP

LOCATIONS

HQ: LoopNet, Inc.
185 Berry St., Ste. 4000, San Francisco, CA 94107
Phone: 415-243-4200 **Fax:** 415-764-1622
Web: www.loopnet.com

PRODUCTS/OPERATIONS

Selected Offerings

BizBuySell (businesses for sale listings)
CityFeet (online commercial real estate network)
LoopLink (listing integration service)
LoopNet.com (commercial real estate listings)

COMPETITORS

CoStar Group
Fidelity National Financial
First American
First American CoreLogic
Market Leader
PropertyInfo

HISTORICAL FINANCIALS

Company Type: Public

Income Statement
FYE: December 31

	REVENUE ($ mil.)	NET INCOME ($ mil.)	NET PROFIT MARGIN	EMPLOYEES
12/08	86.1	18.3	21.3%	305
12/07	70.7	21.1	29.8%	266
12/06	48.4	15.5	32.0%	198
12/05	31.0	11.7	37.7%	138
12/04	17.0	3.7	21.8%	138
Annual Growth	50.0%	49.1%	—	21.9%

2008 Year-End Financials

Debt ratio: —
Return on equity: 17.1%
Cash ($ mil.): 61.3
Current ratio: 4.33
Long-term debt ($ mil.): —
No. of shares (mil.): 34.5
Dividends
Yield: 0.0%
Payout: 0.0%
Market value ($ mil.): 235.6
R&D as % of sales: —
Advertising as % of sales: —

Stock History
NASDAQ (GM): LOOP

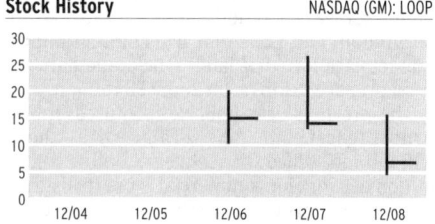

	STOCK PRICE ($) FY Close	P/E High/Low	PER SHARE ($) Earnings	Dividends	Book Value
12/08	6.82	32 10	0.49	0.00	2.68
12/07	14.05	51 25	0.52	0.00	3.53
12/06	14.98	50 26	0.40	0.00	2.61
Annual Growth	(32.5%)	— —	10.7%	—	1.4%

Louisiana Bancorp

Louisiana Bancorp's vault isn't filled with Mardi Gras doubloons, *chère*. The holding company owns the Bank of New Orleans, which offers standard retail banking products to individuals and small businesses, including deposit accounts, loans and mortgages, and credit cards. Residential mortgages represent about half of the bank's loan portfolio; commercial mortgages and land loans make up most of the rest.

Bank of New Orleans operates three locations and a loan office in the Crescent City; a fourth branch has been closed since being damaged by Hurricane Katrina in 2005.

The bank was founded in 1909 as Greater New Orleans Homestead.

EXECUTIVES

Chairman, President, and CEO: Lawrence J. LeBon III, age 60, $283,958 total compensation
CFO and SVP: John P. LeBlanc, age 41, $102,220 total compensation
VP and Installment Loan Manager: Mike Dardis
VP Mortgage Lending: Holly Callia
Marketing Manager: Holly E. Thoede
Commercial Lending Manager: John (Jack) Lyons
Human Resources Manager: Lindsey Gordon
Secretary and Director: Ivan J. Miestchovich, age 59
Manager, Magazine Branch: Diane Dalferes
Manager, Veterans Branch: Pat Berry
Manager, Transcontinental Branch: Phyllis Jacques
Auditors: LaPorte, Sehrt, Romig & Hand

LOCATIONS

HQ: Louisiana Bancorp, Inc.
1600 Veterans Blvd., Metairie, LA 70005
Phone: 504-834-1190
Web: www.bankofneworleans.net

COMPETITORS

Capital One
Citibank
GS Financial
Hancock Holding
Home Bank
IBERIABANK
JPMorgan Chase
Regions Financial
Teche Holding
Whitney Holding

HISTORICAL FINANCIALS

Company Type: Public

Income Statement
FYE: December 31

	ASSETS ($ mil.)	NET INCOME ($ mil.)	INCOME AS % OF ASSETS	EMPLOYEES
12/08	327.4	2.7	0.8%	65
12/07	270.9	2.6	1.0%	60
12/06	219.7	2.0	0.9%	58
Annual Growth	22.1%	16.2%	—	5.9%

2008 Year-End Financials

Equity as % of assets: 26.2%
Return on assets: 0.9%
Return on equity: 3.1%
Long-term debt ($ mil.): 76.7
No. of shares (mil.): 5.1
Market value ($ mil.): 64.7
Dividends
Yield: 0.0%
Payout: —
Sales ($ mil.): 10.4
R&D as % of sales: —
Advertising as % of sales: —

Stock History
NASDAQ (GM): LABC

	STOCK PRICE ($) FY Close	P/E High/Low	PER SHARE ($) Earnings	Dividends	Book Value
12/08	12.80	27 20	0.49	0.00	16.95
12/07	10.49	12 11	0.94	0.00	17.77
Annual Growth	22.0%	— —	(47.9%)	—	(4.6%)

LSB Industries

LSB Industries makes a wide variety of chemicals (including nitric acid) and climate-control products. Its chemicals segment makes nitrate fertilizers and acids for agricultural, mining, and industrial markets. The climate-control division makes hydronic fan coils and a variety of heat pumps. Additionally, its industrial products segment distributes industrial milling, drilling, turning, and fabricating machines. The company's chemical unit accounts for more than half of sales; geographically, pretty much all of its sales are within the US. CEO Jack Golsen and family members own about 40% of the firm, which conducts most of its business through subsidiary ThermaClime.

EXECUTIVES

Chairman and CEO: Jack E. Golsen, age 81, $1,458,200 total compensation
Vice Chairman and President; President, Climate Control Business: Barry H. Golsen, age 59, $681,992 total compensation
EVP Finance, CFO, and Director: Tony M. Shelby, age 68, $409,228 total compensation
EVP, Operations, and Director: David R. Goss, age 69, $359,363 total compensation
SVP and Treasurer: Jimmie D. (Jim) Jones, age 67
SVP, Secretary, and General Counsel: David M. Shear, age 50, $381,572 total compensation
VP and Principal Accounting Officer: Harold L. Rieker Jr., age 49
VP and Corporate Controller: Michael G. Adams, age 59
VP and Managing Counsel: Heidi Brown Shear
Investor Relations: Linda Latman
Auditors: Ernst & Young LLP

LOCATIONS

HQ: LSB Industries, Inc.
16 S. Pennsylvania Ave., Oklahoma City, OK 73107
Phone: 405-235-4546   **Fax:** 405-235-5067
Web: www.lsbindustries.com

2008 Sales

	$ mil.	% of total
US	711.9	95
Other countries	37.1	5
Total	**749.0**	**100**

PRODUCTS/OPERATIONS

2008 Sales

	$ mil.	% of total
Chemical		
Agricultural products	152.8	20
Mining products	108.4	15
Industrial acids & other chemicals	162.9	22
Climate Control		
Geothermal & water source heat pumps	191.0	25
Hydronic fan coils	83.5	11
Other HVAC products	36.9	5
Other	13.5	2
Total	**749.0**	**100**

COMPETITORS

Agrium
Continental Materials
Ercros
ShengdaTech
Terra Industries

HISTORICAL FINANCIALS

Company Type: Public

Income Statement
FYE: December 31

	REVENUE ($ mil.)	NET INCOME ($ mil.)	NET PROFIT MARGIN	EMPLOYEES
12/08	749.0	36.5	4.9%	1,878
12/07	586.4	46.9	8.0%	1,788
12/06	492.0	15.9	3.2%	1,565
12/05	396.7	5.1	1.3%	1,267
12/04	364.1	2.4	0.7%	1,240
Annual Growth	19.8%	97.5%	—	10.9%

2008 Year-End Financials

Debt ratio: 81.5%
Return on equity: 33.4%
Cash ($ mil.): 46.2
Current ratio: 2.58
Long-term debt ($ mil.): 103.6
No. of shares (mil.): 21.5

Dividends
Yield: 0.0%
Payout: —
Market value ($ mil.): 178.9
R&D as % of sales: —
Advertising as % of sales: —

Stock History
NYSE: LXU

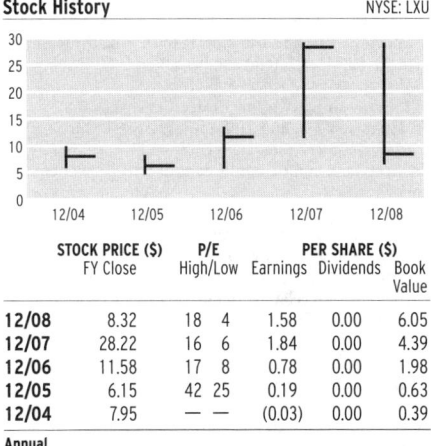

	STOCK PRICE ($) FY Close	P/E High/Low		PER SHARE ($) Earnings	Dividends	Book Value
12/08	8.32	18	4	1.58	0.00	6.05
12/07	28.22	16	6	1.84	0.00	4.39
12/06	11.58	17	8	0.78	0.00	1.98
12/05	6.15	42	25	0.19	0.00	0.63
12/04	7.95	—	—	(0.03)	0.00	0.39
Annual Growth	1.1%	—	—	—	—	98.4%

Lufkin Industries

Lufkin Industries is all geared up to help pump oil. Through its Oil Field division the company manufactures and services pumping units, automation equipment, and foundry castings. It also provides computer control equipment and analytical services used to maximize well efficiency. Through its Power Transmission unit, Lufkin Industries manufactures and services gearboxes (in power levels from 20 to 85,000 horsepower) used in large-scale industrial applications. In 2008 the company exited its commercial truck trailer manufacturing business in order to focus on its core oil field equipment and power transmission businesses.

As part of Lufkin Industries' vertical integration strategy, the Oil Field segment also operates an iron foundry to produce castings for new pumping units, and for third parties.

In 2009, in a move to boost its industry leading beam lift pumping business, Lufkin Industries acquired International Lift Systems, LLC, a Houston-based manufacturer of artificial lift systems for the oil and gas industry. It also bought Rotating Machinery Technology, Inc., a major turbo-machinery company.

EXECUTIVES

Chairman: Douglas V. Smith, age 67, $811,846 total compensation
President, CEO, and Director: John F. (Jay) Glick, age 57, $1,670,734 total compensation
VP, CFO, and Treasurer: Christopher L. (Chris) Boone, age 40, $452,512 total compensation
VP, Power Transmission Division: Terry L. Orr, age 64, $768,081 total compensation
VP, Manufacturing Technology: Scott H. Semlinger, age 56, $1,053,388 total compensation
VP, General Counsel, and Secretary: Paul G. Perez, age 64, $1,252,558 total compensation
VP, Oilfield Division: Mark E. Crews, age 53
Auditors: Deloitte & Touche LLP

LOCATIONS

HQ: Lufkin Industries, Inc.
601 S. Raguet St., Lufkin, TX 75904
Phone: 936-634-2211   **Fax:** 936-637-5272
Web: www.lufkin.com

Lufkin Industries operates manufacturing facilities in Lufkin, Texas, as well as in Argentina, Canada, and France.

2008 Sales

	$ mil.	% of total
North America		
US	469.3	63
Canada	33.3	5
Latin America	97.3	13
Europe	60.5	8
Middle East & North Africa	56.2	8
Other regions	24.6	3
Total	**741.2**	**100**

PRODUCTS/OPERATIONS

2008 Sales

	$ mil.	% of total
Oil field	551.8	74
Power transmission	189.4	26
Total	**741.2**	**100**

COMPETITORS

CE Franklin
Citation Corp.
INTERMET
MAN
Twin Disc
Weatherford International

HISTORICAL FINANCIALS

Company Type: Public

Income Statement
FYE: December 31

	REVENUE ($ mil.)	NET INCOME ($ mil.)	NET PROFIT MARGIN	EMPLOYEES
12/08	741.2	88.2	11.9%	3,000
12/07	597.2	74.2	12.4%	2,700
12/06	605.5	73.0	12.1%	3,000
12/05	492.2	44.5	9.0%	2,700
12/04	356.3	14.4	4.0%	2,300
Annual Growth	20.1%	57.3%	—	6.9%

2008 Year-End Financials

Debt ratio: —
Return on equity: 22.1%
Cash ($ mil.): 107.8
Current ratio: 4.34
Long-term debt ($ mil.): —
No. of shares (mil.): 14.9

Dividends
Yield: 2.9%
Payout: 16.9%
Market value ($ mil.): 513.3
R&D as % of sales: —
Advertising as % of sales: —

Stock History
NASDAQ (GS): LUFK

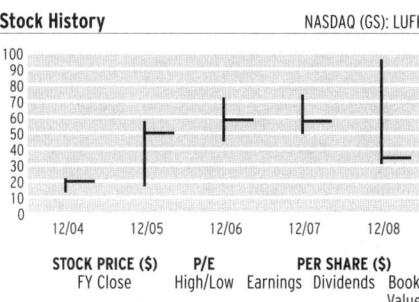

	STOCK PRICE ($) FY Close	P/E High/Low		PER SHARE ($) Earnings	Dividends	Book Value
12/08	34.50	16	5	5.92	1.00	27.82
12/07	57.29	15	10	4.92	0.88	25.85
12/06	58.08	15	9	4.83	0.62	22.06
12/05	49.87	19	6	3.03	0.38	17.55
12/04	19.82	20	13	1.03	0.36	14.04
Annual Growth	14.9%	—	—	54.8%	29.1%	18.6%

Lumber Liquidators

Thanks to the resurgence of hardwoods, Lumber Liquidators is in the money. The nation's largest specialty retailer of hardwood flooring, Lumber Liquidators sells more than 25 domestic and exotic wood species of both pre-finished and unfinished hardwood flooring from about 160 stores in more than 40 states. It also sells antique and reclaimed boards, laminate flooring, and installation accessories. Brands include Bellawood, Builder's Pride, Schön, and more. The company sells its products online, by catalog, and from its Virginia call center. Homeowners represent about 90% of Lumber Liquidators' customer base. The company was founded in 1993 by its chairman, Tom Sullivan.

Lumber Liquidators went public in 2007. Sullivan holds about a 40% stake in the company while Boston-based private equity firm TA Associates owns about 20%. The proceeds from the $110 million offering was used to pay down debt and fund the fast-growing company's expansion.

Lumber Liquidators planned to open about 30 stores in 2009. It added about 35 locations to its network in 2008. As part of its growth plan, the firm looks to open between 30 and 40 stores annually over the next several years. About two-thirds of Lumber Liquidators' stores have opened since 2003.

While about 40% of Lumber Liquidators' products come from the US, another 40% are sourced from the Asia/Pacific region. Bellawood brand products account for about one-quarter of the company's sales.

EXECUTIVES

Chairman: Thomas D. (Tom) Sullivan, age 48, $506,803 total compensation
President, CEO, and Director: Jeffrey W. (Jeff) Griffiths, age 58, $1,453,693 total compensation
CFO: Daniel E. Terrell, age 44, $419,474 total compensation
SVP Human Resources: E. Jean Matherne, age 54
SVP Store Operations: Robert W. Morrison, age 53, $554,628 total compensation
SVP Direct Marketing and Advertising: Marco Q. Pescara, age 44
SVP Merchandising: Andrew P. Shulklapper, age 46

SVP Information Technology and CTO: Seth P. Levy, age 51
SVP Supply Chain: Rick A. Boucher, age 51
SVP Supply Chain: Glenn Sharpe
VP Store Operations: Tyler C. Greenan, age 40, $641,320 total compensation
Secretary and General Corporate Counsel: E. Livingston B. Haskell, age 36
Auditors: Ernst & Young LLP

LOCATIONS

HQ: Lumber Liquidators, Inc.
3000 John Deere Rd., Toano, VA 23168
Phone: 757-259-4280
Web: www.lumberliquidators.com

2008 Stores

	No.
Florida	12
Texas	12
California	11
New York	8
Virginia	7
Georgia	6
Illinois	6
Pennsylvania	6
Michigan	5
Ohio	5
Washington	5
Alabama	4
Colorado	4
Massachusetts	4
New Jersey	4
North Carolina	4
Tennessee	4
Arizona	3
Louisiana	3
Maryland	3
Missouri	3
New Hampshire	3
South Carolina	3
Wisconsin	3
Arkansas	2
Connecticut	2
Indiana	2
Iowa	2
Kansas	2
Kentucky	2
Minnesota	2
Nevada	2
Oklahoma	2
Oregon	2
West Virginia	2
Other states	9
Total	**159**

PRODUCTS/OPERATIONS

2008 Sales

	% of total
Hardwood (solid & engineered)	64
Laminates	13
Bamboo & cork	11
Moldings & accessories	11
Other	1
Total	**100**

COMPETITORS

CCA Global
Floor and Décor Outlets
Flooring America
Home Depot
Lowe's
Master Tile
Sears

HISTORICAL FINANCIALS

Company Type: Public

Income Statement

FYE: December 31

	REVENUE ($ mil.)	NET INCOME ($ mil.)	NET PROFIT MARGIN	EMPLOYEES
12/08	482.2	22.1	4.6%	788
12/07	405.3	11.3	2.8%	670
12/06	332.1	12.9	3.9%	490
12/05	244.9	10.7	4.4%	490
12/04	171.8	8.0	4.7%	—
Annual Growth	**29.4%**	**28.9%**	**—**	**17.2%**

2008 Year-End Financials

Debt ratio: —
Return on equity: 21.4%
Cash ($ mil.): 35.1
Current ratio: 3.64
Long-term debt ($ mil.): —
No. of shares (mil.): 27.2
Dividends
  Yield: 0.0%
  Payout: —
Market value ($ mil.): 287.2
R&D as % of sales: —
Advertising as % of sales: —

Stock History

NYSE: LL

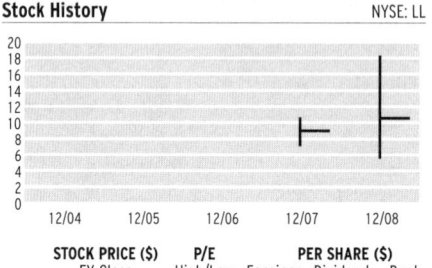

	STOCK PRICE ($) FY Close	P/E High/Low	PER SHARE ($) Earnings	Dividends	Book Value
12/08	10.56	22 7	0.82	0.00	4.21
12/07	8.99	22 15	0.48	0.00	3.39
Annual Growth	**17.5%**	**— —**	**70.8%**	**—**	**24.1%**

Luminex Corporation

Luminex Corporation sheds new light on genetic mysteries. The company's xMAP technology — which consists of instruments, software, and disposable microspheres, or tiny beads on which tests are performed — allows users to run up to 100 bioassays on one drop of fluid. Luminex licenses the technology to other life sciences companies which develop reagent-based tests to go with the instrumentation systems and then distribute them to end users, or use them to perform testing services for their customers. Luminex also develops some assays of its own. Its strategic partners include companies focused on drug discovery and biomedical research (Millipore) and clinical diagnostics (Bio-Rad, Inverness Medical).

The company makes money both on sales of its instrumentation systems to some 60 strategic partners and on royalties on the sales of xMAP-based assays and services developed by those partners. More than 30 companies have commercialized reagent-based tests using the xMAP technology, and they have distributed about 5,000 Luminex instrumentation sets to laboratories around the world. More than 85% of Luminex's sales and customers are in the US.

The company uses its Luminex Bioscience Group (LBG) and Luminex Molecular Diagnostics (LMD) divisions for in-house assay develop-

ment. The LMD segment was formed as a result of the acquisition of Tm Biosciences which has expertise in the areas of human genetic research, personalized medicine, and infectious disease.

In early 2008 the company launched xTAG Respiratory Viral Panel — the first FDA-cleared assay to simultaneously detect and identify 12 viruses and viral subtypes that together are responsible for more than 85% of respiratory viral infections. Going forward, the company intends to continue to develop new assay products to market to its strategic partners.

The company established an office in Shanghai, China, in 2008. The office there serves as the company's center of operations in Asia and expands Luminex's geographic reach.

In 2008 life sciences company Lambda represented about 20% of the company's revenue, while Bio-Rad Laboratories accounted for about 17%.

EXECUTIVES

Chairman: G. Walter Loewenbaum II, age 64
President, CEO, and Director: Patrick J. Balthrop Sr., age 53, $2,343,818 total compensation
SVP Operations: Michael F. Pintek
SVP Assay Group: Jeremy Bridge-Cook, age 40
VP Finance, CFO, and Treasurer: Harriss T. Currie, age 48, $578,782 total compensation
VP, Secretary, and General Counsel: David S. Reiter, age 43
VP Luminex Bioscience Group: Gregory J. Gosch, age 47, $567,547 total compensation
VP Sales and Marketing: Darin Leigh
VP Luminex Technical Operations: Andrew D. Ewing
VP Business Development and Strategic Planning: Russell W. Bradley, age 46, $546,480 total compensation
VP Manufacturing: Steve Back
VP Quality Assurance and Regulatory Affairs: Oliver H. Meek, age 58
VP Systems Research and Development: Timothy R. (Tim) Dehne, age 42
Manager Human Resources: Eddie Chien
Auditors: Ernst & Young LLP

LOCATIONS

HQ: Luminex Corporation
12212 Technology Blvd., Austin, TX 78727
Phone: 512-219-8020   **Fax:** 512-219-5195
Web: www.luminexcorp.com

2008 Sales

	$ mil.	% of total
US	89.4	86
Europe	9.3	9
Canada	2.2	2
Asia	1.2	1
Other	2.3	2
Total	**104.4**	**100**

PRODUCTS/OPERATIONS

2008 Sales

	$ mil.	% of total
Systems	28.1	27
Consumables	31.7	30
Assays	18.7	18
Royalties	14.9	14
Service contracts	5.4	5
Other	5.6	6
Total	**104.4**	**100**

COMPETITORS

Abbott Labs	Illumina
Affymetrix	Johnson & Johnson
Beckman Coulter	Life Technologies
Becton, Dickinson	Orchid Cellmark
Celera	Roche Diagnostics
Cepheid	Sequenom
GE Healthcare	

HISTORICAL FINANCIALS

Company Type: Public

Income Statement

FYE: December 31

	REVENUE ($ mil.)	NET INCOME ($ mil.)	NET PROFIT MARGIN	EMPLOYEES
12/08	104.4	3.1	3.0%	384
12/07	75.0	(2.7)	—	344
12/06	53.0	1.5	2.8%	303
12/05	42.3	(2.7)	—	185
12/04	35.9	(3.6)	—	161
Annual Growth	30.6%	—	—	24.3%

2008 Year-End Financials

Debt ratio: 1.5%
Return on equity: 2.1%
Cash ($ mil.): 81.6
Current ratio: 9.84
Long-term debt ($ mil.): 2.9
No. of shares (mil.): 41.8
Dividends
 Yield: 0.0%
 Payout: —
Market value ($ mil.): 892.8
R&D as % of sales: —
Advertising as % of sales: —

Stock History

NASDAQ (GM): LMNX

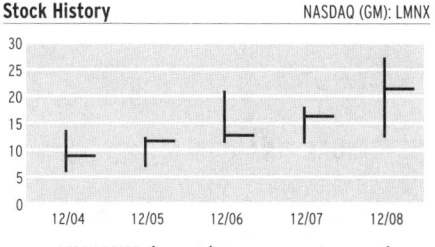

	STOCK PRICE ($) FY Close	P/E High/Low	Earnings	PER SHARE ($) Dividends	Book Value
12/08	21.36	338 157	0.08	0.00	4.65
12/07	16.24	— —	(0.08)	0.00	2.48
12/06	12.70	415 231	0.05	0.00	1.30
12/05	11.62	— —	(0.09)	0.00	1.07
12/04	8.88	— —	(0.12)	0.00	1.07
Annual Growth	24.5%	— —	—	—	44.6%

Mac-Gray Corporation

No change for laundry or copies? Mac-Gray operates debit card- and coin-operated washers and dryers in about 90,000 apartment buildings, condos, dorms, hotels, and public housing complexes in more than 40 states and the District of Columbia. It also supplies card- and coin-operated copiers for college and public libraries, as well as MicroFridge units (combo refrigerator, freezer, and microwave) for academic, military, and other housing facilities. In addition, Mac-Gray distributes equipment to laundromats, hotels, hospitals, and restaurants. Laundry facilities account for the majority of the company's earnings. CEO Stewart MacDonald and his family own about 30% of the firm, which was founded in 1927.

Following a proxy contest in mid-2009, Thomas Bullock was named chairman while MacDonald, who'd held the position since 1992, lost his seat. The clash had precipitated when a group of shareholders expressed their displeasure with the direction of the company, which had grown in size but not profitability. To turn things around, the board elected Bullock, a director since 2000, to take the helm. Bullock had been president and CEO of fruit juice producer Ocean Spray Cranberries before coming to Mac-Gray. He said MacDonald has expressed interest in rejoining the board after devoting time to his duties as CEO.

Although revenues were on the upswing in 2008, the company expects the US recession will cut into profits going forward. Among Mac-Gray's concerns: apartment vacancies are at their highest in more than two decades because of rising unemployment, competition for facilities contracts has surged, and tight credit markets have made financing a challenge for commercial customers. The firm is working to keep cash flowing by paying down its debts; by mid-2009 it had repaid more than $50 million in loans.

Mac-Gray has grown in recent years through several acquisitions. The company expanded its portfolio in 2008 by purchasing Automatic Laundry, the fourth-largest laundry facilities contractor in the US, for about $115 million. Automatic Laundry's operations are primarily located in southern and western states, and the acquisition complements Mac-Gray's business in existing markets. In 2007 the company bought 50-year-old Hof Service for nearly $45 million. Mac-Gray hopes to profit from Hof's operations, which are highly concentrated in Virginia, Baltimore, and Washington, DC.

The company has been phasing out its copier business, as more libraries have turned to offering their patrons electronic versions of reference materials. Copico, Mac-Gray's copier business, accounts for less than 1% of its revenues.

EXECUTIVES

Chairman: Thomas E. Bullock, age 62
CEO: Stewart G. MacDonald Jr., age 59
EVP, CFO, and Treasurer: Michael J. Shea, age 59
EVP Technology and Information Systems: Robert J. (Bob) Tuttle, age 56
EVP Operations: Philip Emma, age 52
EVP Sales: Neil F. MacLellan III, age 49
VP, General Counsel, and Secretary: Linda A. Serafini, age 57
Auditors: PricewaterhouseCoopers LLP

LOCATIONS

HQ: Mac-Gray Corporation
 404 Wyman St., Ste. 400, Waltham, MA 02451
Phone: 781-487-7600 **Fax:** 781-487-7601
Web: www.mac-gray.com

PRODUCTS/OPERATIONS

2008 Sales

	$ mil.	% of total
Laundry facilities management	304.8	84
MicroFridge sales	36.4	10
Laundry equipment sales	21.1	6
Reprographics facilities management	1.3	—
Total	**363.6**	**100**

COMPETITORS

Absocold	GE
Coinmach	PWS
DRYCLEAN USA	SANYO
FedEx Office	Wal-Mart

HISTORICAL FINANCIALS

Company Type: Public

Income Statement

FYE: December 31

	REVENUE ($ mil.)	NET INCOME ($ mil.)	NET PROFIT MARGIN	EMPLOYEES
12/08	363.6	0.5	0.1%	939
12/07	295.9	2.5	0.8%	831
12/06	279.3	0.9	0.3%	737
12/05	260.6	12.1	4.6%	743
12/04	182.7	5.3	2.9%	720
Annual Growth	18.8%	(44.6%)	—	6.9%

2008 Year-End Financials

Debt ratio: 302.0%
Return on equity: 0.5%
Cash ($ mil.): 18.8
Current ratio: 1.00
Long-term debt ($ mil.): 295.8
No. of shares (mil.): 13.6
Dividends
 Yield: —
 Payout: —
Market value ($ mil.): 85.5
R&D as % of sales: —
Advertising as % of sales: —

Stock History

NYSE: TUC

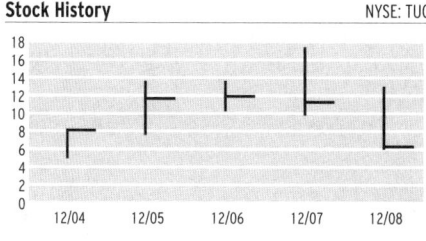

	STOCK PRICE ($) FY Close	P/E High/Low	Earnings	PER SHARE ($) Dividends	Book Value
12/08	6.28	322 153	0.04	—	7.19
12/07	11.26	96 55	0.18	—	7.19
12/06	11.90	225 173	0.06	—	6.73
12/05	11.65	15 8	0.91	—	6.51
12/04	8.09	20 13	0.40	—	5.58
Annual Growth	(6.1%)	— —	(43.8%)	—	6.6%

Mackinac Financial

Mackinac Financial Corporation caters to more than just the *capitalizationally* challenged. The financial institution is the holding company for mBank, which operates about a dozen branches in Michigan's Upper Peninsula and the northern part of the Lower Peninsula, as well as suburban Detroit. The bank provides traditional deposit and lending services to consumers and business clients. Commercial real estate loans account for about half of the company's loan portfolio, which also consists of agricultural, business, construction, and consumer loans. mBank offers treasury management products and services primarily to small to midsized businesses.

EXECUTIVES

Chairman and CEO; Chairman, mBank: Paul D. Tobias, age 58, $276,738 total compensation
President and Director; President and CEO, mBank: Kelly W. George, age 41, $280,758 total compensation
EVP and CFO, Mackinac Financial and mBank: Ernie R. Krueger, age 60, $215,025 total compensation
SVP Information Technology: Jake D. Martin
SVP Branch Administration Officer, mBank: Ann M. Stepp
SVP Branch Management, Retail Banking, and Deposits, mBank: Kevin D. Evans
SVP and Senior Credit Operations Officer, mBank: Tamara R. (Tammy) McDowell
VP Human Resources: Linda Bolda
Regional President, Northern Lower Peninsula, mBank: Andrew P. (Andy) Sabatine
Regional President, Upper Peninsula, mBank: Jack C. Frost
Corporate Secretary: Jennifer Lindroth
Auditors: Plante & Moran, PLLC

LOCATIONS

HQ: Mackinac Financial Corporation, Inc.
130 S. Cedar St., Manistique, MI 49854
Phone: 906-341-8401   **Fax:** 906-341-8578
Web: www.bankmbank.com

PRODUCTS/OPERATIONS

2008 Gross Revenues

	$ mil.	% of total
Interest		
Loans	22.6	77
Securities & other	2.0	7
Noninterest		
Service fees	0.8	3
Other	3.8	13
Total	**29.2**	**100**

COMPETITORS

Baylake
Citizens Republic Bancorp
CNB Corp. (MI)
Community Shores Bank
Fifth Third
Huntington Bancshares

HISTORICAL FINANCIALS

Company Type: Public

Income Statement			FYE: December 31	
	ASSETS ($ mil.)	NET INCOME ($ mil.)	INCOME AS % OF ASSETS	EMPLOYEES
12/08	451.4	1.9	0.4%	104
12/07	408.9	10.2	2.5%	109
12/06	382.8	1.7	0.4%	105
12/05	298.7	(7.4)	—	103
12/04	339.5	(1.6)	—	97
Annual Growth	**7.4%**	**—**	**—**	**1.8%**

2008 Year-End Financials

Equity as % of assets: 9.2%
Return on assets: 0.4%
Return on equity: 4.7%
Long-term debt ($ mil.): 36.2
No. of shares (mil.): 3.4
Market value ($ mil.): 15.0
Dividends
  Yield: 0.0%
  Payout: —
Sales ($ mil.): 17.5
R&D as % of sales: —
Advertising as % of sales: —

Stock History

NASDAQ (CM): MFNC

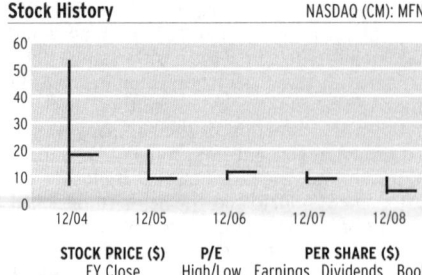

	STOCK PRICE ($) FY Close	P/E High/Low		PER SHARE ($) Earnings	Dividends	Book Value
12/08	4.40	17	7	0.55	0.00	12.15
12/07	8.98	4	3	2.96	0.00	11.50
12/06	11.50	23	18	0.50	0.00	8.42
12/05	9.10	—	—	(2.15)	0.00	7.77
12/04	17.97	—	—	(3.23)	0.00	10.16
Annual Growth	**(29.7%)**	**—**	**—**	**—**	**—**	**4.6%**

Maine & Maritimes Corporation

Maine & Maritimes (MAM, formerly Maine Public Service) is the consumer's main hope for smooth sailing in the waters of regional electricity supply. A holding company formed by electric utility Maine Public Service (MPS), which is now Maine & Maritimes' primary subsidiary, it transmits and distributes electricity to some 35,000 customers in a service area that encompasses 73,000 people in northern Maine. MAM originally operated a range of energy-related businesses but has since refocused on its utility operations. With the liberalization of the state's energy market, Maine & Maritimes has sold its regulated power generation assets.

It also owns former MPS subsidiary Energy Atlantic, which was formed to market power and provide energy-related services to retail customers in Maine's deregulated market; the unit is currently inactive due to a lack of profitability. Discontinued subsidiaries include The Maricor Group (engineering and other energy-related services in the US and Canada) and Maricor Technologies. The company sold the assets of Maricor Technologies in 2007. It also had owned 50% of Maricor Properties (real estate in Canada) but divested that stake in 2008 in another move toward focusing on utility-related businesses.

EXECUTIVES

Chairman: Richard G. (Rick) Daigle, age 62
Vice Chairman: Nathan L. Grass, age 71
President, CEO, and Director: Brent M. Boyles, age 52, $248,938 total compensation
SVP, CFO, Treasurer, and Assistant Secretary: Michael I. Williams, age 42, $187,175 total compensation
VP, General Counsel, Secretary, and Clerk; VP, General Counsel, Secretary, and Clerk, Maine Public Service Company and Director, General Counsel, Secretary, and Clerk, MAM Utility Services: Patrick C. Cannon, age 37, $166,489 total compensation
VP Information Technology and Customer Service: Michael A. (Mike) Eaton, age 45

VP Engineering and Operations; VP Engineering and Operations, Maine & Maritimes Corporation; VP Engineering and Operations, Maine Public Service Company and MAM Utility Service Group: Tim D. Brown, age 49
VP Accounting, Controller, and Assistant Treasurer: Randi J. Arthurs, age 29
Director Communications, Board Relations, and Economic Development: Virginia R. Joles, age 57
Director Human Resources and Risk Management: Frank E. Smith
Director Field Services, Maine Public Service: Stan T. Hartin, age 47
Auditors: Vitale, Caturano & Company, Ltd.

LOCATIONS

HQ: Maine & Maritimes Corporation
209 State St., Presque Isle, ME 04769
Phone: 207-760-2499   **Fax:** 207-760-2419
Web: www.maineandmaritimes.com

PRODUCTS/OPERATIONS

2008 Sales

	$ mil.	% of total
Regulated electric utility	36.9	82
Other	8.4	18
Total	**45.3**	**100**

COMPETITORS

Bangor Hydro-Electric
Bay State Gas
Central Vermont Public Service
Con Edison
Iberdrola USA
Integrys Energy Group
Northeast Utilities
PPL Corporation

HISTORICAL FINANCIALS

Company Type: Public

Income Statement				FYE: December 31
	REVENUE ($ mil.)	NET INCOME ($ mil.)	NET PROFIT MARGIN	EMPLOYEES
12/08	45.3	4.6	10.2%	138
12/07	37.5	1.6	4.3%	131
12/06	35.6	(5.9)	—	218
12/05	40.0	(0.2)	—	219
12/04	37.1	1.3	3.5%	207
Annual Growth	**5.1%**	**37.2%**	**—**	**(9.6%)**

2008 Year-End Financials

Debt ratio: 56.4%
Return on equity: 10.5%
Cash ($ mil.): 1.8
Current ratio: 0.94
Long-term debt ($ mil.): 25.4
No. of shares (mil.): 1.7
Dividends
  Yield: 0.1%
  Payout: 1.8%
Market value ($ mil.): 64.7
R&D as % of sales: —
Advertising as % of sales: —

Stock History

NYSE Alternext: MAM

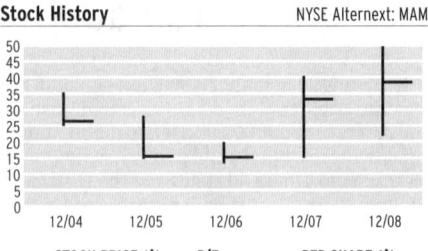

	STOCK PRICE ($) FY Close	P/E High/Low		PER SHARE ($) Earnings	Dividends	Book Value
12/08	38.49	18	8	2.75	0.05	26.78
12/07	33.25	41	16	0.98	0.00	25.53
12/06	15.18	—	—	(3.62)	0.00	24.69
12/05	15.49	—	—	(0.13)	0.75	28.41
12/04	26.35	43	31	0.81	1.34	28.63
Annual Growth	**9.9%**	**—**	**—**	**35.7%**	**(56.0%)**	**(1.7%)**

MainSource Financial

MainSource Financial wants to be the main source of financial services for residents and businesses in Indiana and beyond. It is the holding company of MainSource Bank, MainSource Bank of Illinois, and MainSource Bank — Ohio, which together operate about 80 branches. The banks offers deposit and lending products as well as trust and insurance services. The company also operates some 10 insurance offices in Indiana. Real estate loans account for three-quarters of MainSource Financial's lending portfolio, which also includes other commercial and consumer loans.

The company has made several acquisitions over the years, including the 2005 purchase of National City Corporation's The Madison Bank & Trust Company as well as the 2006 purchase of Union Community Bancorp and a handful of branches from First Financial Corporation. Also in 2006 MainSource Financial entered the Ohio market with the acquisition of Peoples Ohio Financial. The company expanded into Kentucky via the purchase of 1st Independence Financial Group in 2008.

EXECUTIVES

Chairman: Robert E. Hoptry, age 70,
$187,162 total compensation
President, CEO, and Director: Archie M. Brown Jr.,
age 48, $119,777 total compensation
SVP and COO: Jeffrey C. (Jeff) Smith, age 55,
$202,348 total compensation
SVP, CFO, and Secretary: James M. (Jamie) Anderson,
age 35, $204,133 total compensation
SVP and Chief Banking Officer: Daryl R. Tressler,
$254,725 total compensation
Chief Credit Officer: William J. (Bill) Goodwin
**Chairman, President, and CEO, MainSource Bank of
Illinois:** W. Brent Hoptry
**President, MainSource Title; SVP Retail Lending,
MainSource Bank of Indiana:** Mark W. Dunevant
President and CEO, MainSource Bank of Ohio:
David J. Dippold
President and CEO, MainSource Insurance:
Jerry J. Vollmer

LOCATIONS

HQ: MainSource Financial Group, Inc.
2105 N. State Rd. 3 Bypass, Greensburg, IN 47240
Phone: 812-663-6734   **Fax:** 812-663-4812
Web: www.mainsourcefinancial.com

PRODUCTS/OPERATIONS

2008 Gross Revenues

	$ mil.	% of total
Interest		
Loans & fees	118.4	68
Investment securities	26.1	15
Other	0.2	—
Noninterest		
Service charges on deposit accounts	14.6	8
Interchange income	3.6	2
Mortgage banking	2.6	1
Other	8.9	6
Total	**174.4**	**100**

COMPETITORS

Fifth Third
First Merchants
German American Bancorp
Indiana Community Bancorp
Integra Bank
KeyCorp
Old National Bancorp
U.S. Bancorp

HISTORICAL FINANCIALS

Company Type: Public

Income Statement

FYE: December 31

	ASSETS ($ mil.)	NET INCOME ($ mil.)	INCOME AS % OF ASSETS	EMPLOYEES
12/08	2,899.8	19.2	0.7%	915
12/07	2,536.4	21.9	0.9%	805
12/06	2,429.8	22.2	0.9%	829
12/05	1,645.6	16.2	1.0%	617
12/04	1,549.4	16.8	1.1%	645
Annual Growth	**17.0%**	**3.4%**	**—**	**9.1%**

2008 Year-End Financials

Equity as % of assets: 10.3%
Return on assets: 0.7%
Return on equity: 6.8%
Long-term debt ($ mil.): 483.0
No. of shares (mil.): 20.1
Market value ($ mil.): 312.1
Dividends
  Yield: 2.8%
  Payout: 43.0%
Sales ($ mil.): 117.2
R&D as % of sales: —
Advertising as % of sales: —

Stock History

NASDAQ (GS): MSFG

	STOCK PRICE ($) FY Close	P/E High/Low		PER SHARE ($) Earnings	Dividends	Book Value
12/08	15.50	24	12	1.00	0.43	14.90
12/07	15.56	16	12	1.17	0.56	13.12
12/06	16.94	14	12	1.29	0.53	12.58
12/05	17.00	19	13	1.23	0.50	8.00
12/04	22.74	18	11	1.41	0.45	6.12
Annual Growth	**(9.1%)**	**—**	**—**	**(8.2%)**	**(1.1%)**	**24.9%**

Malvern Federal Bancorp

Malvern Federal Bancorp was formed in 2008 to be the holding company for Malvern Federal Savings Bank, which has been in business since 1887. The bank operates seven financial centers in Chester County in southeastern Pennsylvania, west of Philadelphia. It offers standard deposit services such as checking and savings accounts, certificates of deposit, and retirement plans. The community-oriented institution has traditionally been a leading originator of residential home loans in Chester County, but has been shifting its focus toward issuing more commercial real estate, construction, and consumer loans.

EXECUTIVES

Chairman: F. Claire Hughes Jr., age 65,
$163,241 total compensation
Vice Chairman: John B. Yerkes Jr., age 70
President and CEO: Ronald Anderson, age 53,
$262,954 total compensation
EVP and Chief Administrative Officer:
Gerard M. McTear Jr., age 46,
$164,408 total compensation
SVP and CFO: Dennis Boyle, age 57,
$221,936 total compensation
SVP Operations, Malvern Federal Savings Bank:
Richard J. Fuchs, age 59
SVP and Chief Lending Officer: William E. Hughes Jr.,
age 52, $163,241 total compensation
Director Information Technology: Kenneth J. Camarda
Director Marketing: Scott Sterling
VP Deposit Services: Stephanie J. Tagye
VP Consumer Lending: Linda M. Laurent
VP Business Banking: Kyle Stewart

LOCATIONS

HQ: Malvern Federal Bancorp, Inc.
42 E. Lancaster Ave., Paoli, PA 19301
Phone: 610-644-9400   **Fax:** 610-644-1943
Web: www.malvernfederal.com

PRODUCTS/OPERATIONS

2009 Gross Revenues

	$ mil.	% of total
Interest		
Loans	33.7	92
Investment securities	0.9	2
Other	0.1	—
Noninterest		
Service charges & other fees	1.4	4
Other	0.6	2
Total	**36.7**	**100**

COMPETITORS

Bank of America
Bryn Mawr Bank Corp.
Citizens Financial Group
M&T Bank
National Penn Bancshares
PNC Financial
Sovereign Bank

HISTORICAL FINANCIALS

Company Type: Public

Income Statement

FYE: September 30

	REVENUE ($ mil.)	NET INCOME ($ mil.)	NET PROFIT MARGIN	EMPLOYEES
9/09	36.7	1.0	2.7%	95
9/08	35.3	1.4	4.0%	93
9/07	34.2	2.4	7.0%	93
9/06	31.7	3.2	10.1%	85
9/05	27.0	2.5	9.3%	85
Annual Growth	**8.0%**	**(20.5%)**	**—**	**2.8%**

Net Income History

NASDAQ (GM): MLVF

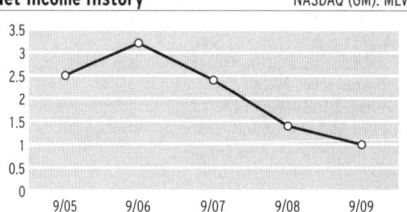

Martek Biosciences

Martek Biosciences' nutritional and pharmaceutical products promote the popularity of pond scum. The firm has developed nutritional oils from microalgae and fungi for use in baby formula (the oils provide fatty acids naturally present in human milk). Its oils, branded *life'sDHA* and *life'sARA*, are made from omega-3 fatty acid DHA (docosahexaenoic acid) and omega-6 fatty acid ARA (arachidonic acid). The company licenses the oils to manufacturers of formula and nutritional products for infants. Martek also licenses its patented oils for use in dietary supplements, nutritional drinks, cereals, and dairy products. It also provides contract manufacturing of specialty chemicals, vitamins, and agricultural products.

Martek's major customers include Mead Johnson (which accounts for more than 35% of sales), Abbott Laboratories, Nestlé, and Pfizer (through the former Wyeth consumer unit). In all, Martek has agreements with about 30 infant formula manufacturers that market products in more than 75 countries. The company is the sole supplier of DHA used in infant formula in the US, and its products are used in about 75% of infant formulas globally.

In 2007 it updated its agreement with Abbott to remain the exclusive supplier of nutritional oils for Abbott's Similac infant formula products until 2011, despite Abbott's having received FDA approval to use fish-oil derived DHA products in its US formulas.

Martek Biosciences has DHA oil manufacturing facilities in Kentucky and South Carolina. Its contract manufacturing operation, located at its South Carolina plant, offers third parties the fermentation capabilities used by the company to grow microalgae used in the production of *life'sDHA*. The company is reducing the scale of its contract manufacturing operations to focus on its more profitable oils business. The company uses a third-party manufacturer, DSM, for most of its ARA oil production.

The company is also researching additional applications for its products, such as investigating the benefits of DHA against neurological, cardiovascular, and vision disorders.

EXECUTIVES

Chairman: Robert J. (Bob) Flanagan, age 52
CEO and Director: Steve Dubin, age 56,
  $1,175,548 total compensation
President: David M. Abramson, age 56,
  $913,091 total compensation
EVP and COO: Peter A. Nitze, age 51,
  $1,055,523 total compensation
EVP Finance and Administration, CFO, and Treasurer:
  Peter L. Buzy, age 49, $912,120 total compensation
SVP, General Counsel, and Secretary: David M. Feitel,
  age 46
SVP Manufacturing: Barney B. Easterling, age 64,
  $742,741 total compensation
VP and Chief Scientific Officer: Norman Salem Jr.
VP Commercial: Angela Tsetsis
VP Administration: Pat Francis
VP Sales and Marketing: Joseph M. Buron
Investor Relations: Kyle Stults
Auditors: Ernst & Young LLP

LOCATIONS

HQ: Martek Biosciences Corporation
  6480 Dobbin Rd., Columbia, MD 21045
Phone: 410-740-0081   **Fax:** 410-740-2985
Web: www.martekbio.com

PRODUCTS/OPERATIONS

2009 Sales

	$ mil.	% of total
Product sales	329.1	95
Contract manufacturing	16.1	5
Total	**345.2**	**100**

COMPETITORS

AMS Health Sciences
BASF SE
Cargill
Cyanotech
DSM
GSK Italy
Lonza
Mera
NAI
Simplexity Health
Suntory Holdings

HISTORICAL FINANCIALS

Company Type: Public

Income Statement

FYE: October 31

	REVENUE ($ mil.)	NET INCOME ($ mil.)	NET PROFIT MARGIN	EMPLOYEES
10/09	345.2	40.6	11.8%	587
10/08	352.4	37.7	10.7%	569
10/07	306.8	32.0	10.4%	515
10/06	270.7	17.8	6.6%	506
10/05	217.9	15.3	7.0%	582
Annual Growth	**12.2%**	**27.6%**	**—**	**0.2%**

2009 Year-End Financials

Debt ratio: 0.1%
Return on equity: 6.6%
Cash ($ mil.): 141.1
Current ratio: 9.74
Long-term debt ($ mil.): 0.4
No. of shares (mil.): 33.3
Dividends
  Yield: —
  Payout: —
Market value ($ mil.): 597.5
R&D as % of sales: —
Advertising as % of sales: —

Stock History

NASDAQ (GS): MATK

	STOCK PRICE ($) FY Close	P/E High/Low		PER SHARE ($) Earnings	Dividends	Book Value
10/09	17.96	26	13	1.22	—	19.12
10/08	29.83	35	20	1.13	—	17.69
10/07	30.55	32	20	0.98	—	15.98
10/06	23.72	68	37	0.55	—	14.89
10/05	30.87	147	59	0.48	—	14.10
Annual Growth	**(12.7%)**	**—**	**—**	**26.3%**	**—**	**7.9%**

Masimo Corporation

Masimo hopes to become a noble in the pulse oximetry monitoring market. The company's Signal Extraction Technology (SET) noninvasively monitors arterial blood-oxygen saturation levels and pulse rates in patients. Masimo's product range offers pulse oximeters in both handheld and stand-alone (bedside) form. Product benefits include provision of real-time information and elimination of signal interference, such as patient movements. The company primarily markets its products globally through direct sales representatives and distributors. It also licenses SET-based products to approximately 50 medical equipment manufacturers, including Cardinal Health, Medtronic, Welch Allyn, and Zoll Medical.

Masimo is using the proceeds from its 2007 IPO on capital and equipment expenses, as well as to develop additional products. Some of the funds may also go towards acquisitions. Product enhancements have included the 2007 launch of a monitoring capability to detect methemoglobin (a form of hemoglobin that can cause a lack of oxygen in the blood), and the 2008 addition of total hemoglobin (oxygen in red blood cells) measurement.

The company is also working to expand its targeted markets outside of its traditional emergency and critical care settings to include general care areas of hospitals, as well as non-hospital environments. While the Americas account for a majority of revenues, Masimo is working to expand its operations in the Americas, Europe, Asia, Africa, Australia, and the Middle East.

Most of the company's sales are conducted through its direct sales force and wholesale distributors like Owens & Minor. Original equipment manufacturers (OEM) that resell or incorporate Masimo's products account for about 20% of sales.

CEO Joe Kiani, who founded Masimo in 1989, holds 9% of the company's stock.

EXECUTIVES

Chairman, CEO, and Acting CTO: Joe E. Kiani, age 44,
  $2,397,778 total compensation
EVP Business Development: David Goodman
EVP and CFO: Mark P. de Raad, age 49,
  $734,100 total compensation
EVP Operations and CIO: Yongsam Lee, age 44,
  $610,074 total compensation
EVP Marketing: Paul R. Jansen
EVP Medical Affairs: Michael O'Reilly, age 56,
  $646,349 total compensation
EVP Engineering: Anand Sampath, age 42
EVP Human Capital, General Counsel and Secretary:
  Stephen M. (Steve) Moran, age 52
VP U.S. Hospital Sales: Stephen Paul, age 38
President, International: Jon Coleman, age 45
President, Masimo Americas: Rick Fishel, age 50
Manager Public Relations: Dana Banks
Auditors: Grant Thornton LLP

LOCATIONS

HQ: Masimo Corporation
40 Parker, Irvine, CA 92618
Phone: 949-297-7000 **Fax:** 949-297-7001
Web: www.masimo.com

PRODUCTS/OPERATIONS

2008 Sales

Product	$ mil.	% of total
North & South America	200.1	65
Europe, Middle East & Africa	37.4	12
Asia & Australia	21.4	7
Royalty & license fees	48.2	16
Total	**307.1**	**100**

Selected OEM Customers

Atom Medical Corporation
Bitmos Medizintechnik GmbH
Cardinal Health
Datascope Corporation
GE Healthcare
GeTeMed GmbH
Invivo Research Incorporated
Ivy Biomedical Corporation
Kohken Medical Co., Ltd.
Medtronic, Inc.
Respironics, Inc.
Schiller AG
Spacelabs Healthcare
Welch Allyn Protocol, Inc.
ZOLL Medical Corporation

Selected Products

IntelliVue
RadLink
RadNet
Rainbow SET oximeters (Radical and Rad series,
    provides CO monitoring)
SafetyNet
SET oximeter sensors
SET oximeters (Radical and Rad series)

COMPETITORS

Bio-logic
Covidien
Criticare
GE Healthcare
Mindray
Philips Healthcare
Siemens Healthcare
Somanetics
Thoratec Corp

HISTORICAL FINANCIALS

Company Type: Public

Income Statement

FYE: December 31

	REVENUE ($ mil.)	NET INCOME ($ mil.)	NET PROFIT MARGIN	EMPLOYEES
12/08	307.1	31.9	10.4%	1,739
12/07	256.3	37.4	14.6%	1,348
12/06	224.3	96.1	42.8%	1,224
12/05	107.9	33.4	31.0%	1,324
12/04	69.4	(3.8)	—	—
Annual Growth	**45.0%**	**—**	**—**	**9.5%**

2008 Year-End Financials

Debt ratio: 0.1%
Return on equity: 17.3%
Cash ($ mil.): 146.9
Current ratio: 3.54
Long-term debt ($ mil.): 0.2
No. of shares (mil.): 57.7
Dividends
  Yield: 0.0%
  Payout: —
Market value ($ mil.): 1,721.4
R&D as % of sales: —
Advertising as % of sales: —

Stock History

NASDAQ (GS): MASI

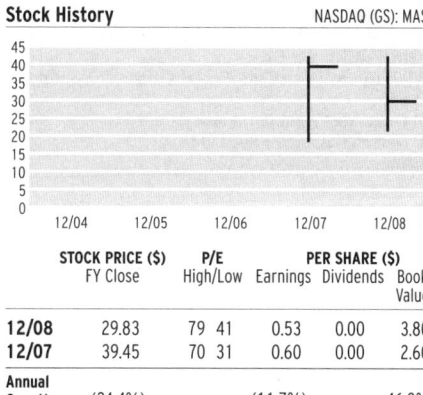

	STOCK PRICE ($) FY Close	P/E High/Low		PER SHARE ($) Earnings	Dividends	Book Value
12/08	29.83	79	41	0.53	0.00	3.80
12/07	39.45	70	31	0.60	0.00	2.60
Annual Growth	**(24.4%)**	**—**	**—**	**(11.7%)**	**—**	**46.2%**

Maxygen, Inc.

Maxygen dedicates itself to maximizing the potential of protein-based pharmaceuticals. The development-stage biotechnology company is creating improved versions of proven protein compounds to treat serious diseases. The company's lead candidate MAXY-4 is being developed in partnership with Astellas Pharma, as a treatment for rheumatoid arthritis and other autoimmune diseases. Another leading candidate, MAXY-G34 is in clinical trials; it is a bio-engineered version of a natural protein that stimulates the production of white blood cells for treatment of neutropenia, or the low white blood cell count often caused by chemotherapy treatments.

Maxygen expanded its relationship with Astellas in 2009 by forming a discovery, research, and development joint venture. Under terms of the agreement most of Maxygen's R&D operations and staff transferred to the new joint venture called Perseid Therapeutics. Maxygen is reducing its corporate and administrative staff as part of the restructuring, with CEO Russell Howard and other key executives leaving the company and director James Sulat taking on the roles of CEO and CFO.

Maxygen owns about 80% of the joint venture, but Astellas has the option to buy all of Maxygen's ownership interest over the next three years. The JV is run by Maxygen's chief business officer, Grant Yonehiro.

The deal with Astellas comes after Maxygen hit a patch of low capital in late 2008. While hunting for a new development partner to share manufacturing costs, the company has announced that it will cut back 30% of its workforce and put further development of the drug on hold.

The company had been working with Roche on two candidates: a hemophilia treatment dubbed MAXY-VII and MAXY-alpha, a potential hepatitis C therapy. Roche bowed out of both deals in 2007, however. Another collaborator, InterMune, halted development of MAXY-gamma, a next-generation version of interferon gamma.

Following the termination of the deals, Maxygen decided to consolidate some R&D activities at its Redwood City, California, facility and shut down research at its Denmark subsidiary.

Maxygen planned to continue development of its MAXY-VII hemophilia treatment on its own, but instead sold the drug to Bayer Healthcare in

2008. Bayer paid $90 million up front (with the potential for $30 million more in milestone payments down the road) for MAXY-VII, as well as the rights to use Maxygen's MolecularBreeding genetic screening technology.

Outside its core protein-based research, Maxygen has a preclinical program aimed at finding a preventative HIV vaccine. The research is funded by grants from the National Institutes of Health and Department of Defense.

Maxygen once had biotech interests in markets besides pharmaceuticals, but it has sold off most of those operations to focus on drug development. It sold plant sciences subsidiary Verdia to DuPont and has divested most of its stake in Codexis, once the company's wholly owned chemicals subsidiary; Maxygen still owns about one-fourth of the company. It also sold Avidia, a biotech company developing peptide drugs for cancer and other conditions, to Amgen in 2006.

Maxygen was spun off from Affymax (which at the time was a subsidiary of what is now GlaxoSmithKline) in 1997. GlaxoSmithKline still owns about 18% of the company.

EXECUTIVES

Chairman: Isaac Stein, age 62
CEO, CFO, and Director: James R. (Jim) Sulat, age 59
Public Relations: Linda Chrisman
Attorney-In-Fact: John M. Borkholder
Auditors: Ernst & Young LLP

LOCATIONS

HQ: Maxygen, Inc.
515 Galveston Dr., Redwood City, CA 94063
Phone: 650-298-5300 **Fax:** 650-364-2715
Web: www.maxygen.com

2008 Sales

	$ mil.	% of total
US	96.3	96
Other countries	4.4	4
Total	**100.7**	**100**

PRODUCTS/OPERATIONS

Selected Product Candidates

MAXY-G34 (neutropenia)
MAXY-VII (hemophilia)

COMPETITORS

Amgen	Novartis
Bristol-Myers Squibb	Novo Nordisk
Eli Lilly	Pfizer
Genentech	Sanofi-Aventis
GlaxoSmithKline	Vical
Human Genome Sciences	ZymoGenetics
Merck	

HISTORICAL FINANCIALS

Company Type: Public

Income Statement

FYE: December 31

	REVENUE ($ mil.)	NET INCOME ($ mil.)	NET PROFIT MARGIN	EMPLOYEES
12/08	100.7	30.3	30.1%	72
12/07	23.2	(49.3)	—	96
12/06	25.0	(16.5)	—	151
12/05	14.5	(35.1)	—	144
12/04	16.3	9.3	57.1%	230
Annual Growth	**57.7%**	**34.4%**	**—**	**(25.2%)**

Debt ratio: —
Return on equity: 17.4%
Cash ($ mil.): 154.9
Current ratio: 13.22
Long-term debt ($ mil.): —
No. of shares (mil.): 38.5

Dividends
  Yield: 0.0%
  Payout: —
  Market value ($ mil.): 343.0
  R&D as % of sales: —
  Advertising as % of sales: —

Stock History   NASDAQ (GM): MAXY

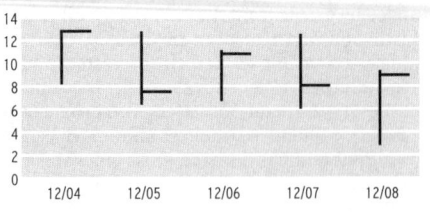

	Stock Price ($) FY Close	P/E High/Low		Per Share ($) Earnings	Dividends	Book Value
12/08	8.92	11	4	0.81	0.00	5.06
12/07	8.03	—	—	(1.34)	0.00	3.99
12/06	10.77	—	—	(0.46)	0.00	4.94
12/05	7.51	—	—	(0.52)	0.00	5.13
12/04	12.79	53	34	0.24	0.00	5.50
Annual Growth	(8.6%)	—	—	35.5%	—	(2.1%)

Meadowbrook Insurance Group

Meadowbrook Insurance, operating through subsidiaries including Star Insurance and Savers Property and Casualty Insurance, provides a variety of alternative risk management programs and services to high-risk or self-insured clients. Focused on the niche of trade groups and associations, the company tailors its products to serve the needs of small to midsized businesses. Along with commercial property/casualty coverage, the company also offers reinsurance brokering, risk management consulting, claims handling, and administrative services. Meadowbrook Insurance companies manage insurance pools for about 1,700 public and municipal government entities in five states.

Meadowbrook focuses its niche coverage on specific regions: It offers commercial auto and multiperil in California, while workers' compensation coverage is limited to New England, Florida, and Nevada; retail property/casualty agencies do business in Michigan, California, and Florida.

The company in 2008 acquired and merged with ProCentury in a deal valued at about $273 million. Meadowbrook's goal is to expand its excess and surplus lines capabilities.

EXECUTIVES

Chairman: Merton J. Segal, age 80
President, CEO, and Director: Robert S. Cubbin, age 51
SVP, CFO, and Chief Accounting Officer:
  Karen M. Spaun, age 44
SVP, Secretary, and General Counsel:
  Michael G. Costello, age 48
SVP and Chief Actuary: Stephen A. Belden, age 53
SVP Field Operations: James M. Mahoney
SVP Insurance Operations: Joseph E. Mattingly, age 49
SVP Business Development: James P. LeRoy

SVP Business Development: Archie S. McIntyre, age 43
SVP; President, Meadowbrook Insurance Agency:
  Kenn R. Allen, age 60
SVP Business Operations: Robert Christopher Spring, age 55
VP Corporate Communications: Carol Ziecik
VP Human Resources: Sue Cubbin
Auditors: Ernst & Young LLP

LOCATIONS

HQ: Meadowbrook Insurance Group, Inc.
  26255 American Dr., Southfield, MI 48034
Phone: 248-358-1100   **Fax:** 248-358-1614
Web: www.meadowbrookinsgrp.com

PRODUCTS/OPERATIONS

2008 Sales

	$ mil.	% of total
Net earned premiums		
Workers' compensation	109.3	24
Commercial multiple peril	78.2	17
Commercial auto liability	62.3	14
Inland marine & other liability	74.5	17
Other	45.4	10
Commissions & fees	42.9	10
Net investment income	36.6	8
Net realized loss	(11.4)	—
Total	**437.8**	**100**

Selected Subsidiaries

American Indemnity Insurance Company, Ltd.
Ameritrust Insurance Corporation
Crest Financial Corporation
Meadowbrook, Inc.
Preferred Insurance Company, Ltd.
Savers Property and Casualty Insurance Company
Star Insurance Company
U.S. Specialty Underwriters, Inc.
Williamsburg National Insurance Company

COMPETITORS

ACE Limited
AIG
Aon
Brown & Brown
Delphi Financial Group
Liberty Mutual
Marsh & McLennan
MetLife
Nationwide
Prudential
Safeco
Travelers Companies
XL Capital

HISTORICAL FINANCIALS

Company Type: Public

Income Statement   FYE: December 31

	ASSETS ($ mil.)	NET INCOME ($ mil.)	INCOME AS % OF ASSETS	EMPLOYEES
12/08	1,813.9	27.4	1.5%	921
12/07	1,114.0	28.0	2.5%	643
12/06	969.0	22.0	2.3%	660
12/05	901.3	17.9	2.0%	648
12/04	801.7	14.1	1.8%	651
Annual Growth	22.6%	18.1%	—	9.1%

2008 Year-End Financials

Equity as % of assets: 24.2%
Return on assets: 1.9%
Return on equity: 7.4%
Long-term debt ($ mil.): 141.2
No. of shares (mil.): 57.1
Market value ($ mil.): 368.0

Dividends
  Yield: 1.2%
  Payout: 13.1%
  Sales ($ mil.): 437.8
  R&D as % of sales: —
  Advertising as % of sales: —

Stock History   NYSE: MIG

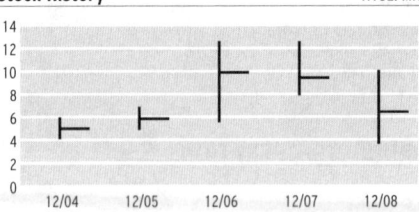

	STOCK PRICE ($) FY Close	P/E High/Low		PER SHARE ($) Earnings	Dividends	Book Value
12/08	6.44	16	6	0.61	0.08	7.67
12/07	9.41	15	9	0.85	0.00	5.28
12/06	9.89	17	8	0.75	0.00	3.53
12/05	5.84	11	8	0.60	0.00	3.10
12/04	4.99	12	9	0.48	0.00	2.93
Annual Growth	6.6%	—	—	6.2%	—	27.2%

Medallion Financial

Medallion Financial turns taxicab licenses, or "medallions," into gold. It makes loans for the purchase of medallions (more than three-quarters of its loan portfolio), which are usually limited in number per city by law. It targets mainly New York City, but also finances medallions in Boston and Cambridge, Massachusetts; Chicago; and Newark, New Jersey. Subsidiary Medallion Bank funds Medallion Financial's taxi and commercial lending activities, as well as originates loans for boats, trailers, and recreational vehicles. Other subsidiaries, including Medallion Capital and Freshstart Venture Capital, also offer commercial financing.

Medallion Business Credit, an originator of loans to small businesses, was merged into Medallion Financial and ceased to exist as a separate legal entity in 2007.

Medallion Financial is organized as a Regulated Investment Company (RIC), and consequently is required to distribute at least 90% of its income to shareholders.

In 2008 the company acquired a portfolio of medallion and other small business loans from Ameritrans Capital Corporation subsidiary Elk Associates Funding for $31 million.

Benefiting from this are chairman and CEO Alvin Murstein and his son, president and director Andrew Murstein, who each own about 10% of Medallion Financial.

EXECUTIVES

Chairman and CEO, Medallion Financial and Medallion Funding: Alvin M. Murstein, age 74,
  $983,674 total compensation
President and Director: Andrew M. Murstein, age 44,
  $1,577,544 total compensation
EVP, Medallion Capital: Dean R. Pickerell
EVP, COO, and Chief Credit Officer: Brian S. O'Leary,
  age 62, $410,860 total compensation
EVP; President, Medallion Funding:
  Michael J. Kowalsky, age 63,
  $396,857 total compensation

SVP and CFO: Larry D. Hall, age 55,
$347,151 total compensation
SVP and Secretary, Medallion Financial and Medallion Funding: Marie Russo, age 83
Chief Compliance Officer and General Counsel:
Jeffrey Yin, age 35
President and CEO, Medallion Bank: John M. Taggart
President, Medallion Capital: Paul Meyering
President, Medallion Business Credit:
Gerald J. Grossman
CEO, Generation Outdoor: Michael Leible
President, Generation Outdoor: Matt Leible
Director, Human Resources: Alexandra (Alex) Gonzales
Auditors: Weiser LLP

LOCATIONS

HQ: Medallion Financial Corp.
437 Madison Ave., 38th Fl., New York, NY 10022
Phone: 212-328-2100   **Fax:** 212-328-2121
Web: www.medallionfinancial.com

PRODUCTS/OPERATIONS

2008 Gross Revenues

	$ mil.	% of total
Interest		
Investments	51.3	91
Lease income	1.0	2
Noninterest		
Other	3.8	7
Total	**56.1**	**100**

Selected Subsidiaries

Freshstart Venture Capital Corp.
Generation Outdoor, Inc.
Medallion Bank
Medallion Capital, Inc.
Medallion Funding Corp.
Medallion Hamptons Holding LLC

COMPETITORS

Allied Capital
Ameritrans Capital
CIT Group

HISTORICAL FINANCIALS

Company Type: Public

Income Statement

FYE: December 31

	ASSETS ($ mil.)	NET INCOME ($ mil.)	INCOME AS % OF ASSETS	EMPLOYEES
12/08	646.7	15.2	2.4%	127
12/07	721.3	15.4	2.1%	118
12/06	631.6	13.1	2.1%	111
12/05	793.0	6.9	0.9%	99
12/04	709.9	22.5	3.2%	102
Annual Growth	**(2.3%)**	**(9.3%)**	**—**	**5.6%**

2008 Year-End Financials

Equity as % of assets: 27.1%
Return on assets: 2.2%
Return on equity: 8.8%
Long-term debt ($ mil.): 462.6
No. of shares (mil.): 17.6
Market value ($ mil.): 134.1

Dividends
Yield: 10.0%
Payout: 88.4%
Sales ($ mil.): 32.4
R&D as % of sales: —
Advertising as % of sales: —

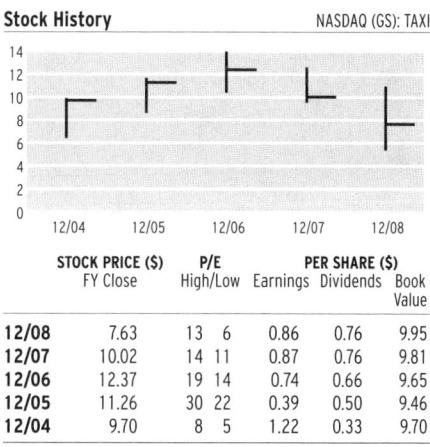

Stock History   NASDAQ (GS): TAXI

	STOCK PRICE ($) FY Close	P/E High/Low		Earnings	Dividends	Book Value
12/08	7.63	13	6	0.86	0.76	9.95
12/07	10.02	14	11	0.87	0.76	9.81
12/06	12.37	19	14	0.74	0.66	9.65
12/05	11.26	30	22	0.39	0.50	9.46
12/04	9.70	8	5	1.22	0.33	9.70
Annual Growth	**(5.8%)**	**—**	**—**	**(8.4%)**	**23.2%**	**0.7%**

MedAssets, Inc.

MedAssets helps hospitals widen their profit margins — or at least not lose quite as much. The company's Spend Management segment operates a group purchasing organization that negotiates prices for hospitals and health systems, which then get better deals on medical supplies and devices. Its Revenue Cycle Management segment provides software and consulting services that help track and analyze a hospital's revenue stream. Such services aim to increase collections and reduce account balances. MedAssets works from about 20 offices nationwide. It counts more than 125 health systems as customers, which have included Christiana Care, Banner Health, and Bon Secours.

The company sells its products and services through an in-house sales team, and maintains a software development group for creating new software products.

Acquisitions are a key part of the company's growth strategy. MedAssets spent over $227 million to acquire revenue management provider Accuro Healthcare Solutions in 2008.

EXECUTIVES

Chairman, President, and CEO: John A. Bardis, age 53,
$841,273 total compensation
Vice Chairman: Terry Mulligan, age 64
Vice Chairman: Bruce F. (Toby) Wesson, age 67
SEVP, COO, Chief Customer Officer, and Director:
Rand A. Ballard, age 54, $669,441 total compensation
EVP and Chief Legal and Administrative Officer:
Jonathan H. Glenn, age 59,
$423,664 total compensation
Chief Information and Technology Officer:
Randy Sparkman
SVP and CFO: L. Neil Hunn, age 37,
$602,934 total compensation
SVP Marketing and Marketing Communications:
Gary Johnson
SVP Human Resources: Lynn Howard
SVP and and Chief Accounting Officer:
Scott E. Gressett, age 41, $450,536 total compensation
Chief Medical Officer: Nicholas J. (Nick) Sears
VP Investor Relations: Robert P. Borchert
Auditors: BDO Seidman, LLP

LOCATIONS

HQ: MedAssets, Inc.
100 N. Point Center East, Ste. 200
Alpharetta, GA 30022
Phone: 678-323-2500   **Fax:** 678-323-2501
Web: www.medassets.com

PRODUCTS/OPERATIONS

2008 Sales

	$ mil.	% of total
Spend Management	151.8	54
Revenue Cycle Management	127.9	46
Total	**279.7**	**100**

Selected Subsidiaries

Aspen Healthcare Metrics LLC
MedAssets Analytical Systems, LLC
MedAssets Net Revenue Systems, LLC
MedAssets Services LLC
MedAssets Supply Chain Systems, LLC
Dominic & Irvine, LLC

COMPETITORS

Broadlane
CareMedic
Eclipsys
HealthTrust
McKesson
MEDITECH
Novation
Premier, Inc.
Siemens Healthcare
SSI Group

HISTORICAL FINANCIALS

Company Type: Public

Income Statement

FYE: December 31

	REVENUE ($ mil.)	NET INCOME ($ mil.)	NET PROFIT MARGIN	EMPLOYEES
12/08	279.7	10.8	3.9%	1,700
12/07	188.5	(9.8)	—	1,200
12/06	146.2	8.8	6.0%	1,100
12/05	98.6	16.5	16.7%	1,150
12/04	75.4	2.1	2.8%	—
Annual Growth	**38.8%**	**50.6%**	**—**	**13.9%**

2008 Year-End Financials

Debt ratio: 58.8%
Return on equity: 3.5%
Cash ($ mil.): 5.4
Current ratio: 0.58
Long-term debt ($ mil.): 225.2
No. of shares (mil.): 56.6

Dividends
Yield: 0.0%
Payout: —
Market value ($ mil.): 826.0
R&D as % of sales: —
Advertising as % of sales: —

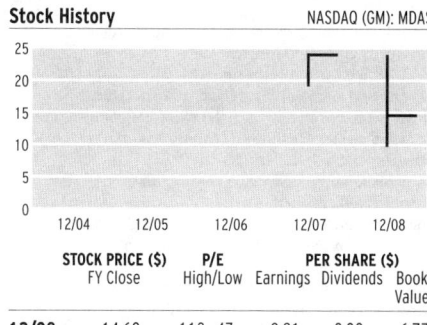

Stock History   NASDAQ (GM): MDAS

	STOCK PRICE ($) FY Close	P/E High/Low		Earnings	Dividends	Book Value
12/08	14.60	113	47	0.21	0.00	6.77
12/07	23.94	—	—	(0.75)	0.00	4.06
Annual Growth	**(39.0%)**	**—**	**—**	**—**	**—**	**66.8%**

Medical Action Industries

Medical Action Industries is cleaning up in the medical products marketplace. The company manufactures, markets, and distributes a wide range of disposable medical products. Some of its main products include wash basins and bedpans, IV start kits, containment systems for medical waste, sterilization products, dressing and surgical sponges, and laboratory products (such as petri dishes and specimen containers). Though it sells primarily to hospitals, Medical Action Industries has expanded its product lines and marketing efforts to target doctors, dentists, veterinarians, outpatient centers, and long-term care facilities. The company's major customers are medical distributors Owens & Minorand Cardinal Health.

Medical Action's products are marketed nationally by direct sales representatives and health care distributors. The company makes some products under private label agreements with other medical suppliers. It operates in the US and some international markets.

In addition to expanding its product lines and finding new markets for existing products, the firm's strategy consists of facilitating international expansion and increasing productivity and efficiency.

It plans to achieve these aims partly through strategic acquisitions. It has bought several smaller companies throughout its history and in 2006 made its largest acquisition to date, purchasing Medegen's Medical Products division for about $80 million. The purchase added a line of patient bedside utensils, as well as some operating room and laboratory products.

Following the purchase of Medegen's Medical Products division, Medical Action announced it would shutter Medegen's manufacturing plant in Colorado and consolidate its operations into the company's Gallaway, Tennessee, facility. That shift continued well into 2008, as the company worked to prepare the infrastructure at the Tennessee facility.

EXECUTIVES

Chairman, President, and CEO: Paul D. Meringolo, age 51, $644,368 total compensation
CFO: Charles L. Kelly Jr., age 49, $347,091 total compensation
VP Information Technology: Carmine Morello
VP Operations: Eric Liu, age 49, $443,922 total compensation
VP, General Counsel, Secretary, and Director: Richard G. Satin, age 54, $488,495 total compensation
Senior Director Business Planning and Market Development: John Kringel
Director Quality Assurance and Regulatory Affairs: Robin Blankenbaker
Director North American Manufacturing and Distribution Operations: Steven Carlson
Director Financial Reporting: Brian Baker
Director Group Marketing: Joe Oberle
Director Health Systems: David Dahle
Director Government Sales and Medegen Marketing: Chuck Adams
Director International Marketing: Peter Meringolo
Director Corporate Human Resources: Laurie Darnaby
Auditors: Grant Thornton LLP

LOCATIONS

HQ: Medical Action Industries Inc.
500 Expressway South, Brentwood, NY 11717
Phone: 631-231-4600
Web: www.medical-action.com

Properties
Arden, North Carolina
    (manufacturing/warehouse/distribution)
Brentwood, New York (executive offices)
Clarksburg, West Virginia
    (manufacturing/warehouse/distribution)
Gallaway, Tennessee
    (manufacturing/warehouse/distribution)
Hauppauge, New York (executive offices — held for sale)
Shanghai, China (general office)

PRODUCTS/OPERATIONS

Selected Products
Absorbent operating room towels
Autoclavable bags
Bedpans
Burn dressings
Central line trays
Disposable laparotomy sponges
Disposable surgical light handle covers
Endoscopic specialty sponges
Gauze sponges
Infectious waste bags
Instrument packs
IV start kits
Laboratory specimen transport bags
Needle counters
Net, padding, and wound care
Patient bedside utensils
Petri dishes
Pitchers and carafes
Specimen containers
Sponge counter bags
Sterility maintenance covers
Sterilization monitoring products
Surgical marking pens

COMPETITORS

Abbott Labs
Alpha Pro Tech
Becton, Dickinson
Cardinal Health
Covidien
Davol
Deroyal Industries
Johnson & Johnson
Kimberly-Clark Health
Medline Industries
Owens & Minor
Patient Safety Technologies
Terumo Medical Corporation

HISTORICAL FINANCIALS
Company Type: Public

Income Statement
FYE: March 31

	REVENUE ($ mil.)	NET INCOME ($ mil.)	NET PROFIT MARGIN	EMPLOYEES
3/09	296.1	5.0	1.7%	854
3/08	290.5	13.2	4.5%	716
3/07	217.3	13.0	6.0%	703
3/06	150.9	11.5	7.6%	385
3/05	141.4	10.7	7.6%	377
Annual Growth	20.3%	(17.3%)	—	22.7%

2009 Year-End Financials
Debt ratio: 43.6%
Return on equity: 4.2%
Cash ($ mil.): 3.5
Current ratio: 2.90
Long-term debt ($ mil.): 53.1
No. of shares (mil.): 16.1
Dividends
  Yield: 0.0%
  Payout: —
Market value ($ mil.): 133.7
R&D as % of sales: —
Advertising as % of sales: —

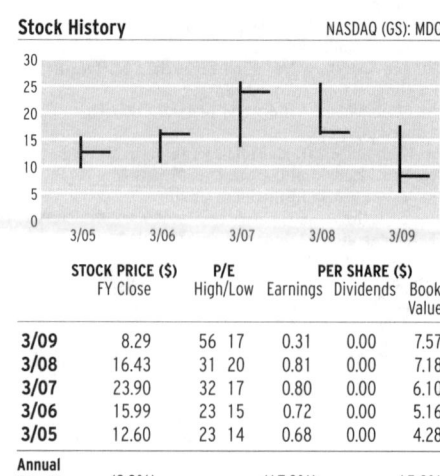

Stock History
NASDAQ (GS): MDCI

	STOCK PRICE ($) FY Close	P/E High/Low		Earnings	PER SHARE ($) Dividends	Book Value
3/09	8.29	56	17	0.31	0.00	7.57
3/08	16.43	31	20	0.81	0.00	7.18
3/07	23.90	32	17	0.80	0.00	6.10
3/06	15.99	23	15	0.72	0.00	5.16
3/05	12.60	23	14	0.68	0.00	4.28
Annual Growth	(9.9%)	—	—	(17.8%)	—	15.3%

Medicis Pharmaceutical

Medicis Pharmaceutical has found a new wrinkle in the pharmaceuticals business. The company sells prescription acne and skin medications in niche markets. Medicis' prescription medications and doctor-dispensed products include oral acne treatment SOLODYN and topical acne therapies TRIAZ and ZIANA, as well as dermal corticosteroid cream VANOS. The company also offers dermal aesthetic treatments including RESTYLANE and PERLANE, which smooth facial wrinkles, lines, and contours. Medicis uses a direct sales force to promote its products mainly to dermatologists, podiatrists, and plastic surgeons, as well as to general practitioners, hospitals, and government agencies in the US and Canada.

Medicis' products are sold primarily through wholesale distributors McKesson (more than half of sales) and Cardinal Health (about 20%), as well as through retail pharmacy chains. Third-party companies handle manufacturing the company's line of nearly 20 products. Medicis' manufacturing partners include AAIPharma and Wellspring Pharmaceutical (for SOLODYN), Contract Pharmaceuticals (TRIAZ, VANOS, and ZIANA), and Q-Med (RESTYLANE and PERLANE).

The company's research and development efforts are a combination of internal efforts and partnerships or licensing agreements with other companies. Medicis is also seeking acquisitions of businesses operating within its niche markets.

In 2007 wrinkle treatment PERLANE was approved by the FDA and launched commercially. The company has also developed and received approval to market wrinkle treatment DYSPORT (formerly RELOXIN) through a partnership with Ipsen in the US. DYSPORT is a potential competitor to Allergan's popular Botox therapy; Medicis plans to expand marketing of the drug into Canada and Japan. Medicis also invested in a similar product being developed by Revance Therapeutics in 2007.

In 2008 the company moved further into the cosmetic surgery market by acquiring body shaping technology firm LipoSonix for $150 million, plus possible milestone payments. LipoSonix markets its noninvasive ultrasound

fat burning system in Europe, and plans to apply for FDA approval of its products.

Later in 2008 the company formed a development partnership with Impax Laboratories to collaborate on several dermatology products. The partnership includes work on a next-generation version of SOLODYN.

Founder and CEO Jonah Shacknai owns about 6% of the company.

HISTORY

Jonah Shacknai, erstwhile lawyer and aide to US congressional FDA committees, founded Medicis in 1988. Later that year the company merged with Innovative Therapeutics to form Medicis Pharmaceutical.

Medicis went public in 1990, and sales surged when it acquired a license to market a generic version of anti-wrinkle cream Retin-A. By 1994 acquisitions of the ESOTERICA line of products and DYNACIN acne antibiotics from SmithKline Beecham (later GlaxoSmithKline) and Schein Pharmaceuticals, respectively, led Medicis to turn a profit, and in 1995 the company moved its headquarters from New York to Arizona.

The company continued its strategy of acquisitions, and bought GenDerm, maker of the topical analgesic Zostrix; it purchased product lines including the LIDEX and SYNALAR lines of topical steroids from Roche subsidiary Syntex, as well as LOPROX and TOPICORT from Marion Roussel (now part of Sanofi-Aventis).

By 1999, however, business forced Medicis to change direction, and the company sold Exorex, a joint venture with IMX Pharmaceuticals, to Bioglan Pharma, and sold most of its over-the-counter product lines so that it could expand its prescription operations.

The company acquired Ascent Pediatrics in 2001, gaining a portfolio of specialty pediatric pharmaceutical products (including ORAPRED, an oral liquid steroid for asthma and other respiratory conditions), as well as a valuable foothold in the pediatrics market into which Medicis was eager to leverage certain of its own products, including LOPROX. (ORAPRED was licensed to BioMarin in 2004.)

In 2002 the company formed a partnership with AAIPharma to develop SOLODYN, a treatment for inflammatory lesions related to severe acne vulgaris. SOLODYN was approved by the FDA in 2006, as was ZIANA, a topical acne gel developed with Dow Pharmaceutical Sciences.

EXECUTIVES

Chairman and CEO: Jonah Shacknai, age 52, $4,140,205 total compensation
EVP and COO: Mark A. Prygocki Sr., age 43, $1,864,368 total compensation
EVP, CFO, and Treasurer: Richard D. Peterson, age 41, $1,140,347 total compensation
EVP and Chief Scientific Officer: Mitchell S. Wortzman, age 59, $1,469,005 total compensation
EVP, General Counsel, and Secretary: Jason D. Hanson, $1,298,274 total compensation
EVP Corporate and Product Development: Joseph P. (Joe) Cooper, age 52, $1,547,576 total compensation
EVP Sales and Marketing: Vincent Ippolito
Auditors: Ernst & Young LLP

LOCATIONS

HQ: Medicis Pharmaceutical Corporation
7720 N. Dobson Rd., Scottsdale, AZ 85256
Phone: 602-808-8800   **Fax:** 602-808-0822
Web: www.medicis.com

PRODUCTS/OPERATIONS

2008 Sales

	$ mil.	% of total
Acne & related dermatological products	325.0	63
Non-acne dermatological products	148.0	29
Non-dermatological products (including contract revenues)	44.8	8
Total	**517.8**	**100**

Selected Products

Acne and Related Dermatological Products
  DYNACIN (oral acne medication)
  PLEXION (topical cleanser for treatment of rosacea)
  SOLODYN (acne vulgaris)
  TRIAZ (acne medicine)
  ZIANA (acne gel)
Non-acne Dermatological Products
  LOPROX (antifungal cream)
  PERLANE (anti-wrinkle gel)
  RESTYLANE (injectible gel for treating facial wrinkles)
  VANOS (corticosteroid cream)
Non-dermatological Products
  AMMONUL (hyperammonemia urea enzyme deficiency)
  BUPHENYL (urea cycle disorders)
  OMNICEF (oral treatment for skin infections)

COMPETITORS

Adamis Pharmaceuticals
Allergan
Anacor
Anika Therapeutics
BioForm
Borghese
Bristol-Myers Squibb
Galderma Laboratories
GlaxoSmithKline
Johnson & Johnson
L'Oréal
Mentor Corporation
Merck
Nycomed US
Ortho Dermatologics
Perrigo
Pfizer
Procter & Gamble
Sanofi-Aventis
Schwarzkopf & Henkel
The Stephan Co.
Stiefel Laboratories
Taro
Valeant
Warner Chilcott

HISTORICAL FINANCIALS

Company Type: Public

Income Statement
FYE: December 31

	REVENUE ($ mil.)	NET INCOME ($ mil.)	NET PROFIT MARGIN	EMPLOYEES
12/08	517.8	10.3	2.0%	578
12/07	464.7	75.1	16.2%	472
12/06*	349.2	(75.8)	—	391
6/05	376.9	65.0	17.2%	359
6/04	303.7	30.8	10.1%	319
Annual Growth	**14.3%**	**(24.0%)**	**—**	**16.0%**

*Fiscal year change

2008 Year-End Financials

Debt ratio: 28.0%	Dividends
Return on equity: 1.7%	Yield: 1.2%
Cash ($ mil.): 86.4	Payout: 88.9%
Current ratio: 2.65	Market value ($ mil.): 826.8
Long-term debt ($ mil.): 169.3	R&D as % of sales: —
No. of shares (mil.): 59.5	Advertising as % of sales: —

Stock History
NYSE: MRX

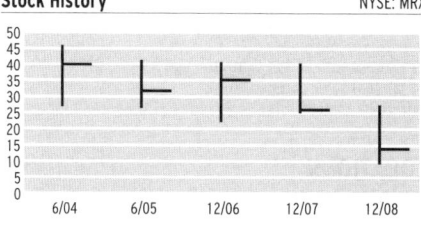

| | 6/04 | 6/05 | 12/06 | 12/07 | 12/08 |

	STOCK PRICE ($) FY Close	P/E High/Low		PER SHARE ($) Earnings	Dividends	Book Value
12/08	13.90	150	54	0.18	0.16	10.15
12/07	25.97	35	22	1.14	0.12	10.46
12/06*	35.13	—	—	(1.39)	0.12	8.57
6/05	31.73	41	27	1.01	0.12	8.18
6/04	39.95	88	52	0.52	0.10	9.34
Annual Growth	**(23.2%)**	**—**	**—**	**(23.3%)**	**12.5%**	**2.1%**

*Fiscal year change

Medifast, Inc.

Medifast is helping people slim down and shape up. The company develops, manufactures, and markets health and diet products under its Medifast brand name. The products, which are manufactured by Medifast subsidiary Jason Pharmaceuticals, include food and beverages (meal replacement shakes, bars), as well as disease management products for diabetics. Medifast sells its wares direct to consumers online and through doctor's offices. Its Take Shape for Life subsidiary distributes the products through a direct marketing and sales network of independent distributors (often people who have had success with Medifast) whom the company calls Health Coaches.

Unlike other companies hawking weight loss, Medifast emphasizes the inclusion of medical practitioners in the development and use of their products. The company is also working to tailor many of its products to the rapidly growing population of diabetics. The company maintains an in-house call center and support staff, with registered dieticians on hand to assist customers.

Medifast also operates a chain of Hi-Energy and Medifast Weight Control centers in Texas and Florida. It has launched a franchise model to expand the number of such centers in order to expand geographically across the US. Franchises have sprouted in California and Maryland.

EXECUTIVES

Chairman: Bradley T. (Brad) MacDonald, age 62, $438,700 total compensation
CEO, CFO, and Director: Michael S. McDevitt, age 31, $662,700 total compensation
President, COO, and Director:
Margaret MacDonald-Sheetz, age 33, $525,000 total compensation
EVP; CEO, Take Shape for Life: Leo V. Willliams III, age 62
VP Finance: Brendan Connors, age 32, $223,000 total compensation
Auditors: Bagell, Josephs, Levine & Company, LLC

LOCATIONS

HQ: Medifast, Inc.
11445 Cronhill Dr., Owings Mills, MD 21117
Phone: 410-581-8042   **Fax:** 410-581-8070
Web: www.medifast.net

PRODUCTS/OPERATIONS

2008 Sales

	$ mil.	% of total
Medifast products	97.1	92
Weight loss centers & other	8.3	8
Total	**105.4**	**100**

COMPETITORS

eDiets.com	Reliv' International
Herbalife Ltd.	Slim-Fast
Jenny Craig	Weight Watchers
NutriSystem	

HISTORICAL FINANCIALS

Company Type: Public

Income Statement

FYE: December 31

	REVENUE ($ mil.)	NET INCOME ($ mil.)	NET PROFIT MARGIN	EMPLOYEES
12/08	105.4	5.4	5.1%	290
12/07	83.8	3.8	4.5%	245
12/06	74.1	5.1	6.9%	265
12/05	40.1	2.4	6.0%	164
12/04	27.3	1.7	6.2%	130
Annual Growth	**40.2%**	**33.5%**	**—**	**22.2%**

2008 Year-End Financials

Debt ratio: 11.3%
Return on equity: 15.3%
Cash ($ mil.): 1.8
Current ratio: 2.48
Long-term debt ($ mil.): 4.3
No. of shares (mil.): 15.4

Dividends
Yield: 0.0%
Payout: —
Market value ($ mil.): 84.9
R&D as % of sales: —
Advertising as % of sales: —

Stock History

NYSE: MED

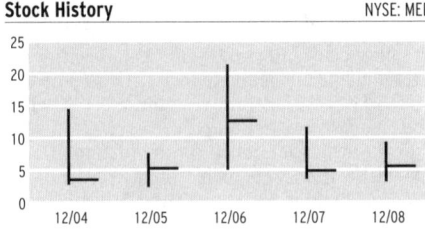

	STOCK PRICE ($) FY Close	P/E High/Low		PER SHARE ($) Earnings	Dividends	Book Value
12/08	5.52	24	9	0.38	0.00	2.48
12/07	4.85	41	13	0.28	0.00	2.11
12/06	12.57	56	14	0.38	0.00	1.83
12/05	5.24	39	14	0.19	0.00	1.43
12/04	3.52	102	21	0.14	0.00	1.25
Annual Growth	**11.9%**	**—**	**—**	**28.4%**	**—**	**18.7%**

MEDNAX, Inc.

MEDNAX made up its new name to reflect its *med*ical focus and *na*tional ambitions, and kept the *x* for nostalgia. The company provides medical practice administration and physician services to hospitals in more than 30 states. Its Pediatrix Medical Group (the company's former name) has more than 1,000 neonatal and pediatric doctors in its stable. Its American Anesthesiology unit employs more than 450 anesthesiologists who practice in hospitals and medical offices. MEDNAX's practice administration services include staffing, billing, and information management.

Pediatrix Medical Group includes physicians in such specialized areas as maternal-fetal heath (for high-risk pregnancies) and pediatric cardiology, as well as other docs who care for critically ill children in intensive care units. It also conducts clinical research and provides additional educational opportunities to its physicians.

MEDNAX's strategy consists of developing regional networks and buying up smaller physicians groups across the US. It markets itself directly to physician groups through advertising as well as through its sales staff.

In 2007 the company set up a network of anesthesiology practices, hoping to reproduce its business model for that specialty. The move signaled a shift in strategy as it broadened its operations from the strictly pediatric. As a result, in late 2008 the company changed its name from Pediatrix Medical Group to MEDNAX and implemented a holding company structure.

EXECUTIVES

Chairman: Cesar L. Alvarez, age 62
CEO and Director: Roger J. Medel, age 63, $4,607,641 total compensation
President and COO: Joseph M. Calabro, age 48, $2,588,333 total compensation
CFO: Vivian LopezBlanco, age 51
SVP and CIO: Robert C. Bryant
SVP Business Development: John F. Rizzo
SVP, General Counsel, and Secretary:
Thomas W. Hawkins, age 48, $1,623,502 total compensation
SVP Operations, Anesthesia Services: William C. Hawk
SVP Research and Education: Alan R. Spitzer
VP Regional Operations, Atlantic Region, Pediatrix Division: Alan Oliver
President, Pediatrix Division: Frederick V. Miller, age 53
President, American Anesthesia Operating Group:
Karl B. Wagner, age 43, $1,937,066 total compensation
Auditors: PricewaterhouseCoopers LLP

LOCATIONS

HQ: MEDNAX, Inc.
1301 Concord Terrace, Sunrise, FL 33323
Phone: 954-384-0175   **Fax:** 954-838-9961
Web: www.mednax.com

PRODUCTS/OPERATIONS

2008 Payors

	% of total
Contracted managed care	65
Government	26
Other third parties	8
Private-pay patients	1
Total	**100**

COMPETITORS

EmCare
IntegraMed America
McKesson
Orion HealthCorp
Physician Staffing
Sheridan Healthcare
Sterling Healthcare
Team Health

HISTORICAL FINANCIALS

Company Type: Public

Income Statement

FYE: December 31

	REVENUE ($ mil.)	NET INCOME ($ mil.)	NET PROFIT MARGIN	EMPLOYEES
12/08	1,068.3	169.2	15.8%	2,532
12/07	917.6	142.7	15.6%	3,914
12/06	818.6	124.5	15.2%	3,378
12/05	693.7	89.0	12.8%	3,013
12/04	619.6	98.3	15.9%	2,826
Annual Growth	**14.6%**	**14.5%**	**—**	**(2.7%)**

2008 Year-End Financials

Debt ratio: 14.5%
Return on equity: 17.6%
Cash ($ mil.): 14.3
Current ratio: 0.90
Long-term debt ($ mil.): 139.9
No. of shares (mil.): 46.5

Dividends
Yield: 0.0%
Payout: —
Market value ($ mil.): 1,475.1
R&D as % of sales: —
Advertising as % of sales: —

Stock History

NYSE: MD

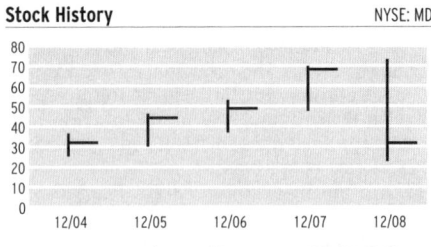

	STOCK PRICE ($) FY Close	P/E High/Low		PER SHARE ($) Earnings	Dividends	Book Value
12/08	31.70	20	7	3.59	0.00	20.74
12/07	68.15	24	17	2.86	0.00	20.61
12/06	48.90	21	15	2.52	0.00	18.61
12/05	44.28	25	17	1.86	0.00	14.87
12/04	32.03	18	13	1.99	0.00	12.27
Annual Growth	**(0.3%)**	**—**	**—**	**15.9%**	**—**	**14.0%**

MEDTOX Scientific

When wooing a customer, MEDTOX Scientific might ask the classic question: "Your place or mine?" The company offers laboratory services, as well as diagnostic and screening tests customers can use on-site. MEDTOX specializes in clinical and forensic toxicology and in heavy metals analysis, offering substance-abuse testing services, hazardous-materials exposure monitoring, and clinical tests for many types of pharmaceuticals through its MEDTOX Laboratories subsidiary (its largest segment). Its MEDTOX Diagnostics subsidiary develops and markets on-site tests used to detect toxic or illegal substances.

EXECUTIVES

Chairman, President, and CEO:
Richard J. (Dick) Braun, age 65,
$797,840 total compensation
VP Finance and Principal Accounting Officer:
Steven J. Schmidt, age 50
VP Quality, Regulatory Affairs, and Human Resources:
Susan E. Puskas, age 58, $329,530 total compensation
VP and CFO; COO, MEDTOX Laboratories:
Kevin J. Wiersma, age 47, $324,530 total compensation
VP Sales and Marketing and Chief Marketing Officer:
James A. Schoonover, age 52,
$338,830 total compensation
VP; COO, MEDTOX Diagnostics: B. Mitchell Owens,
age 52, $312,878 total compensation
Auditors: Deloitte & Touche LLP

LOCATIONS

HQ: MEDTOX Scientific, Inc.
402 W. County Rd. D, St. Paul, MN 55112
Phone: 651-636-7466   **Fax:** 651-636-5351
Web: www.medtox.com

PRODUCTS/OPERATIONS

2008 Sales

	% of total
Laboratory services	77
Product sales	23
Total	**100**

Selected Products and Services

Laboratory Services
  Specialty laboratory services
    Clinical testing for occupational health clinics and
      physicians offices
    Clinical testing for the pharmaceuticals industry
    Clinical toxicology
    Heavy metal, trace element, and solvent analyses
    Logistics, data, and program management services
  Workplace drugs-of-abuse testing

Products
  EZ-SCREEN (breath alcohol test)
  PROFILE-II (urine tests for drug abuse)
  PROFILE-II ER (urine tests for drug abuse)
  PROFILE-III (urine tests for drug abuse)
  SURE-SCREEN (human drug screen)
  VERDICT-II (human drug screen)

COMPETITORS

Abbott Labs
ACON Laboratories
AcuNetx
American Bio Medica
Biosite
Inverness Medical Innovations
Kroll Background Screening
LabCorp
Psychemedics
Quest Diagnostics
Siemens Healthcare Diagnostics

HISTORICAL FINANCIALS

Company Type: Public

Income Statement

FYE: December 31

	REVENUE ($ mil.)	NET INCOME ($ mil.)	NET PROFIT MARGIN	EMPLOYEES
12/08	85.8	5.6	6.5%	582
12/07	80.3	6.7	8.3%	523
12/06	69.8	4.5	6.4%	460
12/05	63.0	3.3	5.2%	402
12/04	56.7	1.8	3.2%	415
Annual Growth	**10.9%**	**32.8%**	**—**	**8.8%**

2008 Year-End Financials

Debt ratio: 0.5%
Return on equity: 9.6%
Cash ($ mil.): 4.1
Current ratio: 2.81
Long-term debt ($ mil.): 0.3
No. of shares (mil.): 8.6
Dividends
  Yield: 0.0%
  Payout: —
Market value ($ mil.): 70.3
R&D as % of sales: —
Advertising as % of sales: —

Stock History

NASDAQ (GM): MTOX

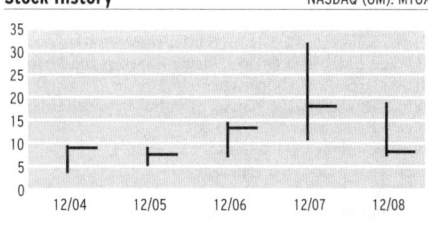

	STOCK PRICE ($) FY Close	P/E High/Low		PER SHARE ($) Earnings	Dividends	Book Value
12/08	8.22	30	12	0.62	0.00	7.07
12/07	18.08	42	15	0.75	0.00	6.50
12/06	13.33	28	14	0.52	0.00	5.60
12/05	7.58	22	13	0.40	0.00	5.24
12/04	9.00	40	16	0.23	0.00	4.42
Annual Growth	**(2.2%)**	**—**	**—**	**28.1%**	**—**	**12.5%**

Mesa Laboratories

Mesa Laboratories is reaching a plateau in the field of measurements. The company makes niche-market electronic measurement, testing, and recording instruments for medical, food processing, electronics, and aerospace applications. Mesa's products include sensors that record temperature, humidity, and pressure levels; flow meters for water treatment, polymerization, and chemical processing applications; and sonic concentration analyzers. The company also makes kidney hemodialysis treatment products, including metering equipment and machines that clean dialyzers (or filters) for reuse. It also provides repair, recalibration, and certification services. Customers in the US make up about three-quarters of sales.

Late in 2009 Mesa Labs bought the bottle cap torque testing business of Vibrac LLC, a privately held maker of automated and manual precision test systems. The bottle cap testing products expands Mesa Lab's DataTrace logging instruments; both product lines are used in the food and beverage and pharmaceutical industries for quality control applications.

Mesa Labs acquired Raven Biological Laboratories in 2006 for nearly $7 million in cash and stock. Raven Labs manufactures biological indicators and provides sterilization validation services. Raven's products are used by dental offices and hospitals and by manufacturers of medical devices and pharmaceuticals for quality control testing in sterilization processes. Mesa Labs paid $3.5 million in cash and exchanged 223,243 shares of common stock to acquire Raven Labs.

In 2009 president John Sullivan took the reins as CEO, replacing Luke Schmieder, who had been CEO since founding the company in 1982. Still chairman of the board, Schmieder owns about 9% of Mesa Laboratories.

EXECUTIVES

Chairman: Luke R. Schmieder, age 67,
$111,315 total compensation
President, CEO, and Director: John J. Sullivan, age 57,
$321,000 total compensation
VP Sales and Marketing: Glenn E. Adriance, age 55,
$161,592 total compensation
**VP Finance, CFO, Chief Accounting Officer, and
Secretary:** Steven W. Peterson, age 54,
$158,406 total compensation
Auditors: Ehrhardt Keefe Steiner & Hottman PC

LOCATIONS

HQ: Mesa Laboratories, Inc.
12100 W. 6th Ave., Lakewood, CO 80228
Phone: 303-987-8000   **Fax:** 303-987-8989
Web: www.mesalabs.com

Mesa Laboratories has facilities in Colorado and Nebraska.

2009 Sales

	$ mil.	% of total
US	15.5	72
Other countries	6.0	28
Total	**21.5**	**100**

PRODUCTS/OPERATIONS

2009 Sales

	$ mil.	% of total
Product sales	17.9	83
Parts & service	3.6	17
Total	**21.5**	**100**

Selected Products

Biological and chemical indicators (Raven Biological
  Laboratories)
Electronic thermal sensors
  DATATRACE
  DATATRACE Micropack Tracers
  ELOGG
  Flatpack Tracers
  FRB Tracers
Hemodialysis products (Automata)
  Database management software (Reuse Data
    Management System)
  Dialyzer reprocessors (ECHO MM-1000)
  Meters (Western Meters)
Sonic fluid measurement products (NuSonics)
  Sonic concentration analyzers
  Sonic flowmeters

COMPETITORS

3M Health Care
Badger Meter
Cantel Medical
Danaher
Ellab
Emerson Electric
Euro Tech
Gambro AB
GE
K-Tron
Mikron Infrared
Minntech
Rockwell Medical
Siemens Corp.
Siemens Water Technologies
STERIS
Teledyne Isco
Thermo Fisher Scientific
Velocys

HISTORICAL FINANCIALS

Company Type: Public

Income Statement

FYE: March 31

	REVENUE ($ mil.)	NET INCOME ($ mil.)	NET PROFIT MARGIN	EMPLOYEES
3/09	21.5	4.8	22.3%	111
3/08	19.6	4.6	23.5%	113
3/07	17.2	4.0	23.3%	100
3/06	11.6	2.8	24.1%	52
3/05	10.0	2.3	23.0%	47
Annual Growth	21.1%	20.2%	—	24.0%

2009 Year-End Financials

Debt ratio: —
Return on equity: 18.7%
Cash ($ mil.): 9.1
Current ratio: 12.53
Long-term debt ($ mil.): —
No. of shares (mil.): 3.2

Dividends
Yield: 2.5%
Payout: 27.0%
Market value ($ mil.): 51.1
R&D as % of sales: —
Advertising as % of sales: —

Stock History

NASDAQ (GM): MLAB

	STOCK PRICE ($) FY Close	P/E High/Low		PER SHARE ($) Earnings	Dividends	Book Value
3/09	16.00	17	10	1.48	0.40	8.65
3/08	21.93	19	13	1.41	0.36	7.44
3/07	19.00	19	11	1.22	0.30	6.49
3/06	14.11	18	12	0.92	0.26	4.67
3/05	13.75	20	12	0.74	0.22	4.82
Annual Growth	3.9%	—	—	18.9%	16.1%	15.7%

Metro Bancorp

Metro Bancorp (formerly Pennsylvania Commerce Bancorp) is the holding company for Metro Bank (formerly Commerce Bank/Harrisburg), which has more than 30 branches in south-central Pennsylvania. The bank provides standard services such as checking, savings, and money market accounts; CDs; IRAs; and credit cards. Commercial mortgages and lines of credit, business loans, and consumer loans make up most of its loan portfolio. Metro Bancorp plans to acquire Philadelphia-based Republic First Bancorp. The combined firm will have about 45 branches stretching from Harrisburg to Philadelphia in southeastern Pennsylvania.

The merger was announced in 2008 after Canadian bank Toronto-Dominion acquired Commerce Bancorp (now part of TD Bank), which had owned more than 10% of Pennsylvania Commerce Bancorp and shared branding.

Directors and executive officers collectively own about 25% of Pennsylvania Commerce Bancorp; of that, CEO Gary Nalbandian owns more than 8%.

EXECUTIVES

Chairman, President, and CEO: Gary L. Nalbandian, age 66, $714,877 total compensation
Vice Chairman: Harry D. Madonna, age 66
EVP and COO: Mark A. Ritter, age 50, $250,469 total compensation
EVP and CFO, Metro Bancorp and Metro Bank: Mark A. Zody, age 45, $335,272 total compensation
Chief Credit Officer, Metro Bancorp and Metro Bank: James Ridd, age 47, $216,108 total compensation
SVP and Chief Risk Officer, Metro Bancorp and Metro Bank: D. Scott Huggins, age 58
SVP; SVP and Market Manager Central Pennsylvania, Metro Bank: Steve Solk, age 54
SVP Operations, Metro Bank: Victoria G. (Vicki) Chieppa, age 60
Public Relations: Jason S. Kirsch
Shareholder Relations: Sherry Richart

LOCATIONS

HQ: Metro Bancorp Inc.
3801 Paxton St., Harrisburg, PA 17111
Phone: 717-412-6301   **Fax:** 717-412-6171
Web: www.mymetrobank.com

PRODUCTS/OPERATIONS

2008 Gross Revenues

	$ mil.	% of total
Interest		
Loans receivable, including fees	82.7	61
Securities	28.5	21
Noninterest		
Service charges & other fees	23.9	17
Other	1.6	1
Total	136.7	100

COMPETITORS

Abington Bancorp Inc
Bryn Mawr Bank Corp.
Codorus Valley Bancorp
Fulton Financial
M&T Bank
Pennsylvania State Employees Credit Union
PNC Financial
Sovereign Bank
Stonebridge Financial

HISTORICAL FINANCIALS

Company Type: Public

Income Statement

FYE: December 31

	ASSETS ($ mil.)	NET INCOME ($ mil.)	INCOME AS % OF ASSETS	EMPLOYEES
12/08	2,140.5	12.9	0.6%	1,077
12/07	1,979.0	7.0	0.4%	922
12/06	1,866.5	7.3	0.4%	909
12/05	1,641.1	8.8	0.5%	787
12/04	1,277.4	8.6	0.7%	710
Annual Growth	13.8%	10.7%	—	11.0%

2008 Year-End Financials

Equity as % of assets: 5.3%
Return on assets: 0.6%
Return on equity: 11.4%
Long-term debt ($ mil.): 79.4
No. of shares (mil.): 13.4
Market value ($ mil.): 358.0

Dividends
Yield: 0.0%
Payout: —
Sales ($ mil.): 104.1
R&D as % of sales: —
Advertising as % of sales: —

Stock History

NASDAQ (GS): METR

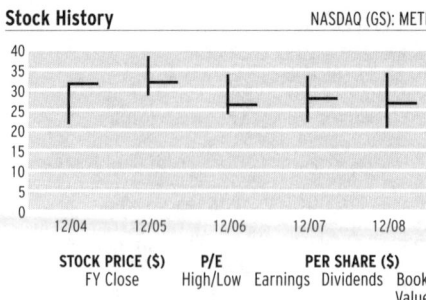

	STOCK PRICE ($) FY Close	P/E High/Low		PER SHARE ($) Earnings	Dividends	Book Value
12/08	26.66	17	11	1.97	0.00	8.52
12/07	27.85	31	21	1.07	0.00	8.37
12/06	26.30	30	22	1.12	0.00	7.53
12/05	31.85	28	21	1.38	0.00	6.82
12/04	31.50	19	13	1.63	0.00	6.33
Annual Growth	(4.1%)	—	—	4.9%	—	7.7%

MFRI, Inc.

MFRI's motto could be: "Pipe down, take a deep breath, and chill out." The company makes piping systems, air filter elements, and industrial process coolant systems (liquid chillers) through subsidiaries Perma-Pipe, Midwesco Filter, and Thermal Care, respectively. Perma-Pipe's specialty piping systems are used on college campuses, military bases, and other large sites. Midwesco provides products and services for industrial air filtration, while Thermal Care's heat transfer equipment is used primarily by the plastics industry. MFRI products are sold worldwide, but the US accounts for the bulk of the company's revenue.

A global player, in 2008 MFRI's Perma-Pipe unit and Jindal Saw, Ltd. of Mumbai, India, received an order to factory insulate and jacket 375 miles of heavy crude oil pipeline in India. In 2009 Perma-Pipe and partner Bayou Companies acquired Garneau's pipe coating and insulation facility and associated assets in Camrose, Alberta.

EXECUTIVES

Chairman and CEO: David Unger, age 75, $682,088 total compensation
President, COO, and Director: Bradley E. (Brad) Mautner, age 54
SVP Fabric Filter Products: G. Keith Ogilvie
SVP Midwesco Filter Resources, Inc.: Joe Marcinski
SVP Cartridge Filter Products: McLeod Stephens
VP; President and COO, Perma-Pipe: Fati A. Elgendy, age 59, $1,107,808 total compensation
VP, CFO, Secretary, Treasurer, and Director: Michael D. Bennett, age 64, $682,088 total compensation
VP; Director Sales and Marketing, Perma-Pipe: Robert A. Maffei, age 61, $555,721 total compensation
VP and Director Production, Perma-Pipe, Inc.: Billy E. Ervin, age 64, $469,148 total compensation
VP Human Resources: Timothy P. Murphy
VP Sales and Marketing, Thermal Care, Inc.: Thomas A. Benson, age 56
President, Thermal Care: Stephen C. Buck, age 61
President and COO, Midwesco Mechanical and Energy: Edward A. Crylen, age 58
President, Midwesco Filter Resources, Inc.: John M. Foster, age 47
President, Oil & Gas, Perma Pipe: John Carusiello
Auditors: Grant Thornton LLP

LOCATIONS

HQ: MFRI, Inc.
7720 N. Lehigh Ave., Niles, IL 60714
Phone: 847-966-1000 **Fax:** 847-966-8563
Web: www.mfri.com

2009 Sales

	$ mil.	% of total
US	197.3	65
Asia	69.7	23
Europe	24.9	8
Mexico, South America, Central America & the Caribbean	4.9	2
Canada	4.7	2
Africa	1.0	—
Other regions	0.6	—
Total	**303.1**	**100**

PRODUCTS/OPERATIONS

2009 Sales

	$ mil.	% of total
Piping systems	151.8	50
Filtration products	105.4	35
Industrial process cooling equipment	31.7	10
Other	14.2	5
Total	**303.1**	**100**

Selected Operations and Products

Midwesco Filter Resources, Inc.
Filter elements, including filter bags and cartridges, and related parts and services

Perma-Pipe, Inc.
Containment piping systems
Insulated and jacketed heating and cooling piping systems
Oil and gas flowlines

Thermal Care, Inc.
Cooling towers
Liquid chillers
Mold temperature controllers
Plant circulating systems

COMPETITORS

Arizona Instrument
CLARCOR
Clyde Bergemann EEC
Donaldson Company
Shaw Industries
Tyco
United Air Specialists
Vario Construction Company
W.L. Gore

HISTORICAL FINANCIALS

Company Type: Public

Income Statement

FYE: January 31

	REVENUE ($ mil.)	NET INCOME ($ mil.)	NET PROFIT MARGIN	EMPLOYEES
1/09	303.1	6.7	2.2%	1,501
1/08	239.5	(0.3)	—	1,263
1/07	213.5	4.6	2.2%	1,058
1/06	154.6	0.5	0.3%	760
1/05	145.1	2.8	1.9%	760
Annual Growth	**20.2%**	**24.4%**	**—**	**18.5%**

2009 Year-End Financials

Debt ratio: 65.6%
Return on equity: 10.8%
Cash ($ mil.): 2.7
Current ratio: 1.83
Long-term debt ($ mil.): 42.1
No. of shares (mil.): 6.8
Dividends
Yield: —
Payout: —
Market value ($ mil.): 33.8
R&D as % of sales: —
Advertising as % of sales: —

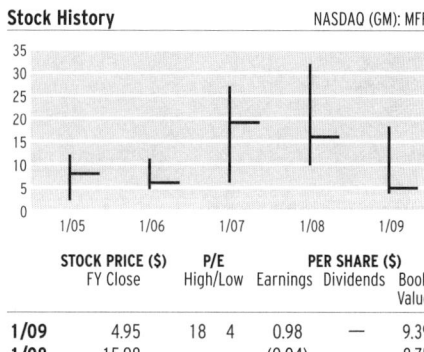

	STOCK PRICE ($) FY Close	P/E High/Low		PER SHARE ($) Earnings	Dividends	Book Value
1/09	4.95	18	4	0.98	—	9.39
1/08	15.98	—	—	(0.04)	—	8.75
1/07	19.10	33	8	0.82	—	5.68
1/06	6.05	110	50	0.10	—	4.66
1/05	8.00	22	5	0.54	—	4.58
Annual Growth	**(11.3%)**	**—**	**—**	**16.1%**	**—**	**19.7%**

MicroFinancial Incorporated

MicroFinancial thinks big when it comes to leasing small-ticket commercial items to small and midsized businesses. Through subsidiary TimePayment, MicroFinancial leases items that are generally valued between $500 and $15,000. Although the "microticket" leaser provides financing for a variety of office and commercial equipment, the majority of the contracts in its portfolio are for point-of-sale authorization systems for debit and credit cards. It doesn't lease and rent equipment directly, but through a network of independent dealers across the US. Internet-based TimePaymentDirect processes applications and approves credit; Insta-Lease provides the same services via telephone, fax, and e-mail.

Until 2002 the company operated primarily through subsidiary Leasecomm. That unit ran into legal difficulties over its business practices and lost its credit facility. MicroFinancial resumed lease-financing originations in 2004 primarily under the TimePayment subsidiary. Chairman Peter Bleyleben and directors Brian Boyle and Torrence Harder each own more than 10% of MicroFinancial.

EXECUTIVES

Chairman: Peter R. Bleyleben, age 57
President, CEO, Secretary, Treasurer, Clerk, and Director: Richard F. Latour, age 56, $516,988 total compensation
VP Legal and Vendor, Lessee Relations: Steven J. LaCreta, age 50, $168,433 total compensation
VP and CFO: James R. Jackson Jr., age 48, $289,919 total compensation
VP Human Resources: Stephen J. Constantino, age 50, $158,208 total compensation
VP Sales, TimePayment: Mark Sullivan
Auditors: Vitale, Caturano & Company PC

LOCATIONS

HQ: MicroFinancial Incorporated
10M Commerce Way, Woburn, MA 01801
Phone: 781-994-4800 **Fax:** 781-994-4710
Web: www.microfinancial.com

PRODUCTS/OPERATIONS

2008 Sales

	$ mil.	% of total
Financing leases	23.1	59
Rental income	9.8	25
Loss & damage waiver fees	3.2	8
Service contracts	0.9	2
Service fees & other	2.5	6
Total	**39.5**	**100**

COMPETITORS

CalFirst
CIT Group
ECHO, Inc.
Electro Rent
Fiserv

HISTORICAL FINANCIALS

Company Type: Public

Income Statement

FYE: December 31

	ASSETS ($ mil.)	NET INCOME ($ mil.)	INCOME AS % OF ASSETS	EMPLOYEES
12/08	104.8	5.9	5.6%	103
12/07	71.0	6.2	8.7%	78
12/06	59.7	3.9	6.5%	67
12/05	65.2	(1.7)	—	87
12/04	71.3	(10.2)	—	103
Annual Growth	**10.1%**	**—**	**—**	**0.0%**

2008 Year-End Financials

Equity as % of assets: 61.4%
Return on assets: 6.7%
Return on equity: 9.4%
Long-term debt ($ mil.): —
No. of shares (mil.): 14.2
Market value ($ mil.): 28.6
Dividends
Yield: 9.9%
Payout: 47.6%
Sales ($ mil.): 39.5
R&D as % of sales: —
Advertising as % of sales: —

Stock History

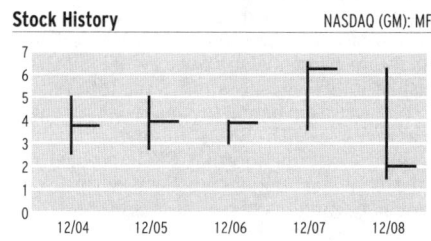

	STOCK PRICE ($) FY Close	P/E High/Low		PER SHARE ($) Earnings	Dividends	Book Value
12/08	2.02	15	4	0.42	0.20	4.54
12/07	6.25	15	8	0.44	0.20	4.29
12/06	3.89	14	11	0.28	0.20	3.96
12/05	3.94	—	—	(0.12)	0.25	3.86
12/04	3.75	—	—	(0.77)	0.00	4.38
Annual Growth	**(14.3%)**	**—**	**—**	**—**	**—**	**0.9%**

Microtune, Inc.

Microtune wants to be your cable (chip) company. As it returns to its origins as a maker of cable tuner chips, the company divested its wireless communication chip business. Microtune's chips enable broadband voice, data, and video communications in electronic gear such as car radios, cable modems and set-top boxes, digital TVs, DVRs, and PCs. Microtune expanded into the wireless area with its purchase of Transilica, but later exited the business. Microtune's customers include Cisco Systems (29% of sales), Unihan (a subsidiary of ASUSTeK Computer that assembles products for ARRIS Group, 13%), Panasonic (12%), Motorola, and Samsung Electronics. The company gets about two-thirds of its sales outside North America.

Microtune was hoping to see increased business from the US conversion to digital TV broadcasts in 2009, but that business may not materialize. The company supplies amplifier and tuner chips that go into the converter boxes being sold to help owners of analog TV sets make the transition to digital TV broadcasts. Microtune designs chips for digital TVs, HDTVs, and accessories for such video equipment. Semiconductors for digital-to-analog converter boxes represented 7% of the company's sales in 2008.

Aiming, however, to transition from a purveyor of pure-play tuners to a developer of integrated radio-frequency-to-bits chips, Microtune acquired privately held Auvitek International in July 2009. The Shanghai-based firm caters a lineup of advanced DTV demodulator integrated circuits (ICs) for the HDTV and TV-enabled accessories markets. Microtune will pay about $9 million in cash and stock for Auvitek.

Microtune outsources production of its silicon and silicon germanium wafers to IBM Microelectronics, Jazz Semiconductor, and X-FAB Silicon Foundries.

In 2008 the company reached a settlement with the SEC on its historical practices in granting stock options. Without admitting or denying the allegations in the commission's complaint, Microtune consented to a permanent injunction against future violations of US securities laws, and escaped from having to pay a penalty or damages in the case. The SEC still is pursuing a suit against Microtune's former CEO and CFO related to the stock options practices, and the company is helping pay the legal fees of those two former executives.

EXECUTIVES

President, CEO, and Director: James A. (Jim) Fontaine, age 51, $987,879 total compensation
EVP; Managing Director, Microtune GmbH: Barry F. Koch, age 43, $460,011 total compensation
VP and Interim CFO: Justin M. Chapman, age 35
VP Worldwide Sales: Robert S. Kirk, age 48, $530,277 total compensation
General Counsel: Phillip D. Peterson, age 39
Auditors: Ernst & Young LLP

LOCATIONS

HQ: Microtune, Inc.
    2201 10th St., Plano, TX 75074
Phone: 972-673-1600   **Fax:** 972-673-1602
Web: www.microtune.com

Microtune has offices in China, Germany, Japan, South Korea, Taiwan, the UK, and the US.

2008 Sales

	$ mil.	% of total
Asia/Pacific	47.5	44
North America	34.6	32
Europe	23.3	22
Other regions	2.6	2
Total	**108.0**	**100**

PRODUCTS/OPERATIONS

2008 Sales

	$ mil.	% of total
Silicon	81.3	75
Modules	26.5	25
Other	0.2	—
Total	**108.0**	**100**

Selected Products

Automotive electronics
    Radio-frequency (RF) automotive tuner subsystems
Broadband communications
    Broadband amplifiers
    Single-chip RF tuners (MicroTuner)
    Subsystems (RF modules and MicroModules)

COMPETITORS

Alps Electric
ANADIGICS
Analog Devices
Broadcom
BroadLogic
Entropic Communications
Freescale Semiconductor
Infineon Technologies
Integrated Device Technology
Intel
LG Electronics
Maxim Integrated Products
Mitsumi Electric
Murata Manufacturing
NXP
Panasonic Corp
RF Micro Devices
Samsung Electronics
SANYO Semiconductor
Sharp Corp.
Silicon Labs
Sony
STMicroelectronics
Texas Instruments
THOMSON
Toshiba Semiconductor
Zarlink

HISTORICAL FINANCIALS

Company Type: Public

Income Statement

FYE: December 31

	REVENUE ($ mil.)	NET INCOME ($ mil.)	NET PROFIT MARGIN	EMPLOYEES
12/08	108.0	6.4	5.9%	220
12/07	91.1	1.1	1.2%	206
12/06	69.2	(5.2)	—	204
12/05	57.0	(1.8)	—	178
12/04	56.2	5.5	9.8%	164
Annual Growth	17.7%	3.9%	—	7.6%

2008 Year-End Financials

Debt ratio: —
Return on equity: 6.0%
Cash ($ mil.): 46.1
Current ratio: 11.96
Long-term debt ($ mil.): —
No. of shares (mil.): 53.5
Dividends
    Yield: —
    Payout: —
Market value ($ mil.): 109.1
R&D as % of sales: —
Advertising as % of sales: —

Stock History

NASDAQ (GM): TUNE

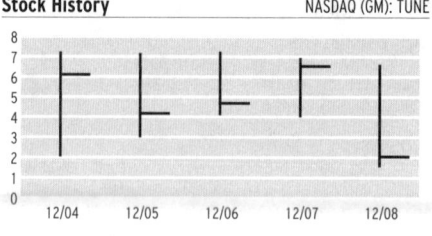

	STOCK PRICE ($) FY Close	P/E High/Low	Earnings	Dividends	Book Value
12/08	2.04	55 13	0.12	—	2.04
12/07	6.53	344 203	0.02	—	1.97
12/06	4.70	— —	(0.10)	—	1.80
12/05	4.17	— —	(0.03)	—	1.77
12/04	6.11	72 21	0.10	—	1.77
Annual Growth	(24.0%)	— —	4.7%	—	3.6%

Middleburg Financial

Middleburg Financial is the holding company for Middleburg Bank, which serves individuals and small to midsized businesses through about 10 branches in northern Virginia. The bank offers standard deposit products such as checking and savings accounts, money market and NOW accounts, CDs, and IRAs. Middleburg Bank focuses heavily on real estate lending: Commercial, agricultural, and residential mortgages account for about three-quarters of its loan portfolio; real estate construction loans add another 15%. Business and consumer installment loans round out the company's loan book.

Middleburg Financial also owns Middleburg Investment Group, which offers investment products to the bank's customers. Along with its Middleburg Trust Company division and fixed-income money manager Middleburg Investment Advisors, which serves clients in two dozen states (although it primarily operates in the DC area), the company has more than $500 million of assets under management.

Director Millicent West owns 10% of Middleburg Financial.

EXECUTIVES

Chairman and CEO: Joseph L. (Joe) Boling, age 64, $720,066 total compensation
EVP and COO: Jeffery H. Culver, age 41
EVP and CFO: Raj Mehra, age 48
EVP and Senior Loan Officer, Middleburg Bank: Arch A. Moore III, age 57, $318,780 total compensation
SVP Human Resources and Organizational Development: Suzanne Withers, age 58
SVP Retail Banking and Marketing: Robert S. Miller, age 52
President, Middleburg Investment Advisors: James H. Patterson, age 68, $480,597 total compensation
President and CEO, Middleburg Trust Company: John Mason L. Antrim, age 58
President and Director; President and CEO, Middleburg Bank: Gary R. Shook, age 44, $349,321 total compensation
Auditors: Yount, Hyde & Barbour, P.C.

LOCATIONS

HQ: Middleburg Financial Corporation
  111 W. Washington St., Middleburg, VA 20117
Phone: 703-777-6327   **Fax:** 703-737-3426
Web: www.middleburgbank.com

PRODUCTS/OPERATIONS

Selected Subsidiaries

Middleburg Bank
  Middleburg Bank Service Corporation

Middleburg Investment Group, Inc.
  Middleburg Investment Advisors, Inc.
  Middleburg Trust Company

COMPETITORS

BB&T
Chevy Chase Bank
M&T Bank
PNC Financial
SunTrust

HISTORICAL FINANCIALS

Company Type: Public

Income Statement

FYE: December 31

	ASSETS ($ mil.)	NET INCOME ($ mil.)	INCOME AS % OF ASSETS	EMPLOYEES
12/08	985.2	2.6	0.3%	333
12/07	841.4	3.1	0.4%	176
12/06	772.3	8.0	1.0%	168
12/05	739.9	7.2	1.0%	165
12/04	606.1	7.1	1.2%	171
Annual Growth	12.9%	(22.2%)	—	18.1%

2008 Year-End Financials

Equity as % of assets: 7.7%
Return on assets: 0.3%
Return on equity: 3.4%
Long-term debt ($ mil.): 89.2
No. of shares (mil.): 6.9
Market value ($ mil.): 100.7
Dividends
  Yield: 3.9%
  Payout: 101.8%
Sales ($ mil.): 50.1
R&D as % of sales: —
Advertising as % of sales: —

Stock History

NASDAQ (CM): MBRG

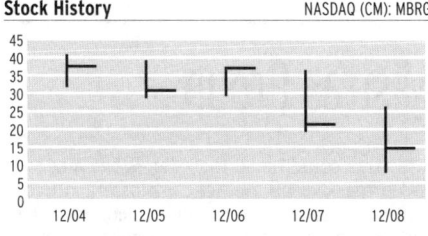

	STOCK PRICE ($) FY Close	P/E High/Low		PER SHARE ($) Earnings	Dividends	Book Value
12/08	14.59	46	14	0.56	0.57	10.96
12/07	21.32	54	29	0.67	0.76	11.29
12/06	36.99	19	16	1.90	0.76	11.29
12/05	30.75	21	16	1.84	0.76	7.75
12/04	37.50	22	18	1.81	0.76	7.47
Annual Growth	(21.0%)	—	—	(25.4%)	(6.9%)	10.1%

The Middleby Corporation

The Middleby Corporation certainly can stand the heat — its commercial and institutional foodservice equipment can be found in kitchens in more than 100 countries. Middleby makes equipment for restaurants, retail outlets, and hotels. The company is made up of three groups: Food Processing Equipment, Commercial Foodservice Equipment, and Middleby Worldwide (international). The company manufactures conveyor cooking equipment (Middleby Marshall, Blodgett, and CTX); heavy-duty gas equipment, like ranges, broilers, and fryers (Pitco Frialator, Nu-Vu, and Southbend); and light- and medium-duty electric cooking equipment, such as toasters and convection ovens (Toastmaster).

The company achieves its growth by acquiring cooking-focused companies that hold patented technologies and well-branded positions in their respective markets. The additions are typically subsumed as brands under Middleby's existing portfolio of innovative technologies. By offering an enhanced lineup, the company aims to reach a broader customer base.

Middleby enjoyed an acquisition binge in 2007. Five companies were taken in, including high-end commercial cooking equipment maker Jade Products, heated-cabinet specialist Carter-Hoffman, food-processing equipment producer MP Equipment, electric cooking products peddler Wells/Bloomfield, and maker of foodservice equipment for bakery café markets New Star Holdings.

In 2008 the company also acquired the net assets and related business operations of Frifri, a leading European frying systems supplier. Middleby subsequently bought range and oven manufacturer GIGA Grandi Cucine. During the first quarter of 2009 the company picked up Turbo-Chef Technologies, a US-based manufacturer of high-speed commercial and residential ovens; CookTek, a manufacturer of commercial induction cooking and warming systems; and all of the assets of Anetsberger Brothers, a griddle, fryer, and dough-roller equipment maker. Late in 2009 Middleby acquired Doyon Equipment, which makes baking ovens for the commercial foodservice market, expanding the company's brands in the warming and cooking segments and providing a number of new customers in the pizza and bakery chain restaurant markets.

The Commercial Foodservice Equipment group has a hot portfolio of ovens, ranges, broilers, fryers, steam equipment, toasters, coffee and tea brewers, and other cooking equipment. Middleby is cooking up new products, too, including the Rocket Fryer (advanced filtration) and the Blodgett Hydrovection oven. The cookware is marketed under brand names, including Houno, Lang, and Wells, to name a few. Customers include hotels, schools, hospitals, correctional facilities, stadiums, military facilities, government agencies, and restaurants (Cracker Barrel, McDonald's, Olive Garden, and Panda Express). Products are manufactured in the US, China, Denmark, Italy, and the Philippines.

The Food Processing Equipment group offers a broad buffet of products designed for the food processing industry, from batch ovens to mixing and slicing machines, packaging, and food safety equipment. The group has manufacturing facilities in the US. A large portion of revenues is generated from producers of pre-cooked meat products.

The International Distribution Division (Middleby Worldwide) offers customers a complete package of kitchen equipment, delivered and installed in over 100 countries. It has regional export management companies in Asia, Europe, and Latin America.

EXECUTIVES

Chairman, President, and CEO; President and CEO, Middleby Marshall, Inc.: Selim A. Bassoul, age 53, $12,463,278 total compensation
EVP Food Processing Group: Magdy Albert, age 58, $583,490 total compensation
VP and CFO, Middleby Corporation and Middleby Marshall: Timothy J. Fitzgerald, age 40, $2,580,286 total compensation
VP Supply Chain; President, Huono A/S, Middleby Philippines Corporation, Giga Grandi Cuicine S.r.l and Frifri: Ousama Sidani, age 52
COO Commercial Cooking Group: David Brewer, age 53
President, Star Manufacturing International: Frank Ricchio, age 57
President, Blodgett Oven Company: Gary Mick, age 48, $561,784 total compensation
President, Jade Range: Ray Williams, age 45
President, Middleby Cooking Systems Group: Mark A. Sieron, age 61, $649,508 total compensation
President, Southbend: Nazih Ibrahim, age 56
President, Pitco Frialator: Paul Angrick, age 52
Investor and Public Relations: Darcy Bretz
Treasurer: Martin M. Lindsay, age 45
Auditors: Deloitte & Touche LLP

LOCATIONS

HQ: The Middleby Corporation
  1400 Toastmaster Dr., Elgin, IL 60120
Phone: 847-741-3300   **Fax:** 847-741-0015
Web: www.middleby.com

2008 Sales

	$ mil.	% of total
US & Canada	529.6	81
Europe & Middle East	69.1	11
Asia	34.5	5
Latin America	18.7	3
Total	**651.9**	**100**

PRODUCTS/OPERATIONS

2008 Sales

	$ mil.	% of total
Commercial foodservice	547.4	80
Food processing	78.5	11
International distribution	62.4	9
Adjustments	(36.4)	—
Total	**651.9**	**100**

Selected Products and Brands

Commercial Foodservice Equipment Group
  Blodgett (convection and combi-ovens)
Bloomfield (coffee and tea brewers, beverage dispensing equipment)
Carter-Hoffmann (heated cabinets, rethermalizing and foodservice equipment)
CTX (conveyor oven equipment)
Frifri (fryers and frying systems)
GIGA Grandi Cucine (ranges, steam cooking equipment, and ovens)
Holman (high-speed, conveyorized toasting equipment)
Houno (combi-ovens and baking ovens)
Jade (specialty cooking equipment)
Lang (gas and electric solutions for commercial and marine applications)
MagiKitch'n (charbroiling products)
Middleby Marshall (conveyor oven equipment)
Nu-Vu (on-premise baking equipment)
Pito Frialator (fryers)
Southbend (heavy-duty, gas-fired equipment)

Star (equipment for fast food and concessions)
Toastmaster (conveyor toasters, hot food servers, griddles)
Wells (countertop and drop-in warmers)
Food Processing Equipment Group
  Alkar (batch and belt ovens, conveyorized cooking systems)
MP Equipment (breading, battering, mixing, forming, and slicing machines)
RapidPak (packaging and food safety equipment)

COMPETITORS

Aga Rangemaster
Ali SpA
Alto-Shaam
Bally Refrigerated Boxes
Cleveland Range
Dover Corp.
Electrolux
Franke Group
Frymaster
Gold Medal Products
Heat and Control
Hobart Corp.
Illinois Tool Works
Ingersoll-Rand
Krack
Lincoln Foodservice
Manitowoc Foodservice
Perfect Fry
Standex
Strategic Equipment and Supply
Vulcan-Hart

HISTORICAL FINANCIALS

Company Type: Public

Income Statement				FYE: Saturday nearest December 31
	REVENUE ($ mil.)	NET INCOME ($ mil.)	NET PROFIT MARGIN	EMPLOYEES
12/08	651.9	63.9	9.8%	1,779
12/07	500.5	52.6	10.5%	1,681
12/06	403.1	42.4	10.5%	1,282
12/05	316.7	32.2	10.2%	1,258
12/04	271.1	23.6	8.7%	992
Annual Growth	24.5%	28.3%	—	15.7%

2008 Year-End Financials

Debt ratio: 100.2%
Return on equity: 31.1%
Cash ($ mil.): 6.1
Current ratio: 1.48
Long-term debt ($ mil.): 228.3
No. of shares (mil.): 18.6
Dividends
  Yield: 0.0%
  Payout: —
Market value ($ mil.): 506.0
R&D as % of sales: —
Advertising as % of sales: —

Stock History   NASDAQ (GS): MIDD

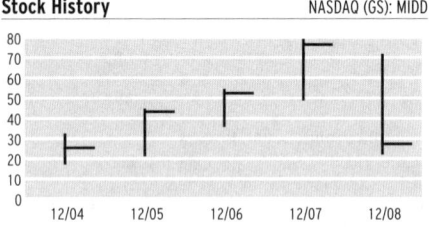

	STOCK PRICE ($) FY Close	P/E High/Low		PER SHARE ($) Earnings	Dividends	Book Value
12/08	27.27	19	6	3.75	0.00	12.28
12/07	76.62	25	16	3.11	0.00	9.86
12/06	52.33	21	14	2.57	0.00	5.42
12/05	43.25	22	11	1.99	0.00	2.61
12/04	25.36	27	15	1.19	0.00	0.39
Annual Growth	1.8%	—	—	33.2%	—	137.1%

MidSouth Bancorp

For banking in the Deep South, try out Mid-South. MidSouth Bancorp is the holding company for MidSouth Bank, which operates some 35 branches in South Louisiana and Southeast Texas. Targeting individuals and local business customers, the bank offers such standard retail services as checking and savings accounts, savings bonds, investment accounts, and credit card services. It also writes real estate mortgages (about 35% of its loan portfolio), and commercial (more than 30%), consumer, and construction loans. MidSouth also offers lease-financing loans for business equipment.

The company expanded into Texas with its 2004 purchase of Beaumont-based Lamar Bancshares. It changed the name of its Lamar Bank branches to MidSouth Bank-TX, then merged the two banks under the MidSouth Bank brand in 2008.

A group of 17 officers and directors owns about a third of MidSouth Bancorp.

EXECUTIVES

Chairman, MidSouth Bancorp and MidSouth LA: Will G. Charbonnet Sr., age 61
Vice Chairman: J. B. Hargroder, age 78
President, CEO, and Director, MidSouth Bancorp and MidSouth LA: C. R. (Rusty) Cloutier, age 61, $400,008 total compensation
SEVP and CFO: James R. McLemore, age 49
EVP; SVP and Senior Loan Officer, MidSouth LA: Donald R. (Donnie) Landry, age 52, $227,761 total compensation
SVP, Principal Accounting Officer, and Controller: Teri S. Stelly, age 49
Secretary, Treasurer, and Director; SEVP and COO, MidSouth LA: Karen L. Hail, age 55, $287,102 total compensation
VP and Chief Retail Officer: Carolyn Ray
Assistant VP Investor Relations: Sally D. Gary
Auditors: Porter Keadle Moore, LLP

LOCATIONS

HQ: MidSouth Bancorp, Inc.
  102 Versailles Blvd., Lafayette, LA 70501
Phone: 337-237-8343   **Fax:** 337-267-4434
Web: www.midsouthbank.com

PRODUCTS/OPERATIONS

2008 Gross Revenues

	$ mil.	% of total
Interest		
Loans	45.5	64
Securities	9.1	13
Other	0.8	1
Noninterest		
Deposit account service charges	10.3	15
Other	4.9	7
Total	70.6	100

COMPETITORS

American Bancorp
Bank of America
Capital One
Encore Bancshares
Hancock Holding
Henderson Citizens Bancshares
Home Bank
IBERIABANK
Regions Financial
Teche Holding
Whitney Holding

HISTORICAL FINANCIALS

Company Type: Public

Income Statement				FYE: December 31
	ASSETS ($ mil.)	NET INCOME ($ mil.)	INCOME AS % OF ASSETS	EMPLOYEES
12/08	936.8	5.5	0.6%	419
12/07	854.1	8.8	1.0%	410
12/06	805.0	8.2	1.0%	371
12/05	698.8	7.3	1.0%	337
12/04	610.1	7.0	1.1%	300
Annual Growth	11.3%	(5.9%)	—	8.7%

2008 Year-End Financials

Equity as % of assets: 7.8%
Return on assets: 0.6%
Return on equity: 7.8%
Long-term debt ($ mil.): 51.5
No. of shares (mil.): 6.6
Market value ($ mil.): 84.4
Dividends
  Yield: 2.5%
  Payout: 38.6%
Sales ($ mil.): 54.5
R&D as % of sales: —
Advertising as % of sales: —

Stock History   NYSE Alternext: MSL

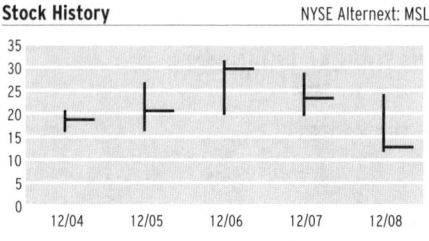

	STOCK PRICE ($) FY Close	P/E High/Low		PER SHARE ($) Earnings	Dividends	Book Value
12/08	12.75	29	14	0.83	0.32	11.04
12/07	23.30	22	15	1.32	0.25	10.35
12/06	29.68	25	16	1.24	0.19	9.03
12/05	20.56	24	15	1.10	0.17	8.04
12/04	18.70	18	14	1.13	0.14	7.34
Annual Growth	(9.1%)	—	—	(7.4%)	23.0%	10.7%

Mistras Group

Mistras could be all that stands between you and a massive oil refinery explosion, nuclear facility meltdown, or big bridge collapse. The engineering services company conducts non-destructive testing on critical equipment and processes used by petroleum (the majority), aerospace, infrastructure, power generation, and chemical manufacturing companies worldwide. It checks plant infrastructure for defects and problems without interrupting production; inspections take place during facility design, build, maintenance, and operation phases. Mistras works from nearly 50 offices in 15 nations to serve clients that include Alcan, Honeywell, Bechtel, BP, Dow Chemical, Airbus, and federal and state governments.

The company, which filed to go public in mid-2008, used its initial IPO proceeds to whittle down debt and for general corporate purposes, including the purchase and manufacturing of testing equipment, investments in software and existing equipment, and possible acquisitions. It also plans to expand into health care, construction, and port infrastructure testing.

In addition to its on-site testing services, the company also offers testing equipment, instruments, and software through its Software and Products division. Services performed in North and Central America, primarily the US, account for the majority of revenue. Testing services include mechanical integrity, above ground storage tank, and visual testing, along with digital radiography, ground penetrating radar, and infrared and ultrasonic sensor testing. Mistras' software offerings include databases and enterprise software to store and analyze testing data, planning software, and on-line monitoring systems.

Chairman, president, and CEO Sotirios Vahaviolos owns about 60% of Mistras pre-IPO.

EXECUTIVES

Chairman, President, and CEO: Sotirios J. Vahaviolos, age 63
CFO and Secretary: Paul (Pete) Peterik, age 59
Group EVP, Services and Director: Michael J. Lange, age 49
Group EVP, Software and Products: Mark F. Carlos, age 58
Group EVP, International: Phillip T. Cole, age 56
Group VP, Nuclear Products and Services: Fred Klorczyk
Marketing Director: Katie Monte
Auditors: PricewaterhouseCoopers LLP

LOCATIONS

HQ: Mistras Group, Inc.
195 Clarksville Rd., Princeton Junction, NJ 08550
Phone: 609-716-4000 **Fax:** 609-716-4145
Web: www.mistrasgroup.com

2009 Sales

	% of total
US	78
Other countries	22
Total	**100**

PRODUCTS/OPERATIONS

2009 Sales

	% of total
Oil & gas	58
Fossil & nuclear power generation & transmission	10
Industrial	10
Chemicals, food & pharmaceuticals	8
Aerospace, public infrastructure & other	14
Total	**100**

COMPETITORS

The Carlyle Group
GE Inspection Technologies
Lloyd's Register
SGS
Siemens AG
Team

HISTORICAL FINANCIALS

Company Type: Public

Income Statement

	REVENUE ($ mil.)	NET INCOME ($ mil.)	NET PROFIT MARGIN	EMPLOYEES	FYE: May 31
5/09	209.1	5.5	2.6%	2,000	
5/08	152.3	7.4	4.9%	1,500	
5/07	122.2	5.4	4.4%	1,500	
5/06	93.7	0.5	0.5%	—	
5/05	80.8	(4.1)	—	—	
Annual Growth	**26.8%**	**—**	**—**	**15.5%**	

2009 Year-End Financials

Debt ratio: —   Current ratio: 1.44
Return on equity: —   Long-term debt ($ mil.): 61.4
Cash ($ mil.): 5.7

Net Income History   NYSE: MG

Mobile Mini

Mobile Mini knows that storing stuff means big business. The company manufactures, leases, and sells portable storage containers and mobile offices. Mobile Mini's line includes steel and wood office units in various sizes, with a selection of shelving, wiring, and locking features. Small to big retailers, construction companies, and medical centers in the US and UK are Mobile Mini's primary customers. Other customers are the military, municipal agencies, and schools. Storage units are both manufactured and refurbished (using old oceangoing containers) by Mobile Mini. The company touts a leasing fleet of 273,700-plus portable storage units and offices. Its leasing operation accounts for some 90% of total sales.

Looking to expand its leasing footprint, the company acquired California-based Mobile Storage Group (MSG) for just over $700 million in 2008. The deal gives Mobile Mini access to a dominating share of the portable storage market in the US and UK. Its purchase fell on the heels of picking up three companies in 2006 from the Royal Wolf Group, part of Triton CSA International B.V., and some of the business of A-One Storage LLC in 2005.

Since its founding in 1983 Mobile Mini has been entrenched in a broad swath of work segments needing temporary storage and work space. According to the company, its move to lay off about 25% of its workforce in 2009 reflects weakening demand along with the costs associated with retrofitting its manufacturing operations and buying MSG.

Private equity firm Welsh, Carson, Anderson & Stowe (WCAS) plays an active role in managing Mobile Mini. It owns a controlling stake of over 75%.

EXECUTIVES

Chairman, President, and CEO: Steven G. Bunger, age 47, $1,261,221 total compensation
EVP and CFO: Mark E. Funk, age 47, $95,035 total compensation
EVP and COO: Jody E. Miller, age 42
SVP and General Counsel: Christopher J. Miner, age 37
SVP Operations: Jon D. Keating, age 39
SVP and Chief Accounting Officer: Deborah K. Keeley, age 44, $400,689 total compensation
SVP, Eastern Division: Kyle G. Blackwell, age 45
SVP, Southeastern Division: William E. Armstead, age 45
SVP, Central Division: Ronald E. Marshall, age 58, $312,539 total compensation

SVP and Managing Director, Europe: Ron Halchishak, age 61
SVP, Western Division: Russell C. Lemley, age 51, $468,338 total compensation
COO, Integration: Douglas A. Waugaman
Auditors: Ernst & Young LLP

LOCATIONS

HQ: Mobile Mini, Inc.
7420 S. Kyrene Rd., Ste. 101, Tempe, AZ 85283
Phone: 480-894-6311 **Fax:** 480-894-6433
Web: www.mobilemini.com

2008 Sales

	$ mil.	% of total
North America	356.3	86
UK	53.1	13
Netherlands	6.0	1
Total	**415.4**	**100**

PRODUCTS/OPERATIONS

2008 Sales

	$ mil.	% of total
Leasing	371.5	89
Sales	41.3	10
Other	2.6	1
Total	**415.4**	**100**

2008 Leasing Customers

	% of total
Construction	36
Consumer service & retail business	30
Industrial & commercial	13
Government & institutions	10
Consumers	4
Other	7
Total	**100**

Selected Products

Mobile offices
Portable storage products
   Manufactured storage units
   Records storage units
   Refurbished storage units

COMPETITORS

AMERCO
GE
McGrath RentCorp
Modtech
Public Storage
Williams Scotsman

HISTORICAL FINANCIALS

Company Type: Public

Income Statement

	REVENUE ($ mil.)	NET INCOME ($ mil.)	NET PROFIT MARGIN	EMPLOYEES	FYE: December 31
12/08	415.4	29.0	7.0%	2,155	
12/07	318.3	44.2	13.9%	2,095	
12/06	273.4	42.8	15.7%	1,943	
12/05	207.2	34.0	16.4%	1,650	
12/04	168.3	20.7	12.3%	1,556	
Annual Growth	**25.3%**	**8.8%**	**—**	**8.5%**	

2008 Year-End Financials

Debt ratio: 71.0%   Dividends
Return on equity: 6.1%   Yield: 0.0%
Cash ($ mil.): 3.2   Payout: —
Current ratio: 0.14   Market value ($ mil.): 512.2
Long-term debt ($ mil.): 351.6   R&D as % of sales: —
No. of shares (mil.): 35.5   Advertising as % of sales: —

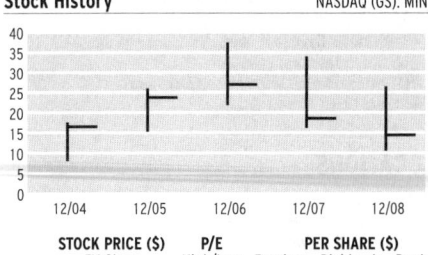

Stock History

NASDAQ (GS): MINI

	STOCK PRICE ($) FY Close	P/E High/Low		PER SHARE ($) Earnings	Dividends	Book Value
12/08	14.42	35	15	0.75	0.00	18.28
12/07	18.54	28	14	1.22	0.00	12.89
12/06	26.94	31	18	1.21	0.00	12.44
12/05	23.70	23	14	1.10	0.00	7.54
12/04	16.52	25	12	0.70	0.00	6.09
Annual Growth	(3.3%)	—	—	1.7%	—	31.6%

Monarch Financial Holdings

Money rules at Monarch Financial Holdings. The holding company serves the South Hampton Roads area of southeastern Virginia through Monarch Bank, Monarch Mortgage, Monarch Capital, Monarch Investment, and OBXBank. With about 10 offices, Monarch Bank offers standard services, including savings and checking accounts, IRAs, and CDS. Bank subsidiary Monarch Mortgage, formed in 2007, has about a dozen offices. Other divisions sell insurance, title, and investment products. Single-family mortgages make up the largest portion of the company's loan portfolio, which also includes commercial, construction, and land development loans. Monarch Bank division OBX Bank operates in North Carolina's Outer Banks area.

EXECUTIVES

Chairman: Jeffrey F. Benson, age 47, $13,715 total compensation
Vice Chairman: Lawton H. Baker, age 65, $9,775 total compensation
President, CEO, and Director:
 William F. (Bill) Rountree Jr., age 65, $542,180 total compensation
EVP, COO, CFO, Secretary, and Director; CEO, Monarch Bank: Brad E. Schwartz, age 46, $270,684 total compensation
EVP and Senior Operations Officer: Barbara N. Lane, age 59
SVP and Chief Accounting Officer; SVP and CFO, Monarch Bank: Lynette P. Harris
SVP and Chief Credit Officer: Andrew N. Lock, age 45
SVP Marketing: Nancy B. Porter, age 40
President, Real Estate and Construction:
 James R. (Jim) Ferber, age 52
President OBX Bank: David McGlaughon, age 51
President and CEO, Monarch Mortgage:
 Edward O. Yoder, age 43, $294,782 total compensation
President, Monarch Bank, Norfolk: Donald F. Price
President, Monarch Bank, Virginia Beach Region:
 W. Craig Reilly, age 33
President, Virginia Asset Group: Darin M. Ely, age 37
President, Chesapeake: Barry A. Mathias, age 59
President, Monarch Bank and Director:
 E. Neal Crawford, age 46
Auditors: Goodman & Company, L.L.P.

LOCATIONS

HQ: Monarch Financial Holdings, Inc.
 750 Volvo Pkwy., Chesapeake, VA 23320
Phone: 757-222-2100   **Fax:** 757-222-2101
Web: www.monarchbank.com

PRODUCTS/OPERATIONS

2008 Gross Revenues

	$ mil.	% of total
Interest		
Loans, including fees	29.9	76
Securities	0.6	2
Other	0.3	1
Noninterest		
Mortgage banking	5.1	13
Service charges & fees	1.2	3
Other	2.0	5
Total	**39.1**	**100**

COMPETITORS

Bank of America
BB&T
Commonwealth Bankshares
Hampton Roads Bankshares
RBC Bank
SunTrust

HISTORICAL FINANCIALS

Company Type: Public

Income Statement

FYE: December 31

	ASSETS ($ mil.)	NET INCOME ($ mil.)	INCOME AS % OF ASSETS	EMPLOYEES
12/08	597.2	1.1	0.2%	295
12/07	503.2	3.2	0.6%	254
12/06	407.7	3.6	0.9%	126
12/05	331.2	2.1	0.6%	101
12/04	226.9	0.8	0.4%	84
Annual Growth	27.4%	8.3%	—	36.9%

2008 Year-End Financials

Equity as % of assets: 7.6%
Return on assets: 0.2%
Return on equity: 2.7%
Long-term debt ($ mil.): 27.7
No. of shares (mil.): 5.8
Market value ($ mil.): 39.1
Dividends
 Yield: 0.0%
 Payout: —
Sales ($ mil.): 36.0
R&D as % of sales: —
Advertising as % of sales: —

Stock History

NASDAQ (CM): MNRK

	STOCK PRICE ($) FY Close	P/E High/Low		PER SHARE ($) Earnings	Dividends	Book Value
12/08	6.75	54	30	0.21	0.00	10.32
12/07	9.50	26	15	0.63	0.00	6.31
12/06	14.35	23	14	0.73	0.00	5.87
12/05	10.57	24	18	0.46	0.00	5.15
12/04	8.67	51	41	0.18	0.00	3.65
Annual Growth	(6.1%)	—	—	3.9%	—	29.7%

Monolithic Power Systems

Monolithic Power Systems (MPS) doesn't make enormous electrical equipment, but rather tiny silicon chips. The fabless semiconductor company offers analog and mixed-signal microchips — especially chips for lighting displays — that are used in digital still cameras, wireless LAN equipment, wireless phones, and other electronic devices. MPS outsources production of its chips to China-based silicon foundry ASMC. The company's products are incorporated into electronic gear from tech heavyweights, such as Dell, Hewlett-Packard, Motorola, Samsung Electronics, and Sony. MPS gets most of its sales in the Asia/Pacific region, primarily from China.

In 2008 Taiwan Semiconductor Manufacturing Co. (TSMC) acquired an equity stake of nearly 6% in Monolithic Power. The company has no foundry services relationship with TSMC, the world's largest contract semiconductor manufacturer. Monolithic Power relies on ASMC to make its semiconductors, while occasionally contracting some fabrication work to Seiko Epson.

Litigation with competitors such as Linear Technology, Micrel, Microsemi, and O2Micro International is a big portion of Monolithic Power's spending budget, consuming 20% of 2005 sales — more than it spent on R&D that year. The figures were reversed in 2006, with MPS spending about 14% of sales on litigation and 21% on R&D (including stock-based compensation). The company reached settlements with Micrel and Microsemi in 2006, paying $3 million to Micrel.

In 2007 MPS spent about 20% of sales on R&D. The company settled its patent litigation with Taiwan Sumida Electronics and put aside $9.8 million to cover that settlement.

For 2008 MPS set aside about $6.7 million for litigation, or around 4% of sales, while designating $34.85 million for R&D expenditures, or nearly 22% of sales.

EXECUTIVES

President, CEO, and Director: Michael R. Hsing, age 49, $1,574,004 total compensation
SVP Worldwide Sales and Tactical Marketing:
 Maurice Sciammas, age 49, $1,112,380 total compensation
SVP Finance and CFO: Richard (Rick) Neely Jr., age 54, $998,630 total compensation
SVP Engineering: Paul Ueunten, age 54
Chief Design Engineer and Director:
 James C. (Jim) Moyer, age 67
VP and General Counsel: Saria Tseng, age 36
President, Asia Operations: Deming Xiao, age 46, $1,171,718 total compensation
Auditors: Deloitte & Touche LLP

LOCATIONS

HQ: Monolithic Power Systems, Inc.
 6409 Guadalupe Mines Rd., San Jose, CA 95120
Phone: 408-826-0600   **Fax:** 408-826-0601
Web: www.monolithicpower.com

Monolithic Power Systems has offices in China, Japan, South Korea, Taiwan, and the US.

2008 Sales

	$ mil.	% of total
Asia/Pacific		
China	72.4	45
South Korea	25.7	16
Taiwan	22.0	13
Japan	15.6	10
Europe	12.9	8
US	4.3	3
Other regions	7.6	5
Total	**160.5**	**100**

PRODUCTS/OPERATIONS

2008 Sales

	$ mil.	% of total
DC-to-DC converters	115.4	72
LCD backlight inverters	32.3	20
Audio amplifiers	12.8	8
Total	**160.5**	**100**

COMPETITORS

Analog Devices	Microsemi
BCD Semiconductor	National Semiconductor
Fairchild Semiconductor	O2Micro
Intersil	ROHM
iWatt	Semtech
Linear Technology	STMicroelectronics
Maxim Integrated Products	Texas Instruments
Micrel	

HISTORICAL FINANCIALS

Company Type: Public

Income Statement

FYE: December 31

	REVENUE ($ mil.)	NET INCOME ($ mil.)	NET PROFIT MARGIN	EMPLOYEES
12/08	160.5	24.2	15.1%	579
12/07	134.0	9.3	6.9%	500
12/06	105.0	(2.9)	—	393
12/05	99.1	5.1	5.1%	240
12/04	47.6	(5.6)	—	154
Annual Growth	**35.5%**	**—**	**—**	**39.2%**

2008 Year-End Financials

Debt ratio: —
Return on equity: 16.0%
Cash ($ mil.): 83.3
Current ratio: 5.53
Long-term debt ($ mil.): —
No. of shares (mil.): 34.9

Dividends
  Yield: 0.0%
  Payout: —
Market value ($ mil.): 440.1
R&D as % of sales: —
Advertising as % of sales: —

Stock History

NASDAQ (GM): MPWR

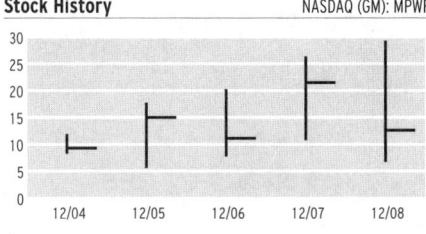

	STOCK PRICE ($) FY Close	P/E High/Low		PER SHARE ($) Earnings	Dividends	Book Value
12/08	12.61	43	10	0.67	0.00	4.72
12/07	21.47	101	42	0.26	0.00	3.93
12/06	11.11	—	—	(0.10)	0.00	2.72
12/05	14.99	103	34	0.17	0.00	2.24
12/04	9.30	—	—	(0.62)	0.00	1.82
Annual Growth	**7.9%**	**—**	**—**	**—**	**—**	**26.9%**

Monotype Imaging

Monotype Imaging may be to thank if you're reading this on a mobile device or a printed page. The company's text-imaging software is integrated into applications and embedded in electronics ranging from mobile phones to laser printers. Its applications manage compression, scaling, color, and layout. Allowing customers access to thousands of typefaces, the company generates most of its revenue from OEM sales, though it also licenses its fonts to creative and business professionals. Customers include Nokia, JVC, Sony, Hewlett-Packard, and Microsoft. TA Associates owns more than half of the company.

Monotype Imaging was formed when a group of investors, including TA Associates, acquired Agfa Monotype (then a subsidiary of Agfa) in 2004.

The company does business as International Typeface Corporation or ITC in the US; China Type Design, Monotype Imaging, and Monotype Japan in Asia; and Monotype UK and Linotype in Europe.

In late 2009 it purchased Planetweb for about $2 million. PlanetWeb provides user interface software and developer tools for the consumer electronics industry.

EXECUTIVES

Chairman: Robert M. Givens, age 65
President, CEO, and Director: Douglas J. (Doug) Shaw, age 54, $830,273 total compensation
EVP: John L. Seguin, age 55, $566,715 total compensation
SVP, CFO, Treasurer, and Assistant Secretary: Scott Landers, age 38, $410,404 total compensation
General Counsel and Secretary: Janet M. Dunlap, age 44, $452,488 total compensation
VP Business Development: Daniel T. (Dan) Gerron, age 43
VP Human Resources: Patricia J. Money, age 53
VP New Type Technology: Geoffrey W. Greve, age 52
VP and General Manager, Creative Professional: David R. DeWitt, age 52
VP Marketing: Christopher J. Roberts, age 43
VP and Chief Technologist: Jack P. Murphy, age 61
VP Engineering and Development: Steven R. Martin, age 47
VP and General Manager, OEM Sales: David L. McCarthy, age 52
Director Words and Letters: Allan Haley
Auditors: Ernst & Young LLP

LOCATIONS

HQ: Monotype Imaging Holdings Inc.
500 Unicorn Park Dr., Woburn, MA 01801
Phone: 781-970-6000   **Fax:** 781-970-6001
Web: www.monotypeimaging.com

2008 Sales

	$ mil.	% of total
Asia	42.7	39
US	36.0	32
Germany	19.3	17
UK	12.9	12
Total	**110.9**	**100**

PRODUCTS/OPERATIONS

2008 Sales

	$ mil.	% of total
OEM	77.8	70
Creative professional	33.1	30
Total	**110.9**	**100**

HISTORICAL FINANCIALS

Company Type: Public

Income Statement

FYE: December 31

	REVENUE ($ mil.)	NET INCOME ($ mil.)	NET PROFIT MARGIN	EMPLOYEES
12/08	110.9	15.4	13.9%	238
12/07	105.2	(25.0)	—	243
12/06	86.2	(17.3)	—	239
12/05	73.8	7.1	9.6%	237
12/04	65.0	(3.7)	—	—
Annual Growth	**14.3%**	**—**	**—**	**0.1%**

2008 Year-End Financials

Debt ratio: 79.3%
Return on equity: 13.8%
Cash ($ mil.): 31.9
Current ratio: 1.08
Long-term debt ($ mil.): 95.8
No. of shares (mil.): 34.7

Dividends
  Yield: 0.0%
  Payout: —
Market value ($ mil.): 201.0
R&D as % of sales: —
Advertising as % of sales: —

Stock History

NASDAQ (GM): TYPE

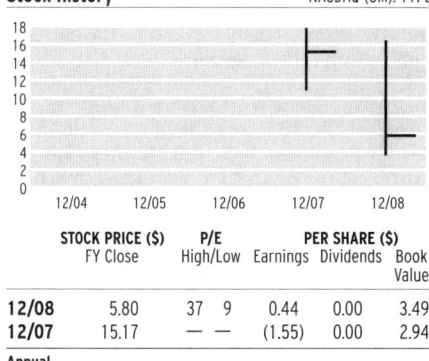

	STOCK PRICE ($) FY Close	P/E High/Low		PER SHARE ($) Earnings	Dividends	Book Value
12/08	5.80	37	9	0.44	0.00	3.49
12/07	15.17	—	—	(1.55)	0.00	2.94
Annual Growth	**(61.8%)**	**—**	**—**	**—**	**—**	**18.5%**

Morningstar, Inc.

Morningstar offers a smorgasbord of financial information to individual, professional, and institutional investors via Internet, software, and print-based products. The company provides data on more than 300,000 investment products, including stocks and mutual funds. It also provides real-time global market data on more than 4 million equities, indexes, futures, options, and commodities. Its Morningstar Style Box, which provides a visual summary of a mutual fund's underlying investment style, and Morningstar Ratings, which rate past performance based on risk- and cost-adjusted returns, have become fixtures on the investment landscape.

Chairman and CEO Joe Mansueto owns about 60% of Morningstar.

The company has three major Internet-based platforms. Its Morningstar.com features content for individual investors on portfolio planning, mutual funds, and stocks. In addition, its Morningstar Advisor Workstation is a Web-based investment planning system for financial advisors, while Morningstar Direct is a product for institutional investment researchers. Other key Morningstar products include Licensed Data, a set of investment data spanning eight core databases, and the Principia product line, a CD-ROM-based investment research and planning application for financial planners. The company's

Morningstar Mutual Funds is a reference publication featuring one-page reports on some 1,500 mutual funds.

Key to the company's strategy is a continued focus on these offerings by expanding their functionality, selling more subscriptions, and reaching new market segments. Morningstar also plans to emphasize its independent investment research offerings and expand its global reach. (The company has operations in some 20 countries.) As a result of the declining economic environment, in 2009 Morningstar took cost-cutting measures, such as reducing employee benefits and bonuses.

Despite a challenging economy, the acquisitive company continues to invest in the business. In 2009 it expanded its operations internationally with the purchase of Intech Pty Ltd, a provider of multimanager and investment portfolio solutions in Sydney, Australia. Later that year Morningstar entered a new distribution channel with the nearly $52 million buy of Logical Information Machines, a provider of market pricing data and data management services to the agricultural, energy, and financial sectors.

A significant acquisition for Morningstar was the 2008 purchase of 10-K Wizard, an electronic provider of SEC filing documents, for $12.5 million. The purchase bolstered Morningstar's research capabilities and aids in the company's goal of providing greater transparency to equity investments. Other 2008 purchases included London market data firm Tenfore Systems for £13.5 million ($20.9 million). Tenfore provides information on stocks, commodities, derivatives, and other investments, and the deal allows Morningstar to bundle real-time data such as stock prices with its research. The company purchased Fundamental Data Limited, a provider of data on closed-end funds in the UK, for some £11 million (approximately $19 million), as well as the Hemscott data, media, and investor relations Web site businesses from Ipreo for about $52 million.

HISTORY

Joseph Mansueto founded Morningstar in 1984, using a line borrowed from Thoreau's *Walden* ("The sun is but a morning star"). Armed with an MBA and experience culled from a stint as a securities analyst for Harris Associates, Mansueto published *Mutual Fund Sourcebook*, a tome outlining performance histories and other information on 400 stock mutual funds. The boom in mutual funds during the early 1980s spurred interest in Morningstar's product and prompted the company to add a second publication, *Morningstar Mutual Funds*, two years later.

The company's 1994 acquisition of MarketBase helped the firm add stock information to its coverage. A 5% staff cut in 1996 and the cessation of some of its publications helped reverse Morningstar's sagging fortunes. It took to cyberspace the next year when it launched Morningstar.net (now Morningstar.com). That year the company partnered with SOFTBANK to create Morningstar Japan and present financial information to investors in that country.

Don Phillips, who had joined Morningstar as its first analyst in 1986, was appointed CEO in 1998. The company began offering a subscription-based premium service feature for its Web site to provide users with expanded financial coverage.

In 1999 Morningstar extended its reach, partnering with FPG Research to offer financial information to residents of Australia and New Zealand. Later that year SOFTBANK invested $91 million in Morningstar.

In 2000 Morningstar established Web site MorningstarAdvisor.com, relaunched its flagship site with additional information and tools, and opened offices in the UK, Hong Kong, and South Korea. Founder and chairman Joe Mansueto also assumed the role of CEO in 2000 and made Phillips a managing director of the company.

The following year the company launched its Web site in Germany, Italy, the Netherlands, Spain, and the UK. Morningstar added Australian financial publisher Aspect Huntley to its stable in 2006. It paid nearly $23 million for the provider of equity information, research, and financial trade publishing in order to expand outside the US. In 2007 Morningstar paid some $58 million for the mutual fund data business from Standard & Poor's. The following year it purchased Hemscott and 10-K Wizard.

In 2008 Morningstar launched four new investment newsletters (*Morningstar Healthcare-Observer, Morningstar InternationalInvestor, Morningstar OptionInvestor,* and *Morningstar Opportunistic Investor*).

EXECUTIVES

Chairman and CEO: Joseph (Joe) Mansueto, age 52, $106,145 total compensation
COO: Tao Huang, age 47, $2,514,189 total compensation
CFO: Scott Cooley, age 41, $890,674 total compensation
Chief Investment Officer Investment Services: Jeffrey Ptak
Chief of Securities Research: Haywood Kelly
SVP Corporate Sales: Kishore Gangwani
VP Quantitative Research: Paul D. Kaplan
Director Corporate Systems: John Tipton
Director Equity Research: Patrick Dorsey
Director Corporate Communications: Margaret Kirch Cohen
Director Mergers and Acquisitions: Dan Piscatelli
Managing Director, Intech Pty Ltd.: Anthony Serhan
Managing Director Corporate Strategy, Research, and Corporate Communications and Director; President Fund Research: Don Phillips, age 46
President and Chief Investment Officer, Ibbotson Associates: Peng Chen, age 39
President Individual Investor Software: Kunal Kapoor, age 33
President Equity Research: Catherine G. Odelbo, age 47
President Morningstar Associates: Patrick Reinkemeyer, age 44, $2,127,446 total compensation
President Advisor Software: Chris Boruff, age 44, $1,205,873 total compensation
President Data Services Business: Elizabeth (Liz) Kirscher, age 45
President International Division and Institutional Software: Bevin Desmond, age 43
General Counsel and Corporate Secretary: Richard E. Robbins, age 47
Auditors: Ernst & Young LLP

LOCATIONS

HQ: Morningstar, Inc.
22 W. Washington St., Chicago, IL 60602
Phone: 312-696-6000 **Fax:** 312-696-6001
Web: www.morningstar.com

2008 Sales

	$ mil.	% of total
US	381.1	76
International	121.4	24
Total	**502.5**	**100**

PRODUCTS/OPERATIONS

2008 Sales

	$ mil.	% of total
Institutional	276.8	54
Advisor	127.6	25
Individual	107.6	21
Adjustments	(9.5)	—
Total	**502.5**	**100**

Selected Products and Services

Morningstar Advisor Workstation (Web-based investment planning software)
Morningstar FundInvestor (monthly mutual fund newsletter)
Morningstar Licensed Data (electronic investment data feeds)
Morningstar Mutual Funds (semimonthly information on 1,600 mutual funds)
Morningstar Principia (CD-ROM-based investment planning software)
Morningstar StockInvestor (monthly stock newsletter)
MorningstarAdvisor.com (market analysis, stock and fund information, portfolio tools, and investment research for advisors)
Morningstar.com (market analysis, stock and fund information, portfolio tools, and investment research for individuals)

COMPETITORS

Bankrate	McGraw-Hill
Bloomberg L.P.	Motley Fool
Dow Jones	PCQuote.com
Financial Engines	TheStreet.com
Intuit	Thomson Reuters
Ipreo	Value Line
MarketWatch	WisdomTree Investments

HISTORICAL FINANCIALS

Company Type: Public

Income Statement

FYE: December 31

	REVENUE ($ mil.)	NET INCOME ($ mil.)	NET PROFIT MARGIN	EMPLOYEES
12/08	502.5	92.5	18.4%	2,375
12/07	435.1	73.9	17.0%	1,720
12/06	315.2	51.5	16.3%	1,440
12/05	227.1	31.1	13.7%	1,130
12/04	179.7	8.8	4.9%	1,000
Annual Growth	**29.3%**	**80.1%**	**—**	**24.1%**

2008 Year-End Financials

Debt ratio: —
Return on equity: 19.6%
Cash ($ mil.): 173.9
Current ratio: 1.77
Long-term debt ($ mil.): —
No. of shares (mil.): 48.6

Dividends
 Yield: —
 Payout: —
Market value ($ mil.): 1,724.9
R&D as % of sales: —
Advertising as % of sales: —

Stock History

NASDAQ (GS): MORN

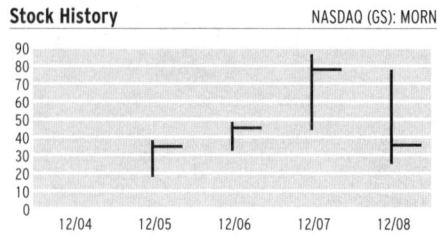

	STOCK PRICE ($) FY Close	P/E High/Low		PER SHARE ($) Earnings	Dividends	Book Value
12/08	35.50	41	14	1.88	—	11.02
12/07	77.75	56	29	1.53	—	8.40
12/06	45.05	43	30	1.11	—	5.55
12/05	34.64	53	26	0.70	—	3.58
Annual Growth	**0.8%**	**—**	**—**	**73.0%**	**—**	**69.8%**

MSCI Inc.

You ask your asset manager how your portfolio is doing, but who does he ask? Probably MSCI. The company, formerly Morgan Stanley Capital International (and doing business as MSCI Barra), creates equity, fixed income, and hedge fund indices, and offers risk management and portfolio analysis tools for large asset management firms. The company's products are marketed under four categories: equity indices (such as MSCI), equity portfolio analytics (such as Barra Aegis), multi-asset class portfolio analytics (such as BarraOne), and other products (including FEA for energy and commodity asset valuation analytics). Financial services powerhouse Morgan Stanley owns about 30% of MSCI and controls 66% of its votes.

MSCI was spun off from Morgan Stanley in 2007. In order to raise capital in the severe economic downturn, in 2009 Morgan Stanley announced plans to sell its remaining stake — worth some $650 million — in MSCI.

In 2008 the company experienced growth in subscriptions across all of its MSCI Global Investable Market Indices products, including developed market, emerging market, and small cap indices, as well as sales of historical index data. The following year it expanded its presence in the Americas with the opening of a new office in Boston.

Looking to the Muslim world for growth, the company opened an office in Dubai and launched its Islamic indices in 2007. Its MSCI Global Islamic Indices product incorporates allowances for Sharia or Islamic law. The company also has plans to open an office in Monterrey, Mexico.

The company's largest client is Barclays, which accounts for about 11% of revenues. MSCI has more than 3,100 clients across some 65 countries, and nearly half of the company's revenues come from outside the Americas. All total, it has about 20 offices worldwide, including headquarters in New York and sales offices in San Francisco, Chicago, and São Paulo, Brazil.

The company filed an IPO in 2007; proceeds from the public offering are being used to pay debt MSCI owes to Morgan Stanley.

EXECUTIVES

Chairman, President, and CEO: Henry A. Fernandez, age 51, $12,069,762 total compensation
COO: David C. Brierwood
CFO: Michael K. Neborak, $6,016,176 total compensation
Head Strategy and Business Development and Chief Administrative Officer: Gary Retelny, $2,936,016 total compensation
Head Client Coverage: C.D. Baer Pettit, $3,746,385 total compensation
Investor Relations: Lisa Monaco
Auditors: Deloitte & Touche LLP

LOCATIONS

HQ: MSCI Inc.
Wall Street Plaza, 88 Pine St., 2nd Fl.
New York, NY 10005
Phone: 212-804-3900   **Fax:** 212-804-2919
Web: www.mscibarra.com

2008 Sales

	$ mil.	% of total
Americas	222.0	51
Europe, Middle East & Africa	141.4	33
Asia & Australia	67.6	16
Total	**431.0**	**100**

PRODUCTS/OPERATIONS

2008 Sales

	$ mil.	% of total
Equity indices	239.5	55
Equity portfolio analytics	132.4	31
Multi-asset class portfolio analytics	34.8	8
Other products	24.3	6
Total	**431.0**	**100**

Selected Products

Barra Aegis (Equity Portfolio Analytics)
BarraOne (Multi-Asset Class Portfolio Analytics)
FEA (Entergy and Commodity Asset Valuation Analytics)
MSCI Domestic Equity Indices
MSCI International Equity Indices

COMPETITORS

Algorithmics
Deutsche Börse
Dow Jones
FactSet
FTSE Group
Nomura Securities
Northwestern Mutual
RiskMetrics
S&P

HISTORICAL FINANCIALS

Company Type: Public

Income Statement

FYE: November 30

	REVENUE ($ mil.)	NET INCOME ($ mil.)	NET PROFIT MARGIN	EMPLOYEES
11/08	431.0	68.3	15.8%	887
11/07	369.9	81.1	21.9%	681
11/06	310.7	71.4	23.0%	705
11/05	278.5	54.2	19.5%	—
11/04	178.4	20.9	11.7%	—
Annual Growth	24.7%	34.5%	—	12.2%

2008 Year-End Financials

Debt ratio: 132.6%
Return on equity: 28.1%
Cash ($ mil.): 268.1
Current ratio: 1.35
Long-term debt ($ mil.): 379.7
No. of shares (mil.): 100.2
Dividends
 Yield: —
 Payout: —
Market value ($ mil.): 1,545.6
R&D as % of sales: —
Advertising as % of sales: —

Stock History

NYSE: MXB

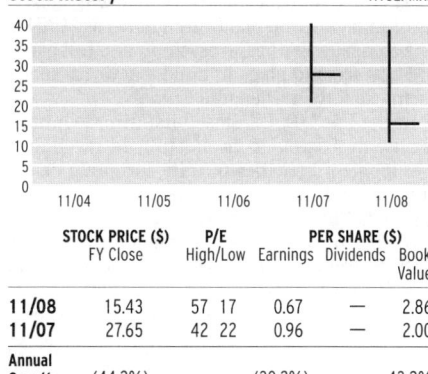

	STOCK PRICE ($) FY Close	P/E High/Low		PER SHARE ($) Earnings	Dividends	Book Value
11/08	15.43	57	17	0.67	—	2.86
11/07	27.65	42	22	0.96	—	2.00
Annual Growth	(44.2%)	—	—	(30.2%)	—	43.2%

Multi-Color Corporation

Multi-Color wants consumers to read its labels. The company produces printed labels for goods, such as food and beverage products, and health and beauty aids in about a dozen locations in the US, Australia, and South Africa. Heat transfer, resealable, shrink wrap, and pressure sensitive are among the label types the firm prints and affixes to glass and plastic containers. Multi-Color also offers gravure printing and injection in-mold labels. Procter & Gamble accounts for about a third of its sales, with Miller Brewing representing 18%. Founded in 1916, the firm expanded overseas in 2008 with its acquisition of Australia's Collotype International Holdings, a maker of pressure sensitive labels for wine and spirits.

The $189 million purchase of Collotype closed in February 2008. It was the firm's largest acquisition to date and extended Multi-Color Corp's customer base to more than 2,400 clients in North and South America, Australia, South Africa, and New Zealand.

In 2009 Multi-Color shuttered its heat transfer label plant in Framingham, Massachusetts, and consolidated its operations with existing facilities. Later that year it relocated its corporate headquarters in Ohio from Sharonville to Batavia. The firm also announced that Frank Gerace, its president and CEO, plans to retire on March 31, 2011, kickstarting Multi-Color's executive succession plans.

Previous purchases include the acquisition of NorthStar Print Group (label printing business) from Journal Communications in January 2005 for $27 million in cash, adding glue-applied label technology to its offerings. The purchase of The NorthStar Print Group (NSPG) bolstered the company's product portfolio and client roster. As a result, cut-and-stack label technology (the ability for labels to be pasted to containers during the labeling process) and the ability to introduce promotional products such as scratch-off coupons, shelf tags, and static clings are now offered by Multi-Color.

In mid-2007, Multi-Color sold its Packaging Services division (about 13% of sales) to NFI Industries for $19.2 million, in order to focus on its core label business.

EXECUTIVES

Chairman: Lorrence T. Kellar, age 72
COO: Nigel A. Vinecombe, age 45
SVP Finance, CFO, and Secretary: Dawn H. Bertsche, age 52
VP Information Technology: Gregory L. Myers
VP Finance, International: Sharon E. Birkett
VP P&G Relationship: Michael A. Laurianti
VP and Treasurer: Mary T. Fetch
VP, Controller, and Chief Accounting Officer: James H. Reynolds, age 43
VP Human Resources: Lesha K. Spahr
VP Sales and Marketing, Decorating Solutions Division: Mark J. Tangry
Director Marketing: Dirk Edwards
President, CEO, and Director; Interim President, North American Business Unit: Francis D. (Frank) Gerace, age 56
President, Wine and Spirits Group, North America: David G. Buse
President, Consumer Products Group, North America: Floyd E. Needham, age 40
Auditors: Grant Thornton LLP

LOCATIONS

HQ: Multi-Color Corporation
 4053 Clough Woods Dr., Batavia, OH 45103
Phone: 513-381-1480   **Fax:** 513-381-2813
Web: www.multicolorcorp.com

2009 Sales

	$ mil.	% of total
US	218.8	75
Australia	59.5	21
South Africa	11.5	4
Total	**289.8**	**100**

PRODUCTS/OPERATIONS

Selected Products and Services

Labels
 Heat transfer
 In-mold
 Neck bands
 Peel-away
 Pressure sensitive
 Resealable
 Shrink sleeve

COMPETITORS

Convergent Label Technology
Fort Dearborn
H. S. Crocker
Jordan Industries
Outlook Group
WS Packaging Group
YORK Label

HISTORICAL FINANCIALS

Company Type: Public

Income Statement

FYE: Sunday nearest March 31

	REVENUE ($ mil.)	NET INCOME ($ mil.)	NET PROFIT MARGIN	EMPLOYEES
3/09	289.8	11.3	3.9%	1,252
3/08	210.3	23.0	10.9%	1,346
3/07	222.4	11.0	4.9%	829
3/06	205.3	9.6	4.7%	1,066
3/05	139.5	8.0	5.7%	826
Annual Growth	**20.1%**	**9.0%**	**—**	**11.0%**

2009 Year-End Financials

Debt ratio: 89.6%
Return on equity: 10.1%
Cash ($ mil.): 3.2
Current ratio: 1.32
Long-term debt ($ mil.): 92.3
No. of shares (mil.): 12.2

Dividends
 Yield: 1.2%
 Payout: 16.3%
Market value ($ mil.): 149.4
R&D as % of sales: —
Advertising as % of sales: —

Stock History

NASDAQ (GM): LABL

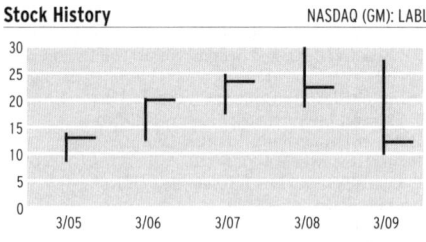

	STOCK PRICE ($) FY Close	P/E High/Low	PER SHARE ($) Earnings	Dividends	Book Value
3/09	12.23	30 11	0.92	0.15	8.44
3/08	22.36	14 9	2.18	0.17	9.82
3/07	23.43	23 13	1.08	0.13	5.27
3/06	20.03	21 13	0.95	0.13	4.34
3/05	13.03	17 11	0.81	0.03	3.53
Annual Growth	**(1.6%)**	**— —**	**3.2%**	**49.5%**	**24.3%**

Multi-Fineline Electronix

Multi-Fineline Electronix offers a multitude of fine electronic parts. The company, which does business as MFLEX, makes a wide variety of flexible printed circuit boards and circuit assemblies. These devices are used to connect other components in various kinds of electronics, such as mobile phones, smart phones, laptop computers, medical devices, and portable bar code scanners. Directly and through subcontractors, Apple, Motorola, Research in Motion, and Sony Ericsson in combination account for more than 95% of the company's sales. MFLEX gets about 70% of sales from outside North America, with most of that coming from China, Hong Kong, Malaysia, and Singapore.

MFLEX's business strategy involves functioning as a fully integrated, end-to-end contract manufacturer, providing design and application engineering, prototyping, high-volume manufacturing, materials acquisition, turnkey component assembly, and testing. With most of its customers clustered in the wireless communications sector, the company is looking to diversify its customer base. It wants to extend its flexible circuit technology to other markets in the electronics industry, such as consumer electronics and portable medical devices, where size and weight are among the primary considerations in new product development.

Toward the end of 2008, the company acquired display component maker Pelikon Limited for about $11 million. Pelikon's SmartInk and MorphPad technologies are used in reconfigurable keypads like those found in smart phone touchpads, where the "buttons" change based on whether the user is texting, using the phone, or taking a picture. The purchase provided MFLEX with display technology for handheld consumer electronics, a market that made up about 25% of the company's sales in 2009. Toshiba uses Morphpad technology in its Biblio e-book reader mobile phone.

MFLEX is restructuring its operations in Asia/Pacific — adding manufacturing capacity in the region and transitioning its international business functions to Singapore — in order to meet changing demands in the market. The company is building a third plant (known as MFC3) in Suzhou, China, scheduled to go on line in the second half of 2010, which will replace its original Suzhou plant (designated as MFC1). The company also has an assembly and test plant in Malaysia, and plans to build a new manufacturing facility in Chengdu, China.

In the US, MFLEX closed its Aurora Optical facility in Arizona, consolidating research and development activities into its corporate headquarters and transferring product manufacturing to its China subsidiary.

Singapore-based investment holding company WBL Corporation owns about 59% of Multi-Fineline Electronix.

EXECUTIVES

Chairman: Philip A. Harding, age 77
President, CEO, and Director: Reza Meshgin, age 46
EVP and CFO: Thomas Liguori, age 50
EVP Operations: Thomas (Tom) Lee, age 50
VP and CTO: William (Bill) Beckenbaugh
VP, General Counsel, and Secretary: Christine Besnard
VP Sales and Marketing: Don Pucci
VP and Managing Director, China Operations: Lance Jin
VP Corporate Development and Chief Strategy Officer:
 Matthew (Matt) Wolk
VP and Corporate Controller: Craig Riedel, age 53
VP Global Human Resources: Hedley Lawson Jr.
Auditors: PricewaterhouseCoopers LLP

LOCATIONS

HQ: Multi-Fineline Electronix, Inc.
 3140 E. Coronado St., Ste. A, Anaheim, CA 92806
Phone: 714-238-1488
Web: www.mflex.com

2009 Sales

	$ mil.	% of total
Asia/Pacific		
China	321.7	42
Hong Kong	106.5	14
Malaysia	18.6	2
Other countries	7.3	1
North America	225.3	30
Europe	84.9	11
Other regions	0.1	—
Total	**764.4**	**100**

PRODUCTS/OPERATIONS

2009 Sales by Market

	% of total
Wireless communications	72
Consumer electronics	25
Other industries	3
Total	**100**

COMPETITORS

Flextronics
Fujikura Ltd.
Hon Hai
Innovex
Nitto Denko
Parlex
Sumitomo

HISTORICAL FINANCIALS

Company Type: Public

Income Statement

FYE: September 30

	REVENUE ($ mil.)	NET INCOME ($ mil.)	NET PROFIT MARGIN	EMPLOYEES
9/09	764.4	46.1	6.0%	15,400
9/08	728.8	40.5	5.6%	18,200
9/07	508.1	3.0	0.6%	17,178
9/06	504.2	40.4	8.0%	12,019
9/05	357.1	37.2	10.4%	10,190
Annual Growth	**21.0%**	**5.5%**	**—**	**10.9%**

2009 Year-End Financials

Debt ratio: 3.0%
Return on equity: 13.8%
Cash ($ mil.): 139.7
Current ratio: 2.38
Long-term debt ($ mil.): 10.9
No. of shares (mil.): 25.2

Dividends
 Yield: —
 Payout: —
Market value ($ mil.): 723.5
R&D as % of sales: —
Advertising as % of sales: —

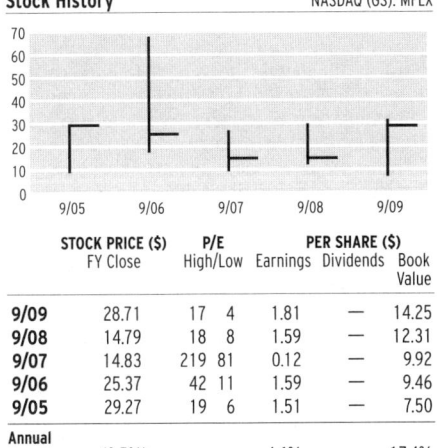

	STOCK PRICE ($)	P/E		PER SHARE ($)		
	FY Close	High/Low		Earnings	Dividends	Book Value
9/09	28.71	17	4	1.81	—	14.25
9/08	14.79	18	8	1.59	—	12.31
9/07	14.83	219	81	0.12	—	9.92
9/06	25.37	42	11	1.59	—	9.46
9/05	29.27	19	6	1.51	—	7.50
Annual Growth	(0.5%)	—	—	4.6%	—	17.4%

MWI Veterinary Supply

It could stand for Mastiff, Weimaraner, and Irish Setter, but MWI Veterinary Supply is actually named after founder and veterinarian, Millard Wallace Ickes. The veterinary products distributor supplies drugs, diagnostics, equipment, and other medical supplies for companion animals and livestock. It serves tens of thousands of veterinary practices from about a dozen distribution centers across the US. The firm offers some 30,000 products from more than 500 vendors. In addition to medical supplies and equipment, MWI distributes pet food and nutritional products. The firm, in business since 1976, also offers customers online ordering, tools to manage inventory, consultation for equipment, and pet cremation services.

The company publishes product catalogs and monthly magazines, which are often used by customers as reference tools for ordering. While sales people and printed materials are vital to its marketing strategy, online ordering is becoming a significant sales channel, generating about 30% of MWI's product sales in 2009.

MWI has grown by acquiring regional suppliers, including AAHA Services, Securos, and Northland Veterinary Supply. The company then absorbs their operations into its own. Other growth measures include improved technology systems (its e-commerce platform) and ever-increasing numbers of sales representatives.

The company has also undergone expansion or new construction of distribution centers; it operates facilities in the West, Southwest, and Midwest US. Geographic areas targeted for growth include the northeastern, midwestern, and southeastern US.

The company has hundreds of sales and marketing representatives serving its clients. Its largest customers are Medical Management International (known as Banfield, the nation's largest private veterinary practice with nearly 1,000 vet hospitals), and Feeders' Advantage, a buying group formed by feedlot operators. MWI owns half of the membership interests in Feeders' Advantage. More than 95% of the company's product sales are from the sale of pharmaceuticals and supplies to veterinary practices.

MWI's pharmaceutical products include anesthetics, analgesics, antibiotics, ophthalmics, and hormones. Its vaccine products are primarily comprised of small animal, equine, and production animal biologicals. Parasiticides are used for control of fleas, ticks, flies, mosquitoes, and internal parasites.

The company does not manufacture the vast majority of its products, instead relying on suppliers that include Pfizer, Boehringer Ingelheim, Merial, and Fort Dodge Animal Health.

MWI became an independent company in 2002 when venture capital firm Bruckmann, Rosser, Sherrill & Co. bought the firm from Agri Beef Co. Bruckmann, Rosser, Sherrill & Co. has gradually sold off its shares in MWI, while Agri Beef retains a small minority (about 6%) stake of the publicly-traded company.

The majority shareholder in MWI is investment manager Neuberger Berman with about 12%. CEO James Cleary is at the company's helm; he also serves on the board of directors and holds about 2% of MWI's shares.

EXECUTIVES

Chairman: John F. McNamara, age 74
President, CEO, and Director: James F. (Jim) Cleary Jr., age 46, $639,918 total compensation
SVP Finance and Administration and CFO: Mary Patricia B. Thompson, age 46, $344,381 total compensation
VP and CIO: James S. Hay, age 66, $226,628 total compensation
VP Marketing: John R. Ryan, age 40
VP Operations: Bryan P. Mooney, age 41
VP and General Manager, Specialty Resource Group: John J. Francis, age 56, $300,710 total compensation
VP Sales: Jeffrey J. Danielson, age 49, $271,144 total compensation
VP Inventory Management: James W. Culpepper, age 55
Auditors: Deloitte & Touche LLP

LOCATIONS

HQ: MWI Veterinary Supply, Inc.
651 S. Stratford Dr., Ste. 100, Meridian, ID 83642
Phone: 208-955-8930   **Fax:** 208-955-8902
Web: www.mwivet.com

PRODUCTS/OPERATIONS

2009 Sales

	$ mil.	% of total
Product sales	880.7	94
Related party product sales	46.4	5
Commissions	14.2	1
Total	**941.3**	**100**

2009 Product Sales

	% of total
Pharmaceuticals	41
Vaccines	18
Diagnostic	8
Parasiticide	7
Capital equipment	3
Other supplies	23
Total	**100**

Selected Products

Analgesics
Anesthesia machines
Anesthetics
Antibiotics
Bandages
Cages
Dental machines
Dietary supplements
Feline leukemia diagnostics
Grooming materials
Heartworm diagnostics
Hormones
Lyme diagnostics
Ophthalmics
Parasiticides
Parvovirus diagnostics
Premium pet foods
Specialty treats
Surgical monitors
Syringes
X-ray machines
Vaccines
Vitamins

COMPETITORS

A.C. Graham	IVESCO
Animal Health	Lambriar Animal Health
Central Garden & Pet	Patterson Companies
Darby Dental	PetMed
The Harvard Drug Group	Professional Veterinary
Henry Schein	Product
Intervet/Schering-Plough	TW Medical

HISTORICAL FINANCIALS

Company Type: Public

Income Statement

FYE: September 30

	REVENUE ($ mil.)	NET INCOME ($ mil.)	NET PROFIT MARGIN	EMPLOYEES
9/09	941.3	24.9	2.6%	887
9/08	831.4	19.9	2.4%	881
9/07	710.1	16.9	2.4%	800
9/06	606.2	13.8	2.3%	719
9/05	496.7	4.6	0.9%	596
Annual Growth	17.3%	52.5%	—	10.5%

2009 Year-End Financials

Debt ratio: 0.0%
Return on equity: 12.8%
Cash ($ mil.): 14.3
Current ratio: 2.16
Long-term debt ($ mil.): 0.0
No. of shares (mil.): 12.2

Dividends
  Yield: —
  Payout: —
Market value ($ mil.): 487.8
R&D as % of sales: —
Advertising as % of sales: —

Stock History

NASDAQ (GS): MWIV

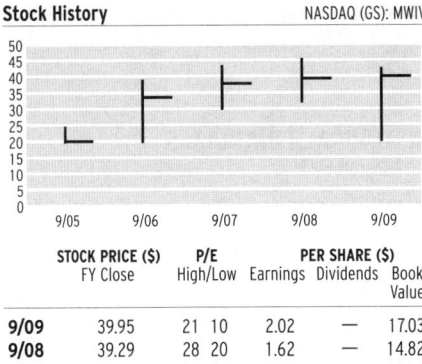

	STOCK PRICE ($)	P/E		PER SHARE ($)		
	FY Close	High/Low		Earnings	Dividends	Book Value
9/09	39.95	21	10	2.02	—	17.03
9/08	39.29	28	20	1.62	—	14.82
9/07	37.75	31	21	1.40	—	13.11
9/06	33.53	31	16	1.25	—	10.62
9/05	19.95	36	29	0.68	—	7.10
Annual Growth	19.0%	—	—	31.3%	—	24.4%

NASB Financial

NASB Financial is the holding company for North American Savings Bank, which operates about 15 branches and loan offices in the Kansas City area. Established in 1927, the bank offers a range of deposit products to retail and commercial customers, including checking, savings, and money market accounts and CDs. Its lending activities are fairly evenly split among mortgages secured by residential, commercial, and development properties. Subsidiary Nor-Am sells annuities, mutual funds, and credit life and disability insurance. Chairman David Hancock and his wife Linda (a board member) own a majority of NASB Financial.

EXECUTIVES

Chairman and CEO, NASB Financial and North American Savings Bank; Chairman, Nor-Am: David H. Hancock, age 63
President and Director; President, North American Savings Bank: Keith B. Cox, age 47
Corporate Secretary, NASB Financial and North American Savings Bank: Shauna Olson
VP and Treasurer; SVP and CFO, North American Savings Bank: Rhonda Nyhus, age 43
VP; SVP Commercial Real Estate Lending, North American Savings Bank: Wade Hall, age 41
VP and Director; EVP and Chief Credit Officer, North American Savings Bank: Paul L. Thomas, age 41
VP; SVP and Chief Investment Officer, North American Savings Bank: John M. Nesselrode, age 49
VP; SVP Retail Banking, North American Savings Bank: Dena Sanders, age 40
VP; EVP Banking Compliance, North American Savings Bank: James A. Watson, age 61
VP; SVP Residential Lending, North American Savings Bank: Bruce J. Thielen, age 48
VP Information Technology, North American Savings Bank: Jeff Jackson
Auditors: BKD, LLP

LOCATIONS

HQ: NASB Financial, Inc.
12498 S. Hwy. 71, Grandview, MO 64030
Phone: 816-765-2200 **Fax:** 816-316-4504
Web: www.nasb.com

COMPETITORS

Bank of America
Commerce Bancshares
Dickinson Financial
Guaranty Federal
UMB Financial
U.S. Bancorp

HISTORICAL FINANCIALS

Company Type: Public

Income Statement

FYE: September 30

	ASSETS ($ mil.)	NET INCOME ($ mil.)	INCOME AS % OF ASSETS	EMPLOYEES
9/09	1,559.6	18.7	1.2%	383
9/08	1,516.8	9.3	0.6%	339
9/07	1,506.5	15.3	1.0%	328
9/06	1,524.8	20.8	1.4%	362
9/05	1,556.3	25.8	1.7%	441
Annual Growth	0.1%	(7.7%)	—	(3.5%)

2009 Year-End Financials

Equity as % of assets: 10.7%
Return on assets: 1.2%
Return on equity: 11.7%
Long-term debt ($ mil.): 466.8
No. of shares (mil.): 7.9
Market value ($ mil.): 206.9
Dividends
Yield: 3.4%
Payout: 37.8%
Sales ($ mil.): 87.9
R&D as % of sales: —
Advertising as % of sales: —

Stock History

NASDAQ (CM): NASB

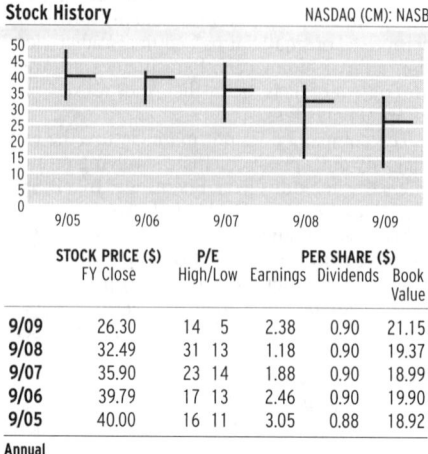

	STOCK PRICE ($) FY Close	P/E High/Low		PER SHARE ($) Earnings	Dividends	Book Value
9/09	26.30	14	5	2.38	0.90	21.15
9/08	32.49	31	13	1.18	0.90	19.37
9/07	35.90	23	14	1.88	0.90	18.99
9/06	39.79	17	13	2.46	0.90	19.90
9/05	40.00	16	11	3.05	0.88	18.92
Annual Growth	(10.0%)	—	—	(6.0%)	0.6%	2.8%

National CineMedia

National CineMedia puts on its show before the previews of coming attractions. The company provides in-theater advertising, selling time on more than 17,000 movie screens (90% of those are digital) in about 45 US states. It produces and distributes pre-show entertainment features (including the entertainment industry infomercial *FirstLook*) and distributes other media content to theater screens, including live entertainment (through its Fathom division). Additionally, the company's CineMeetings business promotes live and pre-recorded corporate events located at movie theaters. Major investors in the company include theater operators Regal Entertainment (37%), AMC Entertainment (30%), and Cinemark (25%).

The proceeds of National CineMedia's February 2007 IPO primarily went to Regal, AMC, and Cinemark for payment obligations related to exhibitor services agreements.

With a diverse client mix, National CineMedia stands to weather the troubles most advertising companies are facing with the economic downturn. Also, in-theater advertising seems to be getting a boost as shrinking budgets prompt advertisers to reach the widest audience possible.

Some critics have blamed pre-screening advertising for some of the recent downturn in box office sales. In response, and to make its "advertainment" programming more appealing to moviegoers, National CineMedia replaced its flagship program *The 2wenty* with *FirstLook*, a pre-show program offering more movie industry insider content and a softer marketing tone. The show's content partners include such heavy hitters in the programming industry as Discovery, NBC Universal, and Turner Broadcasting System. In 2008, *FirstLook* expanded its list of partners even further with the addition of A&E, History Channel, Warner Brothers, and Disney.

Through its Lobby Entertainment Network, CineMedia provides content for high-definition plasma screens and televisions in the foyers of about 1,100 movie theaters. The screens are placed in high-traffic areas such as near concession stands and in waiting areas and run a 30-minute loop of advertising.

The company has grown through its CineMeetings and Fathom divisions. Fathom offers content including live and pre-recorded concerts, Broadway plays, and live sports. Fathom's agreement with the New York Metropolitan Opera to show live and pre-recorded performances has been a hit with patrons.

National CineMedia increased its market coverage when AMC acquired the Loews theater circuit, adding more than 100 theaters and 1,334 screens. The company also got a boost when Cinemark bought the Century theatre circuit, an operator of 77 theaters and 1,017 screens. National CineMedia is taking advantage of the digital revolution by growing through the number of digital theaters being opened by its founding companies. The company also plans to offer financing assistance to help exhibitors upgrade their theaters with digital cinema equipment.

AMC and Regal merged their cinema screen advertising businesses (National Cinema Network and Regal CineMedia, respectively) to launch National CineMedia in 2005. Cinemark acquired its stake in the business later that year.

EXECUTIVES

Chairman, President, and CEO: Kurt C. Hall, age 49, $2,097,876 total compensation
President Sales and Chief Marketing Officer: Clifford E. (Cliff) Marks, age 48, $1,460,402 total compensation
EVP, COO, and CTO: Thomas C. (Tom) Galley, age 53, $948,748 total compensation
EVP and CFO: Gary W. Ferrera, age 46, $889,259 total compensation
EVP and General Counsel: Ralph E. Hardy, age 58, $441,814 total compensation
EVP Sales and Marketing: Dave Kupiec
SVP East Coast Sales: Beth Hoff
SVP Central Division Sales: Pam Biederman
SVP West Coast Sales: Doug Gellerman
SVP Public Relations and Communications: Lauren Leff
SVP Online and Mobile Advertising: Jeffrey Mahl
Auditors: Deloitte & Touche LLP

LOCATIONS

HQ: National CineMedia, Inc.
9110 E. Nichols Ave., Ste. 200
Centennial, CO 80112
Phone: 303-792-3600 **Fax:** 303-792-8800
Web: www.ncm.com

PRODUCTS/OPERATIONS

2008 Sales

	$ mil.	% of total
Advertising	330.3	89
Meetings	38.9	11
Other	0.3	—
Total	**369.5**	**100**

Selected Content Partners (FirstLook)

A&E Television Networks
Discovery Communications
History Channel
NBC Universal
Sony Pictures Entertainment
Turner Broadcasting System Inc.
Universal City Studios
Walt Disney Studios
Warner Brothers

HISTORICAL FINANCIALS

Company Type: Public

Income Statement

FYE: December 31

	REVENUE ($ mil.)	NET INCOME ($ mil.)	NET PROFIT MARGIN	EMPLOYEES
12/08	369.5	15.9	4.3%	598
12/07	331.9	20.6	6.2%	535
12/06	219.3	(10.5)	—	463
12/05	116.6	(5.2)	—	435
12/04	95.3	20.6	21.6%	—
Annual Growth	40.3%	(6.3%)	—	11.2%

2008 Year-End Financials

Debt ratio: —
Return on equity: —
Cash ($ mil.): 69.2
Current ratio: 2.33
Long-term debt ($ mil.): 917.9
No. of shares (mil.): 42.1

Dividends
  Yield: 6.1%
  Payout: 163.2%
Market value ($ mil.): 427.1
R&D as % of sales: —
Advertising as % of sales: —

Stock History

NASDAQ (GS): NCMI

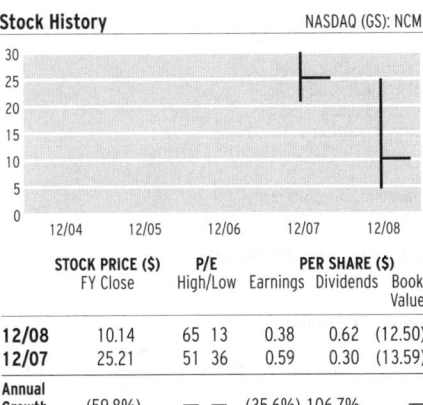

	STOCK PRICE ($) FY Close	P/E High/Low	PER SHARE ($) Earnings	PER SHARE ($) Dividends	PER SHARE ($) Book Value
12/08	10.14	65 13	0.38	0.62	(12.50)
12/07	25.21	51 36	0.59	0.30	(13.59)
Annual Growth	(59.8%)	— —	(35.6%)	106.7%	—

National Instruments

National Instruments (NI) knows you like to take tests. The company's instrumentation hardware and graphical software convert standard PCs into industrial automation and test and measurement systems. These "virtual instruments" can observe, measure, and control electrical signals and physical attributes such as voltage and pressure. The company also offers programming environments (LabVIEW and Measurement Studio) for creating customizable graphical interfaces, controlling instruments, and capturing and analyzing data. In addition, NI provides test management software for running automated factory test systems. Customers outside the Americas account for more than half of sales.

National Instruments is tightening its belt in response to the global economic downturn and credit crisis. While the company grew sales by about 11% in 2008, profits failed to grow for the first time in six years, although the margin of profit was a healthy 10%. Still, NI plans to spend on acquisitions, intellectual property litigation, manufacturing, marketing, product development, and sales during 2009. The company notes that it is dependent on key suppliers for certain components and subassemblies, and may experience component shortages, delays in component deliveries, and quality problems with components from sole-source suppliers.

NI's diverse customer base includes companies in the automotive, semiconductor, and telecommunications industries, as well as chemical and health care firms.

Throughout its history NI relied on relentless promotion and publicity to get its name out in front of engineers and researchers. It advertised heavily in trade publications from Cahners Publishing (now Reed Business Information US), CMP Media, Penton Media, and other publishers, while unleashing barrages of product press releases on trade editors on an almost daily basis.

The company also promotes itself through technical seminars and conferences presented around the world and over the Internet. Its biggest event is the annual NIWeek conference, staged each summer at the Austin Convention Center, near NI's headquarters. Held every year since 1995, NIWeek attracts thousands of attendees from all over the world.

Not hiding its lamp under a bushel, National Instruments has won a number of accolades. *FORTUNE* magazine has named NI one of its top 100 US employers for 10 years running.

Chairman, president, and CEO James Truchard owns about 22% of National Instruments. Cofounder and director Jeffrey Kodosky holds around 5% of the company.

HISTORY

In the 1970s James Truchard, working at the University of Texas Applied Research Laboratory, was frustrated by the lack of connectivity between the lab's computers and testing equipment. Truchard, who as a kid built homemade radios, founded National Instruments in 1976 with fellow lab employees Jeffrey Kodosky and William Nowlin. The trio raised $13,000, which included part of Truchard's teacher retirement fund savings, and set up camp in a room behind Truchard's garage.

Using Hewlett-Packard's technology for collecting test and measurement data from its own machines, the trio created the general-purpose interface bus (GPIB), a device that links computers to scientific instruments. The devices eliminated the practice of using paper, pencils, and rulers to track instruments. The colleagues' vigor kept the company busy if small. Truchard designed hardware and wrote press releases. Kodosky developed programs and handled customer support.

National Instruments thrived as PCs became popular. LabVIEW, introduced in 1986, used graphics to simulate the dials of an engineering instrument's control panel. Users worked the controls simply by moving the mouse. The company expanded internationally in 1987, opening an office in Tokyo. It suffered a loss for 1989 after expanding into Europe.

In 1990 NASA used one of the company's programs to trace fuel system leaks affecting Space Shuttle launches. National Instruments went public in 1995 and intensified product development. It also began acquiring small businesses to expand its technology base, buying industrial automation specialist Georgetown Systems (1996) and motion control equipment maker nuLogic (1997).

In 1998 National Instruments bought two German makers of data acquisition tools, DATALOG and DASYtec. The next year the company and computer maker Dell joined forces to market a scientific measuring and testing workstation. National Instruments also launched an online store, then followed that in 2000 with the NI Developer Zone, a resource for information on automation and measurement systems.

In 2001 NI established a subsidiary in Russia. The following year it opened a manufacturing facility in Hungary. The company acquired Hyperception, a provider of graphical development tools for digital signal processing, in 2003.

NI expanded its product offerings with its 2005 purchases of data acquisition instrumentation makers Measurement Computing and IOtech. In 2007 chairman, president, and CEO James Truchard was elected to the National Academy of Engineering. The following year the company purchased microLEX Systems A/S, a Danish instrumentation firm.

EXECUTIVES

Chairman, President, and CEO: James J. Truchard, age 65, $338,140 total compensation
SVP, IT, Manufacturing Operations, CFO, and Treasurer: Alexander M. (Alex) Davern, age 42, $760,772 total compensation
SVP Research and Development: Phil D. Hester
SVP Sales and Marketing: Peter (Pete) Zogas Jr., age 47, $665,904 total compensation
VP, Marketing, Customer Operations, and Investor Relations: John M. Graff, age 42, $535,197 total compensation
VP Product Marketing and Academic Relations: Raymond C. (Ray) Almgren, age 42, $512,618 total compensation
VP Applications Engineering: Tony Vento
VP Global Information Technology: Arleene Porterfield
VP Quality and Continuous Improvement: Andrew Krupp
VP Finance: John Roiko
VP Human Resources: Mark A. Finger, age 50
VP Industrial and Embedded Product Lines: John Hanks
VP, General Counsel, and Secretary: David G. Hugley, age 44
VP Manufacturing: Robert R. (Rob) Porterfield, age 41
Communications and Investor Relations Manager: Julie Betts
Auditors: Ernst & Young LLP

LOCATIONS

HQ: National Instruments Corporation
11500 N. MoPac Expwy., Austin, TX 78759
Phone: 512-338-9119   **Fax:** 512-683-5759
Web: www.ni.com

National Instruments has offices in more than 40 countries.

2008 Sales

	$ mil.	% of total
Americas	355.9	43
Europe	267.3	33
Asia/Pacific	197.3	24
Total	**820.5**	**100**

PRODUCTS/OPERATIONS

Selected Products

Measurement and Automation Software
  LabVIEW
  Measurement Studio
  LabWindows/CVI
  Switch Executive
  TestStand
  VI Logger
Measurement Hardware
  Counters and timers
  Data acquisition (DAQ) hardware
  Digital input and output devices
  Digital multimeters
  Dynamic signal acquisition devices
  Dynamic signal analyzers
  High-speed digitizers
  Radio-frequency measurement devices
  Signal sources

COMPETITORS

Advantest
Agilent Technologies
Cognex
Fluke Corporation
Keithley Instruments
LeCroy
MathWorks
Rohde & Schwarz
Tektronix
Teradyne
Thermo Fisher Scientific
Wolfram Research

HISTORICAL FINANCIALS

Company Type: Public

Income Statement

FYE: December 31

	REVENUE ($ mil.)	NET INCOME ($ mil.)	NET PROFIT MARGIN	EMPLOYEES
12/08	820.5	84.8	10.3%	5,157
12/07	740.4	107.0	14.5%	4,647
12/06	660.4	72.7	11.0%	4,149
12/05	571.8	61.5	10.8%	3,812
12/04	514.1	48.6	9.5%	3,465
Annual Growth	**12.4%**	**14.9%**	**—**	**10.5%**

2008 Year-End Financials

Debt ratio: —
Return on equity: 12.8%
Cash ($ mil.): 229.4
Current ratio: 4.05
Long-term debt ($ mil.): —
No. of shares (mil.): 77.7
Dividends
  Yield: 1.8%
  Payout: 41.1%
Market value ($ mil.): 1,893.4
R&D as % of sales: —
Advertising as % of sales: —

Stock History

NASDAQ (GS): NATI

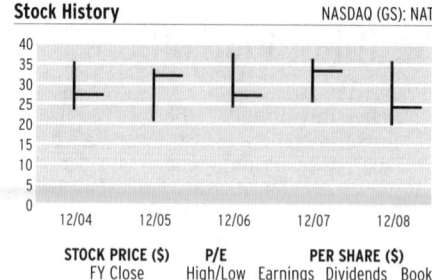

	STOCK PRICE ($) FY Close	P/E High/Low		PER SHARE ($) Earnings	Dividends	Book Value
12/08	24.36	33	19	1.07	0.44	8.55
12/07	33.33	27	20	1.32	0.34	8.51
12/06	27.24	42	27	0.89	0.24	7.68
12/05	32.05	44	28	0.76	0.20	6.48
12/04	27.25	60	40	0.59	0.18	6.26
Annual Growth	**(2.8%)**	**—**	**—**	**16.0%**	**25.0%**	**8.1%**

National Interstate

National Interstate is a specialty property/casualty insurer that concentrates on the transportation market. One of the nation's largest insurers of truck and passenger transportation fleets, the company also provides personal lines of coverage for recreational vehicles, watercraft, and campsite liability. Additionally, National Interstate offers general commercial insurance for small businesses in Alaska and Hawaii. The company distributes its products through both affiliated and independent agents and brokers. National Interstate was spun off in 2005 by its former parent company American Financial Group, which continues to control the company through a 53% stake held by its Great American Insurance Company.

National Interstate insures charter bus companies, school bus fleets, limousine companies, and public transportation operations, as well as other passenger transportation and cargo truck fleets. It offers services to its commercial transportation customers under two models: alternative risk transfer and traditional coverage.

Under the alternative risk transfer model (which accounts for the majority of the company's commercial transportation policies) the company provides underwriting and other services for captive insurance programs that are owned or rented by its customers; in such an arrangement the client participates in assuming risks and sharing in underwriting profits.

National Interstate operates primarily through four property/casualty subsidiaries: National Interstate Insurance Company, Hudson Indemnity, Triumphe Casualty, and National Interstate Insurance Company of Hawaii. It is licensed to operate in all 50 states and Washington, DC, but business is concentrated in California (more than 15% of premiums written) and in Florida, Hawaii, New York, North Carolina, and Texas (over 30% of premiums written, collectively).

Founder and chairman Alan Spachman owns 12% of the company.

EXECUTIVES

Chairman: Alan R. Spachman, age 61
President, CEO, and Director: David W. Michelson, age 51, $1,283,923 total compensation
SVP: Terry E. Phillips, age 59, $539,128 total compensation
VP, CFO, and Treasurer: Julie A. McGraw, age 45, $392,144 total compensation
VP and Chief Investment Officer: Gary N. Monda, age 52, $359,515 total compensation
VP, General Counsel, and Secretary: Arthur J. Gonzales, age 49
Auditors: Ernst & Young LLP

LOCATIONS

HQ: National Interstate Corporation
3250 Interstate Dr., Richfield, OH 44286
Phone: 330-659-8900   **Fax:** 330-659-8901
Web: www.nationalinterstate.com

PRODUCTS/OPERATIONS

2008 Sales

	$ mil.	% of total
Premiums earned		
Alternative risk transfer	137.3	43
Transportation	75.5	24
Specialty personal lines	54.8	17
Hawaii & Alaska	17.6	6
Other	5.5	2
Net investment income	22.5	7
Realized losses on investments	(22.4)	—
Other	2.9	1
Total	**293.7**	**100**

Selected Subsidiaries

American Highways Insurance Agency, Inc.
Explorer RV Insurance Agency, Inc.
Hudson Indemnity, Ltd. (Cayman Islands)
Hudson Management Group, Ltd.
National Interstate Insurance Agency, Inc.
National Interstate Insurance Company
  National Interstate Insurance Company of Hawaii, Inc.
  Triumphe Casualty Company
Safety, Claims & Litigation Services, Inc.

COMPETITORS

American Modern Insurance
Canal Insurance
Clarendon Insurance Group
Great West Casualty
Island Insurance
Kingsway
Lancer Insurance
Progressive Corporation
RLI
Travelers Companies

HISTORICAL FINANCIALS

Company Type: Public

Income Statement

FYE: December 31

	ASSETS ($ mil.)	NET INCOME ($ mil.)	INCOME AS % OF ASSETS	EMPLOYEES
12/08	990.8	10.7	1.1%	358
12/07	898.6	43.6	4.9%	333
12/06	806.2	35.7	4.4%	309
12/05	523.0	30.3	5.8%	285
12/04	401.2	22.8	5.7%	248
Annual Growth	**25.4%**	**(17.2%)**	**—**	**9.6%**

2008 Year-End Financials

Equity as % of assets: 21.8%
Return on assets: 1.1%
Return on equity: 5.0%
Long-term debt ($ mil.): 15.0
No. of shares (mil.): 19.4
Market value ($ mil.): 346.6
Dividends
  Yield: 1.3%
  Payout: 43.6%
Sales ($ mil.): 293.7
R&D as % of sales: —
Advertising as % of sales: —

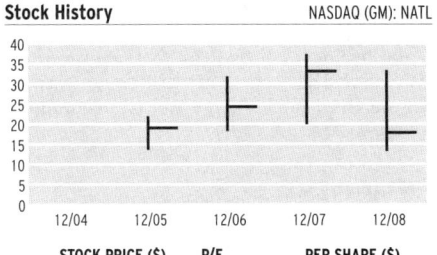

	STOCK PRICE ($)	P/E		PER SHARE ($)		
	FY Close	High/Low	Earnings	Dividends	Book Value
12/08	17.87	60 25	0.55	0.24	11.14
12/07	33.10	16 9	2.25	0.20	10.97
12/06	24.30	17 10	1.85	0.16	8.96
12/05	19.07	14 9	1.60	0.08	7.19
Annual Growth	(2.1%)	— —	(21.8%)	44.2%	31.3%

National Penn Bancshares

Pennies or Benjamins, it's all good to National Penn Bancshares, the holding company for National Penn Bank. Through about 130 branches, almost all of them in eastern Pennsylvania, the bank concentrates on serving small to midsized business customers, with standard offerings such as deposit products and loans. Business loans, leases, and lines of credit make up nearly half of the bank's loan portfolio, which also includes commercial real estate loans (almost 20%), residential mortgages, and consumer loans. Subsidiaries offer trust, investment management, insurance, equipment leasing, and other services.

National Penn Bancshares bought KNBT Bancorp and its Keystone Nazareth Bank & Trust subsidiary in 2008. The deal added some 50 branches in eastern Pennsylvania to National Penn's network.

Acquisitions have either strengthened National Penn in existing markets or moved the bank into new ones; the 2006 purchase of Nittany Financial moved the company into Central Pennsylvania. In 2008 it acquired Christiana Bank & Trust, giving it two offices in Delaware. The latter institution retained its name, while Keystone Nazareth Bank and Nittany Bank were merged into National Penn Bank.

The bank has also been concentrating on niches to supplement its standard commercial and consumer banking lines; these include groups devoted to the manufacturing industry, international banking, and government banking.

EXECUTIVES

Chairman: Thomas A. Beaver, age 57
Vice Chairman: Jeffrey P. (Jeff) Feather, age 66
President, CEO, and Director: Glenn E. Moyer, age 57, $1,624,552 total compensation
SEVP and COO; President and CEO National Penn Bank: Scott V. Fainor, age 47, $415,996 total compensation
CFO; EVP National Penn Bank: Michael J. (Mike) Hughes, age 53
Group EVP and Chief Risk Officer: Sandra L. Bodnyk, age 57

Group EVP Corporate Banking and Chief Lending Officer: Paul W. McGloin, age 61, $349,880 total compensation
Group EVP Enterprisewide Image and Human Resources: Bruce G. Kilroy, age 59, $346,144 total compensation
Group EVP Operations and Technology: Carl F. Kovacs, age 58
Group EVP Wealth, Asset, Trust, Investment Management; Vice Chairman, National Penn Investors Trust Company; Chairman Christiana Bank & Trust; EVP National Penn Bank; Chairman First Service Bank Division: Donald P. Worthington, age 64
EVP and Chief Accounting Officer; CFO National Penn Bank: Gary L. Rhoads, age 54
EVP and CIO National Penn Bank: P. Robert Keeley
EVP, Corporate Secretary, and Investor Relations Officer; SVP National Penn Bank: Michelle H. Debkowski, age 40
EVP and Treasurer: Michael R. Reinhard, age 51, $349,880 total compensation
Public Relations Specialist: Jamie L. Della Croce
Auditors: Grant Thornton LLP

LOCATIONS

HQ: National Penn Bancshares, Inc.
Philadelphia and Reading Avenues
Boyertown, PA 19512
Phone: 610-367-6001 **Fax:** 610-369-6118
Web: www.natpennbank.com

PRODUCTS/OPERATIONS

2008 Gross Revenues

	$ mil.	% of total
Interest		
Loans & leases, including fees	377.7	64
Investment securities	87.9	15
Other	0.6	—
Noninterest		
Wealth management	31.9	5
Service charges on deposit accounts	25.2	4
Insurance commissions & fees	15.4	3
Cash management & electronic banking fees	14.4	3
Other	35.4	6
Total	**588.5**	**100**

Selected Subsidiaries and Affiliates

Christiana Bank & Trust Company
National Penn Bank
  Caruso Benefits Group, Inc.
  Higgins Insurance Associates
  Institutional Advisors, LLC
  Link Financial Services, Inc.
  National Penn Capital Advisors
  National Penn Insurance Agency, Inc.
  National Penn Investors Trust Company
  National Penn Leasing Company
  Vantage Investment Advisors, LLC
National Penn Life Insurance Company
National Penn Investment Company

COMPETITORS

Bank of America
Bryn Mawr Bank Corp.
First Commonwealth Financial
First Keystone Financial
Fulton Financial
Harleysville National
PNC Financial
Royal Bancshares
Sovereign Bank
TD Bank USA
Univest
VIST Financial

HISTORICAL FINANCIALS
Company Type: Public

Income Statement
FYE: December 31

	ASSETS ($ mil.)	NET INCOME ($ mil.)	INCOME AS % OF ASSETS	EMPLOYEES
12/08	9,403.4	32.3	0.3%	1,941
12/07	5,824.4	65.2	1.1%	1,289
12/06	5,452.3	64.1	1.2%	1,247
12/05	4,600.6	59.8	1.3%	1,247
12/04	4,478.8	47.9	1.1%	1,287
Annual Growth	20.4%	(9.4%)	—	10.8%

2008 Year-End Financials

Equity as % of assets: 11.0%
Return on assets: 0.4%
Return on equity: 4.0%
Long-term debt ($ mil.): 1,084.0
No. of shares (mil.): 125.7
Market value ($ mil.): 1,823.8
Dividends
  Yield: 4.7%
  Payout: 161.9%
Sales ($ mil.): 275.5
R&D as % of sales: —
Advertising as % of sales: —

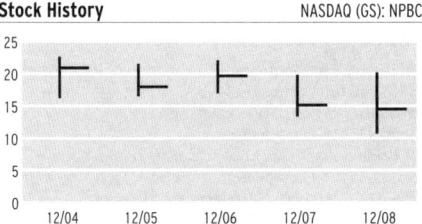

	STOCK PRICE ($)	P/E		PER SHARE ($)		
	FY Close	High/Low	Earnings	Dividends	Book Value
12/08	14.51	48 26	0.42	0.68	9.39
12/07	15.14	15 10	1.31	0.66	4.49
12/06	19.66	17 13	1.29	0.63	4.32
12/05	17.96	17 13	1.28	0.61	3.54
12/04	20.89	21 15	1.09	0.59	3.41
Annual Growth	(8.7%)	— —	(21.2%)	3.6%	28.8%

National Presto Industries

The heat is on at National Presto Industries, but it's thermostatically controlled for even cooking on nonstick surfaces. Under the Presto brand, the company makes and distributes small appliances and housewares, including pressure cookers, fry pans, deep fryers, griddles, coffeemakers, can openers, electric knives, and pizza ovens. The company pours itself into defense work, too, supplying ammo, cartridge cases, electromechanical assemblies, and Load, Assemble, and Pack (LAP) setup for regulated goods. Adding to the bottom line, its absorbent products unit makes diapers and incontinence items. The company sells through US retailers, primarily mass outlets. Wal-Mart Stores account for about 10% of sales.

National Presto adopts a diversified posture for its business growth. The independent company's direction has been fueled by acquisitions into promising arenas such as defense contracts and absorbent products. Defense products are delivered through the company's subsidiary AMTEC Corporation, AMTEC's cartridge case

manufacturing division Amron, and Spectra Technologies (a subsidiary of AMTEC). The US Department of Defense (DOD), the Army, and DOD contractors are primary customers.

National Presto's absorbent products unit, which makes and markets private-label diapers, was formed when the company acquired Presto Absorbent Products and NCN Hygienic Products. These purchases allowed Presto to move its products outside the small appliance realm, minimizing its exposure to cyclical economic trends. Medline Industries Holdings contributes to over 10% of this unit's sales.

Guided by former chairman Melvin Cohen, National Presto rolled out numerous consumer gadgets under the Presto label — some winners (FryBaby and SaladShooter), some duds (ChipShot potato slicer) — along with a steady backlog of ammunitions for the US military. His daughter, Maryjo, current chairman and CEO, owns about 30% of National Presto Industries.

EXECUTIVES

Chairman, President, and CEO: Maryjo Cohen, age 56, $414,946 total compensation
VP Sales: Donald E. Hoeschen, age 61, $255,739 total compensation
VP Engineering: Lawrence J. (Larry) Tienor, age 60, $245,630 total compensation
VP, CFO, Treasurer, Secretary, and Director: Randy F. Lieble, age 55, $92,596 total compensation
Human Resources Manager: Darcy Holman
Advertising Manager: Steve Kjaarsgard
Auditors: BDO Seidman, LLP

LOCATIONS

HQ: National Presto Industries, Inc.
3925 N. Hastings Way, Eau Claire, WI 54703
Phone: 715-839-2121   **Fax:** 715-839-2122
Web: www.gopresto.com

PRODUCTS/OPERATIONS

2008 Sales

	$ mil.	% of total
Defense products	238.7	53
Housewares/small appliances	136.8	31
Absorbent products	72.7	16
Total	**448.2**	**100**

Selected Products

Defense Products
Precision mechanical and electromechanical assemblies
Load, assemble, and pack operations on ordnance-related products
Housewares/Small Appliances
Can openers
Electric knife sharpeners
Electric knives
Electric tea kettles
Fry pans, griddles, and multipurpose cookers
Pizza ovens
Pressure cookers and canners
Slicer/shredders
Absorbent Products
Adult incontinence products
Private-label diapers

COMPETITORS

Cardinal Health Medical	Lockheed Martin
GE Consumer & Industrial	Northrop Grumman
Global-Tech	Procter & Gamble
Hamilton Beach	Salton
Johnson & Johnson	SEB
Kimberly-Clark	

HISTORICAL FINANCIALS

Company Type: Public

Income Statement

FYE: December 31

	REVENUE ($ mil.)	NET INCOME ($ mil.)	NET PROFIT MARGIN	EMPLOYEES
12/08	448.2	44.2	9.9%	996
12/07	420.7	38.6	9.2%	1,032
12/06	304.7	28.0	9.2%	988
12/05	184.6	19.0	10.3%	552
12/04	159.0	15.4	9.7%	551
Annual Growth	**29.6%**	**30.2%**	**—**	**16.0%**

2008 Year-End Financials

Debt ratio: —
Return on equity: 14.6%
Cash ($ mil.): 24.7
Current ratio: 5.77
Long-term debt ($ mil.): —
No. of shares (mil.): 6.9
Dividends
 Yield: 1.3%
 Payout: 15.5%
Market value ($ mil.): 528.0
R&D as % of sales: —
Advertising as % of sales: —

Stock History

NYSE: NPK

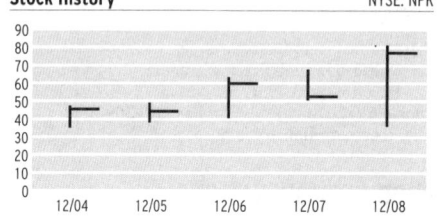

	STOCK PRICE ($) FY Close	P/E High/Low		Earnings	PER SHARE ($) Dividends	Book Value
12/08	77.00	12	6	6.45	1.00	45.30
12/07	52.66	12	9	5.65	0.95	42.97
12/06	59.87	15	10	4.09	0.92	38.13
12/05	44.35	17	14	2.78	0.92	38.36
12/04	45.50	21	16	2.26	0.92	37.26
Annual Growth	**14.1%**	**—**	**—**	**30.0%**	**2.1%**	**5.0%**

Natural Gas Services

The pressure is on to enhance oil and gas well production. Natural Gas Services Group (NGS) manufactures and leases natural gas compressors used to boost oil and gas well production levels. The company also provides flare tip burners, ignition systems, and components used to combust waste gases before they enter the atmosphere. NGS leases compressors to third parties in Colorado, Kansas, Louisiana, Michigan, New Mexico, Oklahoma, Texas, and Wyoming. In early 2008 some 1,194 units of its rental fleet of 1,353 compressors were rented out to clients. Its main customer, XTO Energy, accounted for 40% of sales in 2007.

Founded in 1998, NGS has grown through a number of acquisitions. Its organic business model has fueled its growth, too. The top provider of small to medium-sized horsepower compression equipment to the natural gas industry, the company focuses on serving the non-conventional natural gas production market, the largest and fastest-growing gas produc-

tion segment in the US. While NGS makes and sells compressors and related equipment, its rental business allows it to generate revenues from oil and gas companies that do not wish to put out the capital outlay required in compressor purchases.

EXECUTIVES

Chairman, President, and CEO: Stephen C. Taylor, age 56, $406,615 total compensation
VP Accounting and Treasurer: Earl R. Wait, age 66, $169,970 total compensation
VP Technical Services: James R. Hazlett, age 54, $158,689 total compensation
Investor Relations: Kimberly Huckaba
Auditors: Hein & Associates LLP

LOCATIONS

HQ: Natural Gas Services Group, Inc.
508 W. Wall St., Ste. 550, Midland, TX 79701
Phone: 432-262-2700   **Fax:** 432-262-2701
Web: www.ngsgi.com

PRODUCTS/OPERATIONS

2008 Sales

	$ mil.	% of total
Rental	42.8	50
Sales	41.4	49
Service & maintenance	1.1	1
Total	**85.3**	**100**

COMPETITORS

Baker Hughes
BJ Services
CARBO Ceramics
Compressor Systems
Enerflex
Exterran
Flotek
Miller Petroleum
Oilgear
Production Operators
Weatherford International

HISTORICAL FINANCIALS

Company Type: Public

Income Statement

FYE: December 31

	REVENUE ($ mil.)	NET INCOME ($ mil.)	NET PROFIT MARGIN	EMPLOYEES
12/08	85.3	15.6	18.3%	309
12/07	72.5	12.3	17.0%	270
12/06	62.7	7.6	12.1%	266
12/05	49.3	4.4	8.9%	236
12/04	16.0	3.3	20.6%	111
Annual Growth	**52.0%**	**47.5%**	**—**	**29.2%**

2008 Year-End Financials

Debt ratio: 10.1%
Return on equity: 12.7%
Cash ($ mil.): 1.1
Current ratio: 2.95
Long-term debt ($ mil.): 13.2
No. of shares (mil.): 12.1
Dividends
 Yield: 0.0%
 Payout: —
Market value ($ mil.): 122.5
R&D as % of sales: —
Advertising as % of sales: —

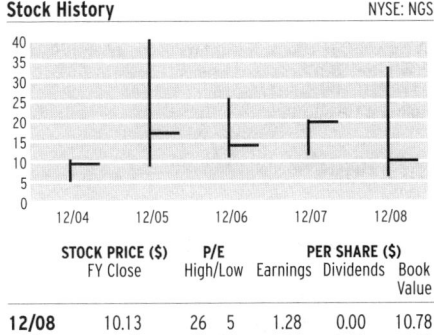

	STOCK PRICE ($) FY Close	P/E High/Low		PER SHARE ($) Earnings	Dividends	Book Value
12/08	10.13	26	5	1.28	0.00	10.78
12/07	19.61	20	12	1.01	0.00	9.46
12/06	13.90	38	17	0.66	0.00	8.37
12/05	16.96	77	17	0.52	0.00	3.78
12/04	9.43	20	10	0.52	0.00	1.89
Annual Growth	1.8%	—	—	25.3%	—	54.5%

Natural Resource Partners

Natural Resource Partners (NRP) makes money from coal without getting its hands dirty. Rather than mining the coal itself, NRP leases properties to coal producers. The company's properties — mainly in Appalachia but also in the Northern Powder River Basin and the Illinois Basin — contain proved and probable reserves of about 2 billion tons of coal. NRP was formed as a partnership between WPP Group (Western Pocahontas Properties, New Gauley Coal, and Great Northern Properties) and Arch Coal. Arch Coal has sold its stake in NRP but remains one of the company's top lessees, along with Alpha Natural Resources. Chairman and CEO Corbin Robertson controls about 35% of NRP, primarily through WPP Group.

In 2005 NRP acquired the mineral rights to approximately 85 million tons of coal reserves from Plum Creek Timber Company for about $21 million. In addition, NRP bought 179 million tons of coal reserves in Ohio and Pennsylvania for $29 million. It then paid $105 million for interests in 145 million tons of coal in the Illinois Basin, and continued the streak of acquisitions by buying the D.D. Shepard property in West Virginia for $110 million.

NRP leases its properties to more than 70 companies who produce more than 50 million tons of coal each year.

EXECUTIVES

Chairman and CEO: Corbin J. Robertson Jr., age 62
President and COO: Nick Carter, age 63
CFO and Treasurer: Dwight L. Dunlap, age 56
EVP Operations: Kevin F. Wall, age 53,
$292,113 total compensation
VP Aggregates: Dennis F. Coker
VP Investor Relations: Kathy F. Roberts, age 58
VP Business Development: Kevin J. Craig, age 41
VP, General Counsel, and Secretary: Wyatt L. Hogan,
age 38
Controller: Kenneth Hudson, age 55
Auditors: Ernst & Young LLP

LOCATIONS

HQ: Natural Resource Partners L.P.
601 Jefferson St., Ste. 3600, Houston, TX 77002
Phone: 713-751-7507
Web: www.nrplp.com

PRODUCTS/OPERATIONS

2008 Sales

	$ mil.	% of total
Coal royalties	259.3	89
Property taxes	9.8	3
Aggregate royalties	9.1	3
Oil & gas royalties	7.9	3
Other	5.6	2
Total	**291.7**	**100**

COMPETITORS

Cloud Peak Energy
CONSOL Energy
Peabody Energy
Westmoreland Coal

HISTORICAL FINANCIALS

Company Type: Public

Income Statement FYE: December 31

	REVENUE ($ mil.)	NET INCOME ($ mil.)	NET PROFIT MARGIN	EMPLOYEES
12/08	291.7	170.0	58.3%	0
12/07	215.0	81.0	37.7%	0
12/06	170.7	88.2	51.7%	0
12/05	159.1	85.9	54.0%	0
12/04	121.4	57.0	47.0%	—
Annual Growth	24.5%	31.4%	—	—

2008 Year-End Financials

Debt ratio: —	Dividends
Return on equity: —	Yield: 11.6%
Cash ($ mil.): 89.9	Payout: 102.5%
Current ratio: 3.63	Market value ($ mil.): 1,211.9
Long-term debt ($ mil.): 478.8	R&D as % of sales: —
No. of shares (mil.): 69.5	Advertising as % of sales: —

Stock History NYSE: NRP

	STOCK PRICE ($) FY Close	P/E High/Low		PER SHARE ($) Earnings	Dividends	Book Value
12/08	17.45	21	6	1.97	2.02	—
12/07	32.46	34	21	1.26	1.84	—
12/06	28.98	17	14	1.74	1.61	—
12/05	25.13	20	14	1.70	1.40	—
12/04	28.83	25	15	1.14	1.19	—
Annual Growth	(11.8%)	—	—	14.7%	14.1%	—

Natus Medical

Natus Medical designs and manufactures audiological and neurological diagnostic and screening products. While the company's focus has historically been on infants (newborn hearing screening, neonatal monitoring), it has expanded its product line to include an array of screening and diagnostic systems for use with older children and adults. Its systems detect such neurological conditions as epilepsy and balance and sleep disorders. Natus also manufactures newborn and infant care products to diagnose and treat brain injury and jaundice. Natus Medical sells its wares in more than 100 countries through a direct sales force and distributors.

About two-thirds of Natus Medical's sales are in the US, where it uses a direct sales force for most of its product lines. Sales to members of group purchasing organization Novation account for 10% of revenues in 2008. Internationally, the company relies mostly on distributors.

Originally, Natus Medical was focused on medical products for the neonatal market. However, beginning in 2003 the company began broadening its product lines through a steady stream of acquisitions, which brought it audiological screening products, neurology and sleep diagnostic systems, and treatments for newborn brain injury and jaundice. Its 2007 acquisition of Canada-based Excel-Tech, in a deal worth about $64 million, brought in more electro-diagnostic systems to detect neurological problems such as epilepsy and sleep disorders, as well as systems used to monitor patients during surgery.

In an effort to streamline its operations following all these acquisitions, in 2008 the company announced a restructuring that included consolidation of its R&D operations into three main locations, as well as the elimination of some field sales positions. It also reduced its manufacturing capacity by increasing its use of contract manufacturers.

While simultaneously restructuring, Natus continued its growth strategy in 2008 by acquiring Massachusetts-based SonaMed, a maker of newborn hearing screening products, and the neurology division of Germany-based Schwarzer, to add more electrodiagnostic systems. It also purchased NeuroCom, a maker of diagnostic equipment for balance and mobility disorders. To prove that it still held a soft spot for babies, Natus spent $2.9 million in 2009 to acquire Massachusetts-based Hawaii Medical, a manufacturer of single-use disposable products for newborn care.

To further strengthen its neurology holdings, in 2009 Natus paid $43.2 million to acquire Alpine Biomed Holdings. The US-based company (which Natus absorbed into its operations) brought with it a range of electromyography diagnostic systems, epilepsy monitoring systems, and disposable products used during neurological diagnostics sold under the Dantech, Stellate, and Alpine brands in the US, Canada, and Europe.

EXECUTIVES

Chairman: Robert A. (Bob) Gunst, age 61
President, CEO, and Director: James B. Hawkins,
age 53, $1,170,498 total compensation
VP Finance and CFO: Steven J. (Steve) Murphy, age 57,
$492,979 total compensation

VP Medical Affairs, Research and Development, and Engineering: D. Christopher Chung, age 45, $479,448 total compensation
VP Operations: William L. Mince, age 57, $505,379 total compensation
VP Marketing and Sales: Kenneth M. Traverso, age 48, $529,967 total compensation
Auditors: Deloitte & Touche LLP

LOCATIONS

HQ: Natus Medical Incorporated
1501 Industrial Rd., San Carlos, CA 94070
Phone: 650-802-0400   **Fax:** 650-802-0401
Web: www.natus.com

2008 Sales

	$ mil.	% of total
US	112.6	70
Other countries	49.2	30
Total	**161.8**	**100**

PRODUCTS/OPERATIONS

2008 Sales

	% of total
Hearing	41
Neurology monitoring systems	34
Newborn care	19
Other	6
Total	**100**

2008 Sales

	% of total
Devices & systems	63
Supplies & services	35
Other	2
Total	**100**

Selected Products

ALGO (newborn hearing screeners)
ABaer (newborn hearing screener)
Ceegraph VISION (neurodiagnostic monitor)
Echo-Screen (hearing screener)
EquiTest (balance disorder devices)
Kortex (diagnostic electroencephalograph monitors)
Navigator PRO (diagnostic hearing system)
neoBLUE (treatment for newborn jaundice)
Olympic CFM-6000 (newborn brain injury diagnostic system)
Olympic Cool-Cap (newborn brain cooling system)
Sleepscan (diagnostic sleep analysis system)

Selected Subsidiaries

Deltamed S.A. (France)
Excel Tech Ltd. (aka Xltek)
NeuroCom International, Inc.

COMPETITORS

Cardinal Health
Cleveland Medical
GE Healthcare
Johnson & Johnson
Medela, Inc.
ResMed
Welch Allyn

HISTORICAL FINANCIALS

Company Type: Public

Income Statement

FYE: December 31

	REVENUE ($ mil.)	NET INCOME ($ mil.)	NET PROFIT MARGIN	EMPLOYEES
12/08	161.8	17.5	10.8%	500
12/07	118.4	9.8	8.3%	435
12/06	89.9	(0.9)	—	360
12/05	43.0	6.2	14.4%	117
12/04	36.5	(2.4)	—	119
Annual Growth	**45.1%**	**—**	**—**	**43.2%**

2008 Year-End Financials

Debt ratio: 0.5%
Return on equity: 10.2%
Cash ($ mil.): 56.9
Current ratio: 5.39
Long-term debt ($ mil.): 1.1
No. of shares (mil.): 28.4
Dividends
  Yield: 0.0%
  Payout: —
Market value ($ mil.): 367.7
R&D as % of sales: —
Advertising as % of sales: —

Stock History

NASDAQ (GM): BABY

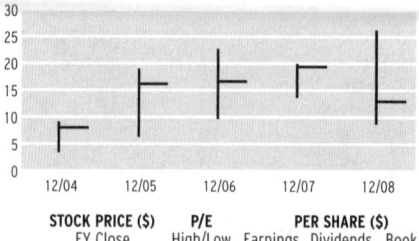

	STOCK PRICE ($) FY Close	P/E High/Low		PER SHARE ($) Earnings	Dividends	Book Value
12/08	12.95	39	14	0.66	0.00	7.98
12/07	19.35	46	32	0.43	0.00	4.08
12/06	16.61	—	—	(0.05)	0.00	3.56
12/05	16.14	57	20	0.33	0.00	2.43
12/04	8.00	—	—	(0.14)	0.00	1.86
Annual Growth	**12.8%**	**—**	**—**	**—**	**—**	**44.0%**

The Navigators Group

The Navigators Group writes specialty lines of insurance and reinsurance to clients whom it hopes are good navigators themselves. The company's various subsidiaries write marine, liability, and other lines of business, primarily in the US and the UK. Navigators Insurance and Navigators Underwriting Agency, which is a member of Lloyd's of London, write ocean and marine insurance, including hull, energy, and cargo insurance, as well as property insurance for onshore energy concerns. The Navigators Agencies are also involved in professional liability, especially directors' and officers' coverage. Navigators Specialty primarily provides general liability for contractors.

Chairman Terence Deeks and his family own about 20% of The Navigators Group.

EXECUTIVES

Chairman: Terence N. Deeks, age 69, $672,145 total compensation
President, CEO, and Director; Chairman Navigators Management: Stanley A. (Stan) Galanski, age 50, $1,837,600 total compensation
SVP and CFO: Francis W. (Frank) McDonnell, age 52, $853,005 total compensation
SVP and Chief Administrative Officer: R. Scott Eisdorfer, age 45
SVP, Chief Compliance Officer, and General Counsel: Bruce J. Byrnes, age 42
SVP and Chief Claims Officer: Jane E. Keller, age 56
SVP and Chief Risk and Compiance Officer: Bradley D. Wiley, age 56
SVP and Chief Underwriting Officer: H. Clay Bassett Jr., age 43
President and CEO, Navigators Management: Christopher C. (Chris) Duca, $1,710,658 total compensation

EVP and COO, Navigators Management: Michael L. Civisca, $813,662 total compensation
EVP Field Operations, Navigators Management; Head, Navigators Business Development: Noel Higgitt, $818,326 total compensation
Auditors: KPMG LLP

LOCATIONS

HQ: The Navigators Group, Inc.
1 Penn Plaza, 32nd Fl., New York, NY 10119
Phone: 212-244-2333   **Fax:** 212-244-4077
Web: www.navg.com

PRODUCTS/OPERATIONS

2008 Sales

	$ mil.	% of total
Net earned premiums		
Insurance companies	463.3	64
Lloyd's operations	180.7	25
Net investment income	63.5	9
Commission income	2.1	—
Net realized capital loss	(37.8)	—
Other income	11.6	2
Total	**683.7**	**100**

COMPETITORS

Allianz Global Risks
Amica Mutual
AXA Corporate Solutions
Chubb Corp
CNA Financial
NYMAGIC
RLI
Safeco
Specialty Underwriters'
Travelers Companies

HISTORICAL FINANCIALS

Company Type: Public

Income Statement

FYE: December 31

	ASSETS ($ mil.)	NET INCOME ($ mil.)	INCOME AS % OF ASSETS	EMPLOYEES
12/08	3,349.6	51.7	1.5%	445
12/07	3,143.8	95.6	3.0%	401
12/06	2,956.7	72.6	2.5%	342
12/05	2,583.2	23.6	0.9%	275
12/04	1,756.7	34.9	2.0%	264
Annual Growth	**17.5%**	**10.3%**	**—**	**13.9%**

2008 Year-End Financials

Equity as % of assets: 20.6%
Return on assets: 1.6%
Return on equity: 7.7%
Long-term debt ($ mil.): 123.8
No. of shares (mil.): 17.0
Market value ($ mil.): 932.7
Dividends
  Yield: 0.0%
  Payout: —
Sales ($ mil.): 683.7
R&D as % of sales: —
Advertising as % of sales: —

Stock History

NASDAQ (GS): NAVG

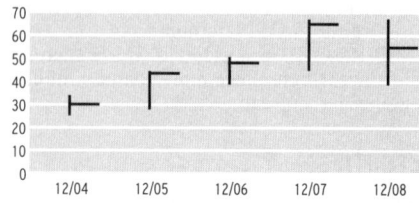

	STOCK PRICE ($) FY Close	P/E High/Low		PER SHARE ($) Earnings	Dividends	Book Value
12/08	54.91	22	13	3.04	0.00	40.58
12/07	65.00	12	8	5.62	0.00	38.98
12/06	48.18	12	9	4.30	0.00	32.46
12/05	43.61	25	16	1.73	0.00	27.68
12/04	30.11	12	9	2.74	0.00	19.34
Annual Growth	**16.2%**	**—**	**—**	**2.6%**	**—**	**20.3%**

NBT Bancorp

The customer is the star at NBT Bancorp, owner of NBT Bank and its Pennstar Bank division, which together operate about 120 branches in central and upstate New York and northeastern Pennsylvania. The banks offer such standard products and services as checking, savings, and money market accounts; CDs; and trust services. The company's lending activities are dominated by business and commercial real estate loans. NBT Bank subsidiaries offer financial and retirement planning, investment products, and automobile and equipment leasing. Its NBT Capital subsidiary provides venture funding to area businesses. The company acquired New York thrift CNB Bancorp in 2006.

NBT Bancorp merged CNB Bancorp's City National Bank and Trust subsidiary (with nine branches) into NBT Bank. The company is looking at several other growth areas, including the Capital Region and Pennsylvania's Luzerne and Monroe counties.

EXECUTIVES

Chairman, NBT Bancorp and NBT Bank: Daryl R. Forsythe, age 66
President, CEO, and Director; President and CEO, NBT Bank: Martin A. Dietrich, age 53, $1,679,129 total compensation
SEVP, CFO, and Secretary, NBT Bancorp and NBT Bank: Michael J. Chewens, age 47, $992,290 total compensation
EVP; President, Commercial Banking, NBT Bank and President, Capital Region: Jeffrey M. Levy, age 47, $470,550 total compensation
EVP and Director Human Resources: Catherine M. Scarlett
SVP and Regional Manager, NBT Bank: Patricia Garrow
Corporate SVP and CIO: Joseph A. Stagliano
SVP and Chief Trust Officer, NBT Bank: Timothy Handy
SVP and Regional Corporate Banking Manager, NBT Bank: John Buffa
President, Retail Banking, NBT Bank; President and CEO, Pennstar Bank: David E. Raven, age 46, $952,268 total compensation
President, EPIC Advisors: Robert F. Judd
Auditors: KPMG LLP

LOCATIONS

HQ: NBT Bancorp Inc.
52 S. Broad St., Norwich, NY 13815
Phone: 607-337-2265   **Fax:** 607-336-6545
Web: www.nbtbancorp.com

NBT Bank operates in New York's Albany, Broome, Chenango, Clinton, Delaware, Essex, Franklin, Fulton, Hamilton, Herkimer, Montgomery, Oneida, Otsego, Saratoga, Schenectady, Schoharie, St. Lawrence, Tioga, and Warren counties. It also operates in Pennsylvania's Lackawanna, Luzerne, Monroe, Pike, Susquehanna, and Wayne counties.

PRODUCTS/OPERATIONS

Selected Subsidiaries

Hathaway Agency, Inc.
NBT Bank, National Association
NBT Financial Services, Inc.

2008 Gross Revenues

	$ mil.	% of total
Interest		
Loans & leases	232.2	64
Securities	59.6	16
Other	2.6	1
Noninterest		
Service charges on deposit accounts	28.1	8
ATM fees	8.8	2
Broker/dealer & insurance revenue	8.7	2
Trust	7.3	2
Retirement plan administration fees	6.3	2
Other	12.4	3
Total	**366.1**	**100**

COMPETITORS

Astoria Financial
Comm Bancorp
Community Bank System
First Niagara Financial
HSBC USA
KeyCorp
M&T Bank
Sovereign Bank
TrustCo Bank Corp NY

HISTORICAL FINANCIALS

Company Type: Public

Income Statement

FYE: December 31

	ASSETS ($ mil.)	NET INCOME ($ mil.)	INCOME AS % OF ASSETS	EMPLOYEES
12/08	5,336.1	58.4	1.1%	1,411
12/07	5,201.8	50.3	1.0%	1,253
12/06	5,087.6	55.9	1.1%	1,314
12/05	4,426.8	52.4	1.2%	1,184
12/04	4,212.3	50.0	1.2%	1,218
Annual Growth	**6.1%**	**4.0%**	**—**	**3.7%**

2008 Year-End Financials

Equity as % of assets: 8.1%	Dividends
Return on assets: 1.1%	Yield: 2.9%
Return on equity: 14.1%	Payout: 44.4%
Long-term debt ($ mil.): 632.2	Sales ($ mil.): 257.8
No. of shares (mil.): 34.3	R&D as % of sales: —
Market value ($ mil.): 960.1	Advertising as % of sales: —

Stock History

NASDAQ (GS): NBTB

	STOCK PRICE ($) FY Close	P/E High/Low		PER SHARE ($) Earnings	Dividends	Book Value
12/08	27.96	20	10	1.80	0.80	12.58
12/07	22.82	17	11	1.51	0.79	11.57
12/06	25.51	16	13	1.64	0.76	11.76
12/05	21.59	16	13	1.60	0.76	9.73
12/04	25.72	18	13	1.51	0.74	9.68
Annual Growth	**2.1%**	**—**	**—**	**4.5%**	**2.0%**	**6.8%**

NCI, Inc.

NCI takes great pride in information technology. The company, through its operating subsidiary NCI Information Systems, provides a variety of information technology (IT) services primarily to US government agencies. NCI's services include enterprise systems management, systems integration, consulting, legacy migration, implementation, maintenance, network design, application development, and network engineering. About 80% of the company's 2007 revenues came from defense and intelligence agencies, including the US Army, US Air Force, and the Defense Logistics Agency. Chairman and CEO Charles Narang controls 87% of the company's voting power.

The company also provides services to federal civilian agencies, including NASA and the Department of Energy. A very small portion of its work is in the commercial sector and for state and local agencies.

NCI added to its holdings in 2007, acquiring Operational Technologies Services, a provider of engineering and professional services to the FAA. It also acquired engineering and IT services firm Karta Technologies in 2007.

NCI was incorporated in 2005 to hold the stock of NCI Information Systems, which was formed in 1989.

EXECUTIVES

Chairman and CEO: Charles K. Narang, age 67, $934,798 total compensation
President and Director: Terry W. Glasgow, age 65, $801,037 total compensation
CFO and Treasurer: Judith L. (Judy) Bjornaas, age 47, $568,803 total compensation
SVP and CTO: Karl J. Leatham
SVP and General Counsel: Michele R. Cappello, age 58, $437,368 total compensation
SVP and General Manager, Army Programs Group: Clarence D. Johnson
SVP and General Manager, Civilian Programs Group: Frederic A. (Fred) Zafran
SVP and General Manager, Air Force and Technology Services: Richard L. Riney III
SVP and General Manager, National Security Group: William J. (Bill) Britton
SVP Human Resources and Administration: W. Norman (Norm) Pierce
SVP Business Development and Capture Management: Christopher M. (Chris) Bishop
Auditors: Ernst & Young LLP

LOCATIONS

HQ: NCI, Inc.
11730 Plaza America Dr., Reston, VA 20190
Phone: 703-707-6900   **Fax:** 703-707-6901
Web: www.nciinc.com

COMPETITORS

BAE Systems Inc.
Booz Allen
CACI International
General Dynamics
HP Enterprise Services
IBM
Lockheed Martin
Northrop Grumman
SAIC
SRA International

HISTORICAL FINANCIALS

Company Type: Public

Income Statement				FYE: December 31
	REVENUE ($ mil.)	NET INCOME ($ mil.)	NET PROFIT MARGIN	EMPLOYEES
12/08	390.6	17.0	4.4%	2,500
12/07	304.4	12.6	4.1%	2,000
12/06	218.3	9.3	4.3%	1,400
12/05	191.3	12.3	6.4%	1,400
12/04	171.3	6.1	3.6%	1,450
Annual Growth	22.9%	29.2%	—	14.6%

2008 Year-End Financials

Debt ratio: 40.5%
Return on equity: 19.0%
Cash ($ mil.): 1.3
Current ratio: 1.72
Long-term debt ($ mil.): 40.0
No. of shares (mil.): 13.5

Dividends
  Yield: 0.0%
  Payout: —
Market value ($ mil.): 406.2
R&D as % of sales: —
Advertising as % of sales: —

Stock History

NASDAQ (GM): NCIT

	STOCK PRICE ($) FY Close	P/E High/Low	PER SHARE ($) Earnings	Dividends	Book Value
12/08	30.13	24 11	1.25	0.00	7.33
12/07	17.11	22 14	0.93	0.00	5.95
12/06	15.29	24 15	0.69	0.00	4.94
12/05	13.73	10 7	1.41	0.00	4.24
Annual Growth	29.9%	— —	11.1%	—	57.6%

Neogen Corporation

Bacteriophobes have a friend in Neogen, a maker of products for the food safety and animal health markets. Its food safety testing products are used by the food industry to make sure food is clean, unspoiled, and free of toxins, pathogens, and allergens. In Canada, the US, and Europe, Neogen reaches end users (including dairies, meat processors, and animal feed producers) through a direct sales force; it uses distributors elsewhere. On the animal health front, Neogen produces drugs, vaccines, diagnostics, and instruments for the veterinary market; it also makes rat poisons and disinfectants used in animal production plants and diagnostic products for research laboratories.

The firm's animal products are sold to distributors around the world, as well as through farm supply retailers in North America.

The company is on the lookout for acquisitions that expand its product portfolio and market share. It has, for instance, bought the dairy antibiotic testing operations of UCB and Eastman Chemical's former Centrus International unit, which added food-borne bacteria testing

products. In 2008 Neogen acquired a line of animal health products from DuPont Animal Health Solutions, a unit of chemicals giant DuPont. That purchase included disinfectants and cleaners intended for farm production markets.

Though the company has used the acquisitions to achieve relatively rapid growth, it is also looking for organic growth over the longer term through new product introductions, higher sales of existing products, and international expansion efforts.

EXECUTIVES

Chairman and CEO: James L. Herbert, age 69, $647,705 total compensation
President, COO, and Director: Lon M. Bohannon, age 56, $493,646 total compensation
VP, CFO, and Secretary: Richard R. Current, age 65, $304,551 total compensation
VP Food Safety Operations: Edward L. Bradley, age 49, $293,167 total compensation
VP Animal Safety Operations: Terri A. Morrical, age 44, $283,310 total compensation
VP Corporate Development: Anthony E. Maltese, age 66
VP Scientific Affairs: Joseph M. Madden, age 60
VP Research and Development: Mark A. Mozola, age 53
VP Manufacturing: Kenneth V. Kodilla, age 52
Senior Scientific Officer: Jennifer Rice
VP Basic and Exploratory Research: Paul S. Satoh, age 72
Auditors: Ernst & Young LLP

LOCATIONS

HQ: Neogen Corporation
620 Lesher Place, Lansing, MI 48912
Phone: 517-372-9200   **Fax:** 517-372-2006
Web: www.neogen.com

2009 Sales

	% of total
US	62
Other countries	38
Total	100

PRODUCTS/OPERATIONS

2009 Sales

	$ mil.	% of total
Food safety	61.0	51
Animal safety	57.7	49
Total	118.7	100

Selected Products

Food safety
  AccuPoint (rapid sanitation test)
  AgriScreen (detects mycotoxins)
  Alert (detects food-borne bacteria, food allergens)
  Beta Star (detects antibiotics in milk)
  Gene-Trak (detects foodborne bacteria)
  Penzyme (detects antibiotics in milk)
  Reveal (detects food-borne bacteria, food allergens, ruminant by-products)
  Soleris (detects spoilage organisms)
  Veratox (detects mycotoxins, food allergens)
Animal safety
  AmVet veterinary products
    PanaKare (digestive aid)
    Natural Vitamin E-AD (vitamin supplement)
    RenaKare (potassium supplement)
  DC&R (disinfectant)
  Equine products
    BotVax B (Shaker Foal Syndrome vaccine)
    EqStim (immunostimulant)
    Ideal (veterinary instruments)
  K-Blue and K-Gold (research diagnostics)
  NeogenVet veterinary products
    Vita-15 (nutritional product for horses)
    Liver 7 (nutritional product for horses)
  Rodenticides (Ramik, Havoc, Prozap)

Selected Subsidiaries

Acumedia Manufacturers, Inc.
Centrus International, Inc.
Hacco, Inc.
Hess & Clark, Inc.
Ideal Instruments, Inc.
Neogen Europe Limited (UK)

COMPETITORS

Bayer Animal Health
Bioniche Life Sciences
Celldex Therapeutics
Ecolab
Eurofins Scientific
Heska
IDEXX Labs
Intervet/Schering-Plough Animal Health
Life Technologies Corporation
Merck
Merial
Novartis
Orchid Cellmark
Pfizer
Silliker
Strategic Diagnostics
Synbiotics
Virbac Corporation
Warnex

HISTORICAL FINANCIALS

Company Type: Public

Income Statement				FYE: May 31
	REVENUE ($ mil.)	NET INCOME ($ mil.)	NET PROFIT MARGIN	EMPLOYEES
5/09	118.7	13.9	11.7%	515
5/08	102.4	12.1	11.8%	447
5/07	86.1	9.1	10.6%	427
5/06	72.4	7.9	10.9%	393
5/05	62.8	5.9	9.4%	363
Annual Growth	17.3%	23.9%	—	9.1%

2009 Year-End Financials

Debt ratio: —
Return on equity: 11.6%
Cash ($ mil.): 13.8
Current ratio: 7.76
Long-term debt ($ mil.): —
No. of shares (mil.): 22.5

Dividends
  Yield: —
  Payout: —
Market value ($ mil.): 330.5
R&D as % of sales: —
Advertising as % of sales: —

Stock History

NASDAQ (GS): NEOG

	STOCK PRICE ($) FY Close	P/E High/Low	PER SHARE ($) Earnings	Dividends	Book Value
5/09	14.69	35 18	0.61	—	5.72
5/08	17.56	35 21	0.54	—	4.95
5/07	12.17	28 18	0.43	—	4.09
5/06	9.07	27 15	0.41	—	2.87
5/05	6.44	33 18	0.31	—	2.44
Annual Growth	22.9%	— —	18.4%	—	23.8%

Netezza Corporation

Netezza understands that there's no point in storing your data if you can't find it again. The company provides data warehouse appliances used to manage large databases. Targeted toward government agencies and companies in data-intensive fields such as financial services and health care, Netezza's appliances integrate database, server, and storage functions, allowing customers to quickly analyze huge amounts of data. Netezza sells its products worldwide, primarily utilizing a direct sales force.

Customers in North America account for about three-quarters of the company's sales; they include Acxiom, Amazon.com, The American Red Cross, AOL, ClarityBlue, Neiman Marcus, and Shoppers Drug Mart. Netezza generates approximately a quarter of its revenue from maintenance and support services.

The company competes against entrenched providers such as Oracle and Teradata in the data warehousing market. Netezza cites the performance and operational costs of its appliances as competitive advantages.

The company has also looked to acquisitions to bolster its competitive position. Netezza acquired Tizor Systems, a provider of data auditing products, in 2009. The purchase added complementary technology that lets Netezza's customers monitor and analyze years of data for compliance requirements. In 2008 the company bought NuTech Solutions, a supplier of business intelligence software for the automotive, consumer goods, financial services, national security, and petroleum industries.

EXECUTIVES

President, CEO, and Director: James (Jim) Baum, age 46, $1,449,132 total compensation
SVP, CFO, and Treasurer: Patrick J. Scannell Jr., age 55, $891,172 total compensation
SVP Worldwide Sales: Raymond (Ray) Tacoma, age 60, $776,351 total compensation
CTO: Justin Lindsey
Chief Strategy Officer: David Flaxman
VP Worldwide Customer Support and Manufacturing: Patricia (Tricia) Cotter, age 51, $466,159 total compensation
VP International: Jon O. Niess
VP Corporate Marketing: Tim Young
VP Hardware Technology: Michael Sporer
VP Product Management and Marketing: Philip Francisco
VP Product Strategy: John Metzger
Director Marketing Communications: Virginia Lux
Director: J. Chris Scalet, age 50
Auditors: PricewaterhouseCoopers LLP

LOCATIONS

HQ: Netezza Corporation
26 Forest St., Marlborough, MA 01752
Phone: 508-382-8200 **Fax:** 508-382-8300
Web: www.netezza.com

2009 Sales

	$ mil.	% of total
North America	146.2	78
Other regions	41.6	22
Total	**187.8**	**100**

PRODUCTS/OPERATIONS

2009 Sales

	$ mil.	% of total
Products	143.5	76
Services	44.3	24
Total	**187.8**	**100**

COMPETITORS

EMC	SAS Institute
Hewlett-Packard	Sun Microsystems
IBM	Sybase
Oracle	Teradata
SAND Technology	

HISTORICAL FINANCIALS

Company Type: Public

Income Statement

FYE: January 31

	REVENUE ($ mil.)	NET INCOME ($ mil.)	NET PROFIT MARGIN	EMPLOYEES
1/09	187.8	31.5	16.8%	381
1/08	126.7	2.0	1.6%	276
1/07	79.6	(8.0)	—	225
1/06	53.9	(13.8)	—	179
1/05	36.2	(3.0)	—	140
Annual Growth	**50.9%**	**—**	**—**	**28.4%**

2009 Year-End Financials

Debt ratio: —
Return on equity: 20.1%
Cash ($ mil.): 111.6
Current ratio: 2.68
Long-term debt ($ mil.): —
No. of shares (mil.): 60.8
Dividends
　Yield: —
　Payout: —
Market value ($ mil.): 369.3
R&D as % of sales: —
Advertising as % of sales: —

Stock History

NYSE Arca: NZ

	STOCK PRICE ($) FY Close	P/E High/Low	PER SHARE ($) Earnings	Dividends	Book Value
1/09	6.07	28 10	0.50	—	2.90
1/08	9.86	— —	(0.03)	—	2.24
Annual Growth	**(38.4%)**	**— —**	**—**	**—**	**29.4%**

NETGEAR, Inc.

NETGEAR keeps consumers and small businesses wired and wireless. The company designs a range of networking equipment — hubs, routers, switches, servers, and interfaces — for connecting PCs in home and small business settings to each other and the Internet. It also supplies network-attached storage (NAS) systems, VPN firewalls, and digital media receivers. NETGEAR sells through distributors, including Ingram Micro (14% of sales in 2008) and Tech Data (11%); to retailers such as Best Buy, Fry's Electronics, and RadioShack; and directly through its online store. The company uses third-party manufacturing services contractors in China and Taiwan to produce its equipment.

NETGEAR has expanded its international sales presence in recent years, looking to emerging markets such as China and India for growth. The company generates more than half of sales from international markets.

In 2008 NETGEAR acquired assets, including technology and engineers, from security appliance developer CP Secure. The purchase of CP Secure's assets expanded its security offerings for small and midsized businesses.

Originally spun off from communications equipment giant Nortel Networks in 2000, NETGEAR bought out Nortel's remaining stake in 2002.

EXECUTIVES

Chairman and CEO: Patrick C.S. Lo, age 52, $1,927,177 total compensation
CFO: Christine M. Gorjanc, age 52, $634,671 total compensation
CIO: Thomas (Tom) Holt
CTO: Mark G. Merrill, age 54
SVP Worldwide Sales: David S. Soares, age 42, $797,254 total compensation
SVP Operations: Michael F. Falcon, age 52, $557,337 total compensation
SVP Engineering: Charles T. (Chuck) Olson, age 53
VP Product Marketing: Vivek Pathela
VP Legal and Corporate Development and Company Secretary: Andrew W. Kim, age 38
VP Engineering Multimedia Products: Michael Spilo
VP Asia/Pacific Sales: Ian McClean, age 47
VP Americas Sales: Michael A. Werdann, age 40, $547,825 total compensation
VP Human Resources: Tamesa Rogers
Senior Director Worldwide Marketing Communications: Judy Hoffmann
Auditors: PricewaterhouseCoopers LLP

LOCATIONS

HQ: NETGEAR, Inc.
350 E. Plumeria Dr., San Jose, CA 95134
Phone: 408-907-8000 **Fax:** 408-907-8097
Web: www.netgear.com

2008 Sales

	$ mil.	% of total
US	297.6	40
Europe, Middle East & Africa		
UK	121.0	16
Other countries	233.1	32
Other regions	91.6	12
Total	**743.3**	**100**

PRODUCTS/OPERATIONS

Selected Products

Broadband access
　Gateways (routers with integrated modems, wireless)
　IP telephony
　Routers
Ethernet networking
　Adapters
　Bridges
　Network interface cards (NICs)
　Peripheral servers
　Switches
　VPN firewalls
Network connectivity
　Media adapters
　Network-attached storage (NAS)
　Powerline adapters and bridges
　Wi-fi phones
　Wireless access points
　Wireless NICs and adapters

COMPETITORS

2Wire	Dell
3Com	D-Link
Actiontec	Hewlett-Packard
Allied Telesis	Huawei Technologies
Apple Inc.	Motorola, Inc.
ARRIS	NetApp
Barracuda Networks	Nokia Siemens Networks
Belkin	Nortel Networks
Buffalo Technology	SonicWALL
Cisco CBG	THOMSON
Cisco Systems	WatchGuard Technologies

HISTORICAL FINANCIALS

Company Type: Public

Income Statement

FYE: December 31

	REVENUE ($ mil.)	NET INCOME ($ mil.)	NET PROFIT MARGIN	EMPLOYEES
12/08	743.3	18.0	2.4%	579
12/07	727.8	46.0	6.3%	518
12/06	573.6	41.1	7.2%	388
12/05	449.6	33.6	7.5%	307
12/04	383.1	23.5	6.1%	269
Annual Growth	18.0%	(6.4%)	—	21.1%

2008 Year-End Financials

Debt ratio: —
Return on equity: 4.7%
Cash ($ mil.): 192.8
Current ratio: 2.77
Long-term debt ($ mil.): —
No. of shares (mil.): 34.6

Dividends
  Yield: —
  Payout: —
Market value ($ mil.): 395.1
R&D as % of sales: —
Advertising as % of sales: —

Stock History

NASDAQ (GS): NTGR

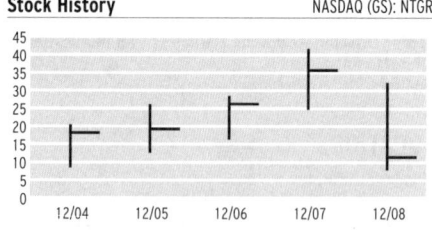

	STOCK PRICE ($) FY Close	P/E High/Low		PER SHARE ($) Earnings	Dividends	Book Value
12/08	11.41	63	16	0.51	—	11.29
12/07	35.67	32	20	1.28	—	10.73
12/06	26.25	24	14	1.19	—	8.50
12/05	19.25	26	13	0.99	—	6.82
12/04	18.16	28	12	0.72	—	5.35
Annual Growth	(11.0%)	—	—	(8.3%)	—	20.5%

NetLogic Microsystems

NetLogic Microsystems' chips logically address the content of the Internet. The company designs and sells what it calls knowledge-based processors, which are used in routers and other devices to optimize speed and search capabilities over the Internet. NetLogic's customers include networking giants Alcatel-Lucent (12% of sales), Cisco Systems (38% of sales, including Cisco's contract electronics manufacturers), Fujitsu, Hitachi, Huawei Technologies, and Juniper Networks. The company's semiconductors are principally produced by Taiwan Semiconductor Manufacturing and United Microelectronics.

NetLogic Microsystems gets two-thirds of its sales outside the US.

Knowledge-based processors are the company's stock in trade and main line of business. They are chips used in processing packets in computer networks; they are said to operate faster and more securely than comparable processors. NetLogic was able to increase sales in 2008, a down year in general for semiconductor vendors, due to products acquired in 2007. The company has a limited number of customers, although it is reducing its dependence on Cisco as its largest customer. The company has grown rapidly in this decade, and must carefully manage its growth.

In 2009 the company acquired assets from the network search engine product line of Integrated Device Technology (IDT). The acquisition included IDT's search accelerator, network search engine and route accelerator product families, and related patents and intellectual property. These products and technologies complement NetLogic's existing portfolio of knowledge-based processors, NETLite processors, and network search engines. NetLogic paid $100 million in cash for the IDT assets.

Also that year the company agreed to merge with RMI Corporation, a developer of low-power processors for Internet protocol networks, for about $175 million in cash and stock. RMI counts Alcatel-Lucent, Cisco, IBM, NEC, Samsung Electronics, and ZTE among its customers.

In 2007 NetLogic acquired Aeluros, a developer of 10-Gigabit Ethernet interface technologies and semiconductors, for $57 million in cash. The firm's products expanded NetLogic's portfolio in knowledge-based processors, especially in the area of low-power, multi-gigabit interface technology.

In 2006 NetLogic acquired the network search engine products of Cypress Semiconductor.

NetLogic Microsystems was backed by investors including Sevin Rosen Funds. The fabless semiconductor company was founded by former CEO Norman Godinho (who owns about 13% of NetLogic) and VP/CTO Varad Srinivasan.

EXECUTIVES

Chairman: Leonard C. (Len) Perham, age 65
President, CEO and Director: Ronald (Ron) Jankov, age 50, $2,123,696 total compensation
SVP Worldwide Sales: Marcia Zander, age 46, $1,100,293 total compensation
SVP Worldwide Business Operations: Ibrahim (Abe) Korgav, age 60
VP and CFO: Michael T. (Mike) Tate, age 43, $1,403,755 total compensation
VP Product Development and CTO: Varadarajan (Varad) Srinivasan, age 58, $859,275 total compensation
VP Worldwide Manufacturing: Mozafar (Mo) Maghsoudnia, age 42, $684,477 total compensation
VP, General Counsel, and Secretary: Roland Cortes, age 44
VP Marketing: Chris O'Reilly, age 36
VP Engineering: Dimitrios Dimitrelis, age 51
VP Corporate Development: Niall Bartlett
Auditors: PricewaterhouseCoopers LLP

LOCATIONS

HQ: NetLogic Microsystems, Inc.
  1875 Charleston Rd., Mountain View, CA 94043
Phone: 650-961-6676   **Fax:** 650-961-1092
Web: www.netlogicmicro.com

NetLogic Microsystems has offices in India and the US.

2008 Sales

	$ mil.	% of total
US	46.3	33
Malaysia	42.4	30
China	30.4	22
Other countries	20.8	15
Total	**139.9**	**100**

PRODUCTS/OPERATIONS

Selected Products

Classification and forwarding processors
Network search engines
Software development kits
Ternary content-addressable memory (TCAM) search
  accelerators

COMPETITORS

Applied Micro Circuits
Broadcom
Cavium Networks
EZchip
Integrated Device Technology
LSI Corp.
Marvell Technology
Mellanox
MOSAID Technologies
Renesas Technology
TranSwitch
Vitesse Semiconductor

HISTORICAL FINANCIALS

Company Type: Public

Income Statement

FYE: December 31

	REVENUE ($ mil.)	NET INCOME ($ mil.)	NET PROFIT MARGIN	EMPLOYEES
12/08	139.9	3.6	2.6%	255
12/07	109.0	2.6	2.4%	225
12/06	96.8	0.6	0.6%	170
12/05	81.8	16.4	20.0%	110
12/04	47.8	(12.0)	—	75
Annual Growth	30.8%	—	—	35.8%

2008 Year-End Financials

Debt ratio: —
Return on equity: 1.9%
Cash ($ mil.): 83.5
Current ratio: 3.45
Long-term debt ($ mil.): —
No. of shares (mil.): 22.4

Dividends
  Yield: —
  Payout: —
Market value ($ mil.): 493.9
R&D as % of sales: —
Advertising as % of sales: —

Stock History

NASDAQ (GM): NETL

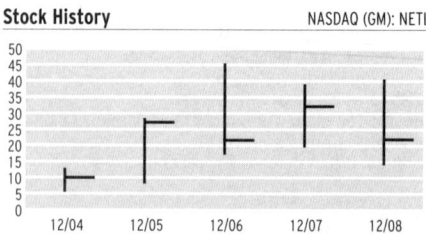

	STOCK PRICE ($) FY Close	P/E High/Low		PER SHARE ($) Earnings	Dividends	Book Value
12/08	22.01	252	90	0.16	—	8.93
12/07	32.20	322	167	0.12	—	7.66
12/06	21.69	1,501	585	0.03	—	6.35
12/05	27.24	32	10	0.87	—	3.06
12/04	10.00	—	—	(1.17)	—	2.14
Annual Growth	21.8%	—	—	—	—	42.8%

NetScout Systems

NetScout Systems helps network administrators stay prepared. The company provides systems that monitor and report on the performance of software applications and the networks on which they run. The company's probes — monitoring appliances that can be placed throughout a network — allow administrators to collect information about traffic flow and to optimize application and network performance. Its nGenius Performance Management System monitors systems ranging from voice-over-IP communications to customer relationship management applications. NetScout sells directly and through resellers and distributors to corporate and government customers.

Generating about 60% of its revenues through indirect sales channels, NetScout primarily markets to midsized and large corporate customers. Target industries include financial services, health care, manufacturing, retail, technology, telecommunications, and utilities.

In 2007 NetScout purchased competitor Network General, developer of the Sniffer line of performance and security analysis tools, for $206 million. NetScout, which developed products based on Sniffer technology prior to the acquisition, more than doubled its revenue with the purchase.

EXECUTIVES

Chairman, President, CEO, and Treasurer:
  Anil K. Singhal, age 55, $1,392,597 total compensation
COO: Michael Szabados, age 57,
  $805,846 total compensation
SVP General Operations and CFO: David P. Sommers,
  age 62, $658,053 total compensation
SVP Worldwide Sales Operations: John W. Downing,
  age 51, $623,445 total compensation
SVP Research and Development: Ashwani Singhal
SVP Services and CIO: Ken Boyd
VP and CTO: Bruce Kelley Jr.
VP Finance and Chief Accounting Officer:
  Jeffrey R. (Jeff) Wakely, age 45,
  $340,947 total compensation
VP Human Resources: Victor P. (Vic) Becker, age 57
VP and General Counsel: Jeff Levinson
VP Marketing NetScout Systems: Steven Shalita
VP Business Development: Bruce Sweet
VP Corporate Development: Z. Alan Fink
Manager Analyst and Public Relations:
  Christine Johansen
Director Investor Relations: Catherine (Cathy) Taylor
Auditors: PricewaterhouseCoopers LLP

LOCATIONS

HQ: NetScout Systems, Inc.
  310 Littleton Rd., Westford, MA 01886
Phone: 978-614-4000   **Fax:** 978-614-4004
Web: www.netscout.com

2009 Sales

	$ mil.	% of total
Americas		
US	199.7	75
Other countries	17.3	6
Europe, Middle East & Africa	37.6	14
Asia/Pacific	13.0	5
Total	**267.6**	**100**

PRODUCTS/OPERATIONS

2009 Sales

	$ mil.	% of total
Products	154.2	58
Services	113.4	42
Total	**267.6**	**100**

2009 Sales by Channel

	$ mil.	% of total
Indirect	158.2	59
Direct	109.4	41
Total	**267.6**	**100**

COMPETITORS

Agilent Technologies
CA, Inc.
Fluke Networks
InfoVista
NetQoS
NIKSUN
OPNET
Resonate, Inc.
SolarWinds
Tektronix
Telcordia
Teltronics
Tivoli Software
TTI Team Telecom

HISTORICAL FINANCIALS

Company Type: Public

Income Statement

FYE: March 31

	REVENUE ($ mil.)	NET INCOME ($ mil.)	NET PROFIT MARGIN	EMPLOYEES
3/09	267.6	20.0	7.5%	788
3/08	169.0	(2.1)	—	790
3/07	102.5	7.7	7.5%	364
3/06	97.9	5.8	5.9%	367
3/05	85.2	2.9	3.4%	359
Annual Growth	**33.1%**	**62.1%**	**—**	**21.7%**

2009 Year-End Financials

Debt ratio: 36.5%
Return on equity: 9.5%
Cash ($ mil.): 82.2
Current ratio: 1.44
Long-term debt ($ mil.): 82.5
No. of shares (mil.): 40.7
Dividends
  Yield: 0.0%
  Payout: —
Market value ($ mil.): 291.2
R&D as % of sales: —
Advertising as % of sales: —

Stock History

NASDAQ (GS): NTCT

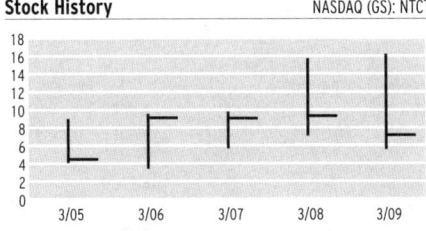

	STOCK PRICE ($) FY Close	P/E High/Low		PER SHARE ($) Earnings	Dividends	Book Value
3/09	7.16	33	12	0.49	0.00	5.55
3/08	9.30	—	—	(0.06)	0.00	4.85
3/07	9.05	42	25	0.23	0.00	3.40
3/06	9.10	52	20	0.18	0.00	3.11
3/05	4.45	98	47	0.09	0.00	2.89
Annual Growth	**12.6%**	**—**	**—**	**52.8%**	**—**	**17.7%**

NeuStar, Inc.

NeuStar shines as a key provider of registry and clearinghouse services used in telecommunications and Internet networks. NeuStar manages the registry of North American area codes and telephone numbers and the database used by telecom carriers (including Verizon, Sprint Nextel, and AT&T) and cable companies (Comcast and tw telecom) to route phone calls. The company also operates an Internet registry supporting domain addresses. NeuStar is a leading provider of operations support systems (OSS) clearinghouse services that provide ordering, service provisioning, billing, and customer service functions for telecom carriers and other companies. The company gets most of its revenues in North America.

NeuStar is the contracted North American Numbering Plan Administrator, the National Pooling Administrator, the administrator of local number portability for communications carriers in North America, and the lone industry registry for US Common Short Codes.

NeuStar is expanding operations through acquisitions. In 2006 the company bought UltraDNS, a Reston, Virginia-based provider of Domain Name System (DNS) and directory services, in a cash deal valued at $61.8 million. It additionally purchased Followap, a mobile instant messaging services provider, for $139 million that year. NeuStar acquired Webmetrics, a provider of Web and network performance testing services, in 2008 for $12.5 million in cash.

EXECUTIVES

Chairman and CEO: Jeffrey E. (Jeff) Ganek, age 57,
  $2,028,045 total compensation
President and COO: Lisa A. Hook, age 51,
  $1,355,383 total compensation
SVP and CFO: Paul S. Lalljie, age 36
CTO: Eric W. Burger
SVP Marketing: Steve Johnson
SVP Sales and Business Development:
  Raymond A. (Ray) Saulino, age 58
SVP Human Resources: Douglas (Doug) Arnold,
  $613,177 total compensation
SVP External Affairs: Gerald (Jerry) Kovach
SVP and Senior Technologist: Rodney Joffe
SVP, General Counsel, and Secretary: Martin K. Lowen,
  age 45
VP Finance and Corporate Treasurer: Steve Boyce
CEO, Webmetrics: Tim Drees
Director Finance and Investor Relations: Brandon Pugh
Auditors: Ernst & Young LLP

LOCATIONS

HQ: NeuStar, Inc.
  46000 Center Oak Plaza, Sterling, VA 20166
Phone: 571-434-5400   **Fax:** 571-434-5401
Web: www.neustar.biz

2008 Sales

	$ mil.	% of total
North America	443.9	91
Europe, Middle East & Africa	34.3	7
Other regions	10.6	2
Total	**488.8**	**100**

PRODUCTS/OPERATIONS

2008 Sales

	$ mil.	% of total
Addressing	130.7	27
Interoperability	64.3	13
Infrastructure & other	293.8	60
Total	**488.8**	**100**

2008 Sales by Services

	$ mil.	% of total
Clearinghouse services	474.1	97
NGM services	14.7	3
Total	**488.8**	**100**

COMPETITORS

Accenture	Keynote Systems
Akamai	NetCracker Technology
Amdocs	Nokia
Billing Services Group	Oracle
BSG Clearing Solutions	Perot Systems
CGI Group	Register.com
Evolving Systems	Sodalia North America
F5 Networks	Synchronoss
Gomez, Inc.	Syniverse
Hewlett-Packard	Telcordia
HP Enterprise Services	Tucows
IBM	VeriSign
ICANN	XIUS-bcgi
Infoblox	

HISTORICAL FINANCIALS

Company Type: Public

Income Statement

FYE: December 31

	REVENUE ($ mil.)	NET INCOME ($ mil.)	NET PROFIT MARGIN	EMPLOYEES
12/08	488.8	4.3	0.9%	966
12/07	429.2	92.3	21.5%	960
12/06	333.0	73.9	22.2%	822
12/05	242.5	51.1	21.1%	502
12/04	165.0	35.6	21.6%	413
Annual Growth	**31.2%**	**(41.0%)**	**—**	**23.7%**

2008 Year-End Financials

Debt ratio: 3.1%
Return on equity: 1.0%
Cash ($ mil.): 150.8
Current ratio: 2.58
Long-term debt ($ mil.): 11.9
No. of shares (mil.): 74.4

Dividends
  Yield: —
  Payout: —
Market value ($ mil.): 1,422.6
R&D as % of sales: —
Advertising as % of sales: —

Stock History

NYSE: NSR

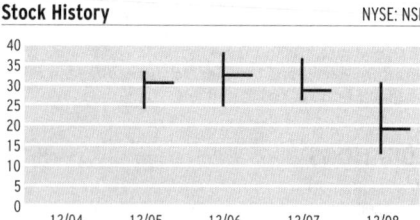

	STOCK PRICE ($) FY Close	P/E High/Low		PER SHARE ($) Earnings	Dividends	Book Value
12/08	19.13	509	221	0.06	—	5.20
12/07	28.68	31	23	1.17	—	6.46
12/06	32.44	40	27	0.94	—	4.59
12/05	30.49	46	34	0.72	—	2.50
Annual Growth	**(14.4%)**	**—**	**—**	**(47.5%)**	**—**	**37.4%**

Neutral Tandem

Neutral Tandem helps telecom providers stay in sync with customers. The company provides third-party interconnection services to competitive carriers via tandem switches, which allow wireline, wireless, and broadband phone providers to exchange traffic between networks without direct connections. Marketed as an alternative to incumbent local exchange carriers (ILECs), Neutral Tandem offers services in more than 60 US metropolitan markets. The company's customers include Sprint Nextel, Comcast Cable, and AT&T. Doll Capital Management and New Enterprise Associates each own about 18% of the company.

Wireless carriers accounted for about 60% of the company's revenue in 2007, while wireline carriers accounted for about 20%; cable companies and non-carriers accounted for the rest.

EXECUTIVES

Chairman: James P. Hynes, age 61
President, CEO, and Director: Rian J. Wren, age 52, $1,330,363 total compensation
EVP and COO: Surendra Saboo, age 50, $853,190 total compensation
EVP and CFO: Robert M. (Rob) Junkroski, age 44, $677,217 total compensation
SVP External Affairs, General Counsel, and Secretary: Richard Monto, age 44, $517,090 total compensation
SVP Sales: David A. Lopez, age 45, $463,621 total compensation
Media Contact: Gerard Laurain
Auditors: Deloitte & Touche LLP

LOCATIONS

HQ: Neutral Tandem, Inc.
  1 S. Wacker Dr., Ste. 200, Chicago, IL 60606
Phone: 312-384-8000   **Fax:** 312-346-3276
Web: www.neutraltandem.com

COMPETITORS

AT&T
Level 3 Communications
Qwest Communications
Verizon

HISTORICAL FINANCIALS

Company Type: Public

Income Statement

FYE: December 31

	REVENUE ($ mil.)	NET INCOME ($ mil.)	NET PROFIT MARGIN	EMPLOYEES
12/08	120.9	24.0	19.9%	137
12/07	85.6	6.3	7.4%	126
12/06	52.9	4.7	8.9%	110
12/05	28.0	0.2	0.7%	110
12/04	3.4	(5.2)	—	—
Annual Growth	**144.2%**	**—**	**—**	**7.6%**

2008 Year-End Financials

Debt ratio: 0.1%
Return on equity: 14.8%
Cash ($ mil.): 110.4
Current ratio: 12.04
Long-term debt ($ mil.): 0.2
No. of shares (mil.): 33.5

Dividends
  Yield: 0.0%
  Payout: —
Market value ($ mil.): 544.2
R&D as % of sales: —
Advertising as % of sales: —

Stock History

NASDAQ (GM): TNDM

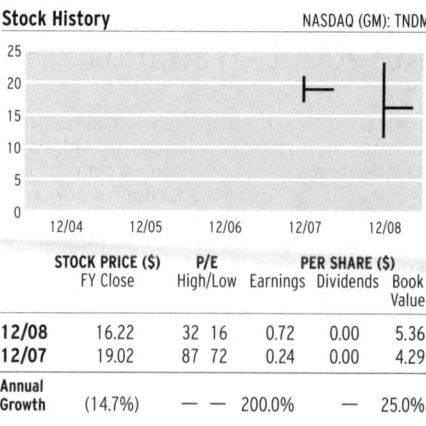

	STOCK PRICE ($) FY Close	P/E High/Low		PER SHARE ($) Earnings	Dividends	Book Value
12/08	16.22	32	16	0.72	0.00	5.36
12/07	19.02	87	72	0.24	0.00	4.29
Annual Growth	**(14.7%)**	**—**	**—**	**200.0%**	**—**	**25.0%**

New Hampshire Thrift Bancshares

New Hampshire Thrift Bancshares is the holding company for Lake Sunapee Bank, which operates more than 25 branches in western and central New Hampshire and western Vermont. Targeting individuals and local businesses, the bank provides such traditional services as checking and savings accounts, money market and NOW accounts, CDs, and IRAs. It mainly uses funds from deposits to originate a variety of loan products, mainly conventional and commercial mortgages, as well as construction, business, consumer, and municipal loans. New Hampshire Thrift Bancshares expanded into Vermont with the 2007 acquisition of First Brandon National Bank, which now operates as a division of Lake Sunapee Bank.

EXECUTIVES

Chairman, President, and CEO; Vice Chairman, President, and CEO, Lake Sunapee Bank: Stephen W. Ensign, age 61, $399,032 total compensation
Vice Chairman, EVP, Secretary, and CFO; EVP, COO, and CFO, Lake Sunapee Bank: Stephen R. Theroux, age 59, $283,198 total compensation
SVP Commercial Lending, Lake Sunapee Bank: Scott W. Laughinghouse
SVP Business Development and Marketing, Lake Sunapee Bank: Robert C. O'Brien
SVP Mortgage Lending, Lake Sunapee Bank: Sharon L. Whitaker
SVP Compliance and Internal Audit, Lake Sunapee Bank: H. Bliss Dayton
SVP Retail Banking and CIO, Lake Sunapee Bank: William J. McIver
SVP Human Resources, Lake Sunapee Bank: Frances E. Clow
Auditors: Shatswell, MacLeod & Company, P.C.

LOCATIONS

HQ: New Hampshire Thrift Bancshares, Inc.
  9 Main St., Newport, NH 03773
Phone: 603-863-5772   **Fax:** 603-863-5025
Web: www.lakesunbank.com

COMPETITORS

Citizens Financial Group
Northway Financial
People's United Financial
TD Bank USA

HISTORICAL FINANCIALS

Company Type: Public

Income Statement

FYE: December 31

	ASSETS ($ mil.)	NET INCOME ($ mil.)	INCOME AS % OF ASSETS	EMPLOYEES
12/08	843.2	5.7	0.7%	226
12/07	834.2	4.5	0.5%	248
12/06	672.0	5.0	0.7%	203
12/05	650.2	5.5	0.8%	188
12/04	595.5	5.1	0.9%	171
Annual Growth	9.1%	2.8%	—	7.2%

2008 Year-End Financials

Equity as % of assets: 8.9%
Return on assets: 0.7%
Return on equity: 7.7%
Long-term debt ($ mil.): 89.1
No. of shares (mil.): 5.8
Market value ($ mil.): 44.5

Dividends
 Yield: 6.7%
 Payout: 52.5%
Sales ($ mil.): 33.6
R&D as % of sales: —
Advertising as % of sales: —

Stock History

NASDAQ (GM): NHTB

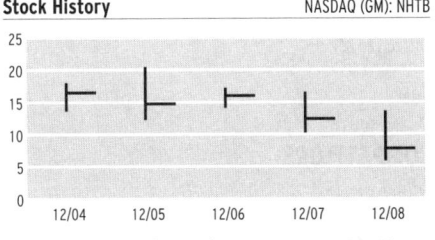

	STOCK PRICE ($) FY Close	P/E High/Low		PER SHARE ($) Earnings	Dividends	Book Value
12/08	7.72	14	6	0.99	0.52	12.94
12/07	12.40	18	11	0.92	0.52	12.59
12/06	16.00	15	12	1.17	0.51	8.39
12/05	14.74	16	10	1.29	0.50	8.10
12/04	16.50	15	12	1.20	0.45	7.59
Annual Growth	(17.3%)	—	—	(4.7%)	3.7%	14.2%

Newpark Resources

Oil field waste is gold for environmental services alchemist Newpark Resources. The company provides integrated environmental and drilling fluid and engineering services to oil and gas drillers. Newpark Resources also supplies prefab work platforms and provides mat-based temporary access roads (through its Newpark Mats & Integrated Services unit), processes and disposes of oil field waste (injecting it underground or recycling it into drilling fluids), and performs fluid processing and recycling on site at rigs. It also processes and disposes of nonhazardous industrial waste.

In 2007 the company began to explore strategic alternatives with regards to its environmental services business, including the possible sale of this segment. In 2008 it agreed to sell its U.S. Environmental Services business to Canada-based waste services firm CCS, Inc., but the FTC blocked the deal as anticompetitive. Newpark

Resources subsequently reincorporated the environmental services operations as a core part of its business portfolio.

In 2008 the company expanded its fluid service operations with a $144 million contract with Petrobras to serve an offshore Brazil project.

EXECUTIVES

Chairman: Jerry W. Box, age 70
President, CEO, and Director: Paul L. Howes, age 54, $2,238,366 total compensation
VP and CFO: James E. (Jim) Braun, age 49, $888,501 total compensation
VP, General Counsel, Chief Administrative Officer, and Secretary: Mark J. Airola, age 50, $851,048 total compensation
VP; President, Mats and Integrated Services: William D. (Bill) Moss, age 56, $445,244 total compensation
VP; President, Environmental Services: Samuel L. (Sammy) Cooper, age 52
VP; President, Fluids Systems and Engineering: Bruce C. Smith, age 57, $1,160,019 total compensation
VP Technical Services: Frank Lyon
VP, Controller, and Chief Accounting Officer: Gregg Piontek, age 38
President. Excalibar Minerals: Tom Eisenman
Auditors: Ernst & Young LLP

LOCATIONS

HQ: Newpark Resources, Inc.
 2700 Research Forest Dr., Ste. 100
 The Woodlands, TX 77381
Phone: 281-362-6800 **Fax:** 281-362-6801
Web: www.newpark.com

2008 Sales

	$ mil.	% of total
US	692.2	81
Mediterranean countries	123.2	14
Canada	26.6	3
Mexico & Brazil	16.3	2
Total	**858.3**	**100**

PRODUCTS/OPERATIONS

2008 Sales

	$ mil.	% of total
Fluids sales & engineering	706.3	82
Mat & integrated services	89.6	11
Environmental services	62.4	7
Total	**858.3**	**100**

COMPETITORS

Baker Hughes
BJ Services
Halliburton
Philip Services
Schlumberger

HISTORICAL FINANCIALS

Company Type: Public

Income Statement

FYE: December 31

	REVENUE ($ mil.)	NET INCOME ($ mil.)	NET PROFIT MARGIN	EMPLOYEES
12/08	858.3	38.5	4.5%	2,119
12/07	612.8	26.7	4.4%	1,987
12/06	668.2	(32.3)	—	1,816
12/05	557.0	21.6	3.9%	1,732
12/04	433.4	4.0	0.9%	1,452
Annual Growth	18.6%	76.1%	—	9.9%

2008 Year-End Financials

Debt ratio: 44.1%
Return on equity: 10.4%
Cash ($ mil.): 8.3
Current ratio: 2.69
Long-term debt ($ mil.): 166.5
No. of shares (mil.): 88.9

Dividends
 Yield: 0.0%
 Payout: —
Market value ($ mil.): 329.1
R&D as % of sales: —
Advertising as % of sales: —

Stock History

NYSE: NR

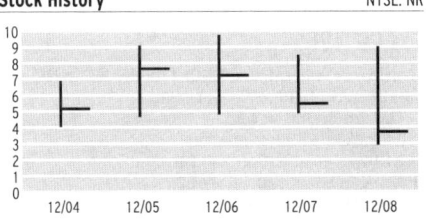

	STOCK PRICE ($) FY Close	P/E High/Low		PER SHARE ($) Earnings	Dividends	Book Value
12/08	3.70	21	7	0.43	0.00	4.25
12/07	5.45	29	17	0.29	0.00	4.06
12/06	7.21	—	—	(0.36)	0.00	3.63
12/05	7.63	36	19	0.25	0.00	3.94
12/04	5.15	136	82	0.05	0.00	3.63
Annual Growth	(7.9%)	—	—	71.2%	—	4.0%

NewStar Financial

Midsized companies can get the loans they need from NewStar Financial. The company provides a variety of loans (primarily senior debt) for refinancing, acquisitions, consolidations, and commercial real estate purchases (primarily office and multifamily residential). Other areas of focus include structured products for specialty finance companies. It serves clients in industries including retail, consumer products, media, and business services; customers include TIDI Products, Oak Street Financial, and Excelligence Learning Corporation. The company has offices in California, Connecticut, Illinois, Massachusetts, and South Carolina. NewStar has applied to convert to a commercial bank holding company.

By converting, the company hopes to be able to build its funding reserves through deposits. NewStar initially planned to form a new national bank, but instead agreed to buy Southern Commerce Bank, which operates about a dozen branches in Florida, from Dickinson Financial Corporation. It later scrapped those plans too, after determining it would have difficulty restructuring the combined firms' balance sheet. NewStar continues to seek other bank acquisitions.

In 2008 the company ceased the origination of structured products, focusing its lending operations on mid-market corporate and commercial real estate. The company is eyeing new products, but has suspended the development of its collateralized loan obligation (CLO) unit.

In 2009 NewStar was part of a group of investors who bought online survey provider Survey Monkey. Also in on the deal was Spectrum

Equity Investors, Bank of America, CIT Group, and Bain Capital Ventures.

Investment funds managed by JPMorgan Chase and Corsair Capital own some 20% of NewStar Financial. Hedge fund OZ Management holds about 15% and Capital Z Management owns more than 10%.

EXECUTIVES

Chairman, President, and CEO: Timothy J. Conway, age 54, $2,972,110 total compensation
CFO: John K. Bray, age 52, $1,302,824 total compensation
Chief Investment Officer and Director: Peter A. Schmidt-Fellner, age 52, $2,245,203 total compensation
Managing Director and Chief Credit Officer Commercial Real Estate: William G. Mallon, age 62
Managing Director and Chief Credit Officer Middle Market and Structured Products: Robert T. Clemmens, age 58, $1,286,932 total compensation
VP Investor Relations and Corporate Communications: Anne G. Bork
VP Operations: Brian Forde
VP Information Technology: Steven T. Hohl
Group Head and Managing Director: Timothy C. Shoyer, age 43
Group Head and Managing Director Middle Market: David R. Dobies, age 43, $1,256,519 total compensation
Managing Director and Head Commercial Real Estate: J. Daniel Adkinson, age 53
Managing Director and Head of Strategy and Corporate Development: Robert K. Brown
Managing Director and Head Sales and Trading: R. Scott Poirier, age 46
Director Accounting and Finance: Daniel K. Crowley
Director Human Resources: Colleen M. Banse
Auditors: KPMG LLP

LOCATIONS

HQ: NewStar Financial, Inc.
500 Boylston St., Ste. 1600, Boston, MA 02116
Phone: 617-848-2500　　**Fax:** 617-848-4300
Web: www.newstarfin.com

PRODUCTS/OPERATIONS

2008 Lending Portfolio

	% of total
Middle Market Corporate	84
Commercial Real Estate	16
Total	**100**

COMPETITORS

Bank of America
Bank of the West
CIT Group
Citigroup
GE Commercial Finance
JPMorgan Chase

HISTORICAL FINANCIALS

Company Type: Public

Income Statement

FYE: December 31

	ASSETS ($ mil.)	NET INCOME ($ mil.)	INCOME AS % OF ASSETS	EMPLOYEES
12/08	2,571.5	22.4	0.9%	94
12/07	2,622.8	(8.6)	—	132
12/06	1,915.2	(27.2)	—	101
12/05	789.5	(5.9)	—	96
12/04	120.3	(5.5)	—	38
Annual Growth	**115.0%**	**—**	**—**	**25.4%**

2008 Year-End Financials

Equity as % of assets: 22.6%　Dividends
Return on assets: 0.9%　　　　Yield: 0.0%
Return on equity: 4.1%　　　　Payout: —
Long-term debt ($ mil.): 1,935.4　Sales ($ mil.): 121.5
No. of shares (mil.): 49.2　　R&D as % of sales: —
Market value ($ mil.): 196.1　Advertising as % of sales: —

Stock History

NASDAQ (GM): NEWS

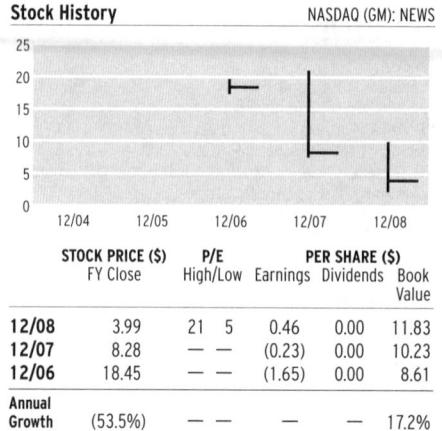

	STOCK PRICE ($) FY Close	P/E High/Low		PER SHARE ($) Earnings	Dividends	Book Value
12/08	3.99	21	5	0.46	0.00	11.83
12/07	8.28	—	—	(0.23)	0.00	10.23
12/06	18.45	—	—	(1.65)	0.00	8.61
Annual Growth	**(53.5%)**	—	—	—	—	**17.2%**

NIC Inc.

So people can do business with government agencies, NIC helps government agencies plug in to the Internet. The company is a leading provider of outsourced Web portal services for state and local governments. It designs, implements, and operates Web sites under contracts with government entities in about 20 states. NIC generates much of its revenue from transaction fees for such services as online license renewals and for providing data on motor vehicle titles and business licenses to insurance companies, lenders, and other authorized organizations. Insurance information provider ChoicePoint accounts for about 40% of the company's sales.

To grow, NIC is striving to renew its existing contracts, which typically run for three- to five-year terms, and to win new business. In addition, the company hopes to develop new applications for government Web sites from which it can generate transaction fees, especially outside the realm of motor vehicle records.

Along with its Web portal outsourcing business, the company sells back-office software designed to help government agencies manage corporate filings and campaign finance reports.

A trust controlled by co-founder and chairman Jeffery Fraser and director Ross Hartley owns about one-third of NIC. Fraser, formerly the company's CEO, retired from that position in February 2008 after an internal review of the company's expense reimbursement practices that was accompanied by an informal SEC inquiry. In separate transactions before and after the review, Fraser returned more than $280,000 in expenses to NIC in order to bring expense reporting into compliance with company policies.

Fraser was succeeded as CEO by Harry Herington, a company employee since 1995 and its president since 2006.

Formerly National Information Consortium, the company was formed through the combination of five different Web services businesses in 1997. It went public during the Internet boom in 1999 and was renamed NIC in 2002.

EXECUTIVES

Chairman and CEO: Harry H. Herington, age 49
COO, General Counsel, and Secretary: William F. (Brad) Bradley Jr., age 54
CFO: Stephen M. (Steve) Kovzan, age 40
EVP Portal Operations: Robert Knapp, age 40
VP Business Development: Elizabeth Proudfit
VP Marketing: Christopher (Chris) Neff
Director Partnerships and Alliances: Candy Irven
Director Communications and Investor Relations: Nancy S. Beaton
Auditors: PricewaterhouseCoopers LLP

LOCATIONS

HQ: NIC Inc.
25501 W. Valley Pkwy., Ste. 300, Olathe, KS 66061
Phone: 877-234-3468　　**Fax:** 913-498-3472
Web: www.nicusa.com

PRODUCTS/OPERATIONS

2008 Sales

	$ mil.	% of total
Outsourced portals	96.8	96
Software & services	3.8	4
Total	**100.6**	**100**

COMPETITORS

Accenture
Affiliated Computer Services
Agency.com
Automated License Systems
BearingPoint
CGI Group
Computer Sciences Corp.
HP Enterprise Services
IBM Global Services
Idea Integration
Manatron
MAXIMUS
Microsoft
Official Payments
Oracle
SAIC
Tyler Technologies
Unisys
USTI

HISTORICAL FINANCIALS

Company Type: Public

Income Statement

FYE: December 31

	REVENUE ($ mil.)	NET INCOME ($ mil.)	NET PROFIT MARGIN	EMPLOYEES
12/08	100.6	11.9	11.8%	473
12/07	85.8	12.0	14.0%	418
12/06	71.4	10.7	15.0%	339
12/05	59.2	6.4	10.8%	305
12/04	55.8	7.1	12.7%	288
Annual Growth	**15.9%**	**13.8%**	**—**	**13.2%**

2008 Year-End Financials

Debt ratio: —　　　　　　　　Dividends
Return on equity: 17.7%　　　Yield: 0.0%
Cash ($ mil.): 60.4　　　　　Payout: —
Current ratio: 2.04　　　　　Market value ($ mil.): 290.7
Long-term debt ($ mil.): —　　R&D as % of sales: —
No. of shares (mil.): 63.2　　Advertising as % of sales: —

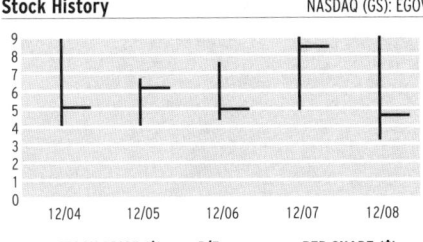
NightHawk Radiology

When local radiologists are fast asleep, NightHawk is waiting for the call. NightHawk Radiology Holdings, through its NightHawk Radiology Services subsidiary, remotely interprets diagnostic imaging scans (like those produced by MRI or X-ray machines) for understaffed hospitals and radiology groups across the US. Here's how it works: During off-hours, a hospital transmits digital diagnostic scans to one of NightHawk's facilities in Australia, Switzerland, or the US, where the images are repackaged and delivered to affiliated NightHawk radiologists for interpretation and diagnosis. The firm has more than 750 customers in the US; its affiliated radiologists are located in different time zones all over the world.

NightHawk, the leader in teleradiology services, has specialized in providing "preliminary reads," the initial, quick report that allows after-hours hospital personnel to begin treatment. But it has been expanding the breadth of its service offerings through both acquisitions and internal development. It has moved beyond its core service to include the provision of more detailed sub-specialty and final reads, as well as specialized cardiac interpretation services, such as 3D imaging. Its expanded service offering is available during daytime hours, as well as at night and on weekends.

Additionally, the company's NightHawk Business Services unit, built on the 2007 acquisition of Midwest Physician Services, provides billing and coding services, medical records management, transcription, staffing services, and other business services to radiology groups. And it has introduced a proprietary technology solution, called Talon, which helps radiology practices manage information.

The company acquired a couple of teleradiology firms in 2007, expanding its size and geographic reach. It also opened two new centralized facilities in San Francisco and Austin, Texas, and grew its base of affiliated radiologists.

NightHawk has benefited from the growing use of diagnostic imaging, coupled with a shortage of radiologists to interpret the scans. It continues to look for ways to capitalize on those favorable conditions by diversifying its service offering and customer base, selling more to existing customers, and pursuing complementary acquisitions.

Chairman Paul Berger and his son Jon founded the company and collectively own more than 15% of its stock.

EXECUTIVES

President, CEO, and Director: David M. (Dave) Engert, age 58, $148,898 total compensation
EVP and COO: Timothy E. (Tim) Murnane, age 59, $643,547 total compensation
SVP and Chief Medical Officer: Timothy V. Myers, age 51
SVP, General Counsel, and Secretary: Paul E. Cartee, age 36
SVP and CFO: David M. Sankaran, age 42, $429,685 total compensation
VP Finance and Corporate Treasurer: Andrea M. Clegg, age 42
Auditors: Deloitte & Touche LLP

LOCATIONS

HQ: NightHawk Radiology Holdings, Inc.
  601 Front Ave., Ste. 502, Coeur d'Alene, ID 83814
Phone: 208-676-8321   **Fax:** 208-664-2720
Web: www.nighthawkrad.net

PRODUCTS/OPERATIONS

Selected Services

Business services
  Accounting and tax services
  Billing and collection
  Coding
  Health plan contract negotiation
  Physician recruitment and staffing
  Practice management services
  Transcription
Talon Clinical Workflow Solution (workflow
  management software)
Teleradiology services
  Preliminary interpretations
  Final interpretations

COMPETITORS

American HealthChoice
Team Health
Virtual Radiologic

HISTORICAL FINANCIALS

Company Type: Public

Income Statement				FYE: December 31
	REVENUE ($ mil.)	NET INCOME ($ mil.)	NET PROFIT MARGIN	EMPLOYEES
12/08	167.6	9.4	5.6%	494
12/07	151.7	14.7	9.7%	503
12/06	92.2	(28.5)	—	223
12/05	64.1	(36.5)	—	232
12/04	39.3	2.6	6.6%	172
Annual Growth	43.7%	37.9%	—	30.2%

2008 Year-End Financials

Debt ratio: 71.8%
Return on equity: 7.1%
Cash ($ mil.): 47.2
Current ratio: 5.36
Long-term debt ($ mil.): 93.1
No. of shares (mil.): 23.5

Dividends
  Yield: 0.0%
  Payout: —
Market value ($ mil.): 114.4
R&D as % of sales: —
Advertising as % of sales: —

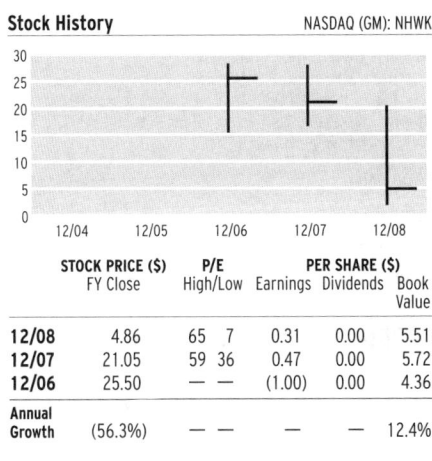
Northwest Pipe

Northwest Pipe's compass points in more than one direction. The company makes welded-steel water transmission lines that are used to form the circulatory systems of water suppliers. Its transmission pipes, some large enough to walk through, are made to transport water under pressure and are sold to government agencies and water districts. Northwest Pipe also manufactures tubular products with diameters of one-half inch to 16 inches for construction, agriculture, and energy purposes, as well as for water well casings, traffic signpost systems, and mechanical tubing.

Enlarging its customer base, Northwest Pipe acquired Utah-based Continental Pipe Manufacturing and traffic signpost maker S Square Tube Products, based in Colorado, in 2007. A couple of years later the company bought the Singapore-based company Byard, which manufactures spiral pipe mills for pipe manufacturers, including many for Northwest itself. The acquisitions are in line with Northwest Pipe's plans to expand its geographic footprint.

EXECUTIVES

Chairman: William R. (Bill) Tagmyer, age 71
President, CEO, and Director: Brian W. Dunham, age 51, $1,881,097 total compensation
SVP, CFO, and Corporate Secretary: Stephanie J. Welty, age 53, $617,429 total compensation
SVP Water Transmission Group: Gary A. Stokes, age 56, $697,738 total compensation
SVP Tubular Products: Robert L. (Bob) Mahoney, age 47, $784,295 total compensation
VP Human Resources: Winsor J.E. Jenkins, $467,529 total compensation
VP Operations, Bossier City, Louisiana: Greg Wilck
VP Quality Assurance: Gary Stone
VP Purchasing: Greg Carrier, age 54
Auditors: Deloitte & Touche LLP

LOCATIONS

HQ: Northwest Pipe Company
 5721 S.E. Columbia Way, Ste. 200
 Vancouver, WA 98661
Phone: 360-397-6250 **Fax:** 360-397-6257
Web: www.nwpipe.com

2008 Sales

	$ mil.	% of total
US	386.4	88
Other countries	53.3	12
Total	**439.7**	**100**

PRODUCTS/OPERATIONS

2008 Sales

	$ mil.	% of total
Water transmission	271.9	62
Tubular products	167.8	38
Total	**439.7**	**100**

COMPETITORS

Allied Tube and Conduit
American Cast Iron Pipe
Ameron
McWane
Mueller Water Products
Tenaris
U.S. Steel Canada
Valmont Industries

HISTORICAL FINANCIALS

Company Type: Public

Income Statement

FYE: December 31

	REVENUE ($ mil.)	NET INCOME ($ mil.)	NET PROFIT MARGIN	EMPLOYEES
12/08	439.7	32.3	7.3%	1,217
12/07	382.8	20.8	5.4%	1,260
12/06	346.6	20.0	5.8%	1,185
12/05	329.0	13.4	4.1%	1,231
12/04	291.9	12.4	4.2%	1,091
Annual Growth	10.8%	27.0%	—	2.8%

2008 Year-End Financials

Debt ratio: 39.3%
Return on equity: 11.8%
Cash ($ mil.): 0.1
Current ratio: 4.80
Long-term debt ($ mil.): 114.4
No. of shares (mil.): 9.2
Dividends
 Yield: 0.0%
 Payout: —
Market value ($ mil.): 393.6
R&D as % of sales: —
Advertising as % of sales: —

Stock History

NASDAQ (GS): NWPX

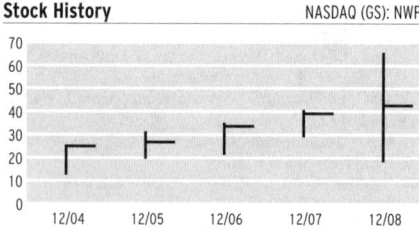

	STOCK PRICE ($) FY Close	P/E High/Low		PER SHARE ($) Earnings	Dividends	Book Value
12/08	42.61	19	5	3.46	0.00	31.57
12/07	39.14	18	13	2.26	0.00	27.75
12/06	33.62	13	8	2.69	0.00	24.99
12/05	26.76	16	11	1.90	0.00	17.26
12/04	24.95	14	7	1.83	0.00	15.61
Annual Growth	14.3%	—	—	17.3%	—	19.3%

NovaMed, Inc.

NovaMed believes that the eyes are the windows to the pocketbook. As more Americans seek convenient fixes for eye problems, the company has cashed in by acquiring and managing ambulatory surgical centers (ASCs) across the US. It operates more than 35 centers, with an emphasis on ophthalmologic surgery such as cataract and refractive eye surgery and laser vision correction (LASIK and other procedures). Other company centers offer health care services in areas such as orthopedics, pain management, and outpatient surgery including plastic surgery and general surgery. The company also rents optical equipment and operates optical labs (finishing of contact and eyeglass lenses) and an optical products purchasing organization.

Most of NovaMed's centers are owned jointly with the physicians who work in them, with NovaMed owning a majority interest. A handful of the centers are wholly owned by the company.

Historically, NovaMed focused only on eye-care services, but it has been expanding its offerings into other medical specialties. The company is growing by acquiring new ambulatory surgery centers and expanding the types of services its new and existing centers provide.

Over the past few years the company has acquired more than a dozen new multi-surgical centers offering a range of medical specialties including orthopedics, pain management, gastroenterology, urology, otolaryngology (ear, nose, throat), plastic surgery, and gynecology.

Along with operating ASCs, the company provides management services to two eye care practices under long-term service agreements. Under the agreements, NovaMed provides business, information technology, administrative, and financial services to these practices in exchange for a management fee.

Practice management is not the company's focus however; NovaMed's strategy for the future is centered on acquiring and developing new ASCs. NovaMed operates in 19 states throughout the US.

EXECUTIVES

President, CEO, and Chairman: Thomas S. Hall, age 49, $1,780,195 total compensation
EVP and CFO: Scott T. Macomber, age 55, $530,507 total compensation
EVP Operations: Graham B. Cherrington, age 46, $359,036 total compensation
SVP and General Counsel: John W. Lawrence Jr.
SVP Business Development: William J. L. Kennedy
SVP Operations: Cassandra T. Speier
VP and Corporate Controller: John P. Hart
VP Optical Services Group: Frank L. Soppa
President, Patient Education Concepts:
 Robert D. Watson
Director Human Resources: Lainie Kennedy
Auditors: BDO Seidman, LLP

LOCATIONS

HQ: NovaMed, Inc.
 980 N. Michigan Ave., Ste. 1620, Chicago, IL 60611
Phone: 312-664-4100 **Fax:** 312-664-4250
Web: www.novamed.com

2008 Ambulatory Surgery Center Locations

	No.
Florida	4
Illinois	4
Missouri	4
Indiana	3
Texas	3
Colorado	2
Michigan	2
New Hampshire	2
Pennsylvania	2
Tennessee	2
Arkansas	1
California	1
Georgia	1
Kansas	1
Louisiana	1
Nebraska	1
Ohio	1
Virginia	1
Wisconsin	1
Total	**37**

PRODUCTS/OPERATIONS

2008 Sales

	$ mil.	% of total
Surgical facilities	116.4	82
Products & other	24.8	18
Total	**141.2**	**100**

COMPETITORS

Abbott Medical Optics	OptiCare
AmSurg	Symbion
HCA	TLC Vision
LCA	United Surgical Partners

HISTORICAL FINANCIALS

Company Type: Public

Income Statement

FYE: December 31

	REVENUE ($ mil.)	NET INCOME ($ mil.)	NET PROFIT MARGIN	EMPLOYEES
12/08	141.2	9.6	6.8%	810
12/07	128.6	(5.6)	—	691
12/06	108.4	5.7	5.3%	666
12/05	81.2	5.6	6.9%	568
12/04	64.6	4.5	7.0%	457
Annual Growth	21.6%	20.9%	—	15.4%

2008 Year-End Financials

Debt ratio: 194.4%
Return on equity: 13.9%
Cash ($ mil.): 4.9
Current ratio: 1.62
Long-term debt ($ mil.): 140.9
No. of shares (mil.): 23.1
Dividends
 Yield: 0.0%
 Payout: —
Market value ($ mil.): 80.0
R&D as % of sales: —
Advertising as % of sales: —

Stock History

NASDAQ (GS): NOVA

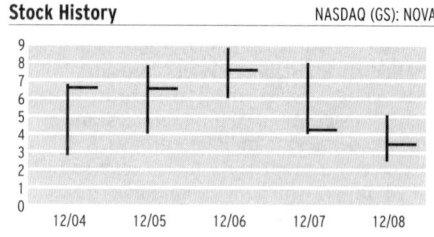

	STOCK PRICE ($) FY Close	P/E High/Low		PER SHARE ($) Earnings	Dividends	Book Value
12/08	3.46	13	7	0.38	0.00	3.14
12/07	4.25	—	—	(0.22)	0.00	2.82
12/06	7.57	38	26	0.23	0.00	2.95
12/05	6.53	34	18	0.23	0.00	2.54
12/04	6.58	35	15	0.19	0.00	2.36
Annual Growth	(14.8%)	—	—	18.9%	—	7.3%

NTELOS Holdings

NTELOS Holdings communicates over the hills and through the woods of the Virginias. The company serves more than 400,000 wireless subscribers in Virginia and West Virginia. Its wireless operations include its NTELOS-branded retail business, as well as a wholesale business it operates under a contract with Sprint Nextel. NTELOS's wireline operations include two rural local-exchange carriers (RLECs) that supply phone service and Internet access to residents and businesses. Since 1998 NTELOS has also operated as a competitive local-exchange carrier (CLEC) in areas outside its RLEC service area. NTELOS also serves portions of Kentucky, Maryland, North Carolina, Ohio, and Tennessee.

The company bought fiber-optic network assets and other related operations from Allegheny Energy for $27 million in late 2009. The deal, a part of the company's strategy of reorganizing its wireline business around broadband services instead of voice calling, nearly doubled the physical size of NTELOS network. The company expanded its wireless service options earlier that year with the launch of a budget-minded prepaid calling plan under a new brand: Frawg Unlimited Wireless.

Chairman and CEO James Quarforth resigned in 2009. James Hyde, the company's president and COO, was promoted to CEO to succeed him. Michael Huber, a director of NTELOS since 2005, was appointed nonexecutive chairman of the board.

NTELOS's wireless business accounted for about three-quarters of its revenues in 2008. The rest of its sales were roughly split between its RLEC and CLEC operations.

Quadrangle Capital Partners owns more than a quarter of NTELOS.

EXECUTIVES

Chairman: Michael Huber, age 40
CEO and Director: James A. (Jim) Hyde, age 45
EVP, CFO, Treasurer, and Secretary:
  Michael B. Moneymaker, age 51,
  $1,306,631 total compensation
EVP; President, Wireless: Frank C. Guido
EVP; President, Wireline: Frank Berry, age 44
SVP Legal and Regulatory Affairs: Mary McDermott, age 54, $641,620 total compensation
SVP Sales and Customer Care, Wireline: David J. Keller, age 43
SVP Wireless Marketing: David McNaughton
Director Creative Services and Public Relations:
  Mike Minnis
Director Investor Relations: Wesley B. (Wes) Wampler
Auditors: KPMG LLP

LOCATIONS

HQ: NTELOS Holdings Corp.
  401 Spring Ln., Ste. 300, Waynesboro, VA 22980
Phone: 540-946-3500   **Fax:** 540-946-3595
Web: www.ntelos.com

PRODUCTS/OPERATIONS

2008 Sales

	$ mil.	% of total
Wireless PCS	415.9	77
Competitive wireline	63.9	12
RLEC	59.5	11
Other	0.5	—
Total	**539.8**	**100**

Selected Services

Wireless communications
  Digital PCS (personal communications service)
  Wholesale wireless services
Wireline communications
  Internet access (dial-up, dedicated, and broadband)
  Local-exchange access
  Long-distance (domestic and international)
  Web hosting
Other communications
  Equipment sales and leasing
  Paging

COMPETITORS

AT&T Mobility
Charter Communications
Comcast
Cox Communications
FiberNet Telecom
Level 3 Communications
PAETEC
Shenandoah Telecommunications
Sprint Nextel
T-Mobile USA
U.S. Cellular
Verizon
Vonage

HISTORICAL FINANCIALS

Company Type: Public

Income Statement

FYE: December 31

	REVENUE ($ mil.)	NET INCOME ($ mil.)	NET PROFIT MARGIN	EMPLOYEES
12/08	539.8	47.2	8.7%	1,454
12/07	500.4	32.5	6.5%	1,355
12/06	440.1	(37.2)	—	1,337
12/05*	264.5	1.1	0.4%	1,274
6/05	63.2	(0.8)	—	1,276
Annual Growth	**71.0%**	**—**	**—**	**3.3%**

*Fiscal year change

2008 Year-End Financials

Debt ratio: 359.9%
Return on equity: 27.9%
Cash ($ mil.): 65.7
Current ratio: 1.62
Long-term debt ($ mil.): 601.2
No. of shares (mil.): 42.3
Dividends
  Yield: 3.6%
  Payout: 79.5%
Market value ($ mil.): 1,043.0
R&D as % of sales: —
Advertising as % of sales: —

Stock History

NASDAQ (GM): NTLS

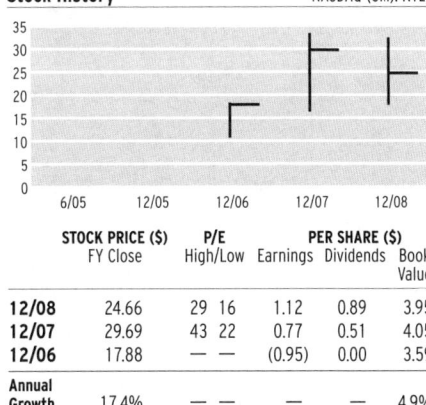

	STOCK PRICE ($) FY Close	P/E High/Low		PER SHARE ($) Earnings	Dividends	Book Value
12/08	24.66	29	16	1.12	0.89	3.95
12/07	29.69	43	22	0.77	0.51	4.05
12/06	17.88	—	—	(0.95)	0.00	3.59
Annual Growth	**17.4%**	**—**	**—**	**—**	**—**	**4.9%**

NuStar GP Holdings

NuStar GP Holdings (formerly Valero GP Holdings) owns an almost 20% limited partner interest in NuStar Energy, which operates independent terminals and petroleum liquids pipeline systems. In the US, NuStar Energy operates 8,303 miles of refined product and ammonia pipelines, 812 miles of crude oil pipelines, 58 refined product terminal facilities, and one crude oil storage facility. It also operates terminals in Canada, Mexico, the Netherlands, Netherlands Antilles, and the UK. Valero GP Holdings was controlled by Valero Energy. Following Valero GP Holdings' 2006 IPO, Valero Energy sold its interest in both Valero L.P. and NuStar GP Holdings.

In 2007 Valero GP Holdings changed its name to NuStar GP Holdings, LLC.

EXECUTIVES

Chairman: William E. Greenhey, age 73
President, CEO, and Director:
  Curtis V. (Curt) Anastasio, age 53
SVP, General Counsel, and Secretary:
  Bradley C. (Brad) Barron, age 44
SVP, CFO, and Treasurer: Steven A. (Steve) Blank, age 55
VP Investor Relations: Mark Meador
VP and Controller: Thomas R. (Tom) Shoaf, age 51
Corporate Secretary: Amy L. Perry
Auditors: KPMG LLP

LOCATIONS

HQ: NuStar GP Holdings, LLC
  2330 N. Loop 1604 West, San Antonio, TX 78248
Phone: 210-345-2000   **Fax:** 210-345-2646
Web: www.nustargpholdings.com

COMPETITORS

BP
Enbridge (U.S.)
Kinder Morgan
Marathon Petroleum
Shell Pipeline
TransCanada

HISTORICAL FINANCIALS

Company Type: Public

Income Statement

FYE: December 31

	REVENUE ($ mil.)	NET INCOME ($ mil.)	NET PROFIT MARGIN	EMPLOYEES
12/08	69.6	66.3	95.3%	1,340
12/07	46.2	43.3	93.7%	1,104
12/06	43.0	30.7	71.4%	1,305
12/05	37.6	20.3	54.0%	—
12/04	35.3	18.4	52.1%	—
Annual Growth	**18.5%**	**37.8%**	**—**	**1.3%**

2008 Year-End Financials

Debt ratio: 0.0%
Return on equity: 12.1%
Cash ($ mil.): 1.8
Current ratio: 0.59
Long-term debt ($ mil.): 0.0
No. of shares (mil.): 42.5
Dividends
  Yield: 8.5%
  Payout: 96.8%
Market value ($ mil.): 752.3
R&D as % of sales: —
Advertising as % of sales: —

Stock History

NYSE: NSH

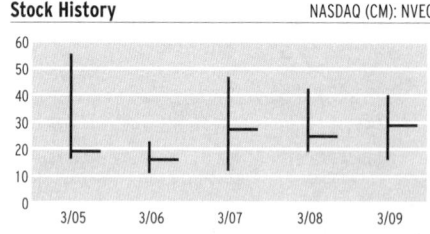

	STOCK PRICE ($) FY Close	P/E High/Low		PER SHARE ($) Earnings	Dividends	Book Value
12/08	17.68	19	8	1.56	1.51	12.77
12/07	28.55	38	23	1.02	1.34	13.02
12/06	24.82	35	26	0.72	0.26	13.06
Annual Growth	(15.6%)	—	—	47.2%	141.0%	(1.1%)

NVE Corporation

NVE is putting a magnetic spin on sensors. The company develops sensors incorporating spintronic (short for spin-based electronic) materials called giant magnetoresistors (GMR). Spintronics differ from conventional electronics in that they use the spin — rather than the charge — of electrons to store and transmit data. The company's sensors are used in aerospace, automotive, currency verification, and factory automation applications. In addition to analog and digital GMR sensors, NVE offers magnetic couplers, magnetic random-access memory (MRAM), and custom-designed modules. Customers include the US government, Avago Technologies, St. Jude Medical, and Starkey Laboratories. Half of sales come from the US.

While 10% of the company's sales continues to come from contract research and development projects, primarily funded by the US government, NVE is actively pursuing distribution channels for its products.

The company was founded as Nonvolatile Electronics, Inc. — hence NVE. It changed its name to NVE Corporation in 2000.

EXECUTIVES

Chairman: Terrence W. Glarner, age 66
President, CEO, and Director: Daniel A. Baker, age 51, $302,044 total compensation
CFO and Treasurer: Curt A. Reynders, age 46, $151,205 total compensation
VP Sensor Business Unit: Jay L. Brown, age 50
VP Advanced Technology: John K. Myers, age 60
Auditors: Ernst & Young LLP

LOCATIONS

HQ: NVE Corporation
11409 Valley View Rd., Eden Prairie, MN 55344
Phone: 952-829-9217 **Fax:** 952-829-9189
Web: www.nve.com

2009 Sales

	$ mil.	% of total
US	12.4	53
Europe	8.2	35
Asia	2.3	10
Other regions	0.5	2
Total	**23.4**	**100**

PRODUCTS/OPERATIONS

2009 Sales

	$ mil.	% of total
Product sales	19.7	84
Contract research & development	3.7	16
Total	**23.4**	**100**

Selected Products

Sensors
  Analog magnetic field sensors
  Differential magnetic field sensors
  Digital magnetic field sensors
Couplers
  Digital signal isolators
  Isolated bus transceivers
Magnetic random-access memory (MRAM)

COMPETITORS

Allegro MicroSystems	NEC Electronics
Analog Devices	Numonyx
Arnold Magnetics	NXP
Avago Technologies	Ovonyx
Elpida Memory	Qimonda
Fairchild Semiconductor	Ramtron International
Freescale Semiconductor	Samsung Electronics
Honeywell International	Sharp Electronics
Linear Technology	Silicon Labs
Macronix International	Spansion
Maxim Integrated Products	Texas Instruments
MEMSCAP	Toshiba Semiconductor
Micromem Technologies	Vishay Intertechnology

HISTORICAL FINANCIALS

Company Type: Public

Income Statement

FYE: March 31

	REVENUE ($ mil.)	NET INCOME ($ mil.)	NET PROFIT MARGIN	EMPLOYEES
3/09	23.4	9.8	41.9%	50
3/08	20.5	7.2	35.1%	50
3/07	16.5	4.8	29.1%	48
3/06	12.2	1.8	14.8%	50
3/05	11.6	1.8	15.5%	64
Annual Growth	19.2%	52.8%	—	(6.0%)

2009 Year-End Financials

Debt ratio: —
Return on equity: 26.8%
Cash ($ mil.): 1.9
Current ratio: 8.84
Long-term debt ($ mil.): —
No. of shares (mil.): 4.7
Dividends
  Yield: 0.0%
  Payout: —
Market value ($ mil.): 135.4
R&D as % of sales: —
Advertising as % of sales: —

Stock History

NASDAQ (CM): NVEC

	STOCK PRICE ($) FY Close	P/E High/Low		PER SHARE ($) Earnings	Dividends	Book Value
3/09	28.81	19	8	2.04	0.00	8.84
3/08	24.70	28	13	1.51	0.00	6.70
3/07	27.25	46	12	1.00	0.00	5.08
3/06	16.02	57	29	0.39	0.00	3.57
3/05	19.02	148	45	0.37	0.00	2.77
Annual Growth	10.9%	—	—	53.2%	—	33.6%

Oak Ridge Financial Services

Boys, Oak Ridge Financial Services is the holding company for Bank of Oak Ridge, which serves individuals and businesses in North Carolina's Guilford County. Through five branches, the bank offers standard retail products such as checking and savings accounts, CDs, money market accounts, health savings accounts, and credit cards. Real estate loans, including residential mortgages and construction and development loans, account for more than half of the company's loan portfolio; commercial and industrial loans are around 40%. Bank of Oak Ridge also provides financial planning services, investments, and life and long-term care insurance.

Established in 2000, the bank converted to a holding company form of ownership in 2007.

As a group, executive officers and board members of Oak Ridge Financial Services own more than a quarter of the company.

EXECUTIVES

Chairman: Douglas G. Boike, age 60
President, CEO, and Director; President and CEO, Bank of Oak Ridge: Ronald O. (Ron) Black, age 60, $373,940 total compensation
SVP and CFO: Thomas W. (Tom) Wayne, age 46, $183,238 total compensation
SVP and Chief Credit Officer, Bank of Oak Ridge: L. William (Bill) Vasaly III, age 56, $230,639 total compensation
VP, Bank of Oak Ridge: Katherine Garst
VP and Retail Bank Manager, Bank of Oak Ridge: Richard Long
Auditors: Elliott Davis LLC

LOCATIONS

HQ: Oak Ridge Financial Services, Inc.
2211 Oak Ridge Rd., Oak Ridge, NC 27310
Phone: 336-644-9944 **Fax:** 336-644-6644
Web: www.bankofoakridge.com

PRODUCTS/OPERATIONS

2008 Gross Revenues

	$ mil.	% of total
Interest		
Loans, including fees	15.7	74
Taxable investment securities	2.0	9
Other	0.3	1
Noninterest		
Investment & insurance commissions	0.8	4
Service charges on deposit accounts	0.8	4
Other	1.7	8
Total	**21.3**	**100**

COMPETITORS

Bank of America
Bank of the Carolinas
BB&T
First Citizens BancShares
NewBridge Bancorp
RBC Bank
SunTrust

HISTORICAL FINANCIALS

Company Type: Public

Income Statement

	ASSETS ($ mil.)	NET INCOME ($ mil.)	INCOME AS % OF ASSETS	EMPLOYEES
12/08	320.7	1.0	0.3%	80
12/07	262.2	1.0	0.4%	66
12/06	207.1	1.3	0.6%	71
12/05	172.5	0.8	0.5%	39
12/04	134.4	0.4	0.3%	34
Annual Growth	24.3%	25.7%	—	23.9%

FYE: December 31

2008 Year-End Financials

Equity as % of assets: 5.7%
Return on assets: 0.3%
Return on equity: 5.6%
Long-term debt ($ mil.): 15.0
No. of shares (mil.): 1.8
Market value ($ mil.): 14.0

Dividends
  Yield: 0.0%
  Payout: —
Sales ($ mil.): 12.1
R&D as % of sales: —
Advertising as % of sales: —

Stock History

NASDAQ (CM): BKOR

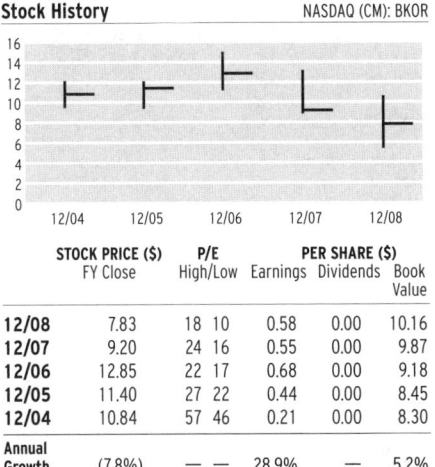

	STOCK PRICE ($) FY Close	P/E High/Low		PER SHARE ($) Earnings	Dividends	Book Value
12/08	7.83	18	10	0.58	0.00	10.16
12/07	9.20	24	16	0.55	0.00	9.87
12/06	12.85	22	17	0.68	0.00	9.18
12/05	11.40	27	22	0.44	0.00	8.45
12/04	10.84	57	46	0.21	0.00	8.30
Annual Growth	(7.8%)	—	—	28.9%	—	5.2%

Oak Valley Bancorp

Oak Valley Bancorp was formed in 2008 to be the holding company for Oak Valley Community Bank, which serves individuals and local businesses through about 10 branches in California's Central Valley. Eastern Sierra Community Bank, a division of Oak Valley, has three locations. The banks provide standard deposit products services such as savings, checking, and retirement accounts and CDs. Their lending activities consist of commercial real estate loans (more than half of their combined loan portfolio) and business, real estate construction, agricultural, residential mortgage, and consumer loans. Investment products and services are offered through an agreement with PrimeVest Financial Services.

EXECUTIVES

Chairman; Chairman, Oak Valley Community Bank:
  Michael Q. Jones, age 63
Vice Chairman; Vice Chairman, Oak Valley Community Bank: Roger M. Schrimp, age 67
CEO and Director; CEO and Director, Oak Valley Community Bank: Ronald C. (Ron) Martin, age 62
President and Director; President and Director, Oak Valley Community Bank:
  Christopher M. (Chris) Courtney, age 46
EVP, CFO, and Chief Administrative Officer:
  Richard A. (Rick) McCarty
EVP Retail Banking; EVP and Retail Banking Group Manager, Oak Valley Bank: Wendy Burth
EVP and Chief Credit Officer, Oak Valley Community Bank: Michael J. (Mike) Rodrigues
EVP Commercial Banking; EVP Commercial Banking, Oak Valley Community Bank: David S. (Dave) Harvey
SVP and Risk Management Officer: Janis Powers
SVP and Credit Administrator, Oak Valley Community Bank, Oakdale/Sonora/Excalon/Stockton:
  Gary Stephens
SVP and Senior Credit Officer: Ron Briw
Corporate Secretary and Director: Arne J. Knudsen, age 70
Auditors: Moss Adams, LLP

LOCATIONS

HQ: Oak Valley Bancorp
  125 N. 3rd Ave., Oakdale, CA 95361
Phone: 209-848-2265   **Fax:** 209-848-1929
Web: www.ovcb.com

PRODUCTS/OPERATIONS

2008 Gross Revenues

	$ mil.	% of total
Interest		
Loans, including fees	27.6	87
Securities & other	1.6	5
Noninterest		
Service charges on deposits	1.3	4
Other	1.3	4
Total	**31.8**	**100**

COMPETITORS

Bank of America
Bank of the West
Citibank
UnionBanCal
U.S. Bancorp
Wells Fargo
Westamerica

HISTORICAL FINANCIALS

Company Type: Public

Income Statement

	ASSETS ($ mil.)	NET INCOME ($ mil.)	INCOME AS % OF ASSETS	EMPLOYEES
12/08	508.2	2.2	0.4%	123
12/07	454.4	4.0	0.9%	125
12/06	455.2	3.8	0.8%	112
12/05	382.1	3.9	1.0%	101
12/04	313.1	3.3	1.1%	77
Annual Growth	12.9%	(9.6%)	—	12.4%

FYE: December 31

2008 Year-End Financials

Equity as % of assets: 8.9%
Return on assets: 0.5%
Return on equity: 5.0%
Long-term debt ($ mil.): 69.0
No. of shares (mil.): 7.7
Market value ($ mil.): 46.1

Dividends
  Yield: 1.3%
  Payout: 29.6%
Sales ($ mil.): 23.0
R&D as % of sales: —
Advertising as % of sales: —

Stock History

NASDAQ (CM): OVLY

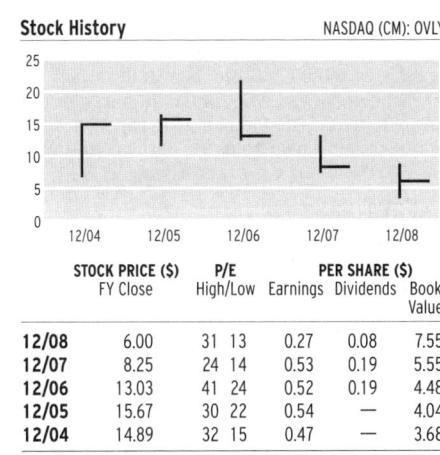

	STOCK PRICE ($) FY Close	P/E High/Low		PER SHARE ($) Earnings	Dividends	Book Value
12/08	6.00	31	13	0.27	0.08	7.55
12/07	8.25	24	14	0.53	0.19	5.55
12/06	13.03	41	24	0.52	0.19	4.48
12/05	15.67	30	22	0.54	—	4.04
12/04	14.89	32	15	0.47	—	3.68
Annual Growth	(20.3%)	—	—	(12.9%)	(35.1%)	19.7%

Obagi Medical Products

Obagi Medical Products is dedicated to the body's largest organ. The company develops and distributes topical skin care and restoration products. These include prescription creams and liquids to treat sun damage and minimize wrinkles. Its Nu-Derm System products are based on its proprietary technology which allows already-approved active ingredients to penetrate the skin more deeply. Obagi products are used to prepare skin for procedures such as laser resurfacing and chemical peels, reduce scarring after skin cancer treatments, and as follow-up to Botox injections. Beyond wrinkles, it also offers products designed to treat acne, rosacea, sun damage, and saggy skin.

Obagi markets its products through an in-house sales force. Obagi's products are sold through more than 8,000 cosmetic surgeons, dermatologists, and other medical specialists in the US.

Internationally, its products are sold in more than 40 countries in Asia, Europe, the Middle East, and South America. As in the US, most of its products are distributed through physicians. However, in Japan a line of Obagi products, manufactured by Rohto Pharmaceutical, are sold in drug stores, spas, and other skin care retailers.

By applying its technology to already-approved active ingredients, the company is able to sidestep the expensive and lengthy clinical development process. While Obagi has historically worked with OTC active ingredients, it also intends to use its skin-penetrating know-how to improve the efficacy of existing prescription active ingredients. To expand its reach, Obagi plans on taking its products into other medical specialties, beyond dermatology. It also has plans to enter the salon and spa markets with new products that won't directly compete with its physician-distributed products.

With an eye to expanding its distribution, in 2009 Obagi launched the sale of a prescription topical acne treatment through pharmacy retailers instead of through doctor's offices. However, the experiment proved too costly, and the company yanked the program. This disappointment

also came at the same time that consumers shied away from aesthetic procedures and cosmetic purchases, which cut into its overall sales.

The company's 2006 initial public offering brought in funds that were used to pay down debt. Founder Zein Obagi holds 9% of the company.

EXECUTIVES

Chairman: Albert J. Fitzgibbons III, age 63
President, CEO, and Director:
 Steven R. (Steve) Carlson, age 52,
 $495,861 total compensation
EVP Global Sales and Field Marketing:
 David S. Goldstein, $440,615 total compensation
EVP Finance, Operations, and Administration and CFO: Preston S. Romm, age 55,
 $259,848 total compensation
VP, General Counsel, and Secretary: Laura B. Hunter,
 $113,277 total compensation
SVP Product Development: Judith C. (Judy) Hattendorf
Auditors: PricewaterhouseCoopers LLP

LOCATIONS

HQ: Obagi Medical Products, Inc.
 310 Golden Shore, 1st Fl., Long Beach, CA 90802
Phone: 562-628-1007   **Fax:** 562-628-1008
Web: www.obagi.com

2008 Sales

	$ mil.	% of total
US	87.5	84
International	17.1	16
Total	**104.6**	**100**

PRODUCTS/OPERATIONS

2008 Sales

	$ mil.	% of total
Physician dispensed		
Nu-Derm	58.4	56
Vitamin C	12.4	12
Elasticity	11.6	11
Therapeutic	6.1	6
Other	11.1	11
Pharmacy Rx	0.2	—
Licensing fees	4.8	4
Total	**104.6**	**100**

COMPETITORS

Allergan
Estée Lauder
Galderma Laboratories
Johnson & Johnson
L'Oréal
Medicis Pharmaceutical
PhotoMedex
Procter & Gamble
Shiseido Americas
SkinMedica
Stiefel Laboratories
Unilever NV
Valeant

HISTORICAL FINANCIALS

Company Type: Public

Income Statement

FYE: December 31

	REVENUE ($ mil.)	NET INCOME ($ mil.)	NET PROFIT MARGIN	EMPLOYEES
12/08	104.6	12.6	12.0%	218
12/07	102.6	15.2	14.8%	182
12/06	78.0	6.1	7.8%	153
12/05	64.9	8.8	13.6%	132
12/04	56.3	14.1	25.0%	—
Annual Growth	**16.7%**	**(2.8%)**	**—**	**18.2%**

2008 Year-End Financials

Debt ratio: 0.0%
Return on equity: 22.9%
Cash ($ mil.): 13.9
Current ratio: 5.33
Long-term debt ($ mil.): 0.0
No. of shares (mil.): 21.9
Dividends
 Yield: 0.0%
 Payout: —
Market value ($ mil.): 163.5
R&D as % of sales: —
Advertising as % of sales: —

Stock History

NASDAQ (GM): OMPI

	STOCK PRICE ($) FY Close	P/E High/Low		PER SHARE ($) Earnings	Dividends	Book Value
12/08	7.46	34	9	0.56	0.00	2.76
12/07	18.33	37	13	0.69	0.00	2.27
12/06	10.31	34	28	0.34	0.00	0.82
Annual Growth	**(14.9%)**	**—**	**—**	**28.3%**	**—**	**83.8%**

Odyssey HealthCare

Odyssey HealthCare helps provide comfort for patients in the final stages of life's journey. One of the nation's largest hospice care providers, the company operates about 100 for-profit hospice programs in some 30 states. Odyssey HealthCare offers a full range of hospice care services, including pain and symptom management, medical social services, personal care, spiritual support and counseling, and daily living assistance. It serves patients in their homes, and in hospitals and nursing facilities; it also operates about 20 of its own inpatient hospice facilities.

Odyssey, which was formed in 1996 with a single hospice program, has grown largely by acquiring local hospices and, to a lesser extent, starting up its own programs in new communities. During 2008 it spent nearly $150 million to acquire VistaCare, which brought in more than 40 new home hospice agencies in 14 states. Two smaller deals in 2009 allowed Odyssey to expand into parts of central Michigan and the Chicago metro area when it bought Avalon Hospice and Generations Healthcare.

The company depends on payments from Medicare for the vast majority of its revenue, and so is sensitive to alterations in government reimbursement schedules. It also depends on doctors, nursing homes, and other health care providers for referrals of patients in need of hospice care; its marketing efforts, as a result, are focused on maintaining strong relationships with those referral sources and educating them about hospice care and the services the company provides.

Odyssey HealthCare serves patients primarily in their residences (including in nursing homes), but it also contracts with hospitals to provide palliative care and also operates about 20 inpatient hospice facilities in seven states. About half of its patients reside in nursing homes and other long-term care facilities.

EXECUTIVES

Chairman: Richard R. Burnham, age 67
President, CEO, and Director: Robert A. (Bob) Lefton,
 age 52, $2,220,635 total compensation
SVP and COO: Craig P. Goguen, age 40,
 $1,009,875 total compensation
SVP, CFO, Assistant Secretary and Treasurer:
 R. Dirk Allison, age 53, $1,073,177 total compensation
SVP Sales and Marketing: Frank W. Anastasio, age 63
SVP Clinical and Regulatory Affairs: Sally A. Parnell,
 age 53
SVP Human Resources: Brenda A. Belger, age 54,
 $491,183 total compensation
SVP, Secretary, and General Counsel:
 W. Bradley Bickham, age 46,
 $896,149 total compensation
VP Information Systems: James G. Zoccoli
VP and Controller: Gregory P. Flynn
VP and Chief Compliance Officer: Sandra K. Banfield
Auditors: Ernst & Young LLP

LOCATIONS

HQ: Odyssey HealthCare, Inc.
 717 N. Harwood St., Ste. 1500, Dallas, TX 75201
Phone: 214-922-9711   **Fax:** 214-922-9752
Web: www.odyssey-health care.com

2008 Sales

	$ mil.	% of total
VistaCare West/North	76.5	12
Texas	73.8	12
Mountain	73.6	12
Southeast	72.0	12
West	71.0	11
Northeast	65.6	11
Midwest	61.3	10
VistaCare Central	48.6	8
VistaCare South	37.8	6
South Central	36.8	6
Adjustments	(1.0)	—
Total	**616.0**	**100**

COMPETITORS

Amedisys
Five Star Quality Care
Gentiva
Girling Health Care
Golden Horizons
Hospice of Michigan
Manor Care
Skilled Healthcare Group
Valley Health System
VITAS Healthcare

HISTORICAL FINANCIALS

Company Type: Public

Income Statement

FYE: December 31

	REVENUE ($ mil.)	NET INCOME ($ mil.)	NET PROFIT MARGIN	EMPLOYEES
12/08	616.0	14.4	2.3%	6,207
12/07	404.9	12.1	3.0%	4,834
12/06	409.8	19.7	4.8%	5,033
12/05	381.6	18.6	4.9%	5,089
12/04	350.3	35.0	10.0%	4,113
Annual Growth	**15.2%**	**(19.9%)**	**—**	**10.8%**

2008 Year-End Financials

Debt ratio: 58.3%
Return on equity: 7.5%
Cash ($ mil.): 56.0
Current ratio: 1.66
Long-term debt ($ mil.): 116.7
No. of shares (mil.): 33.1
Dividends
 Yield: —
 Payout: —
Market value ($ mil.): 306.5
R&D as % of sales: —
Advertising as % of sales: —

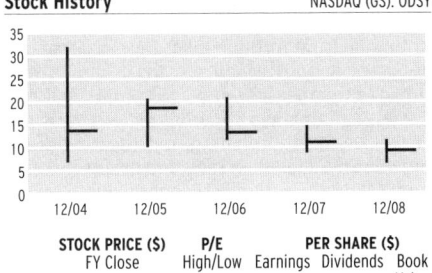

	STOCK PRICE ($)	P/E		PER SHARE ($)		
	FY Close	High/Low	Earnings	Dividends	Book Value
12/08	9.25	26 16	0.43	—	6.04
12/07	11.06	40 25	0.36	—	5.52
12/06	13.26	36 21	0.57	—	5.42
12/05	18.64	39 20	0.53	—	5.05
12/04	13.68	34 8	0.93	—	4.89
Annual Growth	(9.3%)	— —	(17.5%)	—	5.4%

Old Line Bancshares

Old Line Bancshares is the holding company for Old Line Bank, serving consumers, businesses, and high-net-worth individuals in the Old Line State (Maryland) and in the Washington, DC, area. From about a half-dozen banking locations in Maryland's Charles and Prince George's counties, the bank offers standard retail products, including checking and savings accounts, CDs, NOW accounts, and credit and debit cards. The company uses funds from deposits to write business and consumer loans; commercial real estate loans make up more than 45% of the bank's loan portfolio. Old Line Bank also offers luxury boat financing. Old Line Bancshares owns a 50% interest in real estate firm Pointer Ridge Office Investment.

EXECUTIVES

Chairman, Old Line Bancshares and Old Line Bank: Craig E. Clark, age 67
Vice Chairman, Old Line Bancshares and Old Line Bank: Frank Lucente Jr., age 67
President and CEO, Old Line Bancshares and Old Line Bank: James W. Cornelsen, age 54, $396,855 total compensation
EVP; EVP and Chief Lending Officer, Old Line Bank: Joseph E. Burnett, age 63, $263,779 total compensation
EVP, CFO, and Secretary; EVP, CFO, Chief Credit Officer, and Secretary, Old Line Bank: Christine M. (Chris) Rush, age 53, $230,337 total compensation
SVP, Old Line Bank: Sandi F. Burnett, age 51
SVP and Treasurer, Old Line Bank: Erin G. Lyddane, age 35
SVP Branch Operations, Old Line Bank: Jeffrey Franklin, age 43
SVP, Old Line Bank: William J. Bush
Auditors: Rowles & Company, LLP

LOCATIONS

HQ: Old Line Bancshares, Inc.
1525 Pointer Ridge Place, Bowie, MD 20716
Phone: 301-430-2500   **Fax:** 301-932-5458
Web: www.oldlinebank.com

Old Line Bancshares has branches in Accokeek, Clinton, and Waldorf (2), Maryland.

PRODUCTS/OPERATIONS

2008 Gross Revenues

	$ mil.	% of total
Interest income		
Loans, including fees	14.2	87
Securities	0.7	4
Federal funds sold	0.3	2
Other	0.2	1
Noninterest income		
Earnings on bank-owned life insurance	0.4	2
Service charges on deposit accounts	0.3	2
Other fees & commissions	0.3	2
Total	**16.4**	**100**

COMPETITORS

Bank of America
BB&T
First Mariner Bancorp
M&T Bank
PNC Financial
Tri-County Financial

HISTORICAL FINANCIALS

Company Type: Public

Income Statement   FYE: December 31

	ASSETS ($ mil.)	NET INCOME ($ mil.)	INCOME AS % OF ASSETS	EMPLOYEES
12/08	317.7	1.8	0.6%	67
12/07	245.2	1.6	0.7%	53
12/06	218.1	1.6	0.7%	56
12/05	169.0	1.1	0.7%	49
12/04	113.6	0.8	0.7%	33
Annual Growth	29.3%	22.5%	—	19.4%

2008 Year-End Financials

Equity as % of assets: 11.0%	Dividends
Return on assets: 0.6%	Yield: 2.0%
Return on equity: 5.2%	Payout: 27.3%
Long-term debt ($ mil.): 21.5	Sales ($ mil.): 10.5
No. of shares (mil.): 3.9	R&D as % of sales: —
Market value ($ mil.): 23.4	Advertising as % of sales: —

Stock History   NASDAQ (CM): OLBK

	STOCK PRICE ($)	P/E		PER SHARE ($)		
	FY Close	High/Low	Earnings	Dividends	Book Value
12/08	6.07	21 13	0.44	0.12	10.79
12/07	8.05	30 20	0.37	0.12	8.97
12/06	10.61	32 28	0.37	0.12	9.01
12/05	10.44	28 20	0.44	0.10	8.68
12/04	9.82	28 20	0.38	0.10	3.52
Annual Growth	(11.3%)	— —	3.7%	4.7%	32.4%

Old Second Bancorp

Old Second isn't a thrift shop, but it *does* cater to the thrifty. Old Second Bancorp is the holding company for Old Second National Bank, which operates about 35 bank and lending offices in Chicago and its suburbs. The bank provides a variety of business, retail, and trust services to individual and business customers, including demand, savings, time deposit, and retirement accounts; and a range of consumer and commercial lending, as well as credit card and investment services. Bank subsidiary Old Second Affordable Housing Fund provides home buying assistance to lower income customers. Bancorp subsidiary Old Second Financial provides insurance products and services.

Old Second Bancorp, which serves Cook, Kane, Kendall, DeKalb, DuPage, LaSalle, and Will counties, has been expanding by opening new branches and acquiring competitors. It bought HeritageBanc, the holding company for Heritage Bank, for some $86 million in 2008.

The previous year the bancorp merged former subsidiaries, Old Second Bank — Kane County and Old Second Bank — Yorkville, into The Old Second National Bank of Aurora, which it then renamed Old Second National Bank.

Commercial real estate loans and residential mortgages each make up about one-third of Old Second Bancorp's loan portfolio. Construction lending comprises another 20%, and business and consumer loans round out the company's lending activities.

A group of nearly 20 officers and directors owns about 10% of Old Second Bancorp. The company's profit sharing plan and Chicago's The Banc Funds Company each own just over a 5% stake.

EXECUTIVES

Chairman, President, and CEO; Chairman, Old Second National Bank: William B. Skoglund, age 59, $720,536 total compensation
EVP, COO, and Director; President and CEO, Old Second National Bank: James L. Eccher, age 44, $406,155 total compensation
EVP, CFO, and Director: J. Douglas Cheatham, age 53, $333,352 total compensation
EVP and Chief Risk Officer; Senior Lending Officer, Old Second National Bank: Rodney L. Sloan, age 49, $341,972 total compensation
SVP, Marketing and Retail Services: Robert Valaitis
VP, Human Resources: Robert DiCosola
VP, Administration, and Corporate Secretary: Robin Hodgson
President, Old Second Bank — Kane County: David C. Ott
President, Old Second Mortgage: Al Scionti
Auditors: Grant Thornton LLP

LOCATIONS

HQ: Old Second Bancorp, Inc.
37 S. River St., Aurora, IL 60507
Phone: 630-892-0202   **Fax:** 630-892-9630
Web: www.o2bancorp.com

PRODUCTS/OPERATIONS

2008 Gross Revenues

	$ mil.	% of total
Interest		
Loans	136.0	70
Securities	20.7	11
Federal funds sold & other	1.2	1
Noninterest		
Trust income	8.1	4
Service charges on deposits	9.3	5
Gain on sale of mortgage loans	5.9	3
Other	12.0	6
Total	**193.2**	**100**

Selected Subsidiaries

Old Second Financial, Inc.
Old Second National Bank
  Old Second Affordable Housing Fund, L.L.C.
  Old Second Management, LLC
    Old Second Realty, LLC

COMPETITORS

Bank of America
BankFinancial
Citigroup
First Midwest Bancorp
Harris Bankcorp
MB Financial
Midwest Banc Holdings
Princeton National Bancorp
U.S. Bancorp

HISTORICAL FINANCIALS

Company Type: Public

Income Statement

FYE: December 31

	ASSETS ($ mil.)	NET INCOME ($ mil.)	INCOME AS % OF ASSETS	EMPLOYEES
12/08	2,984.6	11.8	0.4%	615
12/07	2,658.6	24.0	0.9%	541
12/06	2,459.1	23.7	1.0%	582
12/05	2,367.8	27.7	1.2%	548
12/04	2,102.3	26.3	1.3%	550
Annual Growth	**9.2%**	**(18.2%)**	**—**	**2.8%**

2008 Year-End Financials

Equity as % of assets: 6.5%
Return on assets: 0.4%
Return on equity: 6.9%
Long-term debt ($ mil.): 103.4
No. of shares (mil.): 13.8
Market value ($ mil.): 160.4
Dividends
  Yield: 5.4%
  Payout: 73.3%
Sales ($ mil.): 124.8
R&D as % of sales: —
Advertising as % of sales: —

Stock History

NASDAQ (GS): OSBC

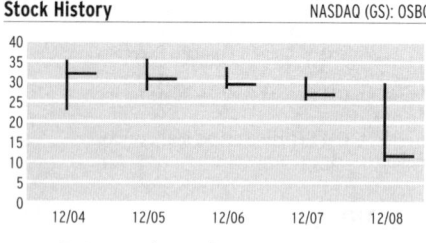

	STOCK PRICE ($) FY Close	P/E High/Low	PER SHARE ($) Earnings	Dividends	Book Value
12/08	11.60	34 12	0.86	0.63	13.97
12/07	26.79	16 14	1.89	0.59	10.84
12/06	29.30	19 16	1.75	0.55	11.47
12/05	30.57	17 14	2.03	0.51	11.01
12/04	31.88	18 12	1.94	0.46	9.77
Annual Growth	**(22.3%)**	**— —**	**(18.4%)**	**8.2%**	**9.4%**

Omega Protein

Omega Protein is the alpha dog of the fish-meal industry. With four US processing plants, a fleet of 58 fishing vessels, and 32 spotter aircraft, the company is the largest US producer of fish meal and fish oil, both of which are derived from menhaden (an inedible fish caught in the Gulf of Mexico and along the East Coast). Animal-feed makers and livestock ranchers use Omega Protein's fish meal for protein additives in feed, while the fish oil is used in Europe in margarine and shortening and for industrial uses. Rich in Omega-3 fatty acids (reputed to provide health benefits), fish oil is also used as a human food supplement.

Omega has about 600 domestic and foreign customers. They are made up primarily of feed producers, who use Omega's fish products to manufacture feed for swine and dairy cattle, as well as for domestic pets. An increasing percentage of the company's products are being used by the aquaculture industry, reflecting the growth of the practice of aquaculture worldwide. The company's primary non-US customers are located in Norway, Canada, Chile, China, and Japan.

Its fish meal brands include Special Select and LeaLac and its fish oil brands include Virginia Prime and OmegaPure. The company also makes fertilizer (OmegaGrow) and a fungicide/insecticide (SeaCide).

In 2007 the company opened a technical center in Houston (The OmegaPure Technology and Innovation Center) to research and develop new Omega-3 products.

Omega Protein was 33% owned by investor and then Omega chairman Avram Glazer's family, which maintained its shares through Zapata Corporation. However, Zapata sold its holdings in Omega in 2006, at which time Glazer stepped down as chairman and president and CEO Joseph von Rosenberg replaced Glazer.

Wellington Management owns about 9% of the company; AXA Financial owns some 8%; AWM Investment and Franklin Resources each own about 6% and Dimensional Fund Advisors owns approximately 5%.

HISTORY

Omega Protein's predecessor dates back to a fish processing operation founded in Reedville, Virginia, by John and Thomas Haynie in 1878. (The site currently is home to the company's largest plant.) Almost a century later, Zapata, an oil and gas firm co-founded by George H.W. Bush, acquired Haynie Products.

The division became known as Zapata Haynie. The company spent the late 1980s and 1990s fighting for FDA approval of refined menhaden oil for human consumption (the oil contains high levels of Omega-3 fatty acids touted as having health benefits); approval was finally granted in 1997.

Financier Malcolm Glazer first acquired a stake in Zapata in 1992. That year Zapata acquired 60% of Venture Milling, a Delaware-based blender of animal protein products. Two years later the division was renamed Zapata Protein, to reflect its expansion into animal feed. Zapata sold most of the assets of Venture Milling in 1997 and acquired two of its four US rivals: Chesapeake Bay area-based American Protein and Louisiana-based Gulf Protein. Also that year it renamed the division Marine Genetics.

In 1998 Zapata changed Marine Genetics' name to Omega Protein and spun off about 40% in that division to the public. Despite an active hurricane season that crimped the fishing season, Omega Protein reported record profits in 1998. However, dramatic price drops for fish meal and fish oil (caused by a global glut in those markets) squeezed the life out of sales and profits in 1999. Omega Protein responded by mothballing part of its fleet for the 2000 fishing season.

In 2003 Omega received two separate unsolicited takeover offers — the first at $45 per share by merger and acquisition firm Hollingsworth, Rothwell & Roxford; the second at $9.50 per share from Australia-based Ferrari Investments and unidentified US partners.

Omega completed a processing facility in 2004 in Reedsville, Virginia, that tripled its existing refined fish-oil production capacity. The factory also expanded capacity for oils used in leather, drilling fluid, and animal food.

The company shut down its sales office in Mexico in 2005 and consolidated its functions with those at its Houston headquarters. The company's Moss Point processing facility and its shipyard in Mississippi were severely damaged due to Hurricane Katrina in August 2005. Its Cameron and Abbeville plants in Louisiana were shut down that September due to damage sustained from Hurricane Rita. Moss Point and Abbeville were reopened in mid-October. The Cameron facility was rebuilt and back in operation by 2006.

EXECUTIVES

President, CEO, and Director: Joseph L. von Rosenberg III, age 50, $1,092,345 total compensation
EVP, General Counsel, and Secretary: John D. Held, age 46, $696,557 total compensation
EVP and CFO: Robert W. Stockton, age 58, $723,981 total compensation
SVP Sales and Marketing: J. Scott Herbert, age 43, $361,934 total compensation
SVP Operations: Joseph E. Kadi, age 48
VP Operations: Thomas R. Wittmann, age 59, $204,642 total compensation
VP Marine Operations; President, Omega Shipyard: Michael E. Wilson, age 58
VP and Corporate Controller: Gregory P. Toups, age 33
VP Human Resources: Barton J. Shacklock, age 57
Auditors: PricewaterhouseCoopers LLP

LOCATIONS

HQ: Omega Protein Corporation
2101 City West Blvd., Bldg. 3, Ste. 500
Houston, TX 77042
Phone: 713-623-0060   **Fax:** 713-940-6122
Web: www.omegaproteininc.com

2008 Sales

	$ mil.	% of total
North America		
US	96.3	54
Canada	12.9	7
Mexico	4.8	3
Asia	26.7	15
Europe	26.2	15
Central & South America	10.5	6
Total	**177.4**	**100**

PRODUCTS/OPERATIONS

Selected Products

Menhaden fish meal (used in aquaculture, livestock, pet, and poultry feeds)
Menhaden fish oil (used in margarine and shortening)
Menhaden fish solubles (used in animal feeds and fertilizer)

COMPETITORS

ADM	Dow AgroSciences
ADM Alliance Nutrition	Griffin Industries
Ag Processing	Kodiak Fishmeal
American Seafoods	Land O'Lakes Purina Feed
Bayer CropScience	Marubeni
Blue Seal Feeds	Nippon Suisan
Bunge Limited	Nutreco
Cargill	Scotts Miracle-Gro
CHS	Scoular
Corn Products	Westward Seafoods

HISTORICAL FINANCIALS

Company Type: Public

Income Statement

FYE: December 31

	REVENUE ($ mil.)	NET INCOME ($ mil.)	NET PROFIT MARGIN	EMPLOYEES
12/08	177.4	12.6	7.1%	653
12/07	157.1	12.1	7.7%	571
12/06	139.8	4.6	3.3%	567
12/05	109.9	(7.2)	—	410
12/04	119.6	3.2	2.7%	470
Annual Growth	10.4%	40.9%	—	8.6%

2008 Year-End Financials

Debt ratio: 37.9%
Return on equity: 9.8%
Cash ($ mil.): 14.0
Current ratio: 4.61
Long-term debt ($ mil.): 52.9
No. of shares (mil.): 18.7

Dividends
Yield: 0.0%
Payout: —
Market value ($ mil.): 75.1
R&D as % of sales: —
Advertising as % of sales: —

Stock History

NYSE: OME

	STOCK PRICE ($) FY Close	P/E High/Low		PER SHARE ($) Earnings	Dividends	Book Value
12/08	4.01	27	5	0.68	0.00	7.45
12/07	9.29	15	9	0.70	0.00	6.33
12/06	7.73	44	28	0.18	0.00	5.40
12/05	6.71	—	—	(0.29)	0.00	7.60
12/04	8.60	98	55	0.12	0.00	7.99
Annual Growth	(17.4%)	—	—	54.3%	—	(1.7%)

Omnicell, Inc.

To err is human, and Omnicell strives to take the err out of dispensing drugs to patients. A developer of specialized software and hardware products, Omnicell makes mobile cabinets and workstations that are equipped with computer system hardware, software, and storage space capacity (drawers for pharmaceuticals and related items). The cabinets are used by nurses, pharmacists, and doctors to manage data and automatically dispense doses of medication to patients. The company also makes systems that manage pharmaceutical inventories, patient profiles, and supply chains. It markets its products to hospitals, nursing homes, and other health care facil-

ities. Omnicell was founded in 1992 by CEO Randall A. Lipps.

The company primarily targets hospitals with more than 50 beds, including community, regional, and national hospitals. It sells its products directly in the US and through distributors in Asia, Australia, Europe, and the Middle East.

The company's growth strategy centers on developing new products and enhancing existing products. Although it does not routinely pursue acquisitions as a means of bolstering its offerings, Omnicell does make strategic acquisitions of product technologies and assets from time to time.

EXECUTIVES

Chairman, President, and CEO: Randall A. Lipps, age 51, $1,993,731 total compensation
SVP Operations: J. Christopher (Chris) Drew, age 43, $1,122,378 total compensation
VP Finance and CFO: Robin G. (Rob) Seim, age 49, $843,339 total compensation
VP and General Counsel: Dan S. Johnston, age 45, $581,250 total compensation
VP Corporate Sales and International: Gary Robinson
VP Strategy and Business Development: Nhat H. Ngo, age 36
VP Marketing: Marga Ortigas-Wedekind, age 47
VP Engineering: Peter Fisher, age 48
VP Human Resources, Employee Learning, and Performance: John G. Choma, age 55
Senior Director, Marketing and Communications: Deborah Reinert
Executive Assistant and Investor Relations: Michelle Smith
Auditors: Ernst & Young LLP

LOCATIONS

HQ: Omnicell, Inc.
1201 Charleston Rd., Mountain View, CA 94043
Phone: 650-251-6100   **Fax:** 650-251-6266
Web: www.omnicell.com

PRODUCTS/OPERATIONS

2008 Sales

	$ mil.	% of total
Products	210.7	84
Services & other	41.2	16
Total	251.9	100

Selected Products

DecisionCenter (data analysis and decision support for inventory management)
Hospital inventory management systems (ScanREQ)
Pharmacy dispensing automation systems
  Anesthesia Workstation (operating room anesthesia supply dispensing system)
  OmniCenter (server for managing automated supply systems)
  OmniLinkRx (physician order management system)
  Patient Medication Profiling (software for patient-specific medication information)
  SafetyMed (system for ensuring that patients get the correct medications on time)
  SecureVault (dispensing and storage system for controlled substances)
  SinglePointe (dispensing and storage system)
  WorkflowRX (inventory management)
Supply dispensing automation systems
  Omnicell Supply (automated supply dispensing systems)

COMPETITORS

AmerisourceBergen	Eclipsys
Baxter International	McKesson
BravoSolution US	SciQuest
Cardinal Health	Siemens Healthcare
Cerner	

HISTORICAL FINANCIALS

Company Type: Public

Income Statement

FYE: December 31

	REVENUE ($ mil.)	NET INCOME ($ mil.)	NET PROFIT MARGIN	EMPLOYEES
12/08	251.9	12.7	5.0%	844
12/07	213.1	43.3	20.3%	806
12/06	154.7	10.4	6.7%	626
12/05	121.5	(2.1)	—	514
12/04	123.9	10.6	8.6%	488
Annual Growth	19.4%	4.6%	—	14.7%

2008 Year-End Financials

Debt ratio: —
Return on equity: 5.2%
Cash ($ mil.): 120.4
Current ratio: 3.92
Long-term debt ($ mil.): —
No. of shares (mil.): 31.9

Dividends
Yield: 0.0%
Payout: —
Market value ($ mil.): 389.7
R&D as % of sales: —
Advertising as % of sales: —

Stock History

NASDAQ (GM): OMCL

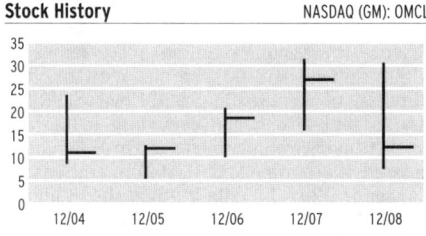

	STOCK PRICE ($) FY Close	P/E High/Low		PER SHARE ($) Earnings	Dividends	Book Value
12/08	12.21	80	20	0.38	0.00	7.32
12/07	26.93	24	13	1.28	0.00	7.98
12/06	18.63	57	29	0.36	0.00	2.82
12/05	11.95	—	—	(0.08)	0.00	1.73
12/04	11.00	61	23	0.38	0.00	1.68
Annual Growth	2.6%	—	—	0.0%	—	44.4%

On Assignment

Attention, scientists: Tired of unreliable assistants? Try On Assignment. The specialist staffing agency places scientists and other professionals, from lab assistants to nurses, for clients in need of temporary help. The company has four divisions: Healthcare Staffing (nurse travel, clinical lab, and diagnostic and imaging staffing services); Life Sciences (scientists, chemists, technicians, etc.); IT and Engineering (engineering and specialized high-end consultants); and Physician (short- and long-term physician staffing). Established in 1985, On Assignment operates from about 80 offices in Belgium, Canada, Ireland, the Netherlands, the UK, and the US.

Key acquisitions in 2007 helped On Assignment weather the economic downturn in 2008. The company acquired Oxford Global Resources in 2007, significantly broadening On Assignment's product offerings as the company entered the IT staffing market. The company also entered the physician staffing sector with the purchase of VISTA Staffing Solutions in 2007. VISTA works with a pool of about 1,300 physicians specializing in 30 different medical practices.

Demand increased in 2008 for On Assignment's IT and Engineering, Healthcare, and Physician segments, while Life Sciences suffered. The company plans to tightly control operating costs in 2009 to offset potential losses.

HISTORY

Chemists Bruce Culver and Raf Dahlquist concocted the company in 1985. Lab Support (its original name) got off to a good start, but the founders were scientists, not business strategists; by 1989 the company was losing steam. The firm's venture investors took over, installing new management under Tom Buelter, who had developed Kelly Services' home care division. He refocused operations to temporary scientific services and turned the company around. It went public in 1992 as On Assignment.

In 1994 On Assignment bought 1st Choice Personnel and Sklar Resource Group, which specialized in temporary placement of financial professionals. The next year it started its Advanced Science Professionals unit to place temps in highly skilled scientific positions. With the 1996 purchase of Minneapolis-based EnviroStaff, On Assignment also began providing temporary workers in environmental fields. On Assignment crossed the border and started operations in Canada in 1997. In 1999 it established Clinical Lab Staff as its fourth division. Also by 1999 the company had opened the first three of several planned European offices in the UK.

In 2001 Buelter relinquished the CEO position to Joe Peterson. (Buelter resigned as chairman early the following year.) Also in 2002 the company acquired Health Personnel Options Corporation, a provider of temporary travel nurses and other health care professionals. The end of 2003 saw the appointment of Peter Dameris as the president and CEO of On Assignment.

In 2007 On Assignment reached new levels of growth with the key acquisitions of IT and engineering staffing provider Oxford Global Resources and physician staffing firm VISTA Staffing Solutions.

EXECUTIVES

Chairman: Jeremy M. Jones, age 67
President, CEO, and Director: Peter T. Dameris, age 49, $4,161,068 total compensation
SVP Finance and CFO: James L. Brill, age 57, $1,132,643 total compensation
SVP Shared Services and CIO: Michael C. Payne
VP Business Development: Garrett Hunt
VP Human Resources: Angela Kolarek
VP Support Services: Karen Keppel
VP Finance and Corporate Controller: Christina Gibson
VP and General Counsel: Samanthe Beck
VP Recruiting: Carol McNamara
Director Marketing: Alison Richmond
Director Regulatory Affairs: Eric Radke
President, Oxford Global Resources:
 Michael J. McGowan, age 56, $1,158,935 total compensation
President, VISTA Staffing Solutions: Mark S. Brouse, age 55, $596,955 total compensation
President, Life Sciences and Allied Divisions:
 Emmett B. McGrath, age 47, $1,051,858 total compensation
Auditors: Deloitte & Touche LLP

LOCATIONS

HQ: On Assignment, Inc.
 26651 W. Agoura Rd., Calabasas, CA 91302
Phone: 818-878-7900   **Fax:** 818-878-7930
Web: www.onassignment.com

2008 Sales

	$ mil.	% of total
US	584.3	95
Other countries	33.8	5
Total	**618.1**	**100**

PRODUCTS/OPERATIONS

2008 Sales

	$ mil.	% of total
IT & Engineering	218.7	36
Healthcare Staffing	180.7	29
Life Sciences	129.5	21
Physician	89.2	14
Total	**618.1**	**100**

COMPETITORS

Accenture
Adecco
AMN Healthcare
ATC Healthcare
CHG Healthcare
Cross Country Healthcare
Day & Zimmermann
The Everhart Group
IBM
Kelly Services
Kforce
Manpower
Medical Staffing Network
MPS
Professional Staff
RehabCare
Robert Half

HISTORICAL FINANCIALS

Company Type: Public

Income Statement

FYE: December 31

	REVENUE ($ mil.)	NET INCOME ($ mil.)	NET PROFIT MARGIN	EMPLOYEES
12/08	618.1	19.0	3.1%	17,373
12/07	567.2	9.3	1.6%	20,350
12/06	287.6	11.0	3.8%	13,760
12/05	237.9	(0.1)	—	12,140
12/04	193.6	(42.4)	—	11,025
Annual Growth	**33.7%**	**—**	**—**	**12.0%**

2008 Year-End Financials

Debt ratio: 57.6%
Return on equity: 9.2%
Cash ($ mil.): 46.3
Current ratio: 2.70
Long-term debt ($ mil.): 125.9
No. of shares (mil.): 36.1

Dividends
 Yield: 0.0%
 Payout: —
Market value ($ mil.): 204.7
R&D as % of sales: —
Advertising as % of sales: —

Stock History

NASDAQ (GM): ASGN

	STOCK PRICE ($) FY Close	P/E High/Low		PER SHARE ($) Earnings	Dividends	Book Value
12/08	5.67	18	8	0.53	0.00	6.05
12/07	7.01	53	22	0.26	0.00	5.35
12/06	11.75	35	21	0.39	0.00	4.60
12/05	10.91	—	—	0.00	0.00	2.12
12/04	5.19	—	—	(1.68)	0.00	2.06
Annual Growth	**2.2%**	**—**	**—**	**—**	**—**	**30.9%**

Online Resources

Financial institutions looking for a Web commerce presence can take Online Resources' systems to the bank. The company enables banks and credit unions to offer their account holders online and mobile access to such financial services as remote banking, funds transfer, and electronic bill payment. It also offers e-commerce services to credit card issuers that allow cardholders to access accounts, view transactions, and set up payments. Founded in 1989, Online Resources serves some 2,000 banks, credit unions, card issuers, billers, and other financial institutions in the US, primarily small to mid-sized providers that lack the capital or expertise to maintain these Web-based services in-house.

Online Resources processes approximately $100 billion in bill payments per year. Online Resources derives approximately 80% of revenues from payments and 20% from other services including account presentation, relationship management, professional services, and custom software solutions.

Typically, Online Resources' clients are regional and community-based financial services providers that have under $10 billion in assets. The firm is attempting to grow its client base in this bracket, while adding value-added services to existing clients, to help them keep pace with larger financial institutions. Acquisitions of Princeton eCom and Internet Transaction Solutions (ITS) have supported this strategy by allowing Online Resources to acquire new account presentation and online payment software products that it can cross-sell to its existing banking and e-commerce clients. Among the many clients that have signed multi-year agreements to adopt the company's services are Kinecta Federal Credit Union, MB Financial Bank, and Fifth Third Bancorp.

In 2009 the company's largest stockholder, Tennenbaum Capital Partners, won a proxy fight and elected three of its candidates to the 10-member Online Resources board. Online Resources management had fought the bid, but Tennenbaum successfully convinced shareholders that the current board had allowed the stock price to drop too far, weakening the company.

Tennenbaum Capital Partners has a 22% stake in the company; chairman Matthew Lawlor owns 5%.

EXECUTIVES

Chairman: Matthew P. Lawlor, age 61, $935,017 total compensation
President, COO, and Interim CEO:
 Raymond T. (Ray) Crosier, age 54, $471,203 total compensation
EVP and CFO: Catherine A. (Cathy) Graham, age 48, $408,406 total compensation
EVP and General Manager, Community Bank and Credit Union Services: Ronald J. (Ron) Bergamesca
EVP and General Manager, Banking CSP Payments:
 Sheila Narayan
EVP and General Manager, eCommerce Services:
 Robert R. Craig
SVP Strategic Development: Daniel M. (Dan) Thomas
SVP Banking Technology Services and CTO:
 Paul A. Franko
VP Human Resources: Sherry Mullin
Senior Director Corporate Communications:
 Beth Halloran
Auditors: KPMG LLP

LOCATIONS

HQ: Online Resources Corporation
4795 Meadow Wood Ln., Ste. 300
Chantilly, VA 20151
Phone: 703-653-3100 **Fax:** 703-653-3105
Web: www.orcc.com

PRODUCTS/OPERATIONS

2008 Sales

	$ mil.	% of total
Banking	94.6	62
eCommerce	57.0	38
Total	**151.6**	**100**

2008 Sales by Service Type

	$ mil.	% of total
Payment services	122.3	81
Professional services & other	13.4	9
Relationship management services	8.0	5
Account presentation services	7.9	5
Total	**151.6**	**100**

COMPETITORS

Chase Paymentech Solutions
Corillian
Digital Insight
First Data
Fiserv
Intuit
Jack Henry
Open Solutions
Payment Data Systems
S1 Corp.
Sybase

HISTORICAL FINANCIALS

Company Type: Public

Income Statement
FYE: December 31

	REVENUE ($ mil.)	NET INCOME ($ mil.)	NET PROFIT MARGIN	EMPLOYEES
12/08	151.6	1.9	1.3%	619
12/07	135.1	10.9	8.1%	626
12/06	91.7	4.6	5.0%	600
12/05	60.5	22.7	37.5%	421
12/04	42.3	5.0	11.8%	335
Annual Growth	**37.6%**	**(21.5%)**	**—**	**16.6%**

2008 Year-End Financials

Debt ratio: 43.1%
Return on equity: 1.4%
Cash ($ mil.): 23.0
Current ratio: 1.86
Long-term debt ($ mil.): 59.5
No. of shares (mil.): 30.1
Dividends
　Yield: 0.0%
　Payout: —
Market value ($ mil.): 142.5
R&D as % of sales: —
Advertising as % of sales: —

Stock History
NASDAQ (GS): ORCC

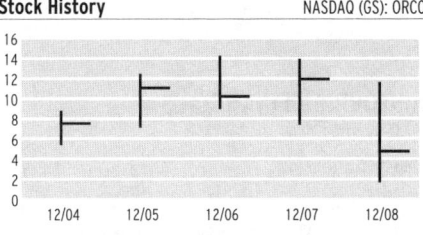

	STOCK PRICE ($) FY Close	P/E High/Low	PER SHARE ($) Earnings	Dividends	Book Value
12/08	4.74	— —	(0.24)	0.00	7.63
12/07	11.92	153 83	0.09	0.00	4.59
12/06	10.21	— —	(0.16)	0.00	5.83
12/05	11.05	14 8	0.88	0.00	3.43
12/04	7.53	35 22	0.25	0.00	1.21
Annual Growth	**(10.9%)**	**— —**	**—**	**—**	**58.4%**

Onyx Pharmaceuticals

Onyx Pharmaceuticals' cancer drug could turn out to be a real gem. Working with health care behemoth Bayer, the biotechnology company developed Nexavar, an FDA-approved treatment for advanced kidney cancer and liver cancer. The partners are jointly promoting the drug in the US, while Bayer handles marketing duties in the European Union (where Nexavar was initially approved in 2006) and elsewhere. Onyx and Bayer are also testing the drug as a possible treatment for other kinds of cancer, both alone and in combination with other cancer therapies. Nexavar received approval as a liver cancer treatment in 2007. The company is seeking to widen into additional areas of drug development.

The company's success is almost entirely dependent on the performance of Nexavar, both in the market and in further clinical trials. Onyx terminated its therapeutic virus program in 2003 in order to focus on developing Nexavar, and it licensed another of its anti-cancer compounds to Pfizer subsidiary Warner-Lambert for further development. It has no other compounds in its pipeline, or for that matter, any internal research and preclinical development staff to refill it.

In 2008 Onyx and Bayer halted a late-stage clinical trial testing Nexavar in patients with non-small cell lung cancer because it failed to improve survival rates.

Early the following year the company made a move to reduce its dependence on Nexavar when it acquired the option to license two development compounds from Singapore biotech firm S*BIO. The compounds have potential applications in cancer and autoimmune disease treatments. Onyx paid S*BIO $25 million for the option; if exercised, Onyx will pay S*BIO additional milestone and royalty payments and will take over development of the drugs for the North American and European markets.

Late in 2009 Onyx diversified further with its acquisition of private biotech firm Proteolix for $275 million, plus another $535 million in potential milestone payments. Proteolix brought with it therapies under development for hematology applications including multiple myeloma (a blood cancer) and other types of cancer malignancies and tumors.

EXECUTIVES

President, CEO, and Director: N. Anthony (Tony) Coles, age 48, $2,770,807 total compensation
EVP and COO: Laura A. Brege, age 51
EVP and CFO: Matthew K. (Matt) Fust, age 44
SVP U.S. Commercial Operations: Randy A. Kelley, age 53
SVP Product Strategy: Barry Flannelly
SVP Corporate Development: Jürgen Lasowski, age 51, $1,003,402 total compensation
VP and Chief Compliance Officer: Paul K. Ross
VP Organizational Learning, Development, and Human Resources: Judy Batlin, age 55, $937,491 total compensation
VP Program Leadership: Courtland Lavallee
VP Clinical Development: Todd J. Yancey
VP Regulatory Affairs: Patricia A. Oto, age 48
VP Corporate Communications and Investor Relations: Julianna R. (Julie) Wood, age 53
VP and Chief Legal Counsel: Gregory J. Giotta, age 62
Secretary: Robert L. Jones
Auditors: Ernst & Young LLP

LOCATIONS

HQ: Onyx Pharmaceuticals, Inc.
2100 Powell St., Emeryville, CA 94608
Phone: 510-597-6500 **Fax:** 510-597-6600
Web: www.onyx-pharm.com

COMPETITORS

Amgen
AstraZeneca
Bristol-Myers Squibb
Genentech
ImClone
Novartis
OSI Pharmaceuticals
Pfizer
Progen Pharmaceuticals

HISTORICAL FINANCIALS

Company Type: Public

Income Statement
FYE: December 31

	REVENUE ($ mil.)	NET INCOME ($ mil.)	NET PROFIT MARGIN	EMPLOYEES
12/08	194.3	1.9	1.0%	197
12/07	0.0	(34.2)	—	153
12/06	0.3	(92.7)	—	125
12/05	1.0	(95.2)	—	100
12/04	0.5	(46.8)	—	30
Annual Growth	**344.0%**	**—**	**—**	**60.1%**

2008 Year-End Financials

Debt ratio: —
Return on equity: 0.4%
Cash ($ mil.): 235.2
Current ratio: 13.87
Long-term debt ($ mil.): —
No. of shares (mil.): 62.1
Dividends
　Yield: 0.0%
　Payout: —
Market value ($ mil.): 2,122.5
R&D as % of sales: —
Advertising as % of sales: —

Stock History
NASDAQ (GM): ONXX

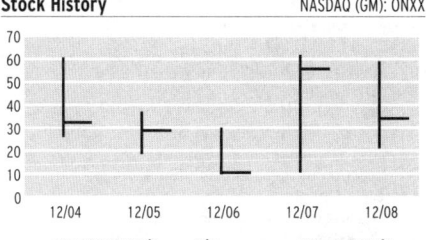

	STOCK PRICE ($) FY Close	P/E High/Low	PER SHARE ($) Earnings	Dividends	Book Value
12/08	34.16	1,945 722	0.03	0.00	7.65
12/07	55.62	— —	(0.67)	0.00	6.96
12/06	10.58	— —	(2.20)	0.00	3.59
12/05	28.80	— —	(2.64)	0.00	3.59
12/04	32.39	— —	(1.36)	0.00	2.90
Annual Growth	**1.3%**	**— —**	**—**	**—**	**27.5%**

OPNET Technologies

OPNET Technologies has made its name in network optimization. The company makes network management software for designing, building, and operating networks. Its offerings include applications to automate the processes of network design, provisioning, and performance analysis. OPNET's software lets designers evaluate how networks will perform under simulated conditions, analyze collected data, and resolve performance problems such as network congestion, configuration errors, and application bugs. The company also offers services such as consulting, maintenance, and training.

Though it sells to service providers and network equipment manufacturers, the company primarily targets large corporate clients and US government agencies. OPNET counts BNP Paribas, Cox Communications, the FBI, GEICO, IBM Global Services, the IRS, and Research In Motion among its clients.

Most of OPNET's revenues are generated by a direct sales force, but in 2008 the company launched a reseller program designed to help OPNET grow its sales to midsized companies. The company utilizes both direct sales and resale and distribution channels internationally. Customers outside the US accounted for about 20% of its sales in fiscal 2009.

Co-founders and brothers Marc Cohen (CEO) and Alain Cohen (president) together own more than a third of the company.

EXECUTIVES

Chairman and CEO: Marc A. Cohen, age 46, $385,396 total compensation
President and CTO: Alain J. Cohen, age 43, $382,396 total compensation
SVP Applications Engineering and Training: Eric S. Nudelman
SVP and Chief Scientist: Edward A. Sykes
SVP Information Systems and CIO: Alberto Morales
SVP Core Technologies: Yevgeny Gurevich
SVP Network Management Solutions Group: Pradeep K. Singh
SVP International Sales: Joseph J. Lenz
VP and CFO: Melvin F. (Mel) Wesley III, age 38, $275,768 total compensation
VP and General Counsel: Dennis R. McCoy
Auditors: Deloitte & Touche LLP

LOCATIONS

HQ: OPNET Technologies, Inc.
7255 Woodmont Ave., Bethesda, MD 20814
Phone: 240-497-3000   **Fax:** 240-497-3001
Web: www.opnet.com

2009 Sales

	$ mil.	% of total
US	96.9	79
Other countries	26.0	21
Total	**122.9**	**100**

PRODUCTS/OPERATIONS

2009 Sales

	$ mil.	% of total
New software licenses	51.2	42
Software license updates & support	43.1	35
Professional services	28.6	23
Total	**122.9**	**100**

COMPETITORS

CA, Inc.	NetScout Systems
Compuware	Quest Software
NetQoS	Tivoli Software

HISTORICAL FINANCIALS
Company Type: Public

Income Statement
FYE: March 31

	REVENUE ($ mil.)	NET INCOME ($ mil.)	NET PROFIT MARGIN	EMPLOYEES
3/09	122.9	4.7	3.8%	593
3/08	101.3	0.5	0.5%	560
3/07	95.1	8.0	8.4%	490
3/06	76.1	2.1	2.8%	433
3/05	64.2	2.1	3.3%	376
Annual Growth	**17.6%**	**22.3%**	**—**	**12.1%**

2009 Year-End Financials

Debt ratio: —
Return on equity: 4.1%
Cash ($ mil.): 91.0
Current ratio: 2.91
Long-term debt ($ mil.): —
No. of shares (mil.): 20.8
Dividends
  Yield: 0.0%
  Payout: —
Market value ($ mil.): 180.0
R&D as % of sales: —
Advertising as % of sales: —

Stock History
NASDAQ (GS): OPNT

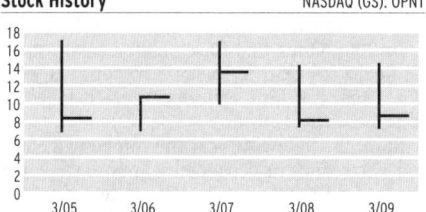

	STOCK PRICE ($) FY Close	P/E High/Low	PER SHARE ($) Earnings	Dividends	Book Value
3/09	8.67	63 32	0.23	0.00	5.61
3/08	8.14	472 251	0.03	0.00	5.33
3/07	13.51	44 26	0.38	0.00	5.44
3/06	10.72	107 71	0.10	0.00	4.79
3/05	8.36	169 69	0.10	0.00	4.82
Annual Growth	**0.9%**	**— —**	**23.1%**	**—**	**3.9%**

Optical Cable

Optical Cable isn't in it for the long haul. Its high-bandwidth fiber-optic communication cables transmit data, video, and audio over short to moderate distances of up to about 10 miles. The company's Ultra-Fox brand fiber-optic cables are made for both indoor and outdoor use. Optical Cable's strands are typically used in local-area networks (LANs) for schools, hospitals, manufacturing plants, and other facilities. The company also produces security cables for use with surveillance cameras and specialty fiber-optic cables with military tactical field applications. Customers include electrical contractors, equipment manufacturers, systems resellers, and distributors.

Founded in 1983, Optical Cable is a leading manufacturer of military ground tactical fiber-optic cable for use by the US military and of fiber-optic cables for the enterprise market. In 2006 the company rejected an unsolicited $36 million acquisition bid from Superior Essex.

Optical Cable is looking to increase its manufacturing capacity and product distribution through process upgrades and the development of strategic alliances. It currently sells its cable products in more than 50 countries. The company strengthened its military customer base in 2007 when it received a crucial qualification status allowing it to provide fiber for the UK military. That same year it inked a lucrative five-year contract with the US military to provide tactical fiber-optic cable assemblies.

In 2008 it further expanded its manufacturing capacity when it acquired SMP Data Communications, which makes fiber-optic and copper connectivity products. The connectivity products allow Optical Cable to offer integrated products to its customers. SMP was operated as a subsidiary of Optical Cable prior to being integrated into the company in 2009.

EXECUTIVES

Chairman, President, and CEO; Chairman and CEO, SMP Data Communications: Neil D. Wilkin Jr., age 45
VP and CFO: Tracy G. Smith, age 40
VP, Sales, International: Michael Newman
Director, Human Resources: Outheria Smith
Auditors: KPMG LLP

LOCATIONS

HQ: Optical Cable Corporation
5290 Concourse Dr., Roanoke, VA 24019
Phone: 540-265-0690   **Fax:** 540-265-0724
Web: www.occfiber.com

2008 Sales

	$ mil.	% of total
US	41.3	68
Other countries	19.7	32
Total	**61.0**	**100**

PRODUCTS/OPERATIONS

Selected Products

Assembly cables
Breakout cables
Distribution cables
Hybrid cables (riser or plenum applications)
Subgrouping cables

COMPETITORS

Alcatel-Lucent	Fujikura Ltd.
Belden	Furukawa Electric
Channell Commercial	General Cable
Cisco Systems	Hitachi
CommScope	Lamson & Sessions
Corning	Nexans
Draka Holding	SWCC SHOWA

HISTORICAL FINANCIALS
Company Type: Public

Income Statement
FYE: October 31

	REVENUE ($ mil.)	NET INCOME ($ mil.)	NET PROFIT MARGIN	EMPLOYEES
10/08	61.0	2.2	3.6%	324
10/07	45.5	1.3	2.9%	198
10/06	45.3	0.4	0.9%	216
10/05	45.9	1.2	2.6%	202
10/04	43.2	0.8	1.9%	182
Annual Growth	**9.0%**	**28.8%**	**—**	**15.5%**

2008 Year-End Financials

Debt ratio: 30.7%
Return on equity: 6.6%
Cash ($ mil.): 3.9
Current ratio: 3.91
Long-term debt ($ mil.): 10.7
No. of shares (mil.): 6.5

Dividends
Yield: 0.0%
Payout: —
Market value ($ mil.): 30.1
R&D as % of sales: —
Advertising as % of sales: —

Stock History

NASDAQ (GM): OCCF

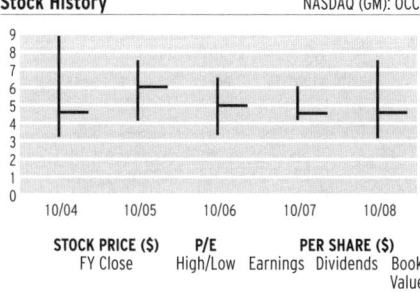

	STOCK PRICE ($) FY Close	P/E High/Low		PER SHARE ($) Earnings	Dividends	Book Value
10/08	4.59	21	9	0.36	0.00	5.32
10/07	4.55	29	20	0.21	0.00	4.88
10/06	4.98	108	57	0.06	0.00	4.65
10/05	6.03	37	21	0.20	0.00	4.48
10/04	4.59	68	25	0.13	0.00	4.23
Annual Growth	**0.0%**	—	—	**29.0%**	—	**5.9%**

Orchids Paper Products

Orchids Paper Products hopes to leave its end users smelling like a rose. The company makes bulk tissue paper and converts it into bathroom tissue, paper napkins, and paper towels for the consumer market. Most of the company's products are sold as private-label items by discount retailers; Orchids Paper products also are sold under the company's Colortex and Velvet brands. Dollar General accounts for nearly 40% of Orchids Paper's sales; other big customers include Big Lots, Dollar Tree, Family Dollar, Fred's, and Variety Wholesalers. Orchids Paper sells most of its products within a 900-mile radius of its manufacturing plant in northeastern Oklahoma.

Orchids has been focused on increasing efficiency, and in 2007 it began producing its own parent rolls, which is the material processed into its other products, such as tissue. The move was a successful effort to limit the the company's reliance on outside sources for parent rolls and the subsequent price fluctuations that have characterized that market in recent years.

Going forward, the company plans to maximize production with its older equipment in a strategic move that deviates from typical paper product makers that have been shutting down older equipment. Orchids has also invested in new equipment. The result of these efforts will be an increase in capacity that the company hopes to sell through new channels, namely grocery and drug store chains.

EXECUTIVES

Chairman: Jay Shuster, age 54
President, CEO, and Director: Robert A. Snyder, age 60, $595,117 total compensation
CFO and Secretary: Keith R. Schroeder, age 53, $306,598 total compensation
VP Sales and Marketing: Dan Daniels
Director Engineering and Reliability: Lonnie Harper

Supervisor, Accounts Receivable and Credit: Margie King
Manager Reliability Improvement, Converting Operations: Don Branson
Plant Manager Converting Operations: Royce Norton
Manager Human Resources: Gary Creekmore
Auditors: Hoganttaylor LLP

LOCATIONS

HQ: Orchids Paper Products Company
4826 Hunt St., Pryor, OK 74361
Phone: 918-825-0616   **Fax:** 918-825-0060
Web: www.orchidspaper.com

PRODUCTS/OPERATIONS

2008 Sales

	% of total
Paper towels	45
Bathroom tissue	31
Parent rolls	17
Paper napkins	7
Total	**100**

COMPETITORS

Cascades Tissue Group
Georgia-Pacific
Irving Tissue
Kimberly-Clark
Potlatch
Wausau Paper

HISTORICAL FINANCIALS

Company Type: Public

Income Statement

FYE: December 31

	REVENUE ($ mil.)	NET INCOME ($ mil.)	NET PROFIT MARGIN	EMPLOYEES
12/08	90.2	5.2	5.8%	306
12/07	74.6	2.6	3.5%	345
12/06	60.2	0.7	1.2%	310
12/05	57.7	1.4	2.4%	264
12/04	47.6	1.0	2.1%	260
Annual Growth	**17.3%**	**51.0%**	—	**4.2%**

2008 Year-End Financials

Debt ratio: 62.8%
Return on equity: 16.9%
Cash ($ mil.): 0.0
Current ratio: 1.34
Long-term debt ($ mil.): 21.1
No. of shares (mil.): 7.4

Dividends
Yield: 0.0%
Payout: —
Market value ($ mil.): 64.7
R&D as % of sales: —
Advertising as % of sales: —

Stock History

NYSE Alternext: TIS

	STOCK PRICE ($) FY Close	P/E High/Low		PER SHARE ($) Earnings	Dividends	Book Value
12/08	8.75	11	8	0.79	0.00	4.54
12/07	9.10	26	12	0.40	0.00	3.79
12/06	8.53	105	61	0.11	0.00	3.34
12/05	6.83	24	18	0.30	0.00	3.21
Annual Growth	**8.6%**	—	—	**17.1%**	—	**48.3%**

Ormat Technologies

Ormat Technologies is on an environmentally safe power trip. The company builds geothermal as well as recovered energy power plants. Geothermal technology extracts hot water or steam that is vaporized and used to drive turbines. The fluid is then cooled and recycled back through the process, making it a clean and renewable energy source. Recovered energy utilizes heat produced in other industrial processes. The company, set up by Israel-based Ormat Industries, also sells power units for both types of plants. Ormat operates geothermal plants (with a total of 410 MW of power) in Guatemala (2), Kenya, Nicaragua, and the US (7). The Bronicki family owns about 35% of the company.

In 2006 Ormat Technologies acquired (from an unrelated third party) a 51% stake in Orzunil I de Electricidad, Limitada (Orzunil), which owns the Zunil Geothermal Project in Guatemala, increasing its ownership stake in the Zunil Project to 72% (and later to 100%).

In 2007 the company signed a 20-year power purchase agreement with Southern California Edison for the sale of energy to be produced by a new 100 MW plant that will be built in Imperial Valley, California.

EXECUTIVES

Chairman and CTO: Lucien Y. Bronicki, age 76, $580,922 total compensation
CEO and Director: Yehudit (Dita) Bronicki, age 68, $621,104 total compensation
President, COO, and Director: Yoram Bronicki, age 43, $625,138 total compensation
CFO: Joseph Tenne, age 54, $600,702 total compensation
EVP Operations: Nadav Amir, age 59, $743,313 total compensation
EVP Project Management: Zvi Reiss, age 59, $667,052 total compensation
EVP Marketing and Sales, Rest of the World: Joseph Shiloah, age 63
SVP Electrical and Conceptual Engineering: Shimon Hatzir, age 47
SVP Contract Management and Corporate Secretary: Etty Rosner, age 54
VP Geothermal Engineering: Zvi Krieger, age 53
VP Operations, Rest of the World and Product Support: Aaron Choresh, age 63
Investor Relations: Smadar Lavi
Auditors: PricewaterhouseCoopers LLP

LOCATIONS

HQ: Ormat Technologies, Inc.
6225 Neil Rd., Ste. 300, Reno, NV 89511
Phone: 775-356-9029   **Fax:** 775-356-9039
Web: www.ormat.com

2008 Sales

	$ mil.	% of total
North America	252.5	73
Latin America	33.9	10
Pacific Rim	21.3	6
Europe	20.4	6
Africa	10.7	3
Asia	6.0	2
Total	**344.8**	**100**

PRODUCTS/OPERATIONS

2008 Sales

	$ mil.	% of total
Electricity	252.2	73
Products	92.6	27
Total	**344.8**	**100**

COMPETITORS

ALSTOM	GE
Calpine	Mitsubishi Electric
Enel	Siemens AG
Fuji Electric	Toshiba

HISTORICAL FINANCIALS

Company Type: Public

Income Statement

FYE: December 31

	REVENUE ($ mil.)	NET INCOME ($ mil.)	NET PROFIT MARGIN	EMPLOYEES
12/08	344.8	49.8	14.4%	1,069
12/07	295.9	27.4	9.3%	899
12/06	268.9	34.4	12.8%	774
12/05	238.0	15.2	6.4%	733
12/04	219.2	17.8	8.1%	677
Annual Growth	12.0%	29.3%	—	12.1%

2008 Year-End Financials

Debt ratio: 43.7%
Return on equity: 6.8%
Cash ($ mil.): 34.4
Current ratio: 1.02
Long-term debt ($ mil.): 369.5
No. of shares (mil.): 45.4

Dividends
  Yield: 0.6%
  Payout: 17.9%
Market value ($ mil.): 1,447.6
R&D as % of sales: —
Advertising as % of sales: —

Stock History

NYSE: ORA

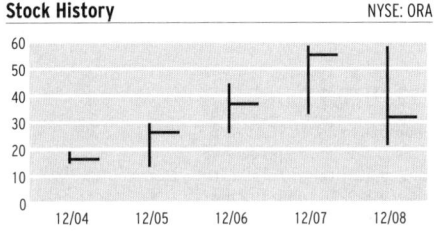

	STOCK PRICE ($) FY Close	P/E High/Low		PER SHARE ($) Earnings	Dividends	Book Value
12/08	31.87	52	19	1.12	0.20	18.63
12/07	55.01	83	48	0.70	0.22	13.61
12/06	36.82	44	27	0.99	0.15	9.70
12/05	26.14	61	29	0.48	0.12	4.01
12/04	16.28	26	21	0.72	0.00	3.70
Annual Growth	18.3%	—	—	11.7%	—	49.8%

Otelco Inc.

Otelco makes sure rural areas enjoy all the modern communications conveniences. The company operates six incumbent rural local-exchange carriers (RLECs) that provide local and long-distance phone services. Other services include high-speed and dial-up Internet access, as well as cable television. Otelco has four RLECs in north central Alabama, one in central Missouri, and one adjacent to Bangor, Maine. It maintains more than 69,000 access lines, and has more than 4,000 cable-TV customers. Otelco has made a business of acquiring RLECs, including assets from Oneonta Telephone that were used to create Otelco Telephone in 1999.

Other acquisitions include Hopper Telecommunications (1999), Brindlee Mountain Telephone (2000), Blountsville Telephone (2003), Mid-Missouri Telephone (2004), and Mid-Maine Communications (2006).

EXECUTIVES

Chairman, President, and CEO: Michael D. Weaver, age 56, $424,221 total compensation
CFO and Secretary: Curtis L. Garner Jr., age 61, $252,754 total compensation
SVP and General Manager, Alabama: Dennis K. Andrews, age 52, $214,497 total compensation
SVP and General Manager, New England: Nicholas A. Winchester, age 39, $172,994 total compensation
VP and General Manager, Missouri: Gary B. Romig, age 58
VP and Controller: Jerry C. Boles, age 56, $172,763 total compensation
VP Operations, New England: Robert J. Souza, age 55
Auditors: BDO Seidman, LLP

LOCATIONS

HQ: Otelco Inc.
  505 3rd Ave. East, Oneonta, AL 35121
Phone: 205-625-3574   **Fax:** 205-625-3523
Web: www.otelco.net

PRODUCTS/OPERATIONS

2008 Sales

	$ mil.	% of total
Local services	30.0	39
Network access	27.3	35
Internet	12.4	16
Transport services	5.0	7
Cable television	2.4	3
Total	**77.1**	**100**

COMPETITORS

AT&T
Cellco
Charter Communications
DIRECTV
DISH Network
EarthLink
Socket Internet
Sprint Nextel
Time Warner Cable
Verizon

HISTORICAL FINANCIALS

Company Type: Public

Income Statement

FYE: December 31

	REVENUE ($ mil.)	NET INCOME ($ mil.)	NET PROFIT MARGIN	EMPLOYEES
12/08	77.1	0.2	0.3%	327
12/07	69.7	0.2	0.3%	215
12/06	57.6	1.2	2.1%	220
12/05	47.0	1.8	3.8%	137
12/04	37.3	6.1	16.4%	—
Annual Growth	19.9%	(57.4%)	—	33.6%

2008 Year-End Financials

Debt ratio: 1,939.0%
Return on equity: 1.1%
Cash ($ mil.): 13.5
Current ratio: 2.70
Long-term debt ($ mil.): 278.8
No. of shares (mil.): 13.2

Dividends
  Yield: 19.0%
  Payout: —
Market value ($ mil.): 100.1
R&D as % of sales: —
Advertising as % of sales: —

Stock History

NASDAQ (GM): OTT

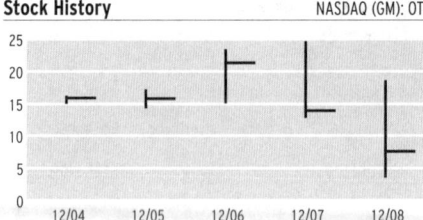

	STOCK PRICE ($) FY Close	P/E High/Low		PER SHARE ($) Earnings	Dividends	Book Value
12/08	7.57	—	—	(0.03)	1.44	1.09
12/07	13.92	—	—	(0.10)	0.71	1.76
12/06	21.32	129	85	0.18	0.71	0.01
12/05	15.79	142	121	0.12	0.71	0.44
12/04	15.89	23	21	0.71	0.00	0.76
Annual Growth	(16.9%)	—	—	—	—	9.5%

Park National Corporation

Customers can park their money with Park National. Through about a dozen community banking divisions, the company operates about 130 bank branches in central and southern portions of Ohio, plus nearly 20 more in Alabama and Florida. The banks provide an array of consumer and business banking services, including traditional savings and checking accounts and CDs, as well as trust services. Business loans, including commercial mortgages, account for about 40% of the company's loan portfolio. The banks also originate consumer, residential real estate, and construction loans. Subsidiary Guardian Finance provides consumer finance services. Scope Leasing offers aircraft financing.

In 2007 Park National expanded into Alabama and Florida with the acquisition of Vision Bancshares. Vision Bancshares Financial Group, which came over in the purchase, offers fixed and variable annuities; life, property, and casualty insurance; and investment products. Prior to this, the company's expansion was limited to its home state of Ohio. It acquired Anderson Bank Company and its two branches in 2006, First Clermont Bank in 2005, and First Federal Bancorp in 2004.

EXECUTIVES

Chairman and CEO, Park National Corporation and Park National Bank: C. Daniel (Dan) DeLawder, age 59, $733,972 total compensation
Vice Chairman; Chairman, Security National Bank: Harry O. Egger, age 69
President, Secretary, and Director; President, Park National Bank: David L. Trautman, age 47, $417,456 total compensation
CFO; SVP and CFO, Park National Bank: John W. Kozak, age 53, $298,281 total compensation
President, Security National Bank: William C. (Bill) Fralick
President, United Bank: Donald R. Stone
President, Citizens National Bank: Jeffrey (Jeff) Darding
President, Unity National Bank: John A. Brown
President, Vision Bank, Florida: John Whitlock
President, Scope Aircraft Finance: Robert N. (Bob) Kent

President, Guardian Financial: Earl W. Osborne
President, Vision Bank, Alabama: Diane Anderson
President, Farmers and Saving Bank:
  James S. Lingenfelter
President, Richland Bank: David J. Gooch
President, Fairfield National Bank:
  Stephen G. (Steve) Wells
President, Second National Bank: John E. Swallow
President, Century National Bank: Thomas M. Lyall
President, Park National Bank Southwest Ohio and
  Northern Kentucky: K. Douglas (Doug) Compton
President, First-Knox National Bank: Gordon E. Yance
Auditors: Crowe Horwath LLP

LOCATIONS

HQ: Park National Corporation
  50 N. 3rd St., Newark, OH 43058
Phone: 740-349-8451   Fax: 740-349-3765
Web: www.parknationalcorp.com

PRODUCTS/OPERATIONS

2008 Gross Revenues

	$ mil.	% of total
Interest		
Loans, including fees	301.2	63
Securities, including dividends	89.9	19
Other	0.3	—
Noninterest		
Service charges on deposit accounts	24.3	5
Fiduciary activities	13.9	3
Other	46.6	10
Total	**476.2**	**100**

COMPETITORS

Camco Financial
Fifth Third
First Place Financial
FirstMerit
Huntington Bancshares
JPMorgan Chase
PNC Financial
Wayne Savings Bancshares

HISTORICAL FINANCIALS

Company Type: Public

Income Statement

FYE: December 31

	ASSETS ($ mil.)	NET INCOME ($ mil.)	INCOME AS % OF ASSETS	EMPLOYEES
12/08	7,070.7	13.7	0.2%	2,051
12/07	6,501.1	22.7	0.3%	2,066
12/06	5,470.9	94.1	1.7%	1,892
12/05	5,436.0	95.2	1.8%	1,824
12/04	5,412.6	91.5	1.7%	1,749
Annual Growth	**6.9%**	**(37.8%)**	**—**	**4.1%**

2008 Year-End Financials

Equity as % of assets: 7.7%
Return on assets: 0.2%
Return on equity: 2.4%
Long-term debt ($ mil.): 895.6
No. of shares (mil.): 14.3
Market value ($ mil.): 1,023.2

Dividends
  Yield: 5.3%
  Payout: 388.7%
Sales ($ mil.): 340.7
R&D as % of sales: —
Advertising as % of sales: —

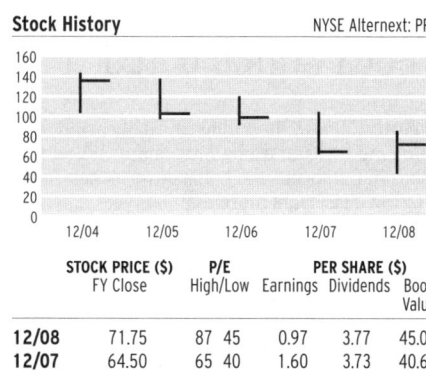

Stock History

NYSE Alternext: PRK

	STOCK PRICE ($) FY Close	P/E High/Low		PER SHARE ($) Earnings	Dividends	Book Value
12/08	71.75	87	45	0.97	3.77	45.07
12/07	64.50	65	40	1.60	3.73	40.67
12/06	99.00	18	14	6.74	3.69	40.00
12/05	102.64	21	15	6.64	3.62	39.16
12/04	135.50	22	17	6.32	3.41	39.45
Annual Growth	**(14.7%)**	**—**	**—**	**(37.4%)**	**2.5%**	**3.4%**

Parker Drilling

Parker Drilling parks its oil rigs off the beaten path. Its helicopter-transportable rigs allow the drilling contractor to work in otherwise inaccessible desert, mountain, and remote jungle locations. Its barge rigs allow the company to drill in transition zones (such as bays and marshes). Parker Drilling owns 28 land rigs and 17 US-based barge drilling and workover rigs. The company drills worldwide (in nine countries in 2008) and has worked in 54 countries since its founding. Subsidiary Quail Tools provides rental tools for oil and gas drilling and workover activities, with operations in the Gulf Coast, the Rocky Mountains, and West Texas regions. Parker Drilling also has a drilling rig construction unit.

In recent years the company has been targeting international markets. A pioneer in arctic drilling, Parker Drilling is marketing its services to operators in the harsh environments of the Caspian Sea, Western Siberia, and Sakhalin Island. Its land drilling operations are focused primarily in the Asia/Pacific region, and the Commonwealth of Independent States (formerly the Soviet Union). Its barge drilling operations are located mainly in the Gulf of Mexico and the Caspian Sea.

In 2008 the company operated 15 rigs in the Gulf of Mexico, nine land rigs in the Commonwealth of Independent States, eight land rigs in the Asia/Pacific region, and nine land rigs in Latin America. That year Exxon Mobil accounted for 13% of Parker Drilling's revenues.

HISTORY

Gifford Parker founded Parker Drilling in 1934, and a year later the firm pioneered the use of diesel-powered electric rigs. By the late 1940s the company was also operating five rigs in Venezuela and 12 in Canada. Robert Parker bought the firm in 1954 and committed it to new drilling techniques. By the mid-1960s it had eight deep-drilling rigs. The firm went public in 1969, and Robert Parker Jr. became president in 1977.

Parker Drilling became the first American land-drilling contractor in mainland China (1980) and in the former Soviet Union (1991). In 1995 it moved into New Zealand and began geothermal drilling in Indonesia.

In 1996 the company moved into offshore drilling by buying Mallard Drilling and doubled in size by buying equipment rental company Quail Tools. The following year it acquired Bolifor (a Bolivian drilling contractor) and Houston-based Hercules Offshore and Hercules Rig. The Hercules deal added 10 Gulf of Mexico drilling rigs to Parker's inventory. In 1998 Parker announced it would merge with Superior Energy Services, an oil field tool rental company, but the deal fell through.

Meanwhile, the company was hit hard as oil prices crashed in 1998. Amid losses the next year, Parker began unloading assets. It sold all of its US land rigs to raise cash and to focus on offshore drilling in international markets. In keeping with its emphasis on offshore activities, the company moved its headquarters from Tulsa, Oklahoma, to Houston in 2001.

That year Parker and Russia's Tyumen Oil formed a joint venture to provide contract-drilling services across Russia. In 2002 Parker secured contracts to build and operate a rig to drill on Russia's Sakhalin Island.

In 2007 the company sold two barge-mounted workover rigs and related equipment to Basic Energy Services for $26 million.

EXECUTIVES

Chairman Emeritus: Robert L. Parker Sr., age 85
Chairman: Robert L. (Bobby) Parker Jr., age 60,
  $2,111,858 total compensation
CEO and Director: David C. Mannon, age 51,
  $1,292,133 total compensation
SVP and CFO: W. Kirk Brassfield, age 53,
  $842,299 total compensation
VP Operations: Michael D. Drennon, age 53
VP Engineering: Denis J. Graham, age 59,
  $696,011 total compensation
VP and General Counsel: Jon-Al Duplantier, age 42
VP Finance and Administration, Quail Tools:
  Keith M. White
VP Business Development, Quail Tools:
  Robert N. White
VP Operations, Quail Tools: R. Marc Whites
Principal Accounting Officer and Corporate Controller:
  Philip Schlom, age 45
Managing Director International Operations:
  Greg Helmen
Director Business Development and Global Sales:
  David McCann
Director Investor Relations: Richard Bajenski
Manager Public Relations: Rose Maltby
Treasurer: David W. Tucker, age 53
Auditors: Melton & Melton LLP

LOCATIONS

HQ: Parker Drilling Company
  1401 Enclave Pkwy., Ste. 600, Houston, TX 77077
Phone: 281-406-2000   Fax: 281-406-2001
Web: www.parkerdrilling.com

2008 Sales

	$ mil.	% of total
US	400.0	48
Commonwealth of Independent States	210.3	25
Latin America	122.5	15
Asia/Pacific	57.0	7
Africa & Middle East	40.0	5
Total	**829.8**	**100**

PRODUCTS/OPERATIONS

2008 Sales

	$ mil.	% of total
International drilling	325.1	39
US drilling	173.6	21
Rental tools	171.6	21
Project management & engineering services	110.1	13
Contruction contract	49.4	6
Total	**829.8**	**100**

Selected Services
Helicopter-transportable rigs
Land drilling
Offshore drilling
Rental tools
Transition zone drilling

Selected Subsidiaries
Parker Drilling Company International Limited
Parker Technology, Inc. (rig design, manufacturing, modification, and servicing)
Quail Tools LLP (oil field tool rentals)

COMPETITORS

Atwood Oceanics
Baker Hughes
BJ Services
Diamond Offshore
Halliburton
Helmerich & Payne
Hercules Offshore
Nabors Industries
Noble
Pride International
Schlumberger
Transocean

HISTORICAL FINANCIALS

Company Type: Public

Income Statement				FYE: December 31
	REVENUE ($ mil.)	NET INCOME ($ mil.)	NET PROFIT MARGIN	EMPLOYEES
12/08	829.8	25.6	3.1%	2,766
12/07	654.6	104.1	15.9%	3,087
12/06	586.4	81.0	13.8%	2,628
12/05	531.7	98.9	18.6%	3,040
12/04	376.5	(47.1)	—	3,014
Annual Growth	**21.8%**	—	—	**(2.1%)**

2008 Year-End Financials
Debt ratio: 79.8%
Return on equity: 4.6%
Cash ($ mil.): 172.3
Current ratio: 2.99
Long-term debt ($ mil.): 455.1
No. of shares (mil.): 116.2
Dividends
Yield: 0.0%
Payout: —
Market value ($ mil.): 336.9
R&D as % of sales: —
Advertising as % of sales: —

| Stock History | | | | NYSE: PKD |

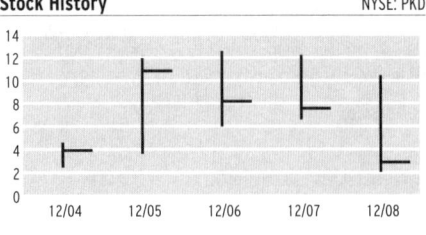

	STOCK PRICE ($) FY Close	P/E High/Low		PER SHARE ($) Earnings	Dividends	Book Value
12/08	2.90	45	9	0.23	0.00	4.91
12/07	7.55	13	7	0.94	0.00	4.60
12/06	8.17	17	8	0.75	0.00	3.95
12/05	10.83	12	4	1.02	0.00	2.24
12/04	3.93	—	—	(0.50)	0.00	1.28
Annual Growth	**(7.3%)**	—	—	—	—	**39.9%**

Peet's Coffee & Tea

Peet's Coffee & Tea enjoys the daily grind. The company owns and operates about 190 coffee shops in California and half a dozen other states offering java lovers more than 20 types of whole bean and fresh ground coffee, including about 15 blends. Its teas run the spectrum from India black to herbal blends. The stores also offer fresh brewed coffee, biscotti, and other pastries, along with mugs and brewing equipment. In addition to its retail operation, Peet's sells coffee through retail grocery chains such as Safeway and Whole Foods, and through its own online mail order operations. The company also supplies coffee to foodservice operators.

Unlike its chief rival Starbucks, Peet's has built its chain without the aid of franchising or licensing. The strategy allows the company to have greater control over its local operations, but it has meant slower growth than franchised concepts. During 2008 Peet's opened more than 20 new locations, down from about 30 new shops opened the previous year.

Peet's is also keen to expand its wholesale coffee roasting business. The company offered to buy out coffee wholesaler Diedrich Coffee for more than $210 million, but the deal sparked a bidding war with Green Mountain Coffee Roasters, which eventually carried the day with a $290 million buyout bid. Both Peet's and Green Mountain were attracted by Diedrich's lucrative manufacturing of K-Cup single serving portion packs, produced under license for Keurig's popular brewing system. (Keurig is a subsidiary of Green Mountain.)

Peet's namesake, Alfred Peet, founded the company in 1966. Starbucks' co-founders Gerald Baldwin and Gordon Bowker bought the company in 1984. (They sold their stakes in Starbucks in 1987.)

EXECUTIVES

Chairman: Jean-Michel Valette, age 50
President, CEO, and Director: Patrick J. (Pat) O'Dea, age 46, $875,836 total compensation
VP, CFO, and Secretary: Thomas P. Cawley, age 48, $566,587 total compensation
VP and General Manager, Consumer Business: P. Christine (Chris) Lansing, age 45, $663,909 total compensation
VP Retail Operations: Kay L. Bogeajis, age 54, $500,701 total compensation
VP Operations and Information Systems: James E. (Jim) Grimes, age 53, $414,689 total compensation
VP Coffee: Doug Welsh, age 46
Roastmaster Emeritus: James A. (Jim) Reynolds
Auditors: Deloitte & Touche LLP

LOCATIONS

HQ: Peet's Coffee & Tea, Inc.
1400 Park Ave., Emeryville, CA 94608
Phone: 510-594-2100 **Fax:** 510-594-2180
Web: www.peets.com

2008 Locations

	No.
California	162
Oregon	8
Washington	7
Massachusetts	6
Colorado	3
Illinois	2
Total	**188**

PRODUCTS/OPERATIONS

2008 Sales

	$ mil.	% of total
Retail stores	187.7	66
Specialty	97.1	34
Total	**284.8**	**100**

2008 Sales

	% of total
Whole bean coffee & related products	53
Beverages & pastries	47
Total	**100**

Selected Operations
Retail coffee shops
Specialty sales channels
  Foodservice distribution
  Home delivery
  Retail grocery sales

COMPETITORS

Bruegger's
Caribou Coffee
The Coffee Bean
Community Coffee
Dunkin
Einstein Noah
Farmer Bros.
Green Mountain Coffee
illy
It's A Grind
Nestlé
Starbucks
Tully's Coffee

HISTORICAL FINANCIALS

Company Type: Public

Income Statement				FYE: Sunday nearest December 31
	REVENUE ($ mil.)	NET INCOME ($ mil.)	NET PROFIT MARGIN	EMPLOYEES
12/08	284.8	11.2	3.9%	3,750
12/07	249.4	8.4	3.4%	3,678
12/06	210.5	7.8	3.7%	3,169
12/05	175.2	10.7	6.1%	2,813
12/04	145.7	8.8	6.0%	2,127
Annual Growth	**18.2%**	**6.2%**	—	**15.2%**

2008 Year-End Financials
Debt ratio: —
Return on equity: 7.7%
Cash ($ mil.): 4.7
Current ratio: 2.45
Long-term debt ($ mil.): —
No. of shares (mil.): 13.0
Dividends
Yield: —
Payout: —
Market value ($ mil.): 302.1
R&D as % of sales: —
Advertising as % of sales: —

| Stock History | | | NASDAQ (GS): PEET |

	STOCK PRICE ($) FY Close	P/E High/Low		PER SHARE ($) Earnings	Dividends	Book Value
12/08	23.25	37	22	0.80	—	11.07
12/07	29.07	51	39	0.59	—	11.33
12/06	26.24	60	44	0.55	—	9.81
12/05	30.35	50	31	0.74	—	9.70
12/04	26.47	44	26	0.63	—	8.40
Annual Growth	**(3.2%)**	—	—	**6.2%**	—	**7.2%**

Pegasystems Inc.

Pegasystems helps companies soar through business changes without being tied down by their old processes. The company provides rules-driven business process management software designed to help clients in the financial services, insurance, and health care industries update their operations and systems to reflect changes to business goals and strategies. Pegasystems offers tools for analyzing and simulating processes, integrating enterprise applications and portals, managing content integration, and managing processes for customer service, claims resolution, and transaction processing. Established in 1983, its customers have included Aetna, WellPoint, Bank of America, and Credit Suisse.

Financial services and health care companies are Pegasystems' primary markets, but the company also sells to clients in the manufacturing, government, travel and hospitality, retail, consumer packaged goods, and telecommunications industries. Pegasystems sells its products through its direct sales force, as well as through distributors and resellers.

Founder and CEO Alan Trefler owns more than 55% of Pegasystems.

EXECUTIVES

Chairman and CEO: Alan Trefler, age 52, $488,496 total compensation
Vice Chairman: Richard H. (Rick) Jones, age 57
SVP Engineering Product Development:
Michael R. (Mike) Pyle, age 54, $464,979 total compensation
SVP and CFO: Craig A. Dynes, age 53, $571,010 total compensation
SVP Corporate Development: Max Mayer, $446,532 total compensation
Chief Marketing Officer: Grant E. Johnson
VP Global Services: Douglas I. (Doug) Kra, age 46, $492,948 total compensation
VP Finance and Chief Accounting Officer: Efstathios A. (Stathis) Kouninis, age 48
VP Industry Marketing: Willy Fox
VP, General Counsel, and Secretary: Shawn S. Hoyt
VP Human Capital: Jeff Yanagi
Manager Public Relations and Communications, Europe, Middle East, and Africa: Joanna Baker
Auditors: Deloitte & Touche LLP

LOCATIONS

HQ: Pegasystems Inc.
101 Main St., Cambridge, MA 02142
Phone: 617-374-9600   **Fax:** 617-374-9620
Web: www.pega.com

2008 Sales

	% of total
US	62
UK	19
Europe	13
Other	6
Total	**100**

PRODUCTS/OPERATIONS

Selected Software

PegaRULES (business rule development)
Pegasystems SmartBPM Suite (rules-driven business process management)

COMPETITORS

Chordiant Software	Oracle
IBM	SAP
ILOG	Savvion
Lombardi Software	TIBCO Software
Metastorm	Trintech
Microsoft Dynamics	

HISTORICAL FINANCIALS

Company Type: Public

Income Statement

FYE: December 31

	REVENUE ($ mil.)	NET INCOME ($ mil.)	NET PROFIT MARGIN	EMPLOYEES
12/08	211.6	11.0	5.2%	825
12/07	161.9	6.6	4.1%	657
12/06	126.0	1.8	1.4%	547
12/05	102.0	4.7	4.6%	458
12/04	96.5	7.6	7.9%	406
Annual Growth	**21.7%**	**9.7%**	**—**	**19.4%**

2008 Year-End Financials

Debt ratio: —
Return on equity: 6.4%
Cash ($ mil.): 36.1
Current ratio: 3.45
Long-term debt ($ mil.): —
No. of shares (mil.): 36.7
Dividends
Yield: 1.0%
Payout: 41.4%
Market value ($ mil.): 453.3
R&D as % of sales: —
Advertising as % of sales: —

Stock History

NASDAQ (GS): PEGA

	STOCK PRICE ($) FY Close	P/E High/Low	PER SHARE ($) Earnings	Dividends	Book Value
12/08	12.36	52 30	0.29	0.12	4.72
12/07	11.93	73 45	0.18	0.15	4.72
12/06	9.87	212 124	0.05	0.06	4.53
12/05	7.31	70 37	0.13	0.00	4.52
12/04	8.53	59 29	0.20	0.00	4.50
Annual Growth	**9.7%**	**— —**	**9.7%**	**—**	**1.2%**

Penn Virginia Resource Partners

The motto for Penn Virginia Resource Partners (PVR) could be "Baby, it's *coal* outside." PVR was formed by energy company Penn Virginia Corporation to manage its coal properties. PVR leases mining rights on its properties to third-party mine operators, collecting royalties based on the amount of coal produced and the price at which it is sold. Its land contains more than 800 million tons of proven or probable reserves (mostly low-sulfur bituminous coal). PVR also sells timber from its properties and charges fees to mine operators for use of its coal preparation and transportation facilities. Penn Virginia GP Holdings controls some 40% of the firm.

Although PVR continues to expand its holdings in Appalachia, the company has made acquisitions in other regions of the US. A purchase in the Illinois Basin area increased the company's coal reserves by nearly 15% in 2005. Eliminating the third party that had performed the task previously, PVR began marketing its natural gas production in Louisiana, Oklahoma, and Texas in 2006. In an effort to increase its production of natural gas in the region, PVR purchased pipeline assets in the Anadarko Basin area of Texas and Oklahoma in 2008.

In 2007 PVR acquired roughly 62,000 acres of West Virginia forestland from packaging and paper manufacturer MeadWestvaco for approximately $93 million. The following year, the company acquired some 29 million tons of coal reserves and 56 million board feet of hardwood timber in Virginia and Kentucky. The deals significantly expanded PVR's timber operations.

EXECUTIVES

Chairman and CEO: A. James (Jim) Dearlove, age 62, $818,661 total compensation
Co-President and COO, Midstream:
Ronald K. (Ron) Page, age 59, $755,751 total compensation
Co-President and COO, Coal: Keith D. Horton, age 56, $821,631 total compensation
VP, CFO, and Director: Frank A. Pici, age 53, $341,313 total compensation
VP, Chief Administrative Officer, General Counsel, and Director: Nancy M. Snyder, age 55, $362,887 total compensation
Auditors: KPMG LLP

LOCATIONS

HQ: Penn Virginia Resource Partners, L.P.
3 Radnor Corporate Ctr., Ste. 300
100 Matsonford Rd., Radnor, PA 19087
Phone: 610-687-8900   **Fax:** 610-687-3688
Web: www.pvresource.com

PRODUCTS/OPERATIONS

2008 Sales

	$ mil.	% of total
Natural gas midstream		
Residue gas	452.5	51
Natural gas liquids	229.8	26
Condensate	26.0	3
Gathering & transportation fees	11.7	1
Coal royalties	122.8	14
Coal services	7.4	1
Other	31.4	4
Total	**881.6**	**100**

COMPETITORS

Alliance Resource	Massey Energy
Arch Coal	Peabody Energy
Bridgeline	Westmoreland Coal
CONSOL Energy	

HISTORICAL FINANCIALS

Company Type: Public

Income Statement

FYE: December 31

	REVENUE ($ mil.)	NET INCOME ($ mil.)	NET PROFIT MARGIN	EMPLOYEES
12/08	881.6	104.5	11.9%	0
12/07	549.4	44.2	8.0%	0
12/06	517.9	65.6	12.7%	0
12/05	446.3	51.2	11.5%	0
12/04	75.6	34.3	45.4%	32
Annual Growth	**84.8%**	**32.1%**	**—**	**—**

2008 Year-End Financials

Debt ratio: —
Return on equity: —
Cash ($ mil.): 9.5
Current ratio: 1.31
Long-term debt ($ mil.): 568.1
No. of shares (mil.): 51.8

Dividends
Yield: 16.0%
Payout: 109.0%
Market value ($ mil.): 589.0
R&D as % of sales: —
Advertising as % of sales: —

Stock History

NYSE: PVR

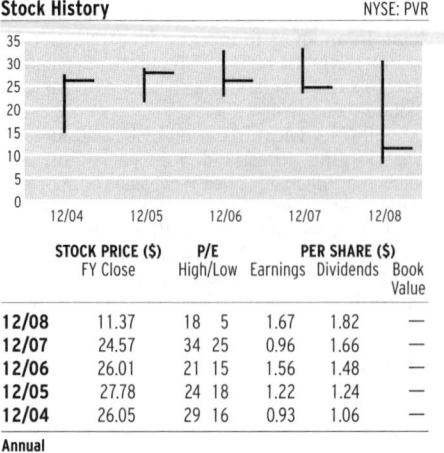

	STOCK PRICE ($) FY Close	P/E High/Low		PER SHARE ($) Earnings	Dividends	Book Value
12/08	11.37	18	5	1.67	1.82	—
12/07	24.57	34	25	0.96	1.66	—
12/06	26.01	21	15	1.56	1.48	—
12/05	27.78	24	18	1.22	1.24	—
12/04	26.05	29	16	0.93	1.06	—
Annual Growth	(18.7%)	—	—	15.8%	14.5%	—

Pennichuck Corporation

How much water would Pennichuck pump if Pennichuck could pump water? Well, Pennichuck does pump water, to about 33,200 customers (about 120,000 people) in New Hampshire and Massachusetts. Its water utility subsidiaries — Pennichuck Water Works, Pennichuck East Utility, and Pittsfield Aqueduct — distribute water in about 28 communities, including the city of Nashua. Most of the company's water comes from a system of ponds. Nonregulated subsidiary The Southwood Corporation develops and sells real estate, and Pennichuck Water Service offers contract maintenance, testing, and billing services. The City of Nashua is trying to acquire Pennichuck Water Works by eminent domain.

Nashua originally sought to take over all three of Pennichuck's utility units after Aqua America (formerly Philadelphia Suburban) agreed to acquire Pennichuck in 2002. The deal was terminated after Nashua residents voted in 2003 to pursue a municipal takeover of the utilities in order to keep them from being acquired by an out-of-state entity.

Pennichuck opposed Nashua's eminent domain petition, which went before the New Hampshire Public Utilities Commission. In 2004 the commission ruled that Nashua could not take over Pennichuck East Utility or Pittsfield Aqueduct Company, which do not serve the city. In 2008 the commission ruled that Nashua could acquire Pennichuck Water Works, the company's largest unit, for $203 million. Pennichuck protested and announced that it was willing to take the dispute to the New Hampshire Supreme Court.

EXECUTIVES

Chairman: John R. Kreick, age 64
President, CEO, and Director: Duane C. Montopoli, age 60, $343,838 total compensation
EVP; President, Pennichuck Water Service: Stephen J. Densberger, age 58
SVP Finance, CFO, and Treasurer: Thomas C. (Tom) Leonard, age 54, $153,010 total compensation
VP Engineering; President, Pennichuck Water Works and other Water Utilities; SVP Operations and Chief Engineer, Pennichuck Water Works, VP and Director, Pennichuck Water Service Corporation, Pennichuck East Utility, and Pittsfield Aqueduct Company: Donald L. Ware, age 52, $233,501 total compensation
VP Administration and Regulatory Affairs, Pennichuck Corporation, Pennichuck Water Works, Pennichuck East Utility, and Pittsfield Aqueduct Company; Director, Pennichuck East Utility and Pittsfield Aqueduct Company; VP Administration and Director, Pennichuck Water Service Corporation: Bonalyn J. Hartley, age 64, $201,312 total compensation
VP Sales and Service, Pennichuck Water Service: Bernard (Bernie) Rousseau
General Counsel and Corporate Secretary; President, The Southwood Corporation: Roland E. Olivier, age 63
Office and Human Resources Manager: Pamela Gorman
Auditors: Beard Miller Company LLP

LOCATIONS

HQ: Pennichuck Corporation
25 Manchester St., Merrimack, NH 03054
Phone: 603-882-5191   **Fax:** 603-882-4125
Web: www.pennichuck.com

PRODUCTS/OPERATIONS

2008 Sales

	$ mil.	% of total
Water utility	28.3	92
Water management & other	2.7	8
Total	**31.0**	**100**

Selected Subsidiaries

Pennichuck East Utility, Inc. (water utility)
Pennichuck Water Service Corporation (contract operations)
Pennichuck Water Works, Inc. (water utility)
Pittsfield Aqueduct Company, Inc. (water utility)
The Southwood Corporation (real estate development)

COMPETITORS

American Water
Aqua America
Aquarion
Connecticut Water Service
Middlesex Water
United Water Inc.

HISTORICAL FINANCIALS

Company Type: Public

Income Statement

FYE: December 31

	REVENUE ($ mil.)	NET INCOME ($ mil.)	NET PROFIT MARGIN	EMPLOYEES
12/08	31.0	4.7	15.2%	102
12/07	29.5	3.6	12.2%	98
12/06	24.5	0.6	2.4%	101
12/05	23.8	0.5	2.1%	95
12/04	23.0	1.8	7.8%	88
Annual Growth	7.7%	27.1%	—	3.8%

2008 Year-End Financials

Debt ratio: 124.7%
Return on equity: 10.1%
Cash ($ mil.): 0.1
Current ratio: 0.82
Long-term debt ($ mil.): 59.6
No. of shares (mil.): 4.3

Dividends
Yield: 3.2%
Payout: 59.5%
Market value ($ mil.): 87.5
R&D as % of sales: —
Advertising as % of sales: —

Stock History

NASDAQ (GM): PNNW

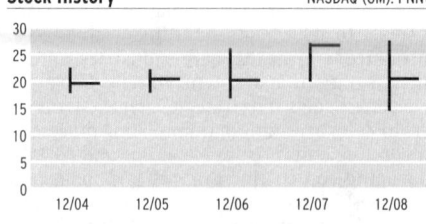

	STOCK PRICE ($) FY Close	P/E High/Low		PER SHARE ($) Earnings	Dividends	Book Value
12/08	20.53	25	13	1.11	0.66	11.21
12/07	26.71	32	24	0.84	0.66	10.69
12/06	20.23	185	121	0.14	0.66	10.46
12/05	20.45	169	139	0.13	0.66	10.71
12/04	19.58	39	32	0.57	0.65	7.08
Annual Growth	1.2%	—	—	18.1%	0.4%	12.2%

People's United Financial

People who need People's need banking and related financial services. People's United Financial is the holding company for People's United Bank (formerly People's Bank). Founded in 1842, the bank has more than 300 locations (including traditional branches, supermarket branches, commercial banking offices, investment and brokerage offices, and equipment leasing offices) in New England and New York. In addition to deposit and trust services, the bank originates commercial real estate loans (more than a third of its portfolio), commercial and industrial loans, residential mortgages, and consumer loans. The company acquired multibank holding company Chittenden Corporation in early 2008.

The deal expanded People's United Financial's reach beyond Connecticut and New York into other states. Chittenden's six banking divisions — Chittenden Trust (Vermont), Flagship Bank and Trust (Massachusetts), Maine Bank & Trust, Merrill Merchants Bank (Maine), Ocean Bank (New Hampshire), and The Bank of Western Massachusetts — continue to operate under the same names as subsidiaries of People's United Bank.

Other divisions of People's United include insurance brokerage R.C. Knox and Company, People's Securities (brokerage and investment services), and People's Capital and Leasing.

People's United Financial demutualized and converted to a stock holding company in 2007.

EXECUTIVES

Chairman: George P. Carter, age 72
President, CEO, and Director: Philip R. Sherringham, age 56, $5,628,871 total compensation
SEVP Commercial Banking; EVP Commercial Banking, People's United Bank: Brian F. Dreyer, age 62, $3,072,135 total compensation
SEVP and CFO: Paul D. Burner, age 56, $730,942 total compensation
SEVP Retail and Small Business Banking; EVP Marketing and Regional Banking, People's United Bank: Robert R. (Bob) D'Amore, age 56, $3,298,831 total compensation
SEVP Wealth Management: Louise T. Sandberg, age 57
SEVP and Chief Administrative Officer, People's United Bank: John P. (Jack) Barnes, age 53
EVP Organizational Effectiveness, People's United Bank: Henry R. (Hank) Mandel, age 64, $2,183,551 total compensation
EVP and General Counsel, People's United Bank and People's United Financial: Robert E. Trautmann, age 55
EVP and Chief Credit Officer, People's United Bank: David A. Bodor, age 62
SVP and CTO: David S. Marsh
SVP and CIO: Lee C. Powlus
SVP and Chief Investment Officer: Matthew C. O'Reilly
SVP Human Resources: Maria A. Stolfi
SVP Investor Relations and Mergers and Acquisitions: Jared D. Shaw
First VP Corporate Communications: Valerie C. Carlson
Auditors: KPMG LLP

LOCATIONS

HQ: People's United Financial, Inc.
850 Main St., Bridgeport, CT 06604
Phone: 203-338-7171   **Fax:** 203-338-2310
Web: www.peoples.com

PRODUCTS/OPERATIONS

2008 Sales

	% of total
Interest & dividends	
Loans	
Commercial real estate	25
Commercial	19
Residential mortgage	16
Consumer	9
Securities & short-term investments	7
Noninterest	
Bank service charges	10
Wealth management	7
Merchant services	2
Other	5
Total	**100**

COMPETITORS

Bank of America
Bar Harbor Bankshares
Citizens Financial Group
Community Bancorp (VT)
Fairfield County Bank
First Litchfield Financial
Liberty Bank
Merchants Bancshares
Naugatuck Valley Financial
New England Bancshares
NewAlliance Bancshares
Patriot National Bancorp
PSB Holdings, Inc.
Rivergreen Bank
Rockville Financial
SI Financial
Southern Connecticut Bancorp
Sovereign Bank
TD Bank USA
Union Bankshares
Washington Trust Bancorp
Webster Financial

HISTORICAL FINANCIALS

Company Type: Public

Income Statement

FYE: December 31

	ASSETS ($ mil.)	NET INCOME ($ mil.)	INCOME AS % OF ASSETS	EMPLOYEES
12/08	20,167.7	139.5	0.7%	4,754
12/07	13,554.8	150.7	1.1%	2,856
12/06	10,686.9	124.0	1.2%	2,861
12/05	10,932.5	137.1	1.3%	2,655
12/04	10,717.9	199.7	1.9%	2,689
Annual Growth	**17.1%**	**(8.6%)**	**—**	**15.3%**

2008 Year-End Financials

Equity as % of assets: —
Return on assets: 0.8%
Return on equity: —
Long-term debt ($ mil.): 195.6
No. of shares (mil.): 348.3
Market value ($ mil.): 6,209.4
Dividends
  Yield: 3.3%
  Payout: 138.1%
Sales ($ mil.): 940.0
R&D as % of sales: —
Advertising as % of sales: —

Stock History

NASDAQ (GS): PBCT

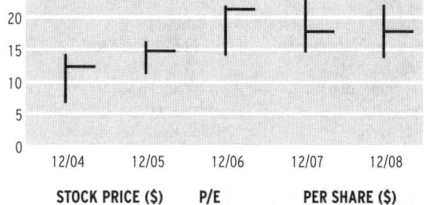

	STOCK PRICE ($) FY Close	P/E High/Low	PER SHARE ($) Earnings	Dividends	Book Value
12/08	17.83	52 33	0.42	0.58	14.86
12/07	17.80	44 28	0.52	0.52	12.76
12/06	21.25	52 34	0.41	0.46	3.85
12/05	14.79	35 25	0.46	0.41	3.70
12/04	12.35	21 10	0.68	0.36	3.45
Annual Growth	**9.6%**	**— —**	**(11.3%)**	**12.7%**	**44.1%**

Perficient, Inc.

Perficient is proficient in helping its customers use Internet-based technologies to their advantage. The IT consulting firm's services include software development, systems integration, consulting, and support. The company specializes in developing middleware applications that are used to integrate and modernize legacy computer hardware and software. Perficient integrates and supports applications from vendors including IBM, EMC, Microsoft, Oracle, Software AG, and TIBCO Software. Its customers have included Anheuser-Busch, AT&T Mobility, and Wachovia.

The company primarily serves customers in the US, though it does some business in Europe. Perficient has traditionally been an aggressive acquirer — it purchased 12 consulting firms between 2004 and 2007 — but a flagging economy led the company to suspend that strategy.

Perficient's expertise encompasses enterprise portals, content management systems, CRM applications, business process integration, service oriented architectures, business intelligence, e-commerce, wireless communication, and custom applications. Looking to expand its revenue opportunities, the company launched industry-focused practices aimed at the health care and communications sectors in 2008. Perficient has identified consumer product goods, energy, financial services, and manufacturing as other sectors where it holds substantial expertise.

EXECUTIVES

Chairman: John T. (Jack) McDonald, age 46, $1,813,997 total compensation
President and CEO: Jeffrey S. (Jeff) Davis, age 45, $1,572,802 total compensation
CFO, Treasurer, and Secretary: Paul E. Martin, age 49, $579,677 total compensation
VP Finance and Administration and Controller: Richard T. (Dick) Kalbfleish, age 54, $213,241 total compensation
VP Client Development: Timothy J. (Tim) Thompson, age 49, $408,823 total compensation
VP Corporate Operations: Kathy Henely
VP Field Operations: John Jenkins
VP Field Operations: Thomas (Tom) Pash
VP Field Operations: Chris Gianattasio
Human Resources Manager: Tracy Robinson
Auditors: BDO Seidman, LLP

LOCATIONS

HQ: Perficient, Inc.
520 Maryville Centre Dr., Ste. 400
St. Louis, MO 63141
Phone: 314-529-3600   **Fax:** 314-529-3640
Web: www.perficient.com

PRODUCTS/OPERATIONS

2008 Sales

	$ mil.	% of total
Services	207.5	90
Software & hardware revenues	10.7	5
Reimbursable expenses	13.3	5
Total	**231.5**	**100**

COMPETITORS

Accenture
BearingPoint
CIBER
Cognizant Tech Solutions
Deloitte LLP
HP Enterprise Services
Infosys
Sapient
Wipro

HISTORICAL FINANCIALS

Company Type: Public

Income Statement

FYE: December 31

	REVENUE ($ mil.)	NET INCOME ($ mil.)	NET PROFIT MARGIN	EMPLOYEES
12/08	231.5	10.0	4.3%	1,186
12/07	218.1	16.2	7.4%	1,427
12/06	160.9	9.6	6.0%	972
12/05	97.0	7.2	7.4%	580
12/04	58.8	3.9	6.6%	424
Annual Growth	**40.9%**	**26.5%**	**—**	**29.3%**

2008 Year-End Financials

Debt ratio: —
Return on equity: 5.9%
Cash ($ mil.): 22.9
Current ratio: 3.98
Long-term debt ($ mil.): —
No. of shares (mil.): 30.7
Dividends
  Yield: 0.0%
  Payout: —
Market value ($ mil.): 146.6
R&D as % of sales: —
Advertising as % of sales: —

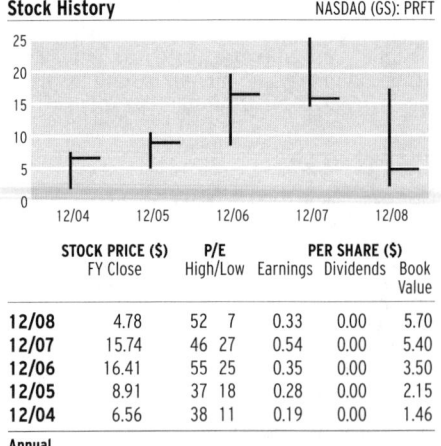

	STOCK PRICE ($) FY Close	P/E High/Low		PER SHARE ($) Earnings	Dividends	Book Value
12/08	4.78	52	7	0.33	0.00	5.70
12/07	15.74	46	27	0.54	0.00	5.40
12/06	16.41	55	25	0.35	0.00	3.50
12/05	8.91	37	18	0.28	0.00	2.15
12/04	6.56	38	11	0.19	0.00	1.46
Annual Growth	(7.6%)	—	—	14.8%	—	40.7%

PetMed Express

Convenience is king to PetMed Express, which bills itself as America's largest pet pharmacy. Through 1-800-PetMeds and 1800petmeds.com, as well as a catalog with hundreds of items, PetMed Express offers prescription and non-prescription medicines for your calico, collie, or colt. Founded in 1996, the company purchases its products at wholesale prices and ships directly to customers. Non-prescription items, such as flea and tick medications and health and nutritional supplements, account for about two-thirds of PetMed's total sales. The company makes the majority of its sales via its Web site. It also offers pet health information on a separate Web site, PetHealth101.com, which it began sponsoring in 2006.

The growing popularity of e-commerce and an increase in pet-related spending have helped to propel PetMed's sales, which have more than doubled since 2005. More than 800,000 new customers did business with the online pet pharmacy in fiscal 2009 vs. an increase of 710,000 new customers in 2008.

While most of the company's customers are individuals, PetMed Express also wholesales non-prescription medications to businesses, including pet stores, groomers, and other US retailers. (In fiscal 2009 less than 1% of the sales were made to wholesale customers.)

EXECUTIVES

Chairman and CFO: Bruce S. Rosenbloom, age 40, $365,431 total compensation
President, CEO, and Director: Menderes Akdag, age 48, $978,081 total compensation
General Counsel and Corporate Secretary: Alison Berges
Auditors: McGladrey & Pullen, LLP

LOCATIONS

HQ: PetMed Express, Inc.
1441 SW 29th Ave., Pompano Beach, FL 33069
Phone: 954-979-5995 **Fax:** 954-971-0544
Web: www.1800petmeds.com

PRODUCTS/OPERATIONS

2009 Sales

	% of total
Non-prescription medications	68
Prescription medications	31
Shipping, handling & other	1
Total	**100**

Selected Products

Non-prescription medications
  Flea & tick control
  Bone & joint care
  Hygiene
  Nutritional supplements
  Vitamins
Prescription medications
  Arthritis medications
  Heartworm preventatives
  Thyroid medications

COMPETITORS

Drs. Foster & Smith	PETCO
drugstore.com	PetSmart
KV Vet	Professional Veterinary
Lambriar Animal Health	Product
Medical Management	United Pharmacal
International	VCA Antech
Pet Supermarket	Virbac Corporation
Pet Valu	Walgreen
PetCareRx	Wal-Mart

HISTORICAL FINANCIALS

Company Type: Public

Income Statement
FYE: March 31

	REVENUE ($ mil.)	NET INCOME ($ mil.)	NET PROFIT MARGIN	EMPLOYEES
3/09	219.4	23.0	10.5%	248
3/08	188.3	20.0	10.6%	256
3/07	162.2	14.4	8.9%	216
3/06	137.6	12.1	8.8%	213
3/05	108.4	8.0	7.4%	180
Annual Growth	19.3%	30.2%	—	8.3%

2009 Year-End Financials

Debt ratio: —
Return on equity: 32.4%
Cash ($ mil.): 30.1
Current ratio: 8.81
Long-term debt ($ mil.): —
No. of shares (mil.): 22.8
Dividends
  Yield: 0.0%
  Payout: —
Market value ($ mil.): 376.4
R&D as % of sales: —
Advertising as % of sales: —

	STOCK PRICE ($) FY Close	P/E High/Low		PER SHARE ($) Earnings	Dividends	Book Value
3/09	16.48	19	11	0.98	0.00	3.28
3/08	11.09	19	13	0.82	0.00	2.93
3/07	11.85	30	16	0.60	0.00	2.36
3/06	17.77	40	13	0.50	0.00	1.65
3/05	7.41	37	12	0.34	0.00	1.06
Annual Growth	22.1%	—	—	30.3%	—	32.6%

Petroleum Development

The hills are alive with opportunity for Petroleum Development, which produces natural gas that it finds in the Rocky Mountains and the Appalachian Basin; the independent also has operations in the Michigan Basin. The company owns interests in 4,354 wells and in 2007 reported net proved reserves of 686 billion cu. ft. of natural gas equivalent. Petroleum Development also drills and operates wells for its partners, and often sets up public limited partnerships to fund its well-drilling program. Subsidiary Riley Natural Gas markets natural gas for the company and others in Appalachia.

Petroleum Development began in 1969 with a focus on Appalachian Basin operations in Ohio, Pennsylvania, Tennessee, and West Virginia. The company expanded its geographic scope in 1997 to include Michigan, and in 1999, the Rocky Mountains.

The company's strategy is to grow reserves, production, net income, and cash flow by maintaining an active drilling program that focuses on low-risk development of company-owned oil and natural gas reserves, limited exploratory drilling, and the purchase of producing properties with significant development potential.

In 2006 it acquired energy company Unioil, which had operations in Colorado and Wyoming, for about $18 million.

In 2007 the company acquired assets from EXCO Resources in the Wattenberg Field area of the DJ Basin, Colorado, for $132 million.

EXECUTIVES

Chairman, President, and CEO:
Richard W. (Rick) McCullough, age 58,
$1,453,929 total compensation
CFO: Gysle R. Shellum, $54,922 total compensation
SVP Exploration and Production:
Barton R. (Bart) Brookman,
$857,576 total compensation
General Counsel and Secretary:
Daniel W. (Dan) Amidon, age 50,
$678,631 total compensation
Chief Accounting Officer: R. Scott Meyers, age 34
Director Information Technology: Karen Griffin
Director Human Resources: John A. DeLawder
VP Special Projects: Ersel E. Morgan Jr.
VP Finance and Treasurer: Peter G. Schreck, age 42
VP Operations: Scott J. Reasoner, age 45
VP Natural Gas and Oil Marketing: Tina R. Smith
VP Acquisitions and Divestures: Dewey W. Gerdom
Manager Investor Relations: Marti Dowling
Auditors: PricewaterhouseCoopers LLP

LOCATIONS

HQ: Petroleum Development Corporation
120 Genesis Blvd., Bridgeport, WV 26330
Phone: 304-842-3597 **Fax:** 304-842-0913
Web: www.petd.com

PRODUCTS/OPERATIONS

2008 Sales

	$ mil.	% of total
Oil & gas	449.7	74
Gas marketing	140.3	23
Well operations & pipelines	11.5	2
Oil & gas well drilling	7.6	1
Other	0.3	—
Total	**609.4**	**100**

COMPETITORS

Belden & Blake
Cabot Oil & Gas
EQT Corporation
Penn Virginia
Quicksilver Resources
Range Resources

HISTORICAL FINANCIALS

Company Type: Public

Income Statement			FYE: December 31
	REVENUE ($ mil.)	NET INCOME ($ mil.)	NET PROFIT MARGIN	EMPLOYEES
12/08	609.4	113.3	18.6%	317
12/07	305.2	33.2	10.9%	256
12/06	286.5	237.8	83.0%	189
12/05	343.1	41.5	12.1%	150
12/04	290.7	34.1	11.7%	120
Annual Growth	20.3%	35.0%	—	27.5%

2008 Year-End Financials

Debt ratio: 77.2%
Return on equity: 25.0%
Cash ($ mil.): 51.0
Current ratio: 1.14
Long-term debt ($ mil.): 394.9
No. of shares (mil.): 19.2

Dividends
 Yield: —
 Payout: —
Market value ($ mil.): 462.7
R&D as % of sales: —
Advertising as % of sales: —

Stock History

NASDAQ (GS): PETD

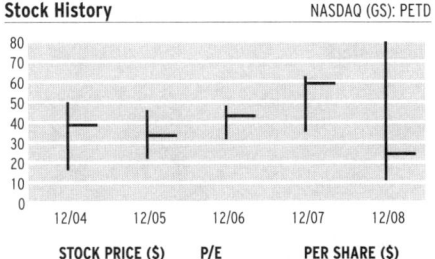

	STOCK PRICE ($) FY Close	P/E High/Low		PER SHARE ($) Earnings	Dividends	Book Value
12/08	24.07	10	2	7.63	—	26.61
12/07	59.13	28	16	2.24	—	20.57
12/06	43.05	3	2	15.11	—	18.73
12/05	33.34	18	9	2.52	—	9.79
12/04	38.57	24	8	2.05	—	8.57
Annual Growth	(11.1%)	—	—	38.9%	—	32.8%

Phase Forward Incorporated

There are many phases in clinical testing, and Phase Forward wants to be one of them. The company provides software that electronically captures data (EDC), manages clinical data (CDM), and automates adverse event reporting (AER). Customers for its products include pharmaceutical and biotechnology companies, medical device makers, academic institutions, and clinical research organizations. With a customer base of nearly 300 companies — including Eli Lilly, GlaxoSmithKline, and Genzyme — Phase Forward boasts that its software has been used in more than 10,000 different clinical trials.

In August 2009 the company acquired the Interactive Voice and Web Response Services (IVRS/IWRS) business of Covance for $10 million in cash. The companies also entered into a marketing agreement to provide Phase Forward's InForm and Clarix applications to Covance clients.

Previously in July 2009 the company purchased Maaguzi LLC, a provider of Web-based electronic patient reported outcomes (ePRO) for $11 million in cash. The deal helped Phase Forward expand its clinical research products as well as entering the ePRO and observational studies markets.

Earlier in 2009 the company purchased Waban Software, a provider of technology for the automation and compliance of clinical data analysis and reporting.

EXECUTIVES

Chairman, President, and CEO: Robert K. (Bob) Weiler, age 59, $2,217,147 total compensation
SVP, General Counsel, and Secretary: D. Ari Buchler, age 45, $796,142 total compensation
SVP, CFO, Chief Accounting Officer, and Treasurer: Christopher (Chris) Menard
SVP Worldwide Sales: Stephen J. (Steve) Powell, age 51, $1,181,115 total compensation
SVP: Steven J. (Steve) Rosenberg, age 54, $1,047,155 total compensation
SVP Human Resources and Administration: Russell J. (Russ) Campanello, age 53
CTO: Tim Rochford
Chief Privacy Officer: Michael P. Owings, age 54
VP Corporate Development and Marketing: Martin A. Young, age 49
President, Lincoln Technologies: Channing H. (Chan) Russell, age 62
Auditors: Ernst & Young LLP

LOCATIONS

HQ: Phase Forward Incorporated
880 Winter St., Waltham, MA 02451
Phone: 781-890-7878   **Fax:** 781-890-4848
Web: www.phaseforward.com

2008 Sales

	$ mil.	% of total
US	94.6	56
UK	51.4	30
France	15.1	9
Asia/Pacific	9.1	5
Total	**170.2**	**100**

PRODUCTS/OPERATIONS

2008 Sales

	$ mil.	% of total
Services	117.5	69
Licensing	52.7	31
Total	**170.2**	**100**

Selected Software

Clinical data management (Clintrial)
Drug safety (Empirica Trace)
Electronic data capture (InForm)

COMPETITORS

DATATRAK International
DrugLogic
eResearchTechnology
etrials Worldwide
Kofax plc
Medidata Solutions
OmniComm
Oracle
Perceptive Informatics
Sparta Systems

HISTORICAL FINANCIALS

Company Type: Public

Income Statement			FYE: December 31
	REVENUE ($ mil.)	NET INCOME ($ mil.)	NET PROFIT MARGIN	EMPLOYEES
12/08	170.2	13.8	8.1%	718
12/07	134.3	29.2	21.7%	509
12/06	106.6	12.3	11.5%	450
12/05	87.1	3.3	3.8%	409
12/04	73.7	(7.1)	—	361
Annual Growth	23.3%	—	—	18.8%

2008 Year-End Financials

Debt ratio: 3.0%
Return on equity: 6.1%
Cash ($ mil.): 131.6
Current ratio: 2.01
Long-term debt ($ mil.): 7.2
No. of shares (mil.): 43.3

Dividends
 Yield: 0.0%
 Payout: —
Market value ($ mil.): 542.0
R&D as % of sales: —
Advertising as % of sales: —

Stock History

NASDAQ (GM): PFWD

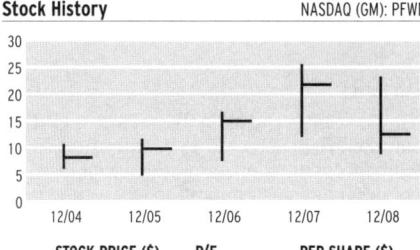

	STOCK PRICE ($) FY Close	P/E High/Low		PER SHARE ($) Earnings	Dividends	Book Value
12/08	12.52	72	28	0.32	0.00	5.49
12/07	21.75	35	17	0.72	0.00	5.00
12/06	14.98	47	22	0.35	0.00	2.03
12/05	9.75	114	50	0.10	0.00	1.54
12/04	8.17	—	—	(0.43)	0.00	1.37
Annual Growth	11.3%	—	—	—	—	41.5%

PHI, Inc.

Whirlybird wizard PHI transports people and equipment, mainly for oil and gas companies. One of the world's top commercial helicopter operators, PHI maintains a fleet of about 250 aircraft and provides contract transportation services across the US and in Africa. Its fleet is primarily made up of helicopters but also includes fixed-wing aircraft. The company is a leading provider of helicopter transport services in the Gulf of Mexico. In addition to its energy-related operations, PHI provides air transportation services to hospitals and other medical facilities and overhauls and maintains airframes, engines, and components. Chairman, president, and CEO Al Gonsoulin owns a controlling stake in PHI.

To reduce its dependence on business from the oil and gas industry, PHI has been expanding its air medical operations, which it provides in about 20 states. At the same time, the company is investing in its fleet by replacing older aircraft with newer ones. PHI's fleet consists of mainly Bell helicopters but also includes aircraft by Eurocopter and Sikorsky.

Combining its oil and gas business with its air medical operations, in 2009 PHI began offering

emergency medical air transportation to offshore oil and gas workers in the Gulf of Mexico.

It hasn't been all smooth sailing for PHI. Tragedy struck in January 2009 as a PHI oil and gas chopper crashed in a Louisiana swamp killing eight people. One person aboard survived and the accident has spawned multiple lawsuits. Investigation is ongoing but the National Transportation Safety Board has found some evidence that a bird collided with the helicopter before it crashed.

Hurricane Gustav and Hurricane Ike battered the Gulf of Mexico coast in September 2008 and cost PHI some $3.3 million in repair costs, evacuation of aircraft at affected bases, and relocation of operations. The hurricanes also caused flight hours and revenues to dip in PHI's oil and gas unit in Louisiana and Texas, as well as its Air Medical segment in Texas.

PHI continues to cooperate with the US Department of Justice's ongoing grand jury investigation launched in 2005 of potential antitrust violations by providers of helicopter transportation services in the Gulf of Mexico.

HISTORY

Robert Suggs and M. M. Bayon formed Petroleum Bell Helicopters in 1949 with three small Bell helicopters. Pioneering the use of helicopters in oil and gas exploration, the young firm served an oil exploration firm working in hard-to-reach areas of the Louisiana swamps. Previously, a 15-man team had to wade through waist-high swamps for more than a day to perform one seismic test. PHI enabled several field tests to be conducted in one day, with much less discomfort to the surveyors.

As its fleet expanded, the company dropped the "Bell" from its name in the 1950s. In 1967 Petroleum Helicopters, Inc. (PHI) stepped out internationally with operations in Angola and Saudi Arabia. It branched into aeromedical services in 1981, providing helicopter ambulance and other transport services for hospitals and medical units.

Suggs died in 1989, and his wife, Carroll, was appointed chairman, president, and CEO the next year. After an acrimonious and highly public family feud with her late husband's children from a previous marriage, Carroll Suggs was awarded half the estate. She went on to control the company.

The downturn in the Gulf of Mexico oil and gas markets hurt revenues in the early 1990s, prompting PHI to diversify. In 1994 the firm was chosen to patrol the Haiti-Dominican Republic border during the Haiti embargo; it was the first appointment of a civilian company for such a mission. The next year PHI added five new aircraft to its aeromedical services segment, its fastest-growing unit. Also in 1995 it acquired a 49% interest in Irish Helicopters Limited, of Dublin.

PHI's pilots voted against joining a union in 1997. Also that year the firm continued to diversify, fighting forest fires for the US Forestry Service and creating Acadian Composites to repair and overhaul helicopter composite panels (for PHI aircraft and third parties). The company ramped up its medical transportation service with the 1997 acquisition of Arizona-based Samaritan AirEvac, an aeromedical unit with six aircraft, from Banner Health.

A depressed oil market and bad weather suppressed demand for PHI's helicopters in the Gulf in 1999, but the company looked forward to bouncing back with higher oil prices.

In 2000 Gulf Coast engineering and construction industry veteran Lance Bospflug became PHI president, taking the reins from Suggs. Also that year, the company's pilots unionized. PHI narrowly averted a pilot strike the following year and reached an agreement with pilots that would allow them to voluntarily pay union dues for a three-year period after which dues would become mandatory.

Also in 2001, one of the company's helicopters crashed off the Texas coast. Much of the aircraft was recovered, but the pilot was not found. Bospflug was named CEO in 2001, replacing Suggs, who remained as chairman. Also that year, Suggs sold her 52% stake in the company to oil industry veteran Al Gonsoulin. Suggs then retired from the company, and Gonsoulin became chairman. PHI also moved its headquarters from Metairie, Louisiana, to Lafayette, Louisiana.

Gonsoulin took over as president and CEO in 2004 after Bospflug stepped down. Hurricanes Katrina and Rita damaged several of the company's facilities along the Gulf of Mexico in 2005. All but one of the PHI bases were back in service by the end of the year, however.

The company officially changed its name from Petroleum Helicopters, Inc., to PHI, Inc., in 2006 in an effort to better align its corporate identity with its mix of business activities.

EXECUTIVES

Chairman and CEO: Al A. Gonsoulin, age 66, $681,179 total compensation
COO and Director: Lance F. Bospflug, age 54
CFO and Secretary: Michael J. McCann, age 61, $299,941 total compensation
Chief Administrative Officer and Director Human Resources: Richard A. Rovinelli, age 61, $266,741 total compensation
Chief Pilot: Michael C. (Mike) Hurst
Director Operations: Carlin N. Craig
Director, PHI Air Medical Group: Howard Ragsdale
Director Material: Robert D. DesRosiers
Director Training: Jerry Loviglio
Director Safety, Environmental, and Auditing: Robert P. Bouillion
Director Corporate Business Development: William P. (Pete) Sorenson, age 59, $253,094 total compensation
Director Engine Overhaul: Mike Block
Director Maintenance: Glendon R. (Glen) Cornett
Regional Director, PHI Air Medical Group: David Motzkin
Auditors: Deloitte & Touche LLP

LOCATIONS

HQ: PHI, Inc.
2001 SE Evangeline Thruway, Lafayette, LA 70508
Phone: 337-235-2452   **Fax:** 337-232-6537
Web: www.phihelico.com

2008 Sales

	$ mil.	% of total
US	489.6	95
International	19.9	4
Other	5.0	1
Total	**514.5**	**100**

PRODUCTS/OPERATIONS

2008 Sales

	$ mil.	% of total
Oil & gas	324.2	63
Air medical	174.7	34
Technical services	10.6	2
Other	5.0	1
Total	**514.5**	**100**

COMPETITORS

Air Methods
Bristow Group Inc
CHC Helicopter
Evergreen Holdings
SEACOR

HISTORICAL FINANCIALS

Company Type: Public

Income Statement

FYE: December 31

	REVENUE ($ mil.)	NET INCOME ($ mil.)	NET PROFIT MARGIN	EMPLOYEES
12/08	514.5	23.5	4.6%	2,382
12/07	446.4	28.2	6.3%	2,299
12/06	423.1	(0.7)	—	2,167
12/05	366.8	14.2	3.9%	2,175
12/04	294.3	4.0	1.4%	1,903
Annual Growth	**15.0%**	**55.7%**	**—**	**5.8%**

2008 Year-End Financials

Debt ratio: 44.9%
Return on equity: 5.3%
Cash ($ mil.): 1.2
Current ratio: 4.44
Long-term debt ($ mil.): 203.0
No. of shares (mil.): 15.3
Dividends
Yield: 0.0%
Payout: —
Market value ($ mil.): 214.5
R&D as % of sales: —
Advertising as % of sales: —

Stock History

NASDAQ (GM): PHIIK

	STOCK PRICE ($) FY Close	P/E High/Low		PER SHARE ($) Earnings	Dividends	Book Value
12/08	14.01	9	8	1.54	0.00	29.55

Pinnacle Financial Partners

Pinnacle Financial Partners wants to be at the top of community banking in central Tennessee. It's the holding company for Pinnacle National Bank, which primarily targets small businesses through more than 30 branches, largely in the Nashville area. The bank's deposit products include checking, money market, and savings accounts and CDs. Business loans, including commercial mortgage and construction loans, make up about 75% of its portfolio, which also includes residential real estate and consumer loans. The company provides investment and trust services through Pinnacle Asset Management, and insurance through Miller and Loughry Insurance Services.

Pinnacle Financial Partners acquired Cavalry Bank in 2006. The following year it bought Mid-America Bancshares, the holding company for Nashville-area banks PrimeTrust Bank and Bank of the South.

Both purchases significantly increased the company's presence in growing Tennessee counties. The three banks (and their 15 branches) have since been rebranded as Pinnacle National banks. The company has also been growing through the opening of de novo branches, particularly in the Knoxville area.

With those bank purchases, though, Pinnacle Financial Partners also gained some nonperforming loans. It profits fell in early 2009 and banking regulators put pressure on the company to strengthen its capital position.

EXECUTIVES

Chairman: Robert A. (Rob) McCabe Jr., age 58, $1,109,126 total compensation
Vice Chairman: Ed C. Loughry Jr., age 66
President and CEO and Director; President and CEO, Pinnacle Bank: M. Terry Turner, age 53, $1,193,088 total compensation
EVP and CFO: Harold R. Carpenter Jr., age 50, $499,386 total compensation
EVP and Chief Administrative Officer: Hugh M. Queener, age 53, $582,966 total compensation
EVP and Manager Client Services: Joanne B. Jackson, age 52
EVP and Senior Credit Officer: Charles B. (Charlie) McMahan, age 62, $345,721 total compensation
EVP and Senior Lending Officer: J. Edward (Ed) White, age 56
Chief People Officer: Rachel West
SVP and Manager Client Services, Rutherford/Bedford: Ron Carter
SVP and Credit Officer: G. Glenn Layne
SVP and Manager Client Advisory Group, Rutherford County: R. Dale Floyd
SVP and Manager Client Services: Larry Whisenant
Chairman and Senior Credit Officer, Pinnacle Knoxville: Harvey White
Auditors: KPMG LLP

LOCATIONS

HQ: Pinnacle Financial Partners, Inc.
211 Commerce St., Ste. 300, Nashville, TN 37201
Phone: 615-744-3700   **Fax:** 615-744-3861
Web: www.mypinnacle.com

PRODUCTS/OPERATIONS

2008 Sales

	% of total
Interest	
Loans	73
Securities	12
Federal funds sold & other	1
Noninterest	
Service charges on deposit accounts	4
Investment services	2
Gains on loans & loan participations sold	2
Insurance sales commissions	1
Trust fees	1
Other	4
Total	**100**

COMPETITORS

Bank of America
BB&T
Fifth Third
First Horizon
Regions Financial
SunTrust
U.S. Bancorp

HISTORICAL FINANCIALS
Company Type: Public

Income Statement   FYE: December 31

	ASSETS ($ mil.)	NET INCOME ($ mil.)	INCOME AS % OF ASSETS	EMPLOYEES
12/08	4,754.1	30.9	0.6%	729
12/07	3,794.2	23.0	0.6%	732
12/06	2,142.2	17.9	0.8%	438
12/05	1,016.8	8.1	0.8%	159
12/04	727.1	5.3	0.7%	126
Annual Growth	**59.9%**	**55.4%**	**—**	**55.1%**

2008 Year-End Financials

Equity as % of assets: 11.3%
Return on assets: 0.7%
Return on equity: 6.1%
Long-term debt ($ mil.): 299.4
No. of shares (mil.): 33.0
Market value ($ mil.): 982.4

Dividends
  Yield: 0.0%
  Payout: —
Sales ($ mil.): 148.9
R&D as % of sales: —
Advertising as % of sales: —

Stock History   NASDAQ (GS): PNFP

	STOCK PRICE ($) FY Close	P/E High/Low	PER SHARE ($) Earnings	Dividends	Book Value
12/08	29.81	29 15	1.27	0.00	19.03
12/07	25.42	25 16	1.34	0.00	14.16
12/06	33.18	32 21	1.18	0.00	7.77
12/05	24.98	31 24	0.85	0.00	1.92
12/04	22.62	41 19	0.61	0.00	1.76
Annual Growth	**7.1%**	**— —**	**20.1%**	**—**	**81.4%**

Pioneer Southwest Energy Partners

It may not be as hip as the Beatles' version, but Pioneer Southwest Energy Partners is hoping for *Spraberry Fields Forever*. In the Spraberry field (in the Permian Basin), Pioneer Southwest Energy Partners reported proved reserves in 2008 of 22.7 million barrels of oil equivalent and an average production of more than 4,810 barrels per day. The oil and gas exploration company's properties consist of non-operated working interests in 1,100 producing wells. The limited partnership was formed by exploration and production firm Pioneer Natural Resources in 2007 to own and acquire oil and gas properties in Texas and eight counties in southeastern New Mexico. Pioneer Natural Resources controls 68% of the company.

According to the Energy Information Administration the Spraberry field is the fifth-largest oil field in the US and the 15th-largest natural gas field. In 2009 it acquired assets in the Spraberry field from Pioneer Natural Resources for $171.2 million.

Following a 2008 IPO, Pioneer Southwest Energy Partners formed Pioneer Southwest Energy Partners USA LLC to own and operate its oil and gas properties in the Spraberry field. The primary strategy of Pioneer Southwest Energy Partners is to maintain quarterly cash distributions to its unitholders.

EXECUTIVES

Chairman and CEO: Scott D. Sheffield, age 56
President and COO: Timothy L. (Tim) Dove, age 52
EVP, CFO, Director and Treasurer: Richard P. (Rich) Dealy, age 43
EVP Business Development: William F. (Bill) Hannes, age 49
EVP Geoscience: Chris J. Cheatwood, age 48
EVP and General Counsel: Mark S. Berg, age 50
EVP and Director: Danny L. Kellum, age 54
VP and Chief Compliance Officer: Mark H. Kleinman, age 43
Secretary: Thomas J. Murphy
Investor Relations: Frank E. Hopkins
Corporate Communications: Susan A. Spratlen
Auditors: Ernst & Young LLP

LOCATIONS

HQ: Pioneer Southwest Energy Partners L.P.
5205 N. O'Connor Blvd., Ste. 200, Irving, TX 75039
Phone: 972-444-9001   **Fax:** 972-969-3516
Web: www.pioneersouthwest.com

PRODUCTS/OPERATIONS

2008 Sales

	% of total
Plains Marketing LP	62
TEPPCO Crude Oil	11
ONEOK Inc.	8
Other customers	19
Total	**100**

COMPETITORS

Anadarko Petroleum
Apache
Chesapeake Energy
Edge Petroleum
Newfield Exploration
Noble Energy
Southwestern Energy

HISTORICAL FINANCIALS
Company Type: Public

Income Statement   FYE: December 31

	REVENUE ($ mil.)	NET INCOME ($ mil.)	NET PROFIT MARGIN	EMPLOYEES
12/08	153.0	94.8	62.0%	1,800
12/07	104.6	61.7	59.0%	0
12/06	101.3	61.8	61.0%	—
12/05	90.3	55.2	61.1%	—
Annual Growth	**19.2%**	**19.8%**	**—**	**—**

2008 Year-End Financials

Debt ratio: —
Return on equity: —
Cash ($ mil.): 29.9
Current ratio: 8.00
Long-term debt ($ mil.): —
No. of shares (mil.): 30.0

Dividends
  Yield: 3.6%
  Payout: 24.8%
Market value ($ mil.): 411.1
R&D as % of sales: —
Advertising as % of sales: —

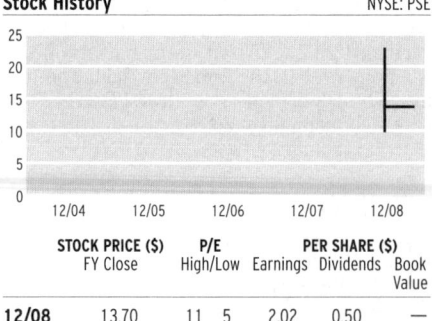
PMC-Sierra

For PMC-Sierra, success is all about networking. PMC's 350 communications and storage semiconductors and microprocessors make the connection for a broad marketplace — metro, access, fiber to the home, wireless infrastructure, storage, laser printers, and fiber access gateway equipment. OEM customers include Alcatel-Lucent, Cisco Systems, EMC, Fujitsu, Hewlett-Packard, and ZTE. PMC's switches, mappers, multiplexers, and other chips handle an alphabet soup of protocols — IP, PON, SONET, SDH, WDM SAS, SATA, SAN, and NAS. The fabless semiconductor company outsources production of its chips primarily to independent Asian foundries such as Chartered Semiconductor and Taiwan Semiconductor.

The majority of PMC's devices are sold to OEMs who in turn supply their equipment principally to communications network service providers and enterprises. Sales to the metro and access markets account for approximately 50% of revenue. Storage, enterprise, and customer premise sales make up the remaining 50%. PMC sells its products to end customers directly (either contract manufacturers selected by OEMs, or OEM customers) and through distributors and independent manufacturer representatives.

PMC has built a reputation for speed — both in the chips it designs and in its obsessive focus on helping its customers achieve tough time-to-market goals. Pushing the market's innovation curve, it has launched numerous industry product firsts. When telecommunications boomed, it was equally aggressive in acquiring smaller chip companies to achieve dominance in various sectors of the communications chip market. For example, PMC pocketed Passave in 2006, a fabless system-on-chip market force in developing technology for broadband fiber access systems.

PMC has typically tapped the profit margins and longer product life cycles of high-end chips that are critical to wide area and access networks. Consequently the company looks to profitably expand its overall business within these traditional service markets. Nevertheless, spurred by the benefits of its 2006 purchase of the storage semiconductor business of Avago Technologies, PMC has shifted markedly into the newer enterprise stor-

age systems marketplace. To support these goals, R&D resources are plowed into developing solutions for the business growth areas of its service provider customers, as well as into broadening its storage and enterprise product offerings. PMC tied up a multiyear joint development agreement in 2008 with IBM for RAID technology.

HISTORY

In 1984 James Diller, a veteran of Fairchild Semiconductor and National Semiconductor, started Sierra Semiconductor. At first the Silicon Valley company made custom analog chips; Diller switched course in the late 1980s toward chips used in PCs and peripherals. At the same time, Sierra sold off its fabrication plants and began outsourcing production to Asian silicon foundries. (Diller was an original board member of Chartered Semiconductor.)

Meanwhile, PMC (for Pacific Microelectronic Center) had been formed in 1984 as a chip design unit within the research arm of BCTel, British Columbia's telephone company. PMC remained small and often struggled throughout the 1980s. In 1991 it started making chips for ATM switching applications. The next year PMC approached Sierra for the funding that helped it spin off from BCTel.

In 1993 Diller recruited Robert Bailey, who had headed an AT&T chip division (later part of Agere, which was acquired in 2007 by LSI Corp.), to be president of PMC. During the mid-1990s, the growth of the Internet helped fuel demand for PMC's networking chips, while bitter competition in the PC chip business slowed Sierra's progress.

In 1996 Diller led Sierra through a tumultuous reinvention: Sierra scrapped its PC businesses in graphics and modem chips to focus on networking applications. The company laid off 300 workers and moved much of its operations 1,000 miles north, to Burnaby, British Columbia, home of the PMC networking operation.

The 1996 upheaval led to a $69 million restructuring charge (in part because Diller had insisted on generous severance packages for Sierra's laid-off employees). In 1997 the company was formally reborn as PMC-Sierra; Bailey became president and CEO, while Diller remained chairman.

PMC-Sierra went on a buying spree during the late 1990s, making a series of acquisitions to beef up the range and depth of its offerings. With industry competition intensifying — and its stock valuations soaring — PMC-Sierra began a series of major purchases in 1999 when it bought Abrizio ($435 million, switching fabrics).

In 2000 PMC-Sierra spent almost $4.5 billion to acquire companies, including AANetcom ($965 million, high-speed interconnect chips) and Quantum Effect Devices ($2.3 billion, embedded processors). That year Diller stepped down as chairman; Bailey succeeded him. (Diller remained vice chairman.)

In 2001 the company cut its workforce by 230 jobs — about 13% of its workforce at the time. Later that year, amid continuing bad news throughout the telecom industry, PMC-Sierra announced further layoffs of about 350 employees. Early in 2003 long-time company director Alexandre Balkanski succeeded Bailey as chairman; Bailey remained president and CEO. (Balkanski left the board in 2005 and Bailey became chairman again.)

In 2005 PMC-Sierra undertook a restructuring of operations that resulted in a 10% reduction in force, with about 90 employees losing their jobs.

In 2006 PMC-Sierra made its Avago acquisition for approximately $425 million in cash. Avago was the chip unit of Agilent Technologies, bought by the private equity firms of Kohlberg Kravis Roberts and Silver Lake Partners in late 2005. The combination added Avago's Tachyon line of Fibre Channel controller chips to PMC's portfolio. The former Avago unit was also developing multiple-protocol controllers supporting a variety of data interface formats for storage systems.

PMC-Sierra also purchased Passave, a developer of passive optical networking components for broadband communications to the home, in 2006.

In late 2007 Bob Bailey set plans to retire as president and CEO once a successor could be named. In April 2008 the company appointed Greg Lang, the former president and CEO of competitor Integrated Device Technology (IDT), as the new president and CEO of PMC-Sierra. Bailey remained chairman of the company following his retirement from management.

EXECUTIVES

Chairman: Robert L. (Bob) Bailey, age 52, $704,338 total compensation
Vice Chairman: James V. (Jim) Diller Sr., age 73
President, CEO, and Director: Gregory S. (Greg) Lang, age 45, $2,019,079 total compensation
VP and COO: Colin C. Harris, age 51, $641,005 total compensation
VP and CFO: Michael W. (Mike) Zellner, age 54, $683,178 total compensation
VP, Worldwide Sales: Robert M. (Rob) Liszt, age 51, $558,542 total compensation
VP and General Manager, Enterprise and Storage Division: Mark C. Stibitz, age 50, $530,596 total compensation
VP and Co-General Manager, Fiber to the Home: Ofer Bar-Or
VP and General Manager, Broadband Wireless Division: Thomas (Tom) Sun, age 47
VP and General Manager, Communication Products Division: Travis Karr, age 37
VP and General Manager Microprocessor Products: Ra'ed O. Elmurib, age 49
VP Corporate Strategy and Technology Office: O. Daryn Lau, age 44
VP Worldwide Human Resources: Lee Rhodes
VP, General Counsel, and Secretary: Alinka Flaminia, age 47
VP and Fellow, Research and Development: Brian Gerson
VP Marketing, Fiber to the Home: Raphael Sankar
VP Marketing Communications: David Climie
Auditors: Deloitte & Touche LLP

LOCATIONS

HQ: PMC-Sierra, Inc.
   3975 Freedom Cir., Santa Clara, CA 95054
Phone: 408-239-8000   **Fax:** 408-492-9192
Web: www.pmc-sierra.com

2008 Sales

	$ mil.	% of total
Asia/Pacific		
China	155.5	30
Japan	95.0	18
Taiwan	39.0	7
Singapore	28.9	6
Other countries	66.3	13
US	103.5	20
Europe & Middle East	27.1	5
Other regions	9.8	1
Total	**525.1**	**100**

PRODUCTS/OPERATIONS

Selected Product Applications

Local-Area Network (LAN)
  Network interface cards
  Switches/routers
Wide-Area Network (WAN)
  Remote-access equipment
    Access multiplexers/DSL access multiplexers
     (DSLAMs)
    Digital loop carriers
    Frame relay access devices
    Frame relay switches
    Internet access concentrators
    Voice switches
    Wireless base stations
  Transmission and switching equipment
    Add-drop multiplexers
    Digital cross-connects
    Routers
    Terminal multiplexers
    WAN core switches
    WAN edge switches

COMPETITORS

Applied Micro Circuits
Broadcom
Conexant Systems
Cypress Semiconductor
Emulex
Exar
EZchip
Freescale Semiconductor
IBM Microelectronics
Ikanos
Infineon Technologies
Infinera
Integrated Device Technology
Intel
LSI Corp.
Marvell Technology
Maxim Integrated Products
Mellanox
Metalink
Mindspeed
Teknovus
Texas Instruments
TranSwitch
Vitesse Semiconductor
Zarlink

HISTORICAL FINANCIALS

Company Type: Public

Income Statement

FYE: Last Sunday in December

	REVENUE ($ mil.)	NET INCOME ($ mil.)	NET PROFIT MARGIN	EMPLOYEES
12/08	525.1	133.9	25.5%	1,064
12/07	449.4	(49.1)	—	1,027
12/06	425.0	(99.9)	—	1,183
12/05	291.4	28.0	9.6%	875
12/04	297.4	51.7	17.4%	951
Annual Growth	15.3%	26.9%	—	2.8%

2008 Year-End Financials

Debt ratio: 9.0%
Return on equity: 19.7%
Cash ($ mil.): 97.8
Current ratio: 3.56
Long-term debt ($ mil.): 68.8
No. of shares (mil.): 227.5
Dividends
  Yield: 0.0%
  Payout: —
Market value ($ mil.): 1,105.6
R&D as % of sales: —
Advertising as % of sales: —

Stock History

NASDAQ (GS): PMCS

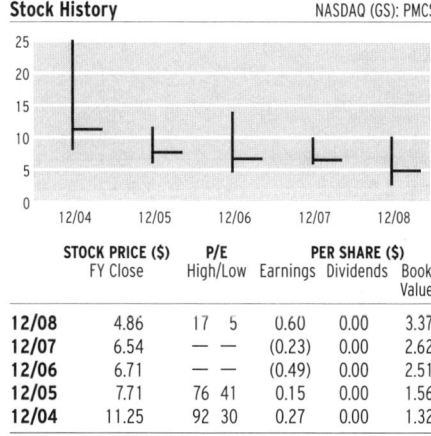

	STOCK PRICE ($) FY Close	P/E High/Low		PER SHARE ($) Earnings	Dividends	Book Value
12/08	4.86	17	5	0.60	0.00	3.37
12/07	6.54	—	—	(0.23)	0.00	2.62
12/06	6.71	—	—	(0.49)	0.00	2.51
12/05	7.71	76	41	0.15	0.00	1.56
12/04	11.25	92	30	0.27	0.00	1.32
Annual Growth	(18.9%)	—	—	22.1%	—	26.5%

PMFG, Inc.

PMFG (formerly Peerless Mfg.) is without peer when it comes to producing products that remove contaminants. The company's separation filtration systems are used to remove solid and liquid contaminants from natural gas and to remove saltwater aerosols from the air intakes of marine gas turbine and diesel engines. Customers include natural gas producers and shipbuilders. Products of PMFG's other business segment, environmental systems, include selective catalytic reduction (SCR) systems, which are used to convert nitrogen oxide produced by the burning of fossil fuels into nitrogen and water vapor. The company has sold some 700 SCR systems to power producers, construction companies, and refineries.

PMFG's business strategy is to seek out opportunities in high-growth international markets, use technological innovation to address a broader range of pollutants, expand its technical expertise and manufacturing processes, and seek strategic acquisitions.

In 2007 PMFG was awarded a contract valued at $14 million for the design and supply of Separation Equipment for multiple compressor stations along the East-West gas transmission pipeline project in India.

In 2008 the company bought Nitram Energy, the parent company of Burgess-Manning, Bos-Hatten, and Alco Products, for $63 million. The deal helped to double PMFG's revenues and broaden the company's range of products.

EXECUTIVES

Chairman: Sherrill Stone, age 73
President, CEO, and Director: Peter J. Burlage, age 45
VP and COO: Warren R. Hayslip, age 55
CFO: Henry G. (Hank) Schopfer III, age 62
VP and General Counsel: Melissa G. Beare
VP Manufacturing and Supply Chain Management:
  Charles G. (Chuck) Mogged Jr.
VP Pressure Products: Jon P. Segelhorst, age 39
VP Separation Systems and Asia/Pacific Operations:
  David Taylor, age 44

VP Environmental Systems: Sean P. McMenamin,
  age 44
Managing Director, Peerless Europe Limited:
  Barry Nesbit
Auditors: Grant Thornton LLP

LOCATIONS

HQ: PMFG, Inc.
  14651 N. Dallas Pkwy., Ste. 500, Dallas, TX 75254
Phone: 214-357-6181   **Fax:** 214-351-0194
Web: www.peerlessmfg.com

2009 Sales

	$ mil.	% of total
US	133.9	85
Other countries	24.1	15
Total	**158.0**	**100**

PRODUCTS/OPERATIONS

2009 Sales

	$ mil.	% of total
Separation filtration systems	123.3	78
Environmental systems	34.7	22
Total	**158.0**	**100**

COMPETITORS

CLARCOR
CUNO
Donaldson Company
ESCO Technologies
Met-Pro
Millipore
Pall Corporation
Siemens Water
  Technologies

HISTORICAL FINANCIALS

Company Type: Public

Income Statement

FYE: June 30

	REVENUE ($ mil.)	NET INCOME ($ mil.)	NET PROFIT MARGIN	EMPLOYEES
6/09	158.0	2.9	1.8%	418
6/08	140.5	8.4	6.0%	407
6/07	75.1	5.9	7.9%	210
6/06	63.4	0.4	0.6%	169
6/05	51.1	(0.6)	—	166
Annual Growth	32.6%	—	—	26.0%

2009 Year-End Financials

Debt ratio: 107.0%
Return on equity: 6.5%
Cash ($ mil.): 17.7
Current ratio: 1.85
Long-term debt ($ mil.): 49.2
No. of shares (mil.): 13.2
Dividends
  Yield: 0.0%
  Payout: —
Market value ($ mil.): 118.4
R&D as % of sales: —
Advertising as % of sales: —

Stock History

NASDAQ (GM): PMFG

	STOCK PRICE ($) FY Close	P/E High/Low		PER SHARE ($) Earnings	Dividends	Book Value
6/09	8.95	140	18	0.22	0.00	3.47
6/08	23.43	39	13	0.64	0.00	3.24
6/07	10.34	24	11	0.46	0.00	2.53
6/06	5.99	171	101	0.04	0.00	1.96
6/05	3.63	—	—	(0.05)	0.00	1.84
Annual Growth	25.3%	—	—	—	—	17.3%

Polycom, Inc.

Polycom can make a real production out of your next meeting. Its videoconferencing devices combine a camera, microphone, computer network connections, and external audio and video devices. Polycom's software enables users to manage a directory of conferencing locations and connect with them using ISDN and IP connections. It also provides audio-conferencing speakerphone systems. The company's services include consulting and integration. Polycom sells its products directly and through resellers, distributors, retailers, and communications services providers; channel partners include Ingram Micro, Tech Data, and Westcon Group. The company outsources the manufacturing of its systems, primarily to Celestica.

Polycom's video solutions segment accounted for more than half of its sales in 2008; the video solutions business was formed the previous year when the company combined its network systems and video communications segments. Polycom makes almost half of its sales outside of North America.

Early in 2007 Polycom acquired Destiny Conferencing, a developer of high-end teleconferencing systems utilizing Polycom technology, for approximately $48 million in cash. The company also acquired wireless telephony systems provider SpectraLink for $220 million in cash in 2007. The SpectraLink purchase added Wi-Fi-based phone systems to its product portfolio.

Polycom has benefitted from a trend away from circuit-switched telephone networks to IP technology, a shift that continues to drive its business. Like its competitors, the company has also identified the weakness in the economy as an opportunity for its business, as customers look to cut costs by reducing travel expenses.

EXECUTIVES

Chairman, President, CEO, and Head of Worldwide Sales: Robert C. (Bob) Hagerty, age 57, $2,959,935 total compensation
EVP Global Field Operations: Andrew M. Miller
SVP and Chief Marketing Officer: Heidi Melin
SVP and General Manager, Global Services: Geno J. Alissi, age 59, $1,074,583 total compensation
SVP Human Resources: Gary M. Ziesés
SVP, Chief Administrative Officer, General Counsel, and Secretary: Sayed M. Darwish, age 43
SVP Worldwide Operations: Robert B. Steele
SVP and General Manager, Video Solutions: Joseph A. (Joe) Sigrist, age 47, $1,045,984 total compensation
SVP Finance and Administration, CFO, and Director: Michael R. Kourey, age 50, $1,564,374 total compensation
SVP and General Manager, Voice Communications: Sunil K. Bhalla, age 52, $1,432,998 total compensation
VP and Corporate Treasurer: Garth B. Hobden
VP, Worldwide Controller, and Principal Accounting Officer: Laura J. Durr, age 48
Auditors: PricewaterhouseCoopers LLP

LOCATIONS

HQ: Polycom, Inc.
4750 Willow Rd., Pleasanton, CA 94588
Phone: 925-924-6000   **Fax:** 925-924-6100
Web: www.polycom.com

2008 Sales

	$ mil.	% of total
North America		
US	512.1	48
Canada	51.9	5
Europe, Middle East & Africa	281.2	26
Asia	189.0	18
Caribbean & Latin America	35.1	3
Total	**1,069.3**	**100**

PRODUCTS/OPERATIONS

2008 Sales

	$ mil.	% of total
Video solutions	560.1	52
Voice communications	353.7	33
Services	155.5	15
Total	**1,069.3**	**100**

Selected Products

Video solutions
  Desktop video communications appliances
  Network systems
    Call processing server
    Network control units
    Office software
    Web-based video network management software
  Videoconferencing systems
  Video peripherals
Voice communications
  Multichannel acoustic echo and noise cancellation systems
  Videoconferencing speakerphones
  Voice conferencing products

COMPETITORS

Aethra
Alcatel-Lucent
Avaya
Avistar Communications
Cisco CBG
Cisco Systems
ClearOne
D-Link
Emblaze-VCON
Hewlett-Packard
Hitachi Cable
Huawei Technologies
IBM
Microsoft
Mitel Networks
NEC
Nortel Networks
Panasonic Corporation of North America
Radvision
Samsung Electronics
Sony
TANDBERG
WebEx
ZTE

HISTORICAL FINANCIALS

Company Type: Public

Income Statement

	REVENUE ($ mil.)	NET INCOME ($ mil.)	NET PROFIT MARGIN	EMPLOYEES	FYE: December 31
12/08	1,069.3	75.7	7.1%	2,648	
12/07	929.9	62.9	6.8%	2,478	
12/06	682.4	71.9	10.5%	1,727	
12/05	580.7	62.7	10.8%	1,636	
12/04	540.3	35.3	6.5%	1,437	
Annual Growth	**18.6%**	**21.0%**	**—**	**16.5%**	

2008 Year-End Financials

Debt ratio: —
Return on equity: 7.6%
Cash ($ mil.): 165.7
Current ratio: 2.79
Long-term debt ($ mil.): —
No. of shares (mil.): 84.4
Dividends
  Yield: 0.0%
  Payout: —
Market value ($ mil.): 1,140.2
R&D as % of sales: —
Advertising as % of sales: —

Stock History

NASDAQ (GS): PLCM

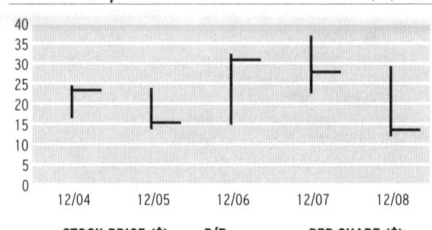

	STOCK PRICE ($) FY Close	P/E High/Low		Earnings	PER SHARE ($) Dividends	Book Value
12/08	13.51	33	14	0.87	0.00	11.47
12/07	27.78	55	34	0.67	0.00	12.13
12/06	30.91	40	19	0.80	0.00	11.22
12/05	15.30	36	21	0.65	0.00	10.15
12/04	23.32	69	48	0.35	0.00	11.43
Annual Growth	**(12.8%)**	**—**	**—**	**25.6%**	**—**	**0.1%**

Porter Bancorp

Porter Bancorp is a stout evaluator of what "ales" your finances. It is the holding company for PBI Bank, which serves local residents and businesses through about 20 offices in Louisville and other central and south-central Kentucky locations. The company also operates Ascencia, a nationwide online banking platform. Deposit services include checking, savings, and money market accounts, as well as CDs. Loans collateralized by real estate such as commercial mortgages (about 35%), construction loans (approximately 25%), and residential mortgages (another 25%), comprise the lion's share of the company's loan portfolio.

Porter Bancorp used the proceeds from its 2006 IPO to expand its presence in Kentucky. It opened new loan offices in 2007 and bought Ohio County Bancshares, holding company of the six-branch Kentucky Trust Bank. The following year it acquired the Paramount Bank (with one office in Lexington) for $5 million in cash. Both Kentucky Trust Bank and Paramount Bank were re-branded as PBI Bank.

In 2009 Porter Bancorp raised its stakes in another Kentucky bank, Citizens First Corporation, to about 20%. Porter placed an unsolicited bid to acquire the rest of the bank's shares, but withdrew the offer when it was rejected by Citizens First management.

Chairman J. Chester Porter, a lawyer, and CEO Maria Bouvett own a combined two-thirds of Porter Bancorp. The Porters also own stakes in two other community banks in Kentucky.

EXECUTIVES

Chairman and General Counsel, Porter Bancorp and PBI Bank: J. Chester Porter, age 68, $472,762 total compensation
President, CEO, and Director, Porter Bancorp and PBI Bank: Maria L. Bouvette, age 52, $465,047 total compensation
CFO; Chief Strategic Officer, PBI Bank: David B. Pierce, age 49, $384,571 total compensation
EVP and Corporate General Counsel: C. Bradford Harris, age 39, $190,515 total compensation
Head Technology; CTO, PBI Bank: Eric J. Satterly
President Southern Region, PBI Bank: Avery K. Matney Jr.
President Northern Region, PBI Bank: Fred Catlett
President, Bullitt County Market, PBI Bank: Keith Griffee Jr.
COO, PBI Bank: E. Todd Young
CFO, PBI Bank: Phil W. Barnhouse
Chief Business Development Officer, PBI Bank: Charles R. Darst
Auditors: Crowe Horwath, LLP

LOCATIONS

HQ: Porter Bancorp, Inc.
2500 Eastpoint Pkwy., Louisville, KY 40223
Phone: 502-499-4800   **Fax:** 502-499-4811
Web: www.pbibank.com

PRODUCTS/OPERATIONS

2008 Sales

	% of total
Interest	
Loans, including fees	87
Securities	5
Federal funds sold & other	1
Noninterest	
Service charges on deposit accounts	3
Secondary market brokerage fees	1
Other	3
Total	**100**

COMPETITORS

BB&T
Fifth Third
JPMorgan Chase
PNC Financial
Republic Bancorp
S.Y. Bancorp
U.S. Bancorp

HISTORICAL FINANCIALS

Company Type: Public

Income Statement

FYE: December 31

	ASSETS ($ mil.)	NET INCOME ($ mil.)	INCOME AS % OF ASSETS	EMPLOYEES
12/08	1,647.9	14.0	0.8%	276
12/07	1,456.0	14.2	1.0%	273
12/06	1,051.0	14.3	1.4%	203
12/05	991.5	14.6	1.5%	195
12/04	887.2	10.9	1.2%	220
Annual Growth	**16.7%**	**6.5%**	**—**	**5.8%**

2008 Year-End Financials

Equity as % of assets: 7.9%
Return on assets: 0.9%
Return on equity: 11.1%
Long-term debt ($ mil.): 176.8
No. of shares (mil.): 8.8
Market value ($ mil.): 131.8
Dividends
  Yield: 5.1%
  Payout: 48.1%
Sales ($ mil.): 54.1
R&D as % of sales: —
Advertising as % of sales: —

Stock History

NASDAQ (GM): PBIB

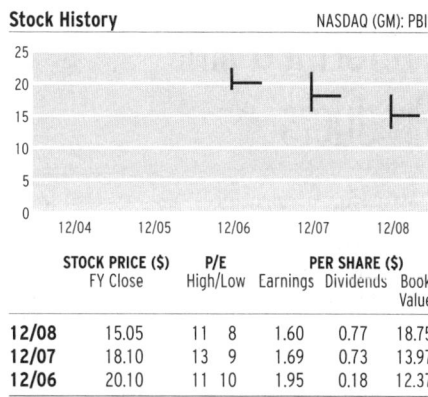

	STOCK PRICE ($) FY Close	P/E High/Low		PER SHARE ($) Earnings	Dividends	Book Value
12/08	15.05	11	8	1.60	0.77	18.75
12/07	18.10	13	9	1.69	0.73	13.97
12/06	20.10	11	10	1.95	0.18	12.37
Annual Growth	**(13.5%)**	**—**	**—**	**(9.4%)**	**106.8%**	**23.1%**

Power Integrations

Power Integrations has an integrated approach to power conversion. The company makes high-voltage analog integrated circuits (ICs) that convert alternating current (AC) to lower-voltage direct current (DC). Power Integrations' high-voltage analog semiconductors, which account for virtually all of the company's sales, are used in PCs, cell phones, cable boxes, and other consumer and industrial electronics. The TOPSwitch line features products made with the company's environmentally friendly EcoSmart technology, which reduces energy waste. The company's wares are used by such electronics manufacturers as Dell, Nokia, and Samsung Electronics. Power Integrations gets nearly all of its sales from overseas.

Four silicon foundries (contract semiconductor manufacturers) fabricate the company's chips: Oki Semiconductor, Panasonic, Seiko Epson, and X-FAB Silicon Foundries. Distributor Avnet accounts for 16% of sales. Distributors handle nearly two-thirds of the company's sales.

Power Integrations doesn't have any long-term contracts with its customers, and so it is subject to market conditions and even just the whim of a customer on orders. The semiconductor industry remains highly cyclical, and lower sales of consumer electronics due to the global recession is generally driving down sales for chip makers. The company was able to grow sales in 2008, although profitability was severely dented. The high-voltage power supply industry is subject to intense competition and characterized by significant price sensitivity; Power Integration may see lower average selling prices and sales volume as a result.

At the end of 2007 Power Integrations acquired Potentia Semiconductor, a Canadian developer of controller chips for high-power AC-DC power supplies. The company paid about $5.5 million in cash for Potentia.

In another example of the widening corporate scandals on options backdating, where executives and board members have skirted US regulations on the timing and purchasing of stock-option grants, Power Integrations reported in 2006 that its board of directors formed a special committee of independent directors to investigate company practices related to stock-option grants to executives and board members. Chairman Howard Earhart, a former CEO of Power Integrations, and CFO John Cobb resigned. The board soon after named Steven Sharp as non-executive chairman to succeed Earhart. Power Integrations later restated financial results for 2001 through 2004, and for the first three quarters of 2005.

The SEC's staff notified the company in 2007 that the commission's investigation into its past practices in granting stock options ended, without any enforcement action recommended against Power Integrations. The company still faces a probe by the US Department of Justice regarding stock options. In addition, Power Integrations is being audited by the Internal Revenue Service.

EXECUTIVES

Chairman: Steven J. (Steve) Sharp, age 67
President, CEO, and Director: Balu Balakrishnan, age 54, $3,663,598 total compensation
VP Engineering and Technology: Derek Bell, age 65, $975,887 total compensation
VP Marketing: Douglas (Doug) Bailey, age 42
VP Worldwide Sales: Bruce Renouard, age 48, $1,122,731 total compensation
VP Operations: John Tomlin, age 61, $1,370,205 total compensation
VP Corporate Development: Clifford J. Walker, age 57
Product Marketing Manager: Andrew Smith
VP Finance and Administration, CFO, and Secretary: Bill Roeschlein, age 40, $1,460,753 total compensation
Director, Investor Relations and Corporate Communications: Joe Shiffler
Auditors: Deloitte & Touche LLP

LOCATIONS

HQ: Power Integrations, Inc.
5245 Hellyer Ave., San Jose, CA 95138
Phone: 408-414-9200   **Fax:** 408-414-9201
Web: www.powerint.com

Power Integrations has offices in China, Germany, India, Italy, Japan, Singapore, South Korea, Taiwan, the UK, and the US.

2008 Sales

	% of total
Asia/Pacific	
China & Hong Kong	35
Taiwan	23
South Korea	16
Japan	5
Singapore	2
Europe	
Germany	4
Other countries	10
Americas	4
Other regions	1
Total	**100**

PRODUCTS/OPERATIONS

2008 Sales

	% of total
TinySwitch	44
LinkSwitch	29
TOPSwitch	25
DPA-Switch	2
Total	**100**

2008 Sales by Market

	% of total
Consumer	30
Communications	28
Computer	21
Industrial electronics	15
Other	6
Total	**100**

Selected Products

AC-to-DC power conversion products (LinkSwitch)
DC-to-DC power conversion products (DPA-Switch)
High-voltage analog ICs for power conversion
  (TOPSwitch, TinySwitch)

COMPETITORS

Allegro MicroSystems
BCD Semiconductor
Fairchild Semiconductor
Infineon Technologies
iWatt
Maxim Integrated Products
Micrel
NXP
ON Semiconductor
Samsung Electronics
Sanken Electric
Semtech
STMicroelectronics
Vishay Intertechnology

HISTORICAL FINANCIALS

Company Type: Public

Income Statement

FYE: December 31

	REVENUE ($ mil.)	NET INCOME ($ mil.)	NET PROFIT MARGIN	EMPLOYEES
12/08	201.7	1.8	0.9%	402
12/07	191.0	26.6	13.9%	385
12/06	162.4	9.4	5.8%	354
12/05	143.1	15.7	11.0%	342
12/04	136.6	20.4	14.9%	310
Annual Growth	10.2%	(45.5%)	—	6.7%

2008 Year-End Financials

Debt ratio: —
Return on equity: —
Cash ($ mil.): 167.5
Current ratio: 7.10
Long-term debt ($ mil.): —
No. of shares (mil.): 27.0

Dividends
  Yield: 0.1%
  Payout: 50.0%
Market value ($ mil.): 537.2
R&D as % of sales: —
Advertising as % of sales: —

Stock History

NASDAQ (GS): POWI

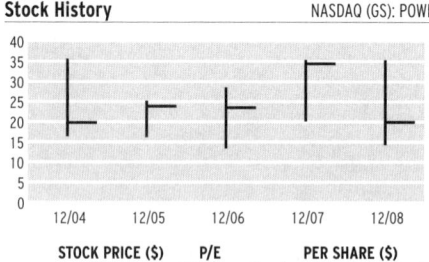

	STOCK PRICE ($) FY Close	P/E High/Low	PER SHARE ($) Earnings	Dividends	Book Value
12/08	19.88	583 243	0.06	0.03	9.61
12/07	34.43	41 24	0.85	0.00	10.71
12/06	23.45	91 44	0.31	0.00	8.17
12/05	23.81	49 32	0.51	0.00	7.75
12/04	19.78	56 26	0.63	0.00	7.86
Annual Growth	0.1%	— —	(44.4%)	—	5.1%

Preformed Line Products

Masterful "preformances" are expected from Preformed Line Products by its audience in the energy and communications industries. The company designs and manufactures components and systems used by utility crews and others to construct, repair, and maintain overhead and underground networks for energy, communications, and broadband network companies. Products include formed wire products (which are used mainly in maintenance construction to revitalize aging plant infrastructures), protective fiber-optic closures and splice cases, and data communication interconnect devices and enclosures for data communications networks. Chairman Robert Ruhlman and his family own approximately 40% of the company.

Preformed Line Products, which was founded in 1947, operates subsidiaries throughout the world. The company pioneered the manufacture of helically shaped armor rods to protect electrical conductors on overhead power lines.

The company entered the alternative energy market in 2007 when it acquired solar power systems manufacturer and installer Direct Power and Water. Preformed Line Products formed a new division, PLP Solar, following the acquisition.

Preformed Line Products has been focusing its efforts on the energy and communications markets, both of which have been undergoing consolidation. Sales to energy customers increased in 2007, but it anticipates those sales to slow in 2008 and has increased its US sales efforts toward the communications markets.

Internationally, however, the company continues to focus on the energy markets, especially in developing nations. In December 2009 Preformed Line Products picked up the Dulmison Business operations, crossing Australia, Thailand, Indonesia, Malaysia, China, Mexico, and the US, from Tyco Electronics. The deal, which includes Dulmison's competencies in designing, manufacturing, and marketing vibration control products and pole line hardware, marks an up shift in Preformed Line Products' portfolio and presence for targeting the global electrical utility industry.

EXECUTIVES

Chairman, President, and CEO: Robert G. Ruhlman, age 52, $1,717,118 total compensation
VP Finance and CFO: Eric R. Graef, age 57, $654,153 total compensation
VP International Operations: William H. Haag III, age 45, $550,039 total compensation
VP Marketing and Business Development: Dennis F. McKenna, age 42, $533,356 total compensation
VP Human Resources: J. Cecil Curlee Jr., age 52, $415,594 total compensation
VP Research and Engineering and Manufacturing: David C. Sunkle, age 50
General Counsel and Corporate Secretary: Caroline S. Vaccariello, age 42
Auditors: Ernst & Young LLP

LOCATIONS

HQ: Preformed Line Products Company
  660 Beta Dr., Mayfield Village, OH 44143
Phone: 440-461-5200   **Fax:** 440-442-8816
Web: www.preformed.com

2008 Sales

	$ mil.	% of total
US	111.7	41
Brazil	30.3	11
Australia	27.2	10
Poland	20.6	8
Canada	10.0	4
South Africa	9.5	4
Other countries	60.4	22
Total	**269.7**	**100**

COMPETITORS

3M
Corning Cable Systems
General Cable
Kyocera
Kyocera Solar
Maysteel
Rio Tinto Alcan
Sumitomo Electric
SWCC SHOWA
Tyco

HISTORICAL FINANCIALS

Company Type: Public

Income Statement

FYE: December 31

	REVENUE ($ mil.)	NET INCOME ($ mil.)	NET PROFIT MARGIN	EMPLOYEES
12/08	269.7	17.6	6.5%	1,858
12/07	254.6	14.2	5.6%	1,936
12/06	216.9	12.1	5.6%	1,528
12/05	205.8	12.0	5.8%	1,583
12/04	183.1	13.0	7.1%	1,395
Annual Growth	10.2%	7.9%	—	7.4%

2008 Year-End Financials

Debt ratio: 1.9%
Return on equity: 12.3%
Cash ($ mil.): 19.9
Current ratio: 3.20
Long-term debt ($ mil.): 2.7
No. of shares (mil.): 5.2

Dividends
  Yield: 1.7%
  Payout: 24.2%
Market value ($ mil.): 241.0
R&D as % of sales: —
Advertising as % of sales: —

Stock History

NASDAQ (GM): PLPC

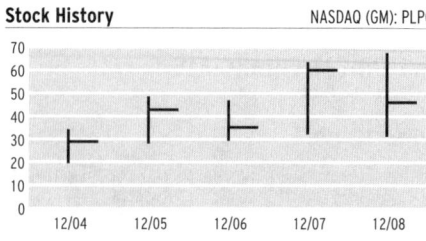

	STOCK PRICE ($) FY Close	P/E High/Low	PER SHARE ($) Earnings	Dividends	Book Value
12/08	46.04	20 10	3.30	0.80	26.03
12/07	59.97	24 13	2.61	0.80	28.60
12/06	35.25	22 14	2.13	0.80	25.01
12/05	42.79	23 14	2.07	0.80	25.51
12/04	28.98	15 9	2.25	0.80	24.52
Annual Growth	12.3%	— —	10.0%	0.0%	1.5%

Premier Financial Bancorp

Premier Financial Bancorp is the holding company for a handful of rural and small-town banks in Kentucky, Ohio, and West Virginia, including Citizens Deposit Bank, Farmers Deposit Bank, Ohio River Bank, Boone County Bank, and First Central Bank. It added to its stable in 2008 with the purchases of Citizens First Bank and Traders Bank. Altogether, Premier's banks have about 35 branches. They offer standard deposit products, such as checking and savings accounts and CDs. The bulk of Premier's loan portfolio is made up of residential mortgages (about 40%) and commercial real estate loans (some 30%). In 2009 the company acquired Washington, DC-based Abigail Adams National Bancorp, which operated about 10 branches.

The deal was worth approximately $11 million. Premier CEO Robert Walker was named chairman and CEO of Abigail Adams a few months before the acquisition was announced. Investor Marshall Reynolds, who specializes in troubled banks, was the largest shareholder of both Premier Financial and Abigail Adams.

In April 2009, Premier Financial received approval for $24 million from the US Treasury from its Capital Purchase Program. Participation in the program was a condition of completing the merger with Abigail Adams.

EXECUTIVES

Chairman: Marshall T. Reynolds, age 72
President, CEO, and Director: Robert W. Walker, age 62, $279,350 total compensation
EVP and COO, Citizens Deposit Bank & Trust: Karen Ravencraft
SVP; CEO, First Central Bank: Dennis Klingensmith, age 55, $152,021 total compensation
SVP and CFO: Brien M. Chase, age 44, $134,326 total compensation
VP Credit Administration: Scot A. Kelley, age 52
VP Human Resources: Katrina Whitt, age 34
President, Ohio River Bank: Daniel Wiley
President, Citizens Deposit Bank & Trust: Mike Mineer
President, Farmers Deposit Bank: Carol Yates
President, Boone County Bank: Emma Byrnside
Secretary and Director: E. V. Holder Jr., age 77
Auditors: Crowe Horwath, LLP

LOCATIONS

HQ: Premier Financial Bancorp, Inc.
   2883 Fifth Ave., Huntington, WV 25702
Phone: 304-525-1600   **Fax:** 304-525-9701

PRODUCTS/OPERATIONS

2008 Sales

	% of total
Interest	
Loans	69
Securities	17
Federal funds sold	2
Noninterest	
Service charges	7
Other	5
Total	**100**

COMPETITORS

Allegheny Bancshares	Fifth Third
ASB Financial	Huntington Bancshares
BB&T	Ohio Valley Banc
Camco Financial	Porter Bancorp
City Holding	S.Y. Bancorp
Community Trust	United Bancorp
Farmers Capital Bank	United Bankshares

HISTORICAL FINANCIALS

Company Type: Public

Income Statement

FYE: December 31

	ASSETS ($ mil.)	NET INCOME ($ mil.)	INCOME AS % OF ASSETS	EMPLOYEES
12/08	724.5	7.5	1.0%	270
12/07	549.3	7.1	1.3%	226
12/06	535.5	6.5	1.2%	225
12/05	528.3	4.4	0.8%	215
12/04	537.3	6.7	1.2%	223
Annual Growth	**7.8%**	**2.9%**	**—**	**4.9%**

2008 Year-End Financials

Equity as % of assets: 12.3%
Return on assets: 1.2%
Return on equity: 9.6%
Long-term debt ($ mil.): 23.2
No. of shares (mil.): 7.9
Market value ($ mil.): 55.8
Dividends
   Yield: 6.1%
   Payout: 34.4%
Sales ($ mil.): 31.3
R&D as % of sales: —
Advertising as % of sales: —

Stock History

NASDAQ (GM): PFBI

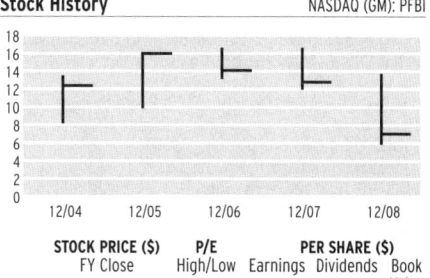

	STOCK PRICE ($) FY Close	P/E High/Low		PER SHARE ($) Earnings	Dividends	Book Value
12/08	7.03	11	5	1.25	0.43	11.27
12/07	12.78	12	9	1.35	0.40	8.49
12/06	14.07	13	11	1.24	0.10	7.69
12/05	15.98	19	12	0.84	0.00	6.84
12/04	12.35	10	6	1.28	0.00	6.43
Annual Growth	**(13.1%)**	**—**	**—**	**(0.6%)**	**—**	**15.1%**

Premiere Global Services

Premiere Global Services provides teleconferencing and Web-conferencing software and services to small and midsized businesses, as well as larger corporate clients. The company's Premiere Global Communications Operating System products include applications that enable operator-assisted and automated teleconferencing, as well as Web-based software tools used for document sharing. Other products automate communications and business process activities such as confirmation of scheduled appointments

or notification of past-due bills, and applications used to automate online marketing campaigns. Premiere Global Services provides its software as a hosted service.

Premiere's conferencing and collaboration service, PGiMeet, accounts for about 70% of its revenues. In 2008 the company began offering PGiMeet on a subscription-based model, but the company still generates most of its revenue using its traditional per-minute pricing model.

Premiere Global Services does about 60% of its business in North America, with the rest roughly split between Europe and the Asia/Pacific region. As part of an international growth strategy, the company has expanded into China and India in recent years.

In late 2009 the company sold its e-mail marketing business to Mansell Group; the deal includes the Campaign Accelerator suite of software tools.

EXECUTIVES

Chairman, CEO, and Director: Boland T. Jones, age 48, $4,518,712 total compensation
President: Theodore P. Schrafft, age 53, $2,032,779 total compensation
CFO: David E. Trine, age 48
CTO: David M. Guthrie, age 42, $1,393,235 total compensation
Corporate Compliance Officer and General Counsel: Scott Askins Leonard
Chief Marketing Officer: Jacqueline Yeaney
Chief People Officer: Erik Petrik
EVP Sales and Marketing: Mark K. Alexander
EVP European Operations: John D. Stone
SVP Human Resources: Alison Sheehan
SVP Global Financial Planning and Analysis: Kevin McAdams
SVP Finance: Michael E. (Mike) Havener, age 41, $788,461 total compensation
SVP Corporate Sales: Frank Gorkis
SVP Small Medium Business Sales: Kraig Brown
Director Human Resources: Kim Pettibone
Investor Relations: Sean P. O'Brien
Auditors: Deloitte & Touche LLP

LOCATIONS

HQ: Premiere Global Services, Inc.
   3280 Peachtree Rd., NW, Ste. 1000
   Atlanta, GA 30305
Phone: 404-262-8400   **Fax:** 404-262-8525
Web: www.premiereglobal.com

2008 Sales

	$ mil.	% of total
North America	384.8	62
Europe	122.5	20
Asia/Pacific	116.9	18
Total	**624.2**	**100**

PRODUCTS/OPERATIONS

Selected Services
Automated conference calling
Automated messaging (fax, e-mail, phone, and SMS)
Electronic invoicing and data management
Fax broadcasting
Operator-assisted conference calling
Special event conference call preparation and consultation
Web presentations

HISTORICAL FINANCIALS

Company Type: Public

Income Statement

FYE: December 31

	REVENUE ($ mil.)	NET INCOME ($ mil.)	NET PROFIT MARGIN	EMPLOYEES
12/08	624.2	36.1	5.8%	2,650
12/07	559.7	33.4	6.0%	2,430
12/06	496.5	25.5	5.1%	2,350
12/05	497.5	47.4	9.5%	2,225
12/04	449.4	41.9	9.3%	2,230
Annual Growth	8.6%	(3.7%)	—	4.4%

2008 Year-End Financials

Debt ratio: 106.0%
Return on equity: 14.6%
Cash ($ mil.): 27.5
Current ratio: 1.42
Long-term debt ($ mil.): 269.0
No. of shares (mil.): 60.1

Dividends
  Yield: —
  Payout: —
Market value ($ mil.): 517.4
R&D as % of sales: —
Advertising as % of sales: —

Stock History

NYSE: PGI

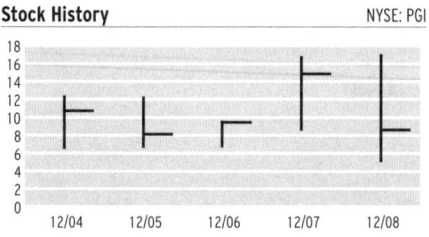

	STOCK PRICE ($) FY Close	P/E High/Low		PER SHARE ($) Earnings	Dividends	Book Value
12/08	8.61	28	9	0.60	—	4.22
12/07	14.85	32	17	0.52	—	4.03
12/06	9.44	26	18	0.37	—	5.26
12/05	8.13	18	10	0.66	—	5.05
12/04	10.71	20	11	0.60	—	4.44
Annual Growth	(5.3%)	—	—	0.0%	—	(1.2%)

PrimeEnergy Corporation

PrimeEnergy hopes to keep the pump primed with its oil and gas exploration and production activities, which take place primarily in Colorado, Louisiana, New Mexico, Oklahoma, Texas, West Virginia, and the Gulf of Mexico. The company has proved reserves of 87 billion cu. ft. of natural gas equivalent. It operates 1,500 wells and owns interests in 850 non-operating wells. Its PrimeEnergy Management unit is the managing general partner of 18 oil and gas limited partnerships and two trusts. Subsidiary Southwest Oilfield Construction provides site preparation and construction services for PrimeEnergy and third parties. CEO Charles Drimal owns 32% of the firm.

PrimeEnergy's strategy is to develop a mixed portfolio of drilling prospects that balance lower risk/medium return wells with higher risk wells with higher economic return potential. In 2008, the company drilled 71 gross (42 net) wells.

The oil and gas company, which was founded in 1973, owns and operates properties in the Gulf of Mexico through subsidiary Prime Offshore.

EXECUTIVES

President and Director, PrimeEnergy Corporation and PrimeEnergy Management: Charles E. Drimal Jr., age 60, $1,650,205 total compensation
EVP, Treasurer, and Director; EVP, PrimeEnergy Management: Beverly A. Cummings, age 55, $874,405 total compensation
Controller: Lynne Pizor, age 49, $198,097 total compensation
Secretary: James F. Gilbert, age 75
Auditors: Pustorino, Puglisi & Co., LLP

LOCATIONS

HQ: PrimeEnergy Corporation
  1 Landmark Sq., Stamford, CT 06901
Phone: 203-358-5700   **Fax:** 203-358-5786
Web: www.primeenergy.com

PrimeEnergy operates in Colorado, Louisiana, Montana, Nebraska, North Dakota, Oklahoma, Texas, West Virginia, and Wyoming, and in the Gulf of Mexico.

PRODUCTS/OPERATIONS

2008 Sales

	$ mil.	% of total
Oil & gas	135.0	80
Field service	24.7	15
Other	9.6	5
Total	**169.3**	**100**

Selected Subsidiaries

Chase Energy L.L.C.
Eastern Oil Well Service Company
EOWS Midland Company
PrimeEnergy Management Corporation
Prime Offshore L.L.C
Prime Operating Company
Southwest Oilfield Construction Company

COMPETITORS

Abraxas Petroleum
Anadarko Petroleum
Brigham Exploration
Cabot Oil & Gas
Forest Oil
Pioneer Natural Resources

HISTORICAL FINANCIALS

Company Type: Public

Income Statement

FYE: December 31

	REVENUE ($ mil.)	NET INCOME ($ mil.)	NET PROFIT MARGIN	EMPLOYEES
12/08	169.3	0.5	0.3%	249
12/07	146.5	7.6	5.2%	245
12/06	92.4	18.3	19.8%	243
12/05	75.9	26.0	34.3%	217
12/04	62.4	7.3	11.7%	196
Annual Growth	28.3%	(48.8%)	—	6.2%

2008 Year-End Financials

Debt ratio: 217.4%
Return on equity: 1.0%
Cash ($ mil.): 11.8
Current ratio: 0.82
Long-term debt ($ mil.): 107.2
No. of shares (mil.): 3.0

Dividends
  Yield: 0.0%
  Payout: —
Market value ($ mil.): 157.7
R&D as % of sales: —
Advertising as % of sales: —

Stock History

NASDAQ (CM): PNRG

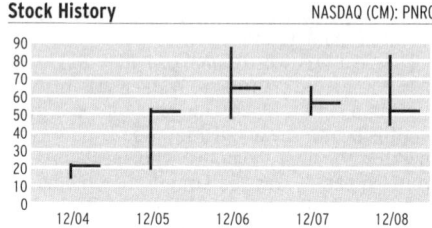

	STOCK PRICE ($) FY Close	P/E High/Low		PER SHARE ($) Earnings	Dividends	Book Value
12/08	51.95	588	317	0.14	0.00	16.24
12/07	56.25	34	26	1.93	0.00	16.57
12/06	64.50	19	11	4.50	0.00	18.02
12/05	51.40	8	3	6.27	0.00	13.09
12/04	20.87	13	8	1.70	0.00	6.01
Annual Growth	25.6%	—	—	(46.4%)	—	28.2%

PROS Holdings

PROS Holdings can help you squeeze the most out of every single penny. The company provides price and revenue optimization software that customers use for tasks such as forecasting demand, optimizing inventory allocation, modeling price elasticity, and monitoring transaction profitability. PROS' customers, in more than 40 countries, come from industries including distribution, manufacturing, services, and air travel. The company also offers professional services such as consulting, support, maintenance, and implementation. PROS was founded in 1985.

EXECUTIVES

Chairman, President, and CEO:
  Albert E. (Bert) Winemiller, age 66, $776,192 total compensation
EVP and CFO: Charles H. (Charlie) Murphy, age 64, $645,635 total compensation
EVP Product Development: Andres D. Reiner, age 38, $334,992 total compensation
EVP Strategic Business Planning and Director:
  Ronald F. (Ron) Woestemeyer, age 63, $340,030 total compensation
Chief Sales Officer, Manufacturing, Distribution, and Services: Chris J. Jones

SVP Pricing Solutions: Jeffrey E. (Jeff) Robinson, age 42, $338,795 total compensation
SVP Product Management: Surain R. Adyanthaya
SVP Business Development: Benson B. Yuen
SVP Professional Services: Peter P (Pete) Kiernan
VP Product Development: Oscar Moreno
Auditors: PricewaterhouseCoopers LLP

LOCATIONS

HQ: PROS Holdings, Inc.
3100 Main St., Ste. 900, Houston, TX 77002
Phone: 713-335-5151   **Fax:** 713-335-8144
Web: www.prospricing.com

PRODUCTS/OPERATIONS

2008 Sales

	$ mil.	% of total
License & implementation	53.9	71
Maintenance & support	21.7	29
Total	**75.6**	**100**

COMPETITORS

JDA Software
Oracle
SAP
Symphony-Metreo
Zilliant

HISTORICAL FINANCIALS

Company Type: Public

Income Statement				FYE: December 31
	REVENUE ($ mil.)	NET INCOME ($ mil.)	NET PROFIT MARGIN	EMPLOYEES
12/08	75.6	10.8	14.3%	381
12/07	62.1	10.4	16.7%	342
12/06	46.0	7.5	16.3%	311
12/05	35.1	3.4	9.7%	311
12/04	32.4	3.7	11.4%	—
Annual Growth	**23.6%**	**30.7%**	**—**	**7.0%**

2008 Year-End Financials

Debt ratio: —
Return on equity: 27.9%
Cash ($ mil.): 52.0
Current ratio: 2.41
Long-term debt ($ mil.): —
No. of shares (mil.): 25.7
Dividends
Yield: —
Payout: —
Market value ($ mil.): 147.9
R&D as % of sales: —
Advertising as % of sales: —

Stock History

NYSE: PRO

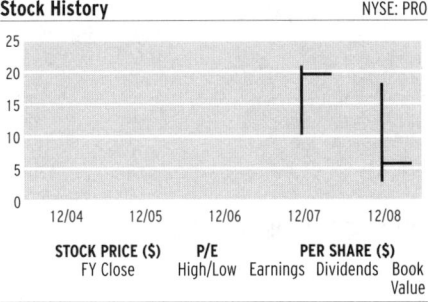

	STOCK PRICE ($) FY Close	P/E High/Low		PER SHARE ($) Earnings	Dividends	Book Value
12/08	5.75	45	8	0.40	—	1.70
12/07	19.62	46	23	0.45	—	1.31
Annual Growth	**(70.7%)**	**—**	**—**	**(11.1%)**	**—**	**29.9%**

Prospect Capital

Prospect Capital (formerly Prospect Energy) is a closed-end investment company focused on prospecting for . . . riches! The company was founded by fomer senior managers of Merrill Lynch with an interest in underperforming energy-related businesses. However, it changed its name from Prospect Energy in 2007 to reflect a broadening interest in non-energy investments. (It has since then invested in food and health care technology companies, among others.) Prospect targets middle-market companies with annual revenues of less than $500 million, typically participating in transactions of no greater than $250 million. It invests in mezzanine loans and equity securities of private or thinly traded public companies.

To protect its assets, Prospect Capital avoids directly investing in any energy companies exclusively engaged in oil and gas exploration, or in speculative development and trading in oil, gas, and/or other commodities.

In 2009 the company arranged to buy publicly traded, middle-market investment firm Patriot Capital Funding for nearly $200 million.

EXECUTIVES

Chairman and CEO: John F. Barry III, age 57
President, COO, and Director: M. Grier Eliasek, age 36
CFO, Chief Compliance Officer, and Secretary:
Brian H. Oswald
Investment Management and Research: Amir Friedman
Investment Origination and Execution:
W. Montgomery Cook
Investment Banking: Bart J. de Bie
Attorney and Portfolio Manager: Kurt W. Rieke
Private Equity and Investment Banking: Mark Hull
Energy Finance: James A. Flores
Private Equity and Restructuring: Robert S. Everett, age 45
Managing Director and Head of Oil and Gas Investments: David L. Belzer
Operations, Finance, and Investor Relations:
Daria Becker
Auditors: BDO Seidman, LLP

LOCATIONS

HQ: Prospect Capital Corporation
10 E. 40th St., 44th Fl., New York, NY 10016
Phone: 212-448-0702   **Fax:** 212-448-9652
Web: www.prospectstreet.com

PRODUCTS/OPERATIONS

2009 Sales

	$ mil.	% of total
Interest	62.9	62
Dividends	22.8	23
Other	14.8	15
Total	**100.5**	**100**

Selected Investment Companies

Advanced Rig Services, LLC (oilfield services)
Appalachian Energy Holdings LLC
BNN Holdings Corp. (dba Biotronic NeuroNetwork, neurophysiological monitoring services)
Castro Cheese Company, Inc. (Hispanic cheeses and creams)
Charlevoix Energy Trading, LLC
Genesis Coal Corporation
Maverick Healthcare, Inc. (dba Preferred Homecare)
Stryker Energy, LLC
TriZetto Group (health care information technology)
Wind River Resources Corp. (oil and gas production)

COMPETITORS

ACI Capital
Broadpoint.Gleacher
First Reserve
GFI Energy Ventures
Katalyst
NGPC
Stephens Group
TPG
Venrock

HISTORICAL FINANCIALS

Company Type: Public

Income Statement				FYE: June 30
	REVENUE ($ mil.)	NET INCOME ($ mil.)	NET PROFIT MARGIN	EMPLOYEES
6/09	100.5	35.1	34.9%	22
6/08	79.4	27.6	34.8%	19
6/07	40.7	23.1	56.8%	19
6/06	16.9	12.9	76.3%	12
6/05	8.1	8.8	108.6%	6
Annual Growth	**87.7%**	**41.3%**	**—**	**38.4%**

2009 Year-End Financials

Debt ratio: —
Return on equity: 7.3%
Cash ($ mil.): 9.9
Current ratio: 0.16
Long-term debt ($ mil.): —
No. of shares (mil.): 54.9
Dividends
Yield: 13.2%
Payout: 109.0%
Market value ($ mil.): 505.1
R&D as % of sales: —
Advertising as % of sales: —

Stock History

NASDAQ (GM): PSEC

	STOCK PRICE ($) FY Close	P/E High/Low		PER SHARE ($) Earnings	Dividends	Book Value
6/09	9.20	13	5	1.11	1.21	9.70
6/08	13.18	16	10	1.17	1.59	7.82
6/07	17.47	18	14	1.06	1.54	5.46
6/06	16.99	—	—	—	1.12	1.97
6/05	12.60	—	—	—	0.38	1.88
Annual Growth	**(7.6%)**	**—**	**—**	**2.3%**	**33.6%**	**50.8%**

Prospect Medical Holdings

Prospect Medical Holdings sees the possibilities in managed health care. The company owns and manages four community hospitals and more than a dozen independent physicians associations (IPAs) in Southern California. It also owns a majority stake in the 420-bed Brotman Medical Center. Prospect Medical's IPAs in turn provide health care to about 200,000 HMO enrollees for fixed monthly fees paid by the managed care organization to which they belong. Two subsidiaries, Prospect Medical Systems and ProMed Health Care Administrators, provide management services to the IPAs.

Prospect Medical Holdings has grown, in part, through acquisitions of independent physicians

associations. It gained two California IPAs (called Pomona Valley Medical Group and Upland Medical Group) in 2007 when it acquired ProMed Health Services.

Also in 2007 the company added four hospitals to its portfolio with the acquisition of Alta Healthcare System, a for-profit health care facility operator. Combined, the hospitals contain about 340 beds and provide general medical, surgical, and outpatient care. One of the hospitals also provides inpatient and outpatient psychiatric services.

The acquisition allows Prospect Medical to provide services that integrate hospital services with physician care and negotiate richer contracts with its managed care clients. The company intends to continue looking for both hospital and IPA acquisitions to strengthen its network of health care providers.

Prospect Medical expanded its hospital operations again in 2009 by becoming the majority owner of the Brotman Medical Center, increasing its stake in the facility from 33% to 72%. The hospital emerged from bankruptcy protection when the ownership transaction was completed. Prospect Medical had bought its minority stake in Brotman Medical Center (which was formerly owned by Tenet Healthcare) in 2005 with the hopes of turning around the hospital's fortunes, but Brotman Medical eventually filed for Chapter 11 bankruptcy in 2007.

Chairman and CEO Samuel Lee owns 30% of Prospect Medical. Former CEO Jacob Terner, who left the company in 2008, controls about 7%. The David & Alexa Topper Family Trust owns a 25% stake in the company.

EXECUTIVES

Chairman and CEO; CEO, Alta Hospitals System:
Samuel S. (Sam) Lee, age 43
CFO: Mike Heather, age 50
EVP Prospect Medical Holdings: Linda B. Hodges, age 64
SVP Finance and Development, Prospect Medical Holdings: R. Stewart Kahn, age 57
SVP Finance and Operations; Interim CEO, Prospect Medical Systems: Dan Frank
VP Information Technology: Terri Holmes
VP Medical Management, Prospect Medical Systems: Rosa Catalano
VP Finance Prospect Medical Holdings: Donna Vigil, age 60
Secretary, Prospect Medical Holdings: Ellen Shin
Director Human Resources: Caryn Loomis
Auditors: BDO Seidman, LLP

LOCATIONS

HQ: Prospect Medical Holdings, Inc.
10780 Santa Monica Blvd., Ste. 400
Los Angeles, CA 90025
Phone: 310-943-4500   **Fax:** 310-943-4501
Web: www.prospectmedicalholdings.com

PRODUCTS/OPERATIONS

2008 Sales

	$ mil.	% of total
IPA management	202.8	62
Hospital services	126.7	38
Total	**329.5**	**100**

COMPETITORS

Beaver Medical Group	Kaiser Permanente
Catholic Healthcare West	Los Angeles County Health
HCA	Department
Health Central	Orion HealthCorp
HealthCare Partners	St. Joseph Health System
Hill Physicians Medical Group	Tenet Healthcare

HISTORICAL FINANCIALS

Company Type: Public

Income Statement

FYE: September 30

	REVENUE ($ mil.)	NET INCOME ($ mil.)	NET PROFIT MARGIN	EMPLOYEES
9/08	329.5	4.2	1.3%	285
9/07	180.7	(33.5)	—	1,853
9/06	135.8	4.9	3.6%	367
9/05*	133.5	4.1	3.1%	349
12/04	129.5	5.1	3.9%	348
Annual Growth	**26.3%**	**(4.7%)**	**—**	**(4.9%)**

*Fiscal year change

2008 Year-End Financials

Debt ratio: 181.8%
Return on equity: 5.9%
Cash ($ mil.): 33.6
Current ratio: 1.20
Long-term debt ($ mil.): 132.4
No. of shares (mil.): 20.6

Dividends
Yield: —
Payout: —
Market value ($ mil.): 51.4
R&D as % of sales: —
Advertising as % of sales: —

Stock History

NYSE Alternext: PZZ

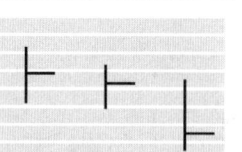

	STOCK PRICE ($) FY Close	P/E High/Low		PER SHARE ($) Earnings	Dividends	Book Value
9/08	2.50	—	—	(0.20)	—	3.54
9/07	5.29	—	—	(3.94)	—	3.38
9/06	5.85	12	7	0.60	—	1.64
9/05*	4.97	17	0	0.48	—	1.31
12/04	7.60	13	0	0.68	—	1.11
Annual Growth	**(24.3%)**	**—**	**—**	**—**	**—**	**33.6%**

*Fiscal year change

Prosperity Bancshares

Feeling prosperous? Prosperity Bancshares wants to help you manage your riches. The company operates 168 Prosperity Bank branches in and around major Texas cities, as well as eastern and southern portions of the state. The bank offers traditional deposit and cash management services. Commercial mortgages make up the largest segment (more than 33%) of the company's loan portfolio, which also includes residential mortgage, construction, home equity, business, and agricultural loans. The acquisitive company has been buying up small banks in Texas. It acquired six branches in Houston from Banco Popular

North America in early 2008 and then bought Houston's two-branch 1st Choice Bancorp.

Later that year Prosperity Bancshares picked up the deposits and all 45 branches of the failed Franklin Bank. The bank said it would continue to operate 35 of the former Franklin branches, and consolidate the rest with existing Prosperity branches.

Other recent acquisitions include Texas United Bancshares and the single-branch Bank of Novasota (2007), SNB Bancshares (2006), and South Texas' FirstCapital Bankers and Grapeland Bancshares (2005).

EXECUTIVES

Senior Chairman and CEO: David Zalman, age 52, $1,012,135 total compensation
Vice Chairman, President, and Director; Chairman and COO, Prosperity Bank: H. E. (Tim) Timanus Jr., age 65, $593,632 total compensation
President, COO, and Director; President, Prosperity Bank: James D. (Dan) Rollins III, age 50, $656,210 total compensation
CFO; EVP and CFO, Prosperity Bank: David Hollaway, age 53, $434,061 total compensation
General Counsel; Vice Chairman and General Counsel, Prosperity Bank: Peter E. Fisher, age 62, $329,501 total compensation
Chief Credit Officer, Prosperity Bank: Chris Bagley
Chief Lending Officer, Prosperity Bank: Randy D. Hester
Chairman, Houston Area Banking Centers: Robert L. Benter
Chairman, Central Texas Centers: Edward Z. (Eddie) Safady
Chairman, Bryan/College Station Area: Mark D. Humphrey
Chairman, South Texas Area Banking Centers: Steve Hipes
President, Houston Area: Chris J. Delaup
President, Dallas/Fort Worth and East Texas Area: Deke Hayes
President, South Texas Area Banking Centers: Bob Kuhn
President, Houston Area Banking Center: Randall Reeves
Auditors: Deloitte & Touche LLP

LOCATIONS

HQ: Prosperity Bancshares, Inc.
4295 San Felipe, Houston, TX 77027
Phone: 281-269-7199   **Fax:** 281-269-7222
Web: www.prosperitybanktx.com

2008 Branches by Region

	Branches	Deposits ($ mil.)
Houston metro area	53	3,225.0
Central Texas area	43	1,584.5
Corpus Christi/South Texas	27	884.7
Dallas/Ft. Worth metro area	24	787.0
East Texas area	21	820.8
Total	**168**	**7,302.0**

PRODUCTS/OPERATIONS

2008 Sales

	% of total
Interest income	
Loans, including fees	57
Securities	30
Federal funds sold	1
Noninterest income	
Service charges on deposit accounts	11
Other	2
Total	**100**

HISTORICAL FINANCIALS

Company Type: Public

Income Statement				FYE: December 31
	ASSETS ($ mil.)	NET INCOME ($ mil.)	INCOME AS % OF ASSETS	EMPLOYEES
12/08	9,072.4	84.5	0.9%	1,734
12/07	6,372.3	84.2	1.3%	1,359
12/06	4,586.8	61.7	1.3%	908
12/05	3,586.0	47.9	1.3%	859
12/04	2,697.2	34.7	1.3%	653
Annual Growth	35.4%	24.9%	—	27.7%

2008 Year-End Financials

Equity as % of assets: 13.8%
Return on assets: 1.1%
Return on equity: 7.1%
Long-term debt ($ mil.): 321.7
No. of shares (mil.): 46.4
Market value ($ mil.): 1,372.8
Dividends
Yield: 1.7%
Payout: 27.4%
Sales ($ mil.): 280.1
R&D as % of sales: —
Advertising as % of sales: —

Stock History

NASDAQ (GS): PRSP

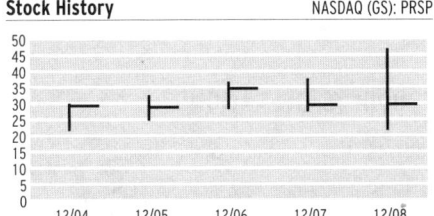

	STOCK PRICE ($) FY Close	P/E High/Low	PER SHARE ($) Earnings	PER SHARE ($) Dividends	PER SHARE ($) Book Value
12/08	29.59	25 12	1.86	0.51	27.05
12/07	29.39	19 14	1.94	0.35	24.30
12/06	34.51	19 15	1.94	0.41	14.32
12/05	28.74	18 14	1.77	0.35	10.02
12/04	29.21	19 14	1.59	0.31	5.94
Annual Growth	0.3%	— —	4.0%	13.3%	46.1%

QC Holdings

Need cash PDQ? Call QC. QC Holdings owns about 585 payday loan stores operating mostly as Quik Cash or National Quik Cash, but also under about a half dozen other brands, including California Budget Finance, First Payday Loans, Nationwide Budget Finance, and QC Financial Services. Targeting working-class individuals, its stores provide short-term loans, typically ranging from $100 to $500, for a fee between 15%-20% of the loan. The company also offers check cashing services, title loans, and Western Union money orders and transfers. QC Holdings, which operates in about two dozen states, closes stores as they become unprofitable or are affected by unfavorable regulatory changes.

Overall, though, the company continues to grow. During the past five years, it has expanded from 258 branches to 585 through a combination of acquisitions and new branch openings. It opened about 20 more de novo branches in 2008.

QC Holdings is also adding alternative products to its offerings. In 2007 the company purchased assets from an automotive retailer and finance company focused exclusively on the "buy-here/pay-here" segment of the used car market. It now operates one such location in Missouri and plans to open one or two additional buy-here/pay-here locations in the coming year.

Chairman and CEO Don Early owns 44% of the company; investor Gregory L. Smith owns 19%; and director Murray Indick owns around 10%.

EXECUTIVES

Chairman and CEO: Don Early, age 66, $1,041,066 total compensation
Vice Chairman and Secretary: Mary Lou Early, age 64, $756,503 total compensation
President and COO: Darrin J. Andersen, age 40, $1,177,366 total compensation
CFO: Douglas E. Nickerson, age 43, $603,329 total compensation
VP Operations, Eastern U.S.: Wayne S. Wood, age 46
VP Operations: Michael O. Walrod, age 42, $419,174 total compensation
VP Operations, Western U.S.: D. Scott Smith, age 48
VP and General Counsel: Matthew J. Wiltanger, age 38
Director Corporate Communications: Tom Linafelt
Auditors: Grant Thornton LLP

LOCATIONS

HQ: QC Holdings, Inc.
9401 Indian Creek Pkwy., Ste. 1500
Overland Park, KS 66210
Phone: 913-234-5000　　**Fax:** 913-234-5500
Web: www.qcholdings.com

2008 Locations

	No.
Missouri	107
California	81
South Carolina	62
Arizona	39
Washington	31
Texas	27
Illinois	24
Oklahoma	23
Virginia	22
Kansas	21
New Mexico	20
Utah	19
Ohio	18
Idaho	14
Kentucky	13
Alabama	12
Colorado	11
Nebraska	9
Nevada	9
Mississippi	7
Wisconsin	7
Louisiana	4
Montana	4
Indiana	1
Total	**585**

PRODUCTS/OPERATIONS

2008 Sales

	$ mil.	% of total
Payday loan fees	181.3	80
Installment loans fees	19.0	8
Credit service fees	8.8	4
Buy-here, pay-here revenue	6.1	3
Check cashing fees	5.8	2
Title loan fees	3.7	2
Other fees	3.0	1
Total	**227.7**	**100**

HISTORICAL FINANCIALS

Company Type: Public

Income Statement				FYE: December 31
	ASSETS ($ mil.)	NET INCOME ($ mil.)	INCOME AS % OF ASSETS	EMPLOYEES
12/08	143.0	13.6	9.5%	2,015
12/07	149.6	14.6	9.8%	2,074
12/06	142.9	9.2	6.4%	2,017
12/05	128.1	5.4	4.2%	1,820
12/04	118.4	18.5	15.6%	1,355
Annual Growth	4.8%	(7.4%)	—	10.4%

2008 Year-End Financials

Equity as % of assets: 34.6%
Return on assets: 9.3%
Return on equity: 26.8%
Long-term debt ($ mil.): 37.6
No. of shares (mil.): 17.4
Market value ($ mil.): 66.0
Dividends
Yield: 5.3%
Payout: 26.3%
Sales ($ mil.): 227.7
R&D as % of sales: —
Advertising as % of sales: —

Stock History

NASDAQ (GM): QCCO

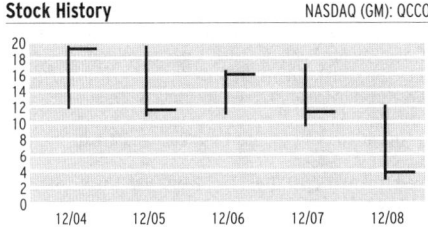

	STOCK PRICE ($) FY Close	P/E High/Low	PER SHARE ($) Earnings	PER SHARE ($) Dividends	PER SHARE ($) Book Value
12/08	3.79	16 4	0.76	0.20	2.84
12/07	11.25	23 13	0.75	0.40	3.00
12/06	15.96	36 25	0.45	0.00	6.02
12/05	11.53	77 44	0.25	0.00	6.37
12/04	19.16	20 12	0.96	0.00	6.11
Annual Growth	(33.3%)	— —	(5.7%)	—	(17.4%)

QCR Holdings

Quad City is muscling in on the community banking scene in the Midwest. QCR Holdings is the holding company for Quad City Bank and Trust, Cedar Rapids Bank and Trust, Rockford Bank and Trust, and First Wisconsin Bank and Trust. Together, the banks have about 10 offices serving the Quad City area of Illinois and Iowa, as well as the communities of Cedar Rapids, Iowa; Rockford, Illinois; and Milwaukee. The banks offer traditional deposit products and services and concentrate their lending activities on local businesses: Commercial real estate loans make up nearly half of the loan portfolio; commercial loans and leases make up another third.

QCR Holdings' Bancard subsidiary provides credit card processing services; its majority-owned M2 Lease Funds leases machinery and equipment to businesses.

QCR Holdings has grown by launching operations in new geographic markets and then building upon them. In 2007 the company acquired its fourth bank charter (First Wisconsin Bank & Trust) and began operating in the Milwaukee metropolitan area, but announced plans to sell the bank to Iowa-based National Bancshares, Inc., the following year.

Company executives and board members collectively own 12% of QCR Holdings; bank investor Jeffrey Gendell owns 7% through Tontine Financial Partners.

EXECUTIVES

Chairman: James J. Brownson, age 63
President, CEO, and Director:
 Douglas M. (Doug) Hultquist, age 54,
 $692,842 total compensation
EVP Funds Management: Victor J. Quinn
EVP and CFO: Todd A. Gipple,
 $459,950 total compensation
EVP and Chief Credit Officer: William M. Tank Jr.
EVP Deposit Operations and Informational Services:
 John A. Rodriguez
SVP and Senior Lending Officer: John Bradley
SVP Deposit Operations: Kathleen M. (Kathy) Francque
SVP and Director Human Resources: Jill A. DeKeyser
SVP and Director Internal Audit: R. Timothy Harding
SVP and Director Finance and Budgeting:
 Shellee R. Showalter
VP and CTO: Michael J. Wyffels
Director; Chief Lending Officer; President and CEO, Cedar Rapids Bank & Trust: Larry J. Helling, age 53,
 $453,966 total compensation
Director; Chairman, Quad City Bank & Trust:
 Mark C. Kilmer, age 50
President and CEO, Quad City Bank and Trust:
 John H. Anderson
President and CEO, Rockford Bank and Trust:
 Thomas Budd
Auditors: McGladrey & Pullen, LLP

LOCATIONS

HQ: QCR Holdings, Inc.
 3551 7th St., Ste. 204, Moline, IL 61265
Phone: 309-736-3580   **Fax:** 309-743-7705
Web: http://-
 www.snl.com/irweblinkx/corporateprofile.aspx?iid=
 1024092

PRODUCTS/OPERATIONS

2008 Gross Revenues

	$ mil.	% of total
Interest		
Loans, including fees	73.4	74
Securities	11.8	12
Other	0.3	—
Noninterest		
Trust department	3.3	4
Service fees on deposit accounts	3.1	3
Other	7.2	7
Total	**99.1**	**100**

2007 Gross Revenues by Segment

	$ mil.	% of total
Commercial banking		
Quad Bank & Trust	59.5	56
Cedar Rapids Bank & Trust	27.3	26
Rockford Bank & Trust	12.0	12
Trust management	3.3	3
Credit card processing	1.0	1
Other	2.6	2
Adjustments	(6.6)	—
Total	**99.1**	**100**

COMPETITORS

AMCORE Financial	First National of Nebraska
Bank of America	MidWestOne
Blackhawk Bancorp	U.S. Bancorp
First Business Financial	Wachovia Corp
First Midwest Bancorp	

HISTORICAL FINANCIALS

Company Type: Public

Income Statement

FYE: December 31

	ASSETS ($ mil.)	NET INCOME ($ mil.)	INCOME AS % OF ASSETS	EMPLOYEES
12/08	1,605.6	6.7	0.4%	345
12/07	1,476.6	4.7	0.3%	329
12/06	1,271.7	2.6	0.2%	351
12/05	1,042.6	4.8	0.5%	305
12/04	870.1	5.2	0.6%	208
Annual Growth	16.6%	6.5%	—	13.5%

2008 Year-End Financials

Equity as % of assets: 5.6%
Return on assets: 0.4%
Return on equity: 7.6%
Long-term debt ($ mil.): 330.4
No. of shares (mil.): 4.6
Market value ($ mil.): 45.5

Dividends
 Yield: 0.8%
 Payout: 7.5%
Sales ($ mil.): 58.6
R&D as % of sales: —
Advertising as % of sales: —

Stock History

NASDAQ (CM): QCRH

	STOCK PRICE ($) FY Close	P/E High/Low		PER SHARE ($) Earnings	Dividends	Book Value
12/08	10.00	16	9	1.06	0.08	19.91
12/07	14.25	18	13	1.02	0.08	18.90
12/06	17.66	35	28	0.57	0.08	15.57
12/05	19.70	23	17	1.04	0.08	11.96
12/04	21.00	18	14	1.20	0.08	11.15
Annual Growth	(16.9%)	—	—	(3.1%)	0.0%	15.6%

Quaker Chemical

Rolling lubricants, like rolled oats, have a Quaker as a maker. This Quaker — Quaker Chemical — rolls out specialty chemicals for industrial and manufacturing processes. Its rolling lubricants are used in making rolled aluminum products and hot- and cold-rolled steel products. Quaker Chemical also makes corrosion preventives, metal finishing compounds, hydraulic fluids, and machining, grinding, and forming compounds. Other products and services include aerospace milling compounds, metal and concrete coatings, and chemical management services. Quaker Chemical's subsidiaries and joint ventures operate worldwide, although it sells primarily to the steel, auto, and appliance industries in the US and Europe.

EXECUTIVES

Chairman and CEO: Michael F. Barry, age 51,
 $908,732 total compensation
VP, CFO, and Treasurer: Mark A. Featherstone, age 47,
 $317,317 total compensation
VP and Managing Director, Asia Pacific: Jan F. Nieman,
 age 48
VP and Managing Director, South America:
 José Luiz Bregolato, age 63,
 $439,643 total compensation
VP and Managing Director, Europe: Wilbert Platzer,
 age 47, $506,465 total compensation
VP Global Strategy, General Counsel, and Secretary:
 D. Jeffry Benoliel, age 50, $458,782 total compensation
Director Human Resources: Ronald S. (Ron) Ettinger
Global Controller: George H. Hill, age 34
General Tax Counsel and Tax Officer: Frank R. Olah
Auditors: PricewaterhouseCoopers LLP

LOCATIONS

HQ: Quaker Chemical Corporation
 1 Quaker Park, 901 Hector St.
 Conshohocken, PA 19428
Phone: 610-832-4000   **Fax:** 610-832-8682
Web: www.quakerchem.com

2008 Sales

	$ mil.	% of total
US	239.5	41
Europe	175.7	30
Asia/Pacific	98.2	17
South America	65.0	11
South Africa	3.2	1
Total	**581.6**	**100**

PRODUCTS/OPERATIONS

2008 Sales

	$ mil.	% of total
Metalworking process chemicals	540.1	93
Coatings	37.3	6
Other	4.2	1
Total	**581.6**	**100**

Selected Products and Services

Chemical management services
Coatings (chemical milling maskants used by the
 aerospace industry, temporary and permanent coatings
 for metal and concrete products)
Construction products (flexible sealants and protective
 coatings)
Corrosion preventives (used to protect metal during
 manufacture, storage, and shipment)
Forming compounds (used to facilitate the drawing and
 extrusion of metal products)
Hydraulic fluids (for hydraulically activated equipment
 used by steel and metalworking companies)
Machining and grinding compounds (used in cutting,
 shaping, and grinding metal parts)
Metal finishing compounds (used to prepare metal
 surfaces for special treatments and processes)
Rolling lubricants (used in the hot and cold rolling of
 steel and in the hot rolling of aluminum)
Technology for the removal of hydrogen sulfide in
 industrial applications

COMPETITORS

Afton Chemical
Daubert Industries
DoALL
FUCHS
General Magnaplate
Houghton International
Infineum
Lubrizol
Milacron
Tilley Chemical Company

HISTORICAL FINANCIALS
Company Type: Public

Income Statement
FYE: December 31

	REVENUE ($ mil.)	NET INCOME ($ mil.)	NET PROFIT MARGIN	EMPLOYEES
12/08	581.6	11.1	1.9%	1,377
12/07	545.6	15.5	2.8%	1,335
12/06	460.5	11.7	2.5%	1,287
12/05	424.0	1.7	0.4%	1,381
12/04	400.7	9.0	2.2%	1,235
Annual Growth	9.8%	5.4%	—	2.8%

2008 Year-End Financials
Debt ratio: 66.9%
Return on equity: 8.7%
Cash ($ mil.): 20.9
Current ratio: 2.39
Long-term debt ($ mil.): 84.2
No. of shares (mil.): 11.1

Dividends
Yield: 5.5%
Payout: 85.7%
Market value ($ mil.): 182.1
R&D as % of sales: —
Advertising as % of sales: —

Stock History
NYSE: KWR

	STOCK PRICE ($) FY Close	P/E High/Low	PER SHARE ($) Earnings	Dividends	Book Value
12/08	16.45	32 10	1.05	0.90	11.37
12/07	21.97	16 13	1.53	0.86	11.78
12/06	22.07	19 14	1.18	0.86	10.01
12/05	19.23	147 93	0.17	0.86	9.56
12/04	24.84	34 24	0.90	0.86	11.07
Annual Growth	(9.8%)	— —	3.9%	1.1%	0.7%

Quality Systems

Quality Systems raises doctors' IQs when it comes to health care information technology. The company provides information management software for medical and dental practices, ambulatory care centers, community health centers, and medical and dental schools. Its NextGen Healthcare Information Systems division focuses on medical practices, makes electronic medical records and practice management systems for managing patient information, appointments, billing, referrals, and insurance claims. Through its QSI division, the company offers practice management software for dental and niche medical practices.

The company's two divisions operate as standalone operations, with each maintaining its own product lines, development teams, and sales and marketing operations. They do, however, share the same corporate office, which handles administrative and accounting functions for both. Its QSI division has clients throughout the US, while its NextGen division primarily operates in Pennsylvania, Georgia, Missouri, and Maryland.

While Quality Systems had its start as a provider of dental practice software, the company has been growing through its NextGen medical practice software division, to the point that NextGen represents 94% of its total sales. The company expanded its NextGen operations through the 2008 purchases of Practice Management Partners (a provider of full-service heath care revenue cycle management products) and health care revenue management provider Lackland Acquisition II, LLC (which does business as Healthcare Strategic Initiatives).

Quality Systems hopes to profit from the American Recovery and Reinvestment Act (ARRA) that was signed into law in the US in early 2009, with $20 billion earmarked in that legislation to spur health care providers in upgrading their IT assets and technology infrastructures.

While nearly all of its current system sales come from a traditional software licensing model, the company has moved to embrace the Software-as-a-Service delivery model, rolling out SaaS offerings for select products in April 2009.

EXECUTIVES
Chairman: Sheldon Razin, age 71
CEO and Director: Steven T. Plochocki, age 57, $388,355 total compensation
President and Chief Strategy Officer: Patrick B. Cline, age 48, $1,036,428 total compensation
COO and Director: Philip N. (Phil) Kaplan, age 42
CFO, Secretary, and Controller: Paul A. Holt, age 43, $426,772 total compensation
EVP and General Manager, QSI Dental Division: Donn E. Neufeld, age 52, $265,810 total compensation
President, NextGen Healthcare Information Systems: Scott Decker
VP, QSI Dental Division: Kathleen Noll
Auditors: Grant Thornton LLP

LOCATIONS
HQ: Quality Systems, Inc.
18111 Von Karman Ave., Ste. 600, Irvine, CA 92612
Phone: 949-255-2600 **Fax:** 949-255-2605
Web: www.qsii.com

PRODUCTS/OPERATIONS
2009 Sales

	% of total
System sales	40
Maintenance, EDI & other services	60
Total	**100**

Selected Products
Clinical data management software
Dental charting software
Dental practice management systems
Internet-based consumer health portal
Medical records storage software
Medical practice management systems

COMPETITORS
Allscripts
AMICAS
CareCentric
Cerner
CPSI
Eclipsys
Epic Systems Corporation
GE Healthcare
Global Med
McKesson
MEDITECH
QuadraMed

HISTORICAL FINANCIALS
Company Type: Public

Income Statement
FYE: March 31

	REVENUE ($ mil.)	NET INCOME ($ mil.)	NET PROFIT MARGIN	EMPLOYEES
3/09	245.5	46.1	18.8%	1,263
3/08	186.5	40.1	21.5%	704
3/07	157.2	33.2	21.1%	661
3/06	119.3	23.3	19.5%	538
3/05	89.0	16.1	18.1%	418
Annual Growth	28.9%	30.1%	—	31.8%

2009 Year-End Financials
Debt ratio: —
Return on equity: 34.2%
Cash ($ mil.): 70.2
Current ratio: 2.24
Long-term debt ($ mil.): —
No. of shares (mil.): 28.6

Dividends
Yield: 2.5%
Payout: 71.0%
Market value ($ mil.): 1,296.1
R&D as % of sales: —
Advertising as % of sales: —

Stock History
NASDAQ (GS): QSII

	STOCK PRICE ($) FY Close	P/E High/Low	PER SHARE ($) Earnings	Dividends	Book Value
3/09	45.25	30 16	1.62	1.15	5.43
3/08	29.87	31 18	1.44	1.00	3.97
3/07	40.00	38 23	1.21	0.00	3.19
3/06	33.10	54 24	0.85	0.00	2.53
3/05	21.17	40 16	0.61	0.00	2.19
Annual Growth	20.9%	— —	27.7%	—	25.5%

Quest Software

Quest Software has made enterprise systems management its personal mission. The company provides application and database management software designed to guarantee application performance and monitor the delivery of information via corporate networks and the Internet. Its software, which is compatible with Oracle, Microsoft, and IBM databases, is used for such functions as database diagnostics, network monitoring, application deployment, problem detection and resolution, and data replication in the event of system failures. Quest also offers desktop and server-side virtualization applications.

Quest's products are used to manage a variety of enterprise software, including enterprise resource planning (ERP) platforms, customer relationship management (CRM) systems, databases, e-commerce exchanges, and corporate

messaging applications. The company's customers come from fields such as telecommunications, manufacturing, energy and utilities, and the public sector.

Quest built its virtualization management software line with the 2007 purchases of Invirtus and Provision Networks. Quest also acquired ScriptLogic, a developer of systems lifecycle management software, for $90 million in cash in 2007.

Chairman Vincent Smith and his family own about a third of the company.

EXECUTIVES

Chairman: Vincent C. (Vinny) Smith, age 45, $3,722,973 total compensation
President, CEO, and Director: Douglas F. (Doug) Garn, age 50, $2,923,534 total compensation
SVP and CFO: Scott J. Davidson, $621,445 total compensation
SVP Product Management and Marketing: Steve Dickson
SVP Worldwide Sales: Alan Fudge
VP, General Counsel, and Secretary: David P. Cramer
VP Global Information Services: Carol Fawcett
VP Unified Communications and Collaboration: David Waugh
VP Research and Development: Alan D. Kucheck, age 57
VP Business Operations: Matthew Gless
VP Corporate Development: Mike Coffman
VP and Corporate Controller: Scott H. Reasoner, age 37
VP Global Marketing: Steve Kahan
VP Human Resources: John Ganley Jr.
CEO, ScriptLogic: Jason Judge, age 39
Public/Analyst Relations, Corporate Communications: Joe Horine
Auditors: Deloitte & Touche LLP

LOCATIONS

HQ: Quest Software, Inc.
5 Polaris Way, Aliso Viejo, CA 92656
Phone: 949-754-8000   **Fax:** 949-754-8999
Web: www.quest.com

2008 Sales

	$ mil.	% of total
US	430.2	58
UK	85.5	12
Other countries	219.7	30
Total	**735.4**	**100**

PRODUCTS/OPERATIONS

2008 Sales

	$ mil.	% of total
Services	401.3	55
Licenses	334.1	45
Total	**735.4**	**100**

Selected Products

Application management (Foglight, JClass, JProbe, PerformaSure, Stat)
Database management (LiteSpeed, Spotlight, Toad)
Windows management
Virtualization management (Vizioncore, vWorkspace)

COMPETITORS

BMC Software
CA, Inc.
Compuware
Embarcadero Technologies
IBM
Microsoft
NetIQ
Oracle
Symantec
VMware

HISTORICAL FINANCIALS

Company Type: Public

Income Statement

FYE: December 31

	REVENUE ($ mil.)	NET INCOME ($ mil.)	NET PROFIT MARGIN	EMPLOYEES
12/08	735.4	68.0	9.2%	3,477
12/07	631.0	63.1	10.0%	3,346
12/06	561.6	59.0	10.5%	2,843
12/05	476.4	41.8	8.8%	2,763
12/04	389.5	47.2	12.1%	2,257
Annual Growth	**17.2%**	**9.6%**	**—**	**11.4%**

2008 Year-End Financials

Debt ratio: 4.7%
Return on equity: 7.7%
Cash ($ mil.): 215.9
Current ratio: 1.13
Long-term debt ($ mil.): 40.8
No. of shares (mil.): 90.4
Dividends
  Yield: 0.0%
  Payout: —
Market value ($ mil.): 1,137.7
R&D as % of sales: —
Advertising as % of sales: —

Stock History

NASDAQ (GS): QSFT

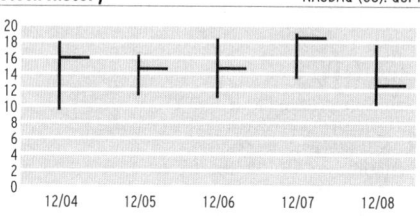

	STOCK PRICE ($) FY Close	P/E High/Low		PER SHARE ($) Earnings	Dividends	Book Value
12/08	12.59	27	16	0.64	0.00	9.67
12/07	18.44	31	23	0.60	0.00	9.93
12/06	14.65	32	20	0.57	0.00	9.06
12/05	14.59	39	28	0.41	0.00	7.70
12/04	15.95	37	20	0.48	0.00	6.72
Annual Growth	**(5.7%)**	**—**	**—**	**7.5%**	**—**	**9.5%**

Questcor Pharmaceuticals

Questcor Pharmaceuticals is on a quest for better health for patients and profitability for itself. The company makes and develops drugs for neurological conditions. Most of its revenue comes from the sale of H.P. Acthar Gel (or Acthar), a drug approved for the treatment of multiple sclerosis flare-ups. However, the drug is mostly prescribed off-label to treat infantile spasms, a rare form of epilepsy; the company is seeking FDA approval for that indication. Questcor also sells insomnia treatment Doral and is developing QSC-001, a pain medication in the form of an orally disintegrating tablet. All of the company's manufacturing is outsourced to contract manufacturers.

Questcor has had some difficulties winning FDA approval for Acthar as a treatment for infantile spasms, although it is the most-often prescribed treatment for the rare condition. The FDA rejected an application for approval in 2007, prompting the company to rethink its strategy for the drug.

Sales of Acthar account for almost all of the company's revenue, but Questcor at one time was losing money on the drug, which it acquired in 2001 from Aventis. In an effort to regain profitability, in 2007 the company raised prices on Acthar fourteen-fold, from about $1,650 per vial to $23,000 per vial, bringing the total cost of a typical course of treatment to around $100,000. To counter protests from health care providers and patients, Questcor expanded efforts to provide financial assistance to uninsured and underinsured patients.

That same year the company's interim president Don Bailey was appointed as CEO. He established a new strategic plan for Acthar, including the price increase, as well as a reduction in the company's sales force of about 70%. Questcor also changed its distribution strategy for the drug, switching from multiple distributors to a single specialty pharmaceutical distributor.

To sharpen its focus on nervous system conditions, the company previously divested several of its marketed products. These included Nascobal, a treatment for vitamin B-12 deficiencies; Ethamolin, which treated esophageal bleeding associated with liver disease; and Glofil-125, a diagnostic agent used to assess kidney function. Subsequently, it acquired the rights to Doral from Meda Pharmaceuticals (formerly MedPointe).

EXECUTIVES

Chairman: Virgil D. Thompson, age 69
President, CEO, and Director: Don M. Bailey, age 63, $1,380,251 total compensation
EVP Corporate Development: Stephen L. (Steve) Cartt, age 46, $852,298 total compensation
SVP Clinical and Regulatory Affairs: Steven C. Halladay, age 61, $401,881 total compensation
SVP Finance and CFO: Gary M. Sawka, age 62, $147,397 total compensation
SVP Pharmaceutical Operations: David J. (Dave) Medeiros, age 57, $639,811 total compensation
Chief Scientific Officer: David Young, age 56
VP Regulatory Affairs: Sian E. Bigora
VP Commercial Operations: Eldon Mayer
VP Contract Manufacturing: Timothy O'Neill
Auditors: Odenberg, Ullakko, Muranishi & Co. LLP

LOCATIONS

HQ: Questcor Pharmaceuticals, Inc.
3260 Whipple Rd., Union City, CA 94587
Phone: 510-400-0700   **Fax:** 510-400-0799
Web: www.questcor.com

PRODUCTS/OPERATIONS

2008 Sales

	$ mil.	% of total
H.P. Acthar Gel	94.4	99
Doral	0.8	1
Total	**95.2**	**100**

Selected Products

Marketed
  Doral (insomnia)
  H.P. Acthar Gel (multiple sclerosis)
In development
  QSC-001 (pain)

COMPETITORS

Cephalon
GlaxoSmithKline
H. Lundbeck
Lundbeck Inc.
Neurocrine Biosciences
Neurogen
Novartis
Sanofi-Aventis
Sepracor
Somaxon

HISTORICAL FINANCIALS

Company Type: Public

Income Statement
FYE: December 31

	REVENUE ($ mil.)	NET INCOME ($ mil.)	NET PROFIT MARGIN	EMPLOYEES
12/08	95.2	40.5	42.5%	46
12/07	49.8	37.6	75.5%	32
12/06	12.8	(10.1)	—	70
12/05	14.2	7.4	52.1%	50
12/04	18.4	(0.8)	—	41
Annual Growth	50.8%	—	—	2.9%

2008 Year-End Financials

Debt ratio: —
Return on equity: 65.0%
Cash ($ mil.): 13.3
Current ratio: 4.00
Long-term debt ($ mil.): —
No. of shares (mil.): 64.2

Dividends
 Yield: 0.0%
 Payout: —
Market value ($ mil.): 597.4
R&D as % of sales: —
Advertising as % of sales: —

Stock History
NASDAQ (GM): QCOR

	STOCK PRICE ($) FY Close	P/E High/Low	PER SHARE ($) Earnings	Dividends	Book Value
12/08	9.31	20 8	0.49	0.00	1.06

Quicksilver Gas Services

It may not be the fastest process ever but Quicksilver Gas Services does it best. The company gathers and processes natural gas and natural gas liquids from the Barnett Shale formation near Fort Worth, Texas, for Quicksilver Resources, its parent (which has proved reserves of 1.2 trillion cu. ft. of natural gas equivalent, and average annual production of 33 billion cu. ft. equivalent). Quicksilver Gas Services' assets include a pipeline and a processing plant with 200 million cu. ft. a day capacity, a processing unit at the existing plant, extensions to the existing pipeline, and pipelines in other drilling areas in Texas. Quicksilver Resources owns about 72% of Quicksilver Gas Services.

The company's strategy is to grow organically, attract interest from third parties, and pursue midstream acquisitions. Boosting its midstream assets, in 2010 Quicksilver Gas Services acquired the Alliance gathering and treating properties (including natural gas gathering systems and compression facilities) from its parent for $95 million.

EXECUTIVES

Chairman: Glenn M. Darden, age 53
President, CEO, and Director:
 Thomas F. (Toby) Darden, age 55
EVP, COO and Director: Paul J. Cook, age 53
SVP, CFO, and Director: Philip W. Cook, age 48
SVP and General Counsel: John C. (Chris) Cirone, age 60
VP and Treasurer: Vanessa Gomez, age 32
VP Chief Accounting Officer: John C. Regan, age 39
Auditors: Deloitte & Touche LLP

LOCATIONS

HQ: Quicksilver Gas Services LP
 777 W. Rosedale St., Fort Worth, TX 76104
Phone: 817-665-8620   **Fax:** 817-665-5008
Web: www.kgslp.com

PRODUCTS/OPERATIONS

2008 Sales

	$ mil.	% of total
Gathering & transportation		
For parent	36.1	46
Revenue	5.6	7
Gas processing		
For parent	30.1	39
Revenue	5.4	7
Other	0.9	1
Total	**78.1**	**100**

COMPETITORS

Crosstex Energy
DCP Midstream Partners
Energy Transfer Equity
Enterprise Products
Penn Virginia
Plains All American
Regency Energy
Southern Natural Gas
Texas Gas Transmission

HISTORICAL FINANCIALS

Company Type: Public

Income Statement
FYE: December 31

	REVENUE ($ mil.)	NET INCOME ($ mil.)	NET PROFIT MARGIN	EMPLOYEES
12/08	78.1	26.4	33.8%	0
12/07	35.9	8.3	23.1%	0
12/06	13.9	2.4	17.3%	0
12/05	4.9	1.6	32.7%	—
12/04	0.0	0.0	—	—
Annual Growth	—	—	—	—

2008 Year-End Financials

Debt ratio: —
Return on equity: —
Cash ($ mil.): 0.3
Current ratio: 0.10
Long-term debt ($ mil.): 227.2
No. of shares (mil.): 12.3

Dividends
 Yield: 6.5%
 Payout: 64.6%
Market value ($ mil.): 116.7
R&D as % of sales: —
Advertising as % of sales: —

Stock History
NYSE Arca: KGS

	STOCK PRICE ($) FY Close	P/E High/Low	PER SHARE ($) Earnings	Dividends	Book Value
12/08	9.48	28 5	0.96	0.62	—
12/07	25.02	129 101	0.20	0.17	—
Annual Growth	(62.1%)	—	380.0%	264.7%	—

Rackspace Hosting

Rackspace may be fanatically focused on hosting services, but sometimes it has its head in the clouds. The company provides a range of Web hosting and managed network services for businesses. It primarily offers traditional hosting services with dedicated servers, but it has expanded into cloud hosting, which lets customers utilize pooled server resources on an on-demand basis. Rackspace also provides hosted collaboration, e-mail, and file back-up applications. The company markets its service operations under the name Fanatical Support. It has more than 50,000 enterprise customers and operates nine data centers located in the US, Hong Kong, and the UK.

Rackspace generates most of its revenues from hosting subscription fees, but a small portion is derived from professional services and other nonrecurring charges. Its international operations accounted for about 30% of its revenues in 2008.

Rackspace has invested in internal development and acquisitions to build its cloud hosting business, which accounted for about 5% of its revenues in 2008. The company purchased cloud storage specialist Jungle Disk and cloud hosting service provider Slicehost in 2008. Rackspace also offers a suite of combined dedicated and cloud computing services called Hybrid Hosting.

EXECUTIVES

Chairman: Graham M. Weston, age 45
President, CEO, and Director: A. Lanham Napier, age 38, $1,095,574 total compensation
President, The Rackspace Cloud and Chief Strategy Officer: Lew Moorman, age 38, $556,963 total compensation
COO: Mark Roenigk
CTO: John Engates
SVP, CFO, and Treasurer: Bruce R. Knooihuizen, age 53, $1,328,171 total compensation
SVP Customer Support: John Lionato, age 46, $665,374 total compensation
SVP Worldwide Sales: Jim Lewandowski, age 48
SVP, General Counsel, and Secretary:
 Alan Schoenbaum, age 51
VP Information Technology: Kiprian (Kip) Miles, age 47
VP Fanatical Support — Managed: Frederick Mendler
VP Marketing and Product Development: Klee Kleber, age 41
VP Human Resources: Wayne Roberts, age 46
Director, Corporate Communications: Annalie Drusch
Auditors: KPMG LLP

LOCATIONS

HQ: Rackspace Hosting, Inc.
 9725 Datapoint Dr., Ste. 100
 San Antonio, TX 78229
Phone: 210-447-4000   **Fax:** 210-447-4300
Web: www.rackspace.com

2008 Sales

	$ mil.	% of total
US	383.5	72
Other countries	148.4	28
Total	**531.9**	**100**

PRODUCTS/OPERATIONS

2008 Sales

	$ mil.	% of total
Managed hosting	506.8	95
Cloud	25.1	5
Total	**531.9**	**100**

COMPETITORS

Amazon.com	NetNation
AT&T	Communications
BT	Planet Internet Services
Cable & Wireless	Qwest Communications
Computer Sciences Corp.	SAVVIS
Critical Path	Switch and Data Facilities
Equinix	Terremark Worldwide
Google	USinternetworking
HP Enterprise Services	Verio
IBM	Verizon
Microsoft	XO Holdings

HISTORICAL FINANCIALS

Company Type: Public

Income Statement — FYE: December 31

	REVENUE ($ mil.)	NET INCOME ($ mil.)	NET PROFIT MARGIN	EMPLOYEES
12/08	531.9	21.7	4.1%	2,611
12/07	362.0	17.8	4.9%	2,021
Annual Growth	46.9%	21.9%	—	29.2%

2008 Year-End Financials

Debt ratio: 94.8%
Return on equity: 11.8%
Cash ($ mil.): 238.4
Current ratio: 2.21
Long-term debt ($ mil.): 255.6
No. of shares (mil.): 122.5

Dividends
  Yield: —
  Payout: —
Market value ($ mil.): 659.1
R&D as % of sales: —
Advertising as % of sales: —

Stock History — NYSE: RAX

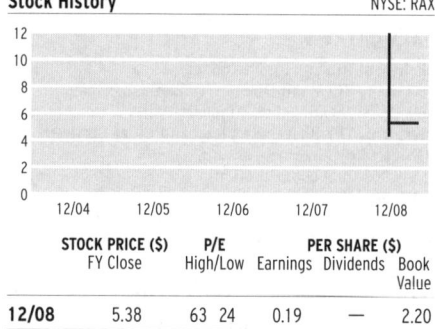

	STOCK PRICE ($) FY Close	P/E High/Low	PER SHARE ($) Earnings	Dividends	Book Value
12/08	5.38	63 24	0.19	—	2.20

Radiant Systems

Radiant Systems helps businesses provide shining service. Its touch-screen point-of-sale (POS) systems are used in cinemas, gas stations, and restaurants. The company's hardware and software link point-of-sale data with centralized merchandising functions like ordering and scheduling. Radiant also offers consulting and systems integration services. Radiant Systems markets directly and through resellers, primarily to large organizations, but it also sells to small businesses. It counts 7-Eleven, BP, ConocoPhillips, Exxon Mobil, Kroger, and The Home Depot among its customers.

Radiant's bread-and-butter client base is made up of organizations with more than 50 locations or sites with more than 50 POS systems. However, the company has teamed with resellers to better serve small and midsized businesses, and

it has generated an increasing percentage of revenues from small businesses in recent years.

The company sees growth opportunities in its international operations. Radiant has operations in North America, Asia, Australia, and Europe. International customers accounted for about 15% of its revenues in 2008. Most of its international business has been in its retail segment, but it plans to expand in both the retail and hospitality markets. Radiant cites its growing number of multinational clients as a key advantage in this endeavor.

Radiant has used acquisitions to expand into new markets and product lines. It bought Quest Retail Technology in 2008. With the Quest acquisition, Radiant gained point-of-sale and back office systems used in restaurants, bars, stadiums, arenas, convention centers, race courses, and theme parks. Also in 2008, the company expanded its presence in Europe with the acquisition of Orderman, an Austria-based maker of handheld ordering and payment devices for the hospitality industry, for about $31 million.

EXECUTIVES

Chairman and CTO: Alon Goren, age 43, $506,308 total compensation
CEO and Director: John H. Heyman, age 47, $1,587,832 total compensation
COO; President, Retail Division: Andrew S. (Andy) Heyman, age 45, $1,158,792 total compensation
CFO: Mark E. Haidet, age 41, $587,183 total compensation
President, Sports and Entertainment Group: Scott Kingsfield
President, Hospitality Division: Paul Langenbahn
President, Hardware Division: Carlyle M. Taylor, age 54
President, International Division: Mark Schoen
VP Accounting: Robert R. Ellis
VP Human Resources: Keith Hicks
VP Retail Division: Chris Lybeer
Director Investor Relations: Karen Minster
Media Relations: Sherry Spreter
Auditors: Deloitte & Touche LLP

LOCATIONS

HQ: Radiant Systems, Inc.
  3925 Brookside Pkwy., Alpharetta, GA 30022
Phone: 770-576-6000   **Fax:** 770-754-7790
Web: www.radiantsystems.com

2008 Sales

	$ mil.	% of total
US	259.1	86
Other countries	42.5	14
Total	**301.6**	**100**

PRODUCTS/OPERATIONS

2008 Sales

	$ mil.	% of total
Systems	155.7	52
Maintenance, subscription & transaction services	108.9	36
Professional services	37.0	12
Total	**301.6**	**100**

2008 Sales

	$ mil.	% of total
Hospitality	225.0	75
Retail	73.1	24
Other	3.5	1
Total	**301.6**	**100**

Selected Products

Kiosks
Point-of-sale terminals
Peripherals
Servers

COMPETITORS

Accenture
Agilysys
Alphameric
CAM Commerce Solutions
Capgemini
Casio America
Clarity Commerce
Danaher
Dell
Dresser Wayne
Epicor Software
HP Enterprise Services
Hypercom
IBM
Ingenico
JDA Software
MICROS Systems
NCR
Panasonic Corp
PAR Technology
Retalix
VeriFone

HISTORICAL FINANCIALS

Company Type: Public

Income Statement — FYE: December 31

	REVENUE ($ mil.)	NET INCOME ($ mil.)	NET PROFIT MARGIN	EMPLOYEES
12/08	301.6	11.0	3.6%	1,354
12/07	253.2	11.8	4.7%	1,033
12/06	222.3	18.4	8.3%	1,032
12/05	172.0	5.6	3.3%	904
12/04	134.9	4.2	3.1%	798
Annual Growth	22.3%	27.2%	—	14.1%

2008 Year-End Financials

Debt ratio: 66.8%
Return on equity: 7.8%
Cash ($ mil.): 16.5
Current ratio: 1.68
Long-term debt ($ mil.): 93.7
No. of shares (mil.): 32.9

Dividends
  Yield: 0.0%
  Payout: —
Market value ($ mil.): 111.0
R&D as % of sales: —
Advertising as % of sales: —

Stock History — NASDAQ (GS): RADS

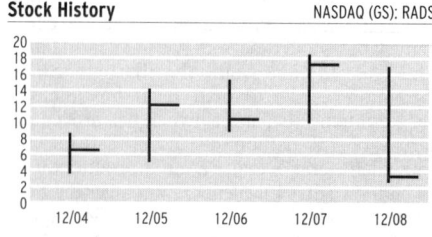

	STOCK PRICE ($) FY Close	P/E High/Low	PER SHARE ($) Earnings	Dividends	Book Value
12/08	3.37	51 8	0.33	0.00	4.26
12/07	17.23	51 28	0.36	0.00	4.31
12/06	10.44	27 16	0.56	0.00	3.52
12/05	12.16	78 29	0.18	0.00	2.56
12/04	6.51	61 27	0.14	0.00	2.23
Annual Growth	(15.2%)	— —	23.9%	—	17.6%

Raven Industries

Quoth the Raven, "Reinforced plastic, electronics, flow control devices, and balloons!" Raven Industries' engineered films division does make reinforced plastic sheeting for various applications, including hot air balloons. Its electronic systems division offers electronic manufacturing services, as well as design support, material procurement and management, and eco stress testing. An applied technology leg manufactures high-tech agricultural aids, from global positioning system (GPS)-based chemical spray equipment to field computers and steering systems. Raven's Aerostar subsidiary produces high altitude research balloons, parachutes, and protective wear used by the agencies. Goodrich is a major customer.

Raven Industries announced in October 2009 that it has agreed to buy almost all the assets of Canadian-held Ranchview. Terms of the agreement were not disclosed. Ranchview develops products that deliver real-time corrections to GPS equipment using cellular networks instead of radio systems.

Confronting the tough economic environment of 2008-09, Raven Industries maneuvered for growth from a diversified, four-legged stance. Sales from its engineered films leg were exposed to weak demand from oil field and construction projects. Each of these two arenas accounts for 40% of sales. Ramping up its cast extruders in 2009, Raven competed for industrial customers demanding geomembrane and composite construction films by peddling a higher-quality product at a comparable industry price.

Piggybacking on promising agricultural markets, the company's applied technology division is expanding its distribution channel. Raven tied the knot with John Deere to have Raven's precision agriculture lineup offered through Deere's branches in the US, Canada, and Australia. Growth in this division is also being fueled by new products, featured as more effective and efficient for increasing farm production. Collaborative agreements are central to developing a slate of technology and information services. Raven has inked a deal with Seed Hawk to improve air-seeder technology. Teaming with AutoFarm, Raven has launched several firsts. In 2008 a new GPS system product, FarmPRO, was marketed. The tool provides steering and an application control system on one screen.

Raven's electronic systems division, however, has struggled to perform amidst the crumbling residential and home remodeling arena. Sales of electronic bed controls, a core line offered to builders, have plunged. Blunting the fall, Raven continues to cultivate demand in the avionics and secure communications markets for its printed circuit boards. (Avionics comprises more than 50% of the division's revenue.) The company's position as a reliable supplier is intended to counter the lower prices of Asian rivals.

Aerostar, Raven's fourth leg of operations, is looking up, literally. Its tethered research balloons (aerostats) are booking an array of contracts, from homeland security to NASA, and universities. Moreover Aerostar parachutes and specialty protective wear are netting a stable of military, commercial, and scientific customers.

Tom Everist has been named chairman, replacing Conrad Hoigaard, who remains a director.

EXECUTIVES

Chairman: Thomas S. Everist, age 59
President, CEO, and Director: Ronald M. Moquist, age 63, $743,946 total compensation
EVP and General Manager, Flow Controls, and Director: Daniel A. Rykhus, age 44, $378,068 total compensation
VP, CFO, and Secretary: Thomas J. Iacarella, age 55, $348,648 total compensation
VP Administration: Barbara K. (Barb) Ohme, age 61
Division VP and General Manager, Electronic Systems Division: David R. Bair, age 52
Division VP and General Manager, Engineered Films Division: James D. Groninger, age 50, $259,523 total compensation
President, Aerostar International: Mark L. West, age 55, $277,509 total compensation
Auditors: PricewaterhouseCoopers LLP

LOCATIONS

HQ: Raven Industries, Inc.
205 E. 6th St., Sioux Falls, SD 57117
Phone: 605-336-2750   **Fax:** 605-335-0268
Web: www.ravenind.com

PRODUCTS/OPERATIONS

2009 Sales

	$ mil.	% of total
Applied Technology	103.1	36
Engineered Films	89.9	32
Electronic Systems	62.0	22
Aerostar	27.2	10
Adjustments	(2.3)	—
Total	**279.9**	**100**

Selected Products and Divisions

Engineered Films (high-performance plastic sheeting for agricultural, construction, geomembrane, industrial, and oil field applications)
Electronic Systems (electronics contract manufacturer of electronic bed controls, printed circuit boards, and secure communication devices)
Applied Technology (data collection, GPS steering devices, and planting and spraying controls)
Aerostar (parachutes, protective outerwear, and aerostats)

COMPETITORS

Astronautics
Cohesant
Denali
Emerson Electric
Flowserve
Graco
Sigma Plastics
Spartech
Williamson-Dickie Manufacturing

HISTORICAL FINANCIALS

Company Type: Public

Income Statement

FYE: January 31

	REVENUE ($ mil.)	NET INCOME ($ mil.)	NET PROFIT MARGIN	EMPLOYEES
1/09	279.9	30.8	11.0%	1,020
1/08	234.0	27.8	11.9%	970
1/07	217.5	25.4	11.7%	910
1/06	204.5	24.3	11.9%	885
1/05	168.1	17.9	10.6%	860
Annual Growth	**13.6%**	**14.5%**	**—**	**4.4%**

2009 Year-End Financials

Debt ratio: —	Dividends
Return on equity: 26.6%	Yield: 2.4%
Cash ($ mil.): 16.3	Payout: 30.6%
Current ratio: 4.21	Market value ($ mil.): 393.1
Long-term debt ($ mil.): —	R&D as % of sales: —
No. of shares (mil.): 18.0	Advertising as % of sales: —

Stock History

NASDAQ (GS): RAVN

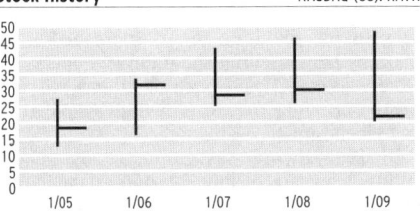

	STOCK PRICE ($) FY Close	P/E High/Low	PER SHARE ($) Earnings	Dividends	Book Value
1/09	21.81	28 12	1.70	0.52	6.30
1/08	30.02	30 17	1.53	0.44	6.56
1/07	28.43	31 18	1.39	0.36	5.45
1/06	31.60	25 12	1.34	0.28	4.68
1/05	18.38	28 13	0.97	0.22	3.67
Annual Growth	**4.4%**	**— —**	**15.1%**	**24.0%**	**14.5%**

Red Hat

Red Hat hopes that businesses are ready to try open-source operating systems on for size. Red Hat dominates the market for Linux, the open-source computer operating system (OS) that is the chief rival to Microsoft's Windows operating systems. In addition to its Red Hat Enterprise Linux OS, the company's product line includes database, content, and collaboration management applications; server and embedded operating systems; and software development tools. Red Hat also provides consulting, custom software development, support, and training services. The company's business model is a mix of providing free, open-source software paired with subscription-based support, training, and integration services.

Although Red Hat originally offered support for consumer-oriented Linux products, the company has shifted its focus entirely to supporting and servicing Linux technologies in enterprise environments. While Linux has failed to gain any traction versus Microsoft's Windows operating system in the consumer space, Linux has been much more successful in corporate environments, especially for managing data center operations such as virtualization, server management, and enterprise application integration.

Red Hat's acquisition of JBoss added middleware tools to its product line, which are used to develop and deploy applications throughout an enterprise that are accessible via the Internet, intranets, extranets, and virtual private networks. JBoss (which operates as a division of Red Hat) specializes in open-source middleware software including application servers and messaging systems. Red Hat continued to round out its services offerings with the 2008 purchase of Amentra, a provider of systems integrations services.

HISTORY

Finnish graduate student Linus Torvalds created the Linux operating system in 1991 as a hobby. When Torvalds released its programming code free over the Internet for anyone to revise, Linux quickly attracted a core base of devoted programmers — including Marc Ewing. A programmer for IBM by day, Ewing developed improvements to Linux in his spare bedroom. Soon he began selling the improved operating system as Red Hat — named after a red and white Cornell lacrosse cap Ewing's grandfather had given him.

In 1994 Ewing was contacted by Robert Young, who after selling typewriters and running a computer leasing company had started a UNIX newsletter. But Young saw better profit margins in catalog sales. Young's ACC Corp. bought the rights to Ewing's creation and the two went into business together. ACC Corp. was renamed Red Hat Software, Inc.

The company compiled Linux's most significant improvements and distributed them on a CD-ROM and through the budding Internet. Their revenues actually came from manuals and technical support sold to new users and businesses who were challenged by the software's ever-changing source code.

By 1997 Linux — and Red Hat's package — were known only among the most militant programmers who sought alternatives to Microsoft's Windows. Hundreds of developers had continually doctored Linux online to create an operating system known for its speed and reliability.

Red Hat exploded in popularity in 1998 after Intel and Netscape both made minor investments in the company. In 1999 Compaq, IBM, Novell, Oracle, and SAP invested in Red Hat. The company went public later that year.

In 2000 Red Hat used its soaring stock as currency to acquire embedded programming specialist Cygnus Solutions for $674 million and Hell's Kitchen Systems (HKS), a maker of payment processing software. President Matthew Szulik replaced Young as CEO and Ewing stepped down as CTO.

Red Hat expanded its software products in 2001 to include database applications and an e-commerce software suite designed for mid-sized businesses. The following year Szulik assumed the additional role of chairman.

Red Hat in late 2003 acquired Sistina Software, a supplier of data storage infrastructure software for Linux operating systems, for about $31 million in stock.

Early in 2005 the company established a government business unit; Red Hat US government customers include the Department of Energy and the Federal Aviation Administration. In 2006 the company acquired open source middleware developer JBoss for about $350 million.

In 2007 the company expanded its middleware offerings through the acquisition of MetaMatrix. The following year the company purchased Qumranet, an Israel-based virtualization software provider, for $107 million. Also in 2008 James Whitehurst took the CEO reins from Szulik.

EXECUTIVES

Chairman: Matthew J. (Matt) Szulik, age 52
President, CEO, and Director:
 James M. (Jim) Whitehurst, age 42,
 $5,004,600 total compensation
EVP and CFO: Charles E. (Charlie) Peters Jr., age 57,
 $2,750,354 total compensation
EVP Corporate Affairs: Tom Rabon

EVP and General Counsel: Michael R. Cunningham, age 49, $2,166,274 total compensation
EVP Engineering and President, Products and Technologies: Paul J. Cormier, age 52, $3,899,699 total compensation
EVP and President, Global Sales, Services, and Field Marketing: Alex Pinchev, age 59, $2,490,101 total compensation
SVP People and Brand: DeLisa Alexander
CIO: Lee Congdon
VP Engineering and CTO: Brian Stevens
VP and General Manager Government Sales Operations: Paul Smith
VP Corporate Development: Michael (Mike) Evans
VP Open Source Affairs: Michael (Mike) Tiemann, age 44
VP Platform Business Unit: Scott Crenshaw
VP Management Solutions Business Unit: Katrinka B. McCallum, age 35
VP Middleware Business Unit: Craig Muzilla
VP Global Operations and Senior Transformation Executive: Nicholas (Nick) Van Wyk
Auditors: PricewaterhouseCoopers

LOCATIONS

HQ: Red Hat, Inc.
 1801 Varsity Dr., Raleigh, NC 27606
Phone: 919-754-3700   **Fax:** 919-754-3701
Web: www.redhat.com

2009 Sales

	$ mil.	% of total
Americas	422.0	65
EMEA	141.7	22
Asia/Pacific	88.9	13
Total	**652.6**	**100**

PRODUCTS/OPERATIONS

2009 Sales

	$ mil.	% of total
Subscriptions	541.2	83
Training & services	111.4	17
Total	**652.6**	**100**

Selected Software

Red Hat Enterprise
Red Hat Network
Red Hat Applications
 Red Hat Cluster Suite
 Red Hat Developer Suite
 Red Hat Content Management System
 Red Hat Portal Server

Selected Services

Consulting
Custom development
Technical support
Training

COMPETITORS

Apple Inc.
BMC Software
CA, Inc.
Hewlett-Packard
IBM
Mandriva
Microsoft
Novell
Oracle
Sun Microsystems
Unisys
Xandros

HISTORICAL FINANCIALS

Company Type: Public

Income Statement

FYE: February 28

	REVENUE ($ mil.)	NET INCOME ($ mil.)	NET PROFIT MARGIN	EMPLOYEES
2/09	652.6	78.7	12.1%	2,800
2/08	523.0	76.7	14.7%	2,200
2/07	400.6	59.9	15.0%	1,800
2/06	278.3	79.7	28.6%	1,100
2/05	196.5	45.4	23.1%	940
Annual Growth	**35.0%**	**14.7%**	**—**	**31.4%**

2009 Year-End Financials

Debt ratio: 3.2%
Return on equity: 7.7%
Cash ($ mil.): 515.5
Current ratio: 1.99
Long-term debt ($ mil.): 35.4
No. of shares (mil.): 187.8
Dividends
 Yield: —
 Payout: —
Market value ($ mil.): 2,570.7
R&D as % of sales: —
Advertising as % of sales: —

Stock History

NYSE: RHT

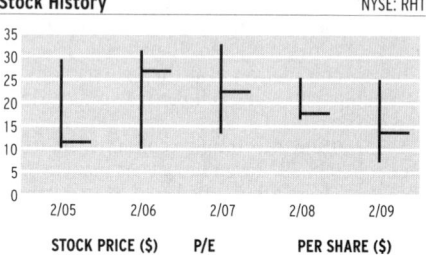

	STOCK PRICE ($) FY Close	P/E High/Low	PER SHARE ($)		
			Earnings	Dividends	Book Value
2/09	13.69	64 19	0.39	—	5.89
2/08	17.83	70 47	0.36	—	5.07
2/07	22.45	112 47	0.29	—	4.37
2/06	26.87	76 25	0.41	—	2.54
2/05	11.47	121 43	0.24	—	1.93
Annual Growth	**4.5%**	**— —**	**12.9%**	**—**	**32.2%**

Red Robin Gourmet Burgers

Hamburger fans are chirping about Red Robin Gourmet Burgers. The company operates a chain of more than 420 casual-dining restaurants in 40 states and Canada that specialize in high-end hamburgers. Its menu features more than 20 different twists on the American classic, including the Banzai Burger (marinated in teriyaki), Bleu Ribbon Burger, and the jalapeño-charged 5 Alarm Burger. The signature Royal Red Robin Burger features bacon and a fried egg on top of the beef. Red Robin also serves chicken, seafood, and turkey burgers, as well as vegetarian alternatives. Non-burger entrées include salads, pasta, seafood, and fajitas. The company operates more than 300 of its locations and franchises the rest.

Red Robin's restaurants are typically free-standing units in retail areas and near entertainment centers. The company has continued to expand its chain despite a downturn in the economy, opening more than 40 locations during 2008, mostly corporate-run eateries. That pace

was up from the previous year when about 25 restaurants were added to the chain.

Former CEO Michael Snyder, who resigned in 2005 after questions were raised about corporate travel expenditures, owns close to 10% of the company.

EXECUTIVES

Chairman and CEO: Dennis B. Mullen, age 65, $3,188,864 total compensation
President and COO: Eric C. Houseman, age 41, $821,974 total compensation
SVP and Chief Development Officer: Todd A. Brighton, age 51, $544,644 total compensation
SVP and Chief Marketing Officer: Susan Lintonsmith, age 44, $450,423 total compensation
SVP, Chief Legal Officer, and Secretary: Annita M. Menogan, age 54, $469,347 total compensation
SVP and CFO: Katherine L. (Katie) Scherping, age 49, $527,437 total compensation
SVP Enterprise Services: Jonathon W. James, age 39
Director Communications: Kevin Caulfield
Auditors: Deloitte & Touche LLP

LOCATIONS

HQ: Red Robin Gourmet Burgers, Inc.
6312 S. Fiddler's Green Cir., Ste. 200N
Greenwood Village, CO 80111
Phone: 303-846-6000 **Fax:** 303-846-6048
Web: www.redrobin.com

2008 Locations

	No.
Company-owned	294
Franchised	129
Total	**423**

PRODUCTS/OPERATIONS

2008 Sales

	$ mil.	% of total
Restaurants	854.7	98
Franchising & other	14.5	2
Total	**869.2**	**100**

COMPETITORS

Applebee's
Brinker
California Pizza Kitchen
Carlson Restaurants
Cheesecake Factory
Chipotle
Cracker Barrel
Darden
Denny's
Fuddruckers
Hooters
Johnny Rockets
Max & Erma's Restaurants
Ruby Tuesday
Steak n Shake

HISTORICAL FINANCIALS

Company Type: Public

Income Statement
FYE: December 31

	REVENUE ($ mil.)	NET INCOME ($ mil.)	NET PROFIT MARGIN	EMPLOYEES
12/08	869.2	27.1	3.1%	27,089
12/07	763.5	30.7	4.0%	25,285
12/06	618.7	29.4	4.8%	21,535
12/05	486.0	27.4	5.6%	16,545
12/04	409.1	23.4	5.7%	13,000
Annual Growth	20.7%	3.7%	—	20.1%

2008 Year-End Financials

Debt ratio: 78.7%
Return on equity: 9.8%
Cash ($ mil.): 11.2
Current ratio: 0.54
Long-term debt ($ mil.): 211.6
No. of shares (mil.): 15.6
Dividends
Yield: 0.0%
Payout: —
Market value ($ mil.): 262.2
R&D as % of sales: —
Advertising as % of sales: —

Stock History
NASDAQ (GS): RRGB

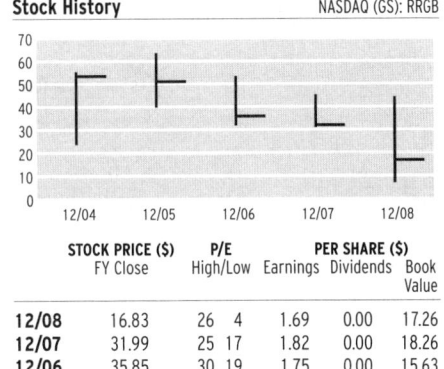

	STOCK PRICE ($) FY Close	P/E High/Low		PER SHARE ($) Earnings	Dividends	Book Value
12/08	16.83	26	4	1.69	0.00	17.26
12/07	31.99	25	17	1.82	0.00	18.26
12/06	35.85	30	19	1.75	0.00	15.63
12/05	50.96	38	25	1.64	0.00	13.15
12/04	53.47	38	17	1.43	0.00	10.38
Annual Growth	(25.1%)	—	—	4.3%	—	13.6%

Renasant Corporation

Those who want to see their wealth reborn (or born, for that matter) might bank at Renasant Corporation. Formerly The Peoples Holding Company, Renasant is the parent of Renasant Bank and Renasant Insurance. Through about 70 branches in Alabama, Mississippi, and Tennessee, the bank provides a range of services to individuals and local businesses, including checking and savings accounts, loans, and investment products. Lending activities account for about 70% of the company's annual revenue; nearly 70% of its loan portfolio consists of residential and commercial real estate loans. The bank also offers agricultural, business, and consumer loans, and lease financing. Renasant Insurance offers personal and business insurance.

After entering the Tennessee market with its purchase of Renasant Bancshares in 2004, The Peoples Holding Company in mid-2005 adopted the Renasant name.

Renasant gained a foothold in northern and central Alabama through its 2005 acquisition of Heritage Financial Holding Corporation and its subsidiary Heritage Bank. In 2007 it expanded its presence in Tennessee with the acquisition of Nashville, Tennessee-based Capital Bancorp for about $135 million.

A group of some 30 directors and executive officers controls nearly 10% of Renasant.

EXECUTIVES

Chairman, President, and CEO; President and CEO, Renasant Bank: E. Robinson (Robin) McGraw, age 62, $649,177 total compensation
Vice Chairman: J. Larry Young, age 70
EVP; SEVP, CFO, and Cashier, Renasant Bank: Stuart R. Johnson, age 56, $345,379 total compensation
EVP; SEVP and Chief Administrative Officer, Renasant Bank: C. Mitchell (Mitch) Waycaster, age 51, $346,822 total compensation

EVP and General Counsel; SEVP and General Counsel, Renasant Bank: Stephen M. Corban, age 54
EVP; SEVP and Chief Credit Policy Officer, Renasant Bank: Claude H. Springfield III, age 62
EVP; SEVP and Strategic Planning Director, Renasant Bank: James W. Gray, age 53
EVP and Director; President Tennessee Division, Renasant Bank: R. Rick Hart, age 61, $847,359 total compensation
EVP; President, Alabama Division: Mike Ross, age 45
EVP; President, Mississippi Division, Renasant Bank: J. Scott Cochran, age 46
EVP; SEVP and Chief Credit Officer, Renasant Bank Alabama Division: Harold H. Livingston, age 61
Auditors: Horne LLP

LOCATIONS

HQ: Renasant Corporation
209 Troy St., Tupelo, MS 38802
Phone: 662-680-1001 **Fax:** 662-680-1234
Web: www.renasantbank.com

PRODUCTS/OPERATIONS

2008 Gross Revenues

	$ mil.	% of total
Interest		
Loans	167.6	66
Securities & other	33.4	13
Noninterest		
Service charges on deposit accounts	22.6	9
Fees & commissions	16.1	6
Other	15.3	6
Total	**255.0**	**100**

Selected Subsidiaries

Renasant Bank
Primeco, Inc.
Renasant Insurance, Inc.
Renasant Leasing Corp.
Renasant Investment Corp.
Renasant Capital Corp.

COMPETITORS

BancorpSouth
Cadence Financial Corporation
Citizens Holding
Compass Bancshares
First Horizon
Hancock Holding
Regions Financial
Trustmark

HISTORICAL FINANCIALS

Company Type: Public

Income Statement
FYE: December 31

	ASSETS ($ mil.)	NET INCOME ($ mil.)	INCOME AS % OF ASSETS	EMPLOYEES
12/08	3,716.0	24.1	0.6%	866
12/07	3,612.3	31.1	0.9%	880
12/06	2,611.4	27.1	1.0%	813
12/05	2,397.7	24.2	1.0%	789
12/04	1,707.5	18.4	1.1%	703
Annual Growth	21.5%	7.0%	—	5.4%

2008 Year-End Financials

Equity as % of assets: 10.8%
Return on assets: 0.7%
Return on equity: 6.0%
Long-term debt ($ mil.): 619.4
No. of shares (mil.): 21.1
Market value ($ mil.): 359.0
Dividends
Yield: 4.0%
Payout: 59.6%
Sales ($ mil.): 163.5
R&D as % of sales: —
Advertising as % of sales: —

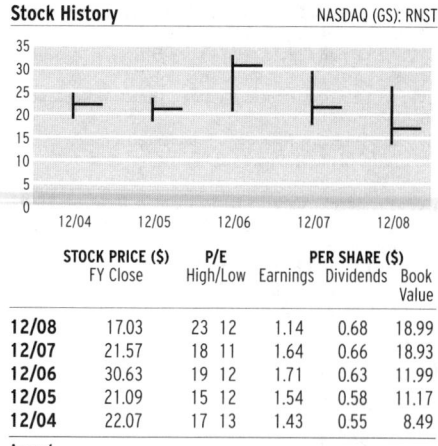

Stock History   NASDAQ (GS): RNST

	STOCK PRICE ($) FY Close	P/E High/Low		PER SHARE ($) Earnings	Dividends	Book Value
12/08	17.03	23	12	1.14	0.68	18.99
12/07	21.57	18	11	1.64	0.66	18.93
12/06	30.63	19	12	1.71	0.63	11.99
12/05	21.09	15	12	1.54	0.58	11.17
12/04	22.07	17	13	1.43	0.55	8.49
Annual Growth	(6.3%)	—	—	(5.5%)	5.4%	22.3%

Repligen Corporation

Repligen looks out for the kids. The firm develops drugs for neurological and autoimmune disorders, including diseases that strike children. The company is developing treatments for Friedrich's ataxia, a debilitating early adulthood disease, and bipolar disorder. Repligen is also developing secretin, a gastrointestinal hormone, to enhance MRI images of the pancreas. The firm holds the rights to recombinant Protein A, which it sells to medical firms and biotechs such as GE Healthcare and Applied Biosystems (now part of Life Technologies Corporation) to mass produce therapeutic antibodies and perform R&D.

Repligen focuses on developing its products through early stages and then licensing the late-stage development and commercialization rights to larger pharmaceutical partners. The company receives royalty payments from Bristol-Myers Squibb (BMS) on sales of BMS's Orencia rheumatoid arthritis drug.

Until its supplier ChiRhoClin ended shipments in 2008, Repligen sold SecreFlo, another secretin-based substance used to assess pancreas function and diagnose gastrinoma, a gastroenterological cancer.

EXECUTIVES

Chairman: Alexander Rich, age 84
President, CEO, and Director: Walter C. Herlihy, age 57, $612,682 total compensation
SVP Research and Development: James R. Rusche, age 55, $357,123 total compensation
VP Market Development: Laura Whitehouse Pew
VP Operations: Daniel P. Witt, age 62, $298,363 total compensation
VP Finance and Administration: William J. Kelly, age 38, $319,663 total compensation
Auditors: Ernst & Young LLP

LOCATIONS

HQ: Repligen Corporation
41 Seyon St., Bldg. 1, Ste. 100, Waltham, MA 02453
Phone: 781-250-0111   **Fax:** 781-250-0115
Web: www.repligen.com

2009 Sales

	% of total
US	59
Sweden	33
Other countries	4
Total	**100**

PRODUCTS/OPERATIONS

2009 Sales

	$ mil.	% of total
Products		
Protein A	14.4	49
SecreFlo	0.2	1
Royalties & other	14.8	50
Total	**29.4**	**100**

COMPETITORS

Abbott Labs
Bio-Rad Labs
Cangene
Human Genome Sciences
Incyte
Life Technologies Corporation
NeuroNova
PDL BioPharma
Teva Neuroscience

HISTORICAL FINANCIALS

Company Type: Public

Income Statement

     FYE: March 31

	REVENUE ($ mil.)	NET INCOME ($ mil.)	NET PROFIT MARGIN	EMPLOYEES
3/09	29.4	5.7	19.4%	69
3/08	19.3	37.1	192.2%	56
3/07	14.1	(0.9)	—	45
3/06	12.9	0.7	5.4%	43
3/05	9.4	(3.0)	—	37
Annual Growth	33.0%	—		16.9%

2009 Year-End Financials

Debt ratio: —
Return on equity: 8.6%
Cash ($ mil.): 5.0
Current ratio: 12.04
Long-term debt ($ mil.): —
No. of shares (mil.): 30.8

Dividends
  Yield: —
  Payout: —
Market value ($ mil.): 147.3
R&D as % of sales: —
Advertising as % of sales: —

Stock History

      NASDAQ (GM): RGEN

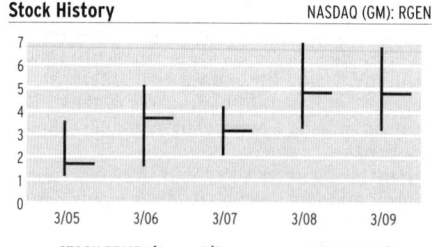

	STOCK PRICE ($) FY Close	P/E High/Low		PER SHARE ($) Earnings	Dividends	Book Value
3/09	4.79	37	18	0.18	—	2.25
3/08	4.82	6	3	1.18	—	2.08
3/07	3.16	—	—	(0.03)	—	0.83
3/06	3.70	254	83	0.02	—	0.83
3/05	1.70	—	—	(0.10)	—	0.79
Annual Growth	29.6%	—	—	—	—	29.9%

Republic Bancorp

If Old Kentucky is *your* home, perhaps you bank at Republic Bancorp. It's the largest Kentucky-based bank holding company, and parent to Republic Bank & Trust, which has about 40 branches in central Kentucky and southern Indiana. In 2006 the company entered Florida, where it has four branches, via its purchase of Tampa's GulfStream Bank, since renamed Republic Bank. The banks offer checking and savings accounts, investment management, and trust services. Their lending activities mainly consist of residential mortgages (about half of the company's loan portfolio) and commercial real estate loans (almost 30%).

Republic Bancorp originates subprime consumer loans through its Republic Finance subsidiary, and offers loans secured by income tax refunds throughout the US.

The company is growing by opening new branches. It plans to merge Republic Bank into Republic Bank & Trust.

The Trager family, including chairman Bernard, vice chairman Scott, and CEO Steven, controls a majority of Republic Bancorp.

EXECUTIVES

Chairman: Bernard M. Trager, age 80, $794,988 total compensation
Vice Chairman; President, Republic Bank & Trust: A. Scott Trager, age 56, $816,456 total compensation
President, CEO, and Director; Chairman and CEO, Republic Bank & Trust: Steven E. (Steve) Trager, age 48, $545,089 total compensation
EVP and Chief Lending and Deposit Officer, Republic Bank & Trust: David Vest, age 49
EVP, CFO, Chief Accounting Officer, Treasurer, and Controller; EVP, CFO, and Treasurer, Republic Bank & Trust: Kevin Sipes, age 37, $663,200 total compensation
SVP, Secretary, and General Counsel: Michael A. (Mike) Ringswald
SVP and Managing Director, Finance: Mike Beckwith
SVP and Chief Investment Officer, Republic Bank & Trust: Greg Williams
SVP Marketing, Republic Bank & Trust: Michael Sadofsky
SVP Information Technology, Republic Bank & Trust: Roger Batsel
SVP Human Resources, Republic Bank & Trust Company: Margaret Wendler
President, Tax Refund Solutions, Republic Bank & Trust: William R. (Bill) Nelson, $643,635 total compensation
President, Central Kentucky Market, Republic Bank & Trust: Bo Henry
President, Florida Market, Republic Bank & Trust: Doug Winton
President, Northern Kentucky Market, Republic Bank & Trust: Steve Brunson
Auditors: Crowe Horwath, LLP

LOCATIONS

HQ: Republic Bancorp, Inc.
601 W. Market St., Louisville, KY 40202
Phone: 502-584-3600   **Fax:** 502-584-3753
Web: www.republicbank.com

PRODUCTS/OPERATIONS

2008 Gross Revenues

	$ mil.	% of total
Interest		
Loans	170.6	65
Securities	27.2	10
Other	4.4	2
Noninterest		
Service charges on deposit accounts	19.4	7
Electronic refund check fees	17.8	7
Debit card interchange fees	4.8	2
Other	18.3	7
Total	**262.5**	**100**

COMPETITORS

BB&T
Citizens First
Farmers Capital Bank
Fifth Third
PNC Financial
S.Y. Bancorp
U.S. Bancorp

HISTORICAL FINANCIALS

Company Type: Public

Income Statement

FYE: December 31

	ASSETS ($ mil.)	NET INCOME ($ mil.)	INCOME AS % OF ASSETS	EMPLOYEES
12/08	3,939.4	33.7	0.9%	724
12/07	3,165.4	24.9	0.8%	727
12/06	3,046.8	28.4	0.9%	739
Annual Growth	13.7%	8.9%	—	(1.0%)

2008 Year-End Financials

Equity as % of assets: 7.0%
Return on assets: 0.9%
Return on equity: 12.8%
Long-term debt ($ mil.): 556.5
No. of shares (mil.): 20.8
Market value ($ mil.): 565.7
Dividends
Yield: 1.7%
Payout: 29.0%
Sales ($ mil.): 175.6
R&D as % of sales: —
Advertising as % of sales: —

Stock History

NASDAQ (GS): RBCAA

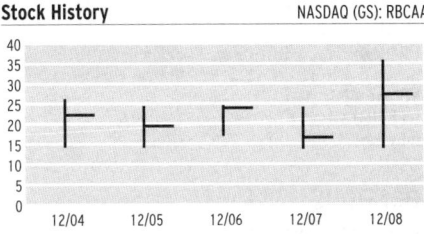

	STOCK PRICE ($) FY Close	P/E High/Low		PER SHARE ($) Earnings	Dividends	Book Value
12/08	27.20	22	9	1.62	0.47	13.27
12/07	16.53	20	12	1.20	0.42	11.97
12/06	23.90	18	13	1.35	0.36	11.41
12/05	19.46	16	9	1.55	0.31	—
12/04	22.20	17	10	1.51	0.25	9.43
Annual Growth	5.2%	—	—	1.8%	17.1%	8.9%

ResMed Inc.

Breathe easy, because you won't lose any sleep while using ResMed's products. ResMed makes and distributes medical equipment used to diagnose and treat respiratory disorders that occur during sleep, such as sleep apnea. Most of its products treat obstructive sleep apnea (OSA), a condition in which a patient's air flow is periodically obstructed, causing multiple disruptions during sleep that lead to daytime sleepiness and possibly other conditions such as high blood pressure. Its products include air-flow generators, face masks, diagnostic products, and accessories. ResMed sells directly and through distributors worldwide to home health equipment dealers, sleep clinics, and hospitals.

The company's main products are continuous positive airway pressure (CPAP) systems that deliver pressurized air from an airflow generator through a nasal mask or pillow, keeping the upper airway open during sleep. It also makes variable positive airway pressure (VPAP) systems, which operate on the same principle but deliver different air pressures for inhalation and exhalation.

ResMed manufactures its products primarily at its Australian facility, though it has additional production plants in France and the US. It sells them in about 70 countries through its own subsidiaries (mainly in the US, Europe, and Australia) and through independent distributors. The US and Germany account for nearly 70% of sales.

The company has been focused on expanding its geographic reach, acquiring a number of medical equipment makers and distributors in Europe and elsewhere. It bolstered its European operations and expanded its product line, for example, with the purchase of Saime, a French maker of home ventilation products.

ResMed then added to its OSA product line with the 2009 buy of Laboratoires Narval, a French maker of a mandibular repositioning device (MRD) designed for patients who snore or have OSA problems. The device is said to reduce symptoms related to OSA or snoring by repositioning the temporomandibular joint that connects the lower jaw (mandible) to the skull (temporal bone) thereby relieving some of the pressure in that area.

Building on research showing linkages between sleep-disordered breathing and conditions such as hypertension, stroke, heart disease, and even diabetes, ResMed is expanding its own research activities in these clinical areas and in 2009 alone invested nearly 10% of its revenue in research and development.

ResMed also won FDA approval for a device (called Adapt SV) used to treat central sleep apnea, a form of the disorder in which the brain temporarily fails to tell the appropriate muscles to breathe.

Getting patients to wear the bulky masks and headgear that treat sleep apnea has proved a barrier to selling the products, and another focus of ResMed's product development efforts is creating devices that are not only more effective, but also more comfortable and convenient. The company introduced two mask products — dubbed Mirage Quattro and Mirage Liberty — that are designed for comfort and allow for greater movement during sleep. Additionally, it launched the Mirage Micro nasal mask, which allows patients to adjust the mask for a more personalized fit.

HISTORY

ResMed was founded as ResCare in 1989 after Peter Farrell led a management buyout of Baxter Healthcare's respiratory technology unit. ResCare initially developed the SULLIVAN nasal CPAP systems (named after inventor Colin Sullivan) in Australia. In 1991 it introduced the Bubble Mask and the APD2 portable CPAP device. Three years later ResCare began marketing its first VPAP, which applied different air pressures for inhalation and exhalation, in the US.

In 1995 the company went public, changing its name to ResMed (its former name was already taken by another medical company). Over the next two years, ResMed expended a lot of oxygen in court suing rival Respironics for patent infringements; judgments in 1997 and 1998 found in favor of Respironics, but ResMed made plans to appeal. In 1998 the firm received FDA approval to market its VPAP device as a critical-care treatment for lung diseases.

In 1999 the firm's listing was switched from the Nasdaq to the NYSE to stabilize stock prices after court losses against Respironics; it also listed on the Australian Stock Exchange. The introduction of two new products, the AutoSet CPAP unit and the Mirage face mask, boosted sales that year. In 2001 ResMed bought MAP Medizin-Technologie, a German manufacturer of sleep-disordered breathing treatment devices. The acquisition enhanced ResMed's position in Germany, which is the company's second-biggest market for its products.

In 2004 ResMed bought its Dutch distributor Resprecare and snapped up Scandinavian, German, and Austrian distributors the following year. Also in 2005, it bought Saime, a French maker of home ventilation products.

The company voluntarily recalled some 300,000 units of a major line of flow generators in 2007, after determining that there was a slight risk of short circuiting in the products. The action significantly hurt profits that year, but the company had largely recovered by the following year, buoyed by strong sales of its newer products.

EXECUTIVES

Chairman: Peter C. Farrell, age 67, $2,811,011 total compensation
President, CEO, and Director: Kieran T. Gallahue, age 46, $3,437,719 total compensation
COO, Asia/Pacific: Robert (Rob) Douglas, age 50, $1,123,703 total compensation
COO, Europe: Stein Jacobsen, age 44
CFO: Brett Sandercock, age 42, $1,237,430 total compensation
SVP Organizational Development and General Counsel: David Pendarvis, age 50, $1,354,527 total compensation
SVP Sleep Strategic Business Unit: Michael J. Farrell
VP US Regulatory and Clinical Affairs: David D'Cruz
VP Clinical Education and Training: Ann Tisthammer
VP Human Resources, Americas: Lenita Maljan
Director Healthcare Ecomonics: Matthew Borer
Auditors: KPMG LLP

LOCATIONS

HQ: ResMed Inc.
9001 Spectrum Center Blvd., San Diego, CA 92123
Phone: 858-836-5000 **Fax:** 858-836-5501
Web: www.resmed.com

2009 Sales

	$ mil.	% of total
US	493.4	54
Germany	132.2	14
France	106.4	12
Australia	21.0	2
Other countries	167.7	18
Total	**920.7**	**100**

PRODUCTS/OPERATIONS

Selected Products

Autotitration devices (automatically adjust CPAP pressure)
  AutoSet CS (for Cheyne-Stokes patients)
  AutoSet Respond
  AutoSet Spirit
  AutoSet T
  Magellan
  S8 Autoset II

CPAP (continuous positive airway pressure) devices
  C-Series Tango
  Max IInCPAP
  Mini Max nCPAP
  ResMed S6 Series
  ResMed S7 Series
  ResMed S8 Series
  ResMed S8 Series II

Diagnostic products
  ApneaLink (sleep apnea screening device)
  Embla (digital sleep recorder for sleep labs)
  Embletta (portable digital sleep recorder)
  MEPAL Diagnostic System (sleep lab diagnostic system)
  Poly-MESAM Portable Diagnostic System (cardio-respiratory polygraphy system)

Mask systems
  Hospital full face mask
  Meridian nasal Mask
  Mirage masks
  Papillon Mask
  Swift LT
  Swift LT for Her

Ventilators
  Elisee
  Eole 3 XLS
  Helia 2
  VS Integra
  VS Serena
  VS Ultra

VPAP (variable positive airway pressure) devices
  Adapt SV (for central sleep apnea)
  Comfort
  Moritz
  VPAP II
  VPAP III
  VPAP Malibu

COMPETITORS

Allied Healthcare Products
Covidien
Lincare Holdings
Omnicare
Philips Healthcare
Respironics
Sunrise Medical
Vanda
Vital Signs

HISTORICAL FINANCIALS

Company Type: Public

Income Statement

FYE: June 30

	REVENUE ($ mil.)	NET INCOME ($ mil.)	NET PROFIT MARGIN	EMPLOYEES
6/09	920.7	146.4	15.9%	2,900
6/08	835.4	110.3	13.2%	2,700
6/07	716.3	66.3	9.3%	2,700
6/06	607.0	88.2	14.5%	2,500
6/05	425.5	64.8	15.2%	1,927
Annual Growth	**21.3%**	**22.6%**	**—**	**10.8%**

2009 Year-End Financials

Debt ratio: 8.4%
Return on equity: 13.3%
Cash ($ mil.): 415.6
Current ratio: 3.17
Long-term debt ($ mil.): 94.2
No. of shares (mil.): 75.0

Dividends
  Yield: —
  Payout: —
Market value ($ mil.): 3,053.0
R&D as % of sales: —
Advertising as % of sales: —

Stock History

NYSE: RMD

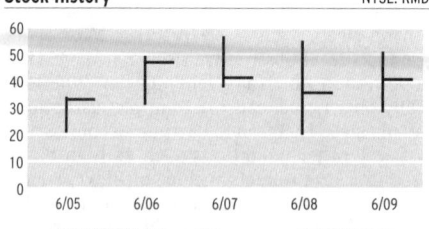

	STOCK PRICE ($) FY Close	P/E High/Low		PER SHARE ($) Earnings	Dividends	Book Value
6/09	40.73	27	15	1.90	—	14.88
6/08	35.74	39	15	1.40	—	14.43
6/07	41.26	66	45	0.85	—	12.42
6/06	46.95	42	27	1.16	—	9.85
6/05	32.99	37	23	0.91	—	6.32
Annual Growth	**5.4%**	**—**	**—**	**20.2%**	**—**	**23.8%**

Rewards Network

Rewards Network can hook ya up. Formerly iDine Rewards Network, the company offers its 3 million members discounts at almost 10,000 restaurants, a large network of hotels, and with all major airlines nationwide. Rewards Network contracts with participating merchants for services at a discounted price and then remarkets those discounts to members who register a major credit card and pay an upfront annual fee of about $50. Members receive loyalty rewards such as rebates, frequent flier miles, and other discounts on food, lodging, travel, gifts, and entertainment. The company was initially founded in 1983.

The "right-to-receive" credits Rewards Network receives are usually redeemable for food and beverages equal to twice the amount of working capital it loaned the restaurant. When the firm sells those rights, the coupons offer the holders a discount for products or services of usually about 20%. In addition to card fees, the company pockets the spread between what it paid for the credits and the price paid by members.

The company's strategy for growth involves increasing its restaurant base while also expanding upon its portfolio of dining credits. To achieve this, Rewards Network is fortifying its sales force team and also acquiring additional dining credits from a selected list of what it deems as "more desirable" restaurants.

Investment vehicle Samstock LLC and its affiliates own about 25% of the company. Samstock is indirectly owned by trusts led by Rewards Network chairman Don Liebentritt.

HISTORY

Melvin Chasen formed Rewards Network as Transmedia Network in 1983 to allow restaurants to swap meal credits for media exposure. In 1985 Transmedia began offering cash advances to restaurants in return for meal credits and began issuing discount cards to consumers. The firm became profitable during the late-1980s recession, when penny-pinching became more prevalent.

Chasen franchised the concept in the US and began licensing the program in Europe and Asia in 1993 (reclaiming these rights in 2000). In 1995 Transmedia began offering credits on purchases that could be used to buy airline tickets. In the late 1990s Transmedia began phasing out franchising.

As the economy boomed, card use dropped and the cost of buying back franchises hurt profits. "Grave dancer" Sam Zell infused cash for a major stake in the firm. Merger plans with Reunion Group failed in late 1998, but the firm bought Montgomery Ward's Dining A La Card program, its top rival, in 1999. It phased out its own branded credit card in favor of having customers register a major credit card with the company.

In 2002 the company changed its name to iDine Rewards Network from Transmedia Network, Inc., to better reflect its business plan. A fourth quarter shake-up in management saw Sheli Rosenberg stepping down from her position as chairman (replaced by none other than financier Zell) and the appointment of director George Wiedemann to president and CEO, accompanied by the resignation of Gene Henderson. Wiedemann lasted just over two years before he resigned in early 2005. He was replaced by Ronald L. Blake.

In December 2003 the company dropped the "iDine" from its name to emphasize the fact it's expanding beyond just dining discounts.

EXECUTIVES

Chairman: Donald J. (Don) Liebentritt, age 58
President, CEO, and Director: Ronald L. (Ron) Blake, age 53, $2,089,924 total compensation
SVP, CFO, and Treasurer: Christopher J. (Chris) Locke, age 39, $495,686 total compensation
SVP, General Counsel, Secretary, and Chief Privacy Officer: Roya Behnia, age 42, $455,000 total compensation
SVP Marketing and Business Development: Megan E. Flynn, age 42, $462,972 total compensation
SVP and CIO: Mario Cruz, age 38
Chief Marketing Officer: Bruce W. Mainzer
Auditors: KPMG LLP

LOCATIONS

HQ: Rewards Network Inc.
  2 N. Riverside Plaza, Ste. 950, Chicago, IL 60606
Phone: 312-521-6767   **Fax:** 312-521-6769
Web: www.rewardsnetwork.com

PRODUCTS/OPERATIONS

Selected Subsidiaries

iDine Media Group Inc.
Rewards Network Canada GP Corporation
Rewards Network Canada LP
Rewards Network Establishment Services Inc.
Rewards Network International, Inc.
Rewards Network Services Inc.
RTR Funding LLC
TMNI International Inc.

COMPETITORS

American Express
Hospitality Marketing Concepts
MasterCard
Passport Unlimited
Provell
Vertrue
Visa Inc

HISTORICAL FINANCIALS

Company Type: Public

Income Statement

FYE: December 31

	REVENUE ($ mil.)	NET INCOME ($ mil.)	NET PROFIT MARGIN	EMPLOYEES
12/08	246.2	4.8	1.9%	397
12/07	225.1	7.0	3.1%	400
12/06	81.4	(15.2)	—	429
12/05	77.1	(0.6)	—	400
12/04	93.2	14.9	16.0%	431
Annual Growth	27.5%	(24.7%)	—	(2.0%)

2008 Year-End Financials

Debt ratio: —
Return on equity: 5.0%
Cash ($ mil.): 9.0
Current ratio: 4.24
Long-term debt ($ mil.): —
No. of shares (mil.): 8.7
Dividends
  Yield: 0.0%
  Payout: —
Market value ($ mil.): 67.7
R&D as % of sales: —
Advertising as % of sales: —

Stock History

NASDAQ (CM): DINE

	STOCK PRICE ($) FY Close	P/E High/Low	PER SHARE ($) Earnings	Dividends	Book Value
12/08	7.77	31 11	0.54	0.00	11.39
12/07	14.91	26 11	0.78	0.00	10.65
12/06	20.85	— —	(1.71)	0.00	9.72
12/05	19.20	— —	(0.06)	0.00	10.80
12/04	21.00	24 10	1.50	0.00	10.60
Annual Growth	(22.0%)	— —	(22.5%)	—	1.8%

Rick's Cabaret

Far from Casablanca, these night clubs offer topless entertainment as part of the floor show. Rick's Cabaret International operates about 19 adult night clubs in Florida, Minnesota, New York, North Carolina, and Texas. Most of the gentlemen's clubs are run under the Rick's Cabaret name, while others operate under such banners as Club Onyx and XTC. Rick's caters to highbrow patrons with dough to blow: It offers VIP memberships for individual and corporate clients that can cost hundreds of dollars annually. In addition to its night clubs, Rick's operates adult Web sites and an auction site for adult entertainment products.

The company added Dallas to its sphere of operations with the 2008 purchase of that city's adult nightclub The Executive Club for $9.5 million. That year it added another Dallas club with the purchase of Platinum Club II.

Also in 2008, Rick's launched itself into print and online media when it acquired trade publisher ED Publications for a little more than $1 million. The deal included such adult industry titles as *Adult Store Buyer* and *Exotic Dancer*, as well as trade shows and Web sites.

CEO Eric Langan owns about 19% of Rick's.

HISTORY

Dallas Fontenot and Salah Izzedin founded Trumps in 1982. The following year they bought a disco and turned it into a swank topless bar called Rick's Cabaret (the name came from an encounter with a drunk in a taxi who was looking for "Rick's"). Izzedin's attorney Robert Watters bought a 10% interest in Trumps in 1987, the same year that the company opened the first members-only VIP room in Houston. The partnership of Fontenot, Izzedin, and Watters soured in 1989 with allegations that Izzedin pocketed unreported money, supplied narcotics to waitresses and dancers, and forced some of them to have sex with him.

Watters took over as CEO in 1991 and became sole owner in 1993. He converted Trumps into Rick's Cabaret International the next year and made Rick's the first topless bar to go public in 1995. The company expanded to New Orleans the following year, opening a club on Bourbon Street. Rick's opened a new club in Minneapolis in 1998 and bought a 93% stake in Taurus Entertainment. Watters resigned in 1999, sold his stock in the company to new CEO Eric Langan and his investment partner, Ralph McElroy, and acquired the firm's New Orleans location, which operated as a Rick's Cabaret under a licensing agreement. (The company sold it the same year.) Later in 1999 Rick's launched its adult Web sites.

In 2000 the company bought a third topless bar in Houston, as well as another adult Web site, xxxPasswords.com. It also began selling prepaid debit cards that allow customers to anonymously buy access to adult entertainment Web sites. Rick's purchased the Chesapeake Bay Cabaret, an upscale club in Houston, in November. Later that year the company inked a deal with adult Web site operator Entertainment Network to offer its content through CandidCam.com.

In 2001 Rick's launched NaughtyBids.com, an auction site for adult products. It also began buying a number of porn auction sites, including Pornauction.com and XXXbids.com, in an effort to enhance the products available on NaughtyBids.com. Late that year it opened Encounters, an upscale club for swinging couples in Houston.

During 2003 Rick's acquired a 51% stake in Houston's Wild Horse Cabaret and opened a sports bar called Hummers (later renamed under the Club Onyx brand). It also acquired the XTC clubs outright from Taurus Entertainment and reorganized some of its other holdings, leaving it with a 51% stake in Encounters (sold in 2004).

The company in 2004 converted its original Rick's Cabaret nightclub in Houston into Club Onyx, an upscale venue that caters to urban professionals, businessmen, and professional athletes. It also bought a new location in Manhattan near Madison Square Garden. The following year the company closed on its acquisition of a three-in-one complex in North Carolina that included a men's club, a male revue for women, and a traditional night club. Also in 2005 it bought swingers-oriented dating Web site CouplesClick.net.

During 2006 Rick's purchased four new nightclubs in Texas. The following year it inked a licensing deal with a subsidiary of Argentina-based Latin Entertainment to open adult clubs in Buenos Aires and other Latin American cities under the Rick's Cabaret name.

EXECUTIVES

Chairman, President, and CEO: Eric S. Langan, age 41, $637,160 total compensation
CFO: Phillip K. (Phil) Marshall, age 60, $259,137 total compensation
VP, Director Technology, and Director: Travis Reese, age 40, $202,403 total compensation
General Counsel: Brenda Stanfield
Investor Relations Officer and Corporate Communications: Allan Priaulx
Auditors: Whitley Penn

LOCATIONS

HQ: Rick's Cabaret International, Inc.
 10959 Cutten Rd., Houston, TX 77066
Phone: 281-397-6730   **Fax:** 281-820-1445
Web: www.ricks.com

PRODUCTS/OPERATIONS

2009 Sales

	$ mil.	% of total
Nightclubs		
Services	36.1	48
Alcohol	28.3	38
Food & merchandise	6.2	8
Media	1.4	2
Internet	0.6	1
Other	2.5	3
Total	**75.1**	**100**

Selected Operations

Nightclubs
  Club Onyx (adult entertainment for urban professionals and professional athletes)
  Rick's Cabaret
  Rick's Sports Cabaret
  Tootsie's Cabaret
  XTC
Media
  Club Bulletin (trade magazine for adult clubs)
  Storerotica (trade magazine for adult stores and products)
  VIP Guide (directory of clubs, industry vendors, entertainers)
Internet
  CouplesClick.net (85%, adult content and online dating)
  CouplesTouch.com (85%, adult content and online dating)
  NaughtyBids.com (adult auction Web site)
  xxxPassword.com (adult content)

COMPETITORS

FriendFinder Networks
Galardi South
LFP
Million Dollar Saloon
New Frontier Media
Playboy.com
Private Media Group
Scores Holding
Vivid Entertainment

HISTORICAL FINANCIALS

Company Type: Public

Income Statement

FYE: September 30

	REVENUE ($ mil.)	NET INCOME ($ mil.)	NET PROFIT MARGIN	EMPLOYEES
9/09	75.1	5.2	6.9%	1,000
9/08	59.9	7.7	12.9%	1,100
9/07	32.0	3.1	9.7%	696
9/06	24.5	1.8	7.3%	560
9/05	14.8	(0.2)	—	443
Annual Growth	50.1%	—	—	22.6%

2009 Year-End Financials

Debt ratio: 45.6%
Return on equity: 7.8%
Cash ($ mil.): 12.8
Current ratio: 1.59
Long-term debt ($ mil.): 32.0
No. of shares (mil.): 9.4

Dividends
 Yield: —
 Payout: —
Market value ($ mil.): 80.5
R&D as % of sales: —
Advertising as % of sales: —

Stock History

NASDAQ (GM): RICK

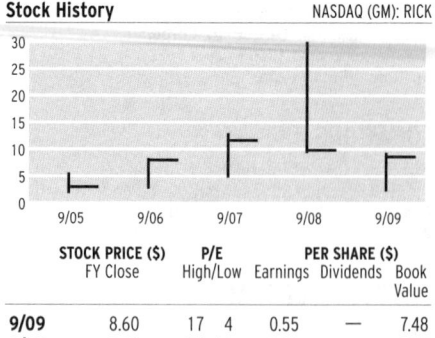

	STOCK PRICE ($) FY Close	P/E High/Low		PER SHARE ($) Earnings	Dividends	Book Value
9/09	8.60	17	4	0.55	—	7.48
9/08	9.82	33	10	0.91	—	6.73
9/07	11.64	25	10	0.50	—	2.57
9/06	7.97	23	8	0.35	—	1.49
9/05	3.01	—	—	(0.05)	—	1.02
Annual Growth	30.0%	—	—	—	—	64.5%

River Valley Bancorp

This River wants to help manage your revenue stream. River Valley Bancorp is a savings and loan holding company for River Valley Financial Bank. Founded in 1875, the bank serves customers through seven offices located in Jefferson and Clark counties, Indiana, and Carroll County, Kentucky. Deposit products include CDs and NOW, savings, and individual retirement accounts. One- to four-family residential mortgage loans are the major focus of the bank's lending activities, representing about 45% of its total loan book. It also offers multifamily mortgage, nonresidential real estate, land, construction, commercial, and consumer loans. Subsidiary Madison First Service is a land holding company.

EXECUTIVES

Chairman, River Valley Bancorp and River Valley Bank: Fred W. Koehler, age 68
President and CEO, River Valley Bancorp and River Valley Bank: Matthew P. Forrester, age 52, $268,329 total compensation
EVP and VP Loan Administration, River Valley Financial Bank: Anthony D. Brandon, age 37, $131,228 total compensation
Treasurer; VP Finance, River Valley Financial Bank: Vickie L. Grimes, age 53
Secretary, River Valley Bancorp and River Valley Financial Bank: Lonnie D. Collins, age 60

VP Loan Services: Mark A. Goley, age 53
VP Business Development, Clark & Floyd County: Robert Kleehamer
VP Business Development and Lending Officer, Clark and Floyd County: Gregory T. (Greg) Siegrist
VP Data Services, River Valley Financial Bank: Deanna Liter, age 45
VP Retail Banking, River Valley Financial Bank: Barb Eades
VP Wealth Management, River Valley Financial Bank: William H. (Bill) Hensler, age 45
VP Human Resources, River Valley Financial Bank: Loy M. Skirvin, age 60
VP and Trust Officer, River Valley Financial Bank: John Muessel, age 56
Auditors: BKD, LLP

LOCATIONS

HQ: River Valley Bancorp
 430 Clifty Dr., Madison, IN 47250
Phone: 812-273-4949   **Fax:** 812-273-4944
Web: www.rvfbank.com

COMPETITORS

Community Trust
First Merchants
First Savings Financial
Indiana Community Bancorp
MainSource Financial
PNC Financial

HISTORICAL FINANCIALS

Company Type: Public

Income Statement

FYE: December 31

	ASSETS ($ mil.)	NET INCOME ($ mil.)	INCOME AS % OF ASSETS	EMPLOYEES
12/08	372.3	2.5	0.7%	97
12/07	350.1	2.2	0.6%	78
12/06	342.2	1.9	0.6%	88
12/05	328.7	2.1	0.6%	72
12/04	289.4	2.3	0.8%	80
Annual Growth	6.5%	2.1%	—	4.9%

2008 Year-End Financials

Equity as % of assets: 6.6%
Return on assets: 0.7%
Return on equity: 10.0%
Long-term debt ($ mil.): 97.2
No. of shares (mil.): 1.5
Market value ($ mil.): 18.9

Dividends
 Yield: 6.7%
 Payout: 54.9%
Sales ($ mil.): 12.7
R&D as % of sales: —
Advertising as % of sales: —

Stock History

NASDAQ (CM): RIVR

	STOCK PRICE ($) FY Close	P/E High/Low		PER SHARE ($) Earnings	Dividends	Book Value
12/08	12.55	12	7	1.53	0.84	16.31
12/07	14.30	15	10	1.34	0.81	17.07
12/06	18.05	17	15	1.18	0.79	16.05
12/05	19.05	19	14	1.27	0.77	15.30
12/04	22.50	21	14	1.42	0.72	14.88
Annual Growth	(13.6%)	—	—	1.9%	3.9%	2.3%

Riverbed Technology

Riverbed Technology makes sure applications flow swiftly over networks. The company develops hardware and software that improves the performance of applications that are shared over networks. Its Steelhead network appliances can be scaled to fit customers ranging from small businesses to global enterprises. Riverbed's Steelhead Central Management Console software keeps track of Steelhead appliances across WANs, managing up to 500 appliances on one network. Riverbed's largest shareholders include Accel Partners (20%) and Lightspeed Venture Partners (20%).

The company sells directly and through resellers, distributors, and systems integrators. More than 90% of its sales were through resellers in fiscal 2008.

Early in 2009 Riverbed acquired network analysis software developer Mazu Networks for about $25 million. The purchase fit its strategy of enhancing the features of its product line. The company intends to extend the functionality of its network optimization products with Mazu's technology for reporting and analytics.

EXECUTIVES

Chairman, President, and CEO: Jerry M. Kennelly, age 59, $3,156,546 total compensation
CTO and Director: Steven (Steve) McCanne, age 40, $2,760,283 total compensation
SVP Marketing and Business Development: Eric Wolford, age 43, $1,848,960 total compensation
SVP Business Services and CFO: Randy S. Gottfried, age 44, $1,227,611 total compensation
SVP Worldwide Sales: Dave M. Peranich, age 48, $1,491,066 total compensation
CIO: Thomas Bakewell
Chief Scientist: Mark S. Day
VP Technical Operations: Stephen R. Smoot, age 42
VP Engineering: Gordon Chaffee, age 40
VP Corporate and Legal Affairs, General Counsel, and Secretary: Brett A. Nissenberg, age 36
Investor Relations: Renee Lyall
Auditors: Ernst & Young LLP

LOCATIONS

HQ: Riverbed Technology, Inc.
 199 Fremont St., San Francisco, CA 94105
Phone: 415-247-8800   **Fax:** 415-247-8801
Web: www.riverbed.com

2008 Sales

	$ mil.	% of total
US	193.2	58
Europe, Middle East & Africa	87.4	26
Other regions	52.7	16
Total	**333.3**	**100**

PRODUCTS/OPERATIONS

2008 Sales

	$ mil.	% of total
Products	252.9	76
Support & services	80.4	24
Total	**333.3**	**100**

Selected Products

Appliances (Steelhead)
Embedded software (RiOS)
Management software (Central Management Control)

COMPETITORS

Blue Coat
Cisco Systems
Citrix Systems
Expand Networks
F5 Networks
Juniper Networks

HISTORICAL FINANCIALS

Company Type: Public

Income Statement			FYE: December 31
	REVENUE ($ mil.)	NET INCOME ($ mil.)	NET PROFIT MARGIN	EMPLOYEES
12/08	333.3	10.6	3.2%	857
12/07	236.4	14.8	6.3%	623
12/06	90.2	(15.8)	—	325
12/05	22.9	(17.1)	—	271
Annual Growth	144.2%	—	—	46.8%

2008 Year-End Financials

Debt ratio: —
Return on equity: 3.8%
Cash ($ mil.): 95.4
Current ratio: 3.76
Long-term debt ($ mil.): —
No. of shares (mil.): 69.2

Dividends
  Yield: 0.0%
  Payout: —
Market value ($ mil.): 788.2
R&D as % of sales: —
Advertising as % of sales: —

Stock History

NASDAQ (GM): RVBD

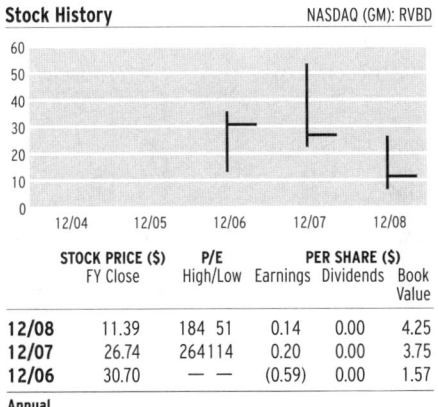

	STOCK PRICE ($) FY Close	P/E High/Low	PER SHARE ($) Earnings	Dividends	Book Value
12/08	11.39	184 51	0.14	0.00	4.25
12/07	26.74	264 114	0.20	0.00	3.75
12/06	30.70	— —	(0.59)	0.00	1.57
Annual Growth	(39.1%)	— —	—	—	64.2%

Rosetta Stone

Who needs translators when you have the Rosetta Stone? Founded in 1991, Rosetta Stone (formerly Fairfield Language Technologies) provides language-learning software via CD-ROM and the Internet. The company's Rosetta Stone Language Library combines educational techniques and interactive technologies to replicate the way children learn their native languages, helping users learn new languages more quickly and effectively. With customers in more than 150 countries, Rosetta Stone offers software for about 30 languages. Its products are available at major retailers such as Amazon.com, Barnes & Noble, and Borders.

About 85% of the company's sales comes from direct sales channels, which include call centers, kiosks, Web sites, and institutional sales forces.

The company's strategy includes developing a Web-based service to offer customers the chance to practice their new language skills with dedicated language conversation coaches, as well as extending its products to handheld devices.

Rosetta Stone also plans to expand the scope of its US marketing efforts, including increased television, print, radio, and online advertising. The company is also eyeing expanding international sales, which currently account for just 5% of revenues.

Fairfield Language Technologies was begun by Allen Stolzfus and his brother-in-law John Fairfield in 1992, with capital provided when Stolzfus' mother mortgaged her house. Family members ran the whole show until Stolzfus' death in 2002. Fairfield Language Technologies was sold to investment firms ABS Capital Partners and Northwest Equity Partners in 2002; the company officially took on the name of its Rosetta Stone software shortly after.

EXECUTIVES

Chairman: Laura L. Witt, age 41
President, CEO, and Director: Tom P. H. Adams, age 37, $1,592,775 total compensation
COO: Eric Eichmann, age 42, $601,947 total compensation
CFO: Brian D. Helman, age 39, $507,345 total compensation
General Counsel and Secretary: Michael C. Wu, age 42, $363,078 total compensation
CTO: Greg Keim
CIO: Jay Topper
Chief Product Officer: Gregory W. Long, age 50, $471,803 total compensation
SVP International Development: Pamela Mulder
SVP Technology and Labs: Mike Fulkerson
VP Institutional Sales and Marketing: Pete Rumpel
Public Relations Manager, North America: Megan Richter
President, Rosetta Stone Japan: Tak Shiohama
Auditors: Deloitte & Touche LLP

LOCATIONS

HQ: Rosetta Stone Inc.
  1919 N. Lynn St, 7th Fl., Arlington, VA 22209
Phone: 800-788-0822
Web: www.rosettastone.com

2008 Sales

	% of total
US	95
Other countries	5
Total	**100**

PRODUCTS/OPERATIONS

2008 Sales

	$ mil.	% of total
Products	184.2	88
Subscription & service	25.2	12
Total	**209.4**	**100**

COMPETITORS

Berlitz
Disney Publishing
McGraw-Hill Education
Renaissance Learning
Simon & Schuster
Transparent Language

HISTORICAL FINANCIALS

Company Type: Public

Income Statement			FYE: December 31
	REVENUE ($ mil.)	NET INCOME ($ mil.)	NET PROFIT MARGIN	EMPLOYEES
12/08	209.4	13.9	6.6%	1,218
12/07	137.3	2.6	1.9%	1,100
12/06	91.6	(15.2)	—	658
12/05	48.4	6.8	14.0%	—
Annual Growth	62.9%	26.9%	—	36.1%

2008 Year-End Financials

Debt ratio: 16.5%
Return on equity: —
Cash ($ mil.): 30.6
Current ratio: 1.37
Long-term debt ($ mil.): 5.7

Net Income History

NYSE: RST

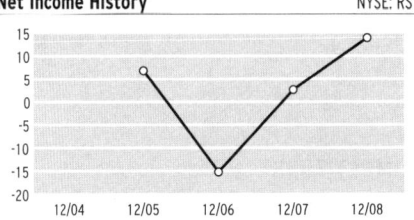

Royal Gold

Royal Gold deals only with royalty. Rather than operating gold mines, the company buys the right to collect royalties from mine operators. This strategy allows Royal Gold to minimize its exposure to the costs of mineral exploration and development. More than one-third of the company's revenue comes from its royalty interests related to the Cortez Pipeline Mining Complex, a project in Nevada, operated by Barrick; the Robinson mine operated by Quadra accounts for 24%. Royal Gold holds royalty stakes in other producing properties elsewhere in the Americas, as well as in Africa. The company also owns interests in exploration- and development-stage projects in the US and in Argentina, Finland, and Russia.

Royal Gold is expanding its portfolio. The company has invested $35 million in the construction and development of High River Gold Mines' Taparko open pit gold project in Burkina Faso, in West Africa. Since 2006 Royal Gold has acquired royalty stakes in projects operated by Kennecott Minerals (in projects in Nevada and Mexico), Nevada Star Resource Corp. (a smelter return royalty), Minefinders (a smelter return royalty interest on a Mexican property), Kennecott Exploration (Mexico), and Barrick.

It added another acquisition in 2009 when it paid Teck $100 million for a percentage of a Chilean gold mine's output. Late that year it reached an agreement to buy International Royalty for about C$750 million ($700 million US). International Royalty owns percentage stakes in mines in Australia, Canada, and Chile.

EXECUTIVES

Chairman: Stanley Dempsey, age 70
President, CEO, and Director: Tony Jensen, age 47
CFO: Stefan L. Wenger, age 36
VP Operations: William M. Zisch, age 51
VP Corporate Development: William Heissenbuttel, age 44
VP and General Counsel: Bruce Kirchhoff, age 50
VP and Corporate Secretary: Karen P. Gross, age 55
Auditors: PricewaterhouseCoopers LLP

LOCATIONS

HQ: Royal Gold, Inc.
1660 Wynkoop St., Ste. 1000, Denver, CO 80202
Phone: 303-573-1660   **Fax:** 303-595-9385
Web: www.royalgold.com

2009 Royalty Revenue

	% of total
US	56
Africa	21
Mexico	15
Other regions	8
Total	**100**

COMPETITORS

Anglo American
BHP Billiton
Rio Tinto Limited

HISTORICAL FINANCIALS

Company Type: Public

Income Statement				FYE: June 30
	REVENUE ($ mil.)	NET INCOME ($ mil.)	NET PROFIT MARGIN	EMPLOYEES
6/09	73.8	38.3	51.9%	17
6/08	69.4	26.1	37.6%	16
6/07	48.4	19.7	40.7%	15
6/06	28.4	11.4	40.1%	14
6/05	25.3	11.5	45.5%	14
Annual Growth	**30.7%**	**35.1%**	**—**	**5.0%**

2009 Year-End Financials

Debt ratio: 2.6%
Return on equity: 6.2%
Cash ($ mil.): 294.6
Current ratio: 51.50
Long-term debt ($ mil.): 19.3
No. of shares (mil.): 40.8
Dividends
　Yield: 0.7%
　Payout: 29.0%
Market value ($ mil.): 1,700.0
R&D as % of sales: —
Advertising as % of sales: —

Stock History

NASDAQ (GS): RGLD

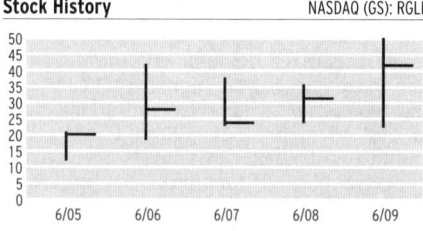

	STOCK PRICE ($) FY Close	P/E High/Low		PER SHARE ($) Earnings	Dividends	Book Value
6/09	41.69	47	21	1.07	0.31	18.38
6/08	31.36	52	35	0.68	—	11.90
6/07	23.77	47	29	0.79	—	7.82
6/06	27.82	85	38	0.49	—	3.96
6/05	20.09	38	23	0.54	—	2.25
Annual Growth	**20.0%**	**—**	**—**	**18.6%**	**—**	**69.1%**

RPC, Inc.

RPC helps to grease the wheels of oil and gas production. Through its Cudd Energy Services division, the company provides oil industry consulting and technical services including snubbing, coiled tubing, nitrogen services, and well control. Another unit, Patterson Rental and Fishing Tools, rents specialized tools and equipment such as drill pipe, tubing, and blowout preventers. RPC also provides maintenance, emergency services, and storage and inspection services for offshore and inland vessels. The company operates in most of the world's major oil producing regions. Chairman R. Randall Rollins and his brother Gary own about 67% of RPC.

RPC provides both technical services (such as pressure pumping services, snubbing services, coiled tubing services, nitrogen service, firefighting, and well control) and support services (the rental of drill pipe and other specialized oilfield equipment, downhole tool rentals, pipe inspection and storage services, and oilfield training services).

The company has built its portfolio of technical and support services through a series of acquisitions, and anticipates that a rebounding world economy, with its increased demand for oil and gas operations, will open up further opportunities.

EXECUTIVES

Chairman: R. Randall Rollins, age 77, $2,262,720 total compensation
President, CEO, and Director: Richard A. Hubbell, age 65, $2,057,500 total compensation
VP, CFO, and Treasurer: Ben M. Palmer, age 49, $799,950 total compensation
VP, Secretary, and Director: Linda H. Graham, age 73, $547,310 total compensation
VP and General Manager, Patterson Rental Tools: Jim Daniel
VP Corporate Finance: James C. (Jim) Landers
Manager Investor Relations and Corporate Communications: Natasha L. Coleman
Auditors: Grant Thornton LLP

LOCATIONS

HQ: RPC, Inc.
2170 Piedmont Rd. NE, Atlanta, GA 30324
Phone: 404-321-2140   **Fax:** 404-321-5483
Web: www.rpc.net

2008 Sales

	$ mil.	% of total
US	846.2	96
Other countries	30.8	4
Total	**877.0**	**100**

PRODUCTS/OPERATIONS

2008 Sales

	$ mil.	% of total
Technical services	746.0	85
Support services	131.0	15
Total	**877.0**	**100**

COMPETITORS

Baker Hughes	Halliburton
BJ Services	Precision Drilling
Boots & Coots	Schlumberger
Ensign Energy Services	Transocean
Exterran	Weatherford International

HISTORICAL FINANCIALS

Company Type: Public

Income Statement				FYE: December 31
	REVENUE ($ mil.)	NET INCOME ($ mil.)	NET PROFIT MARGIN	EMPLOYEES
12/08	877.0	83.4	9.5%	2,532
12/07	690.2	87.0	12.6%	2,370
12/06	596.6	110.8	18.6%	2,000
12/05	427.6	66.5	15.6%	1,649
12/04	339.8	34.8	10.2%	1,596
Annual Growth	**26.7%**	**24.4%**	**—**	**12.2%**

2008 Year-End Financials

Debt ratio: 38.8%
Return on equity: 19.4%
Cash ($ mil.): 3.0
Current ratio: 3.17
Long-term debt ($ mil.): 174.4
No. of shares (mil.): 98.4
Dividends
　Yield: 2.5%
　Payout: 28.2%
Market value ($ mil.): 960.3
R&D as % of sales: —
Advertising as % of sales: —

Stock History

NYSE: RES

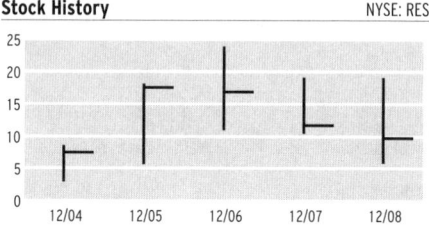

	STOCK PRICE ($) FY Close	P/E High/Low		PER SHARE ($) Earnings	Dividends	Book Value
12/08	9.76	22	7	0.85	0.24	4.56
12/07	11.71	21	12	0.89	0.20	4.16
12/06	16.88	21	10	1.13	0.13	3.41
12/05	17.56	27	9	0.67	0.07	2.36
12/04	7.44	24	9	0.36	0.04	1.84
Annual Growth	**7.0%**	**—**	**—**	**24.0%**	**56.5%**	**25.4%**

Rubicon Technology

Rubicon Technology says *Alea iacta est* (The die is cast) and crosses over into the empire of advanced technology. Using proprietary crystal growth technology, Rubicon makes sapphire materials, wafers, and components for a variety of products. In the the field of optoelectronics, Rubicon makes sapphire components for light-emitting diodes (LEDs) used in cell phones, video screens, and other items. Rubicon's sapphire materials are also used for compound semiconductor manufacturing and laser imaging. In the telecom sector, the company's silicon materials are in demand for the silicon-on-sapphire (SOS) components of cellular and fiber-optics products. Asian customers account for more than half of Rubicon's sales.

The global economic crisis resulted in weak demand for the company's LED and SOS products in 2008, significantly reducing orders for sapphire substrates. Rubicon is counting on increased acceptance of LED-based lighting to create demand for its LED-related products, which account for nearly two-thirds of sales. Sapphire cores represented the rest of revenues.

The LEDs made with Rubicon's sapphire materials provide colored lighting for mobile phone

display screens. LEDs made with sapphire also equip the backlighting units of notebook computers, desktop monitors, and LCD TVs. LEDs are additionally being used more for automobile headlights, taillights, and even interior lighting. Another growing market for LEDs — and Rubicon's sapphire — is large and outdoor commercial signage.

Radio-frequency integrated circuits (RFICs) that need sapphire to be manufactured offer more opportunities for Rubicon's materials. Among the products that use RFICs needing Rubicon's sapphire are mobile phones, broadband television set-top boxes, and satellites.

Rubicon has additionally discovered a window of opportunity in the transportation and military sectors. Its sapphire and fluoride materials are in demand for transparent armor in military vehicles and for special windows used for steering aircraft in conditions of low visibility.

Another application of sapphire materials is for blue laser diodes, which are increasingly being used in Blu-ray DVD players and advanced video game systems.

To grow with its market, Rubicon is developing larger sapphire wafers that will be needed for producing next-generation LEDs and RFICs. Rubicon also projects more demand as the electronics and optical industries create new products that require sapphire and other single-crystal products for manufacturing. Additionally Rubicon sees more market opportunities in the aerospace, petroleum, and laser industries, which are replacing glass and quartz with sapphire for high-performance and harsh-environment uses.

Rubicon is healthily increasing sales and made an annual profit for the first time in 2008. The company has an accumulated deficit of about $149 million.

Through Cross Atlantic Capital Partners, director Donald Caldwell controls about 31% of Rubicon Technology.

EXECUTIVES

Chairman: Don N. Aquilano, age 42
President, CEO, and Director: Raja M. Parvez, age 51, $652,117 total compensation
CFO, Secretary, and Treasurer: William F. (Bill) Weissman, age 50, $331,509 total compensation
Chief Scientist: Elena Dobrovinskaya
SVP Sales and Marketing: Sunil B. Phatak
VP Operations: Faisal Nabulsi
VP Quality and Supply Line Management: Akhtar Zaman
Auditors: Grant Thornton LLP

LOCATIONS

HQ: Rubicon Technology, Inc.
9931 Franklin Ave., Franklin Park, IL 60131
Phone: 847-295-7000 **Fax:** 847-295-7555
Web: www.rubicon-es2.com

2008 Sales

	$ mil.	% of total
Asia	20.0	53
North America	16.5	44
Europe	1.3	3
Total	**37.8**	**100**

COMPETITORS

Cree
Nichia
Soitec

HISTORICAL FINANCIALS

Company Type: Public

Income Statement

FYE: December 31

	REVENUE ($ mil.)	NET INCOME ($ mil.)	NET PROFIT MARGIN	EMPLOYEES
12/08	37.8	4.4	11.6%	99
12/07	34.1	(2.9)	—	144
12/06	20.8	(7.4)	—	122
12/05	16.3	(12.1)	—	127
12/04	16.0	(5.4)	—	—
Annual Growth	**24.0%**	**—**	**—**	**(8.0%)**

2008 Year-End Financials

Debt ratio: —
Return on equity: 4.1%
Cash ($ mil.): 7.6
Current ratio: 15.26
Long-term debt ($ mil.): —
No. of shares (mil.): 20.1
Dividends
Yield: 0.0%
Payout: —
Market value ($ mil.): 85.4
R&D as % of sales: —
Advertising as % of sales: —

Stock History

NASDAQ (GM): RBCN

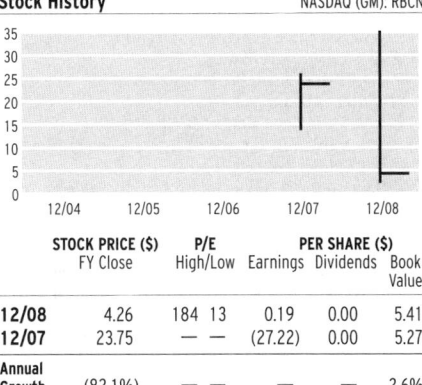

	STOCK PRICE ($) FY Close	P/E High/Low	PER SHARE ($) Earnings	Dividends	Book Value
12/08	4.26	184 13	0.19	0.00	5.41
12/07	23.75	— —	(27.22)	0.00	5.27
Annual Growth	**(82.1%)**	**— —**	**—**	**—**	**2.6%**

rue21, inc.

It's rue21's sincere hope that people, young and old, long to be 21 (again or for the first time). The fast-growing chain sells value-priced apparel and accessories, including jewelry and fragrances, for girls and guys through some 525 stores in malls and strip centers in more than 40 US states. Daily deliveries ensure that the company's stores stock the latest fashion trends and encourage frequent visits by customers. rue21 caters to 11 to 17 year olds and stocks its own rue21 etc!, Carbon, tarea, and rueKicks brands of apparel and footwear. Founded in 1976, rue21 was formerly known as Pennsylvania Fashions. Apax Partners, owner of the teen apparel chain, took rue21 public in fall 2009.

Following the November IPO, which raised about $129 million (including some $29 million for the company), Apax still controls about 58% of rue21's shares. rue21 will use its portion of the proceeds to retire debt.

The youth retailer, which opened its 500th store in July 2009 (up from just about 195 stores in 2005), plans to add 100 new stores in 2010 and could have more than 1,000 shops by 2013. rue21's value-priced, fast-fashion strategy appears well suited to the current retail slump and sales continue to grow despite the downturn in the US economy. (The retailer is hoping to avoid

a repeat of 2002 when the combination of a faltering economy and aggressive expansion by the chain conspired to drive it into Chapter 11 bankruptcy in February 2002. It emerged 15 months later with fewer stores.) Fast-fashion, pioneered by rivals H&M and Forever 21, is a hot retail concept as shoppers are reluctant to spend much money on clothes that will quickly go out of style.

To increase sales, rue21 has been adding in-store etc! departments that greatly expand its accessories offerings, including shoes, jewelry, and handbags. About 300 rue21 stores will have etc! stores-within-stores by the end of 2009. The retailer is also stocking more bras, underwear, and pajama-style apparel, under its tarea private label, in response to the success of such intimates lines as Victoria Secret's Pink and American Eagle's aerie.

The company uses social media marketing (Facebook, MySpace, and Twitter) to stay close to its young clientele. Surprisingly, rue21 does not yet offer online shopping, but says it has plans to offer it in the future.

EXECUTIVES

Chairman, President, and CEO: Robert N. (Bob) Fisch, age 59, $1,558,425 total compensation
SVP and CFO: Keith A. McDonough, age 50, $332,790 total compensation
SVP and General Merchandising Manager: Kim A. Reynolds, age 52, $514,843 total compensation
SVP, Information Technology: Michael A. Holland, age 45, $316,386 total compensation
SVP and Director of Stores: John P. Bugnar, age 60, $382,538 total compensation
SVP, Real Estate: Robert R. Thomson, age 50
SVP, Planning and Allocation: Mark K. J. Chrystal, age 36
Auditors: Ernst & Young LLP

LOCATIONS

HQ: rue21, inc.
800 Commonwealth Dr., Ste. 100
Warrendale, PA 15086
Phone: 724-776-9780 **Fax:** 724-776-4111
Web: www.rue21.com

2009 Stores

	No.
Texas	63
Georgia	37
North Carolina	27
Alabama	26
Pennsylvania	23
Tennessee	22
Florida	20
Louisiana	19
Mississippi	17
South Carolina	17
Illinois	16
California	15
Indiana	14
Michigan	14
Missouri	14
New York	13
Ohio	13
Arizona	12
Oklahoma	12
Virginia	11
Utah	9
Arkansas	8
Kentucky	8
Wisconsin	8
Colorado	7
Iowa	7
New Mexico	7
West Virginia	7
Maryland	6
Other states	33
Total	**505**

PRODUCTS/OPERATIONS

2009 Sales

	% of total
Girls' apparel	58
Girls' accessories	22
Guys' apparel	20
Total	**100**

COMPETITORS

Aéropostale	H&M
American Apparel	J. Crew
American Eagle Outfitters	Metropark
The Buckle	Pacific Sunwear
Charlotte Russe Holding	Target
dELiA*s	Urban Outfitters
Forever 21	Wal-Mart
The Gap	Wet Seal

HISTORICAL FINANCIALS
Company Type: Public

Income Statement
FYE: Saturday nearest January 31

	REVENUE ($ mil.)	NET INCOME ($ mil.)	NET PROFIT MARGIN	EMPLOYEES
1/09	391.4	12.6	3.2%	5,927
1/08	296.9	9.1	3.1%	—
1/07	225.6	7.8	3.5%	—
Annual Growth	**31.7%**	**27.1%**	**—**	**—**

2009 Year-End Financials

Debt ratio: 105.9%
Return on equity: —
Cash ($ mil.): 4.6
Current ratio: 1.01
Long-term debt ($ mil.): 19.5

Net Income History
NASDAQ (GS): RUE

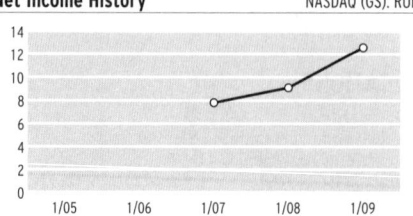

---

salesforce.com

salesforce.com knows the power of good customer relations. The company offers hosted applications that manage customer information for sales, marketing, and customer support, providing clients with a rapidly deployable alternative to buying and maintaining enterprise software. salesforce.com's applications are used by more than 65,000 clients for generating sales leads, maintaining customer information, and tracking customer interactions. The company's applications can be accessed from PCs and mobile devices. salesforce.com's customers come from a variety of industries, including financial services, telecommunications, manufacturing, and entertainment.

salesforce.com continues to bolster its enterprise offerings as part of a push to expand past its core market of small and midsized businesses. The company has also begun to encourage third parties (including customers and independent software vendors) to develop applications that run on salesforce.com's technology platform but are sold separately as modules or add-ons in its AppExchange marketplace.

salesforce.com is embracing (and developing products for) new technologies such as cloud computing, and it was a pioneer in establishing that the Software-as-a-Service (SaaS) business model could be both profitable and scalable. It also offers clients access to application development code on its Force.com platform, which independent software vendors, IT departments, and software developers use to build custom business applications.

In August 2008 the company acquired InStranet, a provider of call center software; salesforce.com integrated InStranet's software into its SaaS platform. The deal was part of a broader strategic move by salesforce.com to extend its product set past core CRM applications to encompass areas such as call center management, partner relationship management, and more.

EXECUTIVES

Chairman and CEO: Marc Benioff, age 45, $343,263 total compensation
EVP and CFO: Graham V. Smith, age 49, $2,186,756 total compensation
EVP, Law, Policy, and Corporate Strategy: Kenneth I. (Ken) Juster, age 54, $2,472,076 total compensation
EVP Marketing and Alliances: George Hu, age 34
EVP Global Corporate Sales: Hilarie Koplow-McAdams
EVP Technology: Parker Harris, age 42
Chief Adoption Officer; President, Global Services: Polly A. Sumner, age 54, $2,196,756 total compensation
Chief Customer Officer; President Worldwide Sales: Jim Steele, age 53, $1,804,381 total compensation
Chief Sales Officer; President Worldwide Sales: Frank R. Van Veenendaal, age 49
Chief Marketing Officer: Kendall Collins
CTO: David (Dave) Moellenhoff, age 38
SVP Service Delivery and CIO: Jim Cavalieri, age 38
SVP and General Counsel: David Schellhase, age 45
Auditors: Ernst & Young LLP

LOCATIONS

HQ: salesforce.com, inc.
The Landmark, 1 Market St., Ste. 300
San Francisco, CA 94105
Phone: 415-901-7000   **Fax:** 415-901-7040
Web: www.salesforce.com

2009 Sales

	$ mil.	% of total
Americas	777	72
Europe	191	18
Asia/Pacific	109	10
Total	**1,077**	**100**

PRODUCTS/OPERATIONS

2009 Sales

	$ mil.	% of total
Subscription & support	985	91
Professional service & other	92	9
Total	**1,077**	**100**

Selected Software and Services

Force.com (application development platform)
Salesforce CRM (customer relationship management)

COMPETITORS

CDC Software	NetSuite
Consona CRM	Oracle
FrontRange Solutions	Pivotal Corp.
IBM	RightNow Technologies
Infor Global	Sage Software
Kana	SAP
Microsoft Dynamics	SugarCRM

HISTORICAL FINANCIALS
Company Type: Public

Income Statement
FYE: January 31

	REVENUE ($ mil.)	NET INCOME ($ mil.)	NET PROFIT MARGIN	EMPLOYEES
1/09	1,076.8	43.4	4.0%	3,566
1/08	748.7	18.4	2.5%	2,606
1/07	497.1	0.5	0.1%	2,070
1/06	309.9	28.5	9.2%	1,304
1/05	176.4	7.3	4.1%	767
Annual Growth	**57.2%**	**56.1%**	**—**	**46.8%**

2009 Year-End Financials

Debt ratio: 3.0%
Return on equity: 7.7%
Cash ($ mil.): 483.8
Current ratio: 1.39
Long-term debt ($ mil.): 20.1
No. of shares (mil.): 124.9
Dividends
　Yield: —
　Payout: —
Market value ($ mil.): 3,323.6
R&D as % of sales: —
Advertising as % of sales: —

Stock History
NYSE: CRM

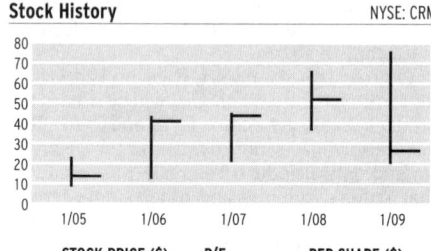

	STOCK PRICE ($) FY Close	P/E High/Low	PER SHARE ($) Earnings	Dividends	Book Value
1/09	26.61	215 59	0.35	—	5.38
1/08	51.91	437 248	0.15	—	3.62
1/07	43.83	— —	0.00	—	2.26
1/06	41.05	179 54	0.24	—	1.57
1/05	13.70	324 129	0.07	—	1.16
Annual Growth	**18.1%**	**— —**	**49.5%**	**—**	**46.7%**

Santander BanCorp

Sea and sand are hallmarks of Puerto Rico's geography, and Santander BanCorp is a hallmark of the island's economy. The holding company owns Banco Santander Puerto Rico, one of the largest banks in the commonwealth, providing commercial, consumer, and mortgage banking services through some 70 branches and more than 150 ATMs on the island, and on the Web. Business loans (about 60% of the bank's loan portfolio) and construction loans (some 20%) dominate the bank's lending activities. Subsidiaries provide securities brokerage, asset management, insurance, consumer lending, and international banking services. It is a subsidiary of Spain's Grupo Santander.

Grupo Santander owns 91% of Santander BanCorp; it has placed an offer to acquire the rest of the company's shares it doesn't already own.

Santander BanCorp expanded into consumer lending with its 2006 acquisition of Island Finance from Wells Fargo Financial. The following year, consumer lending accounted for around

17% of sales, bypassing mortgage lending in revenues. Island Finance has about 70 offices in Puerto Rico.

The company restated its earnings from 2000 to 2005 after the SEC questioned the company's accounting of mortgage loan transactions with other Puerto Rican financial institutions.

EXECUTIVES

Chairman, Santander BanCorp and Banco Santander: Gonzalo de Las Heras, age 69
President, CEO, and Director, Santander BanCorp and Banco Santander Puerto Rico: Juan S. Moreno Blanco, age 44, $1,531,178 total compensation
SEVP, Chief Compliance Officer, and Director: María Calero, age 56, $271,282 total compensation
EVP and Chief Accounting Officer: Roberto Jara, age 49, $376,323 total compensation
EVP and Director Collections and Workouts: Tomás E. Torres, age 46
EVP and Operations and Information Technology Director: José Alvarez, age 52, $1,195,289 total compensation
EVP: Justo Muñoz, age 56
SVP and General Counsel: Rafael S. Bonilla, age 37
SVP, Cost Control, Investor Relations, and Sarbanes-Oxley Officer, Banco Santander: Juan M. Diaz Soutaire
First SVP and Human Resources Director: Ivonna J. Pacheco, age 43
President and CEO, Santander Securities: James A. (Jimmy) Rodríguez, age 52, $833,754 total compensation
President, Santander Insurance Agency: Carlos Acevedo, age 34
President and CEO, Santander Asset Management: Frank Serra, age 38
President, Santander Financial Services: Mario Delgado, age 48
Auditors: Deloitte & Touche LLP

LOCATIONS

HQ: Santander BanCorp
207 Ponce de Leon Ave., Hato Rey, PR 00917
Phone: 787-777-4100 **Fax:** 787-766-1437
Web: www.santandernet.com

PRODUCTS/OPERATIONS

2008 Gross Revenues

	$ mil.	% of total
Interest		
Loans	548.0	73
Securities	47.4	6
Other	5.4	1
Noninterest		
Broker-dealer, asset management & insurance fees	74.8	10
Bank service charges & fees	44.7	6
Other	28.3	4
Total	**748.6**	**100**

2008 Sales

	%
Commercial banking	41
Mortgage banking	30
Treasury & investments	14
Consumer finance	7
Wealth management	2
Other	6
Total	**100**

Selected Subsidiaries

Banco Santander Puerto Rico (commercial banking)
 Santander International Bank of Puerto Rico, Inc.
Santander Financial Services, Inc. (consumer finance)
 Island Finance
Santander Insurance Agency, Inc.
Santander Securities Corporation (broker-dealer)
 Santander Asset Management Corporation

COMPETITORS

Doral Financial
First BanCorp (Puerto Rico)
Oriental Financial
Popular, Inc.
R&G Financial
W Holding

HISTORICAL FINANCIALS

Company Type: Public

Income Statement

FYE: December 31

	ASSETS ($ mil.)	NET INCOME ($ mil.)	INCOME AS % OF ASSETS	EMPLOYEES
12/08	7,897.6	10.5	0.1%	1,768
12/07	9,160.2	(36.2)	—	2,622
12/06	9,188.2	43.2	0.5%	2,338
12/05	8,271.9	79.8	1.0%	1,591
12/04	8,341.8	84.5	1.0%	1,735
Annual Growth	(1.4%)	(40.6%)	—	0.5%

2008 Year-End Financials

Equity as % of assets: 7.0%
Return on assets: 0.1%
Return on equity: 1.9%
Long-term debt ($ mil.): 1,511.4
No. of shares (mil.): 46.6
Market value ($ mil.): 582.5
Dividends
 Yield: 1.6%
 Payout: 87.0%
Sales ($ mil.): 504.2
R&D as % of sales: —
Advertising as % of sales: —

Stock History

NYSE: SBP

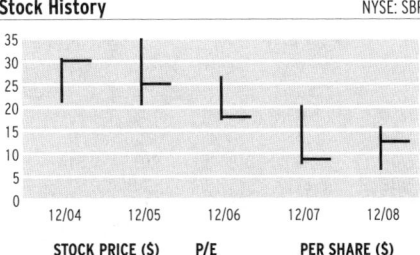

	STOCK PRICE ($) FY Close	P/E High/Low		PER SHARE ($) Earnings	Dividends	Book Value
12/08	12.49	67	29	0.23	0.20	11.83
12/07	8.66	—	—	(0.78)	—	11.50
12/06	17.85	28	19	0.93	—	12.42
12/05	25.12	20	12	1.71	—	12.19
12/04	30.16	17	12	1.81	—	11.92
Annual Growth	(19.8%)	—	—	(40.3%)	—	(0.2%)

Sapient Corporation

Sapient is no sap when it comes to services. A provider of business and technology consulting services, Sapient targets information-based businesses in the financial services, communications and technology, automotive and industrial manufacturing, consumer, public services, health care, energy services, and transportation industries. Customers such as AT&T Mobility, Staples, Janus Capital, and agencies of the US government have used Sapient's consulting, design, implementation, user experience research, and other services for e-commerce, customer relationship management, high-volume transaction processing, online supply chain development, learning and knowledge management, and other processes.

The company acquired Nitro Group in 2009 for $50 million. Nitro provides an advertising

network that serves clients such as Mars, ConAgra, Volvo, and Foot Locker. Sapient hopes the deal will expand its digital marketing presence and client roster. The company's operations are marketed through two focus areas: Sapient Consulting (its traditional consulting business) and Sapient Interactive (the interactive marketing arm that has been expanding through deals such as the Nitro acquisition).

Sapient offers its services primarily on a fixed-price basis, targeting customers that want fast services at low costs. The company relies on its international facilities, which enable development teams to work on projects 24 hours a day, to ensure quick turnaround.

HISTORY

In 1991 information technology systems salesman Jerry Greenberg and software developer Stuart Moore saw a market for providing businesses with fixed-price software systems by a guaranteed delivery date. Greenberg and Moore charged more than $100,000 on their credit cards and used $60,000 of their personal savings to form Sapient.

As the company took off, Moore managed internal operations, such as creating software, and Greenberg handled sales and finance. The two worked closely together and helped establish teamwork as Sapient's most prized trait (as co-CEOs, they shared an office with only inches separating their desks, and they required the same of all senior managers).

The company began specializing in distinct areas such as telecommunications, manufacturing, and energy, and it found a third of its early clients in financial services. Specialization enabled the company to reuse software; coupling that with Sapient's proprietary team-based development process resulted in lower costs and shorter development times.

The company went public in 1996 and started expanding through acquisitions, buying systems integrators and Internet consultants. It opened offices in London in 1998, and in Italy and Australia the next year. Also in 1999 Sapient increased its staff by more than 40% and expanded its consulting services with the purchase of customer behavior specialist E.Lab.

In 2000 Sapient opened an office in India and acquired Human Code, a privately held developer of education, e-commerce, and entertainment software, for about $104 million. The next year, looking to cut costs, the company closed its Australian office, cut its workforce by about 35%, and exited the gaming business. It also began to shift more of its project workload to its office in India in order to take advantage of lower operating costs.

Citing decreased demand for its services in the troubled economic climate, Sapient posted a loss of nearly $190 million for 2001, followed by a loss of nearly $230 million for 2002. The company continued to reduce its workforce in 2002, cutting about 600 more jobs. The following year the company began to see its service revenues pick up, and its workforce size stabilized.

In mid-2005 the company acquired Miami-based Business Information Solutions, a provider of consulting services for companies using enterprise planning software developed by SAP.

Sapient purchased Planning Group International in 2006. Later that year the company sold its stake in its HWT subsidiary for about $5.4 million.

EXECUTIVES

President, CEO, and Director: Alan J. Herrick, age 43, $2,690,195 total compensation
EVP, COO, and Chief Administrative Officer: Preston B. Bradford, age 52
SVP, CFO, and Chief Accounting Officer: Joseph S. (Joe) Tibbetts Jr., age 56, $1,134,786 total compensation
SVP and Managing Director, European Operations: Christian Oversohl, age 41, $807,479 total compensation
SVP, General Counsel, and Secretary: Jane E. Owens, age 55, $520,180 total compensation
SVP and Lead, North American Operations: Alan M. Wexler, age 45, $887,513 total compensation
SVP and Chief Creative Officer: Gaston Legorburu
SVP and Managing Director, Global Trading and Risk Management Practice: Chip Register
VP Corporate Communications: Gail Scibelli
VP Business Development, Sapient Government Services: Leslie Winik
VP Marketing Services, Sapient Interactive: Eric Healy
Director Brand Experience and Innovation: Matt Lindley
Auditors: PricewaterhouseCoopers LLP

LOCATIONS

HQ: Sapient Corporation
131 Dartmouth St., 3rd Fl., Boston, MA 02116
Phone: 617-621-0200 **Fax:** 617-621-1300
Web: www.sapient.com

2008 Sales

	% of total
North America	66
Other regions	34
Total	**100**

PRODUCTS/OPERATIONS

2008 Sales

	$ mil.	% of total
Service revenues	662.4	96
Reimbursable expenses	25.1	4
Total	**687.5**	**100**

Selected Services

Business and operational consulting
Creative design
Interactive marketing
Internet consulting
Internet design
Software implementation
Systems design and integration
Technology development
User experience research

COMPETITORS

Accenture
Booz Allen
Boston Consulting
Capgemini
CIBER
Computer Sciences Corp.
Computer Task Group
Diamond Management & Technology Consultants
HP Enterprise Services
IBM
Inforte
Keane
Perot Systems
Sapiens
Unisys

HISTORICAL FINANCIALS

Company Type: Public

Income Statement

FYE: December 31

	REVENUE ($ mil.)	NET INCOME ($ mil.)	NET PROFIT MARGIN	EMPLOYEES
12/08	687.5	62.5	9.1%	6,360
12/07	566.0	15.2	2.7%	6,217
12/06	421.6	3.0	0.7%	4,952
12/05	333.0	25.7	7.7%	3,017
12/04	266.0	22.8	8.6%	2,314
Annual Growth	**26.8%**	**28.7%**	**—**	**28.8%**

2008 Year-End Financials

Debt ratio: —
Return on equity: 22.2%
Cash ($ mil.): 169.3
Current ratio: 2.55
Long-term debt ($ mil.): —
No. of shares (mil.): 132.7
Dividends
  Yield: 0.0%
  Payout: —
Market value ($ mil.): 589.1
R&D as % of sales: —
Advertising as % of sales: —

Stock History

NASDAQ (GS): SAPE

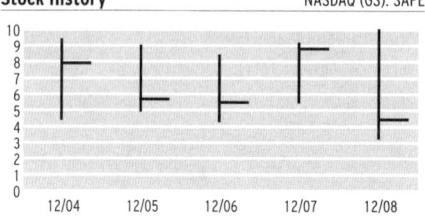

	STOCK PRICE ($) FY Close	P/E High/Low		PER SHARE ($) Earnings	Dividends	Book Value
12/08	4.44	21	7	0.48	0.00	2.28
12/07	8.81	76	46	0.12	0.00	1.96
12/06	5.49	279	145	0.03	0.00	1.62
12/05	5.69	45	25	0.20	0.00	1.53
12/04	7.91	52	25	0.18	0.00	1.40
Annual Growth	**(13.4%)**	**—**	**—**	**27.8%**	**—**	**12.9%**

SeaBright Insurance

SeaBright Insurance Holdings makes smooth sailing of the choppy waters of workers' compensation. Through its SeaBright Insurance subsidiary, it provides a variety of specialty workers' compensation insurance to companies in niche industries, including maritime and construction. The firm also offers coverage to employers that participate in collectively bargained workers' compensation agreements, as well as traditional workers' compensation coverage in some markets. SeaBright sells its products through independent brokers and wholesale subsidiary PointSure Insurance Services. The company was formed in 2003 to facilitate a management buyout of Eagle Pacific Insurance.

SeaBright specializes in providing workers' compensation insurance for customers who require complex, customized coverage or who operate in underserved markets. Maritime customers include shipbuilders and companies involved in marine construction and stevedoring (ship loading and unloading). It also does business in the construction industry with California employers who are engaged in workers' compensation collective bargaining agreements, in which claims are handled through alternative

dispute resolution (ADR). Additionally, the company sells traditional workers' compensation insurance in some underserved markets, including Alaska, Arizona, California, Hawaii, Illinois, Louisiana, and Texas.

California accounts for about 40% of SeaBright's written premiums; other key markets for the company include Alaska, Hawaii, Illinois, and Louisiana. SeaBright used money from its 2005 IPO to write more business in these markets and is also planning to move into new states where it is already licensed to do business (it is licensed in 45 states). It opened an office in the Philadelphia area in 2006 and one in Atlanta the following year to launch expansion in the Northeast and Southeast, respectively.

The company strives to control the medical costs associated with workplace injuries by consulting with employers on workplace safety and accident prevention. It also offers a network of doctors and other health care providers that follow approved treatment guidelines to get injured or ill workers back on the job as quickly as possible.

Late in 2007 the company acquired Total HealthCare Management, a California-based company that provides bill and utilization review, case management, and other services.

EXECUTIVES

Chairman and CEO: John G. Pasqualetto, age 67, $2,003,584 total compensation
President and COO: Richard J. Gergasko, age 51, $1,086,633 total compensation
Acting Principal Financial Officer: M. Philip Romney, age 55, $456,831 total compensation
SVP and Chief Medical Officer: Marc B. Miller, age 53
SVP Policyholder Services; CEO, Total HealthCare Management: Richard W. Seelinger, age 50, $652,217 total compensation
SVP, General Counsel, and Secretary: D. Drue Wax
SVP Underwriting: Jeffrey C. Wanamaker, age 43, $657,015 total compensation
VP and CIO: James L. (Skip) Borland III, age 48
Assistant VP and National Marketing Director: Dean Rappleye
President, PointSure Insurance Services: Craig A. Pankow, age 50
COO, Total HealthCare Management: Jeffrey D. Miller
Auditors: KPMG LLP

LOCATIONS

HQ: SeaBright Insurance Holdings, Inc.
1501 4th Ave., Ste. 2600, Seattle, WA 98101
Phone: 206-269-8500 **Fax:** 206-269-8903
Web: www.sbic.com

PRODUCTS/OPERATIONS

2008 Sales

	$ mil.	% of total
Premiums earned	248.6	89
Investment income	22.6	8
Claims services	1.0	—
Other	8.9	3
Adjustments	(13.8)	—
Total	**267.3**	**100**

COMPETITORS

ACE Limited	PMA Insurance Group
Acuity Mutual	SCF Arizona
AIG	State Compensation
AMERISAFE	Insurance Fund
FCCI	Texas Mutual
First Insurance of Hawaii	Travelers Companies
The Hartford	Zenith National
Liberty Mutual	Zurich American
Louisiana Workers' Compensation	

HISTORICAL FINANCIALS

Company Type: Public

Income Statement
FYE: December 31

	ASSETS ($ mil.)	NET INCOME ($ mil.)	INCOME AS % OF ASSETS	EMPLOYEES
12/08	842.7	29.3	3.5%	316
12/07	755.6	39.9	5.3%	236
12/06	614.3	33.2	5.4%	178
12/05	427.3	18.3	4.3%	152
12/04	226.1	7.2	3.2%	117
Annual Growth	**38.9%**	**42.0%**	**—**	**28.2%**

2008 Year-End Financials

Equity as % of assets: 38.5%
Return on assets: 3.7%
Return on equity: 9.5%
Long-term debt ($ mil.): 12.0
No. of shares (mil.): 21.7
Market value ($ mil.): 254.4

Dividends
  Yield: 0.0%
  Payout: —
Sales ($ mil.): 267.3
R&D as % of sales: —
Advertising as % of sales: —

Stock History
NYSE: SBX

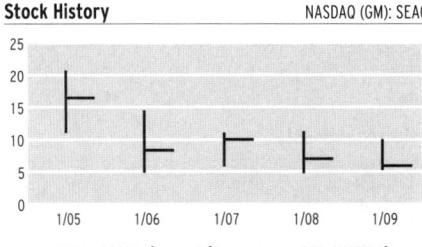

	STOCK PRICE ($) FY Close	P/E High/Low		PER SHARE ($) Earnings	Dividends	Book Value
12/08	11.74	12	6	1.38	0.00	14.99
12/07	15.08	11	7	1.90	0.00	13.58
12/06	18.01	11	8	1.63	0.00	11.49
12/05	16.63	16	9	1.13	0.00	7.18
Annual Growth	**(11.0%)**	**—**	**—**	**8.9%**	**—**	**53.6%**

SeaChange International

SeaChange International sees a change coming in the way we watch television. The company provides video server systems used by TV stations and cable system operators to manage and distribute digital video. Its On Demand products allow operators to offer video-on-demand (VOD) and other interactive services to their subscribers, while its VODlink set-top box middleware allows cable subscribers to access a variety of interactive features. SeaChange's Spot System converts analog video signals, enabling cable TV operators to digitally broadcast and schedule local advertisements for specific markets. The company's Media Services business provides content aggregation and distribution, primarily in Europe.

The company's largest customer, Comcast, accounts for about a third of its revenues. Other customers include Cablevision, DIRECTV, Cox Communications, KDDI, Time Warner Cable, and Virgin Media.

SeaChange generates around a third of its revenues outside North America. It primarily utilizes a direct sales force in the US, relying on both direct sales and distributors in international markets.

In 2009 the company acquired eventIS Group B.V., a Dutch supplier of VOD and linear broadcast software and services, for nearly $37 million in cash, plus earnout and other payments in the following three years. The purchase expands SeaChange's business in Europe. eventIS was profitable on 2008 sales of about $13 million, and its acquisition added around 70 employees to SeaChange's headcount.

The following year SeaChange agreed to buy VividLogic, Inc., a California software developer that markets packages to cable TV service providers, set-top box manufacturers, and consumer electronics suppliers. The company agreed to pay $12 million in cash and other considerations to purchase VividLogic. SeaChange sees the combination of its existing in-home technologies and VividLogic's software helping to capitalize on the market shift to Internet protocol-based content delivery into the home and within the home.

EXECUTIVES

Chairman and CEO: William C. (Bill) Styslinger III, age 63, $1,327,866 total compensation
President and COO: Edward (Ed) Dunbar, age 57
Chief Strategy Officer: Yvette M. Kanouff, age 43, $934,408 total compensation
Chief Marketing Officer: Simon McGrath
CFO, SVP Finance and Administration, Secretary, and Treasurer: Kevin M. Bisson, age 47, $663,014 total compensation
SVP Software Engineering: Steven M. (Steve) Davi, age 45, $559,191 total compensation
SVP: Anthony W. Kelly, age 47
SVP Network Storage Engineering: Bruce E. Mann, age 61
SVP Worldwide Sales: Ira Goldfarb, age 51, $771,552 total compensation
VP Product Marketing and Alliances: Tom Rosenstein
President, SeaChange China and ZQ Interactive: Zheng Gao
Director Investor Relations: Martha Schaefer
Public Relations: Jim Sheehan
Director: Carlo Salvatori, age 68
Auditors: Grant Thornton LLP

LOCATIONS

HQ: SeaChange International, Inc.
50 Nagog Park, Acton, MA 01720
Phone: 978-897-0100   **Fax:** 978-897-0132
Web: www.schange.com

2009 Sales

	$ mil.	% of total
North America	139.4	69
Europe & Middle East	44.1	22
Latin America	4.2	2
Other regions	14.1	7
Total	**201.8**	**100**

PRODUCTS/OPERATIONS

2009 Sales

	$ mil.	% of total
Software	132.2	65
Servers & storage	53.6	27
Media services	16.0	8
Total	**201.8**	**100**

COMPETITORS

ARRIS	Omneon
BigBand Networks	Sony
Cisco Systems	TANDBERG Television
Concurrent Computer	THOMSON
Harris Corp.	TiVo
Motorola, Inc.	

HISTORICAL FINANCIALS

Company Type: Public

Income Statement
FYE: January 31

	REVENUE ($ mil.)	NET INCOME ($ mil.)	NET PROFIT MARGIN	EMPLOYEES
1/09	201.8	10.0	5.0%	1,046
1/08	179.9	2.9	1.6%	861
1/07	161.3	(8.2)	—	811
1/06	126.3	(12.3)	—	671
1/05	157.3	9.9	6.3%	531
Annual Growth	**6.4%**	**0.3%**	**—**	**18.5%**

2009 Year-End Financials

Debt ratio: —
Return on equity: 5.9%
Cash ($ mil.): 62.5
Current ratio: 2.75
Long-term debt ($ mil.): —
No. of shares (mil.): 31.1

Dividends
  Yield: —
  Payout: —
Market value ($ mil.): 184.0
R&D as % of sales: —
Advertising as % of sales: —

Stock History
NASDAQ (GM): SEAC

	STOCK PRICE ($) FY Close	P/E High/Low		PER SHARE ($) Earnings	Dividends	Book Value
1/09	5.92	31	17	0.32	—	5.54
1/08	7.02	111	49	0.10	—	5.32
1/07	10.00	—	—	(0.28)	—	5.06
1/06	8.32	—	—	(0.44)	—	4.95
1/05	16.42	60	33	0.34	—	5.31
Annual Growth	**(22.5%)**	**—**	**—**	**(1.5%)**	**—**	**1.1%**

Servotronics, Inc.

Servotronics knows how to get things moving and cut to the chase. The company makes devices that convert electricity into mechanical movement and cutlery products. Its advanced technology products include servo-control components (torque motors, electromagnetic actuators, and hydraulic and pneumatic valves), which it sells mainly to clients in the aerospace industry. These include Honeywell, United Technologies, and the US government. Servotronics' cutlery unit makes a broad range of products from machetes and bayonets to kitchen knives and putty knives. Customers include retailers, restaurants, and agencies of the US government.

Contracts with agencies of the US government or their prime contractors and subcontractors account for nearly half of sales.

Through a trust, employees own about 34% of Servotronics.

Chairman, president, and CEO Nicholas Trbovich owns about 22% of the company; his son, EVP and director Nicholas Trbovich Jr., owns around 5%. Investor Harvey Houtkin owns approximately 15%.

EXECUTIVES

Chairman, President, and CEO: Nicholas D. Trbovich, age 73, $945,897 total compensation
EVP, COO, and Director: Nicholas D. Trbovich Jr., age 48, $544,810 total compensation
CFO and Treasurer: Cari L. Jaroslawsky, age 40, $235,546 total compensation
VP Marketing: Salvatore San Filippo, age 60
Information Services: Elaine Trbovich
Coporate Secretary: Michael Trobvich, age 46
Director Purchasing: Andy Jakubowski
Auditors: Freed Maxick & Battaglia CPAs, PC

LOCATIONS

HQ: Servotronics, Inc.
1110 Maple St., Elma, NY 14059
Phone: 716-655-5990   **Fax:** 716-655-6012
Web: www.servotronics.com

PRODUCTS/OPERATIONS

2008 Sales

	$ mil.	% of total
Advanced technology group	20.9	61
Consumer products group	13.3	39
Total	**34.2**	**100**

Selected Products

Advanced Technology Products
 Electromagnetic actuators
 Hydraulic valves
 Pneumatic valves
 Proportional solenoids
 Torque motors
Consumer Products
 Bayonets
 Bread knives
 Butcher knives
 Carving forks
 Carving knives
 Field knives
 Linoleum sheet-cutters
 Machetes
 Paring knives
 Pocket knives
 Putty knives
 Sharpeners
 Steak knives
 Survival knives

COMPETITORS

Axsys
Bosch Rexroth Corp.
Buck Knives
Fiskars
GE Fanuc
Gerber Scientific
Guy Degrenne
Hamilton Sundstrand
Hyde Tools
Leatherman Tool
Lifetime Brands
Magnetek
Nook Industries
Numatics
Spyderco
Sun Hydraulics
Victorinox Swiss Army
WKI Holding
W.R. Case & Sons Cutlery
Yaskawa Electric America

HISTORICAL FINANCIALS

Company Type: Public

Income Statement

FYE: December 31

	REVENUE ($ mil.)	NET INCOME ($ mil.)	NET PROFIT MARGIN	EMPLOYEES
12/08	34.2	3.1	9.1%	296
12/07	31.4	2.1	6.7%	265
12/06	24.5	1.1	4.5%	247
12/05	23.1	1.4	6.1%	245
12/04	22.1	0.7	3.2%	226
Annual Growth	**11.5%**	**45.1%**	**—**	**7.0%**

2008 Year-End Financials

Debt ratio: 20.5%
Return on equity: 18.2%
Cash ($ mil.): 4.7
Current ratio: 4.52
Long-term debt ($ mil.): 3.7
No. of shares (mil.): 2.2
Dividends
 Yield: 2.7%
 Payout: 10.3%
Market value ($ mil.): 12.4
R&D as % of sales: —
Advertising as % of sales: —

Stock History

NYSE Alternext: SVT

	STOCK PRICE ($) FY Close	P/E High/Low		PER SHARE ($) Earnings	Dividends	Book Value
12/08	5.52	16	4	1.45	0.15	8.08
12/07	14.50	18	9	0.96	0.00	7.15
12/06	8.35	20	9	0.51	0.00	6.46
12/05	4.70	8	6	0.64	0.00	6.45
12/04	4.85	17	8	0.35	0.00	5.82
Annual Growth	**3.3%**	**—**	**—**	**42.7%**	**—**	**8.5%**

Shutterfly, Inc.

Whether or not you are the consummate shutterbug, you can rely on Shutterfly for digital prints. An e-commerce company specializing in digital photo products and services for the consumer and professional photography markets, the company offers customers the ability to upload, share, store, and edit digital photos through its Web site. In addition to traditional 4-inch by 6-inch prints, Shutterfly offers prints ranging from wallet-sized to jumbo enlargements, and personalized items including mugs, photo books, calendars, magnets, and T-shirts. Users are not required to become members to view shared photos. Silicon Valley icon Jim Clark, who resigned as chairman in 2007, owns more than 20% of the company.

Shutterfly makes about half its revenues during the fourth quarter of the year due to holiday sales. Sales of 4x6 prints account for about 20% of revenues. The company makes additional money through advertising — clients such as Sony, ABC, AT&T, Universal Music, and Proctor & Gamble advertise on its Web site. It has Web site operations, offices, and customer support centers in Redwood City, California, and Mesa,

Arizona, and production facilities in Charlotte, North Carolina, and Phoenix, Arizona.

The company has a growth strategy that includes the acquisition of Tiny Pictures, which develops applications and services for picture and video sharing. And in 2008 it launched Shutterfly Gallery (a community site for photo viewing) and Shutterfly Share Sites (for photo sharing). It also added new designer stationery, notebooks, notepads, address labels, stickers, and calendar posters to its product base that year, and expanded with the acquisition of Nexo Systems for about $15 million in cash and stock. Nexo provides technology that allows users to create their own Web sites. The previous year the company acquired CustomAbility, publisher of customized children's books under the brand name *Make It About Me*.

Shutterfly was founded in 1999 and was funded in part by Clark, a Silicon Valley investor and co-founder of Netscape Communications. The company hired eBay veteran Jeff Housenbold as CEO in 2005 and went public in an IPO the following year.

EXECUTIVES

Chairman: Philip A. (Phil) Marineau, age 62
President, CEO, and Director:
 Jeffrey T. (Jeff) Housenbold, age 39,
 $1,753,978 total compensation
SVP and CTO: Neil Day
SVP and Chief Marketing Officer: Peter C. Elarde, age 44
SVP and CFO: Mark J. Rubash, age 51,
 $1,335,948 total compensation
SVP Business and Corporate Development:
 Douglas J. (Doug) Galen, age 47,
 $664,785 total compensation
SVP Operations: Dwayne A. Black, age 41,
 $556,212 total compensation
VP Internet Operations and CIO: Jeffrey Whitehead
VP Legal: Douglas (Doug) Appleton, age 41
VP Human Resources: Peter Navin
VP Customer Marketing and E-Commerce: Katie Ho
Senior Manager Corporate Communications:
 Gretchen Sloan
Director Investor Relations: Marilyn Lattin
Auditors: PricewaterhouseCoopers LLP

LOCATIONS

HQ: Shutterfly, Inc.
2800 Bridge Pkwy., Ste. 101
Redwood City, CA 94065
Phone: 650-610-5200   **Fax:** 650-654-1299
Web: www.shutterfly.com

PRODUCTS/OPERATIONS

2008 Sales

	% of total
Personalized products & services	61
Print	39
Total	**100**

Selected Products and Services

Online Services
 Edit and enhance
 Organize
 Print
 Share
 Upload
Photo-Based Products
 Greeting cards
 Personalized calendars
 Photo books
 Stationery

COMPETITORS

123Greetings	Rite Aid
AG Interactive	Ritz Camera
Costco Wholesale	Snapfish
CVS Caremark	Walgreen
Google	Wal-Mart
Kodak Imaging Network	Yahoo!
LifePics	

HISTORICAL FINANCIALS

Company Type: Public

Income Statement

FYE: December 31

	REVENUE ($ mil.)	NET INCOME ($ mil.)	NET PROFIT MARGIN	EMPLOYEES
12/08	213.5	4.6	2.2%	514
12/07	186.7	10.1	5.4%	431
12/06	123.4	5.8	4.7%	275
12/05	83.9	28.5	34.0%	208
12/04	54.5	3.7	6.8%	208
Annual Growth	40.7%	5.6%	—	25.4%

2008 Year-End Financials

Debt ratio: 0.0%
Return on equity: 2.6%
Cash ($ mil.): 88.2
Current ratio: 2.28
Long-term debt ($ mil.): 0.0
No. of shares (mil.): 25.7

Dividends
  Yield: 0.0%
  Payout: —
Market value ($ mil.): 179.5
R&D as % of sales: —
Advertising as % of sales: —

Stock History

NASDAQ (GM): SFLY

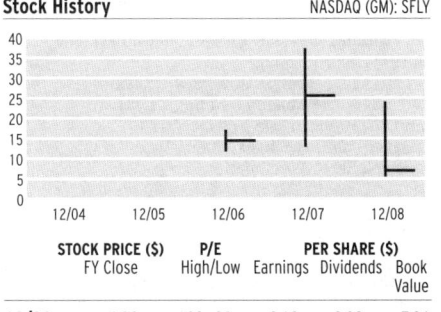

	STOCK PRICE ($) FY Close	P/E High/Low		PER SHARE ($) Earnings	Dividends	Book Value
12/08	6.99	132	32	0.18	0.00	7.26
12/07	25.62	97	35	0.38	0.00	6.64
12/06	14.40	30	22	0.56	0.00	5.89
Annual Growth	(30.3%)	—	—	(43.3%)	—	11.0%

Signature Bank

Signature Bank marks the spot where some professional New Yorkers bank. The institution provides customized banking and financial services to smaller private businesses, their owners, and their top executives through more than 20 locations in the metropolitan area. It attracts deposits by offering money market, savings, and NOW accounts, as well as CDs. Business loans, including commercial mortgages, commercial and industrial loans, and Small Business Administration-guaranteed loans comprise the bulk of the bank's lending activities. Asset management, financial planning, life and disability insurance, and brokerage services are offered through affiliate Signature Securities Group.

Israeli financial institution Bank Hapoalim spun off about 30% of Signature Bank in a 2004 public offering, then divested its majority stake the following year.

EXECUTIVES

Chairman: Scott A. Shay
Vice Chairman: John Tamberlane
President, CEO, and Director: Joseph J. DePaolo
EVP and COO: Mark T. Sigona
EVP and Chief Credit Officer: Michael J. Merlo
EVP, Group Director, and Chairman, Commercial Real Estate Committee: George M. Klett
EVP and Group Director: Randi Schneer
EVP and Group Director: Edwin J. Sirlin
SVP and CTO: Michael Sharkey
SVP and Treasurer: Peter S. Quinlan
SVP and Senior Lender: Steven P. Saporito
Auditors: KPMG LLP

LOCATIONS

HQ: Signature Bank
  565 5th Ave., New York, NY 10017
Phone: 646-822-1500
Web: www.signatureny.com

PRODUCTS/OPERATIONS

2008 Gross Revenues

	$ mil.	% of total
Interest		
Loans	165.7	45
Securities	154.6	42
Other short-term investments	3.1	1
Noninterest		
Commissions	19.9	5
Fees & service charges	13.7	4
Other	10.5	3
Total	367.5	100

COMPETITORS

Apple Bank
Astoria Financial
Bank Leumi USA
Capital One
Citigroup
HSBC USA
JPMorgan Chase
New York Community Bancorp
Safra Bank
TD Bank USA

HISTORICAL FINANCIALS

Company Type: Public

Income Statement

FYE: December 31

	ASSETS ($ mil.)	NET INCOME ($ mil.)	INCOME AS % OF ASSETS	EMPLOYEES
12/08	7,192.2	43.4	0.6%	553
12/07	5,845.2	27.3	0.5%	501
12/06	5,399.4	33.4	0.6%	416
12/05	4,384.9	15.9	0.4%	347
12/04	3,356.4	29.8	0.9%	296
Annual Growth	21.0%	9.9%	—	16.9%

2008 Year-End Financials

Equity as % of assets: 8.2%
Return on assets: 0.7%
Return on equity: 8.6%
Long-term debt ($ mil.): 260.0
No. of shares (mil.): 40.6
Market value ($ mil.): 1,164.6

Dividends
  Yield: 0.0%
  Payout: —
Sales ($ mil.): 222.9
R&D as % of sales: —
Advertising as % of sales: —

Stock History

NASDAQ (GS): SBNY

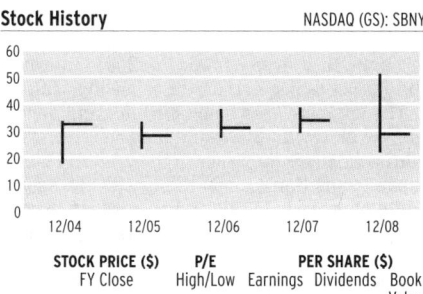

	STOCK PRICE ($) FY Close	P/E High/Low		PER SHARE ($) Earnings	Dividends	Book Value
12/08	28.69	145	64	0.35	0.00	17.20
12/07	33.75	42	33	0.91	0.00	10.49
12/06	31.00	34	25	1.12	0.00	9.67
12/05	28.07	62	44	0.53	0.00	8.65
12/04	32.36	29	16	1.15	0.00	8.35
Annual Growth	(3.0%)	—	—	(25.7%)	—	19.8%

Skilled Healthcare Group

Skilled Healthcare Group (formerly SHG Holding Solutions) doesn't give its elderly clients the fountain of youth, but the nursing home operator does help them live their lives more comfortably. The company operates about 75 skilled nursing facilities and about 20 assisted-living centers in six states; its facilities have some 10,500 beds in all. Through its nursing homes, the company specializes in providing intensive medical care for sicker elderly patients, such as those recovering from stroke or hip replacement surgery. Skilled Healthcare also provides rehabilitation services and hospice care through other divisions. The company is majority owned by investment firm Onex.

The company was previously wholly owned by Onex, but it went public in 2007. Onex owns about 77% of Skilled Healthcare, which used proceeds from its IPO to pay down debt.

Skilled Healthcare owns over 70% of its skilled nursing centers, which are mostly located in large urban or suburban areas. The company's service offerings are geared toward higher-acuity patients, those who require more intensive, skilled care and for whom the company is reimbursed at higher rates. (Medicare and Medicaid account for a majority of revenue.)

The company depends on referrals of such patients from hospitals and doctors, and it has initiated alliances with major medical centers (including Baylor Health Care System in Dallas) to increase desirable referrals. An increasing number of its nursing homes feature Express Recovery units, which are separate rehabilitation wings that provide comprehensive rehab programs for some patients recovering from disease or surgery.

While focused on its long-term care facilities, the company has also been growing its ancillary health care services segment, which includes the operations of rehab therapy provider Hallmark Rehabilitation and hospice services unit Hospice Care of the West. Hallmark serves the company's own nursing homes, as well as more than 120

non-affiliated facilities. Hospice Care of the West operates in California and New Mexico; it entered the New Mexico market in 2007 but exited the Texas hospice market the following year.

The company also bought 10 nursing homes in New Mexico in 2007, and it added several facilities in Missouri earlier in the year. In 2008 it expanded its Kansas operations with the acquisition of several nursing and assisted living centers, and in 2009 it entered the state of Iowa by purchasing a skilled nursing center in Des Moines. The company has historically grown through similar purchases, buying or leasing dozens of nursing facilities since 2003, when it emerged from Chapter 11 bankruptcy. It also occasionally builds new facilities on its own.

EXECUTIVES

Chairman and CEO: Boyd W. Hendrickson, age 65, $1,400,809 total compensation
President, COO, and Director: Jose C. Lynch, age 39, $982,497 total compensation
EVP, CFO, and Treasurer: Devasis (Dev) Ghose, age 56, $824,035 total compensation
EVP, General Counsel, and Secretary: Roland G. Rapp, age 48, $666,566 total compensation
EVP; President, Hallmark Rehabilitation and Hospice Care of the West: Kelly J. Gill, age 54
SVP and Chief Compliance Officer: Susan T. Whittle, age 61
SVP and CIO: Allan Crommett
SVP, Hallmark Rehabilitation: Paul Sumrow
SVP Human Resources: Kristiina Hintgen
SVP Finance and Chief Accounting Officer: Christopher N, Felfe, age 45
SVP Professional Services: Aisha A. Salaam
VP Sales and Marketing, Hallmark Rehabilitation: Velvet Mayes
Auditors: Ernst & Young LLP

LOCATIONS

HQ: Skilled Healthcare Group, Inc.
27442 Portola Pkwy., Ste. 200
Foothill Ranch, CA 92610
Phone: 949-282-5800　　　**Fax:** 949-282-5859
Web: www.skilledhealthcaregroup.com

2008 Sales

	$ mil.	% of total
California	327.1	45
Texas	185.9	25
New Mexico	82.2	11
Missouri	55.9	8
Kansas	51.3	7
Nevada	30.6	4
Other	0.3	—
Total	**733.3**	**100**

PRODUCTS/OPERATIONS

2008 Sales

	$ mil.	% of total
Long-term care services		
Skilled nursing facilities	622.9	85
Assisted living facilities	20.6	3
Ancillary services		
Third-party rehabilitation therapy services	69.9	9
Hospice	19.9	3
Total	**733.3**	**100**

Selected Subsidiaries

Hallmark Investment Group, Inc.
Hallmark Rehabilitation, Inc.
Hospice Care of the West
SHG Resources, LP
Summit Care Corporation

COMPETITORS

Advocat	Kindred Healthcare
Amedisys	Life Care Centers
American HomePatient	Manor Care
Covenant Care	National HealthCare
Ensign Group	Odyssey HealthCare
Extendicare REIT	RehabCare
Five Star Quality Care	Sun Healthcare
Golden Horizons	Tenet Healthcare
HealthSouth	VITAS Healthcare

HISTORICAL FINANCIALS

Company Type: Public

Income Statement

FYE: December 31

	REVENUE ($ mil.)	NET INCOME ($ mil.)	NET PROFIT MARGIN	EMPLOYEES
12/08	733.3	37.2	5.1%	8,492
12/07	634.6	17.1	2.7%	7,446
12/06	531.7	17.3	3.3%	6,980
12/05	462.8	33.9	7.3%	6,689
12/04	371.3	16.5	4.4%	—
Annual Growth	**18.5%**	**22.5%**	**—**	**8.3%**

2008 Year-End Financials

Debt ratio: 112.2%
Return on equity: 9.5%
Cash ($ mil.): 2.0
Current ratio: 1.58
Long-term debt ($ mil.): 462.4
No. of shares (mil.): 37.3
Dividends
　Yield: 0.0%
　Payout: —
Market value ($ mil.): 315.0
R&D as % of sales: —
Advertising as % of sales: —

Stock History

NYSE: SKH

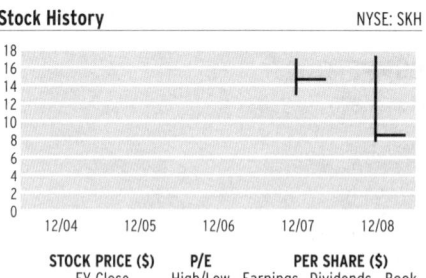

	STOCK PRICE ($) FY Close	P/E High/Low		PER SHARE ($) Earnings	Dividends	Book Value
12/08	8.44	17	8	1.01	0.00	11.04
12/07	14.63	48	37	0.35	0.00	10.03
Annual Growth	**(42.3%)**	**—**	**—**	**188.6%**	**—**	**10.0%**

SkillSoft

SkillSoft provides Internet-based training courses and software for business and information technology (IT) professionals. SkillSoft's more than 6,600 courses include lessons in a variety of business, compliance, safety, and technology topics, while its SkillPort software manages corporate e-learning programs. Its SkillSoft Dialogue product is a virtual classroom that helps clients create and deliver live and on-demand learning sessions. SkillSoft also offers online mentoring for more than 100 IT certification exams. Its subsidiary Books24x7 allows customers to search some 19,000 engineering, IT, and business books online. Columbia Wanger Asset Management owns 20% of SkillSoft.

In addition to its professional courses, the company partners with for-profit colleges including Drexel University and University of Phoenix to provide accredited courses to students as well.

SkillSoft acquired NETg from The Thomson Corporation in 2007 for a reported $270 million. With NETg in its fold, SkillSoft has gained about 1,000 new courses to its repertoire.

Responding to a slow economy, SkillSoft tightened its belt in 2008, laying off about 120 workers system-wide and taking a $1.6 million charge against earnings in its fourth quarter. Management predicted that the move would result in a $7 million increase in revenue for 2009.

SkillSoft outsources much of its content development to third parties.

EXECUTIVES

President, CEO, and Director: Charles E. (Chuck) Moran, age 55, $2,571,690 total compensation
COO: Jerald A. (Jerry) Nine Jr., age 52, $1,531,381 total compensation
EVP, CFO, and Assistant Secretary: Thomas J. (Tom) McDonald, age 60, $1,170,186 total compensation
EVP Content Development: Colm M. Darcy, age 46, $702,986 total compensation
EVP Technology: Mark A. Townsend, age 57, $702,986 total compensation
SVP Marketing: Lee A. Ritze
SVP Strategy, Corporate Development, and Emerging Business: John Ambrose
VP; Managing Director, Europe, Middle East, and Africa: Kevin T. Young
VP; Managing Director, Asia/Pacific: Glenn Nott
VP Finance and Chief Accounting Officer: Anthony P. Amato, age 45
Manager Public Relations: Donna Ayer
Auditors: Ernst & Young LLP

LOCATIONS

HQ: SkillSoft Public Limited Company
107 Northeastern Blvd., Nashua, NH 03062
Phone: 603-324-3000　　　**Fax:** 603-324-3009
Web: www.skillsoft.com

2009 Sales

	$ mil.	% of total
North America		
US	244.0	74
Canada	12.7	4
Europe		
UK	44.7	14
Other countries	7.0	2
Australia/New Zealand	14.0	4
Other regions	6.1	2
Total	**328.5**	**100**

PRODUCTS/OPERATIONS

Selected Subsidiaries

Books24x7.com, Inc.
CBT Technology Limited
NETg Australia Pty Limited
NETg GmbH
NETg SA (France)
SkillSoft Asia Pacific PTE Ltd
SkillSoft Asia Pacific Pty Ltd
SkillSoft Canada Limited
SkillSoft Corporation
SkillSoft Finance Limited
SkillSoft France SARL
SkillSoft Ireland Ltd
SkillSoft NETg Limited
SkillSoft New Zealand Ltd
SkillSoft UK Limited
SmartCertify Direct, Inc.
SmartForce Business Skills Ltd
SS Software Service India Private Limited
Targeted Learning Corporation
Wave Technologies Limited

HISTORICAL FINANCIALS

Company Type: Public

Income Statement

FYE: January 31

	REVENUE ($ mil.)	NET INCOME ($ mil.)	NET PROFIT MARGIN	EMPLOYEES
1/09	328.5	50.8	15.5%	1,124
1/08	281.2	60.0	21.3%	1,133
1/07	225.2	24.2	10.7%	999
1/06	215.6	35.2	16.3%	979
1/05	212.3	(20.1)	—	1,140
Annual Growth	11.5%	—	—	(0.4%)

2009 Year-End Financials

Debt ratio: 59.9%
Return on equity: 24.4%
Cash ($ mil.): 37.9
Current ratio: 0.95
Long-term debt ($ mil.): 122.1
No. of shares (mil.): 98.9

Dividends
  Yield: —
  Payout: —
Market value ($ mil.): 702.1
R&D as % of sales: —
Advertising as % of sales: —

Stock History

NASDAQ (GM): SKIL

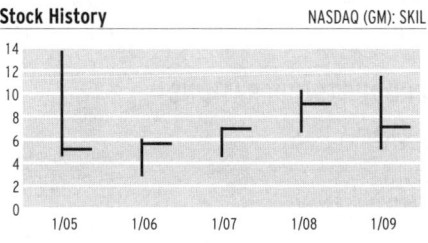

	STOCK PRICE ($) FY Close	P/E High/Low	PER SHARE ($) Earnings	Dividends	Book Value
1/09	7.10	24 11	0.47	—	2.06
1/08	9.11	19 12	0.55	—	2.15
1/07	6.95	30 20	0.23	—	1.39
1/06	5.65	18 9	0.34	—	1.03
1/05	5.17	— —	(0.19)	—	0.86
Annual Growth	8.3%	— —	—	—	24.5%

SmartPros Ltd.

SmartPros counts on accountants and engineers to keep its numbers shipshape. SmartPros offers professional development courses in online, DVD, and CD-ROM formats. Its classes are used by accounting, finance, engineering, legal and business professionals to build skills, keep certifications current, and prepare for certification testing. The company also offers executive workshops, consulting, and e-learning training program development. Among its offerings are courses in auditing, design, compliance, ethics, financial reporting, project management, and safety. CPE (continuing professional education) credits can be earned immediately by passing tests offered at the end of accredited courses.

In addition, SmartPros publishes a news and information Web portal for accounting and finance professionals.

SmartPros has taken steps to expand its offering both by adding content to its e-learning libraries and by expanding its ability to create more proprietary products. SmartPros acquired Sage Online in 2006, adding e-learning courses on topics in banking, securities, and insurance sectors. The company's acquisition of Skye Multimedia in 2006 also added expertise in content development, design and animation, production services, and application development to the company's offerings. The company also added the assets of Cognistar Interactive, a provider of online continuing legal education, to its offerings in 2006.

Growth continued in 2007 with the acquisition of The Selbest Group, which offers consulting for sales, management training, and marketing support in the financial services industry. WatchIT, which provides information technology education and training, and FinancialCampus also joined SmartPros that year.

In 2008 SmartPros acquired Loscalzo, a provider of live accounting and auditing programs, conferences, and seminars. The following year it bought the business and assets of Executive Enterprises Institute, another provider of live conferences and seminars.

Chairman and CEO Allen S. Greene owns about 6% of the company.

EXECUTIVES

Chairman and CEO, SmartPros and SmartPros Legal and Ethics: Allen S. Greene, age 62, $440,899 total compensation
President and Director: Jack Fingerhut, age 58, $288,608 total compensation
CTO: Joseph R. Fish, age 43, $241,490 total compensation
Chief Accounting and Financial Officer and Treasurer; CFO, iReflect: Stanley P. Wirtheim, age 59
SVP Business Development: Michael Fowler, age 45
VP Marketing and eCommerce: Shane Gillispie
VP Engineering and Channel Partners: Mark R. Luciano
VP and Secretary: Karen S. Stolzar, age 60
President, Skye Multimedia and iReflect: Seth Oberman, age 45
President, Loscalzo Associates: Margaret A. Loscalzo, age 59
President, SmartPros Legal and Ethics: Stephen K. (Steve) Henn, age 45
Auditors: Holtz Rubenstein Reminick LLP

LOCATIONS

HQ: SmartPros Ltd.
  12 Skyline Dr., Hawthorne, NY 10532
Phone: 914-345-2620   **Fax:** 914-345-2660
Web: corporate.smartpros.com

COMPETITORS

CPA2Biz
Educational Testing Service
Integrity Interactive
International Institute for Learning
Kaplan
lrn
Prometric
Saba Software
SkillSoft

HISTORICAL FINANCIALS

Company Type: Public

Income Statement

FYE: December 31

	REVENUE ($ mil.)	NET INCOME ($ mil.)	NET PROFIT MARGIN	EMPLOYEES
12/08	18.3	1.6	8.7%	98
12/07	15.2	2.2	14.5%	99
12/06	12.5	1.5	12.0%	77
12/05	10.4	0.7	6.7%	75
12/04	10.2	0.7	6.9%	68
Annual Growth	15.7%	23.0%	—	9.6%

2008 Year-End Financials

Debt ratio: —
Return on equity: 13.9%
Cash ($ mil.): 6.6
Current ratio: 1.31
Long-term debt ($ mil.): —
No. of shares (mil.): 5.1

Dividends
  Yield: 0.0%
  Payout: —
Market value ($ mil.): 12.0
R&D as % of sales: —
Advertising as % of sales: —

Stock History

NASDAQ (CM): SPRO

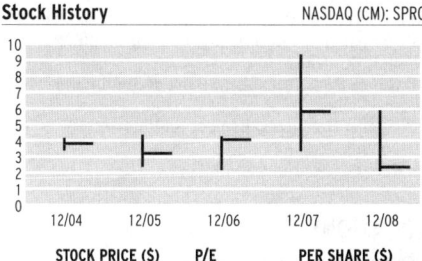

	STOCK PRICE ($) FY Close	P/E High/Low	PER SHARE ($) Earnings	Dividends	Book Value
12/08	2.36	18 7	0.32	0.00	2.39
12/07	5.82	22 8	0.43	0.00	2.14
12/06	4.05	14 7	0.30	0.00	1.63
12/05	3.20	33 19	0.13	0.00	1.37
12/04	3.80	18 15	0.23	0.00	1.26
Annual Growth	(11.2%)	— —	8.6%	—	17.3%

Smithtown Bancorp

Regardless of its name, Smithtown Bancorp is on Long Island (or Paumanok if you're old school). The institution is the holding company for Bank of Smithtown, a community bank founded in 1910. The company touts its one-on-one customer service it offers through about 20 locations on Long Island, New York.

Services include checking and savings accounts, IRAs, and CDs. Through its insurance subsidiary, Seigerman-Mulvey, the bank offers commercial and personal insurance products and financial services.

Commercial mortgages make up more than half of Smithtown Bancorp's loan portfolio, which also includes residential mortgages, commercial and industrial loans, and real estate construction loans.

EXECUTIVES

Chairman, President, and CEO, Smithtown Bancorp and Bank of Smithtown: Bradley E. (Brad) Rock, age 56
President and COO, Smithtown Bancorp and Bank of Smithtown: John A. Romano, age 52
EVP and CFO, Smithtown Bancorp and Bank of Smithtown: Christopher Becker, age 43
EVP and Chief Accounting Officer, Smithtown Bancorp and Bank of Smithtown: Anita M. Florek, age 58
General Counsel and Director: Patricia C. Delaney
Corporate Secretary; Corporate Secretary and Cashier, Bank of Smithtown: Judith Barber
VP Loan Department: Michael J. (Mike) Spolarich
EVP and Chief Lending Officer, Bank of Smithtown: Robert J. Anrig, age 60
SVP Consumer Lending, Bank of Smithtown: Susan Ladone
SVP Operations, Bank of Smithtown: Patricia Guidi
VP Marketing and Advertising, Bank of Smithtown: John P. Schneider
VP Information Technology, Bank of Smithtown: Daniel Viola
VP Human Resources, Bank of Smithtown: Deborah L. McElroy
Auditors: Crowe Horwath LLP

LOCATIONS

HQ: Smithtown Bancorp, Inc.
100 Motor Pkwy., Ste. 160, Hauppauge, NY 11788
Phone: 631-360-9300   **Fax:** 631-360-9373
Web: www.bankofsmithtown.com

PRODUCTS/OPERATIONS

2008 Gross Revenues

	$ mil.	% of total
Interest		
Loans	87.9	87
Securities	3.0	3
Other	0.9	1
Noninterest		
Revenues from insurance agency	3.4	3
Service charges on deposits	2.3	2
Other	3.6	4
Total	**101.1**	**100**

COMPETITORS

Apple Bank
Astoria Financial
Bank of America
Bank of New York Mellon
Bridge Bancorp
Brooklyn Federal Bancorp
Citibank
Dime Community Bancshares
First of Long Island
HSBC USA
JPMorgan Chase
New York Community Bancorp
State Bancorp

HISTORICAL FINANCIALS
Company Type: Public

Income Statement   FYE: December 31

	ASSETS ($ mil.)	NET INCOME ($ mil.)	INCOME AS % OF ASSETS	EMPLOYEES
12/08	1,865.4	15.7	0.8%	243
12/07	1,121.1	14.3	1.3%	198
12/06	1,048.2	14.0	1.3%	188
12/05	878.3	11.1	1.3%	179
12/04	677.0	10.0	1.5%	168
Annual Growth	**28.8%**	**11.9%**	**—**	**9.7%**

2008 Year-End Financials

Equity as % of assets: 6.4%
Return on assets: 1.1%
Return on equity: 15.7%
Long-term debt ($ mil.): 365.3
No. of shares (mil.): 14.9
Market value ($ mil.): 238.2
Dividends
 Yield: 0.7%
 Payout: 7.7%
Sales ($ mil.): 59.6
R&D as % of sales: —
Advertising as % of sales: —

Stock History   NASDAQ (GM): SMTB

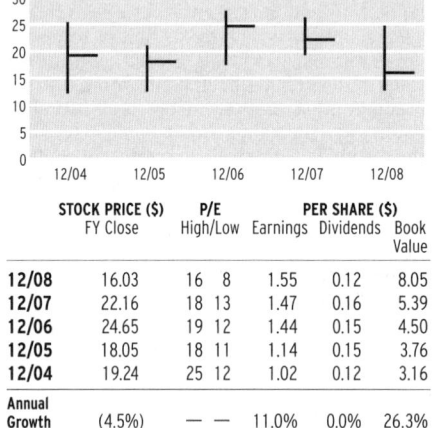

	STOCK PRICE ($) FY Close	P/E High/Low		Earnings	PER SHARE ($) Dividends	Book Value
12/08	16.03	16	8	1.55	0.12	8.05
12/07	22.16	18	13	1.47	0.16	5.39
12/06	24.65	19	12	1.44	0.15	4.50
12/05	18.05	18	11	1.14	0.15	3.76
12/04	19.24	25	12	1.02	0.12	3.16
Annual Growth	**(4.5%)**	**—**	**—**	**11.0%**	**0.0%**	**26.3%**

SolarWinds, Inc.

SolarWinds helps IT professionals improve network management without burning holes in their wallets. The company provides fault and performance management, configuration management and compliance, and troubleshooting applications. Designed to work on single devices or networks with as many as 100,000 machines, its downloadable software can be installed and configured without professional implementation services. The company's customers range from small businesses to large enterprises and government agencies. SolarWinds counts Booz Allen Hamilton, Microsoft, FedEx, Lockheed Martin, and NASA among its customers. In May 2009 SolarWinds went public, raising over $150 million through the IPO.

SolarWinds' competition in the network management software sector includes such heavyweights as CA, Hewlett-Packard, and IBM. The company's strategy has focused on underselling its rivals with products that cost less to configure and maintain. SolarWinds has experienced rapid revenue growth in recent years, building a user base of more than 80,000 customers.

Though it utilizes traditional direct and indirect sales channels, the company's marketing efforts have largely relied on online programs and word of mouth. SolarWinds hosts an online community called Thwack and a blog called GeekSpeak.

SolarWinds generates most of its revenues in North America, but the company's expansion plans include increasing its presence in Asia and Europe. It has offices in the Czech Republic, Ireland, New Zealand, and Singapore.

Bain Capital, Insight Ventures, and co-founder Donald Yonce each hold stakes of more than 20% in the company.

EXECUTIVES

Chairman, President, and CEO: Michael S. Bennett, age 56, $1,888,741 total compensation
COO, CFO, and Treasurer: Kevin B. Thompson, age 44, $728,772 total compensation
SVP and Chief Product Strategist: Kenny L. Van Zant, age 38, $628,155 total compensation
VP Marketing: Rita J. Selvaggi, age 53, $517,640 total compensation
VP Product Development: Douglas G. (Doug) Hibberd, age 44, $468,338 total compensation
VP Worldwide Sales: Paul Strelzick, age 45
VP Finance and Chief Accountant: J. Barton (Bart) Kalsu, age 41
VP, General Counsel, and Secretary: Bryan A. Sims, age 40
VP Corporate and Business Development: Karen L. White, age 46
VP International Sales: Jim Docherty
VP Human Resources and Corporate Infrastructure: Garry D. Strop, age 62
Auditors: PricewaterhouseCoopers LLP

LOCATIONS

HQ: SolarWinds, Inc.
4 Barton Skyway, Ste. 360, 1301 S. MoPac Expwy.
Austin, TX 78746
Phone: 512-682-9300   **Fax:** 512-682-9301
Web: www.solarwinds.com

2008 Sales

	$ mil.	% of total
North America	75.8	81
Other regions	17.3	19
Total	**93.1**	**100**

PRODUCTS/OPERATIONS

2008 Sales

	$ mil.	% of total
License	55.4	60
Maintenance & other	37.7	40
Total	**93.1**	**100**

COMPETITORS

BMC Software
CA, Inc.
Cisco Systems
EMC
Hewlett-Packard
IBM

HISTORICAL FINANCIALS
Company Type: Public

Income Statement   FYE: December 31

	REVENUE ($ mil.)	NET INCOME ($ mil.)	NET PROFIT MARGIN	EMPLOYEES
12/08	93.1	22.3	24.0%	268
12/07	61.7	13.6	22.0%	205
12/06	38.2	9.6	25.1%	—
12/05	27.9	23.3	83.5%	—
Annual Growth	**49.4%**	**(1.5%)**	**—**	**30.7%**

Debt ratio: —
Return on equity: —
Cash ($ mil.): 40.6

Current ratio: 1.41
Long-term debt ($ mil.): 93.9

Net Income History   NYSE: SWI

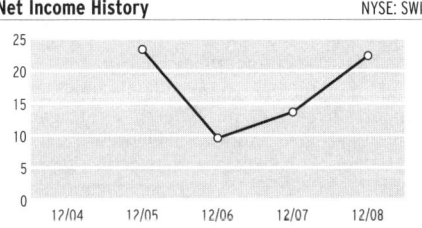

Somanetics Corporation

Somanetics sells the INVOS System, a noninvasive device that monitors blood oxygen levels in the brain, primarily during surgery. Based on Somanetics' *in vivo* optical spectroscopy (INVOS) technology, the device's disposable SomaSensors attach to each side of the patient's forehead, and the firm's proprietary software displays oxygen levels on a computer screen. The company sells the INVOS System through a direct sales force in the US and through distributors abroad such as Covidien (which is its biggest customer, accounting for 14% of revenues) and Edwards Lifesciences. Customers include surgeons, anesthesiologists, and other health care providers in the US and in about 60 countries abroad.

Somanetics has an installed base of more than 2,500 INVOS systems. The majority of its revenue (nearly 75%) comes from sales of disposable SomaSensors to this installed base. Somanetics plans to continue to develop new applications for its INVOS System. It initially marketed the device to cardiac surgeons, but it has expanded its marketing efforts to other critical care areas, such as the pediatric ICU. It is also testing the system with elderly surgical patients with diabetes.

With an eye toward integrating its INVOS technology with other critical care monitoring systems, Somanetics created an interface with Philips Healthcare's VueLink System. Then, in late 2008 the company acquired ICU Data Systems for $2 million. ICU Data Systems' technology integrates data from hospital bedside monitoring devices, including information from INVOS systems. Somanetics then combined the two technologies and launched them as a single product under the name Vital Sync in 2009.

In addition to the INVOS System and related disposables, Somanetics makes the CorRestore patch, an implant made from cow's heart tissue that is used in cardiac repair and reconstruction.

EXECUTIVES

President, CEO, and Director: Bruce J. Barrett, age 49, $899,514 total compensation
SVP Research and Development and Operations: Arik A. Anderson
SVP Sales and Marketing: Dominic J. Spadafore, age 49, $477,569 total compensation
VP, CFO, Controller, and Treasurer: William M. Iacona, age 38, $349,452 total compensation
VP, Chief Administrative Officer, and Secretary: Mary Ann Victor, age 51, $375,355 total compensation
VP Technology and Market Development: Michael D. Wider
VP Medical Affairs: Ronald A. Widman, age 58
VP Quality Assurance: Pamela A. (Pam) Winters, age 50
Auditors: Deloitte & Touche LLP

LOCATIONS

HQ: Somanetics Corporation
1653 E. Maple Rd., Troy, MI 48083
Phone: 248-689-3050   **Fax:** 248-689-4272
Web: www.somanetics.net

2008 Sales

	% of total
US	80
Other countries	20
Total	**100**

PRODUCTS/OPERATIONS

2008 Sales

	% of total
Sensors	73
System monitors	27
Total	**100**

Selected Products

CorRestore System (cardiac implant patch)
INVOS System (patient monitoring system)
SomaSensors (disposable sensors used with the INVOS System)

COMPETITORS

Bio-logic
CAS Medical
Covidien
Criticare
GE Healthcare
Masimo
OSI Systems
Philips Electronics
Respironics
Siemens Healthcare
Welch Allyn

HISTORICAL FINANCIALS

Company Type: Public

Income Statement

	REVENUE ($ mil.)	NET INCOME ($ mil.)	NET PROFIT MARGIN	EMPLOYEES
11/08	47.5	10.4	21.9%	105
11/07	38.6	9.7	25.1%	106
11/06	28.7	10.4	36.2%	89
11/05	20.5	7.8	38.0%	55
11/04	12.6	8.7	69.0%	40
Annual Growth	**39.3%**	**4.6%**	**—**	**27.3%**

FYE: November 30

2008 Year-End Financials

Debt ratio: —
Return on equity: 11.1%
Cash ($ mil.): 37.2
Current ratio: 22.04
Long-term debt ($ mil.): —
No. of shares (mil.): 12.1

Dividends
Yield: 0.0%
Payout: —
Market value ($ mil.): 212.0
R&D as % of sales: —
Advertising as % of sales: —

EXECUTIVES

President, CEO, and Director: Bruce J. Barrett, age 49, $899,514 total compensation
SVP Research and Development and Operations: Arik A. Anderson
SVP Sales and Marketing: Dominic J. Spadafore, age 49, $477,569 total compensation
VP, CFO, Controller, and Treasurer: William M. Iacona, age 38, $349,452 total compensation
VP, Chief Administrative Officer, and Secretary: Mary Ann Victor, age 51, $375,355 total compensation
VP Technology and Market Development: Michael D. Wider
VP Medical Affairs: Ronald A. Widman, age 58
VP Quality Assurance: Pamela A. (Pam) Winters, age 50
Auditors: Deloitte & Touche LLP

Stock History   NASDAQ (GM): SMTS

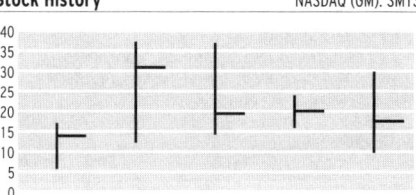

	STOCK PRICE ($) FY Close	P/E High	P/E Low	Earnings	Dividends	Book Value
11/08	17.54	39	13	0.76	0.00	7.02
11/07	20.01	35	24	0.67	0.00	8.45
11/06	19.40	49	19	0.75	0.00	7.46
11/05	30.91	56	19	0.66	0.00	2.30
11/04	13.88	22	8	0.77	0.00	1.45
Annual Growth	**6.0%**	**—**	**—**	**(0.3%)**	**—**	**48.3%**

SonicWALL, Inc.

SonicWALL puts up more than sound barriers — the company provides network security devices and software. Its systems protect communications between headquarters and branch offices, secure broadband Internet access, and filter Web content (blocking a minor's access to adult Web sites, for example). Other products include data backup appliances and related software. It also offers services such as content filtering and intrusion prevention on a subscription basis. SonicWALL sells primarily through distributors, including Tech Data (17% of revenues in 2008), Alternative Technology (16%), and Ingram Micro (16%).

Fees generated from subscriptions and services account for about 60% of the company's revenues. SonicWALL is targeting increased software sales for growth.

International expansion is another element of SonicWALL's strategy. The company's network of resellers and distributors operate in about 50 countries. It generated about a third of its sales outside the US in 2008.

SonicWALL expanded its core product line with the acquisition of virtual private network (VPN) equipment developer Aventail for about $25 million in cash in 2007.

EXECUTIVES

Chairman: John C. Shoemaker, age 66
President, CEO, and Director: Matthew T. (Matt) Medeiros, age 53, $892,759 total compensation
VP and CFO: Robert D. (Rob) Selvi, age 52, $987,690 total compensation
VP Worldwide Sales: Marvin C. Blough, age 49, $831,902 total compensation
VP, Secretary, and General Counsel: Frederick M. Gonzalez, age 59, $385,584 total compensation
VP Finance, Corporate Controller, and Chief Accounting Officer: Robert B. Knauff, age 47
VP Engineering: John Gmuender
VP Human Resources: Dawn Thompson
VP Worldwide Marketing: Steve Franzese
VP Corporate Development: Edward Cohen
Senior Product Marketing Manager: Andrew Klein
Senior Director Public Relations: Colleen Nichols
Auditors: Armanino McKenna LLP

LOCATIONS

HQ: SonicWALL, Inc.
1143 Borregas Ave., Sunnyvale, CA 94089
Phone: 408-745-9600   **Fax:** 408-745-9300
Web: www.sonicwall.com

2008 Sales

	$ mil.	% of total
Americas	150.0	69
Europe, Middle East & Africa	46.1	21
Asia/Pacific	22.5	10
Total	**218.6**	**100**

PRODUCTS/OPERATIONS

2008 Sales

	$ mil.	% of total
License & service	127.8	58
Products	90.8	42
Total	**218.6**	**100**

2008 Sales

	$ mil.	% of total
Unified threat management appliances	164.8	74
Secure content management	23.0	12
SSL	20.6	8
Continuous data protection	10.2	6
Total	**218.6**	**100**

Selected Products

Appliances
  Content filtering
  Data backup
  E-mail security
  SSL VPN
  Unified threat management (UTM)
Applications and services
  Backup and recovery off-site services
  Content filtering
  Enforced anti-virus and anti-spyware
  Gateway anti-virus, anti-spyware, and intrusion
    prevention
  Global VPN client

COMPETITORS

Alcatel-Lucent
Barracuda Networks
CA, Inc.
Check Point Software
Cisco Systems
Fortinet
Hewlett-Packard
Iron Mountain Inc
Juniper Networks
McAfee
Microsoft
Nokia
Quantum Corporation
RSA Security
Seagate Technology
Sony
Symantec
WatchGuard Technologies
Websense

HISTORICAL FINANCIALS

Company Type: Public

Income Statement

FYE: December 31

	REVENUE ($ mil.)	NET INCOME ($ mil.)	NET PROFIT MARGIN	EMPLOYEES
12/08	218.6	4.9	2.2%	820
12/07	199.2	28.6	14.4%	674
12/06	175.5	(10.8)	—	436
12/05	135.3	6.3	4.7%	404
12/04	125.6	(1.3)	—	335
Annual Growth	**14.9%**	**—**	**—**	**25.1%**

2008 Year-End Financials

Debt ratio: —
Return on equity: 1.7%
Cash ($ mil.): 45.1
Current ratio: 1.29
Long-term debt ($ mil.): —
No. of shares (mil.): 54.2
Dividends
  Yield: —
  Payout: —
Market value ($ mil.): 215.9
R&D as % of sales: —
Advertising as % of sales: —

Stock History

NASDAQ (GM): SNWL

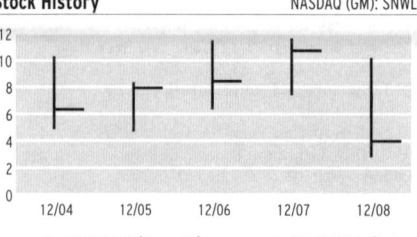

	STOCK PRICE ($) FY Close	P/E High/Low		PER SHARE ($) Earnings	Dividends	Book Value
12/08	3.98	126	36	0.08	—	4.90
12/07	10.72	27	17	0.43	—	6.04
12/06	8.42	—	—	(0.17)	—	5.86
12/05	7.92	92	53	0.09	—	5.90
12/04	6.32	—	—	(0.02)	—	6.21
Annual Growth	**(10.9%)**	**—**	**—**	**—**	**—**	**(5.8%)**

SonoSite, Inc.

Size is everything for SonoSite. The firm makes handheld ultrasonic imaging devices that health care providers can use outside traditional imaging laboratories, for instance, in the ER, at a patient's bedside, or in the doctor's office. Its fourth-generation system, the M-Turbo, has a laptop-sized console and produces imaging quality comparable to larger cart-based systems. Its S Series of products has several customized interfaces for different clinical applications, including the ER or the ICU. SonoSite also sells some older products (its MicroMaxx laptop-style system) and smaller ones; its iLook weighs only three pounds and is designed to provide better visualization during vascular access procedures.

The company markets its products to hospitals, physicians offices, and other health care providers through a direct sales force in North America, Western Europe, Japan, and Australia. It uses distributors elsewhere, selling its products in about 100 countries worldwide. It also sells its handheld devices to the US military, which uses them at front-line hospitals and other military medical facilities.

SonoSite introduced the M-Turbo and S Series products late in 2007; the two lines represent the company's fourth generation of technology on its handheld ultrasound platform. The systems have greater power and higher image quality than its previous iteration, the MicroMaxx system.

The company is expanding its ability to target its sales and marketing direct to physicians' offices. In 2008, it ended an agreement with a third-party sales organization, which was targeting the US physicians' office market, and took over those duties on its own. It later strengthened those resources by acquiring cardiograph monitoring system manufacturer CardioDynamics for $10 million in cash (plus about $2 million in debt assumption) in 2009. Along with the technology platform, SonoSite

---

gained a cardiology-focused direct sales organization used to working directly with doctors' offices through the deal.

SonoSite is also looking for strategic partners that can provide new distribution channels. Partners NAMIC/VA and Nippon Sherwood Medical Industries, for instance, distribute SonoSite's iLook products in the US and Japan.

Additionally, the company is developing new products to expand into different clinical areas. It has developed SonoCalc IMT software, which is used for cardiac disease management applications. And in 2007 the company acquired privately held LumenVu, a Philadelphia-based company that was developing technology to help guide catheters during vascular procedures. SonoSite intends to integrate that technology into a new line of products.

EXECUTIVES

Chairman: Kirby L. Cramer, age 72
President, CEO, and Director: Kevin M. Goodwin, age 51, $2,373,698 total compensation
SVP Product Innovation and Customer Delivery: James M. (Jim) Gilmore, age 44, $673,650 total compensation
SVP Worldwide Sales and Distribution: Graham D. Cox, age 50, $1,075,042 total compensation
SVP Strategic Development and Patient Safety Innovations: John S. Bowers Jr., age 46
VP and CFO: Michael J. (Mike) Schuh, age 48, $676,387 total compensation
CTO: Juin-Jet Hwang
VP and CIO: Cory E. Klatt, age 39
VP and Chief Administration Officer: Marla R. Koreis
VP, General Counsel, and Corporate Secretary: Kathryn (Kathy) Surace-Smith, age 50, $760,875 total compensation
VP US Sales: James N. Branman, age 46, $466,824 total compensation
VP Corporate Development and Growth Planning: Marcus Y. Smith
VP Global Learning: David Levesque
Auditors: KPMG LLP

LOCATIONS

HQ: SonoSite, Inc.
21919 30th Dr. SE, Bothell, WA 98021
Phone: 425-951-1200   **Fax:** 425-951-1201
Web: www.sonosite.com

2008 Sales

	$ mil.	% of total
US	116.7	48
Europe, Africa & Middle East	72.2	30
Asia/Pacific	30.1	12
Latin America & Canada	24.5	10
Total	**243.5**	**100**

PRODUCTS/OPERATIONS

Selected Products

iLook Series (handheld ultrasound system for vascular
  access visualization)
M-Turbo (ultrasound system, multiple applications)
MicroMaxx (ultrasound system, multiple applications)
NanoMaxx (ultrasound system)
S Series Ultrasound Tools (ultrasound system with
  custom interfaces)
  S-Cath (interventional radiology and cardiac
    catheterization)
  S-ICU (critical care)
  S-FAST (emergency medicine)
  S-Nerve (regional anesthesia)
  S-Women's Health (obstetrics/gynecology)
SonoHeart Elite (point-of-care ultrasound system for
  cardiologists)
SonoSite 180PLUS (first-generation handheld
  ultrasound system)
SonoSite TITAN (handheld ultrasound system)

COMPETITORS

Biosound Esaote   Mindray
Esaote   Philips Healthcare
GE Healthcare   Siemens Healthcare

HISTORICAL FINANCIALS

Company Type: Public

Income Statement				FYE: December 31
	REVENUE ($ mil.)	NET INCOME ($ mil.)	NET PROFIT MARGIN	EMPLOYEES
12/08	243.5	20.6	8.5%	640
12/07	205.1	6.9	3.4%	600
12/06	171.1	7.2	4.2%	550
12/05	147.5	5.4	3.7%	500
12/04	115.8	23.0	19.9%	410
Annual Growth	20.4%	(2.7%)	—	11.8%

2008 Year-End Financials

Debt ratio: 63.0%
Return on equity: 9.7%
Cash ($ mil.): 209.3
Current ratio: 9.55
Long-term debt ($ mil.): 144.7
No. of shares (mil.): 17.3

Dividends
  Yield: 0.0%
  Payout: —
Market value ($ mil.): 331.0
R&D as % of sales: —
Advertising as % of sales: —

Stock History

NASDAQ (GM): SONO

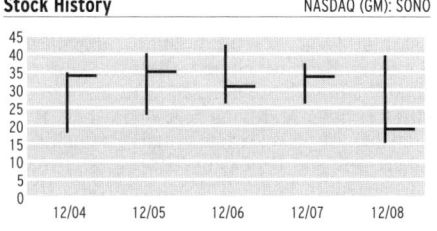

	STOCK PRICE ($) FY Close	P/E High/Low		PER SHARE ($) Earnings	Dividends	Book Value
12/08	19.08	33	13	1.18	0.00	13.25
12/07	33.67	92	66	0.40	0.00	11.12
12/06	30.93	98	62	0.43	0.00	10.44
12/05	35.01	117	69	0.34	0.00	8.76
12/04	33.95	24	13	1.46	0.00	7.68
Annual Growth	(13.4%)	—	—	(5.2%)	—	14.6%

Southern Community Financial

Southern Community Financial is the holding company for Southern Community Bank and Trust, which operates more than 20 branches in the Piedmont Triad region and other parts of North Carolina. Serving area individuals, small and midsized businesses, and homebuilders, the bank offers such retail services as checking and savings accounts, money market accounts, and credit cards. The bulk of Southern Community Financial's loan portfolio is made up of commercial mortgages (about 35%), residential mortgages (25%), construction loans (20%), and commercial and industrial loans (more than 15%). The bank also offers insurance products through an agreement with The Phoenix Companies.

The bank's Southern Community Advisors division offers brokerage services, financial planning, and other investment products and services. VCS Management, a subsidiary of the bank, is the managing general partner of small business investment company Salem Capital Partners.

EXECUTIVES

Chairman and CEO, Southern Community Financial and Southern Community Bank and Trust:
F. Scott Bauer, age 55, $550,757 total compensation
Vice Chairman: James G. (Jimmy) Chrysson, age 54
President, Southern Community Financial and Southern Community Bank and Trust:
Jeffrey T. (Jeff) Clark, age 44,
$330,808 total compensation
EVP and CFO: James Hastings, age 56,
$226,706 total compensation
EVP and Commercial Banking Executive:
Robert L. (Rob) Davis, age 46,
$283,480 total compensation
SVP and Treasurer: James C. (Jim) Monroe Jr., age 59,
$268,352 total compensation
SVP and Manager Commercial Credit: Brian Vannoy
EVP and Senior Operating Officer, Southern Community Bank and Trust: Merle B. Andrews
EVP and Chief Credit Officer, Southern Community Bank and Trust: Paul E. Neil III
SVP and Director Technology & Operations, Southern Community Bank and Trust: Philip M. (Phil) Doerr
SVP and Human Resources Director, Southern Community Bank and Trust: Toby A. Boles
Auditors: Dixon Hughes PLLC

LOCATIONS

HQ: Southern Community Financial Corporation
    4605 Country Club Rd., Winston-Salem, NC 27104
Phone: 336-768-8500   **Fax:** 336-768-2437
Web: www.smallenoughtocare.com

PRODUCTS/OPERATIONS

2008 Gross Revenues

	$ mil.	% of total
Interest		
Loans	82.1	76
Investment securities	14.6	14
Other	0.1	—
Noninterest		
Service charges on deposit accounts	5.9	5
Other	5.4	5
Total	**108.1**	**100**

COMPETITORS

American Community Bancshares
Bank of America
Bank of Oak Ridge
Bank of the Carolinas
BB&T
BNC Bancorp
FNB United
MidCarolina Financial
NewBridge Bancorp
Piedmont Federal
RBC Bank
Surrey Bancorp
Yadkin Valley Financial

HISTORICAL FINANCIALS

Company Type: Public

Income Statement				FYE: December 31
	ASSETS ($ mil.)	NET INCOME ($ mil.)	INCOME AS % OF ASSETS	EMPLOYEES
12/08	1,803.8	5.9	0.3%	337
12/07	1,569.2	7.6	0.5%	337
12/06	1,436.5	4.2	0.3%	326
12/05	1,285.5	8.2	0.6%	299
12/04	1,222.4	8.1	0.7%	271
Annual Growth	10.2%	(7.6%)	—	5.6%

2008 Year-End Financials

Equity as % of assets: 8.2%
Return on assets: 0.3%
Return on equity: 4.1%
Long-term debt ($ mil.): 228.0
No. of shares (mil.): 16.8
Market value ($ mil.): 58.9

Dividends
  Yield: 4.6%
  Payout: 48.5%
Sales ($ mil.): 58.7
R&D as % of sales: —
Advertising as % of sales: —

Stock History

NASDAQ (GS): SCMF

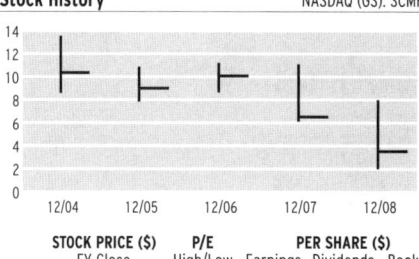

	STOCK PRICE ($) FY Close	P/E High/Low		PER SHARE ($) Earnings	Dividends	Book Value
12/08	3.51	24	6	0.33	0.16	11.18
12/07	6.53	26	15	0.43	0.16	8.48
12/06	10.08	46	37	0.24	0.14	8.11
12/05	9.00	24	18	0.45	0.21	8.06
12/04	10.35	30	19	0.45	0.12	8.15
Annual Growth	(23.7%)	—	—	(7.5%)	7.5%	8.2%

Southern Missouri Bancorp

Southern Missouri Bancorp is the holding company for Southern Bank (formerly Southern Missouri Bank and Trust), which serves local residents and businesses in southeastern Missouri and northeastern Arkansas through more than 10 branches. Residential mortgages account for the largest percentage of the bank's loan portfolio, followed by commercial mortgages and business loans. Construction and consumer loans round out its lending activities. Deposit products include checking, savings and money market accounts, CDs, and IRAs. The bank also offers financial planning and investment services. Originally chartered in 1887, Southern Bank acquired Arkansas-based Southern Bank of Commerce in 2009.

EXECUTIVES

Chairman: Samuel H. Smith, age 71
Vice Chairman: L. Douglas Bagby, age 59
President and CEO: Greg A. Steffens, age 42, $223,970 total compensation
COO and Treasurer: Kimberly A. Capps
CFO: Matt Funke
Chief Lending Officer: William D. (Bill) Hribovsek, $165,857 total compensation
Chief Credit Administration: Lora Daves
Market Area President and Community Bank President: William (Bill) Aslin, $126,246 total compensation
Director Marketing: Christy Frazier
Executive Secretary and Human Resources Officer: Lorna Brannum
Secretary and Director: Ronnie D. Black, age 61
Controller: Lisa Wallis
Auditors: BKD, LLP

LOCATIONS

HQ: Southern Missouri Bancorp, Inc.
531 Vine St., Poplar Bluff, MO 63901
Phone: 573-778-1800   **Fax:** 573-686-2920
Web: www.smbtonline.com

COMPETITORS

Bank of America
Commerce Bancshares
IBERIABANK
Regions Financial
UMB Financial
U.S. Bancorp

HISTORICAL FINANCIALS

Company Type: Public

Income Statement

FYE: June 30

	ASSETS ($ mil.)	NET INCOME ($ mil.)	INCOME AS % OF ASSETS	EMPLOYEES
6/09	465.9	3.8	0.8%	108
6/08	417.8	3.6	0.9%	102
6/07	379.9	2.9	0.8%	96
6/06	350.7	2.8	0.8%	97
6/05	330.4	0.1	0.0%	94
Annual Growth	9.0%	148.3%	—	3.5%

2009 Year-End Financials

Equity as % of assets: 7.0%
Return on assets: 0.9%
Return on equity: 12.0%
Long-term debt ($ mil.): 86.0
No. of shares (mil.): 2.1
Market value ($ mil.): 20.8
Dividends
Yield: 3.6%
Payout: 21.6%
Sales ($ mil.): 15.9
R&D as % of sales: —
Advertising as % of sales: —

Stock History

NASDAQ (GM): SMBC

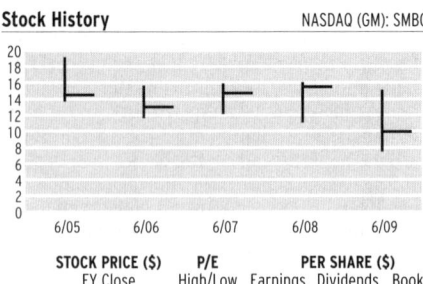

	STOCK PRICE ($) FY Close	P/E High/Low	PER SHARE ($) Earnings	Dividends	Book Value
6/09	9.95	9 5	1.67	0.36	20.12
6/08	15.49	10 7	1.63	0.40	14.59
6/07	14.70	12 10	1.29	0.36	13.75
6/06	13.00	12 10	1.24	0.36	12.72
6/05	14.50	380 277	0.05	0.36	11.97
Annual Growth	(9.0%)	— —	140.4%	0.0%	13.9%

Southern National Bancorp

Southern National Bancorp of Virginia is the holding company for Sonabank, which has more than a dozen locations in central and northern Virginia and another in southern Maryland. Sonabank targets small and midsized businesses, real estate developers, investors, and retail consumers. It offers standard deposit products, including checking, savings, money market accounts, and certificates of deposit. Its lending business focuses on loans secured by commercial real estate, single-family residential construction projects, single-family real estate, and other types of secured and unsecured commercial loans. In 2009 Southern National Bancorp acquired the failed Greater Atlantic Bank in an FDIC-assisted transaction.

EXECUTIVES

Chairman and CEO, SNBV and Sonabank: Georgia S. Derrico, age 64, $364,654 total compensation
Vice Chairman and President and COO, SNBV and Sonabank: R. Roderick Porter, age 63, $292,620 total compensation
EVP, Lending, SNBV and Sonabank: William H. Stevens, age 64, $187,848 total compensation
SVP and CFO, SNBV and Sonabank: William H. Lagos, age 58, $130,344 total compensation
Auditors: BDO Seidman, LLP

LOCATIONS

HQ: Southern National Bancorp of Virginia, Inc.
6830 Old Dominion Dr., McLean, VA 22101
Phone: 703-893-7400   **Fax:** 703-893-7489
Web: www.sonabank.com

COMPETITORS

Bank of America
Bank of Virginia
BB&T
Burke & Herbert Bank
SunTrust
Virginia Commerce Bancorp
Wells Fargo

HISTORICAL FINANCIALS

Company Type: Public

Income Statement

FYE: December 31

	ASSETS ($ mil.)	NET INCOME ($ mil.)	INCOME AS % OF ASSETS	EMPLOYEES
12/08	431.9	1.2	0.3%	65
12/07	377.3	1.7	0.5%	59
12/06	290.6	1.0	0.3%	50
12/05	128.5	0.6	0.5%	31
Annual Growth	49.8%	26.0%	—	28.0%

2008 Year-End Financials

Equity as % of assets: 15.9%
Return on assets: 0.3%
Return on equity: 1.7%
Long-term debt ($ mil.): 30.0
No. of shares (mil.): 11.6
Market value ($ mil.): 68.8
Dividends
Yield: 0.0%
Payout: —
Sales ($ mil.): 12.3
R&D as % of sales: —
Advertising as % of sales: —

Stock History

NASDAQ (GM): SONA

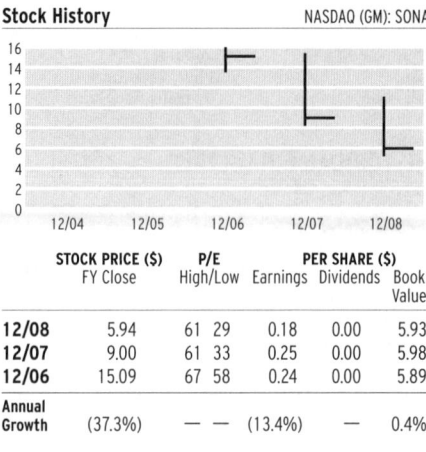

	STOCK PRICE ($) FY Close	P/E High/Low	PER SHARE ($) Earnings	Dividends	Book Value
12/08	5.94	61 29	0.18	0.00	5.93
12/07	9.00	61 33	0.25	0.00	5.98
12/06	15.09	67 58	0.24	0.00	5.89
Annual Growth	(37.3%)	— —	(13.4%)	—	0.4%

Southside Bancshares

Southside Bancshares operates deep in the heart of Texas. It's the holding company for Southside Bank, which serves East Texas through about 35 branches, with a concentration in the cities of Tyler and Longview. About half of its branches are located in supermarkets (including Albertsons and Brookshire stores), and many offer extended hours. The bank provides traditional services such as savings, money market, and checking accounts, CDs, and other deposit products, as well as trust and investment services. Real estate loans make up more than half of the company's loan portfolio, which also includes business, consumer, and municipal loans.

In 2007 Southside Bancshares bought Fort Worth Bancshares, the holding company for Fort Worth National Bank. The deal added three branches in Arlington and Fort Worth, Texas, and a loan production office in Austin to Southside Bancshares' network.

Also in 2007 the company formed a new unit, Southside Financial Group, to acquire portfolios of auto loans from other lenders.

EXECUTIVES

Chairman and CEO, Southside Bancshares and Southside Bank: B. G. Hartley, age 79, $697,389 total compensation
Vice Chairman; Vice Chairman and Chief Administrative Officer, Southside Bank: Robbie N. Edmonson, age 77
President, Secretary, and Director; President, COO, and Director, Southside Bank: Sam Dawson, age 61, $832,216 total compensation
EVP; SEVP and Director, Southside Bank: Jeryl W. Story, age 57, $670,557 total compensation
EVP and CFO; EVP, CFO, and Director, Southside Bank: Lee R. Gibson, age 52, $664,482 total compensation
CEO, Southside Financial Group: Ken Burke
Auditors: PricewaterhouseCoopers LLP

HQ: Southside Bancshares, Inc.
1201 S. Beckham Ave., Tyler, TX 75701
Phone: 903-531-7111   **Fax:** 903-592-3692
Web: www.southside.com

PRODUCTS/OPERATIONS

2008 Gross Revenues

	$ mil.	% of total
Interest		
Loans	73.1	41
Mortgage-backed & related securities	55.5	32
Investment securities	6.6	4
Other	1.0	1
Noninterest		
Deposit services	18.4	10
Gain on sale of securities	12.3	7
Other	9.6	5
Total	**176.5**	**100**

COMPETITORS

Bank of America
Capital One
East Texas Financial
Jacksonville Bancorp of Illinois
Regions Financial

HISTORICAL FINANCIALS

Company Type: Public

Income Statement

FYE: December 31

	ASSETS ($ mil.)	NET INCOME ($ mil.)	INCOME AS % OF ASSETS	EMPLOYEES
12/08	2,700.2	30.7	1.1%	546
12/07	2,196.3	16.7	0.8%	530
12/06	1,891.0	15.0	0.8%	460
12/05	1,783.5	14.6	0.8%	493
12/04	1,619.6	16.1	1.0%	450
Annual Growth	**13.6%**	**17.5%**	**—**	**5.0%**

2008 Year-End Financials

Equity as % of assets: 5.9%
Return on assets: 1.3%
Return on equity: 21.0%
Long-term debt ($ mil.): 715.8
No. of shares (mil.): 14.9
Market value ($ mil.): 334.3
Dividends
  Yield: 2.3%
  Payout: 24.8%
Sales ($ mil.): 116.1
R&D as % of sales: —
Advertising as % of sales: —

Stock History

NASDAQ (GS): SBSI

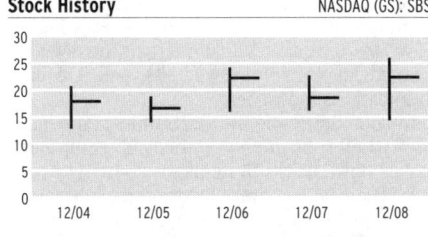

	STOCK PRICE ($) FY Close	P/E High/Low		PER SHARE ($) Earnings	Dividends	Book Value
12/08	22.38	12	7	2.06	0.51	10.75
12/07	18.56	20	15	1.12	0.42	8.86
12/06	22.23	23	16	1.02	0.38	7.41
12/05	16.62	19	14	1.00	0.36	7.32
12/04	17.91	19	12	1.09	0.31	7.01
Annual Growth	**5.7%**	**—**	**—**	**17.2%**	**13.3%**	**11.3%**

Spartan Motors

Even *luxury* motor homes rely on Spartan Motors' products. The company's Spartan Motors Chassis unit makes heavy-duty chassis for motor homes, fire trucks, and specialty vehicles, such as concrete mixers, trolleys, and utility trucks. Spartan Motors also manufactures emergency vehicles and related components through three subsidiaries that make up its Emergency Vehicle Team (EVTeam) segment. Its Crimson Fire and Road Rescue subsidiaries build fire trucks and ambulances, respectively, using chassis from Spartan Motors Chassis and from third parties. Crimson Fire Aerials makes ladder units for fire trucks.

The collapse of the motor home industry in 2008, forced by the recession, volatile fuel prices and the credit crunch, caused the company's sales of motor home chassis to plunge by 58% during the year. Motor home assemblers and marketers Fleetwood Enterprises and Newmar were among Spartan's top customers — but that changed. Fleetwood filed for Chapter 11 protection from creditors in 2009, and Newmar's 2008 sales were dramatically down from the year before. Spartan's response has been vigorous diversification of its lineup.

A considerable portion of Spartan's sales are coming from an uptick in Spartan chassis orders by the military for the Mine Resistant Ambush Protected (MRAP) vehicle program. Sales of these chassis increased by more than 250% in 2007, and doubled in 2008.

The MRAP program, however, is winding down. Demonstrating its flexible capacity, the company is working with military customers to develop alternative mine-resistant vehicles, such as the Multipurpose All-Terrain Vehicle, for deployment in Afghanistan and other war-torn countries.

Spartan also sees potential for growth among its EVTeam of emergency vehicle product offerings. As the US's fleet of emergency vehicles ages and homeland security measures rise, increased demand is anticipated. Aging baby-boomers are expected to drive demand for recreational vehicles, and, less happily, emergency vehicles.

At the same time, Spartan is buffering its exposure to consumer and government-backed military spending by entering micro-niches in North America, such as delivery and service markets. Spartan acquired Utilimaster in late 2009 for $45 million; the deal scoops up expertise in manufacturing specialty vehicles (walk-in and hi-cube vans, and truck bodies) customized to businesses in package and snack delivery, and linen and uniform rental. Spartan also benefits from the Utilimaster's established brand and customer base.

Spartan is looking to recover from legal battles, as well. In 2008 Spartan Motors Chassis pleaded guilty to one charge of making a false statement on the terms and conditions of a military subcontract. Spartan Chassis also reached a settlement with the US Department of Justice in a case involving a former independent contractor who worked for the company and then took a job with Force Protection. That individual had pleaded guilty to a federal charge on financial kickbacks. As a result of its criminal plea and civil settlement, Spartan Chassis will pay a total of $6 million in fines and penalties.

HISTORY

Spartan Motors was founded in 1975 by George Sztykiel, a former lead engineer at Chrysler's heavy truck division, along with William Foster, Jerry Geary, and John Knox. Funded with second mortgages, Spartan started by building chassis for customized fire trucks.

Spartan began producing chassis for high-end motor homes in the late 1980s. The company's breakthrough was a chassis with a rear-mounted diesel engine that cut operating costs and gave Spartan a premium product.

George Sztykiel's son, John, took over day-to-day operations in 1992. The next year the company opened a plant in Mexico to build small, fuel-efficient buses. Spartan made a push to increase product output, but quality suffered and warranty costs jumped, hurting the company's name and its bottom line.

In 1995 a soft market for motor homes caused a drop in sales, prompting the company to begin diversifying. The next year it closed a money-losing Mexican subsidiary. Spartan's operations continued to resemble its name, with Sztykiel emphasizing limited corporate bureaucracy and frugality — he never had a secretary and regularly brown-bagged lunch.

Spartan purchased two fire truck body manufacturers (both longtime customers) in 1997. It also acquired 33% of Carpenter Industries (school bus bodies). Carpenter's poor sales caused Spartan to suffer another loss in 1997. To move into the market for ambulance chassis, the company bought Road Rescue in 1998; Spartan also recapitalized Carpenter to achieve majority ownership.

Spartan joined specialty vehicle maker Federal Signal in a purchasing alliance in 1999. It also signed agreements with RV Holdings, Damon Corporation, and Forest River to supply chassis for the three companies' motor homes. In 2000 Spartan discontinued funding its underperforming Carpenter Industries affiliate.

George Sztykiel announced plans in 2001 to step down as chairman and CEO at the end of the year; George's son, John, assumed the role of CEO in 2002.

In 2003 Spartan combined its Luverne Fire Apparatus and Quality Manufacturing units — both well-known names in the fire truck industry — to form subsidiary Crimson Fire.

EXECUTIVES

Chairman: David R. Wilson, age 73
President, CEO, and Director: John E. Sztykiel, age 52, $1,589,646 total compensation
CFO: Joseph M. Nowicki, age 47
VP Engineering, Spartan Motors Chassis: James L. Logan, $626,733 total compensation
VP and Director: William F. Foster, age 67, $521,772 total compensation
VP and General Counsel: Thomas T. Kivell, age 56, $37,851 total compensation
VP Sales and Marketing: Edward J. (Ed) Dobbs
VP Public Affairs and Brand and Strategic Management and Head, Road Rescue: David L. Reid
VP Operations, Spartan Chassis: Arthur Ickes
President, Crimson Fire: Kevin Crump
President, Road Rescue: Gary DeCosse
COO, Crimson Fire and President, Crimson Fire Aerials: James A. (Jim) Salmi
Auditors: BDO Seidman, LLP

LOCATIONS

HQ: Spartan Motors, Inc.
1100 Reynolds Rd., Charlotte, MI 48813
Phone: 517-543-6400   **Fax:** 517-543-9269
Web: www.spartanmotors.com

PRODUCTS/OPERATIONS

2008 Sales

	$ mil.	% of total
Fire truck chassis	94.0	11
EVTeam products	92.7	11
Motor home chassis	91.1	11
Other	566.6	67
Total	**844.4**	**100**

COMPETITORS

American LaFrance
Collins Industries
Daimler
E-ONE
Federal Signal
Ford Motor
Freightliner Custom Chassis
Mack Trucks
Navistar International
Oshkosh Truck
Pierce Manufacturing
Supreme Industries
Volvo
Workhorse Custom Chassis

HISTORICAL FINANCIALS

Company Type: Public

Income Statement

FYE: December 31

	REVENUE ($ mil.)	NET INCOME ($ mil.)	NET PROFIT MARGIN	EMPLOYEES
12/08	844.4	42.7	5.1%	1,275
12/07	681.9	24.5	3.6%	1,855
12/06	445.4	16.8	3.8%	1,118
12/05	343.0	8.3	2.4%	920
12/04	312.3	5.9	1.9%	880
Annual Growth	**28.2%**	**64.0%**	**—**	**9.7%**

2008 Year-End Financials

Debt ratio: 9.7%
Return on equity: 28.5%
Cash ($ mil.): 13.7
Current ratio: 2.63
Long-term debt ($ mil.): 16.6
No. of shares (mil.): 32.9

Dividends
 Yield: 2.1%
 Payout: 7.6%
Market value ($ mil.): 155.5
R&D as % of sales: —
Advertising as % of sales: —

Stock History

NASDAQ (GS): SPAR

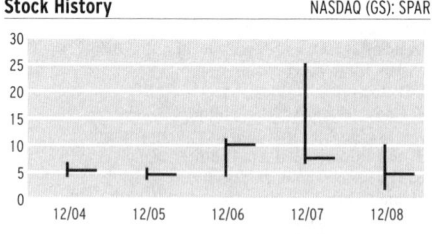

	STOCK PRICE ($) FY Close	P/E High/Low		PER SHARE ($) Earnings	Dividends	Book Value
12/08	4.73	8	2	1.32	0.10	5.19
12/07	7.64	33	9	0.75	0.16	3.93
12/06	10.12	20	8	0.55	0.10	3.14
12/05	4.57	19	13	0.29	0.10	2.21
12/04	5.30	32	21	0.20	0.08	2.05
Annual Growth	**(2.8%)**	**—**	**—**	**60.3%**	**5.7%**	**26.1%**

Spectra Energy Partners

When you take one company's energy holdings and splinter them, you get Spectra Energy Partners. Formed by Spectra Energy out of the former natural gas holdings of Duke Energy, the company is a natural gas pipeline and storage facility operator. Its assets include a liquefied natural gas storage location in Tennessee, 50% of two natural gas storage facilities in Texas and Louisiana, and 25% of Gulfstream Natural Gas System. All told, Spectra Energy Partners has 3,100 miles of natural gas transmission and gathering pipelines capable of moved about 3.3 billion cu. ft. per day. It also has 42.5 billion cu. ft. of gas storage capacity.

The company's core customers include distribution companies and utilities; natural gas producers in Appalachia, the Gulf Coast, and the Mid-Continent; power plants; and major industrial companies.

Spectra Energy Partners' growth plans include expanding its pipeline and storage facilities to meet increased demand. In this regard, in 2009 the company acquired Ozark Gas Transmission and Ozark Gas Gathering Systems from Atlas Pipeline Partners for $300 million.

EXECUTIVES

Chairman: Fred J. Fowler, age 63
President, CEO, and Director: Gregory J. Rizzo
VP and CFO: Laura B. Sayavedra, age 41
Auditors: Deloitte & Touche LLP

LOCATIONS

HQ: Spectra Energy Partners, LP
5400 Westheimer Ct., Houston, TX 77056
Phone: 713-627-5400
Web: www.spectraenergypartners.com

COMPETITORS

AGL Resources
DCP Midstream Partners
Enterprise Products
Exxon Mobil
Florida Gas Transmission
Kinder Morgan
Occidental Petroleum
Quicksilver Gas Services
Transcontinental Gas Pipe Line
Williams Companies

HISTORICAL FINANCIALS

Company Type: Public

Income Statement

FYE: December 31

	REVENUE ($ mil.)	NET INCOME ($ mil.)	NET PROFIT MARGIN	EMPLOYEES
12/08	124.9	101.3	81.1%	77
12/07	100.1	45.3	45.3%	0
12/06	82.6	61.6	74.6%	65
12/05	80.0	57.0	71.3%	—
12/04	81.7	53.2	65.1%	—
Annual Growth	**11.2%**	**17.5%**	**—**	**8.8%**

2008 Year-End Financials

Debt ratio: —
Return on equity: —
Cash ($ mil.): 30.9
Current ratio: 0.69
Long-term debt ($ mil.): 390.0
No. of shares (mil.): 80.3

Dividends
 Yield: 6.8%
 Payout: 95.7%
Market value ($ mil.): 1,589.2
R&D as % of sales: —
Advertising as % of sales: —

Stock History

NYSE: SEP

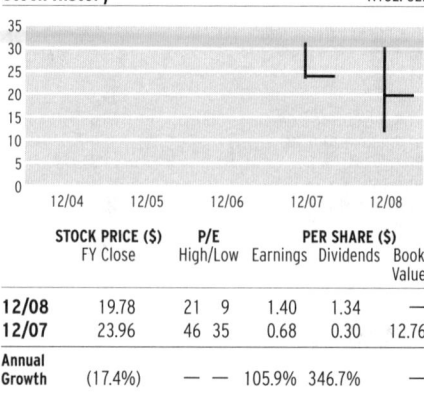

	STOCK PRICE ($) FY Close	P/E High/Low		PER SHARE ($) Earnings	Dividends	Book Value
12/08	19.78	21	9	1.40	1.34	—
12/07	23.96	46	35	0.68	0.30	12.76
Annual Growth	**(17.4%)**	**—**	**—**	**105.9%**	**346.7%**	

Spire Corporation

Life is sweet on the sunny side of the street for Spire. Some 200 factories worldwide use Spire's photovoltaic solar cell manufacturing equipment, including cell testers and assemblers, to produce modules that convert sunlight into electricity. Its solar systems unit uses the equipment to make solar energy modules for buildings and homes. Though Spire's roots are in solar energy, the company also makes medical devices through its Spire Biomedical unit; in addition, the unit uses ion beam technology to resurface artificial valves and grafts to reduce friction and the risk of infection. Spire gets more than half of its sales outside the US.

Another division, Spire Semiconductor (formerly Bandwidth Semiconductor), specializes in wafer epitaxy, thin-film microelectronics, and foundry services. Acquired from Stratos Lightwave, the unit serves customers in the defense, biomedical, consumer products, and telecommunications industries.

In 2009 Spire sold the assets of its hemodialysis catheter business to medical equipment maker Bard Access Systems for about $12 million. The deal lets Spire focus on its solar business and provides the company with capital needed to expand its solar production facilities. Bard Access Systems will also get a license to use Spire's coating and surface modification technology; Spire will retain rights to the technology. As part of the deal, Spire will continue to manufacture and supply certain hemodialysis catheter products to Bard under a distribution agreement.

Spire sells its products primarily using its own sales force, but it also uses distributors and independent sales representatives to market in some international markets.

Spire traditionally struggled with profitability until 2008, when Spire Solar's sales quintupled in the solar energy boom. 2009, however, is presenting challenging economic conditions even for the solar energy sector. Disruptions in the capital and credit markets could have an effect

on the company's operations, cash flows, and financial condition, as well as with Spire's customers and suppliers. The company has a limited number of customers, although it is not dependent on any single customer. Spire must continue to compete by creating or acquiring advanced technology, developing that technology into reliable products, and protecting that technology and those products with copyrights, patents, trademarks, and other means of securing intellectual property rights.

In 2007 the company formed a joint venture with China-based Gloria Solar to design, sell, and install solar photovoltaic systems in the US. Gloria Solar bought Spire's photovoltaic module manufacturing plant, which was used by the joint business, called Gloria Spire Solar. In 2009, however, Gloria Solar and Spire agreed to liquidate the JV after reassessing the strategies for their respective product lines. Spire will take its assets from the business and re-establish it as Spire Solar Systems.

Spire also expanded its solar equipment manufacturing space at its Bedford headquarters in 2007, in order to keep up with increasing demand for its solar cell-making equipment.

Chairman, president, and CEO Roger Little, the founder of the company and an avid triathlete, owns nearly 26% of Spire.

EXECUTIVES

Chairman, President, and CEO: Roger G. Little, age 68, $585,126 total compensation
COO: Rodger W. LaFavre, age 59, $222,580 total compensation
CFO and Treasurer: Christian Dufresne, age 45
Chief Accounting Officer and Corporate Controller: Robert S. Lieberman, age 58
EVP; General Manager, Spire Solar: Stephen J. Hogan, age 57
VP Product Development, Spire Solar: Martin Stein
VP Sales and Marketing: Mark Willingham
Secretary: Michael W. O'Dougherty
Director; CEO, Spire Biomedical: Mark C. Little, age 47, $197,283 total compensation
Auditors: Vitale, Caturano & Company PC

LOCATIONS

HQ: Spire Corporation
1 Patriots Park, Bedford, MA 01730
Phone: 781-275-6000   **Fax:** 781-275-7470
Web: www.spirecorp.com

2008 Sales

	$ mil.	% of total
US	30.4	44
Asia	22.8	33
Europe & Africa	14.7	22
Other regions	0.8	1
Total	**68.7**	**100**

PRODUCTS/OPERATIONS

2008 Sales

	$ mil.	% of total
Spire Solar	51.9	76
Spire Biomedical	11.7	17
Optoelectronics (Spire Semiconductor)	5.1	7
Total	**68.7**	**100**

COMPETITORS

Amtech Systems	Kimal
AngioDynamics	Kyocera Solar
Applied Materials	Merit Medical Systems
B. Braun Melsungen	OTB Group
Bard Access Systems	SCHOTT Solar
BP Solar	Shell Renewables
Entech Solar	SolarWorld
FEI	SunPower
Gambro AB	Suntech Power
GT Solar	SurModics
Implant Sciences	

HISTORICAL FINANCIALS
Company Type: Public

Income Statement
FYE: December 31

	REVENUE ($ mil.)	NET INCOME ($ mil.)	NET PROFIT MARGIN	EMPLOYEES
12/08	68.7	4.8	7.0%	229
12/07	38.4	(3.0)	—	188
12/06	20.1	(8.2)	—	126
12/05	22.4	0.0	—	118
12/04	17.3	(4.1)	—	116
Annual Growth	**41.2%**	**—**	**—**	**18.5%**

2008 Year-End Financials

Debt ratio: 12.8%
Return on equity: 43.2%
Cash ($ mil.): 6.0
Current ratio: 1.13
Long-term debt ($ mil.): 1.7
No. of shares (mil.): 8.3
Dividends
  Yield: 0.0%
  Payout: —
Market value ($ mil.): 42.8
R&D as % of sales: —
Advertising as % of sales: —

Stock History
NASDAQ (GM): SPIR

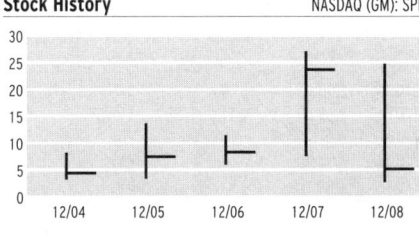

	STOCK PRICE ($) FY Close	P/E High/Low		PER SHARE ($) Earnings	Dividends	Book Value
12/08	5.14	44	5	0.56	0.00	1.62
12/07	23.65	—	—	(0.20)	0.00	1.04
12/06	8.28	—	—	(1.03)	0.00	1.14
12/05	7.45	1,337	360	0.01	0.00	1.11
12/04	4.39	—	—	(0.60)	0.00	0.95
Annual Growth	**4.0%**	**—**	**—**	**—**	**—**	**14.4%**

Stanley, Inc.

Stanley isn't afraid of big government. The company provides IT services — including consulting, systems integration, logistics, outsourcing, and engineering — primarily to military and civilian agencies of the US government. Its clients have included the Library of Congress, the Department of Defense, the Department of Transportation, the Department of Homeland Security, the Department of Justice, the Department of State, NASA, and the Smithsonian Institution. Stanley was started as a consulting firm in 1966 by Admiral Emory Stanley.

The Department of Defense accounted for about 70% of Stanley's revenues in fiscal 2008; it derived the rest from civilian agencies. Stanley provides passport processing and support services under a contract with the US Department of State.

Stanley's revenue growth strategy has relied heavily on acquisitions. It purchased Morgan Research, a technology development firm that supplies engineering and scientific services to government agencies, in 2006. Stanley acquired Techrizon, a provider of IT services to the US Army, in 2007. The company purchased engineering and IT services specialist Oberon Associates for $170 million in 2008. Oberon serves the US Army and other defense and transportation agencies.

EXECUTIVES

Chairman, President, and CEO: Philip O. (Phil) Nolan, age 51, $2,091,591 total compensation
EVP, CFO, and Treasurer: Brian J. Clark, age 39, $1,204,982 total compensation
EVP Corporate Support Organizations: Gregory M. (Greg) Denkler, age 51, $910,301 total compensation
EVP Strategic Operations and Director: George H. Wilson, age 52, $915,139 total compensation
SVP and Group Manager, Technical Programs: Christopher J. (Chris) Torti, age 42, $907,921 total compensation
SVP, General Counsel, and Secretary: Scott D. Chaplin, age 43
SVP Business Operations Group: E. Pat Flannery, age 42
SVP Mission Systems Group: Jim H. Brabston, age 42
Investor Relations Counsel: Lawrence Delaney Jr.
Communications Manager: Joelle Pozza
Auditors: Deloitte & Touche LLP

LOCATIONS

HQ: Stanley, Inc.
3101 Wilson Blvd., Ste. 700, Arlington, VA 22201
Phone: 703-684-1125   **Fax:** 703-683-0039
Web: www.stanleyassociates.com

COMPETITORS

Accenture	HP
Affiliated Computer	IBM Global Services
BearingPoint	ICF International
Boeing	Lockheed Martin
Booz Allen	ManTech
CACI International	NCI
Capgemini	Raytheon
Computer Sciences	SAIC
Dynamics Research	SRA International
General Dynamics	Unisys
GTSI	

HISTORICAL FINANCIALS
Company Type: Public

Income Statement
FYE: March 31

	REVENUE ($ mil.)	NET INCOME ($ mil.)	NET PROFIT MARGIN	EMPLOYEES
3/09	779.7	37.2	4.8%	4,800
3/08	604.3	26.2	4.3%	3,600
3/07	409.4	10.7	2.6%	2,700
3/06	284.8	8.3	2.9%	2,300
3/05	282.5	11.2	4.0%	2,300
Annual Growth	**28.9%**	**35.0%**	**—**	**20.2%**

2009 Year-End Financials

Debt ratio: 15.9%
Return on equity: 19.4%
Cash ($ mil.): 1.8
Current ratio: 1.88
Long-term debt ($ mil.): 34.5
No. of shares (mil.): 24.0

Dividends
Yield: 0.0%
Payout: —
Market value ($ mil.): 610.5
R&D as % of sales: —
Advertising as % of sales: —

Stock History
NYSE: SXE

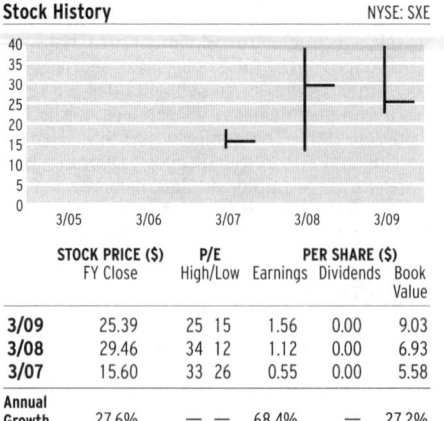

	STOCK PRICE ($) FY Close	P/E High/Low		PER SHARE ($) Earnings	Dividends	Book Value
3/09	25.39	25	15	1.56	0.00	9.03
3/08	29.46	34	12	1.12	0.00	6.93
3/07	15.60	33	26	0.55	0.00	5.58
Annual Growth	27.6%	—	—	68.4%	—	27.2%

StellarOne Corporation

StellarOne hopes to be a shining star in Virginia banking. The holding company for one of the largest banks headquartered in the state, StellarOne is the result of the 2008 merger of Virginia Financial Group and FNB Corporation. The bank has about $3 billion in assets and about 60 locations offering personal, business, and commercial banking services including checking, savings, and money market accounts along with CDs and wealth management services. Its lending activities include commercial and business financing and consumer home, auto, home equity, unsecured, and personal loans. Commercial mortgages make up around three-quarters of StellarOne's loan portfolio.

In what the companies called a merger of equals, Virginia Financial paid about $240 million in stock for FNB. The board has equal representation from both companies with the bank headquarters in FNB's former hometown and the holding company HQ in Virginia Financial Group's former hometown.

StellarOne plans to expand into Richmond and Virginia Beach, and into North Carolina.

EXECUTIVES

Chairman: William P. (Bill) Heath Jr., age 63, $304,319 total compensation
Director, President, and CEO: O. R. (Ed) Barham Jr., age 58, $734,958 total compensation
EVP and COO: Litz H. Van Dyke, age 45, $381,574 total compensation
EVP and CFO: Jeffrey W. Farrar, age 48
Auditors: Grant Thornton LLP

LOCATIONS

HQ: StellarOne Corporation
590 Peter Jefferson Pkwy., Ste. 250
Charlottesville, VA 22911
Phone: 434-964-2211
Web: www.stellarone.com

PRODUCTS/OPERATIONS

2008 Loan Portfolio

	$ mil.	% of total
Real estate-mortgage	1,605.6	71
Real estate-construction	358.6	16
Commercial, financial & agricultural	225.6	10
Consumer	60.1	2
Other	13.4	1
Total	**1,226.6**	**100**

2008 Gross Revenues

	$ mil.	% of total
Interest		
Loans	139.7	77
Invesment securities	15.6	9
Other	1.0	1
Noninterest		
Retail banking fees	14.8	8
Commissions and fees	3.7	2
Mortgage banking-related fees	3.4	2
Other	2.4	1
Total	**180.6**	**100**

COMPETITORS

Bank of America
BB&T
Chevy Chase Bank
JPMorgan Chase
SunTrust
Wells Fargo

HISTORICAL FINANCIALS

Company Type: Public

Income Statement
FYE: December 31

	ASSETS ($ mil.)	NET INCOME ($ mil.)	INCOME AS % OF ASSETS	EMPLOYEES
12/08	2,956.5	9.4	0.3%	846
12/07	1,594.8	17.0	1.1%	496
12/06	1,626.0	19.5	1.2%	580
12/05	1,505.2	18.2	1.2%	480
12/04	1,449.6	15.2	1.0%	512
Annual Growth	19.5%	(11.3%)	—	13.4%

2008 Year-End Financials

Equity as % of assets: 12.4%
Return on assets: 0.4%
Return on equity: 3.6%
Long-term debt ($ mil.): 220.7
No. of shares (mil.): 22.7
Market value ($ mil.): 384.2

Dividends
Yield: 3.8%
Payout: 142.2%
Sales ($ mil.): 122.7
R&D as % of sales: —
Advertising as % of sales: —

Stock History
NASDAQ (GS): STEL

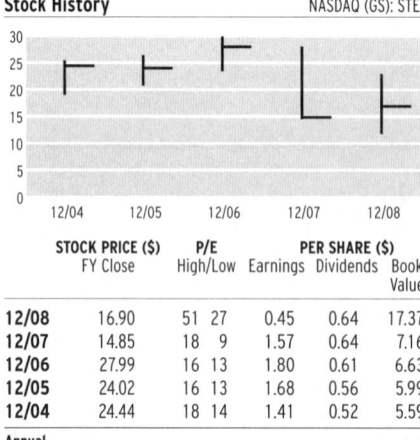

	STOCK PRICE ($) FY Close	P/E High/Low		PER SHARE ($) Earnings	Dividends	Book Value
12/08	16.90	51	27	0.45	0.64	17.37
12/07	14.85	18	9	1.57	0.64	7.16
12/06	27.99	16	13	1.80	0.61	6.63
12/05	24.02	16	13	1.68	0.56	5.99
12/04	24.44	18	14	1.41	0.52	5.59
Annual Growth	(8.8%)	—	—	(24.8%)	5.3%	32.8%

Stericycle, Inc.

Bubble, bubble, toil and trouble, Stericycle treats medical rubble. A leading medical and pharmaceutical waste management company, Stericycle serves about 420,000 clients in North and South America, the UK, and Ireland, including outpatient clinics, hospitals, dental offices, and blood banks. The company, which operates 126 locations in the US, treats waste through autoclaving (using high temperature and pressure to kill pathogens), incineration, and its electro-thermal-deactivation process, which uses low-frequency radio waves to destroy pathogens so the waste can be recycled or used for fuel in waste-to-energy plants. Stericycle also has licensing agreements with firms in Brazil, South Africa, and Japan.

Along with its waste processing operations, Stericycle controls 3CI Complete Compliance, a medical waste transporter. Stericycle took full ownership of 3CI in order to settle a lawsuit filed by 3CI and by minority shareholders of that company.

The company has grown through acquisitions, completing 157 between 1993 and early 2008. During fiscal year 2008 it completed 22 purchases, including 12 regulated waste businesses in the US, and eight regulated waste businesses in Canada, Latin America, and Europe.

In 2009 Stericycle acquired MedServe, which is engaged in the collection, transportation, treatment and disposal of medical waste, hazardous waste, and other wastes, for $185 million.

EXECUTIVES

Chairman, President, and CEO: Mark C. Miller, age 53, $2,297,441 total compensation
EVP and COO: Richard T. Kogler, age 50, $1,064,105 total compensation
EVP and CFO: Frank J. M. ten Brink, age 53, $1,034,243 total compensation
EVP International: Richard L. Foss, age 55, $974,739 total compensation
EVP Mergers and Acquisitions: Richard J. Marasco, age 52
President, Return Management Services Division: Michael J. Collins, age 52, $1,050,320 total compensation
Auditors: Ernst & Young LLP

LOCATIONS

HQ: Stericycle, Inc.
28161 N. Keith Dr., Lake Forest, IL 60045
Phone: 847-367-5910 **Fax:** 847-367-9493
Web: www.stericycle.com

2008 Sales

	$ mil.	% of total
North America		
US	830.8	77
Europe	156.3	14
Other regions	96.6	9
Total	**1,083.7**	**100**

PRODUCTS/OPERATIONS

2008 Sales

	$ mil.	% of total
US		
Regulated waste management services	756.9	70
Regulated returns services	73.9	7
Other countries	252.9	23
Total	**1,083.7**	**100**

Selected Subsidiaries

3CI Complete Compliance Corporation
Biowaste Management Corp.
Bridgeview, Inc.
Ionization Research Co., Inc.
Micro-Med Industries, Inc.
Stericycle Brazil, Ltd. (Brazil)
Stericycle Chile, S.A.
Stericycle Co. Ltd. (Japan)
Stericycle of Washington, Inc.
Stroud Properties, Inc.

COMPETITORS

American Ecology
Ecolab UK
Waste Management

HISTORICAL FINANCIALS

Company Type: Public

Income Statement

FYE: December 31

	REVENUE ($ mil.)	NET INCOME ($ mil.)	NET PROFIT MARGIN	EMPLOYEES
12/08	1,083.7	148.7	13.7%	6,883
12/07	932.8	118.4	12.7%	6,342
12/06	789.6	105.3	13.3%	5,254
12/05	609.5	67.2	11.0%	4,431
12/04	516.2	78.2	15.1%	3,545
Annual Growth	**20.4%**	**17.4%**	**—**	**18.0%**

2008 Year-End Financials

Debt ratio: 112.4%
Return on equity: 21.5%
Cash ($ mil.): 9.1
Current ratio: 1.25
Long-term debt ($ mil.): 753.8
No. of shares (mil.): 84.2
Dividends
  Yield: —
  Payout: —
Market value ($ mil.): 4,386.5
R&D as % of sales: —
Advertising as % of sales: —

Stock History

NASDAQ (GS): SRCL

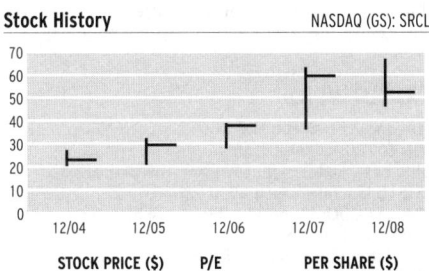

	STOCK PRICE ($) FY Close	P/E High/Low		PER SHARE ($) Earnings	Dividends	Book Value
12/08	52.08	39	28	1.68	—	7.96
12/07	59.40	47	28	1.32	—	8.48
12/06	37.75	33	24	1.16	—	7.42
12/05	29.44	43	29	0.74	—	6.19
12/04	22.98	31	25	0.85	—	5.88
Annual Growth	**22.7%**	**—**	**—**	**18.6%**	**—**	**7.9%**

Sterling Construction

Sterling Construction sees the silver lining even in wastewater. The heavy civil construction company specializes in the building, reconstruction, and repair of transportation and water infrastructure systems. The general contractor primarily serves public sector clients in Texas, Utah, and Nevada. The Texas Department of Transportation accounts for about two-thirds of its business. Transportation projects include excavation and asphalt paving of highways and roads, as well as construction of bridges and light rails. Water projects include work on sewers and storm drainage systems. Clients such as the City of Houston call upon Sterling Construction to collect, treat, and distribute floodwater.

The company has been making efforts to streamline its business by selling off noncore operations while acquiring others that complement its core heavy civil construction business. It sold former Pittsburgh-based subsidiary Steel City Products, which distributed automotive accessories, pet supplies, and lawn and garden products to supermarket chains and other retailers in the Northeast, to The Bostwick-Braun Company.

Meanwhile, it acquired privately owned Road and Highway Builders, LLC (RHB), a Nevada heavy civil construction business. That acquisition gave Sterling Construction RHB's largest customer, the Nevada Department of Transportation, which is responsible for the planning and maintenance of 5,400 miles of state highway and 1,000 bridges.

Sterling further broadened its geographic reach in 2009 by acquiring 80% of Utah-based Ralph L. Wadsworth Construction Company. The company mainly designs and builds bridges, roads, and highways in Utah.

Among major projects it has bid on and won include a $55 million construction contract with the North Texas Toll Road Authority. The project involves excavation and embankment work, installation of storm sewers, and construction of 11 bridges and several miles of highway in Allen, Texas, just north of Dallas.

EXECUTIVES

Chairman and CEO; President and CEO, Texas Sterling Construction Co.: Patrick T. (Pat) Manning, age 63, $599,400 total compensation
President, COO, Treasurer, and Director; SVP, Road and Highway Builders; Treasurer and Director, Texas Sterling Construction Co.: Joseph P. (Joe) Harper Sr., age 63, $599,800 total compensation
EVP Operations and Director, Texas Sterling Construction Co.: Anthony Colombo
EVP Estimating, Texas Sterling Construction Co.: Terry Williamson
EVP, Texas Sterling Construction Co.: Samuel Clark
EVP, Texas Sterling Construction Co.: Jeffrey Manning
SVP, CFO, and Chief Accounting Officer; SVP, CFO, and Treasurer, Road and Highway Builders; EVP, Assistant Secretary/Treasurer, and Director, Texas Sterling Construction Co.: James H. (Jim) Allen Jr., age 68, $362,500 total compensation
SVP, Secretary, and General Counsel; SVP, Secretary, and General Counsel, Road and Highway Builders; Assistant Secretary, Texas Sterling Construction Co.: Roger M. Barzun, $106,800 total compensation
Auditors: Grant Thornton LLP

LOCATIONS

HQ: Sterling Construction Company, Inc.
  20810 Fernbush Ln., Houston, TX 77073
Phone: 281-821-9091   **Fax:** 281-821-2995
Web: www.sterlingconstructionco.com

COMPETITORS

Austin Industries
Bechtel
Boh Bros Construction
Fluor
Furmanite
Holloman
InfrastruX
Insituform Technologies
J.D. Abrams
McCarthy Building
Meadow Valley
Michael Baker
Peter Kiewit Sons'
Shaw Group
Williams Brothers Construction
Zachry Inc.

HISTORICAL FINANCIALS

Company Type: Public

Income Statement

FYE: December 31

	REVENUE ($ mil.)	NET INCOME ($ mil.)	NET PROFIT MARGIN	EMPLOYEES
12/08	415.1	18.1	4.4%	1,200
12/07	306.2	14.4	4.7%	1,200
12/06	249.3	13.3	5.3%	1,025
12/05	219.4	11.1	5.1%	800
12/04	154.2	5.7	3.7%	750
Annual Growth	**28.1%**	**33.5%**	**—**	**12.5%**

2008 Year-End Financials

Debt ratio: 34.9%
Return on equity: 12.2%
Cash ($ mil.): 55.3
Current ratio: 2.65
Long-term debt ($ mil.): 55.5
No. of shares (mil.): 13.3
Dividends
  Yield: —
  Payout: —
Market value ($ mil.): 246.2
R&D as % of sales: —
Advertising as % of sales: —

Stock History

NASDAQ (GS): STRL

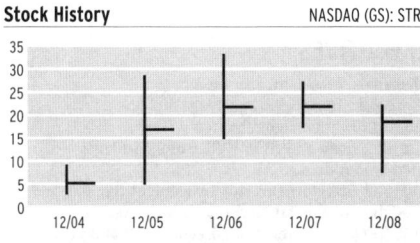

	STOCK PRICE ($) FY Close	P/E High/Low		PER SHARE ($) Earnings	Dividends	Book Value
12/08	18.53	17	6	1.32	—	11.97
12/07	21.82	22	14	1.22	—	10.43
12/06	21.76	29	13	1.14	—	6.85
12/05	16.83	24	4	1.16	—	3.66
12/04	5.19	11	4	0.81	—	2.65
Annual Growth	**37.5%**	**—**	**—**	**13.0%**	**—**	**45.8%**

Stifel Financial

Stifel Financial doesn't repress investors. The company serves individual, corporate, municipal, and institutional investors through about 200 offices in the US, with a concentration in the midwest and mid-Atlantic regions. It also has three offices in Europe. Through subsidiaries Stifel Nicolaus (founded 1890), Century Securities Associates, and others, the company provides securities brokerage, investment products, and financial advice for private clients. Stifel also offers brokerage and mergers and acquisitions advisory services for corporate clients, underwrites corporate and municipal securities, and provides research on US and European equities.

Stifel Financial has been growing vigorously via acquisitions. In 2005 the company acquired virtually all of the capital markets business of Legg Mason from Citigroup and purchased the retail brokerage business of Miller Johnson Steichen Kinnard the following year. In 2007 Stifel Financial bought St. Louis-based FirstService Bank (now Stifel Bank and Trust), which allows it to offer banking services to its clients.

Also in 2007 it added more than 30 offices in the mid-Atlantic region through its purchase of investment bank and brokerage Ryan Beck from BankAtlantic Bancorp. The following year it bought Butler Wick, an advisory firm and brokerage with some two dozen offices in the Ohio Valley region, from United Community Financial, and in 2009 announced plans to acquire 55 wealth management branches from UBS Financial Services. Stifel Financial intends to continue to expand in the Northeast, Southeast, and West.

Hoping to take advantage of the demise of bulge-bracket investment banks such as Bear Stearns and Lehman Brothers, and turmoil in the industry in general, Stifel Financial is expanding its investment banking practice in New York City.

EXECUTIVES

Chairman, President, and CEO:
  Ronald J. (Ron) Kruszewski, age 50,
  $3,924,015 total compensation
Vice Chairman and SVP; EVP, Stifel Nicolaus:
  Ben A. Plotkin, age 53
EVP and Director; Director Investment Banking and Co-Director Capital Markets: Victor J. Nesi, age 49
SVP, CFO, Treasurer, and Director; EVP and Co-COO, Stifel, Nicolaus & Company: James M. Zemlyak, age 49, $1,692,984 total compensation
SVP and Director; EVP and Director Investment Banking, Stifel Nicolaus: Richard J. Himelfarb, age 67, $2,537,034 total compensation
SVP and Director; EVP and Director Equity Capital Markets, Stifel Nicolaus: Thomas P. Mulroy, age 47, $2,924,946 total compensation
SVP and Director; President, Co-COO and Director, Stifel Nicolaus; President, Private Client Group:
  Scott B. McCuaig, age 59,
  $1,619,791 total compensation
SVP and General Counsel, Stifel Financial Corp and Stifel Nicolaus: David M. Minnick, age 52
SVP Operations and Technology; SVP Strategic Planning, and Director, Stifel Nicolaus:
  David D. Sliney, age 39
President, Stifel Bank & Trust:
  Christopher K. (Chris) Reichert, age 45
Auditors: Deloitte & Touche LLP

LOCATIONS

HQ: Stifel Financial Corp.
  501 N. Broadway, St. Louis, MO 63102
Phone: 314-342-2000   **Fax:** 314-342-2151
Web: www.stifel.com

PRODUCTS/OPERATIONS

2008 Sales

	$ mil.	% of total
Commissions	341.1	38
Principal transactions	293.3	33
Asset management & service fees	119.9	14
Investment banking	83.7	9
Interest	50.1	6
Other	0.7	—
Adjustments	(18.5)	—
Total	**870.3**	**100**

COMPETITORS

Bank of America
Charles Schwab
E*TRADE Financial
Edward Jones
Morgan Keegan
Oppenheimer Holdings
Piper Jaffray
Raymond James Financial
Robert W. Baird & Co.
SWS Group
Wells Fargo Advisors

HISTORICAL FINANCIALS

Company Type: Public

Income Statement

FYE: December 31

	REVENUE ($ mil.)	NET INCOME ($ mil.)	NET PROFIT MARGIN	EMPLOYEES
12/08	870.3	55.5	6.4%	3,371
12/07	763.1	32.2	4.2%	2,834
12/06	451.8	15.4	3.4%	2,809
12/05	263.7	19.6	7.4%	1,659
12/04	246.8	23.1	9.4%	1,204
Annual Growth	**37.0%**	**24.5%**	**—**	**29.4%**

2008 Year-End Financials

Debt ratio: 14.9%
Return on equity: 10.9%
Cash ($ mil.): 239.7
Current ratio: —
Long-term debt ($ mil.): 88.5
No. of shares (mil.): 30.3
Dividends
  Yield: 0.0%
  Payout: —
Market value ($ mil.): 1,389.3
R&D as % of sales: —
Advertising as % of sales: —

Stock History

NYSE: SF

	STOCK PRICE ($) FY Close	P/E High/Low		PER SHARE ($) Earnings	Dividends	Book Value
12/08	45.85	31	12	1.98	0.00	19.58
12/07	35.05	34	20	1.25	0.00	14.01
12/06	26.15	40	27	0.74	0.00	7.27
12/05	25.06	25	12	1.04	0.00	5.12
12/04	13.97	13	7	1.25	0.00	4.33
Annual Growth	**34.6%**	**—**	**—**	**12.2%**	**—**	**45.8%**

StoneMor Partners

StoneMor Partners can show you some of the best locations for an extended stay, locations where you may even want to reside permanently. The company operates more than 230 cemeteries and about 60 funeral homes in some two dozen states, primarily along the East Coast but also in Puerto Rico. It also owns most of its properties. StoneMor sells burial lots, lawn and mausoleum crypts, cremation niches, and perpetual care. It offers burial vaults, caskets, grave markers and bases, and memorials. StoneMor, a limited partnership formed by Cornerstone Family Services, is owned by investment firm McCown De Leeuw & Co. IV, L.P., which is managed by George McCown, David De Leeuw, and StoneMor director Robert Hellman.

To keep the company above ground during the economic downturn, StoneMor launched its 2009 Expense Reduction Initiative to reduce its expenses by $5 million that year. As part of the plan, the company slashed its ad spending, sales-incentives programs, commission overrides, and corporate overhead items. It also made personnel cuts by laying off full-time employees.

StoneMor's target customer is 45 to 64 years old. The company sees this group as planners who more typically purchase pre-need products and services than younger age groups. The company buys its caskets from Thacker Caskets through a supply agreement that expires at the end of 2015.

While its growth has slowed to just a handful of acquisitions in 2008 representing a dozen locations total, StoneMor had extended its reach across the US through several large acquisitions during the previous two years. The cemetery operator purchased 21 cemeteries and 14 funeral homes in 2006 from top rival Service Corporation International (SCI) for about $12 million. The deal gave StoneMor properties in Alabama, Colorado, Kansas, Kentucky, Michigan, Missouri, Oregon, Washington, and West Virginia. It boosted its property portfolio again in 2007 when it acquired 45 cemeteries, 30 funeral homes, and a pet cemetery from SCI, again, for $68 million.

EXECUTIVES

Chairman, President, and CEO: Lawrence Miller, age 60, $764,585 total compensation
EVP, CFO, and Director: William R. Shane, age 62, $764,585 total compensation
SVP and COO: Michael L. Stache, age 57, $551,254 total compensation
SVP Sales: Robert Stache, age 60, $551,254 total compensation
VP Business Development: Gregg Strom, age 66, $325,916 total compensation
VP Finance: Paul Waimberg, age 51
Auditors: Deloitte & Touche LLP

LOCATIONS

HQ: StoneMor Partners L.P.
  155 Rittenhouse Cir., Bristol, PA 19007
Phone: 215-826-2800   **Fax:** 215-826-2929
Web: www.stonemor.com

PRODUCTS/OPERATIONS

2008 Sales

	$ mil.	% of total
Cemeteries	159.5	87
Funeral homes	23.9	13
Total	**183.4**	**100**

2008 Sales

	$ mil.	% of total
Merchandise	100.2	55
Services	51.6	28
Investment & other	31.6	17
Total	**183.4**	**100**

COMPETITORS

Carriage Services, Inc.
Service Corporation International
Stewart Enterprises

HISTORICAL FINANCIALS
Company Type: Public

Income Statement
FYE: December 31

	REVENUE ($ mil.)	NET INCOME ($ mil.)	NET PROFIT MARGIN	EMPLOYEES
12/08	183.4	4.6	2.5%	2,307
12/07	145.3	2.8	1.9%	2,169
12/06	115.1	3.0	2.6%	1,634
12/05	99.7	4.1	4.1%	1,352
12/04	89.3	(3.8)	—	1,265
Annual Growth	**19.7%**	**—**	**—**	**16.2%**

2008 Year-End Financials

Debt ratio: —
Return on equity: —
Cash ($ mil.): 7.1
Current ratio: 0.54
Long-term debt ($ mil.): 80.5
No. of shares (mil.): 9.8

Dividends
  Yield: 13.6%
  Payout: 423.7%
Market value ($ mil.): 115.6
R&D as % of sales: —
Advertising as % of sales: —

Stock History
NASDAQ (GM): STON

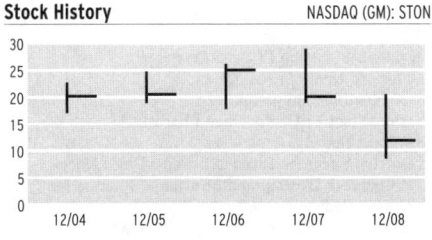

	STOCK PRICE ($) FY Close	P/E High/Low	PER SHARE ($) Earnings	PER SHARE ($) Dividends	PER SHARE ($) Book Value
12/08	11.83	53 23	0.38	1.61	—
12/07	20.05	96 64	0.30	2.03	—
12/06	25.01	76 53	0.34	1.92	—
12/05	20.50	52 41	0.47	1.90	—
12/04	20.17	83 64	0.27	—	—
Annual Growth	**(12.5%)**	**— —**	**8.9%**	**(5.4%)**	**—**

STR Holdings

Think of it as plastic wrap for solar cells. STR Holdings owns Specialized Technology Resources, which manufactures encapsulants: extruded polymer sheet and film used to hold solar modules together and protect the semiconductor circuits from exposure to the elements. The encapsulants are sold on a global basis to solar module manufacturers, including BP Solar, First Solar, and SunPower Corporation. In addition, its quality assurance business provides inspection, testing, and audit services used by consumer products retailers and manufacturers worldwide to ensure their products and facilities

meet applicable international standards. STR Holdings filed to go public in 2009.

The company initially filed an IPO in 2008, but withdrew and refiled its S-1 in 2009 in connection with a corporate reorganization. It plans to use the funds, in part, to terminate the advisory services and monitoring agreement with DLJ Merchant Banking Partners (DLJMB). DLJMB and affiliated investors (including company directors) have a controlling interest in STR Holdings, acquired through an investment in Specialized Technology Resources in 2007. Through the corporate reorganization, the DLJMB equity investment will be turned into common stock of the company.

While the solar energy field is in flux — with a flurry of companies seeking to develop less expensive, more efficient photovoltaic cells — STR is confident that demand for its products will continue to grow; the company is banking on the idea that packaging and protecting circuits in photovoltaic panels will always be necessary before installing them in outdoor environments. Encapsulants are also customized for the customer's manufacturing process, making it more difficult to shop around for cheaper alternatives. The growing solar market in Asia has taken a bite out of STR's US and European customers' market share, however, prompting the company to open a plant in Malaysia to market to new solar manufacturers in the region. STR also has plants in the US and in Spain.

STR's quality assurance business is focused on the consumer products market. As more manufacturers outsource production to developing countries, more retailers want to make sure that the goods they sell meet international quality, safety, regulatory, and social standards. The company provides its services to about 6,000 customers through a network of laboratories and offices in more than 35 countries across the Americas, Asia, Africa, and Europe.

EXECUTIVES

Chairman, President, and CEO: Dennis L. Jilot, age 62
EVP and CFO: Barry A. Morris, age 54
VP and President, STR Solar: Robert S. Yorgensen, age 46
President, STR Quality Assurance: Mark A. Duffy, age 47
Auditors: PricewaterhouseCoopers LLP

LOCATIONS

HQ: STR Holdings, Inc.
  10 Water St., Enfield, CT 06082
Phone: 860-749-8371
Web: www.str-corp.com

2008 Sales

	$ mil.	% of total
US	146.4	51
Spain	89.1	31
Hong Kong	30.4	10
Other countries	22.7	8
Total	**288.6**	**100**

PRODUCTS/OPERATIONS

2008 Sales

	$ mil.	% of total
Solar	182.3	63
Quality assurance	106.3	37
Total	**288.6**	**100**

COMPETITORS

Bridgestone
Bureau Veritas
Dow Corning
Intertek
Mitsui Chemicals
SGS
Underwriters Labs

HISTORICAL FINANCIALS
Company Type: Public

Income Statement
FYE: December 31

	REVENUE ($ mil.)	NET INCOME ($ mil.)	NET PROFIT MARGIN	EMPLOYEES
12/08	288.6	28.1	9.7%	2,100
12/07	174.0	4.8	2.8%	1,700
12/06	130.6	15.3	11.7%	—
12/05	114.9	13.1	11.4%	—
Annual Growth	**35.9%**	**29.0%**	**—**	**23.5%**

2008 Year-End Financials

Debt ratio: 120.5%
Return on equity: 14.1%
Cash ($ mil.): 27.9

Current ratio: 1.92
Long-term debt ($ mil.): 255.5

Net Income History
NYSE: STRI

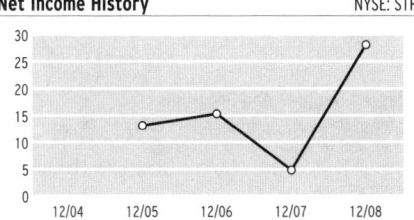

Strayer Education

Students who wander from the traditional learning path can turn to Strayer Education. The company's Strayer University has some 75 campuses in 15 states in the eastern US and Washington, DC. Founded in 1892, the university serves more than 50,000 students, mostly working adults seeking associate's, bachelor's, and master's degrees in fields such as accounting, business administration, computer information systems, and computer networking. Strayer Education also offers Internet-based classes through its Strayer University Online, in which more than 32,000 students are currently enrolled.

Ever expanding, Strayer has been adding almost 10 new campuses a year since 2007, with another 13 openings planned for 2010. Strayer is also investing in its online programs — it opened a second Global Online Operations Center in Salt Lake City in 2009.

Fidelity Management and Research owns almost 13% of the company, while Baron Capital Group owns around 10%.

EXECUTIVES

Chairman and CEO: Robert S. Silberman, age 51,
  $7,987,808 total compensation
President and COO: Karl McDonnell, age 42,
  $1,377,032 total compensation
EVP and Chief Administrative Officer: Lysa A. Hlavinka,
  age 41, $1,131,056 total compensation

EVP and CFO: Mark C. Brown, age 49,
$1,200,936 total compensation
SVP and General Counsel: Gregory Ferenbach, age 49,
$618,093 total compensation
SVP Corporate Communications: Sonya G. Udler, age 41
VP Human Resources: Deborah Keller
VP and CTO: Kevin P. O'Reagan, age 49
President, Strayer University: Sondra F. Stallard, age 59
Provost and Chief Academic Officer, Strayer University:
Joel O. Nwagbaraocha, age 66
SVP Academic Administration, Strayer University:
Randi Reich Cosentino, age 35
VP Admissions, Strayer University: Reginald Rainey,
age 39
Auditors: PricewaterhouseCoopers LLP

LOCATIONS

HQ: Strayer Education, Inc.
1100 Wilson Blvd., Ste. 2500, Arlington, VA 22209
Phone: 703-247-2500   **Fax:** 703-527-0112
Web: www.strayereducation.com

PRODUCTS/OPERATIONS

2008 Enrollment

	Students	% of total
Degree program		
Bachelors	24,273	54
Masters	12,169	27
Associates	4,726	11
Non-degree	3,396	8
Total	**44,564**	**100**

Selected Degrees and Programs

Master of Business Administration (M.B.A.) Degree
Master of Education (M.Ed.) Degree
Master of Health Services Administration (M.H.S.A.)
Degree
Master of Public Administration (M.P.A.) Degree
Master of Science (M.S.) Degree
Information Systems (with multiple concentrations)
Professional Accounting
Executive Graduate Certificate Programs
Business Administration
Information Systems
Professional Accounting
Bachelor of Science (B.S.) Degree
Accounting
Information Systems
Economics
International Business
Criminal Justice
Bachelor of Business Administration (B.B.A.) Degree
Associate in Arts (A.A.) Degree
Accounting
Acquisition and Contract Management
Business Administration
Criminal Justice
Information Systems
Economics
General Studies
Marketing
Diploma Programs
Accounting
Acquisition and Contract Management
Information Systems
Undergraduate Certificate Programs
Accounting
Business Administration
Information Systems

COMPETITORS

Apollo Group
Bridgepoint Education
Career Education
Corinthian Colleges
DeVry
Education Management
ITT Educational
Kaplan

HISTORICAL FINANCIALS

Company Type: Public

Income Statement

FYE: December 31

	REVENUE ($ mil.)	NET INCOME ($ mil.)	NET PROFIT MARGIN	EMPLOYEES
12/08	396.3	80.8	20.4%	2,407
12/07	318.0	64.9	20.4%	1,699
12/06	263.6	52.3	19.8%	2,177
12/05	220.5	48.1	21.8%	2,096
12/04	183.2	39.9	21.8%	1,691
Annual Growth	**21.3%**	**19.3%**	**—**	**9.2%**

2008 Year-End Financials

Debt ratio: —
Return on equity: 44.3%
Cash ($ mil.): 56.4
Current ratio: 1.82
Long-term debt ($ mil.): —
No. of shares (mil.): 14.0

Dividends
Yield: 0.8%
Payout: 28.7%
Market value ($ mil.): 3,003.6
R&D as % of sales: —
Advertising as % of sales: —

Stock History

NASDAQ (GS): STRA

	STOCK PRICE ($) FY Close	P/E High/Low		PER SHARE ($) Earnings	Dividends	Book Value
12/08	214.41	42	25	5.67	1.63	12.57
12/07	170.58	44	23	4.47	1.31	13.46
12/06	106.05	33	24	3.61	1.06	12.24
12/05	93.70	36	24	3.26	0.63	10.84
12/04	109.79	47	30	2.74	0.34	10.63
Annual Growth	**18.2%**	**—**	**—**	**19.9%**	**48.0%**	**4.3%**

Sucampo Pharmaceuticals

Sucampo Pharmaceuticals works to alleviate some of life's more, *ahem*, uncomfortable conditions. Sucampo works with a group of compounds derived from fatty acids called prostones; it uses prostones in the development of therapies for the treatment of age-related gastrointestinal, respiratory, vascular, and central nervous system disorders. Its lead product AMITIZA (lubiprostone) received FDA approval in 2006 for the treatment of chronic constipation in adults. Other applications for AMITIZA, including treatment of irritable bowel syndrome, are in the works. Sucampo is jointly developing and commercializing AMITIZA in the US and Canada with Takeda Pharmaceutical Company.

The product is being marketed to specialist physicians, particularly in the gastrointestinal field, at academic medical centers and long-term care facilities. Beyond North America, the company began pursuing marketing approval for AMITIZA in Europe, but withdrew its request in 2009 to further evaluate the best way to pitch the product for that market. Sucampo's sister company R-Tech Ueno holds the manufacturing rights to AMITIZA.

AMITIZA works by increasing fluid secretion into the intestines by activating specific chloride channels in cells lining the small intestine. The increased fluid level softens the stool, which causes bowel movements. AMITIZA is also in clinical trials to measure its effectiveness in alleviating opioid-induced bowel dysfunction, a common post-surgical complication.

A second product, cobiprostone, is under development for the treatment of ulcers, hypertension, fatty liver disease, chronic obstructive pulmonary disease, and disorders related to cystic fibrosis. A third treatment, SPI-017, is being evaluated to treat peripheral arterial and vascular disease and central nervous system disorders, including Alzheimer's and stroke.

Sucampo went public in 2007, using the proceeds from its IPO to ramp up international sales and marketing efforts for AMITIZA and to fund additional clinical trials for product candidates in its development pipeline.

The company's two founders, husband and wife Ryuji Ueno and Sachiko Kuno, own 95% of the company.

EXECUTIVES

Chairman, CEO, and Chief Scientific Officer:
Ryuji Ueno, age 55, $813,703 total compensation
COO: James J. Egan, age 59
CFO: Jan Smilek, age 42, $271,239 total compensation
SVP Research and Development: Gayle Robert Dolecek,
age 66, $356,112 total compensation
VP Investor Relations and Corporate Communications:
Kathryn (Kate) de Santis
President, Sucampo Pharma Americas:
Stanley G. (Stan) Miele, age 44,
$335,696 total compensation
President and CEO, Sucampo Pharma Ltd.:
Kunihiko Soneoka
President, Sucampo Pharma Europe: David Dodds
SVP Business Development, Sucampo Pharma Ltd.:
Masanori Ueda
Director Human Resources: Susan A. Bach
Director Investor Relations and Public Relations:
P. Curtis (Curtis) Schenck
Auditors: PricewaterhouseCoopers LLP

LOCATIONS

HQ: Sucampo Pharmaceuticals, Inc.
4520 East-West Hwy., Ste. 300, Bethesda, MD 20814
Phone: 301-961-3400   **Fax:** 301-961-3440
Web: www.sucampo.com

PRODUCTS/OPERATIONS

2008 Sales

	$ mil.	% of total
Research & development	72.3	64
Product royalty revenue	34.4	31
Co-promotion revenue	4.8	4
Other	0.6	1
Total	**112.1**	**100**

Selected Products and Product Candidates

Marketed
AMITIZA (chronic idiopathic constipation in adults)
In development
AMITIZA (chronic idiopathic constipation in children,
irritable bowel syndrome with constipation, and
opioid-induced bowel dysfunction)
Cobiprostone (non-steroidal anti-inflammatory drug
induced ulcers, gastrointestinal and respiratory
disorders from cystic fibrosis, portal hypertension,
non-alcoholic fatty liver disease, and chronic
obstructive pulmonary disease)
SPI-017 (peripheral arterial and vascular disease,
stroke, Alzheimer's)

COMPETITORS

Alizyme
Ironwood
Novartis Corporation
Progenics Pharmaceuticals
Solvay Pharmaceuticals
Theravance

HISTORICAL FINANCIALS

Company Type: Public

Income Statement
FYE: December 31

	REVENUE ($ mil.)	NET INCOME ($ mil.)	NET PROFIT MARGIN	EMPLOYEES
12/08	112.1	25.0	22.3%	94
12/07	91.9	13.2	14.4%	104
12/06	59.3	21.8	36.8%	37
12/05	40.2	(0.3)	—	35
12/04	2.2	(19.7)	—	35
Annual Growth	167.2%	—	—	28.0%

2008 Year-End Financials

Debt ratio: —
Return on equity: 25.0%
Cash ($ mil.): 11.5
Current ratio: 4.67
Long-term debt ($ mil.): —
No. of shares (mil.): 41.8
Dividends
  Yield: 0.0%
  Payout: —
Market value ($ mil.): 240.6
R&D as % of sales: —
Advertising as % of sales: —

Stock History
NASDAQ (GM): SCMP

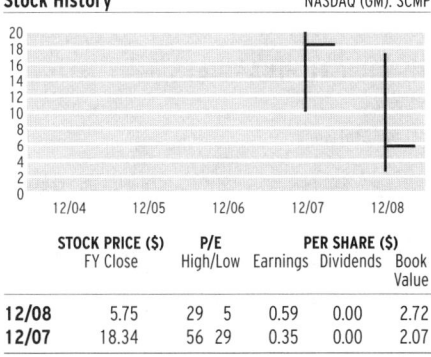

	STOCK PRICE ($) FY Close	P/E High/Low		PER SHARE ($) Earnings	Dividends	Book Value
12/08	5.75	29	5	0.59	0.00	2.72
12/07	18.34	56	29	0.35	0.00	2.07
Annual Growth	(68.6%)	—	—	68.6%	—	31.5%

Summer Infant

Summer Infant makes products for infants and children that can be used in any season. Through its operating subsidiaries, Summer Infant develops and manufactures a line of more than 70 health and wellness products for children from birth to three years old. Some of its products include thermometers, booster seats, audio and video monitors, safety gates, and various bath products. The company earns the majority of its revenue from the US market, selling through retailers like Target, Babies "R" Us, and Wal-Mart. A small percentage of the company's revenue comes from sales in the UK and other European countries. CEO Jason Macari formed Summer Infant in 2001.

Since its inception, the company has pursued a product-centric growth strategy, which includes focusing on the development of new product lines and selling more of its existing products in new retail environments. The company hopes

to eventually move into new geographic markets such as Japan, Mexico, and Australia. It would also like to add new product lines, such as high chairs, car seats, and walkers, to its existing product categories.

Summer Infant has been expanding its products portfolio through acquisitions. In 2009 it acquired Classy Kid, a Las Vegas-based maker of placemats, bibs, and other hygiene products, as well as Butterfly Living, a crib manufacturer based in Pennsylvania. The company purchased children's travel accessories manufacturer Kiddopotamus in 2008, as well as nursery accessories maker Basic Comfort.

Summer Infant operates offices and warehouses in the US, Canada, and the UK.

EXECUTIVES

Chairman and CEO: Jason Macari, age 45, $507,445 total compensation
COO: Jeffrey L. Hale, age 46
CFO and Treasurer: Joseph Driscoll, age 43, $301,116 total compensation
EVP, Product Development and Director: Steven Gibree, age 41, $393,663 total compensation
Human Resource Manager: Kathy Augaitis
General Manager of SIE: Rachelle Harel
Communications Director: Cynthia Barlow
UK Sales Director: Richard Trott
Director: Dan Almagor, age 55
Auditors: McGladrey & Pullen, LLP

LOCATIONS

HQ: Summer Infant, Inc.
1275 Park East Dr., Woonsocket, RI 02895
Phone: 401-671-6550   **Fax:** 401-671-6562
Web: www.summerinfant.com

2008 Sales

	% of total
US	88
Canada	4
UK & other	8
Total	100

PRODUCTS/OPERATIONS

Selected Subsidiaries

Summer Infant (USA), Inc.
Summer Infant Europe, Limited
Summer Infant Asia, Ltd.

COMPETITORS

Dorel Industries
Evenflo
The First Years
Graco Children's Products
Mattel

HISTORICAL FINANCIALS

Company Type: Public

Income Statement
FYE: December 31

	REVENUE ($ mil.)	NET INCOME ($ mil.)	NET PROFIT MARGIN	EMPLOYEES
12/08	132.4	4.9	3.7%	170
12/07	68.1	3.1	4.6%	105
12/06	1.5	0.7	46.7%	3
12/05	0.9	0.3	33.3%	3
Annual Growth	427.9%	153.7%	—	284.1%

2008 Year-End Financials

Debt ratio: 68.0%
Return on equity: 8.5%
Cash ($ mil.): 1.0
Current ratio: 2.56
Long-term debt ($ mil.): 42.3
No. of shares (mil.): 15.6
Dividends
  Yield: 0.0%
  Payout: —
Market value ($ mil.): 33.5
R&D as % of sales: —
Advertising as % of sales: —

Stock History
NASDAQ (CM): SUMR

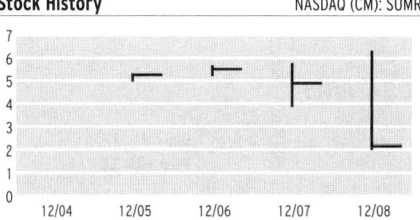

	STOCK PRICE ($) FY Close	P/E High/Low		PER SHARE ($) Earnings	Dividends	Book Value
12/08	2.15	19	6	0.33	0.00	3.99
12/07	4.88	25	17	0.23	0.00	3.41
12/06	5.50	94	87	0.06	0.00	2.67
12/05	5.24	131	125	0.04	0.00	2.62
Annual Growth	(25.7%)	—	—	102.1%	—	15.0%

Sun Hydraulics

It's not solar power that Sun Hydraulics delivers, but fluid power. The company makes screw-in hydraulic cartridge valves and custom manifolds used to control speed, force, and motion in fluid power systems. The cartridge valves are highlighted as unique in the marketplace; their floating design is competitive in pressure capacity, reliability, reduced size, and installation. Applicable in a myriad of industrial and mobile products, Sun Hydraulics' hydraulic valves and manifolds are predominantly sold for use in construction, agricultural, and utility equipment, and to a lesser extent in machine tools and material handling equipment. The company markets its products worldwide through independent distributors.

With a "dividend and conquer" approach, Sun Hydraulics has offered a dividend every quarter since going public in 1997, and reported a profit every year since 1972. Its results are attributed to the company's strategy of sticking to its core product. Sun Hydraulics drives a comprehensive lineup of valves, asserted to have multiple advantages over competing hydraulic valves. The product's placement is key, too; over half of consolidated sales are to customers outside of the US. Operations are planted in the US, UK, Germany, France, Korea, China, and India.

The family of the company's co-founder, Robert Koski, collectively own about 30% of the company.

EXECUTIVES

Chairman: Ferdinand E. Megerlin, age 70
President, CEO, and Director: Allen J. Carlson, age 53, $562,542 total compensation
CFO: Tricia L. Fulton, age 42, $206,643 total compensation
Director Operations: Tim A. Twitty, age 42, $209,089 total compensation

LOCATIONS

HQ: Sun Hydraulics Corporation
1500 W. University Pkwy., Sarasota, FL 34243
Phone: 941-362-1200   **Fax:** 941-355-4497
Web: www.sunhydraulics.com

2008 Sales

	$ mil.	% of total
US	111.2	62
Germany	27.4	15
UK	22.3	13
Korea	17.4	10
Total	**178.3**	**100**

COMPETITORS

Actuant
Bosch Rexroth Corp.
Jet Research Development
Koch Enterprises
Mark IV
Parker Hannifin
Sauer-Danfoss
Servotronics
Textron

HISTORICAL FINANCIALS

Company Type: Public

Income Statement — FYE: Saturday nearest December 31

	REVENUE ($ mil.)	NET INCOME ($ mil.)	NET PROFIT MARGIN	EMPLOYEES
12/08	178.3	25.7	14.4%	682
12/07	167.4	22.1	13.2%	851
12/06	142.3	16.2	11.4%	809
12/05	116.8	12.8	11.0%	597
12/04	94.5	7.8	8.3%	679
Annual Growth	**17.2%**	**34.7%**	**—**	**0.1%**

2008 Year-End Financials

Debt ratio: 0.1%
Return on equity: 25.9%
Cash ($ mil.): 35.2
Current ratio: 5.81
Long-term debt ($ mil.): 0.1
No. of shares (mil.): 16.9

Dividends
Yield: 1.9%
Payout: 23.2%
Market value ($ mil.): 319.0
R&D as % of sales: —
Advertising as % of sales: —

Stock History — NASDAQ (GS): SNHY

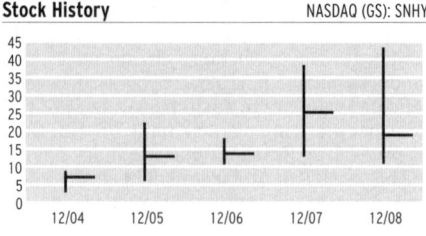

	STOCK PRICE ($) FY Close	P/E High/Low		PER SHARE ($) Earnings	Dividends	Book Value
12/08	18.84	28	7	1.55	0.36	6.29
12/07	25.23	28	10	1.34	0.34	5.43
12/06	13.67	18	11	0.99	0.27	4.18
12/05	12.89	28	8	0.78	0.20	3.33
12/04	7.10	17	6	0.51	0.10	2.68
Annual Growth	**27.6%**	**—**	**—**	**32.0%**	**37.7%**	**23.8%**

SunLink Health Systems

SunLink Health Systems is hoping to shine brightly in the health care business through the management of community hospitals. Through its subsidiaries, the firm operates seven community hospitals with a total of more than 400 beds in Alabama, Georgia, Mississippi, and Missouri. SunLink Health Systems also runs several nursing facilities and home health agencies, which service the geographical areas surrounding the hospitals. The company leases one of its hospitals, Missouri Southern Healthcare, and owns the other six. Each hospital is the only acute care facility in its service area.

SunLink plans to increase the profitability of its existing hospitals by controlling costs, maintaining patient levels, recruiting physicians, and expanding services. It plans to selectively acquire new hospitals that fit the same profile as its existing facilities — that is, hospitals that are primary providers of acute care services in rural areas.

In 2008 SunLink moved into the pharmacy business by acquiring Carmichael's Cashway Pharmacy for $24 million. Carmichael's provides institutional, specialty, and infusion therapy pharmacy services in Louisiana and Texas.

Also in 2008 the company announced that it had hired a strategic advisor to assist in evaluating alternatives for the company, including an acquisition proposal from Resurgence Health Group. The company concluded that it would stick to its existing business plan, while leaving itself open to future alternatives.

The takeover attempt was not the first in SunLink's history: After receiving an unsolicited takeover bid in 2005 from North Atlantic Value LLP, SunLink spent more than a year considering that and other acquisition offers. It decided in late 2006, however, to remain independent. North Atlantic Value owns 17% of the company through director Christopher Mills.

EXECUTIVES

Chairman, President, and CEO: Robert M. Thornton Jr., age 60, $342,243 total compensation
COO: Harry R. Alvis, age 64, $252,410 total compensation
CFO and Principal Accounting Officer: Mark J. Stockslager, age 50, $175,710 total compensation
VP Technical and Compliance Services: Jerome D. Orth, age 61, $166,872 total compensation
VP Hospital Financial Operations: James M. Spurr Jr., age 65, $172,043 total compensation
Secretary: James J. Mulligan, age 85
President, SunLink ScriptsRx: George D. Shaunnessy, age 61, $285,395 total compensation
Auditors: Cherry, Bekaert & Holland, LLP

LOCATIONS

HQ: SunLink Health Systems, Inc.
900 Circle 75 Pkwy., Ste. 1120, Atlanta, GA 30339
Phone: 770-933-7000   **Fax:** 770-933-7010
Web: www.sunlinkhealth.com

PRODUCTS/OPERATIONS

2008 Revenue

	% of total
Medicare	70
Medicaid	10
Private & other sources	20
Total	**100**

Hospitals and Facilities

Callaway Community Hospital (Fulton, MO)
Chestatee Regional Hospital (Dahlonega, GA)
Chilton Medical Center (Clanton, AL)
Memorial Hospital of Adel and Memorial Convalescent Center (Adel, GA)
Missouri Southern Healthcare (Dexter, MO)
North Georgia Medical Center and Gilmer Nursing Home (Elijay, GA)
Trace Regional Hospital and Floy Dyer Manor Nursing Home (Houston, MS)

COMPETITORS

Adventist Health System
Community Health Systems
HCA
Health Management Associates
Northeast Georgia Health System
Saint Joseph's Health System
Southern Regional Medical Center
St. Luke's Hospital (MO)
Tenet Healthcare
Universal Health Services
West Georgia Health System

HISTORICAL FINANCIALS

Company Type: Public

Income Statement — FYE: June 30

	REVENUE ($ mil.)	NET INCOME ($ mil.)	NET PROFIT MARGIN	EMPLOYEES
6/09	199.3	0.9	0.5%	1,851
6/08	158.4	1.6	1.0%	1,845
6/07	143.6	1.4	1.0%	1,752
6/06	135.6	3.9	2.9%	1,622
6/05	128.7	4.5	3.5%	1,555
Annual Growth	**11.6%**	**(33.1%)**	**—**	**4.5%**

2009 Year-End Financials

Debt ratio: 80.0%
Return on equity: 2.2%
Cash ($ mil.): 2.4
Current ratio: 1.46
Long-term debt ($ mil.): 33.4
No. of shares (mil.): 8.0

Dividends
Yield: 0.0%
Payout: —
Market value ($ mil.): 17.5
R&D as % of sales: —
Advertising as % of sales: —

Stock History — NYSE Alternext: SSY

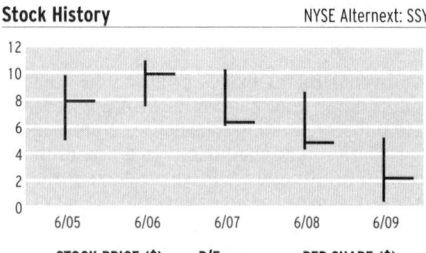

	STOCK PRICE ($) FY Close	P/E High/Low		PER SHARE ($) Earnings	Dividends	Book Value
6/09	2.17	46	5	0.11	0.00	5.19
6/08	4.81	40	21	0.21	0.00	5.00
6/07	6.31	56	34	0.18	0.00	4.48
6/06	9.90	22	15	0.50	0.00	4.27
6/05	7.88	16	9	0.59	0.00	3.64
Annual Growth	**(27.6%)**	**—**	**—**	**(34.3%)**	**—**	**9.3%**

Superior Well Services

It is superior well services, not a superior attitude, that lets Superior Well Services live up to its name. The oil service company provides technical pumping services (stimulation, nitrogen, and cementing) and down-hole surveying services (logging and perforating) that smaller rivals do not provide and at competitive prices to those offered by the big oilfield services companies such as BJ Services and Schlumberger. The bulk of Superior Well Services' customers are regional independent oil and gas companies. The technical pumping services unit owns a fleet of about 1,630 commercial vehicles. The down-hole surveying services unit owns a fleet of 116 trucks. Directors and executives own 41% of the company.

The company has pursued a strategy of becoming a national player in the oil services market by growing through acquisitions. It has expanded from two service centers in the Appalachian region to 36 service centers serving customers in 38 states. Its customer base has grown from 89 in 1999 to more than 1,200 in 2008.

Growing its portfolio of services, in 2008 Superior Well Services acquired Diamondback Energy Services (which has pressure pumping, fluid logistics and completion, production, and rental tools assets) for $225 million.

The company expanded in the mid-continent region in 2007 through the acquisition of ELI Wireline Services, and in North Dakota through the purchase of Madison Wireline Services.

Superior Well Services was founded in 1997 by three former employees of Halliburton Energy Services: David Wallace, Jacob Linaberger, and Rhys Reese.

EXECUTIVES

Chairman and CEO: David E. Wallace, age 55,
$903,071 total compensation
President: Jacob B. Linaberger, age 61,
$730,567 total compensation
EVP, COO, and Secretary: Rhys R. Reese, age 48,
$689,412 total compensation
VP and CFO: Thomas W. Stoelk, age 54,
$490,730 total compensation
VP and Controller: Fred E. Kistner, age 68,
$318,429 total compensation
VP Sales and Marketing: Daniel (Dan) Arnold, age 50,
$508,231 total compensation
VP Operations: Michael Seyman, age 52
VP Western Operations: Arty Straehla, age 55
Auditors: Schneider Downs & Co., Inc.

LOCATIONS

HQ: Superior Well Services, Inc.
1380 East, Ste. 121, Indiana, PA 15701
Phone: 724-465-8904   **Fax:** 724-465-8907
Web: www.superiorwells.com

2008 Sales

	$ mil.	% of total
Appalachia	179.2	34
Mid-Continent	105.6	20
Southeast	93.0	18
Southwest	82.8	16
Rocky Mountains	60.3	12
Total	**520.9**	**100**

PRODUCTS/OPERATIONS

2008 Sales

	$ mil.	% of total
Technical services		
Technical pumping services	463.3	89
Down-hole surveying services	49.1	10
Completion services	2.2	—
Fluid logistics	6.3	1
Total	**520.9**	**100**

COMPETITORS

Baker Hughes
BJ Services
Halliburton
Key Energy
RPC
Schlumberger
Smith International
Weatherford International

HISTORICAL FINANCIALS

Company Type: Public

Income Statement

FYE: December 31

	REVENUE ($ mil.)	NET INCOME ($ mil.)	NET PROFIT MARGIN	EMPLOYEES
12/08	520.9	38.8	7.4%	2,589
12/07	350.8	37.8	10.8%	1,492
12/06	244.6	31.9	13.0%	1,068
12/05	131.7	9.5	7.2%	646
12/04	76.0	9.8	12.9%	502
Annual Growth	**61.8%**	**41.1%**	**—**	**50.7%**

2008 Year-End Financials

Debt ratio: 62.3%
Return on equity: 13.1%
Cash ($ mil.): 1.6
Current ratio: 2.44
Long-term debt ($ mil.): 210.2
No. of shares (mil.): 23.8
Dividends
Yield: —
Payout: —
Market value ($ mil.): 238.0
R&D as % of sales: —
Advertising as % of sales: —

Stock History

NASDAQ (GS): SWSI

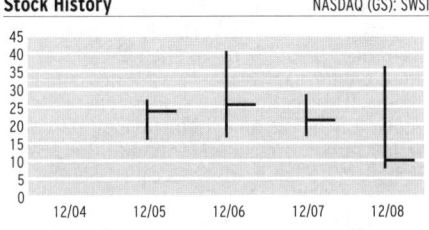

	STOCK PRICE ($) FY Close	P/E High/Low		PER SHARE ($) Earnings	Dividends	Book Value
12/08	10.00	22	5	1.64	—	14.18
12/07	21.22	17	10	1.63	—	10.65
12/06	25.56	25	10	1.63	—	8.99
12/05	23.76	54	33	0.49	—	3.84
Annual Growth	**(25.1%)**	**—**	**—**	**49.6%**	**—**	**54.6%**

Susquehanna Bancshares

Like the river it shares a name with, Susquehanna Bancshares rolls down the eastern seaboard. The multibank holding company serves individuals and regional businesses through more than 230 branches in south-central and southeastern Pennsylvania, Maryland, New Jersey, and West Virginia. Subsidiary Susquehanna Bank offers deposit products, loans, and credit cards. Non-banking subsidiaries provide vehicle leasing, property/casualty insurance, asset management, and brokerage services. Commercial mortgage lending accounts for about 30% of the bank's loan portfolio, while commercial, financial, and agricultural (combined) accounts for some 20%.

The bank's acquisitions have deepened its presence in its existing regions. Its acquisition of Patriot Bank Corp. increased its operations in eastern Pennsylvania, and in 2006 the company acquired Minotola National Bank, nearly doubling its footprint in New Jersey. The following year Susquehanna completed its largest acquisition to date with the purchase of Community Banks; the deal added about 75 branches in southeastern Pennsylvania. Susquehanna Bancshares combined its subsidiary banks into one brand in 2008.

To help fill a service niche in its retirement planning business, Susquehanna acquired Brandywine Benefits Corporation and Rockford Pensions in 2005. It bought Pennsylvania-based investment manager Stratton Holding in 2008. Both acquisitions were folded into Susquehanna wealth management companies, which has some $5 billion in assets under management.

Susquehanna Bancshares has not been immune to the economic recession. In 2009 it announced plans to close 14 branches in Pennsylvania to consolidate operations and cut costs.

EXECUTIVES

Chairman and CEO; Chairman, Susquehanna Bank:
William J. Reuter, age 59,
$1,379,803 total compensation
President and COO, Susquehanna Bancshares and Susquehanna Bank PA, and Director:
Eddie L. Dunklebarger, age 55,
$1,043,476 total compensation
SEVP; COO, Susquehanna Bank D.V. Division:
Dennis W. DiLazzero
SEVP; Managing Director Commercial Sales, Susquehanna Bank MD Division: Christopher D. Holt
EVP, CFO, and Treasurer: Drew K. Hostetter, age 54,
$583,380 total compensation
EVP and Chief Corporate Credit Officer:
Michael M. Quick, age 60, $536,652 total compensation
EVP and Group Executive; Managing Director, Retail Banking Services and Marketing, Susquehanna Bank:
James G. Pierné, age 57
EVP; Managing Director, Commercial/Business Banking Services, Susquehanna Bank:
Jeffrey M. Seibert, age 49
EVP and Chief Administrative Officer:
Edward Balderston Jr., age 61

SVP and Group Executive; President and CEO, Valley Forge Asset Management Corp, Chief Investment Officer of Susquehanna Trust & Investment Company, Chairman, Stratton Management Company and Semper Trust Company, and Director, Stratton Funds: Bernard A. Francis Jr., age 58, $536,652 total compensation
SVP, Secretary, and Counsel: Lisa M. Cavage, age 44
SVP and CTO: Rodney A. Lefever, age 42
VP Investor Relations: Abram G. Koser
Manager Corporate Communications: Stephen Trapnell
Auditors: PricewaterhouseCoopers LLP

LOCATIONS

HQ: Susquehanna Bancshares, Inc.
26 N. Cedar St., Lititz, PA 17543
Phone: 717-626-4721   **Fax:** 717-626-1874
Web: www.susquehanna.net

PRODUCTS/OPERATIONS

2008 Gross Revenues

	$ mil.	% of total
Interest		
Loans & leases, including fees	590.4	69
Securities	104.2	12
Short-term investments	2.4	—
Noninterest		
Service charges on deposit accounts	46.3	5
Asset management fees	25.6	3
Vehicle origination & servicing fees	9.8	1
Commissions on property/casualty insurance sales	12.7	2
Gain on sale of loans & leases	6.5	1
Adjustments	(17.3)	
Other	58.8	7
Total	**839.4**	**100**

COMPETITORS

ACNB
American Bank
AmericasBank
Calvin B. Taylor Bankshares
Carrollton Bancorp
Citizens Financial Group
First Mariner Bancorp
First United
Franklin Financial Services
Fulton Financial
Juniata Valley Financial
Liberty Bell Bank
M&T Bank
Northwest Bancorp
Orrstown Financial
Parke Bancorp
PNC Financial
Sovereign Bank
Sun Bancorp (NJ)
Tower Bancorp

HISTORICAL FINANCIALS

Company Type: Public

Income Statement

FYE: December 31

	ASSETS ($ mil.)	NET INCOME ($ mil.)	INCOME AS % OF ASSETS	EMPLOYEES
12/08	13,683.0	82.6	0.6%	3,271
12/07	13,078.0	69.1	0.5%	3,334
12/06	8,225.1	83.6	1.0%	2,481
12/05	7,466.0	79.6	1.1%	2,211
12/04	7,475.1	70.2	0.9%	2,306
Annual Growth	**16.3%**	**4.2%**	**—**	**9.1%**

2008 Year-End Financials

Equity as % of assets: 12.1%
Return on assets: 0.6%
Return on equity: 4.9%
Long-term debt ($ mil.): 1,517.9
No. of shares (mil.): 86.4
Market value ($ mil.): 1,374.5
Dividends
  Yield: 6.5%
  Payout: 109.5%
Sales ($ mil.): 540.6
R&D as % of sales: —
Advertising as % of sales: —

Stock History

NASDAQ (GS): SUSQ

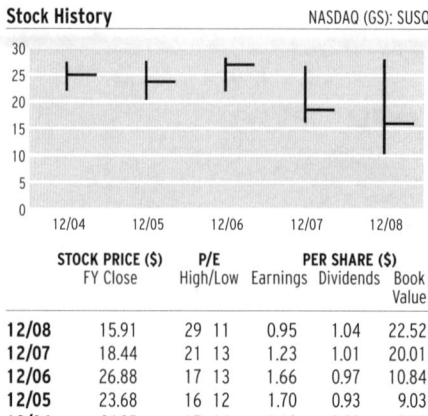

	STOCK PRICE ($) FY Close	P/E High/Low		PER SHARE ($) Earnings	Dividends	Book Value
12/08	15.91	29	11	0.95	1.04	22.52
12/07	18.44	21	13	1.23	1.01	20.01
12/06	26.88	17	13	1.66	0.97	10.84
12/05	23.68	16	12	1.70	0.93	9.03
12/04	24.95	17	14	1.60	0.89	8.70
Annual Growth	**(10.6%)**	**—**	**—**	**(12.2%)**	**4.0%**	**26.8%**

SWS Group

Southwest Securities hopes stock prices go northeast. The primary subsidiary of SWS Group provides securities clearing and brokerage services to retail and institutional clients in more than 30 states, Canada, and Europe. Accounting for nearly three-quarters of SWS Group's revenues, the unit offers private client brokerage services, as well as retail managed accounts and insurance, through more than 20 offices in Texas, California, Nevada, New Mexico, and Oklahoma. It also performs securities underwriting, securities lending, and public finance activities for institutional customers. In addition, SWS Group owns a bank, which is called Southwest Securities, FSB.

The federal savings bank specializes in commercial lending and mortgage banking services through more than 15 branches and loan offices in Texas and New Mexico. Southwest Securities, FSB has plans to grow and aims to open at least two new locations a year.

The company bought Beverly Hills, California-based asset manager and brokerage M.L. Stern & Co. from Pacific Life in 2008. The firm now operates as a division of Southwest Securities and has locations in California and Nevada. The acquisition helped double the size of SWS Group's financial adviser network for private clients.

HISTORY

Don Buchholz and the late Allen Cobb formed MidSouthwest Securities in 1972 ("Mid" was dropped in 1979) after the NYSE began letting members offer discounted commissions to nonmember firms. MidSouthwest Securities specialized in executing orders for nonmember brokerages, expanding after the 1975 deregulation of brokerage commissions. It added clearing services (which soon became its core

business) at the request of independent brokers. The firm expanded through such buys as Pine Securities (1974) and Quinn and Company (1987). It began offering corporate financing in 1978, and in 1987 started underwriting municipal and corporate securities.

The firm formed SWS Technologies in 1996. The next year it launched discount brokerage services through Sovereign Securities. Sovereign's online trading unit, Mydiscountbroker.com, was launched in 1997. By 1999 the online business had eclipsed Sovereign, and the whole unit was renamed Mydiscountbroker.com. In 2000 SWS took advantage of deregulation in the US financial industry by acquiring ASBI Holdings, owner of First Savings Bank in Arlington, Texas.

After suffering a loss in 2002, SWS Group regrouped and returned its focus to banking, brokerage, and clearing. The company sold the accounts of its Mydiscountbroker.com subsidiary to Ameritrade in 2003. It also shuttered the information technology-related services once offered by its SWS Technologies division.

In early 2005 SWS Group agreed to pay $10 million to settle allegations of mutual fund trading abuses. Former Southwest Securities president and CEO Daniel Leland, who stepped down in 2004 amid the investigations, also was fined. Leland remains an executive vice president for the company.

EXECUTIVES

Chairman: Don A. Buchholz, age 80
President, CEO, and Director:
  Donald W. (Don) Hultgren, age 52,
  $1,124,146 total compensation
EVP, CFO, and Treasurer: Kenneth R. Hanks, age 54,
  $694,372 total compensation
EVP and CIO: W. Norman Thompson, age 53
EVP; Chairman, President, and CEO, Southwest Securities, FSB: John L. Holt Jr., age 46
EVP: Daniel R. (Dan) Leland, age 48,
  $3,905,597 total compensation
EVP: Richard H. Litton, age 62,
  $1,182,916 total compensation
EVP: Jeffrey J. Singer, age 40
EVP: Paul D. Vinton, age 60
EVP: Stacy M. Hodges, age 46
VP, General Counsel, and Secretary: Allen R. Tubb, age 55
President, Southwest Securities:
  V. William (Bill) Dolan Jr.
Controller: Laura Leventhal
Auditors: Grant Thornton LLP

LOCATIONS

HQ: SWS Group, Inc.
1201 Elm St., Ste. 3500, Dallas, TX 75270
Phone: 214-859-1800   **Fax:** 214-859-6077
Web: www.swsgroupinc.com

PRODUCTS/OPERATIONS

2009 Gross Revenues

	$ mil.	% of total
Interest	211.9	44
Commissions	179.0	37
Investment banking & other fees	36.4	8
Net gains on principal transactions	34.8	7
Net revenues from clearing operations	11.5	2
Other	12.1	2
Total	**485.7**	**100**

HISTORICAL FINANCIALS

Company Type: Public

Income Statement				FYE: Last Friday in June
	REVENUE ($ mil.)	NET INCOME ($ mil.)	NET PROFIT MARGIN	EMPLOYEES
6/09	381.6	23.6	6.2%	1,170
6/08	301.6	30.9	10.2%	1,193
6/07	273.6	37.6	13.7%	899
6/06	391.6	41.3	10.5%	889
6/05	345.5	31.3	9.1%	1,314
Annual Growth	2.5%	(6.8%)	—	(2.9%)

2009 Year-End Financials

Debt ratio: 34.5%
Return on equity: 7.1%
Cash ($ mil.): 96.3
Current ratio: —
Long-term debt ($ mil.): 117.5
No. of shares (mil.): 27.6

Dividends
  Yield: 2.6%
  Payout: 41.4%
Market value ($ mil.): 385.1
R&D as % of sales: —
Advertising as % of sales: —

Stock History

NYSE: SWS

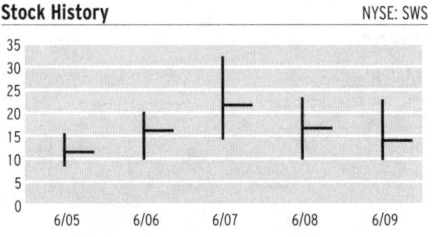

	STOCK PRICE ($) FY Close	P/E High/Low		PER SHARE ($) Earnings	Dividends	Book Value
6/09	13.97	26	12	0.87	0.36	12.35
6/08	16.61	20	9	1.17	0.34	11.72
6/07	21.62	23	10	1.38	0.31	11.12
6/06	16.08	13	7	1.55	0.28	10.50
6/05	11.45	13	7	1.20	0.27	9.64
Annual Growth	5.1%	—	—	(7.7%)	7.5%	6.4%

SXC Health Solutions

SXC Health Solutions helps pharmacists stay on top of their paperwork. A developer of information management software applications, the company provides benefit management software and related IT services to retail and mail-order pharmacies; federal, state, and local government agencies; and payer organizations offering prescription drug benefits services, among others. SXC's software offerings include its online claims processing flagship product RxCLAIM, as well as products for pharmacy data warehousing, rebate management, and Web portal deployment. The company operates primarily in the US but also serves select markets in Canada. SXC was founded in 1993 as Systems Xcellence; it changed its name in 2007.

In 2008 the company acquired pharmacy benefit company National Medical Health Card Systems (NMHC). The acquisition of NMHC's complementary technologies enabled SXC to broaden its core claims processing and other pharmacy benefits management-related offerings. As a result of the acquisition, the company saw a dramatic increase in revenue (from $93 million to $863 million) between 2007 and 2008.

In addition to bolstering its existing businesses, the company hopes to grow through acquisitions that diversify its offerings. In 2008 the company enhanced its product offerings after acquiring the assets of Zynchros, a provider of formulary management products and Medicare Part D compliance-management products.

Other areas of non-core-related expansion include the company's interest in selling resident care management services to long-term care facilities and institutionally based pharmacies.

The company intends to use its growing line of products and services to attract new customers, especially state-level public organizations and small to midsized retail pharmacy companies.

EXECUTIVES

President, CEO, and Director: Mark A. Thierer, age 49
EVP and General Manager, informedRx:
  B. Greg Buscetto, age 47, $588,335 total compensation
EVP Healthcare Information Technology:
  Mike H. Bennof, age 46, $670,419 total compensation
EVP Research Development and CTO: John Romza, age 54, $621,498 total compensation
SVP Finance and CFO: Jeffrey (Jeff) Park, age 38, $983,588 total compensation
SVP, General Counsel, and Corporate Secretary: Clifford E. (Cliff) Berman, age 49
SVP Public Sector and Resident Care Management: Dan Hardin
SVP Industry Relations: Russell Annunziata
SVP Mail and Specialty: Mark A. Adkison, age 46
SVP PBM Operations: Kelly Kettlewell
VP Sales: Mark Mateka
Auditors: KPMG LLP

LOCATIONS

HQ: SXC Health Solutions Corp.
  2441 Warrenville Rd., Ste. 610, Lisle, IL 60532
Phone: 630-577-3100   **Fax:** 630-577-3101
Web: www.sxc.com

PRODUCTS/OPERATIONS

2008 Sales

	% of total
Pharmacy benefit management	89
Healthcare IT (other products & services)	11
Total	**100**

COMPETITORS

Affiliated Computer Services
Argus
Cerner
Express Scripts
First Health Services
Health Management Systems
McKesson
McKesson Canada
Medco Health
Unisys
Unisys Ltd.

HISTORICAL FINANCIALS

Company Type: Public

Income Statement				FYE: December 31
	REVENUE ($ mil.)	NET INCOME ($ mil.)	NET PROFIT MARGIN	EMPLOYEES
12/08	862.9	15.1	1.7%	940
12/07	93.2	13.1	14.1%	429
12/06	80.9	13.5	16.7%	426
12/05	54.1	7.7	14.2%	317
12/04	33.0	2.3	7.0%	260
Annual Growth	126.1%	60.1%	—	37.9%

2008 Year-End Financials

Debt ratio: 22.6%
Return on equity: 9.2%
Cash ($ mil.): 67.7
Current ratio: 1.27
Long-term debt ($ mil.): 43.9
No. of shares (mil.): 30.0

Dividends
  Yield: 0.0%
  Payout: —
Market value ($ mil.): 559.8
R&D as % of sales: —
Advertising as % of sales: —

Stock History

NASDAQ (GS): SXCI

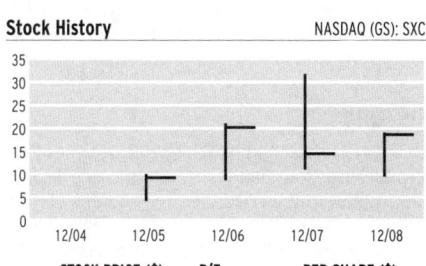

	STOCK PRICE ($) FY Close	P/E High/Low		PER SHARE ($) Earnings	Dividends	Book Value
12/08	18.67	29	15	0.65	0.00	6.48
12/07	14.50	52	19	0.61	0.00	4.42
12/06	20.17	30	13	0.69	0.00	3.72
12/05	9.27	78	36	0.13	0.00	1.98
Annual Growth	26.3%	—	—	89.9%	—	56.3%

Sykes Enterprises

When that software won't install, Sykes can take your call. Sykes Enterprises operates about 45 technical help and customer support centers in Africa, the Americas, Asia, and Europe that use phone, e-mail, and chat to serve those in need of help. Sykes specializes in customer service and inbound technical support and also provides large corporations with technical staffing and consulting relating to customer relationship management. In Europe, the company offers additional fulfillment services such as multilingual order and payment processing and product returns handling. Sykes predominantly serves the communications, consumer, financial services, and technology industries.

In the wake of an earnings restatement and subsequent class-action suit filed by shareholders, Sykes is focusing on its core call center business. Along these lines, it acquired an Argentina-based operator of call centers, Centro de Interaccion Multimedia SA (known as Apex), for $27 million in 2006. It also sold its SHPS subsidiary, which provided employee benefits administration services, to health care industry investment firm Welsh, Carson, Anderson & Stowe.

Sykes' experience and depth in international operations serves the company well as many competitors continue to shift outsourced CRM teleservices overseas to markets with cheaper labor pools. Like most companies in the industry, Sykes' efforts to cut costs have included layoffs and call center closures. Its overall growth strategy includes adding to its call center seat capacity and expanding the number of service lines and markets it serves internationally.

After years of restructuring and optimizing its cost structure, in October 2009, Sykes agreed to acquire rival ICT Group for $263 million. The deal will create a combined company with revenues of more than $1.2 billion and will significantly expand its portfolio of clients. It will also extend its global reach to 23 countries.

Former chairman and CEO John Sykes retains a 14% stake in the company, which he founded in 1977 and which his son Charles Sykes now leads.

HISTORY

Originally based in North Carolina, Sykes Enterprises was founded in 1977 to provide design and engineering services; it often acted as a temp agency for technical professionals. In 1992 Sykes' merger with programming firm Forrest Ford Consultants boosted the company's software services division. The big shift came in 1993, when Sykes moved its headquarters to Florida and refocused its operations on information technology outsourcing services. The company opened two call centers in 1994 and added two more the following year. It went public in 1996.

Targeting Europe as a market for growth, Sykes acquired Scotland's McQueen International Limited, Germany's Telcare, and TAS — all technical support companies — in 1997. In 1998 the company started its employee benefits administration joint venture with HealthPlan Services and soon bought out its partner's interest (it sold all but 7% in 2000 to investment firm Welsh, Carson, Anderson & Stowe).

In early 2000 the company restated 1999 second and third quarter earnings due to irregularities related to delays in the recognition of software revenues. A class-action shareholder lawsuit followed the announcement. In 2001 Iain Macdonald resigned from the board of directors.

Founder, chairman, and CEO John Sykes retired from the company in 2004; his son Charles Sykes was appointed president and CEO. After years of focusing on its core business and reducing costs, the company announced it was acquiring rival ICT Group in late 2009.

EXECUTIVES

Chairman: Paul L. Whiting, age 65
President, CEO, and Director:
Charles E. (Chuck) Sykes, age 46,
$2,321,778 total compensation
SVP and CFO: W. Michael Kipphut, age 55,
$1,294,698 total compensation
SVP Global Sales and Client Management:
Lawrence R. (Lance) Zingale, age 53,
$931,601 total compensation
SVP Global Operations: James C. Hobby, age 58,
$932,866 total compensation
SVP and CIO: David L. Pearson, age 50,
$588,519 total compensation
SVP, General Counsel, and Corporate Secretary:
James T. Holder, age 50
SVP Global Strategy: Daniel L. Hernandez, age 42
SVP Human Resources: Jenna R. Nelson, age 45
VP and Corporate Controller: William N. Rocktoff,
age 46
VP Investor Relations: Subhaash Kumar
President, Sykes Realty: David P. Reule
Director Marketing Communications:
Andrea M. Burnett
Auditors: Deloitte & Touche LLP

LOCATIONS

HQ: Sykes Enterprises, Incorporated
400 N. Ashley Dr., Tampa, FL 33602
Phone: 813-274-1000   **Fax:** 813-273-0148
Web: www.sykes.com

2008 Sales

	$ mil.	% of total
Americas		
Philippines	184.7	22
US	107.5	13
Canada	103.6	13
Costa Rica	62.1	7
Argentina	50.5	6
El Salvador	29.0	4
Other	14.4	2
International		
Germany	74.6	9
UK	64.9	8
Sweden	36.1	4
Spain	33.3	4
The Netherlands	24.3	3
Hungary	13.1	2
Other	21.1	3
Total	**819.2**	**100**

PRODUCTS/OPERATIONS

2008 Sales

	$ mil.	% of total
Outsourced customer contact management services	788.1	96
Fulfillment services	21.0	3
Enterprise support services	10.1	1
Total	**819.2**	**100**

COMPETITORS

24/7 Customer
Accenture
Aegis Communications
Amdocs
APAC Customer Services
Atento Brasil
Atos Origin
Computer Generated Solutions
Computer Sciences Corp.
Concentrix
Convergys
DecisionOne
eTelecare Global Solutions
HP Enterprise Services
ICT Group
Infosys
Keane
NCO
Sitel
Spherion
StarTek
Stream Global Services
Sutherland Global Services
TechTeam
Teleperformance
TeleTech
TRG Customer Solutions
vCustomer
West Corporation
Wipro Infotech

HISTORICAL FINANCIALS

Company Type: Public

Income Statement

FYE: December 31

	REVENUE ($ mil.)	NET INCOME ($ mil.)	NET PROFIT MARGIN	EMPLOYEES
12/08	819.2	60.6	7.4%	32,940
12/07	710.1	39.9	5.6%	29,560
12/06	574.2	42.3	7.4%	26,210
12/05	494.9	23.4	4.7%	18,900
12/04	466.7	10.8	2.3%	17,130
Annual Growth	**15.1%**	**53.9%**	**—**	**17.8%**

2008 Year-End Financials

Debt ratio: —
Return on equity: 16.2%
Cash ($ mil.): 219.1
Current ratio: 3.14
Long-term debt ($ mil.): —
No. of shares (mil.): 41.4

Dividends
  Yield: 0.0%
  Payout: —
Market value ($ mil.): 790.9
R&D as % of sales: —
Advertising as % of sales: —

Stock History

NASDAQ (GS): SYKE

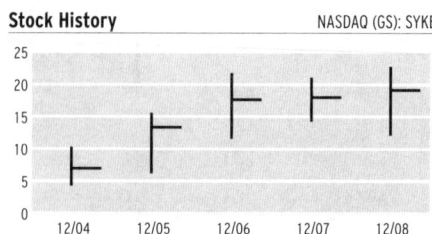

	STOCK PRICE ($) FY Close	P/E High/Low		Earnings	Dividends	Book Value
12/08	19.12	15	8	1.48	0.00	9.28
12/07	18.00	21	15	0.98	0.00	8.83
12/06	17.64	21	11	1.05	0.00	7.05
12/05	13.37	26	11	0.59	0.00	5.47
12/04	6.95	37	16	0.27	0.00	5.08
Annual Growth	**28.8%**	**—**	**—**	**53.0%**	**—**	**16.3%**

Symmetry Medical

Symmetry Medical covers both sides of any orthopedic implant procedure. The company makes orthopedic implants such as hips and knees and the surgical instruments used to insert such devices. In addition to making numerous products for the orthopedic implant market, the company markets its products to physicians who deal with spinal injuries and general trauma, dental work, cardiovascular care, and ophthalmology. Symmetry also manufactures plastic and metal cases to organize, hold, and transport medical devices. Additionally, it makes aerofoils and aircraft engine parts on the side for a few aerospace customers. The company uses a sales and marketing force of about 100 people to promote its products worldwide.

Symmetry tends to grow primarily through acquisitions. In the past few years it has made six strategic buys, including the $46 million purchase of Riley Medical (standard and custom cases, trays, and containers for medical devices), followed by the acquisitions of Everest Metal International (metal fabrication and finishing for orthopedic implants), Specialty Surgical Instrumentation (Ultra brand surgical instruments and containers), TNCO (scopic instruments), and Clamonta, a UK-based machine and finishing company.

Next up, in 2008 Symmetry expanded its orthopedic instrument and device operations through the $45 million purchase of a manufacturing plant previously operated by DePuy Orthopaedics. The sale included a $106 million product-supply agreement with DePuy through 2012. Most of Symmetry's acquisitions have extended the company's reach into new surgical markets where it previously had limited exposure.

Also in 2008 the company announced a plan to invest about $6 million over a two-year period to upgrade two plants in Indiana. The renovations include new equipment and a new design and development center where it is creating prototypes for new devices.

Symmetry sells to nearly 1,900 customers globally, primarily orthopedic device manufacturers. Its two biggest clients, DePuy and Zimmer, account for 33% and 11% of its total revenue, respectively.

EXECUTIVES

Chairman: Craig B. Reynolds, age 60
President, CEO, and Director: Brian S. Moore, age 63, $1,271,208 total compensation
SVP and COO, USA: Michael W. Curtis, age 54, $831,187 total compensation
SVP and COO, Europe: John J. Hynes, age 48, $368,461 total compensation
SVP and CFO: Fred L. Hite, age 42, $991,568 total compensation
SVP Quality Assurance and Regulatory Affairs and Compliance Officer: D. Darin Martin, age 58, $560,933 total compensation
Human Resources Manager: Linda Scalet
Chief Accounting Officer: Ronda L. Harris, age 38
Auditors: Ernst & Young LLP

LOCATIONS

HQ: Symmetry Medical Inc.
3724 N. State Road 15, Warsaw, IN 46582
Phone: 574-268-2252 **Fax:** 574-267-4551
Web: www.symmetrymedical.com

2008 Sales

	$ mil.	% of total
US	302.8	71
UK	55.0	13
Ireland	31.9	8
Other countries	33.7	8
Total	**423.4**	**100**

PRODUCTS/OPERATIONS

2008 Sales

	$ mil.	% of total
Implants	122.6	29
Instruments	177.5	42
Cases	86.4	20
Other products & services	36.9	9
Total	**423.4**	**100**

COMPETITORS

Aesculap, Inc. USA
Biomet
DePuy
DJO
Exactech
MAKO Surgical
Orthofix
Smith & Nephew
Stryker
Synthes
Wright Medical Group
Zimmer Holdings

HISTORICAL FINANCIALS

Company Type: Public

Income Statement				FYE: Saturday nearest December 31
	REVENUE ($ mil.)	NET INCOME ($ mil.)	NET PROFIT MARGIN	EMPLOYEES
12/08	423.4	24.0	5.7%	2,688
12/07	290.9	(1.0)	—	2,449
12/06	253.6	24.1	9.5%	1,795
12/05	263.8	31.8	12.1%	1,862
12/04	205.4	11.7	5.7%	1,673
Annual Growth	**19.8%**	**19.7%**	**—**	**12.6%**

2008 Year-End Financials

Debt ratio: 44.0%
Return on equity: 9.8%
Cash ($ mil.): 10.2
Current ratio: 2.03
Long-term debt ($ mil.): 111.0
No. of shares (mil.): 35.8
Dividends
　Yield: —
　Payout: —
Market value ($ mil.): 285.4
R&D as % of sales: —
Advertising as % of sales: —

Stock History

NYSE: SMA

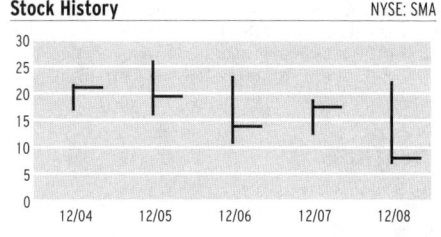

	STOCK PRICE ($) FY Close	P/E High/Low		PER SHARE ($) Earnings	Dividends	Book Value
12/08	7.97	32	10	0.68	—	7.05
12/07	17.43	—	—	0.00	—	6.63
12/06	13.83	33	16	0.69	—	8.12
12/05	19.39	28	18	0.92	—	7.07
12/04	21.05	143	113	0.15	—	6.04
Annual Growth	**(21.6%)**	**—**	**—**	**45.9%**	**—**	**4.0%**

Synalloy Corporation

Since 1945, Synalloy has been signing off on stainless steel. The company focuses on manufacturing welded stainless steel pipe, vessels, and process equipment. Its pipes come in sizes ranging from 1/2 inch to 112 inches in diameter, and are used by customers requiring corrosion resistance or high purity, such as the chemical, petrochemical, and paper industries. Synalloy also produces specialty chemicals (defoamers, surfactants, softening agents) for the textile, chemical, paper, and metals industries. Committed to reducing its debt, the company has been restructuring, consolidating operations, and trimming its workforce.

As part of its cutback and concentrate strategy, Synalloy sold off Blackman Uhler Specialties, a chemical business, to SantoLubes Manufacturing, LLC in 2009. The move aims to shift resources and working capital to its largest business, metals.

The metals division operates primarily through Tennessee-based Bristol Metals, L.P. Synalloy expanded Bristol Metal's capacity in 2009 by acquiring Ram-Fab, Inc. The deal includes a profitable carbon pipe fabrication operation, which is anticipated to complement Bristol Metal's lineup and grow the division's established customer base. Bristol Metal has been producing welded stainless steel pipe since 1946.

EXECUTIVES

Chairman: James G. Lane Jr., age 76
President, CEO, and Director: Ronald H. Braam, age 66
COO: Daniel (Dan) Shauger
EVP and General Manager, Organic Pigments: R. Gary Wulf
VP Finance and CFO: Gregory M. Bowie, age 60, $302,275 total compensation
Secretary: Cheryl C. Carter, age 59, $132,907 total compensation
President, Brismet Pipe Division: J. Kyle Pennington, age 51
President, Piping Systems Division: Michael D. Boling, age 55, $403,556 total compensation
Purchasing and Customer Service Manager, Organic Pigments: Daisy Lugardo
Technical Director, Organic Pigments: Andy Farley
Auditors: Dixon Hughes PLLC

LOCATIONS

HQ: Synalloy Corporation
2155 W. Croft Circle, Spartanburg, SC 29302
Phone: 864-585-3605 **Fax:** 864-596-1501
Web: www.synalloy.com

2008 Sales

	$ mil.	% of total
US	183.9	96
Other countries	8.6	4
Total	**192.5**	**100**

PRODUCTS/OPERATIONS

2008 Sales

	$ mil.	% of total
Metals	131.9	69
Specialty chemicals	60.6	31
Total	**192.5**	**100**

Selected Subsidiaries

Blackman Uhler, LLC
Bristol Metals, LLC
Manufacturers Chemical, LLC
Organic Pigments, LLC

COMPETITORS

AK Steel Holding	Matrix Service
Berg Steel Pipe	Robbins & Myers
Dalmine	Tubacex
Earle M. Jorgensen	Webco

HISTORICAL FINANCIALS

Company Type: Public

Income Statement

FYE: Saturday nearest December 31

	REVENUE ($ mil.)	NET INCOME ($ mil.)	NET PROFIT MARGIN	EMPLOYEES
12/08	192.5	6.0	3.1%	459
12/07	178.3	10.1	5.7%	482
12/06	152.0	7.6	5.0%	437
12/05	128.9	5.0	3.9%	434
12/04	99.8	1.2	1.2%	442
Annual Growth	17.8%	49.5%	—	0.9%

2008 Year-End Financials

Debt ratio: 15.8%
Return on equity: 9.9%
Cash ($ mil.): 0.1
Current ratio: 3.99
Long-term debt ($ mil.): 10.0
No. of shares (mil.): 6.3
Dividends
  Yield: 5.2%
  Payout: 26.3%
Market value ($ mil.): 30.1
R&D as % of sales: —
Advertising as % of sales: —

Stock History

NASDAQ (GM): SYNL

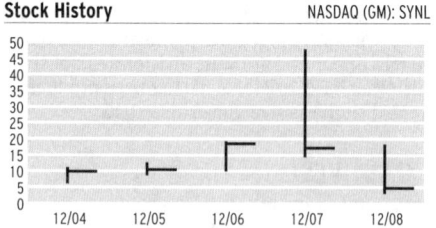

	12/04	12/05	12/06	12/07	12/08

	STOCK PRICE ($) FY Close	P/E High/Low		PER SHARE ($) Earnings	Dividends	Book Value
12/08	4.80	19	4	0.95	0.25	10.03
12/07	17.19	30	9	1.60	0.15	9.28
12/06	18.54	15	9	1.22	0.00	7.52
12/05	10.46	15	11	0.83	0.00	6.27
12/04	9.90	57	34	0.19	0.00	5.41
Annual Growth	(16.6%)	—	—	49.5%	—	16.7%

Synaptics Incorporated

Synaptics keeps you in touch with your electronics. The company develops input products for portable electronic devices, including notebook and handheld computers, digital music players, and mobile phones. Its TouchPad and TouchStyk systems control a computer's cursor, much like a mouse does for desktop PCs. Other products include scroll wheels used to navigate menus on digital music players and remote controls, and the QuickStroke Chinese character recognition and input software. Synaptics utilizes contract manufacturers, including Compal Electronics and Wistron, to make its products. Most of the company's sales are to contract manufacturers in Asia, predominantly in China.

Products used in PCs account for more than half of Synaptics' revenues. End users of its products include PC and peripheral vendors, such as Dell, Hewlett-Packard, Lenovo, and Toshiba. The

company has seen its digital lifestyle product segment grow as a percentage of revenue as it expands beyond its core notebook market into devices such as smartphones and digital music players. While digital music players are forecast to decline in overall sales, video-capable players are seen growing at impressive rates, as are smartphones, an electronics segment that grew in 2009 despite the global recession. Interactive capacitive touchscreens are expected to show the greatest utilization in smartphones, rather than resistive touchscreens or mechanical buttons.

The Nexus One smartphone, unveiled by Google in 2010, uses a ClearPad 2000 capacitive touchscreen sensor supplied by Synaptics. The company is a founding member of the Open Handset Alliance, an industry group utilizing the Android mobile device operating system software created by Google. The Nexus One is manufactured by High Tech Computer (HTC) of Taiwan, long an anonymous contract manufacturer of mobile phones, which began consumer marketing of its brand in the US during 2009.

Synaptics has a limited number of customers. TPK Touch Solutions and Inventec together account for one-quarter of sales. The company's customers do not provide firm, long-term volume purchase commitments; they issue purchase orders as needed. Top customers often change from year to year. Zhan Yun Shanghai Electronics was a leading customer in 2008, but less so in the following year.

After more than a decade as CEO of Synaptics, Francis Lee stepped aside from that post in 2009, while remaining chairman of the company. Thomas Tiernan, president and COO since 2008, was promoted to CEO as a result. Tiernan joined Synaptics in 2006 and previously served as the company's SVP and EVP/GM.

EXECUTIVES

Chairman Emeritus: Federico Faggin, age 67
Chairman: Francis F. Lee, age 57, $3,352,891 total compensation
President, CEO, and Director: Thomas J. Tiernan, age 46, $2,453,729 total compensation
SVP Engineering: Joe D. Montalbo, age 53, $950,417 total compensation
SVP Handheld Business and Corporate Marketing: Gopal K. Garg, age 47
SVP Finance: Kathleen A. Bayless, age 53
VP World Wide Sales: David B. Long, age 48, $833,342 total compensation
VP and CTO: Shawn P. Day, age 43
VP Supply Chain Management: Douglas L. (Doug) Kahn
VP Customer Care and Quality: Ruth Lutes
VP Worldwide Operations: Alex H.C. Wong, age 54
VP Global Human Resources: James B. Harrington
Auditors: KPMG LLP

LOCATIONS

HQ: Synaptics Incorporated
  3120 Scott Blvd., Ste. 130, Santa Clara, CA 95054
Phone: 408-454-5100   **Fax:** 408-454-5200
Web: www.synaptics.com

2009 Sales

	$ mil.	% of total
China	307.8	65
South Korea	70.7	15
Taiwan	46.9	10
Japan	35.8	7
US	3.5	1
Other countries	8.6	2
Total	473.3	100

PRODUCTS/OPERATIONS

2009 Sales

	$ mil.	% of total
PC applications	269.6	57
Digital lifestyle product applications	203.7	43
Total	473.3	100

Selected Products

Chinese-character recognition software (QuickStroke)
Illuminated touch pad (LuxPad)
Mobile phone navigation (MobileTouch)
Notebook computer cursor control pad (TouchPad)
Notebook computer cursor control stick (TouchStyk)
Notebook computer cursor control stick and pad (Dual Pointing)
One-dimensional touch pad (ScrollStrip)
Scrolling wheels (TouchRing)
Touch sensor for displays (ClearPad)

COMPETITORS

Alps Electric
Atmel
Communication Intelligence Corp.
CTS Corp.
Cypress Semiconductor
Elo TouchSystems
Interlink Electronics
Key Tronic
Logitech
Microsoft
Panasonic Corp
Wacom

HISTORICAL FINANCIALS

Company Type: Public

Income Statement

FYE: June 30

	REVENUE ($ mil.)	NET INCOME ($ mil.)	NET PROFIT MARGIN	EMPLOYEES
6/09	473.3	54.3	11.5%	524
6/08	361.1	31.1	8.6%	420
6/07	266.8	26.5	9.9%	312
6/06	184.6	13.7	7.4%	254
6/05	208.1	38.0	18.3%	219
Annual Growth	22.8%	9.3%	—	24.4%

2009 Year-End Financials

Debt ratio: 0.0%
Return on equity: 32.4%
Cash ($ mil.): 169.0
Current ratio: 2.16
Long-term debt ($ mil.): 0.0
No. of shares (mil.): 34.0
Dividends
  Yield: 0.0%
  Payout: —
Market value ($ mil.): 1,314.3
R&D as % of sales: —
Advertising as % of sales: —

Stock History

NASDAQ (GS): SYNA

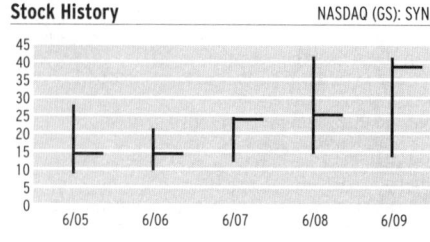

	6/05	6/06	6/07	6/08	6/09

	STOCK PRICE ($) FY Close	P/E High/Low		PER SHARE ($) Earnings	Dividends	Book Value
6/09	38.65	27	9	1.53	0.00	6.51
6/08	25.15	52	19	0.79	0.00	3.35
6/07	23.87	39	20	0.63	0.00	6.12
6/06	14.27	61	29	0.34	0.00	4.91
6/05	14.24	32	10	0.87	0.00	4.25
Annual Growth	28.4%	—	—	15.2%	—	11.2%

Syniverse Holdings

Syniverse Holdings, which operates as Syniverse Technologies, offers business and network engineering services that manage and interconnect voice and data network systems. The company, formerly known as TSI Telecommunication Services, also offers clearing and settlement services, voice and data roaming facilitation, fraud management, and other services to mobile operators, fixed-line carriers, and other telecommunications firms. Customers have included China Unicom, AT&T Mobility (formerly Cingular), Sprint Nextel, Verizon Wireless, and Vodafone Group.

As part of its growth strategy, the company often uses acquisitions as a means to bolster its product offerings. In 2009 it bought Boca Raton, Florida-based Wireless Solutions International (WSI); the deal served to expand the company's roaming service area and added customers to its books. Later that year it acquired VeriSign's messaging business for $175 million. Syniverse hopes to use the acquisition to expand its presence in international markets.

EXECUTIVES

Chairman: Robert J. (Bob) Marino, age 61
President, CEO, and Director: Tony G. Holcombe, age 53, $1,981,738 total compensation
CTO: Jeffrey S. Gordon, age 48, $1,108,391 total compensation
Chief Human Resources Officer: Leigh M. Hennen, age 59
EVP and CFO: David W. Hitchcock, age 48, $958,521 total compensation
EVP and Managing Director, EMEA: Eugene Bergen Henegouwen, age 50, $1,044,727 total compensation
EVP North America: Alfredo T. de Cárdenas, age 46, $928,650 total compensation
EVP and CEO, Asia/Pacific: Raymond Cheung, age 52
EVP and General Manager, Roaming Services and Interworking Line of Business: Lori Gonnu
SVP, General Counsel, and Corporate Secretary: Laura Binion, age 52
SVP and CIO: Ruben P. Lopez
SVP Finance and Chief Accounting Officer: Martin A. (Marty) Picciano, age 43
SVP Corporate Communications and Marketing: Janet Roberts
VP Investor Relations: Jim Huseby
Auditors: Ernst & Young LLP

LOCATIONS

HQ: Syniverse Holdings, Inc.
8125 Highwoods Palm Way, Tampa, FL 33647
Phone: 813-637-5000
Web: www.syniverse.com

2008 Sales

	$ mil.	% of total
North America	361.4	72
EMEA	63.2	12
Asia/Pacific	46.4	10
Caribbean & Latin America	30.7	6
Other	4.7	—
Total	**506.4**	**100**

PRODUCTS/OPERATIONS

2008 Sales

	$ mil.	% of total
Technology Interoperability Services	317.7	63
Network Services	122.5	24
Call Processing Services	29.7	6
Number Portability Services	29.3	6
Off Network Database Queries	4.8	1
Enterprise Solutions	2.4	—
Total	**506.4**	**100**

Selected Services

Network services
 Signaling System 7
Technology interoperability
 Invoicing and settlement
 SMS routing
 Translation
Number portability
 Wireless Local Number Portability (WLNP)
Call processing
 Call handling
 Fraud management
Enterprise services

COMPETITORS

Accenture
AT&T
Authorize.Net
Billing Services Group
BSG Clearing Solutions
Cable & Wireless
Dynamics Research
ECtel
Evolving Systems
France Telecom
Global Crossing
HP Enterprise Services
Intec Telecom
KPN
Logica
NeuStar
Qwest Communications
Swisscom
Sybase
Telcordia
Telesoft
TeliaSonera
VeriSign
Verizon
XIUS-bcgi

HISTORICAL FINANCIALS

Company Type: Public

Income Statement

FYE: December 31

	REVENUE ($ mil.)	NET INCOME ($ mil.)	NET PROFIT MARGIN	EMPLOYEES
12/08	506.4	78.5	15.5%	1,127
12/07	377.5	52.4	13.9%	1,128
12/06	337.0	89.7	26.6%	932
12/05	341.8	5.6	1.6%	797
12/04	332.4	15.1	4.5%	789
Annual Growth	**11.1%**	**51.0%**	**—**	**9.3%**

2008 Year-End Financials

Debt ratio: 95.2%
Return on equity: 15.6%
Cash ($ mil.): 165.6
Current ratio: 3.48
Long-term debt ($ mil.): 510.4
No. of shares (mil.): 69.4
Dividends
 Yield: 0.0%
 Payout: —
Market value ($ mil.): 828.8
R&D as % of sales: —
Advertising as % of sales: —

Stock History

NYSE: SVR

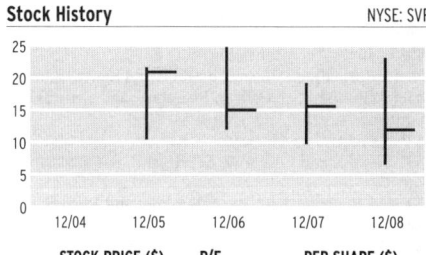

	STOCK PRICE ($) FY Close	P/E High/Low		Earnings	PER SHARE ($) Dividends	Book Value
12/08	11.94	20	6	1.15	0.00	7.72
12/07	15.58	24	13	0.78	0.00	6.78
12/06	14.99	18	9	1.33	0.00	5.98
12/05	20.90	238	118	0.09	0.00	4.65
Annual Growth	**(17.0%)**	**—**	**—**	**—**	**—**	**—**

Syntel, Inc.

Syntel rescues businesses from technology overload. The company provides applications outsourcing, business process outsourcing (BPO), e-business, and information technology (IT) consulting services for large companies and government agencies. Roughly three-quarters of Syntel's sales come from its Applications Outsourcing division, which develops, manages, and maintains business applications. The company's e-Business division specializes in Web applications and data warehousing, and its TeamSourcing division offers short-term IT consulting and staffing. Its BPO services are targeted to financial services, health care, and insurance companies, and include transaction processing and loan servicing.

The company primarily serves large global corporations such as American Express (20% of sales) and State Street (20% of sales). Its traditional strengths include serving clients in industries including financial services, insurance, and health care, where outsourcing of business functions such as claims processing commonly occurs. Syntel's strategic partners include software and hardware providers such as BEA Systems, IBM, Microsoft, TIBCO, and Oracle.

The company has moved to expand its offshore workforce and build business development centers and research parks, primarily in India, where a majority of the company's billable workforce is located. Syntel has also announced plans to transition away from its IT staffing roots, focusing on boosting its applications outsourcing and e-business operations.

Keshav Murugesh was named president and CEO in 2009; Murugesh joined Syntel in 2002.

Co-founding spouses Bharat Desai and Neerja Sethi together own nearly 70% of Syntel.

EXECUTIVES

Chairman: Bharat Desai, age 56, $307,924 total compensation
President, CEO and Director: Keshav R. Murugesh, age 45, $1,003,013 total compensation
President, Banking and Finance Services Business Unit: Rakesh Khanna, age 46, $470,035 total compensation

CFO, Chief Information Security Officer, and Controller: Arvind S. Godbole, age 51, $254,549 total compensation
Chief Information Officer: Muralidharan Ramachandran
Chief Administrative Officer, Secretary, and General Counsel: Daniel M. Moore, age 54
SVP Finance: Dave Mackey
SVP, Finance and Corporate Services: R. S. Ramdas, age 54
SVP and Business Unit Head, Banking and Financial Services: Anil Jain, age 50
SVP Global Human Resources: Srikanth Karra, age 45
VP Corporate Affairs and Director: Neerja Sethi, age 54
VP Sales: Lakshmanan Chidambaram, age 45, $609,594 total compensation
CEO, State Street Syntel Services Private Limited: V. S. Raj, age 45

LOCATIONS

HQ: Syntel, Inc.
525 E. Big Beaver Rd., Ste. 300, Troy, MI 48083
Phone: 248-619-2800 **Fax:** 248-619-2888
Web: www.syntelinc.com

2008 Sales

	$ mil.	% of total
North America	365.5	89
Europe	31.1	8
India	12.1	3
Other regions	1.7	—
Total	**410.4**	**100**

PRODUCTS/OPERATIONS

2008 Sales

	% of total
Applications outsourcing	67
KPO	20
e-Business	11
TeamSourcing	2
Total	**100**

Selected Services

Applications Outsourcing
　Applications development
　Applications maintenance
　Applications management
　Platforms conversion
e-Business
　Customer relationship management services
　Data warehousing and business intelligence
　E-business design, development, implementation, and maintenance
　Enterprise applications outsourcing
　Web architecture
　Web-enablement of legacy applications
　Web portal design
TeamSourcing
　Design
　Development
　Implementation
　Information technology staffing
　Maintenance
　Systems specification
　Technical services
Business Process Outsourcing (BPO)

COMPETITORS

Accenture	IBM Global Services
BearingPoint	Infosys
Capgemini	Keane
Cognizant Tech Solutions	Perot Systems
Computer Sciences Corp.	PricewaterhouseCoopers
Deloitte	TCS America
First Data	Unisys
Getronics	Wipro
HCL Technologies	WNS (Holdings)
HP Enterprise Services	

HISTORICAL FINANCIALS

Company Type: Public

Income Statement

FYE: December 31

	REVENUE ($ mil.)	NET INCOME ($ mil.)	NET PROFIT MARGIN	EMPLOYEES
12/08	410.4	86.7	21.1%	12,363
12/07	337.7	62.9	18.6%	11,709
12/06	270.2	50.9	18.8%	8,364
12/05	226.2	30.3	13.4%	6,093
12/04	186.6	41.0	22.0%	4,527
Annual Growth	**21.8%**	**20.6%**	**—**	**28.6%**

2008 Year-End Financials

Debt ratio: —
Return on equity: 39.9%
Cash ($ mil.): 65.0
Current ratio: 3.28
Long-term debt ($ mil.): —
No. of shares (mil.): 41.5
Dividends
　Yield: 1.0%
　Payout: 11.4%
Market value ($ mil.): 960.4
R&D as % of sales: —
Advertising as % of sales: —

Stock History

NASDAQ (GS): SYNT

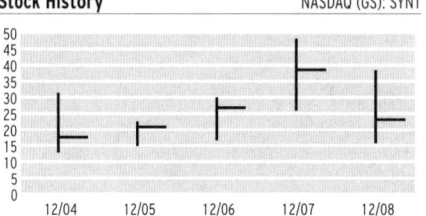

	STOCK PRICE ($) FY Close	P/E High/Low		PER SHARE ($) Earnings	Dividends	Book Value
12/08	23.12	18	8	2.10	0.24	5.46
12/07	38.52	31	17	1.52	0.24	5.00
12/06	26.80	24	14	1.24	0.24	3.60
12/05	20.83	29	20	0.75	0.24	3.67
12/04	17.54	31	13	1.01	0.24	4.59
Annual Growth	**7.1%**	**—**	**—**	**20.1%**	**0.0%**	**4.4%**

T3 Energy Services

T-3 Energy Services (T-3) would like to get a chokehold on the oil and gas industry. The company, formed from the merger of T-3 Energy Services and Industrial Holdings, manufactures and repairs high pressure oilfield equipment including valves, chokes, actuators, blow-out preventers, and wellhead equipment. T-3 refurbishes and repairs pumps, electric motors, and generators; manufactures specialty bolts and fasteners; and fabricates equipment used for oil and gas operations. It also distributes pipes, valves, gaskets, and other products. The company serves oil and gas customers in the US, Canada, Mexico, the Middle East, and India.

T-3 has expanded its portfolio of services through a series of acquisitions. In 2009 the company acquired the surface wellhead business of Azura Energy Systems for $8.1 million. In 2008 it acquired Pinnacle Wellhead, a wellhead service company based in Oklahoma. It acquired Houston-based valve and control makers Energy

Equipment for $72.3 million and HP&T Products for $25.9 million in 2007.

In 2009 the company appointed former board member Steve Krablin as chairman and CEO. Krablin was on T-3's board from 2001 to 2004 and had been CFO at rival National Oilwell Varco until his retirement in 2005.

EXECUTIVES

Chairman, President, and CEO: Steven W. (Steve) Krablin, age 58
SVP and CFO: James M. (Jay) Mitchell, age 41, $356,732 total compensation
SVP Pressure Control: Keith A. Klopfenstein, age 43, $590,737 total compensation
VP Engineering: Gary R. Schaeper
VP Sales: James McMullan
VP Special Projects: Michael T. Mino, age 55
Marketing: Deborah McDonald
Legal: Richard Safier
Human Resources: Pete Skertich
Information Technology: Adam Barrilleaux
Director Quality and EH&S: Michael Rai Anderson
Auditors: Ernst & Young LLP

LOCATIONS

HQ: T-3 Energy Services, Inc.
7135 Ardmore St., Houston, TX 77054
Phone: 713-996-4110 **Fax:** 713-996-4123
Web: www.t3energy.com

T-3 Energy Services operates 18 manufacturing facilities across North America.

PRODUCTS/OPERATIONS

2008 Sales

	$ mil.	% of total
Products	241.3	85
Services	44.0	15
Total	**285.3**	**100**

COMPETITORS

Baker Hughes
Cameron International
FMC Technologies
GE Oil
Lufkin Industries
National Oilwell Varco
Oil States International
Reunion Industries
Smith International

HISTORICAL FINANCIALS

Company Type: Public

Income Statement

FYE: December 31

	REVENUE ($ mil.)	NET INCOME ($ mil.)	NET PROFIT MARGIN	EMPLOYEES
12/08	285.3	13.0	4.6%	748
12/07	217.4	25.3	11.6%	734
12/06	163.1	18.1	11.1%	573
12/05	103.2	4.5	4.4%	465
12/04	110.3	1.5	1.4%	511
Annual Growth	**26.8%**	**71.6%**	**—**	**10.0%**

2008 Year-End Financials

Debt ratio: 8.9%
Return on equity: 6.5%
Cash ($ mil.): 0.8
Current ratio: 2.56
Long-term debt ($ mil.): 18.8
No. of shares (mil.): 13.0
Dividends
　Yield: 0.0%
　Payout: —
Market value ($ mil.): 122.3
R&D as % of sales: —
Advertising as % of sales: —

Stock History

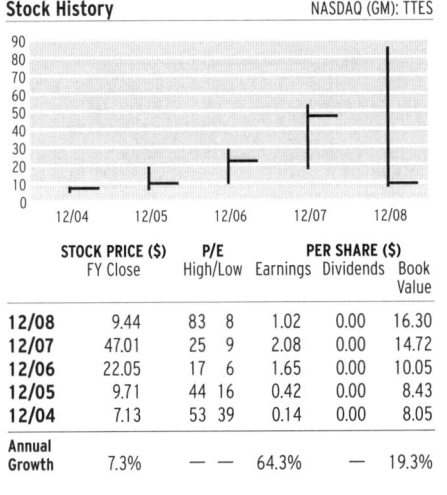

NASDAQ (GM): TTES

	STOCK PRICE ($) FY Close	P/E High/Low		Earnings	PER SHARE ($) Dividends	Book Value
12/08	9.44	83	8	1.02	0.00	16.30
12/07	47.01	25	9	2.08	0.00	14.72
12/06	22.05	17	6	1.65	0.00	10.05
12/05	9.71	44	16	0.42	0.00	8.43
12/04	7.13	53	39	0.14	0.00	8.05
Annual Growth	7.3%	—	—	64.3%	—	19.3%

TAL International

If your freight is going by truck, train, or ship, odds are it might be going in a container owned by TAL International Group. The company is a leading lessor of intermodal freight containers — steel boxes that come in standard sizes and can be used to move goods over the road, over the rails, or over the water. Marine shipping lines are among the company's top customers. TAL International maintains a fleet of more than 680,000 containers, or about 1 million 20-foot equivalent units (TEUs) of capacity. Besides its leasing operations, TAL International sells used containers. Investment firm Jordan Company, through its Resolute Fund affiliate and other entities, controls a 39% stake in TAL International.

The company operates through two business segments. Equipment leasing functions through 20 leasing offices in over 10 countries. Its customers include large shipping lines such as APL-NOL (about 15% of leasing revenues), CMA CGM (about 12%), Mediterranean Shipping Company, NYK Line, and Maersk Line. This segment realized a 7% increase in revenues for 1Q09 compared to 1Q08. The company purchases its containers and chassis in China and then leases them for dry freight, electronics, and apparel; refrigerated containers for perishable items; and special containers for heavy, oversized cargo such as machinery or building products. Additionally, it finances port equipment.

Through its equipment trading segment, the company buys containers from its shipping line customers and resells the containers to traders. The company handles about 37,000 TEUs per year for resale. TAL International has a geographically diverse revenue base, with offices in about a dozen countries and container depot facilities in some 40 countries worldwide.

TAL International announced in mid-2007 that it would review strategic alternatives, including the possible sale of the company. Three months later, the company suspended the strategy review, citing volatility in the capital markets. TAL's board decided to increase the company's stock buyback program, initiated in early 2006, by 1 million shares, authorizing TAL to purchase up to 2.5 million shares of common stock.

EXECUTIVES

President, CEO, and Director: Brian M. Sondey, age 40, $1,131,404 total compensation
SVP and CFO: John Burns, age 47, $432,408 total compensation
SVP Marketing and Sales: Adrian Dunner, age 43, $495,457 total compensation
SVP Asia Pacific: Frederico Baptista, age 61, $536,433 total compensation
VP, General Counsel, Secretary: Marc Pearlin, age 51
Auditors: Ernst & Young LLP

LOCATIONS

HQ: TAL International Group, Inc.
100 Manhattanville Rd., Purchase, NY 10577
Phone: 914-251-9000   **Fax:** 914-697-2886
Web: www.talinternational.com

2008 Sales

	$ mil.	% of total
Asia	190.9	45
Europe	148.8	36
US	45.9	11
Other regions	34.4	8
Total	**420.0**	**100**

PRODUCTS/OPERATIONS

2008 Sales

	$ mil.	% of total
Leasing revenues		
Operating leases	298.9	71
Finance leases	20.4	5
Equipment trading revenue	95.5	22
Management fee income	3.0	1
Other	2.2	1
Total	**420.0**	**100**

Selected Products

Chassis
Flat racks
Generator sets
High cube dry containers
Open tops
Refrigerated containers
Standard dry containers
Tank containers

Selected Services

Chassis (leasing)
Container (leasing)
Container Sales (trader)
Greyslot (logistic services)
SpaceWise (UK container rentals)
Tank container (leasing)

COMPETITORS

CAI International
Chicago Freight Car Leasing
COSCO Pacific
GATX
GE SeaCo
Seacastle
Union Tank Car
XTRA Corp.

HISTORICAL FINANCIALS

Company Type: Public

Income Statement

FYE: December 31

	REVENUE ($ mil.)	NET INCOME ($ mil.)	NET PROFIT MARGIN	EMPLOYEES
12/08	420.0	35.8	8.5%	200
12/07	343.3	38.8	11.3%	214
12/06	303.4	42.1	13.9%	208
12/05	318.5	(10.2)	—	191
12/04	313.0	20.4	6.5%	187
Annual Growth	7.6%	15.1%	—	1.7%

2008 Year-End Financials

Debt ratio: 370.7%	Dividends
Return on equity: 9.4%	Yield: 11.4%
Cash ($ mil.): 57.0	Payout: 147.7%
Current ratio: 1.23	Market value ($ mil.): 432.7
Long-term debt ($ mil.): 1,351.0	R&D as % of sales: —
No. of shares (mil.): 30.7	Advertising as % of sales: —

Stock History

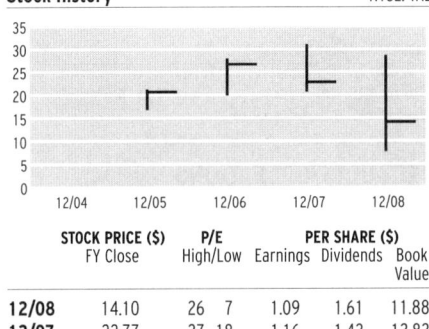

NYSE: TAL

	STOCK PRICE ($) FY Close	P/E High/Low		Earnings	PER SHARE ($) Dividends	Book Value
12/08	14.10	26	7	1.09	1.61	11.88
12/07	22.77	27	18	1.16	1.42	12.82
12/06	26.69	22	16	1.26	0.45	12.99
12/05	20.65	—	—	(0.68)	0.00	12.38
Annual Growth	(11.9%)	—	—	(2.0%)	—	—

Tamalpais Bancorp

Tamalpais Bancorp (formerly Epic Bancorp) is the holding company for Tamalpais Bank, which has about a half-dozen branches in Northern California's tony Marin County. The bank targets individuals, small to midsized businesses, and high-net-worth consumers, offering such services as savings and checking accounts, money market accounts, CDs, and online banking. Its lending activities primarily consist of commercial mortgages (more than half of the company's loan portfolio) and mortgages secured by multifamily housing (about 30%). Financial planning and asset management are provided through subsidiary Tamalpais Wealth Advisors (formerly Epic Wealth Management), which oversees approximately $250 million in assets.

The company also has loan production offices in Santa Rosa and Roseville that focus on Small Business Administration (SBA) loans.

Tamalpais Bancorp is looking to expand its horizons beyond Marin County; it will primarily focus on business customers.

Company executives and board members collectively own 9% of Tamalpais Bancorp.

EXECUTIVES

Chairman and Director; Vice Chairman and Director, Tamalpais Bank: Carolyn B. Horan, age 77
Vice Chairman and Treasurer; Director and Treasurer, Tamalpais Bank: Richard E. Smith, age 71
President, CEO and Director; Chairman and CEO, Tamalpais Bank: Mark Garwood, age 54
EVP; President, Tamalpais Bank: Jamie Williams, age 55
SVP, Chief Accounting Officer, and Interim CFO: Karry Bryan, age 43
SVP and Director Human Resources: Anjana Berde
COO and Chief Economist, Tamalpais Wealth Advisors: William D. Osher
EVP and Chief Credit Officer, Tamalpais Bank: Lawrence (Larry) Cretan
SVP and Chief Marketing Officer, Tamalpais Bank: Mark Chapman

SVP and Loan Operations Manager, Tamalpais Bank:
Karol Watson
SVP, Chief Compliance Officer, and Risk Management
Officer, Tamalpais Bank: Paulette Slack
SVP and Chief Information Officer, Tamalpais Bank:
Richard Lewis
Auditors: Vavrinek, Trine, Day & Co., LLP

LOCATIONS

HQ: Tamalpais Bancorp
630 Las Gallinas Ave., San Rafael, CA 94903
Phone: 415-526-6400   Fax: 415-526-6414
Web: www.tambancorp.com

PRODUCTS/OPERATIONS

2008 Gross Revenues

	$ mil.	% of total
Interest		
Loans, including fees	40.1	88
Investment securities	2.7	6
Other	0.4	1
Noninterest		
Investment advisory services fees	0.6	1
Other	1.6	4
Total	**45.4**	**100**

COMPETITORS

Bank of America
Bank of Marin
First Banks
First Republic (CA)
Umpqua Holdings
UnionBanCal
Westamerica

HISTORICAL FINANCIALS

Company Type: Public

Income Statement   FYE: December 31

	ASSETS ($ mil.)	NET INCOME ($ mil.)	INCOME AS % OF ASSETS	EMPLOYEES
12/08	703.4	4.8	0.7%	80
12/07	556.8	4.2	0.8%	77
12/06	503.5	3.9	0.8%	75
12/05	461.8	4.1	0.9%	73
12/04	425.6	3.4	0.8%	97
Annual Growth	**13.4%**	**9.0%**	**—**	**(4.7%)**

2008 Year-End Financials

Equity as % of assets: 5.3%
Return on assets: 0.8%
Return on equity: 13.7%
Long-term debt ($ mil.): 202.5
No. of shares (mil.): 3.8
Market value ($ mil.): 32.4
Dividends
Yield: 2.6%
Payout: 17.5%
Sales ($ mil.): 25.5
R&D as % of sales: —
Advertising as % of sales: —

Stock History   NASDAQ (CM): TAMB

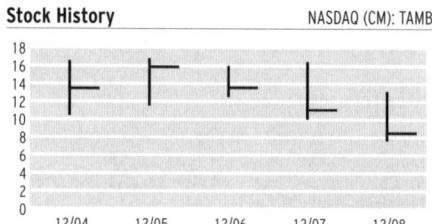

	STOCK PRICE ($) FY Close	P/E High/Low		PER SHARE ($) Earnings	Dividends	Book Value
12/08	8.47	10	6	1.26	0.22	9.77
12/07	11.07	15	9	1.07	0.14	8.61
12/06	13.55	16	13	0.99	0.15	8.08
12/05	15.86	16	12	1.01	0.11	7.02
12/04	13.46	19	12	0.88	0.02	6.06
Annual Growth	**(10.9%)**	**—**	**—**	**9.4%**	**82.1%**	**12.7%**

TC PipeLines

All gassed up and ready to go, TC PipeLines was formed by TransCanada PipeLines to manage the company's US assets. TC PipeLines owns 50% of Northern Border Pipeline, which stretches about 1,250 miles from the Montana-Saskatchewan border to the US Midwest. The company also owns Tuscarora Gas Transmission, a 240-mile pipeline that transports gas from Oregon to Nevada. A third investment is its 46% stake in Great Lakes Gas Transmission Limited Partnership, which owns a 2,115-mile pipeline that moves gas from the Manitoba-Minnesota border to the Ontario-Michigan border. Formed in 1998, the company is managed by general partner TC PipeLines GP, a wholly owned subsidiary of TransCanada.

ONEOK Partners owns the other half of the Northern Border Pipeline. That natural gas pipeline links to facilities of various pipeline companies across the Midwest, including MidAmerican Energy and Northern Indiana Public Service, and local distribution companies. Northern Border Pipeline serves about 40 transportation shippers. A majority of the natural gas transported by Northern Border Pipeline is produced in the Western Canada Sedimentary Basin, which lies within the provinces of Alberta, British Columbia, and Saskatchewan.

Boosting its energy infrastructure portfolio, in 2009 TC Pipelines acquired North Baja Pipeline from TransCanada for about $395 million.

EXECUTIVES

Chairman and CEO: Russell K. (Russ) Girling, age 46
President, General Partner: Mark A. P. Zimmerman, age 44
VP and Treasurer, General Partner: Sean M. Brett, age 61
VP Taxation, General Partner: Terry C. Ofremchuk, age 58
Secretary, General Partner: Donald J. DeGrandis, age 60
Auditors: KPMG LLP

LOCATIONS

HQ: TC PipeLines, LP
13710 FNB Pkwy., Omaha, NE 68154
Phone: 877-290-2772   Fax: 403-920-2457
Web: www.tcpipelineslp.com

COMPETITORS

Alliance Pipeline
Buckeye Partners
El Paso
Enbridge Energy
Great Lakes Gas Transmission
Vector Pipeline
Williams Companies

HISTORICAL FINANCIALS

Company Type: Public

Income Statement   FYE: December 31

	REVENUE ($ mil.)	NET INCOME ($ mil.)	NET PROFIT MARGIN	EMPLOYEES
12/08	154.2	107.7	69.8%	—
12/07	137.4	89.0	64.8%	—
12/06	63.4	44.7	70.5%	—
12/05	53.2	50.2	94.4%	—
12/04	57.5	55.1	95.8%	—
Annual Growth	**28.0%**	**18.2%**	**—**	**—**

2008 Year-End Financials

Debt ratio: —
Return on equity: —
Cash ($ mil.): 8.4
Current ratio: 0.58
Long-term debt ($ mil.): 532.4
No. of shares (mil.): 41.2
Dividends
Yield: 11.9%
Payout: 101.1%
Market value ($ mil.): 958.5
R&D as % of sales: —
Advertising as % of sales: —

Stock History   NASDAQ (GS): TCLP

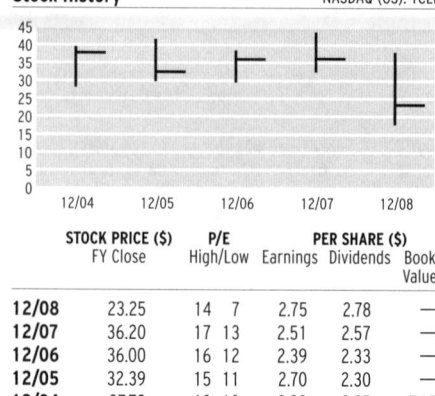

	STOCK PRICE ($) FY Close	P/E High/Low		PER SHARE ($) Earnings	Dividends	Book Value
12/08	23.25	14	7	2.75	2.78	—
12/07	36.20	17	13	2.51	2.57	—
12/06	36.00	16	12	2.39	2.33	—
12/05	32.39	15	11	2.70	2.30	—
12/04	37.79	13	10	2.99	2.25	7.15
Annual Growth	**(11.4%)**	**—**	**—**	**(2.1%)**	**5.4%**	**—**

Team, Inc.

Consider it the A-Team for high-pressure situations. Team provides specialized maintenance services for piping systems, including repairing leaks, hot tapping (adding new connections to pressurized pipelines), and detecting escaping emissions. It also offers field heat treatment and testing and inspection services. The firm makes custom equipment, clamps, and enclosures to augment its standard materials and sealant products. Through two divisions, Team Mechanical Services (TMS) and Team Cooperheat-MQS (TCM), the company serves the chemical and petrochemical, pulp and paper, refining, and steel industries. Team operates from more than 100 locations worldwide; its largest market is the US.

Team has grown rapidly in the past decade, increasing its revenues by more than sevenfold since 2000. It has acquired several other companies in its field and expanded its presence internationally. In 2007 the company acquired Canadian testing and inspection services company Aitec, which contributed to a near-tripling of Canadian revenues and made Team the second-largest inspection provider in the country. The following year, Team acquired pipeline repair company Leak Repairs Specam, one of the largest leak repair companies in the Benelux region, from GTI for $18.5 million.

The global economic crisis had a minor effect on the company in 2008, primarily as a result of decreased spending by Team's customers. With the trend continuing into 2009, Team implemented its own cost-cutting plans which included a workforce reduction.

Company directors and executive officers collectively own 12% of Team.

EXECUTIVES

Chairman and CEO: Philip J. (Phil) Hawk, age 55
SVP, CFO, and Treasurer: Ted W. Owen, age 58
SVP, TCM: Arthur F. (Art) Victorson, age 49
SVP, Commercial Support and Business Development:
  Peter W. Wallace, age 47
SVP, TMS: David C. Palmore, age 54
SVP, Administration, General Counsel and Secretary:
  Andre C. (Butch) Bouchard, age 44
SVP: John P. Kearns, age 53
Auditors: KPMG LLP

LOCATIONS

HQ: Team, Inc.
  200 Hermann Dr., Alvin, TX 77511
Phone: 281-331-6154   **Fax:** 281-331-4107
Web: www.teamindustrialservices.com

2009 Sales

	$ mil.	% of total
US	350.0	70
Canada	112.9	23
Europe	23.5	5
Other	11.2	2
Total	**497.6**	**100**

PRODUCTS/OPERATIONS

2009 Sales

	$ mil.	% of total
Team Mechanical Services	270.4	54
Team Cooperheat-MQS	227.2	46
Total	**497.6**	**100**

Selected Industrial Services

Field heat treating
Field machining
Field valve repair
Fugitive emissions control
Hot tapping
Leak repair
Non-destructive testing
Technical bolting

COMPETITORS

Flowserve
Furmanite
Halliburton
Halma
ITT Corp.
Mistras Group
Schlumberger
T. D. Williamson
Wellstream

HISTORICAL FINANCIALS

Company Type: Public

Income Statement   FYE: May 31

	REVENUE ($ mil.)	NET INCOME ($ mil.)	NET PROFIT MARGIN	EMPLOYEES
5/09	497.6	22.9	4.6%	3,400
5/08	478.5	23.6	4.9%	3,700
5/07	318.3	15.5	4.9%	3,400
5/06	259.8	10.6	4.1%	2,700
5/05	209.0	4.8	2.3%	2,500
Annual Growth	**24.2%**	**47.8%**	**—**	**8.0%**

2009 Year-End Financials

Debt ratio: 52.3%
Return on equity: 17.1%
Cash ($ mil.): 12.6
Current ratio: 3.35
Long-term debt ($ mil.): 76.7
No. of shares (mil.): 18.9
Dividends
  Yield: 0.0%
  Payout: —
Market value ($ mil.): 267.4
R&D as % of sales: —
Advertising as % of sales: —

Stock History   NASDAQ (GS): TISI

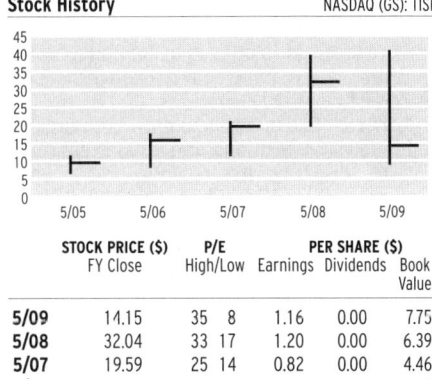

	STOCK PRICE ($) FY Close	P/E High/Low		Earnings	PER SHARE ($) Dividends	Book Value
5/09	14.15	35	8	1.16	0.00	7.75
5/08	32.04	33	17	1.20	0.00	6.39
5/07	19.59	25	14	0.82	0.00	4.46
5/06	15.73	30	15	0.58	0.00	3.38
5/05	9.50	42	26	0.26	0.00	2.59
Annual Growth	**10.5%**	**—**	**—**	**45.3%**	**—**	**31.5%**

TechTarget, Inc.

TechTarget can help you hit the IT professional's bull's-eye. The company operates a network of about 60 Web sites, each of which focuses on a specific information technology sector, such as storage, security, or networking. It offers original, vendor-generated, and user-generated content designed to bring together nearly 8 million registered buyers and sellers of corporate IT products. To further bring these groups together, TechTarget also produces events and industry conferences, and new media offerings (e-mail newsletters, online white papers, Webcasts, and podcasts) aimed at IT professionals. TechTarget generates most of its revenue through online advertising and producing events.

TechTarget's strategy of targeting specific segments within the IT community is designed to make each site more valuable for advertisers, which number more than 1,400. As corporate IT purchases become more complex, the company has worked to establish a subject-matter-expert appeal and to stay ahead of changing technologies.

Recognizing that online advertising provides a far better return on investment than print, the company stopped publishing its *Storage* and *Information Security* magazines in 2008. Costs associated with advertising represent 41% of print revenue versus 28% of online revenue. TechTarget plans to expand its Web sites and move into international markets after launching in the UK in 2008.

The company's 2008 10K was released late; in it, TechTarget said it had reexamined earnings back to 2004 and restated them for 2006 and 2007. A review of its accounting practices showed that the company had inadvertently used an improper method of accounting for Webcast, whitepaper, and promotional e-mail revenues.

Venture capital firms Technology Crossover Ventures and Polaris Venture Partners own 30% and 20% of the company, respectively. Board member Roger Marino, who founded movie studio Revere Pictures, has a 10% stake.

EXECUTIVES

Chairman and CEO: Greg Strakosch, age 46,
  $1,127,650 total compensation
President: Don Hawk, age 38,
  $1,009,156 total compensation
CFO and Treasurer: Eric Sockol, age 47,
  $681,307 total compensation
EVP: Kevin Beam, age 45, $958,439 total compensation
SVP International: Bill Crowley
SVP Sales: Mike Cotoia
SVP Client Services and Corporate Marketing:
  Marilou Barsam
SVP Product Management: Jeff Ramminger
SVP Product Development and Technology:
  Sean Tierney
SVP and Publisher, TechTarget Prosumer Media:
  Michael Carroll
VP and Group Publisher, TechTarget Storage Media:
  Mike Kelly
VP, General Counsel, and Secretary: Rick M. Olin,
  age 52, $302,451 total compensation
VP Human Resources: Arden Port
Auditors: Ernst & Young LLP

LOCATIONS

HQ: TechTarget, Inc.
  117 Kendrick St., Ste. 800, Needham, MA 02494
Phone: 781-657-1000   **Fax:** 781-657-1100
Web: www.techtarget.com

PRODUCTS/OPERATIONS

2008 Sales

	$ mil.	% of total
Online	77.3	74
Events	22.8	22
Print	4.4	4
Total	**104.5**	**100**

Selected Products and Operations

Conferences
  The CIO Decisions Conference
  IT Knowledge Exchange
  The ServerSide Java Symposium
Web sites
  UK
    SearchSecurity.co.uk
    SearchStorage.co.uk
  US
    Ajaxian.com
    Bitpipe.com
    Brighthand.com
    DigitalCameraReview.com
    KnowledgeStorm.com
    NotebookReview.com
    SearchCIO.com
    SearchCRM.com
    SearchDataCenter.com
    SearchDomino.com
    SearchEnterpriseLinux.com
    SearchExchange.com
    SearchMobileComputing.com
    SearchNetworking.com
    SearchOracle.com
    SearchSAP.com
    SearchSecurity.com
    SearchSMB.com
    SearchSQLServer.com
    SearchStorage.com
    SearchVMware.com
    SearchWindowsServer.com
    TheServerSide.com
    TheServerSide.NET
    Whatis.com

COMPETITORS

451 Group	O'Reilly Media
1105 Media	Red Herring
CBS Interactive	SYS-CON Media
CXO Media	Tech Wire Media Group
Forrester Research	United Business Media
Future plc	WebMediaBrands
Gartner	Yankee Group
Information Today	Ziff Davis Media
International Data Group	

HISTORICAL FINANCIALS

Company Type: Public

Income Statement
FYE: December 31

	REVENUE ($ mil.)	NET INCOME ($ mil.)	NET PROFIT MARGIN	EMPLOYEES
12/08	104.5	1.8	1.7%	527
12/07	94.7	8.2	8.7%	584
12/06	79.0	(3.6)	—	474
12/05	66.7	8.9	13.3%	474
12/04	46.7	(3.3)	—	474
Annual Growth	22.3%	—	—	2.7%

2008 Year-End Financials

Debt ratio: 0.0%
Return on equity: 1.0%
Cash ($ mil.): 24.1
Current ratio: 5.00
Long-term debt ($ mil.): 0.0
No. of shares (mil.): 41.6
Dividends
  Yield: 0.0%
  Payout: —
Market value ($ mil.): 179.5
R&D as % of sales: —
Advertising as % of sales: —

Stock History
NASDAQ (GM): TTGT

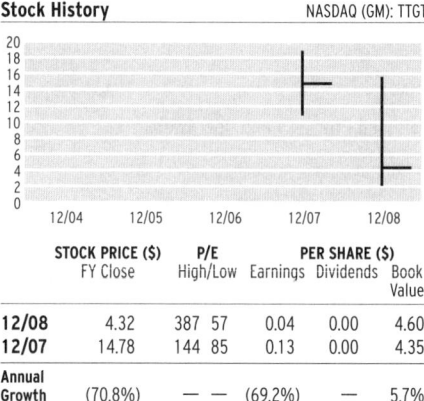

	STOCK PRICE ($) FY Close	P/E High/Low		PER SHARE ($) Earnings	Dividends	Book Value
12/08	4.32	387	57	0.04	0.00	4.60
12/07	14.78	144	85	0.13	0.00	4.35
Annual Growth	(70.8%)	—	—	(69.2%)	—	5.7%

TechTeam Global

When your help desk needs a few more players, TechTeam Global is ready to get in the game. The company's business process outsourcing (BPO) and IT services include consulting, help desk support, systems integration, technical staffing, and training. Among TechTeam Global's customers are *FORTUNE* 1000 companies, government entities, and other organizations. Several US government agencies together account for about 30% of sales; Ford Motor Company alone accounts for about 16%. Outside the US, TechTeam Global maintains help desk facilities in Belgium, Romania, and the Philippines. About a third of the company's sales come from Europe.

In 2008 TechTeam Global shed its subsidiary TechTeam A.N.E., which sold hardware, software, systems integration services, consulting, and IT infrastructure maintenance services primarily to small business customers in Belgium. The divestiture signals a move by TechTeam to focus on its core IT and BPO operations.

TechTeam Global hopes to grow both organically and via acquisitions, and it has been working to diversify its revenue base, both geographically and by customer type. To boost its European revenue, TechTeam Global in 2007 acquired SQM Sverige, a consulting, staffing, and outsourcing services firm based in Sweden. That same year, it bought NewVectors LLC, a consulting and advanced research firm belonging to Altarum Institute. A few months later, TechTeam Global bought RL Phillips Inc., a small provider of government information technology, network engineering, and information assurance services. In 2008 TechTeam Global established help desk facilities in the Philippines by acquiring Onvaio and forming an alliance with Rainmaker Asia.

Early in 2008, TechTeam Global hired Dell veteran Gary Cotshott as a replacement for president and CEO Chris Brown. A short while later, Cotshott guided TechTeam through a period of restructuring, transitioning from a regional operating base to a more global, unified operating structure.

HISTORY

Dr. William Coyro, a dentist who kept his practice through 1994, founded National TechTeam in 1979. Coyro relied on several well-placed investors to get National TechTeam started, including a former Chrysler VP and a former director of General Motors' central purchasing. Focused on support services, National TechTeam went public in 1987. It bought Royalpar (a technical staffing firm) in 1989, and in 1993 it began providing client support for WordPerfect and Corel. The company acquired technical trainer Coup in 1996 and opened a Belgium-based call center with Paratel, a European provider of computer telephony services.

Both good and bad, 1997 was an active year for National TechTeam. The company continued to grow, purchasing Drake Technologies (interactive voice response services), WebCentric Communications (Internet telephony software), and Compuflex (an SAP software consultant). But it also battled rising costs related to that growth, an SEC investigation that led to a restatement of earnings, and shareholder suits. National TechTeam formed the GE TechTeam joint venture with General Electric that year to provide call center operations for GE's warranty programs.

To focus on its corporate help desk business, National TechTeam sold its other OEM call center contracts (including contracts with Hewlett-Packard and 3Com) to GE in 1998, which in turn contributed the business to GE TechTeam. National TechTeam also bought Capricorn Capital Group (now TechTeam Capital Group), which provides the company's leasing services. Coyro handed over the CEO title to president Harry Lewis in early 1999 and resigned the chairman post the following year.

The company sold its stake in GE TechTeam (OEM call center services and equipment leasing) to joint venture partner General Electric Warranty Management in 2000. That year the company restructured TechTeam Capital Group — terminating most of its employees, and ceasing to look for new leases.

In 2001 Coyro returned to the company as CEO. The following year National TechTeam established a subsidiary in Sweden. It also changed its name to TechTeam Global.

TechTeam Global greatly expanded its help desk support services with the 2003 purchase of Digital Support Corporation (DSC), which counts numerous US government agencies as customers, for about $6.5 million. Expansion continued with the 2004 purchase of Advanced Network Engineering (A.N.E.), a Belgium-based IT services company.

Also in 2004, TechTeam Global opened a help desk facility in Romania to take advantage of labor costs lower than those in the US and Western Europe.

Founder Coyro stepped down as president and CEO of the company in 2006. IBM veteran Chris Brown was hired to replace him; however, Brown stepped down in early 2008, with Gary Cotshott named as his successor.

EXECUTIVES

Chairman, President, and CEO: Gary J. Cotshott, age 58, $699,059 total compensation
SVP, Americas: Kevin P. Burke, age 49, $338,786 total compensation
SVP and General Manager, TechTeam Asia/Latin America: Kamran Sokhanvari, age 47
SVP Vector Research Center for Enterprise Performance: Gary T. Mears
Corporate VP, CFO, and Treasurer: Margaret M. (Margo) Loebl, age 49, $139,023 total compensation
VP, General Counsel, and Secretary: Michael A. Sosin, age 49
VP Human Resources: Heidi K. Hagle
VP Client Service Delivery: Robert W. Gumber, age 60, $318,792 total compensation
VP and CIO: Armin Pressler, age 46
VP Client Service Management, Europe, Middle East, and Asia: Ernst Vogtle
VP Business Development: Bill James
CEO, Akela SRL: Lucian Butnaru
President, TechTeam Government Solutions: David A. Kriegman, age 62
Director Business Process Improvement, EMEA: Peter Keane
Director Marketing and Media Contact, Europe, Middle East adn Africa: Dimitry De Schepper
Auditors: Ernst & Young LLP

LOCATIONS

HQ: TechTeam Global, Inc.
27335 W. 11 Mile Rd., Southfield, MI 48033
Phone: 248-357-2866   **Fax:** 248-357-2570
Web: www.techteam.com

2008 Sales

	$ mil.	% of total
US	161.0	62
Europe		
Belgium	43.6	17
Other countries	55.4	21
Total	**260.0**	**100**

PRODUCTS/OPERATIONS

2008 Sales

	$ mil.	% of total
IT outsourcing services	120.2	46
Government technology services	88.6	34
IT consulting & systems integration	27.1	11
Other	24.1	9
Total	**260.0**	**100**

COMPETITORS

Aquent	Computer Sciences Corp.
Bartech	DecisionOne
Butler America	HP
Capgemini	IBM
Capita	Logica
CIBER	Sykes Enterprises
COMFORCE	Technisource

HISTORICAL FINANCIALS

Company Type: Public

Income Statement

FYE: December 31

	REVENUE ($ mil.)	NET INCOME ($ mil.)	NET PROFIT MARGIN	EMPLOYEES
12/08	260.0	3.0	1.2%	2,781
12/07	222.2	6.3	2.8%	2,951
12/06	167.4	1.8	1.1%	2,337
12/05	166.5	5.5	3.3%	2,172
12/04	128.0	4.7	3.7%	1,738
Annual Growth	19.4%	(10.6%)	—	12.5%

2008 Year-End Financials

Debt ratio: 27.6%
Return on equity: 3.1%
Cash ($ mil.): 16.9
Current ratio: 2.10
Long-term debt ($ mil.): 27.2
No. of shares (mil.): 11.1

Dividends
Yield: 0.0%
Payout: —
Market value ($ mil.): 65.1
R&D as % of sales: —
Advertising as % of sales: —

Stock History

NASDAQ (GM): TEAM

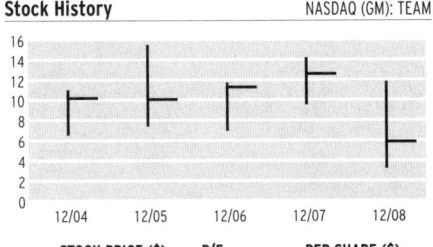

	STOCK PRICE ($) FY Close	P/E High/Low		PER SHARE ($) Earnings	Dividends	Book Value
12/08	5.85	42	12	0.28	0.00	8.87
12/07	12.60	23	16	0.60	0.00	8.72
12/06	11.25	64	39	0.18	0.00	7.75
12/05	10.05	28	14	0.54	0.00	7.03
12/04	10.17	22	14	0.49	0.00	5.99
Annual Growth	(12.9%)	—	—	(13.1%)	—	10.3%

Techwell, Inc.

Techwell designs decoder chips that convert analog video into digital form, and processors used to display digital video, HDTV, and PC data. Mixed-signal semiconductors, which blend analog and digital elements, are in high demand now that popular consumer products, such as cell phones and Apple's iPod, are capable of playing videos downloaded from the Web or from providers of wireless services. Techwell's OEM customers include Fujitsu, LG Electronics, Samsung Electronics, and Toshiba. Almost all of Techwell's sales are to customers in the Asia/Pacific region.

Techwell's chips are finding their way not only into portable consumer electronics products,

such as camcorders and DVD players, but also into automotive display systems and surveillance cameras. Other applications for the company's mixed-signal integrated circuits include advanced TV sets, DVD recorders, set-top boxes, video game consoles, and VCRs.

As a fabless semiconductor company, Techwell relies on contractors to produce its devices. Taiwan Semiconductor Manufacturing Co. (TSMC), the world's largest silicon foundry, makes Techwell's chips, which are then assembled, packaged, and tested by Advanced Semiconductor Engineering (ASE), one of the biggest contractors in that field.

Techwell counted Credit Suisse, Genesis Microchip, Mitsubishi, Panasonic, and Sanyo among its investors. The company raised $43 million in private equity funding.

Technology Crossover Ventures owns about 19% of Techwell. President and CEO Hiro Kozato holds nearly 7% of the company, including stock options.

EXECUTIVES

President, CEO, and Director: Fumihiro (Hiro) Kozato, age 50, $675,214 total compensation
CTO: Feng Kuo, age 52, $700,968 total compensation
VP Finance and Administration and CFO: Mark Voll, age 55, $746,768 total compensation
VP Sales and Marketing: Dong Wook (David) Nam, age 42, $499,571 total compensation
VP Operations: Joe Kamei, age 53
VP Business Development: Tom Krause, age 32
Auditors: Deloitte & Touche LLP

LOCATIONS

HQ: Techwell, Inc.
408 E. Plumeria Dr., San Jose, CA 95134
Phone: 408-435-3888   **Fax:** 408-435-0588
Web: www.techwellinc.com

2008 Sales

	% of total
China	37
Korea	29
Taiwan	27
Japan	5
Other	2
Total	**100**

PRODUCTS/OPERATIONS

2008 Sales

	$ mil.	% of total
Security surveillance	52.7	78
Video decoders	7.6	11
LCD displays	7.1	10
Other	0.2	1
Total	**67.6**	**100**

COMPETITORS

Cirrus Logic
Conexant Systems
Micronas Semiconductor
NVIDIA
NXP
Pixelworks
STMicroelectronics
Texas Instruments
Trident Microsystems
Zoran

HISTORICAL FINANCIALS

Company Type: Public

Income Statement

FYE: December 31

	REVENUE ($ mil.)	NET INCOME ($ mil.)	NET PROFIT MARGIN	EMPLOYEES
12/08	67.6	7.8	11.5%	165
12/07	59.9	14.7	24.5%	142
12/06	53.7	13.2	24.6%	96
12/05	36.1	4.5	12.5%	73
12/04	17.3	(1.7)	—	81
Annual Growth	40.6%	—	—	19.5%

2008 Year-End Financials

Debt ratio: —
Return on equity: 9.1%
Cash ($ mil.): 44.5
Current ratio: 16.46
Long-term debt ($ mil.): —
No. of shares (mil.): 21.7

Dividends
Yield: —
Payout: —
Market value ($ mil.): 140.8
R&D as % of sales: —
Advertising as % of sales: —

Stock History

NASDAQ (GM): TWLL

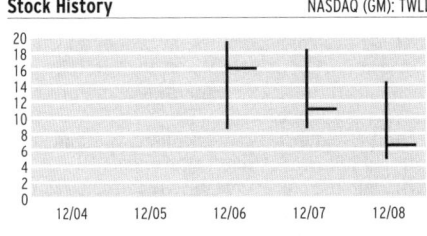

	STOCK PRICE ($) FY Close	P/E High/Low		PER SHARE ($) Earnings	Dividends	Book Value
12/08	6.50	41	14	0.35	—	4.29
12/07	11.01	27	13	0.68	—	3.60
12/06	16.07	30	14	0.64	—	2.64
Annual Growth	(36.4%)	—	—	(26.0%)	—	27.5%

Tejon Ranch

Tejon Ranch took stock and sold the herd. Historically one of the biggest cattle ranches in the US, Tejon Ranch decided its future is in real estate and in 2001 sold the last of its livestock operations. Although livestock accounted for 75% of revenues as recently as 2000, and farming activities still account for about half of its business, the company's approximately 270,000 acres are now the site of residential and commercial development. In 2008 Tejon Ranch struck a deal with major environmental groups to conserve about 90% of the vast chunk of open land, or about 240,000 acres, some 60 miles north of Los Angeles. The company's directors, through equity investment firms, control around 46% of Tejon Ranch.

The landmark conservation plan calls for the permanent conservation of a large portion of the land — and in exchange, the environmental organizations agree not to oppose the company's development plans for approximately 30,000 acres on the western edge of the ranch, which is served by three major highways.

Owner of California's largest privately owned contiguous chunks of land, Tejon Ranch is developing a planned community called Centennial (including a proposed 23,000 homes) and commercial real estate along a 16-mile stretch

of Interstate 5 in Los Angeles County. The Tejon Industrial Complex - West is home to gas stations, restaurants, and distribution warehouses; begun with 350 acres, the park is spreading over an additional 1,100 acres. The West section of the complex sold land to In-N-Out Burger for a restaurant and to Petro Travel Plaza for a convenience stores and gas stations. Tejon Ranch has a 50-50 joint venture with the Rockefeller Group to develop a foreign trade zone within the complex. It also has a joint venture agreement with DMB Associates to develop Tejon Mountain Village, a 23,000-acre residential/resort community.

In addition to the Centennial residential community, the firm is developing Tejon Mountain Village (a golf and spa resort with hundreds of luxury homes planned) and Tejon Industrial Complex-East, located across the freeway from its Tejon Industrial Complex-West counterpart.

The firm's San Joaquin Valley farm operations include the growing of wheat, wine grapes, almonds, pistachios, and walnuts. It also leases land for oil, gas, and mineral production. The movie industry uses the land for filming, and portions are leased for exploration and production of oil and gas.

In 2007 natural-gas company Calpine accounted for 11% of Tejon's revenue.

In 2008 the company launched a men's clothing line, The Tejon Ranch Clothing Collection available at H. Walker's Clothing Co.

HISTORY

In 1843 the Mexican government issued grants for the three ranches and other lands that now make up Tejon Ranch. In 1854 the US government set up an Army post called Fort Tejon (abandoned, 1864). Edward Beale, a government surveyor, acquired Rancho La Liebre in 1855. By 1866 Beale owned all the Tejon Ranch property. A partnership headed by Harry Chandler of the *Los Angeles Times* (then a part of Times Mirror) and land developer Moses Sherman acquired the ranch from Beale's son Truxton in 1912. Tejon Ranch Co. was incorporated in 1936.

Tejon Ranch went public in 1973. During the 1980s, despite a severe drought and a slumping farm economy, the firm resisted the pressure to convert its land to master-planned communities.

It has not, however, resisted publicity. In 1991 Tejon Ranch allowed environmental artist Christo to unfurl 1,700 yellow umbrellas on the ranch for nearly three weeks. It also promotes Fort Tejon as a site of Civil War reenactments. Robert Stine jumped into the saddle as president and CEO in 1996.

Ranch investor Times Mirror sold its 31% stake in the company in 1997 to focus on its media interests. The next year Tejon Ranch built California's largest truck stop with operator Petro Stopping Centers and started selling nonstrategic land, including a parcel to defense contractor Northrop Grumman for a radar test facility.

In 1999 Tejon Ranch started building a 350-acre industrial complex and agreed to build a 4,000-acre planned community.

As part of its commercial real estate development, in 2000 Tejon Ranch sold 80 acres to IKEA for a distribution facility. A 50-acre Petro Travel Plaza was also constructed. That year the company announced plans to sell all of its cattle operations, and use the proceeds to accelerate its real estate development plans.

In 2001 the company formed a joint venture with Dermody Properties to build a 650,000-sq.-ft. distribution building next to the IKEA warehouse. That year it sold the last of its livestock and its Texas feedlot.

Tejon Ranch firmed up plans for its residential development in 2002, entering into an agreement with homebuilders Pardee Homes and Standard Pacific to develop Centennial, an 11,700 acre master planned community complete with 23,000 homes, as well as retail, office, and industrial properties.

In 2004 the company sold its interest in Pacific Almond, its Arizona almond-processing plant.

EXECUTIVES

Chairman: Kent G. Snyder, age 72
President, CEO, and Director: Robert A. (Bob) Stine, age 62
SVP Real Estate: Joseph E. (Joe) Drew, age 67
VP, CFO, Treasurer, and Assistant Secretary: Allen E. Lyda, age 52
VP, General Counsel, and Secretary: Teri Bjorn, age 56
VP Government Affairs: Eileen Reynolds
VP Planning and Entitlements: E. Andrew Daymude
VP Corporate Communications: Barry Zoeller
VP and Controller: Carla Walker
VP Commercial and Industrial Marketing: Barry G. Hibbard
VP Agriculture: Dennis J. Atkinson, age 59
VP, Ranch Operations: Donald N. Geivet
Auditors: Ernst & Young LLP

LOCATIONS

HQ: Tejon Ranch Co.
    4436 Lebec Rd., Lebec, CA 93243
Phone: 661-248-3000
Web: www.tejonranch.com

Tejon Ranch is located on 270,000 contiguous acres in Kern and Los Angeles counties in Southern California.

PRODUCTS/OPERATIONS

2008 Sales

	$ mil.	% of total
Real estate	27.2	68
Farming	12.9	32
Total	**40.1**	**100**

COMPETITORS

Blue Diamond Growers
Calcot
California Coastal Communities
Castle & Cooke
C.J. Segerstrom & Sons
Corky McMillin
Dole Food
Golden West Nuts
Green Valley Pecan
Irvine Company
King Nut Companies
King Ranch
Meridian Nut Growers
ML Macadamia Orchards
Newhall Land
Paramount Farms
Rancho Mission Viejo
Sun World International
Texoma Peanut
Young Pecan

HISTORICAL FINANCIALS

Company Type: Public

Income Statement

FYE: December 31

	REVENUE ($ mil.)	NET INCOME ($ mil.)	NET PROFIT MARGIN	EMPLOYEES
12/08	40.1	4.1	10.2%	142
12/07	32.3	7.3	22.6%	132
12/06	28.4	(2.7)	—	118
12/05	26.4	1.5	5.7%	117
12/04	20.9	0.4	1.9%	104
Annual Growth	17.7%	78.9%	—	8.1%

2008 Year-End Financials

Debt ratio: 0.2%
Return on equity: 2.4%
Cash ($ mil.): 3.0
Current ratio: 10.11
Long-term debt ($ mil.): 0.4
No. of shares (mil.): 17.0
Dividends
  Yield: 0.0%
  Payout: —
Market value ($ mil.): 421.0
R&D as % of sales: —
Advertising as % of sales: —

Stock History

NYSE: TRC

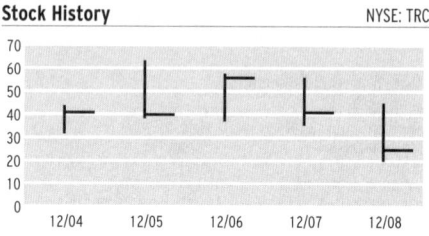

	STOCK PRICE ($) FY Close	P/E High/Low	Earnings	Dividends	Book Value
12/08	24.74	193 89	0.23	0.00	10.18
12/07	40.85	132 85	0.42	0.00	9.70
12/06	55.84	— —	(0.16)	0.00	8.76
12/05	39.92	697 431	0.09	0.00	8.16
12/04	40.80	1,440 1,071	0.03	0.00	7.76
Annual Growth	(11.8%)	— —	66.4%	—	7.0%

Tel-Instrument Electronics

Before airplanes go off into the wild blue yonder, attention must be paid to their avionics. Tel-Instrument Electronics manufactures avionics test equipment for the US Army, the US Navy, and other military and commercial customers. Tel's instruments are used to test navigation and communications equipment installed in aircraft, both on the flight line (known as ramp testers) and in the maintenance shop (bench testers). The US government and military avionics customers (such as Boeing) account for more than two-thirds of sales.

The company is seeking to diversify its product lines with more acquisitions and alliances with other aerospace manufacturers.

Distributors are responsible for about one-third of sales.

Tel-Instrument delved into shipboard and underwater instruments with its acquisition of Innerspace Technology in early 2004. Due to the lack of growth in this market, and the continuing growth of the avionics market, the company

classified Innerspace as a discontinued operation in fiscal 2008 and wrote off the subsidiary's assets.

Chairman, president, and CEO Harold Fletcher owns about 26% of Tel-Instrument Electronics. Director George Leon holds nearly 15%. All directors and officers of Tel-Instrument as a group hold around 59% of the company.

EXECUTIVES

Chairman, President, and CEO: Harold K. Fletcher, age 85, $172,372 total compensation
President and Director: Jeffrey C. (Jeff) O'Hara, age 51, $175,189 total compensation
CFO: Joseph P. (Joe) Macaluso
VP Operations: Marc A. Mastrangelo, age 46, $169,404 total compensation
VP Marketing and Director: Robert J. Melnick, age 76
Secretary: Donald S. Bab
Director Engineering: Ken Filardo
Director Business Development: Chris Allen
Manager Sales Commercial Equipment: Jack Nemeth
Manager Quality: Anthony Gannon
Training, Technical, and Customer Support: Jim Miller
Auditors: BDO Seidman, LLP

LOCATIONS

HQ: Tel-Instrument Electronics Corp.
728 Garden St., Carlstadt, NJ 07072
Phone: 201-933-1600   **Fax:** 201-933-7340
Web: www.telinst.com

2009 Sales

	$ mil.	% of total
US	11.1	85
Other countries	2.0	15
Total	**13.1**	**100**

PRODUCTS/OPERATIONS

2009 Sales

	$ mil.	% of total
Government avionics	11.0	84
Commercial avionics	2.1	16
Total	**13.1**	**100**

COMPETITORS

Aeroflex
L-3 Communications
RADA Electronic Industries

HISTORICAL FINANCIALS

Company Type: Public

Income Statement

FYE: March 31

	REVENUE ($ mil.)	NET INCOME ($ mil.)	NET PROFIT MARGIN	EMPLOYEES
3/09	13.1	0.2	1.5%	24
3/08	11.2	(0.6)	—	60
3/07	7.7	(0.7)	—	62
3/06	11.2	(0.4)	—	52
3/05	10.5	0.0	—	61
Annual Growth	**5.7%**	**—**	**—**	**(20.8%)**

2009 Year-End Financials

Debt ratio: —
Return on equity: 4.5%
Cash ($ mil.): 0.6
Current ratio: 2.15
Long-term debt ($ mil.): —
No. of shares (mil.): 2.6
Dividends
Yield: 0.0%
Payout: —
Market value ($ mil.): 10.8
R&D as % of sales: —
Advertising as % of sales: —

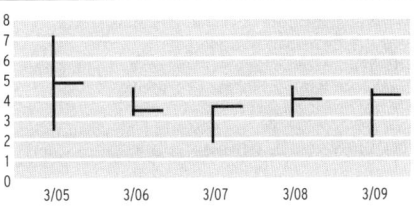

STOCK PRICE ($) FY Close	P/E High/Low	Earnings	Dividends	Book Value
3/09	4.15	55 26	0.08	0.00	1.77
3/08	3.95	— —	(0.25)	0.00	1.62
3/07	3.59	— —	(0.33)	0.00	1.75
3/06	3.40	— —	(0.18)	0.00	1.99
3/05	4.80	— —	(0.01)	0.00	2.05
Annual Growth	**(3.6%)**	**— —**	**—**	**—**	**(3.6%)**

TeleCommunication Systems

TeleCommunication Systems (TCS) enhances the mobile communication experience and keeps government agencies connected. The company develops software and provides services for wireless carriers and voice-over-IP service providers. TCS's software lets carriers deliver enhanced 9-1-1 service, text messaging, location information, and other Internet content to wireless phones. It operates network operation centers (NOCs) that provide its software on a hosted basis. The company also provides the US Department of Defense and other government agencies with communications systems integration and other IT services through its government division. TCS's revenues are roughly split between the commercial and government sectors.

TCS's commercial segment charges customers monthly usage payments for its hosted applications. It also provides software development services. The company plans to focus on messaging and location determination technologies to grow its commercial business. TCS's commercial clients include Verizon, AT&T Wireless, and Hutchison Whampoa.

The company's government sector specializes in satellite communication technology. TCS operates teleports located in Manassas, Virginia that are connected to the public switched phone network. The company resells access to satellite airtime. In addition to the DoD, TCS counts the US Department of Homeland Security, the City of Baltimore, and Northrop Grumman among its government sector clients.

TCS acquired privately held Solvern Solutions, a provider of computer security training and other technology services to the DOD, in 2009. The company said that the purchase was intended to give it a boost in the areas of secure network communications and encryption in support of its satellite communications and wireless

carrier businesses. It also bought Sidereal Solutions, a provider of technology engineering and maintenance services to the satellite industry, that year. TCS will combine Sidereal with its government segment services business. Late in 2009 the company acquired Networks In Motion (NIM), a provider of GPS navigation software for mobile devices, for $170 million. The deal improved the company's ability to offer location-based products and services.

Founder and CEO Maurice Tosé controls almost 40% of TCS's voting power.

EXECUTIVES

Chairman, President, and CEO: Maurice B. Tosé, age 52, $4,343,315 total compensation
EVP, COO, and Director: Richard A. Young, age 62, $2,429,894 total compensation
SVP, CFO, and Director: Thomas M. (Tom) Brandt Jr., age 57, $1,979,722 total compensation
SVP and CTO: Drew A. Morin, age 48, $1,838,526 total compensation
SVP Commercial Sales, Chief Marketing Officer, and Sales Lead, Commercial Sales: Timothy J. (Tim) Lorello, age 51, $1,611,902 total compensation
SVP, General Counsel, and Secretary: Bruce A. White
SVP Government Solutions: Michael D. Bristol Sr.
SVP Service Bureau Operations: Dan A. Allen
Senior Director Corporate Communications: Meredith Allen
Auditors: Ernst & Young LLP

LOCATIONS

HQ: TeleCommunication Systems, Inc.
275 West St., Ste. 400, Annapolis, MD 21401
Phone: 410-263-7616   **Fax:** 410-263-7617
Web: www.telecomsys.com

2008 Sales

	$ mil.	% of total
US	211.5	96
Other countries	8.6	4
Total	**220.1**	**100**

PRODUCTS/OPERATIONS

2008 Sales

	$ mil.	% of total
Government	118.3	54
Commercial	101.8	46
Total	**220.1**	**100**

2008 Sales

	$ mil.	% of total
Systems	118.8	54
Services	101.3	46
Total	**220.1**	**100**

COMPETITORS

CACI International
Computer Sciences Corp.
Comtech Telecommunications
Comverse Technology
Ericsson
General Dynamics
Globecomm
Intrado
Motorola, Inc.
Openwave Systems
Siemens AG
ViaSat

HISTORICAL FINANCIALS

Company Type: Public

Income Statement

FYE: December 31

	REVENUE ($ mil.)	NET INCOME ($ mil.)	NET PROFIT MARGIN	EMPLOYEES
12/08	220.1	57.6	26.2%	585
12/07	144.2	(1.3)	—	500
12/06	124.9	(21.7)	—	600
12/05	102.2	(11.5)	—	629
12/04	142.9	(18.5)	—	588
Annual Growth	11.4%	—	—	(0.1%)

2008 Year-End Financials

Debt ratio: 6.9%
Return on equity: 72.8%
Cash ($ mil.): 39.0
Current ratio: 2.32
Long-term debt ($ mil.): 7.9
No. of shares (mil.): 48.7

Dividends
  Yield: —
  Payout: —
Market value ($ mil.): 418.0
R&D as % of sales: —
Advertising as % of sales: —

Stock History

NASDAQ (GM): TSYS

	STOCK PRICE ($) FY Close	P/E High/Low	PER SHARE ($) Earnings	Dividends	Book Value
12/08	8.59	7 2	1.23	—	2.35
12/07	3.56	— —	(0.03)	—	0.90
12/06	3.10	— —	(0.54)	—	0.72
12/05	2.20	— —	(0.30)	—	1.01
12/04	3.34	— —	(0.56)	—	1.22
Annual Growth	26.6%	— —	—	—	17.7%

Tennessee Commerce Bancorp

Tennessee Commerce Bancorp is doing things a little differently in Music City USA. Founded in 2000, the financial institution is the holding company for Tennessee Commerce Bank. Concentrating on the Greater Nashville area, the bank caters to consumers and members of the service and manufacturing industries, as well as small to midsized businesses. The bank avoids high transaction volume customers such as retail businesses. Instead of creating a network of branch locations, the bank conducts business from one location, utilizes Internet banking, and provides free courier services for deposits. The bank offers traditional services, and commercial loans account for more than 60% of its lending portfolio.

EXECUTIVES

Chairman and CEO: Michael R. (Mike) Sapp, age 55, $882,379 total compensation
COO, Tennessee Commerce Bancorp and Tennessee Commerce Bank: H. Lamar Cox, age 66, $767,727 total compensation
CFO: Frank Perez, age 40, $121,313 total compensation
Chief Administrative Officer: Martin M. Zorn, age 53
Auditors: KraftCPAs PLLC

LOCATIONS

HQ: Tennessee Commerce Bancorp, Inc.
381 Mallory Station Rd., Ste. 207
Franklin, TN 37067
Phone: 615-599-2274   **Fax:** 615-599-2275
Web: www.tncommercebank.com

COMPETITORS

CFB Bancshares
Cornerstone Bancshares
First Horizon
First Pulaski National
First Security Group
Green Bankshares
Pinnacle Financial Partners
Tennessee Valley Financial Holdings

HISTORICAL FINANCIALS

Company Type: Public

Income Statement

FYE: December 31

	ASSETS ($ mil.)	NET INCOME ($ mil.)	INCOME AS % OF ASSETS	EMPLOYEES
12/08	1,218.1	7.8	0.6%	83
12/07	900.2	6.9	0.8%	64
12/06	623.5	4.7	0.8%	50
12/05	404.0	3.1	0.8%	41
12/04	245.9	1.7	0.7%	35
Annual Growth	49.2%	46.4%	—	24.1%

2008 Year-End Financials

Equity as % of assets: 7.1%
Return on assets: 0.7%
Return on equity: 10.4%
Long-term debt ($ mil.): 23.2
No. of shares (mil.): 4.7
Market value ($ mil.): 28.5

Dividends
  Yield: 0.0%
  Payout: —
Sales ($ mil.): 39.2
R&D as % of sales: —
Advertising as % of sales: —

Stock History

NASDAQ (GM): TNCC

	STOCK PRICE ($) FY Close	P/E High/Low	PER SHARE ($) Earnings	Dividends	Book Value
12/08	6.00	16 3	1.60	0.00	21.45
12/07	24.95	22 13	1.41	0.00	13.31
12/06	31.25	28 14	1.14	0.00	10.80
12/05	25.00	40 22	0.87	0.00	5.57
Annual Growth	(37.9%)	— —	31.8%	—	44.1%

Terra Nitrogen

There's a lot of dirt out there on Terra Nitrogen, which produces nitrogen fertilizer products. The company operates a plant in Oklahoma that produces ammonia and urea ammonium nitrate (UAN) solution. Farmers use the company's products to improve both the quantity and the quality of crops. Terra Nitrogen sells its products wholesale to dealers, distributors, and national farm retail chain outlets, primarily in the central and Southern Plains and Corn Belt regions of the US. Agrochemical company Terra Industries is Terra Nitrogen's general partner and owns 75% of the company.

EXECUTIVES

Chairman, President, and CEO, Terra Nitrogen GP Inc. (TNGP): Michael L. (Mike) Bennett, age 56
VP and CFO, Terra Nitrogen GP Inc. (TNGP); SVP and CFO, Terra Industries: Daniel D. (Dan) Greenwell, age 46
VP, Terra Nitrogen GP Inc. (TNGP): Joseph D. Giesler, age 50
VP and Controller, Terra Nitrogen GP Inc. (TNGP); VP and Controller, Terra Industries: Edward J. (Ed) Dillon, age 41
VP Manufacturing, Terra Nitrogen GP Inc. (TNGP): Richard S. Sanders Jr., age 51
VP, General Counsel, and Corporate Secretary, Terra Nitrogen GP Inc. (TNGP): John W. Huey, age 61
VP Investor Relations and Human Resources, Terra Nitrogen GP Inc. (TNGP): Joe A. Ewing, age 58
Manager Communications, Terra Nitrogen GP Inc. (TNGP): Kim Mathers
Auditors: Deloitte & Touche LLP

LOCATIONS

HQ: Terra Nitrogen Company, L.P.
Terra Centre, 600 4th St., Sioux City, IA 51102
Phone: 712-277-1340   **Fax:** 712-277-7386
Web: www.terraindustries.com

COMPETITORS

Agrium
CF Industries
LSB Industries
Mosaic Company
PCS Nitrogen

HISTORICAL FINANCIALS

Company Type: Public

Income Statement

FYE: December 31

	REVENUE ($ mil.)	NET INCOME ($ mil.)	NET PROFIT MARGIN	EMPLOYEES
12/08	903.0	422.4	46.8%	163
12/07	636.3	203.7	32.0%	161
12/06	425.1	45.7	10.8%	160
12/05	455.5	54.7	12.0%	164
12/04	419.6	45.0	10.7%	171
Annual Growth	21.1%	75.0%	—	(1.2%)

2008 Year-End Financials

Debt ratio: —
Return on equity: —
Cash ($ mil.): 154.7
Current ratio: 2.31
Long-term debt ($ mil.): —
No. of shares (mil.): 18.5

Dividends
  Yield: 16.0%
  Payout: 101.2%
Market value ($ mil.): 1,743.8
R&D as % of sales: —
Advertising as % of sales: —

Stock History

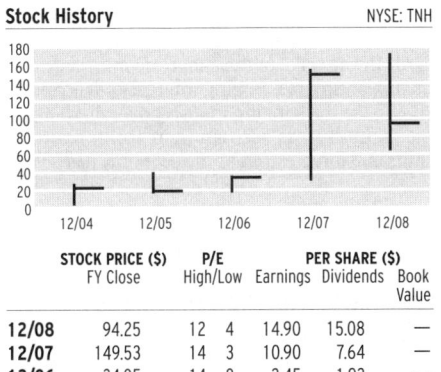

NYSE: TNH

	STOCK PRICE ($) FY Close	P/E High/Low		PER SHARE ($) Earnings	Dividends	Book Value
12/08	94.25	12	4	14.90	15.08	—
12/07	149.53	14	3	10.90	7.64	—
12/06	34.05	14	8	2.45	1.92	—
12/05	19.04	13	6	2.95	2.95	—
12/04	22.31	11	2	2.43	1.75	—
Annual Growth	43.4%	—	—	57.4%	71.3%	—

Texas Capital Bancshares

Texas Capital Bancshares is the holding company for Texas Capital Bank, which has about 10 branches in Austin, Dallas, Fort Worth, Houston, Plano, and San Antonio. Targeting high-net-worth individuals and midddle-market businesses (with a focus on such sectors as heavy construction, petrochemicals, and mining), the bank offers personal and commercial deposit accounts, real estate mortgages, business and consumer loans, Visa credit cards, equipment leasing, wealth management, and trust services. Online banking is offered through its BankDirect division.

Texas Capital Bancshares was formed in 1998 with a Texas-sized bankroll of $80 million, one of the largest ever for a community bank at that time. It believes that its Texas roots give it a competitive advantage over larger competitors that are headquartered out of state.

The company received some $75 million from the federal government as part of the Troubled Asset Relief Program (TARP) for the financial services industry, but the company arranged to repay the funds the following year.

EXECUTIVES

Chairman: James R. (Jim) Holland Jr., age 65
Chairman Emeritus: Joseph M. (Jody) Grant, age 70, $678,284 total compensation
President, CEO, and Director; CEO, Texas Capital Bank: George F. Jones Jr., age 65, $742,511 total compensation
President, COO, Chief Lending Officer, Texas Capital Bank: C. Keith Cargill, age 56, $576,102 total compensation
CFO and Director; CFO, Texas Capital Bank: Peter B. Bartholow, age 60, $607,433 total compensation
EVP and COO: James C. (Jim) White
EVP and Chief Credit Officer: John D. Hudgens
EVP: David L. Cargill
EVP: Russell Hartsfield

President, Houston Region Texas Capital Bank: Jonathan M. (Jon) Clarkson
President, Austin Region Texas Capital Bank: Kerry L. Hall
President, Fort Worth Region Texas Capital Bank: Michael D. Palmer
President, Dallas Region: Vince A. Ackerson
President, San Antonio Region Texas Capital Bank: Mark M. Johnson
President, Texas Capital Bank, Plano: Michael (Mike) Robnett
Investor Relations Contact: Myrna Vance
Controller: Julie Anderson
Media Relations: Patty Sullivan
Auditors: Ernst & Young LLP

LOCATIONS

HQ: Texas Capital Bancshares, Inc.
2100 McKinney Ave., Ste. 900, Dallas, TX 75201
Phone: 214-932-6600   **Fax:** 214-932-6604
Web: www.texascapitalbank.com

PRODUCTS/OPERATIONS

2008 Gross Revenues

	$ mil.	% of total
Interest		
Loans, including fees	231.0	85
Securities	17.7	7
Other	0.2	—
Noninterest		
Equipment rental income	6.0	2
Service charges on deposit accounts	4.7	2
Trust fees	4.7	2
Brokered loan fees	3.2	1
Other	3.9	1
Total	**271.4**	**100**

COMPETITORS

Amegy
Bank of America
BOK Financial
Comerica
Compass Bancshares
Cullen/Frost Bankers
JPMorgan Chase
Prosperity Bancshares
Wells Fargo

HISTORICAL FINANCIALS

Company Type: Public

Income Statement				FYE: December 31
	ASSETS ($ mil.)	NET INCOME ($ mil.)	INCOME AS % OF ASSETS	EMPLOYEES
12/08	5,140.2	24.3	0.5%	547
12/07	4,287.4	29.4	0.7%	510
12/06	3,675.3	28.9	0.8%	503
12/05	3,042.2	27.2	0.9%	709
12/04	2,611.2	19.6	0.8%	510
Annual Growth	18.4%	5.5%	—	1.8%

2008 Year-End Financials

Equity as % of assets: 7.5%	Dividends
Return on assets: 0.5%	Yield: 0.0%
Return on equity: 7.1%	Payout: —
Long-term debt ($ mil.): 40.0	Sales ($ mil.): 174.2
No. of shares (mil.): 35.8	R&D as % of sales: —
Market value ($ mil.): 478.4	Advertising as % of sales: —

Stock History

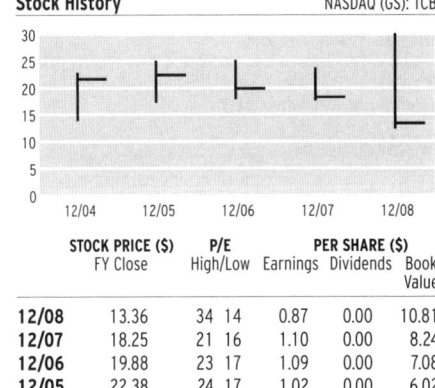

NASDAQ (GS): TCBI

	STOCK PRICE ($) FY Close	P/E High/Low		PER SHARE ($) Earnings	Dividends	Book Value
12/08	13.36	34	14	0.87	0.00	10.81
12/07	18.25	21	16	1.10	0.00	8.24
12/06	19.88	23	17	1.09	0.00	7.08
12/05	22.38	24	17	1.02	0.00	6.02
12/04	21.62	30	19	0.75	0.00	5.45
Annual Growth	(11.3%)	—	—	3.8%	—	18.7%

Texas Roadhouse

Perhaps at this roadhouse, people get rowdy for steaks. Texas Roadhouse operates and franchises more than 325 of its signature steak restaurants in more than 45 states. The Southwest-themed eateries serve a variety of hand-cut steaks, ribs, chicken, and seafood, as well as freshly baked bread and other sides — but only for dinner because most locations are closed on weekday afternoons. More than 250 Texas Roadhouse locations are company-owned, while the rest are franchised. Founder and chairman Kent Taylor has more than 55% control of the company.

The company has followed a vigorous expansion strategy that is heavy on building new corporate-owned locations. After adding more than 30 new eateries, mostly company-owned, during 2007, the company launched more than 20 new locations during 2008. The following year it introduced a new dining concept called Aspen Creek, a lodge-themed restaurant offering hamburgers, pasta dishes, and pizza.

Country singer Willie Nelson, who is a partner in two restaurants located in Austin, Texas, serves as a celebrity spokesperson for Texas Roadhouse. The chain sponsors the popular artist's concert tours and each restaurant features "Willie's Corner" decorated with memorabilia.

Taylor opened the first Texas Roadhouse in 1993. A veteran of the restaurant business, he previously served with such chains as Bennigan's (formerly owned by Metromedia Company), Hooters, and KFC.

EXECUTIVES

Chairman: W. Kent Taylor, age 54, $408,000 total compensation
President, CEO, and Director: G. J. Hart, age 52, $1,498,564 total compensation
COO: Steven L. Ortiz, age 52, $1,095,153 total compensation
CFO: Scott M. Colosi, age 45, $734,452 total compensation
General Counsel and Corporate Secretary: Sheila C. Brown, age 57, $487,718 total compensation
VP Business Development: Juli Hart
Auditors: KPMG LLP

LOCATIONS

HQ: Texas Roadhouse, Inc.
6040 Dutchmans Ln., Ste. 200, Louisville, KY 40205
Phone: 502-426-9984   **Fax:** 502-426-3274
Web: www.texasroadhouse.com

2008 Locations

	No.
Texas	48
Ohio	20
Indiana	19
Pennsylvania	19
Colorado	13
North Carolina	13
Tennessee	13
Michigan	11
Arizona	10
Wisconsin	10
Florida	9
Georgia	9
Kentucky	9
Illinois	8
Massachusetts	7
Virginia	7
Iowa	6
Louisiana	6
Maryland	6
Missouri	6
South Carolina	6
New York	5
Oklahoma	5
Utah	5
Alabama	4
California	3
Delaware	3
Idaho	3
Kansas	3
Nebraska	3
North Dakota	3
West Virginia	3
Other states	19
Total	**314**

2008 Locations

	No.
Company-owned	245
Franchised	69
Total	**314**

PRODUCTS/OPERATIONS

2008 Sales

	$ mil.	% of total
Restaurants	871.6	99
Franchising	8.9	1
Total	**880.5**	**100**

COMPETITORS

Applebee's
Bill Miller Bar-B-Q
Brinker
Carino's Italian Grill
Carlson Restaurants
Cheesecake Factory
Cracker Barrel
Darden
Hooters
Houlihan's
Ignite Restaurant Group
Landry's
Logan's Roadhouse
Lone Star Steakhouse
OSI Restaurant Partners
P.F. Chang's
Romacorp
Ruby Tuesday

HISTORICAL FINANCIALS

Company Type: Public

Income Statement

FYE: Last Tuesday in December

	REVENUE ($ mil.)	NET INCOME ($ mil.)	NET PROFIT MARGIN	EMPLOYEES
12/08	880.5	38.2	4.3%	28,000
12/07	735.1	39.3	5.3%	23,000
12/06	597.1	34.0	5.7%	19,000
12/05	448.3	30.3	6.8%	14,900
12/04	363.0	21.7	6.0%	12,500
Annual Growth	**24.8%**	**15.2%**	**—**	**22.3%**

2008 Year-End Financials

Debt ratio: 36.8%
Return on equity: 10.5%
Cash ($ mil.): 5.3
Current ratio: 0.35
Long-term debt ($ mil.): 132.5
No. of shares (mil.): 70.3
Dividends
  Yield: 0.0%
  Payout: —
Market value ($ mil.): 544.8
R&D as % of sales: —
Advertising as % of sales: —

Stock History

NASDAQ (GS): TXRH

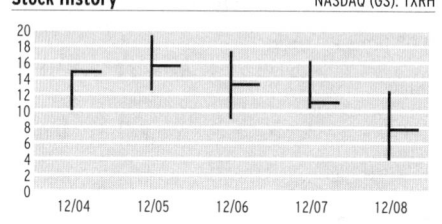

	STOCK PRICE ($) FY Close	P/E High/Low		PER SHARE ($) Earnings	Dividends	Book Value
12/08	7.75	24	8	0.52	0.00	5.12
12/07	11.06	31	21	0.51	0.00	5.23
12/06	13.26	39	21	0.44	0.00	4.54
12/05	15.55	46	30	0.42	0.00	3.29
12/04	14.77	56	38	0.26	0.00	2.46
Annual Growth	**(14.9%)**	**—**	**—**	**18.9%**	**—**	**20.1%**

TFS Financial

TFS Financial is the holding company for Third Federal Savings and Loan, a thrift with some 45 branches and loan production offices in northeastern Ohio and in southern Florida. The bank offers such deposit products as checking, savings, and retirement accounts and CDs. It uses funds from deposits to originate a variety of consumer loans, primarily residential mortgages. Third Federal also offers IRAs, annuities, and mutual funds, as well as retirement and college savings plans. TFS subsidiary Third Capital owns stakes in commercial real estate, private equity funds, and similar investments. Mutual holding company Third Federal Savings and Loan Association of Cleveland owns some three-fourths of TFS Financial.

Third Federal Savings operates in battered housing-market areas in Florida and Ohio. It targets low-income buyers seeking to buy affordable housing, particularly through its Home Today loan program. The bank doesn't categorize the Home Today loans as subprime mortgages, but nevertheless tightened its underwriting standards in the wake of the subprime mortgage crisis. It also stopped issuing interest-only loans in 2009. Like the banking industry overall, though, the company has seen an increase in loan defaults and foreclosures as the economy has fallen.

EXECUTIVES

Chairman, President, and CEO: Marc A. Stefanski, age 55, $4,359,053 total compensation
COO and Chief Accounting Officer: Paul J. Huml, age 50
CFO: David S. (Dave) Huffman, age 57, $765,220 total compensation
CIO: Ralph M. Betters, age 58, $853,534 total compensation
Director; Director Human Resources, Public Relations, Training, Security, and Administrative Services: Marianne V. Piterans, age 55, $798,966 total compensation
Secretary and Director: Bernard S. Kobak, age 81
Director Public Relations: Monica M. Martines
COO, Third Federal Savings and Loan: John P. Ringenbach, age 60, $1,150,926 total compensation
Auditors: Deloitte & Touche LLP

LOCATIONS

HQ: TFS Financial Corporation
7007 Broadway Ave., Cleveland, OH 44105
Phone: 216-441-6000   **Fax:** 216-441-7030
Web: www.thirdfederal.com

PRODUCTS/OPERATIONS

2009 Gross Revenues

	$ mil.	% of total
Interest		
Loans, including fees	455.9	82
Investment securities	29.4	5
Other	1.9	1
Noninterest		
Net gain on sale of loans	32.8	6
Fees & service charges	21.6	4
Bank-owned life insurance contracts	6.6	1
Other	7.2	1
Adjustments	(0.8)	—
Total	**554.6**	**100**

COMPETITORS

Bank of America
Citigroup
Fifth Third
FirstMerit
Huntington Bancshares
JPMorgan Chase
KeyCorp
PNC Financial
RBC Bank
U.S. Bancorp
Wells Fargo

HISTORICAL FINANCIALS

Company Type: Public

Income Statement

FYE: September 30

	ASSETS ($ mil.)	NET INCOME ($ mil.)	INCOME AS % OF ASSETS	EMPLOYEES
9/09	10,598.8	14.4	0.1%	971
9/08	10,786.5	54.5	0.5%	—
9/07	10,278.0	25.6	0.2%	—
9/06	8,595.6	43.5	0.5%	931
9/05	8,913.8	64.5	0.7%	—
Annual Growth	**4.4%**	**(31.3%)**	**—**	**1.4%**

2009 Year-End Financials

Equity as % of assets: 16.5%	Dividends
Return on assets: 0.1%	Yield: 1.6%
Return on equity: 0.8%	Payout: 380.0%
Long-term debt ($ mil.): 70.2	Sales ($ mil.): 297.5
No. of shares (mil.): 308.4	R&D as % of sales: —
Market value ($ mil.): 3,669.7	Advertising as % of sales: —

Stock History

NASDAQ (GS): TFSL

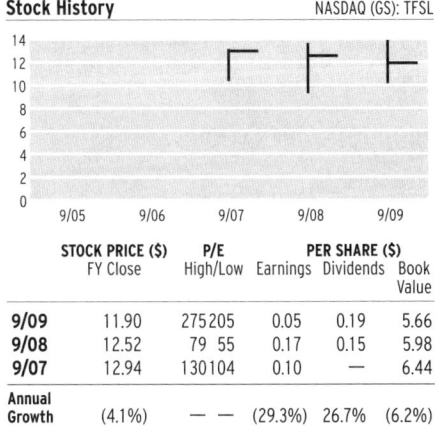

9/05 9/06 9/07 9/08 9/09

	STOCK PRICE ($) FY Close	P/E High/Low	PER SHARE ($) Earnings	PER SHARE ($) Dividends	PER SHARE ($) Book Value
9/09	11.90	275 205	0.05	0.19	5.66
9/08	12.52	79 55	0.17	0.15	5.98
9/07	12.94	130 104	0.10	—	6.44
Annual Growth	(4.1%)	— —	(29.3%)	26.7%	(6.2%)

TheStreet.com, Inc.

If you're looking for investment advice, you might want to check the word on the street. TheStreet.com offers financial news, tools, and analysis, as well as community features such as online chats and message boards, on its advertising supported flagship Web site TheStreet.com and on RealMoney.com, its subscription-based site which also features commentary from market experts. Its MainStreet.com site features content related to personal finance topics. Sales come from advertising and subscriber fees. The company also distributes content through syndication deals with partners such as MSN, AOL, Google, and Yahoo!, and provides equity research and brokerage services to institutional clients.

The company launched a site redesign in 2008, using proceeds from a $55 million cash infusion made by Technology Crossover Ventures in 2007. Also in 2008 in order to cut costs it closed its San Francisco bureau, reduced its headcount by 11%, eliminated 2008 bonuses, and deferred salary increases for 2009. In addition, the company decided to separate the roles of chairman and chief executive; it named Cramer chairman, allowing Thomas J. Clarke Jr., who previously held both positions, to focus more on the CEO job during the economic downturn. However, Clarke failed to boost the company's business, and he left TheStreet.com in 2009 after little more than nine years on the job. As a result of the dismal economy, more layoffs followed, and in 2009 the company cut its work force by 6%.

In addition to its RealMoney site, the company operates several other subscription products for targeted segments of the investing public. These include subscription e-mail newsletters such as *Action Alerts PLUS* (insight on action oriented investment ideas) and *TheStreet.com Top Stocks* (stock charting analysis and trading education). TheStreet.com Ratings offering provides independent ratings and evaluations of stocks, mutual funds, exchange traded funds, and financial institutions such as insurers, health care providers, and banks. Its *TheStreet.com TV* is a free online video network that provides business news and short form feature programs, while its *TheStreet.com Mobile* product offers content to Blackberry users.

TheStreet.com was co-founded by outspoken financial pundit and former hedge-fund manager James Cramer, who still owns more than 10% of the company. He is also the host of the stock market commentary program *Mad Money* that airs on the CNBC cable network. Co-founder Martin Peretz, a former editor-in-chief at *The New Republic*, owns more than 5%.

HISTORY

The charismatic James Cramer has worn more than a few hats (market commentator on *Good Morning America* and contributor to *Worth*, among others), a setup that has sparked questions about potential for conflicts of interest as he juggled journalist/investor roles. While writing for Dow Jones' *SmartMoney* magazine, he was inspired to create TheStreet.com. He took his vision for a financial Web site that provided witty, well-written content on a subscription basis to executives at Dow Jones. They liked the idea, but didn't want to give him a stake in the company, so Cramer pitched it to Martin Peretz, editor in chief and chairman of *The New Republic*, who had helped set Cramer up in the hedge-fund business.

The pair launched TheStreet.com in 1996; the fledgling company attracted advertisers such as American Express, IBM, and MCI. The following year it struck an industry coup by signing with ABC to provide financial news for the broadcaster's new Web site. At the close of 1997, *Barron's* included TheStreet.com on its list of top 10 investment Web sites.

LEXIS-NEXIS veteran Kevin English was named president and CEO of the company in late 1998; he added the chairman title in early 1999. Their relationship growing increasingly acrimonious, Cramer and Peretz gave up running day-to-day operations (they remained directors, with Cramer an active contributor to the site).

The company went public in May 1999. English later resigned as chairman and CEO; board member Fred Wilson took the chairman title, while former president and COO Thomas Clarke was named CEO. TheStreet.com also bought public offering information service ipoPros.com and branched into television with the debut of weekly investing program *TheStreet.com* on the FOX News Channel.

During 2000 the company signed a partnership agreement with News Digital Media (a unit of News Corp.) to expand news coverage and offer sports scores. Its partnership with FOX News went sour that year (FOX objected to Cramer's touting of TheStreet.com's stock on the air), leading to the end of *TheStreet.com* program and a breach of contract lawsuit. (The parties later settled the suit: TheStreet.com donated $10,000 to charity in FOX's name and agreed not to produce another television program until mid-2001.)

With a difficult market for subscription-based content, TheStreet.com recast its flagship site as a free, ad-supported venture and launched RealMoney.com for its subscription-only content. It also inked content deals with online financial network ON24 and book publisher Doubleday. In late 2000 the company acquired SmartPortfolio.com, an e-mail financial newsletter business. However, online ad revenue failed to stem the tide of losses and TheStreet.com was forced to lay off about 20% of its staff.

In 2001 editor-in-chief Dave Kansas, who had been with TheStreet.com since its beginning, resigned. He was replaced by *SmartMoney* editor David Morrow. Also that year, CEO Clarke added chair to his title.

The following year COO James Lonergan was also named president. Also in 2002 TheStreet.com established a subsidiary, Independent Research Group (IRG Research), a proprietary equity research firm and broker-dealer for institutional clients. The company discontinued IRG in 2005.

In 2006 the company acquired Weiss Ratings, and subsequently rebranded it TheStreet.com Ratings. Also that year it launched online video network *TheStreet.com TV*.

In 2007 TheStreet.com purchased Corsis Technology Services, a provider of software and services for advertisers, marketers, and content publishers. Also that year the company acquired Stockpickr.com and Bankers Financial Products Corp. (the owner of BankingMyWay.com and Rate-Watch.com).

Cramer was named chairman in 2008. Clarke left the company in 2009.

EXECUTIVES

Chairman, Markets Commentator, and Advisor to the CEO: James J. (Jim) Cramer, age 54
CEO and Director: Daryl Otte, age 47
EVP Business and Legal Affairs, General Counsel, and Secretary: Gregory Barton, age 47
SVP Advertising Sales: Thomas P. (Tom) O'Regan
SVP Operations: Kurt Tietjen
VP Insurance and Bank Ratings, TheStreet.com Ratings: Melissa Gannon
Chief Accounting Officer: Richard (Rich) Broitman, age 56
Director Research, TheStreet.com Ratings: Donald Lucek
Managing Editor: Michelle Carini
Managing Editor: Michael Gannon
Managing Editor: William Hennelly
Editor: Glenn Hall
General Manager, MainStreet.com: Harleen Kahlon
General Manager, Multimedia: Bill McCandless
Bank Analyst: Philip van Doorn
Investor Relations: Rebecca Updegraph
Auditors: Marcum & Kliegman LLP

LOCATIONS

HQ: TheStreet.com, Inc.
14 Wall St., 15th Fl., New York, NY 10005
Phone: 212-321-5000   **Fax:** 212-321-5015
Web: www.thestreet.com

PRODUCTS/OPERATIONS

2008 Sales

	$ mil.	% of total
Paid services	41.2	57
Marketing services	30.7	43
Total	**71.9**	**100**

Selected Web Site Features

Basic investing information
Commentary
Financial news
Financial tools
Information on tech stocks
International news
Message boards
Online chats
Online video network (*TheStreet.com TV*)
Personal finance content
Portfolio tracker
Ratings (TheStreet.com Ratings)
Stock quotes

HISTORICAL FINANCIALS

Company Type: Public

Income Statement — FYE: December 31

	REVENUE ($ mil.)	NET INCOME ($ mil.)	NET PROFIT MARGIN	EMPLOYEES
12/08	71.9	1.3	1.8%	310
12/07	65.4	31.1	47.6%	349
12/06	50.9	12.9	25.3%	181
12/05	33.7	0.2	0.6%	128
12/04	35.2	(2.2)	—	168
Annual Growth	19.5%	—	—	16.6%

2008 Year-End Financials

Debt ratio: —
Return on equity: 0.9%
Cash ($ mil.): 72.4
Current ratio: 4.72
Long-term debt ($ mil.): —
No. of shares (mil.): 30.6
Dividends
Yield: 3.4%
Payout: 333.3%
Market value ($ mil.): 88.8
R&D as % of sales: —
Advertising as % of sales: —

Stock History

NASDAQ (GM): TSCM

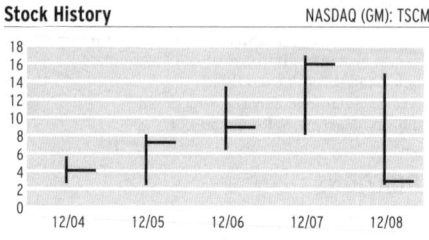

	STOCK PRICE ($) FY Close	P/E High/Low	PER SHARE ($) Earnings	Dividends	Book Value
12/08	2.90	492 89	0.03	0.10	5.00
12/07	15.92	17 8	0.99	0.10	4.98
12/06	8.90	28 14	0.47	0.10	1.44
12/05	7.21	793 259	0.01	—	0.90
12/04	4.08	— —	(0.09)	—	0.83
Annual Growth	(8.2%)	— —	—	0.0%	56.7%

Thoratec Corporation

Suffering from a broken heart? Thoratec's there for the rebound. The company makes ventricular assist devices (VAD) for patients suffering late-stage heart failure, including those awaiting a heart transplant. Thoratec offers external and implantable products that provide circulatory support for both acute and long-term needs. The company's International Technidyne Corporation (ITC) subsidiary sells blood coagulation diagnostic equipment and skin incision devices used for drawing blood. Thoratec also sells Vectra, a graft used in renal hemodialysis. The company works closely with hospitals and cardiac surgery centers primarily in the US and Europe.

Treatments for late-stage heart failure are limited, with a heart transplant typically serving as the only long-term option. While Thoratec's VAD products help many manage their heart disease while awaiting a transplant (known as bridge-to-transplantation), its HeartMate XVE is the only VAD with FDA approval as a permanent treatment (other than medication) for patients who do not qualify for transplantation.

Its HeartMate II device (a smaller, more advanced version of the original HeartMate) was approved for sale in the US in 2008; it was previously approved in Europe. The HeartMate II, the first continuous flow device approved for bridge-to-transplantation applications in the US, is finding success in the cardiac device market, but competitors with similar products in final development stages may bump Thoratec's advantage in coming years. Thoratec has already started designing a HeartMate III device.

The company is also investigating ways to reverse heart failure, particularly in patients diagnosed with acute cardiac disorders. Thoratec's devices are currently used by patients who have experienced acute cardiac failure after heart surgery, and Thoratec expects to grow its VAD use in this patient population.

As part of its plan to offer more alternatives to heart failure patients, in early 2009 the company announced it would pay $282 million for implantable heart pump manufacturer Heart Ware. However, the FTC challenged the deal, citing concerns that it would reduce competition for left ventricle devices in the US, and the two companies cancelled the merger plan several months later.

EXECUTIVES

Chairman: Neil F. Dimick, age 59
President, CEO, and Director:
Gerhard F. (Gary) Burbach, age 46,
$3,121,256 total compensation
EVP and CFO: David V. Smith, age 50,
$1,703,469 total compensation
SVP and General Counsel: David A. Lehman, age 48,
$966,867 total compensation
VP Human Resources: Glen Sunnergren
VP Reimbursement: Robin R. Bostic
VP Marketing: Douglas M. Petty
VP Business Development: Jon R. Shear
VP Technology and Product Development:
Laxmi N. Peri
VP Research and Scientific Affairs: David J. Farrar
VP Sales: Steve Brandt
VP Regulatory Affairs and Quality Assurance:
Donald A. Middlebrook
President, International Technidyne Corporation (ITC):
Lawrence Cohen, age 59, $725,434 total compensation
Auditors: Deloitte & Touche LLP

LOCATIONS

HQ: Thoratec Corporation
6035 Stoneridge Dr., Pleasanton, CA 94588
Phone: 925-847-8600   **Fax:** 925-847-8571
Web: www.thoratec.com

2008 Sales

	$ mil.	% of total
US	232.6	74
Other countries	81.0	26
Total	**313.6**	**100**

PRODUCTS/OPERATIONS

2008 Sales

	$ mil.	% of total
Cardiovascular products	215.0	69
International Technidyne	98.6	31
Total	**313.6**	**100**

Selected Products

Cardiovascular
  HeartMate Left Ventricular Assist System (Heartmate XVE)
  HeartMate II Left Ventricular Assist System (Heartmate II)
  Thoratec Implantable Ventricular Assist Device (IVAD) System
  Thoratec Paracorporeal Ventricular Assist Device (PVAD)
  Thoratec Ventricular Assist Device (VAD) System
  Vectra Vascular Access Graft (VAG)
ITC
  AVOXimeter Whole Blood Co-Oximeter and Oximeter
  HEMOCHRON Whole Blood Coagulation Systems
  Hgb Pro Professional Hemoglobin Testing System
  IRMA TRUpoint Blood Analysis System
  ProTime Microcoagulation System
  Surgicutt Bleeding Time Device
  Tenderfoot Heel Incision Device
  Tenderlett Finger Incision Device

COMPETITORS

Abbott Labs
ABIOMED
AdvanSource
Bard
Becton, Dickinson
Boston Scientific
HeartWare
Instrumentation Laboratory Company
Medtronic
Radiometer Medical
Roche Diagnostics
St. Jude Medical
W.L. Gore
World Heart

HISTORICAL FINANCIALS

Company Type: Public

Income Statement — FYE: Saturday nearest December 31

	REVENUE ($ mil.)	NET INCOME ($ mil.)	NET PROFIT MARGIN	EMPLOYEES
12/08	313.6	22.5	7.2%	1,209
12/07	234.8	3.2	1.4%	1,164
12/06	214.1	4.0	1.9%	934
12/05	201.7	13.2	6.5%	963
12/04	172.3	3.6	2.1%	914
Annual Growth	16.2%	58.1%	—	7.2%

2008 Year-End Financials

Debt ratio: 31.6%
Return on equity: 5.3%
Cash ($ mil.): 107.1
Current ratio: 7.85
Long-term debt ($ mil.): 143.8
No. of shares (mil.): 56.9
Dividends
Yield: 0.0%
Payout: —
Market value ($ mil.): 1,847.7
R&D as % of sales: —
Advertising as % of sales: —

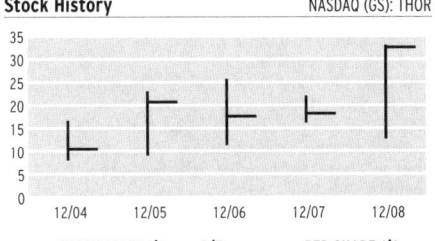

	STOCK PRICE ($) FY Close	P/E High/Low	PER SHARE ($) Earnings	Dividends	Book Value
12/08	32.49	84 33	0.39	0.00	8.00
12/07	18.19	362 274	0.06	0.00	7.00
12/06	17.58	363 165	0.07	0.00	6.42
12/05	20.69	87 36	0.26	0.00	6.12
12/04	10.42	234 118	0.07	0.00	5.14
Annual Growth	32.9%	— —	53.6%	—	11.7%

TIBCO Software

TIBCO Software can help whip your business processes into tip-top shape. The company's business integration software enables customers to integrate, manage, and monitor enterprise applications and information delivery. TIBCO's software includes applications for coordinating business processes and workflows, securely exchanging information with trading partners, creating and maintaining XML-based documents, and managing distributed systems. Customers come from industries including energy, manufacturing, financial services, and health care. The company also offers consulting and support services.

TIBCO acquired business intelligence software developer Spotfire for $195 million in cash in 2007. The following year the company purchased Insightful for about $25 million, with DataSynapse its latest purchase in 2009. The deals strategically expanded TIBCO's product lines, as well as broadening its customer base and exposure to new vertical markets.

EXECUTIVES

Chairman and CEO: Vivek Y. Ranadivé, age 51, $3,484,579 total compensation
EVP and COO: Murray D. Rode, age 45, $1,019,225 total compensation
EVP and CFO: Sydney Carey, age 44
EVP Global Field Operations: Murat Sonmez, age 45, $1,126,393 total compensation
EVP Products and Technology: Thomas J. (Tom) Laffey, age 53, $884,188 total compensation
EVP, General Counsel, and Secretary: William R. (Bill) Hughes, age 49
EVP Organizational Development and Human Resources: Robert P. (Bob) Stefanski, age 45
EVP Worldwide Marketing: Ram Menon, age 43
SVP Europe, Middle East, and Africa: Fabio Pulidori
SVP Americas Field Operations: Robin Gilthorpe
Investor Relations: Matthew Langdon
Media Relations: Phillip Tree
Auditors: PricewaterhouseCoopers LLP

LOCATIONS

HQ: TIBCO Software Inc.
3303 Hillview Ave., Palo Alto, CA 94304
Phone: 650-846-1000   **Fax:** 650-846-1005
Web: www.tibco.com

2008 Sales

	$ mil.	% of total
US	302.0	47
Other countries	342.5	53
Total	**644.5**	**100**

PRODUCTS/OPERATIONS

2008 License Sales by Product Group

	% of total
SOA	56
Business optimization	32
BPM	12
Total	**100**

2008 Sales

	$ mil.	% of total
Service & maintenance	371.1	58
Licenses	273.4	42
Total	**644.5**	**100**

Selected Products Groups

Business optimization
Business process optimization (BPO)
Service-oriented architecture (SOA)

Selected Services

Maintenance and support
Professional (consulting, systems design and integration)
Training

COMPETITORS

DataSynapse
IBM
IONA Technologies
Microsoft
Oracle
Pegasystems
Progress Software
SAP
Software AG
Sun Microsystems
Vitria Technology

HISTORICAL FINANCIALS

Company Type: Public

Income Statement   FYE: November 30

	REVENUE ($ mil.)	NET INCOME ($ mil.)	NET PROFIT MARGIN	EMPLOYEES
11/08	644.5	52.4	8.1%	2,070
11/07	577.4	51.9	9.0%	1,900
11/06	517.3	72.9	14.1%	1,597
11/05	445.9	72.6	16.3%	1,505
11/04	387.2	44.9	11.6%	1,360
Annual Growth	13.6%	3.9%	—	11.1%

2008 Year-End Financials

Debt ratio: 5.7%
Return on equity: 6.6%
Cash ($ mil.): 254.4
Current ratio: 1.77
Long-term debt ($ mil.): 42.5
No. of shares (mil.): 169.5
Dividends
  Yield: —
  Payout: —
Market value ($ mil.): 820.6
R&D as % of sales: —
Advertising as % of sales: —

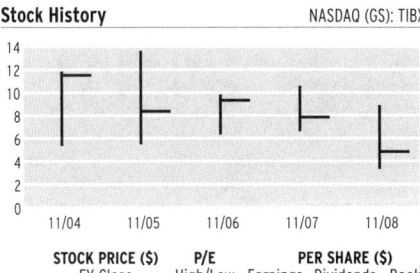

	STOCK PRICE ($) FY Close	P/E High/Low	PER SHARE ($) Earnings	Dividends	Book Value
11/08	4.84	30 12	0.29	—	4.37
11/07	7.83	42 27	0.25	—	5.05
11/06	9.31	29 20	0.33	—	5.58
11/05	8.37	42 18	0.32	—	5.15
11/04	11.50	59 27	0.20	—	4.84
Annual Growth	(19.5%)	— —	9.7%	—	(2.5%)

Titan International

A colossus of off-roads, Titan International makes off-highway steel wheels and tires for the agricultural, construction, mining, and consumer markets. It assembles wheel-tire systems for original equipment manufacturers and aftermarket distributors of tractors, cranes, combines, scrapers, all-terrain vehicles, golf carts, and utility trailers. Other operations include the manufacture and distribution of wheels, rims, and tires to the military for trucks, tanks, and personnel carriers as well as boat and trailer wheels for the consumer. Titan sells its products directly to manufactures and through dealers, distributors, and at its own distribution centers. Agricultural accounts for about 70% of sales.

Deere & Company, Titan's largest customer accounts for 17% of sales; CNH Global N.V. (another maker of agricultural equipment) represents about 11% of Titan's sales. Other customers include Caterpillar, Kubota Corporation, and AGCO Corporation.

Within the company's consumer segment, Titan has exited the OEM business for lawn and garden equipment and all terrain vehicles (ATVs), concentrating instead on the aftermarket for ATV and turf products. The shift marketed an organization-wide strategy to begin focusing on the overall tire aftermarket, which is usually less cyclical that the OEM market.

The company acquired Goodyear's North American farm tire business, significantly growing its production capabilities. It continued to expand its tire operations in 2006 with the acquisition of Continental Tire North America's off-the-road tire operations for about $53 million.

That acquisition helped propel Titan into the giant off-the-road earthmoving market (representing nearly 30% of sales). In 2008 Titan introduced its line of giant mining tires and wheels. The huge "Big Daddy" tires (measuring some 13 feet tall and 12,500 pounds) are used in the mining industry. The startup of production was made possible by a $60 million capital expansion project at its Bryan, Ohio plant. Titan plans to continue growth in the giant tires and wheels market and explore additional acquisitions to help expand in that area.

Increased costs associated with prices for fuel, raw materials, and transportation led the company to implement price increases for its products. The first such increase came late in 2007 and was followed less than six months later with another early in 2008. As materials costs drop Titan expects its prices to follow.

In 2008 Titan International agreed to eventually buy back the UK's Titan Europe, which the company spun off in 2004. At the time of the spin-off Titan International kept a 17% stake. Now it holds about 23% of Titan Europe. The purchase of Titan Europe is part of Titan International's decision to refocus its efforts on large mining vehicle wheels — a market segment it de-emphasized at the time of the spin-off, and one for which Titan Europe has a complementary product mix.

Investment firm Jana Partners owns nearly 23% of the company.

EXECUTIVES

Chairman, President, and CEO:
Maurice M. (Morry) Taylor Jr., age 64, $1,421,719 total compensation
Vice Chairman: Erwin H. (Bill) Billig, age 83
VP Finance and Treasurer: Kent W. Hackamack, age 50, $341,028 total compensation
VP, Secretary, and General Counsel: Cheri T. Holley, age 61, $344,315 total compensation
VP Manufacturing Engineering, Titan Tire Corporation: Jeff Kramer
President, Titan Tire Corporation: Bill Campbell
CEO, Titan Europe and Director: J. Michael A. Akers, age 65
Director Human Resources: Todd Triplett
Auditors: PricewaterhouseCoopers LLP

LOCATIONS

HQ: Titan International, Inc.
2701 Spruce St., Quincy, IL 62301
Phone: 217-228-6011 **Fax:** 217-228-3166
Web: www.titan-intl.com

PRODUCTS/OPERATIONS

2008 Sales

	$ mil.	% of total
Agricultural	729.9	70
Earthmoving & construction	281.0	27
Consumer	25.8	3
Total	**1,036.7**	**100**

COMPETITORS

ArvinMeritor	Hayes Lemmerz
Bridgestone	Michelin
Carlisle Tire & Wheel	Nokian Tyres
Falken Tire	Topy
GKN	Trelleborg

HISTORICAL FINANCIALS
Company Type: Public

Income Statement
FYE: December 31

	REVENUE ($ mil.)	NET INCOME ($ mil.)	NET PROFIT MARGIN	EMPLOYEES
12/08	1,036.7	13.3	1.3%	2,900
12/07	837.0	(7.2)	—	2,700
12/06	679.5	5.1	0.8%	2,700
12/05	470.1	11.0	2.3%	1,800
12/04	510.6	11.1	2.2%	1,800
Annual Growth	**19.4%**	**4.6%**	**—**	**12.7%**

2008 Year-End Financials

Debt ratio: 71.6%	Dividends
Return on equity: 4.8%	Yield: 0.2%
Cash ($ mil.): 61.7	Payout: 5.3%
Current ratio: 2.70	Market value ($ mil.): 290.9
Long-term debt ($ mil.): 200.0	R&D as % of sales: —
No. of shares (mil.): 35.3	Advertising as % of sales: —

Stock History
NYSE: TWI

	STOCK PRICE ($) FY Close	P/E High/Low		PER SHARE ($) Earnings	Dividends	Book Value
12/08	8.25	100	7	0.38	0.02	7.92
12/07	25.01	—	—	(0.22)	0.02	7.73
12/06	16.12	80	62	0.21	0.02	5.31
12/05	13.80	30	21	0.48	0.02	4.76
12/04	12.08	26	5	0.49	0.02	3.03
Annual Growth	**(9.1%)**	**—**	**—**	**(6.2%)**	**0.0%**	**27.1%**

Titan Machinery

For getting the job done, Titan Machinery is titanic. Titan drives one of North America's largest full-service networks supplying construction and agricultural equipment. Its more than 60 dealerships sell and rent new and used machinery and attachments, sell parts, and service equipment. The company represents equipment by CNH's Case IH, New Holland Agriculture, Case Construction, and New Holland Construction. Titan offers excavators, seeders, tillers, and tractors to customers from large-scale farmers to home gardeners. Other products include earthmoving equipment and cranes, used for heavy construction and light industrial jobs, in commercial or residential building, roadwork, forestry, and mining.

Titan's full-service, multi-point dealership approach leverages customer contact and cross-selling opportunities. The company's exposure to economic cycles is reduced moreover by delivering a slate of mixed-use equipment, and recurring parts sales and services.

Titan is growing its business through acquisitions of similar equipment dealerships in predominantly rural locations. The agriculture and construction equipment retailer has bought up more than 20 rivals since 2003, and added some 55 retail operations in the process. In 2009 Titan scored Oskaloosa Implement Co. (Case IH brand equipment dealerships in Pella, and Oskaloosa, Iowa), Lickness Bros. Implement Co. (a Case IH brand dealership in Britton, South Dakota), and Winger Implement (a New Holland brand dealership in Winger, Minnesota). It also picked up nine dealerships in Montana and Wyoming through its acquisition of Western Plains Machinery Co. (Case Construction equipment) and WP Rentals.

Founder, chairman, and CEO David Meyer owns about 20% of the company.

EXECUTIVES

Chairman and CEO: David J. Meyer, age 56, $704,646 total compensation
President, CFO, and Director: Peter Christianson, age 52, $704,646 total compensation
VP Finance and Treasurer: Ted Christianson, $304,559 total compensation
Human Resources Specialist: Josh Koehnen
Auditors: Eide Bailly LLP

LOCATIONS

HQ: Titan Machinery Inc.
4876 Rocking Horse Cr., Fargo, ND 58104
Phone: 701-356-0130 **Fax:** 701-356-0139
Web: titanmachinery.com

PRODUCTS/OPERATIONS

2009 Sales

	$ mil.	% of total
Equipment	540.3	78
Parts	95.0	14
Service	44.2	6
Other	10.9	2
Total	**690.4**	**100**

COMPETITORS

AGCO
Caterpillar
Deere
RDO Equipment

HISTORICAL FINANCIALS
Company Type: Public

Income Statement
FYE: January 31

	REVENUE ($ mil.)	NET INCOME ($ mil.)	NET PROFIT MARGIN	EMPLOYEES
1/09	690.4	18.1	2.6%	1,288
1/08	433.0	5.1	1.2%	716
1/07	292.6	3.6	1.2%	555
1/06	228.5	2.7	1.2%	606
1/05	162.2	1.3	0.8%	—
Annual Growth	**43.6%**	**93.2%**	**—**	**28.6%**

2009 Year-End Financials

Debt ratio: 8.5%	Dividends
Return on equity: 14.5%	Yield: —
Cash ($ mil.): 41.0	Payout: —
Current ratio: 1.62	Market value ($ mil.): 180.4
Long-term debt ($ mil.): 14.8	R&D as % of sales: —
No. of shares (mil.): 17.8	Advertising as % of sales: —

Stock History
NASDAQ (GM): TITN

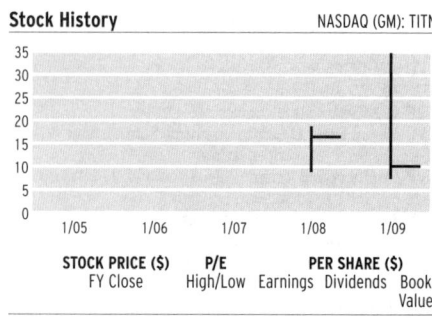

	STOCK PRICE ($) FY Close	P/E High/Low		PER SHARE ($) Earnings	Dividends	Book Value
1/09	10.15	32	7	1.08	—	9.78
1/08	16.48	28	14	0.67	—	4.28
Annual Growth	**(38.4%)**	**—**	**—**	**61.2%**	**—**	**128.3%**

Tower Group

Tower Group is hoping to rise high in the insurance business. Through subsidiaries Tower Insurance Company of New York and Tower National Insurance Company, the firm sells specialty commercial and personal property/casualty insurance to individuals and to small and mid-sized businesses, primarily in the northeastern US. Its commercial products include auto, general liability, and workers' compensation coverage in the retail, wholesale, service, real estate, and construction industries. Its personal insurance lines focus on homeowners policies for modestly priced homes. Policies are distributed through retail and wholesale agents.

Through acquisitions, Tower Group is expanding its operations outside of its core operating territories, as well as into new product segments. The company is looking to purchase small regional insurance companies to create a national presence across the US. Targeted regions for future growth include the West and Southwest.

In 2009 it acquired Hermitage Insurance, a specialty property/casualty provider in the Southeast, from Brookfield Asset Management for $130 million. That purchase expanded Tower Group's network of wholesale agents in the region. It has also agreed to purchase Specialty Underwriters' Alliance, which provides commercial policies for niche industries in the Midwest, for $107 million.

Tower Group also broadened its specialty operations in early 2009 when it acquired reinsurance provider CastlePoint Holdings (which it helped form in 2005). It already owned about 7% of CastlePoint; Tower Group purchased the remaining interest in CastlePoint in a stock and cash transaction worth $490 million. CEO Michael Lee, who owns about 8% of Tower Group, also helms the reinsurance provider. The company aims to expand its revenue sources, increase shareholder value, and cut costs through the deal. CastlePoint will continue to handle reinsurance contracts for Tower Group and other customers.

To grow its insurance business in the Northeast, the company acquired Preserver Insurance Company (and parent entity Preserver Group), which sells small commercial and personal policy lines in eight states, in 2007. In addition to increasing Tower's premium volume, the Preserver acquisition expanded its distribution network of retail agencies in the region.

The company's acquisitive streak began with the 2006 purchase of shell insurance company North American Lumber Insurance, which added licenses in 11 northeastern states and formed the foundation of the present Tower National Insurance Company (TNIC) subsidiary. The company has since organically increased the licensing of both TNIC and Tower Insurance Company of New York (TICNY) to include additional states. The company began writing excess & surplus coverage in Florida and Texas in 2007, and it expanded into California in 2008 through arrangements with wholesale and general agents.

Through its general agency subsidiary Tower Risk Management, Tower Group earns commissions on policies it sells for other providers. Tower Risk Management also provides underwriting, claims administration, and reinsurance intermediary services.

EXECUTIVES

Chairman, President, and CEO: Michael H. Lee, age 51, $1,685,234 total compensation
SVP and COO: Patrick J. Haveron, age 48, $562,568 total compensation
SVP, CFO, Treasurer, and Director: Francis M. (Frank) Colalucci, age 64, $546,824 total compensation
SVP and Chief Underwriting Officer: Gary S. Maier, age 44, $446,931 total compensation
SVP and CIO: Salvatore V. Abano, age 45
SVP Marketing and Distribution: Christian K. Pechmann, age 59
SVP and Chief Accounting Officer: Richard M. Barrow, age 55
SVP, General Counsel, and Secretary: Elliot S. Orol, age 53
SVP Operations: Laurie Ranegar, age 47
SVP: William E. Hitselberger, age 52
Managing Vice President and Chief Accounting Officer: Michael Haines
Managing VP, Northeast Field Management: Bruce Sanderson, $390,405 total compensation
VP Operations: Joe Chamberlain
VP Business Information Technology: Michael J. Mihalik
VP Human Resources: John Marcelliano
Manager Marketing and Corporate Communications: Eugenie M. McKay
Auditors: Johnson Lambert & Co Llp Fal

LOCATIONS

HQ: Tower Group, Inc.
120 Broadway, 31st. Fl., New York, NY 10271
Phone: 212-655-2000   **Fax:** 212-655-2199
Web: www.twrgrp.com

PRODUCTS/OPERATIONS

2008 Sales

	$ mil.	% of total
Net premiums earned	314.6	63
Ceding commission revenue	79.2	16
Insurance services revenue	68.1	14
Net investment income	34.6	7
Policy billing fees	2.3	—
Net realized loss on investments	(14.4)	—
Total	**484.4**	**100**

Selected Subsidiaries

CastlePoint Holdings, Ltd.
Mountain Valley Indemnity Company
North East Insurance Company
Preserver Insurance Company
Tower Insurance Company of New York
Tower National Insurance Company
Tower Risk Management Corp.

COMPETITORS

ACE Limited
AIG
Allstate
Chubb Corp
CNA Financial
Erie Insurance Group
GNY Insurance Companies
Hanover Insurance
Harleysville Group
The Hartford
Magna Carta Companies
Middlesex Mutual
Nationwide
NYCM
OneBeacon
Philadelphia Insurance Companies
Preferred Mutual
Safeco
Selective Insurance
State Farm
Travelers Companies
Utica Mutual Insurance

HISTORICAL FINANCIALS

Company Type: Public

Income Statement

FYE: December 31

	ASSETS ($ mil.)	NET INCOME ($ mil.)	INCOME AS % OF ASSETS	EMPLOYEES
12/08	1,533.0	57.5	3.8%	588
12/07	1,354.6	45.1	3.3%	549
12/06	954.1	36.8	3.9%	403
12/05	657.5	20.8	3.2%	360
12/04	494.1	9.0	1.8%	289
Annual Growth	**32.7%**	**59.0%**	**—**	**19.4%**

2008 Year-End Financials

Equity as % of assets: 21.9%
Return on assets: 4.0%
Return on equity: 17.8%
Long-term debt ($ mil.): 101.0
No. of shares (mil.): 40.5
Market value ($ mil.): 1,141.8
Dividends
  Yield: 0.5%
  Payout: 6.1%
Sales ($ mil.): 484.4
R&D as % of sales: —
Advertising as % of sales: —

Stock History

NASDAQ (GS): TWGP

	STOCK PRICE ($) FY Close	P/E High/Low		PER SHARE ($)		
				Earnings	Dividends	Book Value
12/08	28.21	13	6	2.47	0.15	8.28
12/07	33.40	19	12	1.93	0.15	7.64
12/06	31.07	20	9	1.82	0.10	5.53
12/05	21.98	23	10	1.03	0.10	3.58
12/04	12.00	12	8	1.06	0.03	3.20
Annual Growth	**23.8%**	**—**	**—**	**23.6%**	**49.5%**	**26.9%**

TradeStation Group

TradeStation is chugging along two tracks in the financial services and software markets. The company offers an electronic trading platform to provide commission-based, direct-access online brokerage services. The platform helps investors develop custom trading strategies and executes orders for equities and futures. Subsidiary TradeStation Technologies offers the TradeStation platform as either a hosted subscription-based service or a licensed software package, and it operates an online trading strategy community site. Brothers and co-founders William and Ralph Cruz collectively control just under 50% of the company.

EXECUTIVES

President, CEO, and Director: Salomon Sredni, age 41, $2,019,417 total compensation
COO: John Roberts, age 57
VP Finance, CFO, and Treasurer: David H. Fleischman, age 63, $638,173 total compensation
VP Product Development, TradeStation Technologies: T. Keith Black, age 46, $547,624 total compensation
VP Brokerage Operations; President and COO, TradeStation Securities: William P. Cahill, age 59

VP Corporate Development, General Counsel, and
Secretary; Director, TradeStation Securities,
TradeStation Technologies, and TradeStation Europe:
Marc J. Stone, age 48, $617,361 total compensation
VP Strategic Relations: Janette Perez
Director, Human Resources: Lenia Echemendia
Auditors: Ernst & Young LLP

LOCATIONS

HQ: TradeStation Group, Inc.
8050 SW 10th St., Ste. 4000, Plantation, FL 33324
Phone: 954-652-7000 **Fax:** 954-652-7300
Web: www.tradestation.com

PRODUCTS/OPERATIONS

2008 Sales

	$ mil.	% of total
Brokerage commissions & fees	129.3	81
Interest income	22.8	14
Subscription fees	7.7	5
Other	0.6	—
Total	**160.4**	**100**

COMPETITORS

Bank of America
Charles Schwab
E*TRADE Financial
Interactive Brokers
JPMorgan Chase
Merrill Lynch
TD Ameritrade
Terra Nova Minerals
UBS Financial Services

HISTORICAL FINANCIALS

Company Type: Public

Income Statement

	REVENUE ($ mil.)	NET INCOME ($ mil.)	NET PROFIT MARGIN	EMPLOYEES
				FYE: December 31
12/08	160.4	30.6	19.1%	363
12/07	151.6	35.4	23.4%	318
12/06	128.5	31.0	24.1%	302
12/05	97.0	21.1	21.8%	266
12/04	71.8	14.7	20.5%	256
Annual Growth	**22.3%**	**20.1%**	**—**	**9.1%**

2008 Year-End Financials

Debt ratio: —
Return on equity: 19.8%
Cash ($ mil.): 726.4
Current ratio: —
Long-term debt ($ mil.): —
No. of shares (mil.): 41.4
Dividends
  Yield: 0.0%
  Payout: —
Market value ($ mil.): 266.7
R&D as % of sales: —
Advertising as % of sales: —

Stock History

NASDAQ (GS): TRAD

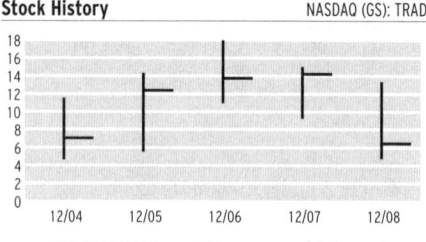

	STOCK PRICE ($) FY Close	P/E High/Low		PER SHARE ($) Earnings	Dividends	Book Value
12/08	6.45	19	7	0.70	0.00	3.99
12/07	14.21	19	12	0.78	0.00	3.48
12/06	13.75	27	17	0.67	0.00	2.86
12/05	12.38	30	12	0.48	0.00	2.00
12/04	7.03	35	14	0.33	0.00	1.19
Annual Growth	**(2.1%)**	**—**	**—**	**20.7%**	**—**	**35.2%**

Transcend Services

Transcend Services helps make sense of doctors' gibberish. The medical transcription company uses Internet-based technology to turn doctors' audio patient records into written text. Its home-based medical transcriptionists convert the physicians' recorded notes (made using either Transcend Services' proprietary BeyondTXT technology or clients' own systems) into text documents. The company is increasingly using speech recognition software to automatically convert voice to text, after which the documents are edited by transcriptionists. Transcend Services counts more than 150 hospitals, clinics, and physician group practices among its customers.

Operating in what is a highly fragmented industry, Transcend Services has grown by acquiring smaller medical transcription businesses including Transcription Relief Services and Medical Dictation Services (2009), DeVenture Global Partners, (doing business as DeVenture Health, 2008) and OTP Technologies (2007).

In addition to acquisitions, the company intends to grow organically by winning new customers, focusing its marketing efforts on community hospitals with between 100 and 600 beds. Transcend also uses partnerships with transcription software companies as a source for customer referrals. The company has started to use Asian providers to process some of its business, and it expects to increase the percentage of its work performed by offshore companies.

Chairman and CEO Larry Gerdes and director Walter Huff Jr. each own about 10% of Transcend Services.

EXECUTIVES

Chairman and CEO: Larry G. Gerdes, age 60, $272,500 total compensation
President and COO: Sue McGrogan, age 43, $622,500 total compensation
EVP Sales and Marketing: E. Leo Cooper, age 63, $578,875 total compensation
CFO: Lance T. Cornell, age 44, $483,050 total compensation
VP, Professional Service: Jeff Felshaw
VP Information Technology: Scott Robertson
Auditors: Miller Ray & Houser LLP

LOCATIONS

HQ: Transcend Services, Inc.
1 Glenlake Pkwy., Ste. 1325, Atlanta, GA 30328
Phone: 678-808-0600 **Fax:** 678-808-0601
Web: www.transcendservices.com

COMPETITORS

3M HIS
Acusis
MedQuist
Nuance
Precyse Solutions
Spheris
SPi Global Solutions
Sten-Tel

HISTORICAL FINANCIALS

Company Type: Public

Income Statement

	REVENUE ($ mil.)	NET INCOME ($ mil.)	NET PROFIT MARGIN	EMPLOYEES
				FYE: December 31
12/08	48.7	5.8	11.9%	1,172
12/07	42.5	11.5	27.1%	1,005
12/06	32.9	1.5	4.6%	877
12/05	25.8	(1.2)	—	916
12/04	15.2	0.3	2.0%	425
Annual Growth	**33.8%**	**109.7%**	**—**	**28.9%**

2008 Year-End Financials

Debt ratio: 1.1%
Return on equity: 29.5%
Cash ($ mil.): 12.3
Current ratio: 4.91
Long-term debt ($ mil.): 0.2
No. of shares (mil.): 8.7
Dividends
  Yield: —
  Payout: —
Market value ($ mil.): 87.3
R&D as % of sales: —
Advertising as % of sales: —

Stock History

NASDAQ (GM): TRCR

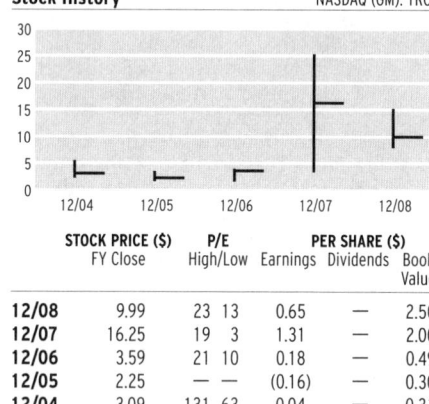

	STOCK PRICE ($) FY Close	P/E High/Low		PER SHARE ($) Earnings	Dividends	Book Value
12/08	9.99	23	13	0.65	—	2.50
12/07	16.25	19	3	1.31	—	2.00
12/06	3.59	21	10	0.18	—	0.49
12/05	2.25	—	—	(0.16)	—	0.30
12/04	3.09	131	63	0.04	—	0.31
Annual Growth	**34.1%**	**—**	**—**	**100.8%**	**—**	**68.2%**

Transcept Pharmaceuticals

Transcept Pharmaceuticals may not make a bitter pill easier to swallow, but it'll make the pill more effective once it's inside. The company's drug delivery technology enhances absorption rates of active drug agents, reducing absorption times, as well as the time it takes for the drug to take effect. The company targets medications where rapid absorption would significantly benefit treatment, including central nervous system and psychiatric disorders. Lead product candidate Intermezzo offers a quick-acting, low-dosage medication for treating insomnia that occurs in the middle of the night. Transcept contracts with third parties for manufacturing and packaging. The company merged with publicly held Novacea in 2009.

The company had changed its name from TransOral Pharmaceuticals in mid-2007. It then agreed to merge with Novacea a year later when Novacea's lead oncology drug candidate, Asentar, failed in clinical trials. After the deal closed in early 2009, former Transcept stockholders held

60% of the combined entity. Now, as a publicly traded company, Transcept plans to conduct itself as a late-state drug development company with an emphasis on psychiatric and sleep medicine.

EXECUTIVES

Chairman: G. Kirk Raab, age 73
President, CEO, and Director: Glenn A. Oclassen, age 66, $628,725 total compensation
SVP Operations and CFO: Thomas P. Soloway, age 42, $358,977 total compensation
SVP and Chief Scientific Officer: Nikhilesh N. Singh, age 50, $395,416 total compensation
VP Pharmaceutical Sciences: Nipun Davar
VP Marketing and Sales: Terrence O. Moore, age 54, $236,824 total compensation
VP, General Counsel, and Secretary: Joseph T. (Joe) Kennedy, age 41
VP Finance: Marilyn E. Wortzman, age 62, $280,698 total compensation
VP Corporate Development: Susan L. Koppy, age 47
VP Regulatory Affairs: Sharon Sakai
VP Operations: Dennie W. Dyer, age 62

LOCATIONS

HQ: Transcept Pharmaceuticals, Inc.
1003 W. Cutting Blvd., Ste. 110
Port Richmond, CA 94804
Phone: 510-215-3500   **Fax:** 510-215-3535
Web: www.transcept.com

COMPETITORS

Biovail	K-V Pharmaceutical
Elan	NexMed
Javelin Pharmaceuticals	Pain Therapeutics

HISTORICAL FINANCIALS
Company Type: Public

Income Statement
FYE: December 31

	REVENUE ($ mil.)	NET INCOME ($ mil.)	NET PROFIT MARGIN	EMPLOYEES
12/08	60.6	34.8	57.4%	33
12/07	16.7	(32.5)	—	64
12/06	0.4	(29.6)	—	59
12/05	0.1	(23.8)	—	51
12/04	1.1	(18.0)	—	51
Annual Growth	172.4%	—	—	(10.3%)

2008 Year-End Financials

Debt ratio: —	Dividends
Return on equity: 53.6%	Yield: 0.0%
Cash ($ mil.): 14.9	Payout: —
Current ratio: 31.74	Market value ($ mil.): 100.3
Long-term debt ($ mil.): —	R&D as % of sales: —
No. of shares (mil.): 13.4	Advertising as % of sales: —

Stock History
NASDAQ (GM): TSPT

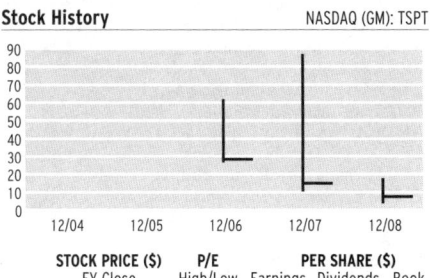

	STOCK PRICE ($) FY Close	P/E High/Low	PER SHARE ($) Earnings	Dividends	Book Value
12/08	7.50	3 1	6.72	0.00	6.28
12/07	14.90	— —	(6.75)	0.00	3.42
12/06	28.30	— —	(9.90)	0.00	4.47
Annual Growth	(48.5%)	— — —	—	—	18.5%

TransDigm Group

Operating through subsidiaries, TransDigm Group makes and distributes a wide range of components for commercial and military aircraft. The company's subsidiaries include AeroControlex (mechanical controls, pumps, valves), Adams Rite Aerospace (cockpit security products, electromechanical controls, interior latches and locks), Marathon Norco Aerospace (batteries, connectors), and Champion Aerospace (ignition systems and components). About 60% of TransDigm's sales come from aftermarket products, mostly for commercial and military aircraft from manufacturers such as Boeing, Bombardier, and Cessna. Military products are used in Northrop Grumman's Hawkeye and Sikorsky's Black Hawk helicopters.

Other subsidiaries include ADS/Transcoil (LCDs, clocks, transducers, brushless motors), Adel Wiggins (clamps, connectors, heaters, refueling systems), and Avionic Instruments (power conversion equipment). Additional subsidiaries include Avtech, which makes flight deck PA systems and cabin lighting and power products; Bruce Aerospace, which offers aircraft interior, exterior, and emergency lighting; CDA InterCorp, a maker of actuators, motors, and gears; and Skurka Aerospace, which provides electric motors, generators, speed transducers, and tachometers.

TransDigm acquires companies that offer niche products that fit well with other subsidiary operations and have significant aftermarket sales. In mid-2009 the company added Acme Aerospace to its fold. Acme makes batteries, chargers, battery back-up, and power conversion systems. A month later TransDigm bought the pneumatic valves and surge suppressor product lines from a subsidiary of Woodward Governor Company. The products fit well with its TransDigm's existing valve offering and are being integrated into its AeroControlex unit.

In December 2009 TransDigm agreed to acquire the assets of California-based Dukes and its subsidiary, Arizona-based GST Industries. The companies make valves, pumps, solenoids, and other components sold primarily to the business jet and military markets. Dukes and TransDigm sell to many of the same customers, including Cessna, Hawker Beechcraft, Bombardier, Lockheed Martin, and Honeywell.

In 2008 TransDigm made two acquisitions from Unison Industries, a subsidiary of General Electric's GE Aviation business unit. In September it picked up Unison's aircraft ignition product line (magnetos, harnesses, and related components for piston aircraft). Three months later, the company bought Aircraft Parts Corporation (starter generators and generator control units for turbine engines) from Unison.

Earlier that year TransDigm bought privately held CEF Industries (actuators, compressors, pumps, and related components). CEF, which also provides contract manufacturing services, sells to many of the same military and business jet customers as TransDigm.

In one of its larger transactions, TransDigm paid $430 million to acquire Aviation Technologies from Odyssey Investment Partners early in 2007. The acquisition of Aviation Technologies gave TransDigm two new divisions — Avtech and ADS/Transicoil; the companies count Airbus, Boeing, and Embraer among their customers.

EXECUTIVES

Chairman and CEO: W. Nicholas (Nick) Howley, age 57
EVP Mergers and Acquisitions: Albert J. Rodriguez, age 49
EVP, TD Group: James Riley, age 43
EVP, CFO, and Secretary: Gregory Rufus, age 53
EVP, TD Group: Robert S. Henderson, age 53
President, AeroControlex Group: Roger V. Jones, age 50
President, Marathon Norco Aerospace: Jack Stiffler
President, Avtech Corporation: Jorge Valladares
President, CEF Industries: Peter Palmer
President, Skurka Aerospace: Thomas J. Sievers
President, Transicoil: Jack Planchak
President, Champion Aerospace: Brent G. Iversen II, age 52
President, Avionic Instruments: Bryce Wiedemann
President and COO, TD Holdings and TransDigm: Raymond F. Laubenthal, age 48
President, Adams Rite Aerospace: John F. Leary, age 62
Investor Relations: Jonathan D. Crandall
Auditors: Ernst & Young LLP

LOCATIONS

HQ: TransDigm Group Incorporated
1301 E. 9th St., Ste. 3710, Cleveland, OH 44114
Phone: 216-706-2960   **Fax:** 216-706-2937
Web: www.transdigm.com

2009 Sales

	$ mil.	% of total
US	611.2	80
Other countries	150.4	20
Total	**761.6**	**100**

PRODUCTS/OPERATIONS

2009 Sales

	$ mil.	% of total
Mechanical/electromechanical actuators & controls	123.2	16
Ignition systems & components	96.8	13
Gear pumps	71.6	9
Power conditioning devices	58.0	8
Specialized valves	55.4	7
AC/DC electric motors	52.8	7
Engineered connectors	46.7	6
Power, lighting & control	40.3	5
Engineered latching & locking devices	34.7	5
Audio systems	33.1	4
Specialized cockpit displays	30.9	4
Rods & locking devices	29.3	4
Lavatory hardware	27.8	4
Nickel cadmium batteries & chargers	25.3	3
Elastometers	21.9	3
Generator controls	13.8	2
Total	**761.6**	**100**

HISTORICAL FINANCIALS
Company Type: Public

Income Statement
FYE: September 30

	REVENUE ($ mil.)	NET INCOME ($ mil.)	NET PROFIT MARGIN	EMPLOYEES
9/09	761.6	162.9	21.4%	2,000
9/08	713.7	133.1	18.6%	2,100
9/07	592.8	88.6	14.9%	2,100
9/06	435.2	25.1	5.8%	1,400
9/05	374.3	34.7	9.3%	1,300
Annual Growth	19.4%	47.2%	—	11.4%

2009 Year-End Financials

Debt ratio: 165.6%	Dividends
Return on equity: 22.1%	Yield: —
Cash ($ mil.): 190.2	Payout: —
Current ratio: 4.96	Market value ($ mil.): 2,439.6
Long-term debt ($ mil.): 1,356.8	R&D as % of sales: —
No. of shares (mil.): 49.0	Advertising as % of sales: —

Stock History

NYSE: TDG

	STOCK PRICE ($) FY Close	P/E High/Low		PER SHARE ($) Earnings	Dividends	Book Value
9/09	49.81	16	7	3.23	—	16.73
9/08	34.23	19	12	2.65	—	13.35
9/07	45.71	26	13	1.83	—	9.95
9/06	24.42	52	40	0.53	—	7.41
Annual Growth	26.8%	—	—	30.6%	—	25.2%

TransMontaigne Partners

TransMontaigne Partners, formed by parent TransMontaigne Inc. in 2005, provides integrated terminaling, storage, and pipeline services for companies engaged in refined petroleum products and crude oil distribution and marketing. Products handled include light refined products (gasolines, heating oils, and jet fuels), heavy refined products (asphalt and residual fuel oils), and crude oil. The company's petroleum products terminaling and transportation operations are located along the Gulf Coast, in Brownsville, Texas, along the Mississippi and Ohio rivers, and in the Midwest.

In late 2007 TransMontaigne Partners acquired 21 refined petroleum products terminaling facilities from TransMontaigne Inc. for $125 million.

EXECUTIVES

Chairman: Stephen R. Munger, age 60
CEO: Charles L. Dunlap
President and COO: Gregory J. Pound, age 57
EVP, CFO, and Treasurer: Frederick W. Boutin, age 54
EVP, Secretary, and General Counsel: Erik B. Carlson, age 62
SVP and Chief Accounting Officer: Deborah A. Davis, age 36
Director Corporate Communications: Judy Kinard
Auditors: KPMG LLP

LOCATIONS

HQ: TransMontaigne Partners L.P.
 1670 Broadway, Ste. 3100, Denver, CO 80202
Phone: 303-626-8200 **Fax:** 303-626-8228
Web: www.transmontaignepartners.com

PRODUCTS/OPERATIONS

2008 Sales

	$ mil.	% of total
Terminaling services fees	111.3	81
Pipeline transportation fees	4.0	3
Management fees	1.9	1
Other	20.9	15
Total	**138.1**	**100**

COMPETITORS

BP	Magellan Midstream
Chevron	Marathon Petroleum
CITGO	Motiva Enterprises
Exxon Mobil	Murphy Oil
Hess Corporation	Sunoco
Holly Corporation	Sunoco Logistics
Holly Energy Partners	Valero Energy
Kinder Morgan Energy	

HISTORICAL FINANCIALS

Company Type: Public

Income Statement

FYE: December 31

	REVENUE ($ mil.)	NET INCOME ($ mil.)	NET PROFIT MARGIN	EMPLOYEES
12/08	138.1	25.6	18.5%	865
12/07	131.7	14.8	11.2%	776
12/06*	56.8	3.2	5.6%	729
6/05	36.1	1.0	2.8%	727
6/04	34.3	10.1	29.4%	635
Annual Growth	41.7%	26.2%	—	8.0%

*Fiscal year change

2008 Year-End Financials

Debt ratio: —
Return on equity: —
Cash ($ mil.): 4.8
Current ratio: 0.74
Long-term debt ($ mil.): 165.5
No. of shares (mil.): 10.8

Dividends
 Yield: 17.0%
 Payout: 114.1%
Market value ($ mil.): 143.4
R&D as % of sales: —
Advertising as % of sales: —

Stock History

NYSE: TLP

	STOCK PRICE ($) FY Close	P/E High/Low		PER SHARE ($) Earnings	Dividends	Book Value
12/08	13.30	17	6	1.98	2.26	—
12/07	28.39	27	19	1.42	1.90	—
12/06*	30.30	75	56	0.44	1.69	—
6/05	25.34	210	182	0.13	—	—
Annual Growth	(19.3%)	—	—	147.9%	15.6%	—

*Fiscal year change

True Religion Apparel

Who knew you could find religion just by throwing open the doors to your closet? True Religion Apparel designs and markets upscale denimwear. The company's apparel offerings — including jeans, skirts, jackets, and tops — are sold under the True Religion Brand Jeans label in about 50 countries spanning North and South America, Europe, Africa, and the Asia/Pacific region. It also markets swimwear, eyewear, footwear, and fragrances. True Religion Apparel peddles its products through upscale retailers such as Barneys New York, Bergdorf Goodman, Neiman Marcus, Nordstrom, Saks Fifth Avenue, and about 900 high-end US boutiques. The com-

pany also operates about 40 stores under the True Religion banner.

The pricey jeans maker has been considering going private to maintain its double-digit sales and earnings gains, as well as expand its store operations. It then would like to re-emerge by taking the company public again.

True Religion in early 2009 added eyewear to its portfolio through a licensing agreement. The company partnered with Revolution Eyewear to make and distribute True Religion-branded sunglasses and other items to be sold in True Religion-branded stores, upscale department stores, and more than 3,000 specialty stores (such as Sunglass Hut). Beyond North America, the licensing agreement reaches Europe, Asia, Australia, and the Middle East. A licensing deal with Pash Industries, inked in 2007, gave True Religion its own branded outerwear and its foot in the door at many exclusive shops where Pash already sells. It also penned an agreement that year with Selective Fragrances to add scents for men and women to its products portfolio.

True Religion intends to maintain its brand image by limiting distribution of its apparel to the more exclusive boutiques, specialty stores, and department stores, as well as its own brand stores. The jeanswear designer expects sales through its True Religion locations to grow substantially, and it plans to add about 25 stores to its network in 2009. Despite efforts to keep its name in high-end shopping hubs, True Religion is moving an increasing amount of its merchandise to off-price retailers and outlet malls. These discount retail channels have helped to boost sales as accounts with some boutique customers become past due because of tightening credit markets and declining consumer spending. In 2008 True Religion opened its first international store in Japan. The company also enlisted Hong Kong-based Bright Unity International to distribute its apparel in Hong Kong, Macao, and China.

Branding its products "Made in the USA," True Religion outsources all of its production to contract manufacturers around the world. Its men's and women's denimwear is sewn and finished by manufacturers in the US, its children's denim and fleece apparel are made in Mexico, and its knit shirts are made in the Far East. To complete production, some apparel is then sent to laundry and finishing centers around Los Angeles.

Columbia Wanger Asset Management holds about a 10% stake in the company.

EXECUTIVES

Chairman, CEO, and Chief Merchant; CEO, Guru Denim: Jeffrey (Jeff) Lubell, age 54, $7,726,524 total compensation
President: Michael F. Buckley, age 46, $4,293,238 total compensation
COO: Lynne Koplin
CFO: Peter F. (Pete) Collins, age 44, $2,008,591 total compensation
SVP Operations: Kelly Gvildys, age 47, $389,600 total compensation
SVP, Merchandising: Rodney Hutton
VP, Real Estate: Marc J. Klein, age 43
VP US Wholesale Sales, True Religion Sales LLC: Sarah Lassek
Marketing Coordinator: Faye Fuji
Design Director: Zihaad Wells, age 33
Director, Marketing and Public Relations: Emilio Fields
Senior Designer, Women's Sportswear: Caius Olowu
Auditors: Deloitte & Touche LLP

LOCATIONS

HQ: True Religion Apparel Inc.
2263 E. Vernon Ave., Vernon, CA 90058
Phone: 323-266-3072   **Fax:** 323-266-8060
Web: www.truereligionbrandjeans.com

2008 Sales

	$ mil.	% of total
US Wholesale	153.2	57
Consumer Direct	75.3	28
International	40.1	15
Other	1.4	—
Total	**270.0**	**100**

COMPETITORS

Abercrombie & Fitch
Armani
Berkshire Partners
Calvin Klein
Diesel SpA
Joe's Jeans
Koos Manufacturing
Levi Strauss
Phat Fashions
Polo Ralph Lauren
Sean John

HISTORICAL FINANCIALS

Company Type: Public

Income Statement · FYE: December 31

	REVENUE ($ mil.)	NET INCOME ($ mil.)	NET PROFIT MARGIN	EMPLOYEES
12/08	270.0	44.4	16.4%	809
12/07	173.3	27.8	16.0%	338
12/06	140.5	21.7	15.4%	163
12/05	102.6	19.5	19.0%	95
12/04	27.7	4.2	15.2%	46
Annual Growth	**76.7%**	**80.3%**	**—**	**104.8%**

2008 Year-End Financials

Debt ratio: —
Return on equity: 37.4%
Cash ($ mil.): 57.2
Current ratio: 7.09
Long-term debt ($ mil.): —
No. of shares (mil.): 25.3
Dividends
 Yield: —
 Payout: —
Market value ($ mil.): 315.3
R&D as % of sales: —
Advertising as % of sales: —

Stock History · NASDAQ (GM): TRLG

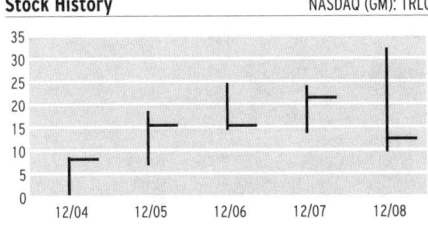

	STOCK PRICE ($) FY Close	P/E High/Low		PER SHARE ($) Earnings	Dividends	Book Value
12/08	12.44	17	5	1.83	—	5.61
12/07	21.35	20	12	1.16	—	3.76
12/06	15.31	26	16	0.92	—	2.53
12/05	15.40	22	8	0.84	—	1.39
12/04	8.10	42	3	0.20	—	0.30
Annual Growth	**11.3%**	**—**	**—**	**73.9%**	**—**	**108.4%**

Tyler Technologies

Tyler Technologies doesn't want local governments tied up in red tape. The company provides information management software and services intended to help state and local government offices operate more efficiently. Specializing in applications for city departments, counties, and public schools, Tyler's products include software for accounting and financial management, posting public records over the Internet, managing judicial cases, recording courtroom proceedings, and automating appraisals and assessments. Its other products include applications that allow citizens to access utility accounts or pay traffic fines online. Tyler complements its product offerings with IT support and maintenance services.

Formerly an auto parts and supplies company established in 1966, Tyler sold its chain of auto parts stores in 1999 and used acquisitions to transform itself into a provider of software for local governments.

Having seen its revenue increase in recent years, the company continues to invest cash in acquisitions and research and development efforts. Some of its recent acquisitions (which are now aimed at enhancing its offerings) include the 2009 purchase of PulseMark, LLC, a provider of data warehousing software for the K-12 school and local government markets, as well as its acquisition the same year of assets from Parker-Lowe & Associates, a software developer that specializes in land records and social services products. In early 2010 the company purchased Wiznet, a provider of electronic document filing software and services for courts and law offices throughout the US.

In addition to acquisitions, the company is expanding its software product line with new offerings and product upgrades, including the Odyssey judicial case management system and public-use Internet portals that enable users to pay property taxes and utility bills and complete other transactions electronically.

Tyler has in recent years relied increasingly on long-term service contracts with customers for revenue.

EXECUTIVES

Chairman: John M. Yeaman, age 68
President, CEO, and Director: John S. Marr Jr., age 49, $1,818,359 total compensation
EVP, Product Strategy; CEO, Courts and Justice and INCODE Divisions: Dustin R. Womble, age 50, $1,526,473 total compensation
EVP, General Counsel, and Secretary:
 H. Lynn Moore Jr., age 41, $857,458 total compensation
SVP, CFO, and Treasurer: Brian K. Miller, age 50, $861,022 total compensation
President, MUNIS: Richard E. Peterson Jr., age 59
President, EDEN Systems: Jeff Green
Auditors: Ernst & Young LLP

LOCATIONS

HQ: Tyler Technologies, Inc.
 5949 Sherry Ln., Ste. 1400, Dallas, TX 75225
Phone: 972-713-3700   **Fax:** 972-713-3741
Web: www.tylerworks.com

PRODUCTS/OPERATIONS

2008 Sales

	$ mil.	% of total
Maintenance	107.4	41
Software services	75.0	28
Software licenses	41.5	16
Appraisal services	19.1	7
Subscriptions	14.4	5
Hardware & other	7.7	3
Total	**265.1**	**100**

Selected Products

Appraisal and assessment software (property appraisal and assessment)
Criminal justice software (court case tracking and management)
Document management and recording software (image storage and retrieval)
Education software
Finance and accounting software
Law enforcement and corrections software (police dispatch, records, and jail management)
Municipal court software (case management)
Odyssey (case and court management)
Public records and content management
Tax collections software (tax collections office operations)
Utility billing software (billing and collections)

Selected Services

Information technology and professional services
Maintenance
Outsourced property appraisals for tax jurisdictions

COMPETITORS

Accenture
Affiliated Computer Services
BearingPoint
CACI International
Constellation Software
Dyntek
HP Enterprise Services
IBM
Lawson Software
Manatron
MAXIMUS
Oracle
SAP
SunGard
Tier Technologies
USTI

HISTORICAL FINANCIALS

Company Type: Public

Income Statement · FYE: December 31

	REVENUE ($ mil.)	NET INCOME ($ mil.)	NET PROFIT MARGIN	EMPLOYEES
12/08	265.1	14.9	5.6%	1,940
12/07	219.8	17.5	8.0%	1,627
12/06	195.3	14.4	7.4%	1,530
12/05	170.5	8.2	4.8%	1,360
12/04	172.3	10.1	5.9%	1,400
Annual Growth	**11.4%**	**10.2%**	**—**	**8.5%**

2008 Year-End Financials

Debt ratio: —
Return on equity: 11.9%
Cash ($ mil.): 1.8
Current ratio: 0.75
Long-term debt ($ mil.): —
No. of shares (mil.): 35.0
Dividends
 Yield: 0.0%
 Payout: —
Market value ($ mil.): 419.1
R&D as % of sales: —
Advertising as % of sales: —

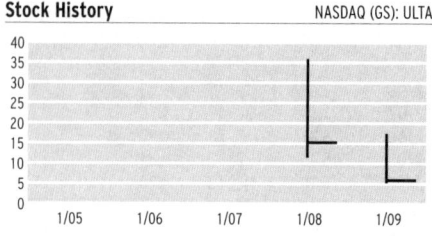

	STOCK PRICE ($) FY Close	P/E High/Low	PER SHARE ($) Earnings	Dividends	Book Value
12/08	11.98	49 26	0.38	0.00	3.27
12/07	12.89	39 27	0.42	0.00	3.92
12/06	14.06	44 25	0.34	0.00	3.60
12/05	8.78	48 28	0.19	0.00	3.21
12/04	8.36	48 33	0.23	0.00	3.38
Annual Growth	9.4%	— —	13.4%	—	(0.9%)

Ulta Salon, Cosmetics & Fragrance

Ulta Salon, Cosmetics & Fragrance wants to be every woman's ultimate beauty stop. Ulta operates about 310 stores in three dozen states. About a third of its stores are located in Illinois, Texas, and California. Ulta stocks more than 21,000 prestige and mass market products, including cosmetics, fragrances, skin and hair care products and appliances, and accessories. All Ulta stores also offer hair salon services, as well as manicures, pedicures, massages, waxing, and other beauty and spa treatments. The company's Web site ULTA.com was upgraded in 2007 to offer about 11,000 products and more than 400 brand names. Ulta, which was founded in 1990 by director Terry Hanson and Dick George, went public in 2007.

Since its IPO, which raised more than $153 million, Ulta has been aggressively opening stores: more than 100 shops since 2007. Ultimately, Ulta hopes to grow to more than 1,000 stores throughout the US. In 2009 the chain slowed down and added only about 35 locations, due to the slowing economy and limited real estate opportunities.

Ulta is aiming to benefit from a change in where women, especially younger women, purchase beauty products. As the department store industry has consolidated and slumped, specialty stores, such as rival Sephora, have been capturing an increasing share of the market for prestige beauty products. To that end, Ulta is focusing on expanding its range of higher-priced "prestige" products, such as Estée Lauder fragrances, Frédéric Fekkai hair care products, and Smashbox cosmetics.

Investment firms Global Retail Partners and Netherlands-based Doublemousse B.V. own about 20% and 19% of Ulta's shares, respectively.

EXECUTIVES

Chairman: Dennis K. Eck, age 65
SVP, General Counsel, and Secretary: Robert S. Guttman, age 55
CFO and Assistant Secretary: Gregg R. Bodnar, age 44, $846,071 total compensation
President, CEO, and Director: Lyn P. Kirby, age 54, $2,489,041 total compensation
Auditors: Ernst & Young LLP

LOCATIONS

HQ: Ulta Salon, Cosmetics & Fragrance, Inc.
1000 Remington Blvd., Ste. 120
Bolingbrook, IL 60440
Phone: 630-410-4800   **Fax:** 630-226-8367
Web: www.ulta.com

2009 Stores

	No.
Texas	42
Illinois	31
California	28
Arizona	22
Florida	22
Georgia	16
North Carolina	13
Pennsylvania	13
Colorado	10
New Jersey	9
New York	9
Virginia	9
Minnesota	6
Michigan	8
Alabama	6
Nevada	6
Oklahoma	6
Indiana	6
Maryland	6
Washington	4
Ohio	6
Missouri	3
Oregon	3
South Carolina	4
Iowa	2
Kentucky	2
Louisiana	2
Massachusetts	4
Tennessee	3
Nebraska	2
Utah	2
Wisconsin	2
Arkansas	1
Delaware	1
Kansas	1
Rhode Island	1
Total	**311**

PRODUCTS/OPERATIONS

Selected Products

Accessories
 Brush sets
 Eyelash curlers
 Flip-flops
 Hair accessories
 Manicure sets
 Yoga accessories
Appliances
 Curling irons
 Flat irons
 Hair dryers
 Microdermabrasion systems
 Shavers
Bath and body
 Aromatherapy
 Body butter
 Body souffle
 Deodorants
 Exfoliators
 Scrubs
 Soaps
Cosmetics
 Blush
 Concealer
 Eye liner
 Eyeshadow
 Lipstick
Fragrance
 Candles
 Cologne
 Perfume
 Potpourri
Hair care
 Coloring
 Conditioner
 Masks
 Shampoo
 Styling creams
Skin care
 Cellulite cream
 De-Aging cream
 Face wash
 Gloves
 Lotions
 Nail strengthening cream
 Sunscreens

COMPETITORS

Bath & Body Works	Merle Norman
Bed Bath & Beyond	Nordstrom
Body Shop	Regis Corporation
CVS Caremark	Sally Beauty
Dillard's	Sephora USA
drugstore.com	Supercuts
J. C. Penney	Target
L'Oréal USA	Walgreen
Lush Ltd.	Wal-Mart
Macy's	

HISTORICAL FINANCIALS

Company Type: Public

Income Statement

FYE: Saturday closest to January 31

	REVENUE ($ mil.)	NET INCOME ($ mil.)	NET PROFIT MARGIN	EMPLOYEES
1/09	1,084.6	25.3	2.3%	9,800
1/08	912.1	14.1	1.5%	7,900
1/07	755.1	8.0	1.1%	7,100
1/06	579.1	16.0	2.8%	7,100
1/05	491.2	9.5	1.9%	—
Annual Growth	21.9%	27.7%	—	11.3%

2009 Year-End Financials

Debt ratio: 35.9%
Return on equity: 11.1%
Cash ($ mil.): 3.6
Current ratio: 2.36
Long-term debt ($ mil.): 88.0
No. of shares (mil.): 58.1

Dividends
 Yield: —
 Payout: —
Market value ($ mil.): 338.7
R&D as % of sales: —
Advertising as % of sales: —

Stock History

NASDAQ (GS): ULTA

	STOCK PRICE ($) FY Close	P/E High/Low	PER SHARE ($) Earnings	Dividends	Book Value
1/09	5.83	40 13	0.43	—	4.22
1/08	15.24	74 25	0.48	—	3.64
Annual Growth	(61.7%)	— —	(10.4%)	—	15.8%

Ultra Petroleum

Ultra Petroleum is ultra-keen in its search for petroleum products. The independent exploration and production company recovers natural gas from Cretaceous sandstone deposits in the Green River Basin of southwestern Wyoming. Ultra Petroleum owns stakes in approximately 19,000 gross developed acres in Wyoming. The Company also owns an interest in 1,000 gross producing wells in this area and is operator of about half of those. The company also has assets in Pennsylvania. In 2008 Ultra Petroleum reported proved reserves of 1.9 trillion cu. ft. of natural gas and 15.5 million barrels of oil.

The oil and gas company expanded into China in 2001 through the acquisition of Pendaries Petroleum, a Houston-based oil and gas exploration company that had large oil assets in Bohai Bay.

Ultra Petroleum subsequently decided to focus its exploration and production efforts in the US, and in 2007 the company sold its assets in China for $223 million. It boosted its reserves in the US in 2009 with an agreement to acquire 80,000 acres in the Pennsylvania Marcellus Shale from a private company.

EXECUTIVES

Chairman, President, and CEO: Michael D. Watford, age 56, $4,152,851 total compensation
CFO: Marshall D. (Mark) Smith, age 50, $1,065,462 total compensation
VP Marketing: Stuart E. Nance, age 50, $562,267 total compensation
VP Operations: William B. (Bill) Picquet, age 58, $1,184,530 total compensation
Corporate Controller and Principal Accounting Officer: Garland Shaw
Manager Investor Relations: Kelly L. Whitley
Auditors: Ernst & Young LLP

LOCATIONS

HQ: Ultra Petroleum Corp.
363 N. Sam Houston Pkwy. East, Ste. 1200
Houston, TX 77060
Phone: 281-876-0120   **Fax:** 281-876-2831
Web: www.ultrapetroleum.com

PRODUCTS/OPERATIONS

2008 Sales

	$ mil.	% of total
Natural gas	986.4	91
Oil	98.0	9
Total	**1,084.4**	**100**

COMPETITORS

BP
Cabot Oil & Gas
ConocoPhillips
EOG
Exxon Mobil
Royal Dutch Shell
Samson Oil
XTO Energy

HISTORICAL FINANCIALS

Company Type: Public

Income Statement

FYE: December 31

	REVENUE ($ mil.)	NET INCOME ($ mil.)	NET PROFIT MARGIN	EMPLOYEES
12/08	1,084.4	414.3	38.2%	86
12/07	566.6	263.0	46.4%	72
12/06	592.7	231.2	39.0%	57
12/05	516.5	228.3	44.2%	57
12/04	258.0	109.1	42.3%	41
Annual Growth	**43.2%**	**39.6%**	**—**	**20.3%**

2008 Year-End Financials

Debt ratio: 52.3%
Return on equity: 42.6%
Cash ($ mil.): 14.2
Current ratio: 0.57
Long-term debt ($ mil.): 570.0
No. of shares (mil.): 151.4
Dividends
  Yield: 0.0%
  Payout: —
Market value ($ mil.): 5,226.3
R&D as % of sales: —
Advertising as % of sales: —

Stock History

NYSE: UPL

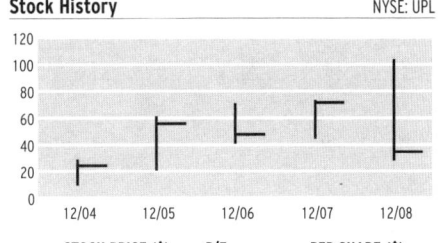

	STOCK PRICE ($) FY Close	P/E High/Low		PER SHARE ($) Earnings	Dividends	Book Value
12/08	34.51	39	11	2.65	0.00	7.20
12/07	71.50	44	27	1.66	0.00	5.64
12/06	47.74	49	29	1.43	0.00	4.15
12/05	55.80	43	15	1.41	0.00	3.77
12/04	24.07	41	15	0.68	0.00	1.77
Annual Growth	**9.4%**	**—**	**—**	**40.5%**	**—**	**42.0%**

Ultralife Corporation

Ultralife isn't just a battery company anymore, but has found new life selling power supply systems for communications equipment. The company continues to design and manufacture rechargeable and non-rechargeable polymer and lithium batteries. However, its quickly expanding business of providing stationary and portable power systems now accounts for more than half of its sales. Ultralife sells its products around the world to original equipment manufactures, distributors, and retailers. The company, under its McDowell Research brand, also sells directly to US and foreign defense departments. Military sales (both directly and indirectly) account for about 75% of Ultralife's revenues.

Ultralife marked its transition from strictly a battery company to a power and communications firm in 2008 when it dropped the word "batteries" from its name.

The company has been busy diversifying itself through a series of acquisitions over the past three years. It began its shopping spree in 2006 when it bought ABLE New Energy Co., a Chinese manufacturer of lithium batteries. ABLE's line of products are used in a diverse range of portable

---

devices such as automotive electronics, medical equipment, and tracking systems.

The company continued to expand in 2007 when it bought RedBlack Communications (formerly Innovative Solutions Consulting), an engineering and technical services firm. Now a division of Ultralife, RedBlack specializes in mobile, modular, and fixed-site communication and electronic systems. Its customers include government agencies, such as the National Security Agency and the Office of Naval Research, and prime military contractors like BAE SYSTEMS and Titan Systems.

Ultralife quickly followed up that deal in 2007 with two more acquisitions that helped diversify the company's product line and geographic reach. The Florida-based Stationary Power Services and Reserve Power Systems joined Ultralife that year. The companies provided infrastructure power management services and lead-acid batteries for standby power systems.

In late 2008 Ultralife acquired certain assets of US Energy Systems and its US Power Services affiliate. US Energy Systems installs and maintains standby power systems, uninterruptible power supply systems, DC power systems, and switchgear/control systems for the telecommunications, utilities, technology, petrochemical, financial, and information services industries.

In 2009 Ultralife bought the assets and assumed the liabilities of SAIC's tactical communications products business. The business makes amplifiers, man-portable systems, cables, power systems, and ancillary communications equipment that will be sold by Ultralife under the current products' brand name, AMTI.

In the past Ultralife has sought to reduce its dependence on the US military market, but research and development efforts continue to have a predominantly military focus. For example, in 2008 Ultralife partnered with Mississippi State University to develop fuel cell-battery portable power systems that would enable lightweight, long-endurance military missions.

Grace Brothers, Ltd. owns about 26% of Ultralife and is represented on the company's board by director Bradford Whitmore, a general partner of Grace Brothers.

EXECUTIVES

Chair: Lt. Gen. Daniel W. Christman, age 65
President, CEO, and Director: John D. Kavazanjian, age 58
COO Stationary Power Services: Philip M. Meek, age 48
CFO and Treasurer: Phillip A. (Phil) Fain, age 55
VP Corporate Strategy and Business Integration: Patrick R. Hanna Jr., age 60
VP Corporate Marketing and Technology: Julius M. Cirin, age 55
VP European Operations: Andrew J. Naukam, age 49
VP Business Operations: James E. Evans, age 60
VP Administration and General Counsel: Peter F. (Pete) Comerford, age 51
Auditors: PricewaterhouseCoopers LLP

LOCATIONS

HQ: Ultralife Corporation
2000 Technology Pkwy., Newark, NY 14513
Phone: 315-332-7100   **Fax:** 315-331-7800
Web: www.ulbi.com

2008 Sales

	$ mil.	% of total
North America		
US	205.4	81
Canada	9.7	4
Europe		
UK	18.1	7
Other countries	8.6	3
Asia/Pacific		
Japan	3.7	1
Australia	1.5	1
Hong Kong	0.9	—
China	2.4	1
Singapore	1.2	1
Other regions	3.2	1
Total	**254.7**	**100**

PRODUCTS/OPERATIONS

2008 Sales

	$ mil.	% of total
Communications systems	136.1	53
Batteries		
Non-rechargeable	68.1	27
Rechargeable	34.7	14
Design & installation services	15.8	6
Total	**254.7**	**100**

Selected Products

Battery Accessories
  Cables
  Chargers
Military Communications
  Battery Chargers
  Headset and push-to-talk systems
  Power systems
  Integrated systems
Primary Lithium Batteries
  3-volt
  9-volt
  Custom design
  HiRate cylindrical
  Lithium/manganese dioxide primary
  Seawater-activated
  Thin cell
Rechargeable Batteries
  Lithium ion
  Lithium polymer

COMPETITORS

Advanced Battery	Lithium Technology
Arotech	Mechanical Technology
China BAK	Micro Power Electronics
Ener1	MTI MicroFuel Cells
Energizer Holdings	Procter & Gamble
Environmental Power	SANYO
GP Batteries	Spectrum Brands
Greatbatch	SunPower Systems
GS Yuasa	Valence Technology

HISTORICAL FINANCIALS

Company Type: Public

Income Statement

FYE: December 31

	REVENUE ($ mil.)	NET INCOME ($ mil.)	NET PROFIT MARGIN	EMPLOYEES
12/08	254.7	13.7	5.4%	1,191
12/07	137.6	5.6	4.1%	1,092
12/06	93.5	(27.5)	—	1,078
12/05	70.5	(4.3)	—	592
12/04	98.2	22.3	22.7%	606
Annual Growth	**26.9%**	**(11.5%)**	**—**	**18.4%**

2008 Year-End Financials

Debt ratio: 5.3%
Return on equity: 18.1%
Cash ($ mil.): 1.9
Current ratio: 2.33
Long-term debt ($ mil.): 4.7
No. of shares (mil.): 17.0

Dividends
  Yield: —
  Payout: —
Market value ($ mil.): 228.2
R&D as % of sales: —
Advertising as % of sales: —

Stock History

NASDAQ (GM): ULBI

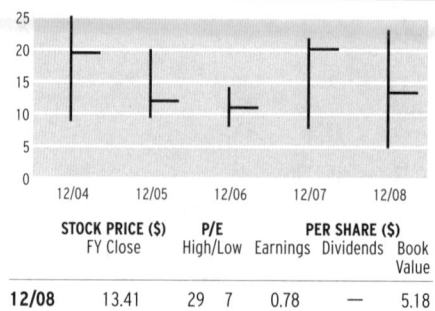

	STOCK PRICE ($) FY Close	P/E High/Low		PER SHARE ($) Earnings	Dividends	Book Value
12/08	13.41	29	7	0.78	—	5.18
12/07	20.15	60	22	0.36	—	3.70
12/06	11.01	—	—	(1.84)	—	2.33
12/05	12.00	—	—	(0.30)	—	3.65
12/04	19.45	17	6	1.48	—	3.74
Annual Growth	**(8.9%)**	**—**	**—**	**(14.8%)**	**—**	**8.5%**

UMB Financial

If money is your mantra, UMB Financial may be the bank for you. The multibank holding company has four UMB-branded banks serving Arizona, Colorado, Illinois, Kansas, Nebraska, Oklahoma, and its home state of Missouri. Through about 140 locations, the banks offer standard services such as checking and savings accounts, credit and debit cards, and trust and investment services. Other subsidiaries of UMB Financial offer insurance, brokerage services, leasing, treasury management, health savings accounts, and proprietary mutual funds. UMB Fund Services performs accounting and administration functions for mutual fund and alternative investment managers.

Commercial, financial, and agricultural loans account for around half of UMB Financial's loan portfolio; real estate mortgages account for another third.

UMB Financial is focused on growing its fee-based businesses, as they are not as dependent on fluctuating interest rates as traditional banking services. The company is less acquisitive than many of its banking peers, though it sometimes makes smaller buys to fill in its market area. It has bought the investment advisory business of TrendStar Advisors, which advises a small-cap fund that will be reorganized and managed by UMB subsidiary Scout Investment Advisors.

In 2009, UMB Financial agreed to buy JD Clark & Company, a privately held, third-party fund service provider to alternative investments firms. It also agreed to buy the Indiana corporate trust business of Harris NA and acquired the corporate trust business of Colorado-based American National Bank. The company did not disclose the purchase price of any of the transactions.

The family of chairman and CEO Mariner Kemper controls about 14% of UMB Financial's stock.

EXECUTIVES

Chairman and CEO; Chairman, UMB Financial and UMB Bank Colorado: J. Mariner Kemper, age 36, $1,474,113 total compensation
Vice Chairman, CFO, and Chief Administrative Officer: Michael D. Hagedorn, age 42, $742,217 total compensation
President, COO, and Director; Chairman and CEO, UMB Bank; Chairman, UMB Fund Services: Peter J. deSilva, age 47, $1,518,420 total compensation
President, Personal Financial Services: Clyde F. Wendel, age 61, $702,330 total compensation
Chief Investment Officer, UMB Financial and UMB Bank: William B. (Bill) Greiner
EVP and Chief Risk Officer: David D. Kling, age 62
EVP and Chief Organizational Effectiveness Officer: Lawrence G. Smith, age 61
EVP Sales, Marketing, and Communication: Heather C. Miller
EVP and Director of Human Resources: Jacqueline A. (Jackie) Witte
Divisional EVP and General Counsel, UMB Financial Director; Chairman and CEO, Perfect Commerce: Alexander C. (Sandy) Kemper, age 43
Vice Chairman, Eastern Region; Chairman and CEO, UMB Bank St. Louis: Peter J. (Pete) Genovese, age 62, $602,214 total compensation
Auditors: Deloitte & Touche LLP

LOCATIONS

HQ: UMB Financial Corporation
  1010 Grand Ave.., Kansas City, MO 64106
Phone: 816-860-7000 **Fax:** 816-860-7610
Web: www.umb.com

PRODUCTS/OPERATIONS

2008 Gross Revenues

	$ mil.	% of total
Interest		
Loans	241.7	35
Securities	136.6	20
Other	9.6	1
Noninterest		
Trust & securities processing	122.3	17
Service charges on deposit accounts	85.0	12
Bank card fees	43.3	6
Trading & investment banking	19.6	3
Brokerage fees	8.6	1
Other	33.8	5
Total	**700.5**	**100**

COMPETITORS

Bank of America
BOK Financial
Capitol Federal Financial
Commerce Bancshares
Dickinson Financial
First National of Nebraska
Great Southern Bancorp
Guaranty Bancorp
TCF Financial
U.S. Bancorp
Zions Bancorporation

HISTORICAL FINANCIALS

Company Type: Public

Income Statement

FYE: December 31

	ASSETS ($ mil.)	NET INCOME ($ mil.)	INCOME AS % OF ASSETS	EMPLOYEES
12/08	10,976.6	98.1	0.9%	3,274
12/07	9,343.0	74.2	0.8%	3,357
12/06	8,917.8	59.8	0.7%	3,432
12/05	8,247.8	56.3	0.7%	3,433
12/04	7,805.0	42.8	0.5%	3,587
Annual Growth	**8.9%**	**23.0%**	**—**	**(2.3%)**

2008 Year-End Financials

Equity as % of assets: 8.9%
Return on assets: 1.0%
Return on equity: 10.5%
Long-term debt ($ mil.): 35.9
No. of shares (mil.): 40.4
Market value ($ mil.): 1,985.5

Dividends
Yield: 1.3%
Payout: 27.3%
Sales ($ mil.): 587.8
R&D as % of sales: —
Advertising as % of sales: —

Stock History

NASDAQ (GS): UMBF

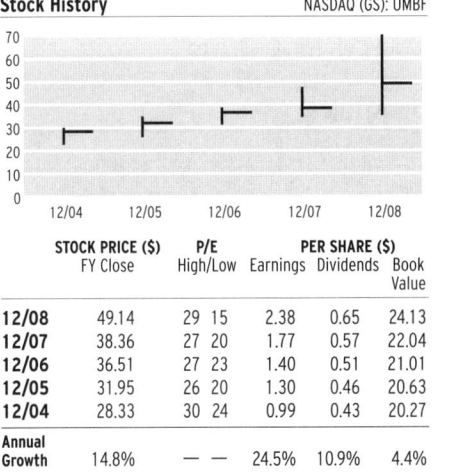

	STOCK PRICE ($) FY Close	P/E High/Low		PER SHARE ($) Earnings	Dividends	Book Value
12/08	49.14	29	15	2.38	0.65	24.13
12/07	38.36	27	20	1.77	0.57	22.04
12/06	36.51	27	23	1.40	0.51	21.01
12/05	31.95	26	20	1.30	0.46	20.63
12/04	28.33	30	24	0.99	0.43	20.27
Annual Growth	14.8%	—	—	24.5%	10.9%	4.4%

Umpqua Holdings

Umpqua Holdings thinks of itself not so much as a bank but as a retailer that sells financial products. Consequently, many of the company's approximately 150 Umpqua Bank "stores" in Oregon, southwestern Washington, and Northern California feature coffee bars and computer cafes. While customers sip Umpqua-branded coffee, read the morning paper, pay bills online, or check out local bands at the bank's online music store, staff members pitch checking and savings accounts, mortgages, loans, investments, and more. Subsidiary Umpqua Investments (formerly Strand, Atkinson, Williams & York) provides retail brokerage services through more than a dozen locations; most are inside Umpqua Bank branches.

As the largest bank headquartered in Oregon, Umpqua Holdings has branches scattered across the state, in addition to two branches in Clark County, Washington. It entered the Northern California market with its 2004 purchase of Humboldt Bancorp.

As part of its strategy to continue expanding along the Interstate 5 corridor from Seattle to Sacramento, California, Umpqua Holdings in 2007 acquired Northern California-based North Bay Bancorp; the branches of North Bay Bancorp's Vintage Bank and its Solano Bank division were rebranded to reflect the new ownership. The previous year, the company acquired another Northern California bank holding company, Western Sierra Bancorp, and merged principal subsidiaries Western Sierra Bank, Central California Bank, Lake Community Bank, and Auburn Community Bank into Umpqua Bank.

In 2009 Umpqua Bank assumed the two branches and other assets of the failed Bank of Clark County in Vancouver, Washington, in an FDIC-assisted transaction.

Unlike many other financial companies that are streamlining operations in turmoiled economic times, Umpqua Holdings has focused on expanding its private banking operations, targeting customers with more than $1 million to invest. The company established a wealth management division in 2009 and later announced plans to offer trust, asset management, and financial planning services.

EXECUTIVES

Chairman: Allyn C. Ford, age 67
Vice Chairman: Dan Giustina, age 59
President, CEO, and Director, Umpqua Holdings and Umpqua Bank: Raymond P. (Ray) Davis, age 59, $3,334,363 total compensation
SEVP and Chief Credit Officer, Umpqua Holdings and Umpqua Bank: Brad F. Copeland, age 60, $1,070,574 total compensation
EVP, CFO, and Principal Financial Officer: Ronald L. (Ron) Farnsworth Jr., age 38, $332,861 total compensation
EVP and Chief Auditor: Gary Neal
EVP Strategic Initiatives: Daniel A. (Dan) Sullivan, age 57, $424,769 total compensation
EVP Asset Management: Kelly Johnson
EVP, Treasurer, and Principal Accounting Officer: Neal McLaughlin, age 41
EVP, Secretary, and General Counsel, Umpqua Holdings and Umpqua Bank: Steven L. Philpott, age 57
Auditors: Moss Adams, LLP

LOCATIONS

HQ: Umpqua Holdings Corporation
1 SW Columbia St., Ste. 1200, Portland, OR 97258
Phone: 866-486-7782   **Fax:** 503-546-2498
Web: www.umpquabank.com

PRODUCTS/OPERATIONS

2008 Gross Revenues

	$ mil.	% of total
Interest		
Loans, including fees	393.9	72
Taxable investment securities	41.2	8
Other	7.4	1
Noninterest		
Junior subordinated debentures	38.9	7
Service charges on deposit accounts	34.8	6
Visa mandatory partial redemption	12.6	2
Brokerage commissions & fees	9.0	2
Other	11.9	2
Total	**549.7**	**100**

COMPETITORS

Bank of America
Bank of the West
KeyCorp
U.S. Bancorp
Washington Federal
Wells Fargo
West Coast Bancorp

HISTORICAL FINANCIALS

Company Type: Public

Income Statement

FYE: December 31

	ASSETS ($ mil.)	NET INCOME ($ mil.)	INCOME AS % OF ASSETS	EMPLOYEES
12/08	8,597.5	51.0	0.6%	1,700
12/07	8,340.1	63.3	0.8%	1,744
12/06	7,344.2	84.4	1.1%	1,530
12/05	5,360.6	69.7	1.3%	1,396
12/04	4,873.0	47.2	1.0%	1,328
Annual Growth	15.3%	2.0%	—	6.4%

2008 Year-End Financials

Equity as % of assets: 14.9%
Return on assets: 0.6%
Return on equity: 4.0%
Long-term debt ($ mil.): 196.2
No. of shares (mil.): 86.8
Market value ($ mil.): 1,255.7

Dividends
Yield: 4.3%
Payout: 75.6%
Sales ($ mil.): 389.1
R&D as % of sales: —
Advertising as % of sales: —

Stock History

NASDAQ (GS): UMPQ

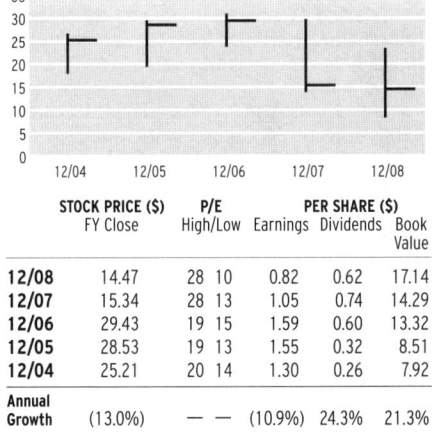

	STOCK PRICE ($) FY Close	P/E High/Low		PER SHARE ($) Earnings	Dividends	Book Value
12/08	14.47	28	10	0.82	0.62	17.14
12/07	15.34	28	13	1.05	0.74	14.29
12/06	29.43	19	15	1.59	0.60	13.32
12/05	28.53	19	13	1.55	0.32	8.51
12/04	25.21	20	14	1.30	0.26	7.92
Annual Growth	(13.0%)	—	—	(10.9%)	24.3%	21.3%

Under Armour

Under Armour is proving its mettle as an apparel warrior. Since its foray into the sporting goods market, the maker of performance athletic undies and apparel has risen to the top of the industry pack, boasting a big portion of the compression garment market. It is gaining a foothold in footwear, too. Under Armour is the official supplier of MLB and the NHL. Specializing in sport-specific garments, the company dresses its consumers from head (COLDGEAR) to toe (Team Sock). Most products are made from its moisture-wicking and heat-dispersing fabrics, able to keep athletes dry during workouts. Under Armour sells its products via the Internet, catalogs, and 17,000 sporting goods stores worldwide.

Its customers include the likes of Cabela's and the Army and Air Force Exchange, as well as Dick's Sporting Goods and The Sports Authority, which as a pair represented 31% of Under Armour's 2008 revenue.

To compete against its larger rivals, such as NIKE, Under Armour spends heavily to promote its products, forming endorsement deals with athletes across multiple sports. The company's latest celebrity tie up is with the mixed martial arts star Georges St-Pierre, who in 2009 signed a multiyear deal to endorse Under Armour's underwear and other apparel for an undisclosed sum.

Under Armour has begun to successfully cater to the footwear niche of the industry by regularly introducing new products each year. It entered the market with football cleats in mid-2006 for the fall season. It expanded its footwear with baseball and softball cleats (2007), launched performance training footwear (2008), and rolled out performance running footwear (2009). From 2007 to 2008 alone, the company boosted its revenue in this segment from 7% of sales to 12%.

Under Armour in 2008 also expanded its distribution at malls through national footwear retailers the likes of Finish Line and Foot Locker. Most of the company's products are manufactured by third parties. Under Armour's four largest suppliers are located in Mexico, China, and Colombia.

Thus far, Under Armour's primary consumer segment has been men, but it is actively working to expand its apparel offerings for women and children. Under Armour sells its product lines to almost 400 women's sports teams at NCAA Division I-A colleges.

In 2008 Under Armour hired David McCreight as its president. McCreight came directly from Sears unit Land's End and has logged experience at Disney Stores and Smith & Hawken.

EXECUTIVES

Chairman and CEO: Kevin A. Plank, age 36, $30,002 total compensation
President: David McCreight, age 46, $1,700,417 total compensation
COO: Wayne A. Marino, age 48, $462,693 total compensation
CFO: Brad Dickerson, age 44, $374,022 total compensation
CIO: Joseph D. Giles
Chief Supply Chain Officer: James E. (Jim) Calo, age 46
SVP Apparel: Suzanne J. Karkus, age 51, $1,093,644 total compensation
SVP Marketing: William J. Kraus
SVP Outdoor and Innovation: Kip J. Fulks, age 36
SVP Footwear: Gene McCarthy
SVP Talent: Melissa A. Wallace, age 50
SVP Retail: J. Scott Plank, age 43
SVP Consumer Insights: Kevin M. Haley, age 40
President and Managing Director, Under Armour Europe B.V.: Peter Mahrer, age 49, $859,794 total compensation
Auditors: PricewaterhouseCoopers LLP

LOCATIONS

HQ: Under Armour, Inc.
1020 Hull St., 3rd Fl., Baltimore, MD 21230
Phone: 410-454-6428   **Fax:** 410-468-2516
Web: www.underarmour.com

2008 Sales

	$ mil.	% of total
US	660.8	91
Canada	31.6	4
Other countries	32.9	5
Total	**725.2**	**100**

PRODUCTS/OPERATIONS

2008 Sales

	$ mil.	% of total
Men's apparel	382.1	53
Women's apparel	140.8	19
Footwear	84.8	12
Youth apparel	56.0	8
Accessories	31.5	4
Licensing	30.0	4
Total	**725.2**	**100**

COMPETITORS

adidas	L.L. Bean
Calvin Klein	NIKE
Columbia Sportswear	North Face
Fruit of the Loom	Patagonia, Inc.
Hanesbrands	Victoria's Secret Stores
Jockey International	Warnaco Swimwear

HISTORICAL FINANCIALS

Company Type: Public

Income Statement

FYE: December 31

	REVENUE ($ mil.)	NET INCOME ($ mil.)	NET PROFIT MARGIN	EMPLOYEES
12/08	725.2	38.2	5.3%	2,200
12/07	606.6	52.6	8.7%	1,400
12/06	430.7	39.0	9.1%	979
12/05	281.1	14.4	5.1%	610
12/04	205.2	14.3	7.0%	574
Annual Growth	**37.1%**	**27.8%**	**—**	**39.9%**

2008 Year-End Financials

Debt ratio: 4.0%
Return on equity: 12.5%
Cash ($ mil.): 102.0
Current ratio: 2.98
Long-term debt ($ mil.): 13.2
No. of shares (mil.): 50.2
Dividends
  Yield: —
  Payout: —
Market value ($ mil.): 1,196.0
R&D as % of sales: —
Advertising as % of sales: —

Stock History

NYSE: UA

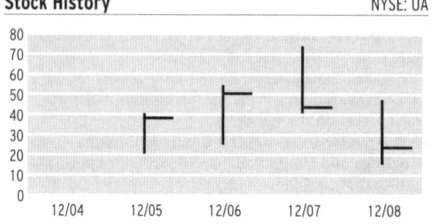

	STOCK PRICE ($) FY Close	P/E High/Low		PER SHARE ($) Earnings	Dividends	Book Value
12/08	23.84	61	21	0.77	—	6.60
12/07	43.67	70	39	1.05	—	5.59
12/06	50.45	68	33	0.79	—	4.27
12/05	38.31	111	59	0.36	—	3.01
Annual Growth	**(14.6%)**	**—**	**—**	**18.5%**	**—**	**98.7%**

Unify Corporation

Unify helps disparate forces such as databases, client/server applications, and the Web exist together in harmony. Software developers, value-added resellers, systems integrators, and IT departments use the company's software to create and deploy applications that integrate data from older legacy systems with newer enterprise applications. Unify also sells client/server development tools and database management software. In mid-2009 the company acquired AXS-One, a provider of integrated content archiving software.

The company has expanded its product lines in recent years to include tools such as Composer for Lotus Notes and Sabertooth; application development product families NXJ Developer, Team Developer, ACCELL, and VISION; and data management software such as SQLBase and DataServer.

EXECUTIVES

Chairman: Steven D. (Steve) Whiteman, age 59
President, CEO, and Director: Todd E. Wille, age 47, $653,525 total compensation
VP, Finance and Administration, and CFO: Steven D. Bonham, age 53, $297,205 total compensation

VP and General Manager, Software Group: Mark T. Bygraves, age 52, $400,355 total compensation
VP Americas, APAC, and Russia Sales: Frank Verardi, age 60, $265,179 total compensation
VP Product Development and CTO: Duane George Sr., age 51, $269,147 total compensation
VP Business Development: Steve L. Soren
VP and General Manager, Composer Solutions: Kevin R. Kane, age 41
Director Strategic Alliances: Jesse Bornfreund
Auditors: Grant Thornton LLP

LOCATIONS

HQ: Unify Corporation
1420 Rocky Ridge Dr., Ste. 380, Roseville, CA 95661
Phone: 916-928-6400   **Fax:** 916-928-6404
Web: www.unify.com

PRODUCTS/OPERATIONS

2009 Sales

	$ mil.	% of total
Services	11.7	57
Software licenses	6.4	31
Migration solutions	2.5	12
Total	**20.6**	**100**

Selected Software

Application development
  Database applications (Accell/SQL)
  Internet integration applications (Accell/Web)
  Integrated development system (Accell/IDS)
  E-commerce applications (VISION)
Business Web applications (Unify NXJ)
Database management
  Enterprise data management system (DataServer)
  Relational database management (DataServer ELS)
  Thin client data access system (DBIntegrator)

Selected Services

Consulting
Maintenance
Training

COMPETITORS

Borland Software
CA, Inc.
Hewlett-Packard
IBM
Information Builders
IONA Technologies
Microsoft
OpenLink
Oracle
Progress Software
Sun Microsystems
Sybase
TIBCO Software

HISTORICAL FINANCIALS

Company Type: Public

Income Statement

FYE: April 30

	REVENUE ($ mil.)	NET INCOME ($ mil.)	NET PROFIT MARGIN	EMPLOYEES
4/09	20.6	2.4	11.7%	89
4/08	19.8	1.6	8.1%	71
4/07	11.2	(2.4)	—	63
4/06	11.2	(0.6)	—	60
4/05	11.3	(2.4)	—	60
Annual Growth	**16.2%**	**—**	**—**	**10.4%**

2009 Year-End Financials

Debt ratio: 9.0%
Return on equity: 32.6%
Cash ($ mil.): 6.1
Current ratio: 1.13
Long-term debt ($ mil.): 0.8
No. of shares (mil.): 10.1
Dividends
  Yield: —
  Payout: —
Market value ($ mil.): 29.7
R&D as % of sales: —
Advertising as % of sales: —

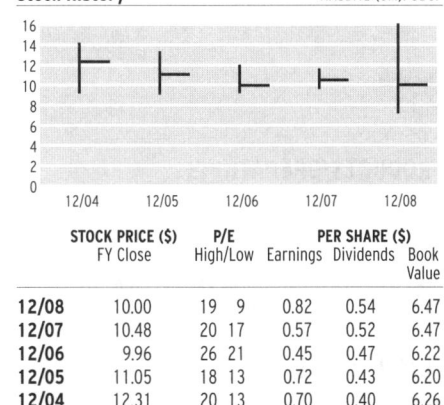

	4/05	4/06	4/07	4/08	4/09

	STOCK PRICE ($) FY Close	P/E High/Low	PER SHARE ($) Earnings	Dividends	Book Value
4/09	2.93	20 4	0.32	—	0.92
4/08	6.40	31 9	0.23	—	0.54
4/07	2.50	— —	(0.41)	—	0.08
4/06	2.20	— —	(0.10)	—	0.22
4/05	2.50	— —	(0.45)	—	0.25
Annual Growth	4.0%	— —	—	—	38.0%

United Bancorp

United Bancorp is the holding company of Ohio's Citizens Savings Bank, which operates as Citizens Savings Bank and The Community Bank. The bank divisions together operate some 20 branches, offering deposit and lending products including savings and checking accounts, commercial and residential mortgages, and consumer installment loans. Commercial loans and mortgages combined account for about 60% of the company's loan portfolio. In 2008 Citizens Savings Bank acquired the deposits of three failed banking offices from the FDIC.

EXECUTIVES

Chairman, President, and CEO; Chairman, The Community Bank and The Citizens Savings Bank, Martins Ferry: James W. Everson, age 71, $350,604 total compensation
SVP, COO, and Director; President and CEO, The Citizens Savings Bank, Martins Ferry: Scott A. Everson, age 39, $289,604 total compensation
SVP, CFO, Secretary, and Treasurer: Randall M. Greenwood, age 43, $163,872 total compensation
VP and Chief Lending Officer; Chief Lending Officer, The Citizens Savings Bank: James A. Lodes, age 62, $147,277 total compensation
VP and Chief Retail Banking Officer: Elmer K. Leeper
VP and CIO: Michael A. Lloyd, age 41
VP and Chief Commercial Banking Officer: Timothy L. Kelley
Auditors: BKD, LLP

LOCATIONS

HQ: United Bancorp, Inc.
201 S. 4th St., Martins Ferry, OH 43935
Phone: 740-633-0445
Web: www.unitedbancorp.com

COMPETITORS

Bank of America	JPMorgan Chase
BB&T	PNC Financial
City Holding	Premier Financial Bancorp
Huntington Bancshares	United Bankshares
Integra Bank	WesBanco

HISTORICAL FINANCIALS
Company Type: Public

Income Statement
FYE: December 31

	ASSETS ($ mil.)	NET INCOME ($ mil.)	INCOME AS % OF ASSETS	EMPLOYEES
12/08	441.8	3.8	0.9%	142
12/07	451.4	2.6	0.6%	219
12/06	421.7	2.1	0.5%	82
12/05	411.9	3.3	0.8%	113
12/04	397.5	3.2	0.8%	81
Annual Growth	2.7%	4.4%	—	15.1%

2008 Year-End Financials

Equity as % of assets: 7.7%
Return on assets: 0.9%
Return on equity: 11.2%
Long-term debt ($ mil.): 47.7
No. of shares (mil.): 5.2
Market value ($ mil.): 52.4
Dividends
  Yield: 5.4%
  Payout: 65.9%
Sales ($ mil.): 18.5
R&D as % of sales: —
Advertising as % of sales: —

	12/04	12/05	12/06	12/07	12/08

	STOCK PRICE ($) FY Close	P/E High/Low	PER SHARE ($) Earnings	Dividends	Book Value
12/08	10.00	19 9	0.82	0.54	6.47
12/07	10.48	20 17	0.57	0.52	6.47
12/06	9.96	26 21	0.45	0.47	6.22
12/05	11.05	18 13	0.72	0.43	6.20
12/04	12.31	20 13	0.70	0.40	6.26
Annual Growth	(5.1%)	— —	4.0%	7.8%	0.8%

United Financial Bancorp

United Financial Bancorp is the holding company for United Bank, which operates about 20 branches serving residents and businesses in western Massachusetts. It offers such standard deposit products as CDs and checking, money market, NOW, retirement, and savings accounts. Deposits are United Bank's primary source of funds for its lending activities, which focus on residential mortgages, commercial real estate loans, and home equity loans. To a lesser extent, the bank provides business, construction, and consumer loans. Its United Wealth Management Group provides investments and financial planning services.

Residential mortgage loans account for some 40% of United Financial's loan portfolio; commercial real estate loans add about 25% more.

Looking to expand, the company in 2009 won a bidding war with Berkshire Hills Bancorp to acquire CNB Financial Corp. and its Commonwealth National Bank subsidiary, which operates six branches in the Worcester, Massachusetts, area. United Financial's $25 million offer trumped Berkshire Hills' $19.5 million bid. Commonwealth National Bank was merged into United Bank.

United Bank was founded in 1882. The company converted from a mutual holding company to a stock holding company in 2007.

EXECUTIVES

President, CEO, and Director, United Bank: Richard B. Collins, age 66, $1,411,754 total compensation
EVP and CFO, United Financial Bancorp and United Bank: Mark A. Roberts, age 46, $353,828 total compensation
EVP Operations and Retail Sales, United Bank: Keith E. Harvey, age 61, $552,848 total compensation
EVP and Chief Lending Officer, United Bank: J. Jeffrey Sullivan, age 45, $420,174 total compensation
SVP Risk Management, United Bank: John J. Patterson, age 62, $306,141 total compensation
SVP Marketing and Community Relations, United Bank: Dena M. Hall, age 35
SVP Residential Lending, United Bank: William Clark
SVP Wealth Management, United Bank: Steven K Daury
Auditors: Grant Thornton LLP

LOCATIONS

HQ: United Financial Bancorp, Inc.
95 Elm St., West Springfield, MA 01089
Phone: 413-787-1700   **Fax:** 413-737-7879
Web: www.bankatunited.com

COMPETITORS

Bank of America	TD Bank USA
Citizens Financial Group	Westfield Financial

HISTORICAL FINANCIALS
Company Type: Public

Income Statement
FYE: December 31

	ASSETS ($ mil.)	NET INCOME ($ mil.)	INCOME AS % OF ASSETS	EMPLOYEES
12/08	1,263.1	7.3	0.6%	223
12/07	1,079.3	4.4	0.4%	207
12/06	1,009.4	4.9	0.5%	198
12/05	906.5	4.4	0.5%	182
12/04	772.0	5.5	0.7%	172
Annual Growth	13.1%	7.3%	—	6.7%

2008 Year-End Financials

Equity as % of assets: 18.0%
Return on assets: 0.6%
Return on equity: 3.2%
Long-term debt ($ mil.): 211.7
No. of shares (mil.): 16.1
Market value ($ mil.): 243.4
Dividends
  Yield: —
  Payout: —
Sales ($ mil.): 45.0
R&D as % of sales: —
Advertising as % of sales: —

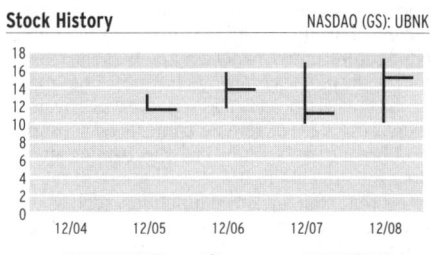

	12/04	12/05	12/06	12/07	12/08

	STOCK PRICE ($) FY Close	P/E High/Low	PER SHARE ($) Earnings	Dividends	Book Value
12/08	15.14	38 23	0.45	—	14.17
12/07	11.10	64 39	0.26	—	14.07
12/06	13.80	52 39	0.30	—	8.57
12/05	11.53	40 35	0.33	—	8.52
Annual Growth	9.5%	— —	(6.1%)	—	38.3%

Universal Electronics

Universal Electronics can help couch potatoes and TV junkies end multiple remote madness. The company makes and markets One For All-branded universal remote controls that are packed with infrared codes, allowing it to operate virtually any remote-capable device, including TVs, DVD players, and set-top boxes. It also produces Nevo-branded remotes and gear for home control systems and wireless networking. Universal Electronics sells and licenses its products and technologies worldwide to consumer electronics and computer manufacturers, as well as to cable and satellite companies such as DirecTV and Comcast. Its One For All remotes are sold by retailers worldwide.

After a similar attempt in early 2008, Universal Electronics in February 2009 acquired a stake in ZiLOG, which makes chips for universal remote controls. The chip maker in 2008 had rejected a $76 million hostile takeover bid made by Universal Electronics alongside ZiLOG investor Riley Investment Management. As part of the 2009 deal, ZiLOG sold its remote control hardware business to Maxim Integrated Products, which together with Universal shares licensed technology and intellectual property. In all, Universal Electronics will benefit from the deals by having access to ZiLOG's remote control software, patents, and other assets. As a result of the agreement, Universal Electronics made plans to retain a key group of ZiLOG's management in the areas of technology, operations, business development, sales, and engineering, as well as ZiLOG's staff in India.

Universal Electronics hopes to grow its share of the retail market in North America. To this end, the company signed an agreement with Audiovox in 2008 to be the exclusive supplier of its embedded microcontrollers and infrared database software, which are used in Audiovox's RCA-branded universal remote controls. Audiovox likewise received the distribution rights for Universal Electronics' One For All remotes sold in North America, Latin America, and the Asia/Pacific region. Also under the agreement, Universal Electronics plans to develop remotes under Audiovox's RCA and Acoustic Research brands.

In addition to researching remote control functionality, the company plans to expand its own product selection. Universal Electronics is extending the One For All name to cover digital antennas, signal boosters, and related audiovisual gear. The move is intended to boost sales in the company's consumer segment, which includes One For All-branded products, because of slightly decreased revenue in 2008. Universal Electronics cited tumultuous financial markets as the reason for the drop. The company's business lines made up for the loss, however, as revenue was driven by increasing sales of remote controls by subscription broadcasters. Universal Electronics attributed the growing figures to rising use of set-top boxes that offer advanced functions, such as digital video recording, video-on-demand, and high-definition TV.

Two business customers account for about a third of the company's sales. DirecTV and its subcontractors were Universal Electronics' top buyers, generating about 20% of sales, while Comcast contributed about 15% in 2008.

EXECUTIVES

Chairman and CEO: Paul D. Arling, age 46, $1,311,555 total compensation
EVP and General Manager, US Operations: Mark S. Kopaskie, age 51, $654,885 total compensation
EVP and Managing Director, Europe: Paul J. M. Bennett, age 53, $731,105 total compensation
SVP and CFO: Bryan M. Hackworth, age 39, $508,375 total compensation
SVP, General Counsel, and Secretary: Richard A. Firehammer Jr., age 51, $474,665 total compensation
SVP Sales: Pamela (Pam) Price
SVP Control and Technology Group, Europe: Olav Pouw
Auditors: Grant Thornton LLP

LOCATIONS

HQ: Universal Electronics Inc.
6101 Gateway Dr., Cypress, CA 90630
Phone: 714-820-1000   **Fax:** 714-820-1010
Web: www.uei.com

2008 Sales

	$ mil.	% of total
US	162.9	57
International	124.2	43
Total	**287.1**	**100**

PRODUCTS/OPERATIONS

2008 Sales

	$ mil.	% of total
Business	231.5	81
Consumer	55.6	19
Total	**287.1**	**100**

COMPETITORS

AMX
Crestron Electronics
Interlink Electronics
Logitech
Motorola, Inc.
Philips Electronics
Sony Electronics
THOMSON

HISTORICAL FINANCIALS

Company Type: Public

Income Statement

FYE: December 31

	REVENUE ($ mil.)	NET INCOME ($ mil.)	NET PROFIT MARGIN	EMPLOYEES
12/08	287.1	15.8	5.5%	433
12/07	272.7	20.2	7.4%	397
12/06	235.8	13.5	5.7%	392
12/05	181.3	9.7	5.4%	329
12/04	158.4	9.1	5.7%	296
Annual Growth	**16.0%**	**14.8%**	**—**	**10.0%**

2008 Year-End Financials

Debt ratio: —
Return on equity: 9.8%
Cash ($ mil.): 75.2
Current ratio: 2.96
Long-term debt ($ mil.): —
No. of shares (mil.): 13.7
Dividends
  Yield: 0.0%
  Payout: —
Market value ($ mil.): 222.1
R&D as % of sales: —
Advertising as % of sales: —

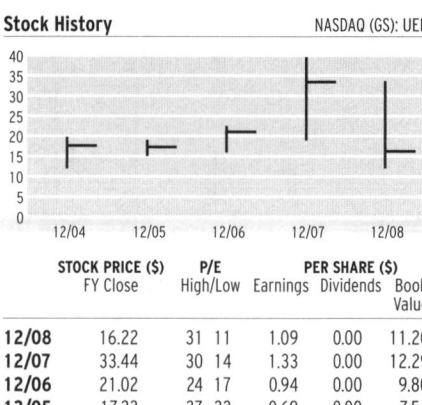

	STOCK PRICE ($) FY Close	P/E High/Low		PER SHARE ($) Earnings	Dividends	Book Value
12/08	16.22	31	11	1.09	0.00	11.20
12/07	33.44	30	14	1.33	0.00	12.29
12/06	21.02	24	17	0.94	0.00	9.80
12/05	17.23	27	22	0.69	0.00	7.54
12/04	17.60	30	19	0.65	0.00	7.59
Annual Growth	**(2.0%)**	**—**	**—**	**13.8%**	**—**	**10.2%**

Universal Power Group

Universal Power Group (UPG) gives customers a charge. The company primarily distributes batteries and electrical parts to manufacturers and retailers in the US. Its products include lithium and nickel-cadmium batteries for such applications as cell phones, camcorders, and motorcycles. UPG also supplies electronic components and other hardware used in security systems, including alarm kits, sirens, and intercoms. In addition, UPG provides logistics services such as warehousing, inventory sourcing, and graphic design. Among the company's customers are Brink's Home Security, Bass Pro Shops, Home Depot Supply, and RadioShack.

As part of its growth strategy, Universal Power Group plans to expand its logistics services by developing new offerings such as freight forwarding and shipping and electronic order entry. The company also intends to provide additional products, as well as enter new markets in Europe and Latin America.

In 2008 Universal Power Group formed a partnership with Amphenol under which Amphenol will develop connectors for UPG's sealed lead-acid batteries. The company will sell the connectors under the UPG UNIVERSAL brand.

Also that year the company agreed to acquire the assets of Monarch Hunting Products, diversifying its product portfolio. The transaction was completed in early 2009. Monarch and UPG expect they will be able to cross-sell products to sporting goods retailers through the combination.

EVP/COO Ian Edmonds was appointed interim president, CEO, and CFO after the departure of several top executives. In mid-2009 he was named president and CEO on a more permanent basis.

Universal Power Group has facilities in Georgia, Nevada, Oklahoma, and Texas.

Zunicom owns 40% of Universal Power Group. Wilen Management holds nearly 14% of the company.

TIVES

n and CEO: Robert L. Gerry III, age 72,
523 total compensation
t, COO, and Director: W. Russell Scheirman,
$1,037,207 total compensation
egory R. (Greg) Hullinger, age 56,
total compensation
Corporate Secretary: Gayla M. Cutrer, age 67,
54 total compensation
: Deloitte & Touche LLP

TIONS

ALCO Energy, Inc.
00 Post Oak Place, Ste. 309, Houston, TX 77027
713-623-0801 **Fax:** 713-623-0982
ww.vaalco.com

) Energy has oil and gas exploration interests in
Gabon, and the US.

UCTS/OPERATIONS

ed Subsidiaries

O Energy (Gabon), Inc.
O Energy (USA), Inc.
O Gabon (Etame), Inc. (90%)
O Production (Gabon), Inc.

PETITORS

Mobil
st Natural Resources
Corporation
ial Oil
Pioneer Natural Resources
Royal Dutch Shell
TOTAL

TORICAL FINANCIALS

ny Type: Public

e Statement FYE: December 31

	REVENUE ($ mil.)	NET INCOME ($ mil.)	NET PROFIT MARGIN	EMPLOYEES
8	169.5	29.7	17.5%	75
7	125.0	19.1	15.3%	35
6	98.3	45.5	46.3%	16
5	84.9	32.8	38.6%	16
4	56.5	26.0	46.0%	12
al th	31.6%	3.4%	—	58.1%

8 Year-End Financials

ratio: 3.0%
n on equity: 19.3%
($ mil.): 125.4
ent ratio: 2.41
-term debt ($ mil.): 5.0
f shares (mil.): 56.6
Dividends
Yield: —
Payout: —
Market value ($ mil.): 421.1
R&D as % of sales: —
Advertising as % of sales: —

ck History NYSE: EGY

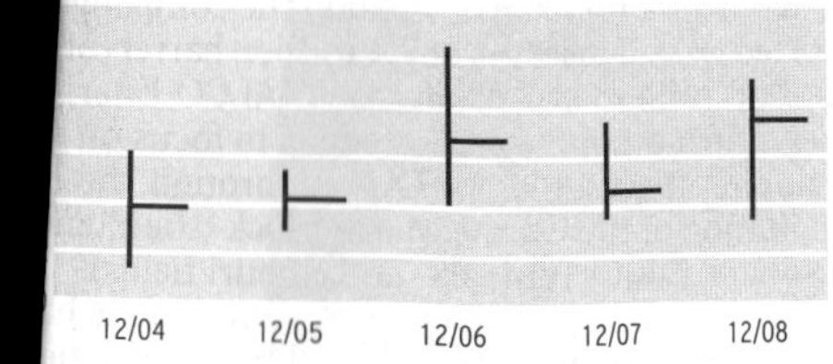

	STOCK PRICE ($) FY Close	P/E High	P/E Low	PER SHARE ($) Earnings	Dividends	Book Value
2/08	7.44	18	7	0.50	—	2.93
2/07	4.65	23	11	0.32	—	2.51
2/06	6.75	16	6	0.67	—	2.16
2/05	4.24	11	6	0.50	—	1.38
2/04	3.88	15	4	0.39	—	0.84
nnual rowth	17.7%	—	—	6.4%	—	36.5%

VASCO Data Security

VASCO Data Security International holds the key to electronic banking. Its Digipass product line features security tokens, handheld devices, and related software used for authenticating a person's identity on computer networks. The company's products incorporate authentication and digital signature security technologies, and can be used to secure intranets and extranets, as well as LANs. In addition to banking, VASCO's products are used to provide remote workers with secure access to corporate networks; other applications include e-commerce transactions. The company, which generates more than 90% of its revenues outside the US, continues to expand internationally.

The company has customers in more than 100 countries. Its European headquarters is located in Zurich, and it has sales subsidiaries in the Americas, the Asia/Pacific region, Europe, and the Middle East.

VASCO utilizes a direct sales force, as well as distribution, reseller, and systems integration channels. Clients include HSBC, Rabobank, VeriSign, and Wachovia.

Banks and other financial institutions remain VASCO's bread-and-butter customer base, but the company is expanding its enterprise security business. It serves the enterprise market exclusively through indirect marketing channels. VASCO's enterprise segment accounts for almost 20% of its revenues.

Chairman and CEO Kendall Hunt owns more than a quarter of the company.

EXECUTIVES

Chairman and CEO: T. Kendall (Ken) Hunt, age 66, $903,711 total compensation
President and COO: Jan Valcke, age 54, $1,107,123 total compensation
EVP, CFO, and Secretary: Clifford K. (Cliff) Bown, age 57, $845,636 total compensation
CIO: Victor Hoogland
Director Contracts and Compliance: Alexandra Spirig
Director Corporate Communications: Jochem Binst
Director Worldwide Human Resources: Bernhard Kolb
Auditors: KPMG LLP

LOCATIONS

HQ: VASCO Data Security International, Inc.
1901 S. Meyers Rd., Ste. 210
Oakbrook Terrace, IL 60180
Phone: 630-932-8844 **Fax:** 630-932-8852
Web: www.vasco.com

2008 Sales

	$ mil.	% of total
Europe, Middle East & Africa	89.5	67
Asia/Pacific	10.1	8
US	7.8	6
Other countries	25.6	19
Total	**133.0**	**100**

PRODUCTS/OPERATIONS

2008 Sales

	$ mil.	% of total
Banking	108.9	82
Enterprise Security	24.1	18
Total	**133.0**	**100**

COMPETITORS

ActivIdentity
Aladdin Knowledge Systems
Entrust
RSA Security
SafeNet

HISTORICAL FINANCIALS

Company Type: Public

Income Statement FYE: December 31

	REVENUE ($ mil.)	NET INCOME ($ mil.)	NET PROFIT MARGIN	EMPLOYEES
12/08	133.0	24.3	18.3%	310
12/07	120.0	21.0	17.5%	240
12/06	76.1	12.6	16.6%	184
12/05	54.6	7.7	14.1%	128
12/04	29.9	3.3	11.0%	112
Annual Growth	45.2%	64.7%	—	29.0%

2008 Year-End Financials

Debt ratio: —
Return on equity: 29.1%
Cash ($ mil.): 57.7
Current ratio: 3.53
Long-term debt ($ mil.): —
No. of shares (mil.): 37.5
Dividends
Yield: 0.0%
Payout: —
Market value ($ mil.): 387.2
R&D as % of sales: —
Advertising as % of sales: —

Stock History NASDAQ (GM): VDSI

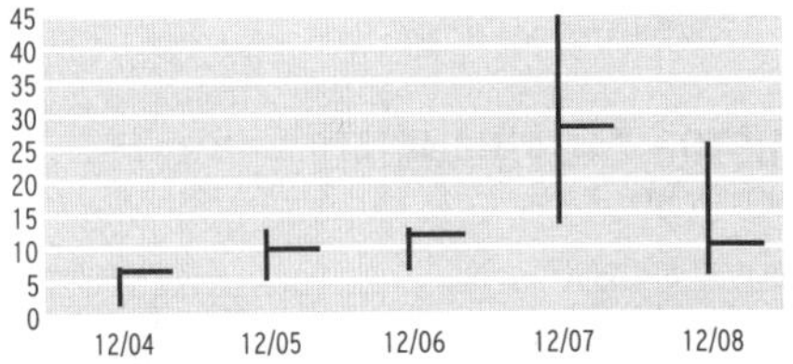

	STOCK PRICE ($) FY Close	P/E High	P/E Low	PER SHARE ($) Earnings	Dividends	Book Value
12/08	10.33	39	10	0.64	0.00	2.54
12/07	27.92	80	25	0.55	0.00	1.91
12/06	11.85	38	21	0.33	0.00	1.13
12/05	9.86	59	26	0.21	0.00	0.68
12/04	6.62	77	20	0.09	0.00	0.35
Annual Growth	11.8%	—	—	63.3%	—	64.4%

Vascular Solutions

Vascular Solutions helps answer the age-old question, "How do you mend a broken heart?" The company develops and markets proprietary blood-clotting bandages, clot-removal catheters, and other products used during vascular medical procedures. The firm makes the D-Stat, a hemostat bandage used to control surgical bleeding. It also makes the Pronto extraction catheter, which removes arterial clots, and the Vari-Lase, a laser system for treating varicose veins. Vascular Solutions markets the devices to interventional cardiologists and radiologists through its own sales team in the US; it uses independent distributors overseas except in Germany, where its Vascular Solutions GmbH subsidiary handles sales.

Other products include specialty catheters such as the Langston catheter, which measures intravascular pressure gradients. In 2006 the

EXECUTIVES

Chairman: William K.W. Tan, age 65
President, CEO, and Director: Ian C. Edmonds, age 37,
  $303,019 total compensation
**SVP Business Development and Marketing and
  Secretary:** Mimi Tan, age 35,
  $222,431 total compensation
SVP Finance and Treasurer: Julie A. Sansom-Reese,
  age 46
SVP Supply Chain and Information Technology:
  Ramin Salehi, age 35
Auditors: KBA Group LLP

LOCATIONS

HQ: Universal Power Group, Inc.
  1720 Hayden Rd., Carrollton, TX 75006
Phone: 469-892-1122   **Fax:** 469-892-1123
Web: www.upgi.com

COMPETITORS

All American Semiconductor
Arrow Electronics
Avnet
C&D Technologies
C.H. Robinson Worldwide
DHL
FedEx
Interstate Batteries
Jaco Electronics
UPS
UTi Worldwide
WESCO International

HISTORICAL FINANCIALS

Company Type: Public

Income Statement

FYE: December 31

	REVENUE ($ mil.)	NET INCOME ($ mil.)	NET PROFIT MARGIN	EMPLOYEES
12/08	117.9	1.2	1.0%	90
12/07	108.5	2.2	2.0%	76
12/06	92.6	0.3	0.3%	66
12/05	81.3	1.1	1.4%	65
12/04	67.2	0.4	0.6%	65
Annual Growth	15.1%	31.6%	—	8.5%

2008 Year-End Financials

Debt ratio: 19.5%
Return on equity: 6.6%
Cash ($ mil.): 0.3
Current ratio: 1.63
Long-term debt ($ mil.): 3.7
No. of shares (mil.): 5.0

Dividends
  Yield: 0.0%
  Payout: —
Market value ($ mil.): 12.9
R&D as % of sales: —
Advertising as % of sales: —

Stock History

NYSE Alternext: UPG

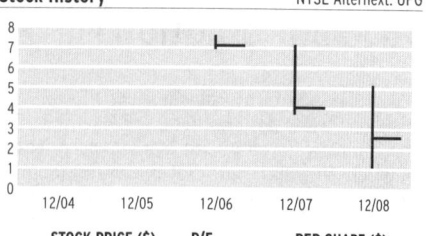

	STOCK PRICE ($) FY Close	P/E High/Low		PER SHARE ($) Earnings	Dividends	Book Value
12/08	2.58	20	5	0.25	0.00	3.74
12/07	4.04	16	9	0.44	0.00	3.53
12/06	7.10	108	100	0.07	0.00	3.06
Annual Growth	(39.7%)	—	—	89.0%	—	10.5%

U.S. Physical Therapy

U.S. Physical Therapy lends a hand to injured workers, athletes, and others in need of some TLC. With about 350 outpatient clinics in more than 40 states, U.S. Physical Therapy provides physical and occupational therapy services for work-related and sports injuries, trauma, and post-surgical rehabilitation. The clinics operate under a number of local or regional brands, including Desert Hand Therapy, Denali Physical Therapy, and Star Physical Therapy. To attract and retain physical therapists, the company offers recruited therapists a stake in their local clinics, either through minority ownership or profit-sharing agreements.

Most of the clinics are joint ventures, in which licensed therapists/clinic managers own a minority stake; others are wholly owned by the company but operated through profit-sharing agreements. The company also manages a handful of physician-owned clinics.

The company relies on its therapist-managers to maintain relationships with local physicians who refer patients to the clinics. Services are paid for by commercial health insurance, managed care programs, Medicare, workers' compensation insurance, or proceeds from personal injury cases.

Historically, U.S. Physical Therapy has grown by developing and opening new clinics, some of them satellites of existing partnerships; it opened 17 clinics in 2007. Since 2005, however, the company has sped up its growth by acquiring other outpatient physical therapy providers. In 2007, for example, it acquired a majority interest in STAR Physical Therapy, an outpatient rehab company operating more than 50 clinics in the southeastern US.

In 2006 the company decided to close 26 money-losing clinics in 13 states, and it closed down another 12 in 2007.

EXECUTIVES

Chairman: Daniel C. Arnold, age 79
Vice Chairman: Mark J. Brookner, age 64
President, CEO, and Director:
  Christopher J. (Chris) Reading, age 45,
  $995,268 total compensation
COO: Glenn D. McDowell, age 53,
  $455,691 total compensation
EVP, CFO, and Director: Lawrance W. (Larry) McAfee,
  age 54, $968,564 total compensation
VP and Controller: Jon C. Bates
Auditors: Grant Thornton LLP

LOCATIONS

HQ: U.S. Physical Therapy, Inc.
  1300 W. Sam Houston Pkwy. South, Ste. 300
  Houston, TX 77042
Phone: 713-297-7000   **Fax:** 713-297-7090
Web: www.usph.com

PRODUCTS/OPERATIONS

2008 Sales

	$ mil.	% of total
Net patient revenue	182.9	97
Management contracts	4.7	3
Total	**187.7**	**100**

HISTORICAL FINAN

Company Type: Public

Income Statement

	REVENUE ($ mil.)	IN(($
12/08	187.7	1
12/07	151.7	
12/06	135.2	(
12/05	132.1	8
12/04	118.3	6
Annual Growth	12.2%	10.5(

2008 Year-End Financials

Debt ratio: 15.2%   D
Return on equity: 13.2%
Cash ($ mil.): 10.1
Current ratio: 2.65   M
Long-term debt ($ mil.): 12.4   R&
No. of shares (mil.): 11.6   Ad

Stock History

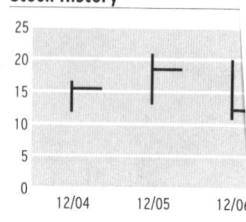

	STOCK PRICE ($) FY Close	P/E High/Low
12/08	13.33	25 11
12/07	14.37	21 16
12/06	12.25	37 20
12/05	18.47	28 18
12/04	15.42	30 22
Annual Growth	(3.6%)	— —

EXECU

Chairma
  $1,258,
Presiden
  age 54,
CFO: G
  $66,30
VP and
  $524,4
Auditor

LOCA

HQ: VA
  46
Phone:
Web: w

VAALCO
Angola

PROD

Selec
VAALC
VAALC
VAALC
VAALC

COM

Exxon
Harve
Hess
Impe

HIS

Comp

Incor

12/0
12/0
12/0
12/0
12/0
Annu Grow

200

Deb
Retu
Casi
Curr
Lon
No.

Sto

12
10
8
6

VAALCO Energy

VAALCO Energy has boldly g players are sure to follow. The s is engaged in the acquisition, e opment, and production of oil a Energy holds exploration asset Gabon, and has interests in the and offshore Louisiana. In 2008 ported proved reserves of 7.4 mill and 30 million cu. ft. of gas. V/ near-term production strategy is veloping its reserves in Gabon t ploitation of the Etame Marin blc Avouma, South Tchibala, and Ebc

VAALCO Energy's long-term st ance its lower-risk domestic drillir potential international prospects.

It sold its high-risk Philippine ho

The company merged with the 1 in a reverse acquisition in 1998. Th managed by Brown Brothers Harri New York, controlled 65% of VAAL its stake in 2005.

company launched two additional specialty catheters, the Twin-Pass and the Skyway, both of which are used during guidewire procedures.

Vascular Solutions inked marketing and supply agreements with King Pharmaceuticals in 2007, giving King marketing rights to the company's ThrombiGel hemostat products in non-interventional cardiology markets.

The company's first product was the Duett device, which uses a balloon catheter and a proprietary blood clotting cocktail of collagen, diluent, and thrombin to seal arterial punctures following such procedures as angiography, angioplasty, and stenting. Competition in the sealing device market led the company to focus on additional medical devices, and the Duett products now make up less than 5% of sales.

EXECUTIVES

CEO and Director: Howard C. Root, age 48, $674,733 total compensation
VP Finance, CFO, and Secretary: James Hennen, age 36, $327,244 total compensation
VP Quality: Brett Demchuk, age 45, $204,476 total compensation
VP International Sales: William (Bill) Rutstein, age 56
VP Sales Operations: Susan Christian, age 40
Auditors: Virchow, Krause & Company, LLP

LOCATIONS

HQ: Vascular Solutions, Inc.
6464 Sycamore Ct., Minneapolis, MN 55369
Phone: 763-656-4300   **Fax:** 763-656-4251
Web: www.vascularsolutions.com

2008 Sales

	% of total
US	87
Other countries	13
Total	**100**

PRODUCTS/OPERATIONS

2008 Sales

	$ mil.	% of total
Products		
Hemostat products	23.5	38
Extraction catheters	15.0	25
Vein products	10.0	16
Access products	5.6	9
Specialty catheters	4.5	8
Other products	1.1	2
License & collaboration	1.5	2
Total	**61.2**	**100**

Selected Products

Hemostat products
D-Stat Dry hemostat bandage
D-Stat Flowable topical hemostat
Duett seal for catheterization procedures
ThrombiGel hemostatic foam

Extraction catheters (Pronto)

Vein products
Auto-Fill anesthetic syringe
Vari-Lase procedure kit

Specialty catheters
Langston catheter
Skyway support catheter
Twin-Pass dual access catheter

Access products
Guardian hemostasis valve
Micro-introducer kits
Specialty guidewires

Other products
Acolysis ultrasound thrombolysis system (international markets only)
MAX-Support abdominal retraction belt (international markets only)

COMPETITORS

Abbott Labs	ev3
AngioDynamics	Johnson & Johnson
Bard	Kensey Nash
Boston Scientific	Medtronic
Dornier	St. Jude Medical

HISTORICAL FINANCIALS

Company Type: Public

Income Statement
FYE: December 31

	REVENUE ($ mil.)	NET INCOME ($ mil.)	NET PROFIT MARGIN	EMPLOYEES
12/08	61.2	16.2	26.5%	252
12/07	52.9	(4.3)	—	242
12/06	43.3	(1.8)	—	210
12/05	32.8	(0.6)	—	179
12/04	22.3	(3.5)	—	144
Annual Growth	**28.7%**	**—**	**—**	**15.0%**

2008 Year-End Financials

Debt ratio: 0.0%
Return on equity: 72.6%
Cash ($ mil.): 7.2
Current ratio: 4.27
Long-term debt ($ mil.): 0.0
No. of shares (mil.): 16.4
Dividends
  Yield: —
  Payout: —
Market value ($ mil.): 147.9
R&D as % of sales: —
Advertising as % of sales: —

Stock History
NASDAQ (GM): VASC

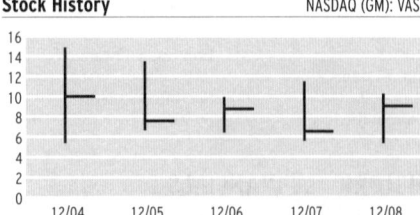

	STOCK PRICE ($) FY Close	P/E High/Low		PER SHARE ($) Earnings	Dividends	Book Value
12/08	9.02	10	5	1.01	—	1.94
12/07	6.50	—	—	(0.28)	—	0.78
12/06	8.73	—	—	(0.12)	—	0.88
12/05	7.56	—	—	(0.04)	—	0.86
12/04	10.02	—	—	(0.25)	—	0.84
Annual Growth	**(2.6%)**	**—**	**—**	**—**	**—**	**23.5%**

Verisk Analytics

Insurance is a risky business, and Verisk Analytics is in the business of helping to manage that risk. The company compiles data designed to detect fraud and predict loss for customers in the US property and casualty insurance, health care, and mortgage industries. Its Risk Assessment unit runs databases that hold billions of records containing statistical and underwriting data used to price insurance policies and write policy language. Its Decision Analytics unit provides health care claims payors and mortgage lenders with predictive models, loss estimation tools, and fraud ID applications. Verisk was created by subsidiary Insurance Services Office (ISO) as a means of going public; Verisk completed its IPO in 2009.

The company went public in October 2009 in one of the largest filings of the year, raising almost $1.9 billion. Minority investors in Verisk who benefited from the IPO included ACE, AIG, Hartford Financial, and Travelers Companies. Warren Buffett's Berkshire Hathaway owns a 10% stake in the company, while Verisk employees own about 20%.

About two-thirds of Verisk's revenue is generated by the US property and casualty insurance industry. Major customers in this category include AIG, Allstate, Hartford, and Liberty Mutual. The company aggregates data about premiums and losses in all 50 states and Puerto Rico to help firms comply with insurance regulators. It sells its products and services through a direct sales force. Customers in the health care, mortgage lending, and government categories include numerous Blue Cross and Blue Shield plans, Wells Fargo, and FEMA.

In an effort to enter new markets and offer new and enhanced products, Verisk Analytics has both an organic and an acquisitive growth strategy. Its product development process incorporates market research, internal software development, and alliances with other information providers and technology companies. Following its IPO, Verisk promptly acquired loss-prevention service provider Enabl-u Technologies in late 2009 to gain access to its data management resources.

EXECUTIVES

Chairman, President, and CEO: Frank J. Coyne, age 60
EVP, Information Services and Government Relations: Carole J. Banfield, age 69
EVP and COO: Scott G. Stephenson, age 52
SVP and CFO: Mark V. Anquillare, age 43
SVP, General Counsel, and Corporate Secretary: Kenneth E. Thompson, age 49
SVP, AISG: Vincent Cialdella, age 58
SVP, Insurance Services: Kevin B. Thompson, age 57
VP, Sales: Neil Spector
VP, Marketing and Corporate Communications: Christopher H. Perini
VP, Business Development: Wayne Lattuca
Auditors: Deloitte & Touche LLP

LOCATIONS

HQ: Verisk Analytics, Inc.
545 Washington Blvd., Jersey City, NJ 07310
Phone: 201-469-3000   **Fax:** 201-748-1472
Web: www.verisk.com

PRODUCTS/OPERATIONS

2008 Sales

	$ mil.	% of total
Risk assessment		
Industry standard insurance programs	329.9	37
Property-specific rating & underwriting	125.7	14
Statistical agency & data services	27.5	3
Actuarial services	21.3	2
Decision analytics		
Fraud identification & detection solutions	214.0	24
Loss prediction solutions	95.1	11
Loss quantification solutions	80.0	9
Total	**893.5**	**100**

COMPETITORS

Computer Sciences Corp.
Deloitte Consulting
DMG Information
Fair Isaac
First American CoreLogic
Ingenix
LexisNexis
McKesson

HISTORICAL FINANCIALS

Company Type: Public

Income Statement

FYE: December 31

	REVENUE ($ mil.)	NET INCOME ($ mil.)	NET PROFIT MARGIN	EMPLOYEES
12/08	893.5	158.2	17.7%	3,731
12/07	802.2	150.4	18.7%	3,404
12/06	730.1	139.0	19.0%	—
Annual Growth	10.6%	6.7%	—	9.6%

2008 Year-End Financials

Debt ratio: —
Return on equity: —
Cash ($ mil.): 33.2
Current ratio: 0.33
Long-term debt ($ mil.): 450.4

Net Income History

NASDAQ (GS): VRSK

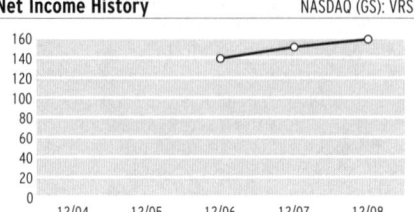

	12/04	12/05	12/06	12/07	12/08

Versant Corporation

Objectivity is the key for Versant. The company's object-oriented (as opposed to relational) database management systems are used primarily by telecommunications and financial services companies for such purposes as real-time data analysis, fraud detection, service activation and assurance, and customer billing. Its products process, store, and distribute information ranging from graphics, video, and unstructured text found in company databases to transactional data from Web-based applications.

In February 2006 the company sold its WebSphere consulting business. In early 2008 Versant bolstered its offerings in the embedded device market by purchasing the database software business of Servo Software.

EXECUTIVES

Chairman: William Henry Delevati, age 60
President, CEO, and Director: Jochen Witte, age 48, $670,119 total compensation
VP Finance, CFO, and Secretary: Jerry Wong, age 58, $340,480 total compensation
VP Product Engineering: Gerhard Klein
VP Open Source Operations: Robert Greene
VP Sales North America: David Ingersoll
VP Software Engineering: Andreas Renner
Media Relations: Thorsten Singhofen
Auditors: Grant Thornton LLP

LOCATIONS

HQ: Versant Corporation
255 Shoreline Dr., Ste. 450
Redwood City, CA 94065
Phone: 650-232-2400 **Fax:** 650-232-2401
Web: www.versant.com

PRODUCTS/OPERATIONS

2008 Sales

	% of total
License	63
Maintenance	36
Professional services	1
Total	**100**

Selected Software

Versant Object Database (object-oriented database)
Versant enJin (deploying Java-based applications)
Versant enJin Tool Integration (integrated tools for IBM and Borland applications)
Versant Fault Tolerant Server (database recovery and restoration application)
Versant Monitoring Console (VMC — real-time systems monitoring software)
Versant Online Database Reorganizer (systems management application)
Versant SQL Suite (supports transition from SQL to VDS or Versant enJin)

Selected Services

Consulting
Maintenance
Mentoring
Technical Support
Training

COMPETITORS

BMC Software	OpenLink
CA, Inc.	Oracle
IBM	Progress Software
InterSystems	SAP
Microsoft	Sun Microsystems
Objectivity, Inc.	Sybase

HISTORICAL FINANCIALS

Company Type: Public

Income Statement

FYE: October 31

	REVENUE ($ mil.)	NET INCOME ($ mil.)	NET PROFIT MARGIN	EMPLOYEES
10/08	25.3	9.5	37.5%	82
10/07	21.1	7.6	36.0%	80
10/06	16.7	3.8	22.8%	76
10/05	20.5	(14.6)	—	100
10/04	22.9	(12.0)	—	126
Annual Growth	2.5%	—	—	(10.2%)

2008 Year-End Financials

Debt ratio: —
Return on equity: 33.7%
Cash ($ mil.): 27.2
Current ratio: 6.05
Long-term debt ($ mil.): —
No. of shares (mil.): 3.6
Dividends
Yield: 0.0%
Payout: —
Market value ($ mil.): 56.9
R&D as % of sales: —
Advertising as % of sales: —

Stock History

NASDAQ (CM): VSNT

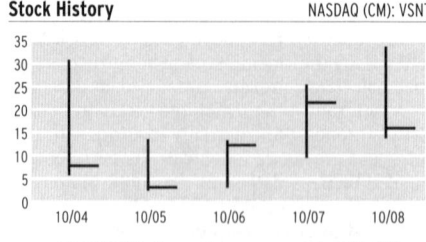

	10/04	10/05	10/06	10/07	10/08

	STOCK PRICE ($) FY Close	P/E High/Low		PER SHARE ($) Earnings	Dividends	Book Value
10/08	15.99	13	6	2.51	0.00	9.32
10/07	21.58	12	5	2.06	0.00	6.51
10/06	12.27	11	3	1.20	0.00	3.88
10/05	3.15	—	—	(4.11)	0.00	2.53
10/04	7.80	—	—	(3.80)	0.00	6.43
Annual Growth	19.7%	—	—	—	—	9.7%

ViaSat, Inc.

ViaSat serves up digital satellite, networking, and signal processing equipment for both government and commercial clients. It makes secure networking products for tactical communications and mobile satellite communications systems designed for military UHF frequencies. For the commercial market, ViaSat produces satellite broadband systems for consumer applications, as well as antenna systems, mobile satellite systems, and very small aperture terminal (VSAT) products used in enterprise telecommunications. The US government is the company's largest client. Other key customers include aerospace and defense contractors such as Boeing, Northrop Grumman, and Raytheon, as well as telecom service providers.

ViaSat's business is heavily weighted toward serving government agencies such as the Department of Defense and its contractors, and the percentage of its total sales to the US government rose to 36% in 2009. However, the company is eyeing the civilian commercial segment as an area of growth. It has said that it sees opportunity in underserved areas of developing nations in particular, where demand for expanded communications infrastructure is on the rise.

To this end, ViaSat acquired broadband satellite Internet provider WildBlue Communications for $568 million in a 2009 bid to add consumer communications services to its sales mix. ViaSat hopes that the launch of a new satellite (slated for early 2011) will make it possible for WildBlue to boost its transmission speeds to levels comparable with those offered by terrestrial cable broadband providers.

EXECUTIVES

Chairman and CEO: Mark D. Dankberg, age 54, $2,036,080 total compensation
President and COO: Richard A. Baldridge, age 51, $1,387,503 total compensation
SVP; President, ViaSat-1: Thomas E. (Tom) Moore
SVP: Gregory D. Monahan
VP and CFO: Ronald G. Wangerin, age 42, $766,364 total compensation
VP and CTO: Steven R. Hart, age 56, $626,467 total compensation
VP and CTO: Mark J. Miller, age 49, $601,468 total compensation
VP, General Counsel, and Secretary: Keven K. Lippert, age 37
VP Human Resources: H. Stephen (Steve) Estes, age 54
Director Marketing Projects: Bruce Rowe
Auditors: PricewaterhouseCoopers LLP

LOCATIONS

HQ: ViaSat, Inc.
6155 El Camino Real, Carlsbad, CA 92009
Phone: 760-476-2200 **Fax:** 760-929-3941
Web: www.viasat.com

2009 Sales

	$ mil.	% of total
North America		
US	528.3	82
Other countries	14.8	5
Europe, Middle East & Africa	49.0	7
Asia/Pacific	30.8	5
Central & Latin America	5.3	1
Total	**628.2**	**100**

PRODUCTS/OPERATIONS

2009 Sales

	$ mil.	% of total
Government systems	388.6	62
Commercial networks	230.9	37
Satellite services	8.7	1
Total	**628.2**	**100**

Selected Products

Government
Mobile military satellite communications
Modems
Terminals
Testing and training equipment
Tactical networking and information security (ViaSat Data Controller)
Tactical radio systems (MIDS)
Commercial
Antenna systems
Consumer broadband systems (SurfBeam)
Very small aperture terminal (VSAT) systems (Linkstar, Skylinx, Linkway, Starwire)

COMPETITORS

Andrew Corporation	Hughes Network
BAE SYSTEMS	iDirect Technologies
Boeing	L-3 Communications
General Dynamics	Lockheed Martin
Gilat Satellite	Northrop Grumman
Harris Corp.	Raytheon

HISTORICAL FINANCIALS

Company Type: Public

Income Statement

FYE: Friday nearest March 31

	REVENUE ($ mil.)	NET INCOME ($ mil.)	NET PROFIT MARGIN	EMPLOYEES
3/09	628.2	38.3	6.1%	1,800
3/08	574.7	33.5	5.8%	1,680
3/07	516.6	30.2	5.8%	1,463
3/06	433.8	23.5	5.4%	1,289
3/05	345.9	19.3	5.6%	1,029
Annual Growth	**16.1%**	**18.7%**	**—**	**15.0%**

2009 Year-End Financials

Debt ratio: —
Return on equity: 8.9%
Cash ($ mil.): 63.5
Current ratio: 2.50
Long-term debt ($ mil.): —
No. of shares (mil.): 31.9
Dividends
Yield: —
Payout: —
Market value ($ mil.): 663.7
R&D as % of sales: —
Advertising as % of sales: —

Stock History

NASDAQ (GS): VSAT

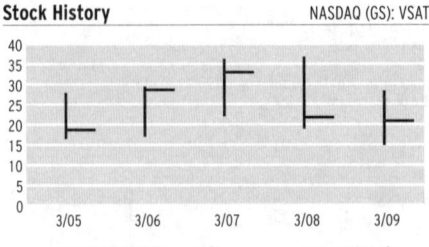

	STOCK PRICE ($) FY Close	P/E High/Low	PER SHARE ($) Earnings	Dividends	Book Value
3/09	20.82	23 13	1.20	—	14.39
3/08	21.72	35 18	1.04	—	12.68
3/07	32.97	37 23	0.98	—	10.94
3/06	28.65	36 21	0.81	—	8.26
3/05	18.69	41 25	0.68	—	7.10
Annual Growth	**2.7%**	**— —**	**15.3%**	**—**	**19.3%**

Village Bank & Trust

Does it take a village to raise a bank? Village Bank & Trust is the holding company for Village Bank, which has about a dozen branches in the suburbs of Richmond, Virginia. It offers standard services, including deposit accounts, loans, and credit cards. Deposit funds are used to write loans for consumers and businesses in the area; commercial real estate loans account for more than 40% of the bank's lending portfolio, which also includes business, construction, residential mortgage, and consumer loans. Village Bank & Trust subsidiaries provide property/casualty insurance, mortgages, and other financial services. In 2008 the bank acquired the three-branch River City Bank in a $20.2 million transaction.

Village Bank & Trust focuses its business in Virginia's Chesterton County; it also has branches in nearby Henrico and Powhatan counties.

It plans to continue launching new branch banking offices in its service area, including one in its new headquarters building, which opened in 2008.

EXECUTIVES

Chairman: Craig D. Bell, age 51
Vice Chairman: Donald J. Balzer Jr., age 53
President, CEO, and Director; President and CEO, Village Bank: Thomas W. Winfree, age 64, $286,388 total compensation
SVP and CFO, Village Bank and Trust Financial and Village Bank: C. Harrill Whitehurst Jr., age 58, $162,712 total compensation
SVP; SVP and COO, Village Bank: Raymond E. Sanders, age 55, $161,651 total compensation
President and CEO, Village Bank Mortgage: Jerry W. Mabry
SVP Lending, Village Bank: Jack M. Robeson Jr., age 60
SVP and Chief Lending Officer, Village Bank: Chris P. Kyriakides, age 46
SVP Commercial Banking, Village Bank: Dennis J. Falk, age 50
SVP Retail Banking, Village Bank: Rebecca L. (Joy) Kline
SVP, Village Bank: William D. (Bill) Stegeman, age 49
VP Information Technology, Village Bank: Bob Thomas
VP and Director Human Resources, Village Bank: Robert R. Staples
Auditors: BDO Seidman, LLP

LOCATIONS

HQ: Village Bank & Trust Financial Corp.
15521 Midlothian Tpke., Ste. 200
Midlothian, VA 23113
Phone: 804-897-3900 **Fax:** 804-897-4750
Web: www.villagebank.com

PRODUCTS/OPERATIONS

2008 Gross Revenues

	$ mil.	% of total
Interest		
Loans	28.1	85
Securities	0.7	2
Other	0.2	1
Noninterest		
Gain on sale of loans	2.4	7
Other	1.8	5
Total	**33.2**	**100**

COMPETITORS

Bank of America	Community Bankers Trust
Bank of McKenney	F & M Bank
Bank of Virginia	First Capital Bancorp
BB&T	SunTrust
C&F Financial	Union Bankshares Corp.
Central Virginia Bankshares	

HISTORICAL FINANCIALS

Company Type: Public

Income Statement

FYE: December 31

	ASSETS ($ mil.)	NET INCOME ($ mil.)	INCOME AS % OF ASSETS	EMPLOYEES
12/08	572.4	0.5	0.1%	167
12/07	393.3	1.0	0.3%	130
12/06	291.2	1.4	0.5%	120
12/05	215.0	1.2	0.6%	101
12/04	160.3	0.9	0.6%	69
Annual Growth	**37.5%**	**(13.7%)**	**—**	**24.7%**

2008 Year-End Financials

Equity as % of assets: 8.1%
Return on assets: 0.1%
Return on equity: 1.4%
Long-term debt ($ mil.): 25.0
No. of shares (mil.): 4.2
Market value ($ mil.): 19.0
Dividends
Yield: 0.0%
Payout: —
Sales ($ mil.): 17.3
R&D as % of sales: —
Advertising as % of sales: —

Stock History

NASDAQ (CM): VBFC

	STOCK PRICE ($) FY Close	P/E High/Low	PER SHARE ($) Earnings	Dividends	Book Value
12/08	4.50	72 21	0.16	0.00	10.91
12/07	10.70	47 26	0.37	0.00	6.36
12/06	14.20	25 20	0.59	0.00	6.06
12/05	12.85	23 18	0.61	0.00	4.05
12/04	11.60	31 24	0.45	0.00	3.54
Annual Growth	**(21.1%)**	**— —**	**(22.8%)**	**—**	**32.5%**

ViroPharma Incorporated

ViroPharma didn't want to wait until its drugs were approved to start making money, so instead it bought an approved one. The development-stage firm discovers drugs to combat RNA viruses, a category that includes cytomegalovirus (CMV) in transplant patients and gastrointestinal infections. To finance its development the company acquired the antibiotic Vancocin, which treats conditions of staph and other infections, from Eli Lilly. Vancocin is distributed through wholesalers in the US. The company also markets Cinryze, a drug made from human plasma to combat angioedema (swelling of the skin or hives).

ViroPharma's products under development include Maribavir for the treatment of CMV and intranasal Peconaril to treat the common cold, which is licensed to Merck & Co.

In 2008 the company acquired Lev Pharmaceuticals, a biotech developer of inflammatory disease treatments, for $443 million (plus potential future milestone payments that could value the deal at over $617 million). The purchase expands ViroPharma's portfolio of serious disease treatments under development for niche customer markets.

Earlier in 2008 the company had discontinued development of investigational hepatitis C drug HCV-796, which it was developing in collaboration with Wyeth (now part of Pfizer), because of safety concerns.

ViroPharma is also seeking other partnership or acquisition opportunities to further expand its product development and marketing operations.

EXECUTIVES

Chairman, President, and CEO:
Vincent J. (Vinnie) Milano, age 45,
$1,576,273 total compensation
VP, COO, and Chief Commercial Officer:
Daniel B. (Dan) Soland, age 50,
$1,145,218 total compensation
VP and CFO: Charles A. (Charlie) Rowland Jr., age 50,
$118,914 total compensation
VP and Chief Scientific Officer: Colin Broom, age 53,
$1,233,370 total compensation
VP Strategic Initiatives: Thomas F. Doyle, age 48,
$1,138,248 total compensation
VP Regulatory Affairs and Quality:
Robert (Bob) Pietrusko, age 60,
$959,753 total compensation
VP Information Technology: Thomas Lembck
VP, General Counsel, and Secretary: J. Peter Wolf,
age 39
VP Corporate Communications: William C. Roberts
VP Human Resources: Carolyn Vanderweghe
Controller and Chief Accounting Officer:
Richard S. Morris, age 35
Manager Corporate Communications and Investor Relations: Robert A. Doody Jr.
Auditors: KPMG LLP

LOCATIONS

HQ: ViroPharma Incorporated
730 Stockton Dr., Exton, PA 19341
Phone: 610-458-7300   **Fax:** 610-458-7380
Web: www.viropharma.com

PRODUCTS/OPERATIONS

Selected Products

Marketed
 Vancocin
 Cinryze
In development
 Maribavir
 NTCD

COMPETITORS

Achillion	Optimer
Amgen	Oscient Pharmaceuticals
AstraZeneca	Pharmasset
Cubist Pharmaceuticals	Roche Holding
Genzyme	Salix Pharmaceuticals
Gilead Sciences	Teva Pharmaceuticals
GlaxoSmithKline	Theravance
Idenix Pharmaceuticals	Valeant
MedImmune	Vertex Pharmaceuticals
Merck	Vical

HISTORICAL FINANCIALS
Company Type: Public

Income Statement
FYE: December 31

	REVENUE ($ mil.)	NET INCOME ($ mil.)	NET PROFIT MARGIN	EMPLOYEES
12/08	232.3	67.6	29.1%	201
12/07	203.8	95.4	46.8%	115
12/06	167.2	66.7	39.9%	67
12/05	132.4	113.7	85.9%	48
12/04	22.4	(19.5)	—	36
Annual Growth	79.5%	—	—	53.7%

2008 Year-End Financials

Debt ratio: 37.8%
Return on equity: 11.7%
Cash ($ mil.): 275.8
Current ratio: 8.30
Long-term debt ($ mil.): 250.0
No. of shares (mil.): 77.4
Dividends
 Yield: 0.0%
 Payout: —
Market value ($ mil.): 1,008.3
R&D as % of sales: —
Advertising as % of sales: —

Stock History
NASDAQ (GS): VPHM

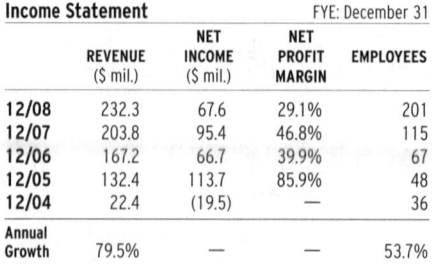

	STOCK PRICE ($) FY Close	P/E High/Low	Earnings	PER SHARE ($) Dividends	Book Value
12/08	13.02	18 10	0.83	0.00	8.54
12/07	7.94	15 6	1.21	0.00	6.41
12/06	14.64	25 7	0.95	0.00	5.32
12/05	18.50	12 1	2.02	0.00	4.22
12/04	3.25	— —	(0.73)	0.00	(0.34)
Annual Growth	41.5%	— —	—	—	—

Virtual Radiologic

Virtual Radiologic diagnoses from a distance. The teleradiology company offers remote diagnostic imaging services, interpreting diagnostic scans made by overworked and understaffed radiology practices throughout the US. It transmits the images and results over a secure broadband network using proprietary workflow management software. Virtual Radiologic operates 24 hours a day, 365 days a year, and reads images made by a number of modalities, including ultrasound, nuclear medicine, computed tomography (CT), and magnetic resonance imaging (MRI). The company serves more than 450 customers.

Virtual Radiologic is using the proceeds of its 2007 IPO for a number of purposes, including paying down debt and expanding its service offering and its radiology staff. It's also using the money for marketing programs, infrastructure improvements, and acquisitions.

The company wasted little time in making acquisitions after its IPO, purchasing Idaho-based Diagna Radiology in 2008. Teleradiology company Diagna brought some subspecialty expertise (in areas such as neuroradiology and nuclear medicine), as well as customers in 17 states.

Former chairman Sean Casey and private investment firm Generation Capital Partners each own more than 25% of Virtual Radiologic.

EXECUTIVES

Chairman and CEO: Robert (Rob) Kill, age 46,
$371,678 total compensation
CFO: Leonard C. (Len) Purkis, age 61,
$1,516,049 total compensation
CTO: Richard W. (Rick) Jennings, age 49,
$362,828 total compensation
Chief Medical Officer and Director: Eduard Michel,
age 48, $519,966 total compensation
VP, General Counsel, and Secretary:
Michael (Mike) Kolar, age 39
Director Investor and Public Relations: Mollie O'Brien
Auditors: PricewaterhouseCoopers LLP

LOCATIONS

HQ: Virtual Radiologic Corporation
5995 Opus Pkwy., Ste. 200, Minnetonka, MN 55343
Phone: 952-392-1100   **Fax:** 952-942-3361
Web: www.virtualrad.net

COMPETITORS

Alliance HealthCare
American HealthChoice
InSight Health
NightHawk Radiology
Philips Remote Cardiac Services
Team Health

HISTORICAL FINANCIALS
Company Type: Public

Income Statement
FYE: December 31

	REVENUE ($ mil.)	NET INCOME ($ mil.)	NET PROFIT MARGIN	EMPLOYEES
12/08	106.6	8.5	8.0%	241
12/07	86.2	(20.3)	—	245
12/06	54.1	(12.0)	—	234
12/05	27.0	(1.5)	—	178
12/04	12.9	(1.4)	—	—
Annual Growth	69.5%	—	—	10.6%

2008 Year-End Financials

Debt ratio: —
Return on equity: 15.9%
Cash ($ mil.): 19.2
Current ratio: 4.12
Long-term debt ($ mil.): —
No. of shares (mil.): 15.9
Dividends
 Yield: —
 Payout: —
Market value ($ mil.): 134.9
R&D as % of sales: —
Advertising as % of sales: —

Stock History
NASDAQ (GM): VRAD

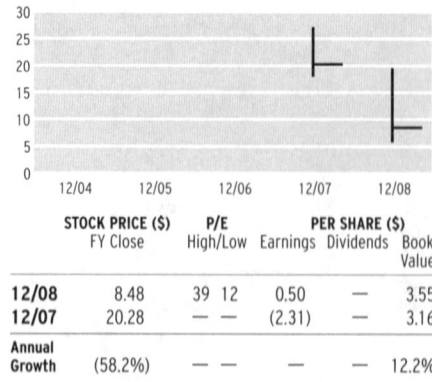

	STOCK PRICE ($) FY Close	P/E High/Low	Earnings	PER SHARE ($) Dividends	Book Value
12/08	8.48	39 12	0.50	—	3.55
12/07	20.28	— —	(2.31)	—	3.16
Annual Growth	(58.2%)	— —	—	—	12.2%

Virtusa Corporation

Virtusa believes that virtually any business can improve its technology. Founded in 1996, the company provides a variety of software development and information technology services, including software engineering, application development, training, maintenance, systems design, and legacy migration. Virtusa's customers come from industries such as financial services, telecommunications, manufacturing, and retail, including BT Group and Vignette. It has operations in the US, the UK, India, and Sri Lanka. Sigma Partners Associates owns about 20% of the company.

Virtusa plans to funnel IPO proceeds toward the construction of a new facility in Hyderabad, India, as well as for other facility expansion efforts, additional personnel, and working capital.

EXECUTIVES

Chairman and CEO: Kris A. Canekeratne, age 43, $502,988 total compensation
EVP Business Development and Client Services: Raj Rajgopal, age 49
EVP Global Services; President, Asia: Roger K. (Keith) Modder, age 45, $244,372 total compensation
EVP Client Services and Business Development: John Gillis
EVP and COO: Thomas R. (Tom) Holler, age 46, $954,137 total compensation
SVP, CFO, Treasurer, and Secretary: Ranjan Kalia, age 49, $299,048 total compensation
SVP Marketing: Doug Mow
SVP Business Development and Head Banking, Financial Services and Insurance Business Unit: Jim Francis
VP, General Counsel, and Assistant Secretary: Paul D. Tutun
VP, Continental Europe: Henk Glazener
Auditors: KPMG LLP

LOCATIONS

HQ: Virtusa Corporation
2000 West Park Dr., Westborough, MA 01581
Phone: 508-389-7300   **Fax:** 508-366-9901
Web: www.virtusa.com

COMPETITORS

Accenture
BearingPoint
Capgemini
Cognizant Tech Solutions
Computer Sciences Corp.
Deloitte Consulting
HCL Technologies
HP Enterprise Services
IBM Global Services
Infosys
Patni Computer Systems
Sapient
Satyam
Tata Consultancy

HISTORICAL FINANCIALS

Company Type: Public

Income Statement

FYE: March 31

	REVENUE ($ mil.)	NET INCOME ($ mil.)	NET PROFIT MARGIN	EMPLOYEES
3/09	172.9	12.1	7.0%	4,048
3/08	165.2	17.8	10.8%	4,265
3/07	124.7	19.0	15.2%	3,576
3/06	76.9	2.0	2.6%	3,576
3/05	60.5	1.1	1.8%	—
Annual Growth	30.0%	82.1%	—	4.2%

2009 Year-End Financials

Debt ratio: —
Return on equity: 7.8%
Cash ($ mil.): 55.7
Current ratio: 4.03
Long-term debt ($ mil.): —
No. of shares (mil.): 23.8
Dividends
Yield: 0.0%
Payout: —
Market value ($ mil.): 147.7
R&D as % of sales: —
Advertising as % of sales: —

Stock History

NASDAQ (GM): VRTU

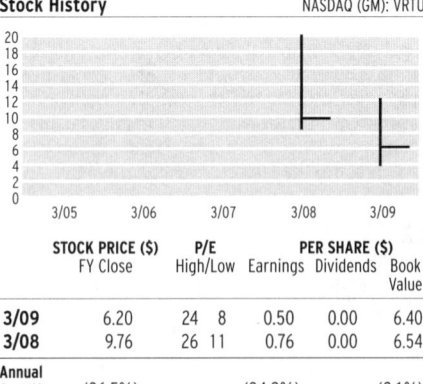

	STOCK PRICE ($) FY Close	P/E High/Low	PER SHARE ($) Earnings	Dividends	Book Value
3/09	6.20	24 8	0.50	0.00	6.40
3/08	9.76	26 11	0.76	0.00	6.54
Annual Growth	(36.5%)	— —	(34.2%)	—	(2.1%)

Vitamin Shoppe

Vitamin Shoppe (formerly VS Holdings) helps vitamin shoppers meet their recommended daily requirements. The company sells vitamins, supplements, and minerals as well as herbal, homeopathic, and personal care products through more than 400 The Vitamin Shoppe stores in about 35 US states and the District of Columbia, a catalog, and the VitaminShoppe.com and BodyTech.com Web sites. Stores offer more than 20,000 items from some 700 national brands plus private-label products. Founded in 1977 as a corner shop in New York City, the company was taken private by Irving Place Capital (formerly Bear Stearns Merchant Banking) in 2002. In 2009 Vitamin Shoppe raised about $155 million in an initial public offering.

Concurrent with its return to the public market, the company changed its name from VS Holdings to the more familiar Vitamin Shoppe moniker. Proceeds from the offering went to the selling shareholders and not to the company. (Irving Place Capital retained a majority stake in Vitamin Shoppe.) Two years prior to its successful IPO the retailer attempted to go public, but the recession and unfavorable market conditions intervened. At the time of the IPO Vitamin Shoppe was the first brick-and-mortar retailer to go public since December 2007.

The fast-growing chain has more than doubled in size since 2003. After opening 62 stores in 2008, the company plans to continue to add stores at a rate of about 30 to 35 new locations per year going forward. It's also entering new markets, including Hawaii, Minnesota, and New Mexico in 2008. The five new Hawaii stores are in resort locations. (Rival Walgreen entered Hawaii in 2007.) In early 2008 the company acquired five Nutrition Depot locations in Florida, which were soon converted to Vitamin Shoppe locations. The company's long-term goal is to operate more than 900 US stores. It prefers to locate shops in freestanding buildings or corner locations in strip malls, rather than traditional shopping malls.

The Vitamin Shoppe also launched a new format — called Eco Shoppe — in Austin, Texas, in May 2009. Eco Shoppe, as its name suggests, sells green-living products including apparel; home, garden, and gift items; office and pet supplies; baby and kids products; and yoga gear. Previously the company launched a new e-commerce site called BodyTech.com, devoted to products for bodybuilders and other athletes.

EXECUTIVES

Chairman and CEO: Richard L. Markee, age 56
President and Chief Merchandising Officer: Anthony N. (Tony) Truesdale, age 47
EVP, COO, and CFO: Michael G. (Mike) Archbold, age 49
Chief Marketing Officer: Louis H. Weiss, age 40
VP, General Counsel, and Corporate Secretary: James M. Sander, age 52
VP Information Technology: Michael Provost
VP Supply Chain Management: Richard Tannenbaum
VP Scientific and Regulatory Affairs: David Morrison
VP Merchandising: Doug Jones
VP Finance: Cosmo La Forgia, age 53
VP Human Resources: Michael Simon
Auditors: Deloitte & Touche LLP

LOCATIONS

HQ: Vitamin Shoppe, Inc.
2101 91st St., North Bergen, NJ 07047
Phone: 201-868-5959   **Fax:** 800-852-7153
Web: www.vitaminshoppe.com

2008 Locations

	No.
New York	58
California	51
Florida	45
Texas	33
New Jersey	22
Virginia	20
Illinois	17
Maryland	13
Pennsylvania	12
North Carolina	11
Massachusetts	10
Michigan	10
Georgia	9
Ohio	9
Colorado	8
Connecticut	7
Arizona	7
Tennessee	6
Wisconsin	6
Indiana	5
Hawaii	5
South Carolina	5
Washington	5
Oregon	4
Louisiana	3
Nevada	3
Other states	17
Total	**401**

PRODUCTS/OPERATIONS

2008 Sales

	$ mil.	% of total
Stores	522.5	87
Direct (catalog & Internet)	79.0	13
Total	**601.5**	**100**

2008 Sales

	$ mil.	% of total
Supplements & sports nutrition	336.4	56
Vitamins, minerals & herbs	209.7	35
Delivery revenue	4.2	—
Other	51.2	9
Total	**601.5**	**100**

Selected Products

Herbal products
Homeopathic products
Personal care products
  Foot care
  Hair care
  Mouth care
  Pet care
  Skin care
  Women's products
Supplements
Vitamins

COMPETITORS

Costco Wholesale
CVS Caremark
drugstore.com
Forever Living
Gaiam
GNC
Herbalife Ltd.
Kmart
Kroger
Medicine Shoppe
MotherNature.com
Nature's Sunshine
NBTY
PureTek
Rite Aid
Safeway
Target
Vitamin World
Walgreen
Wal-Mart
Whole Foods

HISTORICAL FINANCIALS

Company Type: Public

Income Statement			FYE: Last Saturday in December	
	REVENUE ($ mil.)	NET INCOME ($ mil.)	NET PROFIT MARGIN	EMPLOYEES
12/08	601.5	8.2	1.4%	3,114
12/07	537.9	6.8	1.3%	2,880
12/06	486.0	4.8	1.0%	2,612
12/05	436.5	(5.7)	—	—
12/04	387.4	(0.6)	—	—
Annual Growth	**11.6%**	**—**	**—**	**9.2%**

2008 Year-End Financials

Debt ratio: 99.8%
Return on equity: 5.0%
Cash ($ mil.): 1.6
Current ratio: 1.71
Long-term debt ($ mil.): 168.3

Net Income History

NYSE: VSI

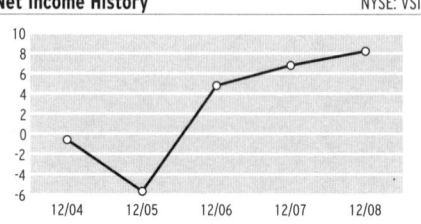

Vocus, Inc.

Vocus' focus is simplifying public and government relations processes. Vocus provides hosted, on-demand software that helps automate a variety of public relations duties; it organizes media contacts, manages news collection, and analyzes public relations effectiveness. Its government relations software offers a state and federal legislative contact list and project management tracking and lobbying analysis tools. Users vary from not-for-profits and the government to corporations and public relations professionals. The company also offers a proprietary information database of over 800,000 journalists, analysts, media outlets, and publicity opportunities.

The company has used acquisitions to expand its offerings, including the purchase of privately held Gnossos Software, which boosted its government relations software business.

Vocus markets its software to small and midsized organizations as a way of tackling public relations tasks that would otherwise require a costly dedicated staff. Its pitch to larger organizations with their own PR staff involves using its tools as a more efficient way of managing content and tracking the success of PR campaigns.

EXECUTIVES

Chairman, President, and CEO:
  Richard (Rick) Rudman, age 48,
  $3,701,778 total compensation
CFO, Secretary, and Treasurer: Stephen (Steve) Vintz,
  age 40, $1,420,674 total compensation
CTO: Mark Heys, age 37
Chief Marketing Officer: William R. (Bill) Wagner,
  age 42, $986,115 total compensation
SVP North American Sales: Norman Weissberg, age 47,
  $1,284,430 total compensation
SVP Customer Services: Darren Stewart, age 40
Managing Director, Vocus International: Andrew Muir,
  age 53, $1,262,404 total compensation
PRWeb Product Manager: Jiyan Wei
Director Product Management: Kye Strance
Media: Robin Lane
Auditors: Ernst & Young LLP

LOCATIONS

HQ: Vocus, Inc.
  4296 Forbes Blvd., Lanham, MD 20706
Phone: 301-459-2590   **Fax:** 301-459-2827
Web: www.vocus.com

COMPETITORS

Biz360
Cision
Medialink
PR Newswire
Reuters
United Business Media

HISTORICAL FINANCIALS

Company Type: Public

Income Statement			FYE: December 31	
	REVENUE ($ mil.)	NET INCOME ($ mil.)	NET PROFIT MARGIN	EMPLOYEES
12/08	77.5	6.9	8.9%	463
12/07	58.1	1.0	1.7%	341
12/06	40.3	0.4	1.0%	317
12/05	28.1	(5.1)	—	220
12/04	20.4	(2.6)	—	170
Annual Growth	**39.6%**	**—**	**—**	**28.5%**

2008 Year-End Financials

Debt ratio: 0.2%
Return on equity: 8.5%
Cash ($ mil.): 65.4
Current ratio: 2.24
Long-term debt ($ mil.): 0.2
No. of shares (mil.): 19.4
Dividends
  Yield: 0.0%
  Payout: —
Market value ($ mil.): 352.7
R&D as % of sales: —
Advertising as % of sales: —

Stock History

NASDAQ (GM): VOCS

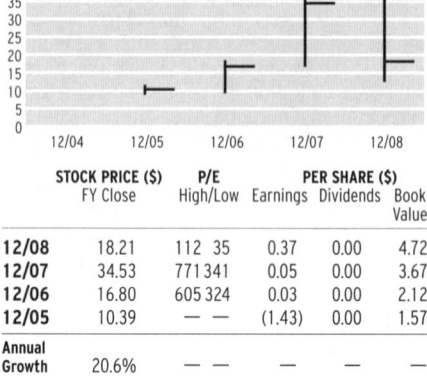

	STOCK PRICE ($) FY Close	P/E High/Low	PER SHARE ($)		
			Earnings	Dividends	Book Value
12/08	18.21	112 35	0.37	0.00	4.72
12/07	34.53	771 341	0.05	0.00	3.67
12/06	16.80	605 324	0.03	0.00	2.12
12/05	10.39	— —	(1.43)	0.00	1.57
Annual Growth	**20.6%**	**— —**	**—**	**—**	**—**

Volcom, Inc.

Volcom says that it's "youth against establishment," and this establishment comes down firmly on the side of youth — skateboarding, surfing, and snowboarding youth in hoodies and chinos. The company designs and makes board sports apparel and accessories for men, women, and kids. It also operates about 20 retail stores in the US and abroad. In addition to Volcom outlets, the firm's gear is available through online retailers, major department stores (Macy's, Nordstrom), and specialty shops (Zumiez, Pacific Sunwear) in the US, Canada, and Puerto Rico. Longtime surfer and former marketer for surf wear giant and rival Quiksilver, Richard Woolcott (chairman and CEO), founded Volcom in 1991. He owns about 15% of the firm.

Volcom is strengthening its brand's global reach through licensing and the extension of its operations. The brand is marketed to about 40 other countries by distributors and licensees in the Asia/Pacific region, Latin America, and South Africa. Upon conclusion of its contract with its European licensee, Volcom set up its own European headquarters in France in 2007. The move has resulted in greater revenues for the firm, spurring it to acquire additional control of its international operations. To this end, Volcom in 2008 took over distribution of its branded products in the UK and Japan.

To bolster its position in the action sports segment that year, Volcom acquired Electric Visual Evolution, a maker of sporty eyewear and apparel, for about $25 million. Electric's products are marketed in about 20 countries.

Besides its own branded outlets, Volcom oversees operations for two Laguna Surf & Sport stores in California. The retailer, which was acquired in 2008, is a prominent surf shop and has had a hand in setting nationwide fashion trends.

Retailer Pacific Sunwear accounts for about 15% of sales while the company's five largest customers contribute to about a third of sales.

Volcom is trying to lessen its dependence on Pac Sun and anticipates its Pac Sun sales will drop in 2009.

Volcom works to keep its logo front and center with antiestablishment youth through sponsorship of concerts, sports events, board-sports athletes, and cyclists. The company also runs film and music divisions.

EXECUTIVES

Chairman and CEO: Richard R. Woolcott, age 43, $445,350 total compensation
President and COO: Jason W. Steris, age 38, $338,640 total compensation
EVP, CFO, Treasurer, and Secretary: Douglas P. Collier, age 46, $336,930 total compensation
EVP Marketing: Troy C. Eckert, age 36, $336,000 total compensation
EVP Sales: Tom D. Ruiz, age 49, $379,894 total compensation
VP Strategic Development and General Counsel: Seth H. (Hoby) Darling
Auditors: Deloitte & Touche LLP

LOCATIONS

HQ: Volcom, Inc.
1740 Monrovia Ave., Costa Mesa, CA 92627
Phone: 949-646-2175   **Fax:** 949-646-5247
Web: www.volcom.com

2008 Sales

	% of total
US	59
Europe	23
Canada	10
Asia/Pacific	4
Other	4
Total	**100**

PRODUCTS/OPERATIONS

2008 Sales

	$ mil.	% of total
Products	332.1	99
Licensing	2.2	1
Total	**334.3**	**100**

Selected Sponsored Athletes

Skateboarding
Mark Appleyard
Rune Glifberg
Geoff Rowley

Snowboarding
Terje Haakonsen
Elena Hight
Janna Meyen

Surfing
Bruce Irons
Dean Morrison
Ozzie Wright

COMPETITORS

Abercrombie & Fitch
Apple Inc.
Billabong
Burton
Columbia Sportswear
DC Shoes
Lost International
Pacific Sunwear
Patagonia, Inc.
Quiksilver
Skechers U.S.A.
Sony Music
Sony USA
Stüssy
Vans

HISTORICAL FINANCIALS

Company Type: Public

Income Statement

FYE: December 31

	REVENUE ($ mil.)	NET INCOME ($ mil.)	NET PROFIT MARGIN	EMPLOYEES
12/08	334.3	21.7	6.5%	490
12/07	268.6	33.3	12.4%	337
12/06	205.3	28.8	14.0%	259
12/05	160.0	29.3	18.3%	181
12/04	113.2	24.6	21.7%	172
Annual Growth	**31.1%**	**(3.1%)**	**—**	**29.9%**

2008 Year-End Financials

Debt ratio: 0.0%
Return on equity: 11.8%
Cash ($ mil.): 79.6
Current ratio: 6.52
Long-term debt ($ mil.): 0.0
No. of shares (mil.): 24.4

Dividends
  Yield: —
  Payout: —
Market value ($ mil.): 265.7
R&D as % of sales: —
Advertising as % of sales: —

Stock History

NASDAQ (GS): VLCM

	STOCK PRICE ($) FY Close	P/E High/Low		PER SHARE ($) Earnings	Dividends	Book Value
12/08	10.90	32	7	0.89	—	7.95
12/07	22.03	37	16	1.37	—	7.09
12/06	29.57	35	15	1.18	—	5.50
12/05	34.01	28	18	1.34	—	4.21
Annual Growth	**(31.6%)**	**—**	**—**	**(58.3%)**	**—**	**60.1%**

Volterra Semiconductor

Volterra Semiconductor aims to usher in a new era in voltage control for microchips. The fabless semiconductor company designs and markets low-voltage power supply chips, including switching regulators for communications and networking applications. Its products are designed to replace several power management components with a single device. IBM, distributor Metatech, and EIL are top customers. The company takes its name from Italian mathematician and physicist Vito Volterra. There is also a Tuscan town named Volterra. Nearly all of Volterra Semiconductor's sales comes from international customers.

Volterra outsources fabrication of its products, primarily to Chartered Semiconductor Manufacturing, Samsung Electronics, and Taiwan Semiconductor Manufacturing.

A former Volterra employee was arrested in early 2005 by federal agents and charged with illegally e-mailing proprietary data sheets to CMSC,

a semiconductor company in Taiwan. The former employee may also have transferred files of proprietary company information to his personal computers. The man, Shin-Guo Tsai, pleaded guilty later that year to a federal felony charge.

Integral Capital Management owns about 9% of Volterra Semiconductor, while William Blair & Company holds nearly 8%. Artis Capital Management has an equity stake of around 7% in the company. T. Rowe Price owns almost 7%. Schroder Investment Management North America, part of Schroders, holds more than 6%. Brown Advisory Holdings has an equity stake of approximately 5%.

EXECUTIVES

Chairman: Christopher B. (Chris) Paisley, age 56
President, CEO, and Director: Jeffrey (Jeff) Staszak, age 56, $1,086,144 total compensation
VP Finance, CFO, Treasurer, and Secretary: Mike Burns, age 43, $474,704 total compensation
VP Marketing: William (Bill) Numann, age 53, $596,158 total compensation
VP Sales and Applications Engineering: Craig Teuscher, age 42, $560,427 total compensation
VP Design Engineering: David Lidsky, age 43, $526,007 total compensation
VP Quality and Reliability: Achilleas Veziris
VP IC Technology and Process Development: Marco Zuniga
VP World Wide Operations: David Ng
Chief Scientist: Anthony Stratakos, age 37
Investor Relations: Heidi Flannery
Auditors: KPMG LLP

LOCATIONS

HQ: Volterra Semiconductor Corporation
47467 Fremont Blvd., Fremont, CA 94538
Phone: 510-743-1200   **Fax:** 510-743-1600
Web: www.volterra.com

Volterra Semiconductor has offices in Japan, Singapore, Taiwan, the UK, and the US.

2008 Sales

	% of total
China	47
Singapore	40
Japan	5
Taiwan	4
US	2
Other countries	2
Total	**100**

PRODUCTS/OPERATIONS

Selected Products

Voltage regulator chipsets (VT1000)
Voltage regulator semiconductors (VT100, VT200)

COMPETITORS

Analog Devices
Analogic Technologies
International Rectifier
Intersil
Linear Technology
Marvell Technology
Maxim Integrated Products
Microsemi
National Semiconductor
ON Semiconductor
Semtech
Texas Instruments

HISTORICAL FINANCIALS
Company Type: Public

Income Statement
FYE: December 31

	REVENUE ($ mil.)	NET INCOME ($ mil.)	NET PROFIT MARGIN	EMPLOYEES
12/08	104.2	14.3	13.7%	182
12/07	74.7	0.6	0.8%	164
12/06	74.6	6.9	9.2%	151
12/05	53.9	5.4	10.0%	121
12/04	43.9	5.1	11.6%	115
Annual Growth	24.1%	29.4%	—	12.2%

2008 Year-End Financials

Debt ratio: —
Return on equity: 20.5%
Cash ($ mil.): 46.9
Current ratio: 6.16
Long-term debt ($ mil.): —
No. of shares (mil.): 25.2

Dividends
  Yield: 0.0%
  Payout: —
Market value ($ mil.): 180.3
R&D as % of sales: —
Advertising as % of sales: —

Stock History
NASDAQ (GM): VLTR

	30 25 20 15 10 5 0
	12/04 12/05 12/06 12/07 12/08

	STOCK PRICE ($) FY Close	P/E High/Low	PER SHARE ($) Earnings	Dividends	Book Value
12/08	7.15	31 11	0.57	0.00	3.01
12/07	11.03	1,675 1,055	0.01	0.00	2.51
12/06	15.00	75 49	0.26	0.00	2.85
12/05	15.00	106 46	0.21	0.00	2.29
12/04	22.16	120 32	0.22	0.00	1.99
Annual Growth	(24.6%)	— —	26.9%	—	10.9%

VSE Corporation

VSE brings military hand-me-downs back into fashion. The company provides engineering, testing, and logistics services for the US Army, the US Navy, and other government agencies on a contract basis. VSE operates through its subsidiaries, which support VSE's Federal Group (engineering, logistics, communications, and management sciences) and its International Group (fleet maintenance and foreign military sales). The International Group's BAV division helps reactivate old Navy ships and transfer them to other countries. VSE generates almost all of its revenues from the Army (60%) and Navy (19%), the US Department of Energy, and other military branches and governmental agencies.

The company depends heavily on just a few large contracts; one of its largest, a ship transfer contract between BAV and the Navy, accounts for about 17% of VSE's revenues. VSE's largest customer is the US Department of Defense (DoD), which includes the Army, Navy, and Air Force.

VSE has three wholly owned subsidiaries. Virginia-based G&B Solutions was acquired in 2008 for almost $20 million. G&B provides clients in the US government with management consulting and information technology services.

The year before, VSE's subsidiary Integrated Concepts & Research Corporation (ICRC) was acquired for almost $12 million in cash. ICRC is a provider of diversified technical and management services, primarily to the US government. The acquisitions of G&B and ICRC have expanded VSE's business into government branches beyond the DoD, such as the Department of Treasury, the Department of Energy, the Department of the Interior, and other federal and civil agencies.

While VSE caters primarily to the government, it additionally serves commercial entities with construction, consulting, engineering, IT, logistics, and program management services. Its third subsidiary Energetics Incorporated is a full-service technical and management consulting company that covers the energy, utility, environmental, transportation, and manufacturing industries.

Relying on government contracts can be a bit like walking a mine field. VSE must be prepared for funding delays, terminations, and political moratoriums. Because the company performs most of its contract work through subcontractors, it must monitor the work closely to ensure compliance with government laws and regulations.

Investor Calvin Koonce, a member of VSE's board, controls a 16% stake in the company. VSE was established in Virginia in 1959 with three employees. Its first contract was to provide the US Navy with a competitive bidding package for missile rocket motors.

EXECUTIVES

Chairman: Donald M. Ervine, age 72, $1,191,807 total compensation
President, CEO, COO, and Director: Maurice A. Gauthier, $1,046,755 total compensation
EVP and CFO: Thomas R. Loftus, age 53, $572,394 total compensation
EVP; President, Federal Group: Thomas G. Dacus, age 63, $641,605 total compensation
EVP, Chief Administrative Officer, and Secretary: Craig S. Weber, age 64
EVP Strategic Initiatives and Business Development: James W. Lexo Jr., age 60, $563,228 total compensation
EVP; President VSE International Group: Michael E. (Mike) Hamerly, age 63
VP Marketing: Randy W. Hollstein
Assistant VP and CIO: David W. Chivers
Director Public Relations, Advertising, and Mass Communications: Sylvia Gethicker
Director Human Resources: Elizabeth M. (Liz) Price
Auditors: Ernst & Young LLP

LOCATIONS

HQ: VSE Corporation
  2550 Huntington Ave., Alexandria, VA 22303
Phone: 703-960-4600   **Fax:** 703-960-2688
Web: www.vsecorp.com

PRODUCTS/OPERATIONS

2008 Sales

	$ mil.	% of total
Federal Group	667.4	64
International Group	220.0	21
Infrastructure Group	106.4	10
IT, Energy & Management Consulting Group	49.9	5
Total	**1,043.7**	**100**

2008 Sales by Customer

	$ mil.	% of total
Government		
Department of Defense		
Army	625.2	60
Navy	195.8	19
Air Force	10.7	1
Department of Transportation	89.9	9
Department of the Treasury	57.0	5
Department of the Interior	19.2	2
Department of Energy	12.8	1
Other agencies	29.7	3
Commercial	3.4	—
Total	**1,043.7**	**100**

Selected Projects

Cross-platform technical data
Energy conservation and advanced technology demonstration projects
Engineering support for military vehicles and combat trailers
Information technology management consulting, services, and solutions
Large-scale port engineering development and construction management
Life cycle support for ships
Logistics management support
Machinery condition analysis
Military equipment refurbishment and modification
Military vehicle ballistic protection systems
Multimedia, computer local area network (LAN), and telecommunications systems
Product data
Ship communication systems
Ship force crew training
Ship maintenance, repair, overhaul planning, and follow-on technical support
Specification preparation for ship alterations and repairs
Technical data package preparation
Technical manual development and support

COMPETITORS

Boeing
General Dynamics
Lockheed Martin
Northrop Grumman
Todd Shipyards

HISTORICAL FINANCIALS
Company Type: Public

Income Statement
FYE: December 31

	REVENUE ($ mil.)	NET INCOME ($ mil.)	NET PROFIT MARGIN	EMPLOYEES
12/08	1,043.7	19.0	1.8%	1,920
12/07	653.2	14.1	2.2%	1,223
12/06	363.7	7.8	2.1%	857
12/05	280.1	6.2	2.2%	716
12/04	216.0	3.4	1.6%	625
Annual Growth	48.3%	53.8%	—	32.4%

2008 Year-End Financials

Debt ratio: —
Return on equity: 28.7%
Cash ($ mil.): 0.6
Current ratio: 1.12
Long-term debt ($ mil.): —
No. of shares (mil.): 5.1

Dividends
  Yield: 0.4%
  Payout: 4.5%
Market value ($ mil.): 201.3
R&D as % of sales: —
Advertising as % of sales: —

Stock History

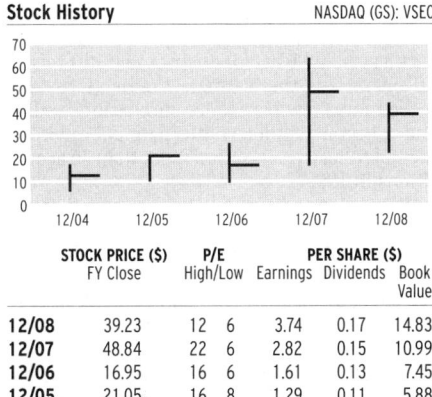

NASDAQ (GS): VSEC

	STOCK PRICE ($) FY Close	P/E High/Low		PER SHARE ($) Earnings	Dividends	Book Value
12/08	39.23	12	6	3.74	0.17	14.83
12/07	48.84	22	6	2.82	0.15	10.99
12/06	16.95	16	6	1.61	0.13	7.45
12/05	21.05	16	8	1.29	0.11	5.88
12/04	12.59	23	8	0.75	0.09	4.49
Annual Growth	32.9%	—	—	49.4%	17.2%	34.8%

Waddell & Reed

Waddell & Reed Financial is one of the oldest mutual fund managers in the US. Subsidiaries administer and distribute more than 75 mutual funds under the names Waddell & Reed Advisors Funds (the company's oldest and largest fund family), Ivy Funds (administered by Ivy Investment Management), and Waddell & Reed InvestEd Portfolios; they also manage accounts for institutional investors and private clients. The company sells annuities and insurance through alliances with third-party providers. Waddell & Reed has more than 450 offices throughout the US, usually in small cities and rural areas.

The company sells its products through a network of more than 2,300 advisors as well as through third-party channels such as brokerages, 401(k) plans, and independent advisors. It has more than $45 billion of assets under management, most of it invested in equities with a focus on long-term performance.

Founded in 1937, Waddell & Reed introduced its first family of mutual funds, The Waddell & Reed Advisors Group, in 1940.

EXECUTIVES

Chairman and CEO: Henry J. (Hank) Herrmann, age 67, $4,150,087 total compensation
President and Chief Investment Officer: Michael L. Avery, age 56, $2,311,395 total compensation
SEVP and National Sales Manager, Waddell & Reed, Inc.: Steve Anderson
EVP and Chief Marketing Officer: Thomas W. Butch, age 51, $1,983,154 total compensation
EVP and Associate National Sales Manager, Waddell & Reed, Inc.: Bradley D. (Brad) Hofmeister

SVP and COO: Michael D. Strohm, age 57
SVP and CFO: Daniel P. Connealy, age 62, $1,385,971 total compensation
SVP and General Counsel: Daniel C. Schulte, age 43, $1,400,800 total compensation
SVP and Chief Administrative Officer — Investments: John E. Sundeen Jr., age 48
SVP Finance, Treasurer, and Principal Accounting Officer: Brent K. Bloss, age 40
SVP and Controller: Mark A. Schieber, age 51
VP, Secretary, and Associate General Counsel: Wendy J. Hills
Director Investor Relations: Nicole McIntosh
Director Communications: Roger Hoadley
Auditors: KPMG LLP

LOCATIONS

HQ: Waddell & Reed Financial, Inc.
6300 Lamar Ave., Overland Park, KS 66202
Phone: 913-236-2000   **Fax:** 913-236-2017
Web: www.waddell.com

PRODUCTS/OPERATIONS

2008 Sales

	$ mil.	% of total
Underwriting & distribution fees	416.7	45
Investment management fees	399.9	44
Shareholder service fees	102.5	11
Total	**919.1**	**100**

COMPETITORS

AllianceBernstein
American Century
BlackRock
Capital Group
Charles Schwab
Davis Advisers
DWS Investments
Eaton Vance
Edward Jones
FMR
Franklin Resources
Invesco
Janus Capital
Legg Mason
MFS
Nuveen
Prudential
Raymond James Financial
RS Investments
Seligman
T. Rowe Price
Van Kampen Investments
The Vanguard Group

HISTORICAL FINANCIALS

Company Type: Public

Income Statement

FYE: December 31

	ASSETS ($ mil.)	NET INCOME ($ mil.)	INCOME AS % OF ASSETS	EMPLOYEES
12/08	775.4	96.2	12.4%	1,678
12/07	893.8	125.5	14.0%	1,702
12/06	662.7	46.1	7.0%	1,606
12/05	632.3	60.1	9.5%	1,573
12/04	619.9	102.2	16.5%	1,516
Annual Growth	5.8%	(1.5%)	—	2.6%

2008 Year-End Financials

Equity as % of assets: 41.3%
Return on assets: 11.5%
Return on equity: 27.4%
Long-term debt ($ mil.): 200.0
No. of shares (mil.): 85.3
Market value ($ mil.): 1,319.3
Dividends
 Yield: 4.9%
 Payout: 66.1%
Sales ($ mil.): 919.1
R&D as % of sales: —
Advertising as % of sales: —

Stock History

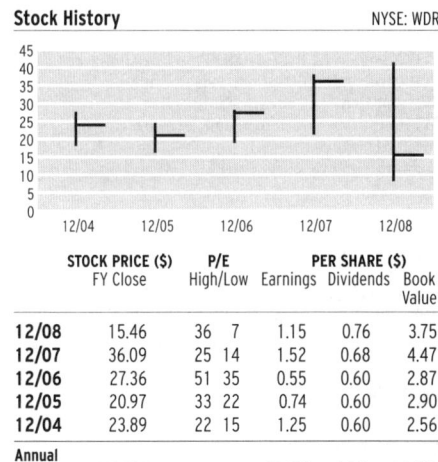

NYSE: WDR

	STOCK PRICE ($) FY Close	P/E High/Low		PER SHARE ($) Earnings	Dividends	Book Value
12/08	15.46	36	7	1.15	0.76	3.75
12/07	36.09	25	14	1.52	0.68	4.47
12/06	27.36	51	35	0.55	0.60	2.87
12/05	20.97	33	22	0.74	0.60	2.90
12/04	23.89	22	15	1.25	0.60	2.56
Annual Growth	(10.3%)	—	—	(2.1%)	6.1%	10.0%

Washington Federal

Washington Federal is the holding company for Washington Federal Savings, which operates about 150 branches in eight western states. The thrift, which was founded in 1917, collects deposits from consumers and business by offering standard products such as CDs, IRAs, and checking, savings, and money market accounts. With these funds, the company mainly originates single-family residential mortgages, which account for about 70% of its loan portfolio. The bank also writes construction, land, and multi-family residential loans. Washington Federal sells life, home, and auto coverage through its First Insurance Agency subsidiary.

The company expanded into New Mexico when it bought First Federal Banc of the Southwest and its First Federal Savings subsidiary in 2007.

The following year Washington Federal bought smaller Seattle-area bank First Mutual Bancshares and its subsidiary First Mutual Bank in a stock-and-cash deal worth $190 million, adding a dozen branches to its network.

Following the two acquisitions, First Federal Savings and First Mutual Bank retained their names and now operate as divisions of Washington Federal Savings. In New Mexico, Gallup Federal Savings and Farmington Savings Bank are divisions of First Federal Savings.

In 2010 Washington Federal acquired all of the branches and virtually all deposits of the failed Horizon Bank, which had been seized by regulators. The FDIC-facilitated transaction added 18 locations — rebranded as Washington Federal — in northwestern Washington to the company's network.

EXECUTIVES

Chairman, President, and CEO: Roy M. Whitehead, age 58
EVP and CFO: Brent J. Beardall, age 39
EVP and Chief Credit Officer: Mark A. Schoonover
EVP Commercial Real Estate: Jack B. Jacobson, age 60
EVP Business Banking: Richard J. (Rick) Collette, age 61
EVP Mortgage and Consumer Lending and Corporate Secretary: Edwin C. Hedlund, age 54
EVP Human Resources and Deposit Operations: Linda S. Brower, age 57

SVP Marketing and Investor Relations: Cathy E. Cooper
SVP Special Assets: Ronald McKenzie
SVP Commercial Real Estate: Fred H. Reininger
SVP Credit Administration: Dale R. Sullivan
SVP and General Counsel: Paul I. Tyler
SVP Corporate Real Estate and Treasurer:
Keith D. Taylor
Auditors: Deloitte & Touche LLP

LOCATIONS

HQ: Washington Federal, Inc.
425 Pike St., Seattle, WA 98101
Phone: 206-624-7930　　**Fax:** 206-624-2334
Web: www.washingtonfederal.com

Washington Federal has branches in Arizona, Idaho, Nevada, New Mexico, Orgeon, Texas, Utah, and Washington.

PRODUCTS/OPERATIONS

2009 Gross Revenues

	$ mil.	% of total
Loans	579.2	81
Mortgage-backed securities	109.5	15
Investment securities	3.0	1
Other	19.0	3
Total	**710.7**	**100**

COMPETITORS

AmericanWest Bancorporation	Sterling Financial (WA)
BancWest	U.S. Bancorp
Bank of America	Washington Banking
Banner Corp	Wells Fargo
KeyCorp	Zions Bancorporation

HISTORICAL FINANCIALS

Company Type: Public

Income Statement

FYE: September 30

	ASSETS ($ mil.)	NET INCOME ($ mil.)	INCOME AS % OF ASSETS	EMPLOYEES
9/09	12,582.5	48.2	0.4%	1,105
9/08	11,796.4	62.3	0.5%	1,095
9/07	10,285.4	135.0	1.3%	886
9/06	9,069.0	143.1	1.6%	765
9/05	8,234.5	145.9	1.8%	749
Annual Growth	11.2%	(24.2%)	—	10.2%

2009 Year-End Financials

Equity as % of assets: 13.9%	Dividends
Return on assets: 0.4%	Yield: 1.2%
Return on equity: 3.1%	Payout: 43.5%
Long-term debt ($ mil.): 2,078.9	Sales ($ mil.): 392.2
No. of shares (mil.): 112.3	R&D as % of sales: —
Market value ($ mil.): 1,892.9	Advertising as % of sales: —

Stock History

NASDAQ (GS): WFSL

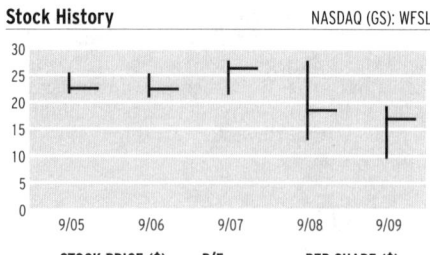

	STOCK PRICE ($) FY Close	P/E High/Low		PER SHARE ($) Earnings	Dividends	Book Value
9/09	16.86	41	21	0.46	0.20	15.55
9/08	18.45	39	19	0.71	0.84	11.87
9/07	26.26	18	14	1.54	0.83	11.74
9/06	22.44	15	13	1.64	0.81	11.25
9/05	22.56	15	13	1.67	0.78	10.58
Annual Growth	(7.0%)	—	—	(27.6%)	(28.8%)	10.1%

Waste Connections

How The Waste Was Won (with apologies to John Ford, et al.) would tell how Waste Connections has come to provide solid waste collection, transfer, disposal, and recycling services to 1.8 million commercial, industrial, and residential customers in 23 states. The integrated solid waste services company does business mainly in smaller markets. It operates primarily in the western US, but also in midwestern and southeastern states. Waste Connections owns or operates about 135 solid waste collection operations, 50 transfer stations, 35 landfills, and another 35 recycling facilities. Along with its garbage operations, Waste Connections offers intermodal logistics services in the Pacific Northwest.

By focusing on acquiring mom-and-pop operations in secondary markets rather than large urban areas, the company has been able to continue riding the crest of a consolidation trend in the waste management industry that began in the 1990s. While other large waste management companies — including major players Waste Management and Republic Services — have slowed or halted their buying sprees, Waste Connections has continued to acquire, although selectively.

For example, in 2007 Waste Connections acquired 15 non-hazardous solid waste collection, transfer, disposal, and recycling businesses, which combined didn't add up to 10% of the company's sales. The following year it made one large acquisition, of Harold LeMay Enterprises in Washington for more than $200 million, and 14 other smaller deals.

Waste Connections stepped outside the solid waste business for the first time in 2004 when it bought Northwest Container Services, a provider of intermodal logistics services in Washington and Oregon. Intermodal logistics involves arranging freight transportation by multiple methods, such as truck and train. The synergy between solid waste and intermodal logistics might not be obvious, but Waste Connections uses its presence in both markets to gain a share of the market for transporting solid waste by rail from the Seattle area to landfills in eastern Washington and eastern Oregon.

HISTORY

When United Waste Systems and USA Waste Services merged in 1997, Ron Mittelstaedt, who was managing United's western operations at the time, saw an opening for mid-market waste haulers created by that consolidation and others. Mittelstaedt put together a group of investors that acquired the Washington operations of Browning-Ferris Industries (BFI) in 1997 and named the firm Waste Connections of Washington. Mittelstaedt, Bradford Bishop, and James Cutler then formed Waste Connections of Idaho and bought BFI operations in eastern Idaho.

In early 1998 Waste Connections of Washington acquired Waste Connections of Idaho. The company expanded into California that year when it purchased Madera Disposal Systems and added Hunter Enterprises, a solid-waste hauler in eastern Idaho. Waste Connections also purchased firms in such midwestern and western states as Kansas, Montana, Nebraska, Oklahoma, Oregon, South Dakota, Texas, and Wyoming.

Waste Connections went public in 1998 and used the money raised to buy more than 75 waste management facilities and service companies.

In 1999 it added the Denver area to its territory after the US Justice Department required merger partners Allied Waste Industries and BFI to sell off operations there. Waste Connections also moved into New Mexico by purchasing landfill and collection company International Environmental Industries — one of more than 35 acquisitions in 1999.

Waste Connections in 2000 swapped some holdings with Allied Waste. Waste Connections sold its Idaho operations to Allied, which in turn sold its operations in Iowa, Montana, and Wyoming to Waste Connections. Later that year Waste Connections purchased some of Allied's Kansas operations.

Consolidation in the waste industry hadn't stopped by 2002. That year Waste Connections made various tuck-in acquisitions in Washington, Oregon, Texas, Tennessee, Oklahoma, and Colorado. One of its largest deals that year was the acquisition of San Luis Garbage Co., of San Luis Obispo, California.

In 2003 Waste Connections bought two companies in California that together annually generated about $29 million. Other purchases that year included two collection and landfill operating companies in Mississippi and tuck-in acquisitions in Iowa, Nebraska, and South Dakota. The company acquired nine nonhazardous solid waste collection and disposal businesses in 2004.

Also in 2004 Waste Connections and Waste Industries USA traded some assets in the southern US. Waste Connections bought Waste Industries' hauling and landfill operations in the greater Memphis market and its hauling and transfer station operation (including an early-stage municipal solid waste landfill development project) in Crossville, Tennessee. Waste Connections sold to Waste Industries its hauling, transfer station, and construction and demolition landfill operations in Atlanta's northern and northwestern suburbs.

EXECUTIVES

Chairman and CEO: Ronald J. (Ron) Mittelstaedt, age 45, $1,783,037 total compensation
President: Steven F. (Steve) Bouck, age 51, $960,010 total compensation
EVP and CFO: Worthing F. Jackman, age 44, $777,311 total compensation
EVP and COO: Darrell W. Chambliss, age 44, $821,813 total compensation
SVP People, Safety, and Development: Eric M. Merrill, age 56, $553,266 total compensation
SVP Administration: Kenneth O. (Ken) Rose, age 60
SVP Sales and Marketing: David M. Hall, age 51
SVP Engineering and Disposal: James M. (Jim) Little, age 47
VP and CIO: Eric O. Hansen, age 43
VP, General Counsel, and Secretary: Patrick J. Shea, age 38
VP and Corporate Controller: David G. Eddie, age 39
VP Employee Relations: Jerri L. Hunt, age 57
Auditors: PricewaterhouseCoopers LLP

LOCATIONS

HQ: Waste Connections, Inc.
35 Iron Point Circle, Ste. 200, Folsom, CA 95630
Phone: 916-608-8200　　**Fax:** 916-351-0249
Web: www.wasteconnections.com

PRODUCTS/OPERATIONS

2008 Sales

	% of total
Collection	66
Disposal & transfer	26
Recycling & other	8
Total	**100**

COMPETITORS

Casella Waste Systems	Republic Services
Hub Group	Veolia ES Solid Waste
IESI-BFC	Waste Industries USA
Pacer International	Waste Management
Recology	Waste Services

HISTORICAL FINANCIALS

Company Type: Public

Income Statement — FYE: December 31

	REVENUE ($ mil.)	NET INCOME ($ mil.)	NET PROFIT MARGIN	EMPLOYEES
12/08	1,049.6	105.6	10.1%	5,379
12/07	958.5	99.1	10.3%	4,978
12/06	824.4	77.4	9.4%	4,310
12/05	721.9	83.9	11.6%	4,104
12/04	629.4	72.3	11.5%	3,768
Annual Growth	13.6%	9.9%	—	9.3%

2008 Year-End Financials

Debt ratio: 66.2%
Return on equity: 10.4%
Cash ($ mil.): 265.3
Current ratio: 1.99
Long-term debt ($ mil.): 830.8
No. of shares (mil.): 78.7

Dividends
  Yield: 0.0%
  Payout: —
Market value ($ mil.): 2,484.5
R&D as % of sales: —
Advertising as % of sales: —

Stock History — NYSE: WCN

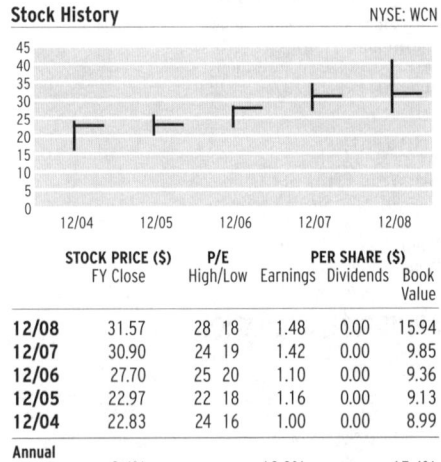

	STOCK PRICE ($) FY Close	P/E High/Low	PER SHARE ($) Earnings	Dividends	Book Value
12/08	31.57	28 18	1.48	0.00	15.94
12/07	30.90	24 19	1.42	0.00	9.85
12/06	27.70	25 20	1.10	0.00	9.36
12/05	22.97	22 18	1.16	0.00	9.13
12/04	22.83	24 16	1.00	0.00	8.99
Annual Growth	8.4%	— —	10.3%	—	15.4%

WebMD Health

House calls are a browser click away thanks to this online doctor. WebMD Health is a leading Web publisher of health information for consumers and health care professionals. Its WebMD.com portal gives consumers information on common health ailments, as well as articles and features on staying healthy through diet and exercise. Doctors and other professionals can access clinical information through WebMD's Medscape offering. All total, The WebMD Health Network (including WebMD.com, Medscape.com, and third-party sites) attracts more than 50 million users.

In 2009 HLTH Corporation acquired the 20% of WebMD Health it didn't already own and completed a reverse merger, with WebMD as the surviving company. Previously a medical practice services provider, HLTH divested most of its other operations to focus on its online content and services business. The merger, worth some $1.2 billion, was intended to reduce costs associated with both WebMD and HLTH operating as publicly traded companies. HLTH and WebMD had previously planned to merge in 2008; that deal, valued at $2.3 billion, was called off due to poor economic conditions and problems with obtaining financing.

WebMD generates the lion's share of its revenue through online advertising as well as marketing sponsorships and licensing. It produces custom versions of its Web content through private portals used by corporations (Wal-Mart, PepsiCo, IBM) and health plans (Cigna, WellPoint). Additionally, WebMD provides branded content to media outlets owned by CBS, and it receives branded content from the Hearst Corporation. Beyond digital media, WebMD Health publishes *WebMD the Magazine* and *The Little Blue Book*, a directory of physician information.

While it seeks to consolidate its domestic business, the company has also been focused on international expansion. WebMD is developing a consumer health information portal in the UK through an agreement with the UK's #1 pharmacy operator Alliance Boots. The health and wellness news and information site will operate in conjunction with in-store promotions at Boots The Chemist drugstore locations.

EXECUTIVES

Chairman: Martin J. (Marty) Wygod, age 69
President and CEO: Wayne T. Gattinella, age 57
COO and CFO: Anthony (Tony) Vuolo, age 51
EVP and CTO: William E. (Bill) Pence, age 46
EVP and General Manager, Health Services: Craig Froude, age 42
EVP Consumer Services: Nan-Kirsten Forte, age 46
EVP, General Counsel, and Secretary: Douglas W. Wamsley, age 50
EVP Professional Services: Steven L. (Steve) Zatz, age 52
SVP: Lewis H. Leicher
WebMD Editorial: Sean Swint
WebMD Publishing and Magazine: Heidi Anderson
Public Relations: Kate Hahn
Investor Relations: Risa Fisher
Director: Kevin M. Cameron, age 43
Auditors: Ernst & Young LLP

LOCATIONS

HQ: WebMD Health Corp.
  111 8th Ave., New York, NY 10011
Phone: 212-624-3700   **Fax:** 212-624-3800
Web: www.wbmd.com

PRODUCTS/OPERATIONS

2008 Sales

	$ mil.	% of total
Online services		
Advertising & promotion	275.8	72
Licensing	89.1	23
Content syndication & other	1.4	—
Publishing services & other	16.4	4
Total	**382.8**	**100**

Selected Offerings

The WebMD Health Network
  TheHeart.org
  MedicineNet.com
  Medscape.com
  RXList.com
  WebMD.com
WebMD Health Services (Online Private Portals)
The WebMD Little Blue Book (physician directory)
WebMD the Magazine

COMPETITORS

A.D.A.M.	Mayo Foundation
Caremark Pharmacy	Medline Industries
EBSCO	New York Academy
HealthStream	of Medicine
Hewitt Associates	Reed Elsevier Group
iVillage	

HISTORICAL FINANCIALS

Company Type: Public

Income Statement — FYE: December 31

	REVENUE ($ mil.)	NET INCOME ($ mil.)	NET PROFIT MARGIN	EMPLOYEES
12/08	382.8	26.7	7.0%	1,300
12/07	332.0	65.9	19.8%	1,175
12/06	253.9	4.5	1.8%	1,025
12/05	168.9	7.7	4.6%	720
12/04	134.1	6.5	4.8%	550
Annual Growth	30.0%	42.4%	—	24.0%

2008 Year-End Financials

Debt ratio: —
Return on equity: 4.3%
Cash ($ mil.): 191.7
Current ratio: 2.66
Long-term debt ($ mil.): —
No. of shares (mil.): 57.7

Dividends
  Yield: —
  Payout: —
Market value ($ mil.): 1,361.5
R&D as % of sales: —
Advertising as % of sales: —

Stock History — NASDAQ (GS): WBMD

	STOCK PRICE ($) FY Close	P/E High/Low	PER SHARE ($) Earnings	Dividends	Book Value
12/08	23.59	93 30	0.45	—	10.98
12/07	41.07	58 35	1.10	—	10.51
12/06	40.02	591 357	0.08	—	8.69
12/05	29.05	219 132	0.15	—	5.19
Annual Growth	(6.7%)	— —	36.4%	—	58.4%

WesBanco, Inc.

WesBanco would like to be "BesBanco" for its customers. The holding company owns WesBanco Bank, which offers banking services through more than 100 branches in West Virginia, Ohio, and western Pennsylvania. In addition to traditional services such as deposits and loans, the bank also offers trust and investment services, including its proprietary WesMark mutual funds. WesBanco Insurance Services is a multiline insurance provider. Commercial real estate loans and residential mortgages each make up approximately one-third of WesBanco's loan portfolio; business, construction, and consumer loans round out its lending activities.

The company bought five branches in Columbus, Ohio, from AmTrust Bank in 2009. The purchase added to WesBanco's presence in that market, a target growth area for the bank. Other

plans include the development of new locations as well as branch consolidations.

The AmTrust deal continued WesBanco's expansion into Ohio, which began with the 2002 purchase of rival American Bancorporation and continued with acquisitions of Western Ohio Financial (2004), Winton Financial (2005), and Oak Hill Financial (2007).

EXECUTIVES

Chairman: James C. (Jim) Gardill, age 63
Vice Chairman: John D. Kidd, age 70
President, CEO, and Director; President and CEO, WesBanco Bank: Paul M. Limbert, age 63, $665,947 total compensation
EVP and COO, WesBanco and WesBanco Bank: Dennis G. Powell, age 60, $410,902 total compensation
EVP and CFO: Robert H. Young, age 53, $369,154 total compensation
EVP Community Relations: Kristine N. Molnar, age 58, $696,153 total compensation
EVP Investments and Trusts: Jerome B. Schmitt, age 60, $385,047 total compensation
EVP and Chief Credit Officer: Peter W. Jaworski, age 54
EVP Commercial Banking: Bernard P. Twigg, age 55
EVP Human Resources: John W. Moore Jr., age 62
EVP Treasury: Brent E. Richmond, age 46
Auditors: Schneider Downs & Co., Inc.

LOCATIONS

HQ: WesBanco, Inc.
1 Bank Plaza, Wheeling, WV 26003
Phone: 304-234-9000 **Fax:** 304-234-9298
Web: www.wesbanco.com

PRODUCTS/OPERATIONS

2008 Gross Revenues

	$ mil.	% of total
Interest		
Loans, including fees	236.9	70
Securities	43.6	13
Other	1.2	—
Noninterest		
Service charges on deposits	24.0	7
Trust fees	14.9	4
Other	18.5	6
Total	**339.1**	**100**

COMPETITORS

1st West Virginia Bancorp	First Century Bankshares
Bank of America	First Community
BB&T	Bancshares
Camco Financial	Huntington Bancshares
Central Federal	Ohio Valley Banc
Cheviot Financial	PNC Financial
Citizens Financial Corp.	United Bancorp
City Holding	United Bankshares
DCB Financial	

HISTORICAL FINANCIALS

Company Type: Public

Income Statement   FYE: December 31

	ASSETS ($ mil.)	NET INCOME ($ mil.)	INCOME AS % OF ASSETS	EMPLOYEES
12/08	5,222.0	38.1	0.7%	1,501
12/07	5,384.3	44.7	0.8%	1,562
12/06	4,098.1	39.0	1.0%	1,168
12/05	4,422.1	42.8	1.0%	1,200
12/04	4,011.4	38.2	1.0%	1,209
Annual Growth	**6.8%**	**(0.1%)**	**—**	**5.6%**

2008 Year-End Financials

Equity as % of assets: 11.2%	Dividends
Return on assets: 0.7%	Yield: 4.1%
Return on equity: 6.5%	Payout: 78.9%
Long-term debt ($ mil.): 708.0	Sales ($ mil.): 217.9
No. of shares (mil.): 26.6	R&D as % of sales: —
Market value ($ mil.): 722.9	Advertising as % of sales: —

Stock History   NASDAQ (GS): WSBC

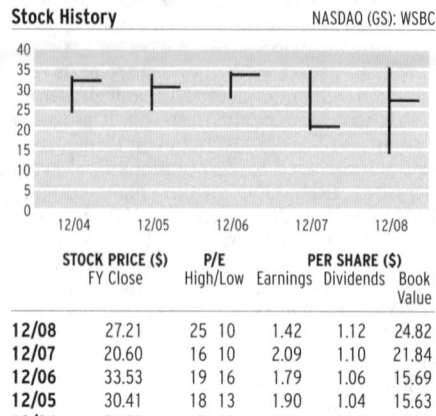

	STOCK PRICE ($) FY Close	P/E High/Low		PER SHARE ($) Earnings	Dividends	Book Value
12/08	27.21	25	10	1.42	1.12	24.82
12/07	20.60	16	10	2.09	1.10	21.84
12/06	33.53	19	16	1.79	1.06	15.69
12/05	30.41	18	13	1.90	1.04	15.63
12/04	31.97	17	13	1.90	1.00	13.93
Annual Growth	**(4.0%)**	**—**	**—**	**(7.0%)**	**2.9%**	**15.5%**

Wesco Financial

Wesco Financial is sort of like Berkshire Hathaway Lite. Charlie Munger, Berkshire vice chairman and a confidant of Warren Buffett, leads Wesco. And like Berkshire, the investment firm provides insurance and reinsurance; in Wesco's case, it does so through subsidiaries Wesco-Financial Insurance Company and Kansas Bankers Surety. It also holds shares in some of the same companies as Berkshire, like Coca-Cola, Kraft, Procter & Gamble, and Wells Fargo. However, Wesco gets more than 40% of its revenue from CORT Business Services, one of the largest providers of rental furniture in the US. It also operates Precision Steel Warehouse, which has steel service centers in Chicago and Charlotte, North Carolina.

Wesco-Financial Insurance occasionally issues "excess-of-loss" or "super-catastrophe" reinsurance, which provides backstop support for primary insurers' coverage of hurricanes, earthquakes, and other disasters. On the other hand, the company's Kansas Bankers Surety subsidiary offers insurance coverage to small and midsized banks in more than 35 states, mainly in the Midwest. It writes policies that cover theft, check-kiting fraud, officers' and directors' liability, and deposits in excess of federal deposit insurance limits. Both insurance subsidiaries are managed by Berkshire's National Indemnity Company.

CORT has grown through the 2008 acquisitions of Roomservice Group (now CORT Business Services UK), which expanded its operations into the UK, and the Corporate Furnishing Division of Aaron's, which added a presence in about a dozen US markets.

Berkshire Hathaway owns some 80% of Wesco.

HISTORY

Wesco Financial is another collaboration between Warren Buffett and Berkshire Hathaway vice chairman Charlie Munger, also Wesco's chairman. In 1973 the two acquired 80% of Wesco (then a savings and loan holding company) from Elizabeth Caspers Peters, daughter of the founder. The company's primary attraction was that it owned 28.8 million Freddie Mac shares. They added Precision Steel in 1979.

In 1993 the firm sold the deposits and loans of subsidiary Mutual Savings and merged it with Wesco-Financial. The savings and loan's foreclosed real estate was shifted into MS Property. In 1996 it bought Kansas Bankers Surety, which was founded in 1909 to underwrite deposit insurance for Kansas banks. Wesco acquired CORT Business Services in 2000.

EXECUTIVES

Chairman, President, and CEO: Charles T. (Charlie) Munger, age 85
VP and CFO, Wesco Financial and MS Property: Jeffrey L. Jacobson, age 61, $286,000 total compensation
VP Building Management and Real Estate; President, MS Property: Robert E. Sahm, age 81, $277,328 total compensation
Secretary: Margaret A. Patrick
Treasurer, Wesco Financial and MS Property: Christopher M. Greco, age 31, $177,600 total compensation
Auditors: Deloitte & Touche LLP

LOCATIONS

HQ: Wesco Financial Corporation
301 E. Colorado Blvd., Ste. 300
Pasadena, CA 91101
Phone: 626-585-6700 **Fax:** 626-449-1455
Web: www.wescofinancial.com

PRODUCTS/OPERATIONS

2008 Sales

	$ mil.	% of total
Furniture rentals	340.2	43
Insurance premiums earned	238.0	30
Sales & services	130.7	16
Dividends & interest	79.1	10
Realized investment gains	7.0	1
Other	4.0	—
Total	**799.0**	**100**

Selected Subsidiaries

MS Property Company
Wesco Holdings Midwest, Inc.
    CORT Business Services Corporation
    Precision Steel Warehouse, Inc.
        Precision Brand Products
    Wesco-Financial Insurance Company
        Kansas Bankers Surety Company

COMPETITORS

Apollo Advisors
Bain Capital
Blackstone Group
The Carlyle Group
Enstar Group
Equity Group Investments
HM Capital Partners
Jordan Company
KKR
Leonard Green
Oaktree Capital
Stone Point Capital
Thomas H. Lee Partners
TPG

HISTORICAL FINANCIALS

Company Type: Public

Income Statement
FYE: December 31

	REVENUE ($ mil.)	NET INCOME ($ mil.)	NET PROFIT MARGIN	EMPLOYEES
12/08	799.0	82.1	10.3%	2,942
12/07	630.9	109.2	17.3%	2,671
12/06	605.7	92.0	15.2%	2,626
12/05	888.3	294.6	33.2%	2,493
12/04	509.3	47.4	9.3%	2,473
Annual Growth	11.9%	14.7%	—	4.4%

2008 Year-End Financials

Debt ratio: 1.7%
Return on equity: 3.3%
Cash ($ mil.): 297.6
Current ratio: —
Long-term debt ($ mil.): 40.4
No. of shares (mil.): 7.1

Dividends
Yield: 0.4%
Payout: 10.0%
Market value ($ mil.): 2,049.8
R&D as % of sales: —
Advertising as % of sales: —

Stock History
NYSE Alternext: WSC

	STOCK PRICE ($) FY Close	P/E High/Low	PER SHARE ($) Earnings	Dividends	Book Value
12/08	287.90	39 21	11.53	1.15	333.96
12/07	407.00	33 24	15.33	1.50	356.03
12/06	460.00	39 28	12.93	1.46	337.14
12/05	385.00	10 8	41.37	1.42	313.27
12/04	393.00	65 49	6.66	1.38	297.33
Annual Growth	(7.5%)	— —	14.7%	(4.5%)	2.9%

Western Gas Partners

Western Gas Partners' style is to gather and go. The company gathers and transports natural gas for its largest customer and parent, Anadarko Petroleum. It pumps about 900 million cu. ft. of gas a day through nine gas gathering systems, six treating facilities, one natural gas liquids pipeline, and one interstate pipeline (totaling more than 4,620 miles across Wyoming, Utah, Texas, Oklahoma, and Kansas). Operating principally under long-term contracts, the company gathers natural gas from individual wells, after which it is compressed, treated, and ultimately delivered to end-users. Anadarko Petroleum spun off Western Gas Partners in 2008 and retains a controlling stake.

Western Gas Partners was formed in August 2007 to handle certain petroleum processing, storage, and transport operations for Anadarko and to make complementary acquisitions. In 2008 some 87% of the company's revenues were generated from transactions with its parent.

In 2009 the company made its first acquisition, when it bought $210 million of midstream assets located in the Powder River Basin from its parent. It later acquired assets in the Uintah Basin in northeastern Utah for $107 million.

In 2010 president Donald Sinclair was promoted to CEO, and former CEO Robert Gwin rose to take on the chairman's role.

EXECUTIVES

Chairman: Robert G. Gwin, age 46,
$879,686 total compensation
President, CEO, and Director: Donald R. Sinclair
SVP and COO: Danny J. Rea,
$351,906 total compensation
SVP and CFO: Benjamin M. (Ben) Fink, age 39
VP and Treasurer: Jeremy M. Smith, age 36,
$173,448 total compensation
VP, General Counsel, and Corporate Secretary:
Amanda M. McMillian, $169,513 total compensation
Investor Relations: Chris Campbell
Auditors: KPMG LLP

LOCATIONS

HQ: Western Gas Partners, LP
1201 Lake Robbins Dr., The Woodlands, TX 77380
Phone: 832-636-6000   **Fax:** 832-636-6001
Web: www.westerngas.com

PRODUCTS/OPERATIONS

2008 Sales

	$ mil.	% of total
Affiliates	271.6	87
Third parties	40.0	13
Total	311.6	100

COMPETITORS

DCP Midstream Partners
Enbridge Energy
Kinder Morgan Energy Partners
ONEOK Partners
Questar
XTO Energy

HISTORICAL FINANCIALS

Company Type: Public

Income Statement
FYE: December 31

	REVENUE ($ mil.)	NET INCOME ($ mil.)	NET PROFIT MARGIN	EMPLOYEES
12/08	311.6	65.3	21.0%	167
12/07	116.1	24.0	20.7%	117
12/06	81.2	9.7	11.9%	120
12/05	71.7	7.1	9.9%	—
12/04	68.0	9.3	13.7%	—
Annual Growth	46.3%	62.8%	—	18.0%

2008 Year-End Financials

Debt ratio: —
Return on equity: —
Cash ($ mil.): 33.3
Current ratio: 2.78
Long-term debt ($ mil.): 175.0
No. of shares (mil.): 29.5

Dividends
Yield: 3.6%
Payout: 59.7%
Market value ($ mil.): 378.2
R&D as % of sales: —
Advertising as % of sales: —

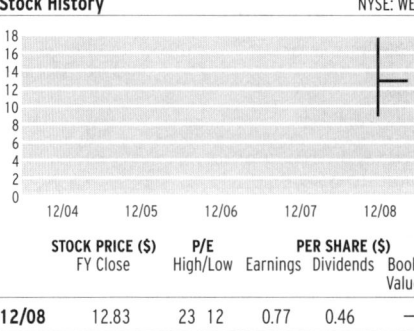

Stock History
NYSE: WES

	STOCK PRICE ($) FY Close	P/E High/Low	PER SHARE ($) Earnings	Dividends	Book Value
12/08	12.83	23 12	0.77	0.46	—

Westfield Financial

Westfield Financial is the holding company for Westfield Bank, which serves western Massachusetts' Hampden County and surrounding areas from more than 10 branch locations. Founded in 1853, the bank has traditionally been a community-oriented provider of retail deposit accounts and loans, but it is placing more emphasis on serving commercial and industrial clients. Commercial real estate loans account for approximately 45% of the company's loan portfolio, and business loans more than 25%. The bank also makes a smaller number of consumer and home equity loans.

Residential mortgages made up more than half of the company's loan portfolio in 2000; the following year, the bank began referring home loan originations to a third-party provider, and such loans now account for less than 20% of its portfolio.

EXECUTIVES

Chairman, Westfield Financial and Westfield Bank:
Donald A. Williams, age 64
President, CEO, and COO, Westfield Financial and Westfield Bank: James C. (Jim) Hagan, age 48
CFO and Treasurer, Westfield Financial and Westfield Bank: Leo R. Sagan Jr., age 46
Chief Investment Officer: Michael J. Janosco Jr., age 62
EVP: Allen J. Miles III, age 46
VP and Manager Operations and Information Systems Department, Westfield Financial and Westfield Bank:
Deborah J. McCarthy, age 49
VP and Residential Loan Officer, Westfield Financial and Westfield Bank: Rebecca S. Kozaczka, age 58
VP, General Counsel, and Director Human Resources, Westfield Financial and Westfield Bank:
Gerald P. Ciejka, age 46
Auditors: Wolf & Company, P.C.

LOCATIONS

HQ: Westfield Financial, Inc.
141 Elm St., Westfield, MA 01085
Phone: 413-568-1911   **Fax:** 413-562-7939
Web: www.westfieldbank.com

Westfield Financial has offices in Agawam, East Longmeadow, Holyoke, Southwick, Springfield (2), West Springfield, and Westfield (4), Massachusetts.

PRODUCTS/OPERATIONS

2008 Gross Revenues

	$ mil.	% of total
Interest		
Debt securities	25.8	44
Residential & commercial real estate loans	18.8	32
Commercial and industrial loans	8.0	14
Federal funds sold	0.6	1
Other	0.9	1
Noninterest		
Service charges & fees	2.4	4
Other	2.4	4
Total	**58.9**	**100**

COMPETITORS

Bank of America
Citizens Financial Group
NewAlliance Bancshares
Sovereign Bank
TD Bank USA

HISTORICAL FINANCIALS

Company Type: Public

Income Statement

FYE: December 31

	ASSETS ($ mil.)	NET INCOME ($ mil.)	INCOME AS % OF ASSETS	EMPLOYEES
12/08	1,109.1	6.7	0.6%	187
12/07	1,039.8	8.7	0.8%	191
12/06	996.8	4.7	0.5%	170
12/05	805.1	6.2	0.8%	151
12/04	796.9	6.3	0.8%	158
Annual Growth	**8.6%**	**1.6%**	**—**	**4.3%**

2008 Year-End Financials

Equity as % of assets: 23.4%
Return on assets: 0.6%
Return on equity: 2.5%
Long-term debt ($ mil.): 173.3
No. of shares (mil.): 30.5
Market value ($ mil.): 314.7
Dividends
 Yield: 1.9%
 Payout: 87.0%
Sales ($ mil.): 35.3
R&D as % of sales: —
Advertising as % of sales: —

Stock History

NASDAQ (GS): WFD

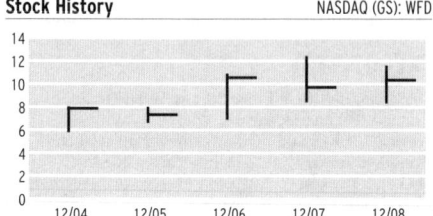

	STOCK PRICE ($) FY Close	P/E High/Low	PER SHARE ($) Earnings	Dividends	Book Value
12/08	10.32	50 37	0.23	0.20	8.52
12/07	9.70	42 29	0.29	0.20	9.40
12/06	10.54	22 14	0.49	0.18	9.49
12/05	7.32	40 35	0.20	0.14	3.80
12/04	7.87	41 30	0.20	0.09	3.87
Annual Growth	**7.0%**	**— —**	**3.6%**	**22.1%**	**21.8%**

Westwood Holdings

Westwood Ho! Westwood Holdings Group is an asset manager spun off from investment bank and brokerage SWS Group in 2002. Through Westwood Trust, the company provides trust, custody, and account management services to companies, institutions, and high-net-worth individuals. Westwood Management is the group's institutional investment management unit, overseeing accounts for corporations, municipalities, and charitable organizations; it is also the administrator of the Westwood family of mutual funds. Westwood Holdings Group has about $8 billion in assets under management.

Westwood in 2006 reduced the minimum required investment for its mutual funds from $100,000 to $5,000.

Susan Byrne, Westwood's chairman and chief investment officer, owns about 15% of the company. GAMCO Investors owns some 17%; Westwood, in turn, owns about 20% of GAMCO Investors' Gabelli Advisers (which distributes the Westwood mutual funds).

EXECUTIVES

Chairman and Chief Investment Officer:
 Susan M. Byrne, age 62, $3,718,973 total compensation
President, CEO, Secretary, and Director:
 Brian O. Casey, age 45, $1,796,825 total compensation
SVP and Portfolio Manager: Mark Freeman
SVP: Richard D. (Dick) Frazar
VP and CFO: William R. (Bill) Hardcastle Jr., age 41, $524,981 total compensation
VP Investment Strategies: David Spika
Auditors: Grant Thornton LLP

LOCATIONS

HQ: Westwood Holdings Group, Inc.
 200 Crescent Ct., Ste. 1200, Dallas, TX 75201
Phone: 214-756-6900   **Fax:** 214-756-6979
Web: www.westwoodgroup.com

PRODUCTS/OPERATIONS

2008 Sales

	$ mil.	% of total
Westwood Management	35.4	76
Westwood Trust	11.1	24
Total	**46.5**	**100**

2008 Assets under Management

	% of total
Separate accounts	43
Subadvisory	23
Commingled funds	16
Managed accounts	5
Westwood funds	4
Private accounts	4
WHG Funds	4
Agency/custody accounts	1
Total	**100**

COMPETITORS

American Century
Atalanta Sosnoff
Duncan-Hurst
Eaton Vance
FAF Advisors
FMR
Franklin Resources
Janus Capital
Martin Capital
Neuberger Berman
NFJ Investment
Nuveen
Oak Associates
Putnam
T. Rowe Price
US Global Investors
Van Kampen Investments
W.P. Stewart

HISTORICAL FINANCIALS

Company Type: Public

Income Statement

FYE: December 31

	ASSETS ($ mil.)	NET INCOME ($ mil.)	INCOME AS % OF ASSETS	EMPLOYEES
12/08	50.8	10.5	20.7%	63
12/07	39.0	7.9	20.3%	52
12/06	28.7	4.5	15.7%	48
12/05	27.3	3.6	13.2%	47
12/04	26.3	3.7	14.1%	45
Annual Growth	**17.9%**	**29.8%**	**—**	**8.8%**

2008 Year-End Financials

Equity as % of assets: 76.4%
Return on assets: 23.4%
Return on equity: 30.8%
Long-term debt ($ mil.): —
No. of shares (mil.): 7.1
Market value ($ mil.): 202.5
Dividends
 Yield: 4.2%
 Payout: 73.6%
Sales ($ mil.): 46.5
R&D as % of sales: —
Advertising as % of sales: —

Stock History

NYSE: WHG

	STOCK PRICE ($) FY Close	P/E High/Low	PER SHARE ($) Earnings	Dividends	Book Value
12/08	28.41	33 14	1.63	1.20	5.44
12/07	37.60	31 17	1.28	0.90	4.12
12/06	23.03	34 23	0.79	0.48	3.19
12/05	18.22	31 24	0.66	0.34	3.02
12/04	19.70	29 24	0.68	0.24	3.04
Annual Growth	**9.6%**	**— —**	**24.4%**	**49.5%**	**15.7%**

Whiting Petroleum

There's nothing fishy about what Whiting Petroleum is all about. The company engages in oil and natural gas exploration and production activities, mainly in the Gulf Coast, Michigan, the mid-continent, Permian Basin, and Rocky Mountain regions. In 2008 it reported proved reserves of 180 million barrels of oil and 354.8 billion cu. ft. of natural gas. That year Whiting Petroleum operated 3,337 net productive wells. It sells oil and gas production to end users, marketers, and other purchasers that have access to nearby pipeline facilities. Where there is no practical access to pipelines, oil is trucked to storage facilities.

The company has grown through the acquisition of reserves and continued field development in its core areas. Whiting Petroleum is pursuing economically attractive oil and gas opportunities to exploit and develop. In 2009 it made two acquisitions in the North Ward Estes field in the Permian Basin for $66 million, boosting its total reserves by about 4%.

In 2007 the company sold a number of non-core properties in Colorado, Louisiana, Michigan, Montana, New Mexico, North Dakota, Oklahoma, Texas, and Wyoming. In 2008 it acquired interests in producing gas wells and development acreage and related assets in the Flat Rock field in Uinta County, Utah, for $365 million.

EXECUTIVES

Chairman, President, and CEO: James J. Volker, age 63, $3,226,838 total compensation
SVP Operations: James T. Brown, age 57, $1,633,623 total compensation
VP Exploration and Development: Mark R. Williams, age 51, $1,672,707 total compensation
VP Reservoir Engineering and Acquisitions: J. Douglas Lang, age 60, $1,505,667 total compensation
VP and CFO: Michael J. Stevens, age 44, $1,481,284 total compensation
VP and National Drilling Manager, Whiting Oil and Gas: Douglas L. Walton
VP Operations: Rick A. Ross
VP Corporate and Government Relations: Jack R. Ekstrom
VP Land: David M. (Dave) Seery, age 55
VP Information Technology: Gale N. Keithline
VP, General Counsel, and Secretary: Bruce R. DeBoer, age 57
Director Investor Relations: John B. Kelso
Controller and Treasurer: Brent P. Jensen, age 38
VP Marketing, Whiting Oil and Gas: Charles (Chuck) LaCouture, age 48
VP Human Resources: Heather M. Duncan, age 39
Auditors: Deloitte & Touche LLP

LOCATIONS

HQ: Whiting Petroleum Corporation
   1700 Broadway, Ste. 2300, Denver, CO 80290
Phone: 303-837-1661   **Fax:** 303-861-4023
Web: www.whiting.com

2008 Proved Reserves

	% of total
Permian Basin	49
Rocky Mountains	27
Mid-continent	21
Gulf Coast	2
Michigan	1
Total	**100**

PRODUCTS/OPERATIONS

2008 Proved Reserves

	% of total
Oil	75
Natural gas	25
Total	**100**

2008 Sales

	% of total
Plains Marketing	15
Valero Energy	14
Other customers	71
Total	**100**

COMPETITORS

Anadarko Petroleum
Black Hills
Cabot Oil & Gas
Frontier Oil
Newfield Exploration
Stone Energy

HISTORICAL FINANCIALS

Company Type: Public

Income Statement

FYE: December 31

	REVENUE ($ mil.)	NET INCOME ($ mil.)	NET PROFIT MARGIN	EMPLOYEES
12/08	1,222.1	252.1	20.6%	470
12/07	818.7	130.6	16.0%	412
12/06	778.8	156.4	20.1%	359
12/05	540.4	121.9	22.6%	309
12/04	282.1	70.0	24.8%	171
Annual Growth	**44.3%**	**37.8%**	**—**	**28.8%**

2008 Year-End Financials

Debt ratio: 68.5%
Return on equity: 15.3%
Cash ($ mil.): 9.6
Current ratio: 0.62
Long-term debt ($ mil.): 1,239.8
No. of shares (mil.): 50.8
Dividends
   Yield: —
   Payout: —
Market value ($ mil.): 1,701.3
R&D as % of sales: —
Advertising as % of sales: —

Stock History

NYSE: WLL

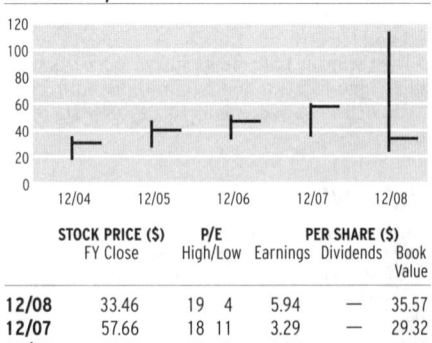

	STOCK PRICE ($) FY Close	P/E High/Low		PER SHARE ($) Earnings	Dividends	Book Value
12/08	33.46	19	4	5.94	—	35.57
12/07	57.66	18	11	3.29	—	29.32
12/06	46.60	12	8	4.25	—	23.34
12/05	40.00	12	7	3.88	—	19.63
12/04	30.25	10	5	3.38	—	12.04
Annual Growth	**2.6%**	**—**	**—**	**15.1%**	**—**	**31.1%**

WHX Corporation

WHX operates a number of businesses through six segments: Precious Metals, Tubing, Engineered Materials, Arlon Electronic Materials, Arlon Coated Materials, and Kasco. The companies operate primarily in the US and provide laminates and substrates, electrical connectors, precision tubing, precious metal fabrication, and fasteners, serving diverse industries such as construction, electronics, telecommunications, medical, aviation, transportation, appliance, semiconductor, signage, utility, and food preparation. WHX, which sells directly and through distributors, has some 30 locations in nine countries.

The company has been impacted by the global economic recession, experiencing a 25% decrease in its first quarter 2009 sales results compared to first quarter 2008. Most all segments reported declines except for Arlon Electronic Materials, which experienced a slight increase in its laminate sales to China and India. The company has been aggressive in its cost controls by reducing compensation and benefits for salaried employees, and making reductions in its workforce across the board. It also temporarily idled

some of its manufacturing operations to match output to demand.

The Precious Metal, Tubing, and Engineered Materials businesses focus on high margin products and new technology. Its Precious Metal segment realizes profits from the processing and fabricating of material, not from the sale of precious metals per se. The Tubing segment manufactures precision seamless small-diameter metal tubing for use in shipbuilding and petrochemical industries as well as the refrigeration, HVAC, and automotive industries. Based on cost vs. profit, WHX divested itself of its welded tubing operations in Europe and closed its Indiana Tube Denmark subsidiary in 2008.

Engineered Materials serves the construction and building, container, and appliance industries with products including fasteners, roofing materials, plastic and steel fittings and connectors for natural gas and water lines, and electro-galvanized steel products.

Bairnco was acquired in 2007, bringing the Arlon and Kasco businesses into the fold. Arlon Electronic Material produces components for the printed circuit board industry, as well as rubber-based insulation materials used by industrial, military, and aerospace customers. The Arlon Coated Materials division makes specialty graphic films under the ArlonFlex and Calon brands as well as adhesive coated vinyl films and fabrics, foils, foams, and papers for consumer and industrial uses. Product applications include thermal and electrical insulation and printing stock. Kasco provides products such as meat grinders and cutting equipment for food processing in supermarkets, meat processing plants, and restaurants.

WHX reorganized under Chapter 11 bankruptcy protection in 2005. The bankruptcy reorganization left the company's creditors in control of WHX. Chairman Warren G. Lichtenstein, through Steel Partners II L.P., owns 75% of WHX.

EXECUTIVES

Chairman: Warren G. Lichtenstein, age 43
Vice Chairman and CEO: Glen M. Kassan, age 66, $628,322 total compensation
SVP and CFO: James F. McCabe, age 46, $589,385 total compensation
SVP; President and CEO, Handy & Harman and Bairnco: Jeffrey A. Svoboda, age 57, $913,707 total compensation
VP and Treasurer: David A. Riposo
VP Human Resources: Pete Marciniak
VP and Director: John J. Quicke, age 60
General Counsel and Secretary: Peter T. Gelfman, age 45
Controller: Lawrence S. Yellin
Patriot Act Compliance Officer: Gerry F. Maturi
Auditors: Grant Thornton LLP

LOCATIONS

HQ: WHX Corporation
   1133 Westchester Ave., Ste. N222
   White Plains, NY 10604
Phone: 914-461-1300   **Fax:** 914-696-8684
Web: www.whxcorp.com

2008 Sales

	$ mil.	% of total
US	639.8	88
Other countries	86.0	12
Total	**725.8**	**100**

PRODUCTS/OPERATIONS

2008 Sales

	$ mil.	% of total
Engineered Materials	246.8	34
Precious Metal	156.9	22
Tubing	118.3	16
Arlon Coated Materials	72.4	10
Kasco	67.2	9
Arlon Electronic Materials	64.2	9
Total	**725.8**	**100**

COMPETITORS

AK Steel Holding Corporation
Allegheny Technologies
Berkel
Brush Engineered Materials
Dietrich Metal Framing
Johnson Matthey Inc.
Macsteel Service Centers USA
MNP Corp.
Nichols Wire
Tokyo Rope Mfg.
Wolverine Tube

HISTORICAL FINANCIALS

Company Type: Public

Income Statement

FYE: December 31

	REVENUE ($ mil.)	NET INCOME ($ mil.)	NET PROFIT MARGIN	EMPLOYEES
12/08	725.8	3.0	0.4%	2,376
12/07	637.9	(20.8)	—	2,552
12/06	461.0	(18.1)	—	1,628
12/05	403.8	(34.7)	—	1,640
12/04	410.9	(140.4)	—	1,788
Annual Growth	15.3%	—	—	7.4%

2008 Year-End Financials

Debt ratio: —
Return on equity: —
Cash ($ mil.): 8.7
Current ratio: 1.37
Long-term debt ($ mil.): 163.3
No. of shares (mil.): 12.2

Dividends
 Yield: 0.0%
 Payout: —
Market value ($ mil.): 97.4
R&D as % of sales: —
Advertising as % of sales: —

Stock History

NASDAQ (CM): WXCO

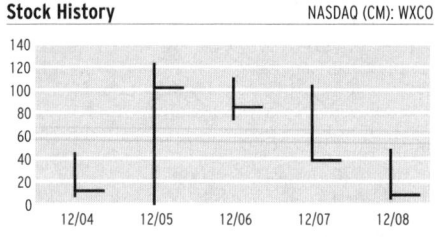

	STOCK PRICE ($) FY Close	P/E High/Low		PER SHARE ($) Earnings	Dividends	Book Value
12/08	8.00	63	7	0.75	0.00	(3.44)
12/07	38.00	—	—	(20.80)	0.00	(5.71)
12/06	84.50	—	—	(18.20)	0.00	(5.24)
12/05	101.50	0	0	303.60	0.00	(4.57)
12/04	11.50	—	—	(293.80)	0.00	(7.96)
Annual Growth	(8.7%)	—	—	—	—	—

Willis Lease Finance

Hey, buddy, got any spare Pratt & Whitneys? Willis Lease Finance buys and sells aircraft engines that it leases to commercial airlines, air cargo carriers, and maintenance and repair organizations in some 30 countries. Its portfolio includes more than 140 aircraft engines and related equipment made by Pratt & Whitney, Rolls-Royce, CFM, GE Aircraft Engines, and International Aero. The engine models in the company's portfolio are used on popular Airbus and Boeing aircraft. The Willis Lease portfolio also includes four de Havilland DHC-8 commuter aircraft.

Some of the company's major customers include Alaska Airlines, American Airlines, Southwest Airlines, and WestJet.

Willis Lease maintains a geographically diversified revenue base. More than 75% of the company's sales come from outside of North America (US and Mexico).

The company has sold its stakes in a parts subsidiary and in a test and repair joint venture.

CEO Charles Willis controls a 38% stake in the company.

EXECUTIVES

Chairman, President, and CEO: Charles F. Willis IV, age 60, $2,636,414 total compensation
EVP, COO, and Director: Jesse V. Crews, age 55
EVP and General Manager Leasing:
 Donald A. Nunemaker, age 61,
 $555,592 total compensation
SVP and CFO: Bradley S. (Brad) Forsyth, age 43,
 $752,472 total compensation
SVP, General Counsel, and Secretary:
 Thomas C. (Tom) Nord, age 68,
 $733,631 total compensation
SVP Technical Services: Judith M. (Judy) Webber,
 age 58, $357,549 total compensation
Director Marketing: Ann Lee
VP Sales, China: Shanfa Yan
VP Sales, US and Canada: Michael Vernon
VP Sales and Pooling Programs: Dave Tegeler
VP Sales, Caribbean, Central and South America, CIS, Mexico, and Russia: George Voskresensky
Auditors: KPMG LLP

LOCATIONS

HQ: Willis Lease Finance Corporation
 773 San Marin Dr., Ste. 2215, Novato, CA 94998
Phone: 415-408-4700   **Fax:** 415-408-4701
Web: www.willislease.com

2008 Lease Revenue

	% of total
Europe	31
Asia	22
North America	
US	20
Mexico	7
Canada	1
South America	14
Middle East	4
Africa	1
Total	**100**

PRODUCTS/OPERATIONS

2008 Sales

	$ mil.	% of total
Lease rent revenue	102.4	67
Maintenance reserve revenue	33.7	22
Gain on sale of leased equipment	12.4	8
Other	3.8	3
Total	**152.3**	**100**

COMPETITORS

AAR Corp.   GE
AerCap   ILFC
AeroCentury   Jetscape
Boeing Capital   Kellstrom Aerospace
CIT Group   SIFCO

HISTORICAL FINANCIALS

Company Type: Public

Income Statement

FYE: December 31

	REVENUE ($ mil.)	NET INCOME ($ mil.)	NET PROFIT MARGIN	EMPLOYEES
12/08	152.3	26.6	17.5%	55
12/07	121.9	14.5	11.9%	52
12/06	85.3	4.3	5.0%	53
12/05	70.5	4.2	6.0%	47
12/04	61.9	3.9	6.3%	44
Annual Growth	25.2%	61.6%	—	5.7%

2008 Year-End Financials

Debt ratio: 400.0%
Return on equity: 17.6%
Cash ($ mil.): 8.6
Current ratio: 1.29
Long-term debt ($ mil.): 641.1
No. of shares (mil.): 9.2

Dividends
 Yield: —
 Payout: —
Market value ($ mil.): 85.1
R&D as % of sales: —
Advertising as % of sales: —

Stock History

NASDAQ (GM): WLFC

	STOCK PRICE ($) FY Close	P/E High/Low		PER SHARE ($) Earnings	Dividends	Book Value
12/08	9.27	5	3	2.68	—	20.95
12/07	12.54	10	6	1.66	—	19.04
12/06	10.32	25	16	0.45	—	16.03
12/05	8.15	25	15	0.44	—	13.24
12/04	7.80	23	15	0.42	—	12.69
Annual Growth	4.4%	—	—	58.9%	—	13.3%

Winmark Corporation

Winmark Corporation loves recycling, but it's not collecting cans and paper. Winmark franchises retail chains that buy, sell, and consign used goods (and some new items) at more than 850 stores. The chains sell sports gear (Play It Again Sports); children's items (Once Upon A Child); teen apparel (Plato's Closet); and musical gear (Music Go Round). Most operations are in the US, but it does have about 60 stores in Canada. Business services and financing falls under the Wirth Business Credit banner. Another subsidiary, Winmark Capital, is in the equipment leasing business. Chairman and CEO John Morgan owns about 25% of Winmark Corp.

The company expanded its business solutions unit by creating the Wirth Business Credit franchise to further assist small businesses with equipment financing. Winmark provides businesses with financing on items ranging from

$5,000 to $250,000. The company has seen its number of Wirth Business Credit franchisees expand steadily.

In 2006 president and COO Stephen Briggs resigned from those positions, as well as from the board of directors. He was replaced by Steve Murphy, VP of Franchise Management.

HISTORY

Jeffrey Dahlberg (son of the founder of Dahlberg, maker of Miracle Ear hearing aids) and Ron Olson started a consulting firm in 1986. Martha Morris, their third client and the founder of Play It Again Sports, showed them how profitable used goods could be. In 1989 the pair bought out Morris, and Olson was named CEO; by 1992 they had built the concept into a chain of 281 stores. The company started franchising stores internationally in 1991.

The firm expanded by acquiring Once Upon a Child (1992); Hi Tech Consignments, which became Music Go Round (1993); and Computer Renaissance (1993). Named Grow Biz International, the company went public in 1993. The following year it acquired CDX Audio, changing the name to Disc Go Round. By the end of 1994, Grow Biz had 765 stores.

By capitalizing on consumers' desire for value and on the growing market trend for recycled goods, the company built its sales from $2.3 million in 1991 to over $100 million in 1995, making it #1 on both the *FORTUNE* and *Inc.* lists of fastest-growing US companies.

Grow Biz opened its 1,000th store in 1996. The next year it bought 40 Video Game Exchange stores, which became the nucleus of what was then its sixth franchise, It's About Games.

In 1998 Grow Biz sold the Disc Go Round franchise and purchased Tool Traders (renaming it ReTool) and the franchise rights to Plato's Closet, sellers of new and used clothing for teens. In late 1998 Dahlberg and Olson offered to take the company private by purchasing the 33% of its stock it didn't already own for about $24 million. They shelved their offer in 1999 after shareholder protests, and soon thereafter Dahlberg took the CEO reigns from Olson. Also in 1999 the company closed It's About Games chain, resulting in a loss for the year.

Dahlberg and Olson left the company in May 2000, retaining 50%. John Morgan, who sold his successful equipment leasing firm to retire, took over as chairman, president, and CEO and soon inducted a new board and shuffled management, vowing to focus the company on stabilizing cash flow. In August 2000 the company sold its Computer Renaissance franchise to Hollis Technologies for $3 million.

In November 2001 the company changed its name to Winmark Corporation. It also ceased franchising its ReTool brand and subsequently terminated relationships with ReTool franchisees.

In late 2002 Winmark formed Winmark Business Solutions to provide more in-depth support to its franchisees. Services include detailed information services, training, and other products and services that are not typically part of a franchise agreement. The company also offers these services to other small businesses.

On December 2, 2003, the company's stock moved from the Nasdaq small cap market to the Nasdaq national market.

Winmark launched its business equipment (computers, POS systems, telecom) leasing services in 2004 and its business financing services in 2005.

EXECUTIVES

Chairman and CEO: John L. Morgan, age 67, $368,961 total compensation
Vice Chairman: Kirk A. MacKenzie, age 70
CFO: Anthony D. (Tony) Ishaug, age 37, $45,100 total compensation
VP Human Resources: Leah A. Goff, age 47
VP Marketing: Merry Beth Hovey, age 45
Director, Music Go Round: Timothy J. (Tim) Kletti
Director, Play It Again Sports: Patrick M. Quinn
Corporate Legal Assistant and Manager Administration and Communications: Kathy Smith
President, Winmark Capital Corporation: Steven C. Zola, age 47, $571,038 total compensation
President Franchising: Steven A. (Steve) Murphy, age 43, $564,708 total compensation
President Finance and Administration and Treasurer: Brett D. Heffes, age 41, $616,182 total compensation
Auditors: Grant Thornton LLP

LOCATIONS

HQ: Winmark Corporation
4200 Dahlberg Dr., Ste. 100
Minneapolis, MN 55422
Phone: 763-520-8500   **Fax:** 763-520-8410
Web: www.winmarkcorporation.com

2008 Franchised Stores

	No.
Play It Again Sports	364
Once Upon A Child	229
Plato's Closet	241
Music Go Round	36
Total	**870**

PRODUCTS/OPERATIONS

2008 Sales

	$ mil.	% of total
Royalties	21.8	62
Leasing	8.1	23
Merchandise	3.3	9
Franchise fees	1.7	5
Other	0.5	1
Total	**35.4**	**100**

Store Formats

Music Go Round (used and new musical instruments, speakers, amplifiers, music-related electronics, and related accessories)
Once Upon a Child (used and new clothing, toys, furniture, and accessories for infants and children up to 12 years of age)
Plato's Closet (used and new clothing and accessories for teenagers)
Play It Again Sports (used and new sporting goods, equipment, and accessories)
Wirth Business Credit (financing for business equipment)

COMPETITORS

Abercrombie & Fitch	Guitar Center
Academy Sports	Gymboree
American Express	Hibbett Sports
Babies "R" Us	Kmart
Cash America	Old Navy
Comerica	Salvation Army
Costco Wholesale	Sam Ash Music
craigslist	Sears
Dick's Sporting Goods	Sports Authority
eBay	T. Rowe Price
EZCORP	Target
The Gap	Wal-Mart
Goodwill Industries	

HISTORICAL FINANCIALS

Company Type: Public

Income Statement

FYE: Last Saturday in December

	REVENUE ($ mil.)	NET INCOME ($ mil.)	NET PROFIT MARGIN	EMPLOYEES
12/08	35.4	1.1	3.1%	106
12/07	31.2	3.0	9.6%	105
12/06	27.4	3.4	12.4%	104
12/05	26.6	2.1	7.9%	102
12/04	27.2	4.1	15.1%	122
Annual Growth	**6.8%**	**(28.0%)**	**—**	**(3.5%)**

2008 Year-End Financials

Debt ratio: 158.8%
Return on equity: 8.3%
Cash ($ mil.): 2.1
Current ratio: 1.33
Long-term debt ($ mil.): 22.1
No. of shares (mil.): 5.2
Dividends
  Yield: —
  Payout: —
Market value ($ mil.): 60.2
R&D as % of sales: —
Advertising as % of sales: —

Stock History

NASDAQ (GM): WINA

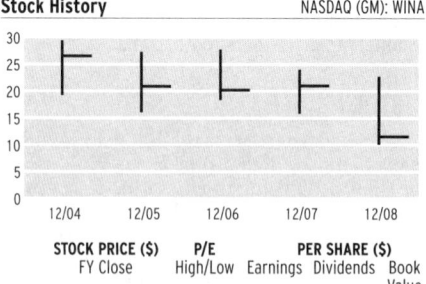

	STOCK PRICE ($) FY Close	P/E High/Low		PER SHARE ($) Earnings	Dividends	Book Value
12/08	11.50	107	49	0.21	—	2.66
12/07	21.00	44	30	0.54	—	2.42
12/06	20.19	48	33	0.57	—	3.01
12/05	20.89	82	49	0.33	—	4.26
12/04	26.50	46	31	0.63	—	4.12
Annual Growth	**(18.8%)**	**—**	**—**	**(24.0%)**	**—**	**(10.4%)**

WMS Industries

The reels keep spinning and the jackpots flow at the casinos thanks to this company. WMS Industries is a leading manufacturer of casino gaming machines and related gaming systems. Its product portfolio includes video poker terminals and video slot machines, as well as traditional mechanical slot machines. It also makes progressive gaming systems offering bonus jackpots and systems that can network multiple games together. Other products include video lottery terminals and casino management software systems. WMS Industries has operations in about 10 countries outside the US.

WMS Industries and its rival gaming machine makers are an important part of the equation for modern casino operators. The company's games are designed to attract attention from players on the busy casino floor with flashing and dancing lights, sounds, and other bells and whistles. Licensing popular and well-known brands for use in its game designs has become a trademark for WMS Industries: Its *Monopoly*-branded machines, produced through an exclusive agreement with toy maker Hasbro, have proven to be among the company's most popular.

Product development in the gaming machine industry has focused more and more around networking technologies to connect multiple games. These systems are used for progressive jackpots and to allow casinos to monitor gamblers for their popular player rewards programs. WMS markets a system called WAGE-NET that combines game monitoring, player loyalty, and other features in one integrated package. The company competes for space on the casino floor with such rivals as International Game Technology and Bally Technologies.

WMS Industries generates revenue through both product sales and leasing agreements in which the company rents games to casinos in return for a share of the money wagered on those machines. The company has more than 10,000 installed machines participating in these shared revenue agreements.

In addition to product development, WMS Industries has been expanding the international sales of its products. In 2009 the company inked a sales partnership with beet Limited to sell its products to customers in Australia.

HISTORY

WMS traces its roots to the Automatic Amusement Company, founded by Harry Williams in the 1930s. Williams produced his first game, called *Advance,* and soon followed it with industry innovations such as the tilt mechanism and, in 1933, electricity. In 1964 his company, Williams Electronics, was bought by jukebox maker Seeburg, which in turn was bought in the 1970s by Xcor, led by Chicago wheeler-dealer Louis Nicastro. Williams went public in 1974. After Seeburg went bankrupt in 1980, it spun off Williams, and Nicastro became CEO.

Williams changed its name to WMS in 1987, and the next year it bought the amusement-game lines of rival Bally/Midway, enhancing its position as a world leader in arcade gaming. In 1990 WMS moved its headquarters from New York City to Chicago and diversified into hotel and casino management.

In 1994 WMS created a joint venture (Williams/Nintendo) to market games for Nintendo platforms and moved into the home video game market with the acquisition of Tradewest Inc. The following year it announced plans to divide into three publicly traded businesses — hotels and casinos (WHG Resorts & Casinos); arcade and video operations (Midway Games); and casino gambling devices, lottery terminals, and pinball games (WMS Industries). In 1998 it spun off its 87% stake in Midway Games, which caused profits to take a hit. WMS's fiscal pain was eased somewhat by the successful debut of its *Monopoly*-themed slot machines in 1998. However, slumping pinball sales prompted the company to cease making pinball machines the following year.

In 2000 WMS announced the release of a series of machines based on popular board and word games such as *Scrabble, Pictionary,* and *Jumble.* Also that year its coin-operated video machines went the way of pinball machines when WMS discontinued their production. In 2001 president and COO Brian Gamache was named CEO. Nicastro stepped back to non-executive chairman. Also that year WMS began expanding outside North America, installing its Jackpot Party video slot machines in Australia.

The company overhauled its technology in 2002 in order to rectify defects in its gaming systems. That year it also launched three new game series (*Hollywood Squares, Survivor,* and *Pac-Man*) and opened an office in Johannesburg, South Africa. In 2004 WMS launched new mechanical reel-spinning game devices along with a new operating system and gaming platform, CPU-NXT.

Continuing its international expansion, WMS acquired in 2006 privately held Orion Gaming, a Netherlands-based manufacturer, for approximately $30 million. (The company closed down the Netherlands facility in 2009, shifting production to other sites.)

EXECUTIVES

Chairman and CEO: Brian R. Gamache, age 50, $7,242,977 total compensation
President: Orrin J. Edidin, age 48, $2,857,422 total compensation
EVP and COO: Kenneth (Ken) Lochiatto, age 46, $1,553,575 total compensation
EVP, CFO, and Treasurer: Scott D. Schweinfurth, age 55, $2,109,842 total compensation
EVP Global Products and Chief Innovation Officer: Larry J. Pacey, age 45, $2,252,329 total compensation
EVP Continuous Improvement: Patricia C. Barten, age 56
VP, General Counsel, and Secretary: Kathleen J. McJohn, age 50
VP, Controller, and Chief Accounting Officer: John P. McNicholas Jr., age 56
VP Investor Relations: William H. (Bill) Pfund
VP Marketing: Robert (Rob) Bone
President, WMS International: Sebastian Salat, age 51
Auditors: Ernst & Young LLP

LOCATIONS

HQ: WMS Industries Inc.
800 S. Northpoint Blvd., Waukegan, IL 60085
Phone: 847-785-3000   **Fax:** 847-785-3058
Web: www.wms.com

PRODUCTS/OPERATIONS

2009 Sales

	$ mil.	% of total
Gaming products	438.5	62
Machine leasing	267.9	38
Total	**706.4**	**100**

COMPETITORS

Aristocrat Leisure
Bally Technologies
GTECH
International Game Technology
Konami
Multimedia Games
Novomatic
Scientific Games

HISTORICAL FINANCIALS

Company Type: Public

Income Statement

FYE: June 30

	REVENUE ($ mil.)	NET INCOME ($ mil.)	NET PROFIT MARGIN	EMPLOYEES
6/09	706.4	92.2	13.1%	1,712
6/08	650.1	67.5	10.4%	1,531
6/07	539.8	48.9	9.1%	1,414
6/06	451.2	33.3	7.4%	1,320
6/05	388.4	21.2	5.5%	1,221
Annual Growth	**16.1%**	**44.4%**	**—**	**8.8%**

2009 Year-End Financials

Debt ratio: 19.4%
Return on equity: 16.7%
Cash ($ mil.): 135.7
Current ratio: 3.89
Long-term debt ($ mil.): 115.0
No. of shares (mil.): 58.7
Dividends
Yield: —
Payout: —
Market value ($ mil.): 1,849.9
R&D as % of sales: —
Advertising as % of sales: —

Stock History

NYSE: WMS

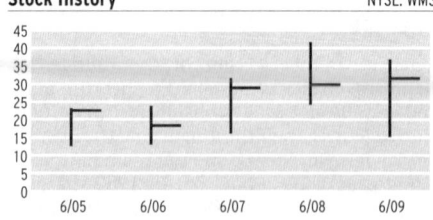

	STOCK PRICE ($) FY Close	P/E High/Low		PER SHARE ($) Earnings	Dividends	Book Value
6/09	31.51	23	10	1.59	—	10.07
6/08	29.77	36	21	1.15	—	8.70
6/07	28.86	36	19	0.86	—	7.39
6/06	18.26	37	21	0.63	—	5.55
6/05	22.50	55	31	0.41	—	4.86
Annual Growth	**8.8%**	**—**	**—**	**40.3%**	**—**	**20.0%**

World Acceptance Corporation

When Junior breaks his leg and you can't bear to part with the velvet Elvis to pay the bill, World Acceptance can help. The consumer finance company offers short-term and medium-term loans and credit insurance to individuals with limited access to other credit sources. Borrowers use the loans of up to $3,000 to meet temporary or unanticipated cash needs, such as car repairs and medical bills. Convenience comes at a price: World Acceptance typically charges the maximum interest rate and related fees allowed by law. The company has more than 800 offices in the US South and Midwest and in Mexico.

World Acceptance sells credit life and other forms of credit insurance, in addition to marketing third-party auto club memberships to borrowers in Alabama, Georgia, Kentucky, New Mexico, and Tennessee. The company also offers income tax preparation services and refund anticipation loans through a third party.

Subsidiary ParaData Financial Systems markets data processing software and related services to other consumer finance companies. Via its World Class Buying Club, World Acceptance markets and finances home electronics and appliances to its customers.

World Acceptance opened more than 100 new office locations in 2007 and 2008. It opened its first office in Mexico in 2005 and has since opened about 40 offices in that country. The company plans to continue its expansion in both countries, including entering new markets as approvals and licenses are gained.

Investment advisor Columbia Wanger Asset Management owns about 15% of the company.

HISTORY

World Acceptance was founded in 1962 by Southern Bancorp. In 1989 president Charles Walters led a management buyout from First Union, which had acquired Southern three years earlier. World Acceptance went public in 1991.

Moving further into its existing markets, primarily in the South, the company began expanding its services. It started marketing auto club memberships to clients in 1993. That year it bought data processing firm ParaData Financial Systems, which in 1995 contracted to provide data processing for Mercury Finance. Also in 1995 World Acceptance began its World Class Buying Club program in Texas and expanded into other states in following years. In 1997 it acquired San Antonio-based Personal Credit Plan, a local consumer lender.

Buoyed by shrinking default rates, the company moved into larger, lower-margin loans in 1998. That year it settled a class-action lawsuit regarding a type of insurance it had used to cover borrowers' collateral; the $5 million settlement hit the company's bottom line. In 1999 World Acceptance launched a pilot program to prepare tax returns and provide loans on anticipated refunds. It expanded the program through most of its network over the next two years.

EXECUTIVES

Chairman and CEO: A. Alexander (Sandy) McLean III, age 58, $1,510,156 total compensation
President, COO, and Director: Mark C. Roland, age 52, $1,129,438 total compensation
SVP, Treasurer, and CFO: Kelly M. Malson, age 38, $651,955 total compensation
SVP, Mexico: Francisco J. (Javier) Sauza Del Pozo, age 56, $648,640 total compensation
SVP, Southern Division: James D. Walters, age 41, $375,162 total compensation
SVP, Western Division: Jeff L. Tinney, age 47
SVP, Central Division: D. Clinton Dyer, age 36
SVP Human Resources: Marilyn M. Messer, age 58
SVP, Secretary, and General Counsel: Judson K. Chapin III, age 63
VP and Director Marketing: Yvette Drake
President, Paradata Financial Systems: James J. Rosenauer
Auditors: KPMG LLP

LOCATIONS

HQ: World Acceptance Corporation
108 Frederick St., Greenville, SC 29607
Phone: 864-298-9800   **Fax:** 864-298-9810
Web: www.worldacceptance.com

2009 Locations

	No.
US	
Texas	223
Georgia	100
South Carolina	93
Tennessee	92
Oklahoma	80
Illinois	61
Kentucky	58
Missouri	57
Alabama	42
Louisiana	38
New Mexico	37
Mexico	63
Total	**944**

PRODUCTS/OPERATIONS

2009 Gross Revenues

	$ mil.	% of total
Interest & fees	331.4	84
Insurance commissions & other	62.3	16
Total	**393.7**	**100**

Selected Subsidiaries

Servicios World Acceptance Corporation de Mexico
WAC Insurance Company, Ltd. (Turks and Caicos Islands)
WFC Limited Partnership
WFC of South Carolina, Inc.
WFC Services, Inc.

COMPETITORS

ACE Cash Express	Check 'n Go
Advance America	Citigroup
AmeriCredit	Dollar Financial
Capital One	EZCORP
Cash America	First Cash Financial
Check Into Cash	HSBC Finance

HISTORICAL FINANCIALS

Company Type: Public

Income Statement

FYE: March 31

	ASSETS ($ mil.)	NET INCOME ($ mil.)	INCOME AS % OF ASSETS	EMPLOYEES
3/09	531.3	60.7	11.4%	3,449
3/08	486.1	53.0	10.9%	3,017
3/07	411.1	47.9	11.7%	2,594
3/06	332.8	38.5	11.6%	2,214
3/05	293.5	34.0	11.6%	2,075
Annual Growth	**16.0%**	**15.6%**	**—**	**13.5%**

2009 Year-End Financials

Equity as % of assets: 54.7%
Return on assets: 11.9%
Return on equity: 23.1%
Long-term debt ($ mil.): 113.3
No. of shares (mil.): 16.2
Market value ($ mil.): 277.9
Dividends
  Yield: 0.0%
  Payout: —
Sales ($ mil.): 383.3
R&D as % of sales: —
Advertising as % of sales: —

Stock History

NASDAQ (GS): WRLD

	STOCK PRICE ($) FY Close	P/E High/Low		PER SHARE ($) Earnings	Dividends	Book Value
3/09	17.10	12	3	3.69	0.00	17.87
3/08	31.85	15	7	3.05	0.00	14.42
3/07	39.95	20	10	2.60	0.00	13.26
3/06	27.40	16	11	2.02	0.00	12.95
3/05	25.52	18	8	1.74	0.00	11.67
Annual Growth	**(9.5%)**	**—**	**—**	**20.7%**	**—**	**11.2%**

World Wrestling Entertainment

The action might be fake, but the business of World Wrestling Entertainment (WWE) is very real. The company is a leading producer and promoter of wrestling matches for TV and live audiences, with more than 300 live events each year, including more than 70 international matches. Its TV programming includes *Monday Night Raw*, a top US cable program on USA Network, *ECW: Extreme Championship Wrestling* on Syfy, and *Friday Night SmackDown!* on MyNetworkTV. WWE also produces about 15 pay-per-view programs, licenses characters for merchandise, and sells videos and DVDs showcasing more than 150 wrestling stars such as Batista, Rey Mysterio, Triple H, and The Undertaker.

While fans don't seem to mind the lack of spontaneity in the "sport," many people and groups have objected to what they see as over-the-top violence in WWE's spectacles. That hasn't stopped the company from capitalizing on its popularity: It publishes a wrestling magazine with a readership of more than 4 million, licenses its characters for use in toy manufacturing and popular video games, and creates books published through a venture with Simon & Schuster.

WWE's bread and butter continues to be live events and television entertainment, which accounts for more than 60% of sales. It inked a new broadcasting deal with upstart network MyNetworkTV (owned by FOX parent News Corporation) to air *Friday Night SmackDown* after The CW Network declined to renew the show in 2008. *SmackDown* had been on The CW since the network launched in 2006. It also launched a new show, *WWE Superstars*, on cable network WGN America in 2009.

Expanding on its popular live events and TV shows, WWE operates an on-demand cable TV service with Cox Communications, Comcast, and other cable carriers that offers subscription access to many of the company's pay-per-view events and other content in its video library. It also distributes content through mobile phone networks. Reaching out to Hollywood, the company's WWE Studios has produced such movies as *The Condemned* and *See No Evil*.

Chairman Vince McMahon has nearly 90% voting control of WWE. He took over as CEO in 2009 when his wife, Linda, resigned to seek a seat in the US Senate.

HISTORY

Jesse McMahon made a name for himself as a boxing promoter in the 1940s before switching to wrestling. His son Vincent joined him in the business, and they founded the World Wide Wrestling Federation in 1963. The company operated in Northeastern cities such as New York, Philadelphia, and Washington, DC, remaining a regional operation until the early 1980s (it dropped Wide from its name in 1979).

Vince McMahon Jr. inherited control of the WWF from his sick father in 1982, changed its name to Titan Sports, and focused on gaining national exposure. McMahon made wrestling hugely popular but angered promoters, as well as some fans, with his nontraditional ideas. He embraced the idea of wrestling as show business instead of sport, involving celebrities such as

Cyndi Lauper and Mr. T, and pursued a presence on cable TV. McMahon also purchased or put out of business many regional promoters as he spread the business across the US.

In the mid-1980s McMahon hit the jackpot with a former bodybuilder named Terry Gene Bollea. Christened Hulk Hogan, he quickly became lord of the ring, making the cover of *Sports Illustrated* and performing for sellout crowds across the US. His likeness spawned toys, clothing, and a Saturday morning cartoon. Titan set a record for attracting the largest indoor crowd (more than 93,000 fans packed Detroit's Pontiac Silverdome for Wrestlemania III) in 1987 and by the following year was selling $80 million in tickets annually.

Titan was body slammed in 1993 when competitor World Championship Wrestling (WCW, formed in 1988 by Ted Turner to broadcast on his TBS network) lured away several major stars, including Hogan. Also that year the US government charged Titan with illegal distribution of steroids. The company was acquitted in 1994, but the bad press, along with the star defections, allowed WCW to take the ratings lead by 1996.

Titan's refashioning of the WWF with more violence and sexual innuendo unleashed a hailstorm of criticism, but returned it to the top spot by mid-1998; meanwhile former WWF star Jesse "The Body" Ventura was elected governor of Minnesota. Titan was named a defendant in a wrongful death suit in 1999 filed by the family of wrestler Owen Hart, who fell to his death during a pay-per-view event (the case was settled in 2000). The company also changed its name to World Wrestling Federation Entertainment (WWFE) and went public that year. The company later licensed the WWF name for a theme restaurant in New York City.

WWFE continued its bone-crunching ways in 2000 by launching XFL, a professional football league that played in the winter following the NFL season. Still smarting from the loss of NFL broadcast rights to CBS, NBC bought half of the new league and broadcast the games on its network. The deal also gave NBC a 3% stake in WWF. The league was a disaster during its first season, and it quickly folded. (The company repurchased NBC's shares in 2002.)

Also in 2000 the company abandoned its broadcasting contract with USA Networks (now IAC/InterActiveCorp) in favor of a more lucrative deal with Viacom, which also took a 3% stake in the company. (Viacom sold the stake back to the company in 2003.) In 2001 WWFE put a headlock on the wrestling world when it bought the WCW from Turner Broadcasting.

In 2002 WWE received the smackdown in a court battle with the World Wildlife Fund, which claimed the company (formerly WWF) lifted the animal preservation group's initials. The company had to change its name from World Wrestling Federation Entertainment to World Wrestling Entertainment as part of a settlement.

After ending its partnership with Viacom's Spike TV in 2005, the WWE cut a deal with NBC Universal to air *Monday Night Raw* on the USA Network and on Spanish-language network Telemundo. The following year, after The WB and the UPN merged to form The CW Network, WWE inked a deal with the upstart broadcaster to air *Friday Night SmackDown*. (The show moved to MyNetworkTV, owned by News Corporation, in 2008.) It also created a new show, *ECW: Extreme Championship Wrestling*, for NBC Universal's SCI FI Channel (now Syfy).

EXECUTIVES

Chairman and CEO: Vincent K. (Vince) McMahon, age 64, $858,880 total compensation
COO and Director: Donna Goldsmith, age 49, $1,041,402 total compensation
CFO: George A. Barrios, age 43, $793,254 total compensation
EVP Marketing: Michelle D. Wilson, age 43
EVP Event Booking and Live Events: Brett Hart
EVP Digital Media: Brian Kalinowski
EVP, General Counsel, and Secretary: Jared F. Bartie, age 40
EVP Global Media: Shane B. McMahon, age 39
EVP WWE Studios: Mike Pavone
EVP Talent Relations: John Laurinatis
EVP Creative Development and Operations: Stephanie McMahon Levesque, age 32
SVP Sales: Joe DelGrosso
SVP Human Resources: Danielle Fisher
SVP Special Events: John P. Saboor
SVP Talent Relations: John Laurinaitis, age 46
SVP Consumer Products: Jim Connelly
VP Information Technology: Michael O'Toole
VP Public Relations and Corporate Communications: Robert Zimmerman
VP Investor Relations and Planning: Michael Weitz
President, WWE Studios: Michael (Mike) Lake, age 66
President, WWE International: Andrew Whitaker
President, Global Business: Carl DeMarco
Auditors: Deloitte & Touche LLP

LOCATIONS

HQ: World Wrestling Entertainment, Inc.
1241 E. Main St., Stamford, CT 06902
Phone: 203-352-8600   **Fax:** 203-359-5151
Web: corporate.wwe.com

PRODUCTS/OPERATIONS

2008 Sales

	$ mil.	% of total
Live & televised entertainment	331.5	63
Consumer products	135.7	26
Digital media	34.8	7
WWE Studios	24.5	5
Total	**526.5**	**100**

Selected Operations

Consumer products
  Home video
  Magazines
  Product licensing
Digital media
  WWE.com
  WWEShop
Live events
  ECW Superstars
  Raw Superstars
  SmackDown
  SmackDown SummerSlam
  Survivor Series
  WWE Live
Pay-per-view events
TV entertainment
  A.M. Raw (USA)
  ECW: Extreme Championship Wrestling (Syfy)
  Friday Night SmackDown (MyNetworkTV)
  Monday Night Raw (USA)
  WWE Superstars (WGN America)
WWE 24/7 (on-demand video service)

COMPETITORS

Harlem Globetrotters
Live Nation
Major League Baseball
NASCAR
NBA
NFL
NHL

HISTORICAL FINANCIALS

Company Type: Public

Income Statement

FYE: December 30

	REVENUE ($ mil.)	NET INCOME ($ mil.)	NET PROFIT MARGIN	EMPLOYEES
12/08	526.5	45.4	8.6%	564
12/07*	485.7	52.1	10.7%	570
4/06	400.1	47.0	11.7%	460
4/05	366.4	39.1	10.7%	412
4/04	374.9	48.2	12.9%	436
Annual Growth	**8.9%**	**(1.5%)**	**—**	**6.6%**

*Fiscal year change

2008 Year-End Financials

Debt ratio: 1.1%
Return on equity: 12.2%
Cash ($ mil.): 119.7
Current ratio: 4.80
Long-term debt ($ mil.): 3.9
No. of shares (mil.): 73.3
Dividends
  Yield: 13.0%
  Payout: 232.3%
Market value ($ mil.): 812.2
R&D as % of sales: —
Advertising as % of sales: —

Stock History

NYSE: WWE

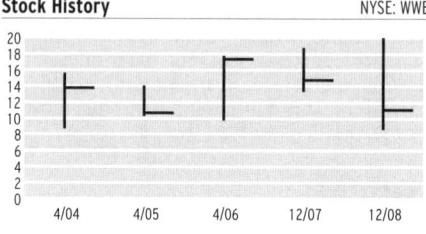

	STOCK PRICE ($) FY Close	P/E High/Low	PER SHARE ($) Earnings	Dividends	Book Value
12/08	11.08	32 14	0.62	1.44	4.91
12/07*	14.76	26 19	0.72	0.96	5.23
4/06	17.34	26 15	0.67	0.72	5.40
4/05	10.69	25 19	0.56	0.36	5.12
4/04	13.76	22 13	0.70	0.16	4.82
Annual Growth	**(5.3%)**	**— —**	**(3.0%)**	**73.2%**	**0.5%**

*Fiscal year change

Wright Express

Wright Express provides payment processing and information management services to nearly 300,000 commercial and government vehicle fleets through a network that tracks purchases made on fleet charge cards at about 180,000 fuel and vehicle maintenance facilities in the US, Canada, and Puerto Rico. The company provides clients with transaction data, analysis tools, and purchase control capabilities for every vehicle in their fleets. Data collected at the point of sale include expenditures, lists of items purchased, odometer readings, and driver, vehicle, and vendor identification. Wright Express also issues corporate MasterCard credit cards.

In 2007 the company bought TelaPoint, which provides supply-chain software to bulk petroleum distributors and retailers. The following year Wright Express bought New Zealand-based fuel card processing software provider Financial Automation Limited, its first foray beyond North America.

Expansion continued in 2008, with the purchase of Pacific Pride Services, an independent fuel distributor network with more than 340 independent fuel franchisees.

Wright Express was spun off by Cendant (now Avis Budget Group) and went public in 2005.

EXECUTIVES

Chairman, President, and CEO: Michael E. Dubyak, age 58, $1,985,288 total compensation
Vice Chairman: Rowland T. (Row) Moriarty, age 62
CFO and EVP Finance and Operations:
  Melissa D. Smith, age 40, $763,577 total compensation
EVP Sales and Marketing: David D. Maxsimic, age 49, $750,008 total compensation
SVP and CIO: George Hogan, age 48
SVP Human Resources: Robert C. Cornett, age 56, $480,746 total compensation
SVP, General Counsel, and Secretary: Hilary A. Rapkin, age 42, $509,115 total compensation
SVP Corporate Payment Solutions: Richard K. Stecklair, age 60
SVP Client Service Operations: Jamie Morin, age 44
VP Investor Relations: Steve Elder
Manager Communications: Jessica Roy
Auditors: Deloitte & Touche LLP

LOCATIONS

HQ: Wright Express Corporation
  97 Darling Ave., South Portland, ME 04106
Phone: 207-773-8171   **Fax:** 207-828-5181
Web: www.wrightexpress.com

PRODUCTS/OPERATIONS

2008 Sales

	$ mil.	% of total
Payment processing	297.4	76
Finance fees	31.0	8
Account servicing	30.7	8
Transaction processing	19.3	4
Product revenues	3.6	1
Other	11.6	3
Total	**393.6**	**100**

COMPETITORS

Comdata
Fleetcor
U.S. Bancorp

HISTORICAL FINANCIALS

Company Type: Public

Income Statement

FYE: December 31

	REVENUE ($ mil.)	NET INCOME ($ mil.)	NET PROFIT MARGIN	EMPLOYEES
12/08	393.6	127.6	32.4%	703
12/07	336.1	51.6	15.4%	694
12/06	291.2	74.6	25.6%	685
12/05	241.3	18.7	7.7%	650
12/04	189.1	51.2	27.1%	620
Annual Growth	**20.1%**	**25.6%**	**—**	**3.2%**

2008 Year-End Financials

Debt ratio: 105.0%
Return on equity: 51.2%
Cash ($ mil.): 183.1
Current ratio: 0.96
Long-term debt ($ mil.): 309.4
No. of shares (mil.): 38.1
Dividends
  Yield: 0.0%
  Payout: —
Market value ($ mil.): 480.5
R&D as % of sales: —
Advertising as % of sales: —

NYSE: WXS

Stock History

	STOCK PRICE ($) FY Close	P/E High/Low		PER SHARE ($) Earnings	Dividends	Book Value
12/08	12.60	11	3	3.22	0.00	7.73
12/07	35.49	32	20	1.27	0.00	5.36
12/06	31.17	18	12	1.81	0.00	4.80
12/05	22.00	54	33	0.46	0.00	1.96
Annual Growth	**(17.0%)**	**—**	**—**	**25.9%**	**—**	**0.9%**

Wright Medical Group

Wright Medical Group wants to make your knees and hips work all right. The company makes reconstructive implants for knees, hips, and other joints. Product lines include the ADVANCE knee system, CONSERVE and PERFECTA hip systems, the OLYMPIA shoulder and trauma system, and Swanson finger and wrist implants. Wright Medical also makes an injectable putty for bone defects as well as bone graft and tissue substitute materials such as OSTEOSET pellets used to regenerate bone. Wright Medical sells its products in more than 60 countries through distributors and a direct sales force that targets customers in the orthopedic surgery market.

Sales of products in the US market account for about 60% of sales, while European countries make up about a quarter of revenues. Wright Medical's traditional products in hip and knee replacement markets account for more than half of sales, but the firm is also establishing a presence in the niche markets of extremity reconstruction and biologics.

The company employs its own research and development staff in an effort to discover new or improved reconstruction products, such as the GLADIATOR bipolar hip implant launched in 2007 and the BIOFOAM knee replacement tibial base introduced in 2008.

Wright Medical also expands its product offerings through acquisitions. The company made several purchases to widen its line of extremity devices in 2008, including the acquisition of INBONE Technologies, a maker of foot and ankle surgical systems, for $24 million. It also acquired the RAYHACK line of wrist reconstruction systems and the endoscopic foot and ankle assets of A.M. Surgical. In 2007 Wright Medical purchased Darco International's foot and ankle implant assets for $17 million.

EXECUTIVES

President, CEO, and Director: Gary D. Henley, age 60, $1,925,113 total compensation
SVP Reseach and Development: Frank S. Bono, age 46, $674,094 total compensation
SVP Government Affairs and Reimbursement:
  Rhonda L. Fellows, age 53

SVP and CFO: Lance A. Berry, age 37
VP North American Sales: Eric A. Stookey, age 38, $729,786 total compensation
VP Business Development: Timothy E. Davis Jr., age 39
VP and Treasurer: Joyce B. Jones, age 55
VP, General Counsel, and Secretary: Jason P. Hood, age 44
VP International Sales and Distribution:
  Karen L. Harris, age 47
VP Sales and Marketing Services: William F. Scott, age 63
VP Human Resources: Edward A. Steiger
Interim President, Europe, Middle East, and Africa:
  Cary P. Hagan, age 42
Auditors: KPMG LLP

LOCATIONS

HQ: Wright Medical Group, Inc.
  5677 Airline Rd., Arlington, TN 38002
Phone: 901-867-9971   **Fax:** 901-867-9534
Web: www.wmt.com

2008 Sales

	$ mil.	% of total
US	282.1	61
Europe	112.7	24
Other regions	70.7	15
Total	**465.5**	**100**

PRODUCTS/OPERATIONS

2008 Sales

	$ mil.	% of total
Hips	160.8	34
Knee	119.9	26
Extremity	88.9	19
Biologics	82.4	18
Other	13.5	3
Total	**465.5**	**100**

COMPETITORS

Biomet
DePuy
Exactech
Integra LifeSciences
Kensey Nash
LifeCell
Lifecore Biomedical
Medtronic Sofamor Danek
OsteoTec
Osteotech
RTI Biologics
Smith & Nephew
Stryker
Symmetry Medical
Zimmer Holdings

HISTORICAL FINANCIALS

Company Type: Public

Income Statement

FYE: December 31

	REVENUE ($ mil.)	NET INCOME ($ mil.)	NET PROFIT MARGIN	EMPLOYEES
12/08	465.5	3.2	0.7%	1,250
12/07	386.9	1.0	0.3%	1,050
12/06	338.9	14.4	4.2%	1,060
12/05	319.1	21.1	6.6%	990
12/04	297.5	24.0	8.1%	899
Annual Growth	**11.8%**	**(39.6%)**	**—**	**8.6%**

2008 Year-End Financials

Debt ratio: 48.6%
Return on equity: 0.8%
Cash ($ mil.): 87.9
Current ratio: 6.33
Long-term debt ($ mil.): 200.1
No. of shares (mil.): 38.6
Dividends
  Yield: —
  Payout: —
Market value ($ mil.): 789.2
R&D as % of sales: —
Advertising as % of sales: —

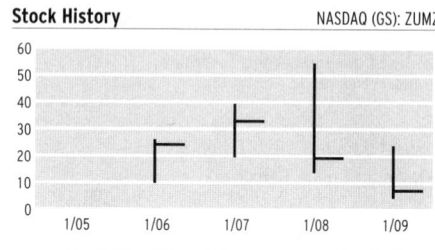

STOCK PRICE ($)	P/E	PER SHARE ($)		
FY Close	High/Low	Earnings	Dividends	Book Value
12/08	20.43	370 169	0.09	—	10.66
12/07	29.17	1,060 699	0.03	—	10.06
12/06	23.28	61 45	0.41	—	8.69
12/05	20.40	48 30	0.60	—	7.56
12/04	28.50	54 31	0.68	—	7.15
Annual Growth	(8.0%)	— —	(39.7%)	—	10.5%

Zumiez Inc.

Zumiez's customers like to zoom. The online and mall-based retailer offers swank swag-like clothing, shoes, accessories, and gear to 12- to 24-year-olds who enjoy such action sports as snowboarding, BMX, skateboarding, and surfing. From about 345 stores in some 30 states, Zumiez sells popular youth brands like Billabong, Burton, Hurley, Quiksilver, Vans, and Spy Optic, as well as private-label goods. Besides the usual hoodies, T-shirts, puffy skater shoes, and snowboarding goggles, stores also sport couches, video games, and sales clerks who really use the gear — all designed to encourage the kids to hang out. Zumiez was founded in 1978 by its chairman Thomas Campion.

Fast-growing Zumiez is expanding by adding new stores and acquiring others. In 2008 it opened 58 new stores (after adding 50 shops in 2007) and entered several new markets, including Hawaii and Virginia. In 2009 it planned to open more than 35 locations in new and existing markets. Zumiez is also increasing the size of its stores and adding more private-label merchandise (about 15% of sales). Despite all that growth, sales at Zumiez's existing stores fell in 2008 along with the economy and consumer confidence. About 20% of Zumiez's stores are located in economically distressed California.

In 2006 the firm acquired the Action Concepts Fast Forward sporting goods chain of 20 stores, mostly in Texas, and has converted them all to the Zumiez nameplate.

Chairman Campion owns about 19% of Zumiez's shares; CEO Richard Brooks owns 12%.

EXECUTIVES

Chairman: Thomas D. Campion, age 60, $267,509 total compensation
CEO and Director: Richard M. Brooks, age 49, $268,226 total compensation
President and General Merchandising Manager: Lynn K. Kilbourne, age 46, $811,394 total compensation
CFO and Secretary: Trevor S. Lang, age 38, $941,292 total compensation
EVP Stores: Ford K. Wright, age 41, $597,894 total compensation
Auditors: Moss Adams, LLP

LOCATIONS

HQ: Zumiez Inc.
   6300 Merrill Creek Pkwy., Ste. B, Everett, WA 98203
Phone: 425-551-1500   **Fax:** 425-551-1555
Web: www.zumiez.com

2009 Stores

	No.
California	69
New York	31
Texas	31
Washington	23
Colorado	17
New Jersey	15
Illinois	14
Arizona	12
Oregon	12
Utah	12
Florida	16
Minnesota	11
Pennsylvania	14
Nevada	8
Wisconsin	8
Maryland	7
Connecticut	6
Idaho	6
Indiana	6
Montana	4
New Mexico	5
Alaska	3
Maine	2
Oklahoma	2
Virginia	2
Wyoming	2
Delaware	1
Hawaii	1
Iowa	1
Rhode Island	1
South Dakota	1
Total	**343**

PRODUCTS/OPERATIONS

2009 Sales

	% of total
Accessories & other	55
Men's apparel	31
Women's apparel	14
Total	**100**

COMPETITORS

Abercrombie & Fitch
Aéropostale
American Eagle Outfitters
Big 5
The Buckle
Charlotte Russe Holding
Claire's Stores
Dick's Sporting Goods
Forever 21
Hot Topic
Old Navy
Pacific Sunwear
Sport Chalet
Sports Authority
Urban Outfitters
Wet Seal

HISTORICAL FINANCIALS

Company Type: Public

Income Statement

FYE: Saturday nearest January 31

	REVENUE ($ mil.)	NET INCOME ($ mil.)	NET PROFIT MARGIN	EMPLOYEES
1/09	408.7	17.2	4.2%	3,650
1/08	381.4	25.3	6.6%	3,300
1/07	298.2	20.9	7.0%	3,006
1/06	205.6	12.9	6.3%	2,273
1/05	153.6	7.3	4.8%	1,502
Annual Growth	27.7%	23.9%	—	24.9%

2009 Year-End Financials

Debt ratio: —   Dividends
Return on equity: 10.3%   Yield: —
Cash ($ mil.): 33.1   Payout: —
Current ratio: 4.59   Market value ($ mil.): 216.3
Long-term debt ($ mil.): —   R&D as % of sales: —
No. of shares (mil.): 30.3   Advertising as % of sales: —

STOCK PRICE ($)	P/E	PER SHARE ($)		
FY Close	High/Low	Earnings	Dividends	Book Value
1/09	7.15	40 8	0.58	—	5.88
1/08	19.23	63 16	0.86	—	5.11
1/07	32.90	53 27	0.73	—	3.46
1/06	24.17	54 22	0.47	—	2.44
Annual Growth	(33.4%)	— —	20.0%	—	62.1%

Hoover's Handbook of

Emerging Companies

Master Index for all
2010 Hoover's Handbooks

Index by Industry

AEROSPACE & DEFENSE

Global Defense Technology E173

Aerospace & Defense Maintenance & Service
VSE Corporation E408

Aerospace & Defense Parts Manufacturing
Astronics Corporation E54
BAE SYSTEMS W57
BE Aerospace A133
CPI Aerostructures E108
Ducommun Incorporated E131
Finmeccanica SpA W142
FLIR Systems E158
Goodrich Corporation A396
Hawk Corporation E187
HEICO Corporation E191
Innovative Solutions E218
ITT Corporation A474
L-3 Communications A517
Ladish Co. E243
LMI Aerospace E250
Lockheed Martin A540
Moog Inc. A596
National Presto Industries E281
Northrop Grumman A634
Rolls-Royce plc W290
Sequa Corporation P449
TransDigm Group E389

Aircraft Leasing
AeroCentury Corp. E22
Aircastle Limited E25
Willis Lease Finance E416

Aircraft Manufacturing
AeroVironment, Inc. E22
Airbus S.A.S. W32
The Boeing Company A156
Bombardier Inc. W75
EADS (European Aeronautic Defence and Space Company EADS N.V.) W124
Textron Inc. A824

Weaponry & Related Product Manufacturing
Alliant Techsystems A65
General Dynamics A383
Raytheon Company A722

AGRICULTURE

Agricultural Support Activities & Products
Ag Processing P29
Alabama Farmers Cooperative P31
Archer Daniels Midland A105
Associated Milk Producers P60
Cargill, Incorporated A188, P113

CHS Inc. A217
Dairylea Cooperative P155
DeBruce Grain P161
Dunavant Enterprises P174
J. D. Heiskell & Company P269
MFA Incorporated P335
Monsanto Company A595
The Scoular Company P446
Southern States Cooperative P465
Staple Cotton Cooperative P471
Wilbur-Ellis Company P546

Animal Production
King Ranch A507

Crop Production
Blue Diamond Growers P92
Calavo Growers E80
Chiquita Brands International A216
Dole Food A298
National Grape Cooperative P352
Sunkist Growers P479

AUTOMOTIVE & TRANSPORT

Auto Manufacturing
BMW (Bayerische Motoren Werke AG) W73
Daimler AG W111
Fiat S.p.A. W140
Ford Motor A364
General Motors A387, P206
Honda Motor Co. W165
Hyundai Motor W169
Mazda Motor W220
Mitsubishi Motors W225
Nissan Motor Co. W242
PSA Peugeot Citroën W262
Renault S.A. W280
Suzuki Motor W331
Toyota Motor W360
Volkswagen AG W374

Auto Parts Manufacturing
Affinia Group P26
Aisin Seiki W33
Allison Transmission P37
ArvinMeritor A108
BorgWarner Inc. A160
Cummins, Inc. A269
Dana Holding A272
Delphi Automotive P163
DENSO CORPORATION W115
Federal-Mogul A350
Flex-N-Gate P194
Fuel Systems Solutions E165
IAC North America (International Automotive Components Group North America) P256
J.B. Poindexter & Co. P269
Johnson Controls A488
Key Safety Systems P281
Magna International W215

Remy International P419
Robert Bosch W285
TA Delaware P483
Tenneco Inc. A816
Tomkins plc W355
United Components P508

Container Leasing
Mobile Mini E271
TAL International E373
TTX Company P503

Motorcycle & Other Small Engine Vehicle Manufacturing
Harley-Davidson A408
Polaris Industries A690

Pleasure Boat Manufacturing
Brunswick Corporation A174

Rail & Trucking Equipment Manufacturing
American Railcar Industries E40
Electro-Motive Diesel P178
Trinity Industries A843

Recreational Vehicle Manufacturing
Thor Industries A828

Truck, Bus & Other Vehicle Manufacturing
AB Volvo W375
Isuzu Motors W180
MAN SE W216
Navistar International A611
Oshkosh Corporation A654
PACCAR Inc A657
Spartan Motors E355

Truck Leasing
Ryder System A742

BANKING

Automated Teller Machine Operators
Global Cash Access E173

Banking – Asia & Australia
Bank of China W60
Commonwealth Bank of Australia W104
Mitsubishi UFJ Financial Group W226
Mizuho Financial W229
National Australia Bank W232

Banking – Canada
Bank of Montreal W61
Canadian Imperial Bank of Commerce W88
Royal Bank of Canada W292
Toronto-Dominion Bank W356

Banking – Europe
Allied Irish Banks W40

Supply Chain Management & Logistics Software

Reynolds and Reynolds P421

CONSTRUCTION

Construction & Design Services

ACS W23
A.G. Spanos (A. G. Spanos Companies) P30
Alberici Corporation P32
Alion Science and Technology P33
Argan, Inc. E52
Austin Industries P65
Barton Malow P73
Beazer Homes USA A134
Bechtel Group A135, P77
Black & Veatch P84
Bouygues SA W77
Brasfield & Gorrie P100
Burns & McDonnell P105
Callison Architecture P108
CH2M HILL Companies P128
Champion Enterprises A208
Clark Enterprises P135
Day & Zimmermann P160
DPR Construction P170
D.R. Horton A306
The Drees Company P171
EMCOR Group A328
ENGlobal Corporation E143
Fagen, Inc. P188
The Flintco Companies P195
Fluor Corporation A360
Foster Wheeler A369
Furmanite Corporation E166
Gilbane, Inc. P211
Great Lakes Dredge & Dock E177
Grupo Ferrovial W139
Henkels & McCoy P243
Hensel Phelps Construction P244
Hill International E195
HOCHTIEF AG W164
Hoffman Corporation P249
Holder Construction P249
Hovnanian Enterprises A443
Jacobs Engineering A477
J.E. Dunn Construction Group P270
J.F. Shea Co. P271
KB Home A496
Layne Christensen E245
Lennar Corporation A525
M. A. Mortenson P306
McCarthy Building Companies P322
McDermott International A572
MWH Global P346
NCI Building Systems A615
NVR, Inc. A642
Parsons Corporation P385
Pepper Construction P392
Peter Kiewit Sons' A677, P395
Pulte Homes A712
Rooney Holdings P427
Ryan Companies US P430
The Ryland Group A744
The Shaw Group A770
SmithGroup, Inc. P460
Sterling Construction E359
Structure Tone P475
Suffolk Construction P476
The Sundt Companies P477
Swinerton Incorporated P482
Tata Group W335
Team, Inc. E374
Toll Brothers A837
Turner Industries P505
URS A867
VINCI W369
Walsh Group P536
Weekley Homes P540

The Weitz Company P541
Whiting-Turner Contracting P545
William Lyon Homes P547
Yates Companies P551
Zachry Holdings P553

Construction Materials

Ameron International E43
Andersen Corporation P50
Atrium Companies P65
Carlisle Companies A190
CEMEX, S.A.B. de C.V. W99
Columbia Forest Products P140
CONTECH P145
Goodman Global P215
Jacuzzi Brands P268
JELD-WEN, inc. P271
Kohler Co. P286
Lafarge S.A. W200
Lennox International A527
Martin Marietta Materials A560
Masco Corporation A561
New NGC P362
NTK Holdings P373
Pella Corporation P389
Pro-Build Holdings P404
Roseburg Forest Products P427
Saint-Gobain (Compagnie de Saint-Gobain) W299
Sierra Pacific Industries P454
Sumitomo Corporation W330
USG Corporation A874
Vulcan Materials A888
Watsco, Inc. A900
Weyerhaeuser Company A913

CONSUMER PRODUCTS MANUFACTURERS

Unilever W365

Apparel

adidas AG W25
Broder Bros. P101
Deckers Outdoor E120
Jones Apparel A489
Kellwood Company P280
Levi Strauss A529, P296
Liz Claiborne A539
New Balance P360
NIKE, Inc. A626
Phillips-Van Heusen A682
Polo Ralph Lauren A691
The Timberland Company A832
True Religion Apparel E390
Under Armour E395
V.F. Corporation A882
Warnaco Group A895
Williamson-Dickie Manufacturing P547

Appliances

AB Electrolux W126
Alliance Laundry P35
Conair Corporation P142
iRobot Corporation E229
Whirlpool Corporation A914

Baby Supplies & Accessories

Summer Infant E363

Cleaning Products

Church & Dwight A219
The Clorox Company A229
Henkel KGaA W161
JohnsonDiversey, Inc. P275
Reckitt Benckiser W278
S.C. Johnson A753, P439
Sun Products P477

Consumer Electronics

Bose Corporation P96
CASIO COMPUTER W96

Harman International A409
Nintendo Co. W238
Panasonic Corporation W255
Philips Electronics (Royal Philips Electronics N.V.) W263
Pioneer Corporation W265
Sony Corporation W325
Universal Electronics E398
VIZIO, Inc. P533

Hand Tools, Power Tools, Lawn & Garden Equipment

Black & Decker A151
MTD Products P345
Snap-on Incorporated A778
The Toro Company A839

Home Furniture

Ashley Furniture P58
Furniture Brands International A376
La-Z-Boy A521
Leggett & Platt A524
Sauder Woodworking P437

Housewares

Newell Rubbermaid A620
Tupperware Brands A846
Visant Holding Corp. P532
Yankee Candle P551

Jewelry & Watch Manufacturing

Fossil, Inc. A368
The Swatch Group W333
Tiffany & Co. A830

Mattress & Bed Manufacturers

Sealy Corporation A766
Simmons Bedding (Simmons Company) P455
Spring Air International P468

Musical Equipment

Gibson Guitar P210
Yamaha Corporation W385

Office & Business Furniture, Fixtures & Equipment

Haworth, Inc. P237
Herman Miller A423
HNI Corporation A435
Kewaunee Scientific E238
Steelcase Inc. A798

Office, School & Art Supplies

Fellowes, Inc. P192

Personal Care Products

Alberto-Culver A58
Alticor Inc. P38
Avon Products A120
Colgate-Palmolive A235
Estée Lauder A338
Inter Parfums E221
Kao Corporation W187
Kimberly-Clark A504
L'Oréal SA W209
MacAndrews & Forbes A547, P307
Mary Kay P316
Melaleuca, Inc. P329
Procter & Gamble A701
Revlon, Inc. A728
Shiseido Company W313

Pet Products

PETCO Animal Supplies P394
PetSmart, Inc. A678
Professional Veterinary Products P404

Photographic & Optical Equipment/Supplies Manufacturers

Eastman Kodak A317
FUJIFILM Holdings W149
Nikon Corporation W237

Sporting Goods & Equipment

Colt's Manufacturing P139
Quiksilver, Inc. A716
Volcom, Inc. E406

Tobacco

Alliance One International A64
Altria Group A67
British American Tobacco W82
Imperial Tobacco W173
Japan Tobacco W184
North Atlantic Trading Company P370
Reynolds American A729
Universal Corporation A864

Toys & Games

Hasbro, Inc. A413
LEGO Holding W203
Mattel, Inc. A565
Ty Inc. P505

CONSUMER SERVICES

Automotive Service & Collision Repair

Pittsburgh Glass Works P397

Car & Truck Rental

AMERCO A71
Avis Budget Group A118
Enterprise Rent-A-Car P181
Frank Consolidated Enterprises P201
Hertz Global Holdings A425

Death Care Products & Services

Service Corporation A769
StoneMor Partners E360

Hair Salons

Regis Corporation A724

Laundry Facilities & Dry Cleaning Services

Mac-Gray Corporation E255

Portrait Photography

Lifetouch Inc. P300

Rent-To-Own

Aaron's, Inc. A29
Rent-A-Center A726

Travel Agencies & Services

Carlson Wagonlit Travel A191
Carnival Corporation A193
priceline.com A698
Royal Caribbean Cruises A739
Sabre Holdings P431
Travelport Limited P497
TUI AG W362

CULTURAL INSTITUTIONS

National Geographic Society P351
Smithsonian Institution P460

EDUCATION

Child Care Services & Elementary & Secondary Schools

Knowledge Learning P284

Colleges & Universities

American Public Education E40
Apollo Group A98
Boston University P98
Bridgepoint Education E74
California State University System P107
City University of New York P134
Columbia University P141
Cornell University P148

Rockwell Automation A734
Siemens AG (Siemens
Aktiengesellschaft) W314

Industrial Contract Manufacturing
Federal Prison Industries P189

Industrial Equipment Leasing
United Rentals A857

Industrial Machinery & Equipment Distribution
Applied Industrial Technologies A100
DXP Enterprises E133
H&E Equipment Services E185
Hillman Companies P246
McJunkin Red Man Holding
Corporation P322
MSC Industrial Direct A601
Titan Machinery E386
W.W. Grainger A924

Industrial Machinery & Equipment Manufacturing
Altra Holdings E33
Amsted Industries P47
Barry-Wehmiller P72
Briggs & Stratton A164
Chart Industries E92
Dover Corporation A303
Energy Recovery E142
Goss International P216
Hitachi, Ltd. W162
Hurco Companies E203
Illinois Tool Works A453
Kennametal Inc. A500
Lincoln Electric Holdings A535
RBS Global P412
Roper Industries A735
Servotronics, Inc. E345
The Timken Company A834
United Technologies A861

Lighting & Other Fixture Manufacturing
Advanced Lighting Technologies P23
AZZ incorporated E58

Material Handling Equipment Manufacturing
Crown Equipment P152
Key Technology E239
NACCO Industries A603

Metal Fabrication
Ampco-Pittsburgh Corporation E44
Commercial Metals A240
Dynamic Materials E134
Euramax International P186
Kaydon Corporation E236
L. B. Foster E246
Precision Castparts A696
Synalloy Corporation E369
WHX Corporation E415

Packaging & Container Manufacturing
Ball Corporation A125
Bemis Company A142
Berry Plastics P80
Crown Holdings A266
Dart Container P157
Graham Packaging P219
Greif, Inc. A401
MeadWestvaco A578
Owens-Illinois A656
Plastipak Holdings P399
Printpack, Inc. P403
Rock-Tenn Company A733
Sealed Air Corp. A764
Solo Cup P463
Sonoco Products A781
Tekni-Plex, Inc. P486
Temple-Inland A813

Paper & Paper Product Manufacturing
Appleton Papers P52
Central National-Gottesman P126
International Paper A465
The Kraft Group P289
The Newark Group P369
Orchids Paper Products E305
Stora Enso Oyj W329

Rubber & Plastic Product Manufacturing
Advanced Drainage Systems P22
Bridgestone Corporation W80
Cooper Tire & Rubber A256
CTI Industries E113
FXI-Foamex Innovations P205
Goodyear Tire & Rubber A397
Michelin (Compagnie Générale des
Établissements Michelin) W222
Nypro Inc. P374
Pirelli & C. W266
Raven Industries E331
Sigma Plastics P455

Textile Manufacturing
Beaulieu Group P76
Hallwood Group E183
Milliken & Company P339
Mohawk Industries A591

Wire & Cable Manufacturing
Belden Inc. A140
CommScope, Inc. A241
General Cable A382
Optical Cable E304
Preformed Line Products E320
Southwire Company P466

INSURANCE
CUNA Mutual P152
Hartford Financial Services A412

Insurance Brokers
AmWINS Group P49
Aon Corporation A95
eHealth, Inc. E138
Lloyd's (Society of Lloyd's) W205
Marsh & McLennan A558

Life Insurance
AEGON N.V. W27
Allianz SE W39
American United Mutual
Insurance P46
Assicurazioni Generali W49
AXA W54
CNP Assurances W103
ERGO Insurance W133
Guardian Life Insurance P228
ING Groep W176
Life Partners Holdings E249
Lincoln National A536
Massachusetts Mutual Life
Insurance A563, P318
MetLife, Inc. A585
Modern Woodmen P341
National Life Insurance P354
New York Life Insurance A618, P364
Nippon Life Insurance W239
Northwestern Mutual Life
Insurance A635, P371
Pacific Mutual P383
Penn Mutual Life Insurance P389
Protective Life A705
Prudential Financial A706
Prudential plc W272
Sammons Enterprises P435
Securian Financial P447
Thrivent Financial P491
Torchmark Corporation A838
Western & Southern Financial P542

Property & Casualty Insurance
Aflac Incorporated A48
The Allstate Corporation A66
American Family Insurance P42
American Financial Group A77
American International Group A80
AmTrust Financial E45
Auto-Owners Insurance Group P66
The Chubb Corporation A218
Cincinnati Financial A222
CNA Financial A231
Conseco, Inc. A246
Factory Mutual Insurance P187
First Mercury Financial E158
Hanover Insurance A407
Liberty Mutual A531, P298
Loews Corporation A542
Main Street America P308
Markel Corporation A554
Meadowbrook Insurance Group E260
Mutual of Omaha P345
National Interstate E280
Nationwide Mutual Insurance A610,
P355
The Navigators Group E284
Progressive Corporation A704
SeaBright Insurance E344
Sentry Insurance P448
State Farm Mutual Automobile
Insurance A796, P471
Tokio Marine W351
Tower Group E387
Travelers Companies A842
Trustmark Mutual Holding
Company P502
Unum Group A865
USAA A872, P526
Zurich Financial Services W387

Reinsurance
Hannover Re (Hannover
Rückversicherung AG) W158
Munich Re Group (Münchener
Rückversicherungs-Gesellschaft
Aktiengesellschaft) W230
Swiss Re W334

Risk Management
Verisk Analytics E401

Surety Insurance
Ambac Financial Group A70
MBIA Inc. A568

Title Insurance
The First American Corporation A355

LEISURE
Carlson Companies P114
Ilitch Holdings P259
It's Just Lunch P267

Entertainment
AMC Entertainment P39
Cinemark Holdings A223
Feld Entertainment P191
Live Nation A537
Rick's Cabaret E337
World Wrestling Entertainment E419

Gambling
Boyd Gaming A162
Connecticut Lottery P143
Georgia Lottery P208
Harrah's Entertainment P234
International Game Technology A464
Jacobs Entertainment P267
Kentucky Lottery P281
Ladbrokes plc W199
Maryland State Lottery P317
Mashantucket Pequot Tribal
Nation P317

Massachusetts State Lottery P319
MGM MIRAGE A587
Mohegan Tribal Gaming
Authority P342
New York State Lottery P366
Pennsylvania Lottery P390
Texas Lottery P489
WMS Industries E417

Lodging
Accor W21
Best Western P81
Club Med W102
Columbia Sussex P140
Hilton Worldwide A433, P247
HVM L.L.C. P255
Hyatt Hotels Corporation A448
Marriott International A555
Starwood Hotels & Resorts A794

Restaurants & Cafes
BJ's Restaurants E68
Bob Evans Farms A155
Brinker International A166
Buffalo Wild Wings E78
Burger King Holdings A176
California Pizza Kitchen E82
The Cheesecake Factory A213
Chick-fil-A P130
Cracker Barrel Old Country
Store A264
Darden Restaurants A275
Denny's Corporation A287
DineEquity, Inc. A294
Domino's Pizza A301
Dunkin' Brands P174
Friendly Ice Cream P204
Harman Management P232
Jack in the Box A476
Johnny Rockets P273
The Krystal Company P289
McDonald's Corporation A573
Metromedia Company P333
Noodles & Company P370
OSI Restaurant Partners P381
Panda Restaurant Group P385
Peet's Coffee & Tea E308
Real Mex Restaurants P414
Red Robin Gourmet Burgers E332
Rock Bottom Restaurants P425
Sbarro, Inc. P439
Starbucks Corporation A793
Subway (Doctor's Associates
Inc.) P475
Texas Roadhouse E381
Uno Restaurants (Uno Restaurant
Holdings Corp.) P521
Waffle House P535
Wendy's/Arby's Group A907
Whataburger P543
White Castle P545
YUM! Brands A931

Sports & Recreation
24 Hour Fitness P16
Anaheim Ducks P49
Atlanta Spirit P64
Boston Red Sox P97
Carolina Hurricanes P116
Cavaliers Operating Company P122
Chicago Bulls (Chicago Professional
Sports Corporation) P130
ClubCorp USA P136
Colorado Avalanche P139
Curves International P153
Dallas Cowboys P155
Dallas Mavericks (Dallas Basketball
Limited) P156
Denver Nuggets P165
Golden State Warriors P214
Green Bay Packers A400, P224
Houston Rockets P253

Index by Headquarters

ARGENTINA

Buenos Aires
YPF W386

AUSTRALIA

Bella Vista
Woolworths Limited W382

Mascot
Qantas Airways W275

Melbourne
BHP Billiton W71
National Australia Bank W232
Rio Tinto Limited W284
Telstra Corporation W345

Perth
Wesfarmers Limited W378

Southbank
Foster's Group (Foster's Group
Limited) W146

Sydney
AMP Limited W43
Commonwealth Bank of
Australia W104

AUSTRIA

Vienna
OMV W252

BELGIUM

Brussels
Dexia NV/SA W122

Leuven
Anheuser-Busch InBev W45

BERMUDA

Pembroke
Bacardi Limited W56

BRAZIL

Rio de Janeiro
PETRÓLEO BRASILEIRO W259
Vale S.A. W366

CANADA

Aurora
Magna International W215

Brampton
Loblaw Companies W207

Calgary
Agrium Inc. W29
Imperial Oil W172

Montreal
Bombardier Inc. W75

Toronto
Bank of Montreal W61
Canadian Imperial Bank of
Commerce W88
George Weston W155
Rogers Communications W288
Royal Bank of Canada W292
Toronto-Dominion Bank W356

CHINA

Beijing
Bank of China W60
China Petroleum & Chemical W102

Shanghai
Sinopec Shanghai
Petrochemical W318

DENMARK

Bagsværd
Novo Nordisk W249

Billund
LEGO Holding W203

Copenhagen
A.P. Møller - Mærsk W46
Carlsberg A/S W92

FINLAND

Espoo
Nokia Corporation W244

Helsinki
Stora Enso Oyj W329

FRANCE

Blagnac
Airbus S.A.S. W32

Boulogne-Billancourt
Renault S.A. W280

Clermont-Ferrand
Michelin (Compagnie Générale des
Établissements Michelin) W222

Clichy
L'Oréal SA W209

Courbevoie
Saint-Gobain (Compagnie de Saint-
Gobain) W299
TOTAL S.A. W359

Croix
Groupe Auchan W53

Évry
Accor W21

Levallois-Perret
ALSTOM W41
Carrefour SA W93

Montigny-le-Bretonneux
Sodexo W322

Paris
Alcatel-Lucent W35
Atos Origin W51
AXA W54
BNP Paribas W74
Capgemini W91
Club Med W102
CNP Assurances W103
Crédit Agricole W106
Electricité de France W125
France Telecom W148
GDF SUEZ W153
Groupe Danone W112
Lafarge S.A. W200
Lagardère SCA W201
LVMH Moët Hennessy Louis
Vuitton W213
Pernod Ricard W257
PPR SA W269
PSA Peugeot Citroën W262
Publicis Groupe W273
Rallye S.A. W277
Sanofi-Aventis W302
SNCF (Société Nationale des Chemins
de Fer Français) W319
Société Générale W320
Veolia Environnement W368
Vivendi W371

Roissy
Air France-KLM W30

Rueil-Malmaison
Schneider Electric W307
VINCI W369

Saint-Étienne
Casino Guichard W95

Saint-Quentin-en-Yvelines
Bouygues SA W77

GERMANY

Berlin
Axel Springer W55
Deutsche Bahn W117

Bonn
Deutsche Post W119
Deutsche Telekom AG W120

Cologne
Lufthansa (Deutsche Lufthansa
AG) W211

Düsseldorf
E.ON AG W132
ERGO Insurance W133
Henkel KGaA W161
METRO AG W221
ThyssenKrupp AG W350

Essen
ALDI Group W37
HOCHTIEF AG W164
RWE W296

Frankfurt
Deutsche Bank W118

Gütersloh
Bertelsmann AG W70

Hamburg
Otto GmbH & Co KG W253

Hannover
Hannover Re (Hannover
Rückversicherung AG) W158
TUI AG W362

Herzogenaurach
adidas AG W25

Leverkusen
Bayer AG W65

Ludwigshafen
BASF SE W63

Mülheim an der Ruhr
Tengelmann W347

Munich
Allianz SE W39
BMW (Bayerische Motoren Werke
AG) W73
MAN SE W216
Munich Re Group (Münchener
Rückversicherungs-Gesellschaft
Aktiengesellschaft) W230
Siemens AG (Siemens
Aktiengesellschaft) W314

INDEX BY HEADQUARTERS LOCATION

Universal City
DreamWorks Studios P170

Ventura
Affinity Group P27

Vernon
Red Chamber Co. P415
True Religion Apparel E390

Visalia
California Dairies Inc. P106

Walnut
J.F. Shea Co. P271
ViewSonic Corporation P532

Walnut Creek
Central Garden & Pet A201

West Sacramento
Raley's P410

Westlake Village
Consolidated Electrical
  Distributors P144
Dole Food A298
Guitar Center P229

Woodland Hills
Advanstar Communications P23
Health Net A417

COLORADO

Boulder
Dynamic Materials E134

Broomfield
Ball Corporation A125
Level 3 Communications A528
MWH Global P346
Noodles & Company P370

Centennial
National CineMedia E278

Denver
Berry Petroleum E63
Bill Barrett Corporation E65
Catholic Health Initiatives P119
Colorado Avalanche P139
Denver Nuggets P165
Double Eagle Petroleum E129
Intrepid Potash E225
Leprino Foods P295
MediaNews Group P325
Molson Coors Brewing A593
Pro-Build Holdings P404
Qwest Communications A717
Royal Gold E339
TransMontaigne Partners E390

Englewood
Air Methods E23
Archstone P53
CH2M HILL Companies P128
CSG Systems International E112
DISH Network A297
IHS Inc. E208
Liberty Media P297
Sports Authority P467

Golden
Health Grades E189
Jacobs Entertainment P267

Greeley
Hensel Phelps Construction P244

Greenwood Village
Newmont Mining A622
Red Robin Gourmet Burgers E332

Lakewood
Mesa Laboratories E265

Longmont
DigitalGlobe, Inc. E126

Louisville
Rock Bottom Restaurants P425

Westminster
Tri-State Generation and
  Transmission P499

CONNECTICUT

Avon
Magellan Health Services A549

Berlin
Northeast Utilities A632

Bridgeport
People's United Financial E310

Bristol
ESPN, Inc. P184

Cheshire
Alexion Pharmaceuticals E27
Bozzuto's Inc. P99

Clinton
Connecticut Water Service E104

Danbury
Praxair, Inc. A695

Darien
North Atlantic Trading
  Company P370

Dayville
United Natural Foods A854

Enfield
STR Holdings E361

Fairfield
General Electric A384

Greenwich
Genesee & Wyoming E169
United Rentals A857

Hartford
Aetna Inc. A46
Hartford Financial Services A412
United Technologies A861

Ledyard
Mashantucket Pequot Tribal
  Nation P317

Milford
Subway (Doctor's Associates
  Inc.) P475

New Haven
Yale New Haven Health System P550
Yale University P551

Norwalk
Affinion Group P27
EMCOR Group A328
FactSet Research Systems E153
IMS Health A455
priceline.com A698
Vertrue Incorporated P532
Webloyalty.com P539
Xerox Corporation A926

Rocky Hill
Connecticut Lottery P143

Stamford
Aircastle Limited E25
Cenveo, Inc. A203
Conair Corporation P142
Crane Co. A265
Frontier Communications A375
Harman International A409

Pitney Bowes A685
PrimeEnergy Corporation E322
Towers Perrin P494
World Wrestling Entertainment E419

Uncasville
Mohegan Tribal Gaming
  Authority P342

West Hartford
Colt's Manufacturing P139

Westport
Terex Corporation A818

Wilton
Sun Products P477

DELAWARE

Dover
Chesapeake Utilities E93

Wilmington
DuPont (E. I. du Pont de Nemours
  and Company) A311

DISTRICT OF COLUMBIA

Washington
AARP P17
Advantis Real Estate Services P24
The Advisory Board Company E21
AFL-CIO P28
Amtrak (National Railroad Passenger
  Corporation) P48
Blackboard Inc. E70
The Carlyle Group P115
Cogent Communications E98
Corporation for Public
  Broadcasting P148
Danaher Corporation A274
DuPont Fabros Technology E133
Environmental Protection Agency (US
  Environmental Protection
  Agency) P182
Federal Prison Industries P189
Federal Reserve System P190
Howard University P254
Marriott International A555
National Geographic Society P351
Pension Benefit Guaranty
  Corporation P390
Pepco Holdings A668
Red Cross (The American National
  Red Cross) P416
Smithsonian Institution P460
Teamsters (International Brotherhood
  of Teamsters) P485
US Postal Service (United States
  Postal Service) A871, P524
Washington Post A897

FLORIDA

Boca Raton
American Media P43
Office Depot A645
Purity Wholesale Grocers P407

Bonita Springs
Source Interlink Companies P463

Bradenton
Beall's Inc. P76

Clearwater
BayCare Health System P76
Lincare Holdings A534
Tech Data Corporation A810

Coconut Grove
Watsco, Inc. A900

Coral Gables
Baptist Health South Florida P71

Daytona Beach
NASCAR (National Association for
  Stock Car Auto Racing, Inc.) P347

Deerfield Beach
JM Family Enterprises P272

Fort Lauderdale
AutoNation, Inc. A114
SEACOR Holdings A762
Spherion Corporation A788

Gainesville
Exactech, Inc. E149

Hollywood
BrandsMart USA (Interbond
  Corporation of America) P99
HEICO Corporation E191

Jacksonville
Arizona Chemical P55
Blue Cross and Blue Shield of
  Florida P87
Crowley Maritime P151
CSX Corporation A268
Gate Petroleum P205
Main Street America P308
MPS Group A600
PSS World Medical A707
VyStar Credit Union P535
Winn-Dixie Stores A919

Juno Beach
FPL Group A372

Lake Mary
FARO Technologies E155

Lakeland
Publix Super Markets A711, P406

Melbourne
Harris Corporation A411

Miami
Brightstar Corp. P100
Burger King Holdings A176
Carnival Corporation A193
Continucare Corporation E106
Greenberg Traurig P225
Lennar Corporation A525
Miami Heat (Basketball Properties,
  Ltd.) P335
The Related Group P418
Royal Caribbean Cruises A739
Ryder System A742
Southern Wine & Spirits P465
World Fuel Services A920

Naples
Health Management Associates A416
Rooney Holdings P427

Orlando
AirTran Holdings A54
Darden Restaurants A275
Gencor Industries E168
Orlando Magic P379
Tupperware Brands A846

Pembroke Pines
Claire's Stores P134

Plantation
TradeStation Group E387

Pompano Beach
PetMed Express E312

St. Petersburg
HSN, Inc. A444

Palatine
Addus HomeCare E18

Park Ridge
Koch Foods P285

Peoria
Caterpillar Inc. A196
OSF Healthcare System P380

Quincy
Titan International E385

River Grove
Follett Corporation P197

Rock Island
Modern Woodmen P341

Rosemont
Reyes Holdings P420
U.S. Foodservice P522

Schaumburg
Motorola, Inc. A599

Skokie
Forsythe Technology P200
Rand McNally P411

Urbana
Flex-N-Gate P194
University of Illinois P513

Vernon Hills
CDW Corporation P123

Warrenville
Navistar International A611

Waukegan
WMS Industries E417

Westmont
Ty Inc. P505

Wheaton
Wheaton Franciscan Services P544

Wheeling
Midland Paper P338

Woodridge
Pabst Brewing P382

INDIANA

Anderson
Remy International P419

Batesville
Hill-Rom Holdings A432

Bloomington
Cook Group P147
Indiana University P260

Bluffton
Franklin Electric E164

Carmel
ADESA, Inc. P20
Conseco, Inc. A246
ITT Educational Services E231

Columbus
Cummins, Inc. A269

Evansville
Berry Plastics P80
United Components P508

Fort Wayne
Do it Best P168

Greensburg
MainSource Financial E257

Indianapolis
Allison Transmission P37

American United Mutual
Insurance P46
Brightpoint Inc. A165
Eli Lilly A325
Hurco Companies E203
Indiana Pacers (Pacers Basketball,
LLC) P260
Interactive Intelligence E223
Marsh Supermarkets P315
National Wine & Spirits P355
Simon Property Group A774
WellPoint, Inc. A904

Madison
River Valley Bancorp E338

Merrillville
NiSource Inc. A627

Michigan City
Horizon Bancorp E200

New Castle
Ameriana Bancorp E34

Warsaw
Biomet, Inc. P83
Lakeland Financial E244
Symmetry Medical E369

IOWA

Ankeny
Casey's General Stores A195

Armstrong
Art's-Way Manufacturing E52

Des Moines
Iowa Health System P266
Principal Financial A700
The Weitz Company P541

Iowa City
University of Iowa Hospitals and
Clinics P514

Muscatine
HNI Corporation A435

Pella
Pella Corporation P389

Sioux City
Terra Industries A820
Terra Nitrogen E380

West Des Moines
Hy-Vee, Inc. P256
Kum & Go P290

KANSAS

Kansas City
Associated Wholesale Grocers P62

Lenexa
Sisters of Charity of Leavenworth
Health System P457
U.S. Central Federal Credit
Union P522

Mission Woods
Layne Christensen E245

Olathe
NIC Inc. E292

Overland Park
Black & Veatch P84
Digital Ally E125
Ferrellgas Partners A353
QC Holdings E325
Sprint Nextel A789
Waddell & Reed E409
YRC Worldwide A930

Shawnee
Perceptive Software P392

Shawnee Mission
Seaboard Corporation A761

Topeka
Capitol Federal Financial E85
Collective Brands A237
Westar Energy A910

Wichita
Koch Industries A511, P285

KENTUCKY

Bowling Green
Houchens Industries P252

Covington
Ashland Inc. A109
Omnicare, Inc. A649

Crestview Hills
Columbia Sussex P140

Fort Mitchell
The Drees Company P171

Highland Heights
General Cable A382

Hopkinsville
HopFed Bancorp E200

Lexington
Lexmark International A530
University of Kentucky P514

Louisville
Almost Family E32
Brown-Forman Corporation A173
Humana Inc. A446
Industrial Services of America E213
Kentucky Lottery P281
Kindred Healthcare A505
Porter Bancorp E318
Republic Bancorp E334
Texas Roadhouse E381
Thorntons Inc. P490
University of Louisville P515
YUM! Brands A931

LOUISIANA

Baton Rouge
Blue Cross (LA) (Blue Cross and Blue
Shield of Louisiana) P89
H&E Equipment Services E185
The Shaw Group A770
Turner Industries P505

Covington
Hornbeck Offshore Services E201

Lafayette
IBERIABANK Corporation E204
LHC Group E247
MidSouth Bancorp E270
PHI, Inc. E313

Metairie
Louisiana Bancorp E252

Monroe
CenturyTel, Inc. A202

New Orleans
Entergy Corporation A332
New Orleans Hornets P362

MAINE

Freeport
L.L. Bean P300

Presque Isle
Maine & Maritimes Corporation E256

South Portland
Wright Express E420

Westbrook
IDEXX Labs (IDEXX Laboratories,
Inc.) E206

MARYLAND

Annapolis
TeleCommunication Systems E379

Baltimore
Constellation Energy Group A251
DLA Piper P167
Johns Hopkins Health System P274
Laureate Education P293
Legg Mason A523
Maryland State Lottery P317
NAACP P347
T. Rowe Price Group A807
Under Armour E395
University of Maryland Medical
System P515
Vertis, Inc. P531
Whiting-Turner Contracting P545

Bethesda
Chevy Chase Bank P130
Chindex International E94
Clark Enterprises P135
Eagle Bancorp E135
Lockheed Martin A540
National Cancer Institute P349
National Institutes of Health P354
OPNET Technologies E304
Sucampo Pharmaceuticals E362
USEC Inc. A873

Bowie
Old Line Bancshares E299

Chevy Chase
Howard Hughes Medical
Institute P253

Columbia
Martek Biosciences E258
MedStar Health P327
W. R. Grace A923

Elkridge
GP Strategies E175

Hampstead
Jos. A. Bank Clothiers E234

Hanover
Allegis Group P34

Lanham
Vocus, Inc. E406

Linthicum
Dialysis Corporation E123

Marriottsville
Bon Secours Health System P94

Owings Mills
Medifast, Inc. E263

Rockville
Argan, Inc. E52
Goodwill Industries P216

Salisbury
Perdue Incorporated P393

Austin
Hormel Foods A441

Bayport
Andersen Corporation P50

Bloomington
Holiday Companies P250
The Toro Company A839

Chanhassen
Datalink Corporation E119
Life Time Fitness E249

Eden Prairie
C.H. Robinson Worldwide A207
Digital River E125
Lifetouch Inc. P300
NVE Corporation E296
SUPERVALU INC. A803

Edina
Universal Hospital Services P510

Granite Falls
Fagen, Inc. P188

Inver Grove Heights
CHS Inc. A217

Marshall
Schwan Food P444

Medina
Polaris Industries A690

Minneapolis
Alliant Techsystems A65
Allina Hospitals P37
Appliance Recycling Centers of America E49
Buffalo Wild Wings E78
Capella Education E84
Carlson Wagonlit Travel A191
Ceridian Corporation P127
Dolan Media E128
Donaldson Company A302
Fairview Health Services P188
General Mills A386
Hawkins, Inc. E188
M. A. Mortenson P306
Medtronic, Inc. A581
Minnesota Timberwolves P340
Nash-Finch Company A607
PepsiAmericas, Inc. A670
Regis Corporation A724
Ryan Companies US P430
Target Corporation A808
University of Minnesota P516
U.S. Bancorp A870
The Valspar Corporation A877
Vascular Solutions E400
Winmark Corporation E416
Xcel Energy A925

Minnetonka
American Medical Systems E38
Carlson Companies P114
Michael Foods P336
UnitedHealth Group A863
Virtual Radiologic E404

Moorhead
American Crystal Sugar P41

New Ulm
Associated Milk Producers P60

North Mankato
Taylor Corporation P484

Oakdale
Imation Corp. A454

Plymouth
AGA Medical Holdings E23
Clearfield, Inc. E97

Richfield
Best Buy A146

Rochester
Mayo Foundation P320

St. Cloud
Coborn's, Incorporated P137

St. Paul
3M Company A26
AgriBank, FCB P31
APi Group P51
Ecolab Inc. A321
Image Sensing Systems E210
MEDTOX Scientific E264
Merrill Corporation P331
Minnesota Wild P340
Patterson Companies A663
St. Jude Medical A747
Securian Financial P447
Travelers Companies A842

Shoreview
Deluxe Corporation A285

Wayzata
Cargill, Incorporated A188, P113

Winona
Fastenal Company A349

MISSISSIPPI

Greenwood
Staple Cotton Cooperative P471

Jackson
Cal-Maine Foods E83
Ergon, Inc. P183

Laurel
Sanderson Farms A748

Philadelphia
Yates Companies P551

Tupelo
Renasant Corporation E333

MISSOURI

Carthage
Leggett & Platt A524

Chesterfield
Kellwood Company P280
Sisters of Mercy Health System P457

Clayton
Apex Oil P51
Enterprise Financial Services E144
Olin Corporation A648

Columbia
MFA Incorporated P335
University of Missouri P516

Des Peres
Jones Financial Companies P276

Fenton
Maritz Inc. P312
UniGroup, Inc. P507

Grandview
NASB Financial E278

Joplin
Empire District Electric E139

Kansas City
AMC Entertainment P39
American Italian Pasta E37
Bartlett and Company P72

Blue Cross and Blue Shield of Kansas City P88
Burns & McDonnell P105
Cerner Corporation A205
Dairy Farmers of America P154
DeBruce Grain P161
Dickinson Financial P166
DST Systems A307
H&R Block A405
Hallmark Cards A404, P231
J.E. Dunn Construction Group P270
Kansas City Southern A495
Midwest Research Institute P338
Russell Stover P429
Sutherland Lumber P480
UMB Financial E394
U.S. Premium Beef P525

Liberty
Liberty Bancorp E248

Poplar Bluff
Southern Missouri Bancorp E353

St. Charles
American Railcar Industries E40
LMI Aerospace E250

St. Louis
Alberici Corporation P32
Ameren Corporation A72
Arch Coal A104
Ascension Health P56
Barry-Wehmiller P72
Belden Inc. A140
Brown Shoe Company A171
CCA Global Partners P123
Center Oil P125
Centric Group P127
Charter Communications A212
Emerson Electric A329
Enterprise Rent-A-Car P181
Express Scripts A345
Furniture Brands International A376
Graybar Electric P221
McCarthy Building Companies P322
Monsanto Company A595
Perficient, Inc. E311
Ralcorp Holdings A719
St. Louis Blues P433
Schnuck Markets P442
Scottrade, Inc. P445
Sigma-Aldrich Corporation A773
Solae, LLC P462
Solutia Inc. A780
SSM Health Care P469
Stifel Financial E360
World Wide Technology P549

Springfield
Associated Electric Cooperative P59
Bass Pro Shops P73

MONTANA

Billings
First Interstate BancSystem P194

Great Falls
Davidson Companies P159

Kalispell
Glacier Bancorp E172

Missoula
Washington Companies P538

NEBRASKA

Kearney
The Buckle, Inc. E77

Lincoln
Crete Carrier P151
Nebraska Book P358
University of Nebraska P516

Omaha
Ag Processing P29
Berkshire Hathaway A144
ConAgra Foods A244
infoGROUP Inc. E215
Mutual of Omaha P345
Peter Kiewit Sons' A677, P395
Professional Veterinary Products P404
The Scoular Company P446
TC PipeLines E374
TD Ameritrade A809
Tenaska, Inc. P487
Union Pacific A852
Werner Enterprises A908

NEVADA

Las Vegas
Allegiant Travel E30
American Pacific E39
Boyd Gaming A162
Global Cash Access E173
Harrah's Entertainment P234
MGM MIRAGE A587
Southwest Gas A787

Reno
AMERCO A71
International Game Technology A464
Ormat Technologies E305

NEW HAMPSHIRE

Keene
C & S Wholesale Grocers P110

Lebanon
New England Alliance for Health P361

Merrimack
Brookstone, Inc. P103
GT Solar E180
PC Connection A665
Pennichuck Corporation E310

Nashua
SkillSoft E348

Newport
New Hampshire Thrift Bancshares E290

Stratham
The Timberland Company A832

NEW JERSEY

Avenel
Bradco Supply P99

Basking Ridge
Avaya Inc. P67
Cellco Partnership P124

Burlington
Burlington Coat Factory Warehouse P104

Camden
Campbell Soup A185

Carlstadt
Tel-Instrument Electronics E378

Clinton
Foster Wheeler A369

Emigrant Bank P179
Enzo Biochem E145
Ernst & Young Global A337, P183, W135
Estée Lauder A338
ExlService Holdings E150
Foot Locker A363
Ford Foundation P198
Forest Laboratories A366
Forstmann Little & Co. P200
Fuel Systems Solutions E165
Genco Shipping & Trading E167
GFI Group E171
Goldman Sachs A395
Gould Paper P217
Guardian Life Insurance P228
Hearst Corporation A420, P240
Hess Corporation A427
HMS Holdings E198
Horizon Media P251
IAC/InterActiveCorp A450
ICC Industries P257
Iconix Brand Group E205
Insight Communications P263
Inter Parfums E221
International Flavors & Fragrances A463
Interpublic Group A467
Investment Technology Group E226
Jefferies Group A481
Jones Apparel A489
JPMorgan Chase A493
The Knot E240
L-3 Communications A517
Latham & Watkins P293
Lefrak Organization P294
Liz Claiborne A539
Loews Corporation A542
MacAndrews & Forbes A547, P307
Major League Baseball P309
Marsh & McLennan A558
Martha Stewart Living A559
McGraw-Hill A575
McKinsey & Company A577, P323
Medallion Financial E260
MetLife, Inc. A585
Metropolitan Transportation Authority P334
Morgan Stanley A598
MSCI Inc. E275
Mutual of America Life Insurance P345
NASDAQ OMX Group A606
National Basketball Association P348
National Football League P350
National Hockey League P352
The Navigators Group E284
NBC Television A613
NBC Universal P357
New York City Health and Hospitals P363
New York Life Insurance A618, P364
New York Times A619
New York University P367
News Corporation A623
NYSE Euronext A643
Omnicom Group A650
Pfizer Inc. A679
Phillips-Van Heusen A682
Polo Ralph Lauren A691
Port Authority of New York and New Jersey P400
PricewaterhouseCoopers International A699, P402, W271
Prospect Capital E323
Red Apple Group P415
The Renco Group P419
Revlon, Inc. A728
Rockefeller Foundation P425
Scarborough Research P441
Scholastic Corporation A758
Sequa Corporation P449

Signature Bank E347
Skadden, Arps A775, P458
Sotheby's A782
Structure Tone P475
TheStreet.com, Inc. E383
Thomson Reuters W349
TIAA-CREF (Teachers Insurance and Annuity Association - College Retirement Equities Fund) A829, P491
Tiffany & Co. A830
Time Warner A833
Tishman Realty & Construction P493
Tower Group E387
Transammonia, Inc. P496
TransPerfect Translations P496
The Trump Organization P501
Univision Communications P521
Verizon Communications A881
Volt Information Sciences A888
Warnaco Group A895
Warner Music Group A896
WebMD Health E411
Weil, Gotshal & Manges P541
White & Case P544
ZelnickMedia P554

Newark
IEC Electronics E207
Ultralife Corporation E393

Norwich
NBT Bancorp E285

Oceanside
American Medical Alert E38

Plainview
New York Islanders P364

Port Washington
Publishers Clearing House P406

Purchase
Central National-Gottesman P126
IntegraMed America E220
MasterCard Incorporated A564
PepsiCo, Inc. A671
TAL International E373

Queensbury
AngioDynamics, Inc. E47

Rochester
Bausch & Lomb P75
Eastman Kodak A317
Paychex, Inc. A664
University of Rochester P517
Wegmans Food Markets P540

Ronkonkoma
NBTY, Inc. A614
Quality King Distributors P408

Schenectady
Golub Corporation P215
New York State Lottery P366

Somers
Pepsi Bottling Group A668

Staten Island
Advance Publications A42, P21
Atlantic Express Transportation P64

Syracuse
Alliance Financial E30

Westfield
National Grape Cooperative P352

White Plains
AboveNet, Inc. E17
Haights Cross Communications P231
ITT Corporation A474

New York Power Authority (Power Authority of the State of New York) P365
Starwood Hotels & Resorts A794
WHX Corporation E415

Whitestone
Kinray Inc. P284

Williamsville
National Fuel Gas A608

Yonkers
Consumers Union P144

NORTH CAROLINA

Cary
Cornerstone Therapeutics E107
SAS Institute P436

Chapel Hill
Blue Cross (NC) (Blue Cross and Blue Shield of North Carolina) P91

Charlotte
AmWINS Group P49
Baker & Taylor P70
Bank of America A126
Belk, Inc. P78
Carlisle Companies A190
Duke Energy A309
Goodrich Corporation A396
New NGC P362
Nucor Corporation A639
SPX Corporation A790

Durham
Cree, Inc. E110
Duke University Health System P173
Quintiles Transnational P409

Greensboro
Carolina Bank Holdings E87
Columbia Forest Products P140
V.F. Corporation A882

Hickory
Alex Lee P33
CommScope, Inc. A241

Huntersville
American Tire Distributors P45

Maiden
Air T, Inc. E24

Matthews
Family Dollar Stores A347

Mooresville
Lowe's Companies A543

Morrisville
Alliance One International A64

Oak Ridge
Oak Ridge Financial Services E296

Raleigh
Carolina Hurricanes P116
General Parts P207
Martin Marietta Materials A560
Progress Energy A703
Red Hat E331

Research Triangle Park
Research Triangle Institute P419

Rocky Mount
Meadowbrook Meat Company P325

Sanford
The Pantry A660

Statesville
Kewaunee Scientific E238

Thomasville
BNC Bancorp E71

Trinity
Sealy Corporation A766

Winston-Salem
BB&T Corporation A132
Novant Health P372
Reynolds American A729
Southern Community Financial E353

NORTH DAKOTA

Carrington
Dakota Growers Pasta P155

Fargo
RDO Equipment P413
Titan Machinery E386

OHIO

Akron
A. Schulman A27
FirstEnergy Corp. A356
Goodyear Tire & Rubber A397

Archbold
Sauder Woodworking P437

Batavia
Multi-Color Corporation E275

Canton
The Timken Company A834

Cincinnati
American Financial Group A77
Catholic Healthcare Partners P120
Chiquita Brands International A216
Cintas Corporation A224
E. W. Scripps A340
Fifth Third Bancorp A353
Hillman Companies P246
Kendle International E237
The Kroger Co. A516
Macy's, Inc. A548
Procter & Gamble A701
Western & Southern Financial P542

Cleveland
American Greetings A79
Applied Industrial Technologies A100
Cavaliers Operating Company P122
Cliffs Natural Resources A228
Eaton Corporation A318
Hawk Corporation E187
Jones Day P276
KeyCorp A502
Lincoln Electric Holdings A535
NACCO Industries A603
Parker Hannifin A661
Sherwin-Williams A771
TFS Financial E382
TransDigm Group E389

Columbus
American Electric Power Company A75
Battelle Memorial Institute P74
Big Lots A147
Bob Evans Farms A155
Diamond Hill Investment E124
Express, LLC P187
Hexion Specialty Chemicals P245
Huntington Bancshares A447
Limited Brands A533
Nationwide Mutual Insurance A610, P355
Ohio State University P377
Schottenstein Stores P443
White Castle P545

Index of Executives

A

Aanestad, Ola M. W327
Aardsma, David A. A899
Aaron, Mark L. A831
Aaron, Roger S. A775, P459
Aasheim, Hilde M. W247
Abano, Salvatore V. E387
Abarca, Jessica A904
Abasolo, Laura W342
Abate, Peter A314, P175
Abbasi, Sohaib E216
Abbot, John P263
Abbott, Gay O. A802
Abbott, Henry J. P126
Abbott, Michael (Palm, Inc.) A660
Abbott, Michael (SUNY) P473
Abbott, Stephen M. P200
Abdelnour, Sam A. A915
Abdul Hamid, Mohamed Ishak W317
Abdul Rahman, Norzilah
  Megawati W317
Abe, Daisaku W229
Abe, Ken W228
Abel, Gregory E. A145
Abel, James E. A694
Abeles, Jon C. P120
Abeles, Philippa A93
Abeles, Robert P518
Abell, Michael E217
Abell, Nancy L. P387
Abenante, Frank W46
Abercrombie, George B. W287
Aberle, Derek A714
Abernathy, Chad E157
Abernathy, Robert E. A504
Abernethy, Hugh E120
Abernethy, Jack A371
Abet, Maurizio W267
Abi-Karam, Leslie R. A686
Abinder, Susan P258
Abington, Bill P327
Able, Brett W. P169
Ables, Buddy P404
Abney, David P. A856
Aboaf, Eric A227
Abood, Denise P304
Abou-Jaoudé, Naïm W122
Abraham, Deborah A896
Abraham, Karen P517
Abraham, Magid M. E102
Abraham, Thomas R. A307
Abramowicz, Daniel A. A267
Abrams, Jim P327
Abrams, Robert A775, P459
Abrams, S. Thomas P464
Abrams, Sarah K. P196
Abramson, David M. E258
Abramson, Richard P469

Abril Pérez, José M. W68
Abril Pérez, Luis W342
Abshire, Richard B. A39
Abud, Joao Jr. A292
Abuhoff, Jack S. E217
Abunaser, Bashar P257
Abzug, Peter P158
Acciari, Luciano W142
Acevedo, William A933
Acharya, Ranjan W379
Achermann, Hubert A514, W194
Acheson, Eleanor D. P48
Acheson Luther, Lisa P88
Achleitner, Paul W40
Ackart, Jennifer C. A721
Acker, Jim P123
Acker, Kevin J. P542
Acker, Stan P510
Ackerman, Jeffrey C. A766
Ackerman, Melinda S. A448
Ackerman, Patricia K. A95
Ackerman, Paul R. A906
Ackerman, Philip C. A608
Ackerman, Steve P438
Ackermann, Josef P143, W119, W315
Ackerson, Vince A. E381
Acklie, Duane W. P151
Acosta, Alan P470
Acosta, Janis N. P257
Acquart, Claude W189
Acquaye, Robert S. P275
Acton, Brian P382
Acton, Elizabeth S. A239
Adachi, Hiroshi W283
Adachi, Toshio W312
Adachi, Yoroku W90
Adair, Marjorie P392
Adam, Bart W310
Adam, Donald F. A143
Adam, Philippe W22
Adamek, Mitch A672
Adami, Norman J. W298
Adams, Alvan P396
Adams, Barry P325
Adams, Bill P543
Adams, Brady P220
Adams, Cathy C. (FHLB Atlanta) P189
Adams, Chuck E262
Adams, Cindi S. P385
Adams, Clint B. P54
Adams, Craig L. A342
Adams, D. Scott A706
Adams, Diana (Ambac) A71
Adams, Diane (Allscripts) E32
Adams, Edward P182
Adams, Fred R. Jr. E84
Adams, Greg G. P374
Adams, J. Dann A335
Adams, J. Michael A61
Adams, Jason P. P464
Adams, Jimmie V. A518
Adams, John L. P131
Adams, Joseph (MWH Global) P347
Adams, Joseph P. Jr. (Aircastle) E25
Adams, Julian E214

Adams, K. S. Jr. A39
Adams, Katherine L. (Honeywell
  International) A440
Adams, Kevin P. P124
Adams, L. Ray E168
Adams, Mark (Equinix) E147
Adams, Mark W. (Micron
  Technology) A589
Adams, Marvin W. (FMR) A363, P196
Adams, Michael G. (LSB
  Industries) E252
Adams, Mike (Bechtel) A136, P77
Adams, Mike (Glazer's Wholesale
  Drug) P211
Adams, Paul (British American
  Tobacco) W83
Adams, Paul (Leprino Foods) P295
Adams, Rex D. A471
Adams, Richard C. P74
Adams, Robin J. A160
Adams, Stephen P28
Adams, Thomas R. (Reynolds
  American) A730
Adams, Timothy M. (athenahealth) E55
Adams, Timothy M. (Macy's) A548
Adams, Tom (Bradco Supply) P99
Adams-Gaston, Javaune P377
Adamson, Geoff P217
Adamson, Grant F. A814
Adamson, Mick P289
Adamson, Terrence B. P352
Adante, David E. P158
Adcock, Robert H. Jr. E199
Adderley, Terence E. A500
Addicks, Mark W. A386
Addison, Brian M. A288
Addison, James E. A755
Adelman, Warren J. P213
Aderhold, Ronald K. A228
Adgate, Brad P252
Adiba, Patrick W52
Adkerson, Richard C. A375
Adkins, Mark A420, P241
Adkins, Norman P466
Adkins, Ralph J. E93
Adkins, Rodney C. A462
Adkison, Mark A. E367
Adler, Edward I. A833
Adler, Jack F. Jr. P270
Adler, Robert L. A322
Adlich, Gregory P465
Adornato, Theodore C. A788
Adrean, Lee A335
Adrian, Merv E161
Adriance, Glenn E. E265
Adu-Gyamfi, R. Siisi A825
Advani, Asheesh W371
Advani, Vijay C. A374
Adyanthaya, Surain R. E323
Afable, Mark V. P43
Afergan, Michael M. E25
Affeldt, Eric L. P137
Africk, Jack P370
Agah, Ray P438
Agan, Dan P421

Agar, Richard A406
Agarwal, Bhikam C. W48
Agata, Atsunobu W28
Agius, Marcus W63
Agnelli, Roger W367
Agnellini, Victor W36
Agnello, Lynn P396
Agnes, Pierre A716
Agnew, Brian P. P296
Agnew, Dan A115
Agnew, Joe P197
Agnew, Nathan W31
Agon, Jean-Paul W210
Agosta, Jeffrey A. A290
Agostinelli, D. D. P65
Agrawal, Vineet W379
Agress, Amy R. E217
Agrusti, Raffaele W50
Aguiñaga Pérez, Héctor W262
Aguirre, Felix E227
Aguirre, Fernando A216
Ahearn, Joseph A547, P307
Ahizoune, Abdeslam W372
Ahlers, Bernd W347
Ahlfeld, Roger C. P521
Ahlstrom, Lee M. A629
Ahmad, Asif P173
Ahmad, Shidah A52
Ahmann, Greg P453
Ahmaogak, Mary Ellen P54
Ahmed, Javed W279, W337
Ahmed, Mumtaz A284, P162, W114
Ahmer, Alan C. E81
Ahn, Hee-bong W170
Ahn, Henry P357
Ahn, Kyung-soo W326
Ahn, Myeong-Kyu W204
Aho, Esko W244
Ahrens, Oliver W23
Ahrnell, Jan Henrik W345
Ahuja, Lalit A808
Aiello, Greg P350
Aijala, Ainar D. Jr. A284, P162, W114
Aikawa, Tetsuro W226
Aiken, Robert (U.S. Foodservice) P523
Aiken, Robert S. (Pinnacle West) A684
Ailes, Roger A371, A624
Ain, Mark S. P289
Ainley, Christopher J. P274
Ainsley, P. Steven A620
Ainsworth, John P510
Airola, Mark J. E291
Aitken, Murray L. A456
Aizawa, Masatoshi W234
Aizawa, Toshihiko W352
Aizawa, Zengo W353
Ajamian, Daniel P483
Ajer, Jeff E66
Akdag, Menderes E312
Akers, J. Michael A. A386
Akhavan, Hamid W121
Akhurst, Bruce J. W346
Akikusa, Fumiyuki W227
Akimoto, Masami W354
Akimova, Tanya E196

Brandenburg, Mark P435
Brandenburger, Larry B. A878
Brandes, Dee W173
Brandes, Mark P125
Brandgaard, Jesper W249
Brandlin, Laura A171
Brandmeyer, Donna E157
Brandolini d'Adda, Tiberto Ruy W139
Brandon, David A. A301
Brandt, Cathy E157
Brandt, Donald E. A684
Brandt, Eric K. A170
Brandt, Paul P266
Brandt, Ron P265
Brandt, Steve E384
Brandt, Werner W304
Brandtzæg, Svein R. W247
Brandtzæg, Svein Richard W247
Branich, Thomas J. E37
Branigan, Craig W384
Branman, James N. E352
Brann, Gentry A771
Brannagan, Douglas T. P220
Brannen, Anna P107
Brannon, Christy P95
Brannum, Lorna E354
Branscum, John E103
Branscum, Stephen P. P514
Branson, Don E305
Branson, James M. A913
Branson, Mark W363
Branson, Richard W371
Branstetter, Matthew E35
Brantley, Mitch P325
Bras, Barbara P82
Brashear, Travis H. A221
Brashears, David F. E168
Brasher, Paul V. A699, W271
Brasher, Richard W. P. W349
Brasier, Barbara L. A457
Brassfield, W. Kirk E307
Braswell, James F. P208
Braswell, Robert T. E87
Bratches, Sean H. R. P185
Brater, D. Craig P260
Brath, Maalfrid A552
Bratman, Fred B. A857
Bratt, Mikael W376
Bratton, Susan M. E178
Brauer, Stephen W147
Brault, Mario E169
Braun, Richard J. E265
Brauner, Susan P92
Braunstein, Sandra F. P191
Brausen, James R. E239
Braverman, Alan N. A894
Bravman, John P470
Brawley, Otis W. P41
Bray, John K. E292
Braz Ferro, Claudio W46
Brazda, Steven J. E80
Bready, Cameron M. E230
Bready, Richard L. P373
Brearton, David A. A515
Breauninger, Gary A394
Breaux, Randall P. A124
Breber, Pierre A215
Brecher, David P502
Brecher, Elliot P263
Breed, John S. A629
Breeden, Frances L. A802
Breeden, Greg P151
Breeden, Kenneth R. A818, P488
Breeden, Mary E. P380
Breeden, Richard C. A406
Breedlove, David P147
Breedlove, James T. A696
Breen, Barry N. P183
Breen, Edward D. Jr. A848
Breene, John P61
Breene, R. Timothy S. A36
Breffort, Jean-Claude W299
Brega, Joao A915
Brege, Laura A. E303
Brégier, Fabrice W32, W125

Bregman, Mark A805
Bregman, Mitchell S. A344
Bregolato, José Luiz E326
Brehm, Eric J. E122
Brehm, Janice L. E35
Breier, Alan A326
Breier, Benjamin A. A506
Breig, Geralyn R. A121
Breitenbach, Randall H. E73
Brekelmans, Harry W295
Brelsford, James A750
Bremer, Bradley S. E49
Bremner, Joseph P104
Bren, Donald L. P267
Brendle, Jim A139
Brenn, James E. A164
Brennan, David R. W51
Brennan, Donald A. A512
Brennan, Edward W214
Brennan, Fran A257
Brennan, John J. (The Vanguard Group) A879, P529
Brennan, John P. (Advent Software) E20
Brennan, Joseph P. A293
Brennan, Michael W57
Brennan, Nora E219
Brennan, Patrick A705
Brennan, Robert A. (Lefrak Organization) P295
Brennan, Robert T. (Iron Mountain Inc) A472
Brennan, Seamus A91
Brennan, Troyen A. A271
Brennan, William P. P200
Brenneman, Rodney K. A762
Brentan, Andrea W129
Brentlinger, David A. P46
Brenton, Ben A779
Breon, Richard C. P467
Brereton, Michael P312
Bresch, Heather A603
Breschan, Matthias W333
Bresciani, Dick P98
Bresky, Steven J. A762
Breslawski, James P. A422
Bresler, Charles A583
Breslin, Brian P329
Bress, Joseph M. P48
Bresten, Theresa M. P254
Bretas, Nancy A728
Brethauer, Craig P76
Breton, Thierry W52
Brett, Sean M. E374
Brettingen, Thomas R. P62
Bretz, Darcy E269
Breu, Raymond W248
Breuche, Rob W86
Breur, Kenneth A. E41
Brewer, Allen E160
Brewer, Mark A764
Brewer, Robert A646
Brewer, W. Keith A865
Brewster, Larry P262
Brezina, Michael P540
Brezovec, Daniel T. A101
Brian, Marjorie E213
Brice, Lee P165
Brickley, Peter W159
Brickman, Christian A. A504
Brickman, David R. E85
Brickman, Jay P151
Brickman, Laurence M. E137
Bridge, Anthony R. A859
Bridge, G. Michael E234
Bridgeford, Gregory M. A543
Bridgers, David P490
Bridges, Marshall H. A436
Bridges, Terrance R. A709
Bridgman, Peter A. A672
Briefs, Wally E99
Brier, Freya R. P177
Brierley, Harold W384
Brierwood, David C. E275
Brigeman, Benjamin L. A210

Briggs, C. John A725
Briggs, John P256
Brigham, Steven P. P103
Bright, Alan E172
Bright, Kimberly P383
Bright, Mary Ann P205
Bright, Michael T. E92
Bright, Nicolas J. A519
Brighton, Todd A. E333
Brill, Ira P201
Brill, James L. E302
Briman, Eran E91
Brimhall, Reed N. A868
Brin, Sergey A399
Brina, Cora A710
Brind'Amour, Yvon W201
Brinded, Malcom W295
Bringhurst, Rory B. P345
Brink, Elaine P187
Brinkley, Alan P141
Brinkley, Charlie W. Jr. A354
Brinkley, Cynthia J. A111
Brinkley, Sterling B. Jr. E152
Brinkman, Dale T. A922
Brinkman, Rob L. P533
Brisco, Robert N. E224
Briscoe, Bill P357
Briscoe, Matthew E194
Brisimitzakis, Angelo C. E101
Briskman, Louis J. A199
Brisky, Lauren J. P528
Brisse, Tom P546
Britanik, Thomas P. A230
Britell, Jenne K. A857
Brito, Carlos W46
Brito, Nuno W130
Britton, Loretta M. P88
Britton, Lynn A457
Britton, William J. E285
Briw, Ron E297
Brkanovic, Tom P456
Brlas, Laurie A228
Broad, Matthew R. A647
Broadbent, Guy A826
Broadbent, Richard W63
Broaddus, Mary A876
Broadhurst, Daniel P. E204
Broadway, Andy E87
Broc Haro, Jean Paul W344
Brock, Benjamin G. E53
Brock, Dan P99
Brock, Graham C. A593
Brock, Heidi Biggs A913
Brock, Ian H. E36
Brock, J. Don E53
Brock, John Franklin A235
Brock, Paul W215
Brock, Roslyn M. P347
Brock, Wayne P98
Brockelmeyer, Scott A353
Brockhaus, Richard T. P461
Brockman, Robert T. P421
Brockman, Vincent C. A760
Brockway, Brian E101
Brockway, Larry T. A859
Brockway, Robert P250
Brodbeck, Howard D. A696
Broderick, Dennis J. A548
Brodin, J. Per P135
Brodsky, Howard P123
Brodsky, Julian A. A238
Brody, Edward J. P328
Brody, Jeffrey P250
Brody, John S. P310
Brody, Paul P342
Brody, Wayne A107
Broeksmit, Robert D. P130
Broerman, Robert A. P448
Brogan, Cynthia D. A772
Brogan, Michael P. A604
Brogan, Stephen J. P276
Brogdon, Jim Jr. A464
Broger, Armin A530
Brogna, Sal E226
Broianigo, Philippe W94

Broidy, Michael P443
Broiles, Randy L. W173
Broitman, Richard E383
Brokatzky-Geiger, Juergen W248
Brolick, Emil J. A932
Broman, Donald E. A779
Bromstad, Angela A613
Bronczek, David J. A352
Bronfin, Kenneth A. A420, P241
Bronfman, Edgar M. Jr. A897
Bronicki, Yehudit E305
Bronson, David M. A708
Bronson, Joyce P418
Bronstein, Phil P241
Bronzo, Neal A. A669
Brook, David E. E241
Brooke, Beth A. A337, P184, W136
Brooke, F. Dixon Jr. P177
Brooker, Thomas G. A742
Brooklier, John L. A453
Brookman, Amber M. E184
Brookman, Barton R. E312
Brookman, Robert S. P487
Brookner, Mark J. E399
Brooks, Bruce W. A152
Brooks, Carolynn A647
Brooks, Douglas H. A167
Brooks, Gail E. P107
Brooks, H. Joseph P105
Brooks, John C. P164
Brooks, Joyce L. A571
Brooks, Kathryn S. E179
Brooks, Michael W147
Brooks, Richard M. E422
Brookshire, Brad P102
Broom, Colin E404
Broome, Anne C. P511
Broome, Lisa E174
Broome, Richard D. A426
Brophy, R. Gregory A419
Broski, Suzanne E112
Brosnahan, Michael P. P542
Brosnan, Timothy J. P310
Bross, Matthew W. W85
Bross, Richard A. A442
Brostowitz, James M. A409
Brothers, Ellen L. A566
Brothers, Gary P156
Brothers, Jeffrey J. P35
Brotherton, Renee W145
Brotman, Jeffrey H. A259
Brotman, Martin P481
Brots, John M. A813
Broughton, Martin F. W82
Broughton, Tim P323
Brous, Maria A711
Brouse, Mark S. E302
Broussard, Bruce D. P524
Broussard, Eric A69
Brouwer, Klaas E217
Brouwer, Wilfried A95
Brova, Jacquelin J. A220
Browchuk, Brett A221
Brower, Caroline P53
Brower, David B. P337
Brown, Adriane M. A440
Brown, Brad P418
Brown, Bruce A702
Brown, Carolyn J. A130
Brown, Cary D. E247
Brown, Charles E. A646
Brown, Christopher A. (Nash-Finch Company) A607
Brown, Colin P272
Brown, Cristopher (DeBruce Grain) P161
Brown, Dan (The Hartford) A413
Brown, Daniel K. (American Tire Distributors) P45
Brown, Danny (CalPERS) A184, P109
Brown, Darrell K. A575
Brown, David A. (HF Financial) E193
Brown, David A. B. (Layne Christensen) E246
Brown, David B. (Dresser, Inc.) P172

C

Desportes, Marc-Henri W52
Desrochers, Robert L. P427
Desrochers, Stacey E76
Desroches, Pascal A833
DesRosier, Thomas J. A390
DesRosiers, Robert D. E314
Dessau, Nigel A44
Desser, John D. E138
Dessing, George W382
d'Estaing, Henri Giscard W103
d'Estais, Jacques W75
DeStefano, Gary M. A626
DeStefano, Joanne M. P148
Deterding, Mark P484
Determan, Bradley D. A436
Detrick, Edwin J. A221
Detry, Richard J. P436
Dette, Franz-Josef A344
Dettinger, Warren W. A292
Deuch, Jeff P345
Deurbroeck, Yvan A581
Dev, Neel A529
DeVaan, Jon S. A590
Devanny, Earl H. III A206
Devany, Steve W179
Devey, Robert W273
DeVey, Tina E208
DeVeydt, Wayne S. A905
Devine, John M. A273
Devine, Ted T. A96
Devine, Thomas P. E148
Devine, Vince P490
Devins, Ferg A594
DeVoe, Darrell A93
DeVoe, David F. A371, A624
DeVore, Donald C. E132
DeVos, Doug P38
DeVos, Richard M. Sr. P380
DeVries, James D. A67
Dew, Lyndol I. A291
Dew, Susan E. P239
Dewald, Steven B. P413
DeWalt, David G. A569
DeWalt, Mike A196
Dewan, Derek E. A601
Dewar, Patrick M. A541
Dewey, Lawrence E. P37
Dewhurst, Moray P. A372
DeWitt, David R. E273
DeWitt, Kenneth A857
DeWitte, Michael D. P436
Deyling, James A. P91
Deyo, Russell C. A487
DeYonker, Alex J. A788
DeYoung, Caitlin A83
DeYoung, Mark W. A66
Dezio, Moreno G. P276
Dhamotharan, Dhamo S. A868
Dhanda, Anuj A689
Dhar, Subhash B. W175
Dhillon, Janet L. A480
Dhillon, Tara A618
D'Hinnin, Dominique W202
D'Hooge, Theresa J. P213
Di Fronzo, Pascal W. A112
Di Giorgio, Mara W69
Di Giovanni, Gianni W131
di Montezemolo, Luca Cordero W141
Di Palma, Dino E18
Di Risio, Derek M. A710
di Sant'Albano, Carlo Barel W139
Di Vaio, Giovanni W69
DiAcri, Michele G. E105
Diamond, A. Patrick A687
Diamond, Bernard P502
Diamond, Greg A568
Diamond, Paul (Addus HomeCare) E19
Diamond, Paul (Tishman) P494
Diamond, Robert E. Jr. W63
Diamond, Ronald T. P142
Diana, Shana A460
DiAngelo, Joe A888
Diaz, Anthony J. A367
Diaz, Mike P380
Diaz, Paul J. A506

Diaz, Yvonne W350
Díaz de León, Raúl P527
Díaz Rato, Enrique W140
Diaz Soutaire, Juan M. E343
DiBartolomeo, Joe A311
Dibbern, Günter W134
Dibble, David E. A929
Dibenedetto, John P207
DiBenedetto, Vincent P532
DiCandilo, Michael D. A85
DiCarmine, Stephen P166
Dice, Ken A626
DiCerchio, Richard D. A259
DiCianni, Joseph A828
Dick, Brian (Golden State Foods) P214
Dick, Brian J. (Affinion Group) P27
Dick, Janet L. E38
Dick, John M. P279
Dick, Melvin A. P466
Dick, Mika E194
Dick, Stratford P201
Dickard, Paul A457
Dicke, James F. II (Crown
    Equipment) P152
Dicke, James F. III (Crown
    Equipment) P152
Dickens, Jim P350
Dickens, Rodney L. A61
Dickerson, Brad E396
Dickerson, Eric P37
Dickerson, Jill P233
Dickerson, Lawrence R. A291
Dickerson, Marshall P302
Dickerson, Michael P. A382
Dickey, John H. A432
Dickey, Nancy W. P489
Dickey, Todd R. P518
Dickinson, Ann K. P166
Dickinson, Burton K. P166
Dickinson, Charles W. A615
Dickinson, Daniel L. P166
Dickinson, Donna W299
Dickinson, Emily D. A679
Dickinson, Lawrence E. E251
Dickinson Holewinski, Amy P166
Dickinson Kress, Jane A. P166
Dickson, Charleen P129
Dickson, David J. A504
Dickson, Eric P514
Dickson, Fred P159
Dickson, Joe A916
Dickson, Robin N. E187
Dickson, Steve E328
DiCola, John F. P120
DiCosola, Robert E299
Dicus, John B. E86
Dicus-Johnson, Coreen P544
Didier, Laura P528
DiDonato, Thomas A74
Diebold, Raymond J. P155
Dieck, Douglas P430
Diedrich, Christian W134
Diedrichs, Carol Pitts P514
Diehr, George A184
Dieker, John K. A402
Diekmann, Michael W40, W64
Diener, Todd E. A167
Dienes, Edward D. A708
Dier, Kelly E. P313
Diercks, Dwight A641
Diercks, Rainer W64
Diercksen, John W. A882
Dierker, David F. A802
Diess, Herbert W73
Dieterman, Jude G. A206
Diethelm, Markus U. W363
Dietiker, Charles P468
Dietrich, E. Joshua P158
Dietrich, Martin A. E285
Dietz, David W. P168
Dietz, Diane M. A745
Dietz, Richard C. A111
Diéval, Alain W107
Diez, John J. A743
DiFilippo, Manny W155

DiFulgentiz, Robert A511, P286
DiGeso, Amy A339
Diggs, James C. A693
DiGiorgio, Tom P446
DiGiorno, Kathy E. A581
DiGiralomo, Sam P38
Dignath, Anne A783
DiGrazia, G. Gino A711
DiLarso, Mike P309
Dildy, Marshall L. P256
DiLiberto, Ernie E119
Diliberto, Lisa A426
Dilks, Charlie P123
Dill, Chris P401
Dill, Cindy A709
Dillard, Alex A293
Dillard, Mike A293
Dillard, Richard P339
Dillard, Tom P471
Dillard, William II (Dillard's) A293
Dillard, William III (Dillard's) A293
Diller, Barry A450
Diller, James V. Sr. E316
Dilley, Shelia A534
Dillman, Rodney J. A563
Dillon, Adrian T. A51
Dillon, Dannie P465
Dillon, David B. A516
Dillon, Donald F. A358
Dillon, Edward J. (Terra
    Industries) A820
Dillon, Edward J. (Terra
    Nitrogen) A820
Dillon, Marcia A497
Dillon, Mary N. A574
Dillon, Rick T. A621
Dillon, Roderick H. Jr. E124
Dillon, Timothy J. P419
Dillon, Veronica A898
Dilorenzo, Michael P353
Dimanche, Conrad P68
DiMenna, Donna P484
DiMicco, Daniel R. A640
Dimick, Neil F. A384
Dimino, Joseph C. A631
Dimitrelis, Dimitrios E288
Dimling, Jack P208
Dimon, James A494
DiMona, Joseph J. P101
Dimond, Randall P405
Dimond, Robert B. A607
Din, Norman P201
Dinan, Curtis L. A652
DiNapoli, Dominic E165
DiNapoli, Mark L. P476
DiNapoli, Mike P476
DiNardo, Sheila S. E49
Dineen, Robert W. A537
Dinesh, Krishnaswamy W175
Dinges, Dan O. E79
Dingle, David K. A193
Dingman, Michael L. P527
Dingus, David H. E58
Diniz Mayer, Rui Maria W152
Dinkel, Richard P286
D'Innocenzi, Thomas A708
Dinsmore, Gordon P228
Dinwoodie, Jason S. P166
Dionis, Javier Bernal W68
Diorio, Marianne A339
DiPietrantonio, Cynthia A490
DiPietro, Erin A859
Dippold, David J. E257
Diradoorian, Raymond H. A63
DiRaimo, Carol A. A477
Dirks, Bob P248
Dirks, Nicholas B. P141
Dirks, Thorsten W196
DiRusso, Lonny R. A740
Disa, John P58
DiSantis, B. Christopher E188
Disclafani, Mary A860
DiSilvestro, Anthony P. A185
Disken, Kenneth J. A541
Diskin, Jeffrey P248

Disney, Anthea A624
Dispenza, Domenico W131
Dissinger, H. Todd A158
Dithmer, Erik A282
Ditkoff, James H. A274
Dittberner, Chad R. A909
Dittmann, Jay A405, P232
Dittmer, Jerald K. A436
Ditzel, David R. A461
Dively, Joseph R. E105
Diver, Jonathan E170
Divers, Jim P38
Dixon, Alicia A200
Dixon, Bradley O. A652
Dixon, Diane B. A117
Dixon, Gregory B. A755
Dixon, Jack E. (Howard Hughes Medical
    Institute) P253
Dixon, James K. (Morgan, Lewis) P343
Dixon, James W. (CompuCom) P142
Dixon, John (Marks & Spencer) W218
Dixon, Joseph A857
Dixon, Lee S. P385
Dixon, Leslie H. P424
Dixon, Robert (Conair) P142
Dixon, Robert (PepsiCo) A672
Dixon, Robert D. (Air Products) A53
Dixon, Simon W186
Dixon, Steven C. A214
Dixon, Tim P165
Dlugopolski, Stephanie P287
Doar, Michael E203
Dobashi, Akio W334
Dobbins, James W. P370
Dobbins, Mark W. A615
Dobbs, Janice A. A290
Dobbs, Kelley J. A57
Dobbs, Robert E. A78
Dobbs, Stephen B. A360
Dobelbower, Peter P249
Dobies, David R. E292
Dobkin, David P. P403
Dobrin, Allan H. P134
Dobrovinskaya, Elena E341
Dobson, David C. A686
Dobson, Thomas E. P543
Docherty, Jim E350
Docherty, Susan E. P206
Doctoroff, Daniel L. P86
Dodd, Patrick P175
Dodd, Timothy J. P155
Dodds, David E362
Dodds, Robert E95
Dodge, Allen E189
Dodge, Daniel R. A625
Dodge, Edward P460
Dodge, Jeffrey L. A335
Dodge, Michael E224
Dodge, Paul J. P404
Dodge, R. Stanton A298
Dodge, Tanith W218
Dodson, Catherine E235
Dodson, J. Marshall A502
Doedtman, David E105
Doeppe, Pamela P435
Doerfler, Ronald J. A420
Doerig, Hans-Ulrich W108
Doering, Richard P164
Doering Meshke, Sheryl P61
Doerr, Kurt D. A334
Doerr, R. Chris P88
Doggett, William B. A319
Doheny, Edward L. II A492
Doheny, Mark A255
Doherty, Colm E. W41
Doherty, John A. E156
Doherty, Kelsey A569
Dohle, Markus W71
Dohnalek, David A157
Doise, Daryl J. E248
Dokoozlian, Nick K. A314, P175
Dolan, Charles F. A180
Dolan, David M. P172
Dolan, Gregory J. P544

COMBINED HOOVER'S HANDBOOK INDEX OF EXECUTIVES

A = AMERICAN BUSINESS
E = EMERGING COMPANIES
P = PRIVATE COMPANIES
W = WORLD BUSINESS

Esparza, Linda A788
Espeland, Curtis E. A316
Espeland, Niels A904
Espinosa, Hamilton P170
Espírito Santo Silva, José Manuel Pinheiro W138
Espírito Santo Silva Salgado, Ricardo W138
Esposito, Angelo S. P366
Esposito, Ann P57
Esposito, Bob P193
Esposito, John (Warner Music) A897
Esposito, John P. (Bacardi) W57
Esposito, Larry P494
Esposito, Lynn P88
Esposito, Rosanne A344
Esquivel, Robert D. A684
Esser, Frank W372
Esser, Patrick J. A262, P150
Essig, Stuart M. E219
Estberg, Edward P411
Estep, Sandra J. A711
Esterow, Kenneth P497
Estes, Bill E58
Estes, H. Stephen E402
Estes, Jena L. P87
Estes, Robey W. Jr. P185
Esteves, Irene M. A724
Estill, Robert E. A553
Estroff, Elizabeth J. A560
Esvelt, Terence G. P95
Esworthy, Bruce P101
Etchart, Eric A551
Etchemendy, John W. P470
Etess, Mitchell Grossinger P342
Etheridge, Arrie P391
Ethier, Mark A444
Ethridge, William T. W257
Etienne, Jean-Michel W274
Etlinger, R. Scott E38
Ettinger, Irwin R. A843
Ettinger, Jeffrey M. A442
Ettinger, Michael S. A422
Ettinger, Ronald S. E326
Eubanks, Bill P31
Eulberg, Joseph R. A155
Euller, Steven C. A189, P113
Eusman, Frans W159
Eustace, Dudley G. W27
Eustace, Robert A. A399
Eustace, Tara P316
Eustis, Mark A. P188
Euteneuer, Joseph J. A718
Evancho, John R. P380
Evangelista, Paul A. E90
Evangelisti, Joseph M. A494
Evanich, Craig P50
Evans, Alastair W206
Evans, Bradley W. P133
Evans, Carol Koh E240
Evans, Charles L. P191
Evans, Dave (Dallas Mavericks) P156
Evans, David C. (Scotts Miracle-Gro) A760
Evans, Dick W285
Evans, Donald L. (Energy Future) P181
Evans, Donald S. (CH2M HILL) P128
Evans, Ian P221
Evans, J. Michael A395
Evans, James E. (American Financial Group) A78
Evans, James E. (Ultralife) E393
Evans, Joan E241
Evans, John (Scottish and Southern Energy) W309
Evans, Jonathan D. (Albany Molecular Research) E27
Evans, Lisa (Novant Health) P373
Evans, Lisa (Southwire Company) P466
Evans, Melody A362
Evans, Michael E332
Evans, Michelle P265
Evans, Robert S. A266
Evans, Russell A. P38
Evans, Scott C. A830, P492

Evans, Simon W174
Evans, Tom A839
Evans, W. Phil P41
Evans-Lombe, Nicholas E. P208
Evanson, Paul J. A61
Evard, John E. Jr. A848
Evens, Deirdre J. E96
Everett, Allison M. A500
Everett, Carole P317
Everett, Robert S. E323
Everett, Roger D. A687
Everett, Stephen W. E123
Everette, Bruce L. A745
Everist, Thomas S. E331
Everitt, David C. A280
Evers, John E. Jr. W315
Eversman, George P168
Everson, James W. E397
Everson, Lloyd K. P524
Every, Robert W378
Every-Burns, Warwick A230
Eves, David L. A926
Evitts, Robin A. A230
Ewert, Douglas S. A583
Ewing, Andrew D. E254
Ewing, Anna M. A606
Ewing, Gary P313
Ewing, Joe A. A820, E380
Ewing, R. Stewart Jr. A202
Ewing, Robyn L. A917
Exline, John A725
Exon, Charles S. A716
Exton, Wayne R. A134
Exum, James F. Jr. P290
Eyerly, Mark P487
Eylar, Paula A163
Eynon, Richard R. A851
Eyrich, Keith P267
Eytchison, Brian R. A264
Ezeta González, Xavier W377

F

Faas, Charles P436
Faber, Emmanuel W113
Faber, Joachim W40
Faber, Terrance A. A92
Faber, Timothy J. A533
Fabrikant, Charles L. A763
Fabrizio, R. W. A84
Fabry, John J. A401
Facchetti, Katia A. A819
Facciani, Jennifer P306
Faccini, M. A191
Fache, Dominique W129
Fadel, Mitchell E. A726
Faeh, Urban E76
Fagan, Janet P449
Fagen, Ron P188
Fagerstal, Dick A763
Fagin, Bari A139
Fagundes, Heather L. A570
Faherty, Gregory T. P65
Fahey, James K. A860
Fahey, John J. (United Rentals) A857
Fahey, John M. Jr. (National Geographic) P352
Fahey, Mike W76
Fahle, Rich A159
Fahn, Larry P454
Fahour, Ahmed W232
Fain, Eric S. A748
Fain, Jonathan D. P486
Fain, Phillip A. E393
Fain, Richard D. A739
Fainé Casas, Isidre W282, W341
Fairbairn, Mark W233
Fairbairn, Sally W309
Fairbank, Richard D. A186
Fairbanks, Joseph C. Jr. E49
Fairfield, Bill L. E215
Fairhead, Alan W388
Fairhead, Rona A. E222, W257

Fairl, William M. A182
Fairleigh, John P525
Faith, David M. P446
Faith, Marshall E. P446
Faivre-Duboz, Michel W281
Faklis, Nick P30
Falcinelli, Richard P. E242
Falck, David P. A684
Falco, Charlie P124
Falcon, Michael F. E287
Faley, David R. A623
Falick, Paul P258
Falk, Dennis J. E403
Falk, Terrell A223
Falk, Thomas J. A504
Falkenburg, Morten W127
Fall, Amadou Gallo P156
Fallick, Patti P353
Falline, Brian A878
Fallis, John P172
Fallon, Charles M. Jr. A176
Fallon, John A. P89
Fallon, Julie E183
Fallon, Patrick W274
Fallon, Thomas J. E214
Fallon, William C. A568
Fallowfield, Tim W183
Falvey, Justin P171
Falvey, Samie Kim A33
Fam, Hany A564
Fan, John C. C. E241
Fanandakis, Nicholas C. A312
Fanelli, Germano A107
Fanjul, Oscar W201
Fanning, Bridie A. A358
Fanning, Michael R. A563
Fanning, Thomas A. A784
Fannon, Diane P423
Fanska, Jerry W. E246
Fant, Sandra P258
Fante, Rich W51
Fantozzi, Joseph P63
Faraci, John V. Jr. A466
Faraci, Philip J. A318
Farage, Christopher M. A662
Farah, John M. Jr. A205
Farandou, Jean-Pierre W320
Farbacher, Elizabeth A. A431
Farber, Evan R. E21
Farber, John J. P258
Farber, Sandra P258
Farber, William E245
Fardell, Jeff A539
Fares, Ed P81
Farhat, Jamal M. A160
Farías, Pablo J. P199
Faricy, Peter A69
Faricy, Robert P260
Faridi, Hamed A571
Farley, Andy E369
Farley, Edward I. P508
Farley, James D. A365
Farley, Stephen P551
Farley, Thomas W. E224
Farman, Christian G. A829
Farmer, Cheryl P202
Farmer, Curtis C. A240
Farmer, David B. P131
Farmer, Ian P. W209
Farmer, Jeremy G. O. A96
Farmer, Richard T. A225
Farmer, Scott D. A225
Farnam, Gregg P340
Farnan, Joseph P175
Farnham, Robert E. A417
Farno, Steve P498
Farnsworth, Alan H. P75
Farnsworth, David E47
Farnsworth, Ronald L. Jr. E395
Farr, David A. (Stewart's Shops) P474
Farr, David N. (Emerson Electric) A330
Farr, Kevin M. A566
Farr, Paul A. A694
Farran, William E218
Farrar, David J. E384

Farrar, Eileen C. A866
Farrar, Jeffrey W. E358
Farrell, Anne V. P418
Farrell, Carl P436
Farrell, David B. E63
Farrell, Edward J. P36
Farrell, Gretchen A. A535
Farrell, James G. P380
Farrell, John M. (Coca-Cola) A233
Farrell, John S. (Bon-Ton Stores) A158
Farrell, Matthew T. A220
Farrell, Michael K. A586
Farrell, Pat (Enterprise Rent-A-Car) P182
Farrell, Patrick V. (University of Wisconsin-Madison) P520
Farrell, Paul E146
Farrell, Peter C. E335
Farrell, Richard M. E178
Farrell, Roger A. A785
Farrell, Thomas G. W201
Farrell, Timothy P431
Farrelly, Joseph W. A467
Farren, Suzy P469
Farrer, James E222
Farrington, Duane P472
Farrington, Thomas M. A676
Farris, G. Steven A97
Farris, Vivian P148
Farris, William K. P526
Farrow, Stephen R. A869
Fartaj, Ali P247
Farver, Charles P389
Farwell, David L. A35
Farwerck, Joost W196
Fasano, Amedeo W279
Fasano, Philip A495, P279
Faske, Steven P252
Fasold, Mark P301
Fassbach, Scott M. E21
Fassbind, Renato W108
Fassino, J.C. P230
Fassino, Rob E240
Fassio, James S. A737
Fast, Eric C. A266
Fastenau, Robert H. J. E156
Fateh, Hossein E133
Fatovic, Robert D. A743
Fattori, Ruth A. A586
Fau, Jean-Francois A823
Fauchet, Philippe W303
Fauci, Anthony S. P354
Faugère, Mireille W320
Faul, Wade P234
Faulkner, Duane H. P227
Faulkner, Roger A829
Fauqueux, Olivier W126
Faury, Guillaume W263
Faust, Drew Gilpin P236
Favre, Michel A. M. W96
Fawaz, Marwan A212
Fawcett, Carol E328
Fawcett, Dan A371
Fawkes, Kurt A718
Fawley, Daniel A. A730
Fay, Edmund A419
Fay, George R. A232
Fay, John P262
Fay, Roger L. P419
Fay, Sharon E. P36
Fayard, Gary P. A233
Fazakas, Stephen P. A110
Fazenda, Nelson A142
Fazzino, Gary A102
Feagin, Susan K. P141
Fealing, Burt M. A803
Fearing, Gregory P. P200
Fearon, Mark W381
Fearon, Richard H. A319
Fears, Douglas E. A421
Feather, Jeffrey P. E281
Featherston, Patricia O. P485
Featherstone, Diane L. A322
Featherstone, Jim P410
Feazell, Trey P64

Fisher, Stephen N. (Pernod Ricard) W258
Fisher, Steven P. (SAIC) A747
Fisher, Tina P156
Fisher, William C. (Polaris Industries) A691
Fishkin, Cory E67
Fishman, Jay S. A843
Fishman, Jerald G. A91
Fishman, Mark C. W248
Fishman, Scot H. P166
Fishman, Steven S. A148
Fiske, Neil S. Jr. P177
Fiske, Roger P323
Fisken, Nik P474
Fitch, Steve P98
Fite, Michele P462
Fitschen, Jürgen W119
Fitting, Alwin W296
Fitts, Clive A716
Fitts, Michael A. P517
Fitzgerald, David E192
Fitzgerald, Douglas W. A742
Fitzgerald, Gabriella P. A77
Fitzgerald, Jeanne A86
Fitzgerald, John J. Jr. A832
Fitzgerald, Michael E163
FitzGerald, Niall W350
FitzGerald, Robert E215
Fitzgerald, Timothy J. E269
Fitzgerald, Walter L. A200
Fitzgibbons, Albert J. III E298
Fitzhenry, Paul A848
Fitzhugh, Michael D. E60
Fitzmaurice, Lisa A. P367
FitzPatrick, Dennis P412
Fitzpatrick, Edward J. A600
Fitzpatrick, Jonathan A176
Fitzpatrick, Timothy A373
Fitzsimmons, Bob P160
Fitzsimmons, Ellen M. A268
Fitzsimmons, Gary P64
Fitzsimmons, Nancy A715
FitzSimons, Ian W258
Fitzwater, Jim A362
Fivel, Steven E. A165
Fjeldheim, Norm A714
Flachman, Jennifer K. A72
Flack, Gregory D. P445
Flack, Robert J. P29
Flagg, Claude A. A821
Flaharty, Gary R. A123
Flaharty, Robert P269
Flaherty, Greg P301
Flaherty, James P. A614
Flaherty, Kathy P382
Flaim, Theresa A. A818
Flaminia, Alinka E316
Flanagan, Kevin P102
Flanagan, Martin L. A471
Flanagan, Robert J. E258, P135
Flanagan, Thomas A86
Flanders, Brent P392
Flanigan, Matthew C. A525
Flanigan, Patrick A390
Flanigan, Richard J. Jr. A206
Flannelly, Barry E303
Flannery, Dion A869
Flannery, Heidi E407
Flannery, Mary Ellen P380
Flannery, Matthew J. A857
Flannigan, John P228
Flatley, Jay T. E210
Flavio, John J. P531
Flaws, James B. A258
Flax, Larry S. E82
Fleckenstein, Robert E. E31
Fleer, Todd P465
Flees, Ralph T. P127
Fleet, Samuel H. P49
Fleischer, Glen A201
Fleischer, Larry A98
Fleischhacker, James E. A593
Fleischmann, Roger (Levi Strauss) P297

Fleischmann, Roger J. Jr. (Central Garden & Pet) A201
Fleisher, Michael D. A897
Fleishman, Ernest B. A759
Fleming, Beverly J. A633
Fleming, Bruce F. A220
Fleming, Candace P141
Fleming, David D. A390
Fleming, John (Ford Motor) A365
Fleming, John E. (Wal-Mart)
Fleming, Mark A383
Fleming, Richard H. A875
Fleming, Samuel C. P148
Fleming, Scott P487
Fleming, Shane D. A272
Fleming Kauffman, Alejandro W262
Flemming, Timothy E. A287
Fletcher, Alan A673
Fletcher, Denise K. P534
Fletcher, Harold K. E379
Fletcher, Jeffrey J. P52
Fletcher, John P405
Fletcher, Karen A. A312
Fletcher, Stan A. A167
Fletcher, Stuart R. W123
Fleury, Edward S. E100
Flexon, Robert C. A638
Flick, Bertolt M. W306
Flint, Charles W. III P195
Flint, Douglas J. W167
Flint, William Jr. P269
Fliss, Tim P442
Flitcraft, Dawn E66
Flitman, David E. A605
Flochel, Patrick J.P. A337, W136
Flocken, Jeffery A815
Flockhart, Alexander A. W167
Floersch, Richard R. A574
Floether, Karl-Heinz A36
Flohn, Thomas A. A535
Flom, Joseph H. A775, P459
Flood, Bryan W. E236
Flood, Gary J. A564
Florczak, James E. A105
Florea, Richard W. A829
Florence, Thad A789
Flores, Amy A52
Flores, Greg III A836
Flores, James A. E323
Flórez, Federico W140
Floriani, Lodovico W50
Florin, Daniel P. P84
Florin, Gerhard A325
Floris, Jean-Pierre W299
Florness, Daniel L. A349
Floum, Joshua R. A886
Flourens, Alain W32
Flower, William C. A728
Flowers, David J. A. A298
Flowers, Garry W. A360
Flowers, John P45
Flowers, Mark P501
Flowers, Robert J. P388
Flowers, Wanda E. A801
Floyd, Allen P335
Floyd, H. Charles A449
Floyd, R. Dale E315
Flückiger, Reto W98
Fluegel, Bradley M. A905
Fluke, Kenneth W. A828
Flur, Dorlisa K. A348
Flynn, Edward B. III A114
Flynn, Jennifer P98
Flynn, Megan E. E336
Flynn, Patrick W177
Flynn, Thomas E. (BMO Financial Group) W61
Flynn, Thomas H. (Foodarama Supermarkets) P198
Flynn, Timothy P. A514, W194
Flynt, Jim D. A502
Foate, Dean A. A688
Foe, Bryan D. A207
Foellmer, Frank P482
Foerderer, Norma P502

Fogarty, Dan P370
Fogarty, James P. A211
Fogarty, W. Tom P143
Fogel, Arthur A538
Fogel, Glenn D. A698
Foggio, Richard S. A121
Fohrer, Alan J. A322
Foil, James P105
Fok, Canning K. N. W168
Folache, José Maria W94
Foland, Jeffrey T. A850
Folch Viadero, Salvi R. W344
Foley, Donald E. (ITT Corp.) A474
Foley, Donald H. (SAIC) A747
Foley, Joseph R. A866
Foley, Richard P367
Folkwein, Kristy J. A110
Folland, Nick W189
Follett, Chuck P197
Folliard, Thomas J. A192
Follo, James M. A620
Folts, Ellen P537
Folz, Jean-Martin W94
Fong, Ivan K. A188
Fong, Russell G. A184
Fonlladosa, Patrice W368
Fontaine, Bryan P96
Fontaine, James A. E268
Fontaine, Jean-Louis W76
Fontaine, Michael W217
Fontaine, R. Richard A378
Fontaine, Richard P. A560
Fontán, Julio P. P131
Fontana, Bernard W48
Fontana, David G. P442
Fontana, James C. P34
Fontana, Mari P338
Fontanes, A. Alexander A532
Fontecedro, Sandro W129
Fontenla-Novoa, Manny W211
Fontham, Elizabeth T. H. P41
Foody, James G. A755
Foote, William C. A875
Foran, Greg W383
Forbes, Glenn S. P321
Forbes, Kathryn A. P416
Forbes, Ricardo P71
Forbes, Stephen J. W89
Forcellini, Anthony L. E238
Ford, Allyn C. (Roseburg Forest Products) P427
Ford, Allyn C. (Umpqua Holdings) E395
Ford, Beth E. A464
Ford, J. W. P26
Ford, Jeffrey J. (GT Solar) E180
Ford, Jeffrey J. (IMS Health) A456
Ford, Judith V. P29
Ford, Ken E232
Ford, Mark P317
Ford, Mary N. E90
Ford, Mike P170
Ford, Monte E. A89
Ford, Robert C. A195
Ford, Rollin Lee A893
Ford, Sabrina P186
Ford, Steven J. A190
Ford, Timothy A. A819
Ford, William C. Jr. A365
Forde, Brian E292
Forde, Richard H. A221
Forehand, J. P. A923
Foreman, Jim P495
Foreman, Robert B. A791
Foreman, Roger L. P88
Forese, James A. A227
Forester, Rich A295
Foresti, Ronaldo A531
Forish, Joseph J. E183
Forker, Jackie E24
Forkovitch, James K. A241
Forlenza, Vincent A. A138
Forman, Gar P130
Formant, Chris (Avaya) P67
Formant, Christopher M. (Avaya) P67

Formella, Nancy P361
Formusa, Joe P472
Fornaro, Carlo W340
Fornaro, Robert L. A55
Forrester, Craig W. A222
Forrester, Matthew P. E338
Forrester, Sean A292
Forsee, Gary D. P516
Forshay, Steven E. E129
Forstall, Scott A99
Forster, Kevin G. A190
Forster, Peter C. P135
Forstmann, Theodore J. P200
Forsythe, Daryl R. E285
Fortanet, Francisco A464
Forte, Deborah A. A759
Forte, Nan-Kirsten E411
Forth, J. Bradford E180
Fortin, Daniel S. A232
Fortin, Mary Jane B. A81
Fortin, Raymond D. A802
Fortune, Christie J. P132
Forward, Frank D. A150
Foschi, Pier Luigi A193
Foshee, Douglas L. A324
Fosler, Gail D. P143
Foss, Donald A. E109
Foss, Eric J. A669
Foss, Karen A73
Foss, Linda L. A110
Foss, Michael E. P394
Foss, Richard L. E358
Fosse, Eric E152
Fossel, Jon S. A866
Fossenier, Patrick J. A254
Foster, Deborah W. P510
Foster, Donald L. A246
Foster, James A230
Foster, John (Kansas City Southern) A496
Foster, John M. (MFRI) E266
Foster, Jonathan F. (New York Power Authority) P366
Foster, Lee B. II E246
Foster, Mark (Accenture) A36
Foster, Martin G. (HCSC) P239
Foster, Melanie P337
Foster, Mickey A352
Foster, Pamela P426
Foster, Randall P446
Foster, Ron (Foster Farms) P201
Foster, Ronald C. (Micron Technology) A589
Foster, Scarlett Lee A596
Foster, W. Kim A362
Foster-Cheek, Kaye I. A487
Fostyk, Michael J. A74
Fotiades, George L. P118
Fotsch, Richard J. P287
Fouad, Sam A337, P184, W136
Foulkes, Helena B. A271
Foulon, Koenraad C. P111
Fouracre, Jenny A301
Fournier, Marcel P117
Fournier, Steve P167
Fourtou, Jean-René W54, W372
Fowke, Benjamin G. S. III A925
Fowler, Cameron W62
Fowler, Fred J. E356
Fowler, John C. P408
Fowler, Richard G. A210
Fowler, W. Randall A333
Fox, Alan M. P521
Fox, Alison (San Antonio Spurs) P435
Fox, Alissa (Blue Cross) P87
Fox, Beverly P117
Fox, Brad A746
Fox, Brent P18
Fox, Carolyn S. P507
Fox, C.H. P381
Fox, Colin A819
Fox, Frank A641
Fox, J. Kenneth P212
Fox, James M. P188
Fox, Keith A575

H

Henkel, Scott M. E84
Henkels, Ginnie P482
Henkels, T. Roderick P243
Henley, Gary D. E421
Henley, Robert W. A642
Henn, Stephen K. E349
Henneberry, Robbie W41
Hennelly, Tim P430
Henneman, John B. III E219
Hennen, Leigh M. E371
Hennequin, Denis A574
Hennessey, Bill P143
Hennessy, John L. E56, P470
Hennessy, Mark J. A462
Hennessy, Paul J. A698
Hennessy, Sean P. A772
Hennig, Jay K. A597
Hennigan, Rob P435
Henning, Gary S. A779
Henningsen, August-Wilhelm W211
Hennon, Armand W258
Hennon-Bell, Lori A707
Henrici, Peter G. A887
Henrikson, C. Robert A586
Henriksson, Ulf W179
Henriques, George L. A664
Henriquez, François G. II P522
Henry, Bo E334
Henry, Brent L. P387
Henry, Brian J. A819
Henry, Daniel T. A77
Henry, J. Warren E106
Henry, Jack (Big Y Foods) P82
Henry, James E. E192
Henry, John K. (Duane Reade) P173
Henry, John W. (Boston Red Sox) P98
Henry, Peter A91
Henry, Pierre W322
Henry, Reed T. E51
Henry, Robert K. A411
Henry, Rona Smyth P424
Henry, Simon W295
Henschel, Laurel E. A775, P459
Hensel, Anthony D. A160
Hensgen, Heinz Ulrich A659
Hensing, John P71
Hensley, Jonathan P417
Hensley, Susan A314, P175
Henson, Christopher L. A132
Hepsworth, Mark E222
Herald, Alice A. A127
Herath, Kirk A611, P356
Herbel, Peter W360
Herbel, Vern D. A838
Herbert, C. Theodore A812
Herbert, James L. E286
Herbert, Jean-Marc W303
Herbert, Jeff A646
Herbert, Peter N. P550
Herbert-Jones, Siân W322
Herbkersman, John P88
Herbst, Lawrence G. P171
Herbstreit, Jack P171
Herdman, Michael D. A126
Heredia, George L. P247
Hereford, James P226
Herglotz, Kevin A746
Herington, Charles M. A121
Herington, Harry H. E292
Herink, Daniel D. A40
Herkert, Craig R. A803
Herkert, Jeffrey P453
Herlihy, Donagh A121
Herman, Fred E. A726
Herman, James L. E114
Herman, Matt P337
Herman, Richard P513
Herman, Roberta P235
Hermance, Ronald E. Jr. E202
Hermann, Tammy P453
Hermanson, Eliot J. P425
Hermelin, Paul W92
Hermiz, Ramzi Y. A351
Hermógenes Rollano, Manuel W282
Hermreck, Immanuel W71

Hernádi, Zsolt W230
Hernandez, Carlos M. (Fluor) A360
Hernandez, Carlos M. (JPMorgan Chase) A494
Hernandez, Daniel L. E368
Hernandez, David P255
Hernandez, Diego W72
Hernandez, Enrique Jr. A630
Hernandez, John P218
Hernandez, William H. A693
Herndon, P. Todd P276
Hernowitz, Ira A414
Herpich, Richard P. A876
Herr, Sandra P71
Herrault, Christian W201
Herrema, Gregory J. A826
Herrera, Ana M. E120
Herrewyn, Jean-Michel W368
Herrick, Alan J. E344
Herrin, Jeff P466
Herring, Carol P. P430
Herring, Donette P119
Herring, James W. P131
Herring, Joseph L. A261
Herring, Joyce P388
Herringer, Maryellen C. A35
Herrington, Terri L. A466
Herrman, Ernie A836
Herrmann, Henry J. E409
Herrmann, Peggy A. A302
Herrmann, Susan A193
Herro, Leslee K. A34
Herro, Lynn M. P369
Herron, Jay P132
Herron, Winell P242
Hersberger, Rodney M. P43
Herschmann, Eric D. A785
Hershenov, Eileen B. P145
Hershenson, Jay P134
Hershhorn, Mark P. P430
Hershman, Lisa A120
Hershman, Wendy P533
Herston, Sam P370
Hertwig, James R. A268
Herz, George W. II P521
Herzig, Bill A276
Herzog, David L. A81
Heshmati, Mo P145
Heske, Gerrit A126
Heskett, Tim P214
Heslop, Julian W156
Hess, Beat W295
Hess, Carl A903
Hess, David P. A862
Hess, Jeffrey P161
Hess, John B. A427
Hess, Peter F. E20
Hesse, Chad F. A292
Hesse, Daniel R. A790
Hesselink, Arent Jan W264
Hessels, Jan-Michiel A644, W264
Hesser, Gregory T. P32
Hesser, Petra W172
Hester, John (Trustmark Mutual Holding Company) P503
Hester, John P. (Southwest Gas) A787
Hester, Phil D. E279
Hester, Randy D. E324
Hester, Stephen A. M. W294
Hester, Troy L. A814
Hetterich, F. Paul A250
Hetzel, R. Andrew P90
Heuer, John J. P517
Heuser, Albert W64
Heussinger, Johann E164
Hevelhorst, Richard P. A209
Hewins, Ward D. P23
Hewitt, Bradford L. P491
Hewitt, Dennis E. A651
Hewlett, Spencer P319
Hexner, Thomas S. P36
Hey, Troy W147
Heyens, David P118
Heyl, Craig E193
Heym, Richard E242

Heyman, John H. E330
Heyman, William H. A843
Heynen, Bruno W248
Heynike, Petraea W236
Heys, Mark E406
Heyse, Richard P. A910
Heystee, Susan A637
Heywood, Graham P. E210
Hiatt, Jonathan P29
Hiatte, Patrick A177
Hibbard, Barry G. E378
Hibbard, Timothy A. A910
Hibbeler, Jeff A149
Hibberd, Douglas G. E350
Hibbs, Kelly P93
Hiber, John P109
Hickcox, W. Thomas P547
Hickerson, Bill P281
Hickerson, M. Neale A437, E199
Hickey, James P160
Hickey, Loughlin A514, P288, W195
Hickey, Michael A. A321
Hickey, Nancy W. A798
Hickey, Simon W275
Hickey, William V. A765
Hickman, Rebecca L. A684
Hicks, Christie A795
Hicks, David G. E189
Hicks, H. Thomas A868
Hicks, Jan P484
Hicks, Jimmy D. E200
Hicks, Kenneth C. A364
Hicks, Kerry R. E189
Hicks, Lucky P63
Hicks, Randall L. A155
Hicok, Gary A641
Hidalgo, Joaquin A626
Hidema, Tomohiro W38
Hidy, Richard J. A870
Hiemstra, Siep W159
Hier-King, Jan A210
Hieronimus, Albert W286
Hiéronimus, Nicolas W210
Hiesinger, Heinrich W315
Higase, Edward T. A394
Higashi, Tetsuro W354
Higdem, Garry M. P128
Higginbotham-Brooks, Renee P254
Higgins, Arthur J. W65
Higgins, Benny W349
Higgins, Bryce A777
Higgins, David J. P482
Higgins, Elizabeth Bush P376
Higgins, Kathy P91
Higgins, Mike E194
Higginson, Alan J. E152
Higginson, Andrew T. W349
Higgs, Jim D. E156
Highley, Duane D. P59
Hight, Eddie L. E42
Hightman, Carrie J. A628
Higson, John Philip A121
Hilado, Tessa A672
Hilburn, Diane E61
Hild, Randy A716
Hildebrand, Phillip J. E239
Hildebrandt, K. Bradley E157
Hildenbrand, Charles V. E212
Hildenbrand, Wilton A180
Hilf, Kristin A722
Hilfman, Dave A253
Hilger, Christopher M. P447
Hilger, James K. A277
Hill, Allen E. A856
Hill, Anne A117
Hill, Barbara B. P193
Hill, Brian A623
Hill, Dan A342
Hill, David (News Corp.) A624
Hill, David F. (International Data Group) P264
Hill, Edwin J. A192
Hill, Elliott A626
Hill, Gareth W279
Hill, George (Office Depot) A646

Hill, George H. (Quaker Chemical) E326
Hill, Gregory P. A427
Hill, Jeff P329
Hill, John (L-3 Communications) A518
Hill, John B. III (Calpine) A184
Hill, John I. (Central Parking) P126
Hill, Johnny (Clearfield) E97
Hill, Kevin N. A665
Hill, P. J. P133
Hill, Paul J. P551
Hill, Ralph A. A917
Hill, Ron E194
Hill, Ruth P432
Hill, Susan E. A149
Hill, Terri L. A611
Hill, Thomas R. W363
Hill, Webster P127
Hill, Willard I. Jr. A568
Hillebrand, Rainer W254
Hillegonds, Paul A308
Hillenius, Dorothy W177
Hilliard, Peter E. E187
Hilliard, R. Glenn A247
Hillinger, Oren W194
Hillman, Bret P269
Hillman, Jeanne M. A913
Hillman, Lori A. A418
Hillman, Max W. Jr. A247
Hillman, Richard P. A247
Hillman, Scot P269
Hills, Bryan P168
Hills, David P92
Hills, Stephen P. A898
Hills, Wendy J. E409
Hillyer, Kim A810
Hilsheimer, Lawrence A. A611, P356
Hilson, Joan Holstein A74
Hilton, Andy A474
Hilton, Bradley J. A708
Hilton, Michael F. A53
Hilton, Timothy T. A363, P196
Hilton, William Barron A433, P248
Hilts, Michael E215
Hiltwein, Mark S. A204
Hilzinger, Matthew F. A342
Himelfarb, Richard J. E360
Hinckley, Clark B. A934
Hindman, Craig A. A453
Hindman, James M. A63
Hinds, Susanna P264
Hine, C. Clarkson A367
Hinerman, Robert E119
Hines, Michael A. P186
Hines, Zoe P474
Hinkie, Sam P253
Hinkle, Allen J. P504
Hinners, Billy A112
Hinrichs, Joseph R. A365
Hinrichs, Liane K. A573
Hinshaw, John A157
Hinshaw, Scott R. A301
Hintgen, Kristiina E348
Hinton, Amy L. P404
Hinton, Leslie F. A624
Hinze, Brant A623
Hioki, Masakatsu W192
Hippler, Jon W. E172
Hirai, Kazuo W326
Hirai, Yoshiiku W188
Hiranandani, Arun P376
Hirani, Sunil G. E224
Hiraoka, John E146
Hirata, Kunio W184
Hirayama, Kizo W241
Hirji, Zabeen W293
Hiroike, Kimio W184
Hirokado, Osamu W251
Hirokawa, Katsumi A593
Hiroki, Kazumasa W109
Hironaka, Kazuo W115
Hironishi, Koichi W151
Hirosaki, Botaro W234
Hirosawa, Takao W332
Hirsberg, Josh A163

Kent, Philip I. A833
Kent, Robert N. E306
Kenworthy, Chris A569
Keogh, Tracy A428
Keough, Philip J. IV A731
Keow, Tong Poh W317
Keown, Michael H. A278
Kepecs, Gábor W27
Kepler, David E. II A305
Keppel, Karen E302
Keppler, Jim P257
Kerger, Paula A. P388
Kerin, Andrew C. A104, P53
Kerin, Joseph E. A74
Kerjouan, Jean-Pierre W303
Kerkhoff, Guido W121
Kerkvliet, Jim R. A392
Kerle, Phillip P273
Kermott, Gary L. A356
Kern, Frank A462
Kern, Howard P. P448
Kern, Paul J. A547, P307
Kernan, Richard T. P172
Kerner, Douglas E. A566
Kerner, Jon D. A601
Kerner, Michael G. W388
Kerper, Mary E. A101
Kerr, Bob P153
Kerr, David J. P152
Kerr, Derek J. A869
Kerr, Graham W72
Kerr, Irene E207
Kerr, James C. A484
Kerr, John O. W295
Kerr, Mary A158
Kerr, Patrick W280
Kerr, Phil P462
Kerr, Woody A128
Kerridge, Jeffrey S. E126
Kerrigan, Robert M. III A785
Kerrigan, Sylvia J. A553
Kerris, Richard P305
Kerschbaum, Manfred A102
Kersh, Steve A257
Kershaw, Michael J. A771
Kersten, Cassidy P396
Kersten, Jeffrey L. P483
Kess, Steven W. A422
Kessel, Richard M. P366
Kessel, Silvia P334
Kessel, Steven A69
Kessel Martínez, Georgina Y. W262
Kessler, Alan C. A872, P525
Kessler, Charles F. A34
Kessler, Lisa E40
Kessler, Mark K. A837
Kessler, Stephen W. A184
Kesteloot, Hendrick P117
Keswick, Adam P. C. W186
Keswick, Benjamin W. W186
Keswick, Henry W186
Keswick, Simon L. W186
Ketchum, L. Craig P322
Ketchum, Mark D. A621
Ketchum, Richard G. A644
Kete, Christopher A109
Ketner, Janet J. E234
Kettenbach, Michael P165
Ketter, Stafan W141
Kettering, Glen L. A628
Ketterson, Robert C. A363, P196
Kettlewell, Kelly E367
Keup, Gregory J. P51
Key, Billy P226
Key, Matthew W341
Key, Scott E209
Keyes, James W. A153
Keyes, Michael J. A173
Keyes, Rick P329
Keyes, Thomas D. A706
Keys, Thomas C. A587
Keys, William M. P139
Keyser, Richard A. A924
Kgosana, Moses A514
Khail, Steven C. A551

Khalighi, Dar P45
Khalvati, Kim A918
Khan, Badar W100
Khan, Ejaz A. A889
Khan, Fareed A, A875
Khan, Mehmood A672
Khan, Rizwan A813
Khan, Shahid P194
Khandros, Natalya E76
Khemani, Rajiv E89
Khemlani, Neeraj A420, P241
Khera, Rajesh E77
Kheradpir, Shaygan A882
Khichi, Samrat S. P118
Khiroun, Ramzi W202
Kho, Julie A101
Khoba, Lyubov W212
Khomyakov, Sergey F, W153
Khosla, Sanjay A515
Khoury, Amin J. A133
Khoury, Kenneth F. A134
Kiani, Joe E. E258
Kiappes, John P344
Kibling, Lew W37
Kibsgaard, Paal A757
Kidd, Doug A471
Kidd, John A. (NetApp) A617
Kidd, John D. (WesBanco) E412
Kidd, Richard E123
Kidd, Steven A314, P175
Kidd, Wyndham Jr. P239
Kiddoo, Bruce E. A567
Kiefer, Jeffrey E145
Kielar, Richard M. P494
Kielholz, Walter B. W335
Kielty, Richard A. E76
Kiely, W. Leo III A594, W298
Kiepura, Michael E. A734
Kierlin, Robert A. A349
Kiernan, Laura A819
Kiernan, Peter P E323
Kierspe, Thomas L. P464
Kiesewetter, George P301
Kifer, Ron A102
Kight, Peter J. A358
Kihn, Jean-Claude A398
Kikis, Peter T. E100
Kikuchi, Kazuyuki W226
Kikuchi, Satoshi W181
Kikumoto, C. David P534
Kilanowski, Mitchell E119
Kilbane, Catherine M. A79
Kile, James A218
Kilgannon, Susan B. A868
Kilgore, Tom D. A818, P488
Kill, Robert E404
Killebrew, Chad E. P482
Killebrew, Flavius C. P489
Killebrew, George P156
Killeen, Paul P213
Killen, James C. Jr. P34
Killian, John F. A882
Killinger, Clayton E. A877
Killingsworth, Cleve L. Jr. P89
Killion, Richard L. A573
Killion, Theophlius A933
Kilmartin, Julian W218
Kilmer, Mark C. E326
Kilpatric, Michael N. A85
Kilpatrick, Emily A714
Kim, Andrew W. E287
Kim, Bong Soo W204
Kim, Clara A297
Kim, David P256
Kim, Dong-Cheol W204
Kim, Dorothy J. A794
Kim, Eric B. A461
Kim, Hoil E180
Kim, James J. A88
Kim, Jeong H. W36
Kim, Jing-Wan W301
Kim, Jin-Il W269
Kim, John Y. (New York Life) A619
Kim, Jong-Eun (LG Group) W204
Kim, Jooho A88

Kim, Kap K. A242
Kim, Matthew M. E93
Kim, Michael C. P64
Kim, Neil Y. A170
Kim, Paul E98
Kim, Peter S. A584
Kim, Sang-Ho (POSCO) W269
Kim, Sang-Young (POSCO) W269
Kim, Sean S.H. W170
Kim, Seung-Nyun W170
Kim, Soo-Kwan W269
Kim, Sun Tae W204
Kim, Yong-Hwan W170
Kimball, Jim P486
Kimball, Walker P77
Kimble, Donald R. A448
Kimbro, Kenneth J. A849
Kimbrough, Brad A724
Kimbrough, Mark A415, P237
Kime, Jeffery L. A829
Kimishima, Tatsumi W239
Kimler, Bill P309
Kimmel, Sidney A490
Kimmel, Steve P34
Kimmet, Pamela O. A235
Kimmitt, Joseph H. A654
Kimura, Hiroshi W185
Kimura, Keiji W326
Kimura, Makoto W237
Kimura, Shigeru W353
Kinard, Lisa P486
Kincaid, Michael J. A431
Kincaid, Steven M. A522
Kinder, David D. P282
Kinder, Jacquelyn P119
Kinder, Richard D. P282
Kindig, Karl W. A247
Kindle, Fred P136
Kindler, Jeffrey B. A680
Kindorf, Rich A35
Kindts, Rudi W83
Kindy, Mark P332
Kinerk, Beth A. A649
King, Andrew S. (Briggs & Stratton) A164
King, Andrew W. (Torchmark) A838
King, Carolyn A706
King, Catherine J. W25
King, Christopher A369
King, David L. (Associated Materials) P60
King, David R. (JDA Software) E234
King, David R. H. (SmithGroup) P460
King, David S. (Halliburton) A404
King, David W. (Tetra Tech) A822
King, Deryk I. W100
King, Diana A661
King, Donald R. P215
King, Edward (California State Board of Equalization) P107
King, Edward M. (Boston University) P98
King, Eileen P387
King, Gale V. P356
King, Ian W58
King, James D. A760
King, Jeffrey P137
King, John E. (Perot Systems) A675
King, John L. (University of Michigan) P516
King, Jon J. (Benchmark Electronics) A144
King, Jon M. (Tiffany & Co.) A831
King, Justin W183
King, Kelly S. A132
King, Kenton J. A775
King, Mark (adidas) W26
King, Mark (Rolls-Royce) W290
King, Mark A. (Diodes) E127
King, Nuala M. A335
King, Pamela E. A515
King, Patrick D. A764
King, Regina P201
King, Richard L. (Associated Food) P60
King, Richie (Foster Farms) P201

King, Robert C. (Pepsi Bottling) A669
King, Robert P. (CONSOL Energy, CNX Gas) A248, E97
King, Roger J. A569
King, Russell W44
King, Scott V. A316
King, Stephen (Alkermes) E29
King, Steve (Isasis Healthcare) P257
King, Thomas A. (Progressive Corporation) A705
King, Thomas B. (National Grid) W233
King, Thomas H. (Allied Systems) P37
King, Tim (Brookshire Grocery) P102
King, Timothy (E. W. Scripps) A341
King, Timothy B. (John Wiley) A486
King, Vivian P429
King, W. Russell A375
King, Wal M. W164
King, William K. A796, P472
Kingan, Michael P517
King-Lavinder, Joyce A235
Kingma, Todd W. A676
Kingo, Lise W249
Kingsbury, Thomas A. P105
Kingsfield, Scott E330
Kingsley, Chris P302
Kingsley, Linda A. A872, P525
Kingsley, Stuart A. A438
Kingston, Michael A93
Kingston, Richard E91
Kingston, Robert W84
Kingswell-Smith, Charles A687
Kinkela, David P218
Kinloch, Leon A253
Kinnaird, Malcolm B. A95
Kinneberg, Eric A375
Kinney, Charles F. A841
Kinoshita, Kenji W192
Kinsella, Liam W41
Kinser, Dennis P63
Kinsey, Jeffrey M. A175
Kinsey, R. Steve A359
Kinsinger, David A518
Kinsley, Brian P140
Kinslow, Anthony D. P457
Kinstle, Mike P329
Kinugawa, Kiyoshi W163
Kinukawa, Jun W224
Kinzel, Donna J. A568
Kinzer, John E70
Kinzey, Cara D. A439
Kinzie, Jack L. P70
Kinzley, Richard W. E69
Kipling, Karen P534
Kipp, Mary E. E139
Kipp, Thomas W120
Kippur, Stephen A. A486
Kiraç, Suna W191
Kiraly, Thomas E. P143
Kirani, Shekhar A880
Kirby, J. Scott A869
Kirby, Lyn P. E392
Kirby, Rex B. P476
Kircher, Chris A244
Kirchhof, Ina W134
Kirchhoff, Bruce E340
Kirchhoff, Wes A71
Kirchman, Kevin P401
Kirchner, Bruce P317
Kiriacoulacos, Peter A238
Kirk, Patricia L. P171
Kirk, Randy P37
Kirk, Robert S. E268
Kirk, Stephen F. A546
Kirk Kristiansen, Kjeld W203
Kirkland, George L. A215
Kirkover, Karen E157
Kirkpatrick, Albert B. A355
Kirkpatrick, Troy A188
Kirksey, Hugh P102
Kirkwood, Karen A. A826
Kirley, Tim P277
Kirloskar, Virendra A509
Kirsch, Jason S. E266

Morita, Karen P225
Morita, Lisa E224
Morita, Masao W326
Morita, Naoyuki W198
Morita, Takashi W33
Moritz, Robert E. A699, W271
Morizono, Hideto W252
Morley, Cheryl P. A596
Morley, Keith R. A904
Moro, Javier W282
Morphy, John M. A665
Morrás Andrés, Esteban W128
Morreau, Jane C. A173
Morrill, R. Layne P59
Morris, Barry A. E361
Morris, Bret A. A418
Morris, Clifton H. Jr. A83
Morris, Darren P383
Morris, Diana P322
Morris, Donna A41
Morris, Douglas W372
Morris, George R. E57
Morris, Greg P453
Morris, Henry L. A778
Morris, Holly J. P491
Morris, James T. (Pacific Mutual) P384
Morris, Jamie P396
Morris, Jeff P336
Morris, Jim (Indiana Pacers) P260
Morris, John L. P73
Morris, Karen P329
Morris, Ken (International Specialty
  Products) P265
Morris, Kenneth C. (Duke University
  Health System) P173
Morris, Kyle E84
Morris, M. Catherine A107
Morris, Maria R. A586
Morris, Michael G. (AEP) A75
Morris, Michael J. (Heritage Oaks
  Bancorp) E193
Morris, R. Steven P23
Morris, Richard S. E404
Morris, Robert L. A503
Morris, William C. (CARBO
  Ceramics) E86
Morris, William M. (Legacy
  Reserves) E247
Morrison, Angela W183
Morrison, Bill (Associated Wholesale
  Grocers) P63
Morrison, Bob (Wolseley) W381
Morrison, Christine A. P37
Morrison, Craig O. P245
Morrison, David (Vitamin
  Shoppe) E405
Morrison, David G. (Viad) A884
Morrison, David H. (Boeing) A157
Morrison, Denise M. A185
Morrison, Gary D. E34
Morrison, Gregory B. A262, P150
Morrison, Harold L. Jr. A219
Morrison, James E. (Kennametal) A501
Morrison, James E. (Teknor Apex) P486
Morrison, John P99
Morrison, Mark A93
Morrison, Michael P159
Morrison, Patricia B. A188
Morrison, Randi Val A294
Morrison, Robert W. (Lumber
  Liquidators) E253
Morrison, Scott C. A126
Morrison, Vanessa A371
Morrison, William L. (Northern
  Trust) A633
Morriss, John P533
Morris-Tyndall, Lucille P482
Morrow, George J. A86
Morrow, Greg A450
Morrow, Ken P364
Morrow, Michael S. A500
Morrow, Phillip Keith A153
Morrow, William A. P151
Morsberger, Michael J. P173
Morsches, Gary J. A668

Morse, David J. P424
Morse, John (Encyclopædia
  Britannica) P180
Morse, John B. Jr. (Washington
  Post) A898
Morse, Paul E. P49
Morse, Phillip H. P98
Morse, Rosemarie P208
Morse, Timothy R. A929
Mortazavi, Minoo E214
Mortensen, Eric J. A529
Mortensen, Steven L. P553
Mortenson, David C. P306
Mortenson, M. A. Jr. P306
Mortenson, Mark A. P306
Mortimer, Jeffrey A210
Mortimer, Mike P410
Mortimore, Sara A520
Morton, John D. P467
Morton, Michael (Golden
  Horizons) P213
Morton, Mike (H.T. Hackney) P255
Morton, Steven D. P494
Morton, Taryn L. W275
Mosbacher, Tim P370
Mosch, James G. A288
Moschella, Frank A659
Moschner, George E. A124
Moscicki, Richard A. A390
Mosconi, Jean-Jacques W360
Moseley, Ellis E. P202
Moseley, Tim S. W89
Moser, Bobby D. P377
Moser, Michael R. P543
Moser, Wayne D. A501
Moses, Alan C. W249
Mosher, Timothy C. A76
Moshier, Arnold P437
Moshouris, Irene A857
Moshovetis, Paul P110
Moskalenko, Anatoly W212
Moskowitz, Paul T. A278
Mosley, Dave A764
Mosley, Jamahl P165
Mosley, Ray E121
Mosonyi, György W230
Moss, Arvid W247
Moss, Jacqueline W89
Moss, Marcia K. P461
Moss, Ralph L. A762
Moss, Sara E. A339
Moss, Stephen F. A455
Moss, Susan E. A506
Moss, William J. A29
Mossbeck, Sheri L. A525
Mossing, Mark T. A798
Mosticchio, Dennis P. P228
Motal, Rebecca P303
Motamed, Thomas F. A232
Motel, George P99
Mothe, Gérard W270
Mott, Daniel C. P42
Mott, Randall D. A429
Motta, Richard P534
Motter, Thomas E70
Mougios, Maureen P. E74
Mouillon, Christian P184, W136
Moullet, Barry B. A276
Moulonguet, Thierry W281
Moulton, John A489
Moulton, Paul G. A259
Mountcastle, Laura L. A231
Mountford, Gordon J. E204
Mounts, L. David A301
Mourad, Sam P462
Mousaw, John E48
Moushey, Nora E. P543
Mousseau, Bradley G. A666
Mow, Doug E405
Mowell, John B. E141
Mowery, Robert A. A922
Moya, P. Robert A98
Moye, Joe W92
Moyer, Glenn E. E281
Moyers, K. Douglass A192

Moyes, Jerry C. P482
Moyes, Kevin P195
Moynihan, Brian T. A127
Mozola, Mark A. E286
Mrachek, William J. E48
Mroz-Bremner, Karen E219
Mucci, Martin A665
Mucci, Paul L. P404
Mucci, Richard L. A619, P365
Muccilo, Robert A249
Mucha, Zenia A894
Mudd, John O. P57, P405
Mudge, Robert A882
Muehlbauer, James L. A146
Muehlhaeuser, Hubertus M. A50
Mueller, Brian (BioMarin
  Pharmaceutical) E66
Mueller, Brian E. (Grand Canyon
  Education) E177
Mueller, Charles E. Jr. P53
Mueller, Donald S. A875
Mueller, Edward A. A718
Mueller, Gene W. P399
Mueller, Jeffrey P287
Mueller, Jim P442
Mueller, Kurt F. A442
Mueller, Margaret L. A522
Mueller, Matt P444
Mueller, Michael G. (Ameren) A73
Mueller, Michael P. (Gerdau
  Ameristeel) A392
Mueller, Paul P442
Mueller, Richard I. E43
Muessel, John E338
Mühlbayer, Michael W111
Muir, Andrew E406
Muir, Glenn P. A438
Muir, Ian W83
Muir, James M. W374
Muir, Nigel D. A696
Muir, William D. Jr. A476
Muirhead, Sophia A. P143
Mulally, Alan R. A365
Mulcahy, Anne M. A927
Mulder, Pamela E339
Mulders, Abbe M. P169
Muldowney, Michael P253
Mulé, Ann C. A801
Muleski, Robert T. A532
Mulhearn, John R. Jr. A394
Mulhern, Carmel W346
Mulhern, James A. P243
Mulhern, Mark F. A703
Mulhern, Pat P523
Mulholland, Michael A205
Mulkeen, Niall P273
Mullaney, Mike W207
Mullaney, William J. A586
Mullen, Dennis B. E333
Mullen, Edward K. P369
Mullen, Jack (ShopKo Stores) P453
Mullen, John P. (Deutsche Post) W120
Mullen, Martin J. A222
Mullen, Michael A435
Mullen, Patrick P217
Mullen, Richard P172
Mullen, Robert H. (The Newark
  Group) P369
Mullen, Robert W. (Structure
  Tone) P475
Mullen, Sue P369
Mullen, Timothy W. A264
Muller, Christophe A434
Muller, Daniel E. A835
Müller, Frank W333
Muller, Frans W.H. W222
Muller, James A. A54
Muller, Peter A241
Müller, Werner W118
Mullett, C. Randal A254
Mulliez, Arnaud W53
Mulliez, Christian W210
Mulliez, Vianney W53
Mulligan, Anne Marie P401
Mulligan, Brian C. W119

Mulligan, Deanna M. P228
Mulligan, Donal Leo (General
  Mills) A386
Mulligan, James J. E364
Mulligan, John A68
Mulligan, Michael J. A383
Mulligan, Terry E261
Mullin, Chris P214
Mullin, Mark W. W27
Mullin, Thomas J. A250
Mullinax, A. R. A309
Mullins, Russell P223
Mullison, Kent P451
Mulloy, Steve P185
Mulrooney, Nina M. P389
Mulroy, Martin V. E16
Mulroy, Thomas P. E360
Mulva, James J. A246
Mulva, Patrick T. A347
Mulyak, Vladimir W212
Mumenthaler, Christian W335
Münchow, Detlef W127
Mundie, Craig J. A590
Mundt, Kevin A. P463
Mundt, Scott P291
Muneoka, Shoji W241
Munganahalli, Deepak A842
Munger, Charles T. A145, E117, E412
Munger, Stephen R. E390
Munick, Paul S. P342
Munir, Naim A701
Munneke, Jeff P340
Munnelly, Joseph M. A104, P53
Muñoz, Frank P431
Munoz, Oscar A268
Munro, Bruce W232
Munro, Ellen K. P304
Munro, Gordon A902
Munsell, William A. A863
Murabito, John M. A221
Murakami, Fumitsune W97
Muraoka, Fumio W358
Murasawa, Atsushi W358
Murashima, Junichi W151
Muraskin, Ben E. A678, P395
Murciano, Jo E130
Murdakes, James E210
Murdoch, James R. A624, W84
Murdoch, K. Rupert A624
Murdock, Carol E190
Murdock, David H. A299
Murdock, Justin M. A299
Murdock, Kent H. P263
Murdock, Wendy J. A564
Murdolo, Frank J. A366
Murguía Orozco, Jorge Eduardo W344
Murillo Soberanis, Marco A. W262
Murin, William J. A432
Murken, Geoff P73
Murnane, Timothy E. E293
Muromachi, Masashi W358
Murphree, Michelle P339
Murphy, Bill P518
Murphy, Bruce D. A503
Murphy, Christopher J. A678, P395
Murphy, Conor A586
Murphy, Corrie P230
Murphy, Daniel (The Kraft
  Group) P289
Murphy, Daniel J. (Alliant
  Techsystems) A66
Murphy, Daniel J. (Unified
  Grocers) P507
Murphy, Daniel M. (Caterpillar) A196
Murphy, David L. A575
Murphy, Elizabeth A. P158
Murphy, Glenn K. A381
Murphy, J. Andrew A638
Murphy, Jack P. (Monotype) E273
Murphy, James J. Jr. (Enterprise
  Financial Services) E145
Murphy, James P. (Costco
  Wholesale) A259

Murphy, Jennifer A523
Murphy, Jeremiah T. P30
Murphy, John (Ernst & Young Global) P184, W136
Murphy, John F. (DIRECTV) A295
Murphy, Judith T. A870
Murphy, Kathy E133
Murphy, Kevin R. A139
Murphy, Mark (ClubCorp) P137
Murphy, Mark H. (Green Bay Packers) A401
Murphy, Matthew (Boston Beer) E73
Murphy, Matthew J. (Maxim Integrated Products) A567
Murphy, Patricia A462
Murphy, Paul B. Jr. A934
Murphy, Peter E. (Harrah's Entertainment) P234
Murphy, Peter F. III (TIAA-CREF) A830
Murphy, Ronald H. P59
Murphy, Steven A. (Winmark) E417
Murphy, Steven J. (Natus Medical) E283
Murphy, Susan H. P148
Murphy, Terrence J. (Legg Mason) A523
Murphy, Terrence J. (NiSource) A628
Murphy, Terry M. (A. O. Smith) A95
Murphy, Thomas D. (Eagle Bancorp (MD)) E135
Murphy, Thomas H. (AmerisourceBergen) A85
Murphy, Timothy H. A564
Murray, Bob P49
Murray, Cathy (Life Care Centers) P300
Murray, David (BHP Billiton) W72
Murray, David (H&R Block) A406
Murray, Diane E74
Murray, Helen J. A76
Murray, James E. (Humana) A446
Murray, James G. (Visa Inc) A886
Murray, James M. (North Atlantic Trading) P370
Murray, John M. P157
Murray, Kathy (ABC Supply) P18
Murray, Michael (D.R. Horton) A306
Murray, Michael A. (Yahoo!) A929
Murray, Patricia A461
Murray, Peter P350
Murray, William P486
Murrell, Adrian P208
Murrell, Rick A625
Murren, James J. A588
Murrin, Jim A430
Murry, Paul Thomas III A683
Murstein, Andrew M. E260
Murtaugh, Timothy M. P391
Murteira Nabo, Francisco L. W152
Murtha, Mark E145
Murthy, D. Krishna W23
Murthy, N. R. Narayana W175
Murtlow, Ann D. A45
Mury, Francis M. E171
Musacchio, Robert A. P44
Muscatel, Dave P412
Muse, John O. E119
Musial, Thomas G. A551
Music, Rick E. A110
Music, Terry P41
Musker, Graeme H. R. W51
Muskovich, John A. P284
Mussat, Joel M. A726
Musser, Jeffrey S. A344
Mustin, Kimberly M. A523
Musto, Frank P337
Musumeche, Rocco P142
Muto, Allan A. E148
Muto, Gary P. A93
Muto, Richard W. A281

Muto, Sakae W353
Mutricy, Alain A600
Mutryn, Thomas A. A182
Muzik, Loreen P528
Muzilla, Craig E332
Myagkov, Pyotr A. W153
Myatt, Bob P45
Myatt, Kevin P550
Mye, H. John III E137
Myer, David F. A38
Myers, C. David A489
Myers, Carolyn A603
Myers, Chris A541
Myers, Donald J. A476
Myers, Glen P38
Myers, Gregory L. E275
Myers, James M. P394
Myers, John K. E296
Myers, Keith G. E248
Myers, Margaret A630
Myers, Robert J. A195
Myers, Terry A106
Myers, Thomas P101
Myers, Timothy V. E293
Myette, Kevin P418
Mylod, Robert J. Jr. A698
Mynott, Stephen A. A117
Myrebøe, Gunnar W327
Myrick, William J. P404
Myron, Robert P. A407
Myrtue, Mark S. E201

N

Naatz, Michael J. A931
Nabi, Youcef W210
Nabulsi, Faisal E341
Nacha, Krishna E150
Nachtigal, Jules P142
Nachtigal, Patricia A457
Nachtsheim, Stephen P. A286
Nachtwey, Peter H. P116
Nachury, Jean-Louis W202
Nadachi, Hirokichi W180
Nadeau, William J. P366
Nadelman, Steven E. A857
Nader, David A443
Nadkarni, Gurudatta A249
Nadler, David A. A558
Nafría Aznar, Vitalino M. W341
Nagai, Eisuke W110
Nagai, Nobuo W239
Nagai, Noriaki W246
Nagamatsu, Shoichi W246
Nagano, Yoshiaki W109
Nagarkatti, Jai P. A773
Nagase, Shin W38
Nagayama, Osamu W287
Nagayasu, Katsunori W227
Naggiar, Caroline D. A831
Nagl, Georg W98
Nagle, Julie F. P200
Nagler, Barry A414
Nagrath, Moheet A702
Nagura, Toshikazu W33
Nahikian, Angela A798
Nahmad, Albert H. A900
Nahmany, Peggy W274
Nahon, Claude W126
Nahrgang, Jim P73
Nail, George P205
Nair, Hari N. A817
Nair, Mohandas P417
Naito, Yoshihiro W353
Nakada, Masafumi W246
Nakagawa, Shunichi W188
Nakahara, Hideto W224
Nakajima, Junzo W163
Nakajima, Kazuhiko W324
Nakamura, Iwao W376
Nakamura, Katsumi W38
Nakamura, Kiyoshi W116
Nakamura, Koji W228

Nakamura, Kuniharu (Sumitomo) W331
Nakamura, Kunio (Panasonic Corp) W255
Nakamura, Masanori W235
Nakamura, Shiro W243
Nakamura, Shunichi W33
Nakamura, Takashi (Ricoh Company) W283
Nakamura, Takashi (Tokyo Electron) W354
Nakamura, Toyoaki W163
Nakanishi, Hiroaki W163
Nakanishi, Shinzo W332
Nakano, Masao W38
Nakano, Takeo W229
Nakaoka, Masaki W90
Nakata, Takuya W386
Nakatani, Yoshitaka W188
Nakayama, Haruhide W251
Nakayama, Takashi W332
Nakis, Dominic J. P25
Nalavadi, O'Neil E217
Nalbandian, Gary L. E266
Nallaiah, Christina W206
Nallathambi, Anand J. A356
Nalley, Rob P421
Nally, Dennis M. A699, P402, W271
Nam, Dong Wook E377
Nam, Yong W204
Namiki, Masao W358
Namini, Yasmin A620
Nance, James L. P522
Nance, Stuart E. E393
Nangle, David J. A535
Nanterme, Pierre A36
Naouri, Jean-Charles (Casino Guichard, Rallye) W96, W277
Naouri, Jean-Yves (Publicis Groupe) W274
Naphtali, Howard C. E226
Napier, Iain J. G. W174
Napoli, Andy P153
Napoli, Irma P457
Napolitano, Fernando Flavio P96
Naqui, Ali E207
Naquin, Michael A. E204
Nara, Hirokazu W197
Narang, Charles K. E285
Narayan, Sheila E302
Narayen, Shantanu A41
Nardone, Lisa P539
Narev, Ian W105
Nargolwala, Kaikhushru S. W108
Narsey, Ramik W383
Nartonis, Robert J. P306
Narum, David H. E156
Nash, Elisabeth G. A770
Nash, Jill A530, P297
Nash, Michael A897
Nash, Ron P408
Nash, Simon W279
Nash, Thomas M. A348
Nash, Winfred D. A573
Naskar, Ben D. E56
Naslund, Charles D. A73
Nassenstein, Chris W31
Nasser, Amin H. W307
Nasser, Jacques A. W72
Nassetta, Christopher J. A433, P248
Nasto, Kristine P424
Natale, James L. A263
Natale, Jo P540
Natale, Marina W365
Natarajan, Prabu A45
Nathan, Don A863
Nathansohn, Alberto W69
Nathanson, Jonathan A542
Nattans, Jeffrey A. A523
Naud, Renee P399
Naughton, Marc G. A206
Naukam, Andrew J. E393
Nauman, J. Michael A593
Nauman, Michael B. P380
Navarre, Christophe W214

Navarri, André W76
Navarro, Benito P490
Navarro, Mary W. A448
Navarro, Ricardo A. (Harris Corp.) A411
Navarro, Richard J. (Albertsons) P33
Navarro Navarro, Carlos W137
Navikas, David B. A693
Navin, Peter E346
Navti, Abigail L. P544
Navulur, Kumar E126
Nawano, Katsuhiko W184
Nawi, Gabriella A843
Nayar, Arun A848
Naylor, Jeffrey G. A836
Naylor, Kevin P260
Nazarian, Robert H. P332
Nazemetz, Patricia M. A927
Neal, Christine P507
Neal, David A613
Neal, Diane L. A533
Neal, Gary E395
Neal, Grant R. P51
Neal, James P243
Neal, Jeffrey T. A24
Neal, Lawrence P. A575
Neal, Michael A. A385
Neal, Patricia W57
Nealon, Thomas M. A480
Nealz, LeAnn A74
Neary, Daniel P. P346
Neary, Michael P475
Neath, Gavin W366
Nebes, Bill A719
Neborak, Michael K. E275
Nebreda, Julian A45
Necessary, Scott E213
Nedelka, Gary T. A370
Neeb, Douglas M. P166
Neeb, Marc W215
Neeb, Michael T. P237
Needham, Floyd E. E275
Needham, Jeffrey R. A676
Neel, David E107
Neeld, James III E84
Neeley, Robert L. P290
Neely, Alfred G. P53
Neely, Lundy W368
Neely, Richard Jr. E272
Neff, Christopher E292
Neff, James D. E200
Neff, Michael F. P481
Negri, Carlo Alessandro Puri W267
Negri, Michael P217
Neihardt, Jonas E. A434
Neil, A. Bruce P419
Neil, Chris C. A909
Neill, George T. A175
Neill, Thomas A. A358
Neilson, Gary L. P96
Neithercut, David J. A336
Neja, Timothy M. E111
Nell, Herman P394
Nell, Ross B. A287
Nelligan, William J. A456
Nelms, Charlie P260
Nelms, David W. A598
Nelson, Bill (Time Warner) A833
Nelson, Brian C. E57
Nelson, David R. P30
Nelson, Debra A588
Nelson, Donnie P156
Nelson, Ed (Whataburger) P543
Nelson, Edward G. (Vanderbilt University Medical Center) P528
Nelson, Erin A282
Nelson, George W. A837
Nelson, Gordon B. A725
Nelson, Gregory M. (Pulte Homes) A712
Nelson, Gregory W. (Eastman Chemical) A316
Nelson, Howard A. P290
Nelson, J. Stephen E60
Nelson, Jean Delaney P447

Nelson, Jenna R. E368
Nelson, Jim P225
Nelson, John (Follett) P197
Nelson, John R. (Altria) A68
Nelson, Joni C. P259
Nelson, Kenneth D. A870
Nelson, Marilyn Carlson P114
Nelson, Micki C. P347
Nelson, Noel P418
Nelson, Peter C. E83
Nelson, Robert C. P70
Nelson, Rodney A757
Nelson, Ronald A. (Lincoln
  Electric) A535
Nelson, Ronald L. (Avis Budget) A119
Nelson, Scott W. P24
Nelson, Shanna Missett P268
Nelson, Stephen C. (Williams-
  Sonoma) A918
Nelson, Stephen E. (Greene County
  Bancorp) E180
Nelson, Steven A. (Diamond
  Offshore) A291
Nelson, Steven H. (UnitedHealth
  Group) A863
Nelson, Thomas C. (AARP) P18
Nelson, Thomas C. (New NGC) P362
Nelson, Thomas N. (BNC Bancorp) E71
Nelson, Tom (Davidson
  Companies) P159
Nelson, William C. (Blue Cross and
  Blue Shield of Kansas City) P88
Nelson, William J. (CHS) A218
Nelson, William R. (Republic
  Bancorp) E334
Nelson-Smith, John W174
Nemec, Thomas S. E174
Nemerov, Jackwyn L. A692
Nemeth, Ken P63
Nepomuceno, Lubin B. W302
Neppl, Christina M. A150
Nerbonne, Daniel J. A687
Nerenberg, Michael I. E170
Nerland, Nairn P148
Nersesian, Ron (Agilent
  Technologies) A52
Nersesian, Ronald S. (Agilent
  Technologies) A51
Nes, Helga W327
Nesbit, Michael A583
Nesbit, Robert F. P341
Nesbitt, Richard W. W89
Nesheim, Geir W93
Nesi, Victor J. E360
Ness, David A721
Nesse, Robert E. P321
Nesselrode, John M. E278
Nesser, John T. III A573
Nestegard, Susan K. A321
Nestor, Dave P182
Nestor, Michael (Port Authority of New
  York and New Jersey) P401
Nestor, Michael J. (IMPAX
  Laboratories) E212
Nesvig, Jon A371
Nethery, Regina C. A446
Nettleship, Clayborne P303
Neu, Christian W113
Neu, David W. A85
Neu, Jim P550
Neubauer, Joseph A104, P53
Neufeld, Donn E. E327
Neufeld, Jane F. P304
Neuger, Win J. A81
Neumaier, Gerhard J. E137
Neumaier, Kevin S. E137
Neuman, Sanford S. E251
Neumann, E. John A874
Neumann, Edwin A. A211
Neumann, Henry W. Jr. P282
Neumann, Horst G. W375
Neumann, Larry A162
Nevels, James E. A425
Neves, Tony P415
Neves de Carvalho, António W130

Neville-Rolfe, Lucy W349
Nevins, Kirk M. E164
Newberry, Stephen G. A519
Newbold, Michael P110
Newborn, Linda E. A280
Newcomb, Sharon P376
Newhouse, Donald E. A42, P22
Newhouse, Samuel I. Jr. A42, P22
Newhouse, Steven A42, P22
Newlands, David B. W356
Newman, Elyse A. A884
Newman, Judith A. A759
Newman, Mark P368
Newman, Michael (Sun
  Healthcare) A800
Newman, Michael D. (Office
  Depot) A646
Newman, Paul R. P173
Newman, Stephen L. (Tenet
  Healthcare) A815
Newman, Steven L. (Transocean
  Inc.) A842
Newmier, Diana M. P160
Newpol, Jonathan S. W350
Newport, Roger K. A56
Newquist, Eddie A884
Newsom, Charles R. P173
Newsome, Gary D. A417
Newsome, Laynie P533
Newsome, Mark P323
Newton, Frederick J. III A98
Newton, Leslie P465
Newton, Richard Y. III P56
Newton, W. Keith P143
Ney, Joseph A. P507
Ney, Nelson A123
Ng, Chin Hwee W318
Ng, David E407
Ng, Kian Wah W318
Ng, Peng Khian W60
Ng, Yu-Kai P496
Ngais, Nelson P374
Ngo, Nhat H. E301
Nguyen, Frank D. E226
Nguyen, Neil H. E122
Nguyen-Phuong, Lam P111
Niblock, Robert A. A543
Nicaise, Claude E28
Nicandrou, Nicolaos W273
Nicastro, Roberto W365
Nicely, Olza M. A145
Nicholas, Danielle A904
Nicholas, Peter M. A162
Nicholls, Katherine P128
Nicholls, Timothy A466
Nichols, Chris A159
Nichols, Colleen E351
Nichols, Georgianna E. A200
Nichols, Holli C. A313
Nichols, J. Larry A289
Nichols, Keith W35
Nichols, Kenneth L. A38, P20
Nichols, Michael C. (SYSCO) A806
Nichols, Michael F. (University of
  Missouri) P516
Nichols, Richard A819
Nichols, Scott G. P98
Nicholson, Bruce J. P491
Nicholson, Larry T. A744
Nicholson, Michael J. A93
Nicholson, Pamela M. P182
Nichting, Tom E112
Nick, Jeffrey M. A327
Nick, Jerry P102
Nickel, Daniel M. P293
Nickel, Daryl A. A556
Nickel, Kenneth M. A860
Nickele, Christopher J. A247
Nickels, Elizabeth A. A423
Nickerson, Douglas E. E325
Nickles, Liz E165
Nicklin, Peter A131
Nickols, David P347
Nicksa, Gary W. P98
Nicol, Jim W356

Nicol, Ron P97
Nicola, Terry A492
Nicolau, Neville F. W44
Nicolelli, Maurizio E153
Nicolet, Patrick W92
Nicoletti, Ralph J. A58
Nicolin, Magnus R. A621
Nicoll, Neil P552
Nicolson, John R. W159
Niden, Howard P319
Nides, Thomas R. A598
Niebruegge, Michael E. P319
Niederauer, Duncan L. A644
Niederhuber, John E. (National Cancer
  Institute) P350
Niederhuber, John E. (NIH) P354
Niedzielski, Vincent P. E232
Niefeld, Kenneth A. P501
Niekamp, Cynthia A. A693
Niekamp, Randall W. P152
Nielsen, Eric A. A819
Nielsen, Erika A160
Nielsen, Finn B. W47
Nielsen, Guy A243
Nielsen, Jane A672
Nielsen, Jim P367
Nielsen, Poul Hartvig W203
Nielsen, Richard E166
Nielson, Jann P329
Nielson, Joani P484
Nieman, Jan F. E326
Niemi, Ilkka W329
Niess, Jon O. E287
Niessen, Linda C. A288
Nieuwenhuys, Gerard P392
Nieves, Anthony A434
Nigam, Hemanshu A624
Nightingale, Anthony J. L. W186
Nightingale, Paul C. P254
Nightingale, Thomas A254
Nihashi, Iwao W361
Niimi, Koji W386
Niimura, Megumi W274
Niinivaara, Mikko W20
Nijhuis, Carolien W196
Nik Abdullah, Nik Muhammad
  Hanafi W317
Nikias, Chrysostomos L. P518
Nikolaev, Nikolay W212
Nila, Anthony P253
Nilekani, Nandan M. P143
Nill, Michael R. A206
Nilles, Richard A508
Nilsson, A. Kenneth E94
Nilsson, Mats W172
Nilsson, Patrik W26
Nilsson, Ronny W145
Nimis, Donald E. A142
Nine, Jerald A. Jr. E348
Ninivaggi, Angelo M. Jr. A688
Nipper, Mads W203
Nisenholtz, Martin A. A620
Nishibori, Satoru W29
Nishida, Atsutoshi W358
Nishigai, Kazuhisa W80
Nishikawa, Koichiro W163
Nishimatsu, Haruka W184
Nishimatsu, Masato W28
Nishimi, Tooru W110
Nishimura, Shigehiro W115
Nishimura, Shozo W251
Nishimura, Tatsuya W109
Nishioka, Akeshi W28
Nishioka, Hiroaki W251
Nishioka, Takashi W226
Nishitani, Yoshiharu W28
Nishiyama, Asahiko W80
Nishiyama, Paul P274
Nishizawa, Masatoshi W224
Nishizawa, Toshio W353
Nislick, David A673
Nissenberg, Brett A. E338
Nissenson, Allen R. A277
Nistal, Miguel P486
Nitschke, Ken A184, P109

Nitta, Jeffrey W. A913
Nitze, Peter A. E258
Nitzkowski, Greg M. P387
Nivet, Steve A724
Niwa, Uichiro W181
Nix, Jerry W. A389
Nix, Rudy A333
Nixon, Dwight C. A445
Nixon, Gordon M. (RBC Financial
  Group) W293
Nixon, Gordon R. (Newmont
  Mining) A623
Nizam, Akif P462
Noack, Achim W65
Nobel, Paul M. A921
Nober, Roger A177
Nobers, Jeff P17
Noble, Anne P143
Nobles, Anne A326
Nobles, John E. P105
Nocella, Andrew P. A869
Noddle, Jeffrey A803
Noe, David P328
Noe, Gregory R. A280
Noé, Peter W164
Noel, Jeffrey A915
Noethen, Todd A. A148
Nogle, Jay P225
Noguchi, Kenji W109
Nogué, François W320
Noir, Jean-Michel W270
Noji, Kunio W192
Nolan, James W. A752
Nolan, Joseph R. Jr. A639
Nolan, Mike A514, P288, W195
Nolan, Patricia W382
Nolan, Paul A571
Nolan, Philip O. E357
Nolan, Susan A675
Noland, Thomas J. Jr. A446
Nolden, Dean J. A551
Noll, Eric W. A606
Noll, Jessica P145
Nollen, Margaret R. A435
Nolop, Bruce P. A340
Nolte, Reed A624
Nomi, Shiro W339
Nomoto, Akinori W38
Nomura, Kiyoshi W80
Nomura, Takeshi W339
Nomura, Toru W181
Nonaka, Hisatsugu W358
Nonaka, Terumoto W283
Nonnengard, James B. A724
Nooitgedagt, Jan W27
Nook, Gregory E. P270
Noonan, Cathy A594
Noonan, James R. E244
Noonan, Thomas M. A266
Noonan, William J. A163
Nooyi, Indra K. A672
Norby, Ronald G. P244
Norcia, Gerardo A308
Norcross, Jeanne A788
Nordeen, Jon K. A512
Norden, Jed L. P450
Nordhoff, Henry L. E170
Nordin, Beth A218
Nordlander, Mats W329
Nordlund, D. Craig A51
Nordlund, H. Marty A909
Nordlund, Jim P133
Nordstrom, Blake W. A630
Nordstrom, Douglas A. A219
Nordstrom, Erik B. A630
Nordström, Gunilla W127
Nordstrom, James F. Jr. A630
Nordstrom, Peter E. A630
Nordyke, Greg P102
Norfleet, Robert G. A478
Norgren, Leslie P431
Norman, John S. A141
Norman, Paul (Kellogg) A498
Norman, Paul E. (Bonneville
  Power) P95

O'Leary, Joseph D. A679
O'Leary, Patrick J. A791
O'Leary, Richard A. A464
O'Leary, Thomas M. (Pepper Construction) P392
O'Leary, Tom (Wesfarmers) W378
Oleksiak, Peter B. A308
Olemaun, Forrest P54
Oler, Debra A924
Oleson, Kenneth A. P553
Oletzky, Torsten W134
Olin, John A. A408
Oliva, Harvey P73
Olivares, Jose A181
Olivares, Santiago W140
Oliveira, Ronald E193
Oliver, David (Colorado Avalanche) P139
Oliver, David M. (SUPERVALU) A803
Oliver, George R. A848
Oliver, Gregory E133
Oliver, H. Lynn A235
Oliver, Kirk R. A61
Oliver, Michael D. W207
Oliver, Robert B. A380
Oliver, Shane W43
Oliver, Walter M. A383
Olivera, Armando J. A373
Olivera, Chris A378
Olivett, John E180
Olivier, Grégoire W263
Olivier, Leon J. A632
Olivier, Roland E. E310
Olivo, Maria A843
Olivo, Roberto E166
Ollari, Frank J. P365
Olli, Amy F. A179
Ollila, Jorma W244, W295
Ollivier, Patrick W22
Ollivier, Pierre W328
Olmos Clavijo, Jesùs W128
Olmsted, Peter J. A382
Olofsson, Lars W94
O'Loughlin, William B. P87
Olowu, Caius E390
Olsem, Douglas J. P445
Olsen, Bradley P295
Olsen, Dave (Starbucks) A794
Olsen, David H. (Daimler) W111
Olsen, Davin P116
Olsen, Eric C. W201
Olsen, George Kirk P257
Olsen, John J. A587
Olsen, Karla A911
Olsen, Michael S. A492
Olsen, Stephen (Fiserv) A358
Olsen, Stephen R. (International Specialty Products) P265
Olsen-Clark, Kim P43
Olson, Charles T. E287
Olson, Don P449
Olson, Gregg M. P401
Olson, James (US Airways) A869
Olson, James D. (Harman Management) P232
Olson, Jayme D. P113
Olson, Jon A. A928
Olson, Kenneth A. E64
Olson, R. Casey A645
Olson, Robert E. A298
Olson, Tim A88
Olson, W. Kregg A97
Olson, Wallace E. E21
Olsovsky, Jo-ann M. A177
Olszewski, Veronica A. E202
Olthoff, Brent R. E193
Olvasó, Árpád W230
Olver, Richard L. W58
Olwig, Robert M. P550
Omae, Suguru W38
O'Malley, David P389
O'Malley, J. Terence P167
O'Malley, James A. A173
O'Malley, John P. P264
O'Malley, Patrick J. A764

O'Malley, Tom W372
Oman, Mark C. A906
O'Mara, Frank A. E56
O'Mealia, Harry A523
O'Meara, John-Paul W26
O'Meara, Vicki A. A686
Omidyar, Pierre M. A320
Omori, Kyota W227
Omtvedt, Craig P. A367
Onda, Yukitoshi W255
Ondricek, Quent P168
O'Neal, Clifton M. P497
O'Neal, Craft P379
O'Neal, Leslie K. A814
O'Neal, Peter J. P507
O'Neal, Rodney P164
O'Neale, Rosalyn T. A185
Oneda, Nobuyuki W326
O'Neil, Kevin W123
O'Neil, Mark F. E120
O'Neil, Scott M. A180
O'Neill, Finbarr J. A575
O'Neill, Jack A191
O'Neill, James R. A635
O'Neill, Kevin P330
O'Neill, Michael P101
O'Neill, Molly K. P173
O'Neill, Sean (Heineken) W159
O'Neill, Sean P. (ENSCO) A331
O'Neill, Terrance P. E104
O'Neill, Thomas (Adecco) W25
O'Neill, Thomas P. (Lincoln Financial Group) A537
O'Neill, Timothy (Questcor Pharmaceuticals) E328
O'Neill, Timothy G. (Cogent Communications) E98
O'Neill, Una A179
O'Neill Odum, Eileen A628
O'Neil-White, Alphonso P240
Onen, Kudret W191
Onetto, Marc A69
Ong, Vincent A144
Ongsiako, Roberto T. W302
Onifer, J. Michael E97
Onikul, Naum J. W383
Onishi, Tetsuo W312
Ono, Hirotaka W332
Ono, Mikio W266
Ono, Takao W234
Onorato, Gianni A193
Onozato, Mitsuru W354
Ontiveros Medrano, Hiram W343
Onuscheck, Michael A162
Oost, Jeff E125
Oosterveer, P.W.B. A360
Oppenheimer, Deanna W. W63
Oppenheimer, Peter A99
Oppenhoff, Michael W36
Opperman, Mary G. P148
Oprins, Michael A159
O'Quinn, Marvin P122
O'Quinn, William L. Jr. A65
Oram, John P258
Oran, Ron P102
Orand, Rebecca P135
Orange, Satia M. P43
Orazem, Ed P196
Orchart, Paul W105
Orcutt, Kim D. A192
Ordemann, William A333
Ordoñez, Francisco A. P164
O'Reilly, Chris E288
O'Reilly, David J. A215
O'Reilly, James F. A274
O'Reilly, John P. W200
O'Reilly, William M. P449
Orellana, Iván W261
Orender, Donna G. P349
Orenstein, Daniel H. E55
Orfanos, Natalia P30
Orlando, David A443
Orlando, Donald P215
Orleck, Sarah P105
Orlinsky, Ethan P310

Orlov, George M. E161
Ormond, Paul A. P311
Orndorff, Cole P306
Ornelas, Gonzalo O. P553
Ornigg, Gwendoline W46
Ornstein, Lawrence H. A427
Orona, Lonny E214
O'Rourke, Lori A539
O'Rourke, Michael P120
O'Rourke, Timothy C. P487
Orpin, Tristan B. E210
Orr, James F. III P426
Orr, John D. W89
Orr, M. Alan A421
Orr, Mark W258
Orr, Michael D. A389
Orr, Robert S. A491
Orr, Susan Packard P159
Orr, Terry L. E253
Orris, Mike W290
Orsi, Bernard P382
Orsoni, Thierry W103
Ortega, César W59
Ortega, Jennifer P411
Ortega, Steven L. P296
Ortenstone, Susan B. A324
Orth, Jerome D. E364
Orthwein, Peter B. A829
Ortigas-Wedekind, Marga E301
Ortiz, Ángel E. W261
Ortiz, Carlos P218
Ortiz, Dionisio E81
Ortiz, Steven L. E381
Ortiz-Tirado, Eduardo P440
Orvos, Adam M. P79
Osanloo, Michael A515
Osawa, Hidetoshi W255
Osborn, William A. A633
Osborne, Carol A. E130
Osborne, Earl W. E307
Osborne, Robert S. A388
Osbourn, Joseph A. A811
Osenbaugh, Jack P549
Oshanani, Edward P101
O'Shanna, Richard J. A605
O'Shaughnessy, Lizbeth S. A798
O'Shea, John A811
O'Shea, Terrence P. E43
O'Shea, William J. A185
Oshima, Akio W251
Oshima, Toshinari W184
Oskvig, O. H. P85
Osorio, António H. W59
Osowski, Henry W. P441
Ossefoort, Doug P404
Ossip, Alon W215
Ostapowicz, Phil P72
Osteraas, John D. E151
Osterberg, Don P442
Osterberg, Mark W. A55
Ostergard, Tonn M. P151
Osterhues, Robin E81
Ostermann, Michael A344
Ostertag, Thomas J. P310
Östling, Leif W374
Ostoich, Vladimir E. E16
Ostrander, Gregg A. P336
Ostrander, Jane A817
Ostrov, Gerald M. P75
Ostrowski, Hartmut W71
Ostrowski, Tad P497
O'Sullivan, Angela P496
O'Sullivan, James J. W220
O'Sullivan, Joe P284
O'Sullivan, Michael B. A737
Oswald, Gerhard W304
Oswald, Kathleen M. P244
Oswald, Robert W64
Oswalt, David S. A762
Ota, Michihiko W219
Otake, Akihito W234
Otani, Susumu W234
Otellini, Paul S. A461
Oti, James A. E219
Otis, Clarence Jr. A276

Oto, Patricia A. E303
O'Toole, Jim P338
O'Toole, Matthew H. W26
Otoshi, Takuma W227
Ott, David C. E299
Ott, Richard A. A334
Otte, Pat A589
Ottensmeyer, Patrick J. A496
Ottenstein, Robert W46
Ottenwaelter, Benoît W321
Ottersgård, Lars A606
Otting, Joseph M. A870
Otto, Frank W. E103
Otto, Kathleen P515
Otto, Martin P242
Otto, Michael W254
Otto, Thomas W217
Otty, Mark A337, W136
Oudéa, Frédéric W321
Ouimette, Bern A878
Oursin, Marc W94
Outlaw, Lucius T. Jr. P528
Outlaw, Penny E229
Outten, M. Cornelia E35
Ouwerkerk, Mike A884
Ouzts, Daniel R. E123
Overbeck, J. Ronald P399
Overbeck, Jolene M. P167
Overbeeke, H. David P26
Overcash, Darrell P316
Overman, Chuck E36
Oversohl, Christian E344
Overton, David A213
Overton, Richard S. A366
Oviatt, Jonathan J. P321
Øvrum, Margareth W327
Ovtchinnikov, Alexander E228
Owada, Yuji W190
Owczarczak, Jack A720
Owen, Angela P418
Owen, Diane B. A435
Owen, John B. (Regions Financial) A724
Owen, John F. (Avon) A121
Owen, Kathleen L. A866
Owen, Kimberly P409
Owen, Marc E. A577
Owen, Rebecca L. P135
Owenby, Johnny A. A417
Owen-Jones, Lindsay W210
Owens, B. Craig A185
Owens, B. Mitchell E265
Owens, Betsy A767
Owens, Bill (Hobby Lobby) P249
Owens, Christine M. A856
Owens, George J. A770
Owens, Jack B. A314, P175
Owens, James W. A196
Owens, Jane E. E344
Owens, Jeffrey J. P164
Owens, Richard W. A503
Owens, Robert W. A801
Owens, Stephen J. P516
Owens, Tom A223
Owens, William A. (CenturyTel) A202
Owings, Peter P166
Ownbey, Michael P269
Ownjazayeri, Vahid A771
Owsley, Larry L. P515
Oxford, Ed P71
Oxford, Randall G. P316
Oxman, Stephen A. P403
Oyinlola, H. Sola A757
Ozaki, Kiyoshi W220
Ozaki, Motoki W188
Ozaki, Yasushi W240
Ozan, Kevin M. A574
Ozawa, Satoshi W361
Ozawa, Takafumi W180
Ozdemir, Aka Gunduz W191
Ozendo, Pierre L. W335
Ozment, Tim P325
Ozzie, Ray A590

A = AMERICAN BUSINESS
E = EMERGING COMPANIES
P = PRIVATE COMPANIES
W = WORLD BUSINESS

P

Paajanen-Sainio, Ulla W329
Pace, Louis M. A141
Pace, Robert J. P434
Pacheco, Brad W. A184, P109
Pacheco, Carlos P165
Pacheco, Ivonna J. E343
Pacheco, Maximo A466
Pacheco, Steve A352
Pachomski, Jamie P188
Pachta-Reyhofen, Georg W217
Paci, Frank G. A661
Pacioni, Mark R. A593
Paciorek, Kara P21
Packard, Julie E. P159
Packard, Ronald J. E236
Packebush, Steve A511, P286
Packer, Jonathan P232
Packer, Karla L. A456
Packman, Scott P333
Padda, Bali W203
Padden, Preston A894
Padgett, Cindy M. A649
Padgett, Pamela A411
Padgett, Robert H. E199
Padovani, Roberto A714
Paeng, Jung-Kook W170
Pagano, Chuck P185
Pagano, Robert J. Jr. A474
Page, Ashley M. A452, P259
Page, Benny P339
Page, G. Ruffner Jr. P325
Page, Gregory R. A189, P113
Page, John P214
Page, Larry E. A399
Page, Malcolm V. P447
Page, Renee P182
Page, Ronald K. E309
Pagel, Keith P61
Pagendarm, William F. E177
Pagliaro, Brian P. P504
Paglione, Lucy J. W155
Pagnutti, Lou P. A337, P184
Pai, Satish A757
Paiano, Robert A413
Paige, J. M. P322
Paik, Woo Hyun W204
Pain, George H. A648
Paisley, Christopher B. E407
Paiva, Roger D. A392
Pajor, Charlie A605
Pajot, Gilles V. J. A456
Pakenham, Barry E. A61
Pakis, Val A. A546
Palacios, Consuelo P239
Palacios, Fernando J. A520
Paladini, Lapo A673
Paladino, Steven A422
Palazzolo, Vincent E109
Palen, Gregory R. A691
Palensky, Frederick J. A26
Palenzona, Fabrizio W365
Palermino, Debra A. A563, P318
Palermo, James P. A128
Paliani, Alfred P408
Paliwal, Dinesh C. A410
Palkovic, Michael W. A295
Pallot, Joseph W. E191
Pallotto, Don P217
Palm, Gregory K. A395
Palm, Risa I. P473
Palmeiro, Laura W113
Palmen, Jan E217
Palmer, Anthony J. A504
Palmer, Dan E52
Palmer, Douglas A29
Palmer, James F. (Northrop
  Grumman) A635

Palmer, James W. (Hill
  International) E195
Palmer, Jeffrey O. W215
Palmer, John (Air New Zealand) W31
Palmer, John M. (New York City Health
  and Hospitals) P363
Palmer, Kay J. A479
Palmer, Mark A. A806
Palmer, Michael D. (Texas Capital
  Bancshares) E381
Palmer, Michael E. (Empire District
  Electric) E140
Palmer, Peter E389
Palmer, Robert P110
Palmer, Steve P465
Palmer-Huggins, Deniese P477
Palmerino, Edward J. P253
Palmiere, Vince A606
Palmisano, Samuel J. A462
Palmore, David C. E375
Palmore, Roderick A. A386
Palmquist, Mark A218
Palmucci, Mark A159
Palo, Christopher E242
Palo, John P186
Paloian, John R. A742
Palombella, Vito J. E214
Palumbo, Fara P91
Palumbo, John A85
Palumbo, Thomas P537
Palus, Jean-François W270
Pambianchi, Christine M. A258
Pampel, Jochen A514, P288, W195
Panadero Illera, Gregorio W68
Panagos, Gregory S. A842
Panattoni, Lisa A737
Panayotopoulos, E. Dimitri A702
Panchenko, Jennifer P484
Panczner, Christopher S. P343
Pandit, Vikram S. A227
Pandolfi, Frances P363
Paneak, Raymond P54
Panega, Andrew B. A742
Panelas, Tom P180
Pangalos, Menelas A680
Pangle, Roger P31
Pankau, David S. P91
Pankow, Craig A. E344
Pannier, David R. A457
Pannucci, Jennifer P267
Pansa, Alessandro W142
Pant, Micky A932
Pantaleoni, Anthony D. A266
Panus, Mark P415
Paoletti, Stephen E. A405, P232
Paolini, Nonce W78
Paolucci, Mike A430
Papa, Carmelo W328
Papa, John A. A487
Papa, Joseph C. A676
Papa, Mark G. A334
Papadatos, Caroline W289
Papadellis, Randy C. P376
Papai, Mike P337
Papaleo, Michael P110
Paparazzo, Phyllis E161
Papazicos, Nicholas E67
Papermaster, Mark A99
Papiasse, Alain W75
Papich, Kim A473
Papier, Alan E140
Pappacena, Edgardo A699, P402, W271
Pappas, Callie A758
Pappas, William D. A65
Pappayliou, George S. W356
Pappert, Gerald J. A205
Paprocki, Ronald J. P518
Paradie, Terrance M. A228
Paradise, Scott E. W215
Paradiso, Dan A760
Paranicas, Dean J. A138
Paranjpe, Girish S. W379
Paravicini, Michael W388
Pardee, Charles M. A342
Pardo, Brian D. E249

Pardo, Emilio P18
Pardun, Thomas E. A912
Pareja Molina, Antonio W128
Paren, Dennis A. A65
Parent, Carolyn J. E122
Parent, Ken P396
Parent, Louise M. A77
Parenti, Marietta P44
Parham, David J. A370
Pariente, Valerie W356
Paris, Joan Marie P380
Paris de Bollardière, Charles W360
Parish, John D. P144
Park, Dennis S. A525
Park, Han-Yong W269
Park, Hyun A682
Park, John (IAC) A450
Park, John J. (Hewitt Associates) A428
Park, Ki-Hong W269
Park, Laure E. A715
Parker, Allen W144
Parker, Chuck P185
Parker, Craig P108
Parker, Dave A877
Parker, Don P436
Parker, Dorothy P518
Parker, Douglas P208
Parker, Gary R. P125
Parker, Gerhard H. E156
Parker, Herbert K. A410
Parker, James J. (Caterpillar) A196
Parker, James T. (WellPoint) A905
Parker, Jan A531
Parker, Jayne A894
Parker, John (Anglo American, National
  Grid) W44, W233
Parker, John G. (Ford Motor) A365
Parker, John R. Jr. (Coca-Cola
  Enterprises) A235
Parker, Kevin (Deutsche Bank) W119
Parker, Kevin T. (Deltek) E122
Parker, Mark G. (NIKE) A626
Parker, Martyn (Swiss Re) W335
Parker, P. W. A870
Parker, Patti A511
Parker, Richard S. P478
Parker, Robert L. Jr. E307
Parker, Ronald C. A672
Parker, Stuart A873, P527
Parker, Todd A904
Parker, W. Douglas A869
Parkes, David (BAE SYSTEMS) W58
Parkes, David (Flintco) P195
Parkes, Jacqueline P310
Parkhurst, Vance C. P380
Parkinson, Richard A. P60
Parkinson, Robert L. Jr. A131
Parks, Larry G. P37
Parks, Wendy E. P275
Parlapiano, Donna A115
Parmelee, William D. P362
Parnell, Sally A. E298
Parneros, Demos A792
Parodi, Dennis R. A74
Parr, Richard A. II P311
Parrell, Mark J. A336
Parrett, William G. P510
Parrish, Al P405
Parrish, Charles S. A821
Parrish, D. Michael A640
Parrish, Daniel P154
Parrish, Rick E146
Parro, Dolph P211
Parrot, Jonathan P151
Parry, David C. (Illinois Tool
  Works) A453
Parry, David M. (Clean Harbors) E96
Parry, Edward J. III P354
Parry, John E24
Parry, Matthew E. A909
Parry, Michael A329
Parry, Peter P68
Parry, Timothy R. A417
Parsky, Barbara J. A322
Parsons, Alex W174

Parsons, Carrie Freeman P202
Parsons, Graham T. W61
Parsons, Richard D. A227
Parsons, Robert R. P213
Parsons, Steve A731
Parsons, William E51
Parsonson, Greg A811
Parthasarathy, Rekha A458
Parthierwill, Stephan W133
Parton, Bruce W31
Partridge, Edward E. P41
Partridge, John M. (Visa Inc) A886
Partridge, John W. Jr. (NiSource) A628
Parulekar, Suneil V. A610
Parvarandeh, Pirooz A567
Parvez, Raja M. E341
Pasakarnis, Pamela E228
Pascal, Philippe W214
Pash, Thomas E311
Pasha, Ahmed A45
Pasquale, James F. P366
Pasqualetto, John G. A344
Passa, Lester M. A268
Passera, Corrado W178
Passerini, Filippo A702
Passig, Theodore O. A237
Passmore, Malinda G. A241
Paster, Howard G. W384
Pastor, Frederick Jr. A710
Pastore, Fred C. A568
Pastorelli, Adolfo W69
Pate, Lisa M. P526
Pate, Thomas R. A264
Patel, Ashvinkumar A929
Patel, Kalendu A146
Patel, Kiran M. A468
Patel, Manesh A751
Patel, Prabhuling P28
Patel, Sanjay J. A813
Patel, Sunit S. A529
Patel, Zarin W67
Pater, Krystian W268
Paterak, Joseph J. Jr. P394
Paterson, John (IBM) A462
Paterson, John (Rolls-Royce) W290
Pathela, Vivek E287
Patineau, Paula J. A66
Patkotak, Crawford P54
Patkowski, Peter P376
Patriacca, Todd B. E33
Patric, Sharon P187
Patrick, Arjay P337
Patrick, Dennis P352
Patrick, George W. A82
Patrick, Joe P333
Patrick, Margaret A. E412
Patrick, Richard A. (FHLB
  Atlanta) P189
Patrick, Richard M. (Washington
  Capitals) P537
Patrick, Shari L. P426
Patrick, Stephen C. A236
Patricot, Hubert A235
Patrone, Anthony P342
Patsalos-Fox, Michael A578, P324
Patt, William P306
Pattakos, Gregory A719
Pattee, Russell S. A697
Patten, Rose M. W61
Patterson, Barry S. P323
Patterson, Chaka A342
Patterson, Dennis M. A802
Patterson, Diane P143
Patterson, Douglas E. A678, P395
Patterson, Elaine A648
Patterson, Gavin W85
Patterson, Ian P446
Patterson, James (Sprint Nextel) A790
Patterson, James H. (Middleburg
  Financial) E268
Patterson, Kevin J. W89
Patterson, L. Leon P385
Patterson, Linda K. E246
Patterson, Neal L. A206
Patterson, Norm P486

Rizk, Emad A577
Rizzo, Daniel C. Jr. A603
Rizzo, Gregory J. E356
Rizzo, John F. E264
Rizzuto, Lee Jr. P142
Roach, Frank W. W381
Roach, Michael P80
Roach, Quentin L. A169
Roach, Randy A. P94
Roach, Stephen S. A599
Roach, Timothy P239
Roark, Stephen R. P268
Robar, Colleen M. P151
Robards, Bill P284
Robb, Charles S. P341
Robb, Curtis P. A266
Robb, Walter E. IV A916
Robbiati, Tarek W346
Robbins, Craig P138
Robbins, Donald P552
Robbins, Glenn F. P515
Robbins, Jeffrey C. E119
Robbins, Richard E. E274
Robbins, Terrence P475
Robbins, W. Clayton P376
Robbins, William T. A805
Robel, Charles J. A569
Roberge, Raymond P. A696
Roberson, Don A537
Roberti, Peter J. P342
Roberts, Beth (Carnival Corporation & plc) A193
Roberts, Beth (NBC) A613
Roberts, Bill (Belk) P79
Roberts, Bonnie P262
Roberts, Brian L. A238
Roberts, Carol L. A466
Roberts, Cecil E. Jr. P29
Roberts, Chris S. (Home BancShares) E199
Roberts, Christopher J. (Monotype) E273
Roberts, David A. (Carlisle Companies) A190
Roberts, David E. Jr. (Marathon Oil) A553
Roberts, Eric P373
Roberts, Glenn E22
Roberts, Gregory B. A518
Roberts, Howard H. Jr. P335
Roberts, J. Michael P393
Roberts, Jeremy W155
Roberts, John (TradeStation) E387
Roberts, John E. (Worthington Industries) A922
Roberts, John N. III (J.B. Hunt) A479
Roberts, Jonathan C. (CVS Caremark) A271
Roberts, Kathy F. E283
Roberts, Kenneth (Rolls-Royce) W290
Roberts, Kenneth (University of Kentucky) P514
Roberts, Kevin (Golden Horizons) P213
Roberts, Kevin J. (Publicis Groupe) W274
Roberts, Mark A. E397
Roberts, Michael P151
Roberts, Neville A146
Roberts, Peter C. A491
Roberts, Ralph J. (Comcast) A238
Roberts, Ralph V. (Worthington Industries) A922
Roberts, Rick L. P129
Roberts, Steve E215
Roberts, Susan A. P75
Roberts, Tim P129
Roberts, Trevor P129
Roberts, Wayne E329
Roberts, William C. (ViroPharma) E404
Roberts, Wyman T. A167
Roberts Myers, Tammy A533
Robertson, Andrew A650
Robertson, Bill P341
Robertson, Brian W167
Robertson, Charles P471

Robertson, Corbin J. Jr. E283
Robertson, David L. A511, P286
Robertson, Eva A706
Robertson, Greg A. (Waste Management) A899
Robertson, Gregg W. (Cyanotech) E115
Robertson, Ian W73
Robertson, James I. A471
Robertson, Julie J. A629
Robertson, Ric P19
Robertson, Russell P471
Robertson, Scott E388
Robertson, Shiela A52
Robertson, Simon W290
Robertson, Thomas S. P517
Robeson, Bradley D. A615
Robillard, Donald P255
Robinette, Leonard P255
Robini, André A370
Robins, Bernard L. A706
Robins, Brian (SunGard) P479
Robins, Brian G. (VeriSign) A880
Robinson, Alan (RWE) W296
Robinson, Allan (Allstate) A67
Robinson, Andrew S. A407
Robinson, Bill (Frank Consolidated Enterprises) P201
Robinson, Brad P382
Robinson, Brian J. A382
Robinson, Brooks A. E90
Robinson, Bruce E. A712
Robinson, C. Marie P459
Robinson, Charles F. P511
Robinson, Dave (Southeastern Freight Lines) P465
Robinson, David E. (athenahealth) E55
Robinson, Deborah C. E35
Robinson, Dorothy K. P551
Robinson, Gary E301
Robinson, Gerald W. P384
Robinson, J. Patrick A621
Robinson, Janet L. A620
Robinson, Jeffrey E. E323
Robinson, John A278
Robinson, Joseph A354
Robinson, Kenneth A. A106
Robinson, Kristi A345
Robinson, M. Trish A563, P318
Robinson, Michael R. E249
Robinson, Patricia (MediaNews) P326
Robinson, Patrick A381
Robinson, Patti (Wyle Laboratories) P550
Robinson, Paul D. (Deloitte) W114
Robinson, Paul L. (SEACOR) A763
Robinson, Paul M. (Warner Music) A897
Robinson, Peter (Innovative Solutions) E219
Robinson, Peter B. (Burger King) A176
Robinson, Phillip W. P363
Robinson, Ralph A. W155
Robinson, Richard (Scholastic) A759
Robinson, Richard S. (William Lyon Homes) P547
Robinson, Rick (Spring Air) P468
Robinson, Robin A749
Robinson, Ronald A. E26
Robinson, Scott D. (Datalink) E119
Robinson, Scott J. (Imation) A455
Robinson, Sonal P. A483
Robinson, Steve A. P131
Robinson, Susannah A181
Robinson, Tracy E311
Robinson, William (Topa Equities) P494
Robish, Annalee P125
Robison, Shane V. A429
Robitaille, Donald B. A563, P318
Roble, Mark A. P424
Robles, Josue Jr. A873, P527
Robling, Sally Genster P397
Robnett, Michael E381
Robo, James L. A372
Robuck, Richard P220

Robusto, Dino E. A219
Rocchetti, Frank W208
Rocco di Torrepadula, Giancarlo W267
Rocha, Noélia W130
Rocha, Roberto S. P418
Rochat, Christian P. P136
Roche, Cathy S. A309
Roche, John C. A407
Roche, Mark A. A367
Roche, Michael J. A67
Roché, Pascal W63
Roche, Pat W381
Roche, Robert P. Jr. A205
Roche, Vincent A91
Rochford, Lloyd T. E51
Rochlin, M. N. P26
Rochon, Donna P362
Rock, Amy Dix E114
Rock, Bradley E. A350
Rock, Rex A. Sr. P54
Rocktoff, William N. E368
Rockwell, Alicia A438
Rockwell, Joseph P165
Rockwell, Richard D. E192
Rockwood, Holly A325
Rodd, Dorothea A619, P365
Roddy, Frank (New York State Lottery) P367
Roddy, Frank J. (Swagelok) P481
Roden, Neil W294
Röder, Peter W231
Roder, W. Troy A370
Roderick, Bill A. P183
Rodero Rodero, Vicente W68
Rodesch, Jean W258
Rodewald, Brett P127
Rodgers, Daniel P200
Rodgers, Darren P239
Rodgers, Griffin P. P354
Rodgers, Mary Anne P159
Rodier, Richard W. A839
Rodin, Judith P426
Rodkin, Gary M. A244
Rodman, Leonard C. P85
Rodono, Nick P362
Rodriguez, Albert J. E389
Rodriguez, Aldo P111
Rodriguez, Antonio A372
Rodriguez, Carlos A. A114
Rodriguez, Darrell P305
Rodriguez, David A. A556
Rodríguez, Dester W261
Rodriguez, Elizabeth P516
Rodríguez, James A. E343
Rodriguez, Javier A277
Rodriguez, Julio W308
Rodriguez, Manuel A217
Rodríguez, Mariana W377
Rodríguez, Oscar A. P418
Rodriguez, Pablo P242
Rodriguez, Ramon P213
Rodriguez, Ray P521
Rodriguez, Rebecca P218
Rodriguez, Steven P127
Rodríguez Fidalgo, Juan W137
Rodríguez Inciarte, Matías W59
Rodriguez-Duran, Dora E107
Rodríguezmacedo Rivera, José L. W377
Roe, Christian (Discount Tire) P167
Roe, Christopher (CUNA Mutual) P153
Roe, Scott A883
Roeder, Susan P50
Roehling, Carl P460
Roehlk, Thomas M. A846
Roelandt, Guy W122
Roell, Stephen A. A489
Roell, Thomas L. P386
Roellig, Mark D. A563, P318
Roemer, Kurt J. P421
Roenigk, Mark E329
Roeschlein, Bill E319
Roeser, Andy P301
Roessner, Karl A. A340
Roeth, George C. A230

Roffman, Howard P305
Rogan, Brian G. A128
Rogan, Michael P. A775
Rogan, Sam A928
Rogan, Thomas I. A862
Rogers, Boyd A883
Rogers, Brent A866
Rogers, Brian C. A807
Rogers, David W. A189
Rogers, Desirée E2
Rogers, Donald I. Jr. A822
Rogers, Edward S. W289
Rogers, Ellen Sheriff A668
Rogers, James E. (Duke Energy) A309
Rogers, James P. (Eastman Chemical) A316
Rogers, James R. (PepsiAmericas Inc.) A671
Rogers, Joe W. Jr. (Waffle House) P535
Rogers, John (Davidson Companies) P159
Rogers, John (J Sainsbury) W183
Rogers, John F. W. (Goldman Sachs) A395
Rogers, Joseph (HVM) P256
Rogers, Karen A352
Rogers, Kathie M. A741
Rogers, Larry (Sinclair Oil) P456
Rogers, Lawrence J. (Sealy) A766
Rogers, Lewis P. E204
Rogers, Marc P442
Rogers, Melinda M. W289
Rogers, Michael C. (MedStar Health) P328
Rogers, Michael D. (Calpine) A184
Rogers, Nancy A. E35
Rogers, Neil W85
Rogers, Phil A44
Rogers, Ralph A. Jr. A49
Rogers, Richard R. P316
Rogers, Rosalie F. E132
Rogers, Ross E. A240
Rogers, T. Gary A530
Rogers, Tamara (Harvard University) P236
Rogers, Tamesa (NETGEAR) E287
Rogers, Terence R. P431
Rogers, William H. Jr. A802
Rogers Saenz, Christine E198
Rogich, Ed A465
Rogus, Mark S. A258
Rohack, J. James P44
Rohan, Karen S. A550
Rohde, Ellen A883
Rohde, Jørn T. W93
Rohde, Michael E. A54
Rohner, Urs W108
Rohr, Brian P. P435
Rohr, James E. A689
Rohr, Jeffrey P. A284, P162, W114
Rohr, Martin W164
Rohr-Dralle, Rondi A735
Rohre, Matt P220
Rohrkaste, Michael K. A654
Roiko, John E279
Roiss, Gerhard W253
Roizin, Philip W. P103
Roland, David P262
Roland, Mike P73
Rolandelli, Pete A890, P536
Rolapp, Brian P350
Rolett, Dan E61
Rolfe, Christopher C. A309
Rolland, Ian M. A628
Rolland, Rodger A68
Rollé, Tammy E. P275
Rollenhagen, Kevin W333
Roller, Mark C. P46
Rolley, Bernard W214
Rollier, Michel W223
Rollier, Philippe R. W201
Rollin, Kenneth B. A301
Rollings, Michael T. A563, P318
Rollins, James D. III E324
Rollins, Jonathan A418

Stanton, William P494
Stanutz, Nicholas G. A448
Stanziano, Don P446
Staple, Alan H. P420
Staples, Cathy Odom A141
Staples, David M. A788
Staples, Joseph A. E223
Stapleton, Brian P53
Stapleton, Larry C. E77
Stapley, Gregory K. E144
Stara, Friedrich W161
Starace, Francesco W129
Starcher, Diana L. A906
Starcher, John M. Jr. P120
Stark, Andrew R. A671
Stark, Arthur A139
Stark, Christoph W74
Stark, David A596
Stark, Jack H. E106
Stark, Mark A414
Stark, Ronald J. A54
Starkey, Russell B. Jr. A874
Starkey, Talia A822
Starkoff, Kathleen P377
Starks, Daniel J. A748
Starling, David L. A496
Starnes, Clarke R. III A132
Starr, Daniel B. P168
Starr, Jason E147
Starr, Judith R. P391
Starr, Loren M. A471
Starr, Rogers F. A478
Starrett, Dave A583
Stasch, Julia M. P308
Stasiewicz, David W. E19
Stasinis, Mark W. E193
Staskiel, James A. P322
Stasse, Dave P203
Stata, Ray A91
Staten, James M. P550
Staten, Reesa M. A733
Staton, Jimmy D. A628
Statton, Tim A136
Statuto, Richard J. P94
Staub, Julie A115
Staubach, Carol P96
Staubach, Roger T. A491
Stausboll, Anne A184, P109
Stautberg, Timothy E. A341
Stavros, Christopher G. A645
Stawski, Ann A654
Stead, Jerre L. E209
Stead, Tatiana A187
Steakley, Joseph N. A415
Stearns, Esther M. P304
Stebbins, Paul H. A921
Stec, Stanley A491
Stecher, Esta E. A395
Stecher, Kenneth W. A222
Stecher, Paul W. A734
Stecher, Steven M. A247
Stecklair, Richard K. E421
Steed, Richard E. A734
Steel, Gary W20
Steele, C. David A105
Steele, Elisa A929
Steele, Gavin W206
Steele, Gordon A621
Steele, John J. (Werner
  Enterprises) A909
Steele, John M. (HCA) A415, P237
Steele, Milton A362
Steele, Patrick S. P164
Steele, Reginald N. P212
Steele, Robert A. (Procter &
  Gamble) A702
Steele, Robert B. (Polycom) E318
Steele, S. K. P26
Steele, Skip P158
Steele, Tammy S. P143
Steeneck, Craig D. P397
Steenrod, Mitch D. P396
Steer, Robert L. A762
Steere, William C. Jr. A680
Steeves, Frank L. A330

Stefanski, Marc A. E382
Steffen, Pierre W32
Steffens, Greg A. E354
Steffes, Gene P523
Steffey, Ken E155
Stegeman, John A. W381
Steier, Larry J. P29
Steiger, Edward A. E421
Steigerwald, Patricia A. E237
Stein, Bradley A739
Stein, Darrell W218
Stein, Isaac E259
Stein, J. C. A427
Stein, Jay A. A438
Stein, Ken A162
Stein, Kevin M. A697
Stein, Laura A230
Stein, Mark J. A450
Stein, Martin E357
Stein, Peter D. A. P513
Stein, Richard M. E76
Steinberg, Christine P201
Steinberg, Gregory M. A80
Steinberg, Julian M. A546
Steinberg, Stuart M. P439
Steinbrenner, Henry G. P368
Steinbrenner, Jessica P368
Steinbrenner, Joan P368
Steinbrink, Jerry P145
Steinebach, Lothar W161
Steiner, Curt P377
Steiner, David P. A899
Steiner, Eva P166
Steiner, Gerald A. A596
Steiner, Kevin P38
Steiner, Lisa P. A173
Steiner, Robert P38
Steinhafel, Art P65
Steinhafel, Gregg W. A808
Steinhorn, Jeff L. A427
Steinkamp, Mark E118
Steinke, Bruce A73
Steinkrauss, Mark A. A812, A858
Steinmetz, Mike A552
Steinour, Stephen D. A448
Steinway, Paul R. P282
Stella, Giovanni W340
Stella, L. Joseph III E100
Stellato, John P231
Stellato, Louis E. A772
Stellio, Vincent P502
Stellmon, John M. P417
Stelly, Donald D. E248
Stelly, Teri S. E270
Stelter, Daniel P97
Stempien, Robert L. P73
Stene, Peter P340
Stenger, Edward J. A273
Stenholt, Colleen J. P429
Sténson, Henry W135
Stensrud, Sara P453
Stephan, Michael J. A115
Stephan, Sharon P516
Stephen, Craig A. A217
Stephens, Bryan P37
Stephens, Gary E297
Stephens, James T. P177
Stephens, Jay B. A722
Stephens, John J. A111
Stephens, Patrick A. A857
Stephens, Randy P330
Stephens, Richard D. A157
Stephens, Shane P471
Stephens, Thomas G. A388, P206
Stephens, Warren A. P474
Stephenson, Kent R. A313
Stephenson, Randall (Boy Scouts of
  America) P98
Stephenson, Randall L. (AT&T) A111
Stephenson, Scott G. E401
Stepp, Ann M. E256
Stepp, Kay P405
Sterbenz, Douglas R. A911
Steris, Jason W. E407
Sterk, Betsy E36

Sterkenburg, Albert A288
Sterling, Donald T. P301
Sterling, Tim A820
Stern, Carl W. P97
Stern, Colin D. A211
Stern, David J. P349
Stern, Gary H. P191
Stern, Jacques W22
Stern, James F. A95
Stern, John A855
Stern, Marc I. W321
Stern, Menachem E91
Stern, Michael A596
Stern, Milford L. P384
Stern, Rachel E153
Stern, Rick A705
Stern, Robert E. A158
Stern, Ron P54
Stern, William A560, E47
Sternad, Ken A856
Sternberg, Elliot B. P432
Sternberg, Paul P143
Sternblitz, David H. A933
Sternschein, Evan A297
Sterrett, Stephen E. A774
Stetz, Gordon M. Jr. A571
Steuert, D. Michael A360
Steuterman, James M. A837
Stevens, Anne L. A194
Stevens, Ben W83
Stevens, Charles R. A909
Stevens, David W. E139
Stevens, Donald B. A659
Stevens, Ellen P100
Stevens, Eric R. P206
Stevens, Jonathan J. P124
Stevens, Matthew A. A316
Stevens, Michael J. (Whiting
  Petroleum) E415
Stevens, Mike (New York Giants) P364
Stevens, Robert J. A541
Stevens, Roberta A. P43
Stevens, Scot P528
Stevens, Simon A863
Stevens, Thomas C. A503
Stevens, William H. (Sonabank) E354
Stevens, William J. (Genuine
  Parts) A389
Stevenson, Robert L. P430
Stewan, Dietmar W37
Steward, David L. P550
Steward, Elaine Weddington P98
Steward, Larry E. A308
Stewart, Darren E406
Stewart, Dwayne T. E73
Stewart, Ian M. P268
Stewart, James W. A149
Stewart, Jason A450
Stewart, John D. (Finmeccanica) W142
Stewart, Jonathan T. (Martin Marietta
  Materials) A561
Stewart, Julia A. A294
Stewart, Kenneth S. A322
Stewart, Kyle E257
Stewart, Laurie K. A53
Stewart, Marta R. (Norfolk
  Southern) A631
Stewart, Martha (Martha Stewart
  Living) A560
Stewart, Michael (McKinsey &
  Company) A578
Stewart, Michael K. (Marathon
  Oil) A553
Stewart, Michael R. (Perrigo) A676
Stewart, Paul W52
Stewart, Peter G. E236
Stewart, Raymond P256
Stewart, Shelley Jr. A848
Stewart, Stacey D. P510
Stewart, Thomas J. P451
Stewart, Timothy M. A712
Steyn, David A. P36
Stice, J. Michael A214
Stickler, Randall G. A448
Stickney, Alexander R. P150

Stiefel, Charles W. W157
Stiehl, William G. A397
Stiffler, Jack E389
Stigler, John N. P403
Stiles, Mark W. A844
Still, Debra W. A712
Still, Jay P. A685
Stiller, Robert P. E179
Stine, Robert A. E378
Stinneford, Mark P91
Stinnett, Donald W. A415, P237
Stinnett, Wayne D. A200
Stinson, Kenneth E. A678, P395
Stinson, Mark A839
Stiritz, William P. A720
Stirling, Steve P243
Stisser, Eric P433
Stith, Brad P401
Stitt, Skip A48
Stitzer, H. Todd W88
Stitzlein, Jim P449
Stobb, Patrick A398
Stock, Alan W. A223
Stock, Keith A830
Stockdale, Bryan K. A730
Stockdale, Caroline A897
Stocker, Michael A. P363
Stocker, Russell W308
Stocking, Richard P482
Stockslager, Mark J. E364
Stockton, Bryan G. A566
Stockton, David J. P191
Stockton, Robert W. E300
Stockwell, Ashley W371
Stockwell, Meri A188
Stoddard, Paul P240
Stoddart, Vanessa W31
Stoddart, William J. A654
Stodder, Mark W. C. E128
Stoe, George P. A922
Stoeckel, Emily Heisley P243
Stoeckel, Howard B. P538
Stoeckert, George I. A311
Stoelk, Thomas W. E365
Stoering, Mark A925
Stoessl, Michael A. A255
Stoffel, Robert E. A856
Stoffels, Paul A487
Stohr, Stan P429
Stokes, Celia E236
Stokes, Charles D. P330
Stokes, Gary A. E293
Stokes, Gemma W233
Stokes, Mark W207
Stokes, Nick A. P93
Stokes, Patrick P100
Stokes, Tom P498
Stolar, Kathleen S. A474
Stolarczyk, Mark A588
Stolfi, Maria A. E311
Stoll, Mark R. A605
Stolle, John R. P332
Stoller, Stuart P. A620
Stoller, William H. P186
Stolzar, Karen S. E349
Stone, Aaron J. P39
Stone, Carolyn J. A313
Stone, David M. P141
Stone, Donald R. E306
Stone, Douglas M. A820
Stone, Erin E146
Stone, Frank A141
Stone, Gary (Northwest Pipe) E293
Stone, Gary B. (Univision) P521
Stone, Jeffrey I. (Brasfield &
  Gorrie) P100
Stone, Jeffrey M. (Progress
  Energy) A703
Stone, Jim P80
Stone, Larry D. A543
Stone, Marc J. (TradeStation) E388
Stone, Mark (Sacramento Kings) P432
Stone, Mark A. (Zale) A933
Stone, Rafael P253

Sutherland, L. Frederick A104, P53
Sutherland, Mark A546
Sutherland, Peter D. W79
Sutherlin, Michael W. A492
Suto, Margaret M. A608
Sutphin, Eric N. A448
Sutten, Mike A739
Sutter, Fred A. A190
Sutter, Terry A. A392
Sutton, Elisabeth P287
Sutton, Mark S. A466
Suver, Susan M. A859
Suwa, Kyoichi W237
Suzman, Mark P83
Suzuki, Eiichi W239
Suzuki, Hiroyuki W246
Suzuki, Kazuo W332
Suzuki, Masatoshi W251
Suzuki, Osamu W332
Suzuki, Takeo W339
Suzuki, Toshihiro W332
Suzuki, Yasuo W192
Suzuki, Yozo W97
Suzuki, Yuji W108
Svanberg, Carl-Henric W79, W135
Svanholm, Poul J. W47
Svärd, Jan W35
Svelto, Annachiara W267
Svensson, Leif W145
Svitil, Torene P19
Svoboda, Frank M. A838
Svoboda, Jeffrey A. E415
Swaback, Ray P327
Swackhamer, Merlin L. P441
Swafford, Preston D. A818, P488
Swain, Kathleen A67
Swaine, Richard P546
Swainson, John A. C. A179
Swallow, John E. E307
Swallow, Michael P484
Swan, Bill P61
Swan, Mara E. A552
Swan, Meghan P278
Swan, Peter A. P421
Swan, Robert H. A320
Swann, Paul E224
Swansen, Russell W. P491
Swanson, Al (Plains All American
   Pipeline) A687
Swanson, Al (U.S. Foodservice) P523
Swanson, David S. P538
Swanson, Eric A. A486
Swanson, Luke W257
Swanson, Stephen L. P41
Swanson, Terry P124
Swanson, William H. A722
Swant, Steven G. P208
Swantee, Olaf W148
Swartz, Brian L. A98
Swartz, Jeffrey B. A832
Swartz, Richard P253
Swartz, Sidney W. A832
Swartz, Steven R. A420, P241
Swartzman, Lisa R. W155, W208
Sweasy, Neil A. A203
Sweatt, Brice P266
Swedowski, Russell D. P43
Sweeney, Alexandra P. A933
Sweeney, Anne M. A33, A894
Sweeney, Don W36
Sweeney, Edward J. A610
Sweeney, Gregory B. P103
Sweeney, Joseph J. A102
Sweeney, Kelly P268
Sweeney, Timothy M. P299
Sweeny, Jack C. A814
Sweere, Lori K. A863
Sweers, Nicholas A718
Sweet, Bruce E289
Sweet, James M. A621
Sweetenham, Paul A836
Sweetman, Mary E. A377
Sweetnam, James E. A273
Sweizer, James M. E40
Swellie, Robert C. A79

Sweney, Elizabeth H. A480
Swenning, J. P514
Swenson, Douglas G. P96
Swenson, Michael L. A926
Swent, James W. III A331
Swetich, Dan W. A604
Swidarski, Thomas W. A292
Swider, John P44
Swiech, Randal P460
Swienton, Gregory T. A743
Swift, Charles W. E62
Swift, David L. P215
Swift, Randy P535
Swift, Stephen T. P240
Swiger, Andrew P. A347
Swihart, Dave A760
Swinburn, Peter A594
Swindal, Jennifer Steinbrenner P368
Swinson, Gwynn P173
Swint, Greg P226
Swint, Sean E411
Swisher, Stephen R. A133
Switzer, James D. A330
Swoboda, Charles M. E110
Swyers, Philip P434
Sykes, Edward A. E304
Sykes, Rebecca P120
Sykes, Russell P460
Sylvester, David C. A798
Symonds, Jonathan R. W248
Synek, Chris A728
Synowicki, Robert E. Jr. A909
Syracuse, Raymond P362
Szabados, Michael E289
Szabo, John E43
Szalay, Maria A. E236
Szczepan, Gregory A. A105
Szczesny, Jeffrey D. P411
Szczupak, David T. A915
Szefel, Dennis J. P161
Szela, Marty A. A31
Szenczy, Catherine P328
Szews, Charles L. A654
Szilagyi, Gary L. E56
Szkutak, Thomas A. A69
Szlauderbach, Stanley J. P181
Sznewajs, John G. A562
Szomjassy, Michael A. P128
Szopinski, Jim P339
Szot, Michael R. A96
Szteinbaum, Sam A429
Sztykiel, John E. A355
Szuch, John S. A354
Szucs, Loretto Dennis E47
Szulc, Jaime Cohen A530
Szulik, Matthew J. E332
Szum, John T. P112
Szygenda, Ralph J. A388
Szyman, Catherine M. A581
Szymanczyk, Michael E. A68
Szymanski, Conrad P76
Szymanski, Mary D. P499

T

Taaffe, Paul W384
Tabak, Natan A890, P536
Tabb, Robert P. A321
Taber, Terry R. A318
Tabolt, David A122
Tabor, Jim A55
Tachibana, Teiji W361
Tachikake, Satoshi W220
Tachner, Adam H. E56
Tacka, David W. A425
Tada, Hitoshi W246
Tadaki, Yoshihiro W180
Taeuber, Annette W211
Taff, Michael S. A573
Taft, Terry P379
Taggarsi, Shyam A336
Taggart, John M. E261
Taggart, Richard G. P36
Tagliaferro, Maria A91

Taglietti, Marco A366
Tagmyer, William R. E293
Tague, John P. A850
Tagye, Stephanie J. E257
Tai, Ichiro W358
Tai, Jackson P. P103
Tai, Luther A249
Takagi, Akinori W97
Takagi, Norihiko W188
Takagi, Shigeru W165
Takahashi, Grégory W322
Takahashi, Koki W80
Takahashi, Minoru W339
Takahashi, Motoki W386
Takahashi, Naoya W163
Takahashi, Shoji W314
Takahashi, Tadao W243
Takahashi, Tatsuo W188
Takahashi, Toru W150
Takahashi, Toshio W150
Takahashi, Yoshiaki W110
Takamori, Tatsuomi W314
Takanami, Koichi W109
Takashige, Mitsuo W314
Takashima, Susumu W97
Takashima, Tatsuyoshi W116, W274
Takasu, Tadashi W97
Takata, Hisashi W283
Takayanagi, Koji W181
Takebuchi, Hiroki W354
Takeda, Genyo W239
Takeda, Munetaka W185
Takeda, Yasuo W241
Takei, Masaru W353
Takeichi, Kouichi W97
Takekuro, Ichiro W353
Takemura, Kaoru W399
Takenaka, Hiroshi W354
Takenaka, Tetsuya W184
Takeuchi, Hideshi W224
Takeuchi, Kazuo W227
Takeuchi, Tatsuo W266
Talamantes, Patrick J. A570
Talán, Mónica P521
Talbert, Marc E. P398
Talbert, Robin P18
Tali, Pietro Franco W131
Tallett-Williams, Michael A537
Talley, Emet C. P46
Talley, Joseph J. P42
Talling-Smith, Simon W82
Talwalkar, Abhijit Y. A545
Talwar, Vikram E150
Tam, Michael A. A159
Tamaddon, Sina A99
Tamagnini, Andrea W178
Tamai, Toshiyuki P108
Tamakoshi, Ryosuke W227
Tamaru, Takuya W386
Tamba, Toshihiro W181
Tambakis, John P152
Tamberlane, John E347
Tamburi, Carlo W129
Tamke, George W. P136
Tammivuori, Jyrki W329
Tamura, Minoru W332
Tan, Benjamin P496
Tan, Chik Quee W318
Tan, Cynara P402
Tan, Ethel M. L. W318
Tan, Larry A823
Tan, Millie P410
Tan, Mimi E399
Tan, Nancy A455
Tan, Pee Teck W318
Tan, Peter (Burger King) A176
Tan, Peter B. H. (Flextronics) W145
Tan, Victor P253
Tan, William K.W. (Universal Power
   Group) E399
Tan, William S. K. (Singapore
   Airlines) W318
Tanabe, Charles Y. P298
Tanabe, Eiichi W224
Tanabe, Hiroyuki W324

Tanaka, Akihito W28
Tanaka, Hiroshi W246
Tanaka, Masakazu W115
Tanaka, Norio W283
Tanaka, Seiichi W228
Tanaka, Takashi W251
Tanaka, Toshizo W90
Tancula, James E. P319
Tandon, Atul P510
Tandon, Sirjang L. A476
Tandy, Bradley P. P84
Tandy, Karen P. A600
Tang, Chengjian W319
Tang, Darin P508
Tang, Edmund E127
Tang, Francis E127
Tang, Paul C. P105
Tang, Sharon E19
Tangeman, Amy J. A344
Tangney, Michael J. A236
Tangoren, Mehmet A490
Tangry, Mark J. E275
Tanigawa, Kazuo W358
Taniguchi, Nobuyuki W312
Taniguchi, Shinichi (Nippon
   Steel) W241
Taniguchi, Shinichi (Sojitz) W324
Tank, Andrew P143
Tank, William M. Jr. E326
Tank Uzun, Ali W191
Tannenbaum, Richard E405
Tanner, Bruce L. A541
Tanner, David A. (ContiGroup) P146
Tanner, David W. (Fortune
   Brands) A367
Tanner, Deborah L. A261
Tanner, Glenn E. E231
Tanner, Gregg A. A278
Tanner, Harold P148
Tanous, Will A897
Tansey, Ellen A808
Tanski, Ronald J. A608
Tansky, Burton M. P359
Tantaquidgeon Zobel, Melissa P342
Tanzberger, Eric D. A770
Tanzer, Martin S. A868
Tapia, Andrés A428
Tapley, Kent P315
Taraborrelli, Angelo W131
Tarantino, Joseph A. A733
Tarapore, Kairus K. P127
Tardanico, Susan M. A825
Tarde, Merv P265
Tardiff, Eric E170
Targhetta, Javier A375
Taride, Michel A426
Tarino, Gary E. A114
Tarkoff, Robert M. A41
Taron, Florence W258
Tarpey, Kenneth E102
Tarr, Jeffrey R. E209
Tarr, Mark J. A419
Tarshis, Andrew E205
Tartaglia, Vince P58
Tasbihgou, Saeed E239
Tashjian, Lee C. A360
Tashma, Lauren S. A367
Tassopoulos, Timothy P. P131
Tata, Ratan N. W336
Tatara, Rich A813
Tataseo, Frank A. A230
Tate, Brenda R. A887
Tate, Christian E130
Tate, G. Truett A207
Tate, Leland E. E57
Tate, Nicola W174
Tate, Paul H. E24
Tate, Wendy P465
Tatelman, Michael A282
Taten, Bruce M. A255
Tatsuta, Yasuto W220
Tattersall, Alan P. E175
Tattersfield, John E180
Tatum, Steve A511, P286
Taub, Stephen A547, P307

Thompson, Mark (DPR Construction) P170
Thompson, Mark E. (Huntington Bancshares) A448
Thompson, Martin W382
Thompson, Matthew A. (Adobe Systems) A41
Thompson, Matthew D. (American CareSource) E35
Thompson, Michael (New Orleans Hornets) P362
Thompson, Michael L. (Cintas) A225
Thompson, Neil A236
Thompson, Norman W31
Thompson, O. L. P464
Thompson, Randy P202
Thompson, Richard L. A527
Thompson, Robert (Fox Entertainment) A371
Thompson, Roger A276
Thompson, Ronald L. A830, P492
Thompson, Rosalind A484
Thompson, Sarah W356
Thompson, Scott A320
Thompson, Ted A401
Thompson, Timothy M. W357
Thompson, Todd A795
Thompson, Tommy G. E23
Thompson, Virgil D. E328
Thompson, Wade F. B. A829
Thompson, William P. (SSM Health Care) P469
Thoms, Jeffrey P35
Thomsen, Mads Krogsgaard W249
Thomson, Caroline W67
Thomson, David K. R. W350
Thomson, Glen P130
Thomson, Michael J. A801
Thomson, Roger F. A167
Thomson, William E103
Thone, William J. P31
Thorburn, Andrew W232
Thoresen, Otto W27
Thorley, Trevor E42
Thormahlen, Stephen C. A689
Thormahlen, Sven W113
Thormodsgard, Diane L. A870
Thorn, Rod P362
Thorn, Stuart P466
Thornbrugh, Mike P409
Thornburg, Eric W. E104
Thornburg, Kirk A55
Thorne, Grant W285
Thorne, James W. E235
Thorne, Michael P551
Thorneman, Michael P68
Thornton, Bert P535
Thornton, Bodley P. A291
Thornton, Craig W86
Thornton, David H. A375
Thornton, Donna P430
Thornton, Matt P490
Thornton, Robert M. Jr. E364
Thornton, Roland R. A718
Thornton, Tom P34
Thorpe, Gregory P379
Thorson, Alan G. P41
Thouret, Claude G. Jr. E135
Thrasher, Kelly P535
Thrasher, Rex C. A329
Thresher, Mark R. A611, P356
Thriffiley, Donald A. Jr. A359
Thrope, Susan A. A619, P365
Thrower, Baron A532, P299
Thueringer, Bob P137
Thulin, Inge G. A26
Thunstrom, Jason E249
Thurber, Lynn C. A491
Thurgood, Keith L. P56
Thurin Rollin, Sara P300
Thurlow, Aaron A610
Thurman, Paul E200
Thurman, Randy H. E87
Thurman, Ronald W. A124
Thurow, Norman P553

Thurston, Mark E218
Thwaites, Christian W. P354
Thygesen, Gert R. E46
Thygesen, Jerome E. A664
Thygesen, Mikael A774
Tiano, Linda V. A418
Tibbils, Kent P58
Tible, Phillippe W189
Tiedemann, Jay P266
Tiedy, Mike A795
Tiefel, William R. A192
Tiemann, Michael E332
Tienor, Lawrence J. E282
Tiernan, Thomas J. E370
Tierney, Brian X. A75
Tierney, Cindy B. A134
Tierney, John F. A294
Tierney, Kate A855
Tierno, Anthony F. P326
Tiesenga, Donald P63
Tietjen, James R. A186
Tietjen, Kurt E383
Tiger, George E148
Tigno, Christopher B. E22
Tikkas, Pantelis W160
Tilden, Bradley D. A57
Tilearcio, Peter P217
Tilevitz, Harris Z. A775, P459
Tilger, Bill P477
Tilghman, Richard H. P392
Tillema, Dowe A364
Tillerson, Rex W. A347, P98
Tilley, Daniel T. P137
Tilley, Glenn W. A884
Tilley, Thomas G. Jr. A377
Tillinghast, Marilyn P110
Tillman, Audrey Boone A49
Tillman, Krista S. P373
Tillman-Taylor, Susan P119
Tillotson, Curt P137
Tilly, Gil C. A88
Tilton, Glenn F. A850
Timanus, H. E. Jr. E324
Timberlake, Edgar F. P484
Timberman, Terri L. A170
Timbie, Mark T. A571
Timken, Ward J. Jr. A835
Timko, Thomas S. P164
Timm, Dan P277
Timm, David W. A302
Timm, Laura A164
Timmel, Timothy L. A222
Timmer, John F. P25
Timmerman, José R. A846
Timmerman, William B. A755
Timmermans, Koos W177
Timmermans, Ted T. A917
Timmins, Paul A904
Timmons, James T. A526
Tindall, Robert J. P108
Ting, Way A660
Tinklepaugh, Williams C. A278
Tinsman, Garrett P437
Tippl, Thomas A38
Tipsord, Michael L. A796, P472
Tira, Peter A570
Tirva, Robert L. A171
Tisch, Andrew H. A542, E236
Tisch, James S. A291, A542
Tisch, Jonathan M. (Loews) A542
Tisch, Jonathan M. (New York Giants) P364
Tisch, Steven P364
Tisdale, T. Mark E96
Tishman, Daniel R. P494
Tison, Ben P410
Tisthammer, Ann E335
Tite, Lynda L. E157
Titlebaum, Mark S. A150
Titzkowski, Tom P523
Titzman, Donna M. A877
Tizatto, Mariângela M. W260
Tjaden, Kurt A436
Tjian, Robert P253
Toben, Edmund D. A236

Tobias, Maura C. P204
Tobias, Paul D. E256
Tobin, Dan A920
Tobin, Glenn P. E108
Tobin, James J. Sr. W215
Tobison, Gary L. A367
Toburen, Rick P465
Tochner, Ira P553
Toczydlowski, Greg A843
Tod, Mike W31
Todaro, Sal A719
Todd, Aaron D. E24
Todd, Bosworth M. P543
Todd, Charles T. Jr. E67
Todd, Christopher R. P289
Todd, Craig E129
Todd, Joseph P404
Todd, Lee T. Jr. P514
Todd, Paul M. A840
Todd, Phil P237
Todd, William K. Jr. A811
Todenhöfer, Tilman W286
Todman, Michael A. A915
Todoroff, Christopher A446
Todorov, Kostadin P125
Todorov, Pierre W22
Toelle, Michael A218
Toevs, Alden W105
Toews, Timothy A646
Toft, Paul E61
Tognazzini, Paul E193
Togneri, Gabriel B. A682
Toida, Kazuhiko W243
Toida, Takashi W109
Tokuda, Hiromi W115
Toland, Marv P177
Toland, Theresa P226
Tolbert, Kirk L. A359
Toledano, Gabrielle A325
Toll, Bruce E. A837
Toll, Robert I. A837
Tolle, Rolf W205
Tolle, Susan E248
Tollerson, Ernest P335
Tollett, Leland E. A849
Tolliver, Joan L. E90
Tolot, Jérôme W154
Tolstedt, Carrie L. A906
Tom, Eric A465
Tom, Laura E51
Toma, Shigeki W180
Tomas, Veneranda M. W302
Tomasky, Susan A76
Tomczyk, Fredric J. A810
Tomé, Carol B. A439
Tomino, Naoki W237
Tomita, Kimio W243
Tomita, Tatsuo W151
Tomita, Tetsuji W197
Tomlin, John E319
Tomlinson, Philip W. A840
Tommasi, Eugene W. P209
Tommasini, Bernard A500
Tomnitz, Donald J. A306
Tompkins, Cathlyn L. A214
Tompkins, Mark P480
Tompkins, P. Kelly A740
Tomshack, James C. A676
Tomsic, Larry P38
Tonelli, Louis W215
Toner, Tom E142
Tonetti, Robert J. P190
Tong, Carlson A514, W194
Tong, Jeffrey K. E214
Tong, Vincent A928
Tongson, Timothy J. A247
Tonne, Gene L. E52
Tonnel, David A842
Tonnesen, Mark A569
Tonoike, Tohru A49
Tonyan, Peter A921
Toohey, Peg P300
Tooker, Jean E. P469
Tookey, Tim J. W. W207
Toole, John J. A393

Toombs, Ross E140
Toomey, Mary W41
Tootle, John S. E83
Topazi, Anthony J. A784
Topel, Bob P199
Topham, H. Scott A566
Topor, Steve P508
Toppe, Ardee P215
Topper, Jay E339
Topper, William L. P215
Toppeta, William J. A586
Topping, Scott E. A786
Torgerson, Francis V. P254
Torgerson, William T. A668
Toriyama, Eiichi W199
Tornaghi, Frank A. A928
Toro, Rafael P218
Torok, Kenneth A. A856
Torp Laursen, Søren W203
Torphy, Theodore J. A487
Torres, John D. A527
Torres, Kathleen P310
Torres, Margaret A. P193
Torres, Tomás E. A343
Torres-Llosa, Eduardo W68
Torsone, Johnna G. A686
Torto, Raymond A198
Tortorella, Anthony A665
Tortorici, Frank P143
Torwirt, Arthur E24
Tosches, Pete P450
Toschi Finn, Linda A630
Tosé, Maurice B. E379
Toshav, Effie P548
Tostivin, Jean-Claude W78
Toub, Christopher M. P36
Touhey, Michael E. A552
Toups, Gregory P. E300
Toups, Roland M. P505
Toups, Stephen M. P505
Tousley, Mike P542
Touyama, Masahiko W110
Tower, Michael J. P64
Towey, Gael A560
Towle, Steven J. A307
Towler, Susan B. P88
Towles, Kelli P260
Townsend, Adam A199
Townsend, Charles H. A42, P22
Townsend, James G. A437, E199
Townsend, Jeffrey A. A206
Townsend, John P124
Townsend, Kent G. E86
Townsend, Lisa P260
Townsend, Mark A. A348
Townsend, Michael J. P366
Townsend, Pegeen P328
Townsend, Ron P74
Townsley, John E. E155
Toya, Hiromichi W38
Toyoda, Akio W361
Toyoda, Kanshiro W33
Toyoda, Shoichiro W361
Toyomasu, Shunichi W243
Toyotani, Akihiko W198
Trachtenberg, Mike P217
Tracy, Christopher E47
Tracy, Dick P168
Tracy, James P. (Hi-Tech Pharmacal) E196
Tracy, James W. (Dot Foods) P168
Tracy, James W. (University of Kentucky) P514
Tracy, Joe P168
Tracy, John J. (Boeing) A157
Tracy, John M. (Dot Foods) P168
Tracy, Patrick F. P168
Tracy, Peggy L. A164
Tracy, Renee P323
Trad, Jeffry J. E200
Traficant, James A. A411
Trager, A. Scott E334
Trager, Bernard M. E334
Trager, Steven E. E334
Trahan, Travis E80

Wendt, Roderick C. P271
Wenger, Brian D. A671
Wenger, Stefan L. E340
Wenig, Devin N. W350
Wenker, Kristen S. A386
Wenner, Jim P452
Wenning, Werner W65
Wennlund, Lloyd A. A633
Wensel, Deborah A. E177
Wentworth, Carol P501
Wentworth, Timothy C. A580
Wenz, Ray P553
Wenzel, Gregory G. P96
Werbelow, Jim M. P418
Werdann, Michael A. E287
Werlein, Ewing Jr. P332
Werlen, Thomas W248
Wermers, Markus A351
Werner, Clarence L. A909
Werner, David P80
Werner, Gary L. A909
Werner, Gregory L. A909
Werner, Jordan P159
Werner, Kevin A. A880
Werner, Thomas C. P98
Werner, Tony G. A238
Wernli, Robert Jr. E74
Wertheim, Ram D. A568
Wertheizer, Gideon E91
Werthman, Ronald J. P274
Wesley, Rosalyn D. A367
Wessler, Alan P335
Wesson, Bruce F. E261
West, David (CommVault) E101
West, David E. (Rent-A-Center) A726
West, David J. (Hershey) A425
West, Elena A733
West, George E. Jr. A658
West, Henry J. P313
West, Marc (Group Health Cooperative (Puget Sound)) P226
West, Mark L. (Raven Industries) E331
West, Mary E. (Datalink) E119
West, Mary Beth (Kraft Foods) A515
West, P. G. P82
West, Richard P. P107
West, Roderick K. A332
West, Ronald A. E245
West, Teresa L. A823
West, Terry R. P535
West, Todd P478
Westberg, Michael E193
Westbrock, Leon E. A218
Westbrook, Greg W145
Westbrook, Maureen P. E104
Westbrook, Sandra J. P409
Westcott, Grant C. W89
Westenfield, Denise M. E119
Wester, Harald J. W141
Westerdahl, Joyce A653
Westerfield, James D. E244
Westerlund, David A. A126
Western, James R. Jr. A659
Westfall, Kevin P. A115
Westfall, Lynn D. A821
Westh, Joakim W135
Westin, David A33
Westlake, W. James W293
Weston, Charles M. A920
Weston, Chris W100
Weston, David W44
Weston, Galen G. W208
Weston, Graham M. E329
Weston, W.G. Galen W155
Weston-Webb, Andy A557, P315
Westphal, Mark W. P336
Westwell, Steve W79
Wetterau, Mark S. P214
Wetzel, Joseph M. A315
Wevik, Stuart E69
Wexler, Alan M. E344
Wexler, Lawrence S. P370
Wexler, Raymond P. A388, P206
Wexner, Leslie H. A533, P377
Wey, Mike P472

Weyandt, Paul J. A496
Weyers, Larry L. A401
Weyhrich, Todd P105
Weyman, Amy A449
Weymouth, Katharine A898
Weynand, Jim A854
Whalen, David (Memorial Hermann Healthcare) P330
Whalen, David (Palm, Inc.) A660
Whalen, Frank E206
Whalen, Jerry W. A872
Whalen, Kevin P394
Whaley, Patricia P413
Whaley, Ruth M. A568
Whalley, Tom A897
Wharton, Shane P303
Whatley, James W. A153
Wheat, William W. A306
Wheatley, Arthur E. A168
Wheeland, Dan P354
Wheeler, Arnold F. P72
Wheeler, Bradley C. P260
Wheeler, E. Valjean P267
Wheeler, Michael J. A631
Wheeler, Penny Ann P37
Wheeler, Robert A829
Wheeler, Steven B. (Booz) P96
Wheeler, Steven M. (Pinnacle West) A684
Wheeler, William J. A586
Wheelock, Pamela P341
Whelan, Daniel E146
Whelan, Karen M. L. A865
Whelan, Michael L. P431
Whelan, William F. E100
Whelley, Eileen G. A413
Whelton, Paul K. P304
Whetstine, Michael J. A678
Whetstone, Rachel A399
Whetstone, Steven P191
Whichard, Marcie P394
Whichard, T.M. III A502
Whipple, Kenneth A231
Whisenant, Larry E315
Whisler, Patricia K. E78
Whisler, Robert E. W199
Whitacre, Bill P278
Whitacre, Edward E. Jr. A388, P206
Whitaker, Corby C. E142
Whitaker, Darla A823
Whitaker, Sharon L. E290
Whitcomb, Laurel P19
Whitcup, Scott M. A63
White, Anthony L. E181
White, B. Joseph P513
White, Bill (Darden) A276
White, Bill (Sprint Nextel) A790
White, Brian P172
White, Brooke A630
White, Bruce A. E379
White, Burt P304
White, Cheryl L. A131
White, Christopher A55
White, Claude E. E220
White, Colleen T. A138
White, David (Advocat) E21
White, David L. (NVIDIA) A641
White, David R. (Campbell Soup) A185
White, David R. (Isasis Healthcare) P257
White, Dennis W156
White, Edward C. (Owens-Illinois) A656
White, Edward W. (Alaska Air) A57
White, George A897
White, Giles W186
White, Graham W205
White, Gregory D. (La-Z-Boy) A522
White, Gregory W. (Old Dominion Electric) P378
White, H. Katherine A765
White, Harvey E315
White, Henry F. Jr. P40
White, J. Edward E315
White, J. Randall A752
White, James H. A321

White, Jane P373
White, John (U.S. Xpress) P526
White, John D. (Texas A&M) P489
White, John T. (Structure Tone) P475
White, Jonathan (Haemonetics) E183
White, Julie M. A906
White, Karen L. E350
White, Keith A381
White, Kyle D. E69
White, Mark (Baker Botts) P70
White, Mark J. (Compass Group) W106
White, Mary L. A212
White, Melinda M. A376
White, Michael D. A672
White, Miles D. A31
White, Patti Reilly A276
White, Richard (World Fuel Services) A921
White, Richard D. (Diodes) E127
White, Richard L. (MPS) A601
White, Robert W. E16
White, Ron A656
White, Spencer D. E169
White, Teresa L. A49
White, Thomas A. H. A866
White, Timothy P. P511
White, Tracy P64
White, Vincent W. A290
White, W. Brett A198
White, Wendy S. P517
White, William (Big Y Foods) P82
Whitehead, Jeffrey E346
Whitehead, John H. A726
Whitehead, Nigel W58
Whitehead, Roy M. E409
Whitehead, Stephen W273
Whitehead, Tracey W72
Whitehouse, Andrew A578, P324
Whitehouse, David R. A376
Whitehouse, Eric E52
Whitehurst, C. Harrill Jr. E403
Whitehurst, E. Kenan A730
Whitehurst, James M. E332
Whiteley, Andrew P. E146
Whiteley, Larry L. P73
Whiteley, Sherry A469
Whiteman, Steven D. E396
Whitescarver, Jack P354
Whitesell, Shirley J. P47
Whitford, Thomas K. A689
Whiting, Paul L. E368
Whitley, Kelly L. E393
Whitlock, Gary L. A200
Whitlock, James R. P169
Whitlock, John (LHC Group) E248
Whitlock, John (Park National) E306
Whitman, David A630
Whitman, William Jr. A574
Whitmer, W. Carl P257
Whitmire, C. Donald Jr. A375
Whitmire, John L. A248
Whitmore, Robert A764
Whitney, Charles W. P376
Whitney, Darren F. P172
Whitney, Paul M. E214
Whitney, Richard K. A277
Whitsett, Peter J. A719
Whitsitt, William F. A289
Whitson, James P. P164
Whitt, Mark J. E487
Whitt, Richard R. III A554
Whitt, Terry P172
Whittaker, Frank R. J. A570
Whitted, J. Michael A791
Whitten, Kyra A509
Whittington, John P. A419
Whittington, Tom P449
Whittle, John E162
Whittle, Susan T. E348
Whitworth, Jonathan P. P538
Whybrow, John W. W381
Whynot, Jeff D. P459
Whyte, James N. E225
Wiard, Nancy Bradley P19
Wibergh, Johan W135

Wichlacz, Wayne A401
Wichmann, David S. A863
Wick, Philip P295
Wickes, Gene H. A903
Wickham, Gregory I. P155
Wickham, Pamela A. A722
Wicks, Franklin D. Jr. A773
Wicks, Timothy A. A931
Widener, Luann E. A286
Widener, Paul P290
Wider, John P18
Widman, Phillip C. A819
Widman, Ronald A. E351
Widmann, Janet P106
Widmann, Werner W145
Widner, Neil C. P42
Wiebe, Robert L. P122
Wied, Jason A401
Wiedemann, Bryce E389
Wiedemann, Kristi P145
Wiedenkeller, Keith P39
Wiederholt, James R. A828
Wiederkehr, Roger P550
Wiehoff, John P. A207
Wieland, Robert A. P37
Wiele, Andreas W55
Wielgus, Wayne W. A739
Wieltsch, Rainer W253
Wieman, Roberta A299
Wiemann, Bradley T. E118
Wiemerslage, Juliane W161
Wierman, Ken P282
Wiersma, Kevin J. E265
Wiertel, Edward A. A367
Wiese, Randy R. E112
Wiese, Ron P446
Wieser, Helmut A60
Wiesheu, Otto W118
Wiest, Barbara G. A452, P259
Wiest, Christian W308
Wiete, Mark P165
Wiewel, Sabrina A406
Wiggins, Michael R. P466
Wiggins, Rocky A55
Wiggins, Stephen K. P91
Wiggins, Timothy J. A813
Wigglesworth, Margaret P138
Wiggs, Steven B. A132
Wight, Marshall A. P70
Wigington, Daryl P80
Wigner, Preston D. A865
Wijers, G. J. W35
Wilansky, Heywood P443
Wilbanks, George E. P172
Wilber, Patricia A894
Wilburne, Douglas R. A825
Wilck, Greg E293
Wilcox, Kim P337
Wilcox, Paul P253
Wild, Dirk J. A771
Wild, Katy P202
Wildeboer, J. W196
Wilder, Lee A30
Wilder, Linda A419
Wilderotter, Mary Agnes A376
Wildhack, John P185
Wildrick, Robert N. E235
Wilens, Michael E. A363
Wiles, Paul M. P373
Wiley, Cliff A711, P407
Wiley, Daniel E321
Wiley, Deborah E. A486
Wiley, Peter Booth A486
Wilf, Leonard A. P367
Wilfley, Michael L. P220
Wilfong, Debra L. A302
Wilgis, E. F. Shaw P328
Wilhelm, Harald W32
Wilhelm, Lance K. A678, P395
Wilhelm, Mike P130
Wilhoite, Randall W. E48
Wilke, Douglas P199
Wilke, Jeffrey A. A69
Wilken, C. H. W186
Wilkerson, Mark A. P46